Employment Law

Visit the *Employment Law, Second Edition* Companion Website at **www.mylawchamber.co.uk/duddingtonemployment** to find valuable **student** learning material including:

- Interactive multiple choice questions to test your knowledge
- Exam-style questions and answer guidance to test your ability to apply knowledge
- Answer guidelines to the questions posed in the book
- Links to useful sites on the web
- Regular updates on major legal changes affecting the book

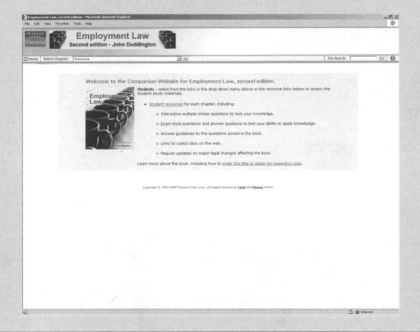

Employment Law

Second Edition

John Duddington

Head of the Law School
Worcester College of Technology

PEARSON
Longman

Harlow, England • London • New York • Boston • San Francisco • Toronto
Sydney • Tokyo • Singapore • Hong Kong • Seoul • Taipei • New Delhi
Cape Town • Madrid • Mexico City • Amsterdam • Munich • Paris • Milan

Pearson Education Limited

Edinburgh Gate
Harlow
Essex CM20 2JE
England

and Associated Companies throughout the world

Visit us on the World Wide Web at:
www.pearsoned.co.uk

———————————

First published 2003
Second edition published 2007

© Pearson Education Limited 2003, 2007

ISBN 978-1-4058-5823-6

British Library Cataloguing-in-Publication Data
A catalogue record for this book is available from the British Library

10 9 8 7 6 5 4 3 2 1
11 10 09 08 07

Typeset in 10.5/12.5pt Minion by 35
Printed and bound in Great Britain by Henry Ling Ltd, Dorchester

The publisher's policy is to use paper manufactured from sustainable forests.

Brief contents

v

Contents

5 The contract of employment

6 Continuity of employment

Part 3   Termination of the employment relationship   273

11   Wrongful and unfair dismissal   275

Supporting resources

Visit **www.mylawchamber.co.uk/duddingtonemployment** to find valuable online resources

Companion Website for students

- Interactive multiple choice questions to test your knowledge
- Exam-style questions and answer guidance to test your ability to apply knowledge
- Answer guidelines to the questions posed in the book
- Links to useful sites on the web
- Regular updates on major legal changes affecting the book

Also: The regularly maintained Companion Website provides the following features:

- Search tool to help locate specific items of content
- E-mail results and profile tools to send results of quizzes to instructors
- Online help and support to assist with website usage and troubleshooting

For more information please contact your local Pearson Education sales representative or visit **www.mylawchamber.co.uk/duddingtonemployment**

Preface

Employment law, like the Roman god Janus, faces two ways. One way points to a seemingly arid mass of regulatory detail which is being added to in a never-ending stream. The other way points, as I hope this book does, to a fascinating subject in which the law blends with history and politics to produce a study full of contemporary relevance. Of all legal subjects this one above all has the combination of practical relevance and a contemporary flavour largely but not entirely unencumbered by the concepts of the past. There are also some tough technical issues for the mind to grapple with.

In writing the second edition of this book, I sought to build on the three aims which I set myself in the first edition: first, to produce an account which is understandable; secondly, to deal adequately with technical and difficult areas; and, thirdly, to attempt to locate employment law in its contemporary setting in society. I have in fact said much more about the social and, where appropriate, political context of employment law than in the first edition, partly, but not exclusively, through the use of the Law in Context sections which are found in all chapters. The introduction of these, together with a much greater use of critical material and the need to keep abreast of the remorseless flow of both statutory and case law, has meant that this is in many ways a new book although I hope that it retains the clarity of exposition which readers kindly remarked that the first edition possessed. As in the first edition I have tried to steer clear of any pro-employer or pro-employee bias. Employment is a partnership between them where the rights and obligations of both must be kept in balance. Thus the task of writers on employment law is to describe that partnership in operation and to be critical if that balance is not maintained. If this book does have a theme it is that employment law has come of age. One senses that the main areas of the subject are well settled and that changes of government are unlikely to alter its shape. Now is the time to focus on the details of the present law and to look to its future development especially in the light of the UK's membership of the European Union, the growing significance of the European Convention on Human Rights and wider trends such as the impact of globalisation.

Employment law is of especial interest to two groups: to lawyers and law students and to personnel officers and others who need a working knowledge of the law. I have tried to deal adequately with all topics which appear in assessments so that the book should be an adequate text for those preparing for degree and professional examinations. I have also included some specimen examination questions to make the book more useful to students. Points for inclusion in answers to these will be found on the accompanying website. In addition I have included summaries at the end of each main chapter and (a new feature) suggestions for further reading. On the other hand, there should be sufficient detail, especially on the newer areas such as family and parental rights, to meet the needs of personnel officers and others. I hope that the inclusion of diagrams and flow charts aids both groups in understanding what has become, in many cases, a very complex branch of the law.

Writing is, as all authors know, a lonely business but I have been sustained in a number of ways. The staff at Pearsons as always provide ideal support and I would like to mention especially Rebecca Taylor, who originally commissioned this edition, Zoë Botterill and Cheryl Cheasley who have seen me through the writing process and who never fail to be helpful and, most important, encouraging.

I once agreed with my wife, Anne, that I would dedicate a book to her with the words: 'To my wife, without whom this would have been a much better book'. Now that I have made good my promise I can say that, far from this being the case, her help and support has in fact been the rock on which this project was built and I could never have written any of my books without her. My daughter, Mary, has been an avid proof reader and custodian of my style and grammar and my son, Christopher, as ever, has remained just an inspiration. It is of course to my family that this book is dedicated. Finally, my colleagues at Worcester Law School have provided cheerful and stimulating company and I have been fortunate to be able to draw on the excellent resources of the Law Library there.

Any preface must contain two essential items: the statement that any errors are my own responsibility and the date at which the information in this book is believed to be correct: in this case it is 25 January 2007 although I have been able to add a few details of cases which have come to my notice since then. The fact that there is a website to this book, which will be updated quarterly, has meant that the usual reluctance of authors to let the proofs of a book go, especially on a subject such as employment law, is tempered by the thought that in this case it can be kept up to date so easily.

The late Nikolaus Pevsner, in his preface to the last of his celebrated 'Buildings of England' series (*Staffordshire*, 1974) wrote, in looking forward to second editions: 'Don't be deceived, gentle reader, the first editions are only *ballons d'essai*; it is the second editions which count.' I now know what he meant!

John Duddington
Worcester, 25 January 2007

Publisher's acknowledgements

We are grateful to the following for permission to reproduce copyright material:

Forms ET1 and ET3 reproduced with permission of Tribunals Service (Employment).

Keeping up to date with employment law

Any book on employment law can only hope to give an indication of likely changes in the law and therefore it is vital to know how to keep up to date. Anyone with access to the internet really has no excuse for not knowing where the law is going as there are several excellent websites, the addresses of which are set out below. Indeed, browsing the net looking for recent legal developments has become a favourite hobby of mine whilst writing this book and I hope that readers will find equal enjoyment!

In addition to the websites, there are the following sources of printed information:

- **The Industrial Relations Law Reports** are published monthly and have the judgments in full of all major employment law cases. There is also a useful commentary at the beginning of each issue on the cases in that issue.

- **The Industrial Cases Reports** are the other main series of reports and are equally useful.

- **The Industrial Law Journal** is the leading journal on employment law. It is published quarterly and contains, besides articles, notes on recent cases and legislation as well as European developments.

- **Income Data Services** publish a fortnightly IDS Brief giving details of current developments which is written in a most readable style. It also publishes handbooks on particular topics, such as unfair dismissal, which are full of useful information.

- **Harvey on Industrial Relations and Employment Law** is a looseleaf encyclopaedia currently running to six parts which is regularly updated and has monthly bulletins which are invaluable as a first point of reference in checking on current developments.

- **Labour Market Trends** is now known (from 15 January 2007) as *Economic and Labour Market Review*. It is published monthly and is full of statistics on current trends as well as containing invaluable articles extrapolating the information in them. This is a must for anyone (surely everyone?) who wishes to evaluate the impact of legislation on the labour market.

Useful websites

Employment law is such a fast-changing subject that the internet is a really useful tool. I have set out the websites which I have found especially useful but it may be that readers find other favourites of their own. As many sites have links to others, it is easy to find more sites.

The most useful sites for keeping up to date are, I think, the following:

www.dti.gov.uk This is the website of the Department of Trade and Industry and has a great deal of information on both recent and proposed changes to the law. Try to look at it once a week.

www.peoplemanagement.co.uk is the website of the Chartered Institute of Personnel and Development and contains a useful section on current legal issues. The other sections of this website are also worth reading, as it is important to look at the total picture of employment relations and not only the law.

www.incomesdata.co.uk Another invaluable resource for keeping up to date on all aspects of employment relations and has some excellent features on, for example, recent cases.

Other invaluable websites are:

www.hmso.gov.uk has the texts of legislation.

www.courtservice.gov.uk has judgments of the courts.

www.bailii.org another source of up-to-date judgments.

www.acas.org.uk ACAS website.

www.eoc.org.uk Equal Opportunities Commission website.

www.cre.gov.uk Commission for Racial Equality website.

www.drc-gb.org Disability Rights Commission.

www.employmentappeals.gov.uk Employment Appeal Tribunal.

www.europa.eu.int European Union.

ilj.oupjournals.org *Industrial Law Journal.*

www.dwp.gov.uk Department for Work and Pensions – useful for updating on social security benefits.

www.dataprotection.gov.uk especially useful at present in view of current developments.

Guided tour

What are the main debates or topical issues within Employment Law?

Law in context boxes highlight controversial areas of the law and encourage an analytical approach to the study of Employment Law.

What are the main points I should know after reading this chapter?

End of chapter summaries draw together the key points you should be aware of following your reading.

Where can I find guidance on answering exam and coursework questions?

Each chapter ends with **exam-style questions** to highlight the sort of questions you could be faced with in your study of Employment Law. Guidance on answering the question can be found on the Companion Website at **www.mylawchamber.co.uk/duddingtonemployment**.

Forgotten the meaning of a legal term?

Turn to the **glossary** at the end of the book to remind yourself of its meaning.

Where can I find out more about the topics in the book?

Use the **further reading list** and **bibliography** at the end of each chapter to point you to further sources which allow you to delve deeper into the subject.

Want to test your knowledge of a subject, practice answering exam-style questions and get useful answer guidance, search the internet for helpful further resources, and stay up to date with all of the major changes in Employment Law?

Visit the Companion Website at **www.mylawchamber.co.uk/duddingtonemployment** to find extensive resources designed to assist you in your study, including: interactive multiple choice questions, answer guidance to the exam style questions contained in the book, additional exam style questions and answer guidance, web links to useful further resources and regular updates on major legal changes in Employment Law.

Table of cases

Table of statutes

International Legislation

Italy

USA

Table of statutory instruments

Table of European and International legislation

CHARTERS, CONVENTIONS AND TREATIES

DIRECTIVES

Table of statutory rights

A large number of statutory rights have been described in this book and readers may find the following table useful as a short guide to the main ones.

Right	Statute	Time limit	Qualifying period	Remedy
Unfair dismissal	Part X, ERA 1996	3 months	One year	Reinstatement, re-engagement, compensation
Unfair dismissal by reason of a business transfer (TUPE)	Transfer of undertakings regulations (2006)	3 months	One year	Reinstatement, re-engagement, compensation
Unfair dismissal for taking part in protected official industrial action	S 238A, TULRCA 1992	6 months	None	Reinstatement, re-engagement, compensation
Unfair dismissal for a reason connected with pregnancy, childbirth maternity leave, parental leave, dependant care leave	S 99, ERA 1996	3 months	None	Reinstatement, re-engagement, compensation
Redundancy payments	Part XI, ERA 1996	6 months	2 years	Statutory redundancy payment
Sex discrimination	SDA 1975	3 months	None	Compensation order declaring rights recommendation
Race discrimination	RRA 1976	3 months	None	As for sex discrimination
Disability discrimination	DDA 1995	3 months	None	As for sex discrimination
Discrimination on the grounds of sexual orientation	Employment Equality (Sexual Orientation) Regulations 2003	3 months	None	As for sex discrimination
Discrimination on the grounds of religion or belief	Employment Equality (Religion or Belief) Regulations 2003	3 months	None	As for sex discrimination

Right	Statute	Time limit	Qualifying period	Remedy
Discrimination on the grounds of age	Employment Equality (Age) Regulations 2006	3 months	None	As for sex discrimination
Equal pay	EqPA 1970	6 months	None	Arrears of pay for up to 2 years
Unlawful deduction from wages	Part II, ERA 1996	3 months	None	Payment of wages deducted
Guarantee payment	Ss 28–35, ERA 1996	3 months	None	Payment of guarantee pay
Right to an itemised statement of employment particulars	Ss 8–12, ERA 1996	3 months	2 months	ET may decide what should be in the particulars or amend inaccurate ones
Right not to suffer detriment as a result of being a union member or taking part in union activities	S 146, TULRCA 1992	3 months	None	Compensation

Note: The phrase 'time limit' in the above table needs clarification, as the time limits run from different starting points.

Unfair dismissal. Time runs from the 'effective date of termination' of employment. This is defined by s 92(6) of ERA 1996 as the date when notice of termination expires, or, where the contract is terminated without notice, when termination takes effect. However, in the case of dismissal for taking part in protected official industrial action, the phrase is 'date of dismissal' (s 238(5) of TULRCA), which has the same meaning. In all of these cases the employment tribunal has power to extend the time limit if it feels that it was not reasonably practicable to present a complaint in time.

Redundancy payments. Time runs from the 'relevant date', which is defined by s 145 of ERA 1996 in identical terms to that of 'effective date of termination'.

Discrimination legislation. The phrase is 'the date of the act complained of' and the employment tribunal has power to extend the time if it considers it just and equitable to do so. In *equal pay claims* the phrase is 'termination of employment'.

Unlawful deduction from wages. Time runs from the date of the last deduction by the employer and this can be extended if the employment tribunal considers that it is just and equitable to do so.

Guarantee payment. Time runs from the day for which payment is claimed with the same extension of time if it is just and equitable.

Right to an itemised statement of employment particulars. Time runs from the day on which employment ceased with the same extension of time if just and equitable.

Right not to suffer for trade union activities etc. Time runs from the last day when there was either an act or a failure to act with the same extension of time if just and equitable.

Abbreviations used when referring to judges

As we shall see, the judgments of individual judges are of great importance both in the interpretation of statutes and other statutory materials, such as Regulations, and also in directly making law through the system of precedent. When referring to the judgments of individual judges, standard abbreviations are used to indicate particular members of the judiciary. These are as follows and the imaginary name of Smith in this context is used to make the examples clearer.

Smith J   Mr or Mrs Justice Smith, a judge of the High Court.

Smith LJ   Lord Justice or Lady Justice Smith, a judge of the Court of Appeal.

Lord Smith   A Law Lord, i.e. a member of the House of Lords who sits as a judge to hear appeals.

Smith P   The President of the Employment Appeal Tribunal, who is also a judge of the High Court.

Smith MR   The Master of the Rolls, the presiding judge of the Court of Appeal, Civil Division.

Smith LCJ   The Lord Chief Justice, the presiding judge of the Court of Appeal, Criminal Division.

Smith LC   The Lord Chancellor used to exercise judicial functions and sit in the House of Lords but, as a result of the Constitutional Reform Act 2005, no longer does so.

Smith VC   Vice-Chancellor. The presiding judge of the Chancery Division of the High Court.

Part 1

Employment law: its history, sources and institutions

This part looks at the context in which employment law operates: the UK legal system, European Union law and human rights law. It also deals with the impact on UK employment law of the Conventions produced by the International Labour Convention. As well as these areas, dispute settlement in employment law is considered with an emphasis on the work of employment tribunals.

1 The context of employment law and its institutions

INTRODUCTION

This chapter looks at the context in which employment law operates in both the legal system and the political world. As such it aims to introduce themes which will appear throughout this book. In addition, many of the central themes will be looked at from a different perspective in Part Five of this book, where the future of employment law is considered.

Employment law is divided into two parts:

(a) The relationship between employers and those who work for them who may be classed as employees or workers (the precise distinction is dealt with in Chapter 4). This is known as individual employment law and includes the law on the right to wages, health and safety, and dismissal, amongst other matters. Parts Two and Three of this book deal with these areas.

(b) The relationship between employers and groups of employees and workers. This is known as collective employment law and includes the law on trade unions and on the calling and conduct of strikes and other industrial action such as go-slows. This is dealt with in Part Four.

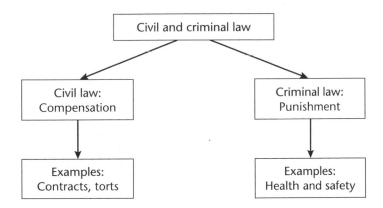

Note: the word 'tort' means a wrong which can be redressed by the payment of compensation or some other civil remedy. The tort featured most often in this book is the tort of negligence, which is fully explained in Chapter 8.

The above examples are oversimplified, but they indicate the fundamental distinction in the law between those matters where it is left to the individual to seek redress and those where the state takes a hand. In general, employment law (or labour law or industrial law as it is sometimes called) is far more concerned with civil matters such as actions for compensation for unfair dismissal and claims for unpaid wages. Criminal law plays a relatively small part, being mainly confined to prosecutions under health and safety legislation.

Before the detail of employment law is considered some preliminary points about the legal system need to be made for the benefit of readers without a legal background. First, the phrase 'English legal system' is generally used, but in fact the legal system extends to Wales also. It is different in Scotland although many of the statutory provisions apply there also.

The other feature of the legal system is that law is made in the following ways:

- By Parliament in the form of statutes and regulations made under them. Codes of practice, e.g. the ACAS Code of Practice on Disciplinary Practice and Procedures, are taken into account in legal proceedings but are not law in the sense that a breach automatically exposes the person in breach to sanctions. Thus a breach of the ACAS Code does not mean that, for example, a dismissal is unfair but is likely to be taken into account by a tribunal which may hold that, partly as a result of the breach, the dismissal is unfair.

- Decisions of the courts have been enormously influential in shaping the law and where the law has been developed by the courts it is known as common law. The fundamental principles of English law, as contained in, for example, the law of contract, owe their origin to the courts, although statute law has built on them. Chapter 5, dealing with the contract of employment, is a good example of the interplay between the courts and statute law.

- Decisions of the courts have also been especially significant in interpreting statutory provisions. Examples are found throughout this book, but an especially good one is *Western Excavating* v *Sharp* (1978), interpreting the part of the law on unfair dismissal known as constructive dismissal (see Chapter 11).

- European Union law (see Chapter 2) and the European Convention on Human Rights (see Chapter 3) are dealt with in subsequent chapters. European Union law has been responsible for most of the development in discrimination law in recent years, such as the introduction of regulations in 2003 prohibiting discrimination on the grounds of sexual orientation and religion or belief, and in 2006 on the grounds of age. It has also been responsible for ensuring that employees do not lose their contractual rights when a business is transferred to new owners, through the Transfer of Undertakings (Protection of Employment) Regulations, dealt with in Chapter 12. The European Convention on Human Rights has had a less direct impact partly because it does not deal with social and political rights such as the right not to be dismissed, but its influence is growing.

THE LEGAL AND POLITICAL CONTEXT OF EMPLOYMENT LAW

Employment law can be viewed on four levels:

- On the individual level, where individuals obtain redress for wrongs done to them, e.g. compensation for unfair dismissal.

- On the collective level, where trade unions take action collectively on behalf of their members such as calling strikes and also where trade unions bargain on behalf of their members and deal with employers and public authorities such as central government.

- On the domestic political level, where the relationship between unions and employers is viewed against central government policies which in the context of employment law are often dictated by the UK's membership of the European Union.

- On the international level, where the domestic political scene now needs to be viewed against global trends such as globalisation and the superpower status of the United States. In employment law it is at this level that international labour standards, in particular those of the International Labour Organization, operate.

The system of employment law in the UK is a very recent one. As the final part of this book attempts to look forward over the next fifty years it is perhaps not a bad start to begin the text by looking back fifty years. In 1957 individual employment law hardly existed. There were no laws prohibiting discrimination and so applicants for jobs could be legitimately rejected on the grounds of sex, race, disability, sexual orientation, religion and belief, and age. Health and safety law was a mass of detailed rules apparently blindly followed with no overriding aim of ensuring health and safety at work. Most significant of all, there was no protection from unfair dismissal and employees could have their employment terminated without reason provided that they were given the notice provided for in their contracts of employment or paid wages in lieu of notice for the period of employment. What is even more surprising is that there was little pressure for change either from employers (not surprisingly) or from unions (surprisingly). The reasons for this will be explained below.

Collective employment law was, in 1957, very different from now. The legal position of trade unions was considerably stronger and remained so until the legislative changes made by the 1979–97 Conservative government and which are discussed in Chapters 13 and 14.

In fact 1957 was a placid era from the viewpoint of employment law. Kahn-Freund (1954), quoted in Davies and Freedland (1993), wrote that 'There is perhaps no major country in the world in which the law has played a less siginificant role in the shaping of (labour management) relations than in Great Britain and in which the law and the legal profession have less to do with the labour relations'. Davies and Freedland (1993) use the term 'collective laissez faire' (title of chapter 1) to describe this attitude and this period. Brodie (2003) has to some extent challenged this notion by drawing attention to the extent of regulation of the employment relationship but it still remains true that there is a completely different feel to the law as it was in 1957. This was due to various factors. In part it was the desire of the then Conservative government to avoid clashes

1

The context of employment law and its institutions

with trade unions (Roberts, 1994) and there is evidence, certainly in the period imme-diately after the Second World War, of a desire on the part of at least some unions not to, as it were, rock the boat. For example, a government White Paper, *Statement on Personal Incomes, Costs and Prices*, published in 1948, recommended what was in effect a wage freeze for the foreseeable future but it was overwhelmingly endorsed by a spe-cial delegate conference of the TUC (Hennessey, 1992, page 382). It is also instructive to turn back yet earlier, by a hundred years, to 1857. Here the striking feature is that, whereas in 1957 employees at least had their contractual entitlements to fall back on, employment law in 1857 (not that it was called by this name) featured the master–servant relationship where manual workers were governed by the Master and Servant Acts under which breach of the service contract was a criminal offence. As Deakin (2006) puts it: 'The nature of the paradigm legal form of the labour relationship under early industrial capitalism in England was statutory and hierarchical, rather than common law and contractual.' Even when the last of the Master and Servant Acts were repealed in 1875 and by the Employers and Workman Act workers were not liable to criminal prosecution, the effects of the old law remained. They do so to this day, as Chapter 5 will show, as many of the implied terms in contracts of employment such as fidelity and obedience, whilst praiseworthy in themselves, have a distinct Victorian flavour to them. In fact, 1875 was a significant year in the history of labour relations as it was the Conspiracy and Protection of Property Act which legalised peaceful picketing (see Chapter 14) and changed the law of conspiracy in favour of trade unions. Previously they had been held to be criminal conspiracies.

The era since 1957 has been one of competing ideologies in employment law. There was undoubtedly a change in atmosphere in industrial relations in the 1960s and what was perceived as a new mood of militancy among trade unions and their members. Thus the number of unofficial strikes increased from 1,400 in 1966 to 3,750 in 1970. There was clearly a need for governments to take action but the climate was still hostile to state intervention in the field of industrial relations. What is surprising is that this hostility was not only present when the government proposed to legislate in the field of workplace disputes, when one would expect the unions to be at least sceptical, but even when government action was proposed to improve the conditions of employees. Davies and Freedland (1993: see especially pages 147–8) describe the reaction of both sides of industry to the initial legislation in modern employment law: the Contracts of Employment Act 1963 and the Redundancy Payments Act 1965. In neither case was there anything more than a lukewarm welcome from the unions and there is the inescapable feeling that there was a too cosy atmosphere which neither wanted to be disturbed. Moreover, there was a political consensus that this state of affairs was hin-dering the development and modernisation of industry. Thus Mr Ray Gunter (quoted in Davies and Freedland, page 148), speaking on the government's proposals in the Industrial Training Bill in 1964, said: 'I again say to the minister that he will have to do the job for them (employers and unions) because he will never get agreement there.'

The climate changed in the later 1960s and the then Labour government appointed a Royal Commission on Trade Unions and Employers' Associations in 1965, the report of which formed the basis of the celebrated White Paper of 1968, *In Place of Strife*, which proposed legal intervention in the conduct of industrial action. The history of this era is explored in Chapter 13 but suffice it for now to note that the 1970s were years of extreme turbulence in the area of industrial relations, with the failure of the Labour government to implement its proposals in *In Place of Strife*, followed by the introduction by the following Conservative government of a detailed piece of legislation, the Industrial Relations Act 1971, which itself provoked conflict and was repealed by the Labour government in 1974. Eventually the Conservative government elected in 1979 embarked on a lengthy programme of legislation in the area of collective employment rights which the present Labour government has largely left in place.

The Industrial Relations Act 1971 also introduced statutory protection against unfair dismissal and the 1974–9 Labour government followed this with a number of individual employment rights, including the outlawing of discrimination on grounds of sex and race, and maternity rights. Thus, in parallel to the politically contentious atmosphere of collective employment law, individual employment law was gradually starting to have an impact. At the same time the influence of European Community law was beginning to be felt. For example, the Acquired Rights Directive was passed in 1977 which obliged all Member States to introduce measures to ensure that on the transfer of a business the contracts of employees were transferred to the new employers and that other acquired rights were also transferred (see Chapter 12). In fact the Conservative government pursued a strategy of individualism which emphasised the rights of individuals but this was seen mainly in terms of protecting individuals against trade union power, which is outlined in Chapter 13. It showed less interest in the individual employment rights as these conflicted with another key strategy, that of deregulation, which meant reducing the burdens on business. Thus, as a simple example, the period of qualifying employment needed before a claim for unfair dismissal could be brought was lengthened from six months to one and then two years. However, the hand of the government was to some extent forced by the growing influence of EC law which required implementation, such as the Acquired Rights Directive (above) which was implemented by the Transfer of Undertakings (Protection of Employment) Regulations 1981.

The strategy of the Labour government elected in 1997 has been to pursue what it calls a 'third way'. This involves striking a balance between the two sides of industry whilst at the same time abandoning the perceived hostility to the European Community of its predecessor. Thus the Working Time Directive, which the Conservative government had opposed, was introduced into UK law by the Working Time Regulations in 1998; but at the same time there was no wholesale repeal of the Conservative government's trade union legislation. Instead there were modest changes to the law on collective employment law, dealing mainly with details, principally in the Employment Relations Acts of 1999 and 2004.

DISPUTE SETTLEMENT IN EMPLOYMENT LAW

Some disputes, for example those involving a breach of a contract or a claim for unpaid wages, go to the civil courts, although claims for a breach of contract of employment can be brought in an employment tribunal, where the amount claimed is £25,000 or less.

Diagram of the civil courts

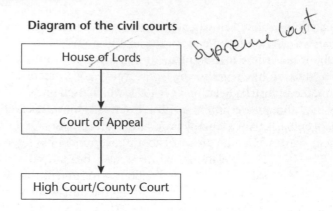

Supreme Court

House of Lords

↓

Court of Appeal

↓

High Court/County Court

Civil claims begin in either the High Court or the County Court, according to their monetary value and their complexity. Appeals go to the Court of Appeal, with a further appeal, generally only on a point of law of general public importance, to the House of Lords. The involvement of the European Court of Justice (ECJ) is dealt with in Chapter 2 and that of the European Court of Human Rights (ECtHR) in Chapter 3.

Claims brought in employment tribunals

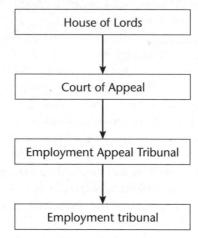

House of Lords

↓

Court of Appeal

↓

Employment Appeal Tribunal

↓

Employment tribunal

Employment tribunals hear all the statutory claims for unfair dismissal, redundancy payments, discrimination and other matters dealt with in these chapters. In addition, they can also hear contract claims as indicated above. The system was administered by the Employment Tribunal Service (ETS) which, from 1 April 2006, became part of the unified tribunal service. The ETS Annual Report and Accounts 2005/6 shows that 115,039 claims were accepted by employment tribunals, an increase from 86,181 in 2004/5 and a figure of only 34,697 in 1990/1. However, the ETS says that this increase was mainly due to the large number of multiple cases which rose from 65,543 as compared to 31,126 in 2004/5. In fact the number of single cases claims declined from just over 55,000 to just fewer than 52,000, which is in line with the trend for the last five years. In addition the ETS believes that the introduction of the new Dispute

Regulations (see Chapter 11) has led to a decrease in the number of claims but in fact the statistical evidence is not yet conclusive. Indeed in the last period covered by the 2005/6 report (November–March) there was an increase of 15% in the number of single claims brought.

The types of claims heard are considered in detail in the relevant chapters but the ETS Annual Report and Accounts 2005/6 gives the following percentage breakdown of claims which gives a flavour of the work of tribunals:

21% for unfair dismissal
18% relating to the Working Time Directive
16% for unauthorised deductions from wages
13% for breach of contract (wrongful dismissal)
11% for discrimination
8% for equal pay
6% for redundancy
7% miscellaneous.

The Report draws attention to the number of claims which covered more than one area. Thus the 115,039 cases covered 201,514 jurisdictional heads which results in an average of 1.8 complaints per claim. Throughout this book attention will be drawn to links between different areas which can result in more than one claim: this is a vital point for both practitioners and students who, when answering problem questions on employment law, should think across the whole subject and look at possible other areas in addition to what may seem to be the main one. An example at the end of this chapter shows how this can occur.

The work of tribunals

Tribunals have a legally qualified chairperson who sits with two others drawn from both sides of industry.

Employment tribunals were originally known as industrial tribunals and their object has been to provide a relatively straightforward means of hearing employment claims. Although to the layperson they do not seem very different from a court, they are not subject to the rules of evidence to the same degree and the procedural rules and forms are simplified from those of the courts.

Employment tribunal procedure

The rules are contained in the Employment Tribunals (Constitution and Rules of Procedure) Regulations 2004 (SI 2004/1861). What follows is not a full account of the procedure but a sketch of the salient points. It is important to note the emphasis which the rules place on whether the claimant (the employee) has already raised the subject of the claim with the employer and the employer's response to it. This links with the statutory disputes procedures considered in Chapter 11. Claims must be brought by the issue of form ET1 (this form is displayed at the end of the chapter) and the person bringing the claim is known as the claimant. Rule 1(4) provides that a claimant must state in the ET1 whether the subject matter of the complaint was raised with the employer at least 28 days prior to the presentation of the claim. If it was not, then the claimant must explain why. However, where the claim is for unfair dismissal this requirement only applies where the claim is for constructive dismissal. One object of the present rules as compared with their predecessor is the increased requirements to state precisely what the claim is about. Thus rule 1(1) specifies that a claim must include all the required information and rule 1(4) amplifies this by providing that this includes details of the claim. Initially, problems arose where claimants did not comply with the strict letter of these rules but the leading authority is now *Grimmer* v *KLM Cityhopper Ltd* (2005). Here the claimant had said on the form that she wished to pursue a complaint in respect of flexible working and the question was whether this contained sufficient information. The Employment Appeal Tribunal (EAT) held that this was enough in itself to enable the employment tribunal to proceed. In a powerful judgment, Prophet J observed that 'there is a danger that executive objectives (i.e. in this case the need for a clear statement of the nature of the claim) may gain precedence over the interests of justice'. In this context it clearly meant not denying a person access to the system of justice where, as here, there was no compelling reason why the merits of the case could not be examined. In *Richardson* v *U Mole Ltd* (2005) the claimant's claim form was not accepted by the tribunal as it did not state that he was an employee of the respondents as required by rule 1(4)(f). It was, however, perfectly clear from other parts of the form that he was an employee. The EAT held that there was no breach of the rule.

Rule 3 gives employment tribunals power to reject claims where no ET1 is used, where it does not include all the required information, where the tribunal does not have jurisdiction to hear the claim and where the grievance was not raised with the employer as above. If all is in order then the respondent must reply to the ET1 by an ET3 (again, this form is displayed at the end of the chapter). This is in the nature of a defence by the employer, which may also make a counterclaim against the employee who is claiming. The ET3 asks the respondent to confirm if the claimant has raised the substance of the claim already, in writing, with the respondent (employer) under a statutory grievance procedure (see Chapter 11). If it has been, then the respondent must state what stage it has reached. If the respondent states that the grievance has not been raised, but the claimant states that he or she has raised it, then the respondent is asked if it did receive this and, if so, to explain why it did not accept it as a grievance. Rule 4(1) provides that a respondent must ensure that the response to the claim reaches the tribunal office within 28 days of the date when the respondent was sent a copy of the ET1 by the Employment Tribunals Office. Rule 6 states when a response will not be accepted: if it is not in the ET3 form, if it does not include all the required information, or if it has not been presented within the time limit. Under rule 8 a default judgment can be entered where a response is not accepted under rule 6 but cannot be made when the respondent has applied for a review of the tribunal's decision not to accept its response. It should be noted that a tribunal can strike out either an ET1 or an ET3 if it considers that the claim is scandalous, frivolous or vexatious and this striking out power also applies where the proceedings are conducted in any such manner.

Under rule 22 there is a fixed period when the parties have the opportunity to reach a settlement through ACAS conciliation. The usual period will be 13 weeks and this will apply to, e.g., unfair dismissal claims, but there is a shorter period of 7 weeks for breach of contract claims (i.e. wrongful dismissal), unlawful deduction from wages, claims under TUPE, etc. There is no period at all for claims based on discrimination or public interest disclosure. The tribunal has the power to order discovery of documents which are relevant to the proceedings and can also order parties who will be called as witnesses to give statements of their evidence in advance. The usual practice is for this to be disclosed to the other side before the hearing. Orders can also be made compelling the attendance of witnesses and, although most witnesses come voluntarily, such orders are useful if a potential witness needs to show a witness order to her employer to gain time off work to attend. Rule 17 allows for case management conferences to be held if the chairperson so decides and will deal with procedural matters and management of the proceedings generally. In addition, where an applicant is considered at a pre-hearing to have no reasonable prospect of success, then a deposit of up to £500 can be required from her as a condition of continuing with the application. Costs can also be awarded where a party has been warned at a pre-hearing that the case has no reasonable prospect of success but still continues.

The actual hearing is less formal than a court in that, for example, robes are not worn and everyone is seated. The party with the burden of proof begins and in dismissal cases this will be the employer, except for constructive dismissal where the employee begins and must prove that the employer's conduct did in fact amount to dismissal. In *Stansbury v Datapulse Ltd* (2004) a lay member of an employment tribunal fell asleep during the hearing of an unfair dismissal claim and was said to have smelt strongly of alcohol. The Court of Appeal allowed an appeal from the decision of the employment tribunal that the applicant had not been unfairly dismissed, on the ground that the behaviour of the tribunal member did not give the appearance of the fair hearing to which every party is entitled.

Rules 38–42 deal with costs orders and provide that tribunals may award costs of up to £1,000 against a party but only if that party was legally represented. Costs may be awarded if a party has in either bringing or conducting the proceedings acted vexatiously, abusively, disruptively, or otherwise unreasonably and this also applies where the representative of a party has acted in these ways when conducting the proceedings. In addition, costs may be awarded when the bringing of the proceedings has been misconceived. The tribunal may take the parties' ability to pay into account when making costs orders. In addition, wasted costs orders may be made against representatives and preparation time orders may now be made in favour of unrepresented litigants. Even so, the fact remains that the rule in actions in the civil courts that the loser is almost always ordered to pay the winner's costs does not apply in tribunal proceedings. Hepple and Morris (2002) were critical of the new powers given to tribunals by these rules to award wasted costs orders and preparation time orders. They pointed out that costs awards were made in only 247 cases out of 130,000 cases and these included cases where the party did not turn up for the hearing. (The latest figures (ETS Annual Report and Accounts 2005/6) show that there were 580 costs orders made in 2005/6 with an average award of £2,256.) Given the low level of costs orders and the low amounts ordered, Hepple and Morris ask: 'What is the mischief which the changes are intended to remedy?' More broadly they feel that the introduction of the power to make wasted costs orders is 'symptomatic of the movement to equate tribunals with the ordinary courts'.

Employment Appeal Tribunal

This hears appeals from employment tribunals and has the same status as the High Court. It is headed by a President who is a High Court judge and cases are heard by a judge and two laypersons from opposite sides of industry. The work of the EAT from October 2002 to July 2005 was considered by Burton J, the then president of the Tribunal (Burton, 2005).

Advisory Conciliation and Arbitration Service (ACAS)

This is a statutory body which has the following general functions:

- Conciliation in individual disputes. Any settlement reached when a claim is brought but then settled after the intervention of ACAS and recorded on the appropriate form is binding and the claim cannot be proceeded with to the tribunal.
- Conciliation in collective disputes between employers and unions.
- Preparation of codes of practice. The most important one is the Code on Disciplinary and Grievance Procedures (see Chapter 11).
- Designating an independent expert to prepare a report in equal value claims (see Chapter 9).
- Providing information and advice on employment matters.

The Employment Rights (Dispute Resolution) Act 1998 contained power for ACAS (see below) to conduct binding arbitrations in unfair dismissal claims provided that the parties agreed. Any decision of the arbitrator is final subject to an appeal on either a point of EC law or the European Convention on Human Rights (ECHR). Power was given to ACAS to prepare a scheme under which the system would operate and this came into effect in May 2001. There is anecdotal evidence that the take-up of it has so far been small. In addition, the provisions of the Employment Act 2002 dealing with statutory disciplinary dismissal and grievance procedures (see Chapter 11) may, as mentioned above, reduce the number of claims. In line with the trend to encourage the settlement of claims by conciliation, s 24 of the Employment Act 2002 provides that tribunals have the power to postpone a hearing in order to give time for conciliation.

Central Arbitration Committee

This is a permanent body, independent of government, employers and unions, which deals with disputes and other matters relating to collective aspects of employment law. It has a major role in trade union recognition matters and applications by unions for the disclosure of information for collective bargaining purposes, discussed in Chapter 13. It also provides voluntary arbitration in industrial disputes. With the revival of trade union recognition and collective aspects of employment law, the Committee has itself been revived from its somewhat moribund state in much of the 1980s and 1990s.

Certification Officer

This officer has the role of certifying whether a trade union is independent (see Chapter 13) and, if so, granting certificates of independence. The grant of such a certificate is a prerequisite to the exercise of most trade union rights.

Commission for Equality and Human Rights

The legislation on sex, race and disability discrimination all provided for bodies with various powers to police the legislation and act in a strategic capacity. These were the Equal Opportunities Commission (EOC), the Commission for Racial Equality (CRE) and the Disability Rights Commission (DRC). These are all to be merged into the Commission for Equality and Human Rights (CEHR) which was established by the Equality Act 2006 and which will also oversee the legislation prohibiting discrimination on the other grounds: sexual orientation, religion or belief, and age. The work of these bodies is dealt with in Chapter 9.

1

The context of employment law and its institutions

LAW IN CONTEXT
Employment law in the United States

Readers may find it interesting, as they go through this book, to compare employment law in Great Britain with the system in the United States. To lawyers accustomed to the British system of detailed regulation of the employment relationship it comes as a surprise to find that US individual employment law as such hardly exists. As the US labour lawyer Estricher (1996) remarks, 'the employment relationship is not pervasively regulated in the United States even to this day. Absent a specific statute or express contract, employment in the United States is considered "at will"; both the employee and the employer are free to terminate the relationship with or without cause'. He points to the economic and social reasons for this: employers benefit from lower labour costs in that they can easily terminate the relationship if it proves unsatisfactory; and workers benefit from being allowed to quit at any time. Thus the British law on unfair dismissal, with its detailed procedures and requirements for a 'fair reason' for the dismissal, finds no counterpart in the US; nor does the redundancy payments legislation (see Chapter 12). However, the majority of courts and tribunals in the US do require employers to adhere to the policies and procedures in their application forms and works manuals and breach of these can lead to an action for damages for past and future lost earnings. There is no provision for reinstatement. (See Chapter 11 for a discussion of the extent to which British law enables an employee who has been unfairly dismissed to claim re-employment.) In addition, a number of states recognise a tort action for terminations of employment which are in violation of public policy. However, to British eyes the situations in which this may be claimed seem minimal:

→

13

examples are dismissal of employees who have indicated that they are available for jury service and dismissal of employees who refuse to commit perjury or refuse to act in breach of professional standards. Health and safety law is, however, developed to a much greater extent. The federal Occupational and Safety Act 1970 requires employers to meet certain standards and there is a general duty (similar to the general duty in our Health and Safety at Work Act 1974) under which employers must maintain a safe workplace and the US Department of Labor sets detailed regulations and inspects workplaces. Other examples where US law intervenes in the employment relationship are to protect workplace privacy and the protection of 'whistle-blowers'. In this last instance there is comparability with UK legislation contained in the Public Interest Disclosure Act 1998 – see Chapter 5.

It is, however, in the area of discrimination law that the British employment lawyer feels most at home. Indeed British discrimination law derived much of its initial inspiration from US law and, in particular, the concept of what we know as indirect discrimination (see Chapter 9) was derived from US law. The foundation of US law is the Civil Rights Act 1964 which all employers with 15 or more employees must comply with and which prohibits discrimination on the grounds of race, colour, religion, national origin and sex. It also enables employees to challenge practices which have a disparate impact on a particular group. This is known in the UK as indirect discrimination (dealt with in Chapter 9): a simple example would be where a job application did not actually state that 'this job is only open to British born persons' (direct discrimination) but said 'only persons born in the UK need apply' which in reality has the same effect. The Age Discrimination in Employment Act 1967 applies to employees aged over 40 and prohibits intentional discrimination where employees are treated differently because of their age. Disability discrimination is also prohibited under the Americans With Disabilities Act 1990 and here an element of positive discrimination is allowed with the obligation on employers to provide 'reasonable accommodation' for persons with a disability which is mirrored in the UK by the duty under the Disability Discrimination Act 1995 to make reasonable adjustments. However, a notable gap compared to British law is the absence of any prohibition of discrimination on the grounds of sexual orientation (see, e.g., *Smith* v *Liberty Mutual Insurance Co.* (1978)). The British Equal Pay Act of 1970 finds its counterpart in the US Equal Pay Act of 1963.

US law on collective bargaining and unions is known as labour law. In most cases unions obtain collective bargaining rights in contested elections administered by a federal agency. (Federal agencies are bodies which carry out functions on behalf of the federal government such as the Bureau of Labor Statistics). There is a division between what is deemed to lie within the realm of collective bargaining and what is within the prerogative of management. Wages and hours of work and working conditions are within collective bargaining, as one would expect, but it is surprising that decisions on, for example, plant closings are within managerial prerogative. The process of collective bargaining is much more strictly regulated than in Britain. Under the National Labor Relations Act 1935 employers and unions have a duty to meet and confer in 'good faith' bargaining although the duty to bargain is limited to the above matters. If the parties cannot agree then notice must be given to the Federal Mediation and

Conciliation Service. After this and after a 60-day cooling-off period has expired the parties may resort to 'self help'. Thus the employer may lock out employees and/or unilaterally implement its final offer to the union. The union may exercise its right to strike. Interestingly the employer, unlike in Britain, is not allowed to terminate the contracts of striking workers but can hire replacements. There are other detailed provisions dealing with the process of collective bargaining which are beyond the scope of this note but one is struck by the contrast between the detailed regulation of this area and the almost complete absence of regulation of the individual employment relationship.

Example: the links between different areas of employment law

Nigel is a single parent with a disabled son of 14. His request to start 30 minutes later in the mornings to wait for his son's school transport is refused by his employer.

Nigel has an obvious claim under the rules dealing with the right to request a flexible working arrangement (see Chapter 10) but he may also have a claim for:

■ Sex discrimination if female employees have been granted a flexible working arrangement in similar circumstances – see Chapter 9.

■ Constructive dismissal if he decides to resign and claim that the employer has repudiated the contract of employment – see Chapter 11.

Another good example of links between different areas is the case of **Horkulak v Cantor Fitzgerald**. This is considered in detail in Chapter 7 as it involved payment of bonuses but it also involved:

■ The application of the duty of mutual trust and confidence – see Chapter 5.

■ Constructive dismissal – see Chapter 11.

1

The context of employment law and its institutions

SUMMARY

This chapter aims to provide a broad sketch of themes which will be more fully developed in later chapters. Thus it begins by distinguishing between individual and collective employment law and it then points out some of the principal features of both English law in general and of employment law in particular. It then considers the contribution made by the courts to the development of the law and that of European Union law and the European Convention on Human Rights. From this it moves to sketch the legal and political context of employment law together with an account of its development.

It then looks at dispute settlement in employment law with particular reference to the work of employment tribunals but also noting the contribution of ACAS, the Central Arbitration Committee and the new Commission for Equality and Human Rights.

Finally it looks, for purposes of comparison, at how the law in the USA tackles the issues raised in this book.

QUESTION

Explain the different methods of dispute settlement which exist in employment law. Do you consider that they provide a satisfactory method of resolving disputes between employers and employees?

FURTHER READING

Annual reports of the Employment Tribunals Service. Reports from 1999–2000 onwards are available on their website: www.employmenttribunals.gov.uk

Gilmour, I. (1997) *Whatever Happened to the Tories*, Fourth Estate: London. (Chapter XI gives a balanced account of what is still a contentious area: the conduct of industrial policy by the Conservative government of 1970–74.)

BIBLIOGRAPHY

Brodie, D. (2003) *A History of British Labour Law 1867–1945*, Hart Publishing: Oxford.

Burton, M. (2005) 'The Employment Appeal Tribunal: October 2002–July 2005', 34 ILJ 273.

Davies, P. and Freedland, M. (1993) *Labour Legislation and Public Policy*, Oxford University Press: Oxford.

Deakin, S. (2006) 'The Comparative Evolution of Employment' in G. Davidov and B. Langille (eds) *Boundaries and Frontiers of Labour Law*, Hart Publishing: Oxford.

Estricher, S. (1996) 'Labor and Employment Law' in A. Morrison (ed.) *Fundamentals of American Law*, Oxford University Press: Oxford.

Hennessey, P. (1992) *Never Again. Britain 1945–1951*, Jonathan Cape: London.

Hepple, B. and Morris, G. (2002) 'The Employment Act 2002 and the Crisis of Individual Employment Rights', 31 ILJ 245.

Kahn-Freund, O. (1954) 'Legal Framework' in A. Flanders and W. Clegg (eds) *The System of Industrial Relations in Great Britain*, Oxford University Press: Oxford.

Roberts, A. (1994) *Eminent Churchillians*, Weidenfel & Nicolson: London. (See especially Chapter Five – 'Walter Monckton and the Retreat from Reality'.)

For further resources and updates please go to the Companion Website accompanying this book at **www.mylawchamber.co.uk/duddingtonemployment**

Claim Form Application

1 Your details

1.1 Title: Mr ☐ Mrs ☐ Miss ☐ Ms ☐ Other ☐

1.2* First name (or names):

1.3* Surname or family name:

1.4 Date of birth (date/month/year): D D - M M - Y Y Y Y Are you: male? ☐ female? ☐

1.5* Address: Number or Name

Street

+ Town/City

County

Postcode

1.6 Phone number **(where we can contact you during normal working hours)**:

1.7 How would you prefer us to communicate with you? E-mail ☐ Post ☐ Fax ☐
(Please tick only one box)

E-mail address:

@

Fax number:

2 Respondent's details

2.1* Give the name of your employer or the organisation you are claiming against.

2.2* Address: Number or Name

Street

Town/City

+ County

Postcode

Phone number:

2.3 If you worked at an address different from the one you have given at 2.2, please give the full address and postcode.

Postcode

Phone number:

2.4● If your complaint is against more than one respondent please give the names, addresses and postcodes of additional respondents.

1

The context of employment law and its institutions

3 Action before making a claim

3.1* Are you, or were you, an employee of the respondent? Yes ☐ No ☐
If 'Yes', please now go straight to section 3.3.

3.2 Are you, or were you, a worker providing services to the respondent? Yes ☐ No ☐
If 'Yes', please now go straight to section 4.
If 'No', please now go straight to section 6.

3.3● Is your claim, or part of it, about a dismissal by the respondent? Yes ☐ No ☐
If 'No', please now go straight to section 3.5.
If your claim is about constructive dismissal, i.e. you resigned because of something
your employer did or failed to do which made you feel you could no longer continue to
work for them, tick the box here **and** the 'Yes' box in section 3.4. ☐

3.4● Is your claim about anything else, in addition to the dismissal? Yes ☐ No ☐
If 'No', please now go straight to section 4.
If 'Yes', please answer questions 3.5 to 3.7 about the
non-dismissal aspects of your claim.

3.5● Have you put your complaint(s) in writing to the respondent?

Yes ☐ Please give the date you put it to them in writing. ☐☐-☐☐-☐☐☐☐

No ☐

If 'No', please now go straight to section 3.7.

3.6● Did you allow at least 28 days between the date you put your Yes ☐ No ☐
complaint in writing to the respondent and the date you sent us this claim?
If 'Yes', please now go straight to section 4.

3.7● Please explain why you did not put your complaint in writing to the respondent or,
if you did, why you did not allow at least 28 days before sending us your claim.
(In most cases, it is a legal requirement to take these procedural steps. Your claim
will not be accepted unless you give a valid reason why you did not have to meet
the requirement in your case. If you are not sure, you may want to get legal advice.)

4   Employment details

4.1   Please give the following information if possible.

When did your employment start?   D D - M M - Y Y Y Y

When did or will it end?   D D - M M - Y Y Y Y

Is your employment continuing?   Yes ☐   No ☐

4.2   Please say what job you do or did.

4.3   How many hours do or did you work each week?   ☐☐☐   hours each week

4.4   How much are or were you paid?

Pay before tax   £ ☐☐☐,☐☐☐.00   Hourly ☐

Normal take-home pay (including   £ ☐☐☐,☐☐☐.00   Weekly ☐
overtime, commission, bonuses and so on)   Monthly ☐
   Yearly ☐

4.5   If your employment has ended, did you work   Yes ☐   No ☐
(or were you paid for) a period of notice?

If 'Yes', how many weeks or months did   ☐☐☐ weeks   ☐☐ months
you work or were you paid for?

5   Unfair dismissal or constructive dismissal

Please fill in this section only if you believe you have been unfairly or constructively dismissed.

5.1 • If you were dismissed by your employer, you should explain why you think your dismissal
was unfair. If you resigned because of something your employer did or failed to do which
made you feel you could no longer continue to work for them (constructive dismissal)
you should explain what happened.

1

The context of employment law and its institutions

5 Unfair dismissal or constructive dismissal continued

5.1 continued

5.2 Were you in your employer's pension scheme? Yes ☐ No ☐

5.3 If you received any other benefits from your employer, please give details.

5.4 Since leaving your employment have you got another job? Yes ☐ No ☐
If 'No', please now go straight to section 5.7.

5.5 Please say when you started (or will start) work.

5.6 Please say how much you are now earning (or will earn). £ ☐☐☐ , ☐☐ .00 each ☐

5.7 Please tick the box to say what you want if your case is successful:

a To get your old job back and compensation (reinstatement) ☐

b To get another job with the same employer and compensation (re-engagement) ☐

c Compensation only ☐

6   Discrimination

Please fill in this section only if you believe you have been discriminated against.

6.1 ● Please tick the box or boxes to indicate what discrimination (including victimisation) you are complaining about:

Sex (including equal pay) ☐   Race ☐

Disability ☐   Religion or belief ☐

Sexual orientation ☐   Age ☐

6.2 ● Please describe the incidents which you believe amounted to discrimination, the dates of these incidents and the people involved.

The context of employment law and its institutions

1

7 Redundancy payments

Please fill in this section only if you believe you are owed a redundancy payment.

7.1 Please explain why you believe you are entitled to this payment and set out the steps you have taken to get it.

8 Other payments you are owed

Please fill in this section only if you believe you are owed other payments.

8.1 Please tick the box or boxes to indicate that money is owed to you for:

unpaid wages?

holiday pay?

notice pay?

other unpaid amounts?

8.2 How much are you claiming? £   ,   .00

Is this: before tax?   after tax?

8.3 Please explain why you believe you are entitled to this payment. If you have specified an amount, please set out how you have worked this out.

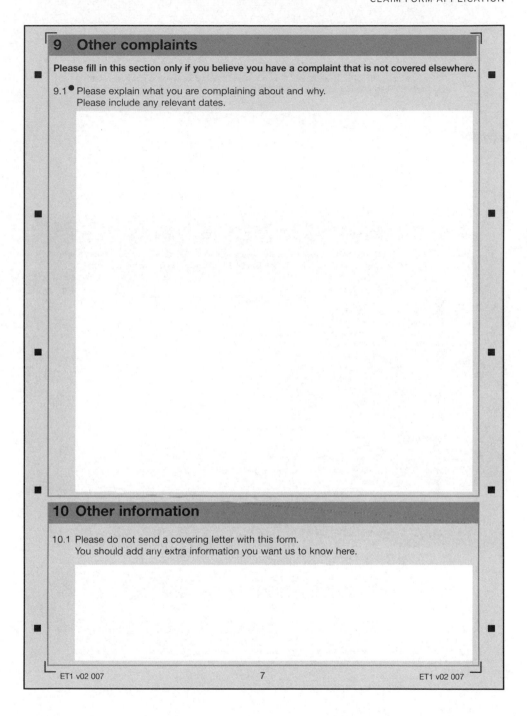

9 Other complaints

Please fill in this section only if you believe you have a complaint that is not covered elsewhere.

9.1 Please explain what you are complaining about and why.
Please include any relevant dates.

10 Other information

10.1 Please do not send a covering letter with this form.
You should add any extra information you want us to know here.

1

The context of employment law and its institutions

11 Disability

11.1 Please tick this box if you consider yourself to have a disability   Yes ☐   No ☐
If 'Yes', please say what this disability is and tell us what assistance, if any, you will need as your claim progresses through the system.

12 Your representative

Please fill in this section only if you have appointed a representative. If you do fill this section in, we will in future only send correspondence to your representative and not to you.

12.1 Representative's name:

12.2 Name of the representative's organisation:

12.3 Address:
+   Number or Name
   Street
   Town/City
   County
   Postcode

12.4 Phone number:

12.5 Reference:

12.6 How would you prefer us to communicate with them? (Please tick only one box)   Post ☐   Fax ☐   E-mail ☐
   Fax number:
   E-mail address: @

13 Multiple cases

13.1 To your knowledge, is your claim one of a number of claims arising from the same or similar circumstances?   Yes ☐   No ☐

Please sign and date here

Signature: Date: D D - M M - Y Y Y Y

ET1 v02 008   8   ET1 v02 008

Source: Employment Tribunals Service

Response Form Application

Case number: ☐☐☐☐☐☐☐☐☐☐☐

1 Name of respondent company or organisation

1.1* Name of your organisation:

Contact name:

1.2* Address   Number or Name

Street

Town/City

+   County

Postcode

1.3 Phone number:

1.4 How would you prefer us to   E-mail ☐   Post ☐   Fax ☐
communicate with you? (Please tick only one box)

    E-mail address:

         @

    Fax number:

1.5 What does this organisation mainly make or do?

1.6 How many people does this organisation employ in Great Britain?

1.7 Does this organisation have more than one site in Great Britain?   Yes ☐   No ☐

1.8 If 'Yes', how many people are employed at the place where the claimant worked?

2 Action before a claim

2.1 Is, or was, the claimant an employee?   Yes ☐   No ☐
If 'Yes', please now go straight to section 2.3.

2.2 Is, or was, the claimant a worker providing services to you?   Yes ☐   No ☐
If 'Yes', please now go straight to section 3.
If 'No', please now go straight to section 5.

2.3 If the claim, or part of it, is about a dismissal,   Yes ☐   No ☐
do you agree that the claimant was dismissed?
If 'Yes', please now go straight to section 2.6.

2.4 If the claim includes something **other than** dismissal,   Yes ☐   No ☐
does it relate to an action you took on
grounds of the claimant's conduct or capability?
If 'Yes', please now go straight to section 2.6.

2.5 Has the substance of this claim been raised by the claimant   Yes ☐   No ☐
in writing under a grievance procedure?

2.6 If 'Yes', please explain below what stage you have reached in the dismissal and disciplinary
procedure or grievance procedure (whichever is applicable).
If 'No' and the claimant says they have raised a grievance with you in writing, please say
whether you received it and explain why you did not accept this as a grievance.

1

The context of employment law and its institutions

3 Employment details

3.1 Are the dates of employment given by the claimant correct?   Yes ☐   No ☐
If 'Yes', please now go straight to section 3.3.

3.2 If 'No', please give dates and say why you disagree with the dates given by the claimant.

When their employment started   D D - M M - Y Y Y Y

When their employment ended or will end   D D - M M - Y Y Y Y

Is their employment continuing?   Yes ☐   No ☐

I disagree with the dates for the following reasons.

3.3 Is the claimant's description of their job or job title correct?   Yes ☐   No ☐
If 'Yes', please now go straight to section 3.5.

3.4 If 'No', please give the details you believe to be correct below.

3.5 Is the information given by the claimant correct about being   Yes ☐   No ☐
paid for, or working, a period of notice?
If 'Yes', please now go straight to section 3.7.

3.6 If 'No', please give the details you believe to be correct below. If you gave them no notice or
didn't pay them instead of letting them work their notice, please explain what happened and why.

3.7 Are the claimant's hours of work correct?   Yes ☐   No ☐
If 'Yes', please now go straight to section 3.9.

3.8 If 'No', please enter the details you believe to be correct.   ☐☐☐ hours each week

3.9 Are the earnings details given by the claimant correct?   Yes ☐   No ☐
If 'Yes', please now go straight to section 4.

3.10 If 'No', please give the details you believe to be correct below.

		Hourly ☐
Pay before tax	£ ☐☐☐ , ☐☐☐ .00	Weekly ☐
Normal take-home pay (including overtime,	£ ☐☐☐ , ☐☐☐ .00	Monthly ☐
commission, bonuses and so on)		Yearly ☐

4 Unfair dismissal or constructive dismissal

4.1 Are the details about pension and other benefits given by the claimant correct? **If 'Yes', please now go straight to section 5.**

Yes ☐   No ☐

4.2 If 'No', please give the details you believe to be correct below.

5 Response

5.1* Do you resist the claim? **If 'No', please now go straight to section 6.**

Yes ☐   No ☐

5.2● If 'Yes', please set out in full the grounds on which you resist the claim.

1

The context of employment law and its institutions

6 Other information

6.1 Please do not send a covering letter with this form. You should add any extra information you want us to know here.

7 Your representative   If you have a representative, please fill in the following.

7.1 Representative's name:

7.2 Name of the representative's organisation:

7.3 Address

+

    Number or Name

    Street

    Town/City

    County

    Postcode

7.4 Phone number:

7.5 Reference:

7.6 How would you prefer us to communicate with them? (Please tick only one box)

    E-mail ☐   Post ☐   Fax ☐

    E-mail address:

    @

    Fax number:

Please sign and date here

Signature: Date: D D M M Y Y Y Y

Data Protection Act 1998. We will send a copy of this form to the claimant and Acas. We will put some of the information you give us on this form onto a computer. This helps us to monitor progress and produce statistics. Information provided on this form is passed to the Department of Trade and Industry to assist research into the use and effectiveness of Employment Tribunals.

ET3 v02 004 URN 05/1442   4   ET3 v02 004 URN 05/1442

Source: Employment Tribunals Service

2

The impact of European Union law and International Labour Standards

EUROPEAN UNION LAW

Introduction

The significance of EU law can be best appreciated by use of the following example, which is based on the case of *Macarthays Ltd* v *Smith* (1980).

Example

Tom, a man, was employed as the manager of a warehouse stockroom at a wage of about £60 per week. He left in October 1975. Four months later, Iris, a woman, was appointed to what was really the same post but on a wage of £50 per week. Could Iris claim equal pay with Tom?

As we shall see in Chapter 9, the Equal Pay Act 1970 gives a right to equal pay for 'like work'. The work of Iris was certainly 'like work' to that done by Tom but the problem was that they were not working at the same time. The Court of Appeal held that the Equal Pay Act did not cover this situation and, had this been the only legal authority, Iris would have lost her claim.

However, the European Court of Justice (ECJ) held that what was Article 119 of the EC Treaties (now Article 141) covered a situation where a woman received less pay than a man who had *previously* worked for the same employer and where they both did equal work. Accordingly, the Court of Appeal decided the case in accordance with the ruling of the ECJ and Iris eventually succeeded in her claim.

This example illustrates the following points:

1 The supremacy of EU law over national law. Where, as here, there is a conflict between the two, then national law must give way. This principle is given statutory force in the UK by s 2 of the European Communities Act 1972. The difference between this straightforward principle and the complex way in which the European Convention on Human Rights is given effect in UK law, as described in the next chapter, is striking.

2 The fact that the basic principles of EU law are derived from the EU Treaties, as explained below.

3 The relationship between national courts and the ECJ. Where, as here, a national court has a case turning on the interpretation of the EU Treaties then, under Article 234 (formerly 177) of the EU Treaty, the national court may refer the question to the ECJ and the national court must then decide the case in accordance with the interpretation given by the ECJ. This is what happened in the above case.

4 The fact that EU law, like continental legal systems, works in broader concepts than UK law. Under Article 119 (now 141) of the EU Treaty, the term used is 'equal work', whereas the Equal Pay Act used the term 'like work', which, as we shall see in Chapter 9, is a rather more technical term.

EU law has had a considerable effect on UK employment law and this is growing. This chapter will first look at the sources of EU law and will then consider the general thrust of EU employment law. Detailed accounts of the impact of EU law will be found in chapters dealing with particular topics.

Sources of EU law

1 The EU Treaties. These are the primary sources of EU law and include the Treaty of Rome (1957), the Maastricht Treaty (1992) and the Treaty of Amsterdam (1997). (More detail about these treaties can be found below.) The treaties provide a framework within which legislation can be implemented.

2 EU Regulations. These are automatically binding in all Member States of the European Union and, in contrast with Directives (see below), they become law without the need for any intervention by Member States, which are effectively bypassed.

3 EU Directives. These lay down particular objectives to be achieved but, in contrast to Regulations, they leave it to Member States to decide how actually to implement them. A good example is the Working Time Directive, which was implemented in the UK by the Working Time Regulations 1998 and 1999. Another is the Framework Directive (2000), under which Member States must introduce legislation prohibiting discrimination on grounds which went further than, for example, existing UK legislation by including age, sexual orientation and religion or belief.

4 EU Decisions. These are addressed to individual Member States, individuals or organisations and are binding on those to whom they are addressed. Examples are decisions on whether proposed mergers are permitted.

The extent to which EU law is binding on individuals and can be relied on by them

In some cases EU law has direct effect in Member States. This means that it can be relied on by individuals. The doctrine of direct effect was developed by the ECJ and is not found in the Treaty itself. A provision will have direct effect if it is clear and unambiguous, unconditional and needs no further action by the European Union itself or national states to come into force beyond implementation by the state. Where a Treaty provision has direct effect, then this means that it can be relied on by individuals both vertically (in actions against the state and organs of the state) and horizontally (in actions against other individuals). A provision in a Directive which has direct effect only has vertical direct effect and cannot be relied on in actions against other individuals.

A good example of direct effect of a Treaty provision in employment law is Article 141, giving the right to equal pay for equal work, dealt with in Chapter 9, and which has had a great influence in moving UK law forward in this area. An example of the direct effect of a Directive is *Marshall* v *Southampton and South West Hampshire AHA* (1986), where the ECJ ruled that different retirement ages for women (60) and men (65) were sexually discriminatory and in breach of the Equal Treatment Directive (76/207), which could be relied on as the health authority was an emanation of the state. The significance of the case was that the relevant UK law, the Sex Discrimination Act 1975, did not, by s 6(4), apply to provisions in relation to retirement. The effect was that, as the Directive had no direct effect horizontally, those who worked for the state or emanations of it were able to rely on this ruling but it had no effect in relation to private employers. This unsatisfactory state of affairs had to be put right and this was done by the Sex Discrimination Act 1986, under which differential retirement ages in all employment was brought within the scope of the sex discrimination legislation.

Where EU law does not have direct effect, it may have indirect effect, which means that the courts will interpret national legislation so as to give effect where possible to the provisions of EU law. A good example is the attitude of the courts to the interpretation of the Transfer of Undertakings (Protection of Employment) Regulations (TUPE) and an instance in this context is the decision of the House of Lords in *Litster* v *Forth Dry Dock and Engineering Co. Ltd* (1989), discussed in Chapter 12. The object of these regulations (which are now contained in similar ones made in 2006) is to transfer the contracts of employment of employees, when an undertaking is transferred, to the transferee (i.e. the new owner). However, the 1981 Regulations only applied where the employees were employed immediately before the transfer. Thus in *Litster* the transferor employer simply dismissed all of the relevant employees one hour before the transfer. If this had been effective the regulations could have been avoided very easily. The House of Lords, however, held that the regulations applied where the 'employees would have been employed if they had not been unfairly dismissed' and so closed a loophole in the wording to make the regulations give effect to the Directive. (It is worth noting that the 2006 Regulations are worded to include provision for what happened in *Litster* and so this interpretation by the courts would not have been necessary today.)

The EU and employment law

The European Union has its genesis in three treaties which were all broadly economic in effect, and which formed the European Coal and Steel Community, Euratom and the European Economic Community, which is now known as the European Union. This point is important, as it shows that EU intervention in social affairs, such as the details of the employment relationship, was not one of the original concerns of the EU. The first piece of EU legislation to have an impact on employment law was Article 119 (discussed above). This was followed by the Equal Treatment Directive of 1976, which established the principle of equal treatment for men and women which meant that, in the words of the Directive, 'there shall be no discrimination whatsoever on grounds of sex' (see Chapter 9). A year later, in 1977, the Acquired Rights Directive gave rights to workers when the ownership of the undertaking which employed them was transferred. These rights were implemented in the UK by the Transfer of Undertakings (Protection of Employment) Regulations 1981 (see Chapter 12). In 1986 the Single European Act inserted a new Article 118a into the Treaty (now Article 137), which provides that Member States must pay particular attention to encouraging improvements in the health and safety of workers. What was also significant was that Article 118a provided for qualified majority voting on its implementation, which meant that individual states, and especially, as it turned out, the UK, could not veto them. This was followed by a number of health and safety Directives, the most important being the Framework Directive of 1989 (see Chapter 8).

Much greater impetus to EU regulation of the employment relationship was given by the adoption in 1989 by 11 Member States (not including the UK) of a Social Charter, which was followed by an Agreement on Social Policy in the form of a Protocol attached to the Maastricht Treaty of 1992. The reason for the Protocol was that the UK government had vetoed the inclusion of the so-called Social Charter in the Treaty itself. This meant that social policy was now firmly at the forefront of EU strategies and in 1997 the incoming Labour government in the UK indicated that it wished to opt into the Agreement on Social Policy. Accordingly, the Treaty of Amsterdam of 1997 incorporated most of the Agreement on Social Policy into the EU Treaty itself, in Articles 136–145. A new Framework Directive on Equal Treatment was agreed in 2000 and a Directive on Rights for Workers Employed on Fixed Term Contracts was agreed in 1999 (99/70). Indeed, it can almost be said that the main impetus today for change in employment law comes from the European Union.

LAW IN CONTEXT
British governments and EU legislation: the Working Time Directive

The origin of legislation on working time is found in a Directive (93/104) adopted on 23 November 1993. The interesting point is that the legal basis of the Directive was Article 118a of the EU Treaty, which requires Member States to pay particular attention to encouraging improvements, especially in the working environment, as regards the health and safety of workers. The linkage between working time and health and safety was crucial because Article 118a (now consolidated in Article 137) gives power to adopt measures to improve the working environment in connection with health and safety by qualified majority voting. Thus there was, according to the Commission, no need for a unanimous vote and the Directive could come into operation without the approval of the then UK (Conservative) government. The UK government did not agree and felt that, as the connection between working time and health and safety was tenuous to say the least, a unanimous vote was required. However, in *UK v EU Council (Working Time)* (1996) the ECJ upheld the view of the Commission that the Directive could be a health and safety measure and in any event the incoming Labour government of 1997 was prepared to adopt the Directive.

INTERNATIONAL LABOUR STANDARDS

The International Labour Organization (ILO) has the general role of promoting fair employment conditions in all member countries, of which there are around 300. It was established in 1919 and now operates as the specialised agency of the United Nations in promoting social justice and human and labour rights. It has so far produced a total of 183 Conventions setting minimum standards on, for example, the right of free association (e.g. right to join a trade union), equal opportunities and hours of work. Although valuable, they are of limited use, as they are not binding on states and can be denounced even when ratified. The UK has ratified 83 Conventions but the Conservative government of 1979–97 denounced some, including the minimum wage fixing machinery. Indeed, a total of 17 Conventions previously ratified have been denounced. However, their effectiveness should not be underestimated, as, for example, Convention No. 100 of 1951 on equal opportunities was taken into account when the Equal Pay Act 1970 was being framed (see Chapter 9). In addition, the ILO provides training and advisory services to both employers' and workers' associations and is generally active in the field of labour relations.

SUMMARY

The theme of this chapter is the impact of International Labour Standards on employment law. This is developed by looking at:

- **European Union law.** Here the object is not to deal in detail with all the ways in which EU law does so, as this is described in appropriate places in the book, but instead to look at the sources of EU law so that readers are clear, in particular, what the terms 'regulations' and 'directives' mean in the context of EU law. This links to the question of precisely how EU law is incorporated into UK law and the development of EU employment law.
- **The International Labour Organization (ILO).** It is noted that this body produces Conventions and examples are given. As with EU law, some actual instances of the impact of the work of the ILO are incorporated into the appropriate chapters.

QUESTION

Select one or more of the following areas of law which are dealt with in this book: discrimination; transfer of undertakings; right to engage in collective action. Estimate the extent to which it has been influenced by European Union law and, in your answer, consider what the position would have been if European Union law had not had an effect.

(You will be able to tackle this when you have read the relevant chapters.)

FURTHER READING

Barnard, C. (2006) *EC Employment Law* (3rd edn), Oxford University Press: Oxford. The standard work.

Bercusson, B. (2006) *European Labour Law* (2nd edn), Cambridge University Press: Cambridge. This is a most valuable book which contains a great deal of background material.

 For further resources and updates please go to the Companion Website accompanying this book at **www.mylawchamber.co.uk/duddingtonemployment**

The impact of human rights law

INTRODUCTION

The European Convention on Human Rights (ECHR) has already had an impact on employment law through its incorporation into UK law by the Human Rights Act 1998 (HRA 1998). However, although this chapter is mainly concerned with the detailed impact of the HRA 1998 on employment law it would be wrong to view the impact of human rights on employment or on any other aspect of law purely through the prism of this Act. The development of the notion of universal human rights and the actual application of the general principles of human rights to particular situations is one of the most significant developments since the end of the Second World War. Thus it is worth pausing to note both the context in which the HRA 1998 operates and the main issues in the ongoing debate on human rights.

LAW IN CONTEXT

Mahoney, writing from the perspective of a philosopher (2006, page x) says: 'The emergence of human rights into human ethical consciousness and their development and now worldwide recognition constitute a moral phenomenon of astonishing scale and unparalleled significance'. The modern idea of human rights dates from the seventeenth and eighteenth centuries but for our purposes the first major events occurred in the years immediately after the end of the Second World War when there was a desire to prevent the horrors which had been endured by the human race in two world wars. Thus one of the first tasks of the newly formed United Nations was to adopt the Universal Declaration on Human Rights in 1948. Although this is not a binding legal document the very fact that there was now a statement of basic human rights gave a vital initial impetus to developments. Two years later, in 1950, the members of the Council of Europe signed a European Convention on Human Rights and the European Court of Human Rights (ECtHR) was established in 1959. The ECHR itself came into effect on 3 September 1953. The mechanism adopted was for countries to sign the Convention as such and to ratify articles of it. Although the UK signed the ECHR in 1950 it did not accept the jurisdiction of the ECtHR until 1966, and only then did the UK accept the right of individual UK citizens to petition the court direct. From 1966 until the Human Rights Act 1998 came into force on 2 October 2000, the UK was in a kind of limbo: whilst it had signed the ECHR and accepted that individuals could

→

petition the ECtHR, the Convention was not actually part of UK law. Therefore, the ECtHR could, and did, rule that the UK was in breach of the Convention but the UK government was not legally obliged to take any notice. It is noteworthy that the Maastricht Treaty of 1992 expressly linked the European Union to the ECHR by providing that the Union must 'respect fundamental rights, as guaranteed by the European Convention for the Protection of Human Rights and Fundamental Freedoms'.

The fact that the ECHR was drafted in the immediate post-war years inevitably means that it emphasised civil and political rights rather than social and economic ones and this is also true of the UN Declaration. The result is that the ECHR says relatively little about employment rights directly and instead its impact on employment law is through the application of particular Articles to employment situations. Indeed the stated reason why the Russian Delegation did not sign the UN Declaration was that it did not say enough on economic, social and cultural rights (Mahoney, 2006, page 50, quoting Roosevelt, 1992). This point is dealt with in more detail below but it is worth, by contrast, examining a more modern statement of human rights contained in the European Union's Charter of Fundamental Rights signed at Nice in 2000 and which is included in the draft Treaty for Establishing a Constitution for Europe. Although there is no immediate prospect of this treaty being brought into force, a glance at those parts of the Charter dealing with employment rights illustrates how far the concept of human rights has moved since the immediate post-war years.

Article 21 of Chapter III (Equality) is worth quoting in full as it prohibits discrimination on grounds which are wider than those in UK or EU law. It prohibits discrimination based on any ground such as sex, race, colour, ethnic or social origin, genetic features, language, religion or belief, political or any other opinion, membership of a national minority, property, birth, disability, age or sexual orientation. Article 23 specifically requires equality between men and women in all areas including employment, work and pay. Chapter IV (Solidarity) contains articles giving workers: the rights to information and consultation within the undertaking (Art 27); the right of collective bargaining and action (Art 28); protection in the event of unjustified dismissal (Art 30); fair and just working conditions including limitation of maximum working hours, daily and weekly rest periods and paid leave (Art 31); rights to paid maternity leave and parental leave and protection from dismissal (Art 33). If the Charter ever became part of UK law in the way the ECHR is then its impact on UK employment law, and especially discrimination law, could be significant. The chances of its becoming part of UK law depend largely on whether the European Constitution is adopted by the EU, which at present seems some way off although there is nothing to stop the UK from simply adopting the Charter without the Constitution.

THE EUROPEAN CONVENTION ON HUMAN RIGHTS

The effect of the Human Rights Act 1998 has been to incorporate most, but not all, of the Convention into UK law. It would be wrong, however, to say that it is part of UK law in the same way as, for example, the Employment Rights Act 1996 is, because:

1 Not all of the ECHR has been incorporated into UK law by the Human Rights Act. Articles 2–12 and 14 have been incorporated and Articles 1–3 of the First Protocol and Articles 1 and 2 of the Sixth Protocol. (Protocols are simply additions to the Convention.)

2 The way in which the ECHR is part of UK law is not straightforward, as explained below.

3 It is possible for states to enter reservations to the Convention. The concept of a reservation means that the state reserves laws or policies so that they cannot be challenged under the Convention.

4 It is also possible, under Article 15, for states to derogate from the ECHR in times of war or public emergency. The UK government has used this in relation to Northern Ireland.

THE ARTICLES OF THE ECHR

Although employment law is affected by only certain articles of the Convention, readers may find it useful to have a summary of all the topics covered by the articles so as to have an idea of the scope of the Convention. They are as follows:

Article 2: Right to life
Article 3: Prohibition of torture
Article 4: Prohibition of forced labour
Article 5: Right to liberty and security
Article 6: Right to a fair trial
Article 7: No punishment without law
Article 8: Right to respect for private and family life
Article 9: Freedom of thought, conscience and religion
Article 10: Freedom of expression
Article 11: Freedom of assembly and association
Article 12: Right to marry
Article 13: Right to an effective remedy
Article 14: Prohibition of discrimination in the exercise of Convention rights.

Furthermore, the Protocols deal with:

Protocol One, Article 1: Protection of property
Protocol One, Article 2: Right to education
Protocol One, Article 3: Right to free elections
Protocol Six: Abolition of the death penalty.

All of the articles are incorporated into UK law by Schedule 1 to the Human Rights Act, with the exception of Article 13. A striking feature, as mentioned above, is the extent to which the articles reflect the prevailing ethos of the post-war period, with the emphasis on political rights and with the need to protect from tyranny very much in mind. What is missing is any clear statement of social and economic rights, such as a right to work, for example, and this inevitably means, as will be seen, that none of the articles deals directly with employment matters. Article 14 might be thought to have a direct bearing on employment law, but this is not so. It does not prohibit discrimination as such but only discrimination in the exercise of Convention rights. This is important, as the article goes much further than UK law does at present because it applies to discrimination not only on the grounds of sex and race but also on grounds of, for example, political or other opinion. However, Article 14 is only internal to the Convention. For example, if the right to education in Protocol One, Article 2 was denied on any of the grounds set out in Article 14, then there would be a breach of the Convention. However, Article 14 does not directly prohibit discrimination in employment on the grounds it sets out. (This topic is considered further in Chapter 9.)

SCOPE OF THE ECHR UNDER THE HUMAN RIGHTS ACT 1998

The Human Rights Act *does not* simply provide that the ECHR has effect in the same way as a statute. Therefore, a person cannot just say that, as their rights under the ECHR have been broken, they are entitled to a remedy and leave it at that. Nor is it true to say that the ECHR is a kind of higher law, as EC law has become, so that any law in conflict with the ECHR is void. This is not so. The position is as follows:

1 All courts and tribunals must take account, where relevant to proceedings before them, of decisions of the ECtHR and its organs (s 2) (see below).

2 So far as is possible, all legislation, whether existing or future, must be read and given effect to in a way which is consistent with the rights in the Convention (s 3).

3 If it is not possible to read primary legislation in a way that gives effect to the Convention, then the High Court or a superior court has the power to declare that a specific provision in an Act is incompatible with the Convention, but such a declaration does not affect the continued operation of that provision (ss 4–5).

4 It is unlawful for a public authority to act in a way which is incompatible with a Convention right unless it could not have acted differently. Public authorities are broadly defined and include not only courts and tribunals but also private persons when exercising functions of a public nature (s 6). Accordingly, s 7 creates a new right, directly enforceable against public bodies, under which it will be a cause of action against them that they have failed to act compatibly with the Convention. However, this will not apply to purely private bodies or to private individuals. A public body is merely defined as a body which exercises public functions (s 6(3)(b)), which is not enlightening, but it is clear that central and local government are public bodies and therefore when acting as employers will be directly subject to the ECHR. Bodies which undertake the functions of the state, such as ACAS and NHS trusts, are also public and so are bodies set up by statute, such as many colleges and universities. In addition, a private employer will cross over and become a public body when it performs public functions. In the House of Lords' debates on the Human Rights Bill, the Lord Chancellor, Lord Irvine, gave as examples where a private security company is engaged to manage security at prisons and where doctors

who work for the NHS also take private patients. Where the security firm is managing the prison and where doctors are working for the NHS, they will be public authorities.

5 When considering whether a state is in breach of the Convention, the courts allow it a 'margin of appreciation' whereby the court should give a certain amount of discretion to the state in achieving its particular policy goals.

Example

Article 11 of the Convention gives the right to form and join trade unions. The UK Parliament passes the (fictitious) Abolition of Trade Unions Act, which prohibits the formation of trade unions. This is obviously contrary to the Convention but the Act is not invalid for this reason. If a prosecution was brought for forming a trade union then the court would make a declaration that the Act was incompatible with the Convention (see point 3 above). It would be up to the government to decide whether or not to ignore this declaration. Clearly, the thinking is that the force of public opinion will in many cases make it difficult for a government to ignore a ruling that it has acted in breach of the Convention.

Example

The UK Parliament passes the (fictitious) Derecognition of Trade Unions Act, under which the recognition provisions of the Employment Relations Act 1999 are abolished. A union complains that the government has refused to recognise it for collective bargaining purposes and that the Act is in breach of Article 11. The union may make a direct complaint against the government as a public body (see point 4 above) but it will almost certainly lose the action, as the ECtHR decided in *National Union of Belgian Police* v *Belgium* (1979) that the right to form trade unions did include the right to be recognised. It is this type of case which is most common where the allegation is not that the statute is directly contradictory to the Convention but that the Convention should be interpreted so that it includes a particular right which the statute infringes.

RELEVANCE OF THE ECHR TO EMPLOYMENT LAW

Although the impact of the ECHR will be examined in detail in the context of individual chapters, the following is an indication of the main areas in which the ECHR has had, or may have, an impact on employment law. It is emphasised that the cases mentioned here are not the only ones where the ECHR has been involved but merely examples. Others are noted in the relevant part of the book.

Article 5 (right to liberty and security)

The argument that a negligent reference could be a breach of Article 5 of the ECHR was raised in *Griffiths* v *Newport Borough Council* (2001) where it was argued that

3

The impact of human rights law

the breach would consist in affecting the employee's security of work. The Court of Appeal did not, however, accept that the terms of Article 5 were applicable (see further Chapter 5 where the possible applicability of other Articles to the giving of reference is discussed).

◾ Article 6 (right to a fair trial)

This affects the procedures of employment tribunals and will have an impact on disciplinary proceedings, as the word 'trial' includes hearings that can determine civil rights or obligations. Thus, where a public authority conducts a hearing, Article 6 will be applicable if that hearing can result in a decision such as suspension or dismissal. If the proceedings are simply investigatory, then Article 6 will not be applicable. An allegation that Article 6 has been broken can be made in judicial review proceedings or the fact of the alleged breach can be relied on in other legal proceedings such as an unfair dismissal claim. Where the employer concerned is a private employer then Article 6 will have relevance only where a statutory provision is relied on which may be alleged to be in breach of the ECHR. The great difference is that it will not be possible to allege that internal disciplinary proceedings conducted by a private employer are illegal because of a breach of Article 6. However, professional disciplinary bodies such as the General Medical Council (*Wickramsinghe* v *UK* (1998)) have been held to come within the scope of Article 6.

◾ Article 8 (right to respect for family and private life)

Article 8 will have an impact on interception of employees' communications and on data protection (see Chapter 5). It may also affect disciplinary proceedings and decisions to dismiss where the private life of the employee is an issue. A good example is *Treganowan* v *Robert Knee* (see Chapter 11).

◾ Article 9 (freedom of thought, conscience and religion)

Article 9 could be relevant where the employer requires employees to hold certain religious beliefs. This is very relevant to Church of England and Roman Catholic Schools, which normally require applicants for teaching posts to be practising members of their faith. Regulation 7(2) and (3) of the Religion or Belief Regulations 2003 expressly allows discrimination on the ground of religion where this is a genuine occupational requirement and so probably meets any possible challenge under this article.

A good example of the application of Article 9 is *Ahmad* v *UK* (1981), where a Muslim teacher wished to have time off to pray at his mosque every Friday but his employer refused. The ECtHR held that Article 9 was not infringed as he had voluntarily accepted a teaching post which prevented his attending prayers; he had not requested time off during his first six years' employment, which could imply that the right to have time off for this purpose was not particularly important to him.

Article 10 (freedom of expression)

Article 10 could have been invoked by 'whistle-blowers' facing dismissal because they had exposed malpractice within their organisation. However, the Public Interest Disclosure Act 1998 probably gives sufficient protection in these cases. This point is discussed further in Chapter 5.

Article 11 (freedom of assembly and association)

This is the one article that has a direct bearing on employment law, as it is of great significance in the area of collective employment rights. It affects the right to join trade unions and thus the tortuous UK legislative provisions on trade union membership and the rules on industrial action and picketing need to be read in the light of it. The impact of the ECHR in this area is demonstrated by the decisions of the ECtHR in the cases of *Wilson* v *UK* (2002) and *Unison* v *UK* (2002). These are considered in Chapters 13 and 14. Another recent decision where the applicability of Article 11 was raised was *Lee* v *ASLEF* (2004) where the issue was the expulsion from ASLEF of Lee on the ground that he was allegedly a member of the British National Party (BNP) – see also Chapter 13. Another example is *Gate Gourmet London* v *TGWU* (2005) – see Chapter 14, which also involved Article 10.

Article 14 (prohibition of discrimination)

As explained above, Article 14 has an unusual status in that it is internal to the Convention, but many of the areas which it covers are also included in the EC Framework Directive (see Chapter 9).

OTHER INTERNATIONAL STANDARDS

The Conventions adopted by the International Labour Organization (ILO) and which were dealt with in Chapter 2 can also be seen as attempts to embed fundamental principles of human rights into employment law. The link between the ILO and other standards of human rights is brought out in Alston (2005).

SUMMARY

This chapter looks at human rights in employment law both from the general viewpoint and from the specific viewpoint of the incorporation of the ECHR into UK law by the Human Rights Act 1998. It makes the point that the ECHR says relatively little about fundamental social and economic rights and, by way of contrast, considers the provisions in the EU's Charter of Fundamental Rights.

3

The impact of human rights law

QUESTION

Consider the impact which the Human Rights Act 1998 has had on employment law up to the present time and estimate the potential which the Act has to bring about further change. Do you consider that the interests of human rights would be better served if the EU's Charter of Fundamental Rights was incorporated into UK law?

FURTHER READING

Allen, R. and Crasnow, R. (2002) *Employment Law and Human Rights* (1st edn; 2nd edn, with A. Beale, 2007), Oxford University Press: Oxford. A very clear and comprehensive guide.

BIBLIOGRAPHY

Alston, P. (ed.) (2005) *Labour Rights as Human Rights*, Oxford University Press: Oxford. This collection of essays looks at human rights in the context of increasing globalisation of the world economy and considers the contribution and effectiveness of transnational standards such as those in ILO and the ECHR.

Mahoney, J. (2006) *The Challenge of Human Rights*, Blackwell Publishing: Oxford. This is an excellent and up-to-date survey of the whole area from a general philosophical viewpoint.

Roosevelt, E. (1992) *The Autobiography of Eleanor Roosevelt*, Da Capo Press: New York. Deals with Eleanor Roosevelt's contribution to the drafting of the Universal Declaration on Human Rights.

For further resources and updates please go to the Companion Website accompanying this book at **www.mylawchamber.co.uk/duddingtonemployment**

Part 2

The employment relationship

This part is really the heart of this book as it considers the employment relationship when it is actually in place and so looks at, for example, the contract of employment, hours of work and pay, and health and safety at work. Part Three, by contrast, looks at the position when it is terminated. Initially it focuses on the parties to the relationship and looks not only at the question of who is an employee/worker but also that of who is an employer. It then moves on to the actual contract of employment and its terms both express and implied. This material links to that in Part Three as the actual terms are of course relevant in considering if a dismissal is wrongful or unfair. The next two chapters deal with specific areas: payment of wages and health and safety. Finally this part looks at discrimination law and the various laws dealing with what are often known as 'family rights' such as maternity, paternity and adoption leave and pay.

4 The employment relationship

INTRODUCTION

This chapter is concerned with the identification of the different types of dependent labour who may claim rights and be subject to obligations under both common law and under statutory employment law. These may be classed under various heads: employees, workers, casual workers, homeworkers, agency workers and so forth. It is also concerned with the identification of those for whom they work – the employer – and, although most of this chapter is concerned with dependent labour, the question of exactly who the employer is needs discussion too.

EMPLOYERS

Introduction

This chapter is to some extent based on a bilateral model of employment relations. This means that the fundamental idea is that there are two parties: the employer and the employee. It has been argued (for instance by Freedland, 2005) that this is often out of date. One area, which will be dealt with later, is in connection with agency workers, who have a relationship both with the agency and the client, known as the end-user. However, with this exception, the employee side of the relationship is usually an identifiable individual. On the other hand, it may be very difficult to find an individual who can be identified as the employer in the sense that he conducts the whole business and to whom the employee is directly responsible. One particular example of how difficult it can be to identify an employer is found in *Cheng Yuen v Hong Kong Golf Club* (1998) which involved a caddie who worked as a casual worker. It was held that he was employed, not by the club, but by individual club members when they hired him. Another example, which will be discussed later, is the issue of whether ministers of religion should have employment rights. If such rights are conferred, then who will be the employer of the minister? Will it be the bishop or a board of finance or another body?

■ Statutory definition of an employer

This is not by itself enlightening: s 230(4) of the ERA 1996 provides that an employer 'in relation to an employee or worker, means the person by whom the employee or worker is . . . employed'. This, of course, begs the question of precisely who does employ the employee.

The decision as to who is an employer is important in two situations:

1 Legal documents, such as a claim for unfair dismissal, need to be served on an employer. In this case there may be the practical question of who the employer is where the employer cannot be identified from any statement of initial employment particulars or written contract of employment because none was issued. In this case the question of who the employer is will come down to a matter of evidence such as who actually engaged the employee and who paid the wages.

2 Various rights under employment law can be claimed only where the employee has a certain length of continuous employment, such as unfair dismissal (normally one year needed) and redundancy (two years needed). Suppose that an employee has changed employers and wishes to add the length of service with one employer to the length of service with the second? This will depend on whether he can count both employers as associated employers.

Example

Sarah began employment with Y Co. on 1 January 2006. On 1 July 2006 she left Y Co. and went to work for Z Co. On 1 January 2007, Sarah was dismissed by Z Co. She wishes to claim unfair dismissal but she has only six months' service with Z Co. However, if she can add the service with Y Co. to that with Z Co. then she will have a year's service. Y Co. and Z Co. are both subsidiaries of the same holding company, W Co.

The details of how to calculate continuous service will be dealt with in Chapter 6 but the important issue for the present is that if both Y Co. and Z Co. count as associated employers then Sarah will be able to add the service with each of the companies together and she will be able to claim for unfair dismissal. Another instance where the question of associated employers is significant is where a redundant employee is made an offer of suitable alternative employment. As will be seen in Chapter 12, the refusal of such an offer can lead to the employee losing any right to a redundancy payment. Section 146(1) of the ERA 1996 has the effect that such an offer may be made by an associated employer as well as by, of course, the actual employer of the employee.

Associated employers

Section 231 of the ERA 1996 provides that two employers shall be treated as associated if either of the following criteria are met:

(a) one is a company of which the other (directly or indirectly) has control; or

(b) both are companies of which a third person (directly or indirectly) has control.

Three issues arise from this:

■ The concept of an associated employer can arise only when at least one of the employers is a company. This was significant in *Gardiner* v *Merton London Borough Council* (1981), where it was held that s 231 did not include local authorities and thus an employee could not add service with, in this case, four local authorities to enable him to calculate compensation for unfair dismissal by reference to his service with all of them. However, local government employees are deemed to have continuous employment for redundancy purposes when they move from one local authority to another.

■ However, the person who controls the company in situation (a) above need not be a company and could be a natural person, an unincorporated association, a partnership or any other form of organisation.

■ Section 231 provides that the test for deciding if employers are associated depends on whether the one not actually employing the employee has control of the other. In *Secretary of State for Employment* v *Newbold* (1981) it was held that control means voting control and thus a person will be in control and thus an associated employer if they control a majority of the votes carried by the shares. An extension to this was suggested in *Zarb and Samuels* v *British and Brazilian Produce Co. (Sales)* (1978), where the EAT accepted an argument that the word 'control' can include a situation where two or more persons act together and between them own more than 50% of the voting shares. However, in *South West Launderettes* v *Laidler* (1986) the Court of Appeal declined to follow the approach in *Zarb*, although later cases (such as *Tice* v *Cartwright* (1999) – a decision of the EAT) have followed *Zarb*. The matter awaits clarification. What can be said is that the concept of control, by focusing on ownership of shares, is narrow and fails to take account of ventures such as franchising and sub-contracting. Furthermore, one may, in practice, control a company without having a majority of the votes at meetings.

DEPENDENT LABOUR

Setting the scene

The present basis of the law

The employment relationship, as seen from the point of view of the worker, is traditionally seen from the point of view of a personal employment relation between employee and employer giving rise to a contract of employment. Thus s 230(1) of the ERA 1996 defines an employee as an individual who has entered into or works under (or, when the employment has ceased, worked under) a contract of employment. It has, however, been argued that this basis is false for two reasons:

1 It assumes that the dependent employment relationship can be understood in one way, that of the contract of employment. Thus it contrasts with those who do not have a contract of employment, who are known as independent contractors and

4

The employment relationship

who do have employment rights (Freedland, 2006). The problem is that, as this chapter will demonstrate, there are many relationships where the worker does not have a contract of employment but there is still a relationship of dependent labour.

2 The other problem is that it is felt too misleading to describe the relationship between the worker and the employer in terms of contract as the idea of contract implies a bargain between equals. Kahn-Freund (1967), in a well-known passage, said of the contract of employment: 'In its inception it is an act of submission, in its operation it is a condition of subordination, however much the submission and subordination may be concealed by that indispensable figment of the legal mind known as "the contract of employment"'. In effect he argues that the phrase 'contract of employment' disguises the inherent servile status of the worker in relation to the employer. Although it could be said that many other contracts today do not result from freely negotiated agreements the point is that in an employment relationship the worker is in a state of dependence on the employer. This dependence is both economic (the worker needs to work for money) and may also, for example, be social, in that the worker looks on work as a means of making friendships and being in a certain position also gives a status to a person. As a footnote to this discussion see Freedland (2006), drawing on the work of Deakin (1998) who explains that the development of the old master and servant relationship into the contract of employment was in fact the product of welfare legislation enacted after the Second World War.

There is undoubtedly pressure for the law to move forward and to deal fully with the question of employment status. The TUC Congress in 2005 noted that 'the lack of progress in resolving the uncertainty over employment status is a particular concern in industries such as construction, where mass self-employment is still a major problem'. The ETUC adopted a resolution on The Coordination of Collective Bargaining in December 2005 which called on its members to pay special attention to dependent self-employment and estimated that there are almost 23 million bogus self-employed in the EC.

The way forward

The problem can be seen from two angles: the law is working with an outdated concept, that of the contract of employment; and the labour market, in response to both social and economic pressures, is fragmenting into many different types of relationships all with the common thread that they involve dependent labour. Before examining the changes in the labour market it will be helpful to look at the possible solutions to the problem of trying to establish a formula for identifying dependent labour.

There are three possible solutions:

1 To retain the contract of employment as the norm with the result that those who do not fall within it do not receive the benefits of employment protection legislation. This, as Davies (2004) points out, is a solution favoured by neoclassical economists who regard labour rights as a burden on business. There was something of this in the policies of the Conservative government of 1979–97.

2 The employee is thought of as having a status rather than a contract. This is to adopt a rights theory and not regard employment protection rights as based on the notion of a contract of employment but instead a particular status is regarded as conferring rights. This was argued by Hepple (1986) who felt that the basis for employment rights should be a broad-based 'employment relationship' between the worker and the undertaking which employs him. It should be noted that in countries where there is a written constitution which incorporates guarantees of individual rights employment protection is frequently seen in terms of rights. Wedderburn (1991) examines the Italian Workers Statute which guarantees rights, for example, to organise trade unions and to strike. One possibility is that the government could adopt the proposals in *Working Life*, published by the Institute of Employment Rights in 1996, which suggests that what it calls the 'core of rights' in the employment relationship should apply to all who work under a contract to personally execute any work or labour and who are economically dependent on the business of the other. The effect would be to apply the wide definition of an employee/worker (see later in this chapter) to all 'core' employment protection rights. Not only this, but it also proposes that equal treatment legislation and certain collective rights should also apply to those who normally work and to those seeking work.

3 To accept that there is no single category which can cover all the employment relationships which exist today and to adopt a piecemeal approach by identifying different types of dependent workers and conferring a varying degree of employment protection rights on each category. This is the approach of UK law. As a kind of offshoot of this, Freedland (2006) suggests that the notion of the personal work contract or personal work nexus rather than the contract of employment can be seen as an explanatory framework for each personal work contract, a kind of tool box with slots for all the kinds of links and connections which exist in the employment relationship.

In fact, the White Paper *Fairness at Work* (1998) signalled the beginning of an attempt to extend a wider definition of who is entitled to employment protection rights, whether the term 'worker' or 'employee' is used. The White Paper said that the government sought views on whether some or all employment protection rights should be extended to 'all those who work for another person'. There was concern about the use of zero hours contracts where a person has no set working hours but is required to be available to the employer even though there is no guarantee that they will be called on to work. One result was the inclusion in the Employment Relations Act 1999 of s 23, which allows the Secretary of State to extend the scope of employment legislation to groups not already covered by it. Thus orders can make provision that individuals be treated as parties to workers contracts or contracts of employment and as to who are to be regarded as the employers of individuals. This power could be used to bring many workers within the scope of employment law whose status is doubtful at present such as casual workers, homeworkers, agency workers and workers on zero hours contracts. So far it has not been used but in *Montgomery* v *Johnson Underwood* (2001) the Court of Appeal felt that it could be used to clarify the status of those who find work through employment agencies, and a DTI Discussion Paper of July 2002 suggested that

4

The employment relationship

s 23 could be used to extend employment rights to various categories of workers including ministers of religion (see below). Nevertheless, it is disappointing that no actual use has been made of s 23 as yet.

Recent legislation has tended to be wider in scope anyway. The National Minimum Wage Act 1998 applies to agency workers and homeworkers (see ss 34 and 35) and the Public Interest Disclosure Act 1998 applies to groups of workers who are not covered by the term as defined by s 230(3) in the ERA 1996 (the wider definition): agency workers; homeworkers; NHS doctors, dentists, ophthalmologists and pharmacists; trainees on vocational or work experience schemes. The Working Time Regulations 1998 also apply to agency workers. However, the definition of an agency worker is different in the Public Interest Disclosure Act than it is in the other two pieces of legislation.

LAW IN CONTEXT
The views of individuals

Before discussing the ways in which UK law seeks to categorise dependent work relationships it is worth noting the study by Burchell, Deakin and Honey (1999) which surveyed attitudes of different types of workers to various patterns of employment status. Some freelance workers and self-employed valued their freedom to organise their own work. A typical quotation (Case Study 8) from a child minder was: 'I like the fact that I am my own boss. To a certain extent you set your own hours . . . it's nice to call the tune basically'. On the other hand, the feeling of being in control was not confined to the self-employed. A viewing assistant, who was an employee, commented on the fact that he felt that he was his own boss because his manager was so flexible with him. On the other hand, the self-employed may come under pressure to meet tight deadlines.

Types of workers

The following examples will show the diversity of employment relationships.

Examples

In all of these examples the employer, Hanbury Manufacturing Co., is a large manufacturing company and each example deals with a particular employee of Hanbury.

Example 1
Sam is employed on the factory floor assembling components. He works a regular 46-hour week.

Example 2
Alice works as the personal assistant to the managing director and works a regular 42-hour week.

Example 3
Denise works as a receptionist at the factory and she works 16 hours a week.

Example 4
Eileen works as and when required to conduct tours around the factory to give parties of schoolchildren an idea of what working life in a factory is like. She has no fixed hours of work.

Example 5
Freda works from home as a designer for the company. She occasionally comes into the office and has no fixed hours of work although her contract provides that she is to work a 44-hour week.

Example 6
Khalid works as a freelancer for Hanbury Manufacturing Co.

Example 7
Gillian is working as a temporary secretary to cover for absence through illness but she was hired through an agency.

Example 8
Hubert runs a taxi hire business which is frequently used by Hanbury Manufacturing Co. to transport both staff and visitors to the station and the airport.

4

The employment relationship

The issue in each case is whether the person is:

- an employee
- a worker
- a professional
- self-employed.

The distinction between the terms 'employee', 'worker' and 'professional' will be explained later but, for the moment, it is important to think in terms of whether the person can be considered an employee or not.

In Examples 1 and 2 it is clear that Sam and Alice are employees. They work regular hours at the employer's place of business. In Example 3 Denise is an employee although she only works part time. It is clear that Hubert in Example 8 is not an employee of Hanbury Manufacturing Co. as he has a business of his own. The difficult ones are Examples 4, 5, 6 and 7. Eileen is a casual worker, Freda is a homeworker, Khalid is a freelancer and Gillian is an agency worker. These categories of worker have expanded greatly in recent years. They may be employees or workers or professionals or self-employed. In this chapter we shall explore how the law has sought to deal with persons in these categories.

■ Terminology

As explained above, the traditional distinction was between an employee and an independent contractor. Thus Sam, Alice and Denise would be employees and Hubert would be an independent contractor. Another way of putting it was to say that an employee had a contract of service whereas an independent contractor had a contract for services. This makes sense in Example 8, where Hubert's taxi firm supplies services in the form of transporting staff and visitors on behalf of Hanbury Manufacturing Co. One problem with this terminology is that the word 'service' can lead to an employee being called a servant. One of the last examples of the use of this term by the courts is that in the judgment of MacKenna J in *Ready Mixed Concrete (South East) Ltd* v *Minister of Pensions and National Insurance* (1968). A recent development is to use the term 'worker' which, as we shall see, is being increasingly used in recent legislation and there is a tendency in EC law to develop the rights of the 'citizen-worker'. In this chapter the term 'employee' will be used unless the context otherwise requires.

■ Why is it important to be able to define who is an employee?

The significance of this was mentioned briefly earlier but the following are the reasons in detail:

- The growth in employment protection legislation since the passage of the Contracts of Employment Act 1963 has given employees vastly increased rights. Not only this, but, as we shall see in Chapter 5, the courts have been active in developing the obligations of the employee at common law.
- Employers also need to know who is an employee particularly as the common law places obligations on employees as well as employers: for instance, the obligation of confidentiality. Clearly it is vital for employers to know whether a particular person is bound by this obligation.
- The change in the composition of the workforce.
- The growth in the impact of EC law has brought with it the challenge of integrating into UK law ideas derived from a legal system with different concepts.

The first two points will become apparent in the course of this book, but we must now look at the last two.

The changing composition of the workforce

The nature of the change

The challenge to employment law is that the traditional pattern of most employees being in full-time jobs, where their status as employees was clear, is changing and, as the examples considered earlier tried to show, it is becoming difficult to fit workers who are in newer patterns of work into the traditional category of employee. As McKendrick (1990) put it:

> The Labour market in Britain is presently undergoing significant structural change. The principal change is a rapid increase in new, flexible forms and patterns of work which

depart radically from the standard employment relationship whereby an employee works regularly (that is, full-time) and consistently for his employer under a contract of employment. This new flexible, 'atypical' workforce consists largely of the self-employed, part-time workers, casual workers, 'temps', homeworkers and those working on government training schemes.

Other examples are those on zero hours contracts, agency workers and seasonal workers. More recent surveys have looked at particular areas. One significant one was by McOrmond (2005) 'Changes in working trends over the past decade', which pointed out that the growth in computer technology and the internet and the shift from a manufacturing-based economy to a service-based one have encouraged changes to the way in which people work so that the old standard model of work from Monday to Friday, nine to five, may no longer be appropriate. However, she points out that this shift is not entirely driven by business needs, but also by the desire for a more healthy work–life balance from both policy makers and the general public. Other surveys on particular areas are considered in relation to that area.

LAW IN CONTEXT
Changing patterns of employment: the statistical evidence

The evidence is that the trend from traditional full-time employment to other patterns of work accelerated greatly in the 1980s. In 'The Changing Composition of the Workforce' Fredman (1997) points out that between 1981 and 1987 the number of full-time jobs of indefinite duration fell by 1.1 million from 70% of total employment to 64%. At the same time non-standard jobs (i.e. of the kind referred to above) increased from 30% to 36% of total employment. Moreover, this trend continued as between 1995 and 1996 the number of part-time and self-employed workers increased by 264,000 and the number of temporary employees by 45,000. It is believed that self-employed workers now make up about 12% of the UK workforce. A recent survey (Guardian, 2006) indicated that the trend to self-employment was likely to rise, with 30% of those surveyed thinking of becoming self-employed. In addition, there is a greater proportion of self-employed among workers over 50 (20%) than workers aged between 25 and 49 (14%) (ONS, 2005).

The impact of EC law

The effect of EC Directives
A number of EC Directives apply to employees: Directive 77/187 on transfers of undertakings, Directive 80/987 on the rights of employees when their employer is insolvent and Directive 91/533 on the information which must be given to employees on their terms and conditions of employment. The term 'employee' is, in principle, to be given the same meaning in a Member State as it has in the national laws of that Member State in accordance with the principle of subsidiarity. However, all of these Directives apply to 'every paid employee having a contract or employment relationship'. As Bercusson (1996) points out, the significant point is the use of the phrase 'employment relationship' which obviously means relationships other than those where there is a contract

of employment. Independent contractors would seem to be included (although the UK government, in a non-binding minute, said that they would be excluded), and Article 1(2)(b) of Directive 91/533 expressly states that the Directive applies to casual and/or specific workers unless its non-application to those categories is justified. Moreover, the Explanatory Memorandum to Directive 91/533 refers to the development of different work patterns leading, as it says, to 'an erosion of the criteria defining the traditional status of an employee'. Quite clearly then the phrase 'employment relationship' was drafted with this problem in mind. It is indeed true that the term 'employee' will be given the same meaning as it already has in each Member State but it is not clear precisely what 'employment relationship' means. As Bercusson points out, the whole idea of Directive 91/533 is to require information, in the words of Article 2(1), of the 'essential aspects of the employment relationship' and therefore the relationship must, by definition, be one where a certain amount of detail is available. Therefore the Directive requires details of, for example, the date when the relationship began, how long it is expected to last, normal working time and remuneration. Thus very casual relationships would be excluded as this detail would not be available.

The concept of the worker in the Treaty of Amsterdam

Article 39 grants the right of free movement to all workers who have nationality in one of the Member States and who have crossed an internal frontier in order to take up an offer of employment. A well-known example is *Union Royal Belge des Sociétés de Football Association ASBL* v *Bosman* (1995) where a footballer successfully argued that this principle of free movement extended to free movement of footballers between clubs in the EC. Furthermore, the ECJ has stated that the concept of a 'worker' must be a Community law concept (*Unger* v *Bestuur* (1964)), unlike the term 'employee', and therefore the term worker has the potential to develop a life of its own. Indeed, as pointed out by Szyszczak (2000), 'a person may also be classed as a worker after having left the paid labour market where, for example, he/she takes up a vocational training course' (at page 59).

The present law

UK law adopts a piecemeal approach to the question of status and there are five different categories. In addition the courts have evolved various tests to decide if a worker fits into a particular one, and these are especially important in deciding whether a person has employee status.

When looking at the tests set out below for deciding whether a person is an employee, a worker or a professional look back to the examples set out above and consider which category each situation falls into.

Employees

The fundamental definition of an employee is found in s 230(1) of the ERA 1996 which, as we saw above, defines an employee as an 'individual who has entered into or works under (or, when the employment has ceased, worked under) a contract of employment'. When one turns to s 230(2) to find out what a contract of employment is the answer turns out to be that a 'contract of employment means a contract of service or apprenticeship, whether express or implied, and (if it is express) whether oral or in writing'. Although this definition has some value, as we shall see later in this chapter, it does not help in defining the term 'employee', which is why the courts have had such an important role in this area. This definition applies to all claims under the ERA 1996 except those under Part II, i.e. it applies to claims for unfair dismissal, redundancy payments, rights to a Statement of Initial Employment Particulars, maternity rights, rights to time off work and guarantee payments. The Health and Safety at Work Act 1974 defines an employee in the narrow sense as used in s 230(1), i.e. someone who works under a contract of service or apprenticeship.

Workers

This is, in effect, an intermediate category between employees and the self-employed. Section 230(3) of the ERA 1996 provides that a worker is either a person who has entered into a contract of employment or who has entered into any other contract 'whereby the individual undertakes to do or perform personally any work or services for another party to the contract whose status is not by virtue of the contract that of a client or customer of any profession or business undertaking carried on by the individual'. In *Byrne Bros* v *Baird* (2002) the use of this definition in the Working Time Regulations (see Chapter 7) was considered and the EAT held that self-employed labour-only sub-contractors were within this definition.

It will be seen that this definition contains three elements:

(a) A worker can be a person who has entered into a contract of employment.
(b) Alternatively, a worker can be a person who, although not having a contract of employment, still undertakes to perform services personally.
(c) A person will not be a worker where he or she is performing services for a professional client. In effect those who run their own businesses are excluded.

The important difference between the two definitions is the inclusion of elements (b) and (c) in the definition of a worker in s 230(3), whereas in the definition of an employee in s 230(1) only (a) is present. This definition of a worker has been used in trade union legislation for some time (see s 296(1) of TULRCA 1992) and workers are also covered by anti-discrimination legislation (see below). In addition, workers are covered by the following:

- the national minimum wage (ss 1 and 54(3) of the National Minimum Wage Act 1998)
- the working time regulations (reg 2(1) of the Working Time Regulations 1998)
- the right not to be discriminated against on the grounds of working part time (see below and note that workers on fixed terms are covered only if they are employees)
- the right to be accompanied at disciplinary and grievance hearings.

The question of who is a worker is discussed by Davidov (2005) who argues that the distinction between employees and workers is that employees are both dependent on the employer and have a democratic deficit in that they are under the control of the employer. Workers, by contrast, may be economically dependent on the employer but do not suffer 'democratic deficits' in that there is not the same degree of control. He argues for a wider understanding of the term 'worker' in the light of this analysis.

Professionals

This term is not used in employment legislation but is used to refer to the provisions of anti-discrimination legislation which protects those who are employed under 'a contract of service or of apprenticeship or a contract personally to execute any work or labour' (see s 1(6)(a) of the Equal Pay Act 1970, s 82(1) of the Sex Discrimination Act 1975, s 78(1) of the Race Relations Act 1976, s 68(1) of the Disability Discrimination Act 1995; reg 2 of the Employment Equality (Sexual Orientation) Regulations 2003 (SI 2003/1661); reg 2 of the Employment Equality (Religion or Belief) Regulations 2003 (SI 2003/1660); and reg 2 of the Employment Equality (Age) Regulations 2006 (SI 2006/1031)). It also applies to claims under Part II of the ERA 1996, which deals with deductions from pay. A good example of its application is *Percy v Church of Scotland Board of National Mission* (below). It should be noted that Article 141 of the Treaty of Amsterdam, which deals with the right to equal pay, refers to employment and occupation and as a result the Employment Equality (Sex Discrimination) Regulations 2005 (SI 2005/2467) were made which made it unlawful to discriminate against office holders. The topic of office holders is discussed below.

The difference from the definition of a worker is that a person can be a professional even if she runs her own business provided that she actually does the work personally. Thus a self-employed electrician would be a professional within this definition provided that he actually did the work rather than sent others to do it.

Note: A further definition is contained in the Transfer of Undertakings (Protection of Employment) Regulations 1981 which defines an employee as a person who works for another 'whether under a contract of service or apprenticeship or otherwise but does not include anyone who provides services under a contract for services'. This is the narrowest of all the definitions.

Self-employed

These are those who run their own business but, unlike professionals, they do not contract to supply their own work or labour. These are outside the scope of employment protection legislation but are covered by certain provisions in the Health and Safety at Work Act (see Chapter 8).

▇ Relationship between the terms 'employees', 'workers' and 'professionals'

It will be seen that, because different definitions are used, it is possible for a person to be able to bring a claim under one part of employment law but not under another. For example, a person will be able to claim under the discrimination legislation provided that he or she works personally for another but an actual contract of employment is needed for a claim for unfair dismissal. A recent example of the interpretation of statutory provisions is found in *Percy* v *Church of Scotland Board of National Mission* (2006), where it was held that a minister of religion came within the provisions of discrimination legislation as she had a contract to personally execute work or labour (see s 230(3) of the ERA 1996 above) but did not come within s 230(1) as she did not have a contract of employment; although, as we shall see, in the later case of *New Testament Church of God* v *Stewart* (2006) the EAT held that ministers of religion can have the status of employees and so can claim for unfair dismissal and the full range of employment rights. (The topic of the employment status of the clergy is dealt with later in this chapter.) An earlier instance is *Loughran and Kelly* v *Northern Ireland Housing Executive* (1998) which involved a claim under the Fair Employment (Northern Ireland) Act 1976 where the phrase 'personally to execute any work or labour' was used. It was held that this covered a solicitor who was a partner in a firm.

It is not easy to see a reason for the different definitions except that Parliament may have felt that, as a matter of policy, discrimination legislation should have the widest possible scope. In the case of trade union legislation the object was to give trade unions immunity from actions in tort (see Chapters 13 and 14) where there was a trade dispute and this could be where the dispute concerned 'workers' as well as employees in the narrow sense.

TESTS USED BY THE COURTS TO ESTABLISH WHETHER AN EMPLOYMENT RELATIONSHIP EXISTS

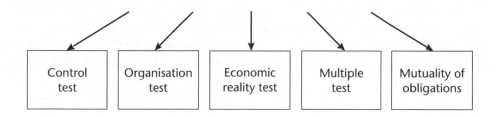

Given that statute does not provide any detailed guidance on when there is an employment relationship the focus naturally shifts to the courts, who have over the years highlighted a number of tests to try to answer this question. All of these tests still tell us something of value and indeed the first test is illustrated by both the oldest case and the newest case which are considered. It should be borne in mind that in cases up to 1968 at least the word 'servant' or 'workman' was sometimes used but, for consistency, the term employee or, where appropriate, worker, will be used throughout.

The tests themselves will first be considered and then the employment status of particular types of workers will be looked at in the light of them.

Control test

In *Walker* v *Crystal Palace Football Club Ltd* (1910) the issue was whether a footballer was employed by the club so as to enable him to claim compensation under the Workmen's Compensation Act 1906 as a result of an accident whilst playing in a match. It was argued for the club that he was not covered by the Act and reliance was placed on the words of Bramwell LJ in *Yewens* v *Noakes* (1880) where he defined an employee as 'a person subject to the command of his master as to the manner in which he shall do his work'. The Court of Appeal in *Walker* nevertheless held that it was enough that he was obliged to obey the general directions of the club even though he clearly exercised his own judgement as to how to play.

These cases can be seen as a reflection of social trends. In *Walker* there was clearly a need for the law to move beyond the outdated concept of control set out in *Yewens* v *Noakes.* In agency cases the court recognised that, if an employee under an agency agreement could not claim unfair dismissal against the client firm, it would be unlikely that he or she could claim successfully against the agency, which would simply say that it had no choice but to comply with the client's request to remove that employee from the client firm.

It should be noted that the recent cases on whether a person who works through an agency is an employee of either the agency or the client/end-user have relied heavily on the extent to which the worker is under the control of either of these. The topic is examined separately below.

The organisation test

In *Stevenson Jordan and Harrison Ltd* v *Macdonald & Evans* (1952) Denning LJ suggested that a person would be an employee if their work was integrated into the business rather than accessory to it. This test has an attractive simplicity to it and was useful in making it clear at the time that skilled professionals, such as doctors in the NHS, were employees. However, it is not satisfactory when dealing with problems of outworkers and workers employed by sub-contractors. Nor does it help in a case where, for example, a highly skilled professional is brought in from outside to do a vital task. It may be, for example, that all the computer systems in a firm have failed and an outsider is brought in to fix them. Although this person is undoubtedly integral to the organisation, she is not an employee nor perhaps a worker either.

The economic reality test

This asks whether the worker is working for himself or herself or is working for another. If the worker takes the risk of making profits or losses then he or she is not likely to be held to be an employee. It appears to originate from decisions in the USA and Canada. In *United States of America* v *Silk* (1946) the Supreme Court said that the test was whether workers 'were employees as a matter of economic reality'. The test was applied in *Market Investigations* v *Minister of Social Security* (1969) which concerned an interviewer who worked for the company part time, carrying out market research.

She could do the work at whatever time she wished provided that it was done within the allotted time. The High Court held that despite the autonomy given to her in how she actually arranged to do the work she was not working for herself but for another and thus she was an employee. Cooke J outlined a number of factors to assist in deciding whether or not a person was in business on his or her own account:

> whether the man performing the services provides his own equipment, whether he hires his own helpers, what degree of financial risk he takes, what degree of responsibility for investment and management he has, and whether and how far he has an opportunity of profiting from sound management in the performance of his task.

Furthermore, Cooke J observed that although it may be easier to apply this test where the worker is running an established business of his or her own a person may still be an independent contractor where he or she does not have an existing business.

Cooke J was, in effect, providing a checklist of factors to decide employee status but the disadvantage of this is that it can encourage a mechanistic approach whereby one simply ticks off factors without looking at the relationship as a whole. Moreover, in *Hall* v *Lorimer* (1994) Nolan LJ pointed out that the question of whether a person is in business on their own account 'may be of little assistance in the case of one carrying on a profession or vocation. A self-employed author working from home or an actor or singer may earn his living without any of the normal trappings of a business'. In this case the worker was a television technician who worked for about 20 television companies, usually for no more than a day at a time. He was held to be self-employed.

In *Lorimer* the question of status arose in the context of tax, but in the context of liability for injuries to the worker at work the courts may reach a different conclusion. In *Lane* v *Shire Roofing Co. (Oxford) Ltd* (1995) a roofer who traded as a one-man firm and who was self employed for tax purposes suffered serious injuries when working for the defendants, who had employed him on a payments by results basis. It was held that he was an employee. Henry J, having outlined various factors in the employee-or-not equation, then remarked that 'these questions must be asked in the context of who is responsible for the overall safety of the men in question'. The decision is therefore clearly a policy one designed to ensure that, so far as possible, those employing staff are responsible for their safety, and is none the worse for that although the fact that the courts can reach different decisions on employee status depending on the nature of the claim does nothing for clarity in this branch of the law.

The multiple test

The leading case is *Ready Mixed Concrete (South East)* v *Minister of Pensions and National Insurance* (1968). The issue was whether the company was liable to pay national insurance contributions for a lorry driver employed by it. The contract between the driver and the company stated that the driver was self-employed and it obliged him to maintain, repair and insure the lorry, to wear the company's uniform and not to use the lorry except on the company's business. If he was unable to work then a replacement had to be hired by him. He was paid by a rate per mile for a specified quantity of cement delivered. It was held that he was an independent contractor because the contract was one of carriage rather than one of employment: 'The ownership of the assets, the chance of profit and the risk of loss in the contract of carriage are his and not the company's'. A significant factor was that the driver could hire a substitute, albeit with the consent of the company and who had to be competent (a point that will be dealt with below), although it must be said that, on the facts, the relationship looks very much like one of employment.

In the course of his judgment, MacKenna J stated that a contract of service existed if:

(a) the employee agreed in consideration of a wage or other remuneration to provide his own work and skill in the performance of some service for his employer;

(b) the employee agreed that in the performance of the service he would be subject to the control of the other party sufficient to make him his master;

(c) the other provisions of the contract were consistent with its being a contract of service.

It may be questioned whether the multiple test and MacKenna J's words really add anything to the law on employee status. The term 'wage or other remuneration' is so general that it excludes nothing and the reiteration of the control test tells us nothing new. The final part appears to add nothing but in *Montgomery* v *Johnson Underwood Ltd* (2001) Buckley J said that it meant that 'all the terms of the agreement must be considered', which brings in the multiple test. The only significant feature is the emphasis on 'his *own* work and skill' (emphasis added) which, as we will see, has led subsequent courts down something of a blind alley. It could be argued that this test says nothing more than is already said by the economic reality test. In essence, the two tests are similar in trying to avoid one all-embracing phrase such as 'control' or 'integration' but they both fall into the trap of appearing to suggest a mechanical 'ticking off of factors' approach. Nevertheless, in a recent decision of the Court of Appeal (*Montgomery* v *Johnson Underwood Ltd* (2001)), MacKenna J's formulation was approved with the explanation that test (i) means mutuality of obligations (see below) and test (ii) means control. If so, then the combination of these two tests may be a useful tool for solving disputes about employment status.

The mutuality of obligations test

This test has gained currency in recent years in dealing with casual workers and other workers, such as homeworkers, who do not fit into the traditional pattern of employment. It focuses on the obligations which the parties owe each other to decide if there is an employment relationship.

It is worth mentioning at the outset that there are three possibilities in cases of these types of workers, especially casual workers:

(a) to decide that the workers are independent contractors;

(b) to decide that the workers are employed each time that they are engaged;

(c) to decide that they have a global contract, i.e. one which continues even though they are not actually engaged.

The starting point is *O'Kelly and others* v *Trusthouse Forte plc* (1983). The applicants were 'regular casuals' employed at a hotel and claimed that they had been unfairly dismissed for being members of a trade union and taking part in its activities. They therefore needed to prove that they were employees. The industrial tribunal listed 18 relevant factors and, of these, the following were in favour of employee status: they were not in business on their own account; they were subject to the conditions of the hotel; and they needed permission to take time off from rostered duties. However, two factors were decisive against their claim:

1 The intention of the parties in the light of custom and practice in the hotel industry was not to create a relationship of employer and employee.

2 Mutuality of obligation was missing. As Ackner LJ put it: 'The "assurance of prefer- ence in the allocation of any available work" which the regulars enjoyed was no more than a firm expectation in practice. It was not a contractual promise'. Had the applicants refused to accept a particular piece of casual work then they would not have been liable for breach of contract. Therefore there could not be, in the termin- ology used above, a global contract of employment.

This decision has been criticised on the ground that the introduction of a requirement of mutual obligations means that employees with irregular or variable contracts will be unable to fulfil this requirement and so lose employee status. It is argued by Leighton (1984) that a flexible approach to the question of employee status with 'evidence of control coupled with *de facto* interdependence' could mean that workers such as cab drivers, homeworkers, building workers and door-to-door salespeople were employees. The requirement of mutuality could mean that this opportunity is lost.

Conversely, in *Wickens* v *Champion Employment* (1984), the mutual obligations test was used to deny employment status to temporary workers engaged by an employ- ment agency because the agency was not bound to make any bookings for them and they were not bound to accept bookings which were made. A more helpful decision for employees was *McMeechan* v *Secretary of State for Employment* (1997), where the Court of Appeal held that an agency worker can have the status of an employee in relation to a particular engagement although there is no employment status under the general terms of the agreement (i.e. no global contract) because of the lack of mutual obligations. On the other hand, in *Clark* v *Oxfordshire Health Authority* (1998) a 'bank nurse' was denied a 'global' contract of employment as the health authority did not guarantee her any work; she was simply available as and when needed. The ques- tion of whether she had a contract of employment each time she worked was remitted to the employment tribunal. The topic of agency workers is considered further on in detail – see also page 50. Note also the tendency of statute law, as mentioned above, to bring agency workers under its protection in a few recent instances.

It had been hoped that the House of Lords would bring much-needed clarity to this area of the law in its decision in *Carmichael* v *National Power plc* (1999) but the oppor- tunity was not taken to review the law in detail and to state any general principles. The applicants were guides at power stations who worked on a 'casual as required' basis. They were offered and accepted work as it arose but there was no guarantee of work nor did they always accept work which was offered. The issue was whether they

4

The employment relationship

were employees so that they were entitled to a statement of initial employment particulars but the House of Lords held that they did not have a 'global' contract of employment. Irvine LC stated that: 'The parties incurred no obligations to accept or provide work but at best assumed moral obligations of loyalty in a context where both recognised that the best interests of each lay in being accommodating to the other.' What is not clear is whether the House of Lords regarded the workers as having contracts each time they acted as guides, and this decision must be regarded as a missed opportunity to bring clarity to this area of the law. A later decision (here, of the ECJ) simply serves to emphasise how unclear the law is. In *Wippel v Peek and Cloppenburg GmbH and Co KG* (2005) it was held that a worker on an 'on demand' contract could still be a worker under the Part-Time Workers Directive.

In *Cornwall County Council v Prater* (2005) the fact that a local authority was not under a continuing obligation to offer work to a home tutor did not prevent the existence of a contract of employment. Once the tutor had accepted particular work then there was a mutuality of obligation: the tutor had to tutor and the local authority had to pay her. Thus she had a contract of employment. (This case also dealt with continuity of employment and is considered further in Chapter 6.)

The difficulty is that after more than 20 years of trying to decide on a suitable test for the existence of an employment relationship on the basis of mutual obligations, the law remains in a confused state. This is particularly unfortunate because this test has been applied in situations, such as agency work, which frequently arise today and where there is accordingly a particular need for clarification. In recent years the courts have recognised that the mutual obligations test has not provided the answer, at least by itself, and have linked it with the test of control, as suggested in *Montgomery* v *Johnson Underwood* (2001).

OTHER POINTS WHICH MAY BE RELEVANT TO THE QUESTION OF EMPLOYMENT STATUS

The description given by the parties to their relationship

In *Ferguson v John Dawson and Partners (Contractors) Ltd* (1976) the plaintiff worked on a building site and was subject to the employer's orders as to what he did and the employer provided tools. However, the site agent said in evidence that when the plaintiff went to work for the company he said to the plaintiff that 'there were no cards. We were working purely as a lump labour force'. (The term 'lump' meant that the workers were paid a lump sum and it was their job to pay tax and national insurance. The term was frequently used in the building trade.) The Court of Appeal held that on the evidence the plaintiff was an employee and that any declaration by the parties to the contrary would be disregarded. Megaw LJ said that: 'I find difficulty in accepting that the parties, by a mere expression of intention as to what the legal relationship should be, can in any way influence the conclusion of law as to what the relationship is.'

However, this robust statement by Megaw LJ may have disguised a policy consideration in that the claim was for injuries sustained at work and to have held that the plaintiff was not an employee would have deprived him of compensation. The decision can thus be viewed in the same light as that in *Lane v Shire Roofing Co. Ltd* (1995), discussed earlier. Support for this view is given by the decision of the Court of Appeal in *Massey v Crown Life Insurance* (1978). Massey was the branch manager of one of the company's offices and asked to change his status from that of an employee to that of an independent contractor as this would be to his advantage from the tax point of view. He was later dismissed and sought to claim unfair dismissal. It was held that he had changed his status and therefore could not do so. No doubt the court was influenced by the fact that Massey clearly wanted both options: it suited him to say that he was self-employed for tax purposes but it suited him to say that he was an employee when he needed to do so to claim unfair dismissal. Clearly this would be wrong in principle and there was also a difference on the facts between this case and that of *Ferguson*: in *Ferguson* the worker was simply presented with a statement about his status, the legal significance of which he probably did not appreciate; in *Massey* the worker knew exactly what he was doing and indeed he suggested the change of status.

One can perhaps sum up the law in this area by saying that where it is obvious that a worker is either an employee or an independent contractor then any label attached to the relationship by the parties will be ignored. If, however, the case is borderline then a label will be taken into account, subject always to the nature of the claim being considered.

The extent to which the worker contracts to perform services personally

Example

John employs Anne and Anne agrees with John that if, for whatever reason, she is unable to perform her duties then she will arrange for someone else to perform them instead. (This will be referred to as a substitution clause.) In all other respects Anne is clearly an employee of John. Does the inclusion of this term mean that she will not, after all, be classed as an employee? The question is really whether the worker is contracting to provide services and not necessarily his or her own service.

The starting point is a statement of MacKenna J in *Ready Mixed Concrete (South East) v Minister of Pensions and National Insurance* (1968), a case discussed above. He stated that: 'Freedom to do a job either by one's own hands or by another's is inconsistent with a contract of service though a limited or occasional power of delegation may not be.' It will be recalled that here the driver could hire a competent substitute with the consent of the company and this was one factor in the decision that he was not an employee.

It will be seen that the power to hire a substitute was not absolute: the substitute had to be competent and the consent of the company was needed. A more extreme example of the power occurred in *Express and Echo Publications Ltd* v *Tanton* (1999). Tanton originally worked for the company as an employee but he was made redundant and he later accepted employment with them as a driver on what he originally accepted was a self-employed basis. A clause in his contract stated: 'In the event that the contractor is unable or unwilling to perform the services personally he shall arrange at his own expense entirely for another suitable person to perform the services.' Tanton never signed the contract but worked according to its terms and on one occasion did arrange for a substitute. Peter Gibson LJ in the Court of Appeal held that 'where, as here, a person who works for another is not required to perform his services personally, then as a matter of law the relationship between that person and the person for whom he works is not that of employer and employee'. In *Commissioners of Inland Revenue* v *Post Office Ltd* (2003) it was held that the existence of a 'substitution' clause also prevented a person having the status of worker under a contract for personal services as the clause prevented there from necessarily being personal services.

The problem with a definite rule that a 'substitution' clause negates both employee and worker status is that it leaves it open to an employer to put such a clause in the contract deliberately to prevent such status from being acquired. However, the subsequent decision in *McFarlane* v *Glasgow City Council* (2001) has modified the principle in *Tanton* by distinguishing it on the facts. In *McFarlane* the applicants were gymnastic instructors and their contracts allowed them, if they were unable to take a class, to arrange for a substitute from a register of instructors maintained by the council. It was held that this was a much more limited power than in *Tanton* as it applied only if the instructor was actually unable to take a class, and otherwise did not apply; thus it would not be possible for the instructors never to turn up, as would theoretically have been the case in *Tanton*. Lindsay J, in the EAT in *McFarlane*, categorised the clause in *Tanton* as 'extreme': 'The individual there, at his own choice, need never turn up for work. He could, moreover, profit from his absence if he could find a cheaper substitute. He could choose the substitute and then, in effect, he would be the master.' This was not the case here. However, although the cases undoubtedly are distinguishable, one cannot help but feel that the EAT in *McFarlane* had no great enthusiasm for *Tanton* and was concerned lest the law got itself into a position where any power to employ a substitute automatically meant that the relationship was not one of employer and employee.

Redrow Homes (Yorkshire) Ltd v *Wright* (2004) is another example of the court, as in *McFarlane*, avoiding the need to hold that the existence of a substitution clause prevents employee or worker status. The claim was under the Working Time Regulations, where a worker is defined as one who agrees to personally perform work or services (see above). The contract here provided that the claimants were 'at all times' to provide sufficient labour. Although these words could be read as allowing them simply to provide labour which need not necessarily be their own, the Court of Appeal held that in reality they were contracting to provide their own labour and so were workers. In *Byrne Brothers* v *Baird* (2002) the existence of a clause in the contracts of workers, allowing them to engage a substitute with the agreement of the contractor and only where he was unable to provide the service, was held not to prevent the workers being classed as such for the purposes of the Working Time Directive.

IS EMPLOYMENT STATUS A QUESTION OF FACT OR LAW?

This point is significant because, as a general point, appeals can be made only on a point of law from the decision of an employment tribunal to an appeal tribunal (the EAT, Court of Appeal or House of Lords) (s 21 of the Employment Tribunals Act 1996). Therefore an appellate tribunal can only interfere with the decision of an employment tribunal where it applies an incorrect test or states the law incorrectly or applies the law in a way which no reasonable tribunal would do. Thus, if a decision on employment status is one of fact then it is not open to challenge on appeal. The disadvantage of this approach is that different tribunals may come to different decisions using the same facts, and so one tribunal may hold that a person is an employee and another may hold that she is self-employed. In *O'Kelly* v *Trusthouse Forte* (1984) the Court of Appeal held that the question of employee status was one of mixed law and fact. This was reinforced in *Lee Ting-Sang* v *Chung Chi-Keung* (1990), where Lord Griffiths said that 'where the relationship has to be determined by an investigation and evaluation of the factual circumstances in which the work is performed', this is a question of fact 'to be determined by the trial court'. The only exception, according to Lord Griffiths, was where the relationship was dependent on the construction of a written document, as in *Davies* v *Presbyterian Church of Wales* (1986), where the employment status of a clergyman was in issue. In such a case the question would be one of law.

The position therefore seems to be that where the question is purely one of applying established rules to the facts, the decision will be one of fact with which the appellate courts cannot interfere. The problem is that it is often difficult to decide precisely what the established rules are in particular cases. A good example is the decision in *O'Kelly* v *Trusthouse Forte*, which left the status of casual workers in doubt. This is why there seems to be no decrease in the number of appeals on the question of employee status.

THE STATUS OF PARTICULAR TYPES OF WORKERS

Homeworkers and teleworkers

Homeworkers have always been a feature of the labour market, traditionally in garment manufacturing, which has been seen as low paid and mainly female. Homeworkers can come under the category of teleworkers, who work from home aided by modern information and communication technologies which enable workers at home to keep in touch with their place of work and with other workers. A survey (Hotopp 2002) showed that the total number of teleworkers in the UK in spring 2001 was 2.2 million and of these 1.8 million could perform their jobs without the use of a computer and a telephone. The total number of teleworkers increased by between 65% and 70% over the period 1997–2001 and there has doubtless been an increase since the date of the survey. Homeworkers are specifically given only one employment protection right,

4

The employment relationship

that of entitlement to the minimum wage, provided that they satisfy the definition of a homeworker in s 35 of the National Minimum Wage Act 1998. This provides that a homeworker 'contracts with a person, for the purpose of that person's business, for the execution of work to be done in a place not under the control or management of that person'.

The decision of the Court of Appeal in *Nethermere (St Neots) Ltd* v *Taverna and Gardiner* (1984) is the main authority on the legal status of traditional homeworkers. The applicants were homeworkers who made garments for the company and the question was the extent to which there were mutual obligations. The workers could fix their hours of work and vary the number of garments which they took but Dillon LJ found that the workers were obliged to take a reasonable amount of work and the company was obliged to provide a reasonable amount of work. Neither of these obligations were written down but the course of dealing between the parties over several years gave rise to mutual obligations on both sides sufficient to lead the court to hold that there was a contract of employment. A similar decision had been reached in the earlier case of *Airfix Footwear Ltd* v *Cope* (1978), where a homeworker who had assembled shoes for the company for seven years was held to be an employee on the basis of the regularity of the relationship over a period of time.

The legal status of the modern teleworker has not been considered by the courts but will fall to be decided by the tests outlined above. Teleworkers are given a measure of protection by the Framework Agreement on Telework. This was concluded by the social partners of the European Union in 2002, but, unusually, it is not to be implemented by a Directive but by agreement between employers and unions. The result in the UK was the Telework Guidance issued by the DTI in 2003. This does not deal with the legal status of teleworkers but provides, for example, that employers should not be able to compel workers to change to telework unless it is part of their job description. It also provides that teleworkers should benefit from the same terms and conditions of employment as workers at the employer's premises.

Volunteers

Debra Morris (1999) has argued there is 'anecdotal evidence that voluntary organisations are denying benefits previously given to volunteers, in order to prevent their gaining employment rights'. As she puts it: 'Voluntary organisations *may* benefit from informal relationships with their volunteers, but is it not appropriate that volunteers should be able to take advantage of *relevant* employment protection legislation?' Recent attempts to argue that volunteers are employees have not met with success. In *South East Sheffield Citizens' Advice Bureau* v *Grayson* (2004) the EAT held that CAB volunteers are not employees. Although they had a 'usual minimum weekly commitment' of six hours a week this did not mean that there was a contractual obligation to do the work, as there was clearly no legal obligation involved. Similarly, in *Melhuish* v *Redbridge Citizens' Advice Bureau* (2005), the EAT held that a volunteer who was simply that (no pay, no obligation to attend work, etc.) is not an employee and does not have a contract at all.

▇ Agency workers

Agency work is a growing sector of employment. The Regulatory Impact Assessment on the Proposal for a Directive on Temporary Agency Workers estimated (2002) that there were 700,000 temporary agency workers, with 26% of agency workers employed in real estate, renting and business activities; 34% of agency workers were engaged in administrative work. There was no real gender imbalance in agency work: just over 51% were men and nearly 49% female. It was estimated that between 10% and 15% of agency workers' postings were of less than six weeks' duration. This last figure is significant as workers with postings estimated to last less than six weeks will be exempted from the proposed EU Directive on Agency Workers (see below).

The problem for employment lawyers is that agency workers do not fit the traditional bilateral employment relationship between employer and temporary worker. Instead the relationship is tripartite. There are two issues:

(a) statutory regulation of the agency relationship; and

(b) the extent to which agency workers have a contractual relationship with the employment agency and the client/end-user.

Statutory regulation of the agency relationship

Employment agencies are regulated by the Employment Agencies Act 1973 and the Conduct of Employment Agencies and Employment Business Regulations 2003 (SI 2003/ 3319). However, these are primarily concerned with regulating agencies themselves and are not concerned with the legal relationship between the agency and the temporary worker. Accordingly they say nothing about the status of the temporary worker in relation to either the agency or the client. The only relevant point is that reg 15(a) of the 2003 Regulations (above) does require the agency to issue the temporary worker with a written statement of terms and conditions which must indicate if the temporary worker is regarded by the agency as employed or self-employed. However, the courts will look behind this at the actual relationship to see whether the temporary worker is in reality employed by the agency or not (see *RNLI* v *Bushaway* (2005) below). The Act and the Regulations are, however, important in dealing with the obligations of the agency. For example, it is a fundamental principle of the Employment Agencies Act 1973 that temporary workers cannot be charged by the agency for work-finding services, the only exceptions being in the modelling and entertainment industries.

In 2002, the European Union published proposals for a Directive which would give agency workers protection from discrimination as compared to workers in the user enterprise in which they work, with a proposed exemption where the agency worker's posting with the user was expected by the agency to be for less than six weeks. The UK government resisted the implementation of this part of the Directive on the ground that agency workers have a triangular relationship with the agency and the client/end-user and equal treatment would mean that agencies would have to apply their clients' pay policies and conditions to their workers. The Directive, which has been shelved for the time being, covered all agency workers and so, as with UK legislation (above), does not provide guidance on the question of whether temporary workers have a legal relationship with the agency and/or the client/end-user.

The extent to which agency workers have a contractual relationship with another party

Given that neither UK legislation nor the UK Directive gives any guidance on this matter it has been left to the courts to grapple with this question. The problem, argues Freedland (2006), is that UK employment law still uses a bilateral model for contracts of employment. This point has been made earlier in relation to complex situations involving employers but Freedland argues that it applies with equal force to the position of agency workers. Before examining this area in detail it is worth emphasising again that it is the courts who decide the status of the worker and they will not take the words of an agreement with the agency as necessarily meaning what they say. A good example of this approach is the decision in *RNLI v Bushaway* (2005), where the issue was the status of an 'entire agreement clause' under which the worker agreed that her contract, which provided that it was not to be construed as constituting an employment relationship, was to be regarded as 'the whole agreement between the parties'. The EAT held that this was not conclusive and that it was permissible to look at what was actually negotiated and at what was actually done by the parties. On this basis it was clear that the claimant was an employee. Similarly, in *Dacas v Brook Street Bureau* (2003) the issue was whether the fact that an agreement stated that the relationship between the worker and either the employment agency or the client (the end-user) was not one of employment decided the matter. The EAT had no difficulty in holding that it did not: the actual label was not decisive.

There are five possibilities for the status of the worker in relation to both the agency and the client/end-user:

1 The worker may not be employed by either. If so, they could be self-employed, or, alternatively, it was suggested in *Construction Industry Training Board* v *Labour Force Ltd* (1970) that agency workers have a '*sui generis*' status where they are neither employed nor self-employed. It is worth emphasising that this decision pre-dated the introduction of employment rights on a wide scale and was concerned with liability on the agency to pay an industrial training levy, which depended on whether the temporary workers were their employees. Nevertheless, the fact that this possibility would result in agency workers having no employment protection makes it an unsatisfactory option and in recent years the courts have striven to construct some employment relationship with either the agency or the client/end-user.

2 The worker may be an employee of the employment agency, as in *McMeechan* v *Secretary of State for Employment* (see above).

3 The worker may be employed by the end-user (i.e. the client of the agency), as in *Dacas* v *Brook Street Bureau* (see below).

4 The worker may have a contract of employment with both the agency and the client/end-user so that the responsibilities of an employer are shared between them, as suggested in *Dacas* (above) by Mummery and Sedley LJJ.

5 The worker may have no status at all, whether as an employee, worker or self-employed contractor. This possibility thankfully seems to have been virtually killed off by the words of Smith LJ in *Cable & Wireless* v *Muscat* (2006): 'We find it hard to imagine a case in which a worker will be found to have no recognised status at all, either as an employee of someone or as a self-employed contractor.'

The worker as an employee of the employment agency

In *Montgomery* v *Johnson Underwood Ltd* (2001) the applicant was registered with an agency but was sent to work for the same client for two years. She subsequently brought unfair dismissal proceedings against both the agency and the client. It was held that the agency did not have sufficient control over the applicant for her to be their employee. The Court of Appeal held that the two essential tests for the existence of a contract of employment were control and mutuality of obligations.

A decision where the lack of control told against an employment relationship with the end-user was *Bunce* v *Postworth Ltd t/a Skyblue* (2005), where the Court of Appeal held on the facts that there was no contract of employment with the agency. A welder, Mr Bunce, claimed unfair dismissal from the agency on the basis that he entered into a contract of employment with them each time he went on an assignment to the end-user even though it was conceded that there was no overall contract between him and the agency. The court rejected this on the basis that the element of control by the alleged employer (here, the agency) needed for a contract of employment with them could not be present when Mr Bunce was working for the end-user. It was the end-user who would control his work. Thus, arguments that the agency is the employer seem likely to fail both on grounds of lack of mutuality of obligations and, more importantly, lack of control.

The worker as an employee of the client/end-user

The first case where the possibility of the worker being an employee was held to be a possibility was *Motorola* v *Davidson and Melville Craig Group Ltd* (2001): the EAT held that where the worker had worked under the control of the client for two years then there could be an employment relationship with the client. The leading authority is now *Dacas* v *Brook Street Bureau* (2004), where the Court of Appeal held that the applicant was, on the facts, employed by the end-user, Wandsworth Council. The significant point is that, by a majority, the court held that where there is an irreducible minimum of mutual obligation, i.e. an obligation to perform work coupled with control, then there is a contract of employment (still referred to by some judges as a contract of service). This was an important restatement of the law in general on employment status and means, in the context of agency workers, that tribunals must consider if there is a contract of employment between the worker and the end-user even though the employee's wages may be paid by the agency. However, this decision must now be read subject to *James* v *Greenwich Council* (overleaf). An employee may claim, for example, unfair dismissal after the relationship with the end-user has lasted one year. This was what the applicant wished to claim *Dacas* and was now able to do although her claim failed on other grounds. The court also pointed out that the worker still had a contract with the agency but it was not one of employment. In *Cable &*

Wireless v *Muscat* (2006) it was emphasised that where there is an obligation on the end-user (the client) to provide the worker with work and the worker is obliged to attend and work under the control of the end-user then a contract of employment can be justified. However, this case had the added feature that the claimant had been employed by the end-user prior to the involvement of the agency.

The decisions in the cases on agency workers were analysed by Leighton and Wynn (2006) who pointed to the problems which can be caused by looking for a solution based on expediency alone; and the decisions in *Dacas* and *Muscat* were strongly criticised by Reynolds (2006) who argued that there is an 'insuperable conceptual difficulty' in finding that there is an implied contract between an agency worker and the end-user where there are no express contractual arrangements between them. Where there is nothing in the conduct of the agency worker and the end-user to suggest that there is a contract between them then there is no room for the implication of a contract.

The criticism by Reynolds seems to have been reflected in the latest case, *James* v *Greenwich Council* (2006), where the EAT gave useful guidance on when a contract can be implied between the agency worker and the end-user:

- Where the end-user cannot insist on the agency supplying a particular worker it is inappropriate to imply a contract.

- It will be rare for a contract to be implied where there was no pre-existing contract between the worker and the end-user (as there was in *Muscat*). The only way in which such a contract could be implied would be if the agency arrangements no longer dictate how the work is to be performed and so the reality of the situation is consistent with a contract.

- The mere fact that the worker may have been working under an agency arrangement with the end-user for a long time does not justify the implication of a contract. It is here that the EAT differs from the remarks of Sedley LJ in *Dacas*.

Agency workers and liability in tort

The question of whether the end-users can be vicariously liable in tort for the actions of the agency worker was raised in *Hawley* v *Luminar Leisure Ltd* (2006). A doorman employed by a security firm badly injured the claimant in an incident outside the nightclub where the doorman was employed. It was held that the nightclub was the 'temporary deemed employer' as it controlled what the doorman did and he was responsible to the club. (See Reynolds (2005) who argues that the contractual relationship between the parties should not be the consideration in deciding whether the employer should be vicariously liable in tort.)

Company directors

Non-executive company directors will not be employees but an executive or managing director could be an employee. If the director works full-time for the company and is paid a salary then there seems to be no reason why he or she should not be an employee (see *Folami* v *Nigerline (UK) Ltd* (1978)) but problems arise where the matter is not so clear-cut. In *Parsons* v *Albert J. Parsons & Sons Ltd* (1979) the director worked full-time but he had no written contract of employment and his remuneration was expressed as 'director's fees'. In the most recent case, *Secretary of State for Trade and Industry* v *Bottrill* (1999), the Court of Appeal held that there was no rule that where a director was the controlling shareholder of a company then he or she could not be an employee. The issue was one of fact in each case. Previously, the EAT had held, in *Buchan* v *Secretary of State for Employment* (1997), that the existence of a controlling shareholding did make a difference as, given that in practice there would be little difference between the director and the company, it would be wrong that such a person should be able to claim unpaid wages from the state when he or she had put the company into liquidation. One can certainly see the force of the argument in *Buchan* but for now it does not represent the law.

Office holders

This category includes those who have a particular status as the holder of an office. In *Great Western Railway Co* v *Bater* (1920) an office was defined as 'a subsisting, permanent, substantive position, which had an existence independently of the person who filled it, and which went on and was filled by successive office holders'. The essence of the idea is that the office itself is either of common law or statutory origin and has a separate existence from whoever holds it.

Much confusion has been caused by failing to distinguish between those who hold what is called 'an office' and those who are office holders in the strict legal sense. Company directors may hold what is called an office but do not come within this definition as their office is not of common law or statutory origin. A clerk to school governors is similarly an employee although often said to hold an office. Office holders in the strict sense are a small category of which some main examples are: police constables; superintendent registrars of births, marriages and deaths; and clergy in the Church of England who hold a benefice. We are concerned only with office holders in the strict sense.

The place of office holders in employment law was reviewed by the House of Lords in *Percy* v *Church of Scotland Board of National Mission* (2005) and, although this decision dealt specifically with ministers of religion (see below), the speeches considered office holders in general. Lady Hale pointed out that before the days of modern employment legislation it was a positive advantage to be an office holder as they had a right, denied to employees, to a hearing before being deprived of their office (*Ridge* v *Baldwin* (1964)). Now, of course, employees have this right (see Chapter 11). However, employees also have the benefit of the multitude of employment protection rights which have sprung up in the last 35 years. If office holders are a separate category, distinct from employees, then they will not have these rights and so in *Percy* the House of Lords held (Lord Hoffmann dissenting) that a person can be both an office holder and an employee so that classification as an office holder will not mean a loss of employment protection rights.

In fact, when one looks at the examples mentioned above, the issue of employment rights is less significant. It is no longer certain that ministers of religion are office

4

The employment relationship

71

holders (see below). Police constables are entitled to public law remedies (see *Ridge v Baldwin* (1964) in Chapter 11) but s 201 of the ERA 1996 provides that they have no rights under employment protection legislation except the right to a statement of initial employment particulars, a minimum notice period and redundancy pay. However, they are covered by anti-discrimination legislation (see Chapter 9) and disciplinary matters come under the Police Regulations. In *Miles v Wakefield Metropolitan District Council* (1987) a Registrar of Births, Marriages and Deaths was in effect treated as an employee to allow him to claim for unpaid salary, although the claim ultimately failed on other grounds (see Chapter 7). It should be noted, as mentioned above, that the Employment Equality (Sex Discrimination) Regulations 2005 now apply sex discrimination legislation to office holders and, in the opinion of Lord Hoffmann in *Percy* (above), Mrs Percy might have succeeded under these regulations had they been in force at the time.

Ministers of religion

As a general rule, ministers of religion were traditionally held not to have employee status although there were attempts to argue the contrary. These floundered on various grounds. In *McMillan v Guest* (1942) it was held that this was a case of an office rather than employment and in *President of the Methodist Conference v Parfitt* (1984) Dillon J said that 'the minister sets out to serve God as his master; I do not think that it is right to say that in the legal sense he is at the point of ordination undertaking by contract to serve the church or the conference as his master throughout the years of his ministry'. As pointed out by Gillian Evans (1997), the issue of control is not clear-cut in the relationship between a member of the clergy and his or her bishop because a bishop theologically has supervision or 'oversight' of his clergy which is, in a way, what she calls a 'personal binding of minister to supervisor'.

In July 2002 a DTI Discussion Paper asked for views (para 78) on using the power in s 23 of the Employment Relations Act (see above) to extend employment protection rights to ministers of religion. There have been a number of responses by the churches to the government's discussion paper. The Roman Catholic Church saw employment status as incompatible with Canon Law whilst the Church of England, whilst not accepting the idea of employment status as such, is looking at ways in which its own internal procedures can give the same rights to the clergy as are enjoyed by others who work. For example, should the clergy have a grievance procedure? A response is expected in 2007. The Methodist Church is also thinking along the same lines and had pointed out that its ministers do already enjoy a substantial number of the rights enjoyed by employees. The government has yet to say how it intends to proceed but some of the churches are clearly hoping that, by demonstrating that their own procedures and the rights they give are comparable with those given to employees, the government will see no need to introduce legislation.

Whilst this consultation was proceeding, the issue of employment rights for the clergy surfaced from another direction. In *Percy v Church of Scotland Board of National Mission* (2006) it was held that a minister of religion came within the provisions of discrimination legislation which apply to workers who are defined as those who enter into a contract to personally execute work or labour (see s 230(3) of the ERA 1996, above). The facts were that Helen Percy was an ordained minister of the Church of Scotland and was an associate minister of a parish in Angus. It was alleged that she had had an affair with an elder in the parish and an enquiry was set up to investigate. It found that there was a case to answer and preparations for a formal trial were put in hand. However, at a mediation meeting she was counselled to resign as a minister and this she did. She accepted that she did not have a contract of employment under s 230(1) of the ERA 1996, so she could not claim for unfair dismissal, but she did claim that she was the victim of sex discrimination contrary to the Sex Discrimination Act 1975 on the basis that in similar circumstances the church had not taken action against male ministers who had been known to have had extramarital sexual relationships in similar circumstances. The truth of the allegations made against her was not decided at this stage but the House of Lords held that as s 82(1) of the SDA 1975 adopted the definition of a worker in s 230(3) of the ERA 1996 (above) she had the right to claim. (See Cranmer and Peterson (2006) and Duddington (2006).)

The effect of this decision was to leave the position of ministers of religion in an unfortunate kind of limbo: they could have rights under discrimination law but not under other parts of employment law, notably unfair dismissal. This gap was swiftly plugged by the decision in *New Testament Church of God* v *Stewart* (2006), where the EAT held that ministers of religion can have the status of employees and so can claim for unfair dismissal and the full range of employment rights. The EAT held that the effect of the *Percy* decision was, according to Ansell J, to cast considerable doubt upon, if not reverse, the presumption against intention to create legal relations in these cases. Thus the question was whether in a particular case the relationship of a minister with their church has the necessary characteristics of a contract of employment. Here the minister performed administrative functions such as the sending in of monthly reporting forms to the National Office and he was subject to the discipline of the National Church and so was held to be an employee. It is important, though, to note that not all ministers of religion may be employees, as the relationship between them and the church may not be the same as in this case. However, it is unlikely that in the case of parish clergy it will be very different and so the likelihood is that parish clergy are, in most cases, in an employment relationship with their church.

Crown servants

Crown servants are simply those in Crown employment and are commonly known as civil servants. There is a doubt as to whether Crown servants have a contract with the Crown and, even if they do, whether that contract is a contract of employment. In *IRC* v *Hambrook* (1956) Goddard LCJ said: 'an established civil servant is appointed to an office . . . so that his employment depends not on a contract with the Crown but on appointment by the Crown'. Other judges have, however, held that Crown servants have a contract even if not a contract of employment (see e.g. *Cresswell* v *Board of Inland Revenue* (1984)). This point is somewhat academic because s 191 of the ERA

4

The employment relationship

1996 provides that all of its provisions extend to Crown servants except those giving the right to a minimum period of notice and the right to a redundancy payment. Therefore, a Crown servant can claim compensation for unfair dismissal but not redundancy pay. Indeed, s 159 of the ERA 1996 expressly states that civil servants have no right to a redundancy payment. However, they are covered by more generous schemes and so this exclusion does not in reality affect them. A special provision is found in s 245 of the TULRCA 1992 whereby Crown servants are deemed to be employees for the purposes of liability for the economic torts. The reason is that trade unions have immunity from actions for the tort of inducement of a breach of contract, one of the economic torts, but this immunity would not exist if a civil servant were not an employee because he or she did not have a contract. This provision therefore protects trade unions rather than civil servants directly. The subject of trade union immunities is dealt with in Chapter 13.

Trainees

Where a trainee has a traditional contract of apprenticeship, he or she will come within employment protection legislation because s 230(2) of the ERA 1996 provides that a contract of apprenticeship is a contract of employment. However, a contract of apprenticeship is a formal agreement between the employer, who agrees to train the apprentice, and the apprentice, who agrees to serve the employer. Not all trainees are apprentices and the number of traditional apprentices is declining because of the increase in training schemes funded by the government. Trainees other than apprentices appear to have no contract (see *Daley* v *Allied Supplier Ltd* (1983)) but trainees are given the protection of equal opportunities and health and safety legislation although they have no rights to, for example, claim for unfair dismissal.

In *Flett* v *Matheson* (2005) the EAT held that a modern apprenticeship scheme is not a traditional contract of apprenticeship and so, although there is no entitlement to damages for breach of contract, if it is terminated before the end of the term, it is a contract of employment. Thus, the appellant was entitled to one week's notice of termination and, as he did not receive this, he was awarded one week's pay.

It should be noted that a modern apprenticeship scheme is tripartite: the employer provides the work experience and a training agent (e.g. a college) provides the training. A traditional apprenticeship is where the obligation to train is on the employer. The judgment of Burton J gives useful guidance on what obligations modern apprenticeship contracts should spell out.

CONTINUITY OF EMPLOYMENT

The main reason why it is important to decide if a worker is an employee is, as we have seen, to decide if he or she is entitled to the benefit of employment protection legislation. However, in certain cases, a person can claim employment protection rights only if, in addition to being an employee, he or she has a certain period of continuous employment. This topic is considered in Chapter 6.

LAW IN CONTEXT
The psychological contract

In addition to the difficulties which the courts face today in deciding the scope of contracts of employment and whether the contract of employment can exist outside the actual period of employment (see above), the concept of the psychological contract has been developed in the field of organisational behaviour.

The basic idea, as set out by Mullins (2005), is that this is not a written document but it 'implies a series of mutual expectations and satisfaction of needs arising from the people–organisation relationship'. Thus it covers a range of expectations of rights and privileges which, to the lawyer, can of course include the implied obligations in a contract of employment (see Chapter 5). Cartwright (2000) (quoted in Mullins) emphasises that mutuality is the basic principle of the psychological contract and here there are obvious echoes of the implied duty of mutual trust and confidence (see Chapter 5). However, the psychological contract goes further than this and covers the implicit expectations of both employers and employees.

Stalker (2000) (again quoted in Mullins) examines the concept of the psychological contract in relation to the ability of the organisation to balance the unwritten needs of the employee with those of the needs of the organisation and suggests a formula of:

- *Caring* – demonstrating a genuine concern for individuals in the workplace

- *Communicating* – talking about what the company hopes to achieve

- *Listening* – hearing not only the words of employees but what lies behind them

- *Knowing* – really knowing the individuals who work for you – their families, their personal wishes, desires and ambitions

- *Rewarding* – remembering that money is not always necessary and that morale can be raised by a thank you or public recognition.

These ideas, whether consciously or unconsciously, are finding their way into the law on the contract of employment. Good examples are not only the duty of mutual trust and confidence but also the law on what constitutes a repudiatory breach of contract sufficient for the employee to claim constructive dismissal. What is clear is that the courts are, in line with good human resources practice, going beyond the narrow interpretation of the implied duties of the employer and the employee.

This idea of the psychological contract can also be seen as throwback to an earlier era when some employers had a different and perhaps more paternalistic relationship with their employees. As Welch, the former head of the General Electric Company, put it (Welch, 1989): 'Like many other large companies in the United States, Europe and Japan, GE had an implicit lifetime psychological contract (with its employees) based on perceived lifetime employment. People were rarely dismissed except for cause or severe business downturns . . . This produced a paternal, feudal, fuzzy kind of loyalty. You put in your time, worked hard and the company took care of you for life.'

4

The employment relationship

SUMMARY

This chapter begins by looking at the traditional model of the employment relationship and considers criticisms of it in the light of current trends such as the growth in self-employment and different forms of employment such as agency workers, homeworkers, casual workers and volunteers. It then looks at the statistical evidence for changing patterns of employment. It considers the influence of EC law on employment status and then looks at the statutory division between employees, workers and professionals. The tests used by the courts to determine employment status are examined both in general and in the light of particular types of employment relationships which are of topical importance, such as agency workers and the recent change in the employment status of ministers of religion.

QUESTION

Ron is a mechanic and has been employed by Mike's Motors, a small lawnmower repair firm, for two years. On 1 February 2007 Mike said to Ron:

'From 1 March you'll be on your own legally. You'll be self-employed. I'm fed up with all of these new employment laws and so I'd like you to sign this, but remember that things won't change bar a few small details. It's all in here.'

Mike then gives Ron a document which states:

I agree that I am a self-employed mechanic. My wages will be paid gross but I will continue to tender my services exclusively to Mike's Mowers. If I am unable, due to sickness, to work on any day then I may engage a substitute. I will provide my own tools and equipment. In consideration of signing this agreement I become entitled to a bonus of £100.

Ron signed the document.

On 1 April Mike came up to Ron and said: 'Sorry old chum but my son is coming into the business and I can't afford to employ you and him. You'll have to go from the end of the week.'

Ron asks you for advice on whether he is able to claim compensation for dismissal.

FURTHER READING

Deakin, S. (1998) 'The Evolution of the Contract of Employment 1900–1950: the influence of the Welfare State' in N. Whiteside and R. Salais (eds) *Governance, Industry and Labour Markets in Britain and France. The modernising state in the mid twentieth century*, Routledge: London.

Freedland, M. (2005) 'Rethinking the Personal Work Contract', 58 *Current Legal Problems* 517. This should be read along with Freedland's other writings on this subject mentioned in the bibliography.

BIBLIOGRAPHY

Bercusson, B. (1996) *European Labour Law*, Butterworths: London (see especially chapter 29 on Contracts and Employment Relationships).

Burchell, B., Deakin, S. and Honey, S. (1999) *The Employment Status of Workers in Non Standard Employment*, EMAR research series 6 (DTI).

Cartwright, J. (2000) *Cultural Transformation*, Financial Times/Prentice Hall: New Jersey (p. 119).

Cranmer, F. and Peterson, S. (2006) 'Employment, Sex Discrimination and the Percy Case', 8 Ecclesiastical LJ 392–405.

Davidov, G. (2005) 'Who is a Worker?' 34 ILJ 57.

Davies, P. (2004) *Perspectives on Labour Law*, Cambridge University Press: Cambridge. (This book examines the economic background to each area of employment law and is most valuable.)

Deakin, S. (2006) 'The Comparative Evolution of Labour Law' in G. Davidov and S. Langille (eds) *Boundaries and Frontiers of Labour Law*, Hart Publishing: Oxford.

Duddington, J. (2006) 'Ministers of Religion and Employment Law: A Story from the Glens of Angus', 156 *Law and Justice* 59.

Evans, G. (1997) 'The Employment Status of Ministers of Religion', 132/133 *Law and Justice* 22.

Fairness at Work (May 1998) (Cm 3968).

Fredman, S. (1997) 'Labour Law in Flux – The Changing Composition of the Workforce', 26 ILJ 337.

Freedland, M. (2005) *The Personal Employment Contract*, Oxford University Press: Oxford.

Freedland, M. (2006) 'From the Personal Work Contract to the Personal Work Nexus', 35 ILJ 1. (This updates the thinking of the author from his book published in 2005.)

Guardian Unlimited (2006) 'Workforce turns to self-employment', 10 October 2006. www. business.guardian.co.uk/story/0,,1891844,00.html (last accessed 29 May 2007).

Hepple, B. (1986) 'Restructuring Employment Rights', 15 ILJ 69.

Hotopp, U. (2002) 'Teleworking in the UK', *Labour Market Trends*, June 2002.

Kahn-Freund, O. (1967) 'A Note on Status and Contract in Modern Labour Law', 30 MLR 635.

Leighton, P. (1984) 'The Contract of Employment', 13 ILJ 62 and especially 65–66. (This is an examination of decisions on the employment status of casual workers.)

Leighton, P. and Wynn, M. (2006) 'Will the Real Employer Stand Up? Agencies, Client Companies and the Employment Status of Temporary Workers', 35 ILJ 301.

McKendrick, E. (1990) 'Vicarious Liability and Independent Contractors – A Re-Examination', 53 MLR 770. (Despite the fact that things have moved on from 1990, this is still a valuable study.)

McOrmond, T. (2004) 'Changes in Working Trends over the Past Decade', Labour Market Trends, January 2004.

Morris, D. (1999) 'Employment Status of Volunteers', 28 ILJ 249.

Mullins, L. (2005) *Management and Organisational Behaviour* (7th edn), Financial Times/ Prentice Hall: New Jersey (p. 37).

Office of National Statistics (ONS): London. 2005.

Reynolds, F. (2005) 'Negligent Workers: Can there be Vicarious Liability?' 34 ILJ 270.

Reynolds, F. (2006) 'The Status of Agency Workers: A Question of Legal Principle', 35 ILJ 320.

Stalker, K. (2000) 'The Individual, the Organisation and the Psychological Contract', *Institute of Administrative Management*, July/August, pp. 28, 34.

4

The employment relationship

Szyszczak, E. (2000) *EC Labour Law*, Longman: Harlow (Chapter 3 is most illuminating on this whole area.)

Wedderburn, K. (1991) *Employment Rights in Britain and Europe: Selected Papers in Labour Law*, Lawrence & Wishart: London.

Welch, C. (1989) 'Speed, Simplicity and Self Confidence: An Interview with Jack Welch', *Harvard Business Review* (Sept–Oct 1989), quoted in V. Stone (2006) 'Employment Protection for Boundaryless Workers' in G. Davidov and S. Langille (eds) *Boundaries and Frontiers of Labour Law*, Hart Publishing: Oxford.

For further resources and updates please go to the Companion Website accompanying this book at **www.mylawchamber.co.uk/duddingtonemployment**

5 The contract of employment

FORM OF THE CONTRACT OF EMPLOYMENT

Introduction

Contracts of employment, with a few exceptions, conform to the general rule that no formalities are required for a contract and therefore a contract of employment can be made orally or in writing. The main exception is contracts of merchant seamen, who must have individual written agreements which must then be collected into crew agreements (see s 25 of the Merchant Shipping Act 1995).

However, all employees are entitled to a written statement of initial employment particulars not later than two months after the beginning of employment. This right was first conferred by the Contracts of Employment Act 1963, the statute that began the modern flow of employment protection rights. The right is now contained in ss 1–7 of the Employment Rights Act 1996 (ERA 1996). (References in this section of the chapter are to the ERA 1996 unless otherwise indicated.) It is of crucial importance to appreciate that the ERA 1996 does not require a written contract of employment but only a written statement of certain terms of employment. The distinction between this statement and a contract will be explored later in this chapter.

Therefore, an employer can do any of the following:

1 Give employees a statement of initial employment particulars with any extra terms, if any, left to an oral agreement.

2 Give employees a written contract of employment which contains the details required to be contained in the statement but also contains other details (see below for examples).

3 Give employees two documents: the statement plus a written contract containing additional matters. This may occur when an employer wishes to insert extra provisions in the contract after the employee has begun work.

In practice, option 2 is quite common, although many employers still just give the statement.

Contents of the statement

Section 1(3) of the ERA 1996 provides that the statement must contain the following details correct at the date of the statement:

(a) the names of the employer and employee;

(b) the date on which the employment began;

(c) the date on which the employee's period of continuous employment began, taking into account any period of employment with a previous employer which counts towards continuity (see Chapter 6 for the details of when this can occur).

Section 1(4) then provides that the statement shall contain the following details, which must be correct at a specified date not more than seven days before the statement is given (the reason for this provision being that a detail might change in the interval between the issuing of the statement and its receipt and therefore without this rule it would be impossible to issue a statement):

(a) the scale or rate of remuneration or the method of calculating it;

(b) the intervals at which it is paid (weekly, monthly, etc.);

(c) any terms and conditions relating to hours of work;

(d) any terms and conditions relating to holidays and holiday pay, sick pay and other terms relating to incapacity for work due to sickness or injury, and pensions and pension schemes;

(e) the length of notice which the employee is entitled to receive and is obliged to give to terminate employment;

(f) the employee's job title or a brief job description;

(g) if the employment is not to be permanent, how long it is to last, or the date when a fixed-term contract ends;

(h) the employee's place of work or an indication that the employee is expected to work at various places if this is so;

(j) any collective agreements which affect the terms and conditions of employment;

(k) where the employee is required to work outside Great Britain for a period of more than one month, the period to be spent abroad, the currency in which remuneration will be paid, any additional remuneration and benefits and any terms and conditions relating to the employee's return to the UK.

Section 3(1)(a) provides that the employer must include a note specifying any disciplinary rules applicable to the employee or referring the employee to a reasonably accessible document containing these. Section 35(2) of the Employment Act 2002 added a s 3(1)(aa) providing that the employer must specify any procedures applicable to the taking of disciplinary decisions or decisions to dismiss or refer the employee to a reasonably accessible document containing these. The addition of para (aa) is intended to support the statutory dispute resolution procedure laid down in ss 29–34 of the Employment Act 2002 and the effect is that procedures for dealing with disciplinary matters must be specified in addition to disciplinary rules. The note specified in s 3 must also specify the person to whom an employee can apply if dissatisfied with a disciplinary decision and a person to whom the employee can apply to seek redress of a grievance. If there are further steps following this application by the employee then the note must specify them, although s 3(2) provides that none of the foregoing applies to rules, disciplinary decisions or grievance procedures relating to health and safety at work and s 35(4) of the Employment Act 2002 adds to this disciplinary decisions to dismiss relating to health and safety. An important provision, which applied only to s 3, was that these details did not need to be given if the total number of employees at the date when the employee's employment began (including those employed by any associated employer) was less than 20. However, s 36 of the Employment Act 2002 removed this exemption.

The following matters, which have to be included in the statement, are worthy of mention at this point:

1 A vital point of employment law, which was stressed in Chapter 1, is that the object of the statutory provisions is to provide a floor of rights. Therefore, the statement can, where statute provides for certain rights, either state that those rights shall apply or that the employee shall be entitled to rights in excess of the statutory minimum. For example, it can provide that the employee shall be entitled to notice periods set out in the ERA 1996 or to extra notice but not to less notice than the ERA provides for. (The topic of notice is dealt with in Chapter 11.)

2 The requirement to state the job title (s 1(4)(f)) needs to be approached with care by an employer because the more specific the job title is, the more difficult it will be to move the employee from one job to another. It should be noted that there is no requirement to give employees a full job description, although this is becoming increasingly common, but only a brief job description as an alternative to a job title. *Land Securities Trillium* v *Thornley* (2005), which is considered later in this chapter, is a good example of the legal effect of a job description. The requirement to state the place of work is also one to be handled with care, as again the designation of a very specific place of work may make it more difficult to move the employee. (This issue is to some extent bound up with redundancy and is dealt with in Chapter 12.)

Points arising from the statement

The particulars must be contained in a single document, with the exception of the following, which can either be contained in the statement or specified in other ways as indicated:

1 the note specifying disciplinary rules (see above);

2 particulars relating to sickness, sick pay and pensions, when the statement may refer to a reasonably accessible document;

3 details of notice periods may be given by referring the employee to the general law or to a reasonably accessible collective agreement.

The intention of the Act is not to require all of the terms to exist but, if a term relating to any of the specified matters does not exist, then s 2(1) requires the statement to point this out. Carried to its extreme, however, this could mean that a statement simply stated that there were no particulars at all. Clearly this cannot be so, because a contract with no terms at all would not be a contract. In *Eagland* v *British Telecommunications* (1990) Wood P, in the EAT, distinguished between mandatory terms (which must be included) and non-mandatory terms (which need not). He found the key to the distinction between mandatory and non-mandatory terms in the

5

The contract of employment

words 'any terms and conditions relating to', which clearly envisaged, by the use of the word 'any', a situation where there were none. As will be seen from the above list, this phrase appears in (c) and (d) dealing with terms relating to hours of work, holidays, sickness and pensions. All of the other terms laid down in s 1(3) and s 1(4)(a), (b), (e) and (f) were mandatory, which clearly makes sense as, for example, it would be strange if the statement declined to say who the employer was. At the date of this case, there was no requirement to give details of terms (g)–(k) but it is probable that (g) (temporary employment) and (h) (place of work) are mandatory, whereas (j) (collective agreements) can apply only if there are any, and (k) (employment abroad) appears to be mandatory with the exception of the final part beginning with the words 'any terms and conditions'. Finally, the requirement to give details of disciplinary and grievance procedures is mandatory.

It is almost certain that, during the time of the employee's employment, some at least of the particulars will change and s 4 provides that, if this is so, then the employer must give employees a statement containing particulars of any changes not later than one month afterwards. Three particular points arise:

1   the changes must be set out in full and may not be given in instalments;
2   where the original details could be specified either in the statement or in other ways (see above) then the same applies to any changes to these details;
3   where only the name or the identity of the employer changes then, although these changes must of course be notified, a whole new statement need not be issued unless continuity of employment is broken.

Enforcement of the obligation to give a statement

There is no right to claim compensation for failure to give a statement, although in an action for, for example, unfair dismissal, the tribunal will not take a favourable view of the employer's case if it emerges during the hearing that no statement was ever provided to the employee.

Instead, if an employer does not give a statement or if the statement the employee is given by the employer is deficient then the employee has the right by s 11 to complain to an employment tribunal.

Section 12(1) allows the tribunal, where either no particulars have been given or the particulars were incomplete, to decide what particulars ought to be included, and s 12(2) gives the tribunal power, where the statement is inaccurate, to amend particulars or substitute other particulars.

These provisions have caused some difficulty in interpretation, particularly the words 'ought to be included'. The courts have not interpreted this phrase in any creative sense so as to give a wide power to tribunals to decide what ought to be in the statement, but have instead reserved any creative power to themselves to use when expanding the concept of implied terms of the contract. Thus in *Construction Industry Training Board* v *Leighton* (1978) Kilner-Brown J, in the EAT, said that tribunals have no power 'to declare what a contract meant or to rectify an error manifest in an otherwise binding contract'. Instead, their function is to find out what has been agreed rather than to invent a term. Thus, in *Leighton* itself, the tribunal had decided that the employee was entitled to a salary increment mentioned in the statement when this was unclear. The EAT held that the tribunal should not have embarked on this exercise and instead left the matter to the civil courts in an action on the contract. A good example of the orthodox view is *Cuthbertson* v *AML Distributors* (1975), where the tribunal refused to state the amount of notice which would have been reasonable when no statement had been given.

However, in *Mears* v *Safecar Security Ltd* (1982) the Court of Appeal held that a tribunal does have jurisdiction to hear a complaint that inaccurate particulars have been given. The distinction between deciding whether particulars are inaccurate and rectifying an error, which the Court of Appeal said in *Leighton* was not permissible, is clearly a fine one and this area awaits clarification in a future decision.

Relationship between the statement and the contract of employment

An employer may, as stated earlier, choose to give a contract of employment which includes the matters that need to be in the statement together with other matters. Obvious examples, which will be considered later in this chapter, are confidentiality clauses, restraint of trade clauses and a clause that the employee must not undertake other work outside working hours without the consent of his or her employer.

The fact that the statement is not by itself the contract of employment is significant because the rule that outside evidence is not normally admissible to add to or vary a written instrument, such as a contract, does not apply to statements. Therefore, it is open to either party to argue that the statement does not reflect what was agreed and this is of particular importance to employees, as the issue of the statement may not have been preceded by any negotiation between the parties.

Therefore, in *System Floors (UK) Ltd* v *Daniel* (1982) the EAT allowed an employer to bring evidence that the correct date when the employee began work was a week later than the statement said. (The point was important in calculating whether the employee had sufficient continuity of employment to claim for unfair dismissal.) As Browne-Wilkinson J put it, the statement 'provides very strong *prima facie* evidence of what were the terms of the contract between the parties, but does not constitute a written contract between the parties'. The employer is placed, he said, under a heavy burden to show that the actual terms are different from those in the statement but the point is that, as the statement is not actually the contract, the employer is at least able to argue that the statement is wrong. So, of course, is the employee. This case was somewhat unusual in that the employer was arguing that his own statement was wrong. In the case of an employee arguing that the statement was wrong the evidential burden would be less as in *Robertson and Jackson* v *British Gas Corporation* (1983), where the employee successfully argued that the details of bonus payments in the statement were wrong.

Set against these authorities is the awkward decision of the Court of Appeal in *Gascol Conversions Ltd* v *Mercer* (1974). The employer gave the employee a new contract of employment dealing with, *inter alia*, hours of work, because the Industrial Relations Act 1971 required these details to be included in statements given to employees, and the employee signed for its receipt as a new contract of employment. The employee later argued that the hours of work stated were wrong. It was held that

5

The contract of employment

83

as he had signed a contract, rather than a statement, he could not later argue that the details were wrong. If it was found that he had simply signed for receipt of the document as a statement then he would not have signed the document as a contract and *could* have argued that the details were wrong. On the facts it is not clear precisely how the parties regarded the effect of the employee's signature but the case stands as a valuable reminder that once a contract is signed as such, it will be very difficult to argue later that any of its contents were wrong.

CAPACITY TO MAKE A CONTRACT OF EMPLOYMENT

The only important restriction here is that minors' contracts of employment are binding provided that, on the whole, they are for their benefit. An illustration is ***De Francesco v Barnum*** (1890), where a contract was so one-sided that it was held to be not binding. Detailed discussion of this topic, however, belongs to textbooks on the law of contract.

CONTENTS OF THE CONTRACT OF EMPLOYMENT

Introduction

The contract of employment, like all other contracts, is made up of terms, which contain the obligations of the parties. Until 1963, and the passage of the Contracts of Employment Act, the terms of the contract as developed by the courts as common law were virtually the only source of employment rights. Now, with the passage of innumerable statutes and other legislation dealing with employment matters, it might seem that the contents of the actual contract are of little significance. This view would be greatly mistaken, as the courts have been most active in developing the common law of employment alongside the statutory developments.

Before looking at the employment contract in detail, it is worth remembering that, as with all other contracts, the parties must actually intend to enter into binding obligations. This point was brought home by the decision in ***Judge v Crown Leisure*** (2005). The claimant was employed as one of three special operations managers and he alleged that at a Christmas party he was promised by a director that he would be put on the same pay scale as a recently appointed manager. The Court of Appeal held that the conversation was too vague to amount to a contractual promise as there was no more than a commitment that the claimant would achieve parity in due course.

Types of contractual terms

Terms come from the following sources:

1 The express terms of the contract as actually contained in the contract, whether orally or written.

84

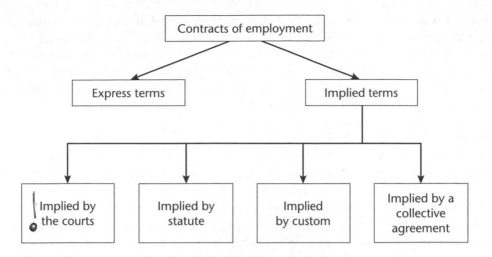

2 The implied terms of the contract. These are not contained in the contract itself but are derived from the following sources:
 (a) statute;
 (b) custom;
 (c) the courts;
 (d) collective agreements.

Not only this, but there is a grey area dealing with such matters as work rules and company policies which may in some cases be sources of contractual terms.

It should be noted that there is a link between implied terms and termination of the contract (see Chapter 11), because a breach of an implied term by the employee may give the employer grounds to dismiss and a breach by the employer may give the employee grounds to claim constructive dismissal as in *Waltons and Morse* v *Dorrington* (1997) and *WA Goold* v *McConnell* (1995) (below).

Each of the above sources of terms will now be considered in turn.

Express terms

This category calls for little comment in itself except to remark that the bald terms of the contract will give little idea of the relationship in practice between the employer and employees nor of how the work is to be done. One can supplement the contract by referring to work rules but work rules are not likely to be held part of the contract, as will appear below. Furthermore, the courts have upheld the idea that there is an area of 'managerial prerogative' which lies beyond the contract and which is seen clearly in cases where the employer wishes to impose changes to the contract on employees. This issue is dealt with in more detail in Chapter 12 in the context of dismissal on a reorganisation of a business.

Terms implied by statute

A straightforward example is provided by s 1(1) of the Equal Pay Act 1970, which provides that every woman's contract of employment is deemed to include an equality clause under which any term in it which is less favourable than that in the contract of a male employee is modified so that it is not less favourable. (Note that in the Act a woman includes a man.) The effect of this, which is explained in detail in Chapter 9, is to give a woman (or a man) a contractual right to equal pay where the work is, in a broad sense, equal. This type of provision is unusual: the normal method of granting statutory rights is to make enforcement of them independent of the contract.

Terms implied by custom

The custom of a trade or business may be a source of a term if it is certain and reasonable and applies throughout a particular trade, business or area. A good, if old, example, is provided by *Sagar* v *Ridehalgh* (1931), where a custom in the Lancashire mills of deducting wages for bad work was held to be binding on an employee. This area of the law needs clarification. For example, Lawrence LJ emphasised that the custom in question had prevailed at the mill where the employee worked for over 30 years, but the essence of custom is that it is observed in a trade rather than just one factory. In addition, Lawrence LJ thought that it did not matter whether the employee knew of the custom or not but in later cases the point has caused a divergence of opinion. In *Marshall* v *English Electric Co. Ltd* (1945) Lord Goddard thought that a custom was automatically incorporated but du Parcq LJ thought that the employee needed to assent. Certainly, a need for assent by the employee is in accord with the trend of modern employment law and it is submitted that it should be required.

Terms implied by the courts and their importance

This is the most important source of implied terms and will be considered in detail. There is no doubt that the importance of the implied terms has increased enormously in recent years, as a glance at some of the cases discussed below will show. Particularly good examples of recent significant decisions are *Johnstone* v *Bloomsbury Area Health Authority* (1991) and *Malik* v *BCCI* (1997). Indeed, in *Johnson* v *Unisys Ltd* (2001) Lord Hoffmann compared the growth in the common law of employment with the growth in statutory regulation of the employment relationship:

> Over the last 30 years or so, the nature of the contract of employment has been transformed. It has been recognised that a person's employment is usually one of the most important things in a person's life . . . Most of the changes have been made by Parliament . . . And the common law has adapted to the new attitudes, proceeding sometimes by analogy with statutory rights . . . The contribution of the common law to the employment revolution has been by the evolution of implied terms in the contract of employment. The most far reaching is the implied term of trust and confidence.

(The term 'trust and confidence' is discussed below.)

Basis on which the courts imply a term

The classic theory is that the courts imply a term to give effect to the intentions of the parties which they have failed to express in the contract. In *The Moorcock* (1889) Bowen LJ said that the courts must imply terms from the intentions of the parties with the object of giving business efficacy to the transaction. This language clearly reflects the preoccupation of contract law in the nineteenth century with business transactions and may be considered hardly appropriate to modern employment law. In **Shirlaw v Southern Foundries Ltd** (1939) McKinnon LJ put forward the 'officious bystander test', the point of which is that a term will be implied only if an officious bystander suggested it to the parties whilst they were negotiating and it was such an obvious suggestion that they replied that 'of course' it was included.

The basis of both these theories, resting as they do on the supposed intentions of the parties, is undoubtedly narrow and leaves no room for any creativity on the part of the courts. In fact, it has long been recognised that the scope of implied terms is much wider than this and in many cases the courts have, whilst acting under the cloak of giving effect to the intentions of the parties, in fact imposed a term which they feel ought to be included. This has, in recent years, been explicitly recognised by the courts, so that the theory that terms are implied only to give effect to the intentions of the parties no longer represents the law. The difficulty is in stating precisely when the courts will imply a term.

One approach is provided by the words of Slade LJ in **Courtaulds Northern Spinning Ltd v Sibson** (1988), who held that, in deciding whether to imply a term as to the place of work, the courts should imply a term if satisfied that the parties would have agreed to it 'if they were being reasonable'. This is a reflection of the decision in **Liverpool City Council v Irwin** (1977), where the House of Lords emphasised that the question was whether the implication of a term was both reasonable and necessary to the contract; although that was not an employment case, this seems to represent the law today. A recent example of where the courts have tried to make the position clear is the speech of Lord Bridge in the House of Lords in **Scally v Southern Health and Social Services Board** (1991), where he contrasted the 'search for an implied term necessary to give business efficacy to a particular contract' and a search for 'a term which the law will imply as a necessary incident of a definable category of contractual relationship'.

The position today is that, especially when the courts feel that the common law of employment needs to be advanced and where they are concerned to limit the powers of employers, they may disregard the search for a solution based narrowly on the intentions of the parties. This is particularly true in the case of the development of the implied term of mutual trust and confidence. On the other hand, even in these cases the courts will not imply a term purely because it would be reasonable in a general sense but will ask whether the implication of a term is necessary to the contract. Where, however, the case deals with more basic issues, such as overtime pay, the courts will try to seek the intentions of the parties.

Implied terms in practice

A good example of an attempt by the courts to imply a term by trying to ascertain the intentions of the parties is **Jones v Associated Tunnelling Co. Ltd** (1981). The employee had been issued with a new written statement, which included a mobility clause that obliged him to work at any place which the employer might decide. He made no protest at the time but when the employers tried to move him to another place of work four years later, he refused and instead claimed that he was redundant. The EAT held that his failure to protest at the time did not necessarily mean that he agreed to the

5

The contract of employment

change, as he might not have wished to come into conflict with his employer. It was clearly necessary to imply a term as to place of work in order to give business efficacy to the contract and, although the employer may have intended a term that the employee could be required to move anywhere in the UK, the employee did not intend this. What the court called the 'lowest common denominator' at which the parties would have agreed if asked was that the employee was to be employed within daily travelling distance of home and this term was therefore implied. Another example is provided by *Ali v Christian Salvesen Food Services Ltd* (1997), where a collective agreement provided that employees were entitled to overtime when they had worked 1,824 hours a year. Ali was dismissed before he had worked these hours in a year and he argued that there was an implied term that he would be paid overtime for every hour worked beyond 40 a week. It was held that the fact that the agreement did not mention a right to this did not mean that it should be implied. The fact that this term was omitted was evidence that the parties did not intend it to apply.

On the other hand, in *United Bank Ltd v Akhtar* (1989) the issue of a mobility clause was seen against the duty of mutual trust and confidence (see below) and a different basis was used for the implication of a term. The employee, a bank clerk, had a contract which contained a mobility clause under which he could be required to move to any branch in the UK. He was given six days' notice to move from Leeds to a branch in Birmingham and he left, claiming constructive dismissal. The EAT held that his claim succeeded as there was an implied term in his contract that he would be given reasonable notice of such a move. In the EAT, Knox J, whilst accepting the traditional view that terms should be implied to achieve business efficacy and to give effect to the parties' intentions, added that 'in the field of employment law it is proper to imply an overriding obligation' of trust and respect which is independent of, and additional to, the actual terms of the contract. Therefore, although the employer in this case was entitled by the actual words of the contract to give the order to move with very little notice, this was in conflict with the overriding obligation and thus in breach of contract. The EAT in *White v Reflecting Roadstuds Ltd* (1991) emphasised that the decision in *Akhtar* did not mean that an employee should not simply allege that the employer's actions were unreasonable but that they were in breach of the implied term to treat the employee with trust and respect.

Relationship between express terms and implied terms

Suppose that an express term of the contract comes into conflict with a term which the courts feel ought to be implied. Which will give way? The question will not normally arise, as terms will not be implied where an express term covers the matter. However, in *United Bank Ltd v Akhtar* (1989), as was seen above, the court held that an express term had to be exercised subject to a fundamental implied term. This, however, was not so much a case of an express term giving way to an implied term but the implied term governing the exercise of the express term.

A clearer case is *Johnstone v Bloomsbury Area Health Authority* (1991). The plaintiff was a junior hospital doctor and his contract provided that, in addition to his standard working week of 40 hours, he should be available on call for an average of another 48 hours a week. He alleged that this was having a detrimental effect on his health, as in some cases he had to work in excess of 100 hours a week, and therefore he sued for damages for a breach by his employers of a duty to take reasonable care for his health and safety. The action was heard on an application by the employers to strike it out as disclosing no reasonable cause of action and the Court of Appeal agreed to allow it to proceed. Stuart-Smith LJ held that the express term should be read subject to an implied term that an employer must take reasonable care for the health and safety of employees. The other judges did not go as far. Leggatt LJ, indeed, did not go far at all, holding that the express terms on hours had primacy over any implied term and he would have struck out the action. Browne-Wilkinson V-C took a middle course and held that the agreement to work overtime simply gave the employer a discretion whether to call on employees to do so and this discretion had to be exercised so as to conform with the implied duty to take reasonable care not to do anything to injure the health of employees. With respect, the view of Stuart-Smith LJ seems preferable, as it boldly faces the issue of a conflict between express and implied terms and clearly holds that in some cases an express term may have to give way.

It seems, therefore, that there are certain fundamental implied terms which override express terms either directly, as in *Johnstone,* or by making the exercise of express terms subject to them, as in *Akhtar.* The *Johnstone* case involved terms as to health and safety but another fundamental implied term is that of mutual trust and confidence, which is considered later in this chapter, and which was really the basis of *Akhtar*. However, the relationship between 'fundamental' implied terms and the express terms of the contract is still being worked out. The extent to which the implied duties of the employer and employee can be affected by express terms is not entirely clear, although some of these are so fundamental that no contract of employment could exist without them.

Unfair terms in employment contracts

There has been discussion on whether the Unfair Contract Terms Act 1977 might be relevant to employment contracts but in the most recent decision (*Commerzbank AG v Keen* (2006)) the Court of Appeal held that the Act was not applicable in the context of rights to claim discretionary bonus payments and possibly in other contexts. As this decision concerned payment of wages it is considered in Chapter 7. In addition, it has been argued that in *Johnstone*, in so far as the express term was in breach of the duty to take reasonable care for employees' health and safety, it could count as a clause negating the employer's duty of care under the tort of negligence and would be void under s 2(1) of the Unfair Contract Terms Act 1977.

The implied terms: duties of the employer and employee

The law has long identified certain duties which will be implied into contracts of employment. The relationship between these and the express terms is, as discussed above, not clear but it is probably true to say that, although the actual contract may well modify the *precise contents* of an implied duty, all of these duties must exist in some form in a contract of employment.

■ Duties of the employer

To pay wages

This duty is considered in detail in Chapter 7. Even so, it needs to be mentioned here if only to emphasise just how fundamental these duties have traditionally been, since clearly there cannot be a contract to work without payment.

To indemnify the employee against liabilities and losses incurred in the course of employment

An example would be the duty to reimburse the employee for travel expenses incurred in the course of employment. The duty does not extend to taking care of employees' property (*Deyong* v *Shenburn* (1946)).

To provide work

The extent of this duty, and whether it even exists, is doubtful. In *Collier v Sunday Referee Publishing Co. Ltd* (1940) Asquith LJ denied that such a duty normally existed: 'Provided I pay my cook her wages regularly, she cannot complain if I choose to take any or all of my meals out.' However, he then recognised certain exceptions to this principle: where payment is by commission or where part of the bargain is publicity for the employee, as with singers or actors. In the latter case, a failure to provide work would mean that the employee might gradually sink into oblivion.

The question is whether there is now a more general duty to provide work. In *Langston* v *AUEW (No. 2)* (1974) Denning MR proposed overruling *Collier* in cases of skilled employees so that there was a duty to provide them with work. However, this view was not shared by the other members of the Court of Appeal and the National Industrial Relations Court (NIRC), in deciding the case on its facts, did not have to address the general issue. The claim resulted from a refusal by an employee to join a union. The other employees took industrial action as a result of this because there was a closed shop in operation, and he was eventually suspended without pay. The NIRC found that, as he was entitled under his contract to be paid premium rates for night shifts and overtime, the denial of the opportunity to work meant the loss of opportunity to earn these, which was a breach of contract by the employers. In *Breach* v *Epsylon Industries Ltd* (1976) the EAT held that there may well be exceptions to the general rule that there is no duty to provide work, although precisely what these might be was not specified by the court.

A more recent example of the right to be provided with work, which may lead to more general developments in this area, arose in the context of a decision by employers to put an employee on 'garden leave'. In *William Hill Organisation Ltd* v *Tucker* (1998) a senior employee of a firm of bookmakers had been engaged in developing spread betting, which was a relatively new form of betting. When he wished to leave, his employer tried to impose a six-month garden leave clause. (Such clauses allow employers to impose a long notice period on employees where they are sent home on full pay with a provision that they cannot do any other work during that time. In effect they are paid whilst their skills and knowledge are getting out of date.) In this case the employee successfully challenged the clause on the ground that he needed the opportunity to work as the skills involved in his work required constant practice. This point could, of course, apply to many other employees and this decision may open the way for an expansion of the right to be provided with work. (It should be noted that the garden leave clause was not expressly contained in the contract but simply imposed by the employer. An express garden leave clause would not be easily upset.)

To take reasonable care for the health and safety of employees

As with the duty to pay wages, this duty is so important that it merits consideration in a separate chapter (Chapter 8), although a clear example is provided by *Johnstone v Bloomsbury AHA* (above). However, it is relevant to mention here that it has been extended to the provision of a working environment which is reasonably safe. In *Waltons and Morse v Dorrington* (1997) the applicant left her employment and claimed constructive dismissal because of the employer's failure to deal adequately with her complaints about being exposed to cigarette smoke from other employees. The EAT upheld her claim and held that the provision of a safe working environment suitable for the performance of contractual duties is an implied term in contracts of employment.

This duty also extends to the taking of reasonable steps to prevent bullying at work and here there is a link with:

(a) constructive dismissal, as a complaint that the employer has breached this duty may lead to a claim for constructive dismissal (see Chapter 11);

(b) sex, race, disability, sexual orientation, religion or belief and age discrimination where the bullying can be said to constitute harassment on any of these grounds (see Chapter 9);

(c) the duty of the employer to take reasonable care for the health and safety of employees (see Chapter 8).

In the context of implied terms, a failure by the employer to deal adequately with bullying can be seen as a breach of the duty of mutual trust and confidence (see below). An interesting point was raised in *McCabe v Chicpak Ltd* (1976), where it was held that if the employee refused to name the alleged bullies then the employer was not liable for failing to take steps other than to speak on general terms to the employee's fellow workers. In *Wigan Borough Council v Davies* (1979) it was held that there was an implied term that employers would take reasonable steps to support employees in their work without harassment or disruption from others and that the onus of proving that no additional steps were practicable lay with the employer. A more recent instance is *Waters v Metropolitan Police Commissioner* (2000), where the House of Lords held that an employer could be liable for psychological harm suffered by an employee when complaints about sexual assaults were not treated seriously and by failing to prevent harassment once the complaint had been made. This case should also be considered alongside the duty of the employer not to subject the employee to undue stress leading to psychological harm, considered in Chapter 8.

To take reasonable care in the giving of references

It was not until the decision of the House of Lords in *Spring v Guardian Assurance plc* (1994) that the courts expressly accepted that a duty of care in negligence could arise in giving a reference. Until then, the giving of references had been subject to the law of defamation, in that the giver of a reference was (and still is) protected from an action for defamation even if it contains defamatory material provided that the person giving it did not act maliciously.

Example

Frank works for Jack and then applies for a job with Leanne. He asks Jack for a reference and Jack falsely states that Frank is 'the worst employee I have ever had. He is both dishonest and incompetent'. This is defamatory and, although the giver of a reference, even if it is false, is protected from an action for defamation, this will not be so if it was given maliciously. In this case Jack makes the defamatory statement as he has a personal grudge against Frank, who he believes has had an affair with Jack's wife.

However, until the decision in *Spring* there was no liability where a reference was only given negligently and, given that malice can be difficult to prove, it was usually difficult before this decision to make any claim when a reference was wrong. It is now easier to make claims but the law here is developing and there are some doubtful areas.

Liability can arise in the following situations:

1 An employer gives a reference negligently which is acted on by a prospective employer who suffers loss. For instance, the reference might say that the employee is trustworthy when she is not and the new employer subsequently suffers loss when they employ this person who then steals. In *Spring* Lord Slynn observed that the employer would be liable under *Hedley Byrne* v *Heller* (1964) for negligent misstatement.

2 An employer gives a reference negligently which means that the employee does not get the job. In effect, whereas the reference in 1 above was too good, this one is too bad. This was the situation in *Spring* and it was here that the House of Lords changed the law by holding that liability can arise.

The facts were that Spring worked in insurance and was given a reference which cast doubt on his honesty and ability and was described by the trial judge as 'the kiss of death' to his insurance career. The House of Lords held that the reference was given negligently and the employers were liable. In addition, three Law Lords held that there was also an implied contractual duty to take due care in the preparation of references.

The following points arise from this decision:

■ As Lord Slynn observed, the referee can quite properly state 'the parameters within which the reference is given', so that the reference is limited to knowledge of a person on certain occasions only. However, a disclaimer of liability (e.g. 'we do not accept liability for the contents of this reference') would be valid only if it satisfied the reasonableness test under s 2 of the Unfair Contract Terms Act 1977.

■ An employer does not have an absolute duty at common law actually to give a reference. In *Spring* Lords Hadley and Woolf thought that there was an implied contractual duty where the employee's (present) contract with the employer is of a kind where a reference is normally required. This contractual test makes the requirement to give a reference depend on the type of job which the employee is actually doing, rather than the type of job he or she is applying for. The law will no doubt develop here. In *Coote v Granada Hospitality* (1999) a refusal to provide a reference was found to be sex discrimination on the ground of victimisation (see Chapter 9). Other employees had been given references and the reason why this employee had not been given one was that she had previously brought a sex discrimination complaint against the employer.

■ An employer may try to safeguard herself by giving a purely factual reference stating certain undoubtedly true facts but no more. In *Bartholomew v Hackney LBC* (1999) the Court of Appeal held that a reference must be in substance true, accurate and fair but not necessarily full and comprehensive. This leaves the point about factual references in doubt: such a reference may be true and accurate but is it fair? In this case the reference stated that disciplinary proceedings for gross misconduct had commenced against the employee when he took voluntary severance but did not state what the misconduct was or that the employee denied it. It was held on the facts that the reference was fair, since knowing the precise details of the misconduct would not have had any effect on a prospective employer and the fact that the employee denied the charge was implicit in the fact that the proceedings were ongoing.

■ What is the position where the employee is being investigated when the reference is given? In *TSB v Harris* (2000) a failure by an employer to tell an employee of complaints about her whilst putting them in a reference was held to be a breach of the duty of trust and confidence. In *Cox v Sun Alliance Life Ltd* (2001) Mummery LJ, in the Court of Appeal, held that any unfavourable statements in a reference should be confined to matters which have been investigated and which the employer had reasonable grounds to believe to be true. The reference to an investigation clearly implies that the matters have been brought to the employee's attention. An interesting point was raised in *Dike v Rickman* (2005) where the High Court held that a reference which stated that an employee had had two complaints made against him of sexual harassment was not given negligently even though it might be that the alleged acts did not come within the statutory definition of sexual harassment.

■ The duty exists only when a reference has been given. In *Legal and General Assurance Ltd v Kirk* (2001) an employee claimed that he had been deterred from applying for a reference because of a false allegation that he owed his employers a debt. It was held that a duty arises only when the reference is being given. The particular feature of this case was that there was a rule of the Regulatory Body that a person owing a debt of more than £1,000 could not be employed in certain capacities. One can see the employee's point: there was no point in even applying for the reference unless the allegation was withdrawn or substantiated.

■ The argument that a negligent reference could be a breach of Article 5 of the European Convention on Human Rights, which gives a right to liberty and security, was raised in *Griffiths v Newport Borough Council* (2001), where it was argued that the breach would consist in affecting the employee's security of work. The Court of Appeal did not accept that the terms of Article 5 could apply to references and in

5

The contract of employment

any event the claim failed as the reference was not given negligently. In *Legal and General Assurance Ltd v Kirk* (2001) another tack was tried: that references are subject to Article 1 of Protocol 1 which entitles persons to the free enjoyment of their possessions. The argument, which did not succeed, was that a negligent reference deprived the employee of his right to trade. Middlemiss (2004) suggests that three other articles have a bearing on the giving or not of references: Article 6 (right to a fair trial) could be breached if the reference refers to internal dispute procedures which are incomplete (as he points out in *Darnell v UK* (1993), it was held that Article 6 is involved only if the claim is of a serious nature and involves civil rights and obligations and this may not be the case here); Article 8 (right to protection of private and family life, home and correspondence) could be breached if the reference provides personal details of the employee to a person who was not an agreed recipient, as where a reference was given without the employee requesting it; Article 10 (right of freedom of expression) which here may give some protection to employers, although the extent of its application in the context of references is as yet untested.

- A final hurdle which an employee needs to surmount is proving that the negligent reference actually caused his or her failure to obtain the job. This issue of causation may be the most significant barrier in the way of a claim.

Does an employee have the right to see references about him or herself? Under the Data Protection Act 1998 (discussed in more detail later in this chapter), although references are personal data to which, by s 7, there is a general right of access, there is a specific exemption in Sch 7, para 1 whereby there is no right of access to references which an employer sends to a prospective employer. An employee could ask the new employer for a copy of a reference supplied to him but this would, under s 7(4), need the consent of the previous employer.

To take reasonable steps to bring to the attention of employees rights of which they could not have been expected to be aware

The starting point is the decision of the House of Lords in *Scally v Southern Health and Social Services Board* (1991). The plaintiffs were doctors employed in the Health Service in Northern Ireland and their employer had failed to tell them of their right to purchase added years to enhance their pension contributions. The House of Lords held that a term would be implied in this case and Lord Bridge laid down the following conditions which need to be satisfied for the implication of such a term:

(a) the terms were not negotiated with the employee but resulted from negotiations with a representative body (e.g. a trade union) or were incorporated by reference;

(b) the employee could avail himself of the right only by taking certain steps himself;

(c) the employee could not, in all the circumstances, reasonably be expected to be aware of the rights unless they were drawn to his attention.

In *Ibekwe v London General Transport Services Ltd* (2003) the employer gave details to employees of their options for their accrued pension rights both in letters in their pay slips and by a notice on the staff notice board. The employee did not see these, as he was off sick. The court held that the employer had taken all reasonable steps to inform employees of their rights. This case is a good example of the way in which the courts have been careful to limit the scope of the duty first imposed by *Scally* which could, in theory, have led to many claims of this kind, which may seem to have little merit.

A duty to care for the economic well-being of employees?

The decision in *Scally* could be seen as a parallel decision to that in *Spring v Guardian Assurance* in that they both imposed a duty on the employer to care for the economic well-being of its employees: in *Spring* in the matter of references and here in the provision of relevant information. Indeed, in *Spring* Lord Woolf expressly linked that decision to *Scally* by observing that 'just as in the earlier authorities the courts were prepared to imply by necessary implication a term imposing a duty on an employer to exercise due care for the physical well being of his employees, so in the appropriate circumstances would the court imply a like duty as to his economic well being'. Moreover, Brodie (1996) regarded the decision in *Scally* as an instance of the 'overarching' obligation of mutual trust and confidence (see below). However, in *Crossley v Faithful and Gould Holdings Ltd* (2004) the Court of Appeal rejected a claim that there is a general implied on the part of an employer to take care for the economic well-being of employees (see Wynn Evans, 2004). In the context of this case, this would have involved holding that there was a breach of duty by the employer in failing to warn an employee of the consequences which resigning would have on the benefits available under a long-term disability scheme. The court, having looked at the decisions in *Spring v Guardian Assurance* and *Scally v Southern Health and Social Services Board*, felt that in neither was there a suggestion that there was an all-embracing duty to care for the economic well-being of employees. For example, in *Scally* the duty arose because the employees would not know of their rights unless their employers told them; and the duty in connection with references in *Spring* is qualified in various ways. Dyson LJ, in *Crossley*, was concerned about the burden which an extension of the duty would place on employers. He gave an example of an employer discussing voluntary redundancy with an employee. Would the employer have a duty to discuss with him the personal consequences of that employee's personal situation following redundancy?

In addition, the court was obviously determined that there should be no general duty on the part of employers to give advice about, e.g., pension rights; and indeed the imposition of such a duty has been rejected in earlier cases such as *Hagan v ICI Chemicals & Polymers Ltd* (2002), where the court rejected the notion of a duty on the employer to ensure that at all times employees are aware of the true position in relation to their pension and other benefits. It would be a different matter if advice was given but was wrong, as happened in *Lennon v Metropolitan Police Commissioner* (2004), where there was liability for negligent misstatement under *Hedley Byrne v Heller* (1964).

The decision in *Scally* thus seems, as the trial judge in *Crossley* vividly put it: 'a bridgehead from which there has been no advance'. Indeed it can be regarded (e.g. by Freedland, 2003) as essentially a procedural rather than a substantive obligation concerned with the correct flow of information and, even in this context, Freedland suggests that its scope is limited to information on pension entitlements.

To deal promptly and effectively with grievances

In *WA Gould (Pearmak) Ltd* v *McConnell* (1995) two salesmen attempted to raise a grievance resulting from a reduction in their commission due to a change in sales methods. There was no procedure laid down nor were they able to discuss it. They resigned and successfully claimed constructive dismissal. Moreover, the EAT held that this term was a fundamental one which may put it alongside the other fundamental terms set out above.

To respect the employee's privacy

This is a recent development and the nature and extent of this duty is not yet clear. In *Dalgleish* v *Lothian and Borders Police Board* (1991) an injunction was granted to prevent disclosure by the Police Board to the local council of the details of council employees who had not paid the community charge. In *Halford* v *United Kingdom* (1997) the European Court of Human Rights was asked to consider the applicability of Article 8 (respect for private and family life) of the European Convention on Human Rights (ECHR) in a situation where an employee claimed that her telephone had been tapped. It was held that this was a breach.

The Data Protection Act 1998

The Data Protection Act 1998 is also relevant in connection with the right of the employee to privacy, although the Act does not refer to privacy as such but regulates the use of information (data) relating to individuals. This Act, which replaces the Data Protection Act 1984 and implements the Data Protection Directive of 1995 (95/46), deals with situations other than employment and refers to data controllers (employers in this context) and data subjects (employees). The terms 'employer' and 'employee' will be used here. The Act applies whenever data is processed, whether electronically (by computer) or manually (e.g. in a filing system) but it should be noted that certain parts of the Act (e.g. in relation to some manual data) will not be completely in force until 23 October 2007.

The Act places two fundamental duties on employers:

1. To comply with the eight 'data protection principles'. These are set out in Schedules to the Act and, in summary, provide that data shall:
   - Be processed lawfully and fairly. In the employment context, one requirement here is that the employee must have consented. An employer clearly needs to keep certain data on employees and the easiest way to obtain consent is for contracts of employment to state that the employer has permission to process certain data and for the employee to sign that he or she agrees.
   - Only be obtained for lawful purposes. The Schedule provides that an employer may specify the purposes in a notice to the employee.

■ Be adequate, relevant and not excessive in relation to the purposes for which they are obtained. Excessively detailed personal records kept on employees could breach this principle.

■ Be accurate and, where necessary, kept up to date. Data on employees will often have been obtained from others, such as previous employers, and an employer may wish to give employees the chance to check that it is correct.

■ Not be kept for longer than necessary. Records relating to employees should always be kept for at least the length of time after employment ends during which an employee could bring an action against the employer (the limitation period): the longest period is three years in the case of personal injury at work. An employer may wish to keep data for longer than this for use if a reference is required.

■ Be processed in accordance with the rights of data subjects set out in the Act. This would be breached if the employer failed to comply with the rights of employees set out below.

■ Take appropriate measures against unauthorised or unlawful processing of data and loss and damage to data. Thus proper security measures are needed and employees with access to records of other employees must maintain confidentiality.

■ Not be transferred to a country outside the European Economic Area (the EU plus Iceland, Norway and Liechtenstein) unless that country has adequate protection for the data.

In the case of 'sensitive personal data' there are further restrictions. This is defined by s 2 as data relating to, for example, racial or ethnic origin, political opinions, religious beliefs, trade union membership, health, sexual life, and commission of an offence. The explicit consent of the employee is needed before such data can be processed and this seems to mean that the employer must gain specific consent to the processing of this data and the general consent referred to earlier will not be enough. The eight principles above also, of course, apply to this data as well and it may be that an employer would not be permitted to process it anyway because, for example, it may not be necessary to keep such data.

(2) To notify the Data Protection Registrar when they are processing computer records, and certain other records, containing personal data. It is a criminal offence to fail to comply.

Employees have the following main rights:

1 To have access to personal data. The employer is only obliged to supply certain information on receipt of a written request and a fee not normally exceeding £10. There are exceptions to this of which one, as explained above, is that an employee does not have a right of access to a reference about him or her. Failure by the employer to comply gives the employee the right to apply to the county court or High Court for an order requiring compliance.

2 To correct personal data which is in breach of the fourth principle by being inaccurate. The Data Protection Commissioner can be asked to intervene if the employer refuses to correct it.

5

The contract of employment

The Act specifically provides in s 56 that it is a criminal offence for a prospective employer to require a prospective employee to obtain any criminal records which they have or any record of non-payment of social security contributions. In effect, the prospective employer cannot say to the employee 'you have a right of access to this information about yourself and you must exercise it and give me the information'.

In *Durant v Financial Services Authority* (2003) the Court of Appeal gave guidance on the two fundamental questions which arise under the Act, although the actual case did not concern employment matters but disclosure of documents by Barclays Bank to Mr Durant, a customer with whom it was in dispute:

- *What is personal data?* The court said that there are two helpful points to bear in mind: Is the data biographical in a significant sense, i.e. is it about the individual (does it name the individual or directly refer to him or her?), or does it just record the participation of the individual in events where that individual is **not** the focus? In the latter case that individual cannot claim that the data is personal to him or her. Secondly, does the information have the data subject as its focus rather than some other person with whom the individual may have been involved?

- *What constitutes a 'relevant filing system' under the Act?* It held that such a system would exist where the files were structured so that it was clear at the outset of a search whether specific information capable of amounting to personal data was held and, if so, in which files.

The Regulation of Investigatory Powers Act 2000

The Regulation of Investigatory Powers Act 2000 provides that it is unlawful to intercept communications in the course of transmission by a telecommunications system. This would make it unlawful for an employer to monitor telephone calls made by employees but there are circumstances where this may be needed, as where it is suspected that an employee is sending emails to another employee which may be sexually harassing. The Telecommunications (Lawful Business Practice) (Interception of Communications) Regulations 2000 (SI 2000/2699), issued under the above Act, allow interception in certain circumstances, one being where the interception is solely for the purpose of monitoring and recording communications relevant to the needs of the business. Here interception is allowed if the employer has made all reasonable efforts to let users know that communications may be intercepted and the equipment is provided wholly or partly for use in the course of the business. An employer could argue that this allowed the monitoring of all telephone calls and emails but this could be contrary to the Human Rights Act 1998, as Article 8 of the ECHR gives a right to respect for private and family life. A test case is awaited!

The Access to Medical Records Act 1988

This is an appropriate place at which to mention the Access to Medical Records Act 1988, which gives employees the right to see medical reports. Although the Data Protection Act also gives this right, it applies only where they are held on computer or on filing systems. The Access to Medical Records Act has no such restriction. Section 1 gives the individual (e.g. employee) access to any medical report relating to him or her which has been prepared by a doctor responsible for his or her medical care. In addition, s 3 provides that an employer shall not request medical reports relating to an individual without that person's consent. Therefore, a prospective employer could not ask for records relating to a job applicant without their consent and an employer could not require an employee's own doctor to supply him with the employee's medical records. However, reports prepared on employees by company doctors or independent doctors, as where an employee may be claiming that he or she is off work through illness, are not within the Act and therefore are available to the employer without the consent of the employee being needed. One exception, however, could be where the company doctor has treated the employee previously, in which case they could be considered responsible for their medical care and would come within s 1 (above). If so, the Act would apply and the individual's consent would be needed before the disclosure of the report.

The duty of mutual trust and confidence

This duty is considered between the duties of the employer and those of the employee as it is a duty which, as its title indicates, could fall on either. Nevertheless, the reality is that the duty has a far greater impact on the employer.

The origin of the duty lies in the law of unfair dismissal and, in particular, in constructive dismissal cases where the issue is whether the employer is guilty of a repudiatory breach of the contract, i.e. the employer no longer intends to be bound by one of the essential terms of the contract (see Chapter 11 and especially *Western Excavating* v *Sharp* (1978)). The courts have developed the law on what constitutes a repudiatory breach so that it encompasses conduct which is a breach of this duty, which really amounts to a duty to treat the employee with respect. The significant point is that now the duty can be used throughout the employer–employee relationship and is not confined to constructive dismissal cases.

One of the earliest examples is in *Isle of Wight Tourist Board* v *Coombes* (1976), where a director said to another employee that his personal secretary was 'an intolerable bitch on a Monday morning'. The secretary resigned and successfully claimed constructive dismissal. It was held that the relationship between a director and his secretary must be one of complete trust and confidence and this had been shattered by the use of these words.

This decision was confined to a particular relationship but the courts soon began to broaden its application. In *Woods* v *WM Car Services Ltd* (1981), which also concerned constructive dismissal, Browne-Wilkinson J said that: 'In our view it is clearly established that there is implied in a contract of employment a term that the employers will not, without proper cause, conduct themselves in a manner calculated or likely to destroy or seriously damage the relationship of confidence and trust between employer and employee'. Further examples of this term in practice are *United Bank* v *Akhtar* (above) and *French* v *Barclays Bank plc* (1998), where a decision by the bank to change the terms of a relocation loan made to an employee was a breach. It also applies in constructive dismissal situations, which are considered in Chapter 11. An important recent case here is *Abbey National plc* v *Fairbrother* (2007).

The implied term was thrust into prominence by the decision of the House of Lords in *Malik v BCCI SA* (1997), which concerned a claim by employees that the conduct of their (former) employers in the way they had run the Bank of Credit and Commerce International had breached this implied term and therefore they were entitled to 'stigma damages', being damages for the damage to their future job prospects by their association with the bank. The claim was upheld in what was certainly the first major decision to deal with the implied term of trust and confidence in a situation other than unfair dismissal. Lord Steyn observed that:

> The evolution of the implied term of mutual trust and confidence is a fact . . . It has proved a workable principle in practice. It has not been the subject of adverse criticism in any decided cases and it has been welcomed in academic writings. I regard the emergence of the implied obligation of mutual trust and confidence as a sound development.

Lord Steyn also held that this term could be broken even if the employer's conduct was not aimed at any individual employee and even if the employee did not know that it was happening. This was so in the *Malik* case because the bank was not fraudulently run in order to target any employee, nor did they all know precisely what was going on.

LAW IN CONTEXT
The implied term of mutual trust and confidence

Freedland (2006, at page 154) argues that 'the construction of employment contracts has been transformed' by the rapid development of what he terms the principle to the effect that contracts of employment 'will be interpreted and applied so as to give effect to a mutual obligation, as between employing entities and workers, upon each contracting party to retain the trust and confidence of the other'. As Freedland observes, its origin was in the law on constructive dismissal where the law, as we shall see in Chapter 11, used a contractual definition of conduct which could constitute constructive dismissal and, as Freedland observes, the implied term of mutual trust and confidence was used to 'give shape' to this contractual basis.

Brodie (2001) notes that this implied term has 'evolved and flourished in an environment where there have been both moves towards good faith playing a greater role in contract law and where employer prerogative has been constrained by employment protection legislation'. Not only this, but Brodie argues that the implied term is, as he puts it, coherent with both common law and statute law and so its future existence should be secure. For example, he points out that in *Johnson v Unisys Ltd* (1999) (see Chapter 11 for a detailed account of this case) it was argued that a dismissal involved a breach of trust and confidence as there was no hearing before the employee was dismissed. This developed the statement of Lord Wilberforce, in *Malloch v Aberdeen Corporation* (1971), who held that 'The right of a man to be heard in his own defence is the most elementary protection of all.' An example of the term being used to control employer prerogative is provided by *Gogay v Hertfordshire CC* (2000) where it was held that a decision by an employer to suspend an employee was in breach of the implied term as the local authority had failed to carry out a proper investigation of the facts before suspending her.

Duties of the employee

To obey orders and instructions permitted by the terms of the contract

The precise terms of the contract are clearly important here, although many contracts contain a very general clause in addition to specific duties. For example, a teacher's contract, in addition to requiring her to teach, mark and set examination papers, etc., will probably also have a clause requiring her to undertake any other tasks associated with the provision of education which her employers may reasonably require. It is this kind of clause which gives rise to difficulties.

The significance of this duty has decreased since the introduction in 1971 of the right to claim for unfair dismissal. Up till then the only claim was for wrongful dismissal and disobedience to a lawful order was, and still is, considered a sufficient breach of contract for summary dismissal. Now the issue, in an unfair dismissal claim, will be the reasonableness of the employer's conduct, a point considered in Chapter 11.

The principle that the employee can be required to obey orders permitted by the contract is subject to two qualifications:

1 The order must not be to perform an illegal act. In *Morrish* v *Henlys* (1973) the employee was dismissed because he refused to acquiesce in a falsification of records. The employer contended that, as it was common practice to do this, the employee's refusal to agree to it was unreasonable. The NIRC, not surprisingly, rejected this and held his dismissal to be unfair.

2 The employer cannot order the employee to do something which would put him or her in danger. In *Ottoman Bank* v *Chakarian* (1930) the employee was held to have been justified in disobeying an order to remain in Constantinople where he had previously been sentenced to death and was in danger of a further arrest. However, in *Walmsley* v *Udec Refrigeration* (1972) an employee was held not to be entitled to refuse an order to go to Eire because of a general fear of IRA activity. The decision in *Chakarian* was referred to by Browne-Wilkinson V-C in the *Johnstone* v *Bloomsbury AHA* case (above) as authority for the proposition that the employer will safeguard the employee's health even if this conflicts with the express terms of the contract.

Although employees have a duty to obey orders permitted under the contract, this goes no further. As Denning MR said in *Secretary of State for Employment* v *ASLEF (No. 2)* (1972): 'a man is not bound to do more for his employer than his contract requires. He can withdraw his goodwill if he pleases.'

To adapt to new methods of carrying out the employer's business

The extent of this duty is not entirely clear, but it was the basis of the decision in *Cresswell* v *Board of Inland Revenue* (1984), where the High Court held that Inland Revenue employees had a duty to adapt to a new computerised system which replaced the manual system of tax coding. Walton J observed that 'an employee is expected to adapt himself to new methods and techniques introduced in the course of employment'. Nevertheless, he also held that the employer was expected to provide training

5

The contract of employment

and, if this involved the acquisition of 'esoteric skills', it might not be reasonable to expect the employee to acquire them.

This topic is related to two others:

1 Dismissal for lack of capability (see Chapter 11).

2 Redundancy, because the question arises whether the changes are such that the employee is being asked to do a new job altogether (see Chapter 12).

To exercise reasonable care and skill in carrying out the contract of employment

The existence of this duty is so obvious that it needs no justification and, again, the main issues now arise in unfair dismissal claims. The only difficult legal issue arises where the employee, in the course of his duties, injures another person who then claims against the employer as being liable for the employee's actions. The employer pays damages and then seeks to recover these from the employee. It was held in *Lister v Romford Ice and Cold Storage Co. Ltd* (1957) that such a claim could be made, as the employee is under an implied contractual duty to exercise reasonable care and therefore is liable for breach of this duty. The effect was that the employee was liable to indemnify the employer for damages which he had paid for the employee's breach of duty.

> ### Example
>
> Patrick is employed by John as a van driver and negligently injures Sarah (who happens to be another employee and his mother, although the same principle would apply if Sarah had been a complete outsider). John pays compensation to Sarah for the negligence of Patrick and then seeks to recover this from Patrick.

These are the facts of *Lister* (above), where it was held that X would be liable. However, it is very rare for an employer to seek to do this, as insurers nearly always pay any damages and they have agreed amongst themselves not to make these claims.

Even so, there is the possibility that an employer might seek an indemnity from the employee but in *Harvey v R.G. O'Dell Ltd* (1958) it was held that the employer's right to do so did not arise where the employee was assisting the employer by performing an act outside normal duties. In this case the employee, who normally worked as a storekeeper, drove his motorcycle on his employer's instructions to do some repair work and was involved in an accident in the course of the journey. It was held that the employee was not obliged to indemnify the employer for damages paid as a result. If there were more claims of this kind it could well be that the courts would limit them by further restrictive decisions such as this.

To exercise good faith in carrying out the contract

This duty has a variety of names, such as 'fidelity' and 'faithfulness', which have a slightly old-fashioned ring to them, and accordingly the term 'good faith' will be used in this book. The remedy for a breach is either dismissal (although if the employee then claims for unfair dismissal the question of reasonableness will arise) or for the employer to claim an account of any secret profits which the employee made through the breach. One example is *Boston Deep Sea Fishing and Ice Co.* v *Ansell* (1888), where a managing director of a company, who had made secret profits out of his position, was liable to account for them to the company.

A modern example of the duty is *British Telecommunications plc* v *Ticehurst* (1992), where a manager took part in action including strikes, work to rules and go-slows. The Court of Appeal held that where an employee has a discretion as to what action to take and exercises it so as to cause disruption and inconvenience then the duty is broken. The fact that the employee was a manager was relevant but it is probable that this principle applies to all employees. Again, in *Secretary of State for Employment* v *ASLEF (No. 2)* (1972) railway workers went on a work to rule and overtime ban in support of a pay claim, causing massive disruption to services, and it was held that this was a breach of contract. Denning MR said that to obey the rule book, if done in good faith without any disruption of services, would be lawful but 'what makes it wrong is the object with which it is done'. Accordingly, the duty can be seen as, in some cases, governing the way in which contractual duties are performed. This decision is criticised by Brodie (2001) on the ground that it improperly 'introduces motive into the question of breach of contract'.

The duty of good faith has a number of aspects, which are almost separate duties of their own. These will now be considered in turn.

Duty not to make secret profits out of the position of an employee

An example is the *Boston Deep Sea Fishing* case (above) but it could be argued that this relates to the special fiduciary duties of company directors. An instance of the duty applying in a more typical case is *Reading* v *Attorney General* (1951), where an army sergeant was paid £20,000 for agreeing to accompany lorries carrying illicit spirits, his uniform guaranteeing that the lorries would not be inspected. He was arrested and imprisoned and the Crown impounded the £20,000. He claimed it back when he was released but it was held that his claim failed. Lord Porter, in the House of Lords, made the point that whether the employer suffered any loss was irrelevant: the liability to account arose simply because the profit had been made.

To disclose misdeeds

There are three distinct issues:

1 Does the employee have a duty to disclose his own misdeeds?
There is no clear authority here, although it could be argued that the duty of trust and confidence implies an openness in the employment relationship which obliges employees to own up to wrongdoings. In *Sybron Corporation* v *Rochem* (1983) the Court of Appeal was bound by the decision of the House of Lords in *Bell* v *Lever Bros* (1932) that there was no such duty, but *Bell* really dealt with the question of mistake at common law and it has been suggested that at least the employee must not actually mislead the employer about the extent of his misdeeds. The distinction is probably between volunteering information about one's misdeeds, which the law does not require, and deliberately misleading the employer when questioned about them.

2 Does the employee have a duty to disclose the misdeeds of fellow employees?

In *Sybron* it was held that there is no general duty to report the misdeeds of fellow employees but the existence of the duty will depend on the circumstances. As Stephenson LJ put it in the Court of Appeal: 'He may be so placed in the hierarchy as to have a duty to report the misconduct of his superior . . . or the misconduct of his inferiors.' An employee may therefore have a duty to report the misconduct of those for whom he is the line manager.

3 The effect of the Public Interest Disclosure Act 1998

This deals with the somewhat different situation where the employee knows of wrong-doing being committed within his or her organisation. There is no positive duty to disclose it, but suppose that the employee does and is then victimised for so doing. In *Initial Services Ltd* v *Putterill* (1968) it was held that an employer could not obtain an injunction to restrain an ex-employee from revealing details to a newspaper of unlawful price protection practices contrary to the Restrictive Trade Practices Act 1956. However, legislation was needed to provide protection to those who were still employees and this came about through the passage of the Public Interest Disclosure Act 1998, which was passed because of widespread alarm about cases where workers had been too frightened to voice their concerns of particular dangers. Indeed, this became apparent in many public inquiries, ranging from the inquiry into the Zeebrugge Ferry tragedy in 1987 to the inquiry into the collapse of BCCI. A notable example was that at Bristol Royal Infirmary, where there was concern about high infant mortality rates but a consultant who spoke out had been forced to give up his NHS career.

The Public Interest Disclosure Act 1998 was passed against this background and also the strong emphasis at that time on higher standards in public life. Lord Borrie, who introduced the bill which led to the Act into the House of Lords, referred to the then recently published report of the Committee on Standards in Public Life (the Nolan Committee), which said:

> All organisations face the risk of things going wrong or of unknowingly harbouring malpractice. Part of the duty of identifying such a situation and taking remedial action may lie with the regulatory body or funding body. But the regulator is usually in the role of detective, determining responsibility after the crime has been discovered. Encouraging a culture of openness within an organisation will help: prevention is better than cure.

(See also Lewis (2005) who argues that whistle-blowers would be in a better position if they were placed under the umbrella of the new Commission for Equality and Human Rights. See Chapter 9 for details of this Commission.)

The Act follows a recent trend by making additions to another Act, in this case the ERA 1996, where additions are made, in particular, to ss 43 and 47.

The scheme of the Act is as follows:

- to provide when a disclosure is 'protected', which means the situations when a worker may make a disclosure and be protected by the Act;

■ assuming that the disclosure is protected, to set out what type of disclosures will be protected;

■ to provide protection for workers who make 'protected disclosures'.

It should be noted that by s 43K of the Act it applies to 'workers' as defined by s 230(3) of the ERA 1996. This includes employees but also those who personally provide services other than in a professional client relationship. However, it goes further and includes those who were introduced or supplied to do that work by a third person, i.e. agency workers.

The 'protected disclosure situations' are set out in s 43B and are those where a worker has a reasonable belief that:

(a) the disclosure tends to show that a criminal offence has been committed;

(b) there has been a failure to comply with a legal obligation;

(c) a miscarriage of justice has occurred;

(d) health and safety has been endangered;

(e) the environment has been endangered;

(f) there is evidence tending to show that information relating to any of the above matters has been concealed.

In addition, a disclosure will be protected in any of the above situations where it relates to a matter which not only *has happened* (as above) but which *is happening* or *is likely to happen in future*. These situations are referred to in the Act as 'relevant failures'. In *Babuld* v *Waltham Forest* (2007) the CA held that, in order for a disclosure to be protected under the Act and thus amount to a 'qualifying disclosure', the worker must have a reasonable belief that the matter he relies on amounts to a criminal act, or found to be a legal obligation, even if it turns out that that belief is wrong.

An obvious problem with situation (a) above is that in fact there may not have been a criminal offence because there may be a particular defence available to the employer. The employee may not have been aware of this when she made the disclosure. Does this mean that it is not protected? In *Kraus* v *Penna Plc* (2004) it was held that an employee does not need to anticipate and evaluate all possible defences available to the employer as this would undermine the protection afforded by the Act.

The protected disclosure situations are those made in good faith to employers or to persons other than the employer who are believed to be responsible; to legal advisers when legal advice is sought; to a Minister of the Crown when the worker's employer is appointed by the Crown; or to any person prescribed by order made by the Secretary of State. In all these cases the disclosure becomes a 'qualifying disclosure'. The idea is that disclosures should normally be made to the person responsible rather than, for instance, to the media, and this makes it advisable that employers should have a policy for dealing with whistle-blowing matters internally.

It may be that the above disclosure situations are not adequate, as where the person to whom disclosure should be made is the person whose conduct should actually be disclosed, such as where the employee wishes to complain about his or her employer

5

The contract of employment

or where the disclosure has been made to the employer who has not taken effective action. In this case the Act provides for two cases where wider disclosures can be made:

1 Where the disclosure is made in good faith, the worker reasonably believes that its contents are true, it is not made for personal gain (i.e. the worker is not receiving sums from newspapers for the disclosure), it is reasonable to make the disclosure (detailed criteria are laid down for deciding this) and any one of the following applies:

    (a) the worker reasonably believes that he would be subject to a detriment by his employer if he made the disclosure to him or to a person prescribed by the Secretary of State (as defined above); or

    (b) if there is no person prescribed then the worker may make the disclosure if he reasonably believes that evidence relating to the relevant failure would be concealed or destroyed if disclosure is made to the employer; or if the worker has previously made a disclosure to the employer or to a prescribed person.

In *Street v Derbyshire Unemployed Workers Centre* (2004) the Court of Appeal held that a disclosure is not made in good faith if the main motive for it is an ulterior motive. Thus if the disclosure is made because of some personal grudge then this will defeat the defence of good faith. The problem is that often disclosures are made from a variety of motives and it can be difficult to disentangle them. Auld LJ held that 'good faith' means more than honesty, which could cause problems: perhaps more helpful is his observation that a person will still be in good faith, whatever reasons he may have for making the disclosure, provided that he is 'still driven by his original concern to right or prevent a wrong'. In *Bolton School v Evans* (2007) the EAT and Court of Appeal considered what was actually meant by a disclosure. An information technology teacher had hacked into the school's computer system in order to show that there was inadequate security. He was disciplined and then resigned claiming constructive dismissal. It was held that s 43B of the Act protected only disclosure and not actions of the employee which were directed to establishing whether his belief in facts was reasonable. In effect the employee was claiming as an investigator and not as a discloser. Thus he was not protected by the Act. This case is considered by Lewis (2006) who draws attention to the link between this Act and the Data Protection Act (see above) and to the Working Party established under Article 29 of Directive 95/46. In its report (February 2006) it pointed out the link between internal whistle-blowing schemes and data protection principles in the fields of, for example, accounting, banking and financial crime.

2 Where the disclosure deals with a 'relevant failure' of an 'exceptionally serious nature'. There is the same provision that it must not be made for personal gain. Here the worker is not obliged to have gone through an internal procedure, such as going to the employer, but can bring the matter straight to the attention of anyone appropriate.

Assuming that the disclosure is protected then the worker is protected by s 47B from being subjected to any detriment as a result. This includes action short of dismissal including refusal of promotion or a pay rise, or being disciplined. In *London Borough of Harrow* v *Knight* (2003) the employer had taken several months to investigate an allegation amounting to a protected disclosure by an employee and the EAT held that this could not *in itself* amount to subjecting the employee to a detriment. It needed to be shown that the employer acted in the way he did because of the protected disclosure. Thus where an employer deliberately delays in investigating an allegation because he or she does not wish to bother investigating it at all, and as a result the employee who made the allegation is subjected to stress, then the employee may have a claim but delay or a slow investigation is not enough by itself.

In addition, any dismissal resulting from making such a disclosure is automatically unfair if the disclosure is the reason for it or the principal reason. There is no qualifying period of employment and no ceiling on compensation.

If a worker comes within the narrow definition of an employee (see above) then if they are dismissed as a result of making a protected disclosure they can claim unfair dismissal. However, if they come within the wider definition and are 'workers' then, if they are dismissed for making a protected disclosure, they will have to claim that their dismissal amounted to a detriment within the Act. The disadvantage here is that they can claim only compensation and not re-employment (see Chapter 11).

Any clause in an agreement, which purports to prevent a worker from making a 'protected disclosure', is void. This is particularly aimed at confidentiality clauses in settlement agreements.

Not to disclose or otherwise misuse confidential information

In *Faccenda Chicken Ltd* v *Fowler* (1986) the employee, a sales manager, left to set up a rival business and his (former) employer claimed that he had used confidential information relating to the needs of customers and the prices which they paid to the detriment of that employer. It was held that the information was not confidential and thus the action failed, but Neill LJ took the opportunity to lay down the following points about the extent and nature of the duty of confidentiality:

1 One should consider any obligations imposed by the express terms of the contract. There were none in *Fowler*.

2 If there are no express terms then one should consider the effect of the implied term of confidentiality. The extent of the duty will vary with the nature of the contract but Neill LJ specifically held that an employee who copies out, or deliberately memorises, a list of customers for use after he leaves will be in breach. (This was the decision in *Robb* v *Green* (1895) and this applies even though there is no contractual restriction on the employee doing business with his former employer's customers.)

3 Where the employment has ended, the duty is restricted to one not to disclose trade secrets. In deciding whether a matter is a trade secret one must look at the nature of the employment, the nature of the information, whether the employer impressed on the employee that the information was confidential and whether the information can easily be isolated from information which can be disclosed.

An employer should always deal with confidentiality by an express clause in the contract and this applies particularly to clauses preventing the use of trade secrets after leaving employment. Another possibility is to include a garden leave clause in the contract (see above). The extent to which such clauses can be enforced is considered in the section below on contracts in restraint of trade.

The employee's duty of good faith and inventions

The common law position is that there is an implied term in employees' contracts that the employer is entitled to the benefit of inventions made by the employee which arise out of employment (**British Syphon Co. Ltd v Homewood** (1956)). This has now been almost entirely overtaken by the provisions of the Patents Act 1977 so that the common law is relevant only where the invention was made before the Act came into force or the employee was not employed in the UK. The Act is considerably more favourable to employees than the common law, which was widely felt to be harsh.

Section 39(1) sets out the circumstances when an invention will belong to the employer:

(a) where the invention was –
   (i) made either in the course of the normal duties of the employee or made in the course of duties which were not normal duties but were specifically assigned to the employee; and
   (ii) an invention might reasonably be expected to result;

(b) where the invention was made in the course of the duties of the employee and, at the time, he had a special obligation to further the interests of the employer's undertaking.

The difference between (a) and (b) is that in (b) the invention belongs to the employer, whether or not an invention might reasonably be expected to result, and it is intended to cover employees such as company directors who have a special obligation to further the interests of the company.

If neither (a) nor (b) apply then s 39(2) provides that the invention shall belong to the employee. Thus the effect of the Act is to replace the previous blanket provisions with two specific cases where the invention shall belong to the employee.

Section 40 of the 1977 Act then deals with two other situations:

(a) where the invention does belong to the employer under (a) or (b) below the employee may claim compensation where it has proved to be of 'outstanding benefit' to the employer;

(b) where the invention belonged to the employee under the rules in s 39 (above) but the employee has assigned it to the employer and has, however, received inadequate benefits from it in relation to the benefits received by the employer.

In both cases the employee may make a claim for compensation to the Patents Court or the Patents Office within a year of the patent expiring and may be awarded a 'fair share' of the actual or anticipated benefits.

Section 41 lays down the criteria for deciding this. In the case of (a) it is:

(i) the nature of the employee's duties, his remuneration and any other advantages which he gained from the invention or from his employment in general;

(ii) the employee's effort and skill in making the invention;

(iii) the effort and skill contributed by any third party;

(iv) the significance of any contribution made by the employer.

In the case of (b) it is:

(i)   any conditions in any licence granted in respect of the invention or patent;

(ii) the extent to which the invention was made jointly between the employee and a third party;

(iii) the significance of any contribution made by the employer.

The 1977 Act contains provisions designed to prevent the employee's rights under it from being taken away by any agreement with the employer. Thus s 42 provides that no contract can take away any of the employee's rights under the Act and s 40(4) provides that the rules on compensation shall likewise not be affected by any agreement made individually by the employee with the employer but that a collective agreement may govern the matter instead. The implication is that an agreement made by the employee's union would be most unlikely to diminish his rights.

In the case of copyright in material, s 11 of the Copyright, Designs and Patents Act 1988 provides that the copyright in works produced by the employee during employment belongs to the employer unless there is any agreement to the contrary. There are no provisions similar to those above dealing with patents and thus an employee who produces a book, film or other work which is copyright is worse off than employees who invent.

The duty not to damage the employer's business when engaging in other work
This duty is best considered in relation to the doctrine of restraint of trade, which is dealt with below.

The doctrine of restraint of trade and other restrictions on work carried out by the employee during or after employment

---

Example

Quicksale Ltd is an advertising agency. It is concerned about the following situations:

(a) Ali works in the accounts department and it is known that at weekends he has assisted at promotional events run by Fastsale Ltd, another agency. What can Quicksale Ltd do?

(b) Barbara manages the advertising accounts of a number of major companies. It is known that she is thinking of leaving and going to work for another advertising agency. What action can Quicksale Ltd take?

● In the case of Ali, as he is still an employee, the answer is to be found in the common law duty of good faith and, in particular, in the duty not to engage in any outside work that could damage the employer's business.

● Barbara's case is more difficult. Her contract might contain a garden leave clause which would put her on very long notice during which she would be paid and still be an employee but would not be working. If such a clause did not already exist then

→

Quicksale Ltd could unilaterally impose one but this might be held to be invalid, as in *William Hill v Tucker* (see above). Even if the garden leave clause was in the contract it might not be entirely effective, as we shall see further on. An alternative is that her contract contains a restraint of trade clause under which, on leaving her employment with Quicksale Ltd, she agrees not to work for any other advertising agency for, perhaps, one year after leaving the employment of Quicksale Ltd. These clauses, if carefully drafted, are effective, but in the absence of such careful drafting they run the risk of being struck down by the courts.

Each of these points will now be considered in turn.

The common law duty not to engage in any outside work which could damage the employer's business

The leading case is ***Hivac Ltd v Park Royal Scientific Instruments Ltd*** (1946), where employees of the plaintiffs, who were engaged on highly skilled work making valves for hearing aids, were employed on exactly the same work for a rival firm outside hours. The two firms were in competition with each other and the court held that an injunction would be granted to restrain the rival firm from employing them in this way. Greene MR observed that 'it would be deplorable if it were laid down that a workman could, consistently with his duty to his employer, knowingly, deliberately and secretly set himself to do in his spare time something which would inflict great harm on his employer's business'. On the other hand, he observed that it would be wrong to place restrictions on employees such as manual workers to make use of their leisure for profit. The vital factors will be the work that the employee does and the pay he receives (see *Nottingham University v Fishel* (2000)). In *Laughton and Hawley v Bapp Industrial Supplies Ltd* (1986) the fact that two employees were intending to leave and set up in competition with their (former) employer was held not to be in breach of the duty of good faith, although there might well be a restraint of trade clause which could apply here. If the employee was, whilst working for his employer, directly soliciting customers to transfer their custom to him when he left, then this could be a ground for dismissal. Clauses restraining employees from working for others may also be expressly inserted into the contract and will be subject to the same principles as stated above.

Garden leave clauses

These have been discussed above and they are a more straightforward method of protecting the employer's interests as the employee in question remains an employee, and is paid wages, throughout the period of garden leave. However, the courts may not enforce them because the usual method of enforcement, through an injunction, is at the courts' discretion. An example is *Provident Financial Group plc v Hayward* (1989), where a six-month garden leave clause imposed on a financial director was not effective to prevent him from taking up another post towards the end of the period. As Dillon J observed: 'The practice of long periods of garden leave is obviously capable of abuse.' If the other business for which the employee wished to leave and work for before the end of the notice period 'had nothing whatever to do with the business of the employers' then the courts would not enforce a garden leave clause. In addition, as in *William Hill* v *Tucker* (above), a garden leave clause may infringe the employee's right to be provided with work.

Contracts in restraint of trade

This somewhat old-fashioned term is a reminder of the fact that these clauses were, and still are, used in quite another connection: where a person has bought a business and paid for the goodwill, he or she may then impose a restraint on the seller of the business preventing him or her from opening a similar business nearby which competes with the one sold. In the employment context, these clauses usually come into force on termination of employment and restrain the employee from engaging in certain work after leaving employment. As such, they have been viewed with suspicion by the courts as infringing a fundamental right to work for whomever one pleases. It is also possible for these clauses to apply *during* employment where the clause restricts the employee from engaging in certain other work. They are sometimes referred to as *covenants* in restraint of trade. A covenant is a promise contained in a deed, and this reminds us that these agreements, especially if they related to the sale of a business, were generally contained in a deed. The term 'contract' should be used where employee restraints are concerned.

These clauses are void unless proved reasonable in the interests of both the parties and the public and the onus of proving this is on the person seeking to enforce the clause (Lord Macnaghten in *Nordenfelt* v *Maxim Nordenfelt Guns and Ammunition Co. Ltd* (1894)). In practice, the courts have stressed the interests of the parties far more than the rather vaguer question of the public interest. However, in *Esso Petroleum Co. Ltd* v *Harper's Garage Ltd* (1968) the question of public interest was to some extent revived by remarks in the House of Lords and has appeared in some recent cases (see below).

A restraint will be held reasonable only if the employer has an enforceable interest to protect. Such an interest will cover knowledge by the employee of trade secrets, cases where the employee has influence over customers, cases where the employee may, on leaving, solicit other employees to join him in a competing business, and other miscellaneous cases dealing mainly with sportsmen and women.

A good, if old, example of knowledge of trade secrets or specialised knowledge of the workings of a business is *Forster and Sons Ltd* v *Suggett* (1918), where a restraint on an employee, who had knowledge of secret glass manufacturing processes, preventing him from working for a similar firm for five years, was held to be valid. In *Littlewoods Organisation Ltd* v *Harris* (1978) knowledge by the executive director of a mail order business of the details of how it worked was held to be an interest capable of protection. The principles set out in *Faccenda Chicken* v *Fowler* (above) may be useful in deciding what information can be protected.

Cases where the employee has influence over customers and where a restraint has been successfully imposed include those on a solicitor's managing clerk (now a legal executive) (*Fitch* v *Dewes* (1921)), an estate agent (*Scorer* v *Seymour Johns* (1966)) and a milkman (*Home Counties Dairies* v *Skilton* (1970)). The employer needs to show that the (former) employee will use his influence over customers to try to persuade

5

The contract of employment

them to transfer their custom to wherever he is going to work in future. Thus in *Home Counties* v *Skilton* the milkman spoke to customers on his milk round telling them that he was leaving Home Counties Dairies and setting up in business on his own, covering exactly the same round. The clear implication was that he hoped that they would follow him. Cases where the employee is leaving to set up or join a competing business and solicits other employees to come with him include *Dawnay, Day and Co. Ltd* v *DeBraconier d'Alphen* (1997), in which it was held that covenants preventing the solicitation of other employees by Eurobond dealers who were leaving to join a competing business were valid. In *TSC (Europe)* v *Massey* (1999) the High Court again expressly recognised that an employer has a legitimate interest in maintaining a stable, trained workforce although here the restraint failed on its facts (see below).

If the employer does not have a legitimate interest to protect, then no restraint can be valid. In *Attwood* v *Lamont* (1920) a restraint on a tailor preventing him from being engaged in various types of outfitters business was invalid, as the only reason for imposing it was that his employer feared him because of his skill and therefore did not want him to work in competition with him. In *Eastham* v *Newcastle United FC* (1964) the retain and transfer system which prevented footballers from moving to other clubs at the end of their contracts was held void and in *Greig* v *Insole* (1977) a ban imposed on English cricketers because they had signed to play in matches in Australia organised by a private promoter was held void, as the matches posed no threat to English cricket. The question of public interest was also raised by the court in that the ban would deprive the public of the chance of seeing the cricketers play. A different situation arose in *Kores Manufacturing Co.* v *Kolok Manufacturing Co.* (1959), where two companies agreed that neither would employ anyone who had been employed by the other for the previous five years, the reason being that it benefited both firms to have a stable workforce. However, the court held that this was unreasonable, although in *Esso Petroleum* v *Harper's Garage* (above) some members of the House of Lords thought that the correct ground for the decision should have been that the agreement was against the public interest as in *Greig* v *Insole* (above).

The relationship between contracts in restraint of trade and garden leave clauses (above) was considered in *TFS Derivatives* v *Morgan* (2005). A covenant in the contract of a City equity broker prevented him from working in a competitive business or one which was similar to that in which he had been employed. He argued that this was unlawful as his employers could instead have put a garden leave clause in his contract and just imposed a longer notice period on him. Cox J in the High Court held, however, that an extended period of garden leave could in fact be more onerous as, for example, the employee would be kept out of a commercial market for a longer period and his skills would atrophy.

Assuming that the employer does have an enforceable interest to protect then the restraint will be valid provided that it is no wider than reasonably necessary to protect the interest. Three issues need to be looked at:

1 the area the restraint covers;
2 the activities it covers;
3 the time it lasts.

> **Example**
>
> Kate works in a hairdresser's business owned by Debbie in Worcester and a clause in her contract states that on leaving the business she must not work as a hairdresser or beautician in Worcestershire for a period of five years.
>
> Although Debbie probably has an enforceable interest to protect, as Kate may well have some influence over customers, the restraint is certainly invalid on each of the three grounds above: the area is too wide (Worcester would probably be as far as it could stretch); it includes work as a beautician as well as a hairdresser; and five years is far too long. Therefore, the restraint would completely fail. Debbie could successfully have imposed some restraint but, as she tried to impose too great a restraint, she ends up with nothing.

In *Greer v Sketchley Ltd* (1979) a restraint was imposed on the director of a dry cleaning company which prevented him, on leaving, from being engaged in a similar dry cleaning business in any part of the UK. As Sketchleys operated only in the Midlands and London, the restraint was too wide, although Denning MR observed that had they operated over the whole of the UK then the restraint might have been upheld. Similarly, in *TSC v Massey* (above) the non-solicitation clause was void as it applied to the solicitation of *any* employee, no matter what their role in the business was, and it applied to those who joined the company after the defendants had left. In *Forshaw v Archcraft Ltd* (2005) the employee had been dismissed for failing to agree to a restrictive covenant which was found on the facts to be unreasonable. The clause provided that certain employees were restrained from working anywhere in the UK for a period of 12 months in a competing business following termination of their employment. This was found to be wider than necessary to protect the legitimate interests of the employer. Even so, an employment tribunal found that the dismissal was fair as there was a justifiable fear that employees would leave to start a new company. The EAT overruled this on the simple ground that if the restraint was unreasonable then dismissal for failing to observe it would also be unreasonable and so unfair. An extreme case of where a dismissal was held to be reasonable is *Fitch v Dewes* (above), where a lifelong restraint on a managing clerk was valid, a possible reason being that it applied only to practice within seven miles of Tamworth Town Hall.

There has been some discussion as to how far, if at all, the courts can interpret a restraint, which may appear to be too wide on its literal interpretation, so that it accords with the intentions of the party imposing it. In *Littlewoods v Harris* (above) the Court of Appeal considered a restraint which covered working for a subsidiary company of the employer and which was on its face too wide, as the employer had many subsidiaries, some of which had completely different businesses to that of mail order, in which the (ex-)employee had worked. The court was prepared to limit the restraint to those subsidiaries concerned with mail order. Two recent decisions have shown a conflicting approach. In *Hollis v Stocks* (2000) the restraint prevented a solicitor from working within ten miles of the firm's office and 'work' was interpreted as 'work as a solicitor'. Yet in *Wincanton Ltd v Cranny* (2000) a restraint which prevented a manager from being engaged in any business which was in competition with that of

5

The contract of employment

his former employer was too wide and the court refused to interpret it so that it was valid. Sedley LJ observed that those who live by these clauses must, if need be, perish by them. If the clause is too wide, so be it!

The doctrine of restraint of trade has also been held to apply to exclusive service contracts where the restraint applies during employment rather than after it. These contracts are found in the music publishing trade and an example is *Schroeder Music Publishing Co. Ltd v Macaulay* (1974), where a contract between a young songwriter and a music publisher provided that the songwriter should give his exclusive services to the publisher for five years without the publisher being under any obligation to publish any of his works. The songwriter was guaranteed only one sum of £50 as an advance against future royalties during that time. The House of Lords held that the agreement was totally one-sided and void. However, as was seen above, restraints on employees during employment can be valid (see e.g. *Hivac v Park Royal Instruments* (1946)), but these are not exclusive service agreements but clauses relating to work which could damage the employer's business.

A contract in restraint of trade may in fact contain more than one restraint and it may be that one or more restraints are valid but others are void. If so, it may be possible to sever the invalid restraint and leave the valid one. A good example is *Scorer v Seymour Johns* (1966), where the problem was that, although the employer had a valid reason for imposing some restraint on an estate agent, the restraint applied not only to the area around the office where he worked but also to the area around another office where he did not work. The second restraint was severed and the one relating to the office where he worked was upheld. The court will not re-write the contract nor will severance be appropriate where the whole restraint is invalid as in *Attwood v Lamont* (above). In *TFS Derivatives v Morgan* (2005) (above) that part of the equity broker's contract which prevented him from working in a similar business to that in which he was employed was severed and the other part was enforced.

If the restraint is valid then it can be enforced by damages, where the activities of the ex-employee in breach of the clause have caused loss, and/or an injunction can be sought enforcing the restraint. One problem for employers is that the courts have a general discretion whether to grant an injunction and it is possible that, even if the restraint is lawful, an injunction could be refused if the court felt that it would serve no useful purpose. However, the general practice is to grant injunctions if the restraint is valid.

If an employee is wrongfully dismissed then a restraint clause, even if otherwise valid, cannot be enforced because the employer, by wrongfully dismissing the employee, has repudiated the whole contract, including the restraint clause, which accordingly falls (*General Billposting Co. v Atkinson* (1909)). In *Rock Refrigeration Ltd v Jones* (1997) the court considered the effect of a clause attempting to avoid the effect of *General Billposting* which stated that a restraint clause applied on termination of the contract 'howsoever caused'. It was held that this was ineffective and the restraint clause still falls. An as yet unanswered question is whether the same applies where the employee claims unfair dismissal, the problem being that a finding of unfair dismissal does not involve a finding of breach of contract. It would seem ludicrous that a wrongfully dismissed employee is not bound by a restraint clause yet an unfairly dismissed employee still is and a possible way forward might be for the courts to say in an unfair dismissal case that the conduct of the employer was not only unreasonable but also a breach of contract so as to disentitle him from relying on the restraint. In constructive dismissal cases there is a finding of breach anyway.

Terms implied by a collective agreement

A collective agreement is one made between an employer or employer's association and a trade union. The object will be to deal with such matters as pay, hours of work and disputes procedures. Such agreements very rarely, if ever, have contractual force (see *Ford Motor Co.* v *AUEW* (1969), where it was felt that such agreements were reached against a background adverse to enforceability) and are, by s 179 of TULRCA, presumed not to be legally binding unless they are in writing and it is expressly stated that they are binding. We are here concerned with whether such an agreement can be incorporated in the contracts of individual employees.

There are two possibilities: express incorporation of the collective agreement into contracts of employment; and implied incorporation of the collective agreement into contracts of employment.

Express incorporation of the collective agreement into contracts of employment

An example is *National Coal Board* v *Galley* (1958), where the contracts of colliery foremen stated that their contracts were to be regulated by national agreements then in force. A new collective agreement was made under which deputies were required to work on such days as might reasonably be required. The defendant refused to work on Saturdays and was held to be in breach of contract. An interesting, if controversial, extension of the principle of express incorporation occurred in *Cadoux* v *Central Regional Council* (1986). The employee's letter of appointment stated that he would be employed subject to national conditions of service, which included a non-contributory pension scheme. The employers then withdrew the scheme and it was held by the Court of Session that they were entitled to do so. Lord Ross said that 'the clear inference from the fact that they are the defendants' rules is that the defendants are entitled to alter them'. The effect was to give the employer the power unilaterally to alter the terms of the contract of employment. On the other hand, in *Robertson* v *British Gas Corporation* (1983) part of a collective agreement which regulated the amounts payable to employees under a bonus scheme was subsequently terminated by the employer. It was held that the employees were still entitled to the bonus payments as any variation had been agreed by the employers. The court in *Cadoux* distinguished *Robertson* on the basis that in *Robertson* the collective agreement had been made between an employer and a trade union, whereas here the agreement was made through consultations locally, but this seems scarcely satisfactory. A further point is that the decision in *Robertson* is also authority for saying that a collective agreement which is not legally enforceable between the parties can still be a source of binding terms in an individual contract. This view was upheld in *Marley* v *Forward Trust Group Ltd* (1986).

Implied incorporation of the collective agreement into contracts of employment

A distinction has been drawn between those terms which are considered suitable for incorporation because it is clear what the parties' intentions are, such as terms relating to hours and pay, and those which are not. In *British Leyland (UK) Ltd* v *McQuilken* (1978) a provision in a collective agreement that an employer would interview employees to establish whether they wished to take redundancy or be retrained was held inappropriate for incorporation. Actual redundancy selection procedures were held not to be incorporated in *Alexander* v *Standard Telephones and Cables Ltd (No. 2)* (1991), but a different view was taken in *Anderson* v *Pringle of Scotland Ltd* (1998), where it was held that a redundancy selection procedure agreement providing that selection would be on the 'last in, first out' principle was suitable for incorporation. It seems that the latter decision is preferable, given the impact that selection procedures have on individuals.

In *Kaur* v *Rover Group Ltd* (2004) the issue was whether a term of a collective agreement, which provided that 'there will be no compulsory redundancies', was incorporated into the contracts of individual employees. The High Court held that it was, and that it therefore overrode an express contractual term allowing the employer to terminate the contracts of employees for any reason. The reasoning was that the express term simply provided for the minimum notice which the employer needed to give in order to terminate: it did not conflict with the term that there would be no compulsory redundancies. The Court of Appeal overruled this, holding that the words of the collective agreement were merely aspirations rather than a binding contractual term.

It is noteworthy that in many cases the terms of a collective agreement are incorporated by implied acceptance by employees. Suppose that a collective agreement grants employees a pay rise but also requires them to work more flexible shift patterns. Once employees have accepted the extra pay they can scarcely reject the part obliging them to work the more flexible shifts. It is not possible to choose which parts of an agreement to observe.

Although a union member may, therefore, find that a collective agreement is a source of contractual terms, what of a non-unionist? The point has caused difficulty. In *Singh* v *British Steel Corporation* (1974) a non-unionist was held not to be bound by a collective agreement, although it has been suggested that the idea that a non-unionist is not bound rests on the theory that the union acts as the agent of its members in making the agreement. This has not always been accepted, as in *Burton Group Ltd* v *Smith* (1977). The law has never devised a satisfactory conceptual basis for the incorporation of implied terms and, as a result, the position of non-unionists is in theory uncertain. In practice they will normally be bound where, as in the above example, the agreement grants a pay rise which they accept.

A final point is that where a collective agreement contains a no strike clause then, by s 180 of TULRCA 1992, this will not form part of individuals' contracts of employment unless:

(a) the collective agreement is made by an independent trade union and is in writing;

(b) it states that the no strike clause may be incorporated into contracts of employment;

(c) it is reasonably accessible during working hours;

(d) the worker's own contract, expressly or impliedly, incorporates it into his contract.

The object is to prevent individual workers from being sued for damages for going on strike when their union, which called them out on strike, could not be because the collective agreement is not legally binding. It would be most unusual to find a situation where a no strike clause *was* incorporated into individual contracts.

ARE WORK RULES, POLICY HANDBOOKS AND OTHER MANAGERIAL DOCUMENTS INCORPORATED INTO INDIVIDUAL CONTRACTS OF EMPLOYMENT?

Such rules may be part of the contract where, for example, a contract of employment expressly states that a certain policy is incorporated. Otherwise they will not be contractual and therefore can be imposed or altered by the management whenever it wishes. Attempts to argue that they are contractual have included the following:

1 *Dryden* v *Greater Glasgow Health Board* (1992), where an employee's claim that the introduction of a non-smoking policy gave grounds for constructive dismissal as being a breach of contract failed because the policy was not contractual and could thus be introduced at will.

2 *Wandsworth BC* v *D'Silva* (1998), where an argument that a code of procedure on staff sickness could not be unilaterally altered by the employer failed as it was not contractual.

3 *Taylor* v *Secretary of State for Scotland* (1999), where an equal opportunities policy stating that the employer would not discriminate on the grounds of, *inter alia*, age was not contractual so that an employee dismissed on this ground could not use it to claim that his dismissal was a breach of contract.

Although the courts have resolutely set their face against incorporation of these documents into the contract, if a claim is brought by an employee for unfair dismissal then, as the basis of the claim is that the employer has acted unreasonably, a failure to observe a code or similar document may well count against the employer.

TO WHAT EXTENT CAN AN EMPLOYER VARY A CONTRACT OF EMPLOYMENT?

The traditional view that a variation needs the consent of both sides is still true and therefore an employer cannot unilaterally vary a contract. However, a failure to agree to a variation may, *in some situations*, give the employer grounds for fairly dismissing the employee. This is explored in Chapter 12 and the case of *RS Components* v *Irwin* (1973) should be particularly noted.

An employer may reserve the power in the contract itself to change the contract. However, in *Wandsworth BC* v *D'Silva* (above) Woolf MR held that clear language was

5

The contract of employment

117

needed to reserve this sort of power and that 'the court is unlikely to favour a variation which does more than enable a party to vary contractual provisions with which that party is required to comply'. A good example of the reluctance of the courts to interpret a contract as giving an employer an unfettered power of variation is *Land Securities Trillium v Thornley* (2005). The appellant's contract of employment contained a clause providing that the employee would 'perform to the best of your abilities all the duties of this post and any other post you may subsequently hold and any other duties which may reasonably be required of you and will at all times obey all reasonable instructions given to you'. The appellant was promoted to what was described in the job description as a senior project leader but later this was changed to that of 'senior architect', which the appellant felt changed her job from that of a hands-on architect to one with a more managerial role. She claimed constructive dismissal (see Chapter 11). The EAT held that the words in her contract 'any other duties which may reasonably be required of you' did not give the employer an absolute power to require her to work any duties which they wished but was subject to a requirement of reasonableness. Moreover, the reference to posts which the employee may subsequently hold did not give the employer the power to change the employee's post without their consent. Cox J observed that job descriptions often fail to accurately represent the actual duties undertaken and so it is necessary to look at the actual work done. Accordingly, on the facts the appellant was constructively dismissed.

The effect of this is that a power to vary provisions to the disadvantage of the employee is unlikely to be accepted unless, at the very least, it is very clearly conferred by the contract.

SUMMARY

This chapter begins by looking at the statement of initial employment particulars: what they must contain, when they must be given, and their relationship to the contract. It then outlines the main types of terms in employment contracts:

- express
- implied.

Implied terms are further divided into those implied by:

- statute
- custom
- courts
- collective agreement.

Much of the chapter deals with terms implied by the courts and within this area it looks at the duties of the employer and the employee and the implied term of mutual trust and confidence. The chapter also looks at a number of statutes which develop particular terms, e.g. the Data Protection Act 1998, the Public Interest Disclosure Act 1998 and the Patents Act 1977. It also looks at the important area of contracts in restraint of trade.

QUESTIONS

1 Select two of the implied terms discussed in this chapter and estimate their importance in employment law today.

2 Sarah is employed as a salesperson by Mouse Ltd, which sells highly specialised computer equipment to large international firms. She earns £50,000 p.a. A clause in her contract states that:

> On termination of your employment for whatever reason you shall not be engaged directly or indirectly in the business of designing or marketing computer equipment anywhere in the world for a period of two years.

Sarah resigns and sets up in business on her own doing the same kind of work as she had done for Mouse Ltd. Mouse Ltd also suspects that, before she left, she copied confidential details of customer accounts.

Advise Mouse Ltd on the following:

(a) whether the above clause in Sarah's contract is enforceable;

(b) whether any action can be taken against her if it is found that she has copied details of customer accounts.

Would it make any difference to your answer if Sarah had been wrongfully dismissed?

FURTHER READING

Brodie, D. (2005) *The Employment Contract*, Oxford University Press: Oxford.

Cabrelli, D. (2005) 'The Implied Duty of Mutual Trust and Confidence: An Emerging Overarching Principle?' 34 ILJ 284.

Working Party established under Article 29 of Directive 95/46 Report (February 2006).

BIBLIOGRAPHY

Brodie, D. (1996) 'The Heart of the Matter. Mutual Trust and Confidence', 25 ILJ 121.

Brodie, D. (2001) 'Legal Coherence and the Employment Revolution', 117 LQR 604 at 607.

Evans, W. (2004) 'Of Portmanteux and Bridgeheads', 33 ILJ 355.

Freedland, M. (2003) *The Personal Employment Contract*, Oxford University Press: Oxford.

Freedland, M. (2006) *The Personal Work Contract*, Oxford University Press: Oxford.

Lewis, D. (2005) 'Providing Rights for Whistleblowers: Would an Anti-Discrimination Model be more Effective?' 34 ILJ 239.

Lewis, D. (2006) 'Whistleblowers, Reasonable Belief and Data Protection', 35 ILJ 324 (drawing attention to the link between the Public Interest Disclosure Act and the Data Protection Act).

Middlemiss, S. (2004) 'The Truth and Nothing but the Truth? The Legal Liability of Employers for Employee References', 33 ILJ 59. This is a most useful survey of an area of great practical importance which has been somewhat neglected by writers on employment law.

 For further resources and updates please go to the Companion Website accompanying this book at **www.mylawchamber.co.uk/duddingtonemployment**

5

The contract of employment

6 Continuity of employment

INTRODUCTION

Some employment rights can be claimed by all employees, such as the rights conferred by sex, race and disabilities legislation. Other rights depend on the employee having a certain amount of continuous employment. One of the main examples is the requirement for an employee claiming unfair dismissal to have one year's continuous employment (although there are exceptions, as we shall see) but there are others: the right to redundancy pay and the amount; the right to a statement of initial employment particulars; and various maternity rights, which all depend on a certain amount of continuous employment.

> ### LAW IN CONTEXT
> #### The qualifying period for unfair dismissal
>
> The reason why certain rights depend on periods of continuous employment whereas others are open to all employees is not easy to find. The origin of the restriction of the right to claim unfair dismissal to employees with a certain amount of qualifying employment appears to be administrative: in 1970, the Department of Employment and Productivity, in *Industrial Relations Bill: Consultative Document*, para 53, stated that the initial two-year qualifying period was needed to prevent industrial tribunals (as employment tribunals were then called) being flooded with claims but that the period would be reduced later. This indeed happened, as the period was reduced to one year in 1974 and to six months in 1975. The Conservative government elected in 1979 then saw the ability to bring claims for unfair dismissal as a bar to firms taking on workers and so the period was raised to a year in 1979 and to two years in 1985.

There was also, until 1995, a requirement that employees should, in certain circumstances, have worked for a minimum number of hours a week. The origin of this appears to be found in the Contracts of Employment Act 1963, which gave a right to receive a written statement of terms and conditions of employment and a right to minimum periods of notice to employees who worked at least 21 hours a week. The intention was to exclude employees with spare time or weekend jobs or where the employment was not of substantial importance to the parties. This was carried through into unfair dismissal legislation and, by the 1990s, unfair dismissal could not be claimed (except in certain cases) by employees working for less than sixteen hours a week or, where the employee had worked for over five years, for at least eight hours a week. However, by the 1990s, the increase in part-time work and the growing importance attached to statutory rights made this restriction seem anachronistic.

In *R v Secretary of State for Employment, ex parte Equal Opportunities Commission* (1995) the House of Lords held that the restriction to employees with certain hours of work a week and the consequent exclusion of many part-time employees constituted unlawful indirect discrimination against women, given that nearly 90% of employees prevented from claiming were women. Therefore the government removed the restriction by the Employment Protection (Part-time Employee) Regulations 1995 (SI 1995/31). The effect is that the restriction on the number of hours worked has gone but the need for a certain number of weeks' continuity of employment remains.

THE RULES ON CONTINUITY OF EMPLOYMENT IN OPERATION

Fundamental rule

This is found in s 212(1) of the ERA 1996, which provides that: 'Any week during the whole or part of which an employee's relations with his employer are governed by a contract of employment counts in computing the employee's period of employment.'

The following points emerge from this provision:

Only weeks during which the employee is actually employed by that employer count in computing continuity in claims against that employer. This is, however, subject to exceptions where in some circumstances weeks of employment with one employer can be carried over and added to weeks of employment with another employer when a business is transferred (see below and Chapter 12).

> ### Example
>
> John was employed by Albert from 1 January 2001 until 1 July 2001. He then left and was employed by Steve from 1 July 2001 until 2 January 2002. Steve then dismissed John and John wished to claim unfair dismissal. He cannot do so (unless he is within the excepted classes) as, although he has over one year's employment, it is not with the same employer. He does not have sufficient continuity of employment.

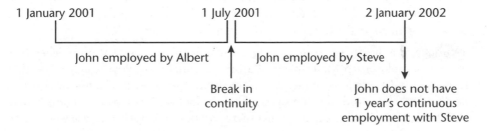

| 1 January 2001 | 1 July 2001 | 2 January 2002 |

John employed by Albert   John employed by Steve

Break in continuity

John does not have 1 year's continuous employment with Steve

6

Continuity of employment

The point that only weeks in which the employee actually has a contract of employment with that employer count is illustrated by *Carmichael v National Power plc* (1999), which was discussed in Chapter 4. Had the power station guides claimed for unfair dismissal on the basis that they had acted as guides for a certain number of years, their claim would have failed because it was held that they did not have a contract of employment when not acting as guides, although they may have had such a contract when they did. In *Hellyer Bros v McLeod* (1987) it was held that trawlermen had no continuity of employment as they were employed on a series of crew agreements which lasted for each voyage but were not employed under a global contract. Therefore, they were not entitled to redundancy payments. This case can be set alongside other cases on employment status such as *Nethermere v Taverna and Gardiner* (1983) and *O'Kelly v Trusthouse Forte* (1983) (see Chapter 4) as an example of the problems which the courts have had in defining employment status. Where, however, there is a contract of employment then continuity is not affected by the fact that the duties may not often be performed. In *Colley v Corkindale* (1995) an employee worked only one shift every fortnight but had continuity as her contract gave her continuity. In *Cornwall CC v Prater* (2005) the fact that a local authority was not under a continuing obligation to offer work to a home tutor did not prevent there from being a contract of employment. Once the tutor had accepted particular work then there was a mutuality of obligation: the tutor had to tutor and the local authority had to pay her. Thus she had a contract of employment. As Davies (2006) points out, the fact that there was no mutuality of obligations *between* contracts was irrelevant: all that the employee had to do was to show that *within* each contract there was mutuality of obligation. As Davies points out, if there was mutuality of obligations between contracts there would be no need to rely on s 212(1) anyway as there would automatically be continuity.

Section 212(1) simply refers to the employee's relations with the employer being governed by 'a' contract of employment and this means that continuity will be preserved even though an employee may have several different contracts with the same employer. The point was well put by Denning MR in *Wood v York City Council* (1978): 'even though a man may change his job from, say, manual work to clerical work, even though he may change the site of his work from one place to another . . . as long as he is with the same employer all the way through, then it is continuous employment.'

Other provisions of the ERA 1996 raise the following points:

1. Section 210(5) of the ERA provides a presumption of continuity and therefore an employer alleging that there is no continuity must prove this. However, in *Secretary of State for Employment v Cohen* (1987) it was held that this applied only to employment with one employer and where the issue related to continuity on the transfer of a business then it was for the tribunal to find whether there was continuity. In effect the burden of proof would be neutral.

2. Section 203 of the ERA prevents any agreement from waiving continuity. Therefore, if a new employer on the transfer of a business made employees agree that their service with the previous employer did not count, then it would be for the courts to decide whether it did and the agreement would have no effect. It is, of course, possible for an employer to agree that there *will* be continuity in a case where there

might not have been, as this will have the opposite effect as it will give employees rights which they might not have had.

WEEKS WHICH COUNT TOWARDS CONTINUITY EVEN THOUGH THERE IS NO CONTRACT OF EMPLOYMENT

Until now, the emphasis has been on the need for employees to show that their contract is continuous for a certain period of time and, conversely, that if there is no contract of employment in existence, then continuity will be broken. However, s 212 of the ERA 1996 then provides that in certain situations continuity will be preserved even though the contract is not in existence. In effect, these are exceptions to the general rule.

The exceptions are as follows:

Employee incapable of work through sickness or injury

Continuity will be preserved in any week in which the employee is incapable of work through sickness or injury (s 212(3)(a)) up to a maximum of 26 weeks (s 212(4)).

Example

David's contract of employment with Arthur began on 1 January 2006. On 1 July 2006 David entered hospital for an operation and Arthur terminated his contract of employment. On 1 January 2007 David returned to work with a new contract of employment but was dismissed the next day. David has one year's continuous employment because his absence did not last for more than 26 weeks even though he actually only had a contract of employment for one day over six months. Had Arthur not terminated David's contract of employment on 1 July 2006 then continuity would not have been affected at all, as his contract would have continued. As it is, David is saved by the exception to the basic rule. If, on the other hand, David had not returned to work until 2 January 2007 and he had not had a contract whilst he was away, then continuity would have been broken as his absence would have lasted more than 26 weeks.

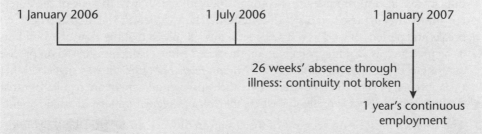

1 January 2006   1 July 2006   1 January 2007

26 weeks' absence through illness: continuity not broken

1 year's continuous employment

Note: Whether Arthur should have terminated David's contract when David entered hospital is, of course, a separate question and the whole topic of termination will be dealt with in Chapter 11.

Employee absent on account of temporary cessation of work

Continuity will also be preserved in any week in which the employee is absent from work on account of a temporary cessation of work (s 212(3)(b)). This time there is no upper limit as there was above and, in theory, the cessation could last for any length of time, although a long cessation would probably not be held as temporary. Once again, it must be remembered that if the contract continues then this provision is not relevant as continuity is preserved anyway.

The following points must be satisfied for this exception to apply:

1   There must be a cessation of work. In *Fitzgerald v Hall, Russell & Co.* (1970) the House of Lords held that the essential requirement is that the employee's actual work must have ceased and this may be even where the employer's business is still continuing.

2   The cessation of work must be temporary. In *Fitzgerald v Hall, Russell & Co.* it was pointed out that this must be looked at with the benefit of hindsight: 'What at the time seems to be permanent may turn out to be temporary, and what at the time seems to be temporary may turn out to be permanent.' Despite this commonsense approach, problems have emerged in deciding whether an absence is temporary. In *Ford v Warwickshire CC* (1983) the applicant was a teacher who had been employed under a series of fixed-term contracts each for the academic year from September to July. It was held that the break between them was only a temporary cessation of work and therefore she had continuity. Lord Diplock said that 'temporary' means 'transient', which itself accords with the general approach in *Fitzgerald*, but he then put forward a somewhat mathematical approach to decide cases where there is seasonal employment followed by breaks such as occur in hotel work. Here he suggested that one should compare the length of the period between the seasonal contracts and the length of the contracts themselves. If the period of the break is short compared with the length of the contract then a cessation could be temporary. In *Flack v Kodak Ltd* (1986) the applicant had been employed for irregular periods of time in the photo-finishing department, with her work varying according to seasonal demand. Woolf LJ, in the Court of Appeal, held that Lord Diplock's mathematical approach was not appropriate to irregular work patterns. Instead, 'it is the whole period of employment which is relevant. In the case of irregular employment, if the periods of employment either side of the dismissal are only looked at, a most misleading comparison would be drawn'. In view of the different approaches in these two cases, the question of how to view the relationship between breaks and periods of work is not settled but it is submitted that the view of Woolf LJ is to be preferred as avoiding what would otherwise be fine distinctions based on precise computations of time. In *Sillars v Charrington Fuels Ltd* (1989) it was suggested that the approach in *Ford* could be used where the gaps in employment are regular but that the approach in *Flack* is preferable where there is an irregular pattern of employment.

3   The absence must be on account of the cessation of work. In *Roach v CSB (Moulds)* (1991) an employee was dismissed by his employers and then worked for another employer for 12 days and was then re-engaged by his previous employers before finally being dismissed by them. It was held that continuity had been broken as the 12 days' absence was not on account of a temporary cessation of work.

Employment regarded as continuing by arrangement or custom

Any week in which by arrangement or custom the employment is regarded as continuing will also count (s 212(3)(c)). An example of this might be where the employee is granted leave of absence on compassionate grounds but without pay so that the contract does continue. However, any arrangement to preserve continuity must be agreed on before the absence begins. In *Lloyds Bank Ltd v Secretary of State for Employment* (1979) this provision was used where the employee's contract provided for employment on a one week on, one week off basis but the employee actually had a contract of employment throughout the time. In *Ford v Warwickshire CC* (1983) it was pointed out that none of these exceptions applies where there is an existing contract and so the correctness of the decision in the *Lloyds Bank* case is suspect. Therefore, it could be argued that the employee fell between two stools: she had a contract all the time and so s 212 was inapplicable but her contract contained breaks and so she did not have continuity.

In *Curr v Marks and Spencer plc* (2003) the EAT held that where a woman was on a company four-year child break scheme then continuity would not be preserved unless the employment was in some way regarded by both parties as continuing. This was not so here and so continuity was not preserved, which emphasises the importance of all agreements and company schemes making the position regarding continuity absolutely clear. In *London Probation Board v Kirkpatrick* (2005) the employee was dismissed and then appealed and was reinstated. However, before he returned to work, his employers decided that the original dismissal should stand. The issue was precisely when he had been dismissed as this determined if his complaint of unfair dismissal was presented in time. It was held that he was dismissed when the employers decided that the dismissal should stand as there was an 'arrangement' implied in the decision of the panel to reinstate him that this continuity of employment would be preserved. Had this not been the case, the dismissal would have taken effect when he was originally dismissed. This decision is, with respect, questionable. The word 'arrangement' implies an agreement of some kind, yet there was no evidence of this. The problem here was that, although the appellant was undoubtedly reinstated as an employee by the decision of the appeal panel, there was a break in continuity, which was why the EAT used s 212(3)(c) of the ERA 1996.

It should be noted that there was a provision that continuity was not affected by absence through pregnancy or childbirth but this has been repealed by the Employment Relations Act 1999, as the contracts of employees now continue through maternity leave.

WEEKS WHICH DO NOT BREAK CONTINUITY ALTHOUGH THEY DO NOT COUNT TOWARDS PERIODS OF CONTINUOUS EMPLOYMENT

In the above examples all the actual breaks in continuity were treated as if they did not exist and therefore not only did they not break continuity but also the weeks actually counted towards continuous employment. However, in the case of employees on strike

6

there is a kind of halfway house under which weeks do not break continuity but they do not themselves actually count in computing continuous employment and the same may apply where there is a lock-out.

The two cases are set out in s 216 and are as follows.

Employee taking part in a strike

Any week, or part of a week, where the employee is taking part in a strike does not break continuity (s 216(2)). A strike is defined for this purpose by s 235(5) as where a body of employees acting in combination cease work or where there is a concerted refusal to continue to work with the aim of compelling the employer to accept or not accept terms or conditions affecting employment. It also includes cases where the strike action is taken to aid other employees. This definition of a strike only applies to the continuity of employment provisions and redundancy payments (see Chapter 12). There is another definition of a strike for the purposes of the law on collective action (see s 246 of TULRCA and Chapter 14).

Employee locked out by employer

Any week, or part of a week, during which an employee is locked out by the employer does not break continuity (s 216(3)). A lock-out is defined for present purposes by s 235(4) as where an employer closes a place of employment, suspends work or refuses to continue to employ employees with the aim of compelling employees to accept or not to accept terms or conditions affecting employment. It also includes situations where the object of the lock-out is to aid another employer.

In the case of a strike s 216(2) is clear: continuity is not broken, although s 216(1) provides that the weeks on strike do not count towards continuity. In the case of a lock-out s 216(3) states that continuity is not broken but nothing is said about whether the weeks count. The reason is probably that, as a strike is normally a breach of contract (see Chapter 14), it was felt that weeks on strike should not count; but, as a lock-out results from action taken by the employer, employees locked out will not normally be in breach. The position is probably that where the contract continues when employees are locked out then weeks will count but where it does not then they will not.

Example

Mary's contract of employment with Y began on 1 January 2006. On 1 February 2006 Mary was called out on strike by her union and did not return to work until 1 March 2006. On 1 February 2007 Mary was dismissed by her employer and asks whether she has one year's continuous employment. The answer is yes. The month on strike did not count but the period before it can be added to the period after it and the result is that Mary has one year's continuous employment.

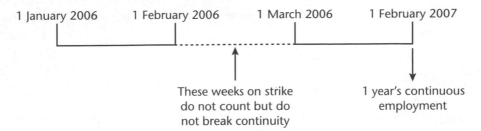

The following other points arise:

1 There is no requirement that the strike be official, although such a distinction is made in deciding whether a dismissal of employees on strike is fair (see Chapter 14).

2 Any period of time after the strike ends but before there is a return to work is likely to be covered by s 212(3)(b) as a temporary cessation of work.

3 Where employees are dismissed whilst on strike continuity will not be affected, as it was held in *Bloomfield* v *Springfield Hosiery Finishing Co. Ltd* (1972) that s 216 applies to all employees employed at the commencement of a strike. Therefore, if employees on strike are dismissed and then re-engaged continuity will not be broken. Furthermore, s 230(1) provides that the term 'employee' in the ERA 1996 includes those who have worked under a contract of employment, which would include employees who have been dismissed in these circumstances.

CASES WHERE CONTINUITY IS PRESERVED WHEN THE EMPLOYER CHANGES

Section 218 of the ERA 1996 deals with continuity in such a case but it is best looked at in conjunction with the Transfer of Undertakings (Protection of Employment) Regulations (TUPE) and the whole topic is considered in Chapter 12.

The effect of maternity leave on continuity of employment is considered in Chapter 10.

ATTEMPTS BY EMPLOYERS TO PREVENT EMPLOYEES GAINING CONTINUITY OF EMPLOYMENT

Although, as we saw earlier, an employer cannot make employees contract out of the rules on continuity (s 203), it is possible for an employer to arrange the contracts of employees so that they do not gain continuity of employment. This happened in *Booth* v *United States of America* (1999), where workers had contracts with two-week breaks between each contract, so that although the contracts added up to over two years they did not have continuity, as none of the exceptions applied. Morrison P, in the EAT, observed that if there was considered to be a loophole in the legislation then it was for Parliament to deal with it and not the courts, although one might observe that on other occasions the courts have quite readily closed loopholes without waiting for Parliament.

SUMMARY

This chapter looks at why the concept of continuity of employment is of fundamental importance in employment law and then moves on to look at the rules on when there will be continuity. It begins with the fundamental rule that any week during the whole or part of which an employee's relations with his employer are governed by a contract of employment counts in computing the employee's period of employment and then looks at whether continuity is preserved when there is no contract of employment. It distinguishes between weeks which count towards periods of continuous employment and those weeks which, although they do not break continuity, do *not* count towards periods of continuous employment.

QUESTION

Debbie began work for Earlsdon College of Arts and Crafts as a part-time lecturer on 1 January 2006. On 1 February 2006 she was away ill and this absence continued until 1 May 2006. On 1 September 2006 she was called out on strike by her union, the Association of Arts and Crafts Teachers, and her absence on strike lasted until 1 October. On 14 February 2007 the College Principal, Anne, caught Debbie sending a Valentine's email to her boyfriend, Hugh, and immediately dismissed her. Debbie feels that she has been unfairly dismissed and wishes to bring a claim for unfair dismissal against the college. She shows you her contract with the college which states that in the summer holiday period (1–31 August) the contracts of all staff are suspended and no salaries are paid.

Advise Debbie on whether she has the required continuity of employment to bring an unfair dismissal claim.

FURTHER READING

Barmes, R. (1996) 'Public Law, EC Law and the Qualifying Period for Unfair Dismissal', 25 ILJ 59.

BIBLIOGRAPHY

Davies, P. (2006) 'Casual Workers and Continuity of Employment', 35 ILJ 196. This looks at the recent case of *Cornwall CC* v *Prater*.

For further resources and updates please go to the Companion Website accompanying this book at **www.mylawchamber.co.uk/duddingtonemployment**

7 Payment of wages and hours of work

PAYMENT OF WAGES

The foundation of the right to receive wages is the contract of employment and indeed in this whole area the common law of employment still holds sway, although there is a certain of amount of statutory regulation. The main instances are the statutory rules governing deductions from wages and statutory sick pay and the National Minimum Wage Act 1998.

The nature of the common law obligations regarding wages was expressed succinctly by Lord Templeman in the House of Lords in *Miles* v *Wakefield MBC* (1987): 'In a contract of employment wages and work go together. The employer pays for work and the worker works for his wages. If the employer declines to pay, the worker need not work. If the worker declines to work, the employer need not pay.'

Although it is clear that an employee who has performed the work is entitled to be paid the wages, two less straightforward issues arise. First, suppose that the employee has failed to complete the work and has instead performed only part of it. Is there a right to part of the wages? The old case of *Cutter* v *Powell* (1795) held that where the employee fails to complete performance there is no right to any remuneration at all. Thus, when a sailor died during a voyage his widow was not entitled to any wages due to his estate. However, this particular case has generated more heat than light as, for one thing, this situation would now come under the Law Reform (Frustrated Contracts) Act 1943 (see Chapter 11). In any event, it applies only where the contract cannot be divided, in that *one* sum was paid for the whole job. In most employment contracts wages can be deemed to accrue from day to day and s 2 of the Apportionment Act 1870 provides that, *inter alia*, all 'periodical payments in the nature of income' shall be considered as accruing from day to day and shall be apportionable accordingly. The language of the Act, which refers to rents, annuities and dividends, suggests that it was not originally intended to apply to contracts of employment, but in *Sim* v *Rotherham MBC* (1987) the High Court thought that it applied to the salaries of monthly paid teachers, which could be considered as accruing day by day.

Suppose that a monthly paid employee stopped working half-way through a month, then there would be a right to payment up to the cessation of work and in any event this would be payable where the cessation was due to the worker's death under the Frustrated Contracts Act. Where the employee was engaged to do a particular job, such as decorating a house, and to be paid a fixed sum on completion, then if performance was not completed the employee might be able to rely on the doctrine of substantial performance as in *Hoenig* v *Isaacs* (1952). Such a right to wages would be counterbalanced by any right of the employer to claim for damages due to loss caused by the employee's failure to complete. For example, failure to decorate rooms in a hotel as agreed could mean that the hotel suffered loss through being unable to let them.

The second issue which arises is where the employee has refused to perform a particular part of the job rather than failing to complete it. In *Cresswell* v *Board of Inland Revenue* (1984) the refusal was to adapt to new methods of work and it was held that in such a case the employee would not be entitled to any wages. In a number of industrial disputes where employees have refused to perform particular duties which they were obliged to perform under their contracts, the employer has deducted wages. There are two possibilities: the employer deducts wages only for the time when the employee has refused to perform the particular contractual duties; or the employer declines to pay any wages *at all* for the time when the employee was refusing to perform the duties. The first solution was adopted in *Miles* v *Wakefield MBC* (1987), where a registrar of births, marriages and deaths refused, as part of industrial action, to conduct weddings on Saturday mornings. He was told that if he was not prepared to work according to his contract on Saturday mornings he need not attend work and would not be paid, but in fact he attended and did other work. The council was entitled to deduct 3/37ths of his salary for the time when he should have been performing weddings. One point, which was left unresolved, was whether he would have a claim in the law of restitution for the value of the work which he *did* perform.

The second solution was adopted in *Wiluszynski* v *Tower Hamlets LBC* (1989). Local authority employees, as part of an industrial dispute, refused to deal with queries from councillors about their constituents' housing problems and the council refused to pay them at all for the time when they were doing this. Two points emerged: the council had told the employees, before the action commenced, that they would not be paid at all unless they were prepared to carry out their duties in full; but the employees argued that the council had, by not physically preventing them from coming to work, impliedly accepted the work which was done. The Court of Appeal held that the council had not accepted the work. As Nicholls LJ put it: 'a person is not treated by the law as having chosen to accept that which is forced down his throat, despite his objection.' The fact that the council had made the position clear in advance was enough and the result was that the employees received no pay for the month when the dispute lasted, even though the backlog of work through not dealing with complaints was cleared in three hours. In *Ticehurst* v *British Telecommunications plc* (1992) a similar decision was reached where the employee had a discretion as to how to exercise her duties (see Chapter 5 for a fuller discussion of this case).

An unresolved issue is where the employer is faced with a go-slow or similar action where the extent of the refusal to perform is difficult to quantify. An employer could deduct a reasonable sum representing duties not performed but the easiest way would be simply to declare that any work done during the dispute will be treated as voluntary, in which case under the *Wiluszynski* decision there is no liability to pay anything at all.

ITEMISED PAY STATEMENT

Section 8 of the ERA 1996 gives employees the right to a written itemised pay statement at or before the payment of wages. This must contain details of the following:

1 The gross amount of wages and salary.

2 The amounts of any variable deductions from that gross amount and the purposes for which they were made. In the case of fixed deductions it is sufficient to give a standing statement containing the details and then the itemised pay statement need only give the aggregate amount of fixed deductions.

3 The net amount of any wages or salary payable.

4 Where different parts are paid in different ways then the amount and method of each part payment must be specified.

A failure to give this statement is dealt with in the same way as a failure to provide the statement of initial employment particulars (see Chapter 5).

DEDUCTIONS FROM WAGES

This topic has a long history, beginning with the passage of the Truck Acts in 1831–40, which were designed to stop the practice of employees being paid in tokens which could only be spent on goods produced by the employer. The present law is contained in Part II (ss 13–27) of the ERA 1996 and it is noteworthy that it applies to workers as defined by s 230(3) of the ERA rather than employees.

The first question is what is meant by wages and this is answered by s 27, which gives a detailed list of what counts as wages. The main category is in s 27(a): 'any fee, bonus, commission, holiday pay, or other emolument referable to the worker's employment, whether payable under his contract or otherwise.'

Three points arise from this:

1 Does it include a payment which is stated to be discretionary or ex-gratia but where the contract contemplated that it would be made? In *Kent Management Services Ltd v Butterfield* (1992) it was held that it did, so that a refusal by an employer to make such a payment could be challenged as an unlawful deduction.

2 Does it apply where no wages at all are paid rather than a deduction from what *is* paid? In *Delaney* v *Staples* (1991) the Court of Appeal held that it did and thus a worker who was dismissed when owed £55.50 holiday pay and accrued commission could claim this under these provisions rather than have to make a separate claim for breach of contract. The effect of this decision has been to increase greatly the number of claims alleging unlawful deductions from wages.

3 Does it apply to a claim for wages due in lieu of notice where the worker is dismissed without proper notice? In *Delaney* v *Staples* (above) the House of Lords answered this in the negative. The worker claimed £82 in lieu of notice and it was held that, as wages are essentially payments due for services rendered and as wages in lieu of

notice are not for this (with one exception), such a claim must be brought in an action for breach of contract. The one exception was where wages are due under a 'garden leave' clause (see Chapter 5), where a failure to pay will count as a deduction. However, it must be emphasised that the issue here is not entitlement to wages in lieu of notice but the correct method of asserting that right.

In *International Packaging Corporation (UK) Ltd* v *Balfour* (2003) the EAT held that where employers unilaterally introduced short-time working then workers affected could claim wages not paid as a result as unauthorised deductions. The EAT held that although there had been agreements in the past to vary working hours this did not amount to an implied term arising from custom and practice authorising short-time working to be introduced unilaterally.

The issue in *Elizabeth Claire Care Management Ltd* v *Francis* (2005) concerned an employee, who, having complained about failure to pay wages on time, was dismissed. The EAT held that the dismissal came within s 104 of the ERA 1996 which provides that a dismissal of an employee for alleging that the employer had infringed a statutory right is automatically unfair.

The other categories of wages in s 27 are sums due under various statutory provisions, for example statutory sick pay, guarantee pay, maternity/paternity/adoption pay and sums payable under orders for reinstatement and re-engagement. The first two are covered later in this chapter, statutory maternity pay etc. in Chapter 10 and the two others in Chapter 11. Certain matters are specifically stated by s 27 not to be wages and thus not subject to the rules on deductions such as pensions and redundancy payments.

Section 13 provides that an employer shall not make a deduction from wages unless:

1 the deduction is required or authorised by statute, e.g. PAYE;

2 the deduction is required or authorised by a provision in the contract provided that the deduction was contained in written terms of the contract of which the employee was made aware, either by being given a copy of the contract or otherwise in writing, before the deduction.

3 the deduction was agreed to by the worker prior to when the deduction is made.

The difference between (2) and (3) is that (2) will usually apply where there is a right under the contract of employment to make the deduction, whereas (3) applies where the worker agrees on the particular occasion to the making of the deduction.

Section 14 then sets out six cases where a deduction can be made even where the requirements in s 13 are not satisfied. Section 14 does not, however, state that deductions in all of the cases below are deemed to be lawful: it was held in *Sunderland Polytechnic* v *Evans* (1993) that whether a deduction is lawful is a separate issue for the civil courts. Therefore lawfulness will depend on each case and in particular the provisions of the worker's contract. The situations in s 14 are as follows:

1 To cover overpayments of wages or expenses (see below).

2 In consequence of disciplinary proceedings held by virtue of a statutory provision. In *Chiltern House* v *Chambers* (1990) Wood P said, *obiter*, that this did not cover disciplinary proceedings held by private employers but only, for example, police and fire services.

3 Where there is a statutory requirement to make deductions from wages and to pay the amount over to a public authority: for example, where the worker has had an attachment of earnings order made against him the sum deducted from wages will be paid to the court for transmission to the creditor.

4 Where the worker has agreed in writing that payments can be made to a third party. Deduction of union subscriptions (known as check-off) is dealt with by s 68 of TULRCA 1992, which provides that all such deductions must be authorised by the worker in writing and that this authorisation can be withdrawn by the worker at any time.

5 A strike or other industrial action in which the worker took part.

6 Deductions made in satisfaction of a court or tribunal order requiring the worker to make a payment to the employer: for example, where the employer has sued the worker for a debt.

The one area in the above which has caused difficulty is overpayments. The law of restitution applies here and this is an area which has developed considerably in recent years and is likely to continue to do so in the future. There is a general right to recover overpayments provided that the worker has not changed his or her position in the belief that he or she was entitled to the money. Thus in *Avon CC v Howlett* (1983) a local authority sued a teacher for wages overpaid when he was off sick. It was held that the employer could not recover as the teacher had spent the money and did not know that it was an overpayment. The moral seems to be to spend your wages quickly! In *Howlett* it was also held that the defence of change of position applied even where the worker had only spent *some* of the overpaid wages, as it would be impossible in practice to establish what actual money had been spent.

In *Gill v Ford Motor Co. Ltd* and *Wong v BAE Systems Operations Ltd* (2004) the issue was jurisdictional. Under s 14 of the ERA 1996 where a deduction from wages is made in respect of an overpayment of wages or where it is made because the worker has taken part in a strike or other industrial action then an employment tribunal has no jurisdiction to decide the legality of the deductions and the worker's remedy is to take proceedings in the civil courts for breach of contract. The point here was whether an employment tribunal has simply to accept the employer's statement that the deduction was made because the worker had taken part in industrial action. The EAT held that it should not. It has the right to investigate the facts to see if the employer's contention is made out.

Where the worker claims that an unlawful deduction has been made, a complaint may be made to an employment tribunal within three months of the last deduction or payment and the tribunal can order repayment of sums wrongly deducted.

BONUS PAYMENTS

What is the position where an employee claims that she is due a bonus payment under her contract and that either:

(a) the employer does not pay it all, or

(b) the amount paid is less than the employee claims that she is entitled to?

Recent cases have involved bonus payments made by banks where a core element of an employee's pay is made up of bonuses. In *Horkulak* v *Cantor Fitzgerald International* (2005) the Court of Appeal based its decision on the application of the implied term of mutual trust and confidence (see Chapter 5) so as to hold that an employer's discretionary decision to withhold a bonus is subject to control by the courts, whilst at the same time it set limits to the extent to which the courts will intervene. An employee's contract entitled him to a discretionary bonus as part of his overall remuneration package and Potter LJ in the Court of Appeal held that the principles were that where, as in this case, there was no formula for the calculation of the bonus then the employee is entitled to a 'bona fide and rational exercise (by the employer) of their discretion as to whether or not to pay him a bonus and in what sum'. Potter LJ observed that to do otherwise would 'fly in the face of the principles of trust and confidence which have been held to underpin the employment relationship'. (This case also involved liability by the employer for constructive dismissal arising over the way in which the employee was treated, which amounted to a breach of the implied duty of mutual trust and confidence. The different issues involved in this litigation are mentioned in Chapter 1.)

In *Commerzbank AG* v *Keen* (2006) the employee rested his claim that his employer (a bank) should have awarded him a larger discretionary bonus than was paid on the basis that the employer had acted in a way which was irrational or perverse and so was a decision which no rational employer would have taken. The reason why the claim rested on this foundation rather than the implied duty of mutual trust and confidence was probably, according to Mummery LJ, that by directly attacking the actual reasons the employee could then require further reasons than those which he was given. The Court of Appeal held that 'the burden of establishing that no rational bank in the City would have paid him a bonus less than his line manger recommended is a very high one' and an 'overwhelming case' was needed. As Mummery LJ emphasised: 'It is for the bank to decide whether to pay a bonus and, if so, in what form. The court is not entitled to substitute itself for the bank.'

In *Coors Brewers* v *Adcock* (2007) employees claimed that they had not been given adequate bonuses under an implied promise by their employer to replicate a share bonus scheme operated by their previous employer. The issue at this stage was the nature of the claim rather than its merits and the Court of Appeal held that this was a claim for unliquidated damages (i.e. an uncertain amount of damages) and not a claim for an unlawful deduction from wages. Wall LJ held that a claim for unlawful deductions from wages is appropriate only where there is a claim to a specific sum of money.

THE EFFECT OF THE UNFAIR CONTRACT TERMS ACT 1977

A further issue raised in the *Commerzbank* litigation was the interesting point of whether s 3 of the Unfair Contract Terms Act 1977 applied in an employment situation. This provides that where a party contracts on written standard terms of business with a consumer any exclusion or restriction of liability is subject to the test of reasonableness. This legislation was introduced to control clauses which, for example, excluded the liability of a supplier of goods for defects in them and there is no doubt that it was not originally intended to affect employment relations. However, it has been argued in more recent years that it can apply. Freedland (2003, page 190) suggests that it is inappropriate for the Act to apply as it is 'not primarily directed at personal work contracts'.

The precise point in *Commerzbank* was that the employee's contract provided that only employees actually employed by the bank at the date of the bonus payment were entitled to bonuses and in this case the employee was not employed by the bank at the relevant date as he had been made redundant earlier in the year. He claimed that this was an exclusion clause and was subject to the statutory requirement of reasonableness in the Unfair Contract Terms Act.

The court held that the Act was not applicable because, as Moses LJ put it, 'An employee does not deal with the employer as a consumer' as is required for s 3 to apply. Furthermore, the contract did not appear to be on 'written standard terms of business' within the meaning of the Unfair Contract Terms Act. This clarification is useful as there had been suggestions in earlier authorities that the Act could apply in employment situations (see e.g. *Brigden* v *American Express Bank Ltd* (2000) and also suggestions made by the Law Commission in its report on unfair terms in contracts (Cm 6464) (February 2005)). However, the question of whether the Act does apply in any relationship is, perhaps, not quite settled and Watson (1995) strongly argues that it should.

RETAIL EMPLOYMENT

Sections 17–22 of the ERA 1996 deal with deductions from the wages of workers in retail employment and provide that any deduction made in respect of cash shortages or stock deficiencies cannot exceed 10% of the gross wages for that day. There appears to be no rule that the deduction can be made only for shortages or deficiencies that are the fault of the employee.

SICK PAY

There is no general implied term in contracts of employment that workers are entitled to sick pay, although in particular cases one might be implied. In *Mears* v *Safecar Security Ltd* (1982) the Court of Appeal found that there was no implied term to this effect, as the employer had never paid sick pay and the employee had never claimed sick pay until he had left employment. In fact the Department for Work and Pensions (DWP) estimates that 90% of employers have their own occupational sick pay schemes (Welfare Reform Green Paper, 2006) which must not fall below the level of protection given by the statutory scheme which is described below. In practice employers' schemes are often more generous and provide, for instance, for six months' absence on full pay and a further six months on half pay.

7

Payment of wages and hours of work

The Statutory Sick Pay (SSP) Scheme was first introduced in 1983 and is now governed by the Social Security Contributions and Benefits Act 1992, as amended by the Statutory Sick Pay Act 1994. The main features of the scheme are as follows:

1. The scheme operates, as do many employment rights, to give a basic entitlement which can be added to by the contract. Therefore, the contract may provide both for pay on top of the amount in the scheme and for pay when the employee is no longer covered by the scheme.

2. Self-employed persons are not entitled to SSP and instead are entitled to incapacity benefit (see below).

3. The employer pays SSP and cannot contract out of liability to pay.

4. The employer cannot recover any of the cost of SSP unless in any income tax month the amount of SSP paid exceeds 13% of the total liability to pay national insurance contributions. If so, the employer can recover the excess over 13%.

5. Employees qualify for SSP if their normal gross weekly wage is at a level to be relevant for national insurance purposes which is currently £84 a week, and they have a contract of employment for over three months. Earnings are averaged over an eight-week period before sickness began to see if the employee is entitled.

6. SSP can be claimed for a 'day of incapacity', which is defined as a day in which the employee is incapable by reason of some specific disease or mental or bodily disablement of doing the work which he can reasonably be expected to do under the contract.

7. Assuming that the day is a 'day of incapacity', SSP is paid if the day falls within a 'period of incapacity', which is a period of at least four consecutive days of incapacity including days of the week when the employee does not work, e.g. weekends and holidays. The object is to restrict SSP to absences for at least four consecutive days.

8. Assuming that the 'day of incapacity' does fall within a 'period of incapacity' then SSP is payable if the absence falls within a 'period of entitlement' which begins with the day on which the illness begins and which ends with the day on which the illness ends, *or* after 28 weeks, *or* the eleventh week before the expected week of a confinement, *or* when the contract is terminated although the employer cannot terminate simply to avoid liability to pay SSP. The main point to remember is that entitlement to SSP for one spell of sickness ends after 28 weeks at the latest. The position thereafter is explained below.

9. However, SSP is not payable for the first three qualifying days (waiting days) unless they fall within a 'linking period', which is where the employee has been sick for two spells separated by not more than two weeks. Here there are no 'waiting days' in the second period.

10. The rule that SSP was paid only to employees aged between 16 and 65 was abolished from October 2006 with the coming into force of the Employment Equality (Age) Regulations 2006 (SI 2006/1031), which are considered in detail in Chapter 9.

11. A final requirement is that the day for which SSP is sought must be a 'qualifying day', i.e. a day when the employee would normally be expected to work.

12 Where the employee is involved in a trade dispute at his or her place of work then there is no right to SSP unless the employee proves that he or she did not participate in the dispute on any day before his or her illness began.

13 The employee claims SSP by notifying his or her employer and the employer may lay down how this is to be done and a time limit for notification. The employer may refuse to pay SSP for the days by which notification is late.

14 The amount of SSP is at present £70.05, which was set in April 2006, but the exact amount will depend on individual circumstances. If absence is for less than a week then the pay is at a daily rate calculated by dividing the weekly rate by the number of qualifying days.

Example

John was absent from 23 January 2006 until 30 January 2006 because of a heavy cold. Is he entitled to SSP? He must prove that he is an employee whose normal weekly wage is at or above the lower limit for NI contributions. All the days will count as days of incapacity but SSP will not be paid for them all, as the first three do not come within a period of incapacity and the period of entitlement to SSP will end on 30 January.

When the employee is no longer entitled to SSP but is still unable to work then he or she is entitled to incapacity benefit, which is paid at different rates depending on whether the incapacity is short term (up to 52 weeks) or long term (over 52 weeks). There are also different rates of short-term and long-term incapacity benefit. As explained above, this benefit is also payable to the self-employed, who are not eligible for SSP. New rules came into force on 8 April 2002 on the extent to which a person can work and still claim incapacity benefit (and some other benefits).

The DWP in its Welfare Reform Green Paper (2006) proposes changes to the SSP system providing for a simpler way for employers to assess entitlement to SSP and so cut down on record keeping. It proposes to abolish the 'waiting days' and, with them, the 'linked periods'. The present rule that sickness periods with a previous employer must be counted will also go.

PAYMENT OF WAGES DURING SUSPENSION, LAY-OFF AND SHORT-TIME

During suspension

What is the position where the employee is suspended from work without pay? Is there a right to wages? In *Hanley* v *Pease and Partners Ltd* (1915) the employee was suspended for one day for not turning up the previous day as he had overslept. His action for damages for wrongful dismissal succeeded. In a remarkably clear and straightforward decision for that era, Lush J had no doubt: 'the employers took upon themselves

7

Payment of wages and hours of work

to suspend for one day; in other words, to deprive the workman of his wages for one day, thereby assessing their own damages for the servant's misconduct at the sum which would be represented by one day's wages. They have no possible right to do that.' The message is clear: deprivation of wages by suspension without pay is not lawful. A disciplinary matter should be dealt with by the proper disciplinary route and not by a simple deduction from wages. The only possible time when this might be justified would be where an employee who could be fairly dismissed is offered as an alternative a period of suspension without wages, as, for example, where the employee had a previously unblemished record and many years' service (see also *Mezey v South West London and St. George's Mental Health NHS Trust* (2007) in Chapter 11). The whole topic of dismissal is considered in Chapters 11 and 12.

During lay-off

The effect of a lay-off is similar to a suspension but, whereas suspension is used in connection with disciplinary matters, a lay-off occurs when the employer has no work for the employee. We have already seen in Chapter 4 that an employee has no general right to be provided with work, but what is the position where employees are laid off? The straightforward answer is that employees who are laid off are entitled to be paid until their contract is terminated by proper notice but the courts have never stated this principle clearly. The starting point is the contract, which may give a right to wages where there is a lay-off, but otherwise the right will depend on an implied term. In *Devonald v Rosser and Sons* (1906) a tinplate factory was closed because of lack of orders and the employees, who were on piecework, were then given notice. It was held that there was an implied term that, as Alverstone CJ put it, 'the master will find a reasonable amount of work up to the expiration of a notice given in accordance with the contract'. Once work was found then it followed that it must be paid for. The link with the provision of work has muddied the waters somewhat but the duty to find work presumably applies only to pieceworkers and the law seems to be that in cases where the employee is on a fixed rate then there is a duty to pay when there is a lay-off even though no work can be found. Even with pieceworkers the duty to find work cannot be absolute but there is a duty to pay.

This last point is shown by the decision in *Minnevitch v Café de Paris Ltd* (1936). Musicians employed at a café were paid according to performance and received nothing when the café closed for six days following the death of King George V. It was held that the owners were entitled to close for two days but the musicians were entitled to payment for the other four days.

A troublesome case is *Browning v Crumlin Valley Collieries Ltd* (1926). Miners were laid off when their mine was closed due to flooding and it was held that the risk of closure of the mine was shared between the mine owner and the miners with the result that there was no right to payment. Greer J said that the question was whether a term should be implied on the basis of *The Moorcock* (1889) (see Chapter 5) and he was satisfied that no employer would have consented to pay wages where the mine was closed through no fault of his. This case has not been followed and it is suggested that a future court might distinguish it by using the more modern tests for implying a term on the basis of what is reasonable and necessary (see Chapter 5) rather than a narrow test of intention as here.

During short-time

There is less authority on this but in principle there seems to be no reason why the law should be any different from that on payment when laid off. Thus where the contract provides for a minimum number of hours' work a week then there is a right to wages for those hours.

Guarantee pay

This is a statutory right contained in ss 28–35 of the ERA 1996. It gives a right to pay when an employee is laid off and is part of the 'floor of rights' philosophy under which statute sets certain minimum standards with the expectation (not always fulfilled) that employers will exceed them. Therefore, contracts and collective agreements may give a right to a higher level of pay than laid down by the Act. Moreover, these provisions are an exception to the rule that it is not possible to contract out of statutory rights because, by s 35(4), the Secretary of State may issue an exemption order where there is either a collective agreement or an agricultural wages order in force giving a right to guaranteed remuneration. Moreover, this may not be as generous as the amount of guarantee pay, although this is unlikely given the modest rates of guarantee pay.

Who is entitled to a guarantee payment?

The right is given to employees under the narrow definition in s 230(1) of the ERA 1996, i.e. a contract of employment is required. Such employees must have a period of continuous employment of at least one month, ending with the day before the day on which guarantee pay is claimed. Where an employee has a fixed-term contract or a specific task contract which is for three months, he or she does not have a right to guarantee pay unless the employee actually works for more than three months.

When is guarantee pay to be paid?

Guarantee pay is payable for a 'workless day' but is subject to a statutory maximum, which is at present (from 1 February 2007) £19.60 a day for any five days in a three-month period, which is hardly generous but fits in with the floor of rights philosophy outlined above. The term 'workless day' is defined by s 28 of the ERA 1996 as a day when the employee is not provided with work by his employer because either:

1 there is a diminution in the requirements of the employer's business for work of the kind which the employee is normally required to do; or

2 for any other reason affecting the normal working of the employer's business in relation to the kind of work which the employee is employed to do.

Reason (1) is self-explanatory but the significance of (2) is seen when one considers the situations where, despite there being a workless day, the employee is not entitled to a guarantee payment. These are set out in s 29 and are as follows:

(a) Where the failure to provide work is in consequence of a strike, lock-out or other industrial action involving the employer or an associated employer. (The meaning of the term 'associated employer' was considered in Chapter 4.) Thus, for example, a strike at a completely separate factory would come under (2) and would mean that the employees would be entitled to a guarantee payment, but not a strike within the employer's own factory nor that of an associated employer. Other possible instances of (2) which would entitle the employee to a guarantee payment are a sudden power failure or, for example, where the premises are shut through floods.

(b) Where the employer has offered suitable alternative work but the employee refuses it. In *Purdy* v *Willowbrook International* (1977) it was held that the alternative work can be work which the employee is not bound to do under his or her contract provided that it is suitable for him or her taking into account the employee's abilities and aptitude for it.

(c) Where the employee fails to comply with a reasonable requirement of the employer designed to ensure that the employee is available for work. For example, supplies of vital materials are late and the employees are asked to wait until they arrive. Some of them, however, do not do so and go home. They would not be entitled to a guarantee payment (see *Meadows* v *Faithful Overalls Ltd* (1977)).

A workless day must be a day when the employee would normally be required to work. Therefore, where an employee works, for example, from Monday to Thursday and the factory is shut down on Friday, there is no right to guarantee pay. What is the position where the employee works a shift that spreads over two days, for example, from 10 p.m. to 6 a.m. and each of those days are workless days? Is he entitled to two guarantee payments? The answer is no. With merciless precision, s 28(5) provides that where the amounts worked on each day are not the same, as here, guarantee pay is payable for the day on which the hours are greater and, if they are equal, then it is paid for the second day.

Calculation of guarantee pay

The complexity of the rules for calculating guarantee pay is out of all proportion to the amounts involved. The basic rule is that the amount is calculated by multiplying the number of normal working hours for that day by the guaranteed hourly rate of pay. The problem is that this is almost bound to produce a figure well in excess of £19.60 and so the calculation is meaningless and it is easier to say that in almost all cases the employee is entitled to £19.60. The only time when this would not be so would be when an employee worked only a few hours and received the minimum rate of pay (see below). If so, they would not be entitled to the maximum and calculations would be needed.

Claims to guarantee pay

Claims must be brought within three months of the last workless day, with the usual exception allowing tribunals to consider late claims. The tribunal has power to order the employer to make the payment.

SUSPENSION FROM WORK ON MEDICAL GROUNDS

Employees who have been suspended from work on specified medical grounds are entitled to their normal pay up to a maximum of 26 weeks. This situation arises where the employee is available for work but the employer cannot provide work because of certain requirements in health and safety enactments. These cover employees engaged on work involving exposure to lead, ionising radiations and some other chemicals together with processes hazardous to health. There are certain exclusions from the right to medical suspension pay:

1 employees who have worked for less than one month or are on a fixed-term contract or a specific task contract for less than three months unless they actually work for more than three months;

2 where the employer has offered suitable alternative work or where the employee has failed to comply with the reasonable requirements of the employer to ensure that his or her services are available.

The similarity of these provisions to those governing guarantee pay will be noted. In addition, there is no right to medical suspension pay where the employee is incapable of work through disease or disablement. The point is not that an employee in these cases will not be paid but that the pay will not be medical suspension pay.

An employee who is dismissed rather than suspended on the above grounds may claim unfair dismissal after one month's continuous employment but the dismissal is not automatically unfair.

NATIONAL MINIMUM WAGE ACT 1998

The background

The history of statutory involvement in the setting of wages is a long one but it has been piecemeal. The main recent example was the Wages Councils set up in industries where collective bargaining was weak and which were empowered to set wage rates in, for example, the hotel and catering industry. Moreover, the Fair Wages Resolution of the House of Commons required government contractors to pay fair wages. This was rescinded in 1982 and Wages Councils were abolished in 1993. The only exception was the Agricultural Wages Board, which continues to set both minimum wages and terms and conditions for those employed in agriculture and related industries.

However, this bonfire of statutory controls was taking place against a movement in quite the opposite direction. In 1989, all the Member States of the EU, with the exception of the UK, adopted the European Charter of Fundamental Rights and Freedoms, Article 5 of which provides that all workers shall be 'fairly remunerated' and that workers shall be assured of an 'equitable wage'. Although not binding on Member States, it undoubtedly helped to create a climate in which the setting of a national minimum wage was seen as a desirable goal of social policy. The introduction of a

7

Payment of wages and hours of work

national minimum wage was promised in the Labour Party manifesto for the 1997 election and the National Minimum Wage Act was duly passed in 1998. It came into force in April 1999 and the original minimum wage was set at £3.60 an hour for employees aged 22 and over and £3.00 an hour for employees aged 18–21. A survey in *Labour Market Trends* (December 1998, page 617) estimated that in spring 1998 up to 2.1 million workers (10.4% of all employees) earned below the national minimum wage (NMW) and part-time workers were more likely to be low paid than full-time workers. Over half of those low paid (i.e. earning below the NMW) were women in part-time jobs and a further 18% were women in full-time jobs. Less than one-third were men. The survey concluded that: 'Low pay is predominantly a female and a part-time phenomenon.' The industries where there was a greater incidence of low pay were catering, personal and protective services and sales. Together these accounted for two-thirds of all low-paid workers. A further survey (*Labour Market Trends*, September 1998, page 463) looked at the experience of countries that already had statutory minimum wages. Although comparisons are not easy because the systems varied, the survey found that, in practice, an NMW need not have an adverse effect on jobs provided that it is set at a reasonable level. This is important, as opponents of the NMW had argued that it could discourage employers from taking on workers. It was also argued by opponents that the introduction of an NMW could have a knock-on effect on other wage rates and thus be inflationary but the survey found that experience abroad was that this was not so.

The Act itself

The Act sets out the broad framework of the legislation with the Secretary of State being given the power to make regulations. It also establishes the Low Pay Commission. This has no powers of action of its own and can act only when the Secretary of State exercises his powers under s 6 and refers a matter to it. The main ongoing task which has been entrusted to the Commission is the monitoring and evaluation of the impact of the NMW. The Commission has only advisory powers but it is not entirely toothless: if the Secretary of State refers a matter to it concerning the setting of the NMW and associated issues and then subsequently the Secretary departs from any recommendations made by the Commission, the Secretary must lay a report before Parliament giving the reasons why the recommendations have not been complied with.

Who is covered by the Act?

The Act, by s 1(2), applies to any 'worker' and thus the wide definition is used rather than the narrow one of 'employee'. The term 'worker', it will be recalled from Chapter 4, covers not only those with a contract of employment but also those who undertake to perform work or services personally. Not only this, but the Act specifically applies to agency workers and homeworkers, a point discussed in more detail in Chapter 4. There are certain exclusions, the main ones being workers under the age of 18, workers employed under a contract of apprenticeship, family workers and *au pairs*. The last two were added by the National Minimum Wage Regulations 1999 (NMWR 1999).

Furthermore, the Secretary of State is given power, by s 3, to provide that certain classes of workers shall not qualify for the NMW and that differential hourly rates of pay may be prescribed. In the event this has been used to prescribe different rates dependent on age (see below) but s 3 specified that this power shall not be used to set rates of pay which differ dependent on area, type of employment, size of employment or occupation.

What is the National Minimum Wage?

This is set by the Secretary of State who, as we saw above, should follow any guidance given by the Low Pay Commission or, if not, explain to Parliament why it is not being followed. The rate is an hourly one and was originally fixed (from April 1999) at £3.60 an hour for workers aged 22 or over and at £3.00 an hour for workers aged 18–22. The present rates (from October 2006) are £5.35 an hour for adult workers and what is now known as a development rate of £4.45 an hour for 18–21-year-olds. The rate for workers under 18 who are not of compulsory school age is £3.30. There is no provision for annual uprating. It should be noted that the lower rate also applies to the first six months of employment for workers aged 22 or over who have agreed to take part in accredited training courses lasting at least 26 days of their first six months of employment (NMWR 1999, reg 13) but, in order to prevent employers simply paying the lower rate without providing the training, the contract must specify what the training is to be.

Where a worker works, say, four hours a week and is aged 22 or over then the calculation is easy: multiply £5.35 by 4. In this situation we are dealing with what the Act and the 1999 Regulations call 'time work', where the worker is paid by reference to a set time when the worker actually worked or was available for work. However, matters are not always so simple.

The Act and the NMWR 1999 provide the following mechanisms for deciding the hourly rate of pay:

The pay reference period

This is the interval between payments of wages up to a maximum of a month. Therefore, wages received during this period must, when averaged against the number of hours worked, be such that the NMR was received. Thus, if a worker aged 22 or over is paid monthly then one month is the pay reference period. If in that month the worker worked a 40-hour week for four weeks then the total number of hours worked would be (40 × 4) 160 hours and the NMR would be 160 × £5.35 = £856.00.

Which payments count towards the NMW?

In the above example it was assumed that all payments counted but this may not be so. The starting point is the actual gross wage and this includes bonuses, incentive payments and any tips paid through the employer. Thus if a waiter or waitress received £2.50 a week but was told by the employer that, as they received at least £10.00 a week in tips there was no obligation to pay them more then that employer would be wrong. If, however, the employer paid the NMW and included in it was a sum representing tips paid into a kitty and shared round by the employer then there would be no objection.

The point is that where the money comes from is irrelevant: the NMR must be paid. Two particular categories must be noted:

1 Certain deductions made by the employer count towards the NMW. These are:
- income tax and NI contributions;
- deductions to cover an advance of wages or an accidental overpayment of wages;
- deductions to cover pension contributions or union subscriptions;
- deductions to pay for shares or securities bought by the worker; and
- deductions, authorised by the worker's contract, for payments imposed for a disciplinary matter.

On this last point it should be noted that any deductions would need to be specifically authorised by the contract: the NMW provisions do not make them lawful but only provide that, if they are lawful by another provision, then they still count towards the NMW. Thus in all these cases the NMW must be paid *inclusive* of these sums: the worker *cannot* claim that he or she is entitled to the NMW when these sums have been deducted.

2 However, the following are examples of items which do not count towards NMW:
- premium payments for overtime and shiftwork;
- allowances which are attributable to a particular aspect of a worker's working arrangements or personal circumstances and which are not consolidated into basic pay, e.g. London weighting, unsocial hours payments, payments for working in unpleasant or dangerous conditions; tips not paid through the payroll;
- payments in kind.

Although payments towards living accommodation are included in the NMW, up to a maximum of £29.05 a week (daily rate £4.15) may be offset against it.

For what time is the NMW to be paid?

There are four categories:

Time work

Time work was referred to in the example above, where the worker is paid according to a set time when he or she was working or available for work. Periods spent travelling in connection with work, although not to work, are included but not time spent 'on call' at home. In *British Nursing Association* v *Inland Revenue* (2002) it was held that employees working from home on an emergency night telephone booking service were working during these shifts even though in between taking calls they could do as they pleased. Accordingly they were on time work.

Salaried hours work

This is where the worker is paid according to set basic hours in a year in return for an annual salary which does not vary with the hours actually worked. The same rules apply as for time workers except that with salaried workers most of the time during the actual salary period is counted for NMW purposes: for example, meal breaks and rest breaks. Therefore, the amount of entitlement to NMW is likely to be higher than with time workers.

Output work

Payment for output work is linked to the amount produced by the worker as in piece-work. Either the worker's time can be assessed by a 'fair estimate' or the worker can just be paid for hours actually worked. A worker is protected, when a 'fair estimate' is made, by a rule that the number of hours agreed as a fair estimate must be not less than four-fifths of the hours that an average worker would take. Any fair estimate agreement must be in writing and made before the work begins.

Unmeasured work

Unmeasured work is work that does not fall into any other category, as where workers are available for work when required. The worker is entitled to pay at the rate of the NMW for hours worked or the parties can agree on a daily average of hours to be worked which then must be paid at the rate of the NMW.

How is the right to the NMW enforced?

The mechanism adopted is that the right to the NMW is a term of each worker's contract and thus s 17 provides that if a worker receives less than the NMW then there is a contractual right to the difference between what was paid and the NMW. This contractual right can either be enforced in a common law action for breach of contract or by a claim under Part II of the ERA 1996 as an unlawful deduction from wages and in any proceedings s 28 reverses the burden of proof so that a person is presumed to qualify (i.e. as a worker) for the NMW unless proved otherwise. In addition, an enforcement notice may be issued against an employer requiring that employer to make payments to workers to bring them up to the NMW. If the notice is not obeyed then the employer can be brought before an employment tribunal which, in addition to ordering payments of the amounts due, can also order the employer to pay a fine equivalent to double the underpayment (see ss 19–21). Finally, it is a criminal offence, punishable by a fine not exceeding level 5 on the Standard Scale, for an employer wilfully to neglect to pay the NMW. The DTI policy is to levy a fine (at present £224.70 per week for each employee) if any minimum wage arrears have not been paid within seven days of service of an enforcement notice.

In *Bebb Travel plc v IRC* (2003) the Court of Appeal held that an enforcement notice to an employer under the Act requiring him or her to make payments to an employee could not, because of the wording of the Act, be issued to require payments to be made to an *ex*-employee. This loophole has now been closed by the National Minimum Wage (Enforcement Notices) Act 2003 which allows notices to be served requiring an employer to pay back pay to ex-employees.

HOURS OF WORK: THE WORKING TIME REGULATIONS

The background

Statutory regulation of hours of work has, in many ways, a similar history to that of the minimum wage. As with the minimum wage, there have been many legislative forays

7

Payment of wages and hours of work

into this area, most notably the Factories Acts in the nineteenth century and the Shops Act 1950. As with the legislation on minimum wages, legislation here was confined to particular industries and then fell foul of the desire of the 1979–97 Conservative government to deregulate as many statutory controls as possible so that the only legislation remaining dealt with hours worked by those under the school leaving age.

The difference between current legislation on hours of work, contained in the Working Time Regulations 1998 (SI 1998/1833) (WTRs) and the National Minimum Wage Act 1998 is that, whereas the genesis of the Minimum Wage Act was domestic political agendas, the WTRs spring from EC law and their gestation was long and complex.

Discussion of the Working Time Regulations centred on what was said, somewhat inaccurately, to be a maximum 48-hour week. Research (published by the European Commission in an Explanatory Memorandum and quoted in Bercusson (1996 at pages 309–10)) showed that the average operating hours of plants in the UK was 76 a week, the highest in the EC after Belgium, with 77, but average working hours in UK industry were 37, equal lowest with Belgium. The Commission was concerned that there could nevertheless be pressure on workers to work longer hours, given the gap between plant opening hours and individual working hours. In the retail trade there was also a gap between weekly opening hours (58) and individual working hours (39). In the UK, a survey in *Labour Market Trends* (1998) showed that an average of 29.8% of male full-time employees and 11.6% of female employees worked more than 48 hours. Moreover, 5% of male and 2% of female employees worked more than 60 hours a week. Looking at occupations, the survey found that managers and administrators among men and professional workers among women were most likely to work over 48 hours a week. Indeed, 6% of professional women workers worked over 60 hours a week, the highest proportion of those working these long hours.

It should be noted that, as these rights emanate from a Directive, the question arises of whether the Directive has direct effect in addition to remedies conferred by the regulations. The point arose in **Gibson v East Riding of Yorkshire CC** (2000), where it was held that the right to four weeks' paid annual leave was not capable of direct effect as the Directive did not contain a sufficiently precise definition of working time.

Useful guidance to the WTRs can be found in *A Guide to the Working Time Regulations* issued by the DTI in 1998 and updated in 2000. It is also available on www.dti.gov.uk/er.

The scheme of the WTRs

Unlike many areas of employment protection law, which set minimum standards that cannot be taken away by the contract of employment, the WTRs set rules which can, in many but not all cases, be modified in a number of ways. Furthermore, it is possible to make what are called 'derogations' in a number of areas, which means that the WTRs will not apply. There is therefore a complex pattern under which the identification of a right will not necessarily mean that that right will apply to a particular worker. However, this should not mask the fact that, for the first time, there is a set of legislative rules governing working time which apply, subject to the modifications and derogations noted above, to all workers and not just to workers in particular sections of industry. It is also worth noting at this point that originally doctors in training were exempt from the WTR but by 2009 their working week will be reduced to the same average of 48 hours as other workers.

◼ Modification of the WTRs by agreements

These agreements are known as 'relevant agreements' and can take three forms: collective agreement; workforce agreement; and individual agreement.

Collective agreement

WTRs can be modified by a collective agreement made between the employer and one or more independent trade unions. However, the terms of any such agreement would have to be incorporated into individual contracts of employment (see Chapter 5).

Workforce agreement

This type of agreement was included to deal with situations where workers do not have their terms and conditions of employment set by a collective agreement and would otherwise not be able collectively to modify the provisions of the WTRs. A workforce agreement is one that is made either with representatives of the workforce or, if on the date when the agreement is made the employer employs less than 20 workers, then it may be signed by a majority of the actual workforce. The agreement may either apply to all the workers or to those who constitute 'a particular group', defined as workers who undertake a particular function, work at a particular place, or work in a particular department or unit. The agreement must be in writing, have been circulated in draft beforehand and be signed by representatives of the workforce or by representatives of the particular group except, as stated above, if there are fewer than 20 workers covered by it, then either by all the representatives or by a majority of the workforce. Once made, the agreement lasts for not more than five years. Not only this, but the regulations lay down detailed provisions on the election of workforce representatives. The employer initially decides the number of representatives to be elected and must ensure that, as far as reasonably practicable, the election is conducted by secret ballot. As the DTI guidance remarks, it would be rare for this not to be possible and it might have been better to have stipulated a secret ballot in all circumstances. The votes must be counted fairly and accurately. Finally, any candidates must be members of the workforce and the employer cannot unreasonably exclude any member of the workforce from standing for election. Before the agreement is eventually signed, copies must be sent to all those affected by it with guidance to enable them to understand it fully.

Workforce representatives are used in other areas such as health and safety and although the same representatives could be used for more than one purpose, the DTI guidance states that it would have to be made clear to those voting that the representatives were being elected for other purposes. Therefore, an employer, having acquired a set of workforce representatives for one purpose, could not simply use them for another purpose.

Individual, legally enforceable, written agreements with workers

The WTRs draw a distinction between agreements individually negotiated between workers and employers which can apply only where it is agreed that the 48-hour a week limit will be excluded (which are not relevant agreements) and agreements contained in contracts of employment with workers but it seems here that such contracts, although made with individuals, would have had to have been agreed by some collective process. It is unfortunate that the regulations, so detailed in other ways, do not make this clear.

The fact that the WTRs allow use to be made of collective agreements in modifying these rules is noteworthy as representing a departure from UK practice. The aim of the Commission was to set minimum standards but at the same time allow for diversity, and Bercusson (1996) describes the focus on collective agreements as: 'The most daring aspect of the Commission's proposal.' The emphasis on collective agreements certainly gives an indirect push to workers to join unions in that, as we shall see, in some cases it may be to the advantage of both employers and workers to modify the regulations and, given the complexities of workplace agreements, a collective agreement may be the easiest way of achieving this.

Who is covered by the WTRs?

The wide definition of worker is adopted, i.e. a worker is a person who either has a contract of employment or who has a contract personally to perform services for another (see s 230(3) of the ERA 1996). However, certain categories are excluded:

- workers in air, rail, road and sea transport together with inland waterways and lake transport;
- sea fishing and other work at sea, e.g. work in the offshore oil and gas industry;
- the activities of doctors in training;
- specific services, e.g. armed services, police, civil protection services.

The Commission has made proposals to amend these exclusions so that all non-mobile workers in transport are included which would, in particular, bring doctors in training within its scope. In *Byrne Brothers* v *Baird* (2002) it was held that self-employed labour sub-contractors were covered by the definition (see also Chapter 4).

The 48-hour week

There is no actual rule that hours of work cannot exceed 48 in a week. Instead, reg 4 provides that an employer must take all reasonable steps to ensure that a worker's working time, including overtime, does not exceed an average of 48 hours for each 7 days in any reference period. The reference period is defined as 17 weeks but it can be raised to 26 or 52 weeks in special cases (see below). Thus it is possible for a worker to work well over 48 hours in a week provided that the average over 17 weeks (or 26/52 weeks) is 48 hours. To enforce this, the employer must keep records, showing whether this rule was obeyed, for up to two years afterwards.

Example

Cheryl works a basic 38-hour working week. However, in 12 weeks of the 17-week reference period she works 10 hours' overtime in each week. Therefore, her total hours worked are:

Standard hours (38 × 17) = 646 hours

Overtime (12 × 10) = 120 hours

Total hours worked in the 17-week reference period: (646 + 120) = 766

Average weekly hours: (766 divided by 17) = 45 hours a week.

Therefore the limit has been complied with.

A crucial question is: what is working time? This is defined by reg 2(1) as any time when the worker is:

1 working at his or her employer's disposal and carrying out his or her duties in accordance with national laws and/or practice;
2 receiving relevant training;
3 at work during any other period which is to be treated as working time under a relevant agreement.

Rest periods are defined as any periods that are not working time. Thus, as the DTI guidance points out, a lunch break would not count unless it was a working lunch.

In the *SIMAP case* (2000) the ECJ held that time spent by doctors on call could be working time if they had to be present at work, as they would be at the disposal of their employer, but not if they could be away from work. As a result of this decision the DTI guidance was amended so that time spent on call only counted where the worker is required to be at his or her place of work. In *Walton v Independent Living Organisation* (2003) the Court of Appeal held that a live-in carer was not entitled to be paid for all the time she was on the premises (72 hours a week) but only for when she was carrying out her duties. The court distinguished *Scottbridge Construction Ltd v Wright* (2003), where a nightwatchman who was required to be on premises in order to respond if the alarm went off was held to be on 'time work', whereas in *Walton* the work was classified as 'unmeasured work'. Even so, it is clear that this area needs clarification.

A particular problem is where a worker has more than one job, as the WTRs impose a 48-hour week on all work which the worker does, not only for one employer. Regulation 4(1) provides that an employer must take all reasonable steps to ensure that the limit is observed and the DTI guidance suggests that an employer should ask the worker if he or she is working elsewhere. If the hours do exceed 48, then an individual opt-out agreement could be made.

There are complex rules dealing with the calculation of average weekly working time. The problem is that account must be taken of days when the worker was absent (e.g. on sick leave, annual leave or maternity leave), and therefore the basic rule is that an equivalent number of days from the next reference period should be added in to make up for the lost days.

7

Payment of wages and hours of work

> ### Example
>
> Shirley works a basic 40-hour 5-day week. She also works overtime for 8 hours a week for the first 10 weeks of the 17-week reference period. In addition, she took 5 days' annual leave in this reference period.
>
> Therefore the total hours worked in the reference period is: 16 weeks at 40 hours = 640 hours. To this is added 10 weeks with 8 hours' overtime: 80 hours. Total = 720 hours. To this is added the time worked for the 5 days of annual leave taken and, as in the first 5 days of the next reference period there was no overtime worked, one adds 5 × 8 (i.e. 5 days at 8 hours a day) = 40 hours. Therefore a grand total of (640 + 80 + 40) = 760 hours. This must be divided by the total number of weeks (17) giving an average number of weekly working hours of 44.7 hours, well within the 48-hour limit.

To what extent is it possible for the rules on the 48-hour week to be modified or excluded?

Modifications or exclusions are possible in four ways:

Agreement with employer

An individual worker may agree with the employer that the 48-hour limit will not apply provided that the worker makes a legally binding agreement to this effect. This is the one situation in the WTRs where individuals can agree to opt out of a particular right. The employer must record the names of those workers who have made such an agreement and the worker can terminate it by giving written notice. The agreement can specify a maximum of three months' notice but, if it is silent on this point, then seven days' notice applies. In *Pfeiffer v Deutsches Rotes Kreuz* (2005) the ECJ held that where a worker has consented to an opt out from the 48-hour working week this consent must be given freely and with full knowledge of all the relevant facts. This could have implications for the practice of giving employees standard opt-out forms which are simply presented to them to sign and it is taken for granted that they *will* sign. It should be noted that the future of the opt-out provisions is uncertain. The European Parliament voted in 2005 to end them but this is being resisted by the UK.

Special cases

The reference period may be extended to 26 weeks if one or more of the special cases listed in reg 21 apply. These special cases are significant under the other parts of the WTRs and the broad principle behind them is that, in these cases, a degree of flexibility is essential on account of the nature of the work. They are set out in reg 21 and are as follows:

1 Where the worker is employed a long distance from home or where the worker has different places of work which are distant from each other. The DTI guidance points out that in these cases it may be desirable for them to work longer hours for a short period to complete the task quickly or continual changes in the location of work make it impractical to set a pattern of work.

2 Where the worker is engaged in security and surveillance activities where, for example, there is a need for a 24-hour presence.

3 Where the worker's activities involve the need for continuity of service or production. Regulation 21 sets out a list of examples, although there may be other cases.
Among those listed are workers in hospitals, prisons, residential institutions, media
work, postal and telecommunications work, public utilities and household refuse
collection and incineration.

4 Where there is a foreseeable surge in activity, as with tourism. Thus a hotel which is
very busy in, for example, July and August may wish to average the working week
over 26 weeks.

5 Where the worker's activities are affected by an occurrence due to unusual and
unforeseen circumstances: for example, where there has been an emergency.

It must again be emphasised that in all of these circumstances the basic rules relating
to the 48-hour week still apply. All that is different is the averaging period.

Extending the reference period

The reference period may be extended to up to 52 weeks by a collective or workforce
agreement.

Where working time cannot be measured

The 48-hour limit does not apply at all where, on account of the specific characteristics of the worker's activity, the worker's working time cannot be measured or
predetermined even by the worker (reg 20). The WTRs give as examples managing
executives, family workers and those who officiate at religious ceremonies. The DTI
guidance suggests that a useful test is to ask whether the worker has discretion over
whether to work on a particular day or if they need to consult their employer. The DTI
guidance suggests that the exemption from the 48-hour week applies only where the
worker has complete control over working hours. This part was amended by the
Working Time Regulations 1999 (SI 1999/3372), reg 4, which provide that where part
of the activities of the worker fall within this category (i.e. they cannot be measured)
then the 48-hour limit will not apply to those activities. This area is still not clear,
however. What is the position where a worker brings work home at night, such as
teachers? Is the time spent at home to be regarded as outside the 48-hour week? The
DTI guidance states that one test is whether the worker can decide whether or not to
work on a particular day without needing to consult their employer but this is only of
help where the worker has a complete discretion and would not apply in the cases of,
for example, teachers.

Enforcement of the 48-hour week provisions

Enforcement of the 48-hour week provisions is by the Health and Safety Executive,
which is responsible, very broadly, for enforcement in industry, schools and hospitals,
and by local authorities which are responsible for enforcement in retailing and services. Employers are liable to a fine for breach. In addition, in *Barber v RJB Mining
(UK) Ltd* (1999) the High Court held that a worker who was made to work in excess
of the 48-hour week by the employer could have an action for breach of contract of
employment, as it is an implied term of the contract that workers will not be required

7

Payment of wages and hours of work

to work in excess of the limit. Moreover, although for the purpose of criminal proceedings the employer is simply obliged to take all reasonable steps to ensure that the 48-hour limit is observed, this qualifying phrase does not apply to civil proceedings. Thus an employer appears to have an absolute duty where there is a civil action. It was held that a worker could claim a declaration and/or an injunction and could refuse to work beyond the 48-hour limit. It remains to be seen whether other parts of the WTRs will also give rise to civil liability.

Records to be kept by the employer

The 1998 Regulations required employers to keep detailed records but this was amended by the 1999 Regulations, so that employers only have to record, as mentioned above, which workers have agreed that the 48-hour week limit will not apply to them.

The limits on night work

An employer is required by reg 6 of the WTRs to take all reasonable steps to ensure that the normal hours of night workers do not exceed an average of 8 hours for each 24 hours averaged over a 17-week period.

Night work is defined as a period of not less than seven hours which must include the period between midnight and 5 a.m. Beyond this there is some flexibility, as a relevant agreement may specify the actual period: for example, it may specify 10 p.m. and 5 a.m., provided that the period is between 10 p.m. and 7 a.m. If no period is specified then the period of night work is between 11 p.m. and 6 a.m.

A night worker is defined as a worker whose daily working time includes at least three hours of night time (as defined above) on the majority of days when they work, or sufficiently often that they can be said to work such hours as a matter of course, or as defined in a relevant agreement. In *R* v *A-G for Northern Ireland, ex parte Burns* (1999) a worker was held to be a night worker where the hours worked were between 9 p.m. and 3 a.m. for one week in three.

Modifications and exclusions of this right

1 The standard reference period of 17 weeks may be extended by a workforce or collective agreement.

2 These limits on night work may be modified or excluded altogether by a workforce agreement.

3 These rules do not apply at all where the worker falls within one or more of the special cases set out in reg 21 (see above) or where the worker's time cannot be measured or determined under reg 20 (see above).

However, where the limits on night work either do not apply or are excluded then the worker must be allowed to take a period of equivalent compensatory rest or, if this is not possible, then there is a right to other appropriate protection. However, these rights do not apply where the worker's time cannot be measured or determined.

The limits on night work are enforced in the same way as the 48-hour week.

Special hazards or heavy mental or physical strain

Where a night worker's work involves special hazards or heavy mental or physical strain, there is a fixed limit, which cannot be modified or excluded, of eight hours' working time. The work that is subject to this limit can either be agreed by a collective or workforce agreement or can be identified as posing a significant risk under a risk assessment conducted by the employer under the Management of Health and Safety at Work Regulations 1992 (SI 1992/2051).

General duty of the employer in organising work patterns

Directive 93/104, the parent of the WTRs, provides, under Article 13, a duty on the employer, when organising shift patterns, to take into account 'the general principle of adapting work to the worker' with a view to, for example, alleviating monotonous work and work at a predetermined work rate. This is based on the principle of 'humanisation of work', a concept borrowed from Germany. This is echoed in reg 8 which, however, applies only where the monotony of the work puts the health and safety of the worker at risk. In this case the employer must organise regular rest breaks, presumably in addition to those provided under the WTRs (see below).

Right to a health assessment

Regulation 7 gives a right to a free health assessment to all night workers and to any worker who is about to become a night worker. The purpose is to assess whether the worker is fit to carry out the designated night work and there is also a right to further assessments at regular intervals. There are no circumstances in which this right can be modified or excluded and it is enforced in the same way as the 48-hour week.

Adult workers' rights to rest periods

An adult worker is one who has attained the age of 18 and there are two provisions:

Daily rest

There is a right to a daily rest period of not less than 11 consecutive hours in each 24-hour period during which the worker works for the employer (reg 10). In *First Hampshire and Dorset plc v Feist and ors* (2007) the EAT held that bus drivers were not entitled to a rigid 11 hours' rest in each 24-hour period nor to compensatory rest (see below) but were entitled to 'adequate rest' under reg 24, which is rest that is not for any defined period but which must be regular and is given to prevent workers injuring themselves or others through fatigue.

In *Gallagher v Alpha Catering Services Ltd* (2005) the Court of Appeal considered the exemption in the WTRs where the right to daily rest breaks does not apply 'where the worker's activities involve the need for continuity of service or production'. The workers in this case were employed to deliver food and drink to aircraft and the employer argued that this activity required such continuity. It held that the exemption

7

Payment of wages and hours of work

153

applied only where the *work* required this. Here there was no reason why the employer could not employ more staff and so allow rest breaks.

Weekly rest

There is a right to an uninterrupted rest period of not less than 24 hours in every 7-day period. This may be averaged at the discretion of the employer over 2 weeks so that the worker has 48 hours' rest every 14 days (reg 11).

Modification and exclusion of these rights

This right does not apply where the worker's working time cannot be measured or determined (see reg 20) nor in the special cases set out in reg 21. Both of these are dealt with above under the 48-hour week. In addition, a collective or workforce agreement may modify or exclude this right. Where the right is modified or excluded then the worker is entitled to compensatory rest or, if this is not possible, to other appropriate protection. This does not apply to workers whose working time cannot be measured or determined.

Adolescent workers' rights to rest periods

An adolescent worker is one under the age of 18 and the rights are as follows:

Daily rest

There is an entitlement to an uninterrupted period of 12 hours' rest in every 24-hour period of work unless the day's work is split up or is of short duration (reg 10).

Weekly rest

There is an entitlement to 48 hours' rest in every 7-day period (reg 11).

Modification and exclusion of these rights

These rights can only be modified or excluded:

1 in cases of unforeseen or unusual circumstances;
2 where the work is temporary and must be performed at once;
3 where no adult worker is available to do the work.

In addition, these rights do not apply where the worker's time is split up over the day: for example, cleaning staff who work in the morning and evening.

Enforcement

The right to rest breaks for all workers is enforced by the worker bringing a complaint to an employment tribunal within three months and compensation may be awarded.

Rights to rest breaks during work

This is contained in reg 12 and, as with rest periods, there are different rights for adult and adolescent workers.

Adult workers

Adult workers are entitled to an uninterrupted break of 20 minutes where daily working time is more than six hours. This is additional to the rest periods. There is nothing in the WTRs about whether workers should be paid and this is a matter for workers' contracts.

Modification and exclusion of these rights

These rights do not apply where the worker's working time cannot be measured or determined (see reg 20) nor in the special cases set out in reg 21. Collective and workforce agreements may exclude or modify these rights. Compensatory rest may be taken instead under the same rules as apply to daily and weekly rest periods.

Adolescent workers

Adolescent workers are entitled to a rest break of 30 minutes where daily working time is more than four-and-a-half hours.

Modification and exclusion of these rights

These rights can only be modified or excluded in the same circumstances as apply to the entitlement to daily and weekly periods.

Enforcement

These rules are enforced in the same way as the entitlement to daily and weekly breaks.

■ Right to paid annual leave

All workers are entitled to four weeks' paid annual leave (reg 13) and this will rise by October 2008 to 28 days. The increase will be in two stages: in October 2007 the entitlement will rise to 4.8 weeks and in October 2008 to 5.6 weeks which gives the full 28 days. It is not additional to bank holidays. The effect is that a worker is entitled to be away from work for a week and so leave should be for the same amount of time as for that worker's working week.

> *Example*
>
> Lyn works a 5-day week – she is entitled to 20 days' annual leave (5 × 4 weeks)
> Sue works a 3-day week – she is entitled to 12 days' annual leave (3 × 4 weeks)

There is a minimum period of qualifying employment of 13 weeks and workers must give notice of when they wish to take leave. The notice period must be at least twice the length of the leave period. The employer may refuse permission to take leave at that time and can set the time when leave is to take place such as a shutdown at Christmas. The entitlement to leave arises in a 'leave year', which normally runs from the date when the worker started work. The leave entitlement cannot be replaced by payment in lieu except where the employment is terminated when the worker has not had the leave for that year. It is a common misconception that this right is additional to rights to leave on public and bank holidays. It is not; the four weeks include these.

7

Payment of wages and hours of work

The right to paid annual leave has given rise to a number of decisions on its interpretation:

Interpretation of the right

(a) Workers on sick leave: does this have an impact on their right to paid annual leave?

In *Kigass Aero Components v Brown* (2002) it was held that a worker on long-term sick leave can still claim annual leave under the WTRs as the only qualification is whether they have been a worker during any part of that year. Thus leave entitlement continues to accrue even though the worker is on sick leave. However, in *Commissioners of Inland Revenue v Ainsworth* (2005) the Court of Appeal held, in a decision of great practical importance, that workers on long-term sick leave who have *exhausted* their right to sick pay are not entitled to four weeks' holiday pay a year under the WTRs. The reasoning is that reg 13 of the WTRs entitles workers to 'leave'. This must mean leave from work. Yet workers who have been on long-term absence from work due to sickness do not, by definition, require leave from work. The Court of Appeal emphasised that the purpose of the WTRs was to lay down standards to protect the health and safety of workers whilst this claim, if it had succeeded, would have done nothing in this direction but would have simply resulted in a windfall for the workers. It should be noted that this decision does not deal with the position of a worker who, having been off sick, then returns to work *before the end* of the holiday year. The law here seems to be that the right to leave remains. In addition it seems that paid holiday leave accrues during sick leave. The other point is that in this case the court decided that any claim to backdated holiday pay can only be for the most recent holiday year. This is a consequence of the fact that a claim for holiday pay under the WTRs is not a claim for unpaid wages. Had it been for unpaid wages then claims for years further back could have been pursued on the basis that they were a series of deductions. The decision of the EAT in *List Design Group Ltd v Douglas* (2003) that a claim could be brought in these circumstances for unpaid wages was held to be wrong.

(b) Rolled up holiday pay

In *Robinson-Steele v RD Retail Services Ltd* (2006) the ECJ has held that the practice of rolled up holiday pay contravenes the Working Time Directive. This is the practice where the employees are given a separate additional payment during the weeks when they work instead of receiving a separate payment when they go on holiday. The reason is that the Working Time Directive is concerned with health and safety and so it requires all employees actually to be paid holiday pay to encourage them to take holiday breaks.

(c) Entitlement to paid days off in lieu

In *McMenemy v Capita Business Services Ltd* (2006) the EAT held that a part-time employee who is not required by her contract to work on the day on which a bank holiday falls is not entitled to an equivalent day off in lieu. Thus if the employee does not normally work on Monday then there is no right to time off on another day when there is a bank holiday on a Monday. The reasoning is that where the employee is full time but is not required to work on, for example, Monday then he would not be given another day off.

(d) Carrying days forward

In *FNV* v *Staat der Nederlanden* (2006) the ECJ held that the Working Time Directive prevents days of annual leave which are carried over to the next leave year being replaced by payment in lieu. The reasoning is the same as in the above case: the Directive is aimed at protecting health and safety and is not primarily about money.

(e) Maternity leave and annual leave

In *Gómez* v *Continental Industrias del Caucho SA* (2004) the ECJ held that where maternity leave coincides with the employer's annual shutdown then maternity leave should be taken at the end of annual leave. The introduction of longer periods of maternity leave, which will rise to a year by 2009, will mean that in some cases a woman who has ended her maternity leave and wishes to add annual leave to this will find that this takes her into a new leave year. This will conflict with the principle that annual leave cannot be carried forward to the next year. This remains to be resolved by the courts. (Maternity leave is considered in detail in Chapter 10.)

Modification and exclusion of this right

This right cannot be excluded or modified and it is enforced by complaint to an employment tribunal, which may award compensation.

THE YOUNG WORKERS DIRECTIVE

The WTRs also implement the Young Workers Directive (94/33). This limits the working time of young workers (those over the minimum school leaving age but under 18) to 8 hours a day or 40 hours a week (with longer hours allowed in certain cases); prohibits night work (again except in certain cases); and provides that young workers shall be adequately supervised.

> **LAW IN CONTEXT**
> **The effect of the Working Time Directive in practice**
>
> A CIPD report, *Working Hours in the UK* (2004; 2006) points out that, according to the Office for National Statistics, the average working week has fallen by over an hour since 1998, when the WTRs were introduced. However, the trend to shorter working hours cannot, the CIPD feels, be attributed entirely to the WTRs as this trend began slightly before they were introduced and is also seen among exempt groups such as the self-employed. A partial explanation may therefore lie in social trends such as the desire to achieve a 'more positive work–life balance'. The hours worked by UK workers are still high by comparison with other EU countries but Australia, Japan and the USA have more 'longer hours workers' than the UK. The 2004 Workplace Employment Relations Survey showed that 11% of employees worked more than 48 hours a week. Working long hours was less common among women than men. Only 11% of men

7

Payment of wages and hours of work

→

worked more than 48 hours a week on average in workplaces where women were in the majority, compared to 21% where women were not in the majority; 54% of employees had worked more than 48 hours a week (Kersley et al., 2006).

Another CIPD report, *Living to Work* (2003), showed that the main reason for long hours was (perhaps not unexpectedly) workload but 50% of workers said that working long hours was their own choice. On the other hand, more than one in four of those who responded to the survey said that long hours had a negative impact on their health and more than two out of five reported a negative impact on relationships. The CIPD report quotes Guest (2002) as finding that, although working long hours may be harmful to health, 'the social support received by those working long hours and their control over their work have a positive effect, mitigating some of the harmful effects'.

SUNDAY WORKING

Retail workers are protected from dismissal for refusing to work on Sundays in certain circumstances, which are contained in ss 40–43 and 45 of the ERA 1996.

Protected shop workers

Shop workers who were employed on 25 August 1994 (when the Sunday Trading Act 1994 came into force) are classified as 'protected shop workers'. They cannot be required to work on Sundays, they cannot be dismissed or selected for redundancy for refusing to work on Sundays and they cannot be subjected to any detriment for refusing to work on Sundays. However, they may lose this protection by:

1 agreeing to work on Sundays; and
2 giving the employer an opting-in notice in writing agreeing to work on Sundays.

Opted-out shop workers

Shop workers who are not protected shop workers, either because they were not employed on the above date or because they gave an opted-in notice, are known as 'opted-out shop workers'. They may give the employer an opted-out notice stating that they object to Sunday working and then after three months from the date of the notice they acquire the same rights as protected shop workers.

A final point is that these provisions do not apply to employees specifically engaged to work on Sundays, although they are still protected under general unfair dismissal law.

RIGHTS TO TIME OFF WORK

Details of the various rights to time off work will be found in the appropriate parts of this book but readers might find it convenient to have a short list of these rights at this point, with an indication of where further details may be found:

1 Right to take time off for trade union duties and activities: see Chapter 13.

2 Right to take time off for employee representatives: see Chapter 12.

3 Right to take time off for public duties: see below.

4 Right to take time off for antenatal care: see Chapter 10.

5 Right to take time off to care for dependants: see Chapter 10.

6 Right to take time off when under threat of dismissal for redundancy: see Chapter 12.

The right to take time off for public duties is for specified duties such as sitting as a magistrate, or as a member of a local council, health authority, education body, prison visiting committee, statutory tribunal or the Environment Agency (ERA 1996, s 50). Time off must be reasonable and ACAS has given guidance in a Code.

It should be noted that these rights are distinct from the rights to maternity, paternity and adoption leave, which are dealt with in Chapter 10.

SUMMARY

This chapter first looks at that part of the employment relationship which concerns the payment of wages. It begins with the law on when wages can be withheld, as where the employee has not completed the work, and then looks at deductions from wages and the situations allowed by statute when deductions are allowed. It then focuses on the topical area of bonuses and when they can, and cannot, be claimed. From here it moves to sick pay and the payment of wages during suspension, lay-off and short-time and the statutory provisions, notably guarantee pay. Discussion of the National Minimum Wage leads on to the rules on working hours and a detailed examination of the Working Time Directive. The chapter ends with a summary of when employees are allowed time off work by statute.

QUESTION

Miranda is employed at a large financial institution and was accused by a fellow employee of harassing her. Miranda was suspended without pay for one week whilst this was investigated and was then told that the allegations had not been proved and so she would be reinstated in her job. Following this she noticed that she had not received the performance bonus which other employees had received and, when she enquired why this was so, she was told that, although she had met the performance criteria for the award of the bonus, there were other aspects of her performance which 'caused disquiet' and these had been taken into account in deciding not to award her a bonus. Miranda wishes to claim:

(a) full pay for the period when she was suspended;

(b) the bonus.

Advise her.

7

Payment of wages and hours of work

FURTHER READING

Department for Work and Pensions (DWP) (2006) (Welfare Reform Green Paper). Chapter 2, 'Helping ill or disabled people', deals with statutory sick pay. DWP: London.

Department of Trade and Industry (DTI) (2004) *Working Time – Widening the Debate: a preliminary consultation on long hours working in the UK and the application and operation of the working time opt-out*. DTI: London.

BIBLIOGRAPHY

Bercusson, B. (1996) *European Labour Law*, Butterworths: London.

CIPD Report (2003) *Living to Work*. CIPD: London.

CIPD Report (2004; updated 2006) *Working Hours in the UK*. CIPD: London.

Freedland, M. (2003) *The Personal Employment Contract*, Oxford University Press: Oxford.

Guest, D. (2002) *Pressure at Work and the Psychological Contract*, CIPD.

Kersley, B. et al. (2006) *Inside the Workplace: Findings from the 2004 Workplace Employment Relations Survey*, Routledge: London.

Labour Market Trends (1998) December, page 599.

Watson, L. (1995) 'Employees and the Unfair Contract Terms Act', 24 ILJ 323.

For further resources and updates please go to the Companion Website accompanying this book at **www.mylawchamber.co.uk/duddingtonemployment**

8 Health and safety

INTRODUCTION

The law on health and safety has several objectives:

1 to prevent accidents at work and to prevent injuries developing as a result of events at work;

2 to encourage a positive attitude to health and safety at work;

3 to provide an effective system of compensation for accidents and injuries at work;

4 to provide, where appropriate, for criminal sanctions for breaches of health and safety laws.

These objectives are achieved through a number of different systems:

1 the common law of negligence, which provides compensation for injuries sustained through work;

2 actions for breach of statutory duty which also aim to provide compensation for injuries at work;

3 actions for breach of an implied term in the contract of employment that the employer will ensure that the working environment is reasonably safe for the performance of contractual duties;

4 the system of state benefits for those injured at work;

5 the Health and Safety at Work Act 1974, which aims to encourage good practice in health and safety but which also provides criminal penalties for breach;

6 European Community Regulations together with the Working Time Regulations, which were discussed in Chapter 7.

Each of these will be considered in turn but the diagram below and examples which follow show their interrelationship.

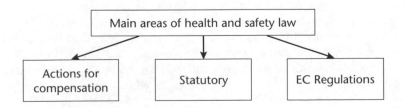

Example

John is injured at the office where he works by some broken glass in a door. His injuries are not serious but he sustained a badly cut hand.

There will have been a breach of the Health and Safety at Work Act 1974 here, although criminal penalties are reserved for serious cases. John may wish to claim some compensation for his injuries under the law of negligence, although the amount would be small, and, if he is away from work, he would receive statutory sick pay (SSP). It is unlikely that he would be away from work for long enough to be eligible for industrial injury benefits. The main result of the accident would probably be a report to the health and safety committee (if there is one) and measures put in place to make sure that this does not happen again.

Example

Jennifer is very seriously burned when some hot liquid escapes from a container. She is away from work for a year. Clearly Jennifer will be entitled to SSP, but she will also be entitled to compensation for the injuries themselves. She could claim incapacity benefit but it is likely that she will wish to claim a higher sum than the amount of benefit and, in any event, entitlement to benefits is linked to other factors (see below). Thus a common law action for negligence is the obvious avenue, although she will have to prove that the employer was negligent. In addition, there is the prospect that the employer will be fined for a breach of the Health and Safety at Work Act 1974.

The other point to make in this introduction is that an injury at work may also, particularly if it is linked to bullying, lead to an action for harassment on the grounds of sex, race or disability if the reason for the actions which caused the injury was discrimination on any of those grounds. A good example is *Jones* v *Tower Boot Co. Ltd* (1997) (see Chapter 9). Furthermore, actions which lead to injury can also give grounds for the employee to claim constructive dismissal, although compensation is far more likely to be sought in an action for negligence.

LAW IN CONTEXT
Health and safety in 2005/6

The statistics on work-related health and safety in Great Britain published by the Office for National Statistics show that 2 million people suffered from an injury which they believed was caused or made worse by their work; 212 workers were killed at work, but the Health and Safety Executive believes that there are about 6,000 deaths each year from occupational cancer (although this is an estimate). In 2004 there were 100 deaths from asbestosis and around 200 from other types of pneumoconiosis, mostly due to coal dust and silica. There is in fact a long-term decline in fatal accidents at work from just under 500 in 1981 to around the 200–300 mark in recent years. However, as types of occupation change so do the types of disease: of the estimated 6,000 cancer deaths, 4,000 of these were from exposure to asbestos, including nearly 2,000 in 2004 from mesothelioma, but these reflect industrial conditions of years ago and deaths from this condition will decrease. Non-fatal injuries reported in 2005/6 numbered 28,605, of which over one-third were caused by slipping and tripping. The target is to reduce the incidence rate of work-related injuries and fatal accidents by 20% between 1999/2000 and 2009/10; the target as at 2005/6 was 12%, so progress is being made.

The message is clear: there is no more vital topic in employment law than this one. (Note that the website of the Health and Safety Commission (www.hse.gov.uk) is a mine of information and really sets the law in context; frequent visits to the website are recommended.)

We will now look in more detail at the various legal systems that apply to health and safety at work.

ACTION FOR COMPENSATION (DAMAGES) IN A COMMON LAW ACTION FOR THE TORT OF NEGLIGENCE

An action for negligence is not, of course, confined to claims arising out of accidents at work (the most common action for negligence is for damages for injuries resulting from a road accident). It should also be noted that actions for negligence are encountered in other areas of employment law: for example, an action arising from what is alleged to be a negligently given reference (see Chapter 5).

In all negligence actions three points must be proved. In relation to an action by an employee against an employer these are:

1 that the employer owed the employee a duty of care;

2 that the employer broke that duty through negligence;

3 that the employee suffered damage as a result which was not too remote a consequence of the employer's negligence.

The following issues are also relevant:

4 Was the employee guilty of contributory negligence?

5 Did the employee consent to the act which caused the injury?

Finally, we must consider whether the employer, rather than owing a direct duty to the employee, is liable for the actions of other employees. This is known as 'vicarious liability'.

◼ The duty of care

The idea of the duty of care is that it defines the situations where the employer *can be* liable to the employee. The standard defines whether there *is* liability. The classic formulation of the duty of care in employment situations is found in *Wilsons and Clyde Coal Co.* v *English* (1938), where Lord Wright said that the duty was threefold:

1 'provision of a competent staff of men';

2 'adequate material';

3 'a proper system and effective supervision', which is really the general duty to provide a safe system of work.

In addition to these categories there is the more recently recognised duty to safeguard the employee from foreseeable psychiatric injury resulting from work.

These will now be looked at in turn, although the duties will be expressed in a more modern way.

Duty to provide competent fellow employees

This clearly means that the employer must provide the employee with fellow employees who are able to do the job and therefore the employer will be in breach of this duty if he fails to provide proper training so that an employee is injured by the negligence of another employee who was not properly trained for the task. A specific instance of this duty being broken is where an employee is injured by practical jokes played by another employee. In *Hudson* v *Ridge Manufacturing Co. Ltd* (1957) an employee had engaged in practical jokes for many years by, for example, tripping other employees up. He had been warned by a foreman but, beyond this, no further action was taken. He then tripped up the plaintiff, a disabled man, and injured him. It was held that the employers were in breach of the duty of care owed to the plaintiff as they were aware of the employee's conduct and had not taken proper steps to put an end to it. Therefore, an employer may find that the only way to deal with a practical joker is to dismiss him or her and such a dismissal may then be fair.

Duty to provide safe plant and equipment

This duty is now one of strict liability, in contrast to the other duties, which require proof of negligence by the employer. In *Davie* v *New Merton Board Mills Ltd* (1959) the House of Lords held that an employer was not liable for defects in equipment which could not have been discovered on a reasonable inspection of equipment supplied from a reputable source. The effect was that an employee might suffer injury from a piece of equipment but be unable to recover any damages where there was a latent defect.

The law was changed by the Employers' Liability (Defective Equipment) Act 1969, which provides that an employer is liable where:

1 the employee suffers personal injury in the course of employment;

2 in consequence of a defect in equipment provided by the employer; and

3 the defect is attributable wholly or partly to the fault of a third party, whether identified or not.

In this case the injury is deemed to be attributable to the negligence of the employer.

Example

Ishmael is injured when operating a drill which fractures when in use. His employer bought the drill from a manufacturer who had often supplied this type of drill in the past, none of which had ever given any trouble. Under the previous law, Ishmael would probably not have succeeded in a claim against the employer for negligence but now the employer will be liable as the 1969 Act creates a presumption that the employer is negligent even though in reality he is not. Had it not been for the Act, Ishmael would have been left to claim against the manufacturer for negligence but if the manufacturer had, for example, ceased business he would have received nothing.

In *Coltman* v *Bibby Tankers Ltd* (1987) a ship sank with all hands and it was alleged that it had been defectively built due to the negligence of the manufacturer. The House of Lords held that the word 'equipment' could include the actual workplace provided by the employer – in this case a ship – as well as equipment in the more usual sense, such as tools.

Duty to provide a safe system of work

This duty includes the provision of a safe workplace, safe methods of working, methods of supervision designed to ensure safety and a generally safe working environment. A good general example is provided by *General Cleaning Contractors Ltd* v *Christmas* (1953), where the employee, a window cleaner, fell when cleaning a window as a result of the sash falling on his hand which made him let go of his hold. Safety belts were provided but there were no hooks to attach them to. The employers were held liable, as it was their responsibility to ensure that there were adequate precautions against injury and the responsibility of deciding how to take precautions should not fall on the employees. The following specific points arise:

Where safety equipment is provided, how far should the employer go in ensuring that employees use it?

The law has changed a great deal since the remark of Lord Simonds in *Smith* v *Austin Lifts* (1959), where he deprecated 'any tendency to treat the relationship of employer and skilled workman as that of a nurse and imbecile child'. His point, albeit very unfortunately expressed, was that employees should be expected to look after themselves to a large extent and not expect the employer to be constantly devising safety precautions. This view was upheld in *McWilliams* v *Arrol* (1962), where a steel erector fell to his death when not wearing a safety belt. Belts were not provided, although they had previously been, but the Court of Appeal found that the employee would not have worn one even if it had been provided. Although there is some truth in what Lord Simonds said, the law has moved on since then. In *Bux* v *Slough Metals Ltd* (1973) a die-caster lost an eye when a piece of molten metal splashed into his eye. Goggles were provided but the employee, on finding that they misted up, told his superintendent that he would not wear them. No attempt was made to persuade him to do so. It was held that the employers were negligent in not giving instructions 'in a reasonable and firm manner . . . followed by supervision'. The decision in *McWilliams* was distinguished on the basis that there the issue was one of causation, in that the employee would not have worn the safety belt even if it had been provided, and the failure to provide them did not cause the injury, but there is no doubt that the decision in *Bux* represented a change of approach. Even so, the law here is still not clear. Suppose the employee refused to wear safety equipment: would the employer have a duty to suspend him or her unless they did so? Would a failure to do this be negligence? Could an employee ultimately be dismissed in such a case? The answer must be that, as a last resort, an employer, provided that he or she acted reasonably, would be held to have acted fairly in dismissing or suspending if this was the only way to protect an employee from injury. The only other guidance comes from *Crouch* v *British Rail Engineering Ltd* (1988), where the employee, a fitter, injured his eye when a piece of metal flew into it. Again, the use of goggles would have prevented the injury and here goggles were available in the storeroom five minutes' walk away. The Court of Appeal held that the employer had a duty actually to provide the goggles to the employee as part of his tool kit. Finally, it is significant that, under s 7 of the Health and Safety at Work Act (see below), employees have a duty to take reasonable care for their own safety. Could a failure to use safety equipment provided be a breach of this Act? Why not?

Does the duty extend to activities away from the employer's premises?

The employer will object that this is unfair, as he or she has no control over safety on premises other than their own. However, the courts have held that the duty does apply here as in *General Cleaning Contractors* v *Christmas* (above). The question then becomes the extent of this duty, a point which is dealt with below. An interesting issue arose in *Reid* v *Rush and Tompkins Group Ltd* (1989), where an employee was injured in a road accident when working for the defendants in Ethiopia, where at that time there was no requirement to have third party insurance. He argued that his employer had a duty either to provide insurance cover where the employee was working or to advise the employee of the risks of being without cover and advise him to obtain it. It was held that the employer's duties did not extend to these matters as there was no duty to warn against the risk of economic loss alone and, in any event, it would be impossible to formulate such a duty in sufficiently precise terms (see also *Square D Ltd* v *Cook* (1992) discussed below).

Duty to safeguard employee from work-related upper limb disorder

The duty has recently been held to extend to a duty to safeguard the employee from what was known as repetitive strain injury (RSI) but is now known as work-related upper limb disorder (WRULD). The initial decision was that in *Pickford* v *ICI plc* (1998), where the employee, a secretary, spent a great deal of her time typing and claimed for what was then RSI. It was held that, in principle, such a claim could succeed but on the facts here it failed as the court was not satisfied on the evidence whether the injury was psychogenic (i.e. in the mind) or physical. The employee had to prove that it was physical and she was not able to do so. Subsequently, in *Alexander v Midland Bank plc* (1999), claims for WRULD were brought by encoders at a bank. Their work involved coding in information at very great speed and there was continual pressure to work faster, with league tables and competitions. The claim was for neck, arm and hand strain. The court held that where on the facts the explanation that the injury was psychogenic was unconvincing, then the injury had to be physical, as it was here. Thus claims for WRULD have been accepted in principle and the issue is one of proof.

Duty to protect the employee from psychiatric illness caused by stress at work

The existence of this duty was recognised in *Walker v Northumberland CC* (1995), one of the most important recent cases in any area of employment law. Mr Walker was a social worker responsible for a team of four. The workload gradually rose but there was no increase in staffing levels. He eventually suffered a nervous breakdown and, before he returned to work, it was agreed that he would be provided with extra assistance. Although extra assistance was forthcoming, it was withdrawn after a month and Mr Walker suffered a second breakdown and was subsequently dismissed on the ground of permanent ill health. The High Court held that his employers were in breach of their duty of care as, once he had suffered one nervous breakdown, there was a foreseeable risk to his mental health and the employers should not have withdrawn the extra assistance provided. The employers had argued that, as their resources were scarce, they had to take this into account when deciding what assistance to allocate, but the court held that a reasonable local authority would have at least continued the extra assistance until Mr Walker's workload was reduced. Furthermore, any argument that scarce resources were relevant in determining the extent of the duty could only be relevant in tort, being derived from the speech of Lord Wilberforce in *Anns v Merton LBC* (1977), and could not apply if the action was brought in contract for breach of an implied term. Given that the scope of the duties in contract and tort were the same (see below), there would be an injustice in imposing a barrier on recovery of damages in one but not the other. It was unfortunate that the decision in *Walker* was not appealed and, although there were many highly publicised cases of considerable amounts of damages being paid for breach of this duty, these resulted from out-of-court settlements.

The adoption by the courts of a tort-based approach centring on causation and foreseeability has led to a number of decisions where the main issue has been the extent to which a reasonable employer ought to foresee this type of injury. A significant decision was that of the Court of Appeal in *Sutherland v Hatton* (and three other conjoined appeals) (2002). Appeals against three awards of damages for psychiatric injury, two to teachers and one to a machine operator, were allowed, and one, of £175,000 to an administrative assistant, was allowed to stand. Hale LJ laid down the following principles:

1 Claims for psychiatric injury were not to be treated differently from claims for personal injury. Therefore, the basic rules of the tort of negligence apply.

2 Claims could be brought only for injury to health and not for stress as such.

167

3 The test is the same in all types of employment, in that no types of work are intrinsically dangerous but relevant factors in deciding if a duty exists are the nature and extent of the work done by the employee and signs of impending harm to health.

4 In considering the standard of care, account should be taken of the size of the operation, the magnitude of the risk and the costs and practicability of preventing it.

5 An employer who offered a confidential counselling or treatment service would be unlikely to be in breach.

6 If the only reasonable step was to dismiss or demote the employee and the employee was not agreeable to this, then the employer would not be in breach of the duty by failing to dismiss.

In considering liability for psychiatric injury caused by work-related stress there are a number of points to consider, not all of them entirely settled:

(a) The extent to which an employer ought to foresee the risk of injury

Barber v *Somerset County Council* (2004) dealt with the vexed question of the point at which an employer is, as it were, put on notice that an employee cannot withstand the usual pressures of the job and thus ought to foresee the risk of psychiatric harm. In *Sutherland* Hale LJ said that unless an employer 'knows of some particular problem or vulnerability, an employer is usually entitled to assume that his employee is up to the normal pressures of the job'. Moreover: 'Generally he is entitled to take what he is told by or on behalf of the employee at face value'. Clearly there are exceptions, as in *Young* v *Post Office* (below) but this was a case where the employee had already had a nervous breakdown. In *Barber* Lord Walker stated that the words of Hale LJ were useful practical guidance but he felt that the best statement of general principle was in the judgment of Swanwick J in *Stokes* v *Guest Keen and Nettlefold* (1968), where he said that 'the overall test is still the conduct of the reasonable and prudent employer, taking positive thought for the safety of his workers in the light of what he knows or ought to know'. The other Lords agreed with this, with the exception of Lord Scott who pointed out that the *Stokes* decision was concerned with liability for physical harm and not psychiatric injury. At bottom, the question is just how far liability for harm caused by work-related stress shall extend and whether an employer is put on notice where, for example, an employee complains about the amount of pressure he or she is under. In *Bonser* v *RJB Mining* (2004), decided before the decision in *Barber*, a manager was subjected to an increasing workload that eventually resulted in his suffering a nervous breakdown. The Court of Appeal held that for there to be liability it must have been reasonably foreseeable to the employer that the employee was, through the strain of the job, vulnerable to a psychiatric breakdown and not just to stress. This was not so here. The fact remains that at present it is difficult for an employee to succeed unless he or she has already suffered a breakdown as a result of work pressures. The question, which is not entirely answered by *Barber*, is whether this will remain the case.

In *Hartman* v *South Essex Mental Health and Community Care NHS Trust* (2005) (and other conjoined appeals) the Court of Appeal considered the decision in *Barber* (above) and adopted the formulation of Hale LJ (now Lady Hale) in the Court of Appeal, and gave less prominence to the slightly conflicting formulation of Lord

Walker in the House of Lords in *Barber*. The Court of Appeal also held that an employer could not be expected to be aware that an employee is vulnerable to stress because she had disclosed health details in a health-screening questionnaire to the employer's occupational health department. The questionnaire had stated that it was 'personal and confidential'. It is interesting that this could affect the employer's liability under the Disability Discrimination Act 1995 (see Chapter 9) to make reasonable adjustments as this applies only where the employer knows that the employee has a disability. (See discussion on this point by Rubenstein (2005) at page 250.) In addition, the Court of Appeal held that where an employee works for only two or three days a week, as was the case in one of the appeals (**Wheeldon v HSBC Bank Ltd**), it will be only in exceptional cases that a claim for psychiatric injury caused by stress will succeed. The court also observed that the mere fact that one employer has foreseen a particular risk does not mean that all other employers in the same field should do so as well. In this connection the test of Swanwick J in *Stokes v Guest, Keen and Nettlefold* (above) can be applied.

(b) Is an employer under a duty to be *proactive* in such cases in enquiring as to the state of the health of employees?

In *Marshall Specialist Vehicles Ltd v Osborne* (2003) the EAT held that the answer is no and emphasised that there must be evidence that the employer should have reasonably foreseen that the employee was under such mental strain as to make intervention by the employer necessary. Here the employee sent an email to her employer at the beginning of June expressing concern about the strain that she and her team were under. The matter was briefly discussed at a meeting on 16 June but no action resulted and on 20 June she left. She had never previously taken up her concerns about the stress she felt she was under and the EAT remitted her claim to the Tribunal, which had previously found in her favour. Although this decision pre-dates that in *Barber* it is suggested that it is in line with the views of Lord Walker in that case.

(c) To what extent can an employer assume that an employee can withstand the usual pressures of the job?

In *Young v Post Office* (2002) a workshop manager who had a nervous breakdown through work-related stress was allowed to return to work on a flexible basis so that he could make his return gradually. Although the understanding was that he was initially under no obligation to work at all, he received little or no support and within seven weeks he was doing the same job which had previously caused the breakdown. It was held that where, as here, the employee has a history of work-related stress then the employer is not only under a duty to take steps to make the working environment less stressful but also under a duty to see that the arrangements made are carried out. It is no answer to the employee's claim to say that the employer is entitled to assume that the employee can withstand the normal pressures of the job.

(d) To what extent will the availability of a counselling service mean that the employer is absolved from liability?

In *Sutherland*, Hale LJ, it will be recalled, stated the principle that an employer who offered a confidential counselling or treatment service would be unlikely to be in breach. As Barrett (2005) points out, it is now clear from the decision in *Hartman* that

8

Health and safety

it is not enough that there is a system of counselling in place. Effective counselling must be offered to the employee.

It is worth noting that a short guide entitled *Work Related Stress* has been jointly produced by the DTI, CBI and the TUC among others. It points out that work-related stress involves 13 million days lost a year, meaning that it is the biggest cause of working days lost through sickness and ill health. The guide contains details of a voluntary agreement designed to provide employers and employees with a framework of measures to deal with work-related stress and draws attention to the Management Standards developed by the Health and Safety Executive to provide a yardstick against which organisations can measure their performance in dealing with work-related stress.

A different question concerning psychiatric harm arose in *White v Chief Constable of South Yorkshire* (1999). The respondents were police officers who had been on duty at Hillsborough Stadium when 96 people were crushed to death and many others were injured. They suffered post-traumatic stress disorder as a result of looking after victims and claimed damages but their claim failed as they were held to be 'secondary victims', i.e. those who fell outside the range of foreseeable injury. In order to recover they would have needed to show that there were close ties of love and affection between them and the victims, which was obviously not the case here. The fact that they were employees was not a reason for treating them as 'primary victims' and allowing them to recover. The difference between the situation in this case and in the *Walker* line of cases (above) is that here the courts were concerned with damage to mental health caused by witnessing a traumatic event rather than through damage to health caused by carrying out their duties under their contract of employment. Nevertheless, Freedland (2006) regrets that the opportunity was not taken to formulate 'a general duty on employing entities to manage work situations and to allocate organizational resources with a higher level of care than had previously been exacted for the mental health of workers'.

Note: This area is one of the many in employment law which cannot be considered in isolation. The link to the Disability Discrimination Act 1995 has already been mentioned and the reader should also note the decision in *Dunnachie v Kingston on Hull Council* (2003) where the House of Lords held that a claim for non-economic loss could not be brought in a claim for unfair dismissal. The relationship between the decision in *Dunnachie* and the duty of care in tort in respect of psychiatric harm is discussed in Chapter 11. Moreover, in *Waters v Metropolitan Police Commissioner* (see Chapter 5) the police commissioner was liable for failure to protect a police officer from harassment or bullying by fellow officers. This decision is dealt with under the contract of employment although the House of Lords held that there could also have been liability in contract. The law in this area is in need of rationalisation. Would a way forward be to treat the principles in the decisions following *Walker* as based on contract rather than tort, which could avoid the problems about foreseeability?

(e) Can the employer claim that the duty of care to employees has been delegated to others with the result that he is not liable?

The courts have rejected this idea, which in effect means that the employer can shift the responsibility for injuries to employees on to someone else. The point was raised in *Wilsons and Clyde Coal Co.* v *English* (1938) (see also above), where an employee was crushed when a haulage system in a mine was negligently operated and the employers argued that they had discharged their duty of care by appointing a qualified manager. Lord Thankerton said that it was a 'fallacy' to say that the duty was discharged by the appointment of a competent person to perform it.

More recently, the decision in *Square D Ltd* v *Cook* (1992) has been put forward as a possible example of an employer successfully delegating the duty. The employee was an electronics engineer in Saudi Arabia. Another company occupied the premises where he worked and yet another company was the main contractor. The employee was injured when his foot was trapped in a floor. The court held that, although the duty of care was not delegable, the duty was always to take reasonable care and one needs to look at all the circumstances, including the degree of control which the employer can reasonably be expected to exercise. The idea that the employer could be responsible for daily events on a site in Saudi Arabia was felt to have an 'air of unreality'. This decision could be considered, despite the words of the court to the contrary, as one where the employer delegated the duty, but it is submitted that a better explanation is that the case deals only with breach of duty rather than the existence of a duty. The court did not suggest that the employer owed no duty at all, only that he did not do so in this particular situation.

The employer broke the duty through negligence

This question arises only when it has been established that a duty was owed and is generally referred to as the question of the 'standard of care'. In effect, the question when considering the *duty* of care is whether this is a situation where the employer *can* be liable. The *standard* of care decides whether the employer *is* liable. The standard of care is broken by negligence and thus we must first decide what negligence is in the context of the relationship between employer and employee.

In many cases it is difficult to separate the questions of duty and breach, as in *Walker* v *Northumberland CC* and *Sutherland* v *Hatton* (above). The judgment of Hale LJ in *Sutherland* inevitably deals with both.

A clear example of where the courts had to assess the standard of care is *Latimer* v *AEC Ltd* (1953). A large factory was flooded in a very heavy rainstorm and the water then mixed with an oily substance which resulted in the floor becoming extremely slippery. The employers had what they believed was enough sawdust to cover any eventualities but it turned out that there was not enough to cover the whole floor. The plaintiff slipped on an untreated part of the floor and injured his ankle. It was held that the question was whether a reasonably prudent employer would have closed down the whole factory rather than run the risk of injury and on the facts it was found that such an employer would not have done so. The degree of risk was too small and thus an employer is entitled to weigh the extent of the risk against the measures necessary to eliminate it.

On the other hand, the duty owed by the employer to employees is a personal one and the special characteristics of each employee must be taken into account. Where an employee is inexperienced, a higher standard of care is owed. Likewise, a high standard

8

Health and safety

of care is owed where the consequences of an injury to a particular employee are much greater than to most employees. In *Paris* v *Stepney BC* (1951) an employee who was blind in one eye was employed as a mechanic. He lost the sight of his other eye when a splinter flew into that eye and it was held that, although there might not have been a duty to supply goggles to fully sighted employees, the consequences of the loss of an eye in this case were much more serious and thus a higher standard of care was owed. Therefore, there was a duty to supply goggles and, as the employers had failed to do so, they were liable for negligence.

An application of this principle is the situation where an employee suffers from a medical condition which is either caused or exacerbated by the work which they do. In *Withers* v *Parry Chain Co. Ltd* (1961) the employee had a severe attack of dermatitis due to the grease used in her job. It was held that her employer was not in breach of duty in employing her on work which it should have known could cause this, as there were no special precautions which could have been taken to protect the employee. In *Pape* v *Cumbria CC* (1991) the employee was a cleaner and suffered dermatitis through coming into contact with chemical cleaning agents. Employees were provided with gloves but hardly ever used them and they were not warned of the danger of dermatitis occurring in this situation. It was held that the employers were in breach of duty, as the dangers were well enough known to make it the duty of a reasonable employer to warn of the risks but not well enough known for the employer to be entitled to assume that employees would know of the risks. In *Withers* the employers were not obliged to even give a warning yet in *Pape* they were under a duty to warn. Although the cases are distinguishable on the ground that in *Withers* there was no means of ensuring safety, they still represent divergent approaches. In *Coxall* v *Goodyear Great Britain Ltd* (2002) the Court of Appeal held that whether a case fell within the *Withers* principle depended on the extent and nature of the risk and there will be cases where the employer is under a duty to dismiss the employee to protect him or her from physical danger. Simon Brown LJ gave as an example where an employee known to suffer from vertigo or epileptic fits is allowed to continue working as a spiderman.

Section 25 of the Health and Safety at Work Act 1974 (HSWA 1974) allows inspectors to seize any articles or substances which pose an imminent danger of serious personal injury and here the fact that the process could not be carried out in any other way would not be relevant. Although the situation in *Withers* might not be what the drafters of s 25 had in mind, there is a good case that it should apply in such a case. Is an employer under a duty in these cases to dismiss an employee who, in the *Withers* type of situation, cannot do the job without injury? As in cases discussed above where the employee would not wear safety equipment, it is submitted that, provided that the employer acts reasonably, dismissal could be fair but the employer would need to show that there was no other work which the employee could do. This conclusion is supported by the remarks of the Court of Appeal in *Sutherland* v *Hatton* (above). However, the employee's injuries may have led to him or her becoming disabled under the Disability Discrimination Act 1995 and the employer would then need to consider whether reasonable adjustments could be made to the job to enable the employee to do it without injury.

■ The employee suffered injuries as a result which were not too remote a consequence of the employer's negligence

This final element in the law of negligence can, in practice, prove the most difficult of all. A good example is a case where an employee claims to have suffered injury to health as a result of stress at work. It may be that there is evidence that the employee was going through difficult personal circumstances at the time and the employer will say that this was the cause. Employees may be aided by the rule established in *Smith* v *Leech Brain and Co. Ltd* (1962) that where the defendant can foresee the type of injury suffered by the claimant then there is liability for all damage which results. An employee was, due to the negligence of his employers, splashed on the lip by a piece of molten metal. Some injury was clearly foreseeable but it was not foreseeable that the employee would die of cancer, as happened. The employers were liable, as they could foresee that he would suffer a burn. Therefore, they were liable for all the consequences. This is often known as the 'thin skull' rule, i.e. that if the defendant (e.g. the employer) knows that the other party (e.g. the employee) has a thin skull (or some personal sensitivity to a particular type of injury) then they are liable for all the damage which results even if it may not be foreseeable.

In *Fairchild* v *Glenhaven Funeral Services Ltd* (2002) an employee claimed that he had suffered from mesothelioma, a form of cancer caused by exposure to asbestos fibres, but, as he had worked for a number of employers during the time when he could have contracted the disease, the Court of Appeal held that it could not be proved that it had occurred whilst he was working for his present employer. This decision was reversed by the House of Lords who held that it was contrary to justice in that where two or more people have committed a wrong then the victim should not be deprived of a remedy only because he or she cannot establish which of them was to blame. Accordingly, the victims were allowed to recover from any of the employers, leaving it to them to seek a contribution from other employers shown to be negligent.

■ Contributory negligence

Where the employer is liable to the employee for negligence, any damages payable may be reduced as it may be held that the employee has been negligent. This provision is found in the Law Reform (Contributory Negligence) Act 1945, s 1(1) of which states that damages 'shall be reduced to such extent as the court thinks just and equitable having regard to the claimant's share in the responsibility for the damage'.

A good example of an employment case where contributory negligence applied is *Crouch* v *British Rail Engineering* (above), where the failure of the employee to wear goggles led to a reduction of 50% in his damages although the employers were negligent in failing to provide them.

■ Consent

This is often known by the Latin name of *volenti non fit injuria* (to those who are willing, no injury is done) and simply means that, if I have consented to what would otherwise be a tort then I lose my right to claim damages for it. A good example is taking part in a game where one consents to running the risks ordinarily associated with it. It differs from contributory negligence in that, if it succeeds, the claimant does not recover any damages at all.

There have been attempts to argue that it should apply in employment cases on the basis that an employee knew of a risk and consented to run it. However, there are two elements in this defence:

1 knowledge of the risk;

2 a free and voluntary consent to run it.

Although knowledge may be present on the part of the employee, it will be difficult to establish that the employee voluntarily consented to run it, as a refusal to do a particular job on the ground of risk could lead to dismissal. In any case there is a strong reluctance on the part of the courts to apply a defence which would result in an employee losing all the damages. In *Bowater* v *Rowley Regis Corporation* (1944) Goddard LCJ said that the defence would hardly ever apply to acts in the course of normal duty and could apply only where the work itself carried an element of danger. A court today would probably be even less in favour of the defence applying.

The only reasonably modern example of where it did apply is *ICI* v *Shatwell* (1965), where X and Y were two shotfirers who carried out testing in the open rather than from behind cover in breach of both statutory duties and their employer's instructions. They were injured but it was held that the employer was not liable as the employees knew of the risk and must be held to have consented to it. This is an unusual decision in that the employees had actually *created* the risk rather than agreed to run a risk created by their employer.

Time limit for bringing actions

Under the Limitation Act 1980, actions for personal injury or death must be commenced within three years of the date when the accident occurred. This period is subject to the following points:

1 Where the claimant only later knew of his or her right to bring an action (e.g. if only later did the claimant find out that the defendant was negligent) then the three-year period runs from when the claimant discovered this or ought reasonably to have done so.

2 The court has a discretion under s 33 to allow an action to proceed out of time where it is equitable to do so.

A more detailed account of these rules will be found in works on civil procedure.

Vicarious liability

In all the above cases we have been concerned with the employer owing a direct duty to the employee. It is also possible for the employer to be liable to the employee because of the negligence of another employee. This situation is known as one of vicarious liability; in other words, the employer is liable, not for his or her own negligence but for that of another. It can be met with in situations other than employment as where, for example, an employee driving a van whilst carrying out his duties injures a pedestrian by negligence. It can also apply to torts other than negligence.

A good example is *Lister v Romford Ice and Cold Storage Co. Ltd* (1957) (also discussed in Chapter 2), where an employer was held liable to pay damages to one employee, X, for the negligent driving of another employee, Y, which had injured X. The fact that X was the father of Y, although legally irrelevant, gave added interest to the case.

In order for an employer to be vicariously liable two conditions must be satisfied. First, the person who was guilty of negligence must be an employee of that employer. Thus, where the tort is committed by an independent contractor, the employee will not usually be liable, although in specific situations liability can arise for the actions of an independent contractor. One instance is where the employer specifically tells the contractor to perform a tort.

Example

A development company, W, knows that a particular piece of land does not belong to it but it wishes to lay a cable across the land and employs John, an independent contractor, actually to lay the cable. This act will be, by itself, a trespass and thus a tort and so W will be liable for the actions of John even though John is not an employee. John could also be sued directly by the owner of the land.

Secondly, the act must be one for which the employer was responsible. The traditional test was to ask whether the employee was performing an act authorised by the employer but doing so in an unlawful manner. This test, which was first suggested by *Salmond on Torts* (now in 21st edition, 1996), was adequate for cases of, for example, negligent driving of the employer's vehicles but was less so in cases of intentional wrongdoing. This point was made by the House of Lords in *Lister v Hesley Hall Ltd* (2001), where the claim was by two pupils at a boarding school for damages resulting from sexual abuse committed by wardens at the school. The employer was held liable and a new test laid down that the employer will be liable if there is a close relationship between the nature of the employment and the wrong. Lord Steyn, in applying this test, considered whether there was a duty owed to the victim by the employer. If so, there would be liability. On the facts here, there was, and so the employer was liable for the acts of the wardens.

▪ Liability of the employer to independent contractors

We have seen above that an employer is not usually liable for the acts of independent contractors, but is an employer liable to an independent contractor who has been injured in the course of working for the employer? The answer is usually that under the common law of negligence there is no duty but under the HSWA 1974, as we shall see, an employer does owe duties to those other than employees. However, where an independent contractor is working on premises occupied by the employer (although not necessarily owned by them) and is injured, then the employer may be liable for breach of the duty of care owed to all lawful visitors under the Occupiers' Liability Act 1957.

ACTIONS FOR BREACH OF STATUTORY DUTY

These are less common than actions under the common law of negligence. The distinction between them is shown by the following example.

Example

Emma works as a secretary for Jones and Co., a firm of solicitors. She is injured when she falls over a bottle of cleaning fluid, which had been carelessly left in the corridor by another employee, Margaret, a cleaner. Emma also suffers injury to her eyesight because of constant exposure to her computer screen and complains that Jones and Co. have failed to monitor the risk or give her proper training. The claim for damages resulting from her fall would be brought in the tort of negligence, whilst any claim resulting from injury to her eyesight could be under the general law of negligence but could also be for breach of statutory duty based on the employer's failure to comply with the Health and Safety (Display Screen Equipment) Regulations 1992 (SI 1992/ 2792). These regulations, which will be discussed in more detail later in this chapter, give a right of action the essence of which is that, because of the breach of a statute or a regulation made under a statute, an employee may claim damages. The interesting point is that the statute will usually impose criminal penalties for its breach and will not primarily be concerned with the possibility of a civil action, which is therefore something of a spin-off. The advantage of an action for breach of statutory duty is that the duty will usually be stricter than that at common law for negligence. (Incidentally, this is also an example of where the employer is not only directly liable to the employee (Emma) but also vicariously liable for the acts of another employee. Had Margaret been an independent contractor then the employer would not have been liable for *her* acts but would still have been liable to Emma for breach of the direct duty owed to her.)

How is it possible to tell whether a civil action can be brought for its breach? In *Groves* v *Lord Wimborne* (1898) it was held that breach of a statutory safety requirement would normally give rise to such an action, although this case concerned sheep on a ship and not employees. This general principle is subject to whether the statute itself gives any indication whether a civil action can be brought for its breach. Section 47 of the HSWA 1974 provides that breach of any of the general duties in ss 2–8 of the Act does not give rise to an action for breach of statutory duty but that regulations made under the Act are to be construed as giving rise to such an action unless the particular regulation states otherwise. The main regulations are those made as a result of EC initiatives in 1992 (known as the 'six pack'), which are explored more fully later in this chapter, and discussion will focus on these. However, it should be noted in passing that actions for breach of statutory duty under industrial safety legislation such as the Factories Act 1961 were, until they were repealed, very important. Of the six pack, only one, the Management of Health and Safety at Work Regulations 1992 (SI 1992/2051), excludes civil liability. Actions for breach of statutory duty are therefore possible under the other five.

Assuming that an action for breach of statutory duty is possible, the other question is what an employee has to prove to succeed. The following five points must be proved:

1 that the statutory duty is owed to the claimant. There is no difficulty with the six-pack regulations, which expressly apply to all employees, even temporary ones;

2 that the duty is placed on the defendant, i.e. in these cases, the employer. This is made explicit in the regulations;

3 that the defendant is in breach of the duty. The precise standard of care has yet to be clarified under all of the regulations but in *Stark v Post Office* (2000) it was held that the requirement to maintain equipment imposed in the Work Equipment Regulations is strict, which means that the employer is liable whether or not there was negligence;

4 that the damage suffered by the claimant was of the type which the statute was designed to prevent. So far there is little on how this will be applied under the regulations but the idea is that damages will not be available where the employee suffers an injury outside the scope of the statute;

5 that the injury was caused by the defendant's breach of the statute. The rules are the same as in the common law of negligence (see above).

In conclusion, actions for breach of statutory duty in health and safety matters are at a crossroads: the well-established rules under the old industrial legislation have gone and, although these actions still have a valuable part to play, how the courts will use them in relation to the six-pack regulations is as yet unclear.

ACTIONS FOR BREACH OF AN IMPLIED TERM IN THE CONTRACT OF EMPLOYMENT

In many cases a claim that the employer is in breach of the duty of care can also be brought as a claim that the employer is in breach of an implied term of the contract of employment to provide a working environment which is reasonably safe for the performance of contractual duties. In *Johnstone v Bloomsbury AHA* (1991) (the junior hospital doctor's case – see Chapter 5) the duty was treated as a contractual one and this was also so in *Waltons and Morse v Dorrington* (1997) (see also Chapter 5). However, there is usually no advantage in bringing the claim in contract and these two cases had features making them more suitable for contractual claims, as we shall see below.

The main reasons for bringing the claim in contract are as follows:

1 where economic loss is claimed, as in *Scally v Southern Health and Social Services Board* (see also Chapter 2), where the claim was for economic loss (loss here of

8

Health and safety

pension rights) rather than personal injury because a claim for pure economic loss cannot normally be brought in tort;

2 where the nature of the claim depends on the construction of the terms of the employee's contract, as in *Johnstone* (above), where the issue was that the term requiring a certain number of hours of work was alleged to have resulted in injury to the plaintiff;

3 where the claim is linked with another contractual issue, as in *Waltons* (above), where the claim was for constructive dismissal, which is based on contract (see Chapter 11), resulting from the alleged failure of the employer to deal adequately with complaints from the employee about exposure to cigarette smoke.

STATE BENEFITS FOR THOSE INJURED AT WORK

Only a brief account of these will be given here as the topic lies more in the area of welfare law. However, any discussion of the law on health and safety would be incomplete without some discussion of state benefits.

The system of state benefits for injuries should be seen as part of a larger system providing a comprehensive scheme of benefits when workers are unable to work through sickness or injury. The initial benefit claimed is statutory sick pay (SSP) (described in more detail in Chapter 7), which provides payments for the first 28 weeks of illness. It is not available to the self-employed, who must claim incapacity benefit. This is also the benefit claimed where an employee is no longer entitled to SSP (also explained in Chapter 7).

Where the employee has suffered longer-term disability as a result of an injury at work then a claim for industrial injuries disablement benefit may be made. The following points should be noted in relation to this type of benefit:

1 it is paid only to 'employed earners' and not to the self-employed;

2 it is paid when an accident is suffered as a result of an injury arising out of and in the course of employment;

3 it is also paid when certain prescribed diseases have been contracted;

4 there is no means test for payment;

5 it is not necessary to establish fault on the part of the employer or anyone else;

6 benefit is paid at set rates and therefore, where the employee has a claim for a substantial sum, an action for negligence will be necessary;

7 payment of benefit does not prevent the claimant from bringing an action for compensation for negligence or breach of statutory duty but any compensation awarded may be subject to compensation recovery under the Social Security (Recovery of Benefits) Act 1997;

8 the essence of the compensation recovery scheme is that any final out-of-court settlement or award by the courts in a personal injury action cannot be made until

the defendant has obtained from the Department for Work and Pensions (DWP) Compensation Recovery Unit a certificate giving the figure of total benefit paid to the claimant. The defendant must then deduct this sum from the damages paid and account for it to the DWP;

9 there are various specific benefits: industrial death benefit; disablement pension; constant attendance allowance; exceptionally severe disablement allowance; reduced earnings allowance; and retirement allowance.

THE HEALTH AND SAFETY AT WORK ACT 1974

Introduction

This Act has two aims, neatly stated in the Report of the Committee on Safety and Health at Work (1972) (known as 'the Robens Committee', after its chairman). This recommended that there should be a new, comprehensive Act dealing with health and safety at work and that 'the Act should contain a clear statement of the general principles of responsibility for safety and health, but otherwise should be mainly enabling in character'.

LAW IN CONTEXT
The background to health and safety regulations

The law on health and safety was, prior to the Health and Safety at Work etc. Act 1974 (HSWA 1974), in a state of some confusion. There was a mass of legislation, passed at different times and in response to different needs. There were some major pieces of legislation, such as the Factories Act 1961, the Mines and Quarries Act 1954 and the Offices, Shops and Railway Premises Act 1961. Added to this there were detailed regulations, with the result that health and safety legislation was, in the words of the Robens Report, a 'haphazard mass of law which is intricate in detail, unprogressive, often too difficult to comprehend and difficult to amend and keep up to date'. The committee therefore recommended (and this is one of the few committees to have its recommendations actually implemented virtually in full) that there should be a new Act (the HSWA 1974) which should contain a clear statement of the basic principles of safety responsibility. One particular merit would be that the Act would cover all activities at work, whereas the previous piecemeal system left many areas uncovered. Furthermore, the existing legislation led to a culture in which health and safety was regarded as a matter of following rules rather than a positive duty which concerned all employees.

An enabling Act

As the proposed Act was to consist of general duties only, there would be a need for detailed regulations and non-statutory codes of practice which would, the committee felt, be the most flexible and practical means of promoting health and safety at work.

8

Health and safety

The previous mass of regulations would be swept away and be replaced by these new regulations and codes.

Machinery of the Act

Although this will be considered in detail later, a mention at this point of the way in which the Act operates may help. As the above introduction has indicated, the emphasis is on self-regulation as far as possible. Nevertheless, the duties in the Act are backed by criminal sanctions and the Health and Safety Executive was set up with overall responsibility for health and safety matters. There is also a system of safety committees and safety representatives.

Main duties laid down by the Act

Section 2(1) sets out the overriding duty: 'It shall be the duty of every employer to ensure, as far as is reasonably practicable, the health, safety and welfare at work of all his employees.'

Section 2(2) then provides that this duty extends to the following matters, although this does not mean that these are the only matters covered:

1 the provision and maintenance of plant and systems of work that are safe and without risks to health;
2 arrangements for ensuring safety and absence of risks to health in connection with the use, handling, storage and transport of articles and substances;
3 the provision of such information, instruction, training and supervision as is necessary to ensure the health and safety at work of employees;
4 as regards any place of work under the employer's control, the maintenance of it in a condition that is safe and without risks to health and the provision and maintenance of means of access to and egress from it that are safe and without such risks;
5 the provision and maintenance of a working environment that is safe, without risks to health, and adequate as regards facilities and arrangements for welfare at work.

In each case these matters are qualified by the phrase 'reasonably practicable'.

'Reasonably practicable'

As with most other safety legislation, the Act does not impose strict liability on the employer. Instead, the above duties require them to do everything reasonably practicable to achieve them. However, where there are criminal proceedings for breaches of the Act, s 40 reverses the burden of proof so that the employer must prove that it was not reasonably practicable to comply with the duty.

The meaning of this phrase, which appeared in s 102(8) of the Coal Mines Act 1911, was considered in *Edwards* v *National Coal Board* (1949). The issue there was whether the NCB had done everything reasonably practicable to make secure a 'travelling road' along which a miner was walking. He had been killed when a large part of the side of the road had fallen and it was held that 'reasonably practicable' meant weighing the risks of an accident against the measures needed to eliminate them. Here, as the risk was considerable, the court would not be prepared to give much weight to considerations such as the cost of preventing them. Although Asquith LJ observed that reasonably practicable is a narrower term than 'physically possible', it does seem clear that it is wider than 'reasonable care' and thus it is wrong to import ideas from the common law of negligence into this Act, a point made in cases considered below.

To whom are the above duties owed?

The Act refers to 'employees' and these are defined by s 53 as those who work 'under a contract of employment or apprenticeship'. However, the Act also affects other persons, as we shall see below.

Other duties under the Act

Duties to those other than employees

Section 3(1) provides that employers have a duty to persons not employed by them (for example, independent contractors and members of the public) to conduct their undertaking so that they are not exposed to risks to their health and safety and this duty is extended by s 3(2) to self-employed persons. In *R v Associated Octel Ltd* (1996) the House of Lords held that the issue in cases brought under s 3 is 'whether the activity in question can be regarded as part of the employer's undertaking' (Lord Hoffmann). The defendants ran a chemical plant and used a specialist firm for repairs. Indeed, the contractor's eight employees were employed virtually full-time working on the defendants' site. One employee of the contractors was badly burned when, whilst he was cleaning a tank, a light bulb broke causing a bucket of highly inflammable acetone to ignite. It was held that the defendants were liable as the cleaning of the tank was clearly an activity which was part of their undertaking. The House of Lords rejected the view put forward in the earlier case of *RMC Roadstone Products v Jester* (1994), where the court had based its approach on the common law of vicarious liability. It had held that the employer was not liable for the acts of independent contractors and that undertaking here would mean the undertaking of the contractors unless the employer exercised control. This attempt to bring concepts from the common law of negligence into the HSWA 1974 was held to be wrong in *Octel*.

The question of risks was considered in *R v Board of Trustees of the Science Museum* (1993), which again shows a conscious break with the principles of the common law. An inspection showed that legionella bacteria in the cooling system of the museum could be dangerous to those outside the building. The museum's defence was that no one had actually been at risk and, in effect, argued that the same rule applied as in actions for negligence: resulting damage must be proved in addition to the breach of duty. The Court of Appeal held that this was wrong: the essence of s 3 is the *exposure* to risk, not necessarily harm resulting from it. Not only this, but the whole philosophy of the HSWA 1974 is that of preventing harm and thus it would be wrong to restrict s 3 to cases where harm has actually occurred.

8

Health and safety

Duties on controllers of premises

Section 4 places a duty on controllers of premises both to those who work there (other than employees, who are covered by s 2) and to those who use plant or substances provided for their use there. The duty extends to ensuring, so far as is reasonably practicable, that the premises, plant and substances are safe and without risks to health. This duty is outside the scope of employment law except for liability to independent contractors and it is of more significance where there are machines on the premises which the public can use, as in a launderette. The very existence of this duty is of interest in showing the scope of the HSWA 1974.

Duties in relation to emissions into the atmosphere

Section 5 imposes duties designed to control and reduce risks resulting from emissions into the atmosphere. This is another example of duties extending beyond the employment relationship. The duty is to use the best means for preventing emissions of noxious or harmful substances and, if any emissions do take place, to render any substances harmless or inoffensive.

Duties on the designer, manufacturer, importer or supplier of articles for use at work

These are laid down in s 6 and the aim is to ensure that, if possible, threats to safety from these articles are removed at a stage before they reach the workplace. The duty extends to four matters:

1 to ensure, so far as is reasonably practicable, that articles are designed and constructed so that they are safe and without risks to health;
2 to carry out such testing and examinations to comply with the duty in 1 above;
3 to ensure that persons who use the article are provided with adequate information about the use for which it was designed or tested, together with information on the conditions necessary both to use it safely and to dismantle or dispose of it safely;
4 to ensure that persons are also supplied with any revisions of information on the matters referred to in 3 above.

Duties laid on employees

Section 7, in line with the philosophy of the Act that safety is everyone's concern, provides that employees have a duty to take reasonable care for their own safety and that of others who may be affected by their acts or omissions at work. In addition, there is a duty to co-operate with others who have duties laid on them to enable them to fulfil *their* duties. Section 7 is obviously important where an employee refuses to use safety equipment provided (see above) and could be used as the basis of disciplinary proceedings against those who have acted in breach of safety rules and caused injury to themselves or others. Section 8 then provides that no person shall interfere with or misuse anything provided in the interests of safety.

Duty not to charge for anything done or provided under these duties

The final duty, set out in s 9, prevents an employer from charging employees for anything done or provided under the Act or any regulations under it.

Can a breach of the Act give rise to civil liability?

The answer is a firm 'no'. Section 47 provides that a breach of any of the above duties shall not give rise to civil liability for, for example, breach of statutory duty.

Liability of the employer

Given that the Act imposes criminal penalties, can a particular employer argue that they should not be liable to them as they had no knowledge of the breach in question? Under the general criminal law, it has been held that a company can be liable only for the acts of someone who can be regarded as its 'directing mind', but in *R v Gateway Foodmarkets Ltd* (1997) it was held by the House of Lords that this was not appropriate to prosecutions under ss 2 or 3 of the Act and the only issue is whether the company was in breach of the duty. Thus in *Gateway Foodmarkets* a company was convicted as the result of breaches of the Act in one of its supermarkets even though the head office had no knowledge of it. The emphasis then switches to the defence of 'reasonable practicability' and it may be that a company could escape liability for a breach of the Act if it had done everything reasonably practicable through training, instructions and other matters to ensure safety.

Administration and enforcement of the Act

This is carried out in three different ways:

1 by the Health and Safety Commission and Executive;
2 by enforcement powers of inspectors backed up by criminal penalties;
3 by safety policies, committees and representatives.

THE HEALTH AND SAFETY COMMISSION

repealed

The powers of the Health and Safety Commission (HSC) are set out in s 11. It is responsible to the Secretary of State for the Department for Work and Pensions and to other Secretaries of State for the administration of the HSWA 1974 throughout Great Britain. Its functions are:

1 to secure the health, safety and welfare of persons at work;
2 to protect the public generally against risks to health or safety arising out of work activities and to control the keeping and use of explosives, highly flammable and other dangerous substances;
3 to conduct and sponsor research; promote training; and provide an information and advisory service;
4 to review the adequacy of health and safety legislation and make proposals to the government for new or revised regulations and approved codes of practice.

8

Health and safety

The Commission has general oversight of the work of the Health and Safety Executive (HSE) and therefore, for example, issues an Enforcement Policy Statement to it (see below). It can delegate any of its functions to the HSE.

The Commission is often asked by the government to conduct inquiries into accidents, examples being the inquiry into 'Obstruction of Railway Lines by Road Vehicles' set up following the accident at Great Heck, near Selby, on 28 February 2001 and the Piper Alpha Oil Installation explosion on 6 July 1988.

THE HEALTH AND SAFETY EXECUTIVE

The Health and Safety Executive (HSE) also derives its powers from s 11 and is responsible for enforcing the Act as well as dealing with questions on safety matters and giving advice. For example, guidance is often sought on matters that should be contained in the safety policies of employers and on particular issues such as which employees who come into contact with VDUs are entitled to an eyesight test.

The Act is enforced by inspectors, who offer advice on safety matters but, in addition, have enforcement powers as follows:

1 Issue of an improvement notice (s 21). This is issued where the inspector believes that one of the statutory provisions is being contravened and that this is likely to be repeated or continued. The notice requires the person named to remedy the contravention within a stated period. An appeal against the issue of an improvement notice may be made to an employment tribunal.

2 Issue of a prohibition notice (s 22). This is issued where the inspector believes that activities are either actually being carried out or are about to be and which involve the risk of serious personal injury. The effect is that the activities cannot be carried out until the matters specified in the notice have been remedied. The notice may take effect immediately or after a stated time. There is the same right of appeal as with an improvement notice.

3 To seize articles or substances which are believed to threaten imminent danger of serious personal injury (s 25).

The number of enforcement notices issued (i.e. 1 and 2 above) was 14,891 in 2004/5 (full figures for 2005/6 are not yet available) as compared with 7,444 in 1996/7; most of these were in the manufacturing and construction industries (Annual Report of the HSC 2006).

In addition, there is a power of prosecution and the HSC, as mentioned above, has laid down guidelines for the HSE in deciding whether to prosecute. These include, for example, the need to target by singling out for prosecution any cases where serious risks were run and whether prosecution is proportionate to the seriousness of the offence. In 2005/6 there were 1,012 prosecutions with 741 convictions, with an average fine of £29,997 (in 2000/1 it was £6,250). In *R v F Howe and Son Ltd* (1999) the Court of Appeal held that the general level of fines was too low and any fine must be large enough to bring home the message that the object of prosecutions is to achieve a safe working environment and to protect the public. Even so, in this instance it held that a fine of £48,000 imposed on a small company was excessive, as more weight should have been given to the means of the company. In addition to fines there is the possibility of imprisonment and there have been five cases of this, all since 1996. Most prosecutions are brought against organisations, as it can be difficult to identify the person responsible, but there are a few cases of actions against individuals. The Offences and Penalties Report for 2000/1 notes that an additional sanction is the disqualification of company directors where there is a conviction under the Company Directors Disqualification Act 1986.

SAFETY COMMITTEES AND SAFETY REPRESENTATIVES

One of the objects of the HSWA 1974 is, as we have seen, to emphasise that safety is not just a matter of following external rules and then leaving it to the management. One way of achieving this is through the mechanism of safety policies, committees and representatives.

Section 2(3) obliges the employer to issue a general statement of health and safety policy together with arrangements for carrying it out.

Safety representatives are appointed either by trade unions where they are recognised by the employer (see Chapter 14) or, where there are no such trade unions, the employer must consult with elected employee safety representatives. (Note the use of employee representatives in a number of situations in employment law, for instance redundancy consultation.) Safety representatives appointed by trade unions can inspect premises, investigate both accidents and complaints from employees, consult inspectors and receive information. There is a right to time off work with pay to perform these duties. Elected employee representatives have similar powers but they have no right of inspection. Another difference is that while a minimum of two trade union representatives can ask the employer to establish a safety committee, and the employer must comply with such a request if made in writing, elected employee representatives do not have this right. However, they are allowed time off work to perform their functions, as with trade union representatives. The Act does not lay down any specific powers for safety committees and the HSC in issued guidance takes the view that arrangements to enable committees to fulfil their functions should evolve from discussion and negotiations with the employer. Thus it is the representatives who have more teeth.

LAW IN CONTEXT
Corporate manslaughter

The crime of manslaughter can be committed when a person is killed by gross negligence and in recent years a number of companies have been prosecuted for manslaughter arising out of accidents. Well-known instances have been the prosecution of P&O Ferries after the sinking of the *Herald of Free Enterprise* in 1987, and the attempted prosecution of Great Western Trains following the Southall train crash in 1997. The problem has been to pin down responsibility on particular individuals. In the *Herald of Free Enterprise* case there was insufficient evidence against any director or senior

8

Health and safety

manager and in the Great Western case the prosecution was brought against the company itself but the court held that the case could not proceed on this basis. The Corporate Manslaughter and Corporate Homicide Bill, which is currently going through Parliament and should become law later in 2007, will introduce a statutory offence of corporate manslaughter and aims to make it easier to bring prosecutions in these cases where a person has been killed and the members of senior management of a company are in breach of a duty of care as a result of the way in which certain activities of the company are managed or organised by its senior managers. The result is to introduce an element of 'senior management failure' as an ingredient of the offence. Although the impetus behind the introduction of this new offence may have been accidents involving the public it is clear that the duty of care will also be owed to employees.

EUROPEAN UNION REGULATIONS ON HEALTH AND SAFETY

The record of the EU in health and safety law has been one of initial inactivity followed by a sudden burst of energy in the late 1980s and early 1990s. The Framework Directive (89/391) was adopted in 1989 and this was followed by the adoption of a Directive on Working Time in 1993, which led to the Working Time Regulations considered in Chapter 7. So far as the Framework Directive is concerned, its adoption led to the adoption of six ensuing Directives which came into effect on 1 January 1993. In the UK these were implemented by regulations, known as the 'six pack'. It was said at the time that 'The European Directives have landed. They have changed the face of British health and safety law' (Redgrave, Hendy and Ford (1993), quoted in Bercusson (1996)). Some have subsequently been amended and reissued or indicated below.

The regulations are as follows:

Management of Health and Safety at Work Regulations 1992

The main duty imposed on employers is that of making assessments of risks to which employees are exposed at work. Regulations were subsequently made (SI 1999/3242) which amended the original ones (SI 1992/2051) by requiring employers to identify any special risks to which new or expectant mothers might be exposed while at work. The regulations are backed by a code of practice, which emphasises that safety arrangements should be integrated with the management system so that, for instance, when priorities are set any risks are, where possible, eliminated by the careful design of facilities.

Workplace (Health, Safety and Welfare) Regulations 1992

These (SI 1992/3004) set out general requirements for, e.g., temperatures, ventilation, lighting, facilities (e.g. toilets) and safe passageways. They are reminiscent of the old Offices, Shops and Railway Premises Act, which they replaced, although too close a comparison should not be drawn.

■ Provision and Use of Work Equipment Regulations 1998

These (SI 1998/2306) set out minimum standards for work equipment and require that, for example, equipment is suitable for its intended use and is maintained in good repair and that there is protection against hazards such as dangerous machinery.

■ Personal Protective Equipment (EC Directive) Regulations 1992

These (SI 1992/3139) require employers to provide suitable equipment, to ensure that it is properly used and to provide information on its use. (It would be interesting to see how a case such as *Bux* v *Slough Metals* (above) would fare under this.)

■ Health and Safety (Display Screen Equipment) Regulations 1992

Under these regulations (SI 1992/2792) employers have a duty to assess risks caused by use of VDUs and reduce them where possible and to provide proper accompanying equipment such as proper workstations.

■ Manual Handling Operations Regulations 1992

These (SI 1992/2793) require the employer to avoid the need, where possible, for manual handling where there are risks and, if it does take place, to ensure that there is a proper risk assessment and that risks are reduced to the lowest practicable level.

These regulations do not confer any civil liability beyond liability for breach of statutory duty (above).

LAW IN CONTEXT
Health and safety law: the future

In 2004, the Health and Safety Executive issued a paper to mark the 30th anniversary of the Health and Safety at Work Act which was entitled 'Thirty years on and Looking Forward'. This charts the changes which have occurred in the law since 1974 and looks forward. It draws attention to the main areas of policy listed in the first annual report: examples are asbestos, fire precautions, dust and the safeguarding of machinery. In 2003/4 the priority programmes included workplace stress, falls from height and health services. What immediately becomes clear is the change in the nature of health and safety at work, reflecting the switch from a manufacturing to a service-based economy. One particular area which, the report points out, is now much more prominent is occupational health and safety and this is part of the strategy for the HSC for 2010. On the other hand, traditional industries – agriculture and construction – account for two of the HSC's nine priority programmes. These are joined as priorities by the newer health-related problems of workplace stress and musculoskeletal disorders.

8

Health and safety

SUMMARY

This chapter looks at the ways in which an employer can be liable to its employees for breaches of health and safety laws and at the corresponding protection given to employees. As this is an area where a number of different legal rules interact, the distinction between civil and criminal liability is therefore stressed. In the field of civil liability detailed consideration is given to the recent cases on liability of the employer for breach of the duty to protect the employee from psychiatric illness caused by stress at work. The chapter also emphasises that health and safety legislation, although part of the criminal law, is about encouraging an atmosphere of safe working practices as much as criminal sanctions. Finally, the impact of the Corporate Manslaughter and Corporate Homicide Bill is considered.

QUESTION

Barry works in a bank in the City of London. He has a team of five but his deputy leaves and is replaced by a junior clerk. Barry complains to Terry, his line manager, that his workload is becoming excessive as he is now doing the work of two but Terry tells him that times are bad and there is no funding for anyone on the salary of a deputy. Barry then sees his doctor, who certifies that he is suffering from hypertension brought on by stress, but Terry simply says: 'Wait a year and then things may improve and we'll look at the situation again.' A week later Barry has a nervous breakdown.

Advise Barry on the possibilities of success in any claim against the bank.

FURTHER READING

James, P. and Walters, D. (2005) *Regulating Health and Safety at Work: an agenda for change?* Institute of Employment Rights: Liverpool. As its title suggests, this is an excellent book for ideas on how the law in this area, which has been neglected by academics, might develop.

Matthews, R. and Agercos, J. (2007) *Health and Safety Enforcement Law and Practice* (2nd edn), Oxford University Press: Oxford.

BIBLIOGRAPHY

Barrett, B. (2005) 'Employer's Liability after *Hatton* v *Sutherland*', 34 ILJ 182.

Bercusson, B. (1996) *European Labour Law*, Butterworths: London.

DTI, CBI & TUC (2005) *Work Related Stress* (booklet). DTI & HSE: London.

Freedland, M. (2006) *The Personal Work Contract*, Oxford University Press: Oxford (especially pp. 143–5 which look at the line of cases beginning with *Walker* v *Northumberland CC*).

Redgrave, A., Hendy, J. and Ford, M. (1993) *Health and Safety* (2nd edn), Butterworths: London.

Rubenstein, M. [2005] IRLR 250 (Commentary).

For further resources and updates please go to the Companion Website accompanying this book at **www.mylawchamber.co.uk/duddingtonemployment**

9 Discrimination law

INTRODUCTION

It is, these days, surprising to note how recently discrimination was embedded in employment relations and that the law did nothing to prevent it. A few examples will suffice.

On 3 December 1919 the Education Committee of the Rhondda Urban District Council passed a resolution that the 'engagements of married women teachers be terminated'. The reason was that newly qualified teachers coming out of training colleges were finding it difficult to find jobs and this would create a good number of vacancies. But clearly the council did not favour married women teachers anyway. In evidence Councillor Abel Jacobs, who proposed the resolution, said that when married women were temporarily absent this was most inconvenient as substitutes had to be found. Moreover, another councillor, Mr Harcombe, stated that in his view 'the employment of married women teachers was detrimental to schools'. The High Court, in *Price* v *Rhondda Urban District Council* (1923) had no difficulty in holding that the council had statutory authority to pass the resolution and so, one presumes, at least 57 employees (for Mrs Price brought the action of behalf of that number of her colleagues) had their employment terminated on the grounds of what was clearly sex discrimination. Two years later, in *Roberts* v *Hopwood* (1925) the scheme of the Poplar Council for paying equal wages to both men and women workers was stigmatised by Lord Atkinson in the House of Lords as being motivated by the 'eccentric principles of socialistic philanthropy, or by a feminist ambition to secure the equality of the sexes' and was of course declared unlawful. Indeed, it was not until 1955 that the government agreed to the principle of equal pay for like work in the non-industrial civil service (Davies and Freedland (1993), page 123) and many women workers had to wait until the Equal Pay Act came into force in 1975 to be given the right to equal pay for like work. Although these examples are drawn from the area of sex discrimination many other examples could be given of discrimination in the other fields now prohibited by law.

PREVENTION OF DISCRIMINATION OR PROMOTION OF EQUALITY?

This topic is sometimes known as 'equal opportunities' but the reason why this term is not used here is that it would imply that the subject matter of this chapter is concerned with equality. In one sense it is, in that the removal of discrimination should ensure greater equality. In another sense, though, there is a gulf between anti-discrimination law and equality as such. Equality, like all abstract concepts, is extremely difficult to pin down. A simple definition would be that it consists in treating everyone in the same way but we know that this is not possible in reality. For example, minors are denied certain legal rights, not in order to discriminate against them but to ensure that they are not taken advantage of. Nor can we say that opportunities are always equal because there will always be cases where some individuals have greater access to particular rights through factors such as birth, wealth and position; it may not be desirable but it is the case. This issue is explored in more detail below.

LAW IN CONTEXT
What should be the aim of discrimination law?

The simple answer, as indicated above, is that it should aim at equality. Thus, for example, in employment matters all applicants should be treated on their merits and preference should not be given to an applicant because of, for example, her sex or race. The essence of this approach, categorised by Fredman (2002) as equality as consistency, is that it is symmetrical in that it aims to treat everyone in exactly the same way. In this sense it is procedural and so, as Barnard and Hepple (2000) point out, it involves the removal of obstacles or barriers such as 'word of mouth recruitment or non job related selection criteria' (although they use the term 'equality of opportunity' to cover both equality as consistency and wider meanings of equality). However, on further examination it becomes apparent that if this aim was pursued then equality would be far from being achieved. For example, suppose that an applicant for a job was partially sighted and explained at the interview that in order to read documents she would need them to be in larger size type. If equal treatment is the absolute aim then the answer must be no, as this would go against the principle of equal treatment as she would be treated more favourably than other employees. Yet the practical result is that this applicant is denied the opportunity of a job. As Fredman points out, the equality as consistency principle in fact only requires that 'two similarly situated individuals be treated alike'. One could say that the emphasis in the UK is starting to move away from formal equality, as evidenced by the Equal Opportunities Commission's Annual Report and Accounts for 2005–6 which uses the phrase 'Women. Men. Different. Equal' and the phrase 'equality and diversity' is often used.

Collins (2003) divides into three the situations where there is in fact a deviation from the principle of equal treatment. These are:

- In particular cases different treatment is required such as that of pregnant women and of disabled persons to enable them to gain access to work and other opportunities.

- Equal treatment is not allowed where it would cause 'unjustifiable indirect discrimination' or 'disparate impact'.

- Where what Collins describes as 'preferential treatment for certain groups in particular circumstances' (generally known as positive discrimination) may be justified.

In each of these cases, on Fredman's principle, the equality as consistency principle is inapplicable as the two individuals are not 'similarly situated'. These situations will be considered in detail later in this chapter but, for now, it is worth pausing to ask, on the assumption that Collins's argument is correct, on what principle can discrimination law be said to rest. To put it simply, what can we replace equal treatment with?

A starting point is the analysis of approaches to equality made by Fredman (2002) into:

- *Equality as consistency,* as outlined above.
- *Equality of results* which requires that the end result shall be equal and aims at substantive equality. As Fredman points out, this goes beyond the 'equality as consistency' principle by recognising that apparently equal treatment can in fact reinforce discrimination because of previous or continuing discrimination. Equality of results is to some extent achieved through the concept of indirect discrimination or, to give it the name used in the USA, disparate impact. Thus Fredman gives the example, based on *Price* v *Civil Service Commission* (1977), of an upper age limit on entry to the civil service of 28. This observes formal equality in that results are clearly consistent as there is the same upper limit on entry for all. However, it will have a disparate impact on women as many women are taking a career break to start their families and, by the time they are ready to consider applying to enter the civil service, they will be past the upper age limit for entry. Therefore this rule was held to be discriminatory. However, Fredman argues that merely focusing on results can embed discriminatory practices. She gives the example of where, as a result of successful equality as consistency and equality of results, women are successful in breaking into, for example, senior posts previously held exclusively by men. Is all that has happened that women have conformed to male working patterns of, for instance, long working hours? In this context it is worth noting that the drive to 'family friendly policies' dealt with in Chapter 10, such as the right to request a flexible working arrangement, can be seen as promoting substantive equality.
- *Equality of opportunity* which, on one meaning, recognises that, once individuals have the ability to compete equally, then formal equality has been achieved. In effect it goes further than equality as consistency as it requires more than just procedural equality; but it does not go as far as requiring equality of results. It is not in fact entirely clear how the concept of equality of opportunity in this sense really differs from the other two meanings of equality discussed above and, as we saw, Barnard and Hepple appear to treat 'equality of opportunity' as a wider concept embracing other types of equality. For example, they see promotion of positive discrimination as promoting equality of opportunity.
- *A value driven approach.* This concept is put forward by Fredman as embodying a broad set of values which discrimination law should seek to promote. These comprise the primacy of individual dignity and, as she points out, the emphasis on dignity in the Charter of Fundamental Freedoms of the European Union (see Chapter 3) where chapter 1 is simply headed 'Dignity'. Barnard and Hepple add the value of fair participation in society as promoted by the fair employment legislation in Northern Ireland (see later in this chapter).

9

Discrimination law

→

The approach of UK law has been to focus on particular groups and to enact legislation that provides that if these groups are discriminated against in particular circumstances then they will have a right to a remedy. If a person does not fall within those groups then, even though they may not have been treated equally, they will not have any remedies. There is no concept either of positive discrimination, with one small exception, although, as we shall see, the impact of EC law may be bringing about a change here. Thus for the moment there is no duty in law to take steps to *promote* equality. Instead, the law is essentially reactive: it operates when there is a complaint of discrimination but does not allow steps to be taken to remove the causes of it. For example, if a firm has a very small number of women employees compared with men and it genuinely wishes to ensure a more equal balance between the sexes, it might advertise positions as open to female candidates only. However, if it did so it would be in breach of the law.

The fundamental issue goes beyond employment law and is concerned with what Allott (1980) has called the 'Limits of Law'. Just how far should the law go in actively promoting particular social goals? Which of these are suitable for legal promotion and which should be promoted by society through example, education, persuasion and other non-legal means? At its heart this is a question, not for the employment lawyer, but for society itself.

The present laws on discrimination borrow a great deal from US legislation, especially the Civil Rights Act 1964 and subsequent decisions of the US courts, in particular that of the Supreme Court in *Griggs* v *Dukes Power Co.* (1971), which paved the way for the concept of indirect discrimination which has done so much to extend the boundaries of the law. At the same time as the first legislation outlawing discrimination was being passed, the UK joined the EC and it is EC legislation which has been the driving force behind the later development of sex discrimination law, following the Directive on Equal Treatment (76/207). EC law has had an impact across the whole spectrum of discrimination law following the introduction of Article 13 into the EC Treaties by the Treaty of Amsterdam in 1997. This provided that the EC may take action against discrimination 'based on sex, racial or ethnic origin, religion or belief, disability, age or sexual orientation'. It was followed by a Directive (2000/43) dealing specifically with race equality and a general Framework Directive (2000/78) prohibiting discrimination on the grounds of religion or belief, disability, age or sexual orientation. Originally these had to be implemented by 2 December 2003 but there was an extension to December 2006 in respect of age and disability. As a result the following regulations were introduced:

1 the Employment Equality (Sexual Orientation) Regulations 2003 (SI 2003/1661), which came into force on 1 December 2003;

2 the Employment Equality (Religion or Belief) Regulations 2003 (SI 2003/1660), which came into force on 2 December 2003;

3 the Employment Equality (Age) Regulations 2006 (SI 2006/1031), which came into force on 1 October 2006;

4   the Race Relations Act 1976 (Amendment) Regulations 2003 (SI 2003/1626), which came into force on 19 July 2003;

5   the Disability Discrimination Act 1995 (Amendment) Regulations 2003 (SI 2003/1673), which came into force on 1 October 2004.

The effect of these changes has been not only to add two new areas of discrimination law but to alter the definition of indirect discrimination to bring it into line with the recently changed definition now applicable to sex discrimination and to alter the definition of harassment. Both of these topics are considered below.

In addition the effect of Article 14 of the ECHR must be borne in mind because, as explained in Chapter 3, it contains a very wide-ranging prohibition against discrimination but which is internal to the ECHR.

DISCRIMINATION LAW CLAIMS

In 2005/6 there were 14,250 claims under the Sex Discrimination Act; 17,268 under the Equal Pay Act; 4,103 under the Race Relations Act; 4,685 under the Disability Discrimination Act, 486 under the Employment Equality (Religion or Belief) Regulations 2003; and 395 under the Employment Equality (Sexual Orientation) Regulations 2003. These statistics all relate to cases where the relevant claim was the main claim.

Levels of compensation in 2005/6 for the three types of discrimination where the greatest number of claims were brought were:

■ sex discrimination: average award £10,807

■ race discrimination: average award £30,361

■ disability discrimination: average award £9,021.

SOURCES OF DISCRIMINATION LAW

As discrimination law is derived from a variety of legislative sources, the following list of the main sources may be helpful.

UK law

■ Sex Discrimination Acts (SDA) 1975 and 1986

■ Equal Pay Act (EqPA) 1970

■ Race Relations Act (RRA) 1976

■ Disability Discrimination Act (DDA) 1995

■ Employment Equality (Sexual Orientation) Regulations 2003

■ Employment Equality (Religion or Belief) Regulations 2003

■ Employment Equality (Age) Regulations 2006.

Note: Acts will be referred to by the above abbreviations in this chapter.

9

Discrimination law

The SDA and the EqPA form a single code dealing with discrimination on the grounds of sex.

EC legislation

EC Treaty (Rome) 1957, as amended by the Treaty of Amsterdam (1997).

Articles of the EC Treaty (Rome), as amended

- Article 13: discrimination.
- Article 141 (formerly 119 until renumbered by the Treaty of Amsterdam): equal pay.

Note: for the sake of clarity, all references in this chapter will be to Article 141 even where the case was decided under what was Article 119.

Main EU Directives

- 75/117 (equal pay)
- 76/207 (equal treatment)
- 92/85 (pregnancy)
- 97/80 (burden of proof in sex discrimination cases)
- 2000/43 (race discrimination)
- 2000/78 (Framework Directive).

European Convention on Human Rights

- Article 14.

Other sources

In addition, the International Labour Organization (ILO) introduced three Conventions dealing with discrimination (in 1958, 1965 and 1980) but they have no binding force. Even so, it was the ILO Convention No. 100 of 1951 which was influential in the framing of the EqPA 1970. Article 2 provides for the principle of equal remuneration between men and women for work of equal value and when the EqPA was passed the UK government felt able to ratify Convention No. 100, although it is interesting to note that the ECJ subsequently held that the Act should specifically include equal value as a head of comparison (see below).

REVIEW OF DISCRIMINATION LAW

As will be seen from this chapter, discrimination law is a complex subject partly because it has grown up piecemeal since the first legislation in this area, the Equal Pay

Act 1970. The government announced a review of discrimination law in February 2005, which has now produced its final report. The review focused on an analysis of the fundamental principles of discrimination law and, in particular, areas where there are inconsistencies in the present law.

Studying discrimination law

This is a complex subject, probably the most complex in the whole of employment law. However, there is a basic structure to the subject and, with few exceptions, each set of laws covering discrimination deals with the following:

- direct discrimination
- indirect discrimination (except in the case of disability discrimination)
- discrimination by victimisation
- discrimination by harassment
- situations where discrimination is permitted
- liability of the employer for discrimination
- remedies for discrimination.

The reader should ensure that he or she is familiar with how each of the above operates in relation to each form of discrimination.

Note: We begin our account of the detailed law on discrimination by looking at sex discrimination, but in some cases the law is the same for each type of discrimination and, when this point is reached for the first time in the discussion on sex discrimination, it will be dealt with for all types of discrimination.

SEX DISCRIMINATION

First, two preliminary issues will be considered:

To whom does the SDA 1975 apply?

Section 82(1) provides that the SDA 1975 applies to employment under either a contract of service or apprenticeship or a contract personally to execute any work or labour. Accordingly, the wider definition of employee applies and the SDA is not confined to those with an actual contract of employment. There are identical provisions in s 78(1) of the RRA 1976; s 68 of the DDA 1995; reg 2 of the Employment Equality (Sexual Orientation) Regulations 2003; reg 2 of the Employment Equality (Religion or Belief) Regulations 2003; and reg 2 of the Employment Equality (Age) Regulations 2006.

9

Discrimination law

When does it apply?

Section 6(1) of the SDA 1975 makes it unlawful to discriminate in the following ways:

1 in arrangements for deciding who should be offered employment (this covers all selection procedures including the interview);
2 in the terms on which employment is offered;
3 by refusing or deliberately omitting to offer employment.

In *Saunders* v *Richmond on Thames LBC* (1978) it was held that it is not necessarily discriminatory to ask a woman candidate at an interview different questions from those addressed to a man, provided that there is no discrimination in the interview process. Nevertheless, the effect of discrimination law is that it has become the practice to ask the same questions of each candidate and this is certainly the best practice.

Once the person is an employee then s 6(2) prohibits discrimination:

1 in the way in which she is afforded access to opportunities for promotion, transfer or training or to any other benefits, facilities or services or by refusing or deliberately omitting to afford her access to them;
2 by dismissing her or subjecting her to any other detriment. Although the legislation does not mention constructive dismissal it has been interpreted to include this.

Catherall v *Michelin Tyre plc* (2003) is a good example of the interaction between different areas of employment law and of the fact that dismissal in this context includes constructive dismissal. It concerned the situation where a disabled employee was given the choice between retirement on medical grounds or redundancy. The EAT held that this was a case of termination of employment as the employee was given no choice about whether employment was to be terminated but only a choice about the method of termination. In addition, it was held that where a redundancy selection procedure was operated so that there was a claim for constructive dismissal it would be open to a tribunal to hold that there was a dismissal within the DDA 1995.

The scheme of the SDA 1975 is to prohibit the following types of discrimination:

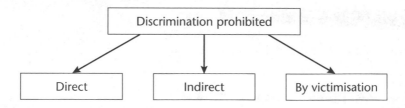

Discrimination on the grounds of marital status is also prohibited.

Direct discrimination

This is defined by s 1(2)(a) of the SDA 1975 as less favourable treatment of a woman on the grounds of her sex.

 The test is objective and intention to discriminate or motive is irrelevant. Thus in *James* v *Eastleigh BC* (1990) the council applied different ages to men and women for qualification to use the swimming pool free: 60 for women and 65 for men. This was held to be discriminatory, even though there had been no intention to discriminate. Nor can discrimination be justified by the payment of some other benefit. In *Ministry of Defence v Jeremiah* (1979) only men were required to do a particularly dirty job and this was held to be discriminatory, even though they were paid extra for the work. This decision has probably laid to rest the much criticised decision in *Peake v Automotive Products Ltd* (1978), where a practice of allowing women to leave work five minutes earlier than men was held not to be discriminatory, according to Denning MR, on the ground of chivalry. This was criticised as 'one redolent of all the values that the SDA had sought to lay to rest' (Wallington, 1978). In *Jeremiah*, Denning MR attempted to justify it on the alternative ground of *de minimis non curat lex* (the law takes no account of trifles), i.e. that five minutes is too small a time to worry about; but the case still remains a blot on the law.

Direct discrimination can also occur when women are treated less favourably because of generalised assumptions based on sexual stereotypes. In *Horsey v Dyfed CC* (1982) a woman was refused permission to go on a training course in Kent as her husband was employed in London and it was thought that she was unlikely to return. This view, based on the idea that women follow their husbands, was clearly discriminatory.

There must be a link between the alleged discriminatory act and the fact that the complainant was of a particular sex. This seems to be the explanation of *Bullock v Alice Ottley School* (1993), where there were different retirement ages for teachers and domestic staff (60) and maintenance staff (65). In practice the first group was largely female and the second entirely male. A claim under the SDA 1975 by an employee from the first group (who had to retire at 60) was rejected on the grounds that the different retirement ages were not discriminatory because there was nothing to stop men from applying for a job in the first group and women in the second. The groups had nothing to do with sex. Although this decision may be correct in theory, it does seem strange as applied in practice.

Dress codes and uniform at work

In *Schmidt v Austicks Bookshops* (1978) it was held that it was not discriminatory for women to be forbidden to wear trousers when there was a dress code for men also, albeit a different one. In *Smith v Safeway Stores plc* (1996) the Court of Appeal held that a prohibition on male employees wearing long hair whilst female employees were permitted to do so was not discriminatory as there were other rules applying to women too in that they had to have their hair tied back. (In the EAT it was held that this rule *was* discriminatory as it affected the employee's appearance outside work as well.) Phillips LJ held that a dress code which made *identical* provision for men and women would have an unfavourable impact, as where men as well as women were required to have 18-inch long hair, lipstick and earrings. Whilst this is doubtless true, it has also been argued that a dress code of the kind in *Schmidt* forces women to conform to an 'appropriate image of femininity' (McColgan, 2000, page 397). A more recent example is *Department for Work and Pensions v Thompson* (2004) which dealt with a complaint by an employee that a requirement that men should wear a collar and tie at work was direct sex discrimination. The claim succeeded before the tribunal partly because

9

Discrimination law

no similar requirement was placed on women. The EAT held that the wrong test had been applied by the employment tribunal and the correct test was whether the overall requirement to achieve a correct level of smartness could only be attained by requiring men to wear a collar and tie. (In passing, it is extraordinary to note that no fewer than 6,950 similar cases were lodged against the Department following this action and awaited a ruling pending the decision here.)

Indirect discrimination

The present definition of indirect discrimination was inserted into the SDA 1975 by the Sex Discrimination (Indirect Discrimination and Burden of Proof) Regulations 2001 (SI 2001/2660) as further amended by the Employment Equality (Sex Discrimination) Regulations 2005 (SI 2005/2467). It is contained in s 1(2)(b) of the SDA 1975.

Note: The same basic definition applies to race discrimination (s 1(1A) of the RRA 1976); sexual orientation (reg 3(1)(b) of the Employment Equality (Sexual Orientation) Regulations 2003); under reg 3(1)(b) of the Employment Equality (Religion or Belief) Regulations 2003: and reg 3(1)(b) of the Employment Equality (Age) Regulations 2006. There is, as mentioned above, no concept of indirect discrimination in the DDA 1995.

Section 1(2)(b) of the SDA 1975 provides that a person indirectly discriminates against a woman where:

> he applies to her a provision, criterion or practice which he applies or would apply equally to a man, but
> (i)   which puts or would put women at a particular disadvantage when compared with men,
> (ii) which puts her at that disadvantage, and
> (iii) which he cannot show to be a proportionate means of achieving a legitimate aim.

This definition of indirect discrimination is noteworthy for the following reasons:

1 It introduces a new test for measuring adverse impact. Previously the test was whether the provision, criterion or practice was a detriment to a considerably larger proportion of women than men. The reason for the change is to get away from over-reliance on statistical evidence.

2 The wording of the justification test is changed. The old test was to ask if the provision, criterion or practice was justifiable irrespective of sex. The new test (see (iii) above) aims to reflect the case law of the ECJ by introducing a test of proportionality.

In *British Airways v Starmer* (2005) the EAT held that a decision in relation to one employee can be a provision. Here the employee had requested that she be allowed to work 50% of full-time hours because of childcare responsibilities but her employers insisted that she should work 75%. The effect is that any employment decision, not necessarily in relation to a group but also in relation to an individual, can be challenged as indirect discrimination if it has an adverse impact. This is new, as the cases on indirect discrimination have previously been concerned with group discrimination. In *Hardys and Hansoms plc v Lax* (2005) the Court of Appeal in effect applied the proportionality principle to the old test of justification, and so this decision may be a useful guide to how the new provisions are interpreted. Pill LJ held that: 'The employer has to show that the proposal . . . is justified objectively notwithstanding its discriminatory effect. The principle of proportionality requires the tribunal to take into account the reasonable needs of the business'. In the end, though, it is for the tribunal to make its own decision. The court rejected the proposition that the band of reasonable responses test, which applies in unfair dismissal, should apply here, and this would certainly be incompatible with the new provisions.

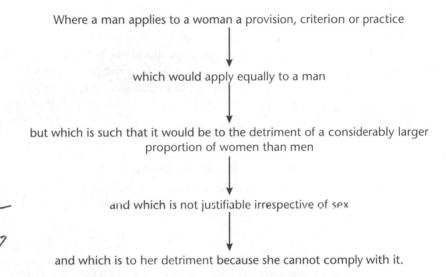

Where a man applies to a woman a provision, criterion or practice

which would apply equally to a man

but which is such that it would be to the detriment of a considerably larger proportion of women than men

and which is not justifiable irrespective of sex

and which is to her detriment because she cannot comply with it.

Each part of this definition will now be examined.

A provision, criterion or practice

This has changed from the previous wording of a 'condition or requirement' as it was felt that the previous wording was too narrow. For example, in *Perera v Civil Service Commission (No. 2)* (1983) identical wording in the Race Relations Act 1976 was held to mean that there must be an absolute requirement. The applicant, a Sri Lankan, had been refused promotion to a post for which he was qualified because criteria such as command of the English language had been taken into account. It was held that, as these were only criteria, their application was not in breach of the RRA 1976. The new definition, which mirrors US law, would mean that the court in a case such as *Perera* would take the criteria into account.

Would be to the detriment of a considerably larger proportion of women than men

This is the heart of the idea of indirect discrimination and is often known as 'adverse impact'. It has been used to attack rules that disadvantage particular groups of workers.

199

In *Price v Civil Service Commission* (1978) a rule of the civil service that applicants for executive officer grade posts had to be between the ages of 17 and 27 was held to be indirect discrimination against women, as fewer women than men could comply with the upper age limit because a larger number women of that age group were having, or bringing up, children. In deciding whether a considerably larger proportion of women than men can comply, the correct pool for comparison is often a crucial factor. This is demonstrated by *Jones v Manchester University* (1993), where an advertisement for a post of careers adviser stated that applicants, amongst other criteria, should preferably be between 27 and 35. The applicant, a mature graduate, was not considered, apparently because she was 46. The tribunal held that there was indirect discrimination as the pool was all mature students graduating after 25. Of this group the proportion of women under 35 was considerably smaller than the proportion of men. The Court of Appeal held that this was the wrong pool. The correct one should be all men and women suitably qualified and here there was no great difference between the number of women capable of satisfying the criteria. This was because the post was open to *all* graduates and not just mature ones. The effect of the decision is that applicants need to be careful in choosing the pool and must not narrow it artificially to suit their case (see diagram below).

The pool for comparison
(based on *Jones v Manchester University*)

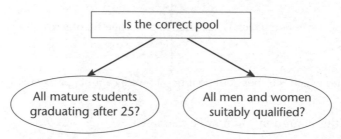

In addition, the question has arisen of what 'considerably smaller' means. Is it something that can be measured with mathematical precision? In *London Underground Ltd v Edwards (No. 2)* (1998) the Court of Appeal held that there was no set number below which the number would not be considerably smaller. Here a complaint that a considerably smaller proportion of women than men could comply with new shift patterns was found to be justified, because out of 2,000 men train drivers all could comply but one woman out of a total of only 21 could not comply. In the USA there has been some attempt by the courts to apply a rule that the success rate of those in the disadvantaged groups should not be more than 80% of those in other groups but there are strong arguments in favour of a broader approach. The concept of indirect discrimination has been applied in a variety of situations. In *Meade-Hill v British Council* (1995) it was held that a job mobility clause in a contract was discriminatory, as a higher proportion of women than men are secondary earners and thus a considerably greater proportion of women than men would find it difficult to move house. A setback was the decision in *Kidd v DRG (UK) Ltd* (1985), where a claim that women found it considerably more difficult than men to work full time because of domestic responsibilities was rejected and thus a challenge to a redundancy selection procedure which targeted part-time workers first failed. The Part-time Workers Regulations 2000 (see below) do not help here, as they do not give a right to insist on a return to work part-time; but the right to request a flexible working arrangement (contained in s 47 of the Employment Act 2002, and see Chapter 10) may assist.

The practice of the courts and tribunals in this area has not been entirely consistent. In *Home Office* v *Holmes* (1984) it was held that a refusal to allow a woman to return to work part-time after maternity leave was indirect discrimination, as she was a single parent and the EAT agreed with the finding of the tribunal that 'despite the changes in the role of women in modern society it is still a fact that the raising of children tends to place a greater burden on them than it does on men'. This decision did not, however, establish as a general principle that it is indirect discrimination to refuse to allow a woman to return to work part-time after maternity leave. Thus in *Greater Glasgow Health Board* v *Carey* (1987) it was held on the facts that a refusal to allow an employee to return to work after being on maternity leave was justifiable on the grounds of efficiency. The most which can be said is that, where an employer is faced with a request to return to work part-time after maternity leave, then reasons for any refusal need to be carefully considered. A blanket refusal on the grounds of company policy would be open to successful attack. However, the new rules on flexible working contained in the Employment Act 2002 will make a significant change here as they give an employee a right to ask their employer to consider a flexible working arrangement in circumstances which will include a return to work following pregnancy and this can include a change in working hours (see Chapter 10 for a fuller discussion of this).

Which is not justifiable irrespective of sex

The defence of justification is now governed by the proportionality test developed by the ECJ in cases such as *Bilka-Kaufhaus* v *Weber von Hartz* (1986). This states that the practice must be capable of justification by reference to a legitimate objective and that the means chosen must be appropriate and necessary to that end. Two cases on the identical provision in the RRA 1976 serve as good examples. In *Panesar* v *Nestlé Co. Ltd* (1980) it was held by the Court of Appeal that a rule which stated that no beards could be worn, thus excluding Sikhs from employment, was justifiable on hygiene grounds. In *Board of Governors of St Matthias CE School* v *Crizzle* (1993) the restriction of a post of headteacher to communicant Christians was justifiable in fostering the ethos of the school, even though a considerably smaller number of Asians were excluded by it.

Which is to her detriment because she cannot comply

This means that there must be some disadvantage to the complainant. Thus it is not a narrow term requiring, for example, financial loss. It is best examined in the context of harassment (see *Thomas* v *Robinson* (below)); but it also must be shown where the claim is for indirect discrimination. In *Gill* v *El Vino Co. Ltd* (1983) the practice at a wine bar of serving women customers sitting at tables whilst men were served standing was held to be discriminatory and the mere fact that customers were treated differently

9

Discrimination law

on grounds of sex was accepted as sufficient detriment. In *Thomas* v *Robinson* (2003) there was a single occasion of a racially insensitive remark, and the EAT held that, although a single incident can be enough to found a claim, there was always a need for detriment and here the applicant should have been cross-examined to establish if she had been upset by the remark. The EAT observed that there are some environments in which, undesirable though it is, racial abuse is taken and given 'in good part' and so detriment must always be shown.

Note: A significant difference between direct and indirect discrimination is that compensation for unintentional indirect sex discrimination is not automatically awarded. This is discussed in the section on remedies.

DISCRIMINATION BY VICTIMISATION

Discrimination by victimisation is defined by s 4 of the SDA 1975 as where a person is treated less favourably because she has brought proceedings under the SDA 1975 or the EqPA 1970; giving evidence is also covered. In the RRA case (under identical provisions) of *Aziz* v *Trinity Street Taxis* (1989) it was emphasised that the victimisation provisions apply only where the acts of victimisation were connected with actions under the relevant discrimination legislation. A taxi driver thought that he was being treated badly by a taxi drivers' association of which he was a member and that their actions amounted to race discrimination. To assist in his claim for race discrimination he tape-recorded conversations with others whom he thought agreed with his views. He was then expelled from the association for doing so but it was held that the reason for the expulsion was not because of race discrimination but because of the tape recordings (see also page 244 where this topic is discussed in the context of equal pay).

DISCRIMINATION ON GROUNDS OF MARITAL STATUS

This is defined as discrimination by s 1(2) but cases on it have been rare. One recent example is *Chief Constable of Bedfordshire* v *Graham* (2002), where a woman police officer was refused promotion to inspector as her husband was the divisional commander. The reason was that in any criminal proceedings against him she would not be a compellable witness for the prosecution. It was held that this was not sufficient to justify refusing her the post. An earlier example is *Skyrail Oceanic* v *Coleman* (1981), where a woman was dismissed from her job on her marriage.

HARASSMENT

Harassment is an aspect of direct discrimination which was first clearly developed by the Court of Session in *Porcelli* v *Strathclyde Regional Council* (1986). The test was whether the harassment was on the grounds of sex. If it is not then there could still be an action at common law for a breach of an implied term of the contract (see

Chapter 4) or for the tort of negligence (see Chapter 8). In addition, an employee could leave and claim constructive dismissal although in that case the amount of compensation is subject to a statutory ceiling, whereas it is not in the case of contract or tort. In *Porcelli* the applicant was employed as a laboratory technician and was subjected to degrading treatment by two male technicians in an eventually successful attempt to force her to leave. Suggestive remarks were repeatedly made to her, the men deliberately brushed against her, her personal belongings were interfered with, information was withheld from her and equipment was put in a place where she could not reach it. It was held that this would not have happened if she had been a man and her claim succeeded. The fact that she had to transfer to another school was sufficient detriment. The problem was that the Court of Session in this case did not actually hold that sexual harassment was in itself sex discrimination. Thus in *Stewart v Cleveland Guest (Engineering) Ltd (1994)* the EAT ruled that a woman who resigned from her job as a result of 'pin ups' had not resigned as a result of sex discrimination as a man might well have found them offensive.

Given that there are now statutory definitions of harassment one might think that this issue is of mere historical interest. However, the statutory definitions will not cover all cases of harassment and so this case law is still relevant, as will be explained below.

The statutory definitions of harassment were introduced as a result of the implementation by the UK of specific Directives (2000/43 – Race Equality; and 2000/78 – Employment Equality) issued under the Equal Treatment Directive. This was amended in 2000 so that it now contains a definition of harassment which provides that it is unwanted conduct related to any of the grounds stated in Article 1 (see below) which takes place with the purpose and effect of violating the dignity of a person and of creating an 'intimidating, hostile, degrading, humiliating or offensive environment'.

▊ Definition of harassment

Note: This is one of the areas where there is a virtually standard definition although it is important to note that the definition in the DDA 1995 is slightly different – see below. Therefore, the definition in the SDA 1975 will be given but the case law will be drawn from any appropriate area of discrimination law.

Section 4A of the SDA 1975 provides that a person subjects a woman to harassment where:

    (a) on the ground of her sex, he engages in unwanted conduct that has the purpose or effect
        (i) of violating her dignity, or
        (ii) of creating an intimidating, hostile, degrading, humiliating or offensive environment for her, or
    (b) he engages in any form of unwanted verbal, non-verbal or physical conduct of a sexual nature that has the purpose or effect
        (i) of violating her dignity, or
        (ii) of creating an intimidating, hostile, degrading, humiliating or offensive environment for her, or

9

Discrimination law

(c) on the ground of her rejection of or submission to unwanted conduct of a kind mentioned in paragraph (a) or (b), he treats her less favourably than he would treat her had she not rejected, or submitted to, the conduct.

It will be seen that there is a distinction between sexual harassment (s 4A(a)) and harassment of a sexual nature (s 4A(b)). IDS *Employment Law Brief* 790 has some examples of the distinction between the two types: male workers placing tools on a shelf which is too high for a female worker to reach would amount to sexual harassment. A newspaper insists on sending a female work experience student to a strip club to research a feature despite her telling them that she is uncomfortable with the idea; she finds the experience distressing and humiliating. This would be harassment of a sexual nature.

In addition, s 4A(2) provides that conduct shall be regarded as having the effect mentioned in (a) or (b) only if, having regard to all the circumstances, including in particular the perception of the woman, it should reasonably be considered as having that effect. The DTI Explanatory notes for the Employment Equality (Sexual Orientation) Regulations 2003 and the Employment Equality (Religion or Belief) Regulations 2003 stated that this test is partly objective and partly subjective, with the subjective element being the perception of the woman. It is designed to reflect the decision in **Driskel v Peninsula Business Services** (2000) where the EAT held that, although the ultimate judgement is an objective one, the tribunal can take into account the 'employee's subjective perception of the subject matter of the complaint as well as the understanding, motive and intention of the alleged discriminator'.

We now have, for the first time, a specific definition of harassment and this area will no longer, except in the situations mentioned below, be left to be decided by case law using the definition of direct discrimination.

Note: There are identical provisions in the following:

- s 4A(3) of the SDA 1975, prohibiting discrimination on the ground that a person intends to undergo, is undergoing or has undergone gender reassignment;

- s 3A of the RRA 1976, prohibiting harassment on grounds of race or ethnic or national origins;

- reg 5 of the Employment Equality (Sexual Orientation) Regulations 2003, prohibiting harassment on grounds of a person's sexual orientation;

- reg 5 of the Employment Equality (Religion or Belief) Regulations 2003, prohibiting harassment on grounds of a person's religion or belief;

- reg 6 of the Employment Equality (Age) Regulations 2006, prohibiting harassment on grounds of a person's age.

However, s 3B of the DDA 1995, which prohibits harassment on grounds of a person's disability, uses the words 'relates to' instead of 'on the grounds of'. The difference between these two phrases may be significant. McColgan (2005, page 58) points out that the phrase 'on the grounds of', which is used in all other areas, may not include harassment of the kind experienced by the claimant in **Pearce v Mayfield School** (2001)

and as a result it may be that the legislation does not adequately implement the Directive. In *Pearce* a claim of harassment by a lesbian teacher who had been forced to resign from her school because of abuse from pupils was held not to fall within the SDA 1975 as it could not have been shown that she was treated less favourably than a gay male teacher who might have been taunted on account of his sexuality. In the words of the present law, the courts were not prepared to hold that she was harassed *on the grounds of* her sexual orientation. On the other hand it could be argued that the harassment certainly '*related to*' her sexual orientation.

It is arguable that there are areas of harassment which are not covered by the statutory definitions. These are as follows:

- Harassment on the grounds of colour or nationality as neither of these are expressly mentioned in the definition of harassment on the ground of race. However, in virtually all cases this will also count as harassment on the grounds of race, ethnic or national origins, which are covered.

- Harassment which comes within the situations mentioned above where the harassment may not be held to be on 'the ground of' where a person who is not of the relevant group would also have been harassed. (See *Stewart* v *Cleveland Guest (Engineering) Ltd* (1994) and *Pearce* v *Mayfield School* (2001).)

The result is that the courts may still have to develop the common law on harassment.

The Race Discrimination Directive uses slightly different language and states that harassment is conduct which violates the dignity of a person and which creates 'an intimidating, hostile, degrading, humiliating or offensive environment' and this was adopted by the regulations which came into force in 2003 as the model for the definition of harassment in cases of discrimination on the grounds of disability, sexual orientation, and religion or belief. It will be seen that there are slight and puzzling differences between the definitions, in that the definition as applied to harassment on grounds of sex simply requires the conduct to *affect* dignity whereas the definition for the other areas requires the conduct to *violate* dignity, which seems to make harassment more difficult to prove. On the other hand, the list of what can constitute a harassing environment is longer in the general definition rather than the definition applicable to sexual harassment. Why not have the same definition?

In *Reed and Bull Information Systems Ltd* v *Stedman* (1999) it was held that the question of whether the complainant suffered harassment is subjective but where a woman appears to be unduly sensitive then the question is whether she has made it clear that she takes exception to such conduct. Accordingly, what may be harassment to one person may not be so to another.

One issue that probably remains unresolved is whether it is necessary to find a male comparator. In *British Telecommunications plc* v *Williams* (1997) the EAT held that sexual harassment, if proved, would always amount to sex discrimination, as the conduct is itself gender specific. The Court of Appeal rejected this view in *Smith* v *Gardner Merchant Ltd* (1998), where it was held that there was still a need to show that the act was sex-based. This means that where an act is indeed offensive to a woman then it still will not be sexual harassment if a man would not have been harassed by it.

9

Discrimination law

205

The solution may lie in legislation and indeed a Private Member's Bill on Dignity at Work was promoted in the 2001/2 session of Parliament which would make harassment and bullying at work unlawful. This is surely the solution because, although harassment on sexual, racial or disability grounds is repugnant, other forms of harassment are equally unpleasant. Such legislation would, however, need careful drafting.

The Protection from Harassment Act 1997

This is an appropriate place to consider the effect of the Protection from Harassment Act 1997 on employment law. This Act was not originally passed to deal with employment situations but with curbing stalking. Harassment itself is not defined by the Act except that it must be a course of conduct (s 1(1)), and so one act cannot suffice. Under s 1(3) an act of harassment may constitute an offence unless it was lawfully and reasonably done to prevent a crime; and, by s 7(2), harassment includes alarming another or causing that person distress and it may consist of speech alone. Section 1(2) provides an objective test for *mens rea*: that a person ought to know that his conduct amounts to harassment if a reasonable person in possession of the same information as is possessed by that person would think that it amounted to harassment. Breach of the Act can lead to either criminal penalties (s 2) or, by s 3, civil remedies in an action for damages for a statutory tort, which can include damages for anxiety caused by the harassment and financial loss. Section 3(4) allows applications to be made for injunctions to restrain acts of harassment.

The Act is discussed in relation to harassment in discrimination law as it is an obvious alternative remedy in this situation. However, the impact of the Protection from Harassment Act 1997 can also be felt in the following areas of employment law where it can provide an alternative course of action:

- the employer's duty to take reasonable care for the health and safety of employees, whether this is founded on contract or tort, including liability for psychiatric injury at work;
- an action for constructive dismissal by an employee.

A good example of where the Act has been applied in an employment situation is *First Global Locums v Cosias* (2005). Here a former employee (X), who had been dismissed for gross misconduct, was restrained by injunction from harassing former fellow employees. X was prone to mood swings and his behaviour was aggressive; and, when he was dismissed as a result, he threatened to have another employee killed. Another example is *Green v DB Group Services (UK) Ltd* (2006) which illustrates the interaction between the Protection from Harassment Act and other forms of liability. A bank employee was subjected to what the court called a 'relentless campaign of mean and spiteful behaviour' by fellow employees but there was no one major incident. The court held that this fact did not bar a claim and one needed to look at the cumulative effect. Accordingly, the employer was liable:

- under the Protection from Harassment Act 1997;
- for the acts of the employees under vicarious liability;

■ for a breach of the duty of care owed by employers to employees, as the employer did not take adequate steps to protect their employee from what was going on, especially as she had raised it at her appraisal.

However, in many cases one employee will be alleging harassment by another employee but will seek to make the employer liable. Thus the question is whether an employer can be vicariously liable for the statutory tort created by s 3.

The question of vicarious liability was considered by the Court of Appeal and the House of Lords in *Majrowski* v *Guy's and St Thomas's Hospitals* (2006). Majrowski was employed as a clinical audit co-ordinator and alleged that whilst working in this post he was bullied, intimidated and harassed by his departmental supervisor because he was gay. He claimed that the hospital was vicariously liable for the manager's breach of statutory duty under the Protection from Harassment Act 1997. (No action was available to him at that date under discrimination law as the events occurred before the Employment Equality (Sexual Orientation) Regulations 2003 were in force.) The House of Lords held that in principle there could be vicarious liability for breaches of a statutory obligation for which damages can be awarded. In the case of actions for breach of statutory duty arising out of this Act, the 'close connection test' was applied: the employee's wrongful act must be so closely connected with what he is authorised to do that it could rightly be regarded as a mode, albeit an improper one, of doing it (see Lord Steyn in *Lister* v *Hesley Hall* (2001), Chapter 8).

Having established that there could be vicarious liability under the Protection from Harassment Act 1997, Lord Nicholls then gave guidance as to what could constitute harassment itself: there is, he said, a boundary between conduct which is unattractive and even unreasonable and conduct which is oppressive and unacceptable. In deciding where this boundary is to be drawn, courts will have in mind that irritations, annoyances, even a measure of upset, arise in everyday dealings and for liability to arise the misconduct must be sufficient for criminal liability under s 2 of the Act. In *Green* v *DB Group Services* (2006) Owen J helpfully divided the elements which must be proved to constitute harassment as conduct:

(a) occurring on at least two occasions (this requirement thus rules out an action based on one incident as in *Banks* v *Ablex Ltd* (2005));

(b) targeted at the claimant;

(c) calculated, in an objective sense, to cause distress;

(d) which is objectively judged to be oppressive and unreasonable.

The result is that there is now a powerful new weapon to deal with workplace bullying which has the following advantages over other roughly parallel causes of action in this area:

■ Liability is strict and so there is no need to establish negligence nor that the claimant suffered injury.

■ Actions under this Act will cover serious cases of bullying where previously the only remedy was a claim for constructive dismissal.

impact lowered

see Recent Cases

9

Discrimination law

- There is no statutory defence that the employer took all reasonable steps to prevent harassment as there is in discrimination law.

- An injunction can be obtained under the Act to restrain the harassment, as in *First Global Locums* v *Cosias* (above).

- Damages can be awarded for anxiety falling short of injury to health, an advance on the present common law position.

- The limitation period in actions brought under s 3 of this Act is six years, whereas under the Limitation Act 1980 there is, of course, a three-year period for actions for personal injury.

POSITIVE DISCRIMINATION

This is allowed only in limited circumstances under ss 47 and 48 of the SDA 1975, where access to facilities for training may be afforded to women only where, at any time in the previous 12 months, the number of women employed in the particular work in Great Britain for which training is offered was nil or comparatively small. It is also lawful to encourage women to take advantage of opportunities for doing that work. Section 48 applies to training by employers and s 47 to training by other bodies. In addition, it is lawful under s 47(3) to run courses specifically for those returning to employment after having spent time discharging domestic or family responsibilities.

There is a similar provision in ss 37 and 38 of the RRA 1976 except that it refers to 'proportions' who are in particular work and there is no reference to 'domestic responsibilities'. There are similar provisions in the Employment Equality (Sexual Orientation) Regulations 2003 (reg 26), the Employment Equality (Religion or Belief) Regulations 2003 (reg 25) and the Employment Equality (Age) Regulations 2006 (reg 29). In each case the situation which allows training is where it reasonably appears to the person doing the act that it prevents or compensates for disadvantages linked to sexual orientation (or religion or belief or age). There is no provision specifically allowing positive discrimination in disability legislation but, as we shall see, some of the provisions of the DDA 1995, especially those imposing a duty on an employer to make reasonable adjustments, do amount to positive discrimination.

It may be that EC law in this area will move further as a result of the insertion in the EC Treaty of a new Article 141(4), which allows Member States to maintain or adopt measures providing for specific advantages to make it easier for underrepresented sexes to pursue careers. This is a radical departure from previous thinking and it has the potential to take discrimination law forward into a new era of actually *promoting* equality. In *Badeck* (2000) the ECJ ruled that measures intended to give preference to women in areas of the public services where they were underrepresented were not in breach of the Treaty, so long as they did not give automatic preference to women candidates. In *Abrahamsson* (2000), however, it was held that Swedish Regulations were contrary to the Treaty as they *required* university appointments to be from the underrepresented sex. In *Lommers* v *Minister van Landbouw* (2002) the Dutch Ministry of Agriculture had a policy of making subsidised nursery places available only to female employees except in emergencies and this was held not to breach EC law, provided that the policy was interpreted to make nursery places available on the same terms to men who are single parents. This decision of the ECJ is noteworthy in upholding a policy which would be certainly not be adopted in the UK and a future source of developments is undoubtedly positive discrimination. However, there are limits as to how far EC law will go. In *EFTA Surveillance Authority* v *Kingdom of Norway* (2003) the EFTA Court, applying the Equal Treatment Directive, which is a part of EC law that is also applicable in the EFTA area, held that a decision of Oslo University to reserve all 20 posts for doctoral research grants for women was in breach of the Directive. The imposition of quotas and reserved places without any room for flexibility went beyond what is permissible.

LAW IN CONTEXT
Affirmative action in Northern Ireland

One part of the United Kingdom where positive discrimination, under the name of affirmative action, is in place is Northern Ireland. The reason is, of course, the perceived discrimination by Protestants against Roman Catholics. This is well documented and dates from the setting up of the Northern Ireland state in 1921. Elliott (2000) quotes Sir Basil Brooke (later Lord Brookeborough and Prime Minister of Northern Ireland) in 1933, speaking of the number of Protestants who employed Roman Catholics and urging them to: 'wherever possible to only employ good Protestant lads and lassies'. This advice was clearly heeded so that as late as 1991 Roman Catholics with the same educational qualifications were twice as likely to be unemployed as Protestants (Fair Employment Commission, 1995). It is fair to say that in recent years the position has improved: for example, the Fair Employment Monitoring Report (2004) shows that, by comparison with the sectors monitored in 1990, the Roman Catholic share of the workforce has increased by 5.9% although the actual growth in the total Roman Catholic workforce since then was only 0.8%. Moreover, given that historically there was considerable discrimination against Roman Catholics in the public sector (see Elliott (above) who quotes the case of even a telephonist at Stormont being transferred on account of her religion (page 389)), the public sector workforce was in 2004 made up of 58% Protestant and nearly 42% Roman Catholics.

It was felt necessary to address the previous discrimination by what was called 'affirmative action'. The first legislation was the Fair Employment Act 1976 and the legislation regarding employment is now contained in the Fair Employment and Treatment (Northern Ireland) Order 1998 (SI 1998/3162 (N.I. 21)). Article 4 defines affirmative action as action designed to secure fair participation in employment matters by members of the Protestant and Roman Catholic community by the adoption of practices which encourage participation and the modification or abandonment of practices which restrict or discourage it. Article 5(3) provides in effect that anything done in furtherance of the policy of affirmative action does not breach the principle of equality of opportunity between members of different religious groups. It has been remarked (McCrudden, 1992) that the concept of affirmative action as set out above is 'remarkably indeterminate' and, apart from the notion of 'fair employment', is not

→

defined. However, there are specific instances in the order where affirmative action is allowed: inviting applications from underrepresented groups, training schemes (art 72) and negotiated redundancies (art 73).

The thrust of this part of the legislation is to eliminate religious discrimination against groups (in practice Roman Catholics) rather than to give specific rights to individuals. Individuals do indeed have rights not to be discriminated against on religious grounds in art 2 but these are put in the same terms as other existing UK legislation. Affirmative action clearly looks at the wider picture. Employers are held responsible for promoting 'fair participation' where there are disparities in the employment of particular religious groups, even where there is no proof that there has been actual discrimination. Hegarty (1995) mentions an instance of the legislation in practice when the Fair Employment Commission (the predecessor of the Equality Commission) placed advertisements in newspapers specifically inviting applications from members of the Protestant community. However, once applications had been received there would be no requirement to give preferential treatment to Protestants.

It is impossible to assess the precise effect of the legislation as the increase in employment participation by Roman Catholics has been achieved against a background of a lessening of antagonism in religious matters generally. However, the increase in Roman Catholic participation must surely owe something to the climate created by the regulations and their predecessors.

PROOF OF DISCRIMINATION

Assuming that discrimination has taken place, the following issues arise:

How is it proved?

Note: This is one of the areas where there is a virtually standard definition although it is important to note that the definition in the DDA 1995 is slightly different – see below. Therefore the definition in the SDA 1975 will be given but the case law will be drawn from any appropriate area of discrimination law.

The proof of discrimination can be difficult because, although it may not be too awkward to show less favourable treatment, this will have to be on the ground of sex or other prohibited grounds.

Example

Jane is interviewed for a post as a teacher. At the interview she is told that 'we do not usually have women teachers here, you know' and she is not appointed, even though she is the only candidate who holds special qualifications in the main subject which is to be taught. She has been treated less favourably but how can she prove that this was on the ground of her sex? The school may say that, for instance, her performance at the interview did not show any real enthusiasm for the job.

The position is now made easier by the Sex Discrimination (Indirect Discrimination and the Burden of Proof) Regulations 2001 (SI 2001/2660), which are now incorporated into the Sex Discrimination Act 1975 by s 63A. Once the claimant proves facts from which the court could conclude, in the absence of an adequate explanation from the respondent, that there has been an act of discrimination then the court shall uphold the claim unless the respondent proves that he has not committed the act. (It should be noted that the same rules on the burden of proof are applied to other forms of discrimination mentioned in this chapter.) Section 63A to some extent builds on the approach of the Court of Appeal in *NW Thames RHA v Noone* (1988) that where the applicant shows less favourable treatment in circumstances which are consistent with discrimination then the tribunal may infer that there has been discrimination unless the employer shows that this was not so. In *Igen v Wong* (2005) the Court of Appeal emphasised that the Burden of Proof Regulations require tribunals to go through a two-stage investigation:

1 The claimant must prove facts from which the tribunal can conclude that, in the absence of a reasonable explanation, discrimination has occurred.

2 Once this initial burden has been discharged, the respondent must prove that it did not commit the act of discrimination.

The first case to consider the effect of the Burden of Proof Regulations 2001 was *Barton v Investec Henderson Crosthwaite Securities Ltd* (2003). Here it was held that the regulations pose the question whether 'it is necessary for the respondent [the employer] to prove, on a balance of probabilities, that the treatment was in any sense whatsoever due to sex' and thus the tribunal must 'assess not merely whether the respondent has proved an explanation for the facts from which such inferences can be drawn, but further that it is adequate to discharge the burden of proof on the balance of probabilities that sex was not any part of the reason for the treatment in question'. There is no doubt that this interpretation goes further than might have been anticipated in throwing the burden of proof on employers. However, in *Chamberlin Solicitors v Emokpae* (2004) the EAT looked at the guidelines in *Barton* (above) and slightly amended them. According to the EAT in this case, it now reads: 'it is necessary for the respondent to prove, on a balance of probabilities, that the treatment was *not significantly influenced* . . . by grounds of sex' (emphasis added). The EAT made the interesting point that the Equal Treatment Directive does not require the eradication altogether of gender in the decision-making process but merely its downgrading. *University of Huddersfield v Wolff* (2004) is at least a useful guide in dealing with cases where discrimination is alleged simply because a person is treated less favourably than another person of a different sex, race, sexual orientation or religion or belief. To put it simply: a woman and a man apply for the same job and the man gets it. Is this enough to throw the burden of proving that there was no discrimination onto the employer? The EAT answered no. There must be some connection between the less favourable treatment and sex or other reason. In legal terms, the question is one of causation. This is helpful but it does not take us far enough: what sort of evidence is needed to put the burden on the employer? The effect of these decisions is discussed by Cunningham (2006) who feels that the effect is that they will operate unfairly on employers and that the reversed burden of proof has created a general duty on employers to 'act with transparent rationality at all times'.

Note: Identical provisions are contained in: s 54A of the RRA 1976; s 17 of the DDA 1995; reg 29 of the Employment Equality (Religion or Belief) Regulations 2003; reg 29 of the Employment Equality (Sexual Orientation) Regulations 2003; and reg 37 of the Employment Equality (Age) Regulations 2006.

The need for a comparator

Unlike the EqPA 1970, neither the SDA 1975 nor the RRA 1976 require that an actual comparator be established. This is because the Acts use the phrase 'treats or *would treat*' (emphasis added) (see s 1 of both the SDA 1975 and the RRA 1976). Instead, there is simply the need to show that the treatment is less favourable than would be given to either an actual or a hypothetical comparator. Although this avoids the difficulties which have arisen with the EqPA 1970, it has thrown up problems of its own. One is that dismissals for pregnancy were not in breach of the SDA 1975 as there could be no male comparator, although this problem has largely been solved (see Chapter 10). Another is in the area of discrimination on grounds of sexual orientation (above). It is noteworthy that in the DDA case of *Clark* v *Novacold* (1999) the Court of Appeal held that in disability cases the comparison should be with an able-bodied person and that less favourable treatment is shown merely by the fact that the disability prevented the person from doing the work. This case rescued the law on the DDA 1995 from becoming enmeshed in possible comparisons between a disabled person and one who was sick but not disabled under the DDA. In *Balmoody* v *UK Central Council for Nursing, Midwifery and Health Visiting* (2002) the Court of Appeal held that the construction of a hypothetical comparator was a question of law to be determined by the tribunal in each case.

Genuine occupational qualifications

Section 7 of the SDA 1975 sets out the genuine occupational qualifications (GOQs) which, if proved, will give a defence to an action under the SDA. These are exhaustive and are as follows:

1 Where the essential nature of the job calls for a man (or woman) for reasons of physiology (excluding physical strength or stamina).

2 Where being a man (or woman) is essential for reasons of authenticity in dramatic or other performances.

3 Where the job involves physical contact with men (or women) where they might reasonably object to it being carried out by a person of the opposite sex.

4 Where the holder of the job is likely to work in circumstances where men (or women) are likely to object to the presence of a person of the opposite sex as they are in a state of undress or using sanitary facilities.

5 Where the employee is expected to live in a private home and objection might be taken to the employment of a man on the grounds of either the degree of actual

contact with others in the home or the knowledge of intimate details of such a person's life which the job entails.

6 Where the employees live in premises provided by the employer and the premises are normally occupied by members of one sex and there are no separate sleeping facilities for members of the opposite sex and it would not be reasonable to expect the employer to provide them.

7 Where the job is in a hospital, prison or other establishment for persons requiring special care and attention who are all of the same sex and it would not be reasonable to employ women.

8 Where the holder of the post provides personal welfare or education services to individuals which can be most effectively provided by a man (or woman).

9 Where the job is in a country where by law the duties could not be performed by a woman.

10 Where the job is one of two to be held by a married couple.

This list has, perhaps because of its detail, caused few difficulties of interpretation. One example is *Etam* v *Rowan* (1989), where the EAT agreed that a job in a woman's clothing shop could come within (3) above. However, the defence failed because of the provisions of s 7(4). These state that none of the GOQs apply where there are sufficient male employees who are capable of carrying out the duties and whom it would be reasonable to employ provided that the numbers are likely to meet the employer's future likely needs without undue inconvenience. In *Etam* v *Rowan* there were sufficient female employees to do the job. A more recent example is *Chief Constable of West Yorkshire* v *A* (2002), where the question was whether the need for police officers to carry out intimate body searches was a bar to the employment of a transsexual: it was held that it was not, as the number of such searches was in practice so low.

Is the employer vicariously liable for acts of discrimination committed by employees?

Note: This is one of the areas where there is a virtually standard definition although it is important to note that the definition in the DDA 1995 is slightly different – see below. Therefore the definition in the SDA 1975 will be given but the case law will be drawn from any appropriate area of discrimination law.

Section 41(1) of the SDA 1975 provides that an employer is liable for acts committed by employees in the course of employment. This is known as vicarious liability, as the employer has not committed discrimination himself but is liable for what others have done. Clearly, where the employer issues discriminatory instructions or has discriminatory practices the employer is directly liable, but s 41(1) is important where there is an allegation of sexual harassment. Is the employer liable in such cases? Section 41(3) provides a defence where the employer can prove that all reasonably practicable steps were taken to prevent employees from discriminating. The problem in relation to sexual and racial harassment cases in particular has been that the worse the acts of

9

Discrimination law

harassment, the more difficult it may be to establish that they were committed in the course of employment. This was recognised in *Jones* v *Tower Boot Co. Ltd* (1997), where acts of racial harassment had consisted in violent acts, including branding the employee with a hot screwdriver, and there was also verbal abuse. On a traditional view, the employer would not have been liable for these as they fell right outside the course of employment. This would, however, mean that the employee would have no remedy. Thus the Court of Appeal held that the phrase 'course of employment' had to be given a 'purposive interpretation' in line with the spirit of the Act, which meant that the words should bear the same meaning as in everyday speech. Accordingly, the employers were liable. What is the position where the acts are committed by persons who are not employees? In this case the only way in which the employer can be liable is if it can be found that he or she was in some way *directly* liable. This occurred in *Burton and Rhule* v *De Vere Hotels* (1997), where waitresses at a dinner were exposed to racist jokes by a speaker. Although the speaker was not employed by the management, so that s 41(1) was inapplicable, it was held that the manager should have ensured that the waitresses were taken from the room if there was a risk of subjection to harassment. In practice it will be very difficult to ensure that this is always done and one wonders if the effect of these two cases is to take us some way along the road to strict liability for employers in cases of harassment on sex, race or disability grounds.

Note: An identical provision is found in: s 32 of the RRA 1976; s 58 of the DDA 1995; reg 22 of the Employment Equality (Religion or Belief) Regulations 2003; reg 22 of the Employment Equality (Sexual Orientation) Regulations 2003; and reg 25 of the Employment Equality (Age) Regulations 2006.

Post-employment discrimination

Can a former employee bring an action for discrimination against the former employer in respect of matters occurring after the termination of employment? In *Relaxion Group* v *Rhys Harper; D'Souza* v *Lambeth LBC; Jones* v *3M Healthcare* (2003) it was held that s 6(2) of the SDA 1975 and similar provisions of the RRA 1976 and the DDA 1995 do not apply only when there is a contract of employment but also when the contract has ended but there is a substantive connection between the discriminatory acts and the employment relationship. One example here was that in *Rhys Harper* where the complaint related to a failure to investigate a claim of sexual harassment properly after the complainant had left employment. There was an obvious connection between this and the employment relationship (see also *Woodward* v *Abbey National plc* (2006)). Future claims can be based on statute as s 20A of the SDA 1975 applies the prohibition against discrimination on grounds of sex to a situation where the relationship (i.e. of employment) has come to an end.

There are similar provisions in: s 27A of the RRA 1976; s 16A of the DDA 1995; reg 21 of the Employment Equality (Sexual Orientation) Regulations 2003; reg 21 of the Employment Equality (Religion or Belief) Regulations 2003; and reg 24 of the Employment Equality (Age) Regulations 2006. However, decisions such as those in *Rhys Harper* are a useful guide as to when an employer may be liable.

REMEDIES FOR DISCRIMINATION

Note: the same basic scheme of remedies is used in the other cases of discrimination with modifications as indicated.

Individual actions

Complaints must be presented by employees or ex-employees within three months of the act complained of, but where the discrimination is continuing then time runs from when the act ends. The remedies as set out in s 65 of the SDA 1975 are as follows:

Compensation

The basic principle is that discrimination claims should proceed as actions for the tort of breach of statutory duty: ss 65(1)(b) and 66(1) of the SDA 1975; ss 56(10)(b) and 57(1) of the RRA 1976; s 17A(3) of the DDA 1995; regs 30(1)(b) and 31(1) of the Employment Equality (Sexual Orientation) Regulations 2003; regs 30(1)(b) and 31(1) of the Employment Equality (Religion or Belief) Regulations 2003; and regs 48(1)(b) and 39(1) of the Employment Equality (Age) Regulations 2006. Thus the fundamental principle is that compensation is awarded to place the claimant in the position she would have been in had there been no unlawful discrimination. In *Essa v Laing Ltd* (2004) the Court of Appeal held, by a majority, that the test to be applied when assessing compensation is not one of reasonable foreseeability but of whether the harm arose naturally and directly from the act of discrimination. This claim was for injury to feelings as a result of racist abuse at work, following which the employee left and never returned. He also lost interest in his amateur boxing career and felt unable to look for other work. The employers claimed that, on the facts, the employee had overreacted and thus they should not be liable for all the loss but the court held that, as the loss flowed from the act of discrimination, they were. However, there appears from the judgments to be some doubt as to whether this test should be applied in all cases of discrimination and further clarification is awaited in future cases.

Compensation can be awarded for both financial loss and for non-pecuniary losses such as psychiatric damage and injury to feelings and of aggravated damages. In *Scott v Inland Revenue Commissioners* (2004) the Court of Appeal emphasised that aggravated damages are different from damages for injury to feelings. Aggravated damages are intended to be awarded where there is conduct which is high-handed, malicious, insulting or oppressive.

In *BT v Reid* (2004) the Court of Appeal held that an award for injury to feelings in a race discrimination claim could include an element for the time taken to resolve the original complaint, and that an award of aggravated damages can reflect the fact that, as happened here, the employee who had made racist remarks was promoted whilst the investigation into the complaint was continuing. Thus the awards made by the tribunal of £6,000 for injury to feelings and £2,000 aggravated damages were allowed to stand.

In addition, exemplary compensation based on punishment of the respondent for anti-social behaviour may be awarded although the circumstances in which this may be so are not clear. In *Kuddus* v *Chief Constable of Leicestershire* (2002) the House of Lords held that an award of exemplary compensation can be awarded if the conduct of the public authority merits this. This, of course, leaves unclear whether it can be awarded in actions against private bodies.

Compensation for unintentional indirect discrimination

Compensation where indirect discrimination is unintentional is subject to a different formula which applies to all cases of discrimination except on grounds of disability where there is no indirect discrimination. The formula requires that it would be just and equitable to order compensation and that the tribunal is satisfied that the power to make a declaration and a recommendation is not an adequate remedy in the circumstances: s 65(1)(b) of the SDA 1975; s 56(1) of the RRA 1976; reg 30(2) of the Employment Equality (Sexual Orientation) Regulations 2003; reg 30(2) of the Employment Equality (Religion or Belief) Regulations 2003; and reg 38(2) of the Employment Equality (Age) Regulations 2006.

Order declaring the rights of the parties

In practice this is almost always granted along with another remedy, usually compensation, and so is of little practical significance.

Recommendation

A recommendation may be made that the respondent takes specified action aimed at reducing or obviating the adverse effect on the complainant of the discrimination complained of. However, a tribunal can only make a recommendation affecting others in the same position as the claimant, such as a recommendation that the employer revise its recruitment procedures. Thus, in *Noone* v *North West Thames RHA (No. 2)* (1988) the employer was found to have rejected a job application on racial grounds and it was held that the tribunal could not recommend that the employer should dispense with the statutory advertisement procedure so that the field would be narrowed. This was because it would affect other potential candidates.

In practice, the orders and recommendations described above are hardly ever awarded and in 1998 the Commission for Racial Equality proposed that in relation to recommendations and the RRA 1976 (which contains identical provisions) there should be a wider power to make recommendations regarding any of the employer's practices and procedures which have been at issue. The Equal Opportunities Commission (EOC) has proposed that tribunals should be given power to order re-employment.

◼ Collective enforcement of discrimination legislation

The legislation on sex, race and disability discrimination all provided for bodies with various powers to police the legislation and act in a strategic capacity: the Equal

Opportunities Commission (EOC); the Commission for Racial Equality (CRE); and the Disability Rights Commission (DRC). These are all to be merged into the Commission for Equality and Human Rights (CEHR) which was established by the Equality Act 2006 and which will also oversee the legislation prohibiting discrimination on the other grounds: sexual orientation, religion or belief, and age. In particular, s 8 of the Equality Act requires the CEHR to: promote understanding of, and encourage good practice in relation to, equality and diversity; promote equality of opportunity; promote awareness and understanding of rights under the equality legislation; and work towards the elimination of unlawful discrimination and harassment. It is expected that the CEHR will work towards the harmonisation of existing legislation on discrimination.

Even though the existing bodies will soon cease to function the CEHR will take over their powers and so consideration of some instances of what the existing bodies can do is still useful. They have powers to, for example, conduct investigations, take action against discriminatory advertisements, and seek injunctions to restrain persistent cases of discrimination. They have also sought judicial review where it was believed that, for example, UK legislation was in breach of EC law. The most spectacularly successful example of this, in the case of the EOC, was the decision in *R v Employment Secretary, ex parte EOC* (1995) that the rule which at that time stated that part-time employees had to wait five years before bringing an unfair dismissal claim compared with two years for full-time employees was indirectly discriminatory as a far higher proportion of part-time employees were women. This led to the removal of the differential limits. The EOC also provides information and advice and works in general to promote equal opportunities. The CRE has similar powers and examples of its work, taken from recent reports, are the elimination of discrimination in education and training, the development of racial equality guidance in youth justice cases and looking at measures to combat the discrimination and poor access to services experienced by racial minorities in rural areas.

The Disability Rights Commission (DRC) was set up by the Disability Rights Commission Act 1999 with similar powers and duties to the EOC and the CRE. It is also responsible for other legislation, such as the Special Educational Needs and Disability Act 2001. Among its activities are a helpline, a disability casework service, the giving of policy advice to the government, and the support of cases in tribunals. An interesting example of its work is given in its 2001 Review. A mobility impaired lady in her eighties was accused of damaging the block of flats where she lived with her motorised wheelchair. She was sent a £60 bill for the damage and she feared that she would have to move out. The intervention of the DRC resulted in an admission that her wheelchair had not caused the damage and she received an apology and £600.

DUTIES OF PUBLIC BODIES

Section 84 of the Equality Act 2006 inserts a new s 76A into the SDA 1975, which imposes a specific duty on public bodies to promote equality of opportunity between men and women; and s 83 inserts a new s 21A into the SDA 1975, which prohibits

9

Discrimination law

public bodies from discriminating in the exercise of their functions. Specific duties on public bodies, which will be set out in detail in regulations, will include identifying gender inequality goals and showing the actions by which public bodies must propose to implement them. This area is considered further in the particular context of race discrimination.

SEXUAL ORIENTATION

The courts held that neither the SDA 1975 nor the then EU legislation applied to discrimination on the ground of sexual orientation. Thus in *Grant v South-West Trains* (1998) it was held by the ECJ that there was no discrimination against a female employee who was refused travel concessions for her lesbian partner. As the condition applied to both men and women employees, it was not based on sex, as a male homosexual would also have been refused the concession. The question of sexual harassment has arisen in cases where male homosexuals or lesbians have been harassed on account of their orientation and here the issue has been one of comparison (see *Pearce v Mayfield School*, above).

However, discrimination on the ground of sexual orientation is now prohibited by the Employment Equality (Sexual Orientation) Regulations 2003. Regulation 2(1) defines discrimination on grounds of sexual orientation as where a person is discriminated against on grounds of orientation to the same sex, the opposite sex, or both. The definition of indirect discrimination in reg 3(1) follows that in the legislation on sex discrimination by providing that it occurs where a provision, criterion or practice which would be applied to a person not of the same sexual orientation puts a person of that sexual orientation at a particular disadvantage and it is not a proportionate means of achieving a legitimate aim.

There are different detailed provisions in reg 7 dealing with when there can be a genuine occupational requirement allowing discrimination. In the case of sexual orientation, it arises in two cases:

1 Where being of a particular sexual orientation is a genuine and determining occupational requirement. The employer must show that it is proportionate to apply the requirement in the particular case and either the person to whom it is applied does not meet it or the employer is not satisfied, and it is reasonable for him not to be satisfied, that the person meets it.

2 Where the employment is for the purposes of an organised religion and the employer applies a requirement relating to sexual orientation either to comply with the doctrines of that religion or because of the nature of the employment and the context in which it is carried out, so as to avoid conflicting with the strongly held religious convictions of a significant number of that religion's followers. The employer must show that either the person to whom it is applied does not meet it or the employer is not satisfied, and it is reasonable for him not to be satisfied, that the person meets it.

In *R (on the application of Amicus – MSF section and others)* v *Secretary of State for Trade and Industry and Christian Action Research Education and others* (2004) the Employment Equality (Sexual Orientation) Regulations 2003 were challenged on the ground that they were not compatible with either the Framework Employment Directive or the European Convention on Human Rights.

The High Court held that the regulations were compatible but the court made a number of interesting observations:

■ Regulation 7(2), (the exception allowing discrimination where being of a particular sexual orientation is a genuine and determining occupational requirement) is compatible with the Directive even though it applies not only where the person does not meet the requirement as to sexual orientation but also where it is reasonable for the employer 'not to be satisfied' that the person meets it. The effect is that the exemption applies where the employer reasonably believes that the person does not meet it even though there is no direct evidence that this is so. The reason is that this avoids the employer having to ask intrusive questions as to the orientation of a person although the employee is safeguarded by the provision that any belief by the employer must be reasonable.

■ Regulation 7(3), which contains a specific exemption from the prohibition on discrimination where the employment is for 'the purposes of an organised religion', is a narrower formula than appears in the Religion or Belief Regulations, which refer to employment for 'the purposes of a religious organisation'. Thus employment as a teacher in a faith school is likely to be covered by the Religion or Belief Regulations but not the Sexual Orientation ones.

Discrimination against those who have undergone gender reassignment

In *P v S and Cornwall CC* (1996) it was held that dismissal of a transsexual who was about to undergo gender reassignment was in breach of the Equal Treatment Directive. The ECJ held that the Directive applied not only where there was discrimination on the basis of a person being of one or the other sex but also where the discrimination is based on the *particular* sex of a person. In doing so they seemed to get away from the need to make comparisons which had prevented the law from outlawing discrimination on the grounds of sexual orientation but this further step was not taken. However, the decision in *P v S* might only have protected those employed by the state or emanations of the state (see Chapter 2) (although in *Chessington World of Adventures Ltd v Reed* (1998) it was applied to private sector employees). The decision in *P v S and Cornwall CC* (1996) led to an amendment to the SDA 1975 (s 2A) coming into force on 1 May 1999 which specifically prohibited discrimination on the ground that a person 'intends to undergo, is undergoing or has undergone gender reassignment'. In addition, harassment on these grounds is prohibited by s 4A(3) of the SDA 1975 which came into force on 1 October 2005. There is no prohibition of indirect discrimination but, as the decision in *Chessington World of Adventures Ltd* v *Reed* (1998) expressly

Discrimination law

9

applied the then SDA to cases of gender reassignment, it is possible to argue that the prohibition of indirect discrimination in the SDA applies here. There are genuine occupational qualifications which allow discrimination on limited grounds laid down in ss 7A and 7B of the SDA 1975 but these do not apply when the person has obtained a full gender recognition certificate. These cover the following:

- where the job entails intimate physical searches authorised by statute
- work in a private home
- where there is shared accommodation and reasonable objection could be taken to the holder of the post sharing accommodation and facilities with the other sex
- where the job entails providing vulnerable individuals with personal services and in the reasonable view of the employer they cannot be provided by a person undergoing gender reassignment.

RACE DISCRIMINATION

This is governed by the RRA 1976 and in many ways the scheme is the same as for the SDA 1975. Indeed, a number of examples in the preceding pages have been from race discrimination law.

Definition of race discrimination

Section 1(1) of the RRA 1976 provides that the Act applies to discrimination on racial grounds which are defined by s 3(1) as grounds relating to colour, race, nationality or ethnic or national origins. Racial group is defined as any group defined by reference to the above grounds. In *Redfearn v Serco Ltd t/a West Yorkshire Transport Service* (2006) the EAT considered the interpretation of the phrase 'racial grounds' in *Showboat Entertainment Centre v Owens* (1984) where it was held that racial grounds covers any reason or action which is based on race. In *Redfearn,* a bus driver who was a BNP candidate for the local council and who drove buses where up to 80% of his passengers were of Asian origin was dismissed when he was elected. The tribunal had held that the dismissal was on health and safety grounds as there was a fear for his safety but the EAT differed and held that the health and safety grounds were influenced by racial considerations. The Court of Appeal held, however, that the dismissal was not on racial grounds. Mummery LJ held that a dismissal was not on racial grounds just because the circumstances included 'a relevant racial consideration' i.e. the policies of the BNP, to which the employee belonged, on racial matters. Therefore the reasoning in the *Showboat* case is not authority for saying that the term 'racial grounds' covers *any* case where the discriminatory act was significantly influenced by racial considerations, even where that race was that of a third party.

Two questions arise:

What is an ethnic group?

In many cases this will be obvious, but what of Sikhs? They are not the inhabitants of a particular country but there seems to be no doubt that any reasonable person would regard them as an ethnic group. In *Mandla v Dowell Lee* (1983) the House of Lords held that they were and Lord Fraser held that to constitute an ethnic group the group must regard itself and be regarded by others as having certain characteristics, including:

(a) a long shared history; and

(b) its own cultural tradition.

In addition, he regarded the following criteria as relevant, although clearly not essential:

■ a common geographical origin or descent from common ancestors

■ a common language, literature and/or religion

■ community.

Jews have been held to constitute an ethnic group (*Seide v Gillette Industries Ltd* (1980)) and also gypsies (*Commission for Racial Equality v Dutton* (1989)). Somewhat controversially, it was held in *Dawkins v Environment Department* (1993) that Rastafarians are not an ethnic group because they have only been identifiable for about 60 years.

What is the meaning of nationality and of national origins?

An instructive case is *Northern Joint Police Board v Power* (1997), where it was held that there was no discrimination on racial grounds when a complaint of discrimination was brought by Scots against English. England and Scotland were held to be part of one nation, Britain, but it was also held that there could be discrimination in this type of case on grounds of national origin, as England and Scotland were once distinct nations. In *Gwynedd CC v Jones* (1986) the EAT held that there could be no discrimination on the grounds of not being able to speak Welsh, as this in itself was not a determining factor in this particular case.

■ Genuine occupational qualifications

The Race Relations Act 1976 (Amendment) Regulations 2003 (SI 2003/1626) provide for a general exemption from the RRA whenever being of a particular race or ethnic or national origin is a genuine occupational qualification. However, as this implements the Race Directive it may not apply to discrimination on grounds of colour or nationality, as this phrase, which is in the RRA 1976, does not appear in the Directive.

Section 5 of the RRA 1976 sets out the following specific genuine occupational qualifications (GOQs) which, if proved, will give a defence to an action under the RRA:

1 the persons of a particular racial group are needed for reasons of authenticity in a dramatic or other performance;

2 the job involves working as a model and persons of a particular racial group are needed for reasons of authenticity;

9

Discrimination law

3 the job involves work in catering and persons of a particular racial group are needed for reasons of authenticity;

4 where the holder of the job provides persons of a particular racial group with personal services which can most effectively be provided by persons of that racial group.

However, as under the SDA, s 5 of the RRA 1976 states that none of the GOQs apply where there are sufficient employees of that racial group who are capable of carrying out the duties and whom it would be reasonable to employ on them provided that the numbers are likely to meet the employer's future likely needs without undue inconvenience.

The RRA 1976 deals with terms and conditions including pay

The difference is simply that under sex discrimination law there are two pieces of legislation: the SDA 1975 and the EqPA 1970. In race relations law there is only the RRA 1976.

Positive obligations on public bodies

Following a review by the CRE in 1998 which recommended that there should be a positive duty on all public bodies to promote equal opportunity and good race relations, the MacPherson Report into the murder of Stephen Lawrence gave an added impetus to the perceived need to combat 'institutional racism'. This resulted in the Race Relations (Amendment) Act 2000, which makes it unlawful for a public body to discriminate in areas not covered by the 1976 Act. Therefore, activities such as law enforcement are now subject to the duty not to discriminate and all public bodies must work towards the elimination of discrimination. This involves, for example, monitoring the number of applicants for jobs against the number shortlisted and the number appointed. There are now similar provisions in other discrimination legislation: see s 76A of the SDA 1975 and s 49A of the DDA 1995. In addition there are specific prohibitions on discrimination by public bodies. However, in *Commissioners of Inland Revenue v Morgan* (2002) the EAT held that the term 'institutional racism' should not form part of a finding by an employment tribunal as there is no offence of a body being institutionally racist. Therefore the tribunal was wrong to hold that there was 'institutionalised racism' in the solicitors' department of the Inland Revenue.

DISCRIMINATION ON GROUNDS OF RELIGION OR BELIEF

The Employment Equality (Religion or Belief) Regulations 2003 cover discrimination on the grounds of religion, religious belief and similar philosophical belief (reg 2(1)). The original definition of religion and belief in these regulations was 'any religion, religious belief or other philosophical belief'. This did not make it clear whether a *lack of* religion and/or belief was covered so that, for example, an atheist would be able to claim as well as a believer. In line with the symmetrical approach of discrimination law one would have thought this to be the case anyway and this is now confirmed by the amendment made to the Religion or Belief Regulations by s 44 of the Equality Act 2006. The effect is to protect not only those with a religion and/or belief from discrimination but those who are discriminated against on the ground that they lack a religion and/or belief. The full amended definition provides that:

(a) religion means any religion;

(b) belief means any religious or philosophical belief;

(c) a reference to religion includes to lack of religion;

(d) a reference to belief includes to lack of belief.

One interesting point which Rubenstein (2004) draws attention to is whether the phrase 'lack of belief' could cover someone who is discriminated against on the ground of 'their weakly held view', i.e. who is 'unsure'. For example, suppose that a teacher in a church school was dismissed as it was felt that her own faith had become tepid and so she could not communicate the faith of the school to the students?

Genuine occupational requirement

There are different detailed provisions in reg 7 dealing with when there can be a genuine occupational requirement allowing discrimination. In the case of religion or belief, it is in two cases:

1 Where being of a particular religion or belief is a genuine and determining occupational requirement.

2 Where the employer has an ethos based on religion or belief and, having regard to that ethos and the nature of the employment or the context in which it is carried out, being of a particular religion or belief is a genuine occupational requirement.

In both (1) and (2) the employer must show that it is proportionate to apply the requirement in that particular case and either the person to whom it is applied does not meet it or the employer is not satisfied, and it is reasonable for him not to be satisfied, that the person meets it.

DISABILITY DISCRIMINATION

The latest figures show that there are 8.6 million disabled people in the UK (Annual Review of the Disability Rights Commission for 2005–6). Given this high number it is surprising that the main statute, the Disability Discrimination Act (DDA) was not passed until 1995. It has, like most discrimination legislation, been amended since it first became law. There was some reluctance on the part of the then government to introduce legislation specifically prohibiting discrimination on the grounds of disability and the scope of the then new legislation is discussed by Doyle (1997). An interim report by Income Data Services on the Act (2000) showed that over 68% of cases concerned dismissal and only 9% recruitment.

Definition of disability

Section 1(1) of the DDA 1995 defines a disability as:

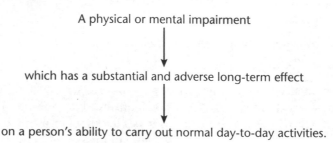

A physical or mental impairment

↓

which has a substantial and adverse long-term effect

↓

on a person's ability to carry out normal day-to-day activities.

The Disability Discrimination Act (DDA) 2005 amended the definition of disability so that the requirement that a mental illness must be clinically well recognised is removed and people who have cancer, HIV infection or MS are deemed to be disabled persons. However, regulations may exclude certain types of cancer from this Act (i.e. so that it will be necessary for those suffering from these types to satisfy the general definition of disability in the DDA 1995). The common feature of the three conditions specified in this Act is that they are progressive.

In addition, the Disability Discrimination (Blind and Partially Sighted Persons) Regulations 2003 (SI 2003/712) provide that a person is deemed to be disabled under the DDA 1995 if they are either certified blind or partially sighted by a consultant ophthalmologist or registered as blind or partially sighted in a register maintained by a local authority.

A useful if basic point made by the ECJ in *Chacón Navas v Eurest Colectividades SA* (2006) was that disability is not the same as sickness in that merely because a person is ill does not mean that they are disabled. On the other hand it must also be pointed out that there is in fact a considerable overlap and it would be a pity if a distinction developed between 'sickness' and 'disability'. In *Hewett v Motorola Ltd* (2004) the EAT held that a person who suffered from Asperger's Syndrome could be disabled as he had a difficulty in understanding. Understanding was given a broader meaning than just an ability to understand instructions and could include in this case an inability to understand 'normal social interaction . . . and/or the subtleties of human non-facial communication'.

Each element of the definition will now be examined in turn, but it should first be pointed out that this definition has been criticised for using what is known as a 'medical' definition of disability, by concentrating on the nature of the impairment, and not a 'social' one, which would focus on the barriers in society to the inclusion of disabled people.

■ Physical or mental impairment

These are not defined, and the DDA 2005 removed the requirement that a mental illness be 'clinically well recognised' in order to count. In *Kapadia* v *Lambeth London Borough Council* (2000) it was held that depression could count as a disability provided that the other conditions under s 1 are met but short-term depressive illness may not count as it is not long term. The Disability Discrimination (Meaning of Disability) Regulations 1996 (SI 1996/1455) provide that certain conditions are not impairments under the Act. These are follows:

(a) addiction to alcohol, nicotine or other substance unless the addiction was origin-ally the result of medically prescribed drugs or medical treatment. However, liver disease resulting from alcohol abuse would count as an impairment given that, provided that the condition comes within the definition of an impairment, it is irrelevant how it was caused;

(b) tendency to set fires; and, perhaps more surprisingly,

(c) tendency to steal;

(d) tendency to physical or sexual abuse of others;

(e) exhibitionism;

(f) voyeurism;

(g) hay fever.

However, what is the position where an employee develops what counts as an impair-ment under the DDA 1995 through an excluded condition? In *Power* v *Panasonic UK Ltd* (2003) the EAT held that where a person suffers an *impairment* through an excluded condition, such as alcohol in this case, then they can come within the DDA 1995. Thus a distinction was drawn between excluded conditions as such and impairments which result from that condition. The effect is that if a person has an impairment within the meaning of the DDA it is not necessary to consider how it was caused. In *Edmund Nuttall Ltd* v *Butterfield* (2005) the employee was dismissed after his employers found that he had committed offences of indecent exposure. This could be classed as 'exhibitionism' which of course is an excluded condition under the DDA. However, here it was alleged that it was the result of depression which could be a mental impairment. The EAT held that one must not always concentrate on the impairment which caused the excluded condition because then, as the EAT points out, the effect would be that the regulations setting out the excluded conditions would be rendered 'nugatory'. Instead, the question is the simple one of causation: what caused the less favourable treatment? If it was the excluded condition, the claim fails, but if it was the impairment then the claimant is within the DDA.

The fact that the Act focuses on the impairment itself led the courts to try to distinguish the *cause* of the impairment from its *effect*. In *Rugamer* v *Sony Music Entertainment* (2001) it was held that the nature of the illness needs to be considered first. A different approach was taken in *College of Ripon and York St John* v *Hobbs* (2002), where a lecturer had muscle cramps resulting from a loss of mobility. Although there was no evidence of any organic disease, it was held by the EAT that the condition could still be physical, as its effects were physical. Clearly, the decision in *Hobbs* will be beneficial where there is undoubtedly some external manifestation of illness but no obvious cause.

Substantial and adverse long-term effect

The Code of Practice states that 'substantial' means more than trivial and the Guidance issued with the Act suggests that, in deciding if it is substantial, account can be taken of, for example, difficulty in going down stairs and 'inability to carry a moderately loaded tray steadily'. However, 'mere clumsiness' is not enough. In *Goodwin* v *Patent Office* (1999) an employee suffered from paranoid schizophrenia and as a result his behaviour at work was bizarre but a tribunal had decided that there was no substantial effect on his ability to carry out day-to-day activities, as he could look after himself at home. The EAT held that the tribunal should have considered his behaviour at work, which inevitably would have led to the conclusion that he was disabled. In *Leonard* v *Southern Derbyshire Chamber of Commerce* (2001) the EAT held that a tribunal should not balance out what a person can and cannot do when deciding whether the effect of the impairment is substantial. The approach should be to see what the applicant can do *only with difficulty*. In *Cruikshank* v *VAW Motorcast* (2002) the applicant had occupational asthma, which was made worse by fumes at work. The EAT held that it was possible to take into account such aggravating factors at work in deciding whether the condition had a substantial and adverse effect. The question was whether the impairment had a substantial and long-term adverse effect on the employee's ability to perform day-to-day tasks both outside work and at work. Accordingly, the EAT rejected the notion that a person is not disabled where he or she can carry out all tasks except very special ones associated with particular employment. The effect, as pointed out by Rubenstein (2002), is that an employee may be disabled for some jobs but not for others, which is not what the DDA 1995 intended.

Long-term effect is defined in Schedule 1 as where the impairment is capable of lasting one year or more or for the rest of a person's life in the case of a terminal illness. Where it ceases but is likely to re-occur then it will be treated as having a long-term effect. An employee who has a progressive condition will be treated as disabled under the Act at the point when the condition has *an* effect on their ability to carry out normal day-to-day activities although at this point it is not substantial. This is to prevent an employer from launching a pre-emptive strike and dismissing them before the person gains the protection of the Act. In *Mowat-Brown* v *University of Surrey* (2002) it was held that a person will come within the protection of the Act when the condition is expected to be substantial although is not yet so.

Ability to carry out normal day-to-day activities

There is an 'exhaustive list' of what constitutes day-to-day activities in Sch 1 to the Act. They are defined as activities involving mobility; manual dexterity; physical co-ordination; continence; ability to lift, carry or move everyday objects; speech, hearing and eyesight; memory or ability to learn, concentrate or understand; perception of the risk of physical danger. In **Kirton v Tetrosyl Ltd** (2003) the applicant suffered from incontinence through measures taken to treat prostate cancer and the EAT held that where an effect on day-to-day activities was caused not by the impairment but by the measures taken to treat it, as here, then the DDA 1995 did not apply. However, the Court of Appeal, in overruling the EAT, sensibly held that where the impairment results from 'the ordinary consequences of an operation to relieve the disease' (Scott-Baker LJ) then it falls within the DDA.

Schedule 1, para 6 provides that, in assessing if the effects on a person's ability to carry out day-to-day activities are substantial, no account shall be taken of any measures to treat or correct the impairment except for the wearing of glasses or contact lenses to correct sight impediments (known as the deduced effects provisions). So a person who has a hearing aid is treated as having a disability even though they may be able to hear very well with it. This is undoubtedly right, as who is to know when the aid might suddenly malfunction? On the other hand, this also has the effect that the Act is applied to those who, on account of the treatment or other aid to correct the impairment, may find that their disability affects them very little in their day-to-day activities. In **Woodrup v Southwark LBC** (2002) Simon Brown LJ called the deduced effects provision 'very benign' and said that those wishing to use this provision should be required to 'prove his or her disability with some particularity'. Here the applicant claimed to be disabled because if her psychotherapy treatment for anxiety neurosis was discontinued then her impairment would have a substantial effect on her day-to-day activities, but the medical evidence was, in any event, not strong enough to establish this.

Schedule 1, para 2(2) provides that where an impairment ceases to have an adverse effect on a person's ability to carry out normal day-to-day activities it is still to be treated as continuing to have that effect provided that the effect is likely to re-occur. In **Swift v Chief Constable of Wiltshire** (2004) the EAT held that the test was whether the *effect* on day-to-day activities was likely to re-occur and not whether the *illness* (the impairment) was likely to re-occur. This is because, as in the case of mental illness, the impairment may indeed not re-occur but it may leave the applicant with an effect that may do so.

A final point on the definition is that, by s 2, it covers those who have had a disability but who have made a full recovery. This is to guard against the person being discriminated against when, for example, applying for a job, as the disability may be revealed on a CV.

When does the DDA 1995 apply in employment?

The Act applies to the same types of employees and to the same types of employment as does the SDA 1975. One provision in the DDA 1995 (s 11) is unique to discrimination law in that where a job advertisement indicates, or might reasonably be taken to indicate, that the employer might discriminate against a disabled applicant then there is a presumption of discrimination. However, this is not as wide as it sounds, because it applies only where the disabled person has applied for and not been offered the

9

Discrimination law

job. Furthermore, the presumption can be rebutted by the employer showing that the reason for the disabled person not being offered the job did not relate to his or her disability.

Definitions of discrimination on the ground of disability

There are two important differences between disability and all other types of discrimination:

not true anymore

1 There is no prohibition of indirect discrimination and so only direct discrimination is prohibited under the DDA 1995.

2 There are three types of direct discrimination and one of these, disability-related discrimination, can be justified. In all other cases of discrimination only indirect discrimination can be justified.

Discrimination on the grounds of disability

This is defined in s 3A(5), which provides that a person discriminates against a disabled person if, on the ground of a person's disability:

■ he treats that person less favourably than he treats or would treat a person not having that particular disability, whose relevant circumstances, including his abilities, are the same as, or not materially different from, the disabled person.

As mentioned above, this type of discrimination cannot be justified. The definition is similar to that for direct discrimination in other cases and the effect is that it is limited to the disability, with the result that it does not apply to the perceived disability of a person nor to discrimination against one person on account of the disability of another.

The phrase 'on the ground of' is clearly a narrow one and will cover only cases where there is a direct link between the disability and the treatment.

Who is the comparator?

The comparator is a person who has the same capabilities as the claimant but who does not have the disability in question.

> ### Example
>
> An employer refuses to employ a person with epilepsy as he believes that she cannot drive safely. The comparison is with a person who cannot drive safely but who does not have epilepsy.

Disability-related discrimination

This is defined by s 3A(1) of the DDA 1995 and the main difference is that here the reason for the less favourable treatment need only be related to the disability instead of 'on the grounds of' as in the case above. The definition is that a person discriminates against a disabled person if:

(a) for a reason related to the disabled person's disability, he treats him less favourably than he treats or would treat others to whom that reason does not or would not apply, and

(b) he cannot show that the treatment in question is justified.

> ### Example
>
> A restaurant refuses admittance to a blind person as it has a 'no dogs' rule. The refusal is not 'on the ground of' the blind person's disability as the actual refusal is on the ground of the 'no dogs' rule. However, the refusal of admittance is certainly 'related to' his disability.

Who is the comparator?

The leading case is *Clark* v *Novocold Ltd* (1999): Clark suffered a back injury at work and was diagnosed as having soft tissue injuries at the base of the spine. He was unable to work as a result and, after four months' absence, he was dismissed. The employers argued that the dismissal was not related to his disability as they would have dismissed any person who was unable to work for such a long period. This like-for-like comparison would be appropriate where, for example, direct sex discrimination is claimed but in this context the Court of Appeal held that it was the wrong test. Instead a comparison should be made with an able-bodied person who can do the job. The issue then becomes whether the disabled person had been subjected to a detriment by reason of their disability. If this is so, then the employer can always attempt to rely on the justification defence. A similar decision is that in *Cosgrove v Caesar and Howie* (2001) where the EAT compared the treatment of the applicant, who had been dismissed when absent for over a year through depression, with that of an employee who had not been absent from work for over a year.

> ### Example
>
> An employer refuses to employ a person with epilepsy as he believes that she cannot drive safely. The comparison is with a person who can drive safely and who does not have epilepsy. The point is that the comparator does not have the reason for the treatment.

A much canvassed question has been whether the employer needs to have knowledge of the disability to be liable. In *O'Neill* v *Symm* (1998) it was held that knowledge was required but this is not now the law. In *Heinz Co. Ltd.* v *Kenrick* (2000) a man was dismissed after a year's absence but before he was confirmed as having ME. The EAT rejected the argument that, as Lindsay J put it, 'the relationship between the disability and the treatment should be adjudged subjectively, through the eyes of the employer'. Instead the test must be an objective one of whether the relationship between the disability and the treatment exists. If the test was subjective then Lindsay J pointed out that the issue would turn on whether 'ignorant or obtuse employers' have recognised a disability or not.

The defence of justification

This, as pointed out above, applies only to disability-related discrimination whilst in the SDA 1975 and the RRA 1976 it applies only to indirect discrimination. The reason for this is that a person may, through a disability, be unable to do a job, but the danger is that the defence could be applied so as to deprive the DDA 1995 of all its force. Section 3A(3) of the DDA provides that a difference in treatment is justified if the reason for it 'is both material to the circumstances of the particular case and substantial'. The Code of Practice amplifies this somewhat by providing that the reason must relate to the individual circumstances in question and must not be trivial or minor. In *Baynton* v *Saurus General Engineers Ltd* (1999) the EAT approved of the idea of applying a balancing exercise between the interests of the disabled employee and those of the employer. Lindsay J in *Clark* v *Novocold*, in the EAT, whilst not precluding this, felt that the limited requirements of s 5(3) should be borne in mind. He pointed to the words of the section and observed that all that is material is that the reason has to relate to the individual concerned and must not be trivial or minor. The Income Data Services report (2000) showed that the two most common reasons claimed by employers as justification were the employee's health and the amount of sick leave taken. In *Jones* v *Post Office* (2001) the Court of Appeal held that where an employer acted on a 'properly conducted risk assessment' then the question was whether a decision was within the range of responses open to a reasonable decision-maker (a similar test to that used in deciding if a decision to dismiss is fair: see Chapter 11) and this must now be taken to be the test. This is, in fact, a low threshold and the reason for this was explained by Arden LJ in this case as being that the DDA 1995 required the needs of the claimant to be balanced against those of fellow employees and the general public.

Discrimination through failure to make reasonable adjustments

This type of discrimination is defined by s 4A(1) of the DDA 1995 as where:

- a provision, criterion or practice applied by or on behalf of an employer, or any physical feature of premises occupied by the employer places the disabled person at a substantial disadvantage as compared with those who are not disabled.

In this case there is a duty on the employer to take such steps as are reasonable in all the circumstances of the case to prevent the provision, criterion or practice having that effect.

In effect there are three issues:

1 When does the duty apply?
2 Who is the comparator?
3 What are 'reasonable steps'?

When does the duty apply?

The amended version of the duty was notable for removing the word 'arrangement' and substituting the phrase 'provision, criterion or practice'. The word 'arrangement' caused difficulties, as in *Archibald v Fife Council* (2004). Here a road sweeper was unable, following a back operation, to continue to do her job and she was offered the chance to apply for office jobs. However, although she was interviewed for over 100 of these she was not selected. The Court of Session held, in effect, that no 'adjustments' could have been made to enable her to do her job as a road sweeper and so the duty did not apply. However, the House of Lords held that the duty to make reasonable adjustments applies whenever an employer's 'arrangements' place the employee at a substantial disadvantage compared with other employees and 'arrangements' include such matters as the job description for the post. The duty to make adjustments may involve transferring the employee to another job, where this is reasonable. Therefore the employer may be under a duty actually to place the disabled employee in another job without advertising it, as distinct from merely giving the employee the chance to apply for it. Lady Hale and Lord Rodger explain the rationale for the duty to make adjustments as being, in effect, positive discrimination. Although the word 'arrangements' has gone, it is submitted that the phrase 'provision, criterion or practice' should be given a similarly wide interpretation.

Who is the comparator?

In *Smith v Churchills Stair Lifts plc* (2006) an applicant for a job who was disabled was rejected for a sales position as he could not carry sample radiator cabinets. The Court of Appeal pointed out that most of us cannot do this and held that the test was whether the applicant was substantially disadvantaged by comparison with the six successful job applicants. Clearly he was, as they got a job and he did not, and so the question of reasonable adjustments arose. The court held that a sample other than a full-sized radiator could have been used and the failure to do this was a failure to make reasonable adjustments.

Meanwhile the decision in *Murphy v Slough Borough Council* (2005) deals with a small but important point: where there is a complaint against a school of a failure to make reasonable adjustments and the issue arises of financial resources, then whose financial resources are relevant – those of the governing body or the LA? The Court of Appeal held that one must ask which employment powers are involved. Here the complaint was that the governors had failed to allow a period of paid leave as a reasonable adjustment and, as the decision on whether to grant this fell within their powers, they were the correct respondents to the action.

What are 'reasonable steps'?

Section 18B(1) provides that the following factors may be taken into account where an employer comes under a duty to make reasonable adjustments:

(a) the extent to which taking the step would prevent the effect (i.e. how much would it actually help?);

(b) the extent to which the step is practicable;

(c) the cost involved and the extent to which taking the step would disrupt other activities;

(d) the employer's financial and other resources;

(e) the availability of financial and other assistance to the employer in taking the step;

(f) the nature of his activities and the size of his undertaking;

(g) where the step would be taken in relation to a private household, the extent to which taking it would disrupt that household or disturb any person residing there.

Section 18B(2) gives a number of examples of possible adjustments which an employer might make: allocating duties to another employee; transferring the employee to another vacancy; altering working hours; arranging training; modifying instructions or reference manuals; providing supervision; assigning him or her to another place of work; acquiring or modifying equipment, etc. In addition, the Code of Practice issued by the Disability Rights Commission suggests other steps which might be reasonable, such as permitting flexible working; conducting a proper assessment of what reasonable adjustments may be required. In *Kenny v Hampshire Constabulary* (1999) it was held that the provision of supervision does not extend to providing a personal carer to assist with the personal requirements of the disabled person at work but this was because it did not fall within the definition of an 'arrangement' (see above) and this might now well be a reasonable adjustment.

Section 4A(3) provides that an employer does not have a duty to make reasonable adjustments if he does not know, and could not reasonably be expected to know, that the person has a disability and is likely to be placed at a substantial disadvantage. In *Ridout* v *TC Group* (1998) Morison J stated that this required tribunals to measure the extent of the duty against the actual or assumed knowledge of the employer both as to the actual disability and the likelihood of its causing the individual substantial disadvantage. In this case a job applicant who suffered from photosensitive epilepsy (a very rare condition) complained at her interview about the bright unscreened lighting and wore sunglasses around her neck. The employer thought that the sunglasses merely explained her condition and took no other steps. It was held that no duty to make adjustments arose.

In *Nottinghamshire CC* v *Meikle* (2004) the EAT held that the duty to pay contractual sick pay is subject to the duty to make reasonable adjustments under the DDA 1995. Thus it *may* be a reasonable adjustment for an employer to continue to pay sick pay (or not to reduce it) if the employee is disabled even though it would have stopped or been reduced for a non-disabled employee. This case concerned a teacher whose sight grew progressively worse but whose requests for adjustments (e.g. enlargement of written notices) were generally ignored. She resigned and it was held that the failure of her employer to make reasonable adjustments was a breach of the duty of mutual trust and confidence and so she could claim constructive dismissal. The EAT held that, if all the reasonable adjustments had been made, then the claimant would not have been absent for the period of over 100 days, at which point the reduction in sick pay took effect. This case is also a good example of the interaction between different remedies in employment law.

In *Southampton City Council* v *Randall* (2006) the EAT held that on the facts it would have been a reasonable adjustment for the employer to consider devising a new post for a disabled employee as the employee's line manager had been given a blank piece of a paper on which to draw a job specification. In addition, there had been no assessment of how to assist the employee to overcome the effect of his disability and this was also a breach of the DDA 1995.

The Income Data Services Report (above) showed that the most common claim for a reasonable adjustment related to a request to be considered for an existing vacancy.

Proving discrimination

See above under sex discrimination.

Remedies under the DDA 1995

These, together with the procedures, are the same as under other discrimination legislation and are dealt with above. Readers should note in particular the decision in *Catherall* v *Michelin Tyre plc.*

AGE DISCRIMINATION

Background to the 2006 Regulations

The Employment Equality (Age) Regulations 2006 came into force on 1 October 2006. The regulations have a similar structure to those in other areas and contain all the basic features of discrimination legislation outlined in the table on page xxx–xxxi.

The legislation on age discrimination has had a long gestation period. When the Labour government came to power in 1997 it was committed to some action on age discrimination but it was not clear whether this would be through legislation or through voluntary action (see Sargeant (2006), from which much of the background material in this section has been drawn). In the event, the government proposed a voluntary Code of Practice in November 1998 but then the EU Framework Directive (2000/78) required legislation to be introduced to prohibit discrimination on the grounds of age, amongst other areas, and the present regulations are the result.

Structure of the 2006 Regulations

As with other legislation dealing with discrimination law, these regulations prohibit direct and indirect discrimination. By reg 3(1)(a) direct discrimination is defined as less favourable treatment on the ground of age or apparent age. Indirect discrimination is defined by reg 3(1)(b) as applying a provision, criterion or practice which is applied to persons not of the same age group but which puts persons of the age group to which the claimant belongs at a particular disadvantage compared to other persons. The defence of justification applies if it can be shown that the difference in treatment is a proportionate means of achieving a legitimate aim. Sargeant (2006) points out that the Framework Directive uses the words 'appropriate and necessary' means of achieving a legitimate aim but the regulations use the word 'proportionate', which is arguably less strong.

The fundamental definitions are the same as in other anti-discrimination legislation but there is one significant difference: the defence of justification (above) applies to both direct and indirect discrimination whereas in other anti-discrimination legislation it applies only to indirect discrimination. The government had proposed, in the draft regulations, that examples would be given of where direct discrimination could be justified, such as the fixing of a maximum age for recruitment or promotion based on both the training requirements of the post and 'the need for a reasonable period in the post before retirement'. One example could have been where a person aged 58 is refused a training contract as a solicitor on the ground that when they were trained they would not serve long enough until retirement. However, in the event no examples appeared, although the Directive has some and these may be relied on by the courts. These are in broad terms and include vocational training objectives and the labour market. The courts will no doubt refer to these and much of the success of the regulations in practice may depend on how widely they are interpreted. In addition, reg 8 provides for discrimination on the ground of age where, 'having regard to the nature of the employment and the context in which it is carried out possessing a characteristic related to age is a genuine and determining occupational requirement'.

Regulation 4 deals with victimisation on the ground of age; reg 6 prohibits harassment on the grounds of age; reg 25 deals with vicarious liability for discriminatory acts on the ground of age; and reg 37 deals with the burden of proof. In all cases, the same terminology is used as in other anti-discrimination legislation. The provisions on remedies are similar to those in other anti-discrimination legislation (reg 38).

◼ Provisions relating to retirement ages

The initial problem with legislation on retirement ages in employment law is that we start from scratch as there is no actual national retirement date in the UK. Instead the retirement ages of employees are often laid down in employee's contracts but in some cases there is no contractual provision and so theoretically they can go on working indefinitely. The issue when the government was consulting on the Age Regulations was whether there should be a default retirement age, i.e. one set in default of any contractual provision. The Framework Directive (para 14 of the preamble) simply says that the Directive shall be 'without prejudice to national provisions laying down retirement ages'. However, it is important to note that Article 8(2) provides that any measures implementing the Directive shall not lessen the protection which already exists against discrimination in each Member State.

Against this background. the government consulted on whether there should be a default retirement age in the regulations with a proposal that it should be set at 70. In the responses to the DTI Consultation (2005) the unions opposed any default retirement age. The TGWU said that the approach should be to emphasise choice and flexibility for older workers. It could not see why discrimination could be allowed against workers who were 70 when it was not allowed when they were in their 60s. However, most employers supported a default retirement age. One reason was that a default retirement age enables careers to be ended with dignity especially where the worker wishes to continue working but is losing his capability. Another reason, which weighed heavily with the government, was that a set retirement age is a necessary part of workforce planning and the government stated in its response to the Consultation (DTI 2005, para 6.1.4) that this was the primary reason for setting a default retirement age.

The result was that a default retirement age of 65 eventually emerged although this will be reviewed in 2011. Meanwhile, the organisation Heyday (which is associated with Age Concern) has been given leave to seek a judicial review of the Age Discrimination Regulations on the ground that the forced retirement age of 65 contravenes the EU Equal Treatment Directive.

Meanwhile, we have the present rules. The default retirement age of 65 is effected by new provisions inserted into the Employment Rights Act 1996 which are numbered ss 98ZA–98ZH. It is worth noting before these are considered in detail that reg 7(4) provides that applicants who would become employees are not protected if they are older than the normal retirement age or, if there is none, 65. In addition, those who would reach the normal retirement age or, in default of one, become 65 within six months of their application, are likewise not protected. The effect is that, if there is no normal retirement age, any applicant for a job can be turned down on the ground of age after reaching 64.5 years.

Under the default retirement age provisions any retirement age below 65 must be objectively justified and, on the other hand, if an employee over 65 is dismissed then he or she has, for the first time, the right to claim that the dismissal was unfair.

The rules on retirement dismissals are set out in new sections added to the Employment Rights Act 1996 (ERA 1996). The effect is that there are two questions to consider:

1 Is the dismissal a retirement dismissal? If not, then it is subject to the normal rules governing dismissals (see Chapter 11).

2 If the dismissal is a retirement dismissal then is it a fair retirement dismissal?

To deal with retirement dismissals a new ground for a potentially fair dismissal is added to s 98 of the ERA 1996: a retirement dismissal.

There are the following possibilities:

1 There is no normal retirement age and the operative date of termination of the contract of employment takes place before the employee reaches the age of 65. The dismissal cannot be a retirement dismissal and so must be considered in the general law of unfair dismissal (s 98ZA).

2 There is no normal retirement age but the operative date of termination is after the date when the employee has reached the age of 65 and the employer has notified the employee of his right to make a request to continue in employment. Here the dismissal shall be a retirement dismissal (s 98ZB).

3 There is a normal retirement age and the operative date of termination takes place before that date. Dismissal cannot be a retirement dismissal (s 98ZC).

4 The normal retirement age is 65 or higher and the employer has notified the employee of his right to make a request to continue in employment. Here the dismissal shall be a retirement dismissal (s 98ZD).

5 The normal retirement age is below 65 and the employer has notified the employee of his right to make a request to continue in employment. Here the dismissal shall be a retirement dismissal (s 98ZE).

Assuming that it is a retirement dismissal, is it a fair dismissal?

Under s 98ZG a retirement dismissal will be unfair in these cases where the employer has failed to comply with a statutory obligation:

(a) failure to comply with the continuing duty to notify the employee of their right to make a request to work beyond their intended retirement date and to notify them of their intended retirement date;

(b) failure to consider a request to continue beyond the intended retirement date;

(c) failure to hold a meeting with the employee;

(d) failure to hold a meeting to consider a request to continue beyond retirement.

If the dismissal is unfair, then the minimum basic award is £6,300.

In the following cases a retirement dismissal is automatically unfair:

(a) the employer has not informed the employee, at least two weeks before the intended retirement date, of any of the following rights: to request to continue working; the intended retirement date;

(b) the retirement dismissal takes place at the time when the employer is still under a duty to consider the employee's request to continue working beyond retirement.

The effect of all these complex rules is that where an employer dismisses an employee on the ground of retirement then the dismissal is fair if:

(a) the reason for retirement is a genuine reason;

(b) the retirement dismissal takes place either on or after the planned retirement date of 65 or any lower age which the employer can objectively justify;

(c) the employer has followed the duty to consider procedure.

The rules on retirement are set out in Sch 6 and are as follows:

(a) The employer must notify the employee in writing of their intended retirement date and of their right to make a request to work beyond that date. This must be done between one year and six months before the intended retirement date. The employer is advised (but is not required) to tell the employee at this stage how the process will be managed.

(b) If the employer does not inform the employee of their rights the employee still has the right to request an extension of working beyond their retirement date.

(c) A request to continue working beyond the retirement date must be made in writing three months before the intended retirement date. It must state if the employee intends to continue working indefinitely, for a stated period or until a stated date.

(d) If such a request is made then the employer must normally hold a meeting with the employee to consider it unless the employer agrees. The employee has a right to be accompanied at the meeting.

(e) If the request is refused then the employee must be given a right of appeal.

(f) No reasons need be given for why an application has been rejected.

(g) If the application is accepted then the outcome will almost certainly be that the employment is continued until a fixed date. If the employee wishes to continue beyond this date the procedure will be put in operation again although it is likely that most employers will have a final date.

EQUAL PAY

The legislation on this is contained in the Equal Pay Act 1970 which has, however, been heavily influenced by what is now Article 141 of the European Treaties. As mentioned above, it forms the counterpart of the SDA 1975 in discrimination on grounds of sex in dealing with discrimination in terms and conditions of employment. The Act has certainly had an effect in improving the pay of women as compared with men but there is strong evidence that, having had a marked initial effect, it now simply prevents the pay of women from falling further behind that of men. Between 1970 and 1977 women's pay as a proportion of men's had risen from 63% to 75.5% but it is now 81% for women full-time workers. The reason why it is not more is that women tend to work in part-time jobs and in areas which are not as well paid as men. Further advance in the pay of women as compared to men may have to wait for changes in society which are beyond the scope of the law to achieve.

The Equal Pay Act 1970 in effect operates alongside Article 141 of the EC Treaty, which provides for equal pay for equal work. As explained in Chapter 3, where there is a conflict between them then Article 141 prevails. In Chapter 3, the best example of this is *Macarthays v Smith* (1980) where, as already explained, it was held that Article 141 enabled a female employee to claim equal pay with a previous male employee although the EqPA 1970 did not provide for this.

The scheme of the Act

Section 1(1) of the EqPA 1970 implies an equality clause into the contracts of employees (as with the SDA 1975 it refers to women but includes men) in the following cases:

Like work   Work rated   Work of
                   as equivalent   equal value

9

Discrimination law

The effect is that where a woman is doing any of these types of work with a man in the same establishment or an associated establishment then her contract automatically contains an equality clause enabling her to claim equal pay with a man. Each of these will now be considered in turn.

Like work

Like work is defined by s 1(4) as work which is broadly similar, and the differences between the work done by a woman and a man are not of practical importance in relation to terms and conditions of employment. The point is that, to be able to claim equal pay, a woman does not have to show that the work done by her and a man is identical. The courts quickly took this point. In *Capper Pass* v *Lawton* (1977) it was held that a woman chef who prepared lunches for the company directors and their guests was employed on like work to two male chefs who served in the factory canteen. In *Dugdale* v *Kraft Foods Ltd* (1976) it was held that the time at which the work is done does not by itself justify a difference in pay, although Phillips J pointed out in *National Coal Board* v *Sherwin* (1978) that this does not mean that both men and women cannot be paid extra for working at night and at weekends. The phrase 'not of practical importance in relation to terms and conditions of employment' was first considered by the Court of Appeal in *Shields* v *E Coomes Holdings Ltd* (1978), where a woman counterhand in a bookmakers was paid less than a male counterhand and, although the work done by them was virtually the same, the man was there partly to deter troublemakers. However, it was found that he was not trained to do this job, nor had he ever done it. Thus the difference between the work of the woman and the man counterhand was not of practical importance in relation to terms and conditions of employment and a difference in pay was not justified. However, in *Thomas* v *NCB* (1987) women canteen assistants claimed equal pay with a man who was on permanent night duty and it was held that their claim failed as the added responsibility *was* of practical importance in relation to terms and conditions.

Work rated as equivalent

This applies only if the work of a woman has been graded as equivalent under a job evaluation scheme. However, here a woman's work is not rated as equivalent then she may challenge the scheme on the ground that it does not fulfil the criteria set out in s 1(5), which provide that the jobs of men and women must have been given an equal value in terms of the demand made on a worker under various heads, such as effort, skill and decision. In *Bromley* v *H&J Quick Ltd* (1988) Dillon LJ held that any job evaluation scheme must be both non-discriminatory and analytical.

Work of equal value

This head was introduced into the EqPA 1970 by the Equal Pay (Amendment) Regulations 1983 (SI 1983/1794) following the decision of the ECJ in *Commission of the EC* v *UK* (1982) that existing legislation on equal pay infringed the Equal Pay Directive

(75/117) in not allowing an equal value claim. This has been the most fruitful area for equal pay claims, as it has enabled women to claim equal pay where there is no similarity on the surface between their job and that of the man.

The first major case was *Hayward v Cammell Laird Shipbuilders Ltd* (1988), where a woman successfully claimed equal pay where she was employed as a canteen cook and her work was held to be of equal value with that of male painters, thermal insulation engineers and joiners employed by the company. Once her claim succeeded, the court then had to decide whether she was entitled to the same basic rate of pay as her male comparator or a comparison of all the terms of her contract including matters such as meal breaks, sickness benefits and holidays. In fact, when all the terms of her contract were taken into account she was actually better off than her male comparators. However, the House of Lords held that she could simply point to a particular clause in her contract which was less favourable and claim that it should be made equally favourable under the equality clause. In *Pickstone v Freemans plc* (1988) a woman employed as a warehouse operative was not barred from claiming equal value with a man employed as a checker operative even though there was a man employed at the warehouse on the same work as her. The House of Lords held that the fact that other men were doing like work or work rated as equivalent did not bar an equal value claim.

In practice, equal value claims require a complicated procedure which, even after it was simplified by the Sex Discrimination and Equal Pay (Miscellaneous Amendments) Regulations 1996 (SI 1996/438), is still lengthy. One reason is that a report from an independent expert is often commissioned by the tribunal and the preparation of this report takes time. The Employment Act 2002 attempts to remedy this by providing in s 42 that the equal pay questionnaire which is used by the applicant to obtain information from the employer is to be shortened and the government estimates that this will result in 10% of applications being withdrawn before a hearing.

Assuming that the woman establishes that she is employed on any of the three types of work outlined above there are two further hurdles to surmount:

1 Is there a genuine material difference between the work of the woman and the man?

YES	NO
↓	↓
Claim fails	Claim moves on
	↓

2 Are the woman and the man in the same employment, i.e. are they employed at the same establishment or at another establishment where common terms and conditions are observed?

The genuine material difference defence

Contained in s 1(3), this defence provides that the equality clause will not apply where a variation in the contracts of men and women is due to a material factor other than

9

Discrimination law

sex. Obvious examples are long service and better qualifications. In *Sharp* v *Caledonia Group Services* (2006) the fundamental point was emphasised that a difference in pay between employees of different sexes must be objectively justified and it is not enough for an employer to show that the difference is not based on sex. Therefore, once one of the three types of work set out in s 1(1) is established there is a prima facie case of discrimination if pay is not equal and so the burden of proof shifts to the employer.

Do service-based pay scales amount to indirect discrimination against women under the Equal Pay Act? There is no doubt that they do so in practice, as the working lives of women are shorter than those of men. In *Cadman* v *Health and Safety Executive* (2006) the ECJ held that the general principle established by the ECJ in the *Danfoss* case still applied (see Table of Cases for full reference): rewarding experience is a legitimate objective of pay policy; and the ECJ held that as a general rule the criterion of length of service is appropriate to achieve that objective. However, the ECJ emphasised that this is a presumption. Therefore the claimant may bring evidence to rebut this by showing on the facts that longer service does not lead to better performance. The result is that payment of higher wages to long-serving workers can, and probably will, come under the genuine material difference defence but it is open to challenge.

In *Bailey* v *Home Office* (2005) the Court of Appeal held that where there is one group which is male dominated and which has a pay advantage as compared to the disadvantaged group which is not male dominated then the burden is on the employers objectively to justify the difference in pay between the two groups on the basis set out in s 1(3) above. As Peter Gibson LJ explained: 'The Employment Tribunal is concerned to determine whether what on its face is a gender neutral practice may be disguising the fact that female employees are being disadvantaged as compared with male employees to an extent that the disparity is prima facie attributable to a difference in sex.'

However, in *Strathclyde Regional Council* v *Wallace* (1998) the House of Lords held that where there is no evidence that the difference in pay is due to grounds of sex then there is no need for the employer to be called on to raise the 'genuine material difference' defence at all. Women in a group of 134 teachers, 81 of whom were men and 53 women, were all doing the work of principal teachers, although not promoted to that position. Nine women in the group claimed equal pay with a male promoted teacher but their claim failed on the ground that there was no evidence of sex discrimination at all. Lord Browne-Wilkinson pointed out that the object of the employees was to achieve equal pay for like work, regardless of sex. That, he pointed out, was not the object of the Act.

By contrast, in *Bailey*, administrative officers in the prison service claimed equal pay with prison governors employed on work rated as equivalent. The comparators (the governors) were male dominated but the disadvantaged group was split evenly between men and women. This was enough to require the employers objectively to justify the difference in pay.

The following considerations have arisen in these cases:

1　Is 'red circling' justified? Red circling means that the pay of an employee who has been moved to a less-well-paid type of work is protected by wages still being paid at the higher rate for the work previously done. This could lead to a claim by women that a man was being paid more than them for work which was the same. In *Snoxell v Vauxhall Motors* (1977) the EAT held that where the red circling was due to a factor based on sex (as here, where the women had not been allowed to enter the grades where the men originally were) then there was a valid claim under the Act. However, in other cases red circling has been allowed only on the basis that it will be phased out in time (see *Outlook Supplies v Parry* (1978)).

2　What if the employer says that it was necessary to pay a man more, as this was the only way in which anyone could be induced the take the post? This is known as the 'market forces defence' and in *Clay Cross (Quarry Services) v Fletcher* (1978) it was rejected as a defence under s 1(3), Denning MR robustly remarking that 'the employer cannot evade his obligations under the Act by saying "I paid him more because he asked for more"'. The law was then muddled somewhat by statements by the House of Lords in *Rainey v Greater Glasgow Health Board* (1987) that the remarks in *Fletcher* were 'unduly restrictive' (per Lord Keith) of the purpose of s 1(3), and so a female prosthetist failed in her claim for equal pay with a man who had been employed on a higher grade because it was necessary to pay recruits at a higher rate to match private sector salaries. In *Enderby v Frenchay Health Authority* (1994) the ECJ held that any difference in pay had to be objectively justified and so even if market forces applied in principle, not all of the difference in pay would necessarily be held to be justified on this ground. The effect is that *any* difference in pay must be shown to be attributable to market forces.

3　In *Jenkins v Kingsgate (Clothing Productions) Ltd (No. 2)* (1981) the EAT held that the payment of differential wages to part-time workers could be justified as a genuine material difference only if it was intended to achieve an object unrelated to sex. In *Bilka-Kaufhaus v Weber* (1986) the ECJ reached a similar conclusion in holding that the exclusion of part-time workers from an occupational pension scheme, which here affected far more women than men, was justifiable only if it could be objectively justified on grounds unrelated to sex. Here the employer, a store, wished to discourage part-time work because part-timers did not want to work in the late afternoon and on Saturdays. These cases are to some extent academic in view of the Part-time Workers (Prevention of Less Favourable Treatment) Regulations 2000 (SI 2000/1551), although the extent to which differential pay rates applicable to part-timers is justified may be a useful guide in the interpretation of the regulations.

4　Can the fact that pay rates are set in separate bargaining processes justify a genuine material difference in pay? In *Enderby v Frenchay HA* (1994) a woman speech therapist claimed that her work was of equal value to that of male pharmacists and clinical psychologists, but their pay had been set in different negotiations. The ECJ held that it was not in itself a justification that pay rates were arrived at in separate negotiations and it is in the actual pay where any justification for a difference must be sought.

9

Discrimination law

■ The comparator

Once the claim to equal pay has been made out and it has been established that the defence under s 1(3) is inapplicable, then we move on to the final stage of showing that there is a comparator. Under the EqPA 1970 an actual comparator must be found and it is provided by s 1(6) that the comparator must be in the same employment as the applicant or at another establishment at which common terms and conditions are observed either generally or for employees of the relevant classes. Thus it is of no avail for a woman to show that she is paid less than a man doing the same job but working for another employer.

The same establishment or the same employer

Where the woman and the man are working at the same establishment then the matter is easy: there will be a right to equal pay. Where they are working at different establishments for the same employer then there is the requirement to show common terms and conditions at each establishment. In *Leverton v Clwyd CC* (1989) the House of Lords held that this means that common terms and conditions must be observed at each establishment and not that the terms and conditions of the comparators must be the same. In *British Coal Corporation v Smith* (1996) a claim succeeded where the terms and conditions of canteen workers and clerical officers were contained in agreements which each applied at the establishments where the men and women worked and the fact that there were variations at a local level was not a reason for holding that there were not common terms and conditions.

Different employers or different organisations

What is the position where the woman and the man are working for different organisations? In principle there is no right to equal pay. However, in *Defrenne v Sabena* (1976) the ECJ held that Article 141 of the EC Treaty allows comparisons between employees in the same service. This is illustrated by *South Ayrshire Council v Morton* (2002) where the Court of Session held that a woman headteacher could compare her pay with that of a male headteacher employed by a different local authority. The court interpreted Article 141 as only giving as an example the fact that a comparison could be made with those in the same establishment or service and that other factors could be relevant in making a comparison such as whether both employees were covered by the same collective agreement. However, in *Lawrence v Regent Office Care Ltd* (2002) the ECJ limited the extent to which comparisons can be made between the pay of workers *not* employed by the same employer or an associated employer by deciding that it is not possible for school catering and cleaning staff who now work for a private employer after contracting out to compare their pay with employees still employed in local government. Although the ECJ accepted that the employees were still in the same service, what was fatal to the claim was the need to find a single source (i.e. a particular body) which was responsible for the inequality and which could restore the equal treatment. However, it is regrettable that the ECJ did not explain what it meant by the phrase 'single source'. There is now a gap opening between the rights of different types of workers where they work in the same service (as distinct from the same employment) as is shown by the successful claim brought by teachers in *South Ayrshire Council* v *Morton* (above). In ***Robertson and others*** v ***DEFRA*** (2005) the Court of Appeal interpreted the phrase 'single source' to rule out a claim for equal pay by civil servants in one government department (DEFRA) with those in another (DETR). The two groups of employees had their terms and conditions of employment negotiated by their own departments and thus each department was the source of them. Accordingly there could not be said to be a 'single source'.

The difficulty with the decision in *Robertson* in particular is that where an organisation changes to a departmental structure then employees may lose a claim for equal pay. If there is no one body responsible for a disparity in pay then, as Fredman (2004) observes, the loss falls on those least at fault (the employees) but there is no reason why this should be so. Steele (2006) suggests that the particular context of the departmentalisation in *Robertson* weighed heavily in the court's mind as the employer had over half a million employees and he points to Mummery LJ's description of the prospect of one civil servant being able to use another civil servant as a comparator as 'extravagant'. In *Lawrence*, Mummery LJ said that in that case the change from central to departmental pay negotiations was 'genuine' and not made in order to avoid the equal pay legislation. However, as Connolly (2006) observes, this approach would involve tribunals in having to consider the motives for a change to pay negotiations with all the complications that this would bring.

Where it is possible to make a comparison then in ***Evesham*** v ***North Hertfordshire HA*** (2000) it was held that a woman has the right to equal pay with her comparator and no more. Here a speech therapist established that she was entitled to be placed on the same pay scale as a clinical psychologist but was not entitled, having crossed over to his pay scale, then at once to climb up it on the ground of her greater experience. The Court of Appeal held that the Act simply requires equal treatment and in this context the choice of a comparator is all-important.

What can be claimed?

The EqPA 1970 applies not only to pay and other benefits or 'perks' such as travel concessions (*Garland* v *BR Engineering* (1982)), but also to occupational pension schemes (see *Bilka* v *Weber* (above)) and in ***Barber*** v ***Guardian Royal Exchange Assurance*** (1991) it was held that men and women are entitled to pension benefits at the same age. Following *Barber* there has been considerable further litigation in the area of pension schemes.

In ***Newcastle upon Tyne City Council*** v ***Allan*** and ***Degnan*** v ***Redcar and Cleveland Borough Council*** (2005) the EAT held that compensation for non-economic loss, such as injury to feelings, cannot be claimed in an equal pay claim. This is in contrast to claims under other discrimination legislation which allow recovery as these are statutory torts and so, as in tort actions, non-economic loss is recoverable. An action for equal pay, by contrast, is one in contract as the scheme of the Equal Pay Act is to insert a statutory implied term into contracts of employment. Given that this takes us into contract law we are then met with the contract rule that only very occasionally can non-economic loss be recovered in contract. Whilst this decision is impeccably orthodox, the logic in terms of discrimination law is hard to see. The Equal Pay Act is part of a scheme of anti-discrimination legislation and there seems to be no good reason for its having a different rule to other areas.

Making a claim

Claims must be brought within six months and under s 2(5) back pay was payable only for a period of two years before the claim. However, in *Jennings v Levez* (1999) the EAT held that this limit was unlawful as it did not correspond to the six-year limit for claiming arrears of pay in contract and so breached the principle of equivalence. As a result a new s 2ZB was inserted into the Equal Pay Act 1970 providing that arrears can now be claimed for up to six years.

Victimisation on the ground that an equal pay claim has been brought

Section 6 of the Equal Pay Act 1970 contains the standard prohibition against victimisation on the ground that an employee has brought a claim under the Act. In *St Helens MBC v Derbyshire* (2004) female catering staff claimed that they were entitled to a bonus scheme similar to that operated for road sweepers on the ground that their work was of equal value. Most claims were settled but some employees proceeded with their claims. Before the tribunal hearing they received letters from a senior officer of the council stating that if they succeeded in their action there could be large-scale redundancies and referring to the impact which the action 'will have on the service and on everyone employed within it'. The EAT held that, to amount to victimisation, it was not necessary that direct threats be made of dismissal or demotion, and that these letters amounted to victimisation. Their tone was such that those to whom they were addressed might have been exposed to reproach and vilification by colleagues and this was sufficient detriment. The House of Lords in upholding the EAT, agreed that the letter actively subjected the employees to a detriment.

DISCRIMINATION AGAINST PARTICULAR TYPES OF WORKERS

Part-time workers

There are around 6 million part-time workers in the UK today, forming a significant part of the labour market. They have a measure of special protection as a result of the Part-time Workers (Prevention of Less Favourable Treatment) Regulations 2000 (SI 2000/1551) which came into force on 1 July 2000. The regulations were passed as a result of the EC Directive on Part-time Work (Directive 97/81 EC) and, as a broad principle, give a part-time worker the right not to be less favourably treated than a full-time worker. One could say that they prohibit discrimination against part-time workers in the same way as equal opportunities legislation prohibits discrimination on the grounds of sex, race and disability. However, the details are different.

Which workers do the regulations apply to?

Regulation 1(2) adopts the definition in s 230(3) of the ERA 1996. Therefore a worker is anyone who either has a contract of employment or undertakes to personally perform work for the other party, with the usual proviso that this does not include situations where the worker is performing services for a professional client.

What is meant by a part-time worker?

The regulations adopt the interesting and novel principle of relying on 'custom and practice' to decide this rather than complex statutory formulae. One suspects that this is the right approach in that, although it will lead to litigation on the question of 'custom and practice', this will be preferable to adding yet more complexity to employment law.

Accordingly, reg 2(2) provides that a worker is part-time where the worker, 'having regard to the custom and practice of the employer in relation to workers employed by the worker's employer under the same type of contract, is not identifiable as a full-time worker'. There is a similar definition of a full-time worker in reg 2(1) (but stating that the worker by custom and practice is regarded as full-time).

Three points should be noted:

(i)   The regulations also add that both sets of workers must be paid wholly or in part by reference to the time they work.

(ii) A comparison can only be made, for custom and practice purposes, between workers who, broadly speaking, are employed by the same employer in the same organisation. This point is dealt with in more detail below but the significant issue here is that the custom and practice of one employer or in a trade or profession generally, is not relevant: what matters is the custom and practice of the employer against whom the claim is being made.

(iii) This appears to be the first time that the phrase 'custom and practice' has been used in statute law and any interpretation of it by the courts will be bound to have an effect on the common law of employment.

How is the comparison to be made?

The regulations do this in two stages:

■ Regulation 1(2) lays down the 'pro-rata' principle, which is to apply unless 'it is inappropriate' (reg 5(3)). Where a full-time worker receives or is entitled to pay or any other benefit then a part-time worker is entitled to receive that benefit pro-rata according to the number of hours worked by him or her in comparison to those worked by the full-time worker. Regulation 2(3) provides that weekly hours shall be calculated without counting overtime and that, where hours vary, the average shall be taken. However, even though the pro-rata principle applies, it is still open to the employer to argue that the difference in treatment is 'objectively justified' (reg 5(2)).

9

Discrimination law

This term is intended to have the same meaning as in the Sex Discrimination and Race Relations Acts and its meaning is discussed above.

■ Regulation 2(4) then sets out which full-time workers are to be the comparators. There is a three-stage test:

(i) The workers must be employed by the same employer under the same type of contract. Regulation 2(3) provides that the following shall be regarded as employed under different types of contract:

(a) employees employed under a contract which is not one of apprenticeship;

(b) employees employed under a contract of apprenticeship;

(c) workers who are not employees;

(d) any other description of worker which it is reasonable for the employer to treat differently from other workers on the ground that workers of that description have a different type of contract.

(ii) They must be engaged in the same or a broadly similar work having regard, where relevant, to whether they have similar qualifications, skills and experience.

(iii) The full-time worker must be based at the same establishment as the part-time worker or, if there is no full-time worker based at that establishment, then a comparison may be made with a full-time worker based at another establishment provided always that both employees are employed by the same employer. Accordingly, a comparison cannot be made with a notional full-time worker. The worker must actually exist. This feature of the regulations is unusual and the only other major area where it occurs is with claims under the Equal Pay Act 1970. It has been suggested by McColgan (2000) that the requirement of an actual comparator will render the regulations 'largely irrelevant to the vast majority of workers'. She quotes figures produced by the government in the consultation process showing that it is likely that only one-sixth of the 6 million part-time workers would be able to find a comparator.

Matthews v Kent and Medway Towns Fire Authority (2006), which was the first time that the regulations had been considered by the courts, involved a claim by retained fire fighters that they were treated less favourably than full-time fire fighters in relation to benefits under a pension scheme, sick pay, and pay for additional responsibilities. The decision of the House of Lords is noteworthy for the purposive interpretation given to the regulations.

There were two issues:

1 Were the two types of workers – part-time and full-time – employed on the same type of contract? (See (i) above.) The House of Lords held that they were. The employment tribunal and the EAT had held that they were not, as the retained fire fighters came under category (d) above. The House of Lords, agreeing with the Court of Appeal, held that category (d) was intended as a residual category, designed to fill any gaps which have been left. Part-time employment is inevitably different from full-time employment and if the 'threshold of comparability is set too high' (Lord Hope) then it will mean that the only claims which will succeed will be those where

full- and part-time workers work in exactly the same way. Thus a comparison could be made between retained part-time fire fighters and full-time fire fighters as their contracts were of the same type.

2 Having established that the two groups were employed under the same type of contract, the second issue was whether they were engaged in the same or broadly similar work (see (ii) above). The House of Lords held that they were. In making the assessment it is important to give weight to the similarities between the work done by the two groups and the importance of that work to the enterprise as a whole, remembering that almost inevitably there will be differences between the work done by the two groups. The error of the employment tribunal was to give undue weight to the different levels of skill and experience between the two groups without assessing the extent to which this affected what the two groups were actually engaged in.

What benefits can be claimed?

Regulation 5 provides that the right to not less favourable treatment extends to:

(a) Treatment according to the terms of the contract. Thus it applies to rates of pay, sick pay and maternity pay, occupational pension schemes, access to training, leave, and career breaks. It also applies to selection for redundancy and therefore part-timers should be treated no less favourably than full-timers (see Chapter 12). (The guidance attached to the regulations is particularly helpful in giving examples.) Overtime is dealt with by a special provision (reg 5(4)) which states that where the part-time worker has completed the number of hours which a full time worker would need to work to qualify for overtime then the part-time worker will be entitled to overtime. This is a particularly helpful change for part-timers, as previously there was no right to overtime once they had worked beyond their normal hours.

(b) A right not to be subjected to any detriment by the employer for exercising their rights under the regulations. This is a similar right to that which exists under other employment protection legislation.

It should be noted, however, that the regulations do not protect applicants for employment.

Other provisions

1 Regulations 4 and 5 deal with the situation where a worker was full-time and then returns to work part-time (whether or not after absence). They provide that a worker in these cases has the right to be treated not less favourably than before although the 'objective justification defence' will apply.

2 Regulation 6 gives a part-time worker who believes that he or she has been treated less favourably under the terms of reg 5 the right to receive a written statement of the reasons for this from the employer within 21 days of the request. A failure by the employer to comply can lead the tribunal to draw inferences, including that the employer has infringed the right in question.

247

3 Regulation 7 gives workers the right to complain to an employment tribunal that his or her rights have been infringed and the tribunal may award compensation as well as make a declaration and recommend that the employer takes action to remedy the adverse effects on the complainant of the unequal treatment, i.e. that the employer treats equally in future. There is no ceiling on compensation. Proceedings must be brought within three months of the date of the less favourable treatment although there is the usual proviso allowing complaints to be considered out of time if it is just and equitable to do so.

4 An employee who is dismissed shall be regarded as having been unfairly dismissed if the reason or principal reason for the dismissal is that the worker asserted his or her rights under these regulations. This provision is found throughout employment law but here it includes the seeking of a written statement under reg 6.

A final point is that the regulations do not give any rights to full-time workers. It would have been possible, for instance, to have provided that full-time workers have a right to request to transfer to part-time work. Instead there is a much more limited right to ask for a flexible working arrangement in certain circumstances (see Chapter 10).

Relationship between the Part-time Workers Regulations and the Sex Discrimination Act

As discussed earlier in this chapter, the Sex Discrimination Act 1975 has been used to establish that discrimination against part-timers amounted to indirect sex discrimination because of the considerably larger number of women compared with men employed in many organisations. In future, such claims can be brought instead under these regulations, with the advantage that there will be no need to prove, as a first stage, that there was an adverse impact on the ground of sex. Therefore claims will be possible where all or most of the workers in an organisation are women or, for that matter, men.

Fixed-term employees

Following on from the above regulations on part-time workers, the Fixed-term Employees (Prevention of Less Favourable Treatment) Regulations 2002 (SI 2002/2034) came into force on 1 October 2002. These were also introduced as a result of an EC Directive, in this case the Fixed-Term Work Directive, and can be seen as part of a process of attempting to ensure that those engaged in atypical work patterns (i.e. other than full-time work on permanent contracts) are not disadvantaged in their employment rights. The proposed directive on agency work (see below) is part of the same pattern.

The Regulatory Impact Assessment on these regulations estimated that the number of those working on fixed-term contracts in the UK is between 1.1 and 1.3 million and a higher proportion (just over half of the total) are in the public sector. The public sector accounts for 70% of those who have been on fixed-term contracts for more than two years.

To whom do the regulations apply?

The striking difference from the Part-time Workers Regulations is that these apply only to employees and not to workers, as the definition adopted is that set out in s 230(1) of the ERA 1996 and not that in s 230(3).

What is meant by a fixed-term employee?

The simple answer is that it is an employee on a fixed-term contract, which is defined under reg 1(2) of the regulations as a contract of employment that, under its provisions determining how it will terminate in the normal course, will terminate:

(a) on the expiry of a fixed term;

(b) on the completion of a particular task; or

(c) on the occurrence or non-occurrence of any other specific event other than the attainment by the employee of any normal and bona fide retiring age in the establishment for an employee holding the position which he holds.

In *Allen* v *National Australia Group Europe Ltd* (2004) it was held that a contract is still fixed term for the purposes of the regulations even though it contains a term which allows it to be terminated earlier by notice. The reasoning of the court was based on the words of reg 1(2) above, which provide that a contract is fixed term if it terminates on the expiry of a fixed term *in the normal course*. Thus a contract could still be fixed term even if in the event it did *not* terminate in the normal course and instead ended, for example, by notice.

Employees whose contracts do not fall within the above definition are defined as permanent and they are the comparators.

The right to not less favourable treatment

This is contained in reg 3 and gives a right not to be less favourably treated than a permanent employee as regards the terms of the contract or being subjected to any other detriment. The general principle for deciding whether less favourable treatment has occurred is the pro-rata one, as for part-time workers, unless it is inappropriate. A fixed-term employee will not be less favourably treated if the difference in treatment is justified on objective grounds (reg 4). This means that an employer will establish justification where the contract of the fixed-term employee is, *taken as a whole*, not less favourable than that given to permanent employees. This 'package approach' differs from that adopted in the Part-time Workers Regulations where a straightforward comparison in terms of the benefits received is made. The intention is to allow the employer and employee to negotiate a total package where greater benefits are received in some areas but less favourable treatment than permanent employees is given elsewhere provided that as a whole there is no less favourable treatment. A possible example would be *less* favourable pension benefits but *more* favourable pay rates. The phrase 'as a whole' could lead to some complex cases unless the courts devise a formula that excludes most decisions in this area from the need for judicial scrutiny.

In *Department for Work and Pensions* v *Webley* (2005) it was held that non-renewal of a fixed-term contract was not less favourable treatment and so the regulations did

9

Discrimination law

not apply to the practice of an employer (here, the Department) of terminating the contracts of employees in job centres after 51 weeks. Obviously, if the contract was terminated after 52 weeks the employees would be able to claim for unfair dismissal.

The following points should also be noted:

- The right to not less favourable treatment has been extended to pay and pensions as a result of provisions in the Employment Act 2002.

- It is specifically provided by reg 3(2) that a fixed-timer must not be treated less favourably as regards any periods of service qualification, the opportunity to receive training and the opportunity to secure permanent employment. So far as the last right is concerned, reg 3(5) provides that a fixed-timer has the right to be informed of any vacancies in the establishment.

- The comparison with a permanent employee is, by reg 2, to be made with one who is employed by the same employer and engaged in the same or broadly similar work having regard, where relevant, to whether they have the same or similar levels of skills, qualifications and experience. The comparator must be based at the same establishment or, where there is no comparator there, then a comparison can be made with a comparator at a different establishment.

- One of the most significant provisions is in reg 8, which provides that where an employee has been employed under one or more fixed-term contracts for four years or more *and* the employment under a fixed-term contract was not justified under objective grounds *then*, if the contract is renewed or if they are re-engaged under a new contract without continuity of employment being broken, the new contract will be a *permanent* one. No period of continuous service before 10 July 2002 counts and so the effect is that the earliest date by which an employee could claim a permanent contract as a result of these provisions is 10 July 2006. It will be possible for a workforce or collective agreement to amend this rule by, for example, specifying different maximum numbers of fixed-term contracts. (See Chapter 6 for details of the rules on continuity of employment and Chapter 7 for details of collective and workforce agreements.)

> ### Example
>
> Terry was employed by Ambridge College of Technology as a lecturer under a series of one-year fixed-term contracts beginning in September 2002. He is offered another one-year fixed-term contract in September 2006. This will now be a permanent contract, as the period for which the fixed-term contracts ran was four years, unless the college establishes an objective justification for the fixed-term contract.
>
> Thus the effect of reg 8 is to put a cap on fixed-term contracts of four years unless objectively justified.

- The regulations abolish waiver clauses under which employees employed under a fixed-term contract for two years or more could waive their right to a redundancy payment under the provisions of s 197(3) of the ERA 1996.

- Provisions relating to the right to receive a written statement of reasons for alleged less favourable treatment, complaint to an employment tribunal and dismissal are the same as those found in the Part-time Workers Regulations.

LAW IN CONTEXT
Discrimination law: new frontiers?

Are there any further areas where it would be appropriate to prohibit discrimination? Two have been suggested:

- Discrimination against those whose pre-employment screening has disclosed a genetic predisposition to, for example, cancer. The Human Genetics and Advisory Commission in its 1999 report recommended that, when and if genetic screening in employment becomes common practice, employees should not be required to take a genetic test or to disclose its results unless there is clear evidence that the results are needed to assess ability to do a job or susceptibility in doing a job (see McColgan (2005), page 575).

- Discrimination against carers. There are 5.6 million people in England, Scotland and Wales providing unpaid care for another adult and 38% of mothers, 11% of fathers and 18% of carers have either left a job or been unable to take one because of difficulties of combining it with caring responsibilities (Report by the Equal Opportunities Commission, 2004). Thus discrimination against carers in the labour market is an issue which deserves more attention than it has received. Suppose that a carer applies for a particular job and at the interview discloses that she is a carer for, for example, her disabled son. The prospective employers decide not to offer her the job as, although she has care arrangements in place, they are concerned about what would happen if they broke down. The carer is not covered by present discrimination law. In *Attridge Law* v *Coleman* (2006) a mother of a four-year-old disabled son resigned after her employer allegedly discriminated against her in the flexible working opportunities which it offered to her by contrast to employees with non-disabled children. The question is whether the DDA 1995 covers discrimination on the ground of the disability of another (the argument being that it is disability *related* discrimination) and the EAT has referred this to the ECJ. If the answer is yes then carers will have protection from discrimination. (It is worth noting at this point that carers do have a right to ask for a flexible working arrangement – see Chapter 10.)

As a final thought on discrimination law, a valuable snapshot of what is actually happening in the workplace in this area is provided by *Inside the Workplace: Findings from the 2004 Workplace Relations Survey* (Kersley et al., 2006). In looking at the statistics it is important to remember that employment legislation not only imposes requirements; it also hopes to encourage good practice. As far as discrimination law is concerned, 73% of workplaces claim to have an Equal Opportunities Policy (EQPS) compared with 64% in 1998. Those without tended to be small organisations which

9

Discrimination law

were in the private sector and non-union. Less than 25% of workplaces undertake monitoring of recruitment, selection and promotion procedures to check for indirect discrimination and for reviewing relative pay rates. When monitoring does occur it is generally of recruitment and selection procedures. It is interesting that the use of informal channels of recruitment continues at a high rate despite the fact that this may not achieve workforce diversity. These methods include word of mouth recommendation and recommendations of existing workers and about two-thirds of all workplaces used one of these methods in the previous 12 months. It seems that not all British workplaces reflect the increasing diversity of society. In 58% of those with at least 10 workers, 75% of employees were of the same sex, 56% did not have any ethnic minority employees and 81% had no disabled employees.

SUMMARY

This chapter deals with three distinct areas which together make up discrimination law:

(a) Discrimination on six grounds which are prohibited: sex, including gender reassignment; sexual orientation; race; religion or belief; disability; and age.

   Within these areas there is a common scheme whereby the following types of discrimination are prohibited:

- direct discrimination;
- indirect discrimination (except in the case of disability discrimination);
- discrimination by victimisation;
- discrimination by harassment.

In addition in each area except disability discrimination there are situations where discrimination is permitted.

   There are also the following common features:

- circumstances when the employer is liable for discrimination;
- remedies for discrimination.

(b) Equal Pay Act 1970. This deals with sex discrimination on the grounds of pay. In the other areas the main statute or regulation deals with discrimination on grounds of pay. For example, the Race Relations Act 1976 deals with discrimination in pay on racial grounds.

(c) Part-time Workers (Prevention of Less Favourable Treatment) Regulations 2000 and the Fixed-term Employees (Prevention of Less Favourable Treatment) Regulations 2002.

QUESTIONS

1 Jane works at a firm of solicitors. Two months ago she was involved in a car accident which has left her with recurring back trouble and also spells when she finds it difficult to concentrate. Medical reports indicate that these conditions will continue for some time.

She has asked to be allowed to work flexible hours and to reduce her total working hours from 38 a week to 30. She has also asked to be provided with a special chair to ease the pain in her back.

Her employers have agreed to provide a chair when the staff move to new offices next year but have refused to agree to the changes in working hours on the ground that all employees need to be at work at the same time and for the same number of hours so as to provide an efficient service to clients.

Advise Jane on any claim which she may have under the Disability Discrimination Act 1995.

2 Catherine is interviewed for a teaching post at a small primary school. She is asked at the interview how many children she has and, when she answers 'five', she is asked, 'how will you manage to get them all off your hands in time for you to get to work?' She says that this will be no problem, but she is not appointed. She has now learnt that a man was appointed who was not asked questions about his children.

Advise Catherine on whether she has any claim under the Sex Discrimination Act 1975.

3 Edith has been appointed as a secretary at a local authority school on a salary of £13,000 for a 21-hour week. She has just learned that, although her predecessor, a woman, was on the same salary, the man who was secretary before her received £13,000 for a 20-hour week. She also finds that a male secretary at a neighbouring school, run by the same local authority, receives £14,000 for a 21-hour week.

Advise Edith on any claim which she could bring.

FURTHER READING

Brownsword, R., Cornish, W. and Llewellyn, W. (1998) *Law and Human Genetics: Regulating a Revolution*, Hart Publishing: Oxford. (Although this book was published some years ago in a fast-moving area it is still valuable and there is a useful discussion on genetics and discrimination in employment at p. 21.)

Cotter, A.-M. (2004) *Gender Injustice: An International Comparative Analysis of Equality in Employment*, Ashgate Press: Aldershot. (A clear and comprehensive guide to sex discrimination and the law in the USA, UK, Australia and New Zealand, Africa, North America and the European Union.)

Lawson, A. and Gooding, C. (2005) *Disability Rights in Europe: From Theory to Practice*, Hart Publishing: Oxford.

BIBLIOGRAPHY

Allott, A. (1980) *The Limits of Law*, Butterworths: London.

Barnard, C. and Hepple, B. (2000) 'Substantive Equality', 59 CLJ 562.

Collins, H. (2003) 'Discrimination, Equality and Social Inclusion', 66 MLR 16.

Connolly, M. (2006) *Discrimination Law*, Sweet & Maxwell: London (p. 254) (This book is an excellent survey of the whole of discrimination law but unfortunately it was published too early to deal with the legislation on age discrimination.)

Cunningham, N. (2006) 'Discrimination Through the Looking Glass; Judicial Guidelines on the Burden of Proof' 35 ILJ 279.

Davies, P. and Freedland, M. (1993) *Labour Legislation and Public Policy*, Oxford University Press: Oxford.

Doyle, B. (1997) 'Enabling Legislation or Dissembling Law? The Disability Discrimination Act 1995', 64 MLR 64.

DTI (2005) *Equality and Diversity: Age Matters*, Age Consultation 2003, Summary of Responses. DTI: London.

Elliott, M. (2000) *The Catholics of Ulster*, Penguin Books: London. (See especially pp. 383–94 on discrimination on religious grounds. This is an admirable book with detailed analysis and explains why there was the need to pursue affirmative action in Northern Ireland.)

Equal Opportunities Commission (2004) *Interim Report into Part-time and Flexible Working*. EOC: London.

Equality Commission for Northern Ireland (2004) *Fair Employment Monitoring Report*. Equality Commission for Northern Ireland: Belfast.

Fair Employment Commission (1995) *The Key Facts: Religion and Community Background in Northern Ireland*. Fair Employment Commission: Belfast.

Fredman, S. (2002) *Discrimination Law*, Oxford University Press: Oxford. (Chapter 1, 'Equality: Concepts and Controversies' has a valuable analysis of approaches to equality.)

Fredman, S. (2004) 'Marginalising Equal Pay Laws', 33 ILJ 281.

Hegarty, A. (1995) 'Examining Equality: The Fair Employment Act (NI) 1989 and its Review', 2 Web JCLI.

Kersley, B. et al. (2006) *Inside the Workplace: Findings from the 2004 Workplace Relations Survey*, Routledge: London.

McColgan, A. (2000) *Discrimination Law: Text, Cases and Materials*, Hart Publishing: Oxford.

McColgan, A. (2005) *Discrimination Law: Text and Materials* (2nd edn), Hart Publishing: Oxford.

McCrudden, C. (1992) 'Affirmative Action and Fair Participation: Interpreting the Fair Employment Act 1989', ILJ 170. (This Act was the predecessor of the present regulations.)

Rubenstein, M. (2002) Commentary, 29 IRLR 2.

Rubenstein, M. (2004) 'Is Lack of Belief Protected?', *Equal Opportunities Review*, p. 128.

Sargeant, M. (2006) 'The Employment Equality (Age) Regulations 2006: A Legitimisation of Age Discrimination in Employment', 35 ILJ 209.

Steele, I. (2006) 'Tracing the Single Source; Choice of Comparators in Equal Pay Claims', ILJ 338.

Wallington, P. (1978) 'Ladies first – how Mr. Peake was piqued', CLJ 37.

For further resources and updates please go to the Companion Website accompanying this book at **www.mylawchamber.co.uk/duddingtonemployment**

10 Employment rights and the family

INTRODUCTION

The first legislation in this area was contained in the Employment Protection Act 1975 which introduced the right not to be dismissed on the ground of pregnancy or maternity together with maternity pay and leave. The Labour Manifesto of 1997 promised to create 'a flexible labour market that serves employers and employees alike' and since 1997 there has been a flood of legislation which has both extended existing rights and introduced new ones. The latest is the Work and Families Act 2006 which has made changes to the system and a number of the changes enabled by this Act are brought into effect by the Maternity and Parental Leave etc. and the Paternity and Adoption Leave (Amendment) Regulations 2006 (SI 2006/2014). The law is described as at 1 April 2007 when the latest changes came into force.

The relationship between the different rights is complex and the following example may help:

Example

Claire is pregnant. She has the right to time off for antenatal care and if she is dismissed on account of pregnancy then this counts as automatically unfair dismissal. She must take two weeks' maternity leave but she will probably wish to have longer and she can take up to 52 weeks' maternity leave. Her husband, John, will be able to take two weeks' paid paternity leave. Claire is also entitled to maternity pay for, at present, 39 weeks of maternity leave.

After the child is born, both parents are entitled to parental leave until the child is five but this is unpaid and they are also entitled to time off for dependent care to deal with domestic emergencies. Finally they may request a flexible working arrangement until the child reaches his or her sixth birthday or, if the child is disabled, for the rest of his or her life or until the disability ceases provided that they remain carers.

ANTENATAL CARE

There is no requirement of a minimum length of service and a woman has a right not to be unfairly denied the right to keep appointments but the employer can ask to see a letter of appointment (s 55 of the ERA 1996).

THE RIGHT NOT TO BE DISMISSED

This right, although originating from UK law, was developed as a result of the EC Pregnant Workers Directive (92/85) and is now contained in s 99 of the ERA 1996 as amended by the Maternity and Parental Leave etc. Regulations 1999 (SI 1999/3312). This provides that it is automatically unfair to dismiss a woman if the reason or principal reason relates to pregnancy, childbirth or maternity, or the taking of ordinary, compulsory or additional maternity leave. The woman does not have to inform the employer when she is offered the job that she is pregnant although at some time the employer must know that she is pregnant (perhaps through a third party) otherwise the reason could not be pregnancy. The words 'relates to' mean that dismissal is also automatically unfair if it is for any reason connected with pregnancy, e.g. a miscarriage. In addition, dismissal is also automatically unfair if it is on the grounds that the employee has taken or agrees or indeed refuses to take paternity leave, adoption leave or parental leave or has taken time off to deal with a domestic emergency. Furthermore, it is unlawful by s 47C of the ERA 1996 to subject an employee to any detriment for any of the above reasons for which dismissal is automatically unfair.

Where a woman is dismissed on these grounds then the employer must, even if not requested to do so, give her a written statement of reasons (s 92(4) of the ERA 1996).

SEX DISCRIMINATION AND PREGNANCY AND MATERNITY

There is, additionally, a right under EC law not to be dismissed on pregnancy grounds as this counts as sex discrimination. Originally, it was not possible for a pregnant woman to claim that a pregnancy dismissal was sex discrimination as there was no comparator; but in *Webb* v *EMO* (1994) the ECJ held that a pregnancy dismissal could be sex discrimination as it was gender related. A claim here has the advantage over a claim under s 99 (above) in that there is no ceiling on compensation, whereas s 99 claims are subject to the normal ceiling on unfair dismissal claims (see Chapter 11). It also, of course, covers situations where the employee is not dismissed but treated less favourably in other ways. The position has now been clarified by a new s 3A, which is inserted into the Sex Discrimination Act 1975 by the Employment Equality (Sex Discrimination) Regulations 2005 (SI 2005/2467). Section 3A provides that a person discriminates against a woman if:

(a) at a time in a protected period, and on the ground of the woman's pregnancy, the person treats her less favourably than he would treat her had she not become pregnant; or

(b) on the ground that the woman is exercising or seeking to exercise, or has exercised or sought to exercise, a statutory right to maternity leave, the person treats her less favourably than he would treat her if she were neither exercising nor seeking to exercise, and had neither exercised nor sought to exercise, such a right.

The term 'protected period' is defined as one which begins each time a woman becomes pregnant and it ends when her ordinary, or, if appropriate, additional maternity leave ends or earlier if she has returned to work. If she is not entitled to maternity leave because she has, for example, had a miscarriage, then the protected period finishes at the end of two weeks from the end of the pregnancy.

Section 3A also provides that where a person's treatment of a woman is on grounds of illness suffered by the woman as a consequence of a pregnancy of hers, that treatment is to be taken to be on the ground of the pregnancy.

THE RIGHT TO MATERNITY LEAVE

This right, from the Maternity and Parental Leave Regulations 1999, has been amended by ss 17 and 18 of the Employment Act 2002 and by the Work and Families Act 2006. A major change is that there is now one period of leave which is for up to 52 weeks; but the previous distinction between ordinary and additional maternity leave is still important in connection with, for example, the employee's return to work and other matters as explained below.

Compulsory maternity leave

This is for two weeks following the birth and it is a criminal offence for an employer to employ a woman in this period (Maternity and Parental Leave Regulations 1999).

Statutory maternity leave

There are two periods of leave: the period of ordinary maternity leave and the period of additional maternity leave. However, the distinction between these is no longer as important, for the following reasons:

- All female employees are entitled to maternity leave as there is no minimum period of qualifying employment whereas previously there was a distinction between ordinary maternity leave, to which all employees were entitled, and additional maternity leave, to which only employees with 26 weeks of continuous employment before the 15th week before the expected week of childbirth (EWC) were entitled. Note that the EWC is defined as the week beginning at midnight between the Saturday and the Sunday in which the birth is expected.
- It is no longer the case that statutory maternity pay (SMP) is paid during ordinary maternity leave but not additional maternity leave because there is now a right to SMP for 39 weeks and this will be extended to 52 weeks in 2009.

It should be noted that the rest of the rules apply to both ordinary and additional maternity leave unless stated otherwise.

10

Employment rights and the family

Entitlement and notice

All female employees are entitled to maternity leave as there is no minimum period of qualifying employment. It can last for *up to 52 weeks* and in order to be entitled to take leave the employee must inform her employer no later than the 15th week before the expected week of childbirth (EWC) of the fact that she is pregnant, when the EWC is and when she wishes maternity leave to start. She can change this date but she must give the employer 28 days' notice of the changed date unless this is not reasonably practicable, as where the baby is born early, in which case she must give as much notice as possible. Whatever date is chosen, leave cannot begin until the 11th week before the EWC. However, if maternity leave has not begun but the employee is absent through a reason related to pregnancy at any time after the fourth week before the expected week of childbirth then this automatically triggers the beginning of leave. The reason is to stop the taking of sick leave rather than maternity leave at this point. The latest day when leave can begin is the day after the day of the birth. If the employee's contract of employment is terminated before leave starts then the right to leave is lost although there is still a right to maternity pay.

The employee's contract of employment

During *ordinary maternity leave* this continues as if she were not absent, apart from terms concerning remuneration. This is because she receives maternity pay. The effect is that employees remain entitled to any other benefits, e.g. cheap mortgages, and holiday leave continues to accrue and continuity of employment is preserved. In *Hoyland* v *Asda Stores Ltd* (2005) the EAT held that it is not unlawful sex discrimination for annual bonuses paid to workers to be reduced pro-rata when the worker is on maternity leave. The point is that a woman who is on maternity leave is treated as not being at work although her status as an employee is protected. Thus in principle she is still entitled to bonuses but they can be reduced to reflect her period of absence. However, the EAT held that bonuses for the two-week period of compulsory maternity leave must be paid. In *Merino Gomez* v *Continental Industrias del Caucho* (2004) (see also Chapter 7) the ECJ held that a woman on maternity leave is entitled to take annual leave guaranteed under the Working Time Directive which has accrued during her absence. This includes a situation where the period of maternity leave coincides with the dates of an annual holiday fixed in advance by a collective agreement, the reason being that the purpose of the Working Time Regulations is to protect the health and safety of workers and maternity leave is not holiday.

During *additional maternity leave* those parts of the employee's contract continue which relate to: the giving of notice of termination of employment; the benefit of disciplinary and grievance procedures; entitlement to redundancy compensation; the employer's implied obligation of mutual trust and confidence; non-disclosure by the employee of confidential information; and the acceptance of gifts by the employee. Continuity of employment does not continue but is not broken.

Pension rights during maternity leave

During *ordinary maternity leave* the employee is entitled to accrue pension benefits based on her normal salary. If *additional maternity leave* is paid then pension benefits continue to accrue but not if it is unpaid because terms of the contract relating to remuneration do not continue. However, as a period of additional maternity leave does not break continuity of employment, pensionable service after leave must be treated as continuous with leave before it.

Contact during maternity leave

A new provision, contained in the Maternity and Parental Leave etc. and the Paternity and Adoption Leave (Amendment) Regulations 2006 is *'keeping in touch days'*. This allows the employee to do up to ten days' work for the employer during maternity leave without losing either SMP or ending the actual leave. On the other hand, any days worked in this way do not extend the actual leave period. The work done by the employee under these provisions is to be by agreement between the parties and so the employer cannot require the employee to work in this way. The regulations do not prescribe whether the work is to be performed in blocks of, for example, three days or individual days and so this is left to the parties to agree. In addition, the above regulations also allow reasonable contact between the parties during leave and this removes the uncertainty felt by employers as to whether they were allowed to contact the employee at all.

Return to work

The employer must, within 28 days of the start of leave, notify the employee of the date on which leave will end, which will normally be at the end of 52 weeks from the start date. If the employee wishes to return earlier, then 8 weeks' notice (previously it was 28 days') of this must be given to the employer. If she does not give this notice then the employer can postpone her return until the full 8 weeks' notice is given. Where the employee is returning after *ordinary maternity leave* (26 weeks) then the right is to return to the previous job on the same terms but if the employee's job is redundant when she is away then she is entitled to be offered a suitable alternative vacancy if it exists. Failure to allow her to return is automatically unfair dismissal unless it was not reasonably practicable to allow the employee, on grounds other than redundancy, to return to a suitable job. If the employee decides that she does not wish to return to work at the end of leave then she must give whatever notice is required to terminate her contract of employment. If she simply does not return to work at the end of leave without having terminated her contract of employment then this does not in itself operate to terminate her contract automatically. Instead she must be treated as any other employee who is absent. If the employee is returning after taking *additional maternity leave* (i.e. absence for more than 26 weeks) then she has the same right to return to the same job unless it is not reasonably practicable to allow her to return to it, in which case she must be offered a similar job on not less favourable terms and conditions.

MATERNITY PAY (SMP)

Maternity pay is governed by the Social Security Contributions and Benefits Act 1992 and regulations made under it, principally the Statutory Maternity Pay (General) Regulations 1986.

Maternity pay is paid for 39 weeks but it is intended that this will increase to 52 weeks by 2009 so that there is an entitlement to pay for the whole period of maternity leave. To qualify a woman must meet the following criteria:

(a) have 26 weeks' continuous service by the end of the 15th week of the EWC. In effect this means that employees who started their employment before they became pregnant will be entitled and there is still an entitlement even though the employee has left work or is dismissed after the 15th week before the EWC;

(b) earn at least £84 a week on average in the calculation period which, if the employee is paid monthly, is the eight weeks up to and including the 15th week before the EWC. If the employee is paid monthly then the calculation period is usually based on the two monthly payments before the 15th week before the EWC.

SMP is paid at an earnings-related rate of 90% of average weekly earnings for the first six weeks and then for the remaining 33 weeks at a flat rate of £111 a week (from April 2007) or 90% of average earnings if this is less. The fact that SMP is earnings related for only the first six weeks is criticised by James (2006), who points out that few women are able to take advantage of their long-term maternity leave entitlement as the rate of SMP thereafter is so low. The employer can, of course, pay more than this. In *Alabaster v Woolwich plc and Secretary of State for Social Security* (2004) the ECJ held that where a woman receives a pay increase before the start of her maternity leave then this must be taken into account in calculating the earnings-related element of her SMP. UK provisions on SMP did not comply with EU law as they allowed for this to be taken into account only where the pay increase was backdated.

The decision in *Alabaster* led to a change in the Maternity Pay Regulations so that any pay rise awarded between the beginning of the reference period used for the calculation of maternity pay and the end of maternity leave must be included. It is interesting to note that the Court of Appeal, to whom the case returned from the ECJ, felt that the Equal Pay Act 1970 was the most appropriate legislation under which to bring such claims but that the principle of requiring a comparator would not apply to this type of claim. The use of the Equal Pay Act may lead to the principle in *Alabaster* being extended to where, for example, a woman employee is paid less than other employees as she had missed training due to being on leave. It ought also to apply to contractual maternity pay.

The Statutory Maternity Pay, Social Security (Maternity Allowance) and Social Security (Overlapping Benefits) (Amendment) Regulations 2006 reg 3 have inserted a new reg 9A into the Statutory Maternity Pay (General) Regulations 1986 allowing a woman's maternity pay to continue when she works on a keeping in touch day.

The employer can recover 92% of SMP from the government but small employers (those whose gross National Insurance contributions are £40,000 or less in the qualifying tax year) can recover all of it.

MATERNITY ALLOWANCE (MA)

This is payable to women employees who do not meet the criteria for SMP and MA is paid to them by the Department for Work and Pensions. The criteria are as follows:

- She is pregnant and has reached the start of the 11th week before the EWC.

- She has been employed as an employed earner or a self-employed earner for at least 26 weeks in the 66 weeks preceding the EWC.

- Her average weekly earnings are not less than the MA threshold which is currently £30 a week.

Maternity allowance is paid for up to 39 weeks at a weekly rate of 90% of average earnings or the prescribed rate which is currently £108.85 a week.

PATERNITY LEAVE

Paternity and Adoption Leave Regulations 2002 (SI 2002/2788) as amended

An employee is entitled to either one or two weeks' leave following the birth of the child provided that he has been continuously employed for 26 weeks ending with the 15th week before the EWC. The other qualification is that he must either be the father of the child or the mother's husband or a person who lives in an 'enduring family relationship' with the mother provided that he is not a relative of the mother. It is possible for paternity leave to be taken by a woman where the partner of the actual birth mother is a woman.

It is important to emphasise that the entitlement is not to a total of two weeks' leave but to a block of one or two weeks and the weeks must be consecutive. Thus an employee cannot take, for example, one week immediately after the child is born and then another week later on. The other requirement is that leave must be taken in the 56 days after the birth. Only one period of leave can be taken even in the case of multiple births. The employee must notify the employer of his intention to take leave not later than the 15th week before the EWC and at this stage should say if one or two weeks' leave will be taken and when it will start. The employee can simply say that it will start when the child is born.

The employee's contract of employment continues during the leave period and the provisions here are identical to those when ordinary maternity leave is taken. Furthermore, it is unlawful either to dismiss an employee or subject him to any detriment because he has taken paternity leave.

ADDITIONAL PATERNITY LEAVE

Section 3 of the Work and Families Act 2006 introduces a new s 80AA into the Employment Rights Act 1996 which allows for additional paternity leave and it is anticipated that this will come into effect at the same time as paid maternity and adoption leave is extended to 52 weeks. It will allow an extra 26 paid weeks' leave beyond the present entitlement to two weeks' leave. It must be taken before the first birthday of the child. The idea is that the mother can, if she wishes, return to work after six months' leave and the father can then take paid leave for the next 26 weeks, thus

10

Employment rights and the family

giving them a total of one year's paid leave. The government put out to consultation options for how the scheme would work and in November 2006 it announced its preferred responses, which are as follows:

- To be eligible a father or partner must have completed 26 weeks' continuous employment at the 15th week before the EWC and must continue in employment until leave is actually taken.
- The earliest date at which leave can begin is to be 20 weeks from the date of the birth of the child.
- Leave can actually begin when the mother has finished her maternity leave period or is no longer receiving statutory maternity pay.
- There can be a gap between the end of maternity leave and the beginning of paternity leave.
- There will be the same rules on the extent to which contractual rights continue and the right to return to work as apply to ordinary maternity leave.
- There will be keeping in touch days.

The DTI estimates that between 9,000 and 16,000 fathers will take advantage of these provisions in their first year of operation.

PATERNITY PAY

Paternity and Adoption Leave Regulations 2002 (SI 2002/2788) as amended

This is available for one or two weeks' paternity leave and the amounts and the qualifications are the same as for SMP. When paternity leave is extended to up to a further 26 weeks there will also be a right to additional paternity pay for this period.

ADOPTION LEAVE

Paternity and Adoption Leave Regulations 2002 (SI 2002/2788) as amended

The scheme is modelled on that for maternity leave and applies when a child aged under 18 is placed for adoption. There are the following identical features:

- There are two periods of leave – ordinary and additional – which last for the same length of time. It is also proposed to extend adoption leave to 52 weeks by 2009.
- Where an employee takes ordinary adoption leave their contract of employment continues during the leave period and the provisions here are identical to those when ordinary maternity leave is taken. Furthermore, it is unlawful either to dismiss an employee or subject her to any detriment because she has taken adoption leave. Similarly, where additional adoption leave is taken there are the same provisions relating to the employee's contract and the same right to return to work as if additional

maternity leave had been taken. Furthermore, it is unlawful to either dismiss an employee or subject her to any detriment because she has taken adoption leave.

■ There are the same rules on keeping in touch days and contact during employment.

The trigger date for the right to take adoption leave is that the employee must have been employed for at least 26 weeks ending with the week in which he was notified of having been matched with the child and has then notified the agency that he agrees that the child should be placed with him and the actual date of placement. In order to take leave the employee must:

■ provide evidence of his entitlement;

■ inform the employer of the date when the child is likely to be placed for adoption and the date the employee has chosen for leave to begin.

The obvious difference between maternity and adoption leave is that with adoption leave it is up to the adopters to decide who is to take the leave and, of course, there is no presumption that it will be the mother. If one adopter, whether the man or the woman, chooses to take adoption leave then the other is entitled to take paternity leave. If two people of the same sex adopt a child then they choose who is to have maternity and who is to have paternity leave.

ADOPTION PAY

Paternity and Adoption Leave Regulations 2002 (SI 2002/2788) as amended

This is paid for 39 weeks but it is intended that this will increase to 52 weeks by 2009 so that there is an entitlement to pay for the whole period of adoption leave. It is necessary to have 26 weeks' continuous service by the week in which the adopter is notified that she has been matched with a child and has agreed a date of placement with an adoption agency (the adoption week). The employee must earn at least £84 a week on average in the calculation period which, if the employee is paid monthly, is the eight weeks up to and including the adoption week. The same rules on recoupment by the employer apply here as do to SMP.

PARENTAL LEAVE

Maternity and Parental Leave etc. Regulations 1999 (SI 1999/3312) as amended

Employees who have been continuously employed for at least one year are entitled to parental leave (although parents of a disabled child may in some circumstances be able to count periods of service with a previous employer), provided that they have responsibility for a child. Responsibility is defined in the same terms as are used in family law as laid down by s 3 of the Children Act 1989 as amended. Thus a mother automatically has parental responsibility and a father will do so if he is married to the child's mother

10

Employment rights and the family

or, if the parties are unmarried, he registers the birth jointly with the mother. Parental responsibility can also be acquired by a court order or by agreement with the mother. This has the effect that adoptive parents and guardians can qualify for parental leave.

Parental leave is until the child reaches the age of 5 or, where the child is in receipt of a disability living allowance, 18, and is for 13 weeks or, in the case of a disabled child, 18 weeks; 21 days' notice to the employer is needed but this is likely to be increased to 28 days.

It is available to both parents but there is a statutory right to pay. Employers and employees may agree a scheme but, if not, the statutory scheme applies. This provides that the employee must give 21 days' notice of the days when leave is being taken and an employee can only take leave for up to four weeks in any year. Leave under the statutory scheme must be taken in blocks of a week. In *South Central Trains Ltd* v *Rodway* (2004) the EAT held that parental leave was required by the regulations to be taken in periods of not less than a week. Thus an employee who took one day's leave off to look after her child was not entitled to do so and her employers were entitled to take disciplinary action against her for taking leave. The effect was that the employee was counted as having taken one whole week off.

During parental leave the employee's terms and conditions of employment continue in the same way as for additional maternity leave but continuity of employment continues. If up to four weeks' leave is taken then the employee is entitled to return to the same job as before; but if the period of parental leave is followed by a period of additional maternity or adoption leave, or where the employer allows it to continue for more than four weeks, then the right to return to work is the same as for additional maternity or adoption leave. The employee has the right not to be dismissed or subjected to any detriment on the ground that he has taken parental leave.

In practice, one of the main uses of these provisions will be to enable families to go on holiday together, but anecdotal evidence suggests that the take-up of this right has been small.

TIME OFF TO CARE FOR DEPENDANTS

This is a right (ss 57A and 57B of the Employment Rights Act 1996) given to all employees to take reasonable time off to:

- provide assistance when a dependant is ill, injured, assaulted or gives birth;
- arrange care for an injured dependant;
- deal with matters in consequence of the death of a dependant;
- deal with an unexpected disruption in arrangements for the care of a dependant or the termination of those arrangements;
- deal with an incident involving a child at school.

A dependant is defined as the employee's wife, husband, child, parent or someone who lives in the same household as the employee but is not their tenant, lodger, boarder or employee.

In *Qua* v *John Ford Morrison Solicitors* (2003) the EAT laid down the following points on the interpretation of this right:

1 It does not apply to enable time off to be taken to provide care for a dependant but only in order to make arrangements for their care, although inevitably in the case of sudden illness the right will apply to deal with care in an immediate crisis.

2 In deciding what is reasonable time off no account should be taken of any disruption to the employer's business.

3 An employee who is on leave does not have to give the employer daily updates on when she may return. The law simply requires that the employer must be told of the reason for the absence and, unless this is not possible, how long it is expected to last.

In *Forster* v *Cartwright Black* (2004) the EAT held that where an employee takes sick leave following the deaths of both of her parents this does not count as taking time off in consequence of the death of a dependant. It only includes, in this context, taking necessary action in consequence of the death, which includes making funeral arrangements but does not give a right to compassionate leave in the circumstances of this case.

The right is not paid as such but it is expected that employers who have paid in the past will continue to do so. There is no requirement to give notice in advance but the employee should tell the employer the reason for the absence as soon as practicable.

LAW IN CONTEXT
Leave arrangements which go beyond the statutory requirements to support employees with caring responsibilities

The 2004 Workplace Employment Relations Survey (WRES) (Kersley et al., 2000) found that of all workplaces:

57% provided fully paid maternity leave
57% provided fully paid paternity or discretionary leave for fathers
25% provided fully paid parental leave or special paid leave for parents
43% provided special paid leave for family emergencies
4% provided leave for carers of older adults.

There were some findings which were probably inevitable: public sector employers were more likely to go beyond the minimum than those in the private sector; and these arrangements were more likely to be found in larger organisations.

RIGHT TO REQUEST A FLEXIBLE WORKING ARRANGEMENT

The statutory provisions relating to this right are in s 47 of the Employment Act 2002 and these are inserted into the Employment Rights Act 1996 as s 47E, ss 80F–80I and s 104C. Detailed provisions are contained in the Flexible Working (Eligibility, Complaints and Remedies) Regulations 2002 (SI 2002/3236) and the Flexible Working (Procedural Requirements) Regulations 2002 (SI 2002/3207).

10

Employment rights and the family

265

Who is covered?

The right to request a flexible working arrangement was originally given to qualifying employees (see below) who care for a child under the age of 6 or a disabled child under 18. Following the coming into force of the Civil Partnerships Act 2004 the right was extended to civil partners. There was then increasing pressure to extend the right to request a flexible working arrangement to all carers and indeed the government estimated in its Response to the Consultation on the Work and Families Bill (DTI, 2006) that nearly 6 million people care for a sick, elderly or disabled person and around 1.8 million are likely to be in work when their caring role begins. In addition, 50% of employees who took time off in the two years up to April 2005 to care did so to care for a partner, parent or other relative. Accordingly, under regulations introduced under the Work and Families Act 2006 this right has been extended to all carers from April 2007.

Thus there are two conditions which must be met in order to qualify as a person who cares for a child:

(a) to be a person who is the mother, father, adopter, guardian or foster parent of the child, or is married to, or is the civil partner of, anyone in these categories; *and*

(b) to be a person who expects to have responsibility for the upbringing of the child.

A carer will be defined for the purposes of claiming this right as any employee who is or who expects to be caring for an adult who falls into any of the following categories:

■ married to the employee or who is the partner or civil partner of the employee;

■ a near relative of the employee (near relative being a parent, parent in law, adult child, adopted adult child, siblings, uncles, aunts, grandparents and step-relatives);

■ not in either of the above categories but living at the same address as the employee.

According to the Employment Relations Minister Jim Fitzpatrick (DTI Press Release, 9 November 2006) the government estimates that this definition will cover about 80% of carers.

Regulation 3 of the Eligibility Regulations (above) provides that the right to make these requests applies to employees as defined by s 230(1) of the ERA 1996 and that they must have at least 26 weeks' continuous service on the date when the application is made.

What is the right?

Employees are not given a right to a flexible working arrangement but, by s 80F, a right to request one of the following changes:

(a) in hours of work;

(b) in times of work;

(c) where, as between his home and the employer's place of business, he is required to work.

The procedure

Under s 80F(2) of the ERA 1996 it is up to the employee to begin the process by making a formal written application which specifies the change requested (see above) and the date when the employee wishes it to take effect. The application must also state what effect the proposed change will have on the employer and how the employer might deal with it. These requirements are mandatory (*Hussain* v *Consumer Credit Counselling* (2004)). Where an application has been rejected another one cannot be made to the same employer for 12 months. There is a right of appeal.

Action by the employer

When the employer has received a request a meeting must be held with the employee within 28 days unless, within that time, the employer decides to agree to the request and sends the employee written notice to this effect. The employee has the right to be accompanied by a companion at this meeting. If there is a meeting then the employer must notify the employee of the decision within 14 days. If the request is refused then the actual ground must be stated (see the grounds below) and it is insufficient just to state that it is for 'business needs' (*Clarke* v *Telewest Communications* (2004)).

Under s 80G(1)(b) an employer may refuse a request for a flexible working arrangement as defined by the Act if any one or more of the following conditions apply:

- the burden of additional costs
- detrimental effect on the ability to meet consumer demand
- inability to reorganise work among existing staff
- inability to recruit additional staff
- detrimental impact on quality
- detrimental impact on performance
- lack of work during the periods when the employee proposes to work
- planned structural changes
- other grounds which the Secretary of State may specify by regulations.

It is not for the tribunal to question a reason put forward by the employer as justifying a refusal of an application. However, under s 80H(1)(b) if the tribunal, having considered the evidence put forward by the employer as justifying the refusal, feels that it does not support this decision then it can hold that the refusal was unjustified. Thus, in *Mehaffy* v *Dunnes Stores* (2003) the claimant asked to work flexibly to spend more time at home with her son following maternity leave. Her application was rejected and the tribunal found that the employer had closed its mind to the possibility of employees working part-time and, although reasons had been given, there was in effect an automatic refusal.

Effect of granting a request

The effect of granting a request is that the employee's contract is varied and, unless otherwise agreed, this is permanent. Thus when the child reaches the age of six or the

10

Employment rights and the family

carer is no longer a carer they do not have the right to revert to their former contract. With this in mind, one suggestion is for employers and employees to have a trial period to see how the variation works in practice; but DTI guidance emphasises that this can only be by agreement between the parties. In such a case, *IDS Brief 801* points out that the parties should ensure that, if the trial period does not work, there is a right to revert to the original arrangement.

Remedies

An employee can complain to a tribunal on the following grounds:

(a) the employer failed to comply with the statutory procedure;

(b) the employer rejected the application on a ground that was not a permitted reason for refusal (see s 80G(1)(b) above);

(c) the employer's decision to reject the application was based on incorrect facts (s 80H(1)(b) above).

The actual remedies are as follows:

- Compensation of up to eight weeks' pay. The upper limit (currently £310) applies to this award.

- The employer reconsiders the decision. However, the tribunal cannot order the employer to agree to the request. Complaints must be brought within three months of the date on which the employee is notified of the refusal and, as usual, there is jurisdiction to extend this if the tribunal considers that it was not reasonably practicable to have brought the complaint in this time.

The tribunal may award both of these remedies.

Relationship with other remedies

- A letter requesting a flexible working arrangement can amount to a grievance for the purposes of the statutory grievance procedure and so where the application is rejected the employee can present a claim for constructive dismissal (*Commotion Ltd* v *Rutty* (2006)). Chapter 11 deals in full with both dismissal and the statutory grievance procedures.

- A claim may be made that refusal of flexible working constitutes indirect sex discrimination (see Chapter 9) and so it will be for the employer to show that the refusal was justified. (See *IDS Brief 802*, April 2006, page 17 for instances of cases where such a claim has succeeded.) It is noteworthy that such a claim can be made even where the employee has not complied with the procedure for requesting a flexible working arrangement as here it is the actual decision which is being challenged.

- Under s 47E of the ERA 1996 an employee has the right not to be subjected to any detriment on the ground that she has exercised her rights under the flexible working legislation.

■ An employee who is dismissed because she has attempted to exercise the right to claim flexible working may claim that she has been dismissed for exercising a statutory right and such a dismissal is automatically unfair under s 104(1) of the ERA 1996.

LAW IN CONTEXT
Flexible working

A CPID survey, *Employment and the Law* (2005), showed that 62% of the respondents felt that, from the employers' point of view, there had been benefits from the legislation on flexible working. The most common examples were improved staff retention, higher morale and a reduction in costs because of hot desking. However, looking at the origin of the responses, there was a marked difference between the public sector, where almost 75% saw the legislation as a driver of good practice, and manufacturing and production, where only 40% saw it in this light. In the manufacturing sector, 23% of respondents saw the right as unnecessary compared with only 5% in the private sector. The government estimated in its Response to the Consultation on the Work and Families Bill (DTI 2006) that 22% of employees with dependent children had requested a flexible working arrangement and over 80% of requests had been accepted in full or in part.

However, there is now a move to extending the right to a flexible working arrangement to all employees. The TUC, in its report *Challenging Times* (November 2005), estimates that over 75% of all workers have no flexibility in their contracts and the Equal Opportunities Commission (in *Britain's Hidden Brain Drain* (September 2005)) points out that there are very few part-time job opportunities at a senior level and feels that an extension of the right to request a flexible working arrangement to all employees would open up more senior posts to women. There is also some interesting data on flexi-time working in general (i.e. not necessarily in the situations covered by the Act) in *Inside the Workplace: Findings from the 2004 Workplace Relations Survey* (Kersley et al., 2006) with significant increases in the proportion of workplaces allowing non-managerial employees to work flexi-time. However, there were low levels of childcare facilities and financial help with childcare, with only 8% of workplaces providing one of these. In addition, it seems that the relatively new statutory provisions on parental and paternity leave have not yet filtered through to all employers, as it is reported that 27% of workplaces do not provide parental leave and 8% do not provide paternity leave.

SUMMARY

This chapter deals with the expanding law on work and families and looks at the various ways in which those at work are given rights to enable them to combine their domestic and caring responsibilities with their duties under their contracts of employment. It also looks specifically at the rights of carers.

There are the following rights, both actual and proposed:

- not to be dismissed on grounds of pregnancy or maternity
- maternity leave, both ordinary and additional
- maternity pay
- paternity leave, both ordinary and additional
- paternity pay
- adoption leave, both ordinary and additional
- adoption pay
- parental leave
- time off for emergencies
- right to ask for a flexible working arrangement.

QUESTION

Alix, who works as a legal secretary at a firm of solicitors, is pregnant. She wishes to remain at work as long as possible until the baby is born so that she has the maximum possible maternity leave afterwards. She also wants to return to the same job when she returns but she hopes that she will be able to work part-time for one year. She then hopes to be able to go back to working full-time. Her husband, Charles, would like to take paid time off after the baby is born for as long as possible as he feels that it is important that fathers are not left out at this time.

Explain to Alix and Charles whether the law will allow all of their wishes to be met.

Would it make any difference to your answer if:

(a) Charles and Alix were not married?

(b) Charles and Alix were adopting a child?

FURTHER READING

Conaglen, J. (2000) 'Women, Work and Family: a British Revolution?' in J. Conaglen, R. M. Fischl and K. Klare (eds) *Labour Law in an Era of Globalisation*, Oxford University Press: Oxford.

Griffiths, J. (2006) 'Flexibility for Parents Helps Business', *People Management*, 16 June 2006.

BIBLIOGRAPHY

CIPD (2005) *Employment and the Law*. CIPD: London.

DTI (2006) *Work and Families: Choice and Flexibility*. DTI: London.

Equal Opportunities Commission (2005) *Britain's Hidden Brain Drain* (September), EOC: London.

IDS (2006) Brief 801, March 2006. Income Data Service: London.

IDS (2006) Brief 802, April 2006. Income Data Service: London.

James, G. (2006) 'The Work and Families Act 2006: Legislation to Improve Choice and Flexibility?' 35 ILJ 272.

Kersley, B. et al. (2006) *Inside the Workplace: Findings from the 2004 Workplace Relations Survey*, Routledge: London. (See also the article on this by Dickens (2006) 'Equality and Working Life Balance. What's Happening at the Workplace' ILJ 445.)

TUC Report (2005) *Challenging Times* (November). TUC: London.

For further resources and updates please go to the Companion Website accompanying this book at **www.mylawchamber.co.uk/duddingtonemployment**

10

Employment rights and the family

Part 3

Termination of the employment relationship

This part looks at the legal position when the contract of employment is terminated. In Chapter 11 we contrast the remedies for dismissal by looking at both wrongful (common law) dismissal and unfair (statutory) dismissal. In addition we look at precisely what dismissal means and consider the economic framework in which the law of dismissal operates. The focus of Chapter 12 is dismissals for economic reasons which include dismissals by reason of redundancy, dismissals on the transfer of an undertaking and some dismissals under the category of 'some other substantial reason'.

11 Wrongful and unfair dismissal

INTRODUCTION

The essence of a claim for wrongful dismissal is that the employee is claiming that the dismissal was in breach of contract. It therefore contrasts with unfair dismissal, where the claim is not based on the contract but on statute. Statistically, unfair dismissal is by far the more important of the two, with 41,832 claims in 2005/6 where the main claim was for unfair dismissal, as compared to 26,230 claims for wrongful dismissal, which the Annual Report of the Employment Tribunals Service shows as breach of contract. In addition, there were 5,630 claims arising out of failure to inform and consult on a redundancy and 899 on failure to inform and consult on a transfer of an undertaking.

However, it is often necessary to discuss the concepts of wrongful and unfair dismissal side by side and therefore the following table may be found useful for reference.

Wrongful dismissal	Unfair dismissal
Based on the contract	Based on statute
Employee must prove claim	Tribunal decides
No claim if contractual notice given	Can still claim even if contractual notice given
No claim for future loss of earnings	Can claim for future loss of earnings
Facts discovered after the dismissal may be used in evidence	Facts discovered after the dismissal cannot be used in evidence
Remedy is compensation	Remedy is compensation or reinstatement or re-engagement
No ceiling on compensation	Statutory ceiling on compensation
Claim can be brought in the county/High Court or in an employment tribunal if it is for £25,000 or less	Claim must be brought in an employment tribunal
No claim if a fixed-term contract is not renewed	May claim if a fixed-term contract is not renewed
No qualifying period of employment	One year's qualifying period of employment in most cases

The other significant differences are found in the procedures of the county court and High Court which, as compared to the procedures of employment tribunals, tend to be more formal (see Chapter 1).

METHODS OF TERMINATION

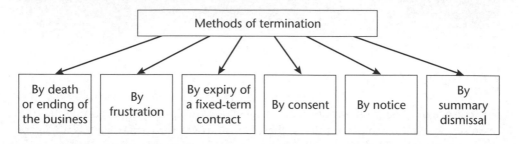

Each of these methods will now be considered in turn under the headings of wrongful and unfair dismissal.

WRONGFUL DISMISSAL

This section will look in more detail at the methods of termination set out above to see whether they give rise to a claim for wrongful dismissal. It will then look at the remedies on the assumption that there is a claim for wrongful dismissal. The methods of termination set out below are, in general, also relevant to a claim for unfair dismissal and they are also discussed later in the context of an unfair dismissal claim.

Termination by death or by the ending of the business

The death of the employer ends the contract of employment at common law but it is important to remember that if the business ends as a consequence of the employer's death then the employees will be entitled to a redundancy payment under the Employment Rights Act 1996 (see Chapter 12). If the business is a company and is wound up compulsorily by the court then this operates as a notice of dismissal to the employees. If it is voluntarily wound up but is to continue in another form, for example by being taken over by another company, then there is no dismissal.

Termination by frustration

The doctrine of frustration applies throughout the law of contract and has the effect of discharging the contract (i.e. bringing it to an end). The result will be that the employee is no longer entitled to wages and no claim for wrongful dismissal can be brought, as there has been no dismissal. Any back pay due may be claimed under the Law Reform (Frustrated Contracts) Act 1943, but there will be no right to compensation for future loss of earnings unless an action can be brought establishing that the employer was at fault in some way. This could be where the conduct of the employer is alleged to have caused the illness which frustrated the contract (see below). However, a person who suffers from illness or incapacity may be entitled to statutory sick pay (SSP) and industrial injuries disablement benefit (see Chapter 7). Nevertheless, these sums will not be large and the effect of the contract of employment being ended by frustration will be to deprive the employee of any chance of receiving any lump sum by way of compensation when their employment ceases. This drastic effect of frustration has led some judges to seek to limit the circumstances in which it can apply to contracts of employment, as we shall see below.

A contract is frustrated when performance of it either becomes impossible or where further performance would involve performing something radically different from what was originally intended. Obvious instances from the employment perspective are the illness or incapacity of the employee, but not all such instances will frustrate the contract. In *Condor v Barron Knights Ltd* (1966) the contract of a drummer in a pop group was frustrated when he was unable to fulfil his contract because of the stress of the work and the resulting illness. In *Marshall v Harland and Wolff Ltd* (1972) Sir John Donaldson set out certain matters which should be considered in deciding whether a contract is frustrated and these were added to by the EAT in *Egg Stores v Leibovici* (1976). A composite list from both cases is as follows:

1 The length of the previous employment.

2 The terms of the contract, including any provision for sick pay.

3 How long it had been expected that the previous employment would continue.

4 The nature of the job.

5 The length, nature and effect of the illness or disabling event.

6 The need of the employer for the work to be done and the necessity for a replacement.

7 The risk to the employer of acquiring obligations in respect of redundancy payments or compensation for unfair dismissal to the replacement employee.

8 Whether wages have continued to be paid.

9 Acts and statements of the employer in relation to the employee, including either the dismissal or failure to dismiss the employee.

10 Whether a reasonable employer could have been expected to wait any longer before ending the employment.

The fact that the application of the doctrine of frustration means that the employee may be left without any compensation for the ending of employment has led some judges to seek to restrict its operation to cases of contracts which are intended to last for a long time and not to be determinable by notice. Where the contract is determinable by notice then it is argued that there is no need for the doctrine of frustration, as the contract can be ended by notice. This view was put forward by Bristow J in *Harman v Flexible Lamps Ltd* (1980) but it was rejected by the Court of Appeal in *Notcutt v Universal Equipment Co. (London) Ltd* (1986), where Dillon LJ pointed out that contracts determinable by notice may be intended to last for a long time and thus the distinction

Wrongful and unfair dismissal

11

drawn by Bristow J between long-term contracts and those determinable by notice was a false one. Not only this, but the decision in *Harman* v *Flexible Lamps* completely ignored the decisions in *Marshall* v *Harland and Wolff* and *Egg Stores* v *Leibovici*.

Even so, in the *Egg Stores* case it was accepted that the doctrine does need to be applied carefully in the case of short-term contracts which can be determined by notice which would at least give the employee the right to wages for the period of notice. This was accepted in *Notcutt* and remains the law. There is a case for looking at whether the doctrine of frustration should apply at all to contracts of employment and to provide that in all cases where the employee is unable to perform the contract through illness or incapacity he or she will be paid wages for the periods of notice to which he or she is entitled. This would avoid requiring the employer to pay a large sum for an occurrence which was not his or her fault, whilst giving the employee some payment.

In *Gryf Lowczowski* v *Hinchingbrooke Healthcare NHS Trust Ltd* (2006) a surgeon was suspended in December 2003 and in November 2004 he was required to attend a reskilling programme as a result of an assessment of his abilities. By August 2005 it had not proved possible to rearrange a reskilling course and so his employer dismissed him on the ground that his contract was frustrated. It was held that this was not so. The issue in this case was not the length of time the employee had been suspended but whether there was a realistic possibility of his being able to attend a reskilling programme and it was found on the facts that this was so.

The other main situation where a contract of employment can be frustrated is where the employee is imprisoned. The problem with applying the doctrine of frustration here is that it can be argued that the act causing the frustration (i.e. the crime for which the employee was imprisoned) was self-induced, in that the employee actually committed the act. Nevertheless, in *Hare* v *Murphy Bros Ltd* (1974) it was held by Denning MR that a contract of employment was frustrated by imprisonment, although Stephenson LJ held simply that imprisonment ended the contract and he was not concerned about the precise label used to describe why this was so. This left some uncertainty in the law, which was eventually resolved by the Court of Appeal in *Shepherd & Co. Ltd* v *Jerrom* (1986), which held that frustration can apply where an employee is imprisoned. The difficulty about the fact that the act was self-induced was met by Balcombe LJ who accepted the view of Denning MR that the frustrating event was the actual imposition of the sentence, which was not, of course, a matter for the employee. There remains the question of whether frustration applies to all sentences of imprisonment. On principle, and accepting the view of Balcombe LJ, it should do so and this may well be the case with actions for wrongful dismissal. Where unfair dismissal is concerned there may be other considerations, as we shall see.

In *Four Seasons Healthcare Ltd* v *Maughan* (2005) the EAT held that a contract of employment was not terminated by frustration where the employee was bailed and so here the employee succeeded in a claim for unpaid wages from when he was bailed until when he was convicted 10 months later. However, it was lawful for the employers, in accord with the disciplinary procedure, to suspend him without pay for an initial period of seven days. The point was that the employee was charged with offences committed at a care home where he worked and it was a condition of bail that he did not enter the home. The EAT pointed out that whereas frustration is an event not foreseen by the parties, here the contractual disciplinary procedure specifically referred to the type of offence (physical abuse of a patient) with which the employee was charged. Thus the conclusion was that he was, after the initial period, suspended on pay.

▮ Termination by expiry of a fixed-term contract

Termination in this way may give rise to an action for wrongful dismissal where the contract was terminated before it expired. Where the contract simply expired and was not renewed then there can be no action for wrongful dismissal because, as explained above, such an action is based on breach of contract and a failure to renew a fixed-term contract which has ended cannot be a breach of it.

Given these consequences, and the growing use of such contracts, it is clearly vital to know precisely what a fixed-term contract is.

> ### Example 1
>
> X is employed as a lecturer by Malvern University for the period 1 September 2002 until 31 August 2003.
>   This appears to be a fixed-term contract, but what if it also provides that it can be ended by one month's notice on either side during this period?
>
> ### Example 2
>
> Y is employed as a carpenter to work on the construction of a new building until it is completed.
>   This is fixed-term in the sense that the duration is not unlimited but is limited by the time it takes to complete a task.

The first problem is that the definition of a fixed-term contract in the law on dismissal covers only contracts for a fixed term as measured by time and not task contracts as in the second of the two examples above. This was held by the Court of Appeal in *Wiltshire CC v NATFHE* (1980) but the Fixed-term Employees (Prevention of Less Favourable Treatment) Regulations 2002 (SI 2002/2034), which came into force on 1 October 2002 (see Chapter 9) specifically include task contracts. Similarly, in *Dixon v BBC* (1979) it was held that a contract could still be fixed-term for the purposes of the law on dismissal even if it contained provision for termination by notice, as in the first example above. The reason was related to the law on unfair dismissal, which will be dealt with later in this chapter. The same rule applies where the Fixed-term Employees Regulations 2002 applies; see *Allen v National Australia Group Europe Ltd* (2004) in Chapter 9. It should be noted that the definition of a fixed-term contract under the regulations does include a task contract, unlike the law on dismissal. Even allowing for the different purposes of the law of dismissal and the regulations, this all seems unsatisfactory.

The other point is that, as explained in Chapter 9, under the regulations it will no longer be possible for the employer to contract out of the obligation to pay a redundancy payment and this, together with the fact that under the regulations fixed-timers may have their contracts converted to full-time, is likely to make these contracts less attractive to employers anyway.

Termination by mutual agreement

Where the employer and employee mutually agree that the employment is at an end, then there can naturally be no dismissal and thus no action for wrongful dismissal. The problem is to distinguish a genuine mutual agreement from the 'resign or be sacked' situation, where the employee may argue that there has been a repudiatory breach of contract by the employer sufficient to justify a claim for wrongful dismissal. Voluntary agreements to take redundancy can be good examples of termination by mutual agreement. In *Birch* v *University of Liverpool* (1985) two lecturers agreed to take early retirement under a scheme which gave very generous compensation in return for employees forgoing their right to (much smaller) statutory payments. They were held to have agreed to terminate their contracts so that it was not open to them to claim later that they had been dismissed. However, each case must be looked at on its own facts. In *Ely* v *YKK Fasteners Ltd* (1994) the employee told his employers that he wanted to leave his job in order to emigrate to Australia. The employers then arranged for a replacement but subsequently the employee changed his mind and said that he intended to stay. The employers, having made the arrangements for the replacement, insisted that he had already resigned. The Court of Appeal held that he had only said that he intended to resign in the future. This was not a resignation as such and, on the facts, it was the employers who had dismissed him.

Termination by notice

It is here that the difference between wrongful and unfair dismissal is seen most clearly because, whereas an employee given due notice can still claim unfair dismissal, as the issue is one of fairness, no claim can be brought for wrongful dismissal in such a case because a wrongful dismissal action depends on establishing a breach of contract by the employer and, by giving due notice, the employer has, far from breaking the contract, kept it. However, the main type of wrongful dismissal claim is where it is alleged that *less than* due notice was given and so the claim is for wages for the period of notice or accrued holiday pay to which the employee was entitled but which was not paid.

At common law an employer is entitled to dismiss on giving notice of the length laid down in the contract but this has been overlaid by the statutory notice provisions now contained in s 86 of the ERA 1996. This provides that employees continuously employed for between one month and two years are entitled to one week's notice and this increases by one week for every year of continuous employment, with a maximum of 12 weeks' notice where employees have more than 12 years' continuous employment.

Employers are only entitled to receive one week's notice where the employee has been employed for at least one week. It must be emphasised that these are only *minimum* periods of notice and, if the contract provides for longer periods of notice, then these must be given. If not, the employee may claim for wages for the period of notice to which he or she was entitled in an action for wrongful dismissal. It is, however, important to establish that notice was actually given. In *Morris* v *Bailey* (1969), where notice was given, not to the employee personally but to his union, this was held to be insufficient. It is also important that any words used make it clear that the employee is actually being given notice.

> ### Example
>
> John works in a newsagent's shop. The owner, Mike, says to him: 'Business is bad. I think that it would be in your best interests to look for another job.' This is not notice and John is still entitled to turn up for work and to receive his wages.

What is the position where the employer wishes to give the employee wages in lieu of notice? In Chapter 7 we saw that a claim for wages in lieu of notice must be brought as a claim for breach of contract (*Delaney* v *Staples* (1991)). The question here is a more fundamental one: can wages in lieu of notice be paid at all or is the employee always entitled to work out notice? The following situations need to be distinguished:

1 Where the contract expressly allows wages to be paid in lieu of notice. There is obviously no difficulty here: the employer may dismiss and pay wages in lieu of notice. In effect, the employee is dismissed with very little warning but does receive wages for whatever period of notice he or she is entitled to. A variation on this theme is the idea of garden leave clauses, where the employee is given a long period of notice during which he or she is paid but is not allowed to work for others during that time. These are dealt with more fully in Chapter 5.

2 Where the employer and employee agree that the employment will terminate immediately and the employee agrees to accept wages in lieu of notice. This will be lawful. The only difference between (1) and (2) is that in (1) the contract expressly provides for this, whereas in (2) it is dealt with by an ad hoc agreement.

3 Where the employer dismisses the employee and offers wages in lieu of notice without the employee agreeing. Here the employee will have a claim for wrongful dismissal but may not be awarded any more than the employer offered.

Termination by summary dismissal

An employer may terminate the contract summarily where the employee has been guilty of a repudiatory breach of the contract of employment. This area has been overtaken by the law on unfair dismissal because where an employee is summarily dismissed an action for unfair dismissal will be preferable, the reason being that a claim for wrongful dismissal can, with limited exceptions, only lead to damages for wages for the period of notice to which the employee was entitled. The only time when a summarily dismissed employee would choose to claim for wrongful dismissal would be if it was not possible to claim for unfair dismissal (see below). With this in mind, treatment of this topic will be brief.

The leading case is *Laws* v *London Chronicle Ltd* (1959), where Evershed MR held that 'the question must be – if summary dismissal is claimed to be justifiable – whether the conduct complained of is such as to show the servant to have disregarded the *essential conditions of the contract of service*'. The words which have been italicised correspond to the phrase 'repudiatory breach' on the part of the employer, in that if the employee has *not* broken an essential condition of the contract then any dismissal will mean that it is the employer who has committed a repudiatory breach and will be liable for wrongful dismissal.

Two contrasting cases on this area concern gardeners, both of whom were dismissed following an altercation with their employer during which the gardener used foul language. In the first, *Pepper* v *Webb* (1969), dismissal was held to be justified as the cause of the dismissal was found to be the failure of the gardener to do the very job which he was employed to do in looking after the garden and greenhouse. This was, to use the words of Evershed MR (above), the disregard of the essential conditions of service. In *Wilson* v *Racher* (1974) the incident in which the foul language was used was an isolated one and dismissal was held not to be justified. Thus the employer committed a repudiatory breach by dismissing the employee.

The whole topic of when an employer is justified in dismissing because of the conduct of the employee is covered in the section below dealing with unfair dismissal. As a general guide, it can be said that occasions when dismissal is fair will normally be sufficient to justify summary dismissal as well. However, in applying these to the law of summary dismissal, the question must always be asked whether the employee had disregarded an essential condition of the contract of employment.

Summary

Thus the only cases where an employee can claim for wrongful dismissal will be where:

1 notice was given but it was not of sufficient length;

2 the dismissal was summary;

3 a fixed-term contract was terminated before the expiry date.

Remedies for wrongful dismissal

Assuming that the employee is able to claim for wrongful dismissal, what remedies may be claimed?

Damages

The general rule is that damages are awarded only for wages due to employees for the period of notice to which they were entitled but did not receive. These are awarded as damages for the employer's breach of contract. The question of what are wages received a restricted reply in *Lavarack* v *Woods of Colchester Ltd* (1967), where an employee was held not to be entitled to discretionary bonuses payable during the notice period precisely because they *were* discretionary and there was no contractual entitlement to them. Where damages are awarded they may be reduced if the employee has failed to mitigate his or her loss by failing to look for and, if offered, accept alternative work. There are, however, the following exceptions where the employee may recover additional payments as damages.

Employee dismissed but employer did not go through contractual disciplinary procedures

In *Gunton* v *Richmond on Thames LBC* (1980) the employee was dismissed without the hearing to which he was entitled under his contract. Damages were awarded for net salary lost for the period for which the procedures should have applied. This will not, however, mean that the employee receives a large extra sum, usually on top of damages for wages in lieu of notice, because the time when any procedures should have operated will not, unless in exceptional cases, exceed a few weeks. The principle in *Gunton* was also applied in *Boyo* v *Lambeth LBC* (1995) but its application is limited to cases where the contract expressly incorporates a right to have specified disciplinary procedures followed before dismissal.

Bonus payments

In *Horkulak* v *Cantor Fitzgerald International* (2004) the Court of Appeal held that an employee is entitled to a rational and bona fide exercise of the employer's discretion as to whether he should receive a bonus. Thus a failure by the employer to exercise a discretion in this way can lead to a claim for damages. (This decision is considered in more detail in Chapter 7.)

Damages (known as stigma damages)

These are claimed for the stigma suffered by the employee in the labour market due to having been associated with a particular employer. In effect the employee is saying that a prospective employer would look at his or her CV and, seeing that they had worked for Firm X, decide that they did not want to employ anyone who had worked for them. The possibility of such a claim was opened up by the decision of the House of Lords in *Malik* v *BCCI* (1997), where it was held that a claim for stigma damages could be brought as a result of a breach by the employers of the implied term of mutual trust and confidence (see Chapter 5). However, the effect of this decision was subject to a restrictive interpretation by both the Court of Appeal and the House of Lords in *Johnson* v *Unisys Ltd* (2001), where it was held that the decision in *Malik* was not authority for the proposition that stigma damages could be awarded in an action for wrongful dismissal. It was pointed out that *Malik* was concerned with an award of damages for breach of an implied term of the contract *during* employment and was not concerned with damages for breach of contract. (The *Johnson* decision is discussed below.) Where damages are awarded, if they exceed £30,000, the excess is taxable (ss 148 and 188 of the Income and Corporation Taxes Act 1988). This does not apply to unfair dismissal compensation.

11

Wrongful and unfair dismissal

Employee is claiming damages for loss of reputation

This seems to be largely confined to cases of actors and actresses, as in *Marbe* v *George Edwardes Ltd* (1928), where an actress was awarded damages for loss of reputation when her contract was broken.

Wrongful dismissal and unfair dismissal

Two factors have led to attempts to extend the heads under which damages can be awarded for wrongful dismissal:

(a) the fact that damages in a wrongful dismissal claim are limited to wages due to employees for the period of notice to which they were entitled but did not receive with the result that damages tend to be low;

(b) the fact that there is a statutory cap on compensation (including the basic award) for unfair dismissal. This will be explained in detail later in this chapter but at present the cap in most cases is set at £69,900.

The result is that where the employee's loss exceeds this figure full compensation will not be received. One particular attempt to claim extra damages failed in *Fraser* v *HLMAD Ltd* (2006): the Court of Appeal held that where damages for wrongful dismissal (limited to £25,000) are recovered in the employment tribunal then a claim for the excess over this sum cannot be brought in the High Court. This is because, under the common law doctrine of merger, once final judgment is given the cause of action is merged in the judgment and is extinguished.

This has now become an anomalous situation because, since the remedy of unfair dismissal was introduced by the Industrial Relations Act 1971, two other possible remedies have emerged where there is no cap on damages:

(a) action for unlawful discrimination – see Chapter 9;

(b) a common law action for breach of the duty to protect the employee from psychiatric illness caused by stress at work – see Chapter 8.

The different attempts that have been made to extend the rules on damages for wrongful dismissal will now be examined but at the outset it must be said that none of them have been successful.

Dismissal has meant that the employee has lost the opportunity to claim for unfair dismissal

---

Example

Jennifer was employed as a teacher by Barset CC from 1 September 2002 but was summarily dismissed on 1 August 2003. As a result she was unable to claim for unfair dismissal, as she did not have the requisite period of one year's continuous employment. She can bring a claim for wrongful dismissal for damages representing wages for the period of notice to which she was entitled but can she add on a claim for damages for the loss of her statutory rights to compensation for unfair dismissal?

In *Harper* v *Virgin Net* (2004) the Court of Appeal held that there can be no claim for damages at common law for loss of opportunity to claim unfair dismissal. It looked at the original provisions (contained in para 10 of Part III of Sch 16 to the Trade Union and Labour Relations Act 1974) which clearly stated that an employee who is dismissed without the statutory notice period will be deemed to have an EDT (effective date of termination) at the end of the statutory notice period. This would have been enough to have disposed of the case but Brooke LJ also referred with approval to the speech of Lord Millett in *Johnson* v *Unisys* (2001). Here he disapproved of any development in the power of the courts to award damages at common law on the basis that a dismissal was not exercised in good faith as the 'creation of the statutory right' (to claim unfair dismissal) has 'made any such development of the common law both unnecessary and undesirable'. The effect is that the courts are trying to stop two alternatives springing up: a statutory action for unfair dismissal and, alongside it, an action for wrongful dismissal where damages can be claimed on a wider basis than at present. The statutory action is felt sufficient.

A claim for damages on the basis that the dismissal was in breach of the duty of mutual trust and confidence

In *Johnson* v *Unisys Ltd* (2001) Johnson worked for a multinational software company and was then summarily dismissed. He was awarded the then maximum amount of compensation of £11,691 but he subsequently claimed in a common law action that he was entitled to a further £400,000 for breach of contract and negligence because, as a result of the manner of his dismissal, he had suffered a mental breakdown which had prevented him from obtaining employment since then. The claim was that the breach of contract was either a breach of the employer's disciplinary procedure which was incorporated into his contract as an express term or a breach of the implied term of mutual trust and confidence. The House of Lords struck out the claim on the ground that it disclosed no reasonable cause of action. The reasons for this decision were, in effect, twofold:

1 The policy reason that a common law claim of this kind would conflict with the statutory claim for unfair dismissal. A dismissed employee would, if the action was allowed, have a choice: either a claim for unfair dismissal under the Employment Rights Act 1996 or a common law claim that the dismissal was wrongful as being in breach of the implied term of mutual trust and confidence. The House felt that such a common law claim would circumvent the statutory one and, indeed, on the facts of this case, that would have been so: as we saw above, the damages sought were far in excess of that which could either then or now be claimed in an unfair dismissal claim; and the claim was presented three and a half years after the dismissal when an unfair dismissal claim must be presented within three months of the effective date of termination of the contract. The reasoning can be summed up simply by saying: why have two types of claim when one will do?

2 The strictly legal reason that the implied duty of mutual trust and confidence applies only to the performance of obligations under the contract and not to the termination of the contract. The majority held that the implied term was better suited to preserving a continuing relationship than being used when that relationship had been terminated. On the face of it there is something in this: if the relationship has

11

Wrongful and unfair dismissal

ended how can there be any mutual trust and confidence? Yet the fallacy behind it was exposed by Lord Steyn (dissenting), who observed that there was no difference between an express term of the contract giving the employer the right to terminate the employee's contract on notice and an implied one that it could not be done in bad faith (i.e. in breach of the duty of mutual trust and confidence).

In *Eastwood* v *Magnox Electric plc/McCabe* v *Cornwall CC* (2004) the House of Lords affirmed the '*Johnson* exclusion area' (per Lord Nicholls). The applicant claimed damages for the way in which his suspension from duty, whilst allegations against him of inappropriate sexual conduct were investigated, was handled. These allegations eventually brought about his dismissal. The House of Lords held that a common law action can be brought only when the cause of action accrued out of facts arising *before* dismissal. This could be, for example, where there is financial loss arising out of suspension or loss arising from psychiatric or other illness occurring before dismissal which could be caused by, for example, unfair disciplinary action taken before dismissal.

Damages for injured feelings resulting from the manner of dismissal

These were claimed in *Addis* v *Gramophone Co. Ltd* (1909) but the House of Lords held that such a claim was inadmissible and this has been the view of the law ever since, despite attempts to argue the contrary. In *Johnson* v *Unisys* the House of Lords found no reason to depart from this rule in wrongful dismissal cases. However, the speech of Lord Hoffmann opened up the possibility of such a claim in unfair dismissal cases as he held that all the matters of which Johnson complained could have been the subject of an unfair dismissal action. As these included compensation for the manner of the dismissal, logically this must be a possible head of claim. The exciting (to some) possibility that tribunals could award compensation for non-economic loss of this and other kinds was, however, squashed by the decision in *Dunnachie* v *Kingston upon Hull Council* (see below).

Direct enforcement of the contract

Given that the circumstances in which damages for wrongful dismissal are limited, is there more mileage in an action asking that the contract should be directly enforced against the employer?

Example

Charles is dismissed from his job as a computer programmer. He is not interested in compensation but simply wants his job back.

As a general rule, such a claim is bound to fail as English law has always set its face against the enforcement of contracts in general and not only employment contracts, preferring to award damages. There are two situations:

(a) the employer wishes to enforce the contract against the employee, i.e. to compel the employee to work;

(b) the employee wishes to enforce the contract against the employer by compelling the employer to continue to give him or her work.

Situation (a) is governed by s 236 of the Trade Union and Labour Relations (Consolidation) Act 1992, which provides (in refreshingly straightforward language) that no court shall by way of any specified court order compel any employee to do any work. Thus there is a statutory bar to an action by an employer in (a) above, although s 236 does not cover independent contractors. However, s 236 is simply a reflection of an equitable principle that the courts will not order anyone, whether an employee or not, to perform a contract of personal service.

Situation (b) holds more interest, although it must be said that even here it is unlikely that in any particular case the employee will succeed in getting a contract of employment enforced against the employer. There is, however, some interesting case law on this subject.

The starting point is the decision of the Court of Appeal in *Hill* v *CA Parsons & Co. Ltd* (1971), where the Court of Appeal held that an injunction would be granted to restrain the dismissal of an employee. The case was unusual, and the circumstances will not reoccur, in that the Industrial Relations Act 1971 was about to come into force. The reason for the dismissal was that Hill refused to join a union where there was a closed shop agreement and the effect of the Act would be to render dismissals for this reason automatically unfair. The effect of the injunction was that Hill remained an employee until the Act came into force and could then claim under its provisions. There was, however, a point of more general interest in that the relationship between the parties had not broken down and mutual trust and confidence remained.

In *Irani* v *Southampton and SW Hampshire Health Authority* (1985) the employee was dismissed in breach of agreed procedures and an injunction was granted to restrain the dismissal until these had been gone through. The case was similar to *Hill* in two ways: the enforcement of the contract of employment was a means to a particular end and there was no question of the employee actually returning to work; and the relationship between the parties had not broken down. In *Irani* the cause of the dismissal was that Irani and a consultant at the hospital where he was employed could not work together but there was no complaint about his work.

In more recent cases the courts have gone further and actually restrained the employer from breaking the contract. In *Powell* v *Brent LBC* (1987) the council, having promoted the employee to a more senior post, then revoked this on the grounds that it had been alleged that the council's equal opportunities policy had been broken in making the appointment. The court granted an injunction which restrained the council from re-advertising the post until the main action had been tried. Once more it was emphasised that there had been no breakdown in relationships between the parties.

A more striking case is *Jones* v *Gwent CC* (1992), where the employee, a lecturer, had been through two disciplinary procedures when allegations of misconduct were found to be groundless but she was still dismissed by the college governors. The reason given was that it was felt that her return to the college would cause a breakdown in relationships due to her past behaviour. The court granted an interim injunction preventing dismissal in breach of the procedures laid down in the employee's contract and a permanent injunction restraining any dismissal on the basis of the governors' decision. It is this second limb of the decision which marks a new departure and it will

11

Wrongful and unfair dismissal

be interesting to see how far the courts are prepared to travel along this road. An interesting recent example of injunctions in a slightly different context is proved by *Mezey* v *South West London and St. George's Mental Health NHS Trust* (2007), where an employer was restrained from suspending an employee without pay pending the outcome of disciplinary proceedings.

Public law remedies and dismissal

The distinction between public and private law is not easy to state with absolute precision but the basic point is fairly easy to grasp. Whilst private law is concerned with adjusting rights and duties between individuals (including organisations), public law deals with matters which affect either the whole community or at least a sizeable proportion of it. Thus the actions of central and local government are matters of public law, whereas disputes between employers and employees are matters of private law. Nevertheless, there have been numerous attempts, some successful, to argue that an employee has rights under public law and thus to seek judicial review. Why?

There are three main reasons:

1 Public law emphasises that when a decision is taken, the rules of natural justice must be observed. There are two rules:

   (a) that the decision-maker must not be biased; and
   (b) that there must be a fair hearing.

   Although the requirements of a fair procedure loom large in the law of unfair dismissal (see below), they are much less prominent in actions for wrongful dismissal unless, as discussed above, there is a disciplinary procedure incorporated into the contract. Thus a claim in public law can bring in some fundamental procedural safeguards for the employee.

2 The remedies for a breach of public law deal directly with the decision itself, which can lead to the employee being able to enforce the contract. The relevant ones are:

   (a) a quashing order (formerly known as an order of *certiorari*), which would have the effect of quashing a decision to dismiss; and
   (b) a mandatory order, which requires the performance of a duty.

   These could be combined where the court quashes a decision to dismiss because of a flawed procedure and requires the decision-maker to hold any hearing again.

3 Public law remedies do not depend on proving that the claimant is an employee and are thus available to an independent contractor as well.

A clear example of where an employee was able to claim a public law remedy is *R* v *Liverpool City Council, ex parte Ferguson* (1985), where the council, as part of a dispute with central government, had set a rate that was illegal, as it assumed that the council would be in deficit. Subsequently, the council was compelled to dismiss some employees because it would not have enough money to pay their wages. The court allowed these employees to claim under public law as, although the actual dismissal could be said to be a private law matter, it arose out of a decision to set an illegal rate, which was a public law matter.

This is an unusual case and the courts have been reluctant to allow many claims under public law for the simple reason that it gives those who are able to claim them an advantage over those who cannot. For example, the employees in the *Liverpool* case (above) would not have been able to claim in public law if a private employer had employed them. The difficulty has been to draw a clear dividing line between when a claim will be allowed and when it will not.

It appears that an office holder (see Chapter 4) can claim a public law remedy because the very fact that a public office is held makes the matter one of public law (see *Ridge* v *Baldwin* (1964)). This does not, however, get us very far, given the limited number of office holders. In *R* v *East Berkshire Health Authority, ex parte Walsh* (1984), a nurse who had been dismissed sought judicial review of the decision, arguing that this was a public law matter because the decision to dismiss was in breach of the procedure in the Whitley Council agreement, which dealt with conditions in the NHS and had been approved by the relevant Minister. The Court of Appeal held that this was not a matter of public law and the termination of a contract of employment was a private law matter, even though the employer was a public body. The crucial factor was that the Whitley Council procedures had been incorporated into the applicant's contract of employment. A clear statement of the principles here was provided by Woolf LJ, who held in *McLaren* v *Home Office* (1990) that an employee could seek judicial review where there is some body established by statute or under the royal prerogative which has a sufficient public law element. The rationale of this is that it is in the public interest to ensure that such bodies observe the law. Thus it seems that prison officers will be able to seek judicial review of decisions to dismiss them, as in *R* v *Home Secretary, ex parte Benwell* (1985), where the authority to take action against the officer was based on statute. Unlike *Walsh*, there was no issue of contract, as the matter rested entirely on statute. The other point was that at that date prison officers had no right to claim unfair dismissal (they have been able to do so since 1994) and so judicial review was the only remedy here.

Bringing a claim for wrongful dismissal

There is the choice of either a claim in the civil courts or, where the amount claimed is no more than £25,000 (in respect of any one contract of employment), it may be brought in an employment tribunal. What frequently happens is that a contract claim for wrongful dismissal is added on to an unfair dismissal claim where the latter is the primary remedy. One reason for this is that loss due to the employee not having received the correct (or any) notice can be claimed in the wrongful dismissal claim and therefore the unfair dismissal claim can be used to claim future loss of earnings. The other possibility is that it may be that the unfair dismissal claim fails on the facts but the tribunal may still decide that the employee is entitled to pay for notice which was not given. If a wrongful dismissal claim is brought in a tribunal then the normal three-month period for bringing claims applies (see below). It is increasingly being suggested that the £25,000 limit, which has been unchanged since the introduction of this jurisdiction in 1994, should be raised in line with the significant increases in the amount which can be awarded in unfair dismissal claims.

11

Wrongful and unfair dismissal

UNFAIR DISMISSAL

This is the statutory counterpart of the action for wrongful dismissal and was originally introduced by the Industrial Relations Act 1971. The law is now contained in Part X of the Employment Rights Act 1996.

Methods of termination and unfair dismissal

The methods of termination described above in relation to wrongful dismissal apply to unfair dismissal as follows:

Termination by death or on the ending of a business

The position is the same as for wrongful dismissal.

Termination by frustration

The position is essentially the same because s 95 of the ERA 1996, which sets out the circumstances in which an employee is dismissed for the purposes of unfair dismissal, speaks of termination in three ways but the assumption is that the contract is there to be terminated. If the contract has already been frustrated, then it is no longer alive. Nevertheless, it is vital to look at frustration alongside the question of dismissals for sickness which fall under the head of capability dismissals, and this is explored later in this chapter.

Termination on the expiry of a fixed-term contract

It is here that the first major difference appears between wrongful and unfair dismissal. An unfair dismissal claim can be brought *not only* where an employee is dismissed during a fixed-term contract, as for wrongful dismissal, but also where a fixed-term contract is not renewed. In the latter case there is no action for wrongful dismissal.

Termination by mutual agreement

The position is the same as for wrongful dismissal but the close relationship between this concept and that of constructive dismissal should be noted. Constructive dismissal does not exist as such in the law of wrongful dismissal but in the law of unfair dismissal a forced resignation may amount to constructive dismissal and give rise to a claim. This is examined below under the discussion of constructive dismissal.

Termination by notice

The other major change from wrongful dismissal appears here, in that termination, even with due notice, does not bar a claim for unfair dismissal. (This is explained in detail below.)

Termination by summary dismissal

The law of unfair dismissal does not use the term 'summary dismissal' but instead s 95 of the ERA 1996 speaks of termination *with* or *without notice*. In fact, the law of unfair dismissal has largely taken over this area but the point to note is that here the issue is whether the dismissal is for a fair reason rather than whether there was a repudiatory breach of contract.

Stages in an unfair dismissal claim

The following are the main stages and the flow chart below should be kept in mind when looking at the law on unfair dismissal.

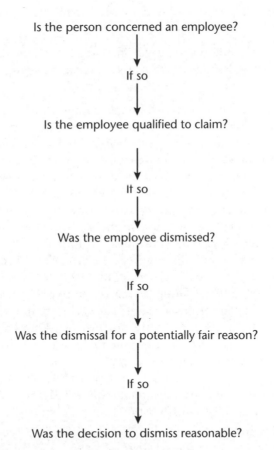

Is the person concerned an employee?

↓

If so

↓

Is the employee qualified to claim?

↓

It so

↓

Was the employee dismissed?

↓

If so

↓

Was the dismissal for a potentially fair reason?

↓

If so

↓

Was the decision to dismiss reasonable?

Is the person concerned an employee?

This topic does not call for greater elaboration here, as the distinction between employees and independent contractors was dealt with in Chapter 4. However, it is vital to reiterate that the right not to be unfairly dismissed applies only to employees, as the foundation of the law here, s 94 of the ERA 1996, states that: 'An *employee* has the right not to be unfairly dismissed by his employer' (emphasis added). Thus an independent contractor is left to claim for breach of contract where, as the relationship is akin to employment, the matter will generally be decided according to the principles of wrongful dismissal.

Is the employee qualified to claim?

The starting point is the phrase 'the effective date of termination'. Section 97 of the ERA 1996 provides that this means:

(a) where notice is given, the date on which it expires;

(b) where there is no notice (i.e. summary dismissal), the date when termination takes effect;

(c) where the employee is employed under a fixed term, the date on which the term expires.

The cases where the employee is not qualified to claim are set out below and thus, if the employee is *not* within any of these classes, it can be assumed that he or she is qualified:

1 Where at the effective date of termination the employee had not been continuously employed for one year. In *Pacitti Jones* v *O'Brien* (2005) the Court of Session held that, in calculating the meaning of a year in connection with claims under the ERA 1996, the day on which an employee starts work is to be counted. (Note that in cases of automatically unfair dismissal there is no qualifying period of a year and claims can be brought from day one of employment except in cases of dismissal on the transfer of an undertaking and for spent convictions (see pp. 301–02).) The qualifying period was reduced to one year in 1999 (and thus applies to dismissals occurring on or after 1 June 1999). Previously, from 1985 onwards, it had been two years and before that, from 1979, one year; before 1979 it had been six months. The reason for the changes was the feeling of the 1979–97 Conservative government that employers were inhibited from taking on employees because of fear of the consequences of an unfair dismissal claim. The change to one year was dictated by a change in the political climate and also the two-year limit had been subject to a lengthy challenge in the courts on the ground that it was sexually discriminatory, as it indirectly discriminated against female employees who were more likely than men to be in jobs for a short time. This litigation (finally under the name of *R* v *Secretary of State for Employment, ex parte Seymour Smith* (1995)) eventually failed but it did build up a certain head of steam against the two-year limit.

2 Before the coming into force of the Employment Equality (Age) Regulations 2006 the law was that where at the effective date of termination the employee was either over the normal retiring age for the job or, if there was none, over 65 then she could not bring a claim. This has, however, now gone and the position is dealt with in Chapter 9 where these regulations are discussed.

3 Where the employee is either a share fisherman (s 199 of ERA 1996) or employed in the police service (s 200 of ERA 1996).

4 Where the employee is governed by a dismissal procedures agreement which has been approved by the Secretary of State as operating in substitution for the statutory scheme (s 110 of ERA 1996). The only one in existence is the agreement between the Electrical Contractors Association and the Electrical, Electronic Telecommunications and Plumbing Union in 1979.

In addition, an employee must work in Great Britain to bring a claim; in *Serco Ltd* v *Lawson and another* (2004) the Court of Appeal held that where an employee carried out all of his work outside Great Britain (on Ascension Island) then there was no jurisdiction to hear a claim for unfair dismissal.

Was the employee dismissed?

This is the next hurdle which the employee has to surmount and the definition of dismissal for the purposes of the law on unfair dismissal is set out in s 95 of the ERA 1996. Dismissal occurs in the following circumstances:

1 The contract is terminated by the employer with or without notice.

2 A fixed-term contract expires without being renewed under the same contract.

3 The employee terminates the contract, with or without notice, in circumstances where he or she is entitled to terminate it without notice because of the employer's conduct. This has come to be known as constructive dismissal but it is important to remember that the Act does not use this phrase and so it is important to apply the statutory phrase.

Category 1 above includes both summary dismissal and dismissal with or without notice and the discussion above under wrongful dismissal of when employment can be said to be terminated and when the employee really leaves by mutual agreement is of particular relevance here. Fixed-term contracts (2 above) have also been dealt with under wrongful dismissal but the significant point here is that where a fixed-term contract expires and is not renewed, then the employer will have to show that the reason for non-renewal was a fair one. In *Terry* v *East Sussex CC* (1976) it was held that a failure to renew a fixed-term contract could come under dismissal for some other substantial reason (see below) and it may be that it is easy for an employer to justify non-renewal as where the need for the services of the employee has ended.

Constructive dismissal

The main category for discussion here is that of constructive dismissal (point 3 above). The legislation gave no guidance on the meaning of the phrase 'entitled to terminate it' and it was not until *Western Excavating v Sharp* (1978) that it was established that this meant that the employee was contractually entitled to terminate the contract. In this case Denning MR held that: 'if the employer is guilty of conduct which is a significant breach going to the root of the contract of employment, or which shows that the employer no longer intends to be bound by one or more of the essential terms of the contract, then the employee is entitled to treat himself as discharged from any further performance.'

This contract test, rather than a more general test of whether the employer has behaved unreasonably, might have been thought to be unduly restrictive. There was,

11

Wrongful and unfair dismissal

however, undoubtedly a fear that the concept of constructive dismissal might get out of hand and be used whenever, for example, the employer and the employee simply had a disagreement. In *Western Excavating* itself the employee resigned when his employer refused to give him an advance against accrued holiday pay. As Denning MR pointed out, there was no breach of contract by the employers at all. The merit of the contract test is that, by focusing on the contract, it provides a means of distinguishing between situations where, in Lawton LJ's phrase in this case, 'the employer is the kind of employer of whom the employee is entitled without notice to rid himself' and those where there is an employer with whom the employee simply happens to disagree.

In the event, the imposition of a contract test has still enabled the law of constructive dismissal to be fruitfully developed. The courts have recognised that an employee will be contractually entitled to terminate for breach of an implied as well as an express term, and have extended the range of implied terms to include a term that the employer will treat the employee with trust and respect, which is really a variation of the implied term of mutual trust and confidence. This was dealt with in Chapter 5 and reference should be made in particular to the judgment of Browne-Wilkinson J in *Woods* v *WM Car Services Ltd* (1981). In *Abbey National plc* v *Fairbrother* (2007), where the claim arose out of an alleged mishandling of a grievance, the EAT made the important point that in a constructive dismissal case the tribunal should consider if the employer had reasonable and proper cause for its conduct *before* going on to ask if that conduct was calculated to destroy or seriously damage the relationship of trust and confidence.

Examples where conduct by the employer has been held to be in breach of this implied term are: *British Aircraft Corporation Ltd* v *Austin* (1978) (failing to investigate a justified health and safety complaint); *BBC* v *Beckett* (1983) (unjustifiable demotion for a minor disciplinary offence); *TSB Bank plc* v *Harris* (2000) (misleading reference); *Wigan BC* v *Davies* (1979) (failure to protect the employee from harassment by other employees). In addition, in *Woods* v *WM Car Services Ltd* (above) it was held that it is possible for a series of incidents over a period of time to amount to a breach. (See *Rossiter* v *Pendragon plc* (2002) (Chapter 12) for an unsuccessful attempt to claim constructive dismissal in connection with transfer of an undertaking.) In *Stanley Cole* v *Sheridan* (2003) the EAT held that where an employee is given a final written warning which is not justified this can amount to a repudiatory breach of contract by the employer which will entitle the employee to resign and claim constructive dismissal. Here a final written warning had been issued as a result of the employee leaving work for half an hour after an argument with another employee which had made her feel ill. It was held that this did not merit such a warning.

What is the position where the employee resigns and claims constructive dismissal but the employer says that the employee did not discuss their complaint with them first? In *Tolson* v *Governing Body of Mixenden Community School* (2003) a teacher resigned from her post at a school on the ground that the way in which timetable changes were implemented was in breach of the implied duty of mutual trust and confidence. The tribunal dismissed her claim on the ground that she had failed to discuss the matter with the headteacher and had not used the grievance procedure but the EAT held that this was wrong: the focus should be on the conduct of the employer and not the employee. It should be noted, however, that since the new statutory grievance

[handwritten marginal note: not anymore can bring a claim without grievance]

procedures came into force in October 2004 (see below), a failure to use them first might prevent a claim for constructive dismissal from being brought.

There may also be a breach by the employer of an express term of the contract giving rise to a claim for constructive dismissal. Obvious examples are a failure to pay wages and a unilateral decision by the employer to change the employee's place of work.

There are, however, three points to bear in mind which may act against the success of a constructive dismissal claim:

1 As the matter is essentially one of contract, the claim cannot succeed if the employer was allowed under the contract to do what was done. For example, where the contract contains a mobility clause then it will not be a breach to require the employee to move. However, even here it may be that this power is exercised in such a way as to breach the implied duty of trust and confidence and thus amount to a breach. Thus in *United Bank Ltd* v *Akhtar* (1989) it was held that the giving of very short notice of a move could be a breach (see also Chapter 5).

2 Where the employee does not resign or at least complain in strong terms soon after a breach by the employer then he may be held to have accepted the breach. (see *Hunt* v *BRB* (1979)). However, if she does complain but stays on until she finds another job this may not count as accepting the breach.

3 The employee must not resign before the employer is actually in breach. In *Kerry Foods Ltd* v *Lynch* (2005) an employee who was in dispute with his employer over a proposed change in the working week from five days to six was given notice by his employers that if he did not agree to the change his contract would end and he would be offered a new contract on terms that he worked a six-day week. He resigned at once, before the notice expired, and claimed constructive dismissal. The EAT held that his claim failed as there was at the time no breach of contract: he should have waited until the notice expired and then claimed that the proposed change was unreasonable.

A final and very important point is that even though the court may find that the employer has been guilty of a breach, it may also find, in accordance with the general law on unfair dismissal, that the employer acted reasonably under s 98(4) (below). One example is that a unilateral change in contract terms may be held to be justified under the 'some other substantial reason ground' (see below).

Before considering the question of the actual fairness of the dismissal, two other points should be noted:

1 Can it be said that the employee has dismissed himself or herself by his or her conduct and as a result there is no dismissal at all by the employer? This was suggested by Denning MR in *London Transport Executive* v *Clarke* (1981), where a bus driver took seven weeks' absence from work without permission. Although the employee knew that this conduct would result in his being dismissed, the majority of the Court of Appeal held that it was still open to the employer to elect whether to treat the contract as continuing or to repudiate it. The result of applying this elective theory of contract termination is that the courts and tribunals are not debarred in

advance of considering the merits of a claim, even though, as here, it was bound to fail.

2 The employee cannot agree in advance not to claim for unfair dismissal. Section 203(1) of the ERA 1996 renders void any agreement 'to exclude or limit the operation of any provision of any part of this Act' and this has been held to include cases where the employee agrees in advance that he or she will be taken to have resigned in particular circumstances. A good example is *Igbo* v *Johnson Matthey Chemicals Ltd* (1986), where the employee signed an agreement that if she did not return from holiday by a stated date then her employment contract would be deemed to be automatically terminated. This was held to be void under s 203(1), because what was in essence an agreement for self-dismissal was clearly an attempt to exclude the unfair dismissal provisions of the Act.

Was the dismissal for a reason that is potentially fair?

Once it has been established that the employee was dismissed, the claim moves on to two more stages:

1 The employer must show what the reason for the dismissal was.

2 The tribunal must be satisfied that the employer acted reasonably in treating *that* reason as a sufficient reason for dismissing the employee (see s 98(4) (below)).

A distinction is therefore drawn between the *reason* (in 1 above) and *reasonableness* (in 2 above). It is for the employer to show the reason but the tribunal decides reasonableness. Therefore, in 1 the burden of proof is on the employer and he or she must begin by bringing evidence to show the reason, whereas in 2 the burden of proof is said to be neutral in that neither side has to prove or disprove reasonableness and instead the tribunal decides.

The reason for the dismissal: the test for establishing whether the reason was fair

The employer does not have a free choice in deciding which reasons to bring forward in support of his or her contention that the dismissal is fair. Instead, s 98(1) and (2) of the ERA 1996 provide a list of six reasons which are 'potentially fair'. This means that if the employer fails to show that the dismissal was for any of these reasons, then the employee's claim for unfair dismissal will succeed without the tribunal having to consider the issue of reasonableness at all. Furthermore, it may be that the reason for the dismissal was one which statute provides is automatically unfair, as explained above, in which case there will automatically be a finding of unfair dismissal. If, however, the employer shows that the dismissal was for one or more of those reasons then the action moves on to the question of reasonableness. Thus no reason for dismissal can be considered automatically fair, and therefore justified, in advance.

Before considering the reasons in detail it is vital to remember that the tribunal is not to act as an appeal court in deciding whether the reason for the dismissal was a fair one. Instead, the 'range of reasonable responses test' applies. This was expressed by Browne-Wilkinson P in *Iceland Frozen Foods Ltd* v *Jones* (1982) as the tribunal having to start from the words of the statute (now s 98(4)) and 'in many (though not all) cases there is a band of reasonable responses to the employer's conduct within which one employer might reasonably take one view, another quite reasonably take another'.

Example

Joanne is dismissed because she has been late for work on a number of occasions. Joanne states that this is because she has a young child to look after who is often ill. After considering the matter carefully, the tribunal decides that, although many employers would have given a final warning, dismissal is not outside the band of responses which a reasonable employer might make as a result of her actions. Thus the dismissal is for a fair reason.

(It must, however, be emphasised that the reasons are only one aspect and the questions of procedure must also be considered, as in the flow chart on p. 291.)

This test was criticised as allowing a decision to dismiss to be fair even though it may have been at the very edge of fairness. In *Haddon* v *Van der Bergh Foods Ltd* (1999) the test was swept aside by the EAT, which felt that, instead, the words of the statute were enough in themselves and that a gloss such as this test was wrong. This phase did not last long and in *Post Office* v *Foley* (2000) the band of reasonable responses test was restored. The Court of Appeal in *Foley* observed that, as the test in s 98 of the ERA 1996 imposes a standard of reasonableness, it follows that the employer must be judged by what is reasonable. However, one unresolved issue in the decision was that, although Mummery LJ observed that there was an objective standard implicit in the test of reasonableness and that it was higher than that of perversity, he did not elaborate on this. The result is that the test remains subject to criticism in that it allows a dismissal to be fair for being within the band of reasonable responses, whereas under the law of wrongful dismissal it might not be held to be a breach of contract. Collins (2003, page 176) suggests that 'The statutory question of whether the employer acted reasonably becomes transmuted into the lower test of whether the employer acted unreasonably'. Moreover, he argues that unreasonableness in this context is simply conduct which is not perverse or irrational. The fact that unreasonableness is a concept used to control the activities of public bodies is not the point. They are bodies entrusted by statute with a good deal of discretion. Here we are dealing with a dispute between individuals, where it is suggested that different considerations should apply. As an alternative, Collins (2003, page 174) proposes a test of whether the dismissal was required in the legitimate business interests of the employer and if this was sufficient to justify the interference with the job security of the employee and the need for the employee to be treated with respect.

In *Sainsbury's Supermarkets* v *Hitt* (2003) the Court of Appeal held that the range of reasonable responses test applies not only to the employer's decision to dismiss but also to the question of whether the employer's investigation into suspected misconduct was a reasonable one in the circumstances. Thus when a tribunal applies the test in *BHS* v *Burchell* to decide if an employer has carried out a reasonable investigation, the employer is judged by what Mummery LJ in *Hitt* calls 'the objective standards of the reasonable employer'. The effect is that an employer is given greater latitude in conducting an investigation into alleged misconduct and, although there is still a need actually to hold an investigation and give the employee the opportunity of explaining his or her conduct, an employer will be given discretion in, for example, the enquiries which are made before dismissing. One could say that this decision, along with the downgrading of procedural requirements by the new statutory dismissal, disciplinary and grievance procedures in the Employment Act 2002, is another example of a successful assault on what was once the impregnable fortress of the principle in the *Polkey* case (see p. 303).

An example of the 'range of reasonable responses' test in action is provided by *Strouthos* v *London Underground Ltd* (2004). The employee was secretary of the London Transport pistol club and took one of his employer's vehicles to Belgium, without permission, for a shooting competition. He was dismissed for this. The tribunal held that this was unfair as not being within the range of reasonable responses but the EAT held that it was fair. However, the Court of Appeal held that the dismissal was outside the range of reasonable responses and therefore unfair. It pointed out that the disciplinary charge did not mention dishonesty but merely that the vehicle had been taken to Belgium without permission. Even had dishonesty been alleged, the court felt that the tribunal had been entitled to conclude that dismissal on these facts was not within the range of reasonable responses.

There are therefore three possibilities:

1 If the employer fails to show that the reason was one of the potentially fair reasons, the employee's claim will normally succeed.

2 If the reason was one which is automatically unfair, the employee's claim will automatically succeed.

3 If the employer shows that the reason was one of the potentially fair reasons, the action continues to the reasonableness stage.

The six potentially fair reasons set out in s 98(2) of the ERA 1996 are widely drawn and in most instances an employer will have no difficulty in showing that the dismissal was for one or more of them. There is, however, an additional requirement that they must be substantial and thus a trivial instance would not be enough.

The potentially fair reasons

(a) a reason relating to the capability or qualifications of the employee for performing work of the kind he or she was employed to do;

(b) a reason related to the employee's conduct;

(c) the retirement of the employee;

(d) the redundancy of the employee;

(e) the employee could not continue to work in the position he or she held without breaking a statutory provision;

(f) some other substantial reason of a kind justifying dismissal.

Note: Retirement dismissals are dealt with in Chapter 9 under the rest of the provisions on age discrimination.

Capability or qualifications

'Capability' is stated by s 98(3) of the ERA 1996 to be assessed by reference to 'skill, aptitude, health or any other mental or physical quality'. The most common instance under this head is ill health. In *East Lindsey DC* v *Daubney* (1977) it was held that consultation with the employee should be the first step and cases have emphasised that the employer should weigh the needs of the business for the employee's job to be done against the expected time when the employee is likely to be away and the prospect of a full recovery. The doctrine of frustration is relevant in that where there is no prospect of a recovery at all then the contract is frustrated and automatically ends, with no issue as to the fairness of the dismissal. Where the issue is incompetence and the employee was dismissed for not being able to do the job then the question of what training was given is vital. In *Davison* v *Kent Meters* (1975) dismissal for assembling 471 out of 500 components in the wrong order was unfair as there was no evidence that training had been given in how to assemble them correctly. 'Qualifications' is defined by s 9 as referring to academic, technical or professional qualifications and dismissal could be fair where an employee is required to obtain certain qualifications but does not do so. Even so, the question of reasonableness is relevant because the employee may argue that he or she was not given time off work to enable him or her to study for the relevant qualifications.

Conduct

The ACAS Code gives examples of where an employee may be dismissed for gross misconduct including (para 7) theft, fraud, violence at work, harassment, serious negligence or breach of confidence and deliberate damage to property. In *BHS* v *Burchell* (1978) it was held that an employer should first show that he or she honestly and on reasonable grounds believed that the employee had committed the offence and that at that stage he or she had carried out as full an investigation as was reasonable. The employer is not bound to wait for the outcome of a criminal trial before dismissing, although it is common practice to wait until then and suspend beforehand. It has been pointed out that the *Burchell* test can lead to confusion, as the burden of proof states that the employer must show a reasonable belief in the guilt of the employee. In *Boys and Girls Welfare Society* v *McDonald* (1996) it was emphasised that the application of this test did not alter the statutory rule that the burden of proof rests neither with the employer nor the employee but is neutral. What is the position where the employer is not certain which of the members of a group were guilty of dishonesty? Can they all be dismissed? In *Whitbread & Co.* v *Thomas* (1988) the EAT held that, provided the act would justify dismissal if committed by one employee, then dismissal of the whole group can be fair so long as a proper investigation has been made to try to identify who was individually responsible and that the act was committed by one or more members of the group.

Redundancy

See Chapter 12.

Continued employment would be a breach of the law

Examples where the employee could not work in his or her position without contravention of a legislative provision have been few. However, an obvious example would be where an employee who is employed to drive a vehicle is disqualified and there is no alternative work.

Some other substantial reason (SOSR)

This category of potentially fair reasons for dismissal is a residual one which can include any reason not included in the other five specific reasons. It has been used in cases involving reorganisations (see Chapter 12) and other aspects are considered here.

In *RS Components* v *Irwin* (1974) Sir John Brightman explained the rationale as follows:

> Parliament may well have intended to set out . . . the common reasons for a dismissal but can have hardly have hoped to produce an exact catalogue of all the circumstances in which a company would be justified in terminating the services of an employee.

Furthermore, he held that this head is to be considered as an independent head of dismissal and is not to be confined to reasons which are *ejusdem generis* (i.e. of a similar kind) to the specific reasons.

There are, in effect, two issues to consider when deciding if a dismissal is fair under this ground although clearly these are interrelated:

1 Was the reason a substantial one? In *Harper* v *National Coal Board* (1980) Lord McDonald said that what he called 'a whimsical or capricious reason which no person of ordinary sense would entertain' would not be substantial.

2 Did the employer have a genuine belief that the reason was substantial? In *Harper* Lord McDonald said that one factor would be whether 'most employers would be expected to adopt' the view that the reason was a substantial one.

In practice, a number of decisions on SOSR have had the effect of widening the powers of employers to dismiss. Some of these are dealt with in Chapter 12, which looks at dismissals on reorganisations, and this includes *RS Components* v *Irwin* (above). The operation of SOSR has been criticised by Bowers and Clarke (1981), who feel that: 'Other substantial reason could not fail to be a wide categorisation but that it would provide so wide a ragbag of gateways to fair dismissal surely could not have been foreseen, nor that so few employers would fail to prove that their reason was substantial.' They suggest that a more extensive definition of reasons could mean that the need for SOSR disappeared. However, this suggestion was made in 1981 and SOSR is still with us.

The following are the main types of situations where SOSR has been held to be a potentially fair reason for dismissal:

Refusal by an employee to agree to changes in the contract of employment
See Chapter 12.

Dismissals arising out of reorganisation falling short of redundancy
See Chapter 12.

Personality differences between the dismissed employee and other employees

In *Treganowan* v *Robert Knee & Co. Ltd* (1975) the working atmosphere in an office had become intolerable due to a difference of opinion between Treganowan and other employees about the merits of the permissive society. This was affecting the company's business and it was held that the dismissal of Treganowan was for SOSR. However, in *Turner* v *Vestric Ltd* (1981) it was held that an employer should make every effort to improve the working relationship before considering dismissal.

Dismissal because of pressure from a third party

The third party might, for example, be a major customer. The justification put forward by the employer will be that the business would be affected if the customer withdrew their custom and therefore there was no alternative to dismissing the employee. However, in *Dobie* v *Burns International Security Services (UK) Ltd* (1984), the Court of Appeal held that an employer must also take into account injustice to the employee, looking at, for example, the length of service of the employee and the employee's record.

Dismissal of a temporary employee where it was made clear that the employment was temporary

This may be the explanation of *Priddle* v *Dibble* (1978), where the applicant, a farm worker, was dismissed to make way for his employer's son. The dismissal was held fair. Bristow J found that the applicant had known that the son would be likely to work on the farm and it was 'natural and reasonable for a farmer to want to employ his son'. One could add that this is not in doubt, but, with respect, it should not be seen as a justification for dismissal. A decision of this kind could be seen as supporting the argument of Bowers and Clarke (above) that this head of dismissal should be reconsidered.

Automatically unfair reasons for dismissal

In the following cases the dismissal is automatically unfair and so there is no room for the test of reasonableness. However, it is for the employee to establish that the reason fell within these grounds:

- reasons related to trade union membership or activities (see Chapter 13);
- reasons related to the assertion of a statutory right (s 104 of the ERA 1996), e.g. where the employee has asserted any right in the ERA, the Working Time Directive or the right to minimum notice of termination of employment;
- where the employee has taken leave for family reasons (see Chapter 10);
- reasons related to health and safety, e.g. where the employee was carrying out duties as a health and safety representative or a member of a health and safety committee (see Chapter 8);
- refusing to work on Sundays (s 35(5) and (6) of the ERA 1996);
- making a protected disclosure under the Public Interest Disclosure Act 1998 (see Chapter 5);
- taking part in protected industrial action (see Chapter 14);
- dismissal in connection with the transfer of the undertaking (see Chapter 12);

- for spent convictions (Rehabilitation of Offenders Act 1974);
- for carrying out the functions of pension fund trustees (s 102 of the ERA 1996);
- for carrying out the functions of employee representatives in relation to redundancy or transfers of undertakings (see Chapter 12);
- where the employer had failed to follow the statutory dismissal and disciplinary procedures in dismissing an employee (Employment Act 2002) – see later in this chapter.

It is also relevant to mention that under s 92 the employee is entitled to be provided on demand with a written statement of the reasons for dismissal and, if this is not given within 14 days, the employee is entitled, on complaint to a tribunal, to be awarded an extra two weeks' pay. The significance here is that once the employer has stated the reason in writing then this is admissible in evidence at any hearing and, although the employer is at liberty to give a different reason later, it will be necessary to explain why there was a change. In *Abernethy* v *Mott, Hay and Anderson* (1974) Cairns LJ gave some examples of where a tribunal might accept a different reason from that given at the time, such as where a different reason is given out of kindness, or where the employer misdescribes the reason so that, although in reality it falls within the six reasons set out above, it did not appear at first to do so and as a result it is later clarified. A more robust approach was taken in *Hotson* v *Wisbech Conservative Club* (1984), where the reason given in the employer's notice of appearance to the tribunal was that the employee was inefficient but it became clear at the hearing that it was because the employee was suspected of dishonesty. It was held to be unfair to dismiss for a reason which was not the real reason.

Was the dismissal reasonable? Procedural fairness

This is the heart of the law on unfair dismissal and it is contained in s 98(4) of the ERA 1996 in words which should be very carefully noted by anyone connected with employment law:

> the determination of the question whether the dismissal is fair or unfair (having regard to the reason shown by the employer) –
> (a) depends on whether in the circumstances (including the size and administrative resources of the employer's undertaking) the employer acted reasonably or unreasonably in treating it as a sufficient reason for dismissing the employee, and
> (b) shall be determined in accordance with equity and the substantial merits of the case.

The following points arise.

Facts discovered afterwards cannot be relied on

It is the reason shown by the employer when dismissing which is considered and it is not possible for the employer to rely on facts discovered afterwards to justify the fairness of the dismissal. This was established by the House of Lords in *W Devis and Sons Ltd* v *Atkins* (1977), in contrast to the position in a wrongful dismissal claim, where facts discovered afterwards can be relied on.

> **Example**
>
> Joan is dismissed on suspicion of pilfering from the shop where she works. After she was dismissed, proof comes that she was indeed pilfering. This cannot be used to justify the fairness of the dismissal, although it may well be relevant to the amount of compensation that Joan will receive. If Joan had brought a claim for wrongful dismissal then the employer would have been able to rely on the facts discovered afterwards as a defence to her claim.

Did the employer act reasonably?

The previous law: Polkey test

Although this test is now of lesser significance, it has been such a central feature of the law of unfair dismissal for so long and is still referred to so often that it needs explanation. The test, which derives from the decision in *Polkey* v *AE Dayton Services Ltd* (1988), emphasised that the issue is the reasonableness of the employer's conduct and not injustice suffered by the employee. This meant that the focus is on the conduct of the employer and that correct procedures were vitally important. The genesis of the emphasis on procedure can be traced to early cases such as *Earl* v *Slater and Wheeler (Airlyne) Ltd* (1973). The employee was off sick and when he was away it was discovered that he seemed not to be carrying out his work satisfactorily. When he returned he was handed a letter of dismissal but he had no opportunity to answer the allegations. The tribunal held that the dismissal was fair, as the allegations appeared to be true and so no injury had been done to him. Donaldson P held that this was not the point: 'Good industrial relations depend on management not only acting fairly but being manifestly seen to act fairly.' Here in a nutshell is the present law.

This branch of the law has not, however, had a straightforward passage. In *British Labour Pump Co. Ltd* v *Byrne* (1979) it was held that in spite of the failure by an employer to use the proper procedures, the dismissal would still be fair if it could be proved on a balance of probabilities that, even if they had been properly followed, the employee would still have been dismissed. This decision was much criticised for allowing the employer the benefit of hindsight and the House of Lords in *Polkey* v *AE Dayton Services Ltd* (1988) overruled it. Here the employee was made redundant without warning and the tribunal held that his claim for unfair dismissal failed, as it could not be shown that consultation would have made any difference. The House of Lords held that this was the wrong approach and instead the question should be whether the employer acted reasonably in deciding not to issue any warning. Mackay LC emphasised that a failure to follow the procedure laid down need not make a dismissal unfair provided that a decision not to follow a particular aspect of the procedure (for example, to consult the employee) was a reasonable one. He envisaged circumstances where a failure might not be unfair, such as when failure to consult was caused by an impending redundancy situation. On the other hand, it is difficult to see how the failure in the *Earl* case (above) could ever be considered fair.

The new procedures

The government wished employers to establish proper disputes resolution procedures and, at the same time, to discourage employees from resorting to a tribunal before using those procedures (the background to this is considered in the 'Law in context' box below). The solution was felt to be to lay down basic procedures for dealing with both dismissals and some types of disciplinary action on the one hand and for grievances on the other. These would be pitched at such a simple and basic level that it would be reasonable to expect compliance in all but a few cases but the price to be paid for this simplicity was that compliance would, in nearly every case, be mandatory. The result was ss 29–34 of the Employment Act 2002 which lay down the general principles behind the statutory dismissal and disciplinary procedures (DDPs) and statutory grievance procedures (GPs). The actual Statutory Dispute Resolution Procedures are set out in Sch 2 to the Employment Act 2002 but this must be read together with the Employment Act 2002 (Dispute Resolution) Regulations 2004 (SI 2004/752), which have prescribed additional rules, as indicated below. It may be noted in passing that the introduction of what are designed as simple procedures has been brought about by remarkably complex legislation. In **Shergold v Fieldway Medical Centre** (2006) Burton P stated the principle behind the procedures: 'It is quite plain that the purpose of the legislation was to encourage conciliation, agreement, compromise and settlement rather than the precipitate issue of proceedings. It is not unlike the system of pre-action protocols in relation to High Court and County Court litigation although hopefully it is even more likely to succeed because of the relationship, or the immediately preceding relationship, between the parties to the dispute.'

The procedures are, by s 30 of the Employment Act 2002, implied into all contracts of employment and they cannot be excluded by agreement between the employer and employee.

Effect of failure to comply with procedural requirements

There are now two possibilities:

(a) Failure to comply with the statutory procedures. Section 98A(1) of the ERA 1996 provides that a dismissal in breach of the DDP will be automatically unfair, although the Secretary of State is given power to grant exemptions from some of the requirements of the statutory procedures in certain circumstances and reg 4 of the Employment Act 2002 (Dispute Resolution) Regulations 2004 (below) provides that they do not apply in certain special cases. There is also an effect on both the basic and compensatory award which is dealt with later.

(b) Failure to comply with other procedures. This is dealt with by s 98A(2) which provides that the dismissal of an employee shall not be regarded in itself as making the employer's action unreasonable *if he shows that he would have decided to dismiss the employee if he had followed the procedure* (emphasis added).

What is meant by 'other procedures'?

In **Alexander v Brigden Enterprises Ltd** (2006) Elias J held that this provision applies when an employer fails to comply with either its own established procedures (which is obvious) and also any other procedures which the tribunal considers in fairness the employer ought to have complied with. In this case counsel for the employee sought unsuccessfully to draw a distinction between 'procedural' and 'substantive' defects and argued that a failure to consult (on a redundancy) was a substantive defect with the result that the *Polkey* principle still applied.

Thus, provided that the employer has complied with the DDP, the *Polkey* test will not apply. Instead, the *British Labour Pump* test is effectively resurrected. The reason for this change is that the government felt that tribunals have been concentrating too much on the minutiae of procedures and not enough on the merits of the case. It has also pointed out that many firms do not have internal disputes procedures and these changes will at least ensure that all employees will have certain basic procedural safeguards in their contracts.

The effect of s 98A(2)

The effect of s 98A(2) is that tribunals must make predictions based on what would have happened if a dismissal which had procedural defects had been conducted in a procedurally fair way: see Elias J in *Software 2000 Ltd* v *Andrews and others* (2007). In this case Elias J laid down the following possibilities to guide tribunals in assessing the award, if any, of compensation to make:

- If fair procedures had been followed the employer has satisfied the tribunal that on the balance of probabilities the dismissal would have occurred in any event.
- Was there a less than 50% chance of dismissal? If so, any compensation should be reduced accordingly.
- Employment would have continued but only for a limited fixed time. Thus in *O'Donoghue* v *Redcar and Cleveland Borough Council* (2001) the Court of Appeal held that a tribunal was entitled to find that an employee who was unfairly dismissed by reason of sex would have been fairly dismissed six months later because of her antagonistic and intransigent attitude.
- Employment would have continued indefinitely. However, Elias J held that this conclusion should be reached only if the evidence that it might have terminated earlier is 'so scanty that it can effectively be ignored'.

In *Scope* v *Thornett* (2006) the Court of Appeal held that tribunals, in this situation and in all cases when assessing compensation for unfair dismissal, should not avoid making reductions to a compensatory award merely because it would involve speculation (see also 'Remedies' below).

The Disciplinary and Dismissal Procedures

These are set out in Part 2 of Sch 1 to the Employment Act 2002. The situations when they apply and the consequences of failure to comply are set out in the Employment Act 2002 (Dispute Resolution) Regulations 2004.

The Standard Disciplinary and Dismissal Procedure

When does it apply?

The vital point is that the procedure applies not only when dismissal is contemplated but also to certain types of disciplinary action, known as relevant disciplinary action, short of dismissal. Dismissal has the same meaning as for the rest of law on unfair dismissal (see s 95 of the ERA 1996 above) and the procedure applies when a dismissal is for any reason. Relevant disciplinary action is defined by reg 2 of the Employment Act 2002 (Dispute Resolution) Regulations 2004 as action short of dismissal which the employer asserts is based wholly or mainly on the employee's conduct or capability, other than suspension on full pay or the issue of oral or written warnings. This therefore has two elements:

(a) It applies only if the reason is conduct or capability and does not apply to disciplinary action on the other potentially fair grounds set out in s 98 of the ERA 1996.

(b) It applies only in certain limited cases of disciplinary action: not where a warning is contemplated or where there is suspension on full pay. Thus it *will* apply to suspension on reduced or no pay or to disciplinary transfer. The rationale for this was explained in the DTI Guidance on the Employment Act 2002 (Dispute Resolution) Regulations 2004 at para 7. It is that the procedures are not intended to apply to actions which are part of a workplace procedure and this includes oral or written warnings or suspension on full pay. However, disciplinary suspension on reduced or no pay will be subject to the statutory procedure because disciplinary suspension is a 'conduct or capability related action additional to the suspension itself'. Investigatory suspension on full pay is not subject to the statutory procedure but, as the DTI Guidance points out, an employee could bring a grievance procedure in relation to this.

What does it involve?

Chapter 1 of Part 1 of Sch 2 to the Employment Act 2002 sets this out as follows:

Step 1: statement of grounds for action and invitation to meeting
1 (1) The employer must set out in writing the employee's alleged conduct or characteristics, or other circumstances, which lead him to contemplate dismissing or taking disciplinary action against the employee.
(2) The employer must send the statement or a copy of it to the employee and invite the employee to attend a meeting to discuss the matter.

Step 2: meeting
2 (1) The meeting must take place before action is taken, except in the case where the disciplinary action consists of suspension.
(2) The meeting must not take place unless –
(a) the employer has informed the employee what the basis was for [the grounds given in the statement issued in step 1];
(b) the employee has had a reasonable opportunity to consider his response to that information.
(3) The employee must take all reasonable steps to attend the meeting.
(4) After the meeting, the employer must inform the employee of his decision and notify him of the right to appeal against it if he is not satisfied with it.

Step 3: appeal
3 (1) If the employee wishes to appeal, he must inform the employer.
(2) The employer must then invite the employee to attend a meeting.

(3) The employee must take all reasonable steps to attend the meeting.

(4) The dismissal or disciplinary action can take effect before the appeal takes place.

(5) After the appeal meeting, the employer must notify the employee of the final decision.

Paragraph 13(3) of Sch 2 to the Employment Act 2002 provides that at the appeal the employer should, as far as is reasonably practicable, be represented by a more senior manager than attended the first meeting, unless this person attended the first meeting. This also applies to appeals under the modified procedure and under the grievance procedure.

The modified procedure

When does it apply?

Regulation 3(2) of the Employment Act 2002 (Dispute Resolution) Regulations 2004 provides that this will be in relation to a dismissal where:

(a) the employer dismissed the employee without notice because of his conduct;

(b) the dismissal occurred at the time the employer became aware of the employee's conduct or immediately thereafter;

(c) the employer was entitled, in the circumstances, to dismiss the employee before enquiring into the circumstances in which the conduct took place and it was reasonable for him to do so. (The effect is that it applies where the dismissal was for gross misconduct but the regulations do not clarify when dismissal without notice is justified.)

What does it involve?

Step 1: statement of grounds for action

The employer must:

(a) set out in writing:
   (i) the employee's alleged misconduct which has led to the dismissal,
   (ii) what the basis was for thinking at the time of the dismissal that the employee was guilty of the alleged misconduct, and
   (iii) the employee's right to appeal against the dismissal and

(b) send a copy of this to the employee.

Step 2: appeal

[This is the same as in the standard procedure.]

Situations where the procedures do not apply

Neither the standard nor the modified procedure applies in the circumstances set out in reg 4 of the Employment Act 2002 (Dispute Resolution) Regulations 2004. These are as follows:

(a) All the employees of a description or in a category to which the employee belongs are dismissed, provided that the employer offers to re-engage all the employees so dismissed either before or upon the termination of their contracts. This would cover, for example, a reorganisation where all affected employees are dismissed and then re-engaged on different terms and conditions.

11

Wrongful and unfair dismissal

(b) The dismissal is one of a number of dismissals in respect of which the duty in s 188 of the Trade Union and Labour Relations (Consolidation) Act 1992 applies. Section 188 provides that the employer has a duty to consult representatives when proposing to dismiss as redundant a certain number of employees; it is considered in Chapter 12 but the effect is that the employer is under a statutory duty to consult where it is proposed to dismiss at least 20 employees within a certain time.

(c) At the time of the employee's dismissal he is taking part in –

(i) an unofficial strike or other unofficial industrial action, or

(ii) any other strike or other industrial action which is not protected industrial action unless the employer either dismisses employees selectively or offers re-engagement selectively and therefore, by virtue of s 238(2) of the Trade Union and Labour Relations (Consolidation) Act 1992, an employment tribunal is entitled to determine whether the dismissal was fair or unfair. (This topic, and, in particular, the terms 'unofficial' and 'official strike' and 'protected industrial action', are considered in Chapter 14.)

(d) The reason (or, if more than one, the principal reason) for the dismissal is that the employee took protected industrial action and the dismissal would be regarded, by virtue of s 238A(2) of the Trade Union and Labour Relations (Consolidation) Act 1992, as automatically unfair.

(e) The employer's business suddenly ceases to function, because of an event unforeseen by the employer, with the result that it is impractical for him to employ any employees.

(f) The reason (or, if more than one, the principal reason) for the dismissal is that the employee could not continue to work in the position which he held without contravention (either on his part or on that of his employer) of a duty or restriction imposed by or under any enactment.

(g) The employee is one to whom a dismissal procedures agreement designated by an order under s 110 of the Employment Rights Act 1996 applies at the date of dismissal.

The grievance procedures

These are set out in Part 2 of Sch 1 to the Employment Act 2002. The situations when they apply and the consequences of failure to comply are set out in the Employment Act 2002 (Dispute Resolution) Regulations 2004.

The standard grievance procedure

When does it apply?

A grievance is defined in reg 2 as 'a complaint by an employee about action which the employer has taken or is contemplating against him'. It also covers the situation where the grievance concerns the actions of a third party where the employer could be vicariously liable for their actions. The actual procedures apply in relation to any grievance about action by the employer which could form the basis of a claim by the employee to an employment tribunal in specified situations laid down in Schs 3 and 4 to the regulations. These encompass all the statutory claims: unfair dismissal, wrongful dismissal, unauthorised deductions from wages, redundancy payments where the claim is based on constructive dismissal, equal pay, discrimination, claims under the Working Time Regulations, subjecting an employee to a detriment in relation to the exercise of trade union rights, etc. The grievance procedures apply to 'protected disclosures' under the Public Interest Disclosure Act 1998 (see Chapter 5) only if the information relates to a matter which could be raised as a grievance and the employee intended that the disclosure should count as raising the matter with the employer as a grievance (para 15(2) of Sch 2 to the Employment Act 2002). The effect is that the employee has a choice: raise it as a grievance or as a protected disclosure.

Effect of a failure to comply with the grievance procedures

(a) Where the employee does not comply with the first step of the procedure: the employee cannot present a complaint on a matter covered by the procedure (see above) to a tribunal if she has failed to send the employer a copy of the grievance and wait for a minimum of 28 days for the employer's response.

(b) Where the employee begins proceedings before the procedure has been completed and the failure to complete it was due wholly or mainly to the employee's failure either to comply with a requirement of the procedure or to institute an appeal under it, then a tribunal must reduce any award made to the employee by 10% and there is a discretion to reduce it by up to 50% unless there are exceptional circumstances which make it unjust or inequitable to make any reduction. This point is considered further at p. 319.

What does it involve?

Step 1: statement of grievance
The employee must set out the grievance in writing and send the statement or a copy of it to the employer.

Step 2: meeting
(1) The employer must invite the employee to attend a meeting to discuss the grievance.
(2) The meeting must not take place unless –
   (a) the employee has informed the employer what the basis for the grievance was when he made the statement under [step 1], and
   (b) the employer has had a reasonable opportunity to consider his response to that information.
(3) The employee must take all reasonable steps to attend the meeting.
(4) After the meeting, the employer must inform the employee of his decision in response to the grievance and notify him of the right to appeal against the decision if he is not satisfied with it.

Step 3: appeal
(1) If the employee wishes to appeal, he must inform the employer.
(2) The employer must then invite the employee to attend a meeting.
(3) The employee must take all reasonable steps to attend the meeting.
(4) After the appeal meeting, the employer must [notify the employee of the] final decision.

The modified procedure

When does it apply?
Regulation 6(3) of the Employment Act 2002 (Dispute Resolution) Regulations 2004 provides that it will apply where:

(a) the employee is no longer employed by the employer and either:
  (i) the employer was unaware of the grievance before the employment ceased, or
  (ii) the employer was aware of it but the standard grievance procedure was not commenced or completed before the last day of the employee's employment, and
(b) the parties have agreed in writing that the modified procedure shall apply. (However, it is not possible to agree this in advance: the agreement must be made after the employer became aware of the grievance.)

What does it involve?
The employee must:

(a) set out in writing the grievance and the basis for it;
(b) send the statement and a copy of it to the employer.

Situations where the procedures do not apply

Neither the standard nor the modified grievance procedure applies in the following circumstances:

(a) the employee has ceased to be employed by the employer;
(b) neither procedure has been commenced, and
(c) since the employee ceased to be employed it has ceased to be reasonably practicable to comply with the procedure;
(d) there are three general exclusions where the procedure does not apply:
  (i)   where the procedure is not commenced because a party reasonably believes that to commence the procedure would result in a significant threat to persons or property;
  (ii) where a party has been subjected to harassment and has reasonable grounds to believe that to commence the procedure would result in further harassment;
  (iii) it is not reasonably practicable to commence proceedings in a reasonable period.

There are finally five cases where the statutory procedure is treated as having been complied with even though it has not been completed. Here the employee may as a result have an extended time to apply to a tribunal:

(a) where the standard procedure applies *and* the employee has ceased to be employed by the employer *and* the employee has complied with the first step and it is no longer practicable to comply with the other steps;
(b) where the grievance was originally dealt with under a collective grievance procedure;
(c) where the grievance was originally dealt with under a dispute resolution procedure developed by employers and unions;

(d) where the employer has invited the employee to a meeting which was suddenly rearranged and the rearranged meeting was itself unforeseeably cancelled;

(e) where the procedure was begun but the employee did not comply with a subsequent requirement on the grounds of threats or harassment resulting from the behaviour of another employee or the employer.

There could have been an overlap between the disciplinary and dismissal procedures on the one hand and the grievance procedure on the other where the employee commences a grievance procedure at the same time as the employer is commencing the disciplinary procedure. However, reg 6(5) and (6) provides that there is no requirement for an employee to follow a grievance procedure if the employer has dismissed or is contemplating dismissing the employee or if the employer has taken or is contemplating taking some relevant disciplinary action based on conduct or capability. (This term was defined earlier in the discussion of the standard disciplinary and dismissal procedure). There is an exception to this in reg 7 where the employer is contemplating action of the kind stated above and the grievance is that this action would amount to unlawful discrimination or that the grounds on which the employer is taking action, or is contemplating doing so, are in fact unrelated to the grounds asserted. An example would be where the employee asserts that the employer is actually dismissing him for misconduct but in fact he wants the employee's job for his own son.

Case law on the new procedures

(a) *Which employees do they apply to?* In **Scott-Davies** v **Redgate Medical Services** (2006) it was held that they apply only to those with at least one year's qualifying employment. Judge McMullen pointed out that the policy of the statutory procedures was that there would be fewer tribunal claims. It therefore followed that there was no justification for allowing those who could not present an unfair dismissal claim to a tribunal to be covered by the procedures.

(b) *What information should the employer provide at Step 1?* In **Alexander** v **Brigden Enterprises Ltd** (2006) the EAT held, in a case involving redundancy dismissals, that an employer must do more than just identify why it has been decided to effect redundancies. Elias J held that the words in step 2 'the basis for including in the statement the ground or grounds given in it' require that an explanation should be given as to why the employer is contemplating dismissing that employee at all. In a redundancy situation information should be given as to why there is a redundancy situation and why the employee is being selected. In **YMCA Training** v **Stewart** (2006) it was held by the EAT that the requirement to state the 'basis' for an allegation did not mean all the detailed evidence that might be relied on but a 'sufficiently detailed statement of the case against him (the employee) to enable him to properly put his side of the story' (Underhill J). In this case a witness statement from another making allegations about the conduct of the employee and which formed the basis of the allegations was held to be enough.

(c) In **YWCA Training** v **Stewart** it was pointed out *the statutory procedure permits the employer to present his case in two stages*: stating the grounds in step 1 and the basis

11

Wrongful and unfair dismissal

for them in step 2. However, the EAT held that it did not matter that both of these were addressed in the same letter (or letter and enclosure).

(d) *When should the employer announce his decision?* In *YMCA Training* v *Stewart*, Underhill J held that 'it is inherent in the requirements of step 2 . . . that the employer should not announce any decision (or – still less – take any action) until the employee has had the opportunity to put his case at the meeting'. However, the procedures do not mean that the employer has to wait until after the meeting has ended to announce his decision: instead it can be announced at a later stage in the actual meeting. Underhill J was thus prepared to interpret the words 'after the meeting' as including 'at the end of the meeting'. Whilst this may be sound, employers who follow this advice must beware of announcing so suddenly at the end of the meeting that it seems that they have not considered the employee's response to the employer's own statement.

(e) *What constitutes a grievance letter?* Decisions have taken a broad view of what constitutes a grievance letter and a determination not to impose strict conditions on what can and cannot amount to one. A good example is *Shergold* v *Fieldway Medical Centre* (2005) where the EAT held that a written grievance for the purposes of the regulations can be contained in a letter of resignation. Burton J observed that the 'statutory requirements . . . are minimal in terms of what is required'. He held that there is no need in the writing to make it plain that it is a grievance or an invocation of a grievance procedure. In *Galaxy Showers* v *Wilson* (2006) the EAT rejected an attempt by the employer to argue that a grievance, to count as part of the statutory process, must indicate that it is intended to be taken further. Instead a straightforward complaint will do.

Another example is *Commotion* v *Rutty* (2005), where a letter from an employee applying for a variation in her working pattern under the flexible working provisions in s 80F of the ERA 1996 (see Chapter 10) was held to be a grievance letter. The reasoning was in itself common sense: why should an employee have to present two letters both saying the same thing: one formally applying for a flexible working on the basis of her grievance that this had not been allowed, and the other repeating this grievance for the purposes of claiming constructive dismissal? However, in *Canary Wharf Management Ltd* v *Edebi* (2006) the EAT held that a *generalised* complaint from an employee about working conditions and the effect they were having on his health did not amount to raising a grievance for the purpose of the statutory procedures.

(f) *Conduct of grievance procedures.* Although the decision in *Abbey National Plc* v *Fairbrother* (2007) did not concern the operation of the statutory grievance procedure the EAT made the important point that the general conduct of grievance procedures by the employer is subject to the test of reasonable responses.

Hepple and Morris (2002) criticise the above statutory procedures on the ground that they do not provide adequate safeguards for employees. For instance, there is no provision for graded sanctions related to the seriousness of the offence and whether any prior warning has been issued. Additionally, the employer is not obliged to keep records of any disciplinary action taken.

LAW IN CONTEXT
The background to the dispute resolution procedures

In the background, as ever, was the question of costs. The DTI (in *Routes to Resolution*, 2001) estimated that the cost to the taxpayer of employment tribunals was £51.7 million, and the average cost to each employee of each application was £2,000. These figures were regarded as high 'relative to the types of problems handled and the compensation to individuals that is at stake'. Furthermore, the number of unfair dismissal applications rose from 41,914 in 1998/9 to 49,401 in 2000/1. The benefits to the taxpayer were estimated in the Regulatory Impact Assessment at £65–£90 million once the effect of the changes was seen in reduced applications to employment tribunals.

Hepple and Morris (2002 at page 249) argue that these calculations do not take into account the fact that employment rights are part of an exchange under which the government and employers give recompense or give recognition to the rights of workers for their cooperation in wealth creation and to compensate them for the inequality of outcomes of the employment relationship.

Note: As a footnote to this, the Gibbons Report (2007) has recommended the abolition of the procedures.

Procedural considerations

Given that under s 98(4) of the ERA 1996 any decision to dismiss must be reasonable, how has this been applied? The starting point is the ACAS Code of Practice on Disciplinary and Grievance Procedures, reissued in September 2004. This does not take the place of a disciplinary or grievance procedure but recommends what should be contained in one. Although it does not have legal force, s 207 of TULRCA 1992 provides that it is admissible in legal proceedings and any relevant parts shall be taken into account. In effect, any departure from its provisions will have to be justified. However, where there is a DDP or GP which is applicable under the Employment Act 2002 (see above) then the employer has to observe it, otherwise a dismissal is automatically unfair.

The ACAS Code

The ACAS Code itself provides that disciplinary procedures should not be viewed as a means of imposing sanctions but as a means of helping and encouraging improvement amongst workers whose performance is unsatisfactory (para 58). The main features are as follows but it is emphasised that the following must be read in the light of the statutory dispute resolution procedures.

Oral and written warnings

Oral warnings are appropriate for minor offences but for more serious matters a formal written warning should be given. This should set out the nature of the offence and state that a final written warning will be considered if there is no satisfactory sustained improvement or change (paras 21 and 22). A note of oral warnings should be kept, but the Code suggests that they should be disregarded after six months for a first formal warning and one year after a final written warning (paras 20, 22 and 24). A warning given for one offence should not normally be used in a disciplinary procedure in relation to another offence, although there may come a point where different warnings can be taken together, as in *Auguste Noel* v *Curtis* (1990). Here a number of warnings for different offences could be said to be part of an overall pattern of misconduct. The need to be careful about when warnings were given and when they expire was illustrated in *Bevan Ashford* v *Malin* (1995). A final written warning was given, to last 12 months, but the employee was dismissed for a similar act on the very day *after* the warning had expired. The dismissal was held unfair.

Disciplinary proceedings

Where disciplinary proceedings are needed then the Code recommends that before making any decision about disciplinary action the employer should consider the employee's disciplinary and general record, length of service, actions taken in previous similar cases, explanations given by the employee and what is reasonable in the circumstances (para 17). Paragraph 43 states that commission of a criminal offence outside work is not suggested as an automatic reason for dismissal and the issue is whether it makes the employee unsuitable for the work. In *Taylor* v *OCS Group Ltd* (2006) the Court of Appeal held that where there is a defect in the initial disciplinary procedures then there is no automatic rule that this can only be cured by a rehearing rather than a review. The issue in each case is whether the disciplinary process as a whole was fair, notwithstanding the earlier defect. It should of course be emphasised that where the statutory disciplinary procedure applies (this case pre-dated these) then *any* failure to follow this procedure makes the dismissal automatically unfair. In *Airbus UK* v *Webb* (2007) the EAT held that expired warnings can never be taken into account in deciding whether to dismiss an employee.

In *Ramsay* v *Walkers Snack Foods Ltd* (2004) the EAT considered the position where allegations about an employee's conduct are made by an informant who wishes to remain anonymous. The guidelines are contained in *Linfood Cash and Carry* v *Thomson* (1989) and provide that a balance must be struck between the need to protect informants who are genuinely in fear and the need to give a fair hearing to those accused of misconduct. *Ramsay* involved dismissals for alleged theft by employees of money which had been put into crisp packets as part of a sales promotion. Statements made were unsigned and did not contain enough detail which might have revealed who the informants were. Nor did managers personally interview the informants to see what weight should be given to the information. Even so, the EAT held that the statements could be used in the proceedings. The informants were unwilling to sign any statement unless it was edited to remove any possibility of identification.

Right to be accompanied

A worker has the statutory right under ss 10–15 of the Employment Relations Act 1999 to be accompanied by a 'worker's companion' in three basic situations:

(a) at a disciplinary hearing where a formal warning could be imposed or confirmed,

(b) at a disciplinary hearing where the employer could take some other action or this could be confirmed,

(c) at a grievance hearing, which is defined by s 13(5) as a hearing which concerns the performance of a duty owed by the employer to the worker. This does not include the situation where the worker wishes to change terms and conditions of employment.

The right is given to workers as defined in s 230(3) of the ERA 1996, as distinct from employees, and also applies to agency workers and homeworkers (s 13(1)) and so a worker who is not classed as an employee and who cannot therefore claim for unfair dismissal can still claim this right to be accompanied.

Under this right, a worker may request to be accompanied by a fellow worker, a union official employed by the employer or by a union official who has been certified by the union as having received training in acting as a worker's companion. Employers do not have to notify employees of this right but the ACAS Code of Practice, paras 13 and 77 recommend that they should. The original provision was that the companion could address the hearing and confer with the worker during it but was not to be able to answer questions on behalf of the worker. Sections 37–38 of the Employment Relations Act 2004 attempted to clarify the role of a worker's companion in disciplinary and grievance hearings. The rule is now that the companion can put forward the worker's case and sum it up. The companion may also respond on behalf of the worker to any view expressed at the hearing. This last provision clarifies the law as, although, as previously, the companion is not able to answer questions on the worker's behalf, the companion can now respond to a view expressed at the hearing. Whether this rather nice distinction can be observed at a hearing at which no one knowledgeable in employment law may be present remains to be seen! EATs have a right to hear appeals in relation to the right to be accompanied. If the employer refuses to allow a worker to exercise the statutory right to be accompanied then the employee can complain to a tribunal, which must order the payment of up to two weeks' pay to the employee (s 11).

Proportionality of penalty

Any penalty imposed should be proportionate to the nature of the offence, the degree of wilfulness and the position of the employee, including seniority. The final step should be dismissal, disciplinary transfer or demotion (paras 15–18).

Time limits for bringing a claim

Section 111 of the ERA 1996 provides that claims for unfair dismissal must be brought within three months of the effective date of termination of the contract but there is power to extend this where the tribunal considers that it was not reasonably practicable for the complaint to be presented in that time. In *Fitzgerald* v *University of Kent at Canterbury* (2004) the Court of Appeal held that the effective date of termination (EDT) cannot be varied retrospectively by an agreement between the employer and employee. The employee had accepted early retirement on 2 March 2001 but the date when it took effect had been agreed as 28 February. If the date of 2 March was the EDT then her complaint of unfair dismissal was presented in time but if it was 28 February it was out of time. The court held that it was 2 March and felt that a principle was at stake here: the parties could not vary when an actual event had occurred (the EDT) so that one of them might gain an advantage. In the result, the claim for unfair dismissal was in time.

The time limit for presenting a claim is extended in some cases where the statutory disputes procedures apply by reg 15 of the Employment Act 2002 (Dispute Procedure) Regulations 2004.

(a) *Where there is a statutory disciplinary or dismissal procedure.* If a dismissed employee presents a claim after the three-month period has expired then the time limit is extended for a further three months provided that the employee had reasonable grounds for believing, when the initial period expired, that a disciplinary or dismissal procedure, whether statutory or otherwise, was being followed in relation to the matters which included the substance of the claim.

(b) *Where there is a statutory grievance procedure.* The time limit is extended by a further three months in two cases:

   (i) where the employee presents a complaint to the tribunal but has not complied with the first step of the procedure or before 28 days have passed since a copy of the grievance was sent to the employer. The employee then has the opportunity to present the claim in the extended time period;

   (ii) where the employee complied with the first step within the normal time period of three months but the actual complaint to the tribunal was presented after the three-month period had expired.

Human Rights Act 1998 and unfair dismissal

The impact of Article 8 of the ECHR (respect for private and family life) on a dismissal was considered by the Court of Appeal in *X v Y* (2004). A charity youth worker was dismissed after failing to tell his employers that he had been cautioned for indecency in a public toilet. The court rejected his claim that the dismissal was in breach of Article 8 as a public toilet is, by definition, a public place and so private life was not involved. However, the court accepted that a dismissal because of conduct in an employee's private life could be in breach of Article 8 and a tribunal would be obliged to take note of the HRA 1998 as by Article 3 it must give effect to the provisions of the Employment Rights Act 1996 in a way which is compatible with the ECHR.

Remedies for unfair dismissal

There are three remedies for unfair dismissal:

1 compensation,

2 re-engagement,

3 reinstatement.

Remedies 2 and 3 are often known together as 're-employment'.

Compensation is the remedy sought in nearly all cases. In 2005/6 the number of cases where re-employment was ordered was 8 (0.1%) out of 7,419 cases proceeding to a hearing. Compensation was awarded in 2,410 (32.5%), the remedy was left to the parties in 255 cases, no award was made in 752 cases, and 3,994 cases were dismissed. The percentage success rate of those which proceeded to a hearing was 46.1% and 53.9% of claims were dismissed. However, when the law of unfair dismissal was introduced in 1972, re-employment was intended to be the primary remedy.

Re-employment orders

The orders are made under ss 114 and 115 of the ERA 1996 and the effect of a reinstatement order is that the complainant must be treated as if he had never been dismissed. Back pay must be made for the period when he was not employed and in all respects he must be treated as if the dismissal had never taken place. Re-engagement involves being re-employed in a job which is comparable to the previous one. The award is discretionary and it is made only if the tribunal is satisfied not only that it would be practicable for the employer to comply but also that it would be just. Section 116(5) provides that if a permanent replacement has been engaged in place of the dismissed employee then the tribunal shall not take this into account if the circumstances in s 116(6) apply. These are that the employer shows both that it was not practicable to arrange for the employee's work to be done without engaging a permanent replacement and that the replacement was engaged after a reasonable time had elapsed when the employer had not heard that the dismissed employee wished to be re-employed. In other situations the tribunal had a discretion in deciding whether re-employment is practicable or just. Thus, in *Enessy* v *Minoprio* (1978)) it was held that re-employment would not be ordered in a small firm where the parties were in a close personal relationship which had broken down; and in ***Wood Group Heavy Industries Turbines Ltd v Crossan*** (1998) it was not ordered where the dismissal was for misconduct and where this meant that the relationship of mutual trust and confidence between the parties had broken down.

An employer cannot be compelled to comply with an order for re-employment: instead, an order can be made that he or she is ordered to pay an additional award to the complainant. The additional award is a minimum of 26 weeks' pay or £8,060, whichever is the lower, and the maximum is 52 weeks' pay or £16,120, whichever is the lower.

Compensation

This consists of the following:

A basic award

Note: The limits on the amount of compensation are set yearly by the Employment Rights (Increase of Limits Orders) and take effect in February each year. The limits given below are those in force from 1 February 2007.

The basic award is calculated on the same basis as redundancy compensation (see Chapter 12) and is awarded for loss of accrued continuity of employment rights consequent on the dismissal. The current maximum is £9,300 and the maximum week's wage taken into account is £310. It is reduced by the amount of any redundancy payment received but where the employee is dismissed in circumstances that he or she does not qualify for a redundancy payment then two weeks' basic pay is payable. There is a minimum basic award of £4,200 where an employee is dismissed on grounds of trade union membership or activities, health and safety reasons, carrying out the functions of a pension fund trustee, carrying out statutory functions as an employee representative and asserting a statutory right under the Working Time Regulations (s 120(1A) of the ERA 1996). Where the dismissal was automatically unfair under s 98A(1) because the employer had failed to comply with the statutory disciplinary procedure then the employee is entitled to a minimum of four weeks' basic pay unless the tribunal considers that such an increase would result in injustice to the employer.

The basic award may be reduced where the employee has contributed by his or her conduct to the dismissal and this may be so even where the misconduct is discovered only *after* the dismissal. It will be recalled that in *Devis* v *Atkins* (1977) it was held that misconduct discovered after the dismissal could not affect the decision on whether the dismissal was fair but it can be taken into account here and it may be that the employee receives nothing.

Example

John is dismissed for suspected pilfering at work. The tribunal finds that at the time of the dismissal this was not fair on the evidence available. However, ten minutes after the dismissal, proof comes to light that John was indeed guilty. Although John's dismissal was held unfair he may well not receive any compensation under either the basic award or the compensatory award (below).

Compensatory award

The maximum unfair dismissal compensation is now £60,900 except for the cases where there is no limit: where the employee is dismissed or selected for redundancy for health and safety reasons or for making an authorised disclosure under the Public Interest Disclosure Act 1998. In 2005/6 the maximum award of compensation was £477,603 but the Annual Report of the Employment Tribunals Service (from which all these figures are taken) does not explain how this was arrived at. The median award was £4,228 and the average award was £8,679. The greatest number of awards (over 30%) were in the range of £1,000 to £4,000 and only 2.6% were near the statutory limit by being over £50,000.

The basic principle in deciding the actual award is set out in s 123(1) of the ERA 1996: it must be such an amount as the tribunal considers 'just and equitable having regard to the loss sustained by the complainant in so far as that loss is attributable to action taken by the employer'.

The heads of loss were set out in *Norton Tool Co.* v *Tewson* (1973) as follows:

- *Immediate loss of wages up to the time of the tribunal hearing*. This includes net wages and overtime if worked regularly, together with bonus payments and tips. It is therefore a wider calculation than is made for damages for wrongful dismissal.

- *Manner of dismissal*. An award will be made under this head only if the manner of dismissal made it more difficult to find another job.

- *Future loss of earnings.* These will be awarded on the basis of the difference in wages between the job from which the employee was dismissed and any new job already obtained. If the employee is still out of work then the tribunal must have some evidence based on the labour market and local conditions, taking into account the employee's age and state of health.

- *Loss of future employment protection rights.* The employee has lost any continuity of employment. As this is also compensated in the basic award, a sum of £100 is normally awarded here.

- *Loss of pension rights.* This head was added subsequently.

As stated earlier, the award can be reduced to take account of the employee's conduct.

Under s 31(3) of the Employment Act 2002 compensation will be *increased* by 10–50% where an employer unreasonably fails to follow the statutory disciplinary procedure set out in the Act unless there are exceptional circumstances which make it unjust or inequitable to do so. Where it is the employee who has either failed to comply with a requirement of the procedure or to exercise a right of appeal under it, then by s 31(2) the award may be *reduced* by the same figure. In *Alexander v Brigden Enterprises* (2006) the EAT held that, even where the statutory procedures have not been followed and so dismissal is automatically unfair, it may be that there is a 100% likelihood of dismissal and so no compensation is awarded. The obvious example, as here, is where a redundancy procedure is not followed but there is a 100% likelihood of dismissal.

Sums in the notice period

In *Langley and Carter v Burlo* (2006) the Court of Appeal held that if the terms of an employee's contract provide that during sick leave he is entitled only to sick pay, then, if whilst on leave he is dismissed without notice, he is entitled only to compensation based on the amount of statutory sick pay which he was due in the notice period. The principle that compensation for unfair dismissal should not result in the employee receiving a bonus is subject to one exception established in *Norton Tool v Tewson*: that an employee who is dismissed without notice cannot be required to give credit for new earnings received in the notice period. It is likely that the House of Lords will shortly rule on the principles in this area.

Reduction for contributory fault

Section 123(6) of the ERA 1996 provides that where the tribunal finds that the dismissal was to any extent caused or contributed to by the claimant then it shall reduce the amount of compensation by such amount as it thinks just and equitable. In *Nelson v BBC (No. 2)* (1980) it was held that the following matters must be taken into account in deciding whether to reduce an award under these provisions:

- Was the action of the employee culpable or blameworthy? This does not have to be conduct which amounts to a breach of contract or tort. If it does not, then it must be 'perverse or bloody minded' or conduct which is 'unacceptable in the circumstances'.

- Did that action cause or contribute to the dismissal?

- Is it just and equitable to reduce compensation?

Where an employee's conduct is beyond his control, such as ill health, this is not reason for making a reduction (*Slaughter* v *C Brewer & Sons Ltd* (1990)). An early example of where one was made is *Scottish Co-operative Society Ltd* v *Lloyd* (1973) where a dismissal was held to be unfair where an employee had not received any specific warnings about his conduct. However, he had failed, for instance, to reply to complaints about him and had failed to obey instructions.

In *Scope* v *Thornett* (2006) the Court of Appeal held that tribunals, when assessing compensation for unfair dismissal, should not avoid making reductions to a compensatory award merely because it would involve speculation. Some tribunals had considered that the words in s 123(6) (above) allowing a reduction to be made when it was 'just and equitable' prevented them from speculating as to the extent of a future loss but this was not so.

Can non-economic loss be recovered in an action for unfair dismissal?

In *Dunnachie* v *Kingston upon Hull City Council* (2004) the Court of Appeal held that damages could be awarded in an action for unfair dismissal for non-pecuniary losses such as distress, humiliation, damage to reputation and to family life, and for psychiatric injury. The basis of the decision was that s 123 of the ERA 1996, which provides that compensation can be awarded for unfair dismissal of such amount as the tribunal considers just and equitable, is wide enough to cover non-pecuniary losses caused by the dismissal.

At the time of this decision there was speculation that the courts might be attempting to make claims for unfair dismissal more attractive in the light of their attempt to restrict the development of a parallel action for wrongful dismissal for general losses flowing from the dismissal. (See also *Johnson* v *Unisys* earlier in this chapter.) However, the House of Lords then overruled this judgment and held that in unfair dismissal cases a tribunal cannot award compensation for injury to feelings. It held that the word 'loss' in s 123 of the ERA 1996 covers only pecuniary loss. Lord Steyn emphasised that in 1971, when the original legislation was passed, there could have been no question of including compensation for injury to feelings as a head of loss. However, as Rubenstein (2004) observes, this takes no account of the fact that when unfair dismissal legislation was adopted 'there was no discrimination legislation, damages for psychiatric injury were unknown, and the implied term of mutual trust and confidence had yet to be developed'. In particular, if the dismissal was the result of unlawful discrimination, then if an action for discrimination was brought, a claim for damages for non-economic loss could be brought (see Chapter 9). However, if the dismissal did not involve discrimination then these cannot be claimed. It is very difficult to see the logic of this but Lord Steyn pointed out in his speech in *Dunnachie* that the Donovan Commission (1968) had recommended that compensation should be allowed for non-economic loss. Thus the issue was a live one in 1971 when the unfair dismissal legislation was first enacted in the Industrial Relations Act and Parliament must have decided to exclude it.

Bowers and Lewis (2005) suggest that there might still be scope for claims for non-economic loss in unfair dismissal cases. They point out that there is no statutory guidance on the factors to be considered when a tribunal increases an award of compensation because of failure by the employer to comply with the statutory disciplinary and dismissal procedures. In addition they point out that, unlike s 123 of the ERA 1996 which refers to loss, here tribunals are merely directed to assess what uplift of damages is 'just and equitable in the circumstances'. It will be interesting to see what a tribunal makes of this argument when it is advanced before it.

LAW IN CONTEXT
The concept of property rights in the job

This has been a feature of the dialogue about dismissal for some years. The concept that an employee has a proprietary right in the job must not of course be confused with the concept of proprietary interests in property law. Instead it points out that an employee has, largely through the law of unfair dismissal, a right in the job itself. Collins (1992) explained that the assertion of property rights in the job expressed 'the idea that employees should enjoy greater job security than that accorded to them by the common law's doctrine of termination at will'. Thus it can be seen as marking out the vital difference between the statutory right to claim unfair dismissal with its emphasis on procedural safeguards for the employee and the concept of a fair dismissal with the common law doctrine that any contract of employment can be terminated simply on giving notice. (Davies and Freedland (1984) provide what is still one of the best analyses of the development of the concept.)

However, as Anderman (2004) points out, it is possible to identify judicial pronouncements which hold that an employer also has a property right which 'underpins an acceptance of managerial prerogatives'. He instances the words of Lord Steyn in *Malik v BCCI* who, when discussing the implied obligation of mutual trust and confidence, observed that a balance needed to be struck between 'the employer's interest in managing his business as he sees fit and the employee's interest in not being unfairly and improperly exploited'. Anderman suggests that the 'reasonable responses test' for judging the fairness of the reason for the dismissal is an example of the employer's property in the job and another one is the case law on dismissals on a reorganisation such as *Hollister v NFU*, which are dealt with in Chapter 12. What is essential for the student of employment law is to identify the extent to which the property rights of both employer and employee are recognised and to assess the extent to which both are justified.

SUMMARY

This chapter first looks at the ways in which the employment relationship can be terminated:

- death or on the ending of the business
- frustration
- expiry of a fixed-term contract
- mutual agreement

- notice
- summary dismissal.

It then looks at the two remedies which employees have on termination:

- wrongful dismissal – contractual
- unfair dismissal – statutory.

Wrongful dismissal is first examined and the remedies in both private and public law are considered.

The discussion of unfair dismissal is organised around the following topic:

- who is entitled to claim?
- what is meant by 'dismissal'?
- fair reasons for dismissal
- procedural fairness – including the statutory dispute procedures
- remedies.

In addition, the growing case law on the relationship between wrongful and unfair dismissal is highlighted where appropriate.

QUESTION

'It is important that the operation of the legislation in relation to unfair dismissal should not impede employers unreasonably in the efficient management of their business, which must be in the interests of all.' (Phillips J in *Cook* v *Thomas Linnell and Sons Ltd* (1977).)

(a) Do you agree with this statement?

(b) Do you consider that it accurately reflects the aims of the legislation and the attitudes of the courts when interpreting it?

FURTHER READING

Collins, H. (2001) 'Claim for Unfair Dismissal', 30 ILJ 305. (This is a case note on *Johnson* v *Unisys*.)

BIBLIOGRAPHY

Anderman, S. (2004) 'Termination of Employment: Whose Property Rights?' in C. Barnard, S. Deakin and G. Morris (eds) *The Future of Labour Law*, Hart Publishing: Oxford. (Pages 111–22 discuss unfair dismissal in a property rights perspective and consider the test of reasonable responses both in this context and in general.)

Bowers, J. and Clarke, A. (1981) 'Managerial Prerogative: a study in some other substantive reasons' 10 ILJ 34 (article critical of decisions under the ground of 'some other substantial reason').

Bowers, J. and Lewis, M. (2005) 'Non Economic Damage in Unfair Dismissal Cases: What's Left after *Dunnachie*?' 34 ILJ 83.

Collins, H. (1992) *Justice in Dismissal: The Law of Termination of Employment*, Oxford University Press: Oxford.

Collins, H. (2003) *Employment Law*, Oxford University Press: Oxford.

Davies, P. and Freedland, M. (1984) *Labour Law Text and Materials* (2nd edn), Oxford University Press: Oxford. (See pp. 428–32: 'The Rise and Fall of Job Property?')

Donovan, Lord (1968) *Report of the Royal Commission on Trade Unions and Employers Associations*, Cmnd 3623.

DTI (2001) *Routes to Resolution: Improving Dispute Resolution in Britain*. DTI consultation paper: London.

Gibbons, M. (2007) *A Review of Employment Dispute Resolution in Great Britain*. DTI: London.

Hepple, B. and Morris, G. (2002) 'The Employment Act 2002 and the Crisis of Individual Employment Rights', 31 ILJ 245. (This article looks at the future of employment law in the light of the growth of individual employment rights and pp. 255–69 focus on the new statutory disciplinary procedures.)

Rubenstein, M. (2004) 'Commentary [in the Industrial Relations Law Reports] on the decision in *Dunnachie v Kingston upon Hull City Council*', IRLR 669.

For further resources and updates please go to the Companion Website accompanying this book at **www.mylawchamber.co.uk/duddingtonemployment**

11

Wrongful and unfair dismissal

12 Dismissal for economic reasons

INTRODUCTION

This chapter looks at dismissals where the reason for the dismissal is, broadly speaking, not a personal one connected with the employee *per se* but results from the ending of the employee's job, the reorganisation of the business, or the transfer of the business to another employer. These three reasons correspond, in general terms, to the three areas that will be examined in this chapter. However, the principles of the law on unfair dismissal which were outlined in Chapter 11 are also relevant and will be referred to extensively here.

REDUNDANCY

Significance of redundancy today

Redundancy is a topic which, although remaining in importance in employment law, no longer occupies the central place which it once did. This is for two reasons, one legal and one social.

- The legal reason is that the level of compensation for unfair dismissal is so far in advance of redundancy pay that it is financially advantageous for employees to claim that they have been unfairly dismissed and not made redundant. The details will be discussed later but, to keep a general sense of perspective in mind, the maximum redundancy pay that can be claimed is £9,300 whereas unfair dismissal compensation stands (including the basic award) presently at a maximum of £69,900.

- The social reason is that the number of redundancies is declining. The latest survey (DTI, 2006) shows that annual redundancy rates are falling and have been for the past few years. This is so for both men and women. In addition, the number of manufacturing employees made redundant in recent years has been only around half of that seen in the late 1990s. The actual figures are based on what are termed 'job separations' and show that the percentage of the job separations which are involuntary as opposed to voluntary has dropped from 37% in 1995 to around 28% in 2005. The survey points out that even this figure is likely to be inflated as the Office of National Statistics (ONS) definition counts both voluntary redundancies and the end of temporary jobs as being involuntary.

LAW IN CONTEXT
The purpose of redundancy legislation

The core idea of redundancy is, as Davies and Freedland (1993) put it, that 'the employer had ceased to have a business need for the job that the employee in question had been doing and had accordingly decided to dismiss the employee'. The original legislation was the Redundancy Payments Act 1965, but the law is now contained in Part XI of the Employment Rights Act 1996.

The Redundancy Payments Act 1965 has been described as 'crossing the Rubicon as far as employment protection legislation was concerned' (Davies and Freedland, 1984). The reason is that this was the first piece of statutory regulation of the employment relationship itself. Previous legislation, as we have seen, tinkered with the edges of the contract of employment (see Chapter 4), whereas in the 1965 Act, for the first time, Parliament enacted a comprehensive code dealing with a particular area. It has never been clear whether Parliament meant this to be the forerunner of the flood of statutory regulation which then followed, marking the end of 'voluntarism', or whether it was seen simply as a response to a particular problem.

The answer may well be the latter. It was felt in the early 1960s that industrial change needed to happen more rapidly and that one way of doing this was to encourage greater labour mobility. There were already voluntary schemes in existence whereby workers who had been made redundant were given lump sum payments but these were not especially generous, nor did they cover many workers. Accordingly, the Redundancy Payments Act made it a statutory requirement to make these payments. What then happened was doubtless unforeseen at the time. In 1971 Parliament passed the Industrial Relations Act, which gave a statutory right to protection from unfair dismissal and, ever since, the redundancy payments legislation has been a poor relation of it mainly because the compensation levels are so much greater with unfair dismissal. This is particularly so at present, with, as we saw above, the maximum compensation for unfair dismissal (including the basic award) standing at £69,900, whereas the maximum for redundancy is £9,300. Accordingly – and this is of crucial importance in appreciating the relationship between different areas of law here – an employee will prefer to argue, if possible, that he has been unfairly dismissed, whereas an employer will argue instead that the employee has been made redundant. A good recent example is *High Table Ltd v Horst* (1997), discussed below. When considering the cases, one needs to distinguish between those decided in the golden age of redundancy payments legislation from 1965 to 1971, when it held the field unchallenged and was the only means of dismissed employees gaining any statutory compensation, and those decided after the coming into force of the Industrial Relations Act 1971 when it became, and has remained, a decided second best to unfair dismissal.

Redundancy payments legislation has been described by a leading authority (Grunfeld, 1989) as having 'helped, in some degree . . . to enable British industry and commerce to take on the growing international competition'. Be that as it may, the Act was strongly criticised by Fryer (1973) as having perpetuated several myths adding up to the belief that the Act 'has done something, even too much, to redress the gross imbalance between capital and labour'. In Fryer's view, the Act did not, in spite of a 'myth' to the contrary, restrict managerial discretion.

$\rightarrow$

12

Dismissal for economic reasons

One point stressed by both Grunfeld and Fryer is that the Act did not confer any kind of job security. It simply gives compensation for loss of a job through redundancy. The purpose of the Act was described by Denning MR in *Lloyd* v *Brassey* (1969) as 'in a real sense compensation for long service'. He also stressed that: 'It is not unemployment pay. Repeat "not". Even if he gets another job straightaway he is nevertheless entitled to redundancy pay.'

Impact of European Union law

The main impact of EU law has been in the area of redundancy consultation procedures and not on the substantive law of redundancy.

Role of the courts

In *Moon* v *Homeworthy Furniture (Northern) Ltd* (1977) the EAT decisively rejected an attempt to make the courts the arbiters of whether a redundancy was justified. A factory had been closed down and the whole workforce was made redundant. The employees argued that the employer's contention that the factory was not economically viable was wrong. The EAT held that, provided there was a cessation of work, which there was here, the court could not investigate whether this could have been avoided. As Kilner-Brown put it: 'The employees were and are seeking to use the industrial tribunal and the EAT as a platform for the ventilation of an industrial dispute.' One can see this attitude as an example of the unwillingness of the courts to interfere in matters considered to be within the scope of managerial prerogative, a point to which we shall return in the discussion of dismissals resulting from a reorganisation (see later in this chapter). It has been suggested in Ewing (1996), that a court should be able to refer the question of whether a redundancy was necessary to a Labour Inspector. However, as things stand at present, the role of the courts is confined to dealing with whether a factual situation actually constitutes redundancy.

Summary

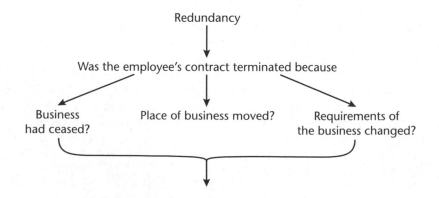

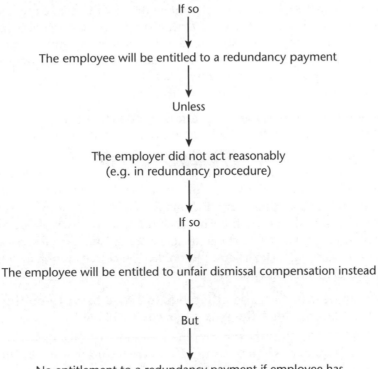

If so

↓

The employee will be entitled to a redundancy payment

↓

Unless

↓

The employer did not act reasonably
(e.g. in redundancy procedure)

↓

If so

↓

The employee will be entitled to unfair dismissal compensation instead

↓

But

↓

No entitlement to a redundancy payment if employee has
unreasonably refused an offer of suitable alternative employment

Definition of redundancy

✓ Redundancy is defined in s 139 of the ERA 1996 as where a dismissal is wholly or mainly attributable to:

(a) the fact that the employer has ceased or intends to cease:

    (i) to carry on the business for the purposes for which the employee was employed,

    (ii) to carry on the business in the place where the employee was employed,

(b) the fact that the requirements of the business for employees to carry out work of a particular kind have ceased or diminished or are expected to.

✓ It will be seen that the Act envisages redundancy occurring in three situations:

1 The business closes down.

2 The business continues but the employee is required to move his or her place of work.

3 The business continues but the need for work done by that employee ceases or diminishes.

It must be emphasised that, in all cases of redundancy, the issue is not, strictly speaking, whether an employee is redundant but whether that employee's *post* is redundant.

The focus is not on the employee personally but on the post that that employee holds. Furthermore, this emphasis on the post rather than the person reminds us that a redundancy situation must not be used as a cover to get rid of an employee whom the employer wants to be rid of for other reasons: for example, allegations of misconduct. The way to deal with this is by a dismissal procedure.

We will look at each of these situations in turn.

Where the employer has ceased or intends to cease to carry on the business for the purposes for which the employee was employed

The term 'business' is defined by s 235 of the ERA 1996 as including a trade or profession and any activity carried on by a body of persons whether corporate or incorporate. The only other point worthy of note is that the employer does not have to be the actual owner of the business. In *Thomas* v *Jones* (1978) a sub-postmistress retired and, as a result, the post office which she ran closed. An employee who had worked in the post office was held to be entitled to a redundancy payment because the actual business of running that particular post office had ceased even though the post office itself, of course, still continued.

Where the employer has ceased or intends to cease to carry on the business in the place where the employee was employed

The situation here is that either the entire business has moved or that there is no longer any need for the employee's services at the place where he or she worked. The courts originally evolved a contractual test for deciding this but now what can be called a 'geographical test' holds sway.

The contractual test

This asked whether an employee could be contractually bound to move his place of work. Therefore, if there was an express term in the employee's contract that, for example, an employee could be required to work anywhere in the United Kingdom, then an employee who worked in London could not claim a redundancy payment if his or her place of work was moved to Manchester. (Note, however, that the employer must act reasonably when requiring the employee to move: see *United Bank* v *Akhtar* (1989) – see Chapter 5.) Suppose that there was no express mobility clause. In that case the courts would ask whether a term could be implied into the employee's contract that, for example, the employee should be employed within daily travelling distance of home. If so, and employees were being required to travel beyond this, then they would be entitled to refuse to do so and claim a redundancy payment. Conversely, if the distance was within daily travelling, then, if they refused, they would themselves be in breach of contract. In *O'Brien* v *Associated Fire Alarms* (1968) employees who were employed in Liverpool were required to work in Barrow, about 150 miles away. The Court of Appeal held that they were redundant, as Barrow was clearly not within daily travelling distance of their homes. This approach was confirmed in *Courtaulds Northern Spinning Ltd* v *Sibson* (1988), where the Court of Appeal, in a case involving a claim for constructive dismissal (see Chapter 11), upheld the decision in *O'Brien* and rejected an attempt by the industrial tribunal to impose a requirement that a request to the employee to move must be reasonable.

328

The geographical test

This looks at where the employee actually works rather than at where he or she could be required to work under a mobility clause. This approach was first applied in **Bass Leisure Ltd v Thomas** (1994). The applicant worked at a depot in Coventry and her employer, in accordance with a term in her contract, required her to work at another depot 20 miles away. She did not wish to do so. The EAT held that she was entitled to a redundancy payment as her actual place of work could not include a depot 20 miles away. The Court of Appeal approved this approach in **High Table Ltd v Horst** (1997). The respondent was employed as a waitress by the appellant, which provided waitress services for a number of firms in the City of London. Her letter of appointment specified that she was appointed as a waitress to a particular firm but, after five years, cuts in the budget of that firm meant that she was no longer needed there. The appellant's staff handbook, which formed part of the respondent's contract of employment, gave the appellant the right to move the respondent to another location, which would, wherever possible, be within daily travelling distance of work. The court held that the respondent was redundant. Peter Gibson J held that the contract of employment cannot be 'the sole determinant' of where the employee's place of work is and the question of where the employee works 'is one to be answered primarily by a consideration of the factual circumstances which obtained until the dismissal'. There is a slight difference in approach between this decision and that in *Bass Leisure*, which appeared to reject any reliance at all on a mobility clause. Here the Court of Appeal simply relegated such a clause to *evidence* of the position and held, on the facts, that the respondent's place of work was the actual firm where she worked.

The decision in *High Table* is interesting for two further reasons:

1 Peter Gibson J mentioned that a mobility clause could still be invoked by an employer to require employees to move their place of work and, if an employee refused to move under the terms of a mobility clause, then this may be grounds for a fair dismissal. He observed that 'the issues of dismissal, redundancy and reasonableness in the actions of an employer should be kept distinct'.

2 The decision neatly illustrates how redundancy now works in the opposite way from what was originally intended. The employee (the respondent) did not want to be made redundant but wished to claim unfair dismissal, presumably on the basis that the employer should have redeployed her. The employer wished to claim redundancy, as the amount of compensation payable is less.

In the result, employees lose under both the above tests. Mobility clauses can be used against employees but the courts are not now prepared to use the existence of a mobility clause to say that there is no redundancy and therefore open up a claim for unfair dismissal.

Where the requirements of the business for employees to carry out work of a particular kind have ceased or diminished or are expected to do so

This has proved to be the most difficult part of the definition of redundancy to apply. It also seems from the statistics quoted at the beginning of this chapter to be very common in practice, as these showed that over half of redundancies were due to staff cutbacks rather than the actual closing down of the business. The typical situation is where the business is continuing but the need for employees whose work is of a particular kind has either ceased or is diminishing. Although this may not have been so in all of the cases referred to in the above figures, it will have been so in a considerable number.

The nature of the problem

Example

Pete has worked as a typist for Gradgrind Ltd for 25 years. His work is excellent. Gradgrind Ltd require all their typists to use word processors but Pete refuses, saying that 'he will not get used to new tricks'.

This situation neatly illustrates the relationship between redundancy and unfair dismissal. If Gradgrind Ltd failed to act reasonably by, for example, offering training and otherwise attempting to meet Pete's concerns, then Pete could have a claim for redundancy under s 98(4) of the ERA. If, however, Gradgrind Ltd has acted reasonably then the focus switches to whether Pete was redundant on the ground that the requirement for typists was 'work of a particular kind'.

The approach of the courts

The first major case to deal with this issue was *North Riding Garages Ltd* v *Butterwick* (1966). The applicant had been employed at a garage as a workshop manager in charge of the repairs workshop. He also spent some time in actual mechanical work on vehicles. The new owners wished him to do more work on the sales side and more paperwork. They also introduced new working methods to which the applicant found it difficult to adapt, and he was dismissed. Widgery J held that 'an employee who remains in the same kind of work is expected to adapt himself to new methods and techniques'. However, 'if new methods alter the nature of the work required to be done' then employees may be redundant. In this case no particular kind of work had ceased or diminished and therefore the applicant was not redundant.

Similarly, in *Vaux and Associated Breweries Ltd* v *Ward* (1968) a barmaid in a hotel was dismissed because it was felt that she would not fit in with a new image which was being introduced in the hotel. It was held that she was not redundant, as the requirement for her work had not changed: her replacement did the same work as she did.

Once again, in *Hindle* v *Percival Boats Ltd* (1968), a highly skilled boatbuilder was dismissed as he was 'too good and too slow'. The Court of Appeal held that he was not redundant, as the requirement for his work had not ceased or diminished. The fact that he had not been replaced did not assist him because, as Sachs LJ put it: 'an employer is entitled to come to a genuine conclusion that despite the requirements of his business he prefers to have a vacancy in his staff rather than to take on an unsuitable replacement.'

All these three cases show a broad view being taken by the courts as to what is work of a particular kind and a corresponding emphasis on the duty of employees to adapt to new methods of work. A slightly different approach was seen in *Murphy* v *Epsom*

College (1984). The applicant was one of two plumbers employed by the school. The school modernised its heating system and decided that it needed a heating technician rather than two plumbers. The applicant was selected for dismissal and it was held that he was redundant, as plumbing was a particular kind of work and this had diminished. The irony was that the applicant wished to claim unfair dismissal but was thus unable to do so, whereas in the three earlier cases the applicants who were held not to be redundant might have had a good chance of succeeding in an unfair dismissal claim but at the time that remedy was not, of course, available.

The position where the employee's contract enables the employer to require the employee to move to other work if the present work ceases or diminishes

Until recently, the law appeared to be that in such a situation the employee was not redundant. In *Nelson v BBC* (1977) the employee's contract required him to work 'when how and where' the BBC required. Therefore, he was not redundant when the Caribbean service in which he worked was cut back, since he could be transferred to another post. In effect, the Court of Appeal preferred the 'contract' test to the 'function' test, which asks what work the employee was required to do and actually did. In *Cowen v Haden Ltd* (1983) this approach was approved but the Court of Appeal managed to achieve a different result on the facts. A divisional contracts surveyor's own contract enabled his employer to require him to perform any duties 'which reasonably fall within the scope of his capabilities'. It was held that these wide words only related to work that reasonably came within the function of a divisional contracts surveyor. Therefore, he was held to be redundant because there was, in fact, no longer work of this particular kind.

This emphasis on the words of the employee's contract was decisively rejected by the House of Lords in *Murray v Foyle Meats Ltd* (1999). The applicants were employed as meat plant operatives. They normally worked in the slaughter hall but, under their contracts of employment, they could be required to work elsewhere and occasionally did so. Fewer employees were required in the hall due to falling business and the applicants were dismissed. They brought proceedings for unfair dismissal and the employers contended that the dismissals were due to redundancy as there was a diminution in the requirements for employees to carry out work of a particular kind, i.e. in the slaughter hall. (The relevant statute was the Contracts of Employment and Redundancy Payments Act (Northern Ireland) 1965, with identical wording to what is now the Employment Rights Act.)

Irvine LC, with whom the other Law Lords agreed, held that both the contract and the function tests miss the point. He considered that:

> the language of [s 139(1)(b)] is simplicity itself. It asks two questions of fact. The first is whether one or other of various states of economic affairs exists. In this case, the relevant one is whether the requirements of the business for employees to carry out work of a particular kind have diminished. The second question is whether the dismissal is attributable, wholly or mainly, to that state of affairs.

Applying this test, he held that 'the tribunal found on the facts that the requirements for employees to work in the slaughter hall had diminished. Secondly, they found that

12

Dismissal for economic reasons

that state of affairs had led to the applicants being dismissed. That, in my opinion, is the end of the matter.' Accordingly, the applicants were redundant.

The difficulty with this deceptively simple approach is that, as has been pointed out (by Barnard (2000)), it 'effectively air brushes the words "work of a particular kind" from the statute: the statute does not say "there is a redundancy whenever a dismissal is attributable to a diminution in the employer's requirement for employees" but that is the effect of the Lord Chancellor's approach.'

Another view is to regard the decision as bringing welcome clarification to this area by saying, in effect, that an employee whose dismissal is attributable to redundancy has been dismissed by reason of redundancy. The effect of the decision is that in cases where the employee's contract covers a wider range of duties than those actually performed, then the work actually performed will, in effect, be 'work of a particular kind'. The practical result will be to make it more difficult for employees to claim unfair dismissal and easier for employers to say that they are redundant.

Example

Eileen's contract requires her to work 'in any capacity' for her employers, Digs Ltd, who run a garden centre. Eileen has worked for many years selling garden furniture but Digs Ltd decide to discontinue this and dismiss Eileen. She claims that she has been unfairly dismissed. Digs Ltd claims that she is redundant. Under the law as established in *Nelson v BBC*, Eileen could argue that she was not redundant as she could, under the terms of her contract, be required to work elsewhere. Therefore, by dismissing her, Digs Ltd is liable for unfair dismissal. However, the effect of *Murray v Foyle Meats* is that, as the requirement for Eileen to work in the section selling garden furniture has ceased, she is therefore redundant.

The decision in *Murray v Foyle Meats* means that *Nelson v BBC* is now no longer good law but that *Cowen v Haden* is probably still correct on its facts.

In *Shawkat v Nottingham City Hospitals Trust (No. 2)* (2001) the applicant was employed as a thoracic surgeon but, following a reorganisation, he was required to carry out cardiac work as well as thoracic work. He declined to do so. The Court of Appeal held that he was not redundant because there was no diminution in the requirements for the work of a particular kind which the applicant was doing, i.e. thoracic surgery. The reorganisation did not result in the applicant's redundancy. This decision can be seen as an application of Irvine LC's words in *Murray* when he emphasised that a redundancy must be attributable to a diminution in the requirements for employees to carry out a particular kind of work. Here the requirements had not declined. Instead, the applicant was left to claim that unreasonable duties had been imposed on him and therefore he was unfairly dismissed.

Bumped redundancies

> ### Example
>
> In **Safeway Stores v Burrell** (1997) Judge Peter Clark gave the following example:
> An employee is employed to work as a fork-lift truck driver, delivering materials to six production machines on the shop floor. Each machine has its own operator. The employer decides that it needs to run only five machines and that one machine operator must go. Selection for dismissal is done on the principle of who is the least qualified within the department. The fork-lift truck driver has the fewest qualifications. Accordingly, one machine operator is transferred to driving the truck: the short service truck driver is dismissed. Is he dismissed by reason of redundancy? The answer is yes.
>
> (*Note*: redundancy selection procedures are dealt with later in this chapter.)

The reason given by the judge was that there was a diminution in the requirement for employees to carry out the work of operators and this caused the dismissal. Therefore, there does not have to be a diminution in the requirement for the work actually done by the dismissed employee.

This reasoning was applied in this case where the applicant, a petrol station manager, lost his post in a reorganisation where all posts of petrol station managers were replaced by petrol filling station controllers. He was told that he could apply for one of these posts but he declined. It was held that he was redundant. As was pointed out by Judge Clark, the Act refers to 'employees' and not 'employee' and the fact was that a redundancy had come about and, as a result, he was redundant.

This reasoning was rejected in **Church v West Lancashire NHS Trust** (1998), also a decision of the EAT. It was held that the phrase 'work of a particular kind' means work of a particular kind which the actual employee was employed to do and therefore in a bumping situation the bumped dismissal will not be redundancy. In the fork-lift truck example, the truck driver would not be redundant because there was no diminution in the requirement for *his* work.

This controversy seems to have been settled by **Murray v Foyle Meats** (above) and it is within this context that the decision makes most sense. The words of Irvine LC clearly indicate that the test in *Safeway Stores v Burrell* is correct. As will be recalled, he stated that, provided the requirements for work of a particular kind have ceased or diminished *and* the employee is redundant as a result, then that is redundancy.

Redundancies, terms of the contract and reorganisations

A number of cases have dealt with the situation where employers have altered the terms on which employees were employed and these employees have claimed that this change amounted to redundancy. A straightforward decision is **Chapman v Goonvean and Rostrowrack China Clay Co. Ltd** (1973), where the withdrawal of free transport to work was held not to make affected employees redundant. The argument that the requirements of the business for their work would have ceased if this change had not been made was rejected. Denning MR pointed out that the requirements for their work continued as before.

This was followed by *Johnson v Nottinghamshire Combined Police Authority* (1974), where a change in shift patterns was similarly held not to amount to redundancy. In *Lesney Products v Nolan* (1977) a change in shift systems resulted in reduced opportunities for overtime but, once again, this was held not to amount to redundancy. Although the actual decision was fairly straightforward, Denning MR's emphasis on the right of employers to reorganise their business was an important indicator of judicial attitudes in an area to which we shall return later in this chapter: 'it is important that nothing should be done to impair the ability of employers to re-organise their work force and their times and conditions of work so as to improve efficiency'.

◼ Redundancy selection procedures

Assuming that the dismissal of an employee falls within the definition of redundancy then that employee will be entitled to a redundancy payment. However, as has been pointed out, the maximum compensation for unfair dismissal is far higher and it is this which makes redundancy selection procedures so significant. Therefore, an employee will seek, if possible, to bring the claim under unfair dismissal rather than redundancy.

Relationship between redundancy and unfair dismissal

Example

Fred works in a shop owned by Molly. Fred's contract simply states that he is employed by Molly. Molly decides that the shop does not need so many employees as business is falling off and issues Fred with a notice of dismissal by reason of redundancy.
  Fred may decide to:

◼ challenge the need for redundancy at all on the basis, for example, that the shop was profitable. However, as we have seen, the courts will not concern themselves with this issue (see *Moon v Homeworthy Furniture* (above));

◼ argue that the definition of redundancy does not apply to him. This will involve a consideration of whether the requirement for Fred's particular kind of work had ceased or diminished. If it has, then Fred is redundant. If not, then he will have a good claim for unfair dismissal;

◼ argue that, although his post *may* be redundant, the redundancy selection procedure was unfairly carried out. For instance, Molly may have decided to make 20 employees redundant and Fred objects to the fact that he was chosen. Here Fred's claim will be founded on unfair dismissal.

It is the last of these points to which we will now turn. In the following cases an employee whose dismissal was due to redundancy will nevertheless be held to have been dismissed unfairly and thus entitled to compensation for unfair dismissal.

Redundancy as an excuse

This provision deals with where an employee is selected for dismissal ostensibly because of redundancy but in reality for another reason. Redundancy is just the excuse. The employee is unfairly dismissed where all the following conditions are satisfied:

1 the employee is dismissed by reason of redundancy; and

2 he or she can show that the circumstances constituting the redundancy applied equally to other employees in similar positions in the undertaking who were not dismissed; and

3 the dismissal was for one of the following reasons:

    (a) trade union membership or activities;

    (b) non-membership of a trade union;

    (c) on the grounds of pregnancy or childbirth;

    (d) making health and safety complaints;

    (e) asserting a statutory right;

    (f) being a protected shopworker;

    (g) acting as a pension fund trustee;

    (h) acting as an employee representative; or

    (i) exercising rights under the National Minimum Wage Act 1998, Public Interest Disclosure Act 1998 or Working Time Regulations 1998.

(*Note*: these areas have been explained more fully in other chapters; the statutory basis of these provisions is in ss 99–105 of the ERA 1996 and s 153 of the TULRCA 1992.)

Selection procedure was unfair

The employee may claim in broader terms, as in the above example, that the redundancy selection procedure was unfair. In *British Aerospace plc v Green* (1995) Millett LJ explained that criticism of the redundancy selection procedure may take two forms:

1 A challenge to the fairness of the selection system, e.g. selection criteria or consultation procedures.

2 A challenge to the fairness of the manner in which the system was applied.

The basis of the law here is s 98 of the ERA 1996. As will be recalled, s 98(2)(c) provides that redundancy is a potentially fair reason for dismissal and s 98(4) provides that, as in other cases, the determination of whether the dismissal is fair or unfair depends on whether 'in the circumstances (including the size and administrative resources of the employer's undertaking) the employer acted reasonably . . .' The statutory disciplinary and dismissal procedure discussed in Chapter 11 applies to redundancy dismissals unless the redundancy dismissal is one of a number of collective redundancies to which the statutory consultation procedure in s 188 of TULRCA (see below) applies. A useful summary of the approach of the courts was given by Waite LJ in *British Aerospace plc v Green* (1995). He observed that 'the employer who sets up a system of selection which can reasonably be described as fair and applies it without any overt sign of conduct which mars its fairness will have done all that the law requires of him'.

Main guidelines on fairness

These are not rules as such but, in line with the words of Waite LJ above, simply guidelines.

The guidelines were set out by Browne-Wilkinson J in the EAT in *Williams* v *Compair Maxam Ltd* (1982):

- Employers must give as much warning as possible of impending redundancies.
- Employers must consult unions on the redundancy procedure and will seek to agree the selection criteria with the union.
- Any criteria must be capable of being objectively checked against, for example, attendance records, efficiency records and length of service.
- Selection must be made fairly in accordance with the criteria and employers must consider any representations made by the union as to the selection procedure.
- Employers must seek to offer alternative employment, if possible, rather than redundancy.

Browne-Wilkinson J summed up the approach by saying that:

> The basic approach is that, in the unfortunate circumstances that necessarily attend redundancies, as much as is reasonably possible should be done to mitigate the impact on the workforce and to satisfy them that the selection has been made fairly and not on the basis of personal whim.

(*Note*: these requirements have since been added to by statute (see below).)

Other points to note on redundancy procedures

Changes in selection criteria

Initially many selection criteria were based on 'LIFO' (last in, first out). This was often favoured by unions as a less unfair way of selection but it is likely that the Employment Equality (Age) Regulations 2006 make this unlawful age discrimination and it would be most unwise for an employer to make LIFO the basis of selection. In any event, the emphasis has now switched to more sophisticated criteria, such as those based on skills audits of employees, and their efficiency. This will often lead to employees being assessed on a points system.

Right to see evidence of correct application of criteria

Where an employee has been selected for redundancy, is there a right to see evidence relating to other employees to check whether the criteria have been correctly applied? In *British Aerospace* v *Green* (above) the Court of Appeal held that 'Documents relating to retained employees are not likely to be relevant in any but the most exceptional circumstances'. However, this approach was not applied in two later cases. In *FDR Ltd* v *Holloway* (1995) the court ordered disclosure of documents on employees not selected and in *John Brown Engineering Ltd* v *Brown* (1997) the Scottish EAT held that where disclosure of scores on a points system has not been made by employers then an industrial (now employment) tribunal was entitled to find that the relevant employees had been unfairly dismissed. The law on this area is, for the moment, uncertain but it is hoped that a less rigid approach than in *British Aerospace* may eventually be adopted. Indeed, it may be that *British Aerospace* could eventually be confined to its own facts, as that case involved very large redundancies: 530 employees out of a total of 7,000.

Lower standards of procedure for smaller firms

In smaller firms a lower standard of procedure is set because of the reference in s 98(4) of ERA 1996 to size and administrative resources but, even so, any selection must be based on objective criteria (*Gray* v *Shetland Norse Preserving Co.* (1985)).

Effect on employer of failing to observe procedure

A failure to observe the procedure may not be fatal to an employer, as in *Lloyd* v *Taylor Woodrow Construction* (1999), where a failure to inform the employee of the selection criteria was cured at the appeal stage when he was allowed to challenge the criteria. However, the court emphasised that a defect could be cured only at an appeal which was a complete rehearing rather than simply a review of the decision. This area is not, however, yet settled. Some confusion has derived from the speech of Lord Bridge in *Polkey* v *Dayton* (above), where he said that an employer might act reasonably in taking the view that 'in the exceptional circumstances of the particular case, the procedural steps normally appropriate would have been futile, could not have altered the decision to dismiss and therefore could be dispensed with'. The difficulty was that this left the door open to the sort of interpretation which actually occurred in *Duffy* v *Yeomans and Partners Ltd* (1994), where it was held that an objective test applied, i.e. did the employer, in deciding not to follow a particular procedure, do what a reasonable employer might do? In *Polkey* the test was deliberately subjective and looked at what that *particular* employer did. The danger is that the interpretation in *Duffy* could take us back to the now discredited approach in *British Labour Pump* v *Byrne* (see Chapter 11).

Infringement of equal opportunities legislation

A redundancy selection procedure is open to challenge on the ground that it infringes equal opportunities legislation. In *Clarke* v *Eley (IMI) Kynoch Ltd* (1982) redundancy criteria which involved making part-time workers redundant first was held to amount to indirect sex discrimination, as the great majority of employees were female. This area has not yet been clarified; for example, are LIFO criteria in breach of the Sex Discrimination Act 1975 because women are statistically less likely to have long service than men as a result of career breaks? The point was left open in the *Clarke* case but in *Brook* v *London Borough of Haringey* (1992) it was felt that the fact that LIFO was widely used would tend to negate any finding of discrimination. However, LIFO is less widely used now. The other possibility is that redundancy selection procedures may infringe the Part-time Workers (Prevention of Less Favourable Treatment) Regulations 2000, which prohibit discrimination against part-timers unless there is objective justification (see Chapter 9). This may prove to be more effective than a challenge under the Sex Discrimination Act, as there is no need to prove that there was adverse impact.

Advance consultation

In *Elkouil* v *Coney Island Ltd* (2002) the EAT held that where a redundancy dismissal is unfair through a failure to consult in advance then the starting point should be what the likely outcome would have been if there had been proper consultation. Here the consultation process should have started ten weeks before the notice of dismissal and thus the applicant would have had ten weeks to look for another job. Therefore, the applicant lost the chance of being re-employed much earlier than he was and an award of ten weeks' pay was made.

Statutory consultation procedures

In addition to the above rules on consultation and, to some extent, running parallel with them, there are statutory procedures which apply when an employer is proposing to make 20 or more employees redundant. The origin of these rules is in European Community law and specifically in Directive 75/129 of 1975. The impetus for this was, according to Bercusson (1996), the 'economic dislocation of Western Europe consequent on the rise in oil prices following the 1973 Middle East War'. The same reason applied to the legislation on transfer of undertakings (see later in this chapter). The current EC Directive is 98/59. The UK legislation is in s 188 of the Trade Union and Labour Relations (Consolidation) Act 1992, supplemented by the Collective Redundancies and Transfers of Undertakings (Protection of Employment) (Amendment) Regulations 1995 (SI 1995/2581) and 1999 (SI 1999/1925).

There is an extended definition of redundancy, which is applicable here only, and which is now contained in s 195 of the Trade Union and Labour Relations (Consolidation) Act 1992. This provides that redundancy is a 'dismissal for a reason not related to the individual concerned or for a number of reasons all of which are not so related'. The effect is to include, within the definition of redundancy, dismissals from reorganisation of a business; and which could have applied in, for example, *Shawkat* v *Nottingham City Hospital NHS Trust* (above). There is also a statutory presumption that any dismissal is for redundancy (s 195(2)).

Relationship between the statutory consultation procedures and redundancy selection procedures

Breach of the statutory procedures can lead to the making of a 'protective award', which results in a payment of wages to employees concerned (see below). However, unlike breach of the selection procedures, it does not lead to a finding of unfair dismissal, although in *Rowell* v *Hubbard Group Services Ltd* (1995) the EAT felt that in an unfair dismissal case a tribunal should follow the general approach of the statutory procedures and therefore, indirectly, they can be said to be relevant to an unfair dismissal claim.

The statutory consultation procedures in detail

These procedures apply when an employer is proposing to dismiss as redundant 20 or more employees at one establishment within 90 days or less. In *Hardy* v *Tourism South*

East (2005) the EAT held that when calculating the figure of employees whom it is proposed to make redundant it is necessary to include those whom it is proposed to redeploy. This can affect whether the total is 20 or more, which of course brings the statutory consultation procedure into play.

Section 188 provides that, in deciding the number involved, no account shall be taken of those in respect of whose dismissals consultation has already begun.

The employer is required to consult appropriate representatives of affected employees. These are as follows:

1 Representatives of an independent trade union recognised by the employer if the employees are 'of a description' in respect of which the union is recognised by the employer. The employees do not have to actually be members of the union, a point stressed in *Governing Body of the Northern Ireland Hotel and Catering College* v *NATFHE* (1995).

2 If 1 above does not apply then the employer must consult employee representatives who have already been elected or appointed and who have authority from the employees to act in this case or, if none exist, then employee representatives must be specifically elected for this purpose.

The consultation must begin in good time (see below) and in any event not less than 30 days before the first dismissal takes effect. However, where the employer proposes to dismiss 100 or more employees, the 30-day period is increased to at least 90 days. The consultation must be genuine, as s 188 specifically provides that it 'shall be undertaken by the employer with a view to reaching agreement with the appropriate representatives'. In *R v British Coal Corporation and Secretary of State for Trade and Industry, ex parte Price* (1994) Glidewell LJ said that adequate information must be provided, adequate time allowed for responses and conscientious consideration of these responses. It is common for a meeting to be held when unions or employee representatives put forward their reasons why the redundancies should not happen; and the effect of this decision is that an employer should then take time to consider these reasons rather than respond at once. In *Middlesbrough BC v TGWU* (2002) the employers had already decided that there would be redundancies before the redundancy consultation began and it was held that this meant that the consultation could not be genuine.

The consultation must include ways of avoiding the dismissals, reducing the numbers to be dismissed and mitigating the consequences of dismissals. The following information must be disclosed to the unions or representatives:

1 reasons for the proposals;

2 numbers and descriptions of employees to be made redundant;

3 total number of such employees at the establishment;

4 proposed method of selection;

5 proposed method of carrying out the dismissals and over what period they are to take effect;

6 proposed method of calculating redundancy payments.

12

Dismissal for economic reasons

339

It may be that in a particular case extra information should be provided in line with Glidewell LJ's remarks above that 'adequate information should be provided'. This could include details of employees not selected for redundancy, as discussed above.

The following issues have arisen in the interpretation of these provisions:

When exactly must consultation begin?

There is a conflict between the words of s 188, which says that consultation must begin when the employer is 'proposing to dismiss', and Directive 75/129 (the mainspring of these rules), which uses the words 'contemplating redundancies', a wider term. In *APAC* v *Kirvin Ltd* (1978) it was held that the word 'proposing' meant that consultation need only begin when the employer has formed a definite view that redundancies are needed. In *ex parte Price* (above) Glidewell LJ accepted that there was a conflict and, if that view prevails, s 188 will need amending. However, in *Griffin* v *South West Water Services Ltd* (1995) Blackburne J disagreed with Glidewell LJ that there was a conflict and so the point remains open. In *MSF* v *Refuge Assurance plc* (2002) Lindsay J in the EAT considered that there is indeed an inconsistency between these two provisions and therefore it seems that legislation may be needed amending s 188 to bring it into line with EC law. The time when redundancy consultation must begin has now been the subject of a ruling from the ECJ: in *Junk* v *Kuhnel* (2005) it was held that an employer must begin any statutory redundancy consultation procedures, not when individual notices of dismissal are given but before then, when the employer intends to terminate contracts. In *Leicestershire CC* v *Unison* (2005) the EAT explained the effect of *Junk* v *Kuhnel* on UK law. Consultation must begin when the employer 'proposes to give notice of dismissal' and so s 188(1) of TULRCA 1992, which uses the phrase 'proposing to dismiss', must be interpreted in this way. Proposing to give notice of dismissal is less than a decision to dismiss but more than just a possibility that there will be dismissals.

Does the term 'employer' include associated employers?

This may be important when deciding how many employees have been made redundant. In *E Green & Son (Castings) Ltd* v *ASTMS* (1984) it was held that, even though three firms were all subsidiaries of the same holding company and they all operated from the same premises, they were separate employers and so it was not possible to aggregate the total numbers to, in this case, increase the total consultation period from 30 days to 90.

What is meant by 'establishment'?

The point arose in *Clarks of Hove Ltd* v *Bakers' Union* (1978) where a factory, a bakery and shops were all held to constitute one establishment. This enlightened decision is curiously at odds with that under the previous heading above.

Failure to consult

Protective award

A failure to consult can lead to the unions or employee representatives involved or, where there was no consultation machinery, the employees themselves, seeking a protective award from an employment tribunal. This is an order that the employer shall continue to pay wages for a protected period (ss 189 and 190 of TULRCA 1992). The length of the period is such as the tribunal considers just and equitable having regard to the seriousness of the employer's default in complying with the statutory requirement, with a maximum of 90 days. In *Talke Fashions v Amalgamated Society of Textile Workers and Kindred Trades* (1977) the EAT held that the approach should be compensatory and should initially look at how much the employee has lost through the employer not consulting in time. However, in later cases the EAT has allowed other matters to be taken into account so that a punitive element is, in effect, added. In *Spillars-French (Holdings) Ltd v Usdaw* (1979) Slynn J pointed out that there were 'degrees of different gravity'; for example, the fact that some information was given orally to employee representatives when it should have been in writing would not be treated as seriously as a failure to give reasons at all. In *Susie Radin Ltd v GMB* (2004) the employer argued that it should not be liable to pay a protective award imposed because of a failure to consult over proposed redundancies. It argued that the purpose of the award was compensatory and that, as it was clear that consultation would have made no difference, there was no justification for making the award. The Court of Appeal disagreed and held that the purpose of the award is punitive and, although tribunals have a discretion to do what is just and equitable in deciding whether to make one, the focus must always be on the seriousness of the employer's default.

Note three other points:

1 A complaint that an employer has failed to comply with the consultation requirements must be presented to the employment tribunal within three months of the date when the last of the dismissals to which it relates takes effect unless it is not reasonably practicable to do so.

2 An employee may not be entitled to a protective award if he or she unreasonably resigns during the protected period or unreasonably refuses suitable alternative employment.

3 In *TGWU v Brauer Coley* (2006) the EAT held that employees who are not of a description in respect of which their union was recognised by their employer are not entitled to a protective award. There was no entitlement because the duty to consult did not apply to them.

Special circumstances defence

The employer may argue that there were special circumstances which made it not reasonably practicable to comply with the consultation requirements (s 188 (7)). If so, the employer is obliged to take only such steps as are reasonably practicable. If this defence succeeds then there will either be no protective award or, possibly, a reduction in it. In *Clarks of Hove v Bakers' Union* (1978) the employer had been in financial difficulty and, instead of initiating the consultation procedure, sought a buyer for some of its shops to enable it to continue trading. When a potential buyer pulled out, it made all its employees redundant. The Court of Appeal held that insolvency is not by itself a special circumstance; it depends on the cause. Sudden disaster striking a company could be, but if the insolvency was due to a gradual run down of the company (as happened in this case), then it would probably not be. As Geoffrey Lane LJ put it, 'to be special, the event must be something out of the ordinary, something uncommon'.

12

Dismissal for economic reasons

Notification of redundancies to the Secretary of State

In addition to the consultation requirements, an employer who proposes to dismiss as redundant 20 or more employees at one establishment within 30 days must give the Secretary of State written notice of the proposal at least 30 days before the first dismissal takes effect. Where 100 or more employees are to be dismissed within 90 days then notification must be 90 days before. The special circumstances defence applies here also. The penalty is a fine and a copy of the notice must be sent to the employee representatives.

TIME OFF TO LOOK FOR WORK

Section 52 of the ERA 1996 gives an employee under notice of dismissal for redundancy the right to time off work either to look for new employment or to make arrangements for training for new employment. This right applies only to employees with at least two years' continuous employment and it is enforced by complaint to an employment tribunal, which can order the employer to pay the employee an amount equivalent to the pay which would have been received had the time off been allowed but subject to a maximum of two-fifths of a week's pay (usually, in practice, two days' pay).

REDUNDANCY COMPENSATION

The whole object of the law on redundancy is, of course, to enable employees to claim redundancy compensation. This is calculated according to a formula, as laid down in s 162 of the ERA 1996, which has recently been amended by the Employment Equality (Age) Regulations 2006 (reg 33) so that the lower and upper limits for eligibility to claim a redundancy payment have been abolished. The amended rules are as follows:

- one and a half weeks' pay for every year of continuous employment in which the employee was 41 years old and over,

- one week's pay for every year of continuous employment in which the employee was 22 years old but not over 41,

- half a week's pay for every year of continuous employment in which the employee was not over 22.

The maximum amount of pay which can be counted is at present £310.00 and the maximum number of years' continuous employment which can be counted is 20. Thus the maximum is £310 × 20 × 1½, i.e. 20 years at 1½ weeks' pay for every year = £9,300.

Who is not entitled to a redundancy payment?

The following employees are not entitled to a redundancy payment (all references are to the ERA 1996):

- those with less than two years' continuous employment (s 155);
- share fishermen (s 199(2));
- persons ordinarily working outside Great Britain unless at the relevant time they were working in Great Britain on the employer's instructions (s 196(6));
- Crown servants and certain public officials (s 159);
- those employed as a domestic servant by a near relative (as defined in s 161);
- classes of employees excluded by order of the Secretary of State in cases where a collective agreement covers the issue of redundancy (s 157);
- those dismissed for misconduct (see below);
- those who refuse a suitable offer of alternative employment (see below).

Making a claim for a redundancy payment

By s 164 of the ERA 1996 the claim must be made in writing to the employer, although no special form is laid down. An employee will (subject to the exception below) lose the right to a redundancy payment unless within six months of the date of termination of employment one of the following occurs:

1 the payment is agreed and paid;

2 the employee has claimed by notice in writing;

3 a question as to either the right to payment or the amount of payment has been referred to an employment tribunal;

4 the employee has presented a complaint of unfair dismissal to an employment tribunal.

The exception referred to above is that even if the six-month period is not observed then a tribunal may, if it considers it 'just and equitable', still award a redundancy payment if the complaint is made in ways 2 to 4 above in the six-month period immediately following the initial six-month period. There is no requirement that the actual application to the tribunal should be made within any particular time; only that the above rules are observed. An unfortunate rule is that an employee who claims early, i.e. before the actual termination of employment, is prejudiced in that this claim is invalid (*Watts* v *Rubery Owen Conveyancer* (1977)). This rule does not apply to unfair dismissal claims by virtue of the express words of s 111(3) of the ERA 1996.

If the employer refuses to make a redundancy payment after the employee has taken all reasonable steps, short of actually taking proceedings in an employment tribunal, or if the employer is insolvent and the whole or part of the payment is unpaid, then the employee may apply to the Secretary of State for a payment (s 166 of the ERA 1996).

Cases where an employee dismissed by reason of redundancy may not be entitled to a redundancy payment

An offer to renew the employee's contract or to re-engage him or her is unreasonably refused

Where the employer makes an offer to the employee, before the termination of employment, to do either of the following:

1 renew the contract of employment on the same terms, *or*

2 re-engage the employee under different terms and conditions and the offer constitutes suitable employment,

then the employee is not entitled to a redundancy payment if the offer is unreasonably refused, provided that it was to take effect not later than four weeks after the end of employment.

Renewal of the contract is straightforward but re-engagement needs some discussion. Two points must be considered and should initially be kept separate, although Neill LJ in *Spencer* v *Gloucestershire CC* (1985) said that too rigid a distinction should not be made, as the same factors might be common to both.

Was the actual offer of employment suitable for the employee?

In *Carron Co.* v *Robertson* (1967) it was that held that suitability must be looked at objectively and is a question of fact for the tribunal. In *Taylor* v *Kent CC* (1969) Parker LCJ said that suitability means 'employment which is substantively equivalent to the employment which has ceased'. Relevant issues have been pay, location and how long the employment is expected to last. In *Taylor* it was held that an offer to a redundant headteacher of a post as a supply teacher was not suitable because of the loss of status involved.

Offer is found to be unsuitable

If the offer is found to be unsuitable then the matter ends and the employee is entitled to the redundancy payment. If, however, the offer is found suitable then the further question arises of whether the employee unreasonably rejected it. This is a subjective question and personal reasons which relate to the employee must be considered. In *Spencer* v *Gloucestershire CC* (1985) school cleaners were asked to accept fewer hours' work as an economy measure and they refused, saying that the job could not be done properly in the time allowed. It was held that this could be a reasonable reason for refusal. In *Thomas Wragg & Sons Ltd* v *Wood* (1976) an employee under notice for redundancy found another job but, one day before his redundancy notice was due to expire, he was offered an alternative job by his employers. His refusal of his job was held reasonable. Other cases have dealt with, for example, family commitments.

Trial period

An employee who accepts an offer of renewal or re-engagement is, by s 138(2) of the ERA 1996, automatically allowed a trial period of at least four weeks from the end of the old contract. The advantage to the employee is that, merely by starting the new job

344

he or she is not taken to have accepted it, as it may be difficult to say whether it is suitable until it has been tried. If the employee terminates the employment during the trial period for any reason connected with, for example, its unsuitability, then the employee is treated as having been dismissed at the date of termination of the old contract. Although the employer can still argue that the employment was suitable, at least the employee is able to argue that it was not and this is the significance of the trial period.

An employee who has been constructively dismissed because the employer sought to impose a new contract on him or her also has the right to the same trial period. However, a complication has arisen because at common law it had been held, before the statutory trial period was introduced, that an employee has a trial period of a reasonable length unless a specific period was agreed. In *Air Canada* v *Lee* (1978) the EAT held that the statutory period was additional to the common law one, but it is uncertain how one tells when the common law period has ended and the statutory trial period has started.

The employee is guilty of misconduct

These provisions are, unfortunately, extremely complex and care is needed in their application. In principle, there seems to be no need for these rules since an employee dismissed for misconduct is not entitled to redundancy compensation. However, s 140 pre-dates the unfair dismissal legislation and we seem to have a classic case of subsequent legislation failing to dovetail with earlier legislation.

Example

John is employed by Michael. Michael gives John three months' notice on 1 January that he is dismissed for redundancy. John is then discovered to have been stealing and is dismissed on 1 February. Section 140(1) applies.

This provides that John will lose his entitlement to a redundancy payment provided that Michael dismissed John in any one of the following ways:

1 without notice;

2 with shorter notice than John is entitled to;

3 with full notice but with a statement that the employer would have been entitled to dismiss without notice.

There is also a distinction between a single and a double dismissal. A single dismissal is where an employee could have been dismissed for redundancy but is in fact dismissed for misconduct. A double dismissal is illustrated in the above example. It was held in *Simmons* v *Hoover Ltd* (1977) that where there has been a double dismissal then s 140(3) comes into play and the tribunal has the discretion to award an 'appropriate payment' to the employee, presumably all or part of the redundancy payment. This does not apply where there has been a single dismissal. The EAT, in *Simmons*, set out seven situations where s 140 could apply; and further discussion of s 140 can be found in the decision of the NIRC in *Sanders* v *Ernest A. Neale Ltd* (1974).

Dismissal of employees on strike

The effect of s 143 and s 140 is that, where an employee is under notice of dismissal for redundancy and then goes on strike and is dismissed for going on strike, the entitlement to a redundancy payment is not affected, although the employer may serve a notice on the employee (a notice of extension) requiring him or her to make up the time lost by going on strike. Note that the definition of a strike is the same as for continuity purposes and is in s 235 of the ERA 1996 (see Chapter 6). If the employee fails to comply with the notice, a guaranteed right to a redundancy payment is lost, although a tribunal retains a discretion to order an 'appropriate payment' nonetheless. In *Simmons* v *Hoover* (1977) the converse applied and the employee first went on strike and was *then* issued with a redundancy notice. It was held that what is now s 140(2) did not apply and there was no right to a redundancy payment. Therefore, in order to have a right to a redundancy payment the redundancy notice must come before the strike. A final point is that these provisions date from the time when an employee on strike had no right to complain for unfair dismissal and today the idea of a strike as misconduct sits oddly with the provisions of the Employment Relations Act 1999 (see Chapter 14), where in some circumstances the dismissal of an employee on official strike is automatically unfair.

The position of employees laid off or on short-time

In some cases an employee laid off or on short-time may be able to claim a redundancy payment. Again, the provisions, in ss 147 and 148 of the ERA 1996, are complex. The following points arise:

■ Does the employer have the right to lay off the employee or put the employee on short-time? If not, such an action is likely to constitute an unfair dismissal and the employee will be able to claim for this.

■ If the employer does have the right to do either of these then a right to a redundancy payment may arise, provided that the lay-off or short-time satisfies the statutory definition.

■ Lay-off is defined as where the employee for a whole week receives no remuneration under the contract.

■ Short-time is defined as where during a whole week the employee receives less than half the normal week's pay.

■ An employee who is laid off or on short-time as defined above for a period of four or more consecutive weeks may claim a redundancy payment provided that this is done by serving a notice within four weeks of the end of the period.

■ An employee who is laid off or on short-time for a series of six or more weeks in a period of thirteen weeks (of which no more than three were consecutive) may also claim a redundancy payment, provided that the notice is served within four weeks of the last date in the series.

■ The employee must actually terminate the contract by giving the required notice.

- The employer can contest the claim by serving a notice within seven days of the employee's notice stating that within four weeks there will be a period of thirteen weeks without any lay-offs or short-time.

- Where the lay-off or short-time is wholly or mainly attributable to a strike or lock-out, these provisions do not apply (s 154).

DISMISSAL ON A REORGANISATION

Introduction

Dismissal of an employee on a reorganisation of a business can lead to any of the following consequences:

(a) a finding that the employee was redundant because there was no longer work of the particular kind which the employee was employed to do, as explained above;

(b) a finding that the employee was unfairly dismissed;

(c) a finding that the employee was fairly dismissed as the reason for the dismissal fell within the category of dismissal 'for some other substantial reason'.

It is with category (c) and its relationship with categories (a) and (b) that we are concerned in this section. Although the concept of SOSR dismissals has been explained earlier in general terms, SOSR has had a particular impact in this area.

> ### Example
>
> Mary is employed as a manager of a small supermarket and is asked by her employer, Steve, to stay behind for an hour after the other staff have gone in order to stack the shelves and to be responsible for personnel matters. Neither of these duties were in Mary's contract but Steve tells Mary that the national firm which runs the supermarket is in financial difficulties and Mary, along with all the other managers, will need to perform these extra duties in order that staffing costs can be saved.
>
> Mary is clearly not redundant because her job has not altered: her particular kind of work remains the same. (See *Chapman* v *Goonvean and Rostrowrack China Clay Co. Ltd* and *Johnson* v *Nottinghamshire Police Authority* earlier in this chapter.)
>
> Mary will argue that she has the right to refuse to perform the extra duties because her contract cannot be altered without her consent. As a matter of contract law this is true but it may be that, if she refuses, Steve could dismiss her and, instead of Mary having a good claim for unfair dismissal, Steve could argue that Mary's dismissal was for a fair reason: in particular, some other substantial reason.

Dismissal for refusing to agree to changes in the terms of the contract of employment

Although dismissal on a reorganisation covers wider issues than simply refusing to agree to changes in contract terms, this topic is a useful starting point, not least because

12

Dismissal for economic reasons

the first case on it involved this matter. In *R S Components Ltd* v *Irwin* (1974) the employers, who manufactured electrical components, found that a number of their employees were leaving and soliciting customers of the employers to deal with them instead. As a result, the employers were losing business and therefore they required employees to sign a restrictive covenant which prevented them from soliciting customers of their employers for 12 months after leaving their employment. The employee was one of four who refused to accept the covenant and he was dismissed. It was held that the dismissal was fair on the ground that dismissal was for a substantial reason. Brightman J considered that it would be 'unfortunate for the development of industry' if an employer who was considering embarking on a new technical process was unable to require employees to agree to some 'reasonable restriction' on the use of their knowledge. In *Irwin* it appears to have been assumed that the restriction was, in itself, reasonable, as clearly a failure to agree to an unreasonable restriction should not be a ground for a fair dismissal.

Reorganisational redundancy

The idea of reorganisational redundancy

This is really a separate topic from that above and the word redundancy is, of course, strictly incorrect in this context as the situation is not redundancy but possible unfair dismissal. As Bowers and Clarke (1981) point out: 'It is difficult to pinpoint precisely when this notion of "reorganisational redundancy" crystallised.' The initial thinking of the courts was simply to ask whether an employee's work had been reorganised so that he or she was redundant or not. If not, then there was the possibility of a claim by the employee for unfair dismissal (see e.g. *Delanair Ltd* v *Mead* (1976)). Nevertheless, the courts soon began to talk in a way which blurred the line between redundancy and straightforward dismissal. In *Gorman* v *London Computer Training Centre* (1978) Phillips J said that an employer who was overmanned could say that, even though for 'technical reasons the employees were not redundant nevertheless a dismissal could be for some other substantial reason'.

The first case in which reorganisational redundancy was recognised and applied appears to be *Ellis* v *Brighton Co-operative Society* (1976). The employee was required to work longer hours and his duties were increased as a result of a reorganisation of the business. He was not contractually bound to accept these changes and, when he refused to do so, he was dismissed. It was held that his refusal to accept them justified dismissal for some other substantial reason. The EAT held that 'Where there has been a properly consulted-upon reorganisation which, if it is not done, is going to bring the whole business to a standstill, a failure to go along with the new arrangements may well – it is not bound to but may well – constitute some other substantial reason.'

When will a dismissal in cases of 'reorganisational redundancy' be justified?

Although there has been much discussion as to the precise terminology to be used, there is no doubt that the employer must show that the situation was dictated by the needs of the business. The debate has been about the precise threshold to be applied, with some judges stressing the requirement for a pressing business reason and others emphasising the need to uphold managerial prerogative.

The first major case was *Hollister* v *NFU* (1979). Hollister was one of the NFU's group secretaries and the union reorganised its insurance business so that Hollister no longer received any commission on insurance sold. It was found that the total package offered on the reorganisation did not mean a drop in salary but Hollister refused to accept it because taken as a whole it diminished his existing rights. The Court of Appeal held that he was fairly dismissed. Denning MR felt that the test in *Ellis* (above) of whether if there was no reorganisation the business would be brought to a standstill was too restrictive and preferred the test of Arnold J in the EAT in *Ellis* of whether 'there was some sound, good business reason for the reorganisation'.

In later cases the courts have expressed further different formulations of the test. In *Banerjee* v *City and East London AHA* (1979) the EAT used an even looser test than that in *Hollister*: would the proposed changes bring discernible advantages to the organisation and were they 'matters of importance'?

The question of reasonableness

Some emphasis has been placed by the courts on the need for the employer to have acted reasonably and this has, to some extent, acted as a check on the stress laid upon the employer's right to manage. The problem is that the decisions conflict. In *Evans* v *Elementa Holdings Ltd* (1982) the EAT held that the matter should be looked at from the perspective of the employee and a tribunal should ask whether the terms offered were 'objectionable and oppressive'. However, in *Chubb Fire Security Ltd* v *Harper* (1983) the EAT held that the question of reasonableness should be considered from the point of view of both parties: were the employers acting reasonably in deciding that the advantages to them of the proposed reorganisation outweighed any disadvantage which they should have contemplated that their employees might suffer?

In *Richmond Precision Engineering Ltd* v *Pearce* (1985) the approach in *Chubb* was in turn criticised and it was held that the question of weighing advantages and disadvantages was not the only task for a tribunal. Purely because there was a disadvantage to the employee did not mean that the employer had acted unreasonably. It held that the test is whether the terms offered are those which a reasonable employer could offer in the changed circumstances of the employer's business. In *St John of God (Care Service) Ltd* v *Brooks* (1992) it was pointed out that this was wrong in law: the issue is whether the decision to dismiss is reasonable and does not concern a reasonable employer's offer. Not only this, but circumstances surrounding the offer also needed to be considered. In this case the fact that the vast majority of employees had accepted new, and much less favourable, terms and conditions when NHS funding for a care service was reduced was 'highly significant'. One might sum up this area by saying that, given the need for some criteria, the question is, as always, one of reasonableness and no factor should be excluded.

The need for consultation with the employee

In *Hollister* v *NFU* the Court of Appeal held that this was only one of the relevant factors and therefore there was no absolute requirement to consult. As Denning MR put it: 'Negotiation is only one of the factors which has to be taken into account.' In fact Mr Hollister was not consulted at all. However, it is submitted that this no longer represents the law and indeed in the previous case of *Ellis* v *Brighton Co-operative Society* the court had referred to a 'properly consulted-upon reorganisation'. Certainly it seems that the emphasis on fairness to the employee in *Polkey* v *AE Dayton Services Ltd* (1988) (see Chapter 11) means that some degree of consultation is required in cases of reorganisation.

DISMISSAL ON THE TRANSFER OF AN UNDERTAKING

Introduction

Employees may find that the organisation for which they work changes even though their actual work remains the same and indeed there appears to be no difference at all so far as their actual work is concerned. This change can happen in several ways, of which these are examples:

- the ownership of the business may simply change hands;
- one business may be taken over by another;
- two or more businesses may amalgamate;
- the particular work which the employee does may be outsourced to another organisation, such as where, especially in the public sector, work is contracted out;
- the franchisee of a business may change.

The employees acquire new employers but are their rights affected in any way? The common law position was set out in *Nokes* v *Doncaster Amalgamated Collieries Ltd* (1940), when the question arose as to the position of employees in two companies which had been amalgamated. Atkin LJ held that the contracts of employment were not transferred and emphasised that: 'the servant was left with his inalienable right to choose to serve his new master or not'.

This approach was rooted in the contractual idea that obligations under a contract were between the parties and that rights and obligations under them could not be transferred to third parties. The effect was that employees could find that, when the undertaking for which they worked changed hands, their contracts were not taken on by the new owner and their employment was ended without any redress. Even if they were taken on, they had lost continuity of employment. In a world where takeovers and mergers were becoming increasingly common, the continued existence of the common law rule represented a grave threat to job security.

The common law position was advantageous to the transferee of the business which would probably wish to decide for itself those of the workforce to keep and those not to, or which instead might wish to replace all of the workforce with others who would have less favourable terms and conditions of employment. It was, however, most unfavourable to employees who could find that they were dismissed on a transfer and their many years of loyal service counted for nothing. It took a European Community

Directive (Acquired Rights Directive (77/187)) to change matters. This was based on the fundamental principle that the employment rights of employees should not be adversely affected by any change in the ownership of the business for which they work. Thus the object of the Directive is to ensure that when the business is sold the contracts of employment of employees are automatically transferred to the new employer. This is the direct opposite of the common law principle explained above. The Directive was originally given effect to in UK law by the Transfer of Undertakings (Protection of Employment) Regulations 1981 which have now been replaced by the Transfer of Undertakings (Protection of Employment) Regulations 2006 (SI 2006/246). These retain the basic position but make changes of detail. It should also be noted that the Acquired Rights Directive 77/187 has itself been replaced by a similar Directive 2001/23 which consolidates amendments to the original Directive.

The following diagram shows the difference between the common position and that under TUPE.

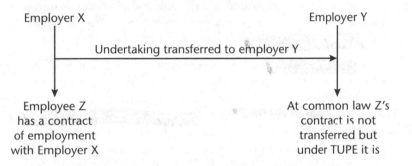

The above example is slightly oversimplified, in that it is not certain that contracts of employees will be transferred under TUPE, but it does illustrate the dramatic difference which TUPE has made when a business is transferred.

The position changed with the enactment of the Transfer of Undertakings (Protection of Employment) Regulations 1981 (the 1981 Regulations) which were passed in order to implement the Acquired Rights Directive. These were amended by the Trade Union Reform and Employment Rights Act 1993 and have now been replaced in their entirety by the Transfer of Undertakings (Protection of Employment) Regulations 2006 (SI 2006/246).

(*Note*: when decisions of the ECJ are discussed in this chapter, references will be to the Directive; and when the decisions are those of UK courts, references will be to TUPE.)

The 1981 Regulations were generally effective in their main objective of ensuring that employees did not lose their rights when a business was transferred but over the years problems arose in deciding whether they applied to situations where services were outsourced as, for example, where a local authority contracted out its services. Thus the 2006 Regulations introduce a new definition of a service transfer and also make the following other changes:

Dismissal for economic reasons

12

- clarify the circumstances in which a transferee employer may lawfully dismiss on a transfer;

- introduce new provisions to ensure that the transferee is aware of the employees' rights together with their own liabilities on a transfer;

- make the transferor and transferee jointly and severally liable for any failure to inform and consult the employees who are being transferred.

The 2006 Regulations will now be explored in detail.

What is a transfer?

The 2006 Regulations apply to 'public and private undertakings engaged in economic activities whether or not they are operating for gain' (reg 3(4)). This clearly covers transfers in the public sector where there is no element of profit involved; but under reg 3(5) some transfers within public administration are not covered because it exempts 'administrative reorganisation of public administrative authorities or the transfer of administrative functions between public administrative authorities'.

There are two types of transfer:

(a) *A transfer to another person of an undertaking, business or part of an undertaking situated immediately before the transfer in the UK where there is a transfer of an economic entity which retains its identity.* (Standard transfers: reg 3(1)(a)). Regulation 3(2)) defines an economic entity as an organised grouping of resources which has the objective of pursuing an economic activity whether this is central to the business or ancillary to it. This provision is intended to deal with where, for example, a manufacturing business is sold. The definition builds on existing case law but one departure is that, as McMullen (2006) points out, the new regulations do not require there to be a stable economic entity. This requirement was fatal to the claim in *Rygaard* v *Stvø Mølle* (1996) where a building contract which had been sub-contracted to Firm X was, by agreement, then sub-contracted to Firm Y and it was held by the ECJ that the Acquired Rights Directive did not apply because it was held that a transfer must relate to a stable economic entity which was not limited to performing a one-off contract. McMullen suggests that, despite the absence of the word 'stable' in the regulations, it should be implied and so the decision in *Rygaard* v *Stvø Mølle* will still be good law. In *Mackie* v *Aberdeen City Council* (2006) a contract between the council and a smart card operator under which the operator would produce a card to be used to gain access to council services was for a fixed price to produce a fixed product and thus was held to be outside TUPE as there was no stable economic entity. McMullen suggests that this will continue to be the case. The other noteworthy point is the phrase 'which retains its identity'. Thus here, unlike the position in transfers which involve a service provision change (below), the entity which is transferred must itself retain its identity.

(b) *A transfer which involves a service provision change.* This is an entirely new provision which aims to clarify just when these transfers are covered by TUPE. They are defined as situations in which any of the following occur:

(i) activities cease to be carried out by a person (a client) on his own behalf and are carried out instead by another person on the client's behalf (the contractor);

(ii) activities cease to be carried out by a contractor on a client's behalf (whether or not those activities had previously been carried out by the client on his own behalf), and are carried out instead by another person on the client's behalf (a subsequent contractor);

(iii) activities cease to be carried out by a contractor (or a subsequent contractor) on a client's behalf (whether or not those activities had previously been carried out by the client on his own behalf), and are carried out instead by the client on his own behalf.

Example

Situations (i), (ii) and (iii) above are illustrated by this example:

Suppose that a local authority decides to contract out its school meals services to Tasty Meals Ltd. **This is situation (i)**: the local authority is the client and Tasty Meals Ltd is the contractor. So the employees of the local authority have their contracts taken over by Tasty Meals Ltd.

When the contract is put out to retendering Tasty Meals Ltd lose it and it goes to Scrumptious Meals Ltd who are the subsequent contractors. **This is situation (ii)**. So the employees of the local authority have their contracts taken over by Scrumptious Meals Ltd.

When the contract ends, the service is now run directly by the local authority once again. **This is situation (iii)**. So the employees are now once again employees of the local authority.

In this situation there is no requirement that activities which are carried on must remain identifiable, unlike in the case of standard transfers. The reason was that the government did not want to prevent TUPE from applying where the new service provider carries out the service in a new or innovative manner.

There are, however, the following conditions laid down in reg 3(3) which must be satisfied for contracts of employment to be transferred under the rules relating to service provision changes:

(a) (i) immediately before the service provision change there is an organised grouping of employees in Great Britain which has as its principal purpose the carrying out of the activities concerned on behalf of the client;

(ii) the client intends that the activities will not be carried out with a single specific event or task of short-term duration. McMullen (2006) argues that the drafting is unclear: does the exemption apply where there is a single specific event and a task of short-term duration or either of these? The latter is suggested as preferable;

(b) the activities do not consist wholly or mainly of the supply of goods for the client's own use.

353

Of these it is (a)(i) which calls for comment because it introduces a new type of test, that of whether there was an organised grouping of employees, to decide if there is a TUPE transfer.

The effect is that the law on service transfers is now specially dealt with in TUPE and so the previous case law will be of academic interest only. In fact, the problem of deciding whether TUPE applied to transfer of services exercised the ECJ on many occasions and, in particular, a distinction was sometimes drawn between labour-intensive functions and where the function was reliant mainly on assets. Thus in *Süzen* v *Zehnacker* (1997) it was held that employees dismissed when a cleaning contract for a school was transferred from one contractor to another could not claim as 'the mere loss of a service contract to a competitor cannot . . . by itself indicate the existence of a transfer'. It was held that 'an entity cannot be reduced to the activity entrusted to it' and that where a service contract was lost to a competitor, the 'service undertaking previously entrusted with the contract does not, on losing a customer, thereby cease fully to exist'. In *Betts* v *Brintel Helicopters* (1997) it was held, applying *Süzen*, that there was no transfer where a contract to provide helicopter transport to workers on oil rigs was transferred, one significant feature being that no employees were taken on and that no assets were transferred. The obvious point here is that it appeared that a transferee could avoid TUPE by the simple method of refusing to take on workers employed by the transferor.

Position of employees when there is a transfer

The cornerstone of the law is reg 4(1), which provides that a relevant transfer shall not operate to terminate the contract of employment of anyone employed by the transferor and assigned to the organised grouping of resources or employees transferred but any such contract shall have effect after the transfer as if it was originally made between the transferee of the undertaking and the employee.

Thus the common law position is reversed and the transfer of an undertaking does not terminate contracts of employment but merely transfers them. Therefore, transferred employees are entitled to retain their existing conditions of employment and the effect is that firms which have absorbed a number of other firms may have employees on a bewildering variety of different conditions. The obvious answer is to harmonise them but legally this can only mean levelling up to the most favourable terms. It is worth noting that TUPE applies not only to transfers of liability but can also transfer liability in tort. In *Bernadone* v *Pall Mall Services Group Ltd* (2000) liability to an employee injured at work was transferred. In addition, reg 5 provides for the transfer of collective agreements and reg 6 for the transfer of trade union recognition.

Regulation 4(1) should be read in conjunction with reg 7, which provides that where either before or after a relevant transfer an employee of the transferor is dismissed then dismissal shall be treated as automatically unfair if the sole reason or principal reason for it was the transfer or a reason connected with it. Accordingly, if Employer Y in the example on p. 353 had refused to take on Employee Z then this would have been an automatically unfair dismissal and Z would have had a claim against Y. It will be seen that reg 7 refers to dismissal either before or after the transfer and the effect is to avoid the problem which occurred under the 1981 Regulations as illustrated by *Litster* v

Forth Dry Dock Engineering Co. Ltd (1989). Under reg 5(3) the 1981 Regulations applied only where the employee was employed *immediately* before the transfer and here all the 12 applicants were dismissed one hour before the transfer. The House of Lords held that they were still protected and read into reg 5(3) the words 'or would have been so employed if they had not been unfairly dismissed'. A decision otherwise would have left a gaping hole in the protection afforded to employees. The improved wording in the 2006 Regulations removes the need for this reasoning.

There is, however, a defence provided by reg 7(2) which states that where the reason or principal reason for the dismissal is an economic, technical or organisational one, entailing changes in the workforce, then the dismissal is deemed to be for some other substantial reason (or by reason of redundancy if this is the case) and therefore attention switches to s 98(4) of the ERA 1996 (see Chapter 11) to determine whether the employer acted reasonably. This is known as the ETO defence. In *Berriman v Delabole Slate Ltd* (1985) the applicant was employed as a quarryman in a business which was transferred. The transferee wished to bring in new conditions of employment so as to bring the contracts of the transferred employee into line with existing employees. The Court of Appeal held that the ETO defence did not apply, as it only covered situations where there are changes in the number or functions of the workforce. The ETO defence did apply in *Whitehouse v Chas Blatchford & Sons Ltd* (1999). The transferee of a business had successfully bid for a contract to supply appliances to a hospital but the bid was made conditional on a reduction in staffing costs. As a result the applicant was made redundant along with 13 others and it was held that the ETO defence covered this. The applicant was still entitled to a redundancy payment but not to a (probably) greater amount of compensation for unfair dismissal.

Constructive dismissal on a transfer

An interesting attempt to challenge a change in working conditions failed in *Rossiter v Pendragon plc* (2002) but the position would now be different under the 2006 Regulations. The employee's contract had been transferred under TUPE but one result was that the commission scheme was much less favourable than before the transfer, resulting in a loss of income of about £3,000 a year. He claimed constructive dismissal but his claim failed, as the Court of Appeal held there was no repudiatory breach of contract (see *Western Excavating v Sharp*, Chapter 11). The fact that he had suffered a detrimental change in his working conditions was not enough in the absence of a repudiatory breach. However, under reg 4(9) of the 2006 Regulations the employee may treat the contract as terminated by the employer if the transfer would involve 'a substantial change in working conditions to the material detriment' of the employee. This was in fact the decision of the EAT in *Rossiter* and will open up the possibility of constructive dismissal claims on a transfer.

The position where an employee refuses a transfer of employment

It may be that an employee does not wish to transfer to a new employer and the right not to do so was recognised by the ECJ in *Katiskas v Konstantinidis* (1993), which held that an employee may object to a transfer. This right is now recognised by reg 4(7) of

12

Dismissal for economic reasons

355

the 2006 Regulations, which provides that the contract of an employee will not be transferred if that employee objects.

TUPE and continuity of employment

The concept of continuity of employment was dealt with in Chapter 6, but there is an overlap with TUPE transfers which is best considered here. Section 218 of the ERA 1996 provides that continuity of employment is preserved where a trade, business or undertaking is transferred. Problems arose in determining precisely what was meant by these terms and it was held in *Woodhouse v Peter Brotherhood Ltd* (1972) that there would be no transfer of the business where there was only a transfer of the physical assets. Section 218 seems to overlap with TUPE, although TUPE does not expressly refer to whether continuity of employment is preserved. However, it is likely that it does do so, as reg 4(2)(a) refers to the transfer of rights under or in connection with the contract and it is submitted that continuity is a right in connection with the contract. In the event that this is not so then s 218 plugs the gap.

The need for the transfer of an actual undertaking, business or part of an undertaking

In order for TUPE to apply there must be an *undertaking* which is *transferred*. The requirement of a transfer was fatal to the employee's claim in *Askew v Governors of Clifton Middle School* (1999), where a teacher at a school which ceased to be maintained by the local authority was made redundant. He applied to work at the school which replaced his old school but was not employed and then claimed that he had been unfairly dismissed as TUPE applied. His claim failed on the simple ground that there had been no change of employer, which remained the local authority. In *Allen v Amalgamated Construction Co. Ltd* (1999), where there were transfers between subsidiary companies in the same group then it was held that TUPE applied provided that the companies were distinct legal persons with separate employment relationships with their employees.

Insolvency of the employer

A particular problem arises when a business is transferred on an insolvency as the transferee will not wish to incur liabilities and as a matter of public policy rescues of insolvent businesses should be encouraged as this means that the employees may keep their jobs. Thus the regulations have special provisions where an insolvent business is transferred.

The Acquired Rights Directives have distinguished between two situations and this is reflected in the UK TUPE Regulations:

(a) where the assets of the transferor are liquidated;

(b) where the business of the transferor is kept intact for sale as a going concern.

Regulation 8 provides that reg 4 (transfers of employment obligations) and reg 7 (protection from dismissal on a transfer) do not apply on a transfer where the transferor is the subject of bankruptcy proceedings or similar proceedings which have been instituted under an insolvency practitioner in order to liquidate the assets.

Situation (a) above is defined as where there are 'relevant insolvency proceedings'. The government considers that this phrase means any collective insolvency proceedings where the whole or any part of the business is transferred as a going concern (McMullen, 2006). In this case TUPE applies but with two modifications:

1 Regulation 8 provides an exception to the general principle that debts owed by the transferor to its employees will pass to the transferee. The debts which will not pass are those identified as the 'relevant statutory schemes' and are arrears of pay, redundancy pay, holiday pay and pay in lieu of notice.

2 Variations to the contracts of employees which are for an ETO reason are permitted under the general principle in reg 4(5)(a) and this will apply where there is an insolvency. However, there is also a particular provision in reg 9 dealing with variations on an insolvency. This allows the transferor or transferee or an insolvency practitioner to agree certain permitted variations to employment contracts by agreement with the appropriate employee representatives. These are either recognised trade union representatives or elected or appointed employee representatives. The only variations which can be made are those designed to safeguard employment opportunities by ensuring that the business that is transferred survives.

Pensions

The 1981 TUPE Regulations did not apply to the transfer of obligations under occupational pension schemes and Article 3(3A) of the Acquired Rights Directive 2001/23 continued this by exempting from transfer rights any supplementary company or intercompany pension schemes that relate to employees' rights to old age, invalidity or survivors' benefits. Reg 10(2) of the 2006 Regulations now provides that benefits other than those specified above (old age, invalidity or survivors' benefits) are liable to transfer. In *Beckman* v *Dynamco Whichloe Macfarlane Ltd* (2002) it was held by the ECJ that the above exemption from TUPE does not cover enhanced benefits on the grounds of early retirement through redundancy and thus the liability to pay falls on the transferee. Furthermore, under the Transfer of Employment (Pension Protection) Regulations 2005 (SI 2005/649) transferees have a limited obligation to make pension provision for transferred employees under ss 257–258 of the Pensions Act 2004 covering the categories of old age, invalidity or survivors' benefits. The transferee must match the contributions of the employees of up to 6% of salary.

Notification of employee liability information

The 2006 TUPE Regulations introduce an obligation on the transferor to notify the transferee of all rights and obligations which will be transferred to the transferee. This provision, which was not contained in the 1981 Regulations, is in reg 11 and requires the transferor to notify the following information to the transferee in respect of each employee 'who is assigned to the organised grouping of resources or employees' that is the subject of the transfer:

- identity and age;
- the matters which must be included in the statement of initial employment particulars required by s 1 of the ERA 1996 (see Chapter 5);
- information on any disciplinary procedures taken against the employee within the past two years under the statutory dispute resolution procedures (see Chapter 11);
- information on any grievance procedures taken by the employee within the past two years under the statutory dispute resolution procedures (see Chapter 11);
- information on any court or tribunal claims brought by the employee against the transferor employer in the previous two years, or which the transferor employer has reasonable grounds to believe that the employee may bring against the transferee employer. There is a condition that any such claims must relate to the employee's employment with the transferor;
- information on any collective agreement which will have effect after the transfer in relation to the employee under reg 5.

This information must be supplied in writing or made available to the transferee in a reasonably accessible form and the information must be correct as at a specified date not more that 14 days before it is notified. There is also a duty to notify any changes in this information not less than 14 days before the actual transfer.

If there is a failure to supply this information a tribunal, on a complaint made to it, may make a declaration to that effect and award compensation subject to a minimum of £500 for each employee unless the tribunal considers it just and equitable to award a smaller amount. In calculating the amount of compensation the tribunal must have regard to both any loss sustained by the transferee because the information was not disclosed and the terms of any contract between the transferor and transferee under which the transferor may be liable to pay compensation for failure to notify this information.

Consultation on the transfer of an undertaking

Regulation 13 provides that where there is a relevant transfer there is a duty to inform and consult 'appropriate representatives', which means either employee representatives elected by the employees or representatives of an independent trade union recognised by the employer. If there is no trade union and no representatives are elected then the information must be provided individually.

The following information must be provided:

1 the fact that the transfer is to take place, the date when it is to take place and the reasons for it;
2 the legal, economic and social implications for the employees;

3 the measures which the employer envisages he will take in relation to the employees. If no measures are envisaged this must be stated;

4 if the employer is the transferor, the measures which the transferor envisages that the transferee will be taking. If no measures are envisaged this must be stated.

Under reg 15 the appropriate representatives may complain to a tribunal of a failure to consult, and affected employees may be awarded a maximum of 13 weeks' pay. The employer may, as with redundancy consultation, put forward the 'special circumstances' defence to a complaint of failure to consult.

Joint and several liability

Transferors and transferees are jointly and severally liable in respect of two obligations:

- under reg 15 – failure to inform and consult;
- under reg 17(2) – liability for personal liability in situations where the transferor employer is not obliged to carry employers' insurance under the Employers' Liability (Compulsory Insurance) Act 1969. This will apply where the transferor is a public sector employer.

12

Dismissal for economic reasons

LAW IN CONTEXT
Employment rights on rescues of businesses

Where there is a rescue of a business with the result that either the whole or part of it is taken over by another business then the rules in TUPE come into play. However, TUPE provisions have been criticised on the basis that they interfere with the rescue process. Armour and Deakin (2001) have suggested that granting employees some control over the situation may be the best answer in some cases so that employees may decide to waive their acquired employment rights in the interests of keeping the business afloat. However, they also argue that it is a corollary of this that effective means of employee representation are in place because it is they who will have to negotiate any waivers of employment rights.

In an earlier article (Armour and Deakin, 2000) the authors point out the effect of TUPE on corporate rescues. On the one hand it increases the cost of rescues by requiring the transferee to take the whole workforce regardless of its own requirements and it cannot easily renegotiate terms and conditions of employment to make them more compatible with its existing employees. If it dismisses employees which it does not need it will be required to pay redundancy compensation. However, it is possible for the transferee to negotiate a reduced price for the business to take account of these liabilities.

Two issues raised in this article have, in fact, been dealt with by the 2006 Regulations. One is the requirement for the transferee to be supplied with employee liability information (see reg 11 above), which will enable the transferee to be in a better position to calculate the costs of the business it is taking over although perhaps not early

→

enough for this to have an effect on the price paid for the business. The other is the provision allowing variations of contracts of employment in an insolvency situation (see reg 9). Will these enable the twin objectives to be achieved of facilitating corporate rescues and at the same time safeguarding the rights of employees affected?

SUMMARY

This chapter brings together three different areas of law which have the common theme of the effect which a reorganisation of a business has on the rights of employees. Thus it first looks at redundancy, then dismissal on a reorganisation where there is no actual redundancy and points out that here there is a gap in the law as employees may be held to have been fairly dismissed for some other substantial reason. The chapter then looks at the position where there is a transfer of the business and contrasts the position at common law with that under the Transfer of Undertakings (Protection of Employment) Regulations. The effects of these are explored in detail and any differences between the present regulations and their predecessor (the 1981 Regulations) are explained.

QUESTION

Danny worked as a school meals supervisor for Barset County Council. The school meals service was then contracted out to a private firm, Best Burgers, and Danny was told two weeks after the change that his post was redundant but that he could apply for a post as a van driver delivering pre-cooked meals to schools. Danny is unhappy about accepting this job as it will mean working further away from home and he needs to be near home as he cares for his elderly mother.

Advise Danny on whether he should accept the new post and, if not, whether he has any claim against Barset County Council and/or Best Burgers.

FURTHER READING

Collins, H., Ewing, K. and McColgan, A. (2005) *Labour Law Text and Materials* (2nd edn), Hart Publishing: Oxford (Chapter 10, 'Restructuring the Business' looks in detail at all of the issues discussed in this chapter. However, care is needed in using the section on transfer of undertakings as it pre-dates the 2006 Regulations.)

BIBLIOGRAPHY

Armour, J. and Deakin, S. (2000) 'The Rover Case (2) Bargaining in the Shadow of TUPE', 29 ILJ 395. (In addition to the general discussion of rights of employees on corporate rescues, this is an invaluable study of the effect of the law on one particular event: the sale of the Rover Group by BMW to the Phoenix Consortium in 2000.)

Armour, J. and Deakin, S. (2001) 'Insolvency, Employment Protection and Corporate Restructuring: The effects of TUPE', Working Paper 202, Centre for Business Research: University of Cambridge.

Barnard, C. (2000) 'Redundant Approaches to Redundancy', *Cambridge Law Journal* 36.

Bercusson, B. (1996) *European Labour Law*, Butterworths: London (especially p. 219).

Bowers, J. and Clarke, A. (1981) 'Unfair Dismissal and Managerial Prerogative: a Study of Some Other Substantial Reason', 10 ILJ 34.

Davies, P. and Freedland, M. (1984) *Labour Law Text and Materials* (2nd edn), Oxford University Press: Oxford (see p. 528).

Davies, P. and Freedland, M. (1993) *Labour Legislation and Public Policy*, Oxford University Press: Oxford (see pp. 145–6).

DTI (2006) 'How Have Employees Fared? Recent UK Trends.' Employment Relations Research Services Paper 56.

Ewing, K. (ed.) (1996) *Working Life*, Lawrence & Wishart: London (see p. 298).

Fryer, R. (1973) 'The Myths of the Redundancy Payments Act', 2 ILJ 1.

Grunfeld, C. (1989) *The Law of Redundancy* (3rd edn), Sweet & Maxwell: London (see p. 3).

McMullen, J. (2006) 'An Analysis of the Transfer of Undertakings (Protection of Employment) Regulations', 35 ILJ 113. (This is invaluable in charting the changes made by the 2006 Regulations.)

12

Dismissal for economic reasons

 For further resources and updates please go to the Companion Website accompanying this book at **www.mylawchamber.co.uk/duddingtonemployment**

Part 4

Collective employment law

There is clearly a different focus in this part of the book from all the preceding ones. Here we are concerned with the collective rather than the individual aspect of employment law. Thus the focus is on the collective enforcement of rights through, for example, collective bargaining and industrial action rather than individual enforcement of rights by an action in an employment tribunal. In Chapter 13 we consider the status of trade unions and their relationship with their members and in Chapter 14 the position of both trade unions and their members who take part in collective action, which in this context means strikes or other industrial action. There is also a detailed examination of the role of trade unions in modern society and how this might develop in the future.

13 Trade unions: their status and their members

INTRODUCTION

The history of the legal relationship between the law and trade unions has not been a happy one. When, at the time of the Industrial Revolution, trade unions in the modern sense began to be formed, they were outlawed by the Combination Acts of 1799 and 1800. This was partly because of fear of bodies of organised labour, inspired to some degree by the French Revolution, partly no doubt because of a general feeling that trade unions as such interfered unduly with the powers of employers, and partly because, from the strictly legal point of view, a trade union was seen as acting in restraint of trade. Thus it came within the definition of criminal conspiracy which, as we shall see later, could make an agreement to do a particular act a criminal offence even though the act was not in itself criminal. This last point retains its significance today for, even though long ago it was declared by statute that the purposes of a union were not unlawful, although technically in restraint of trade (by the Trade Union Act 1871), the fact remains that some of the very activities of a union, such as the calling of a strike, bring it into conflict with the law. Why, then, is there this continued uneasy relationship between the law and trade unions?

A full answer to this question can only be given in a book devoted to history and industrial relations, rather than in a legal textbook such as this, but certain points can validly be made here. The law has traditionally been keen to protect the rights of individuals when these are opposed to a large organisation, but, although this may go some way to explaining what is sometimes perceived as hostility of the law to trade unions, it does not go far enough. There is in fact a noticeable difference between the attitudes of the courts to issues explored in this chapter where, to some extent, the law and unions have worked alongside each other, as compared to the next chapter, where collective industrial action is considered. Not only this, but in the early part of the twentieth century what has been called 'the long sleep of public law' meant that the courts were most reluctant to intervene on the side of individuals in actions against public bodies and this did not really change until *Ridge v Baldwin* (1964).

It may well be that the real explanation can be found in a class analysis, where the judges' attitudes were conditioned by class hostility to unions. Certainly unions have believed this. Memories still exist of the case of the Tolpuddle Martyrs who, in 1834, were convicted and transported to Australia on a charge of taking an illegal oath contrary to the Unlawful Oaths Act 1797. The underlying reason for their conviction was seen as the fact that they were organising a union of agricultural workers. The problems with the law and trade unions has often been contrasted with the way in which the law took up the notion of a company and, by a series of statutes passed in the nineteenth century, gave companies a secure legal framework in which to operate. In fact, it was suggested at that time that unions should also become companies and this was also suggested by the Royal Commission on Trade Unions and Employers' Associations (the Donovan Commission) in 1968. The unions rejected this idea. The Industrial Relations Act 1971 provided that unions who registered under the Act would have corporate status but the consequence of registration was seen by unions as also leading to an unacceptable degree of interference in their internal affairs. The result was that very few unions registered and the idea of corporate status was unnecessarily linked with a political agenda. Is it not time, at a period when, unlike in the 1970s, the subject does not arouse so much heat, to look afresh at a proper legal status for trade unions?

LAW IN CONTEXT
History of trade unions and the law: a brief review

The Combination Acts, which effectively banned trade unions, were repealed in 1825 but this did no more than remove the threat of prosecution for criminal conspiracy. In *Hornby* v *Close* (1867) it was held that the activities of unions were in restraint of trade and it was not until the Trade Union Act 1871 that, as we saw above, this was reversed. This Act was the first piece of legislation to deal with the affairs of unions but it was followed by the Conspiracy and Protection of Property Act 1875, which in effect provided that those engaged in strike action would no longer be liable to prosecution for criminal conspiracy. The interesting point is that the first Act was passed by a Liberal government but the second was passed by a Conservative one. This illustrates the point that, whilst on the whole it has been Liberal and, later, Labour, governments who have been more favourable to unions, this is not universally true. On the other hand, Labour governments, and, in particular, the present one, have not always enjoyed a cosy relationship with trade unions.

It was, however, a Liberal government which acted to remove the next threat to unions, which came about as a result of the decision of the House of Lords in *Taff Vale Railway Co.* v *ASRS* (1901). This had held that a union could be sued in tort for the acts of its officials and thus the funds of the union could be at risk from an action by an employer for damages caused by a strike called by those officials. The result was the Trade Disputes Act 1906, which gave immunity to trade unions from actions in tort. (The law on immunities is explored in the next chapter.) There matters rested for many years as, although it was felt by some that there was a need to look afresh at trade unions and their place in modern society, there was a disinclination to take any action. This state of affairs was particularly prevalent in the early days of the 1951–64 Conservative government, when Walter Monckton was Minister of Labour and his desire to avoid confrontation with organised labour was shared by Churchill (see Roberts, 1994); and the general attitude of the period to industrial relations is also captured in Chapters 2 and 3 of Davies and Freedland, *Labour Legislation and Public Policy* (1993).

The setting up of the Donovan Commission in 1965 was a harbinger of changing times and its report was followed by a White Paper, *In Place of Strife* (1968), which went beyond the recommendations in the report and proposed an Industrial Relations Act with, for example, strike ballots and powers to enforce a 'conciliation pause' where a strike had been called without adequate discussions between employers and unions. These proposed powers were backed by legal sanctions and as such were anathema to the majority of the unions, coming in particular from a Labour government. They were withdrawn and replaced by a set of voluntary proposals but the episode, in addition to the political damage done to the Labour government, led to the introduction by the Conservative government elected in 1970 of a more far-reaching Industrial Relations Bill. The details of this are history but the resulting Act attempted a detailed regulation of trade unions and their affairs with, for example, provision for the imposition of emergency 'cooling off procedures' in industrial disputes and a presumption that collective agreements were legally binding. Trade unions were made liable for 'unfair industrial practices', some of which corresponded with the 'economic torts' so that, to trade unions, the spectre of *Taff Vale* (above) emerged from the shadows of 1901. The requirement on unions to register under the Act proved to be a disastrous mistake, as unions made the campaign against registration the cornerstone of their opposition to the Act. At the same time, the Act introduced new laws giving employees protection against unfair dismissal and these have, of course, survived. In one way, and presumably quite unintentionally, this introduction of new individual employment rights by the Industrial Relations Act turned out to be a far more effective method of changing the nature of trade union action than any of the complicated provisions in the Act relating to industrial disputes. This was because, with the flood of new employment rights of which this was really the precursor, employees have increasingly turned to tribunals and, more recently, arbitration as a means of settling grievances rather than resorting to industrial action.

The Conservative government fell in February 1974 in the middle of a miners' strike, and the incoming Labour government not only repealed the Industrial Relations Act but introduced legislation which greatly buttressed the position of trade unions. In particular, the law on the closed shop was strengthened, unions were given the right to be consulted on impending redundancies and the right to appoint safety representatives with wide powers. This marked the apogee of trade union power, as the Conservative government elected in 1979 embarked on a gradual programme of legislation with major statutes in 1980, 1982, 1984, 1989, 1990 and 1993. Unlike the Industrial Relations Act, the emphasis was not on one all-embracing piece of legislation but on a gradualist approach. There were two themes: first, either bringing what were seen to be unacceptable practices under control or prohibiting them (for example, the outlawing of secondary picketing); and, secondly, giving increased rights to individual union members. A great deal of this legislation is still with us because the Labour government elected in 1997 passed one major employment law statute on this area, the Employment Relations Act 1999, which left most of the legislation of the previous government intact, and made it clear that it would not introduce any more major legislation in this area, although the Employment Relations Act 2004 changed a number of details as we will see. The position was expressed by the then Prime Minister

13

Trade unions: their status and their members

→

367

in his foreword to the White Paper, *Fairness at Work* (1998, Cmnd 3968), which preceded the Employment Relations Act: 'The days of strikes without ballots, mass picketing, closed shops and secondary action are over.'

At the same time, and initially almost unnoticed by the protagonists, the impact of both the European Convention on Human Rights and of European Community (now Union) law was gradually making itself felt in the field of collective employment law; and these may prove to be the most significant influences in the future.

DEFINITION AND LEGAL STATUS OF TRADE UNIONS

Definition of a union

Section 1 of the Trade Union and Labour Relations (Consolidation) Act 1992 (TULRCA 1992) defines a trade union as an organisation consisting wholly or mainly of workers of one or more descriptions and whose principal purposes include the regulation of relations between workers of that description or descriptions and employers or employers' associations. The key elements are that it must be an organisation of workers concerned with relations with employers. Thus in *Midland Cold Storage* v *Turner* (1972) a shop stewards committee in the London docks which acted as a pressure group was not a union as it did not enter into bargaining with the employers.

Legal status of unions

Section 10 of TULRCA 1992 states that a union is not a corporate body but that it can sue and be sued in its own name; it can make contracts; and criminal proceedings can be brought against the union itself. Unions are in a unique legal position: they are theoretically unincorporated associations, which is the same legal status as that possessed by countless small sports and social clubs, yet s 10 of TULRCA 1992 then gives them most of the legal powers and duties of corporations, in allowing them to sue and be sued, etc. This position had already been reached by the courts in *Bonsor* v *Musicians Union* (1956), where it was held that a union was liable to compensate a member who had been expelled wrongly. (See later in this chapter for a further discussion of this case.) However, they do not possess one power of a corporation, as they cannot hold property which must, by s 12, be vested in trustees to be held on their behalf. If a union is sued then that property can be taken in satisfaction of a judgment just as if the union was a corporation.

Example

A union is sued for damages by an employer for calling a strike without holding a secret ballot as required by law. The union is held liable to pay damages and these will come from property held by the trustees.

An important provision is contained in s 11 of TULRCA 1992, which continues the rule first introduced in the Trade Union Act 1871 that the activities of a union are not to be regarded as unlawful simply because they may be technically in restraint of trade. This applies not only to the actual purposes of the union but also to its rules. The reason for this was to avoid the possibility, canvassed by Sachs LJ in *Edwards* v *SOGAT* (1971), that the courts could intervene and strike down a union rule on the grounds that it was oppressive and therefore possibly in restraint of trade. (The relationship between union rules and restraint of trade is dealt with later in this chapter.)

One should also note that, by s 160 of TULRCA 1992, a trade union may be joined in an unfair dismissal action by either the employee or employer where it is alleged that the union put pressure on the employer to dismiss the employee because of non-membership of the union.

▊ Listing of unions and certificates of independence

Section 2 of TULRCA 1992 provides that the Certification Officer shall keep a list of trade unions. There is no legal requirement on unions to be listed but there are a number of advantages: entry on the list is, by s 2(4), conclusive evidence that the organisation is a trade union and there are a number of tax advantages. Moreover, ss 13 and 14 of TULRCA 1992 provide for a simplified procedure for the vesting of property in trustees where the union is listed. There is no similarity between listing and the requirement to register under the Industrial Relations Act and so the vast majority of unions are listed. The main inducement to be listed is that listing is the essential prerequisite to the granting of a certificate of independence, which is essential for the granting of a large number of statutory rights: these are too numerous to list in full here but many rights granted to unions are granted only to those who have certificates of independence. Thus only unions with such a certificate are entitled to be consulted about impending redundancies and other matters and only members of independent trade unions are protected from dismissal on the grounds of union activities.

Applications for certificates of independence are made to the Certification Officer under s 6 of TULRCA 1992 and s 5 sets out the definition of an independent trade union. This is one which is not under the domination or control of an employer or an employers' association and is not liable to interference by the employer or employer's association tending towards control, whether this interference is by the provision of financial or material support or by any other means. The object is to weed out organisations which may appear to be representing the employees but which in fact are simply pawns of the employer.

The criteria for the granting of certificates were set out by the Certification Officer in 1976 and can now be found in their Annual Report. They were approved by the EAT in *Blue Circle Staff Association* v *Certification Officer* (1977) and are as follows:

The strength and sources of the union's finances

Clearly a union which receives finance from the employer will not be considered independent.

The extent of any assistance given by the employer in either establishing or running the organisation

The word 'extent' should be emphasised: it is common practice and good industrial relations for the employer to provide the union with facilities such as notice boards and, if necessary, an office and this is recommended in the ACAS Code of Practice on Time Off for Trade Union Duties and Activities. If, however, the extent of the assistance is such that the union would not be able to function without it then the independence of the union is likely to be jeopardised.

Whether the constitution allows for interference by the employer in the affairs of the union

In the *Blue Circle* case (above) the rules originally allowed management representatives to sit on the committee and, even though this was changed, these representatives helped in the drafting of the new rules. This indicated that the organisation was not independent. In *Squibb UK Staff Association* v *Certification Officer* (1979) the EAT held that where a staff association had been dominated by the employer then it might take some time before it was able to demonstrate that it had shaken this off sufficiently to be granted a certificate of independence.

Is the union a single company one or does its membership come from a broader base?

This is also relevant when considering the extent of any assistance given by the employer (above) because, as the Certification Officer has pointed out in the Guidance on Applications for a Certificate of Independence, if a single company union receives facilities from an employer then it would find it very difficult to survive if those were cut off, whereas a broadly based union which also received them could survive. An instance of a single company union failing to gain a certificate is provided by *Government Communications Staff Federation* v *Certification Officer and CCSU* (1993), where the continued existence of an organisation representing staff at GCHQ (who were not at that time allowed to join a union) depended on the approval of the Director. The EAT felt that the words 'liable to interference' in s 5 meant 'vulnerable to interference' or exposed to the risk of interference so that any matters which indicated a possibility of interference by the employer would mean that the union would not be granted a certificate. Nevertheless, there have been many instances of single company unions which were undoubtedly independent, such as the railway unions when railways were nationalised.

Does the union have a robust attitude in negotiations with the employer?

The negotiating record of the organisation will be looked at, although the amount of industrial action which the organisation has been involved in is not by itself a criterion.

RECOGNITION OF UNIONS

The idea of recognition is that an employer is prepared to negotiate and otherwise deal with a union on matters covered by collective bargaining. In very many cases this has been happening for many years and will happen for a long time in the future. However, it is also true to say that, with the decline in union membership and the shift from national collective bargaining to bargaining on a company basis, union recognition has been in decline.

Voluntary or statutory recognition

Recognition can be voluntary under an express agreement, or it can, under provisions introduced by the Employment Relations Act 1999, be introduced as a result of a statutory procedure. Section 178(3) of TULRCA 1992 provides that a union is recognised 'to any extent' for the purposes of collective bargaining which means negotiations covering:

(a) terms and conditions of employment;

(b) engagement or non-engagement or termination or suspension of either employment or the duties of employment;

(c) allocation of work or duties of employment between employees;

(d) disciplinary matters;

(e) membership or non-membership of a trade union;

(f) facilities for union officials;

(g) machinery for negotiation or consultation on any of the above matters.

The phrase 'to any extent' means that there must be a clear agreement to recognise but that it need not be for all of the above matters. It should be noted that a collective agreement is, by s 179 of TULRCA 1992, presumed not to be legally binding (see Chapter 5). Where a union is recognised as a result of the statutory recognition procedure in the Employment Relations Act, then it covers only negotiations relating to pay, hours and holidays.

Other forms of recognition

Recognition can also be for various purposes scattered around the legislation, such as the receipt of bargaining information, consultation on impending redundancies, consultation on TUPE transfers and appointment of safety representatives. None of these is, of course, covered by the statutory recognition procedure.

Recognition for disciplinary and grievance procedures

An employer may agree to recognise a union only for the purpose of representing its members in disciplinary and grievance procedures. This type of recognition will not entitle the union to claim that it is recognised for the purposes of collective bargaining or any of the matters discussed in 'Other forms of recognition', above (see *USDAW* v *Sketchley Ltd* (1981)).

THE STATUTORY RECOGNITION PROCEDURE

The statutory recognition procedure is extremely detailed and operates by way of insertion by the Employment Relations Act 1999 into TULRCA 1992 of a new Schedule A1.

The procedure in outline

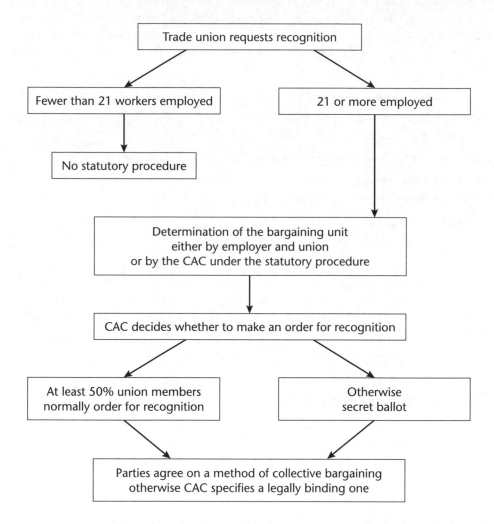

The procedure in detail

This begins with a request by a trade union (or unions, as a joint request may be submitted) for recognition on behalf of a group of workers known as the 'bargaining unit'. There is one vital precondition: the statutory recognition procedure applies only where the employer employs at least 21 workers, although the proposed bargaining unit may be smaller than this. It should also be noted that there is nothing to prevent an employer entering into a voluntary recognition agreement with a non-independent union but the statutory recognition applies only to recognised unions. If the parties agree on recognition at that stage (i.e. voluntary recognition, known in the legislation as 'agreements for recognition') the matter ends. If not, the statutory procedure continues.

Identification of the bargaining unit

The first stage is the identification of the group of workers for whom the union seeks to be recognised by the employer, known as the bargaining unit. This may be a crucial stage, as recognition is likely to depend on the level of support for it in the bargaining unit. It may be that a union has strong support amongst a particular group but does not have the same degree of support amongst the whole workforce. The union will probably try to get the particular group recognised as the bargaining unit and the employer will argue for the whole workforce to be the unit. The parties (the employer and the union) will try to agree what the bargaining unit shall be but if they cannot do so, then the Central Arbitration Committee (CAC) decides. The Employment Relations Act 2004 has amended Sch A1 to TULRCA 1992 with the object of clarifying existing provisions and thus it now provides that, in a situation where the CAC has to determine the bargaining unit, it must first consider the bargaining unit proposed by the union and only if that is not appropriate should it then go on to consider other possible units.

However, the CAC can act only if it is satisfied that members of the union applying for recognition constitute at least 10% of the workers in the proposed unit and that a majority of workers in the unit would be likely to favour recognition. The object is to deter frivolous applications and the White Paper *Fairness at Work* (1998) suggested that a petition presented by at least 10% of the workers would be strong evidence.

Once the CAC has accepted the application then under s 5 of the Employment Relations Act 2004 the union can apply for a 'suitable independent person' to be appointed to handle communications between it and the workers involved. The object is to give the union independent postal access to the workers and, to enable this to take place, the employers must pass names and home addresses of the workers to the independent person. When the CAC begins to determine the bargaining unit, it must take into account the need for the unit to be compatible with effective management, existing bargaining arrangements, the desirability of avoiding small fragmented bargaining units within an undertaking and the characteristics and location of the workers in the proposed unit and other relevant workers. Once the bargaining unit is decided, the parties may agree voluntarily that the union shall be recognised by the employer or the matter may be left to the CAC to decide. The question for the CAC then becomes one of whether the union should be recognised as representing workers in the unit and the procedure for this is outlined below. In *R v CAC, ex parte Kwik-Fit Ltd* (2002) the Court of Appeal held that where the CAC finds that the union's proposed bargaining unit is appropriate then that is the end of this stage. The CAC is not to go further and consider whether the unit is the best one. Any alternative bargaining unit put forward by the employer should not be treated on equal terms with that put forward by the union but can be useful in testing whether the unit put forward by the union is appropriate. In *Graphical Paper and Media Union* v *Derry Print Ltd* (2002) it was held that the statutory recognition procedures can only be used to gain recognition for a bargaining unit covering one employer but where there are two firms which are really one then an exception will be made and recognition can be sought in respect of both of them in one procedure.

Order for recognition

Once the bargaining unit is determined, the question is then whether the union shall be regarded as representing workers in it. The CAC therefore decides whether to make an order for recognition, although it must be emphasised that at any time in the procedure the parties may reach a voluntary agreement. There are two ways in which the CAC can decide whether the union should be recognised:

1 If the CAC is satisfied that at least 50% of the workers in the unit are union members then there will be a declaration that the union shall be recognised unless there are significant doubts about the evidence of union membership, or a significant number of members tell the CAC that they do not want collective bargaining, or the CAC itself considers that a ballot should be held in the interests of good industrial relations.

2 If less than 50% of workers are union members then a secret ballot of the workers in the bargaining unit must be held. If the result of the ballot is that a majority of those support union recognition *and* those voting constitute at least 40% of the workers in the bargaining unit then the application succeeds. If not, it is dismissed.

Method of collective bargaining

Following a declaration of recognition, the parties should agree on a method of conducting collective bargaining but, if they cannot do so, then the CAC may, as a last resort, specify a method which takes effect as a legally enforceable agreement between the parties. The Trade Union Recognition (Method of Collective Bargaining) Order 2000 (SI 2000/1300) specifies a model method with a six-stage process, starting with the submission by the union of a claim and ending with the involvement of ACAS if the parties cannot agree. The model also makes provision for the setting up of a Joint Negotiating Body.

Changes in the bargaining unit

Where either party believes that there have been changes in the bargaining unit after the declaration of recognition then they can apply to the CAC for a determination that the bargaining unit is no longer appropriate. Such an application can be made only if there is evidence that the present unit is no longer appropriate because of changes in the structure of the business or its activities or where there has been a substantial change in the number of workers in the present unit.

Application for derecognition

An application for derecognition can be made after a minimum of three years from the declaration of recognition. This application can be made only on the following grounds:

(a) the employer contends that the size of the workforce has fallen to below 21;

(b) the employer or workers believe that there is no longer majority support for the collective bargaining arrangements;

(c) the original declaration of recognition was made on the basis of 50% union membership and the employer believes that this is now below 50%;

(d) the workers wish to end voluntary recognition of a non-independent union.

The results of the first five years of the statutory recognition procedure are analysed by Gall (2005). The number of applications accepted by the CAC in the period June 2000 to June 2005 was 272 and 55 were rejected. In the determining of the bargaining unit 62% of decisions were pro-union in that they accepted the unit proposed by the union or one close to it and 17% were pro-employer in that the employer's proposed unit was accepted. Automatic awards of recognition were made in 52 cases and awards as a result of a ballot were made in 72 cases. Unions lost ballots in 44 cases and voluntary agreements were reached in 85 cases. The number of workers covered by the process has tended to be small, with an average of 200 workers being involved, and in total 39,000 workers have been brought under union recognition by the statutory recognition procedure. However, Gall draws attention to the 'shadow effect' where the whole idea of union recognition has gained greater acceptance through the introduction of this procedure. Thus in the period under review just under 1,800 new recognition agreements were signed covering just under 800,000 workers.

DISCLOSURE OF BARGAINING INFORMATION TO INDEPENDENT RECOGNISED TRADE UNIONS

Section 181 of TULRCA 1992 provides that an employer has a general duty to disclose information to trade unions, for the purpose of collective bargaining, which is either information without which the union would be impeded in carrying out collective bargaining or information which ought to be disclosed in the interest of good industrial relations. The contrast with the provisions discussed above could not be starker: whilst it might be said that they are over-detailed, these are virtually meaningless. Fortunately, there is a Code of Practice (on Disclosure of Information to Trade Unions for Collective Bargaining Purposes) which gives details of information that should be disclosed. Examples are details of pay and benefits, conditions of service, analysis of the workforce, the performance of the organisation and financial information. Section 182 lays down certain information that need not be disclosed: that which has been communicated to the employer in confidence; information relating specifically to an individual (e.g. details of performance-related pay received by a named individual); and other information which, if disclosed, could cause substantial injury to the undertaking. The Code gives, as examples of the last category, details of marketing and pricing policies and details of how tender prices are made up. A failure to disclose information as required can lead to a complaint by the union to the CAC. If conciliation through ACAS fails then the CAC may hear a claim by the union that the contracts of specified workers should include specified terms and conditions. The CAC cannot, however, give guidance on what should be disclosed in future.

INFORMATION AND CONSULTATION

Employees have various rights to information and consultation through their trade union or elected employee representatives in the following areas:

Health and safety – see Chapter 8;
Redundancy – see Chapter 12;
Transfers of undertakings – see Chapter 12.

There are also non-statutory mechanisms for information and consultation and a survey by the CBI (see Hall, 2005) reported that 49% of companies surveyed had permanent mechanisms, which usually meant a staff council. Another survey by the Labour Research Department (2004) found that there had been a sharp increase in the number of consultation bodies which involved employees who were not union members – from 11% of responses in 2002 to 25% in 2004. It is against this background that we need to consider the Information and Consultation of Employees Regulations 2004 (SI 2004/3426). They were passed as a result of EC Directive 2002/14 and the object is to give rights to employees to be given information about the business they work for and to be consulted about how it is run. However, the regulations apply to employees who work for undertakings with 150 or more employees and this figure will go down to 100 employees in April 2007 and 50 in April 2008. (This will mean that 37,000 undertakings are covered.) The number of employees is determined by taking an average over the previous 12 months, or less if the undertaking has not existed that long. Part-time employees count as full-time if they have worked as such for the whole month for the period of the calculation. The regulations are unlikely to apply to smaller undertakings. An undertaking is defined by reg 1 as a 'public or private undertaking carrying out an economic activity, whether or not operating for gain' and the similarity with the definition of an undertaking for the purposes of transfers of undertakings will be noted.

The process of obtaining an information and consultation agreement (ICA) is laid down in detail. The employer may start it, but if the employees do so, then at least 10% must make the request with a minimum of 15 and a maximum of 2,500. (The double threshold reflected concern by both unions and employers that existing agreements should not be lightly overturned.) If an ICA already exists (see above) then the employer can ballot all the employees on whether they agree to the request for a new ICA. If a majority of those voting agree to the request for an ICA then one must be set up so long as those voting represent 40% of the workforce. Where the employer fails to initiate the process following a valid request from the employees or if the parties cannot reach a negotiated agreement then the default requirements set out in regs 18–20 will apply. These provide that the employer must inform and consult on the following:

(a) recent and probable development of the undertaking (information only);

(b) probable development of employment in the undertaking and any anticipatory measures envisaged where there is a threat to employment (information and consultation);

(c) decisions likely to lead to substantial changes in work organisation or contractual relations (information and consultation with a view to reaching agreement).

In *Moray Council* v *Stewart* (2006) the issue was whether an existing agreement was sufficient or whether there was a requirement for a statutory one. The EAT held that it is possible for an agreement to be regarded as approved by the whole workforce if it is approved by the trade union representatives and the majority of the employees are members of the union. As Elias J put it: 'Whatever the opinion of the non unionists the support of the trade unionists will carry the day.'

If the parties reach agreement then they will decide precisely what the agreement will contain but the default agreement will doubtless serve as a model. The DTI estimates that 35% of undertakings at present without an ICA are likely to have requests for one; but where there is already a non-statutory ICA in place it is estimated that in only 1–3% of cases will a ballot succeed in changing it.

EUROPEAN WORKS COUNCILS

The European Works Council Directive requires organisations with at least 1,000 employees across the European Economic Area (the EU countries plus Norway, Liechtenstein and Iceland) to establish a mechanism for informing and consulting staff on transnational issues. This was implemented in the UK by the creation of the Transnational Information and Consultation of Employees Regulations 1999 (SI 1999/ 3323). These do not apply to organisations which establish such a body voluntarily nor to multinational organisations which are already obliged to establish one because they are subject to legislation in other countries which have already implemented the Directive. If there is no existing body then either the management or 100 employees or their representatives may begin the process leading to the establishment of a works council.

THE RIGHT TO FREEDOM OF ASSOCIATION

Background

The right to freedom of association can be said to date from the repeal of the Combination Acts in 1825 but, as always in UK law, the right was couched in negative terms: it was simply provided that a union was not liable in the criminal law for existing. No positive right to form one was given and the legislators at the time would have been astonished at the suggestion that it should be. Even today, the right to associate is

13

Trade unions: their status and their members

protected in UK law by statutory provisions giving the right, for example, not to be subjected to any detriment on the grounds of union membership. Before these detailed provisions are considered, however, it should be noted that international and, specifically, European legislation does recognise a positive right to associate.

Under international standards

The constitution of the International Labour Organization (ILO), first established in 1919 and whose constitution was revised in 1946, asserts that freedom of association is essential to sustained progress. This right is also given expression in the Universal Declaration of Human Rights, adopted by the United Nations General Assembly in 1948, which declares that 'everyone has the right to form and join trade unions for the protection of his interests'. These statements are not, of course, legally enforceable, although they do set a standard to which states should aspire and, arguably, they could be said to have paved the way for the European principles in this area. The impact of the ILO on employment law is considered more generally in Chapter 1.

Under European principles

The ECHR states in Article 11(1) that: 'Everyone has the right to freedom of peaceful assembly and association with others, including the right to join and form trade unions for the protection of his interests.' It then states in Article 11(2) that no restrictions shall be placed on this right other than are prescribed by law and are necessary in a democratic society in the interests of public safety, for the prevention of disorder or crime, for the protection of health or morals or for the protection of the rights and freedoms of others. The effect of Article 11 was considered by the ECtHR in *X v Ireland* (1971), where it was held that any intimidation of employees to make them give up their functions within a union was in breach of Article 11. As such, this adds nothing to existing UK law and this impression is strengthened by remarks of the judges in *UKAPE v ACAS* (1980), where Lord Scarman, whilst prepared to recognise the effect of Article 11, even though at that date it was not incorporated into UK law, felt that it did not give a right to a union to seek recognition from an employer, a right now provided by statute. Thus it seems that, given that UK law has comprehensive provisions protecting union membership and activities, Article 11 may not add anything beyond possibly applying to self-employed persons who are victimised by employers on the grounds of union membership. This is because UK legislation refers only to 'employees', whereas the Convention has no such restriction. Given the increase in the number of persons who are self-employed this may not be quite as insignificant a point as it seems. The ECtHR has itself adopted a restrictive interpretation of Article 11 and has stated that it does not give a right to trade union recognition or a right to strike (see *Swedish Engine Drivers Union v Sweden* (1980) and *Schmidt and Dahlstrom v Sweden* (1976)). Moreover, the ECtHR has stated that Article 11 is an area where states should enjoy 'a wide margin of appreciation in the choice of means to be employed'. Finally, one must not forget the link between the ECHR and EU law because Article 6 of the Treaty of European Union commits the EU to respect fundamental rights, amongst which those in the ECHR are mentioned. The right of freedom of association was recognised by the ECJ in the *Bosman* decision in 1995 (see p. 54) and the ECJ is prepared to extend the right of association to allow a staff association to do anything which protects the interests of their members (*Union Syndicate* v *EC Council* (1974)). It will be interesting to see whether the ECJ, rather than the ECHR, explicitly rules, as it has already come close to doing, that there is a right to strike.

The right of association in UK law

The right of association is protected by UK law in the following ways.

Protection against being refused employment on grounds of union membership or non-membership

Section 137 of TULRCA 1992 makes it unlawful to refuse employment on the grounds of union membership. The term 'refused' is defined widely as refusals to entertain applications, making a person withdraw an application, refusing to offer employment and offering it on such terms that no reasonable employer would offer. It will be noted that the right to associate (i.e. not to be refused employment on grounds of union membership) is coupled with the right to disassociate (i.e. the right not to be refused employment on grounds of *not* belonging to a union) and this second aspect is related to the closed shop, which is considered below. The likelihood is that s 137 only applies to refusals on the grounds of union *membership* rather than *activities* because the decision of the EAT that it *could* apply to activities (*Harrison* v *KCC* (1995)) may be suspect in view of the later decisions of the House of Lords in *Associated Newspapers Ltd* v *Wilson* and *Associated British Ports* v *Palmer* (1995), which are considered below. Thus an employer who refused employment to a person on the grounds that they were known as union activists would almost certainly not be caught by s 137. A complaint of a breach of s 137 lies to an employment tribunal, which can order compensation up to the limit of compensation for unfair dismissal.

Protection against dismissal on trade union grounds

Section 152(1) of TULRCA 1992 provides that a dismissal of an employee will be automatically unfair if the reason, or principal reason, is that the employee:

(a) was, or proposed to become, a member of an independent trade union;

(b) had taken part, or proposed to take part, in its activities at an appropriate time (defined as either outside working hours or within working hours with the employer's agreement);

(c) was not a member of a trade union or had refused to become or remain a member. (This is an instance of the right to disassociate and is considered below under the closed shop.)

Note that, as with all cases of automatic unfair dismissals, there is no qualifying period of employment before an application can be brought under s 152.

Suppose that a job applicant was a union activist in a previous employment and gains a position with a new employer by concealing this. This is precisely what happened in *City of Birmingham DC* v *Beyer* (1977), where the employee was dismissed when his past as a union activist was found out (about an hour after he started work!).

It was held that because he had concealed his activities the dismissal was fair on the ground of the employee's deceit. However, in *Fitzpatrick* v *British Railways Board* (1990) it was held by the Court of Appeal that where an employer dismisses on the ground that an employee was a union activist in a previous employment then this by itself could be dismissal on grounds of trade union activities. The distinction between the two cases is really the deceit of the employee in *Beyer*. Note that if either of the employees in these cases had been refused employment on the grounds of union activities then s 137 of TULRCA would apply. The distinction between membership and activities has been considered in other cases (above).

The remedies on a complaint that a dismissal was for a s 152 ground are the same as for other unfair dismissal actions (see Chapter 11), except for the following:

1   There is a minimum basic award of £4,200, unlike the normal unfair dismissal cases where there is no minimum.

2   An employee can apply for interim relief under ss 161–166 of TULRCA 1992 where the tribunal, if it thinks that the complaint is likely to be upheld at the full hearing, must first ask the employer if they are willing for the employment to continue until the hearing. If the employer is willing then an order is made that the employment shall continue until then. If not, then the second option is for the tribunal to order that certain parts of the contract of employment shall continue so that the employee will continue to be paid and pension rights and continuity of employment will be preserved. However, other parts of the contract will not continue, such as the employee's obligation to work, and the effect is that an employer who does not comply with the initial request to continue employment will end up paying the employee for doing nothing. A request for interim relief must be made within seven days of the dismissal and where it is for trade union membership or activities it must be supported by a certificate from a union official stating that in their opinion the dismissal was for this reason.

3   Section 160 of TULRCA 1992 allows employers or employees to ask the tribunal to join a trade union or other person to the proceedings where it is claimed that the employer was induced to dismiss the employee as a result of pressure exerted by them because the employee was not a union member. This could work where, for instance, the employer gives in to union pressure and dismisses the employee who then complains of unfair dismissal and joins the union as a co-defendant. Complaints under s 152 must be presented within three months of the dismissal (with the usual proviso for an extension of time beyond this at the employment tribunal's discretion).

Protection against being subject to detriment

Section 146(1) of TULRCA 1992, as amended by para 2(2) of Sch 2 to the Employment Relations Act 1999 and the Employment Relations Act 2004, provides that workers have the right not to be subjected to any detriment as an individual by any act, or deliberate failure to act, by his employer, if the act or failure takes place for the purpose of:

(a) preventing or deterring the employee from being, or seeking to be, a member of an independent trade union or penalising him or her for doing so;

(b) preventing or deterring the employee from taking part in the activities of an independent trade union at an appropriate time or penalising him or her for doing so;

(c) compelling the employee to be or become a member of an independent trade union. (This is again an example of the right to disassociate.)

It is for the employer to show what the purpose was for which it acted or failed to act but it is for the worker to show that the purpose was in breach of the statute in one or more of the three situations above (s 148(1) of TULRCA 1992).

It should be noted that 'workers' are protected as defined by s 296(1) of TULRCA 1992, which adopts the definition in s 230(3) of the ERA 1996 which provides that a worker is either a person who has entered into a contract of employment or who has entered into any other contract 'whereby the individual undertakes to do or perform personally any work or services for another party to the contract whose status is not by virtue of the contract that of a client or customer of any profession or business undertaking carried on by the individual'. It is thus wider than that of an employee for the purposes of claiming unfair dismissal, for example.

Consider these two situations:

1 Duddington Ltd tells its employees that they cannot belong to a trade union and if they do so they will be dismissed. This is covered by s 152 and dismissal would be automatically unfair.

2 Thacker Ltd tells its employees that if they give up their rights to be represented by the union in collective bargaining (not give up actual union membership) then they will be granted a pay rise. This is also now unlawful by s 29 of the Employment Relations Act 2004 (see below).

The careful wording of the meaning of the term 'detriment' (see above) is the result of decisions of the House of Lords in *Associated Newspapers* v *Wilson* and *Associated British Ports* v *Palmer* (1995). In both these cases the employer had offered pay increases to employees who gave up their rights to have their contracts negotiated through collective bargaining and changed to individual contracts. It was held that the employer's decision not to give pay rises to those who did not agree to the new contracts was not an act but just an omission and, as s 146 then covered only situations where the employer actually took action, the acts in these cases were not covered by s 146. On this point these cases are now only of historic interest because of amendments to s 146 which now cover a deliberate failure to act.

These decisions were also of importance because of the consideration which was given by the courts to the word 'purpose' in s 146. To put it simply, it may be that the *effect* of the employer's actions will be to subject an employee to a detriment on trade union grounds but was this the *purpose* of the employer's actions? In the *Wilson* and *Palmer* cases the issue was whether the purpose of the employers in offering a pay rise only to those who signed individual contracts was to penalise those employees who had not signed or to change the system of bargaining from collective to individual agreements. It was held by a majority of the House of Lords that it was the latter. The ECtHR ruled in *Wilson and others* v *UK* (2002) that the giving of 'sweeteners', as in *Wilson* and *Palmer*, to induce employees not to make use of the union's services was in breach of Article 11 of the ECHR because, as the ECtHR observed, no real distinction can be drawn between membership of a union and use of its services.

In response to these decisions of the ECHR, s 29 of the Employment Relations Act 2004 inserted a new s 145B into TULRCA 1992 which provides that a worker has a right not to have an offer made to him by an employer where the employer's sole or main purpose in making it is so that the terms and conditions of employment of workers shall not be determined by collective agreement. Section 145A of TULRCA 1992 (also inserted by s 29) provides that it is unlawful to offer a worker an inducement not to join a non-independent trade union or to participate in its affairs or use its services. This also applies to inducements to join a union.

Another issue, which is relevant to both s 152 and s 146, is the meaning to be given to the words 'membership of a trade union'. Does it cover just membership or the *benefits* of membership? In **Discount Tobacco v Armitage** (1995) an employee was dismissed after her union had written to her employer asking for her to be given a written statement of terms and conditions of employment. The EAT found that she had been dismissed on the grounds of trade union membership, Knox J sensibly pointing out that to confine the term 'union membership' to in effect no more than possession of a membership card would be to 'emasculate the provision altogether'. This wider view can be seen as at variance with the decisions in *Wilson* and *Palmer* because the effect of *Armitage* was to hold that there was no distinction between membership of a union as such and the benefits of membership, yet that was precisely what the employees in the other two cases had lost. Although the decision in *Armitage* was accepted in *Wilson* and *Palmer* as correct on its facts, the House of Lords declined to lay down a general principle that membership of a union should be given the same meaning as using its facilities and so the robust approach of Knox J in *Armitage* has not been followed.

A complaint by a worker of detriment under s 146 must be presented to an employment tribunal within three months (or later if the tribunal finds that it was not reasonably practicable for it to be presented within the time limit) and the tribunal may award compensation which is just and equitable. This can include compensation for injury to feelings, for example, as well as financial loss.

Other protection

Section 144 of TULRCA 1992 provides that a provision in a contract for the supply of goods or services that only non-union labour should be used is void. There is also a statutory duty under s 145 of TULRCA 1992 not to exclude a person from a list of approved suppliers on the ground that it is unlikely that they would be able to meet a requirement to use only non-union labour.

THE RIGHT TO WORK

The recognition by the courts of a 'right to work' can be seen as a counterpart to the right to associate because, if there is no right to work, then the right to associate when at work is meaningless. In **Nagle v Fielden** (1966) the claimant had been refused a licence as a trainer by the Jockey Club because she was a woman. As the club had a monopoly over flat racing, this meant that the claimant could not engage in her profession as a trainer. The Court of Appeal held that she was unlawfully denied a licence. Lord Denning said that 'the common law . . . has for centuries recognised that a man has a right to work at his profession without being unjustly excluded from it'.

This case is also important in the context of the jurisdiction of the courts over union rules and should also be considered in the light of the statutory rules on exclusion from unions. Both of these are dealt with later in this chapter.

THE CLOSED SHOP

The idea of the closed shop is that an agreement is made between an employer and a trade union that the employer will not employ anyone who is not a member of that union. The fact that such an agreement can be made is an instance of the law supporting the right to associate, but equally the fact that such agreements can no longer be enforced is in fact an example of the law upholding the right to disassociate.

There are two ways in which closed shops operate: the *post-entry* closed shop, under which existing employees must belong to a particular union; and the *pre-entry* closed shop, where belonging to a union is a condition of employment. There is nothing unlawful in the making of such an agreement; the issue is whether and how it can be enforced. The high water mark of enforcement of closed shops came with the legislation of the 1974–9 government, culminating in the Trade Union and Labour Relations (Amendment) Act 1976. This made dismissal automatically fair where the reason was that the employee was not a member of an independent trade union unless the employee had a genuine religious objection to membership of any trade union whatsoever. At that time almost 25% of all employees were covered by closed shop agreements, and they were particularly prevalent in the nationalised industries.

The 1979 Conservative government was hostile to the idea of the closed shop and added strength was given to this view by the decision of the ECtHR in *Young, James and Webster* v *UK* (1981). This concerned whether a closed shop agreement in the railway industry was in breach of Article 11 of the ECHR, which provides, as we saw above, that there is a right to join a trade union. A majority of the judges considered that this implied a right *not* to join. On the facts of the case it was held that Article 11 had been violated. The closed shop agreement had been introduced after the employees had begun employment, the employees objected to union membership on principle and the consequence of refusal to join (dismissal and consequent loss of livelihood) was judged particularly harsh. Thus it would seem that the enforcement of a closed shop agreement by dismissal of those who refused to join would be in breach of the ECHR.

The possibility of the ECtHR being asked to rule on a closed shop is most unlikely now that enforcement of closed shops has ceased as a result of legislation. Tony Blair has ruled out the reintroduction of legislation enforcing the closed shop (in his preface to the White Paper *Fairness at Work*, quoted above). The relevant legislation was first contained in the Employment Act 1988, which prevented enforcement of a post-entry closed shop (now in s 152 of TULRCA 1992), and the Employment Act 1990, which

13

Trade unions: their status and their members

prevented enforcement of a pre-entry closed shop (now contained in s 137 of TULRCA 1992, which is noted above). The position now is that it is unlawful either to refuse a person employment or to dismiss an employee on the grounds of failure to be a member of an independent trade union.

RIGHTS TO TIME OFF WORK FOR UNION DUTIES OR ACTIVITIES

These rights are contained in ss 168 and 169 (duties) and s 170 (activities) of TULRCA 1992, together with s 43 of the Employment Act 2002, and are supported by an ACAS Code of Practice.

Right to time off for union duties

This right is with pay and is given to officials of recognised independent trade unions. The right only applies to time off for three purposes:

1 negotiating with the employer;

2 acting on behalf of employees;

3 training which is relevant to the above duties and which is approved by the union or by the TUC.

The ACAS Code of Practice gives guidance on what can be within the scope of the right: negotiating on terms and conditions of employment; consultation on redundancies and transfers of undertakings; and disciplinary and grievance procedures. The Act requires that the duties must be concerned with negotiations with the employer and the courts have held that attendance at meetings and conferences and other activities can be covered if there is a close connection between the activities and the negotiations. Thus in *London Ambulance Service* v *Charlton* (1992) attendance at meetings of a district committee of the ambulance service to prepare for negotiations in connection with collective bargaining were held to be covered and in *Adlington* v *British Bakeries (Northern) Ltd* (1989) attendance at a meeting to discuss the implications of a government proposal to repeal a statute regulating hours of work in the baking industry was also covered. Kerr LJ, in the Court of Appeal, said that there was an 'exceptionally close connection' between the meeting and a bargaining matter with employers. Although this case was decided under the previous law, which had more generous provisions relating to time off, it is likely that it is still good law.

Section 169 of TULRCA 1992 provides that the employee is entitled to be paid the amount which they would have received had they worked at the time. This seems straightforward but what is the position where the duties are performed by a part-time worker at a time when they are not actually at work? In *Hairsine* v *Hull City Council* (1992) it was held that there was no right to paid time off but this may be in conflict with the decision of the ECJ in *Arbeiterwohlfahrt der Stadt Berlin* v *Bötel* (1992). This held that a part-time worker was indirectly discriminated against by a decision that she should receive less pay while on a training course than a full-time worker would.

However, the matter is not entirely clear, as the decision of the ECJ was under what is now Article 141, which refers to 'work' and, although attendance at a training course will count as work in view of the above decision, could the same be said of a negotiating session? The point is not dealt with in the Part-time Workers (Prevention of Less Favourable Treatment) Regulations 2000 (SI 2000/1551).

The remedy is for the tribunal, on a complaint by the employee, to award the amount of pay which should have been received.

Right to time off for union activities

This is without pay and is given to members of recognised independent trade unions. The ACAS Code gives as examples attending union conferences and other meetings as a union representative, voting in union elections, and attending meetings with union officials to discuss matters relevant to the workplace. In *Luce* v *Bexley LBC* (1990) a refusal to allow a teacher time off to attend a lobby of Parliament against the Education Reform Bill was held to be justified as the lobby was concerned with political objections to the Bill and not specifically with union activities.

The remedy is for the tribunal, on a complaint by the employee, to award just and equitable compensation taking into account the blame attaching to the employer and any loss to the employee.

Rights to time off for trade union learning representatives

This was introduced by s 43 of the Employment Act 2002 and gives rights to paid time off to trade union learning representatives who are members of independent recognised trade unions. The right covers time off for analysing training needs, providing information and advice on them, arranging learning and training, promoting the value of it and preparing for learning and training. The representative must have undergone training to prepare for this role and the union must certify to the employer that this has taken place. The government hopes that this new right may be taken up by members of groups who are underrepresented among shop stewards who can claim rights to time off for union activities. Groups mentioned are ethnic minority groups, older men and part-time workers.

RIGHT TO TIME OFF FOR EMPLOYEE REPRESENTATIVES

Section 61 of the ERA 1996 provides that employee representatives are entitled to reasonable paid time off during working hours to perform their functions and to undergo training. The right is thus the same as that given to trade union officials but is, of course, restricted to the specific functions which representatives may perform under statute. There is, unfortunately, no code of practice governing this right, but it is suggested that where the functions of employee representatives parallel those of union officials, the time off should be the same. This is especially important with redundancy consultation. There is the same remedy if time off is refused as for trade union officials.

UNION RULES

Many of the cases to be considered below deal with disciplinary hearings conducted by unions against their members. It is vital to appreciate that there are also statutory provisions governing these, which will be considered after the common law rules, and the two sets of rules have to be understood together.

Basis of the courts' approach

The courts may be asked to intervene when it is alleged that a union has acted in breach of its rules. A preliminary, but important, issue is the way in which the courts construe these rules. It has often been emphasised that the rules should not be subjected to the same minute scrutiny as, for example, statutes. In *Heatons Transport (St Helens) Ltd* v *TGWU* (1972) Lord Wilberforce pointed out that 'union rule books are not drafted by parliamentary draftsmen. Courts of law must resist the temptation to construe them as if they were.' In *Jacques* v *AUEW (Engineering Section)* (1986) Warner J said that the rules of unions are not to be construed like a statute 'but so as to give them a reasonable interpretation which accords with what in the court's view they must have been intended to mean'.

The effect is that the courts will look not only at the rules of the union but also at custom and practice and the result of this approach is to give the courts a good deal of freedom in how they interpret and apply union rules. What seems clear is that when looking at the disciplinary powers of unions the courts favour the rights of the individual member. Lord Denning went further in *Edwards* v *SOGAT* (1971) and put forward the 'by-law theory', under which the rules of the union will be construed as a legislative code and can be struck down if unreasonable. Indeed, he referred to construing the rules *against* the makers, i.e. the union itself. The by-law approach, with its attendant presumptions (which, it must be said, has not found favour with other judges), could be said to be in conflict with the decision of the ECtHR in *Cheall* v *UK* (1985). Here it was held that, although the right of unions to expel or admit members was not unfettered (see below), provided that the union acted according to the principles laid down by the court, they should be free to decide questions of expulsion and admission.

The contract of membership

This is founded on the rules of the union, subject to the above considerations. One obvious point is that it will not, therefore, apply when a person is *applying* to become a member, which is why the court in *Nagle* v *Fielden* (above) rested the common law on membership applications on a right to work.

In *Bonsor* v *Musicians Union* (1956) the contract doctrine was applied to a case of expulsion. Bonsor had failed to pay his subscriptions to the union for a year and a rule provided that if a member was more than six months in arrears with subscriptions then a branch committee could resolve that he be expelled. Instead, Bonsor was told by the branch secretary that he was expelled and this was held to be unlawful, as the rule book was a contract and the expulsion was in breach of the rules.

The courts have intervened on many other occasions, examples being: refusal of a right of appeal given under the rules (**Silvester v National Union of Printing, Bookbinding and Paper Workers** (1966)); irregularities in the holding and conduct of meetings (**MacLelland v NUJ** (1975)); and a strike call in breach of the union's rules (**Taylor v NUM (Derbyshire Area) (No. 1)** (1984)).

The view was taken that the courts would not imply a power into the rules to discipline or expel a member. However, in **McVitae v Unison** (1996) the court held that such a power can be implied where there are compelling reasons for this. Disciplinary proceedings had been taken by NALGO against some of its members for alleged racial and sexist acts but NALGO then merged with NUPE to form UNISON. There was no express power in the rules of UNISON to take disciplinary proceedings against members for acts committed before amalgamation but the court held that a power would be implied, especially as the conduct alleged was contrary to the rules of UNISON.

Where there are disciplinary rules then the courts can, in some cases at least, examine both the rule and the action taken under it to see if the action was justified. In **Esterman v NALGO** (1974) a ballot of NALGO members was held during a dispute with local authorities which showed that 49% were in favour of industrial action. The union then instructed its members not to co-operate in the holding of local government elections. The claimant disobeyed this and was invited to attend a meeting at which her expulsion would be considered on the ground that she was 'unfit for membership'. The court granted an injunction to stop the hearing on the ground that the failure to obtain a majority meant that there was doubt whether the union had power to instruct its members to take action and therefore the claimant could not be 'unfit for membership' in disobeying this instruction. The result of *Esterman* is that the union will not be allowed even to consider the matter at all, as distinct from the court simply reviewing a decision already taken. The draconian nature of this case was somewhat mitigated by the Court of Appeal in **Longley v NUJ** (1987), where it held that an injunction to stop a hearing in advance would only be granted in 'exceptional circumstances' where no reasonable tribunal acting *bona fide* could possibly find against the claimant.

Does a claimant have to exhaust all internal remedies before making an application to the court? In **Leigh v NUR** (1970) the claimant was nominated as a candidate in the election for president of the union but the general secretary refused to approve his candidature. The claimant took action in the courts to rescind this action and the union contended that he should first exhaust the remedies in the union's rule book before taking legal action. Goff J, in the High Court, held that an express clause in the rules that a claimant must first exhaust legal remedies cannot oust the jurisdiction of the courts to hear claims that the rules have been broken, but a claimant must show a good reason why a court should intervene *before* the remedies in the rule book are exhausted.

A related issue is whether the rule in **Foss v Harbottle** (1843), which is applied to companies, also applies to trade unions. The effect of this rule is that if something is done which can be ratified by a simple majority of members then no action can be brought by an individual in respect of it. The rule does not apply where it is alleged that the rights of individuals have been infringed and this obviously means that in many of the cases discussed above the rule could not be applied. In *Taylor* v *NUM (Derbyshire Area) (No. 3)* (1985) the claim was that expenses incurred on a strike were unlawful as the strike was *ultra vires* the union, having been called without a ballot. Accordingly, it was claimed that these expenses should be repaid by the officials concerned. It was held that repayment would not be ordered, partly because a simple majority of the union's members could resolve not to seek repayment and, in effect, ratify the decision to call a strike. Vinelott J observed that: 'The courts are, in principle, reluctant to intervene in the affairs of any association, corporation or unincorporated association . . . you can please yourself whether you call that the rule in *Foss* v *Harbottle* or not.' The point has been urged that this decision is wrong: if the payments were *ultra vires* then the decision to make them could not be ratified because an *ultra vires* act cannot be ratified (*Ashbury Carriage and Iron Railway Co. Ltd* v *Riche* (1875)).

Section 63 of TULRCA 1992 has an impact on the above situations by providing that, where a member applies to the union to have a matter determined, then if the union has failed to determine it within six months the court must ignore any rule requiring internal remedies to be exhausted in deciding whether or not to hear the action. This rule would not prevent a claimant going to the court *before* six months were up and in this situation the remarks of Goff J in *Leigh* v *NUR* (above) are still relevant.

The rules of natural justice

The rules of natural justice are:

1 the rule against bias;
2 the right to a fair hearing.

These rules have been applied to the decisions of trade unions and the following cases serve as good examples of such application.

Rule against bias

In *Taylor* v *National Union of Seamen* (1967) the general secretary of the union had dismissed an official and had then presided over the appeal made by him. Not only this but, during the appeal, he had made interventions which were prejudicial to the official's case. It was held that this was a clear case of bias. (See also *Roebuck* v *NUM (Yorkshire Area) (No. 2)* (1978).)

In *White* v *Kuzych* (1951) the union member objected to the inclusion on a panel hearing a disciplinary charge against him of a member known to be hostile to his views. It was held that this was not by itself evidence of bias. Lord Simon said that members with strong views on policy could still sit on a tribunal, so long as there is 'a will to reach an honest conclusion'. This is an important and realistic decision because where there is an issue on which there are strong feelings (such as, here, the closed shop) then members with views on it can still sit as long as they keep those views out of the meeting. If they were not allowed to sit at all, it could be very difficult at times to find a tribunal able to sit because all potential members would have views one way or the other.

The right to a fair hearing

A good example of the right to a fair hearing is *Radford* v *NATSOPA* (1972). Radford was facing a disciplinary hearing and refused to reveal to the union in advance the nature of his discussions with his own solicitor. He was then expelled forthwith for wilfully taking action against the union. It was held that, as there was no hearing on this charge, the decision to expel him would be quashed as it was in breach of natural justice.

A final point to note is that there is no automatic right to legal representation (*Enderby Town FC Ltd* v *Football Association* (1971)) although, on a practical level, it would be wise to think carefully before deciding whether to turn down a request for this. A request for *some* representation (not necessarily legal) should always be granted on a disciplinary charge especially as this is in line with the right to be represented by a 'worker's companion' at disciplinary hearings conducted by employers (see Chapter 11).

STATUTORY RULES ON EXCLUSION, EXPULSION AND OTHER DISCIPLINARY ACTION TAKEN BY UNIONS AGAINST THEIR MEMBERS

From the passage of the Trade Union Act 1984 onwards a new theme emerged in the legislation introduced by the 1979–97 Conservative governments on trade unions. This was that of 'giving the unions back to their members' and it led to many new rules, not only on disciplinary matters but also on related topics such as union elections.

The rules on disciplinary matters appear in two places: in ss 64–66 of TULRCA 1992 (dealing with unjustifiable disciplining) and in s 174 of TULRCA (dealing with the right not to be excluded or expelled from a union). There is an overlap between the two, as one of the forms of unjustifiable disciplining is expulsion. The reason for this is that s 174 is the successor to legislation which had its genesis in the Employment Act 1980 and which was designed to deal with where an employee had been excluded or expelled where there was a closed shop. Now that closed shops are no longer enforceable, there is a strong case for having a single code of legislation dealing with disciplinary action. Before dealing with the details, three preliminary points should be noted:

1 Section 64(5) expressly preserves the existing common law rights where disciplinary action has been taken by a union. In some cases it will be a question of choice whether to use statute or common law.

2 Where a person is *excluded* from a union then only s 174 can apply.

3 Where there is a complaint of unjustifiable expulsion then s 66(4) provides that the bringing of proceedings under either s 174 or s 66 will bar proceedings under the other head.

13

Trade unions: their status and their members

■ Exclusion or expulsion under s 174 of TULRCA 1992

Exclusion means where a person is refused admission to membership. In *NACODS* v *Gluchowski* (1996) the claimant was suspended from membership of the union but it was held that s 174 applies only to refusal of membership or expulsion and not to suspension.

Section 174(2) provides that the exclusion or expulsion of an individual shall only be permitted on any one of the following grounds:

(a) that the individual does not satisfy, or no longer satisfies, an 'enforceable member-ship requirement' contained in the rules of the union;

(b) that the individual does not qualify for membership, or no longer qualifies, because the union only operates in a particular geographical area;

(c) that the union is a single employer union and the individual either is not, or is no longer, employed by that employer;

(d) that the exclusion or expulsion of the individual is entirely attributable to the con-duct of the individual provided that it is not 'excluded conduct', which is defined below.

The term 'enforceable membership requirement' in (a) above is defined as one which restricts membership by reference solely to the following criteria, which are set out in s 174(3):

(i) employment in a specified trade, industry or profession;

(ii) occupational description;

(iii) possession of specified qualifications or work experience.

Accordingly, it is, for example, unlawful for a union to refuse to admit a person on ground (a) who satisfies any of the above criteria as laid down by the union.

The other significant provision is that found in (d) in s 174(2) (conduct) and here again the Act leaves nothing to chance.

Section 174(4) originally provided that conduct is excluded conduct if it consisted in:

(a) being, or ceasing to be, a member of another trade union or political party or where the individual is employed by a particular employer or at a particular place;

(b) conduct of a type which is specified in s 65 as one where the individual is protected from unjustifiable discipline.

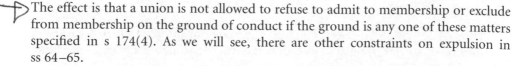

The effect is that a union is not allowed to refuse to admit to membership or exclude from membership on the ground of conduct if the ground is any one of these matters specified in s 174(4). As we will see, there are other constraints on expulsion in ss 64–65.

However, the rule preventing expulsion from membership on the grounds of mem-bership of a political party caused difficulty. In *ASLEF* **v** *Lee* (2004) the union had expelled Lee, who was an active member of the BNP, on the ground that his member-ship brought the union into disrepute. The EAT held that the question was whether the expulsion was attributable to his actual membership of the BNP (unlawful) or to his conduct, which would have been lawful under s 174(2) above. Section 33 of the Employment Relations Act 2004 now provides that exclusion or expulsion from a union is now lawful if it is entirely attributable to the individual's conduct (other than 'excluded conduct' – see above) and the conduct to which it is attributable is not 'protected conduct'. Protected conduct is conduct which consists in the individual's being, or ceasing to be, or having been or ceased to be, a member of a political party.

> ### Example
>
> The Toilers Union expels Jack for his membership of the Worcestershire Independence Party. This is unlawful if the reason was solely for his membership of the party but it is lawful if it was for his political activities even though *a subsidiary factor* was his membership.

13

(See Hendy and Ewing (2005), who discuss these provisions and the decision in *ASLEF v Lee* in the light of Article 11 of the ECHR.)

The remedy for a breach of s 174 is ultimately an award of compensation but the provisions are exceedingly complex. The essence of them is that a complaint is made to an employment tribunal which, if it upholds the claim, makes a declaration to this effect. The union then has a period of time in which to admit the person to membership or rescind the expulsion. If it acts in accordance with the declaration then compensation is awarded by the tribunal, the maximum being the same as for unfair dismissal (maximum compensatory award £60,900, maximum basic award £9,300). If it does not act in accordance with the ruling then the matter goes direct to the EAT (a most unusual procedure), which can award compensation with the same maximum but with a minimum of £6,600. (See *Bradley v NALGO* (1991), discussed below under s 65, for a case dealing with the amount of compensation.)

Note the effect which s 174 has had on the TUC's Bridlington Principles (below).

Unjustifiable disciplining under ss 64–66 of TULRCA 1992

Section 64 sets out the disciplinary sanctions which are caught by these provisions and s 65 sets out the actions by an individual which can lead to these sanctions. The effect is that if a member commits any of the acts listed in s 65 then the union cannot take any of the actions listed under s 64 as a disciplinary measure.

The following are the unjustifiable disciplinary sanctions listed in s 64(2):

(a) expulsion from the union or a branch or section of it;

(b) that a sum should be paid to the union or a branch or section of it;

(c) sums paid as subscriptions shall not be treated as having been paid or as having been paid for a different purpose;

(d) deprivation of some or all of the benefits, services or facilities enjoyed by members;

(e) encouraging or advising another union not to accept the person in question as a member;

(f) subjecting the person to any other detriment.

Trade unions: their status and their members

In *NALGO* v *Killorn* (1990) union members who had crossed a picket line during a strike were suspended and their names were advertised in a circular. The suspension was held to amount to a deprivation of benefits under (d) above and the advertisement of names was held to be subjecting them to a detriment under (f), as it caused them acute embarrassment.

Section 65(2) then lists the actions by individuals that can lead to the imposition of these sanctions. It must be emphasised that in any of these cases the sanctions listed above will amount to unjustifiable discipline. The list is as follows:

(a) failing to take part in or support a strike or other industrial action whether the strike or other action is called by the member's own union or another union;

(b) failing to contravene, for the purpose of the strike or other industrial action, a requirement imposed by the employer under the contract of employment or any other agreement with the employer;

(c) asserting that the union or its officials or trustees have broken the law;

(d) encouraging another to act in the ways set out in (b) or (c) above;

(e) contravening a requirement of the union which is itself an infringement of s 64;

(f) failing to agree to the deduction of membership subscriptions from wages;

(g) resigning or proposing to resign from a union or refusing or proposing to refuse to become a member of a union;

(h) working or proposing to work with persons who are not union members;

(i) working or proposing to work for an employer who uses non-union labour;

(j) requiring the union to fulfil its duties to members under TULRCA, e.g. dealing with ballots.

In addition, seeking assistance from the Certification Officer is also an action for which the disciplinary sanctions listed in s 64 are unjustifiable, under s 65(3).

Although this list might be thought to contain everything which a union member might do, certainly in the course of an industrial dispute, this is not so. In *Knowles* v *Fire Brigades Union* (1996) a fire fighter was expelled for having accepted a 'retained' contract to be available in his spare time although it was against union policy to accept these contracts. The Court of Appeal held that neither (a) nor (b) above were broken as there was no industrial dispute. The matter was simply one of union policy. In this case there would probably be no remedy either under s 174 above because expulsion for conduct cannot be on the grounds defined in s 65, which then leads us back to the point that s 65 did not apply here. The only possible remedy would be at common law.

It is possible that the provisions of s 174 are in breach of Article 11 of the ECHR and of Articles 3 and 5 of ILO Convention No. 87 on freedom of association. Article 11 gives a right of freedom of association (see above) and in *Cheall* v *UK* (1985) the ECtHR held that where a union excluded or expelled a person and the decision was in breach of its rules, or was arbitrary, or the result was that the person lost employment or otherwise suffered exceptional hardship, then the decision could be in breach of the ECHR. It is arguable that these are the only grounds for exclusion or expulsion under the ECHR and that the grounds in s 174 and ss 64–65 should be interpreted in accordance with the ruling in *Cheall*.

The remedies for a breach of ss 64–65 are similar to those laid down for breach of s 174 and are set out in s 66. In *Bradley* v *NALGO* (1991) members who had been expelled for not taking part in a strike were held to have been unjustifiably disciplined but were only awarded the minimum, as there was no evidence that as a result of their expulsion their future job prospects would suffer.

AMALGAMATIONS BETWEEN UNIONS AND DISPUTES BETWEEN UNIONS

Sections 97–106 of TULRCA 1992 provide detailed procedures for amalgamations between unions and transfers by one union of its members and assets to another. The details are beyond the scope of this book but what is of more significance are the 'Bridlington Principles' which have, since 1939, governed disputes between unions over membership. (They are known as the Bridlington Principles as they were first drawn up at the TUC conference held there in 1939.) These originally provided that unions would not accept as members those who were or had been members of another union without making enquiries from that union about the status of the applicant. If a member was found to have been admitted to membership in breach of these rules, the TUC Disputes Committee could either order a union not to admit that person or, if they had been admitted, to expel them. These rules then ran foul of what is now s 174 of TULRCA 1992 (above), dealing with the circumstances in which a person can be expelled from a union, and so the principles were revised in 1993 with the result that, if a person is admitted in breach of them, the remedy is the payment of compensation to the person's former union by the union which admitted that person, and there is no longer a power to order the union to expel the member.

POLITICAL FUNDS OF TRADE UNIONS

Trade unions have traditionally engaged in political activity, one of the main areas being support for Labour Party candidates at elections. These activities are governed by legislation, which was first made necessary by the decision of the House of Lords in *Amalgamated Society of Railway Servants* v *Osborne* (1911), where it was held that expenditure on political objects was *ultra vires* the union. This decision is yet another example of the anomalous status of trade unions, as the *ultra vires* doctrine belongs to company law and unions are not, of course, companies. However, the House of Lords drew an analogy with companies and held that the doctrine applied.

This decision led to the Trade Union Act 1913, which allowed a trade union to establish a political fund, separate from its other funds, and from which individual members would be allowed to opt out. The present legislation is contained in ss 71–87 of TULRCA 1992. This provides that union funds can only be applied to political objects if the members have approved the setting up of a political fund by passing a

13

Trade unions: their status and their members

393

'political resolution' in a secret ballot which has to be held every ten years. The rules for the ballot must be approved by the Certification Officer, voting must be by post, and an independent scrutineer must oversee the ballot.

Section 72 defines 'political objects' as expenditure of money on any of the following matters:

(a) any contribution to the funds of, or on payment of expenditure incurred by, a political party;

(b) the provision of services or property for the use of a political party;

(c) in connection with the registration of electors, the candidature of any person, the selection of a candidate or the holding of a ballot by the union in connection with election to any political office;

(d) the maintenance of any holder of any political office;

(e) the holding of political conferences or meetings;

(f) the production, publication or distribution of literature, film, sound recording or advertisements designed to persuade people either to vote or not to vote for a political party or candidate.

A vital point is that if the expenditure falls within any of these categories then it must be paid for out of the political fund. If there is no money in the fund then the expenditure cannot be made.

In *Paul and Fraser* v *NALGO* (1987) it was held that publication by NALGO of leaflets and posters in a campaign just before the 1987 general election against government spending cuts and their effect on the public services was within (f) above. Browne-Wilkinson J felt that a campaign to change the government itself was within (f) but a campaign just to change the *policy* of the government was not. The distinction between these two is not always easy to draw.

Where a 'political resolution' has been passed then s 82 of TULRCA 1992 provides that a set of rules must be established relating to the fund stating that, for example, any payments under the above categories must come from the political fund and that members who have opted out from making contributions shall not be discriminated against for that reason nor barred from holding any office other than one which relates to the management of the fund.

Whenever a political resolution is passed or renewed then union members must be told of their right to opt out of paying the political levy. Opting out can take place at any time and s 84 provides that if notice of opting out is given within one month of the political resolution being passed or renewed then there is no liability at all to pay the political levy. If notice is given later then the liability ceases from the following 1 January.

ELECTIONS OF UNION OFFICIALS

These are dealt with in ss 46–56 of TULRCA 1992. The object is to ensure that elections are held at regular intervals, that voting is by secret ballot and that no one is unreasonably excluded from standing for union office. Thus s 46 provides that elections must be held at least every five years for the following offices: all members of the executive, whether voting or not; president; and general secretary. Section 47 provides that no person shall be unreasonably excluded from standing for election, but it was held in *Paul and Fraser* v *NALGO* (1987) that a union can require that a candidate must have a certain level of support from the membership as a condition of standing. Section 47 also states that no candidate shall be required to be a member of a political party, but it does allow for the rules of the union to exclude members by class. The effect is that the union could not require candidates to be, for example, members of the Labour Party but it could lay down the negative requirement that no member of the Conservative Party could stand. There are detailed requirements for the conduct of elections: there must be a postal ballot and each candidate must be given the opportunity to have an election address produced and distributed by the union (s 48). The election must be supervised by an independent scrutineer (s 49).

LAW IN CONTEXT
Role of trade unions today

Trade union membership has shown a significant decline since the 1970s. In 1979, 55% of employees were trade union members (Pollert, 2005) but this had dropped to just 26% by the autumn of 2005. Union membership is higher for women than men and higher for older employees. Thus more than one-third of employees aged over 35 were union members compared to 25% of those aged between 25 and 34 (ONS). The number of workers covered by collective bargaining over pay declined from from 70% of employees in 1984 to 35.9% by 2003 (Pollert).

Ewing (2005) suggests that trade unions today have five functions:

Service function. This involves the provision of services and benefits to members and has inevitably increased in importance with the growth in employment rights and their increasing complexity. Nevertheless, this function is not new. Ewing (at p. 7) quotes the speech of the then Prime Minister, Tony Blair, to the TUC Congress in 2004 when he referred to the miners' union in the Durham coalfield which, when established in 1869, provided medical care and pensions to members and looked after legal claims and bereaved families.

Representative function. This means the function of representing members in the workplace, which may involve individual representation such as acting as a worker's companion (see Chapter 11) or collective representation including consultation and bargaining on behalf of the workforce.

Regulatory function. This, as Ewing puts it, 'acknowledges that trade unions are involved in a process of rule making that extends beyond their members or the immediate colleagues of their members'. The union may perform this function as a member of a body which sets terms and conditions for all employees in an industry or sector or by the union being involved in securing legislation which enhances the rights of employees. A good example of the latter is the extent to which the unions influenced the Labour government of 1974–9 to bring forward a mass of employment protection legislation, virtually all of which is still with us today.

13

Trade unions: their status and their members

→

Governmental function. This involves unions engaging with the government in the development of government policy as distinct from purely legislation.

Public administration function. This is to some extent linked to the governmental function but it goes wider. It is demonstrated by the involvement of unions in training the workforce, whether as members of bodies such as Sector Skills Councils or more directly by the Union Learning Fund which was set up to support the role of trade unions in learning. Another example of this function is the introduction of trade union learning representatives (see p. 385). There should be 22,000 of these by 2010 and they are intended to be a new type of union activist who will both identify the training needs of workers and assist in meeting them. A good example of this function and that of the governmental function is found in the response of the TUC to the White Paper, *Further Education: raising skills, improving life chances*, published in 2006. The TUC welcomed the recognition in the White Paper of the role of unions including the development of a union academy and the commitment by the Department for Education and Skills to discuss a TUC proposal to establish workplace collective learning funds. (The response is found on the TUC's website at www.tuc.org.uk/skills/tuc.)

The so-called 'Warwick Agreement' of 2004 is an interesting pointer to future trends. This was an agreement between the unions and the government over Labour policy and trade union law. (Cynics suggested that it was the price paid by the government for trade union contributions to the cost of the Labour Party's 2005 general election campaign.) For example, the government pledged that workers on official strike would be protected from dismissal until twelve weeks after the dispute rather than eight, and this was implemented by the Employment Relations Act 2004 (see Chapter 14). However, as Ewing (2005) points out, the agreement contains a number of omissions such as the lack of a commitment by the government to what Ewing calls 'core labour standards' and the legislation on trade union membership (see later in this chapter) remains in place. Ewing suggests that in reality the government is pushing the unions into the direction of a new 'supply side unionism' where the functions of unions are 'being determined in Whitehall rather than in the workplace'. A 'Warwick 2' is now talked of.

Note: Colling (2006) looks in detail at the services provided by unions to members and at union engagement with the law, by means of two case studies: one focusing on NATFHE (National Association of Teachers in Further and Higher Education) and the other on Prospect, whose members are engineers and technical specialists in the civil service and utility industries.

SUMMARY

This chapter begins by charting the history of the relationship between the law and trade unions and looks at the political background in which the law has developed. It then focuses on the relationship between the union and its members and thus looks at the internal workings of the union. It sets the law in context by considering the functions which trade unions perform in modern society and then the legal status of trade unions, the issuing of certificates of independence to trade unions and the recognition of unions for collective bargaining purposes.

The second part of the chapter looks at the extent to which the right to freedom of association is regulated by the ILO and under European law and then moves on to look at the detailed topic of exactly how the right of freedom of association is regulated in UK law. This leads to a consideration of the legal history of the closed shop and then to rights to time off work for union activities and for union representatives. The chapter ends by looking at how the law regulates the operation of union rules.

QUESTION

The rules of the Toilers Union state that:

(a) Any member or official of the union whose conduct is in the opinion of the union detrimental to the interests of the union shall be disciplined as the committee of the branch to which that member belongs sees fit.

(b) Any member whose membership of a political party, whose aims are, in the opinion of that member's branch committee, incompatible with those of the union shall be expelled from membership.

The Union asks you if these rules are lawful and, if they are not:

(a) what the consequences for the union would be if it acted under them; and

(b) is there any way in which the rules could be amended to make them comply with the law?

FURTHER READING

Brodie, D. (2003) *A History of British Labour Law 1870–1945*, Hart Publishing: Oxford. (Stimulating account which challenges many established ideas.)

Howarth, D. (2005) '*Against Lumley v Gye*', 68 MLR 195.

Mortimer, J. (2005) *The Trade Disputes Act 1906*, Institute of Employment Rights: Liverpool. (Published to mark the centenary of this Act and essential reading for anyone interested in the history of employment law.)

BIBLIOGRAPHY

Ewing, K. D. (2005) 'The Function of Trade Unions', 34 ILJ 1.

Colling, T. (2006) 'What Space for Unions on the Floor of Rights? Trade Unions and the Enforcement of Statutory Employment Rights', 35 ILJ 140. (Useful study of selected instances of how unions function in the enforcement of individual rights as distinct from collective rights.)

Davies, P. and Freedland, M. (1993) *Labour Legislation and Public Policy*, Oxford University Press: Oxford. (Invaluable study of the making of law in this area; some of its conclusions may need to be looked at in the light of Brodie (2003).

13

Trade unions: their status and their members

Donovan, Lord (1968) *Report of the Royal Commission on Trade Unions and Employers' Associations* (Cmnd 3623), HMSO: London.

Fairness at Work (1998, Cm 3968), HMSO: London.

Further Education: Raising Skills, Improving Life Chances (2006, Cm 6768), HMSO: London.

Hall, M. (2005) 'Assessing the Information and Consultation Regulations', 34 ILJ 103.

Hendy, J. and Ewing, K. (2005) 'Trade Unions, Human Rights and the BNP', 34 ILJ 197. (This looks in detail at *Aslef* v *Lee*.)

Gall, G. (2005) 'The First Five Years of Britain's Third Statutory Union Recognition Procedure', 34 ILJ 345.

In Place of Strife (1968, Cmnd 3623), HMSO: London.

Labour Research Department (2004) '*LRD Workplace Report*', Labour Research Department: London.

ONS. 'Labour Market Union Membership', **www.statistics.gov.uk** (these statistics are compiled regularly).

Pollert, A. (2005) 'The Unorganized Worker: the Decline in Collectivism and New Hurdles to Individual Employment Rights', 34 ILJ 217.

Roberts, A. (1994) *Eminent Churchillians*, Weidenfeld & Nicolson: London. (See especially the chapter on Walter Monckton. Pages 266–8 give a revealing picture of the government's desire to avoid a rail strike.)

For further resources and updates please go to the Companion Website accompanying this book at **www.mylawchamber.co.uk/duddingtonemployment**

14 Collective action

INTRODUCTION

INTRODUCTION

The central point of the law on collective action by trade unions is that the taking of such action (such as a strike) almost inevitably involves the commission of a tort and, possibly, a crime.

The history of the law on collective action, which includes strikes, go-slows and works to rule, is one of the law attempting to strike a balance between the right to engage in collective action and the rights of others, notably employers and employees who do not wish to take part in such action. The way in which this has been done is to provide that trade unions and others engaging in collective action shall enjoy certain immunities from being sued in tort or prosecuted under the criminal law. This is a typically British way of doing things. There is no broad principle guaranteeing the freedom to take strike action. The torts and crimes that may be committed remain unaltered. There is simply a limited immunity. However, this may change, as we shall see later in this chapter, when the effect of the ECHR is felt to a greater extent.

LAW IN CONTEXT
Industrial action today

The law on collective action can be appreciated by looking at the statistics on labour disputes which show a dramatic decline in the number of labour disputes in recent years. In 2005 the number of days lost to stoppages of work arising from industrial disputes was 157,400 and these were from 116 industrial disputes (Beardsmore (2006), from which all of these statistics are taken). This compares with the average number of days lost in the 1990s of 666,000, which in themselves showed a considerable decrease from those of 7.2 million in the 1980s and 12.9 million in the 1970s. Brown and Oxenbridge (2004) (at page 67) consider the relationship between strikes and union membership and point out that 'strikes were an inescapable part of collective bargaining in the early years' so that in the period 1893–9 the number of strikes per 1 million union members was 469 whereas in the period 2000–3 it was 22. This, as they point out, demonstrates how vital it was for unions to have immunity from actions in tort when calling industrial action (see below). The change in the attitudes

→

of employers in the 1990s brought about partly by the policies of the 1979–97 Conservative government and partly by changes in the structure of industry has led to the dramatic reduction in the number of strikes, the background to which was explained in more detail in Chapter 1.

One consequence of this lack of thinking from first principles is that UK law has never thought through precisely what, for legal purposes, industrial action is, and when it amounts to a breach of contract. This point is well worth noting at the outset and will be considered more fully later in this chapter in the section on individual employees and industrial disputes. In the discussion on collective action which follows it will generally be assumed that the action involved is a strike, which does obviously amount to a breach of contract, although, as we shall see, there have been attempts even here to argue in some instances that it may not be.

Example

The Union of Nuts and Bolts Operatives decides to call its members out on strike and issues notices to them with the instruction that they are to withdraw their labour from a certain date. The union at this point may have committed three torts:

1 The tort of conspiracy, by deciding to call a strike, although this is doubtful in view of the decision of the House of Lords in *Crofter Hand Woven Harris Tweed Co. Ltd v Veitch* (1942).

2 The tort of inducement of a breach of contract. This has certainly been committed, as the instruction to members to withdraw their labour is an inducement of a breach of contract (see below).

3 The tort of intimidation will have been committed if the union issued a threat to the employer that it would call a strike.

Note: the above torts are together known as the 'economic torts'.

Accordingly, the employer could sue the union for torts (2) and (3) and possibly (1) under the principle in *Taff Vale Rly Co.* v *ASRS* (1901), which held that a union could be sued in tort and its assets taken in satisfaction of a judgment. The effect of this would be that the union could be made bankrupt. Suppose, for example, that the workers at a factory went on strike for two months. Their employer loses £5m in lost orders and sues the union in tort for this. The union cannot pay, it is made bankrupt and it ceases to exist. The right to strike would, for all practical purposes, not exist.

The law prevents this from happening by granting immunity from all of the above torts provided that the action is taken 'in contemplation or furtherance of a trade dispute'. The meaning of this phrase will be considered later, but it can be said for now that the strike call by the union in the above example would have immunity as a trade dispute.

There is, however, one further hurdle which the union will have to surmount in order to gain immunity: the strike must have the support of a ballot which satisfies the statutory requirements.

The following flow chart shows the relevant factors in deciding whether a union is liable for the economic torts.

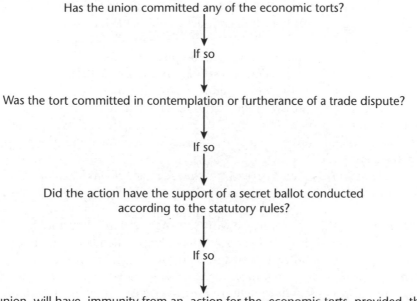

Has the union committed any of the economic torts?

If so

Was the tort committed in contemplation or furtherance of a trade dispute?

If so

Did the action have the support of a secret ballot conducted according to the statutory rules?

If so

The union will have immunity from an action for the economic torts provided that:
(a) the action is not secondary action
and
(b) the action is not taken for a prohibited purpose

14

Collective action

THE LIABILITY OF TRADE UNIONS IN SPECIFIC TORTS

The tort of inducement of a breach of contract

This tort can be committed either by a direct inducement of a breach or by an indirect one.

Direct inducement

The following diagram shows how this tort can be committed:

Union
Induces
Member   To break contract with   Employer
X   Y

The strike call induces X, a union member, to break his contract of employment with Y, his employer

This is where X induces Y to break a contract which Y has made with Z. Its origin is in the decision in *Lumley v Gye* (1853), where the owner of a theatre (X) was liable for inducement by persuading a singer (Y) to break her contract with the manager of another theatre (Z) so that she could sing for X instead. The organisers of industrial action which amounts to a breach of contract will be liable for inducement by calling on employees to take the action.

An essential point is that the actual inducement is aimed at one or more of the parties to the contract. In *Middlebrook Mushrooms Ltd v TGWU* (1993) mushroom growers were in dispute with a union and the union distributed leaflets outside supermarkets supplied by the growers asking customers not to buy the growers' mushrooms. An action for inducement of a breach of contract failed, as the leaflets were not directed at the supermarket, in order to induce it to break its contract with the growers, but only at the customers.

The following points, which derive from the judgment of Jenkins LJ in *DC Thomson & Co. Ltd v Deakin* (1952), must be proved for an action for inducement to succeed:

Defendant must intend to interfere with contractual rights of another

First it must be proved that the defendant (the inducer) intended to interfere with the contractual rights of another. It seems that precise knowledge of the actual terms of the contract is not needed, so long as the defendant knows that a breach of the contract will result from the inducement. In *Emerald Construction Ltd v Lothian* (1966) a building workers' union advised its members, on safety grounds, to take industrial action to force main contractors on sites to cease using sub-contractors. However, if the main contractors did so, they would be liable to the sub-contractors for breach of contract. The union argued that it would not be liable for inducing this breach of contract as it did not know that the only way in which main contractors could end contracts with sub-contractors was by breach. The Court of Appeal held that although the union may not have had precise knowledge of the terms of the contracts, it did have the means of finding out what the terms were and from this it has been argued that recklessness as to whether a breach is induced is enough. This is supported by the county court decision in *Falconer v ASLEF and NUR* (1986), where the union was sued by a season ticket holder for calling strike action which induced a breach of contract by British Rail in not running trains. The county court judge rejected the union's argument that they intended to harm British Rail and not the claimant, as the breach of the claimant's contract was a foreseeable result of the strike action (see also *Mainstream Properties Ltd v Young* (2007)).

Evidence of actual inducement

There must be evidence of actual inducement, such as direct instructions to union members to withdraw their labour, and that these were then acted upon so that a breach resulted. This element could not be proved in *DC Thomson & Co. Ltd v Deakin* (above). The union (NATSOPA) had a recognition dispute with X Co., who were printers and publishers. X was supplied with paper by Bowaters and NATSOPA asked other unions to help in supporting action against X. As a result, lorry drivers employed by Bowaters told their employer that they would object to delivering paper to X and therefore Bowaters did not ask them to do so. X sued NATSOPA for inducing a breach of their contract with Bowaters but the union was not held liable. The union had only asked other unions for help and – a crucial point – they had not induced Bowaters' employees to stop delivering paper.

Indirect inducement

The following diagram shows how this tort can be committed:

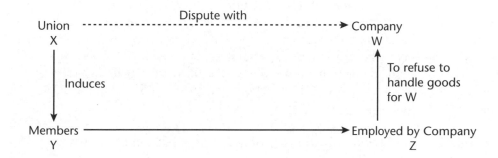

This is where X induces Y to break a contract (e.g. by going on strike) with Z and as a result Z breaks a commercial contract with W. A simple way of appreciating the difference between direct and indirect inducement is to remember that in direct inducement there are three parties but in indirect inducement there are four. Indirect inducement is generally known as secondary action, i.e. where a union (X) has a dispute with W and induces its members (Y) employed by Z to refuse to handle goods delivered for W so as to put pressure on W. The breach of contract between Z and W is indirectly induced by X. This was the situation in *JT Stratford and Sons Ltd* v *Lindley* (1965), where the union induced its members to break their contracts of employment with the result that their employer broke a commercial contract with another firm. The union was held liable to that firm for inducement. The effect of an exclusion clause in the commercial contract was considered in *Torquay Hotel Co. Ltd* v *Cousins* (1969). The defendant, a union official, told Esso that supplies of oil to the hotel would be met by a picket line, as the union was in dispute with the hotel. There was a *force majeure* clause in the contract between the hotel and Esso which excluded the liability of Esso for breach of contract where the failure to deliver oil was due to an industrial dispute. However, Russell LJ, in the Court of Appeal, pointed out that the clause excluded liability *for* a breach of contract; it did not mean that there was no breach. Therefore, the union was liable for inducing a breach of contract between the hotel and Esso. The reasoning of Denning MR was different. He held that the tort of inducement is committed even when a third person only prevents or hinders the performance of a contract, as well as when an actual breach is induced. It is not easy to envisage the circumstances when this will occur and it is submitted that the approach of Russell LJ is to be preferred. Nor is it clear whether this extension of the tort applies to direct as well as indirect inducement. (See also the discussion below on the tort of interference with trade or business, with which the remarks of Denning MR are connected.)

403

Defence of justification

This defence applies to the tort of inducement but there is only one reported case where it has succeeded in actions involving industrial disputes. This was *Brimelow* v *Casson* (1924), where chorus girls who worked for the claimant were paid such low wages that some of them resorted to prostitution in order to earn a decent wage. The union persuaded some theatre owners to refuse to honour contracts with the claimant in an attempt to put pressure on him and it was held that the union had a moral duty to do this and was not liable for inducing a breach of contract. But in *South Wales Miners Federation* v *Glamorgan Coal Co.* (1905) the defence of justification failed where the union persuaded its members only to work intermittently so that less coal would be produced. The argument was that as coal became scarcer its price would rise, the mine owners would make more money and wages would then increase as a result. Although the union thought that this action was justified as being in the best interests of both workers and employers, the court did not agree and held that the defence of justification did not apply.

Immunity from actions for the tort of inducing a breach of contract

Section 219(1)(a) of TULRCA 1992 provides that an act done in contemplation or furtherance of a trade dispute is not a tort only on the ground that it induces another to break a contract. The immunity applies to breaches of any contract, not just contracts of employment, and so in principle the immunity covers both direct and indirect inducement although, as we shall see, immunity for inducement for what constitutes secondary action is severely curtailed by statute. The phrase 'contemplation or furtherance of a trade dispute' is considered after all the economic torts have been outlined.

◼ Liability for inducement of a breach of other legal rights

Although this is a relatively modern development, the potential for an extension of the tort of inducement to areas other than breach of contract was laid down by Lord Macnaghten in *Quinn* v *Leatham* (1901) when he pointed out that any 'violation of a legal right' was a cause of action. Thus in *Meade* v *Haringay LBC* (1979) a school was closed by the local authority as a result of strike action by caretakers and other staff. It was said *obiter* by Denning MR, with whom Eveleigh LJ agreed, that the union involved had induced the local authority to act in breach of its statutory duty by closing the schools and that the statutory immunity (above) did not cover this (as it only applies to breaches of contract). In *Associated British Ports* v *TGWU* (1989) the Court of Appeal agreed that the tort of inducement of a breach of statutory duty could be committed provided that there was an independent right of action to sue for the breach of duty. Some breaches of statutory duty are actionable by individuals (as in *Meade*) but others are not. Discussion of this question more properly belongs in books on administrative law but the general rule is that it is a question of construction of the statute. The position is made clear in relation to one area by the Telecommunications Act 1984, s 16 of which expressly provides that where a licensed operator is in breach of its licence then the Director-General of Telecommunications may issue an enforcement order to the operator. If the operator breaches this order then any person who suffers loss where the contravention was due to industrial action may sue the organiser of that action (e.g. the union involved).

In addition to breach of statutory duty, the tort of inducement has been extended to inducements of equitable obligations, such as the obligation to account as in *Prudential Assurance Co.* v *Lorenz* (1971), where a union induced agents involved in an industrial dispute not to submit premiums, which they had collected, to the company. However, in *Wilson* v *Housing Corporation* (1997) it was not extended to inducing a breach of contract. The significant point is not so much that the tort of inducement exists in these cases, as there is clearly no reason why it should not, but that a union which commits it other than when inducing a breach of contract in circumstances covered by the statutory immunity will be liable. Therefore, whilst the statutory immunity (above) remains, it is gradually being reduced in scope by the development of this part of the law.

The tort of interference with trade or business

The notion of inducement has recently been extended to situations where there is no actual inducement of a breach but instead there is an interference not amounting to a breach. The origin of this may be seen in the words of Denning MR in *Torquay Hotels* v *Cousins* (above), when he referred to acts which hinder or prevent the performance of a contract. The extension of liability to these acts was approved by the House of Lords and, in particular, by Lord Diplock, in *Merkur Island Shipping Corporation* v *Laughton* (1983). The precise scope of this tort remains uncertain and there have been suggestions that a new 'super-tort' is emerging which will embrace not only inducement and interference but also intimidation, which is dealt with below. The problem for unions is that there is no express immunity from interference with a contract as distinct from breach.

The tort of intimidation

This is an old tort, dating from *Tarleton* v *McGawley* (1793). It has traditionally been committed where there is a threat of physical violence to make a person do or not do something but in *Rookes* v *Barnard* (1964) the House of Lords surprisingly extended it to industrial disputes. Rookes (a non-union member) was lawfully dismissed with proper notice as a result of an ultimatum by the union that there would be a strike if he was not. The tort of inducement was not committed, as the dismissal was lawful, but the tort of intimidation *was* held to have been committed, as there was a threat (the intimidation) to break contracts of employment by a strike and this amounted to an unlawful act which was intended to injure Rookes by causing his dismissal. The extension of this tort to industrial disputes was justified by Lord Devlin, who likened threats to clubs and observed that all that matters 'is that, metaphorically speaking, a club has been used'. It did not matter what it was made of, whether it was a physical club or an economic club. The effect is that a union which threatens strike a or other industrial action in breach of contract will commit this tort.

This decision caused alarm among trade unions, as the tort of intimidation in this context was not covered by the statutory immunities, although this was swiftly remedied by the Trade Disputes Act 1965.

Immunity from actions for the tort of intimidation

Section 219(1)(b) of TULRCA 1992 provides that an act done in contemplation or furtherance of a trade dispute is not actionable solely on the ground that it consists in threatening that a contract will be broken or that its performance will be interfered with. This applies, as with the immunity for inducement, to any contract and not just to contracts of employment.

The tort of conspiracy

This can be committed in two ways:

Conspiracy to injure another

Here the essence of the tort is the combining together rather than what is proposed, but it must be proved that the predominant purpose of the combination is to injure a third party and not to advance the interests of the conspirators. It was used in *Quinn v Leathem* (1901) to render a union liable for conspiracy where it had initiated a boycott of an employer's produce in the course of an attempt to enforce a closed shop. It was held that the union's purpose was not to advance the interests of their members but to injure the employer. This development was dangerous to the activities of unions as it struck at lawful activities (a boycott is not by itself unlawful) by labelling them as conspiracy on the basis of their motive. A wider view of the purpose of industrial action was taken in *Crofter Hand Woven Harris Tweed* v *Veitch* (1942). The claimant was a producer of cloth on the island of Lewis who obtained yarn (raw material) from the mainland rather than on the Hebrides, as it was cheaper. The union instructed dockers to refuse to handle this yarn because the imports were threatening the jobs of island workers who also produced yarn but it was held that the union was not liable for conspiracy as its purpose was not to injure the claimant but to protect the interests of their members. On this basis, it is very unlikely that a union would be liable for this type of conspiracy, as the purpose of industrial action is almost always going to be the advancement of members' interests or some other lawful motive, even though damage is caused to the employer's business in the form of lost business. For instance, in *Scala Ballroom* (*Wolverhampton*) *Ltd* v *Ratcliffe* (1958), conspiracy was not committed when a union's object was to force an employer to end a colour bar. Thus a strike call will almost always not be an actionable conspiracy.

Conspiracy to injure another by using unlawful means

The difference between this and conspiracy to injure (above) is that here the actual means proposed are unlawful, whereas there the tort was committed by the combination itself. This form of conspiracy would be committed by, for example, conspiring to cause personal injury and it is part of the general law rather than having a particular application to industrial disputes.

Immunity from actions for the tort of conspiracy

Section 219(2) of TULRCA 1992 provides that an agreement or combination to do an act in contemplation or furtherance of a trade dispute is not actionable provided that the act would, if done by one person, not be actionable. Thus there is immunity from conspiracy to injure another but not from conspiracy to injure another using unlawful means. In any event, in the light of the decision in the *Crofter* case, it is unlikely that a union would commit this tort.

The possibility of actions against unions for economic duress

Actions for economic duress have surfaced since the 1970s and the essence of the action is that a party to a contract was forced to enter it by some form of pressure that went beyond normal commercial pressure. It can be applied to industrial disputes, although its main use is obviously between businesses. An example of its use in industrial disputes is found in *Universe Tankships Inc. of Moravia* v *International Transport Workers Federation* (1982). The ITWF was conducting a campaign against the use of flags of convenience ships and, in pursuance of this, members of the National Union of Seamen refused to handle a ship belonging to the claimant. The union lifted this action only when the claimant made a substantial payment to its welfare fund. It was held that this payment was made as a result of economic duress and therefore the claimant was entitled to restitution of it. The difficulty with economic duress – and not only in cases involving industrial action – is drawing the line between legitimate and illegitimate pressure. The action for restitution for sums paid as a result of economic duress is not in tort and none of the statutory immunities outlined above applies.

Summary of the position on whether action is covered by a statutory immunity

There is statutory immunity for the torts of inducing a breach of contract, intimidation and conspiracy, provided that they are covered by the 'golden formula', explained below. There is no immunity from any other action. It has already been pointed out, but deserves further emphasis, that, as time goes on, the position of trade unions with regard to immunity in tort is gradually weakening. The situations described above, where there is no immunity, show how the law has developed over the last 30 years and how the immunities of unions in tort are thus being gradually eroded.

Does the action take place in contemplation or furtherance of a trade dispute?

The immunity granted from actions for the torts of inducing a breach of contact, intimidation and conspiracy only applies where the action takes place in contemplation or furtherance of a trade dispute. This is the celebrated 'golden formula' and the effect is that two questions have to be asked:

1 Was there a trade dispute?

2 If so, was the action which resulted in one or more of the above torts being committed in contemplation or furtherance of it?

Was there a trade dispute?

The term 'trade dispute' is defined by s 244 of TULRCA 1992 as a dispute between workers and their employer which relates wholly or mainly to one or more matters (see below). Before looking at these matters, there are three significant points to be made:

Definition of 'worker'

The term 'worker' is defined in s 296 of the Act and is the wider definition which includes not only those employed under a contract of employment but also those who undertake to perform work or services personally (see Chapter 4).

Former workers

The dispute can concern former workers if the dispute concerns the termination of their employment (s 244(5) of TULRCA 1992).

Dispute must be between workers and present employer

The dispute must be between workers and their present employer. Thus sympathy strikes are not covered by the statutory immunities, as sympathy strikers do not have a dispute with their employer. In *University College Hospital NHS Trust* v *Unison* (1999) a dispute about the terms which would be offered to employees when the undertaking was transferred to private employers was held by the Court of Appeal not to be covered as it was not a dispute with present employers but with potential future ones. This was partially reversed by the ECtHR in *Unison* v *UK* (2002), where it was held that the restriction on the right to strike had to be justified under Article 11 but in this case it was, as Article 11(2) allows restrictions which are proportionate and necessary in a democratic society. The ECtHR agreed with the UK government that the restriction did not prevent strike action being taken when actual steps were taken to downgrade conditions. Even so, this case is of general interest as an example of the application of the ECHR to collective rights.

This issue also arose in *Dimbleby and Sons Ltd* v *NUJ* (1984), in which the House of Lords refused to hold that there was a trade dispute where there were associated companies and one of these was engaged in a trade dispute but not the other. This reluctance of the courts to concern themselves with where economic power lies and willingness to look only at legal ownership of the organisation has been criticised. For example, Novitz and Skidmore in *Fairness at Work* (2001) point out (at page 140) that workers employed by interconnected companies may wish to take action to establish transnational standards in a group of companies and at present such action would not be covered by the statutory immunities. Wedderburn (1989), who is similarly critical of the present position, has referred to the process of restricting immunities rigidly to disputes with an employer party as 'enterprise confinement'. Moreover, the ILO has argued that workers should be able to participate in sympathy strikes so long as the actual strike is lawful (see Novitz and Skidmore (2001), pages 139–40). So far, the UK government has shown no sign of deviating from the position taken in the White Paper, *Fairness at Work* (1998), that the days of sympathy strikes are over and it must be said that if the law were to be changed to allow *unrestricted* secondary industrial action then unions would soon lose a great deal of goodwill. Is the solution one which, whilst recognising that the days of mass secondary picketing are over, still recognises that the present law does not take sufficient account of the economic realities of business organisation today? Possibly the development of the jurisprudence surrounding Article 11 may take us further.

Matters which can be the subject of a trade dispute

Section 244(1) lists the matters which can be the subject of a trade dispute as follows:

1 Terms and conditions of employment, or the physical conditions in which workers are required to work. In *BBC* v *Hearn* (1977) Denning MR held that the phrase 'terms and conditions' could cover terms which actually applied in practice without their ever being formally incorporated into the contract, but the scope of this is unclear.

2 Engagement or non-engagement, or termination or suspension of employment or the duties of employment of workers. This has been held to include a dispute about possible job losses (*Hadmor Productions Ltd* v *Hamilton* (1982)). However, it does not include cases where the action is in support of the reinstatement of workers who have been on unofficial strike (see below).

3 Allocation of work or the duties of employment between workers or groups of workers. Therefore, demarcation disputes are covered provided that all the workers are employed by the same employer. This was the element that was not present in *Dimbleby* v *NUJ* (above).

4 Matters of discipline.

5 A worker's membership or non-membership of a trade union. However, action taken to enforce union membership is not covered (s 222 of TULRCA 1992 (below)).

6 Facilities for union officials.

7 Machinery for negotiation and consultation and other procedures relating to these matters including union recognition.

The final requirement is that the dispute must relate 'wholly or mainly' to any of the above matters. Therefore disputes which are political will not be covered. In *BBC* v *Hearn* (1977) threatened disruption of the broadcasting of the FA Cup Final (because the broadcasting of it to South Africa would infringe the anti-apartheid policy of the union) was not covered. However, if it can be shown that the action, although having political overtones, is fundamentally concerned with any of the above matters then it will be covered. In *Wandsworth LBC* v *NASUWT* (1994) the issue was whether a boycott by teachers of testing under the national curriculum was covered. The Court of

14

Collective action

409

Appeal held that it was because, although the union was opposed to the principle of testing, the fundamental cause of the dispute was the extra workload which would be placed on teachers. An instance of where the dispute was the other side of the line is *Mercury Telecommunications* v *Scott-Garner* (1984), where action taken to try to prevent the privatisation of British Telecom was held to be motivated by the opposition of the union to privatisation as such rather than by fear of job losses as a result of privatisation.

Is the action in 'contemplation or furtherance' of a trade dispute?

This is the other hurdle which industrial action must surmount in order to be protected under the statutory immunities.

'In contemplation' of a trade dispute means that the dispute, although not actually occurring, must be imminent. In *Health Computing Ltd* v *Meek* (1980) a union sent out a circular instructing its members not to deal with a private company which was attempting to win contracts with health authorities. The reason was that the union feared job losses among its members if this happened. The court accepted the argument of the union that the object of the circular was to prevent a dispute if health authorities did in fact award contracts and so the action was covered. However, in *Bent's Brewery Co. Ltd* v *Hogan* (1945) the union sought information from managers of public houses about their takings prior to formulating a wage claim. The giving of this information would have been a breach of the managers' contracts of employment and it was held that the action by the union was not covered because there was no dispute, although clearly if any claim was not conceded there might be.

'In furtherance' of a trade dispute means that the dispute must actually be happening and thus if it has ended the immunities also end. One example of where the immunities would not apply is where action is taken during a dispute but is motivated solely by personal spite against, for instance, the employer as an individual.

Whether the action is in contemplation or furtherance of a trade dispute is a matter for the subjective judgement of those involved in organising it. The reasonableness of the belief that it *is* is irrelevant. This position was reached in *Express Newspapers* v *McShane* (1979), where the House of Lords overruled the objective test proposed by the Court of Appeal which, by making the courts to some extent the judge of whether the action came within the 'golden formula', had opened up a potentially wide field for judicial involvement in this area and one which was viewed with apprehension by the unions.

Summary of the position so far

Assuming that the actions of the union fall within the statutory immunities and that they are within 'contemplation or furtherance of a trade dispute' one might then assume that the union could safely conclude that it had immunity from actions in tort. Not so, however. Before going on to investigate the further possible legal pitfalls awaiting the organisers of industrial action, it might be helpful to look at an example of how the law works thus far.

> **Example**
>
> The Toilers Union calls a strike amongst its members at the premises of Gradgrind and Co. over a proposed reduction in wages and an increase in working hours. The strike call is a tort as it is an inducement of a breach of contract but, as the action is concerned with terms and conditions of employment, it is one of the matters which can be the subject of a trade dispute and the strike call is clearly in furtherance of this.

Situations where the statutory immunities are lost

The union cannot rest assured that it is safe from legal action because, in the following circumstances, a union can still be liable in tort for having called a strike or other industrial action:

1 where the action is viewed as 'secondary industrial action';
2 where the action does not have the support of a secret ballot conducted according to the statutory requirements;
3 where the action is taken for a purpose prohibited by statute.

These will now be considered in turn.

Secondary industrial action

This covers what are popularly known as 'sympathy strikes' and is defined by s 224(2) of TULRCA 1992 as where a person induces another to break a contract or interferes or induces another to interfere with its performance, or threatens to do so, and the employer who is a party to the contract is not a party to the dispute.

> **Example**
>
> Employees of the Great Worcestershire Railway Company are on strike over a proposal by the management to reduce overtime payments and the dismissal of certain employees for alleged breaches of safety rules. These come within the definition of a trade dispute (categories 1 and 2, p. 409 above) and the action will have the statutory immunities. Employees of the Herefordshire Railway Company come out on strike, also in support of their fellow workers, but this will not attract the statutory immunities, as there is no dispute between them and their employer.
>
> (*Note* that if there was a likelihood that the action by the Worcestershire Railway Company would be a prelude to similar action by other railway companies then the question would be whether the action by the employees of the Herefordshire Railway Company was sufficiently in contemplation of a trade dispute to bring it within the 'golden formula'.)

The removal of the statutory immunities from secondary industrial action was originally contained in legislation passed by the 1979–97 Conservative government but it has remained and the present Labour government has no plans to remove it. The

14

Collective action

present position has already been discussed above (under the heading 'Dispute must be between workers and present employer').

The only situation where secondary industrial action will be protected is where it arises in the course of picketing. Suppose that there is peaceful picketing which is within the law (see below). The pickets persuade a lorry driver who is about to deliver supplies to the factory to turn back. This will result in a breach of the driver's own contract of employment as he or she will have been contractually obliged to make the deliveries. However, the pickets will not be liable for having induced this.

Action which does not have the support of a ballot

The requirement to hold a ballot before industrial action was another change introduced by the last Conservative government which has remained unaltered in essence under the present Labour government. The law is contained in ss 226–235 of TULRCA 1992, supported by a Code of Practice on Industrial Action Ballots and Notification to Employers (2000), which covers 'desirable practices' on ballots. It is generally accepted that ballots are here to stay. Even Novitz and Skidmore (2001), who are critical of much of the present legislation, agree that ballots are right in principle, but they make the valid point that the requirements should not be so complex as to invite frequent legal challenges by employers. Furthermore, the ECtHR accepted in *NATFHE* v *UK* (1998) that the requirements in the legislation on some of the details of the ballot are not in breach of Article 11 of the ECHR (right to freedom of association) and thus by implication it accepted the legitimacy of the requirement of a ballot in itself. Nevertheless, if the procedural requirements are too onerous then this could be a breach of Article 11. In fact, despite some changes made by the Employment Relations Act 1999, the balloting requirements are undeniably complex.

The basic position, as stated by s 226 of TULRCA 1992, is that any act done by a trade union to induce a person to take part, or continue to take part, in industrial action is not protected (i.e. from action in tort) unless the action has the support of a ballot. The phrase 'industrial action' means that action other than a strike, such as an overtime ban or a ban on rest day working, is covered (*Connex South Eastern Ltd* v *RMT* (1999)). The fundamental rule is that a failure to comply with any of the requirements set out below will result in the ballot having no effect and the consequent loss of the statutory immunities in any resulting action. This is subject to one exception, contained in s 232B of TULRCA 1992, which provides that accidental failure to comply with the rules on entitlement to vote and the sending of ballot papers will not invalidate the ballot if the failure is on such a small scale as not to affect the result. One example would be the putting of the wrong address on the envelope containing the ballot paper.

The statutory requirements and other relevant points are set out below.

All members will be entitled to vote

Every member who it is reasonable *for the union* to believe at the time of the ballot will be induced (i.e. by the union) to take part in the industrial action will be entitled to vote (s 227). The words in italics, 'for the union', were inserted by s 23 of the Employment Relations Act 2004 to make it clear that the union does not have to give a right to vote to those members who might take part in the action even though the union itself does not induce them to (see Schiemann LJ in *RMT* v *Midland Mainline* (2001)). The courts have shown some liberality in the interpretation of s 227. In *BRB* v *NUR* (1989) the Court of Appeal held that an inadvertent failure to allow a member to vote by, for example, not supplying a ballot paper, did not invalidate the ballot. The test, imported from s 230, is one of reasonable practicability. In *London Underground* v *RMT* (1995) a particular problem arose: what is the position regarding members who have joined the union since the ballot? Can they still be called on to take industrial action? The Court of Appeal sensibly said that such action would still be protected, pointing out that the words in s 227 refer to those whom the union reasonably believes to be entitled to take part. As Millett LJ put it: '[the union] cannot identify future members'. There is also a requirement in s 228 for separate workplace ballots so that the proposed action must be supported by a majority in each workplace in order to make the action at that workplace protected from liability in tort. The reason is that workers in different workplaces may have different views on whether action should be taken. 'Workplace' is defined by s 228 as premises with which the worker's employment has the closest connection. Nevertheless, it is possible to have one ballot for more than one workplace in the following situations (s 228A):

1 where there is a common interest across workplaces;

2 where there is a common occupation amongst those balloted even though there is more than one employer;

3 where there is a single employer across different workplaces.

Ballot paper must comply with statutory requirements

The ballot paper must comply with the following requirements and a failure to do so will invalidate the result of the ballot:

1 It must contain at least one of the statutory questions, which are whether the member is prepared to take part in a strike or in other industrial action short of a strike. If both types of action are contemplated then the ballot must ask both questions.

2 It must, by s 229(4) of TULRCA 1992, contain what has become known as a 'health warning' which must be in these words:

> If you take part in a strike or other industrial action, you may be in breach of your contract of employment. However, if you are dismissed for taking part in a strike or other industrial action which is called officially and is otherwise lawful, the dismissal will be unfair if it takes place fewer than 12 weeks after you started taking part in the action, and depending on the circumstances may be unfair if it takes place later.

The intention behind this is admirable: to ensure that there is no doubt in the minds of those considering voting in favour of what the legal consequences might be. The problem is that too many of these words are incomprehensible. However, given the need to make the position clear, it is difficult to see what else could have been done. The statement cannot be commented upon in the voting paper and has to go in even if it is likely that the action will not involve a breach of contract, such as a ban on working voluntary overtime (see *Power Packaging Casemakers Ltd* v *Faust* (1983)).

14

Collective action

The ballot paper need not give any details of what the dispute is about, although the Code of Practice recommends that it does.

3 It must give the name(s) of those entitled to call the action in the event of a majority voting in favour. The reason is to prevent a strike call, for example, being made by local officials before the union's head office has given approval.

4 It must contain the name of the independent scrutineer. The scrutineer must report on the ballot within four weeks, stating whether he or she is satisfied with the arrangements for its conduct, although the scrutineer does not oversee the actual ballot (i.e. the counting of votes etc.) itself.

5 The union must provide the employer of those entitled to vote with a sample of the ballot paper at least three days before the voting begins (s 226A(1) of TULRCA 1992). The object is to enable the employer to challenge the ballot if he or she believes that there is an irregularity in it.

Ballot must be conducted according to statutory rules

The ballot must be conducted according to the following rules:

1 It must be by post.

2 Members must be allowed to vote without interference from the union, its members, its officials or its employees (s 230(1) of TULRCA 1992).

3 Voting must be in secret.

4 So far as is reasonably practicable, those voting must incur no direct cost.

5 All votes must be counted fairly and accurately.

6 Voting must be in secret (although the requirement of secrecy will not apply if this is not reasonably practicable).

7 The union must, by s 226A of TULRCA 1992, give seven days' notice of the ballot to employers of those entitled to vote and this notice must also give such information to employers as will help the employer 'to make plans'. The reason for this requirement is that it is felt that an employer needs to know what might happen so that, for example, disruption to customers is minimised. However, in the House of Lords' debates on this clause Lord Wedderburn considered that this was a 'most extraordinary provision' (quoted in Novitz and Skidmore (2001) at page 146) as he felt that it simply provided the employer with the ammunition to reduce the impact of a strike.

The extent of the details which the union should supply to the employer has been a particularly controversial area. The original legislation (contained in the Trade Union Reform and Employment Rights Act 1993) required the union to describe the employees in the notice to the employer. In *Blackpool and Fylde College* v *NATFHE* (1994) this was held to amount to a requirement that the union should supply the employer with the names of all those who were to be balloted. Moreover, as the words of the legislation were unambiguous, the court did not feel able to interpret the legislation so as to give effect to the right to privacy in Article 8 of the ECHR so that the names were not disclosed. The position is now clarified by s 22 of the Employment Relations Act 2004 which amends s 226A of TULRCA 1992, stipulating what information the union needs to supply to an employer to ensure that the rules are complied with: the categories of employees to which the employees being balloted belong and the total number in each category, a list of the workplaces at which they work and the total at each workplace, and the grand total of employees being balloted. Unions must ensure that this information is as accurate as is reasonably practicable.

The actual decision in the *NATFHE* case (above), in any event, was overruled by the provision in s 226A(3A)(c) of TULRCA 1992, as amended by the Employment Relations Act 1999, that a failure to supply names of employees would not be a ground for holding that the ballot was invalid. The Code of Practice states that the information should be such as to enable disruption to customers to be avoided if possible and to ensure health and safety and to safeguard equipment which might suffer from being shut down if left without supervision. It should be noted that the same rules on the information to be disclosed to employers apply when the union gives notice that industrial action will be called; and clearly the same objections also apply.

Possibility of intimidation by either an employer or a union during a ballot

Section 10 of the Employment Relations Act 2004 inserts a new para 27A into Sch A1 to TULRCA 1992 to deal with the possibility of intimidation by either an employer or a union during a ballot. It provides that employers and unions have a duty to refrain from 'unfair practices' during the period of the ballot. Unfair practices are defined as where the employer or union:

(a) offers anything as an inducement to vote or abstain from voting;

(b) coerces or attempts to coerce a worker to disclose voting intentions or how they have voted.

It also covers threats by an employer to dismiss a worker, and also where an employer takes or threatens to take disciplinary action against a worker or to subject a worker to any other detriment in connection with how they will vote or have voted in a ballot.

Action must begin within time limit

If the ballot has resulted in a vote in favour of a strike or other industrial action then the action must begin by a certain date otherwise the ballot loses its effectiveness and another will have to be held. The usual period is four weeks but the employer and the union can agree on an extension of up to another four weeks (s 234(1) of TULRCA 1992). The vital point is that the industrial action must commence within the time limit even though it might continue beyond then. In *Monsanto plc v TGWU* (1986) the action was suspended for two weeks to allow negotiations to take place and then resumed when these broke down. However, this was by then beyond the four-week time limit. The Court of Appeal held that as the action had commenced within the time limit there was no need for a fresh ballot as the resumption was merely a continuation of the action.

Action must be called by a specified person

The actual call for a strike or other industrial action must, as mentioned above, be by a specified person (s 233 of TULRCA 1992). In *Tanks and Drums Ltd v TGWU* (1992)

14

Collective action

the Court of Appeal held that where the specified person was the general secretary of the union then it was lawful for him to instruct a local official that he could actually take the decision to call the strike if negotiations with the employer were unsuccessful. However, the court felt that a decision by the specified person simply to delegate in advance all decisions to call industrial action would be unlawful. Specific delegation in each situation is needed.

Notice must be given

The union must, by s 234A of TULRCA 1992, give at least seven days' notice in writing to the employer of any industrial action following on from a ballot. Notice can be given at any time from the day on which the employer is informed of the result of the ballot. The same rule as to the information to be given applies as in cases where the employer is informed of the intention to hold a ballot: it must be such as to enable the employer to make plans. Moreover, if the action is intended to be continuous then the notice must state when it is to start and if it is to be discontinuous (i.e. only on certain days of the week or certain weeks) then the notice must state all the dates when it is to take place. An exception is where the employer and the union have agreed on a suspension of the action to enable negotiations to take place. In this case it can be resumed without the need for a fresh notice (s 234A(7B)). If a particular employer is not notified then the statutory immunities are lost as against him but not against other employers who *have* been given notice.

Failure to comply with rules

If a union fails to comply with all of the above rules then who can take action? Obviously there is the loss of the statutory immunities but, in addition, any union member can restrain the calling of any industrial action without the support of a ballot (s 62 of TULRCA 1992). An employer who is affected by a ballot called in breach of the statutory requirements can act by seeking an injunction once the action has begun and can use s 235 (below) so long as they are not companies because s 235 refers to 'individuals'. Section 235 is especially aimed at allowing a third party to claim an injunction. If such a party can show that the likely effect of unlawful industrial action would be to prevent or delay the supply of goods or services to them or to reduce the quality of goods or services supplied, they may seek an injunction to prevent it. This applies to any action which amounts to a tort and which is not protected by the statutory immunities (e.g. action not in contemplation or furtherance of a trade dispute, secondary action, etc.) and also to any action taken without the support of a ballot.

All procedures have been exhausted

The Code of Practice exceeds even the extensive requirements described above and, although not legally binding, breach of its provisions may be relevant when a court is deciding whether to grant an injunction in the circumstances described above. The Code suggests that no industrial action should take place until all the agreed procedures have been exhausted and that no industrial action should take place until the report of the scrutineer has been received. In addition, the Code recommends that ballots should not be used simply as a tactical means of, for instance, getting the employer to improve on an earlier offer, and should only be used when industrial action is really contemplated.

LAW IN CONTEXT
The significance of ballots before industrial action

Beardsmore (2006) shows that the number of ballots calling for strike action steadily increased between 2002 and 2004 with a peak of 919 in 2004. However, in 2005 the number decreased to 775. The proportion of ballots in 2005 which called for strike action and which resulted in a 'yes' vote was 86%. The number of ballots calling for action short of a strike was 606 and of these there was a 'yes' vote in 93%. Brown and Oxenbridge (2004) point out (at page 71) that the use of ballots by unions has led to their being an effective alternative to strikes: although, as the above figures show, there was a majority for strike action in the great majority of cases, in the great majority of *these* cases the strike does not occur.

Where the action is taken for a prohibited purpose

This is the third way in which industrial action which is taken in contemplation or furtherance of a trade dispute may nevertheless lose the protection of the statutory immunities. In effect, these are actions which the legislation so strongly disapproves of that those who take them lose the protection of the statutory immunities. Such action will arise in the following cases:

1 Where one or more of the reasons for the action is the fact or belief that the employer has dismissed an employee who took part in unofficial industrial action (s 223 of TULRCA 1992). This is part of the strategy of removing protection from unofficial industrial action. Precisely what such action is will be explained below.

2 Where one or more of the reasons for the industrial action is the fact or belief that the employer has employed or might employ a non-union member or has failed, is failing or might fail, to discriminate against a non-union member (s 222 of TULRCA 1992). The object of these provisions was originally to withdraw immunity from action to enforce the closed shop but the legislation has the effect of removing immunity from any action at all for reasons of non-membership of a union.

3 Where the industrial action is taken in order to induce a person to incorporate a requirement in a (commercial) contract that a union shall be recognised (s 225 of TULRCA 1992). Therefore, industrial action cannot be used as a means of getting union recognition for workers employed by another employer, as distinct from the employer with whom the union is dealing.

PICKETING

The word 'picketing' conjures up a certain image to most people: that of workers, during a strike, standing with banners outside the entrance to a workplace, trying to

14

Collective action

417

persuade fellow workers and others such as lorry drivers not to enter the workplace. Some readers may remember the mass picketing during the 1970s: for example, in the miners' strike. However, in order to begin a discussion of the legal issues surrounding picketing, it would be helpful to have a more precise definition. Unfortunately, this is what we do not have. The only way forward is to start with s 220 of TULRCA 1992 (dealt with in detail later in this chapter), which refers to the 'attendance' of pickets. Nevertheless, the actions of pickets *when* attending may involve breaches of the law and this section is concerned with precisely what pickets can lawfully do and when their actions will be unlawful. The area is a complex one, involving not only statute and common law but also the Code of Practice on Picketing. In addition, the ECHR needs to be considered. In essence the law needs to balance the right of pickets to assemble and put their point of view against the need to prevent civil disorder.

There is no right in English law to picket. However, s 220 of TULRCA 1992 provides that the attendance of pickets is lawful provided that the following conditions are satisfied:

1 The picketing is in contemplation or furtherance of a trade dispute.

2 The pickets are attending at or near their place of work (although trade union officials may attend at or near the place of work of their members).

3 Their only purpose is peacefully to obtain or communicate information or peacefully to persuade a person to work or not to work.

Section 220 does not define what is meant by 'place of work' but the Code of Practice (para 17) states that 'lawful picketing must be limited to attendance at, or near, an entrance or exit from the factory, site or office at which the picket works'.

The effect of s 220 is that any activities *outside* peacefully persuading or communicating in the circumstances set out above may incur civil or criminal liability.

Example

There is a strike at the firm of Nuts and Bolts Ltd and a number of employees are picketing the entrance to it by standing outside. They ask those employees who are going into work not to do so and try to persuade them to join the strike. Some agree to join the strike but others decide to go into work. The activities of the pickets, were it not for s 220, might amount to the following:

(a) the crime of obstruction of the highway;

(b) the torts of public and private nuisance;

(c) the tort of inducement of a breach of contract (committed by inducing others to break *their* contracts of employment by joining the strike). This would also apply if the pickets persuaded an employee of another organisation (e.g. a lorry driver) not to cross picket lines by making deliveries and thus he broke his contract of employment.

However, the protection given to picketing goes no further than this. As Lord Salmon put it in *Broome v DPP* (1974): '. . . it is nothing but the attendance of the pickets at the places specified which is protected; and then only if their attendance is for one of the specified purposes'. Thus in this case the actions of a picket in standing in front of a lorry to stop it entering a site were not protected and he was convicted of obstruction. In *Tynan* v *Balmer* (1967) the actions of pickets in continually walking round in a circle were also outside the immunity. Thus the refusal of the defendant (a union official) to obey the order of a police officer to order this to stop was held to be a wilful obstruction of a police officer in the execution of his duty.

Accordingly, the activities of pickets can give rise to liability in the following ways.

Under the civil law

Inducement of a breach of contract

It is interesting that this is the one occasion when the law still allows what amounts to secondary industrial action because, as the example above showed, the effect of the picketing can be that an employee (in this case the lorry driver) breaks a contract (his own) with *his* employer, who is not a party to the dispute.

Nuisance

This is a doubtful area. There are two torts: public nuisance and private nuisance. Private nuisance is an unlawful interference with a person's (in this context, the employer's) use or enjoyment of land but the courts have differed on the question of whether picketing can constitute a nuisance. In *Hubbard* v *Pitt* (1975) Denning MR had no doubt that 'picketing is not a nuisance in itself'. However, he pointed out that it can be a nuisance when it is 'associated with obstruction, violence, intimidation or threats'. If any of these are committed then it is likely that there will be prosecutions for specific criminal offences rather than simply an action for the tort of private nuisance. Is there any place for actions in private nuisance as in industrial disputes?

In *Mersey Dock and Harbour Co.* v *Verrinder* (1982) it was held that the actions of pickets in standing outside the employer's premises could be a nuisance if these amounted to putting improper pressure on the employer, but since then the Code of Practice has put a virtual maximum of six on the number of pickets, which can hardly be considered improper pressure. The most important decision is that in *Thomas* v *NUM (South Wales Area)* (1985), where Scott J held that mass picketing could amount to a nuisance and that harassment of workers who did wish to go into work could be what he called a 'species of private nuisance'. This extension of private nuisance went against the traditional view that actions for nuisance can only be brought by those with an 'interest in the land' (i.e. an owner or a tenant). This covers employers but not employees and this orthodoxy was reasserted by the House of Lords in *Hunter* v *Canary Wharf Ltd* (1997). Thus actions for nuisance arising out of picketing can, it seems, only be brought by employers. However, the wider question of whether there is an independent tort of harassment is not settled, although actions may now be brought under the Protection from Harassment Act 1997 (below).

Public nuisance is a tort which covers any activities which can cause inconvenience or damage to the public, and an individual who has suffered damage over and above that suffered by the public at large can sue. It is rarely used in relation to picketing but was in *News Group Newspapers Ltd* v *SOGAT* (1986), where the conduct of pickets at

14

Collective action

large demonstrations at Wapping extending over a considerable time was found to constitute public nuisance and *The Times* newspaper, which had lost journalists as a result, was entitled to claim.

Trespass

The tort of trespass is very rarely used in cases involving picketing and the likelihood of it being used at all has decreased since the decision of the House of Lords in *Jones* v *DPP* (1999) (which did not concern picketing but a protest near Stonehenge), that peaceful assemblies could amount to reasonable use of the highway. Previously, it had been thought that any use of the highway other than for passage could be a trespass, and that would have covered picketing, although the s 220 immunity would often have protected it anyway.

Harassment

The statutory tort of harassment, contained in the Protection from Harassment Act 1997, is primarily aimed at activities such as stalking and has, as we saw in Chapter 9, been used in cases of harrassment at work. It can also be applied to picketing. It is committed by a course of conduct which amounts to harassment of another and could have applied, for example, in cases such as *Thomas* v *NUM* and *News Group Newspapers* v *SOGAT* (above), where large numbers were involved.

▇ Under the criminal law

Obstruction of the highway

Obstruction of the highway, contrary to s 137 of the Highways Act 1980, occurred in *Broome* v *DPP* (above) and the difficulty is, of course, determining when a use of the highway becomes an obstruction. The presence of anyone standing on the pavement, for example, is an obstruction in that others will have to walk round that person to continue on their way. However, the courts take the view that to amount to an obstruction the use must be unreasonable and it is probable that picketing within the scope of s 220 and the Code of Practice would not be an obstruction.

Obstructing a police officer

Obstructing a police officer in the execution of his duty (s 89(2) of the Police Act 1996) amounts to a crime where, for example, pickets refuse to obey the instructions of the police to prevent a breach of the peace. In *Piddington* v *Bates* (1960) the police limited the number of pickets outside premises to two and it was held that Piddington had been correctly arrested for obstructing a police officer in the execution of his duty when he repeatedly tried to disobey this instruction in order to join the picket line. In *Moss* v *McLachlan* (1985) police stopped a convoy of miners, coming to join picket lines, about a mile and a half from the actual lines and, when they refused to obey an instruction to turn back, they were arrested. It was held that they had obstructed the police in the execution of their duty, as the police feared that there would be a breach of the peace if the convoy continued. This decision must now be read subject to that of *R* v *Chief Constable of Gloucestershire* (2006).

Specific offence under s 241 of TULRCA 1992

This was originally introduced by the Conspiracy and Protection of Property Act 1875 and makes it an offence for a person, with a view to compelling another to do or not to do an act which they have a right to do, wrongfully and without legal authority to:

(a) use violence to or intimidate that person or his wife or children, or injure his property;

(b) persistently follow that person about from place to place;

(c) hide his tools, clothes or other property or deprive or hinder him in the use of them;

(d) watch or beset his house or other place where he resides, works, carries on business or happens to be;

(e) follow that person with two or more other persons in a disorderly manner along a street or road.

This can be seen as the counterpart of s 220 in that, whilst s 220 confers the one kind of specific immunity which pickets have, s 241 creates the one specific crime which pickets can commit.

It appears that the words 'wrongfully and without legal authority' mean that the act must amount to a tort before it can amount to a crime under s 241. Indeed, in *Ward Lock and Co.* v *Operative Printers Society* (1906) Fletcher Moulton LJ said that s 7 of the Conspiracy and Protection of Property Act 1875 (the predecessor of s 241) 'legalises nothing, and renders nothing wrongful that was not so before'. The most common charge under s 241 is 'watching and besetting' but this will only be committed if the picketing is outside the immunity in s 220.

Public order offences

The Public Order Act 1986 introduced a number of specific offences which can be committed in industrial disputes. They can be grouped into two types:

Those which relate to the control of public meetings, assemblies and processions

Section 11 requires that advance (usually six days') notice of public processions is given to the police; s 12 allows the police to impose conditions on public processions; and s 13 allows the banning of them altogether if the powers in ss 11 and 12 are considered insufficient to prevent serious disorder. In the case of public assemblies (defined as those consisting of 20 or more persons in a public place wholly or partly in the open air), the police can impose conditions as to their duration, place and maximum numbers where the purpose of the organisers is considered to be intimidatory to others or where the assembly may result in serious public disorder, disruption to the life of the community or serious damage to property. Although these provisions are applicable to all public order situations, they clearly have an impact on picketing and this is especially so of s 14.

Those which relate to actual offences which may be committed as a result of public disorder

These are (in descending order of seriousness):

1 riot (s 1), which requires a common purpose on the part of at least 12 persons;

2 violent disorder (s 2), which requires the presence of three or more persons;

3 affray (s 3), which has no minimum number and is simply the use or threat of unlawful violence;

4 threatening, abusive or insulting words or behaviour (s 4);

5 intentional harassment (s 4A); and

6 disorderly behaviour (s 5).

Note that 4 and 5 above are treated equally seriously.

The Code of Practice on Picketing

This, as with all codes of practice, is not legally binding as such but is taken into account by the courts. The best-known provision is the suggested maximum number of six pickets for each entrance to premises, and this has led to six being considered as the normal maximum by the courts (see, for example, Scott J in *Thomas v NUM* (above)). Some other main provisions are that where an entrance is used by workers at other firms then the pickets should not ask them to join the strike; picketing should be confined to locations as near as possible to the place of work; pickets should only be designated as official if the union is prepared to accept responsibility for their actions; and pickets should ensure that essential supplies and services get through.

Picketing and the Human Rights Act 1998

Article 11(1) of the ECHR provides that: 'Everyone shall have the right of freedom of peaceful assembly.' This right has been held to apply to peaceful assemblies but not where the organisers intend disorder to result nor, clearly, where disorder does result (*G v Germany* (1989)). This balance between the right of assembly and the need to prevent public disorder is reflected in UK law and so it seems unlikely that the general thrust of the provisions explained above could be considered in breach of the ECHR, especially in view of 'the margin of appreciation' given to states in the area of public order. In *Gate Gourmet London Ltd v TGWU* (2005) the court considered the principles which should apply when deciding whether to grant an interlocutory injunction limiting the number of pickets and restraining them from approaching employees going to their place of work. It held that the courts must give due weight to the right to peaceful picketing guaranteed by Article 11 of the ECHR and the right to freedom of expression guaranteed by Article 10. However, here there was evidence that the pickets had threatened and abused employees going to work and so an injunction was granted.

Another situation where the present law on picketing could be challenged under the ECHR is this: suppose that there was a peaceful assembly of ten pickets. A police officer requires four of them to go in order to bring the number down to six. They refuse and are arrested for obstructing a police officer in the execution of his duty. What duty? The answer would be 'to prevent breaches of the peace'. But no breach is likely. The other issue is that there is no clear guarantee in UK law of peaceful assembly and indeed the law on what constitutes an obstruction, for example, is so vague that it could, if strictly interpreted, make it impossible to hold an assembly. The decision of the House of Lords in *Jones* v *DPP* (above) is a welcome clarification of the fact that trespass to the highway is not committed by peaceful assemblies, and this seems to bring the law into line with the requirements of the ECHR, although it should be noted that the minority (Lords Hope and Slynn) held that the right was confined to reasonable use as a highway and did not extend to assemblies. This view could well be at variance with the ECHR.

GENERAL LIABILITY OF TRADE UNIONS IN TORT

The discussion above has concentrated on the specific torts which trade unions are likely to commit when organising industrial action. It should not obscure the fact that trade unions are liable in tort as such and, outside the specific immunities dealt with above, they have no immunity at all and are, with regard to liability, in the same position as anyone else. This did not apply from 1906 until 1982, when trade unions had a complete immunity from actions in tort, but this immunity, originally conferred by the Trade Disputes Act 1906, was removed by the Employment Act 1982. Thus injunctions can be sought against unions and they can be liable for damages. This brings the risk that the amount of damages awarded could be such as to bankrupt the union where the employer sues for losses due to a stoppage in production caused by a strike.

To meet this problem, s 22 of TULRCA 1992 provides limits on the amount of damages, based on the number of members which the union has, as follows:

- less than 5,000 members: maximum award £10,000;
- between 5,000 and 25,000 members: maximum award £50,000;
- between 25,000 and 100,000 members: maximum award £125,000;
- over 100,000 members: maximum award £250,000.

Moreover, any award of damages may not be met from the political fund. However, these limits do not apply where the union is sued for damages for personal injury nor where it is sued for breach of duty in connection with the ownership, occupation, possession, control or use of property. The effect is that the limit applies whenever the union is sued in connection with an industrial dispute but not otherwise. For example, if the union owned a vehicle which was involved in a crash whilst being used on union business and driven by an employee of the union, then the union could be liable for the full amount of damages if the negligence of the driver was found to be the cause of the crash.

14

Collective action

This example also illustrates another point: for what actions will the union be liable? Given that the union can only act through individuals, this is of crucial importance. The position is that there are two tests for establishing whether a union is liable for the individual's acts.

Where the action is brought for one or more of the 'economic torts'

Here s 20 of TULRCA 1992 provides that a union will be liable for acts authorised or endorsed by it where the act was done, authorised or endorsed by any of the following: the union's principal executive committee, general secretary or president; any other official or committee; any other person empowered by the rules to do, authorise or endorse these actions. There are detailed rules (contained in s 21) on when and how a union may repudiate actions so as to escape liability. In summary, they are that anyone one from the executive, general secretary or president must give written notice of the repudiation in writing as soon as reasonably practicable to the officials or committee whose actions are repudiated. They must also give notice of repudiation to every union member who might take part in the action which is now repudiated as well as to their employers.

Where the action is brought in respect of any other tort

In this case the test of whether the union is liable is whether the act was authorised by the union, either expressly or by implication. In *Heatons Transport (St Helens) Ltd v TGWU* (1972) the House of Lords held that custom and practice meant that a union was bound by the actions of shop stewards who had instituted the blacking of lorries in the course of an industrial dispute.

THE POSITION OF INDIVIDUAL EMPLOYEES IN EMPLOYMENT DISPUTES

At the outset of this discussion one small but significant point must be made: the legislation on collective action has, up to now, spoken of 'workers' as defined by s 296(1) of TULRCA 1992, which adopts the wider definition contained in s 230(3) of the ERA 1996. Thus it includes not only those who work under a contract of employment but also those who undertake personal services. However, from now on, in relation to the law on unfair dismissal, the narrower definition of employee in s 230(1) of the ERA 1996 is used, which refers only to those working under a contract of employment. It is suggested by Morris and Archer (2000, page 531) that this may be in breach of Article 11 of the ECHR, which states that the right to join a trade union for the protection of their interests is available to everyone. It is argued that a court may in future regard the use of the term 'employee' and not 'worker' in unfair dismissal legislation relating to industrial action as a restriction on this right under Article 11 and amending legislation will be required.

The foundation of much of the law outlined above is the simple fact that a strike is a breach of the contract of employment. In *Morgan v Fry* (1968) Denning MR put forward a different view: that provided that the length of notice of strike action is of at least the length of the notice required to terminate contracts of employment then the strike only suspends the contract and does not break it. This view was not accepted in the later case of *Simmons v Hoover Ltd* (1977), where the orthodox view that a strike is a breach of contract was restated and this has gone unchallenged since then.

It is worth noting the suggestion of Elias (1994) that strikes which are called in response to repudiatory breaches of contract by the employer (e.g. changes in the contract of employment imposed by the employer) should *not* be considered to be breaches of contract by the employees. The breach is that of the employer and not the employees. This view, which seems to accord with orthodox contract principles as well as justice, was not accepted in *Simmons v Hoover Ltd* (1977) (see also *Wilkins v Cantrell and Cochrane (GB) Ltd* (1978)). However, it does have merit. The law on unfair dismissal treats some breaches of contract by employers as repudiatory so as to entitle employees to resign and, on an individual basis, to claim that their contracts have been terminated, thus leading to liability on the employer for constructive dismissal. Why should not repudiation by the employer also entitle employees to make, in effect, a collective resignation? The fact that this is labelled as a strike is irrelevant.

Before considering in detail the position of employees dismissed for taking part in strikes or other industrial action, we need to look at precisely what these terms mean, as this is an area where there is an unfortunate lack of clarity.

Strikes

Strikes are defined by s 246 of TULRCA 1992 as 'any concerted stoppage of work'. This may have made redundant the curious decision in *Lewis and Britton v E Mason and Sons* (1994) that action by one employee can constitute industrial action, although this will depend on whether the action in this case (a refusal by a lorry driver to drive an unheated lorry to Scotland in winter) was a strike or other industrial action. Note that there is a different definition of a strike for continuity purposes in s 235(5) of the ERA 1996 (see Chapter 6).

Industrial action short of a strike

The first question is whether particular industrial action short of a strike is a breach of contract. If it is, then the employer will have the right to withhold wages for the time during which the employee was engaged in the action (see Chapter 7) and may be able fairly to dismiss the employee (see below). What if it is not? In *Faust v Power Packing Casemakers Ltd* (1983) the Court of Appeal held that industrial action need not amount to a breach of contract where the action consisted of the employee 'applying pressure on his employer or of disrupting his business'. The reason given by Stephenson LJ was that to hold otherwise would involve the courts adjudicating on the merits of industrial disputes in unfair dismissal applications. The unhappy result is that whilst any action involving a breach of contract *will* amount to industrial action, one cannot say that the absence of a breach of contract means that there is no industrial action. Nor does the reasoning of Stephenson LJ seem convincing, even adopting his own words. For if the courts are to examine the motives for the action, which is what his words quoted above must inevitably mean, then surely this must involve the courts looking at what the dispute is about, which is not far distant from looking at the merits of the dispute.

Given this confusion, the best way forward is to look at particular forms of industrial action. The following are the main types.

1 refusal to perform duties expressly laid down in the contract;

2 a go-slow;

3 a ban on overtime;

4 a work to rule;

5 a withdrawal of goodwill.

Whether any of these are breaches of contract will depend on several factors:

Whether the action was a breach of an express term of the contract

Where the employee refuses to perform terms expressly laid down in the contract this will be a breach, as in *Miles* v *Wakefield MBC* and *Wilusznski* v *Tower Hamlets LBC* (both cases on withholding of wages – see Chapter 7). Whether a go-slow amounts to a breach is more problematic but it was held to be one in *General Engineering Services Ltd* v *Kingston and St Andrews Corporation* (1988). If overtime is voluntary then one would have thought that such a refusal would not be industrial action but in *Faust* v *Power Packing Casemakers Ltd* (above) it was held, applying the view of the law in that case, discussed above, that refusing to work voluntary overtime could be industrial action even though not a breach of contract. The other two situations are unlikely to involve express breaches of contract, but may be breaches of an implied term (below).

Whether the action amounts to a breach of an implied term of the contract to serve the employer faithfully

The nature of this term was explained in Chapter 5 but it is of particular significance in this context. In *Secretary of State for Employment* v *ASLEF (No. 2)* (1972) the Court of Appeal held that work to rule was a breach and in *Ticehurst* v *British Telecommunications plc* (1992) a withdrawal of goodwill by a manager was also held to be a breach. The deciding factor seems to be the intent with which the act is done. Thus in the *ASLEF* case Denning MR observed that an employee 'can withdraw his goodwill if he pleases. But what he must not do is *wilfully* obstruct the employer' (emphasis added). In *Ticehurst* Ralph Gibson LJ said that there would be a breach if the employee did or omitted to do an act where there was a discretion in the matter 'not in the honest exercise of choice or discretion . . . but in order to disrupt the employer's business or to cause the most inconvenience that can be caused'.

Was the employee taking part in the action?

A further consideration is whether the employee is actually taking part in the strike or industrial action. If not, then there can, of course, be no breach of contract. In *Coates* **v** *Modern Methods and Materials Ltd* (1982) a strike was called and an employee turned up for work but saw pickets at the entrance. She did not go in to work, as she said that she feared abuse if she crossed picket lines, so returned home. She was suffering from back trouble and her doctor gave her a sick note which covered the next two weeks. It was held that she had taken part in the strike as the fact was that she had not crossed the picket lines. Stephenson LJ held that employees must be judged by what they do and not by why they do it: 'those who stay away from work with the strikers without protest' are to be regarded as having taken part in the strike. An interesting example is provided by *Rasool* **v** *Hepworth Pipe Co. (No. 2)* (1980), where attendance at an unauthorised one-hour union meeting was held not to be taking part in industrial action because the meeting was not called with the purpose of putting pressure on the employer. This is an odd decision, illustrating the lack of clear thinking in this area, because taking time off to attend an unauthorised meeting was undoubtedly a breach, although the context was whether employees had been taking part in union activities.

STRIKES AND OTHER INDUSTRIAL ACTION AND DISMISSAL

Note: in the discussion that follows, the word 'strike' will be used to cover both strikes and other industrial action.

The law of contract allows an employer to summarily dismiss an employee who is taking part in a strike, as the strike is a repudiatory breach of contract. Similarly, payment of wages to those taking part in strikes and other industrial action can be withheld (see Chapter 7).

The law on unfair dismissal originally regarded dismissal of employees on strike or taking part in other industrial action as being in a kind of halfway house. Under the Industrial Relations Act 1971, tribunals had no jurisdiction to hear a complaint of unfair dismissal when striking employees were dismissed rather than the dismissal being held fair or unfair, although this was subject to qualifications, as described below. This legislation was, rather surprisingly, continued by the Labour government of 1974–9 and the effect was that dismissal was treated in exactly the same way as if the legislation had said that it was fair, because the employees were not entitled to any remedy. The Conservative government tightened the law in the Employment Act 1990 by removing all protection from employees who were on unofficial strike. The Labour government returned in 1997 was committed to changing the law to give greater protection from dismissal to striking employees but what resulted in the Employment Relations Act 1999 was, in the eyes of many, a somewhat half-hearted gesture in fulfilment of this commitment. The effect is that, *in some circumstances only*, dismissal of striking employees is automatically unfair. The position now is that there is a distinction between official and unofficial industrial action *and* a distinction between certain types of official industrial action. This complex position is the result of the intervention of successive governments in a piecemeal fashion without ever going back to first principles.

SUMMARY OF THE PRESENT LEGISLATION

1 If the action is official which is also protected under s 238A of TULRCA 1992 then dismissal is automatically unfair if the circumstances set out in s 238A(3), (4) and (5) apply. (This is the change made by the Employment Relations Act 1999.)

2 If the action is official which is also protected under s 238A of TULRCA 1992 but the circumstances set out in s 238A(3), (4) and (5) do not apply then the employees will not be able to make a complaint of dismissal if the employer has dismissed all the employees taking part, otherwise it may be unfair. (This is the position as it originally was in the Industrial Relations Act 1971.)

3 If the action is official but not protected then the position is the same as in 2 above.

4 If the action is unofficial then employees who are dismissed have no remedy in any circumstances. (This is the change made by the Employment Act 1990 and left as it is by the Labour government.)

These will now be looked at in detail.

Dismissal of employees who are on official industrial action which is also protected

There are two vital questions: is the action official and, if so, is it protected?

Official

The legislation defines 'official' negatively, in that s 237(2) of TULRCA 1992 provides that action is unofficial in relation to an employee unless *either* the action is authorised or endorsed by the union of which the employee is a member *or* the employee is not a member but others taking part in the action are members of a union which has authorised it. However, if no one taking part in the action is a union member then it is not to be regarded as unofficial. The reason for this last provision is that otherwise, if there was no union representation, then all action would be unofficial, which would, as we shall see, have unfortunate consequences. If action is not unofficial then it must be official and so one needs to look at the converse of the above situations.

Protected

This means that the union authorising or endorsing the action has, by virtue of s 219 of TULRCA 1992, immunity in tort for so doing. This means that:

1 the act involves the commission of one or more of the economic torts (see above);

2 the act is in contemplation or furtherance of a trade dispute;

3 the union has complied with the statutory procedures on balloting;

4 the action is not secondary industrial action;

5 the action is not taken for purposes prohibited by statute.

(The reason for these provisions is that it is felt that it would be wrong if the union was immune from an action in tort for calling the strike but employees could have action taken against them for taking part in it.)

If the action amounts to official protected industrial action then s 238A(2) of TULRCA 1992 provides that any employee shall be regarded as unfairly dismissed if the reason or principal reason for the dismissal is that they took protected industrial action and any one of the following three conditions are satisfied:

1 The dismissal took place within 12 weeks beginning with the day on which the employee started to take protected industrial action. (By s 25 of the Employment Relations Act 2004, days when a worker is locked out do not count to the 12-week period.)

2 The dismissal took place after the end of the 12-week period but the employee had stopped taking protected industrial action. (This is to protect the employee from being subjected to victimisation by the employer after returning to work.)

3 The dismissal took place after the end of the 12-week period and the employee was still taking protected industrial action but the employer had not taken reasonable procedural steps to resolve the dispute. The following factors are laid down by s 238A(6) for deciding whether reasonable steps have been taken by the employer:

   (a) Did the employer or a union comply with procedures laid down in any collective agreement which is applicable?

   (b) Did the employer or a union, after the start of the protected industrial action, offer or agree to commence or resume negotiations or unreasonably refuse a request that conciliation or mediation services be used?

Section 27 of the Employment Relations Act 2004 inserts a new s 238B into TULRCA 1992. This sets out the matters which must be taken into account when deciding if an employer or union has unreasonably refused a request that conciliation or mediation services be used after protected industrial action has begun. These are: did an appropriate person represent the employer/union at meetings, did the employer/union co-operate in arranging the meeting, did they answer reasonable questions and did they take any action that they had agreed to do at the meeting? The significance of this is that if an employer is held to have acted unreasonably in the above situations then employees will have the right to claim automatic unfair dismissal beyond the 12-week period.

However, in determining whether the employer has taken any of these steps, the tribunal shall not take account of the merits of the dispute (s 238A(7)). Thus there will be no point in the employer arguing that the reason why none of the procedural steps was taken was that the strike was so completely unreasonable that there was nothing to negotiate about.

14

Collective action

> ### Example
>
> The Toilers Union calls a strike among its members at Gradgrind & Co. in support of a pay claim. The strike is official as it is called by the union and the action is protected as the strike call amounts to an inducement of a breach of contract for which the union has immunity in tort under s 219 of TULRCA 1992. The action is not secondary industrial action, nor was it called for a prohibited purpose and it had the support of a ballot. Gradgrind dismissed Joan, an employee who was taking part in the strike, two days after it started. The dismissal of Joan is *automatically* unfair.
>
> (Readers may find that it helps in the understanding of a complicated area if situations 2 and 3 on p. 428 are applied to this example.)

◾ Dismissals where the action was official protected industrial action

Where the action was official protected industrial action but the circumstances in 1, 2 and 3 above did not apply, the rules are the same as for dismissals under the heading below.

◾ Dismissals where the action is official but not protected

Where the action is official but not protected, the circumstances in 1, 2 and 3 cannot apply.

The rules are the same under this heading and the one above. As mentioned above, this is the law as it was before the Employment Relations Act 1999 came into force and the basic position is that if all employees taking part in industrial action were dismissed and not re-engaged then s 238 of TULRCA 1992 provides that the 'tribunal shall not determine whether the dismissal was fair or unfair'. Stated slightly more precisely, s 238 provides that the only cases where a tribunal can hear complaints of unfair dismissal are as follows:

1 Where one or more relevant employees were not dismissed ('relevant employees' is defined by s 238(3) for these purposes as employees at the establishment where the employee works who were, at the date of the dismissal, taking part in the strike or other industrial action).

2 Where a relevant employee was, before the expiry of three months beginning with the date of his or her dismissal, offered re-engagement but the complainant was not.

In these cases the dismissal is neither automatically fair nor unfair but the tribunal will consider fairness in the ordinary way. Therefore, the employer must show that the reason for the dismissal was one or more of the potentially fair ones (see Chapter 11) and the tribunal will then proceed to decide reasonableness in accordance with s 98(4) of the ERA 1996. However, if the only reason given by the employer for the dismissal is that the employer was on strike then the dismissal will be unfair, as this is not a potentially fair reason within s 98(4). If the dismissal is held unfair then the House of

Lords held in *Crosville Wales Ltd* v *Tracey (No. 2)* (1997) that compensation cannot be reduced by the mere fact that the employee was participating in the strike, although it was stated *obiter* that conduct apart from participation might go to reduce damages. This could be, for example, where their behaviour was 'over-hasty and inflammatory' (per Lord Nolan).

Where, however, the reason for the selection of the striking employee for dismissal was union membership or activities then the dismissal is automatically unfair (s 152 of TULRCA 1992) and the same applies where the dismissal was for specified health and safety activities, reasons relating to family leave, grounds of pregnancy or childbirth, or acting or standing for election as an employee representative (s 238(2A) of TULRCA 1992).

Where the action is unofficial

Here, as stated above, dismissed employees have no remedy even where the dismissal was selective, except that dismissal on the grounds specified in s 238(2A) above will be automatically unfair.

LOCK-OUTS

Lock-outs require separate discussion because, although they are clearly different in nature from strikes and other industrial action, they are treated in the same way under unfair dismissal legislation.

The definition of a lock-out in s 235(5) of the ERA 1996 is probably applicable to lock-outs in industrial disputes, although it is found in a part of an Act dealing with entitlement to redundancy payments. It defines a lock-out in terms of action taken by an employer rather than action by an employee as in all other cases of industrial action. Such action can, by s 235(5), be the closing of a place of employment, the suspension of work or the refusal by an employer to continue to employ certain employees in consequence of a dispute. As such, a lock-out may well amount to a breach of contract by the employer. The question of whether the lock-out is a repudiatory breach will depend on its length, amongst other factors. The curious point is, however, that employees who leave and claim that they have been dismissed because of the lock-out will find that they are in exactly the same position as employees who are dismissed for taking industrial action where the conditions listed above did not apply or where the action was not protected.

Therefore, the protection afforded by s 238A of TULRCA 1992 to strikers dismissed within the first 12 weeks etc. does not apply to those dismissed as a result of a lock-out and they are left in the position which applied to all official strikers before 1999. Thus an employer can dismiss all employees locked out but if there are selective dismissals then there may be liability for unfair dismissal. The matter is complicated by the fact that the definition of 'relevant employee' differs for lock-outs as compared with strikes or other industrial action. For lock-outs, s 238(3) defines relevant employees as those 'who were directly interested in the dispute'. In *Fisher* v *York Trailer Co. Ltd* (1979) the employers sent a letter to all 34 employees on a shift, as they were concerned that they were 'going slow'. They required all of them to undertake that they would work at a normal pace but seven did not do this and were dismissed. The EAT held that *all* 34 employees were 'directly interested' in the dispute and so they could all be dismissed under the provisions outlined above. This could be a double-edged sword for employers: an employer might see it as an advantage to be able to dismiss all employees involved but then care must be taken actually to dismiss *all*, as if any relevant employees are not dismissed those dismissed could claim that they have been selectively dismissed under s 238 of TULRCA 1992.

The other problem with this area is that the boundary between a strike and a lock-out may be a thin one.

Example

Gradgrind & Co. decide to increase working hours of employees from 40 to 42 a week, together with a new shift pattern consequent on the introduction of new machinery. The company says that the cost of the new machinery has been such that it must be used more intensively than the machinery it replaced. Existing hours of work and shift patterns are written into contracts of employment. The employees decide that they will not return to work until Gradgrind & Co. agrees to negotiate on these matters but Gradgrind reply by saying that the employees will not be allowed into work unless they agree to the new arrangements. If this is a strike then, if it also amounts to official protected industrial action (see above), Gradgrind will not be able to dismiss anyone on strike for the first 12 weeks. If it is a lock-out then Gradgrind can dismiss all those 'directly interested' and will be safe from any action for unfair dismissal provided that *all* are dismissed (see above – s 238 (3) TULRCA 1992).

THE FUTURE OF THE LAW ON DISMISSAL FOR TAKING PART IN STRIKES, LOCK-OUTS AND OTHER INDUSTRIAL ACTION

This branch of the law has always been controversial and remains so. There is pressure for it to be changed so that, as suggested by Novitz and Skidmore (2001, page 178), 'the dismissal of any workers engaged in lawful industrial action is treated as a nullity'. Yet, at the same time, as the authors recognise, the whole idea of strikes, lock-outs and other industrial action is viewed as an anachronism, not least by the present government, with its emphasis on partnership in industrial relations.

Of one thing we can be sure: this part of employment law, like all others, is not static. It will go on developing, sometimes at an alarming pace (especially for those who write books on employment law!). Yet the subject will not cease to fascinate, beguile and, when the courts and the legislators between them have left us in a state of total confusion, as in the law discussed above, infuriate. But dull and predictable employment law will never be and this is one reason among many for studying it.

SUMMARY

This chapter looks at the law on collective action and begins by examining the history of the interaction between the law and organised labour and the fact that the calling of strikes automatically brought trade unions up against three torts:

- inducement of a breach of contract,
- conspiracy,
- intimidation.

It then looks at how the law initially solved this problem by giving unions blanket immunity in tort under the Trade Disputes Act 1906 and the present position under TULRCA 1992 where immunity is given where the action is within the golden formula of 'action in contemplation or furtherance of a trade dispute'.

It then moves on to look at how, even when the action is within the 'golden formula', a union can still be liable in tort for having called a strike or other industrial action:

- where the action is viewed as 'secondary industrial action';
- where the action does not have the support of a secret ballot conducted according to the statutory requirements;
- where the action is taken for a purpose prohibited by statute.

Finally the chapter looks at the position where individual workers go on strike or take other industrial action.

QUESTION

'Without the threat of recourse to industrial action, collective action would amount to little more than "collective begging". Given this, there is a strong case for reform of the current extensive restrictions on industrial action.' (Novitz and Skidmore (2001) *Fairness at Work*, Hart Publishing: Oxford.)

Do you agree with these statements?

FURTHER READING

Bogg, A. (2005) 'The Employment Relations Act 2004: Another False Dawn for Collectivism?' 34 ILJ 72. (A critical look at the provisions of this Act.)

BIBLIOGRAPHY

Beardsmore, R. (2006) 'Labour Disputes in 2005', *Labour Market Trends*, June.
Brown, W. and Oxenbridge, S. (2004) 'Trade Unions and Collective Bargaining' in C. Barnard, S. Deakin and G. Morris (eds) *The Future of Labour Law*, Hart Publishing: Oxford.

14

Collective action

Elias, P. (1994) *The Strike and Breach of Contract: Essays for Paul O'Higgins*, Mansell: London.

Fairness at Work (1998, Cm 3968), HMSO: London.

Morris, G. and Archer, T. (2000) *Collective Labour Law*, Hart Publishing: Oxford. (Although this is now somewhat dated, it is still the best general account of this branch of the law.)

Novitz, T. and Skidmore, P. (2001) *Fairness at Work*, Hart Publishing: Oxford. (This is a critical analysis of the Employment Relations Act 1999 and its treatment of collective rights. Chapter 1 is especially useful in its account of what are now the early days of 'New' Labour.)

Wedderburn, W. (1989) 'Freedom of Association and Philosophies of Labour Law', 18 ILJ, 1–39, p. 27.

For further resources and updates please go to the Companion Website accompanying this book at **www.mylawchamber.co.uk/duddingtonemployment**

Part 5

The future of employment law

In looking at the future of employment law, it is suggested that two fundamental assumptions need to be made:

(a) that any crystal-gazing is meaningful only if it is confined to a period of the next 50 years – any further ahead is impossible to predict;

(b) that the present economic policy of the UK government to ensure full employment within a highly skilled labour force will continue.

On these assumptions we can begin by returning to the four levels on which employment law was viewed at the start of this book. They are, briefly:

- the individual level,
- the collective level,
- the domestic political level,
- the international level.

In any projections about the future of employment law on these levels it is vital to remember that this branch of the law, to a greater extent than most others, is influenced by social, economic and political trends. With the scene thus set, let us look at the future of, first, individual and then collective employment law.

The structure of individual employment law is unlikely to change in that it is impossible to imagine that there will be any attempt to remove the right to claim unfair dismissal, for example. However, trends in the organisation of work may mean that the emphasis does change. There is almost certainly going to be even greater emphasis on flexibility in working patterns with more working from home and flexible working. This will mean that workers will increasingly be seen as individuals and will have less support from others whether these are fellow workers or unions. At the same time this may lead to subtle changes in the interpretation of the legislation on, for example, unfair dismissal, with perhaps greater emphasis on the need for employees to be flexible to meet the needs of the business. The development of some of the case law on 'managerial prerogative' (see Chapter 11) in the law on fair dismissals for 'some other substantive reason' may assist this process. This will obviously impact on collective employment law where it is at present impossible to imagine the unions regaining their traditional role in collective bargaining as the conditions which gave rise to it (large numbers of workers grouped in workplaces with a tradition of organised labour) have gone for ever.

On the wider front, employment relations look like being played out against a background of increasing globalisation with ever larger firms and, politically, the dominance of the USA. In this latter respect it is interesting to note the quite different part played by the law in industrial relations in the USA (see Chapter 1) and the reluctance of the USA to sign up to a number of ILO conventions. The ultimate challenge is to reconcile the traditional structure of employment law with the changes in the structure of the world economy brought about by the increasing liberalisation of trade. The impact of the Charter of Fundamental Rights in the new EC Constitution (see Chapter 2) will, if it ever becomes part of UK law, buttress the existing legal protections afforded to workers; but will it be sufficient in itself to meet the challenges posed by a rapidly changing world economic order?

FURTHER READING

Hepple, B. (2005) *Labour Laws and Global Trade*, Hart Publishing: Oxford.
Kaufman, C. (2007) *Globalisation and Labour Rights*, Hart Publishing: Oxford.
O'Higgins, P. (2004) 'The End of Labour Law as We Have Known It?' in C. Barnard, S. Deakin and G. Morris (eds) *The Future of Labour Law*, Hart Publishing: Oxford.

 For further resources and updates please go to the Companion Website accompanying this book at **www.mylawchamber.co.uk/duddingtonemployment**

Glossary of legal terms

Acts of Parliament Laws made by Parliament.

Appellant The party bringing an appeal.

Applicant The person(s) who bring(s) an action in an employment tribunal.

Civil law That part of English law which regulates the relations between individuals, including companies, as distinct from criminal law, which regulates the relations between individuals and the state.

Claimant The person(s) who bring(s) an action in the civil courts. Until 2000 the term was the 'plaintiff' and law reports until this date use that term.

Codes of practice These are generally issued under the authority of a statute but they are not legally binding. They are, however, taken into account by the courts and in practice one should be prepared to explain and justify a failure to observe the provisions of a code.

Common law That part of English law which has been developed by decisions of the courts as distinct from statute law which is made by Parliament.

Contracts Legally binding agreements.

Crown In practice, this means the executive arm of the state, which administers the country, the term having its origin in the fact that executive acts are carried on in the name of the monarch.

Defendant The person(s) against whom a civil law action is brought.

Ex parte Literally 'from one party' and meaning where only one party is represented on the initial application. This term is used in cases where applications have been made for judicial review against public bodies but the term used for cases brought today is 'from one side' rather than *ex parte*.

Force majeure Where a person acts under an irresistible compulsion.

Injunction A court order which commands a person to do or not to do an act which, if committed, would amount to a crime or a tort.

Obiter (in full, *obiter dicta*) This is used to refer to words spoken by a judge in a judgment which are not strictly necessary for deciding the case but which are said as an indication of the judge's views on a related point. The literal meaning is 'words on the way'.

Regulations In UK law this means laws made under the authority of an Act of Parliament by what is known as delegated legislation by, for example, government ministers. It also means a particular type of EU law (see Chapter 2).

Respondent This term has two meanings: the person against whom an action in an employment tribunal is brought and the party against whom an appeal in a civil action is brought.

Statute law A statute is another name for an Act of Parliament and therefore statute law is simply another name for Acts of Parliament.

Torts Wrongs which involve a breach of the civil law rather than the criminal law and therefore normally lead to an action for damages (compensation).

Ultra vires 'Beyond the powers': where a public body has acted beyond the powers given to it by statute. The result is that such an act is generally void.

Index

THE EMPIRE STOPS HERE

Philip Parker was born in Liverpool in 1965. As a publisher he ran *The Times* books list, which included works such as *Ancient Civilizations* and *The Times History of the World*. He has travelled widely in Europe, North and South America, North Africa, Asia and Australia. He lives in London with his partner and daughter.

THE EMPIRE STOPS HERE

A Journey Along the Frontiers of the Roman World

PHILIP PARKER

PIMLICO

To Tania and Livia

Published by Pimlico 2010

2 4 6 8 10 9 7 5 3 1

Copyright © Philip Parker 2009

Philip Parker has asserted his right under the Copyright, Designs
and Patents Act 1988 to be identified as the author of this work

All internal photographs copyright © Philip Parker 2009

First published in Great Britain in 2009 by
Jonathan Cape

Pimlico
Random House, 20 Vauxhall Bridge Road,
London SW1V 2SA

www.vintage-books.co.uk

Addresses for companies within The Random House Group Limited can be found at:
www.randomhouse.co.uk/offices.htm

The Random House Group Limited Reg. No. 954009

A CIP catalogue record for this book
is available from the British Library

ISBN 9781845950033

The Random House Group Limited supports The Forest Stewardship Council (FSC),
the leading international forest certification organisation. All our titles that are printed on
Greenpeace approved FSC certified paper carry the FSC logo. Our paper procurement
policy can be found at www.rbooks.co.uk/environment

Typeset by Palimpsest Book Production Limited, Falkirk, Stirlingshire
Printed and bound in Great Britain by
Clays Ltd, St Ives PLC

Contents

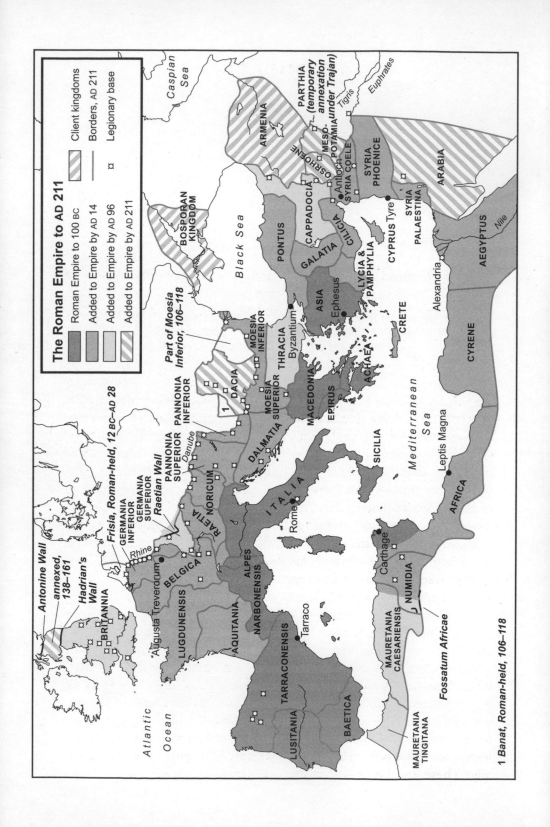

The Roman Empire to AD 211

- Roman Empire to 100 BC
- Added to Empire by AD 14
- Added to Empire by AD 96
- Added to Empire by AD 211

Client kingdoms
Borders, AD 211
⊡ Legionary base

Part of Moesia Inferior, 106–118

Frisia, Roman-held, 12 BC–AD 28

Raetian Wall

Antonine Wall annexed, 138–161

Hadrian's Wall

Fossatum Africae

1 *Banat, Roman-held, 106–118*

Caspian Sea

PARTHIA (temporary annexation under Trajan)

ARMENIA

OSRHOENE

MESO-POTAMIA

Tigris

Euphrates

BOSPORAN KINGDOM

Black Sea

PONTUS

CAPPADOCIA

GALATIA

SYRIA COELE

Antioch

SYRIA PHOENICE

ARABIA

CYPRUS

Tyre

SYRIA PALAESTINA

ASIA

LYCIA & PAMPHYLIA

Ephesus

CILICIA

CRETE

AEGYPTUS

Nile

Alexandria

MOESIA INFERIOR

MOESIA SUPERIOR

THRACIA

Byzantium

MACEDONIA

EPIRUS

ACHAEA

DACIA

PANNONIA INFERIOR

DALMATIA SUPERIOR

Danube

PANNONIA SUPERIOR

NORICUM

RAETIA

ITALIA

Rome

SICILIA

Mediterranean Sea

Leptis Magna

AFRICA

CYRENE

Carthage

NUMIDIA

MAURETANIA CAESARIENSIS

MAURETANIA TINGITANA

BAETICA

LUSITANIA

TARRACONENSIS

Tarraco

AQUITANIA

NARBONENSIS

ALPES

LUGDUNENSIS

BELGICA

GERMANIA SUPERIOR

GERMANIA INFERIOR

Augusta Treverorum

Rhine

BRITANNIA

Atlantic Ocean

INTRODUCTION

limes – frontier   *limites* – the frontiers

An invisible thread connects Carlisle and the Lowlands of Scotland with Hungary, Syria, southern Egypt, Libya and Morocco. A traveller can journey from Newcastle to Cologne, Budapest, Amman and Rabat without once crossing beyond the bounds of this line. This bond is not some Euro-enthusiast's vision of the future, but a common history as frontier regions of the Roman Empire. It is here, at the limits of its territory, that such an empire can speak to us most directly and most poignantly. It is here, along the vast length of its frontier, that I have chosen to investigate the complex entity that was Rome. I have concentrated deliberately on the edge of the Roman world, on the lands that promised victory, booty and glory and yet so often left the bitter taste of compromise or defeat instead. Here, unique societies developed, distinct from that of the mother-city, but which were still intimately influenced by the central authorities' determination of their laws, minting of their money and stationing of their garrisons to ensure internal security and fend off depredations from outsiders.

Rome is familiar and at the same time alien. Its history and heritage loom large in European and European-influenced cultures. But for all Rome's size, longevity and an impressive array of gods, poets, emperors and soldiers, our understanding of it is at best fragmentary. Hadrian's Wall, Julius Caesar, Antony and Cleopatra, Claudius, Attila the Hun: all these have entered our shared culture. Yet how exactly do those familiar characters fit into the vast canvas of Roman time and space? What evidence survives to bring them out of the shadows of myth into a historical world that is the lineal ancestor of our own? How did Rome come to conquer such an enormous territory, and where and why did its expansion halt and fold in upon itself to leave a joint legacy for the citizens of more than thirty modern countries? What is that legacy and how powerfully does it survive, both physically and cultur-ally? These are the questions this book seeks to answer.

If the Roman Empire had survived until today, it would constitute the seventh-largest country in the world, at some 6.5 million square kilometres approaching the area of Australia or Brazil. At their height, Rome's frontiers stretched approximately 10,000 kilometres, almost double the distance from London to New York. The span of time that Roman history covers is just as enormous: more than 2,000 years separate the city's traditional foundation date of 753 BC from the fall of Constantinople, its second capital, in AD 1453 (and the loss of its very last territories within a decade of that).

Rome had humble beginnings; the account of its foundation by Romulus marks the establishment of a small settlement occupying just one of the city's seven hills.[1] For four centuries thereafter, the future superpower struggled for its very survival in the face of invasions from neighbouring Latin tribes,[2] who were just as eager as the Romans for plunder and land into which they could expand. Yet by 200 BC, Roman legions had crushed the armies of their most dangerous opponent, the Carthaginian general Hannibal, and carried their eagle standards throughout the western Mediterranean. By the time of Julius Caesar, Roman forces had broken Gaul and in 55 BC crossed the English Channel to give the Britons a bloody nose.[3] Rome's rise was by now irresistible. The pace did not slacken, and one by one the neighbouring kingdoms fell into its grasp. By around AD 117, under the emperors Vespasian, Domitian and Trajan, yet another string of territories had been subdued: parts of modern Switzerland and Germany; Dacia; Armenia and Mesopotamia. As the legions advanced and more and more territory fell under Roman dominion, there was almost no concept of a frontier. The Roman emperors claimed the whole world as theirs by right. Certain parts of it they did not occupy merely because it was not profitable to do so.

In one sense, the Roman Empire had a series of 'frontiers', each one established at the time of a conquest and then rendered redundant when the line of control moved forward, a process that began at the very start of the city of Rome's existence and carried on until the furthest extent of the Empire's control, then going by stages into reverse until Rome itself fell in 476.

Rome's first frontier was the *pomerium*, by tradition the line that Romulus marked out with a plough as he demarcated the area that would belong to his new foundation. That Rome would long have trouble along its frontiers was tragically foretold by the action of his brother Remus, who leapt over the perimeter in a fit of jealousy that the new city was not being established on a site chosen by him, and was promptly murdered by Romulus. The *pomerium* was marked out by boundary stones – the

oldest of which date from the 1st century AD. This boundary, and therefore the ceremonial area of the city into which serving generals and
foreign sovereigns could not enter, and within which the dead could not
be interred, was extended several times, by the dictator Sulla in 80 BC,[4]
for instance, as well as under the emperors Claudius (AD 41–54) and
Vespasian (69–79), expansions often intended to mirror (and magnify) a
real enlargement of the Empire.[5]

Yet ultimately the pace of expansion slackened, the emperors grew
wary of the ambitions of successful generals, and advance legionary
camps became permanent garrisons. Static defences were constructed
to mark the edge of the Empire and to keep a watchful eye on the
unsubdued tribes and kingdoms beyond. Instead of new provinces to
be subdued, the lands beyond the frontier – known indifferently as
barbaricum – became the domain of barbarian tribes and the source of
occasional terrifying and devastating incursions into imperial territory.
This turning away from an automatic assumption that the Empire would
expand unceasingly had begun even under Augustus, who according
to Tacitus advised his heir (Tiberius) to 'keep the empire within its
boundaries'.[6] This did not, however, stop the imperially favoured poet
Virgil from including the formula 'To the Romans I set no boundaries
in space or time' in his great epic *The Aeneid*.[7] Perhaps it was the disastrous defeat by the Germans at the Battle of Teutoberger Wald in
AD 9 – which caused the loss of three legions – that soured Augustus's
early enthusiasm for territorial aggrandisement. In any case, the acquisitions under his successors were on a lesser scale, save for an attempted
grab of the whole of Mesopotamia by Trajan.

Exactly what the Romans meant by the word *limes* (or *limites* in the
plural) becomes a much more germane point once those frontiers
solidified. It is the term generally used by modern historians (and archaeologists) to denote the boundaries of the Empire and, more specifically,
those that were actively defended by a series of fixed fortifications or a
network of fortified cities. In truth, its earliest use seems to have referred
to a military road, normally employed either as an avenue of penetration into new territory or as a means by which to safeguard rapid
communications just behind the frontier. Only in the 1st to 3rd centuries
AD does the word come to refer to the general land frontier of the
Empire, though not in the modern sense of lines on a map that separate sharply delineated areas of political control. In the later Empire,
from the 4th century, its meaning changed once more to denote a frontier area, rather than the frontier itself, and the territory commanded by
a *dux*, a late-Roman category of military officer.[8] What it never seems

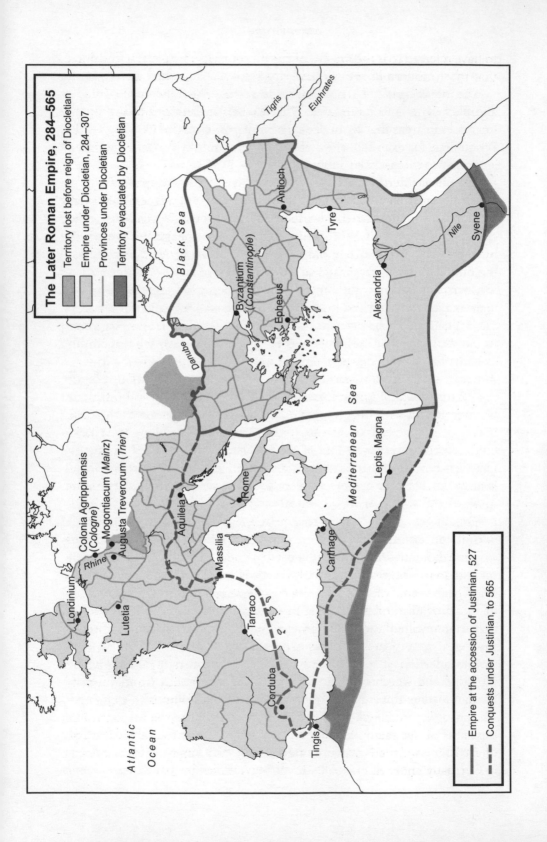

The Later Roman Empire, 284–565

Territory lost before reign of Diocletian
Empire under Diocletian, 284–307
Provinces under Diocletian
Territory evacuated by Diocletian

Empire at the accession of Justinian, 527
Conquests under Justinian, to 565

Black Sea

Tigris
Euphrates

Antioch
Tyre
Byzantium (Constantinople)
Ephesus
Nile
Syene
Alexandria

Danube

Mediterranean Sea

Leptis Magna

Colonia Agrippinensis (Cologne)
Mogontiacum (Mainz)
Augusta Treverorum (Trier)
Rhine
Londinium
Lutetia
Aquileia
Rome
Massilia
Tarraco
Carthage
Corduba
Tingis

Atlantic Ocean

to have referred to is the system of fortifications itself, precisely the usage that most modern historians have, for convenience, taken up.

The influence of the frontier stretched both ways, beyond the Empire and backwards into its interior. The Romans maintained outposts and fortresses in areas that would conventionally be regarded as 'beyond' the Empire (as, for example, at Divitia-Deutz in modern Cologne) and they arrogated to themselves the right to operate in *barbaricum* whenever they felt it in their interests to do so. Only with the Persian Empire, the most politically and militarily potent of Rome's neighbours, were treaties made that actually delimited the frontier and laid down regulations about contacts along it and where fortifications might be permitted to be built by each side.[9] Even if they did not, strictly speaking, lie directly upon the boundary itself, the principal cities in those provinces situated along the *limes* were strongly influenced by their proximity to the frontier. The legions that provided the Empire's principal military strike forces were often garrisoned some way back from the frontier itself, allowing them to move to wherever they were needed, rather than watching impotently as barbarian forces bypassed the frontier positions themselves.

Because of the Romans' own rather elastic notion of what a 'frontier' actually was, I have chosen to look at the history of the Roman frontier provinces, rather than the actual line of the border, whatever that might be determined to be. This allows a certain amount of flexibility regarding the actual date of the frontiers to be examined. In general I have chosen the maximum extension of the Empire, wherever it reached in any particular area, as long as the occupation was more than ephemeral. In North Africa, this includes the advancement of the *limes* towards the desert fringes under Septimius Severus (193–211), whilst in Britain it permits an examination of the occupation of the Scottish Lowlands under Antoninus Pius (138–61) and the building of the Antonine Wall, more than 150 kilometres north of the 'traditional' border along Hadrian's Wall. At the same time, it excludes treatment of the conquests by Trajan of the 'provinces' of Assyria and Mesopotamia in 115–17, on the grounds that they revolted and broke away from the Empire almost as soon as the Emperor returned from his campaigning there.

The question of exactly why the Roman frontiers ended up where they did, and whether there was a self-conscious policy on the part of Roman leaders towards them, has taxed historians almost ever since.[10] The apparent predilection for river frontiers where they were practicable seems to be one factor, for in Europe the *limes* came to occupy the line of the Rhine and the Danube, along much of their length. The campaigns in Germany under Augustus up until the Teutoberger Wald debacle may well have been aimed at extending the Empire's border to run along the Elbe. In the east the Euphrates, and to a lesser extent the Tigris, formed a similar role in demarcating the frontier with the Persian Empire. Although not ideal defensive positions, rivers did form barriers that could only be crossed at certain favourable locations (unless, as was the case in 405–6 with the Rhine, the river actually froze, permitting barbarians to cross over in uncontrollable numbers). They also acted as convenient arteries for trade, a vital advantage in an era when land transportation was costly and slow, and the need to supply large numbers of troops stationed in fixed positions made the rivers or their near vicinity obvious places to build forts to house them.[11]

In North Africa, and indeed in Britain, there was no such obvious river line, and in the case of the former it was the desert that formed a barrier into which the Romans did not, on the whole, cross. Oasis positions such as Bu Ngem and Ghadames in Libya or Castellum Dimmidi in Algeria were garrisoned, but here local conditions permitted the stationing of troops, and there was the added advantage that dominating the water sources meant that the routes along which local tribes could penetrate without risking severe hardship from thirst were already controlled by the Romans. To proceed any further would have meant difficulties in supplying their own forces and, in the case of permanent occupation, would have left an unfriendly environmental belt behind the frontier, which could not undergo the type of economic development or support the building of the network of towns that characterised most Roman provinces.

In Britain, the Highland zone posed a similar – if less daunting – ecological barrier to advancement. Although there would have been a certain logic in occupying the whole of the island of Britain, it was something the Romans came close to, but never quite achieved.[12] Once the resources available to the governors diminished, it never seemed worth the trouble to risk the security of the province to the south in an effort to absorb such mountainous regions that promised little in the way of plunder or produce.

That things were not always so simple is indicated by the case of Germany, where, as early as the reign of Vespasian, the Romans began to creep forward from the lines of the Danube and the Rhine, in part to find positions that would plug the hole where those two rivers do not quite meet in the north-east of modern Switzerland. Yet the final advance of just thirty kilometres under Antoninus Pius left an impressively straight 100-kilometre-long stretch of frontier, but one far removed from the original river line. Here, too, the environment may have played a part, for the heavily forested areas of the German interior offered little in the way of obvious economic benefit and had no tradition of urban culture such as even the hilltop *oppida* (fortified settlements) of Celtic Gaul had presented to Julius Caesar. In the absence of any central authority, the conquest of the German tribes was a will-o'-the-wisp. Once one leader had been beaten, his followers simply melted away into the forests, only for a new war chieftain to emerge elsewhere.

A debate has raged amongst historians since the 1970s as to whether the Romans in fact had a 'Grand Strategy' towards the question of expansion and how best to defend their frontiers. Sparked by Edward Luttwak's *The Grand Strategy of the Roman Empire* (published in 1976), discussion has centred on his thesis that there was a self-conscious and deliberate change of stance after the early phase of expansion. According to Luttwak, this developed into a middle situation of 'forward defence' whereby a maximum of resources was stationed at the frontier. This was then modified, under the uncontainable pressure of barbarians pushing against the borders, to a strategy of 'defence in depth' in which the rigidity of a fixed line held against all-comers was replaced by a deep network of positions extending far back into the frontier, where the intruders would become entangled and finally retreat.[13]

Yet to search for consistency in policy over such a vast period of time is probably fruitless. Doubtless individual emperors understood something of the nature of the challenges facing the Empire and deliberately initiated policies to address them. Thus, it is clear that Hadrian adopted a more defensive stance than his predecessors and did order the building of a set of fixed barriers. He also travelled far more extensively than previous rulers and so, presumably, gained more of an understanding of the real situation on the imperial frontiers than an emperor such as Tiberius, who rarely strayed from the environs of Rome when in power.

However, the Romans lacked the intelligence resources to predict the routes and strengths of the waves of barbarians that crashed against the frontiers from the later 2nd century.[14] Responses to these tended to be re-active and localised. Once a problem had arisen, it had to be solved, but it was rarely foreseen, with a solution devised to head it off. Whilst the rulers of the Roman Empire may well, therefore, have been constantly reassessing their options in the light of events, this hardly amounts to a 'Grand Strategy'. Major initiatives such as the conquest of Britain by Claudius in AD 43 scarcely amount to a strategy at all, conditioned more by the need to demonstrate military prowess and acquire glory than by any desire to promote the security or well-being of the Empire – in fact, Caligula's annexation of a large stretch of North Africa in AD 40 seems to have been prompted by a fit of pique at the dress sense of his cousin, King Ptolemy of Mauretania.[15]

Hadrian ordered the building of his eponymous wall across northern Britain in the early part of the 2nd century AD, and though it was perhaps intended to control movement rather than act as a solid barrier, the fortified Wall has since become an apt symbol of the increasing defensiveness of Rome. In Germany, too, watchtowers were reinforced at this time with more permanent and forbidding obstacles. And then, as if the very fear of retreat had summoned up its own genie, the pace of barbarian pressure against the frontiers increased. The catalogue of barbarian invasions grows ever more dense in the 3rd century, although it is hard to determine which, for example, of the ten recorded incursions between 253 and 298 gravely threatened the security of the Empire.[16] A series of civil wars and a revolving-door procession of short-lived rulers also seriously undermined it, and it was doubtless this weakness that contributed to the Romans' increasing inability to see off the barbarians. Decius was killed in battle against the Goths in 251 – the first emperor to die in combat against an enemy – and in 263 the Romans withdrew from a province in Europe for the first time, when they abandoned the Agri Decumates (part of modern Germany and Switzerland). Dacia (modern Romania) was similarly evacuated soon afterwards, and it was only under Aurelian in the 270s that a sense of equilibrium was restored. The historian Ammianus Marcellinus described the threatening barbarian invasions of this period as 'like a river which had burst its barriers'.[17] The barbarians did not go away, pressed from behind by yet more distant tribes, and in the end the *limes* proved untenable.

At the conclusion of the 3rd century, chastened by its close call in the turmoil of the preceding half-century, the Empire reinvented itself. Although some of his predecessors had undertaken reforms dictated by the desperate necessity of pressing crises, Diocletian (284–305) implemented more wholesale changes. Everything from the central administration to the army, the taxation systems and the long-standing organisation of provinces was modified, resulting, on balance, in a more centralised structure, with more resources immediately available to the Emperor to help him impose his will. In contrast, the government of the early Empire had been largely a matter of the *amici* ('friends') of the Emperor operating in a largely informal system with relatively few bureaucrats, who were in any case principally imperial slaves or freedmen.[18]

Although the process was not entirely straightforward – few of the 'simple' notions about the Roman Empire ever are – Diocletian broadly speaking doubled the number of provinces that the Empire had previously possessed. Thus Britain, which had beforehand been divided into two provinces, Britannia Inferior and Superior,[19] now had four provinces: Britannia Prima, Britannia Secunda, Maxima Caesariensis and Flavia Caesariensis. The resources available to the governors of each of these four provinces, most particularly the local garrison, were thus divided and diminished, so the danger of an overmighty governor recruiting a few of his neighbours and assembling a force that might overthrow the Emperor himself – an occurrence that had become disturbingly commonplace in the 3rd century – was largely removed. The number of bureaucrats necessary to service all these new governors was multiplied by the grouping of several provinces into a diocese, each supervised by a vicar. Thus the Diocese of Africa, which included modern Tunisia, much of Algeria and parts of Libya, comprised the provinces of Zeugitana, Byzacena, Mauretania Caesariensis, Numidia and Tripolitania. In turn, the dioceses were grouped together into praetorian prefectures (generally one for Gaul, including Spain and Britain; one for Italy, including most of North Africa; one for Illyricum, essentially much of the Balkans; and one for the remainder of the Eastern Empire).[20] For the sake of simplicity, I have largely ignored these new provincial boundaries and titles from the reforms of Diocletian, and my chapter divisions reflect earlier usage.

The office of prefect, which had previously designated the supreme army officer of the Empire, was now shorn of its military responsibilities and instead the praetorian prefect became a sort of bureaucratic supremo and, until the later 5th century, theoretically the most important person in the Empire after the Emperor himself. Despite this great increase in administrative personnel, the Empire still had relatively few officials compared to a modern state, and never aspired to the provision of services such as universal education or health-care. Even in the judicial field, much later Roman legislation – such as the setting of tariffs payable by litigants – had as much to do with rationing access to justice through the establishment of financial barriers as with any notion of equity for all.[21]

Even the government of the Later Roman Empire, with its uniformed corps of officials able to extend the reach of the authorities to an extent that had been inconceivable earlier, was not an efficient beast. Policies and laws determined at the centre were often watered down to the point of ineffectiveness by the time they reached the provinces, and even resorting to officials who lay outside the normal structures, such as the *agentes in rebus* – who acted almost as a secret police service in the Later Empire – only marginally increased the Emperor's ability to know what was actually going on in the vast territory over which he ruled. At the frontiers, this problem was magnified by distance; even employing the comparatively speedy journey times permitted by transit along the rivers, it could take a minimum of eleven days to get from southern Germany (near Ulm) to Sirmium (in modern Serbia),[22] while imperial rulings issued in Milan in the 4th century took somewhere between two and ten weeks to travel just as far as Rome. The lag between order and implementation could sometimes have near-comic effects. In AD 40 the Emperor Caligula sent a letter to Publius Petronius, then governor of Syria, ordering him to commit suicide; fortunately it took more than three months to reach him, and by the time it did, the governor already had in his hands another letter that informed him of Caligula's assassination in January 41. Under such circumstances it was extremely difficult, and ultimately pointless, to try to micromanage the border provinces.

The frontier, as established by the time of Trajan, links important places whose Roman provenance can only be guessed at in their current guise – Colonia Agrippinensis (Cologne), which hosted the Roman Rhine fleet; Mogontiacum (Mainz); Vindobona (Vienna), where the Emperor Marcus Aurelius died; Aquincum (Budapest), with its twin military and civilian amphitheatres; Naissus (Niš), which was so comprehensively destroyed by Attila the Hun that a Roman army had to camp outside its walls in a field filled with human bones; and Singidunum (Belgrade), which began life as a legionary camp; and other more brooding ruins, such as Volubilis (in Morocco), Leptis Magna (in Libya) and Petra (in Jordan). After the fall of the Empire, these cities and provinces went their separate ways, but all had shared the rule of Rome for centuries. Their common heritage cries out for recognition.

Roman emperors did not have the luxury, as we have, of looking at the extent of their empire and the course of the *limes* on precisely drawn maps, with towns and forts carefully marked out by neat squares and circles. The Romans were inveterate surveyors, carefully dividing out the land on which they intended to establish cities into neat squares. Yet the skills of the *agrimensores*, the men who performed this task (and equally, the division of the countryside around the towns, establishing the boundaries between segments with stones), were not put to similar use in mapping the Empire. The Romans, when they put their minds to cartography, thought in terms of 'Itineraries', or depictions of routes, showing the distances between stages on a journey rather than a topographically accurate representation of the terrain. The most famous of these, known as the Peutinger Table (or Tabula Peuteringiana),[23] is a medieval copy of a probably late-4th- or early-5th-century original. It is made up of a roll around 7 metres long and 34 centimetres wide, depicting more than 110,000 kilometres of roads, and showing 6,000 marked distances between towns, fort and *mutationes* (stations of the *cursus publicus* or public post).

More than 500 locations are decorated with miniature depictions of towns or other places of interest, which, in the case of the major cities of the Roman world, such as Rome, Constantinople and Antioch (Antakya), are quite elaborate. With its muted colours and stretched-out representation of the Roman provinces, the Peutinger Table forms an attractive mainstay of museums the entire length and breadth of the frontier. That it was not unique is indicated by another source, the *Antonine Itinerary*, a purely written (as opposed to visual) set of routes throughout the Empire, probably dating from the early 3rd century, which may have been prepared for use by the Emperor Caracalla himself.

The Peutinger Table has in particular provided an invaluable treasure trove of information for archaeologists and historians seeking to establish the names (and sometimes the locations) of Roman sites that are not otherwise attested in literary sources. Another equally useful resource (if not, strictly speaking, a map or an itinerary) is the *Notitia Dignitatum*, a list of principal office-holders, both civil and military, in the eastern and western portions of the Empire, together with the junior officials they supervised or the troops they commanded. It has a complex history: probably drawn up around 395, after which its eastern and western portions were then kept up to date haphazardly, with the western section being revised until about 408.[24] As well as information on the deployment of the late-Roman army – if the *Notitia* can be believed to portray this accurately, rather than promote a bureaucratic theory that was not reflected in reality – it also contains priceless indications of the names of garrison stations in the early 5th century. Information contained in it (and in more localised sources) assisted historians and archaeologists in determining the correct names of the forts along Hadrian's Wall, where the names were either not recorded at all by contemporary writers or were referred to in an ambiguous fashion.

By the time of the *Notitia*, the Empire had changed dramatically from the beast it had been at the time of Augustus, the first emperor. The reforms of Diocletian in the late 3rd century had been followed by an equally portentous transformation under Constantine I, who by the Edict of Milan in 313 decreed the toleration of Christianity in the Empire.[25] The urban topography of the Empire now began to shift, with rich benefactors, where they still existed, giving money for the construction of churches rather than temples or theatres, and the bishops emerging as powerful alternative power bases in the cities. Over time, the politics of the Christian Church, and struggles over who was to command obedience within it, began to overshadow power plays over the army and the central administration itself.

For all its success in weathering storms that would have destroyed any lesser state, the Roman Empire's frontiers began to leak badly in the 4th century, and by the early 5th century barbarian groups had come to be established permanently within what had formerly been the borders, many of them as *foederati* claiming a treaty relationship that permitted their otherwise troubling transgression. From the end of the 4th century the Empire's survival was further compromised by its division into eastern and western portions, in theory still part of one unit, but in practice pretty much looking after their respective interests. The last Roman emperors in the West fought vainly to stabilise the situation, with resources progressively compromised by each loss of territory and the destruction of previously productive cities. Once the Vandals became established in North Africa in 429 and the precious grain supply that its provinces had provided to Italy was lost, the game was nearly up. The Western Empire staggered on for nearly fifty years until what was in effect a military *coup d'état* by the Germanic majority in the army over-threw the last emperor in 476. Yet the Eastern Empire survived, and under Justinian (527–65) even managed to reconquer many of the lost provinces in the West, before these ephemeral successes were in turn swept away by another series of crises and invasions as the Lombards, the Avars and then – inspired by the new religion of Islam – the Arabs rolled back the tide of the Byzantine advance.

Although Byzantium[26] – the term by which historians generally refer to the Eastern Empire after the late 5th century – recovered, and indeed flourished once more, only portions of the old *limes*, in eastern Anatolia and along the Danube, remained. In general, where the Roman history of an area had not ended earlier – through its conquest by Germanic or Slav invaders – I have taken the Arab invasions of the 7th century as the point beyond which I will not trace its history. In travelling along the frontier all the way from Bowness-on-Solway in the north of England to Volubilis in Morocco, I have encountered more than five centuries of Roman history, in some twenty-one modern countries, covering a range of climatic variations from a snowstorm in Switzerland to a sandstorm at forty-five degrees Centigrade in Egypt's Dakhleh Oasis, and have covered more than 20,000 kilometres on the ground. Through all this astonishing variation, the staggering fact is that the Roman Empire and its *limes* endured for centuries, where many modern states have barely held on to their conquests for decades. Along the frontier a vibrant and unique culture grew up, which has bequeathed to us many towns and cities that still thrive today and, even where they do not, a legacy of some of the most beautiful and inspiring ruins in the world. In this sense Rome, and more especially its frontiers, are truly eternal.

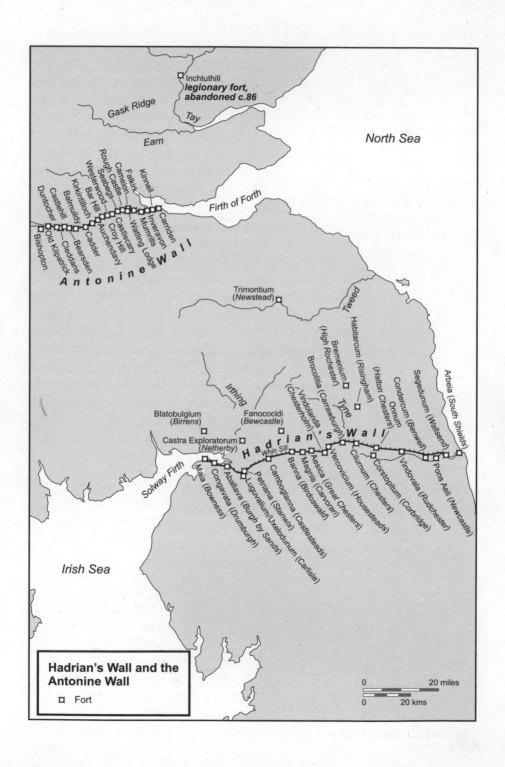

Inchtuthill
legionary fort,
abandoned c.86

Gask Ridge

Tay

Earn

North Sea

Firth of Forth

A n t o n i n e   W a l l

Duntocher
Old Kilpatrick
Bishopton
Cleddans
Castlehill
Bearsden
Balmuildy
Cadder
Kirkintilloch
Bar Hill
Westerwood
Auchendavy
Rough Castle
Seabegs
Croy Hill
Camelon
Castlecary
Falkirk
Watling Lodge
Kinneil
Mumrills
Inveravon
Carriden

Trimontium
(Newstead)

Tweed

Habitancum
(Risingham)

Bremenium
(High Rochester)

Brocolitia *(Carrawburgh)*

Arbeia *(South Shields)*

Segedunum *(Wallsend)*

Condercum *(Benwell)*

Onnum
(Halton Chesters)

Tyne

Irthing

Blatobulgium
(Birrens)

Fanococidi
(Bewcastle)

Castra Exploratorum
(Netherby)

H a d r i a n ' s   W a l l

Whin Sill

Vindolanda
(Chesterholm)

Vercovicium
(Housesteads)

Cilurnum
(Chesters)

Corstopitum
(Corbridge)

Vindovala
(Rudchester)

Pons Aeli
(Newcastle)

Aesica *(Great Chesters)*

Magnis *(Carvoran)*

Banna *(Birdoswald)*

Camboglanna *(Castlesteads)*

Petriana *(Stanwix)*

Luguvalium *(Uxelodunum) (Carlisle)*

Aballava *(Burgh by Sands)*

Congavata *(Drumburgh)*

Maia *(Bownes)*

Solway Firth

Irish Sea

**Hadrian's Wall and the
Antonine Wall**

⌗ Fort

0 _____ 20 miles

0 _____ 20 kms

CHAPTER I

Britannia

The hard road goes on and on – and the wind sings through your helmet-plume – past altars to Legions and Generals forgotten, and broken statues of Gods and Heroes, and thousands of graves where the mountain foxes and hares peep at you . . . Just when you think you are at the world's end, you see a smoke from East to West as far as the eye can turn, and then, under it, also as far as the eye can stretch, houses and temples, shops and theatres, barracks and granaries, trickling along like dice behind – always behind – one long, low, rising and falling, and hiding and showing line of towers. And that is the Wall!

Rudyard Kipling, *Puck of Pook's Hill*[1]

In truth it seems more like an ending than a beginning, the estuary of the Solway Firth wide and tranquil, the sun bouncing off the lazily drifting water, giving a rare sparkle and hint of the Mediterranean in this northern clime. The broad beach is backed by a thick strip of grass and a clump of swaying trees, its mud-water trails winding aimlessly towards a small headland. Across the water, in Scotland, four factory chimneys break the otherwise picture-pretty panorama of fields punctuated by a few low houses. This enticing, if unexceptional, landscape marks the beginning of Hadrian's Wall, one of the defining achievements of Roman military engineering.

For sure, Roman defence works of one kind or another continued on westwards and snaked round the coast of Cumbria to reach Lancashire,[2] but it is here that the Wall, as conceived and ordered by Hadrian, reached its westernmost point. It has impressed scholars, travellers and tourists for centuries, and its magnificent state of preservation – at least in its central section, striking straight and unyielding across crags and low ground alike – has served to awe, but has at the same time bedevilled our understanding of the nature of the Roman frontier. For it is tempting to think that such a linear barrier was intended as a definitive line to be held at all costs against potential invaders, who, suitably cowed, would lurk on their 'barbarian' side of the line, never to be admitted to the Roman 'civilised' side. Unfortunately, both the historical development of the Wall and its engineering give the lie to this oversimplified view. In fact the Wall most probably served as a mix of imperial propaganda – which, in view of its fame close to 2,000 years later, must be judged a success – and a means of economic control.[3]

The answer to exactly how the frontier came to be here lies in the nature of the Roman conquest of Britain. The island had first come into the sights of Rome in 55 BC, when Julius Caesar, flush from having subjugated the best part of Gaul in a freelance campaign that brought him enormous glory and caused not inconsiderable chagrin to his senatorial adversaries, decided that a sally across the 'Ocean' that traditionally marked the end of the world might add a little something to his already sky-high reputation. Although he returned in 54 BC and won a series of encounters with the rather disunited Britons, a revolt in Gaul the next year diverted his attention, after which the greater call of power politics on the central Roman stage meant that he never returned to the frankly rather peripheral island. Yet he may well have made some kind of treaty arrangement with British chiefs, and the expectation really must have been that his successes were a preliminary to the organisation in short order of Britain as a properly constituted Roman province.[4]

It took almost a hundred years for Claudius to despatch Roman arms back across the Channel and to begin the conquest of Britain in earnest. His motivation may have been the desire to win an easy victory, for his elevation to the throne had followed the murder of his nephew Caligula, and he was put forward by the praetorians, the elite imperial bodyguard, as much as a candidate who would not punish them for their involvement in the murder of his predecessor as for any perceived fitness for the job. Indeed, it was precisely his reputation as something between a drooling idiot and an academic stuck in an ivory tower that attracted them; Claudius would, they thought, be a pliable and malleable emperor, easily shaped by the interests of the faction that had promoted him.

Claudius, who was in fact nobody's fool and had feigned idiocy as a ploy to prevent his volatile nephew from having him assassinated, was badly in need of some martial achievements to bolster his position. Landing somewhere in Kent (probably at Rutupiae,[5] modern Richborough), in the summer of AD 43, his forces[6] rapidly secured the south-east, and the Emperor himself was able to make a brief cameo appearance to bask in some of the glory.

Over the next four decades, Roman control pushed inexorably northwards and westwards, weathering on the way a revolt by Boudicca's

Iceni in the early 60s, which nearly brought the whole enterprise of Britannia to a premature end.[7] Finally, by around 74, direct Roman control reached to the edge of modern Scotland. Four years later a new governor of Britannia arrived, who has, thanks to the biography written by his son-in-law Tacitus, become the most famous of them all.

Gnaeus Julius Agricola, who had previous experience in Britain,[8] was to serve an unusually long stint in the post.[9] He conducted a series of six campaigns, which projected Roman power ever further northwards, and looked set to establish the whole island of Britain as Roman territory. The campaigns can only really be followed by seeking to identify the marching camps which the Roman army built each evening as they campaigned, for the information provided by Tacitus is frustratingly imprecise and too vague to determine the exact lines of advance.

It seems, however, that by 80 the Romans had reached the estuary of the Tay, and forts were established along the line of the Forth–Clyde isthmus, the most obvious stopping point short of occupation of the Highlands. Finally, in 83, the Caledonians, the principal tribal group in the area, were pressured into standing and fighting a pitched battle, almost always a serious misjudgement on the part of Rome's barbarian enemies.

The location of this battle at 'Mons Graupius' is uncertain, but may have been somewhere north of Aberdeen.[10] The Caledonians, led by Calgacus, were roundly defeated; Agricola lured them off the high ground they had occupied by weakening his centre, which the disorganised tribesmen then rushed to envelop, leaving them vulnerable to a rout by fresh cavalry regiments that the Roman general had held in reserve. The victory had, unusually, been achieved almost entirely by auxiliary regiments; the elite legionaries had not been engaged. At any rate, some 10,000 Caledonians are said to have died, for the loss of just 360 Romans. Tacitus puts a moving and rather philosophical speech into the mouth of Calgacus after the battle. The Romans, he said, had 'made a desert and called it peace',[11] a taunt which the defeated have levelled at the victors throughout history, but which has always availed them little.

The Romans now settled in for a permanent occupation of Scotland.[12] Although Agricola was withdrawn, most probably in 84, a legionary fortress was built at Inchtuthil, on the Tay, about 25 kilometres to the north of Perth. It was probably destined to be the home of the XX Valeria Victrix legion, but a sudden change of plan altered the destiny both of the fortress and of the whole of Scotland. Some time after 86,[13] the order came to evacuate Inchtuthil, probably prompted by a crisis on the Danube, which called for fresh troops to be transferred there; the fortress was not even completed yet, for no *praetorium* (commander's house) or bathhouse has been located. When the legionaries left, they buried a huge quantity of nails – some one million in all – in an enormous pit, not wanting to cart such a weight of ironwork back south with them, but also wanting to deny the Caledonians the use of such a precious resource, which might be remanufactured into weaponry.[14]

The Romans were now left with insufficient forces to hold down the Highlands of Scotland, and the advance positions were abandoned. A line of towers that had occupied the Gask Ridge, blocking incursions through the surrounding glens, was also evacuated in the early 90s. None of these positions had really constituted a linear frontier; rather they were points from which further advances could be made, and now that any movement forward was not in prospect, the search began for a more sustainable set of strong-points further south. Tacitus sniffily notes that the complete conquest of Britain had in effect been achieved and then allowed to slip away.[15]

The exact stages by which this gradual retreat took place are obscure, but by the end of it, early in the reign of Trajan (98–117), most of the Roman conquests north of the Solway–Tyne isthmus had been abandoned, save for a series of forts, such as Trimontium (Newstead), which acted as outposts in territory that was presumably still notionally allied to the Romans and over which some level of supervision had to be exercised. Trajan's need for troops to carry out his own wars against the Dacians in 101–2 and in 105–6 then ensured that there would be no easy return to the north of Scotland.[16]

A Roman military road, which had been constructed during the governorship of Agricola, ran from Lugovalium, the fort at modern Carlisle in the west, to Corstopitum (Corbridge) almost at the eastern end of the isthmus. This road, which is known to historians by its name in medieval times, the Stanegate (or 'Stone Road'), now in effect became the northern frontier of Britannia. A series of other forts lay along the line,[17] built during the reign of Vespasian, Titus or Domitian,[18] sited around a day's march (or about 20 kilometres) from each other.

These posts did not form a comprehensive frontier system such as Hadrian was about to implement, but instead sat along a route that permitted easy movement of troops and rapid reinforcement. With a concentration of force not far removed from the recently evacuated territories, this enabled the Roman army to turn rapidly from a defensive posture to an offensive one, should imperial policy come to dictate it again.

In 117, Trajan died. He was succeeded by Hadrian, who had received a letter announcing his adoption by the Emperor just a day earlier, thereby making him the heir apparent. There was a great deal of gossip, possibly well founded, that Trajan had not in fact initiated the move, and that it had been concocted by a clique centred around his wife Plotina (who was rumoured to be rather too fond of the young general). In 122, Hadrian visited Britain. It was not an expedition that was widely noted by Roman historians, with only the *Historia Augusta* unambiguously reporting that 'he made for Britain, where he set many things right'.[19] There seems to have been some kind of disturbance in the province at the start of his reign and Hadrian now perhaps came to the far-flung north-west of the Empire to see for himself.[20]

Hadrian's Wall

For such a grand and showy feat of engineering, Hadrian's Wall receives curiously little notice in the sources of the time. Again, it is only the *Historia Augusta* that remarks that Hadrian 'was the first to construct a wall eighty miles in length, which was to separate barbarians and Romans'.[21] Exactly why the Emperor ordered the building of such a permanent barrier is unclear. That he was, as far as the limits of the Empire were concerned, conservative is clear, tending to preserve and reinforce what he already held, rather than hunt for new territories with rash campaigning beyond the frontiers.[22]

He had a few years previously ordered the transformation of the border area between Germania Superior and Raetia, where the gap between the Rhine and Danube rivers left an awkward and vulnerable salient. A palisade of oak posts was erected, running for hundreds of kilometres, symbolically and clearly marking the line of the frontier; the barbarians could make no mistake, or trade on any uncertainty, about where the line went.[23] Beyond that barrier, they would be trespassing on Roman territory.

In northern England, Hadrian went for an altogether more ambitious scheme. Just why Britannia ended up with a stone (or, in parts, turf) wall, when Germania had to make do with a ditch and a wooden barrier, and Raetia only got a stone wall some six decades later,[24] is not obvious. The reason may be as prosaic as the comparative scarcity of sufficient wood in northern Britannia to build a barrier similar to the one in Germania, or it could have been that the shorter stretch of frontier to be covered along the Solway–Tyne isthmus permitted a much grander and – at least for those able to see or hear of it – more prestigious structure to be attempted. Given that Hadrian was not particularly popular to begin with, since his legitimacy was suspect and his reign began with a purge of senators suspected of opposing his accession,[25] the creation of such a striking monument would have been an extremely useful symbol of his power.

The VI Victrix legion was sent north to begin work on the project. For the first 45 Roman miles,[26] the Wall was built in stone, and from the River Irthing to the Solway Firth (another 31 Roman miles) it was constructed out of turf, a decision that may have indicated that stone was less readily available along the western portion of the Wall's route. Initially, too, the plan for the eastern stone section was that it should be 3.1 metres in width and approximately 4 metres in height. The Turf Wall needed to be wider (at around 6.2 metres) to ensure its stability, and was probably just less than 4 metres high. Every (Roman) mile, a miniature fort, or 'milecastle', would be placed and in between each of these there would be two turrets. In front of the Wall, a ditch would be placed as an additional obstacle, varying in length depending on the terrain, though in some places along the Wall this feature was absent.

In the central section, the Wall incorporates the dramatic volcanic outcrop of the Whin Sill, and in general occupies vantage points offering reasonable visibility to the north. Where it does not (as in the region around Great Chesters), the planners did nothing to deviate the Wall to a more convenient route, preferring the geometric simplicity of a straight line to the more mundane advantages of being able to sight intruders before they actually arrived.

The purpose of Hadrian's Wall was almost certainly to exercise a high degree of control over the movements of those entering and leaving the Roman province; the Wall is provided with gateways at regular intervals, with travellers not having to travel more than a kilometre along the Wall at any one point to reach one,[27] not a sensible provision if it had been seen as a purely military barrier. The gates, presumably, mark the points at which those carrying goods for sale into the Roman province would have paid their tolls.

Moreover, the Wall was not intended as a platform from which to fight. Its width – around 10 Roman feet at most – would barely have permitted two armed soldiers to pass one another, and so would have made a most impracticable defensive position. In addition, at whatever point intruders might attack, it would take time for even small units to make their way from the nearest milecastle or turret; and then, should the enemy somehow not already have passed over the Wall, the confined fighting space available would mean that the Roman soliders would not be able to bring their full force to bear. That is, unless the barbarians should choose to attack at one of the forts along the Wall, a most unlikely tactic for those intent merely on quick plundering raids to the south.

The history of the Wall's construction is complex. Building probably commenced north of the existing Stanegate fort at Corstopitum (Corbridge), and one team of legionaries built eastwards towards Pons Aeli (Newcastle), while another worked their way west to the point where the Turf Wall began.[28] Although the Wall was originally planned to sit on a foundation of around 3 metres, only in the section from Newcastle to the North Tyne (known as the Broad Wall) was this actually achieved. Between that point and the Irthing, although the foundations had already been laid, the Wall was actually built to a narrower gauge of 2.4 metres (the Narrow Wall).

Initially, the only troops along the Wall line were stationed at the mile-castles and fortlets, with reinforcements, if needed, having to be summoned from the Stanegate forts to the rear. Before the construction of the barrier was completed, however, there was yet another change of plan and a decision was taken to construct new forts along the Wall itself, with a distance of around 10–14 kilometres between each of them. Eleven in all were attached to the Wall structure,[29] normally with one-third of the fort (and three gates) projecting out into *barbaricum*, an arrangement which again suggests that Roman military planners thought in terms of issuing out of the forts to face the enemy, rather than having to defend those three vulnerable gates against attack.

The Stanegate forts were rendered redundant by these new Wall forts, and were for the most part abandoned, or turned over to civilian use. The system was completed by the digging of another ditch to the rear of the Wall, known to modern archaeology as the Vallum, which may have marked out the limit of the *territorium*, the district under the direct control of the military. 'Outpost' forts were also built north of the Wall line, at Blatobulgium (Birrens) and Fanococidi (Bewcastle), an indication that, whatever the beguiling simplicity of regarding Hadrian's Wall as a fixed and rigid barrier, the Romans had no intention whatsoever of abdicating all control or freedom of manoeuvre in the territory immediately to the north of it.

Inscriptions discovered on the Wall show that the building was undertaken by detachments from all three of Britannia's legions: II Augusta, which came up from Isca (Caerleon) in Wales; XX Valeria Victrix from Deva (Chester); and VI Victrix, which was based at Eboracum (York).[30] The first season of building probably took place in 122,[31] the year of Hadrian's visit, although there would not have been time to make a great deal of progress. By 124, large sections of the Stone Wall were complete and probably all of the Turf Wall.[32] It was possibly then that the decision to bring the forts up to the line of the Wall was taken. The forts themselves, though, were still being built in the 130s, with Magnis (Carvoran) probably not being completed until 136/7. Apart from the inevitable repairs and minor improvements conducted during the life of the Wall, the final changes to the original scheme took place with the rebuilding in stone of part of the turf section late in the reign of Hadrian, and the completion of the same work in the section from milecastle 54 to Bowness around 160, under Antoninus Pius.

The effort required to complete all these works was staggering; including various outpost stations, twenty forts had to be built, together with 100 milecastles and around 200 turrets. The total amount of material required seems to have been in the region of one million cubic metres for the Stone Wall and about four-fifths of that amount for the Turf Wall.[33] When the Wall scholar Collingwood Bruce enlisted the services of Robert Rawlinson, a friendly engineer, to determine the costs of the material used, he based it on a figure of 10,000 men needed to build the Wall and dig the ditch and taking 240 days. The cost, in the mid-19th century, came out at an estimated £1,021,000, barely enough in the early 21st century to purchase a three-bedroom flat in a fashionable part of central London.[34]

The visitor hoping for visible relics of the Wall in its westernmost reaches will be disappointed, as none of the original line is to be seen in place and almost all the stones have long gone. Somewhere in the current main street of Bowness stood the fort of Maia, utterly vanished now, though the point where its internal roadways intersected stands conveniently on the site of the King's Arms pub. The nearby church of Saint Michael, however, does at least incorporate some Roman masonry within it, and these probably represent the last remains of the most westerly fort along the Wall.

Past Drumburgh, which once housed the fort of Congavata, the line of the Wall passes through Burgh-by-Sands, where Aballava stood. Here, again at the church of Saint Michael (who, as a rather militaristic archangel, is an appropriate consumer of recycled Roman army material), some Roman masonry can be seen, patches of red sandstone, presumably cannibalised from the fort and Wall. The rather imposing square tower of the church incorporates arrow slits, for this was long contested territory between England and Scotland, and the need for such defensive installations overrode any ecclesiastical admonitions to love one's neighbour.

The next fort to the east lay on a site that has prospered more since

Roman times. Indeed, Carlisle, or Luguvalium, as it was known, is one of only two main urban centres along the Wall (the other being Pons Aeli/Newcastle at the eastern extremity). A delightful cathedral city, its population of 70,000 hardly competes with other metropolises elsewhere along the Roman frontier, but it is nonetheless a stark contrast to the rural stretches along which the Wall traces its course in this westerly region. An earlier Flavian fort (called Uxelodunum) was built here, probably around 72, but it was later demolished and a new building constructed upon the mound on which now soar up the medieval battlements of Carlisle Castle. This Roman fort was still standing, at least in part, more than two centuries after the province fell from the Empire's grasp in 410, for there is a record of the Northumbrian holy man and bishop, Saint Cuthbert, visiting the place in 685.[35]

It was not just at Luguvalium that the Wall remained substantially intact at the time. The 8th-century monk Bede makes mention of it in his *Ecclesiastical History*, implying that stretches of it may still have existed on the easternmost part of its course, close to his monastery at Jarrow. Bede, though, mistakenly attributes the construction of the Wall to Septimius Severus rather than Hadrian.[36] For those living in an era in which northern England was only just emerging from the chaotic and impoverished world of the first two post-Roman centuries, the remains of the Wall must have seemed an almost impossible achievement. Nowadays, in contrast, apart from a few stones built into the structure of Carlisle Castle, it is only possible to get a real sense of the Roman achievement on the western part of the Wall at Carlisle's Tullie House Museum.

The troops that garrisoned the Wall represented the Roman military machine at the peak of its military effectiveness. In early imperial times, the Roman army overwhelmingly consisted of an annual levy of farmers who exchanged their sickles for swords each year, hoping to return home for harvest time. It was men such as these who had subdued the other peoples of the Italian peninsula, defeated Hannibal and begun the acquisition of Rome's Spanish and Balkan provinces. By the start of the 1st century BC, however, the length of time the soldiers were needed had stretched from months into years, and the civil wars of the middle of that century led to the raising of armies hugely in excess of the legion or two that had been traditional. It also led to increasing professionalisation of the army as the soldiers, and particularly the centurions (the senior NCOs), fought in campaign after campaign and came to form the backbone of a seasoned and effective fighting force.

When Augustus emerged triumphant as sole ruler of the Empire,

having seen off Mark Antony and his Egyptian ally Cleopatra at the
Battle of Actium in 31 BC, he commanded around eighty legions, possibly
in excess of 400,000 men. The expectation, at least of those who held
to the republican way of doing things, might have been that he dismiss
the vast majority of these and then raise fresh troops whenever the
exigencies of future campaigning should demand it. Augustus did
dispense with more than half of the force – it was simply too expensive
to keep them in uniform – but he retained twenty-eight permanent
legions, Rome's first full standing army. The number would vary slightly
over the coming centuries: three legions lost against the Germans in
AD 9, a clutch cashiered in AD 70 for disloyalty,[37] two raised in Italy in 165
to act as a strategic reserve and a further three for Septimius Severus's
expedition against the Parthians in the 190s. The total, however, did not
vary dramatically until the shape of the whole army was modified wholesale in the late 3rd century under external pressures with which the old
system could not cope.

By the time of Hadrian, the organisation of the legions was also set
out on a more formal basis than it had been in the initial years of the
Empire. Every legion was numbered – although confusingly, there were
often several sharing the same designation – and each had a nickname
that identified it more securely, such as the V 'Alaudae' ('the larks') or,
more martially, the XII 'Fulminata' ('the lightning-throwers'). Each legion
was essentially an infantry force, made up of ten cohorts of 480 men,
each in turn subdivided into six 'centuries' of eighty men,[38] reinforced
by a small cavalry force of 120, which together with specialists and officers made a total complement of something over 5,000 soldiers.[39]

All of the men had to be Roman citizens on enlistment, and they
were commanded by a legionary legate, always from the senatorial elite,[40]
often an ambitious politician with at least one prior military posting. He
was assisted by a subordinate tribune, normally only in his twenties but
again of senatorial rank, for whom this would be his first military experience. The effective third in command was the *praefectus castrorum*
(prefect of the camp), normally a long-serving senior centurion, and then
beneath him five junior tribunes, the *tribuni angusticlavii*, recruited from
the equestrian class (the next step down socially from the senatorial order),
who were – though very much subordinate to the senatorial tribune –
likely to be older than him.

The nearest legionaries to the Wall, apart from building parties or at
times when active campaigning was going on, were based well back at
the fortress in Eboracum (York). They were supported by a roughly equal
number of auxiliaries, and it was these who made up the garrison of

Hadrian's Wall. The Romans had long recruited foreign allies to their armies, allies whose fighting styles were often well adapted to the conditions of particular terrains or campaigns. The organisation of these forces was once again regularised under Augustus. They still formed a noncitizen force, but three different types of unit were established. The cohort (*cohors*) was entirely composed of infantry and was either quingenary (480 men) or milliary (800 men). The cavalry were divided into *alae* ('wings'), each either quingenary (512 men) or milliary (768).[41] Further variation was provided by mixed units of cavalry and infantry, termed *cohortes equitatae*. Within these basic designations there was a great deal of flexibility, and units of slingsmen, archers and even, in the East, of camel-borne soldiers are recorded.[42]

Both legionaries and auxiliaries had to sign up for twenty-five years of service – the term had been twenty years early in the imperial period, but was soon extended.[43] Legionaries received a bonus on their retirement, which in AD 5 was set at some 12,000 sesterces, a sum equal to more than twelve years' salary.[44] Instead of a cash payment, the auxiliaries were awarded Roman citizenship on completing their term of service, a privilege that they could pass onto their descendants (although sons actually born during their time of service were excluded, so that they in turn would be forced to join the army if they wanted to enjoy the privilege of Roman citizenship).[45] On being discharged they were given a diploma, inscribed on leaves of bronze, which proved their right to citizenship, a copy of which was supposed to be deposited in Rome. Scores of these diplomas have been found, although representing only a fraction of those originally issued, and the fact that they also list the units and provinces from which the troops were being discharged makes them an invaluable resource for tracking the movements of auxiliary units around the Empire.

The strength of the garrison on the Wall obviously varied somewhat depending on military contingencies. After the principal Roman line of defence was pushed northwards in the 140s to the Antonine Wall on the Forth–Clyde isthmus, it dropped to virtually zero. When Hadrian's Wall was completed in about 138, however, the garrisons of the forts and mile-castles represented up to 8,000 men.[46] By the 3rd century, under Septimius Severus, this number was probably somewhat lower, although by then the troops had to man a greatly reduced number of turrets and mile-castles, many of which had been decommissioned. From this time, there was more stability in the units garrisoning each defensive position, and many of those attested in residence at the start of the 3rd century probably remained in place until the last years of Roman rule in Britain.

The next-door fort to Luguvalium was around 12 kilometres to the east. Petriana, now in the village of Stanwix, housed the biggest and most prestigious unit of all along the entire British frontier, the *Ala Petriana milliaria*, a 1,000-strong cavalry regiment, one of few such double-strength units anywhere in the Empire.[47] To accommodate this number of soldiers, Petriana, whose remains lie beneath yet another church of Saint Michael, was itself the largest fort on the Wall.

The terrain around it is open, ideally suited to operations by cavalry units, and, equally, more vulnerable to large-scale incursions from across the frontier than the broken-up, undulating and craggy sections further to the east. It has also, sadly, militated against the survival of much of the Wall, for the robbing of stones was considerably easier in this area, where the settlements in which they could be reused were much closer at hand.

It is only after a nearly 20-kilometre hike from Stanwix east to Hare Hill that the first extant section of the Wall appears, up a pleasant tree-shaded rise and behind a fine beech hedge. It is also, by chance, the highest section on the whole north-British frontier. Rising up in the shape of an omega truncated at one side, this chunk gives some sense of the scale on which the entire Wall would originally have appeared. Yet it seems strangely domesticated in this tranquil setting, a secret that has integrated itself into the landscape, hidden far away from its military purpose. The facing stones that concealed the rubble core are not the original ones, having been replaced by others found here and there along the Wall by restorationists in the 19th century, enthusiasts who were rather keener on the effect than the authenticity of their work, and who additionally re-erected the upper courses of the Hare Hill section, which had long since fallen into ruin.

The Wall, indeed, has long attracted the interest of antiquarians, being one of the structures that first sparked off real interest in Britain's Roman heritage in the 16th century. Hare Hill was remarked upon by one of the most notable of them all, William Hutton, who in 1802 noted, 'I viewed this relick with admiration. I saw no part higher ... Near this place the Wall is five feet high.'[48]

From Hare Hill it is less than a kilometre east to the first surviving turret at Banks – denominated as 52a, according to the generally accepted numbering system[49] – set beside a little lay-by off the main road. Wings of the Wall head off from either side of the small square turret, reconstructed to around a metre in height, but the main feature of interest is a huge chunk of masonry preserved in the place where it fell when the turret collapsed. The building was occupied at least until the 3rd century, when cutbacks and rationalisations meant that many of the turrets were abandoned.

A few hundred metres away, in a rolling pasture at Pike Hill, lie the ruins of a Roman signal station. Only the fractured remains of the original survive, for it was damaged when the modern road was built in the 1870s, but the view – the reason for which the station was sited here so close to other military buildings – is tremendous. The signal station in fact pre-dated the Wall, and was awkwardly bonded with it, but the vantage point, towards the foothills of the Cheviots to the north, and as far as the northern reaches of the Lake District to the south, made its preservation worthwhile. Inside the ruined structure a platform that led to the upper storeys of the tower can just be made out, a reminder that many of the buildings along the Wall originally rose to far above the level that can be seen today.

For those walking east along the Wall's line, the way here continues to be mercifully flat, past the remains of Lea Hill turret and through an attractive (and cooling) wood from which the grassed-over V-shape of the Vallum can clearly be seen striking across the landscape – a welcome reminder (as the Wall itself here is almost wholly missing) that this is still the course of the frontier. Just beyond this section, between Wall Burn and High House Farm, a rare section of the Turf Wall can be seen, a continuous bumpy ridge that looks as though a burial mound had been seized, stretched and elongated for several hundred metres.

This whole western section of the Wall, which stretched initially from the River Irthing to Bowness – and which was rebuilt in stone in two stages, in the late 130s and then around 160 – lay largely on a foundation of turf, although in places (such as around milecastle 72) this was replaced by cobblestones. The specified size of the turves – according to the military manual of Vegetius[50] – was 18 Roman inches by 12 by 6, although it is hard to tell if the legionary builders on the northern frontier kept to this standard, as insufficient evidence survives to gauge the measurements accurately. Most of the Turf Wall seems to have been destroyed when it was rebuilt in stone, explaining the slightness of the remains that can be seen today.

From this stretch at High House Farm, the way continues northeastwards across flat farmland for a short distance until the walls of the Birdoswald estate come into view. The Romans chose to site the fort of Banna here, to the north of the Irthing gorge, providing a platform from which to strike northwards, rather than the purely defensive location that would have meant constructing the camp to the south of the river. Originally built in timber (probably around 125), it was replaced by a stone fort around 138,[51] and seems to have been in use right until the end of Roman Britain (and quite possibly beyond). The place may well be the Amboglanna of the *Notitia Dignitatum* (which gives as its garrison the *Cohors I Aelia Dacorum*, originally from Dacia in modern Romania).

Birdoswald is the first of the forts along the Wall that survives in anything like its original state, neither robbed wholesale for its stones, nor completely obliterated by the expansion of the urban settlements around it (as at Carlisle), and it displays many of the features of classic early imperial military architecture. Roman forts of this period were normally constructed using a 'playing-card' design – in a rectangular shape, with the corners rounded. In general they had four gates, one at each of the cardinal points, while the strength of the surrounding ditches and earthworks (and whether the wall or internal buildings of the fort were of turf or stone) depended very much on the topography, the materials available, the perceived threat from outsiders and the length of time that the site was occupied.

Defence was not the primary concern in choosing the site because, just as the Wall itself was not intended as a fighting platform, so the legions or auxiliary cohorts were not expected – save in the most unfavourable circumstances – to have to defend themselves from within their forts. The early Roman army was an aggressive strike force and the forts were instead bases from which to dominate land already held and launch invasions to acquire further territory or mount punitive raids on those tribes that might dare to disturb the *pax Romana*.

The placement of the gates and the internal buildings of the fort very much mirrored those of a Roman marching camp; every evening on campaign the troops were expected to construct a temporary fortification, whose design both promoted military discipline and provided some level of protection in the case of unexpected attack. The camps and forts were laid out along two spinal roads; the *via principalis* ran from the gateways at the longer end of the fort, and was joined at right angles by the *via praetoria* at the point where it touched the main headquarters building of the fort, the *principia*.

The *principia* itself was normally composed of a colonnaded courtyard, around which were arrayed offices, and behind which lay a cross-hall or basilica to which the garrison could be summoned for important meetings or ceremonies, and in which may have been displayed statues of the imperial family. At the far wall of the cross-hall normally lay the *aedes*, or temple of the standards, where the unit's symbols and flags were kept, together with its most sacred image, the *aquila* or eagle, whose loss was the worst disgrace that a legion could endure.

Close to the *principia* was situated the *praetorium*, the accommodation for the legate (the commander of a legion) or the prefect in charge of an auxiliary unit. Often a luxurious affair, sometimes with hypocausts to provide under-floor heating, this was a far cry from the provision for the rest of the soldiers. The soldiers' accommodation at least in infantry units, was based upon the eight-man *contubernium* structure. The smallest tactical unit in the army on the march, was a *contubernium* traditionally housed in a single tent (of canvas or leather). In the more permanent fortifications, a pair of rooms was provided for eight men, one of these probably being set aside for the storage of equipment and the other for living and sleeping. At the end of a row of such blocks, a slightly larger unit was normally destined for the use of the centurion or one of the other senior non-commissioned officers.

Apart from the barracks blocks, which often took up most of the area inside the fort, other important buildings included the *valetudinarium* or hospital, for military units were one of the few places where men with less-than-elite status might have access to proper medical care; the *horrea* or granaries, where the unit's supplies were kept; and the bathhouse, an important social amenity which, apart from its undoubted hygienic purpose, acted as a meeting place for the soldiers and helped mitigate the numbing boredom of garrison life.

Much of the middle area of Birdoswald is unexcavated, and so most of these internal structures are visible only through slight contours and bumps.[52] The only significant remains, apart from the gates and the walls, which can be seen above ground are the granaries, built at the start of the 3rd century,[53] following a period of some forty years when the fort had lain abandoned after the move of the frontier line northwards to the Antonine Wall.[54] The bulk of the external curtain wall of Birdoswald, however, still stands, save for the northern section, whose stones were robbed to build a bastle or fortified farmhouse in the 14th century during a time when the Borders, the territory disputed between England and Scotland, were dominated by families of reivers, cattle-raiding clans whose hatred of each other was matched only by a mutual enmity for outsiders.

The fort actually butts against the Wall, although before the Stone Wall replaced the turf construction in about 138, it had projected beyond it. The gates are in reasonable condition, particularly the main west gate or *porta principalis sinistra*, which was originally a double-entrance flanked by two side-towers that may have risen to two storeys. In the 3rd century, this was rebuilt using stonework of a very high quality that was inserted into the more mundane masonry construction of the adjoining wall. Its smooth working, still visible today, seems to come from another structure and is unlike anything found elsewhere on Hadrian's Wall. It is even possible that it was taken from an unknown imperial monument in the vicinity.[55] By the mid-3rd century the southern end of this double-gateway was blocked up, in general taken to be a sign of diminished security or at least lessened confidence, for it made the fort easier to defend, an indication that the garrison now felt this was something it might actually be called upon to do.

There are a large number of inscriptions from the 3rd century, one recording building work on the east gate in 219, but little evidence of trouble from the tribes to the north, and the garrison may even have been removed in the late 3rd century to man new forts on the south coast of England.[56] An inscription from that time records that the commander's residence at the fort needed to be rebuilt as it had 'fallen into ruin'[57] and was covered in earth. Presumably the residence had fallen into disrepair during a period of abandonment, unless military discipline had become so lax as to permit such neglect while a garrison was actually in station.

A small section of wall within the fort marks evidence that the training of the soldiers was taken seriously at Banna. It is the remains of the southern part of a basilical hall, but not one intended for meetings or religious worship. Instead, this was a place for exercise and drill. Such a *basilica exercitaria* is mentioned by Vegetius, who writes that it was intended to allow the troops (presumably infantry) to train when conditions outside were wet or windy.[58] As the country around Hadrian's Wall has more than its fair share of inclement weather, this hall presumably saw extensive use, under the supervision of a centurion who would deploy a wooden vine stick (or *vitis*) to encourage idling or recalcitrant soldiers.

By the 4th century troops had been at Banna for almost 300 years. Now, however, conditions in Britain, which had escaped much of the turmoil that afflicted Rome's mainland European (and particularly her Danubian) frontiers, took a turn for the worse. In 360, the Picts and Scots attacked from the north, and the general Lupicinus[59] was sent to deal with them. But it was not enough; for seven years later a 'barbarian conspiracy'[60] broke out and Britain was attacked simultaneously, in the north by the Picts and from the south by seaborne barbarian raiders. Nectaridus, a senior officer in command of the coastal defences,[61] was killed, and Fullofaudes, a *dux*,[62] was captured by the invaders. The Emperor, Valentinian I, was galvanised into drastic action and despatched his trusted general Theodosius to regain the British provinces. After landing in the spring of 368 at Rutupiae (Richborough) in Kent, he marched on London, rallied the legionary garrisons and then secured the southern part of England, before proceeding north to flush out any remaining bands of raiders who had tarried unduly about the securing of their plunder.[63]

Around the middle of the 4th century, the northern of the two granary buildings at Banna collapsed and was not repaired. In its stead a timber hall was built at the start of the 5th century, which was later replaced by a more substantial wooden long-hall, whose outline is marked out today by wooden poles in the ground. At one end a hearth was built. It all seems more reminiscent of the halls of early medieval kings, or of the Dark Age potentates of the *Beowulf* saga, than anything normally found in a classical Roman fort.

The troops who garrisoned Banna in the last years of its life would have belonged to units referred to collectively as *limitanei*. Until the 3rd century, the principal division in the Roman army had been between the legionaries and the auxiliaries, but during the later Empire this distinction blurred, particularly after 212 when the award of citizenship to all free males meant that the main motive for service in the auxiliaries (the gaining of citizen status after twenty-five years) vanished. The main division now came to be between the *comitatenses*, or field armies – which had their origin in the units that the beleaguered emperors of the second half of the 3rd century gathered about themselves to stave off barbarian invasions or the depredations of rivals to their throne – and the *limitanei*, or border troops, who were assigned to garrison duty on the frontiers.[64]

The army had long been changing to adapt to the very real challenges the Empire faced, and units of around 1,000 men (as opposed to the 5,000 of the traditional legions) began to be more common, whilst from the 3rd century new formations known as *numeri*, which were drawn from particular ethnic groups and did not conform to the normal Roman command structure, appeared in increasing numbers. Units detached from a legion, known as 'vexillations', now tended to serve for long periods apart from their parent unit, whereas previously they had only really done so if needed for a particular campaign.

The command structures of the army also changed. While before the 3rd century the legionary commander, the *legatus legionis*, had normally been a senator progressing upwards on the career ladder for the nobility known as the *cursus honorum*, and which might lead as its next stage to a junior governorship, from around 260 the senatorial legates were replaced by officers of equestrian rank.[65] The next step down in the Roman social hierarchy, this class was originally composed of members of families not very dissimilar to those of the senatorial aristocracy, but less ambitious or able in the quest for power. The property qualification for membership of the equestrian class was also lower, a mere 400,000 sesterces under the early Empire, as opposed to the 1,000,000 sesterces for the senatorial order.[66]

The 3rd century saw other changes in the shape of the army. In the 260s, Gallienus established a mobile cavalry force, a necessary expedient for an emperor who faced the falling away of the western provinces, chaos in the east and significant barbarian threats on all fronts. Exactly whether these new units survived into the 4th century or whether the change was reinvented under Diocletian (284–305) is unclear,[67] but along- side his administrative changes, the new emperor also reformed the army, raising some elite legions (most notably the Ioviani and Herculiani) and a number of lower-strength legionary units, which appear to have had only around 1,000 men.

By 305, the thirty-three legions that had existed under Septimius Severus had been increased to sixty-seven, whilst the number of auxiliary units was correspondingly multiplied.[68] The size of the army was doubtless augmented, probably to the maximum level it ever reached, but what that total was remains unclear. The 6th-century bureaucrat and histor- ian John Lydus gives a worryingly precise number of 389,704 under Diocletian, whilst Agathias, writing a little later, says that the army's strength had been 645,000 in the 4th century.[69]

Under Constantine (306–37) the process went a step further, with the field army of *comitatenses* being increased in size and becoming the most important element in the army. He abolished the old praetorian guard and replaced it with units of *protectores* and *scholae*, which owed a personal loyalty to the Emperor. The historian Zosimus accused Constantine of having ruined the Empire by withdrawing troops from the frontiers, where they had formed a strong barrier, and stationing them in provinces further to the interior that did not need protection.[70] Yet in truth, the larger field army was able to move more quickly to address threats against the frontier, which could come with little warning and at almost any point. Now that the Empire was on the defensive, it was actually better served by a more lightly held perimeter, so that forces to the rear could move more rapidly to plug any breaches of the frontier.

A short stroll to the east down a country lane from Banna lies the first really substantial section of Wall, around half a kilometre long. First, by Harrow Scar, is a section of consolidated Wall, which then leads on to the tranquil shaded haven of Willowford Brook, where a confusing assembly of ruins marks several phases of the abutment of a Roman bridge crossing. The erosion of parts of it in Roman times, and the subsequent shifting of the river's course, has left it looking beached and most unbridge-like in a grassy meadow. Just beyond, set against the barn wall of Willowford Farm, is the unlikely setting of one of the 'centurial stones', markers placed into the walls by the various legionary gangs to signify the completion of each section. This one was erected by the century of Gellius Philippus, which, presumably, was responsible for the nearby section of Wall that strikes down in a lovely line stretching along the river, and which was in part reused for the building of local stone farmhouses and outbuildings.

A kilometre or so away at Poltross Burn (milecastle 48), the Roman ruins are set right against the line of the railway, whose construction caused their partial destruction. Nonetheless, they are some of the most intact along the western sectors of Hadrian's Wall, built on a slight downward slope, which must have been the cause of much cursing by the tired auxiliary troopers on watch as they trudged up and down towards it. The solid southern gate entrance, which survives well, and the bulky thickness of the remaining walls show that even these relatively minor milecastle installations could give good protection to their garrison – in this case the barrack buildings in the interior indicate about sixty-four men – in times of need. Later on, when the true history of the frontier was long forgotten, this ruin became known in folk tradition as the stables of King Arthur.

A nearby stretch of the path features an advert by 'Jefficus', a local Roman re-enactor who has appended a reproduction legionary shield on a shed as publicity for his services, while later on the frontier cuts through a small patch of garden completely filled with an assortment of gnomes (although no legionary gnomes at all were visible – all off on campaign, no doubt). Besides Tipalt Burn, a couple of kilometres to the east, the path touches Thirlwall Castle, a romantic medieval shell, a fortified manor house built in the 14th-century by the local de Thirlwall family and almost entirely composed of masonry acquired from the Roman Wall.

The fort of Magnis lies just a little further on, a few hundred metres south of the line of the Wall. The first military building here was probably erected around 90 under Domitian, but nothing of it, or the subsequent Hadrianic fort, can be seen. It serves as the site, however, of the Roman Army Museum, which details the life of the garrison, the First Cohort of Hamian Archers (from modern Homs, in Syria) who called Magnis their home from around 136–7[71] to at least 163. An inscription to the goddess 'Syria', which was found there, is an unmistakable sign of the eclectic mix of religions that could be found amongst troops who were posted to the frontier from a great variety of provinces throughout the Empire (and who for at least several generations, if their units' posting should last that long, would have conserved the traditions of their homeland).

That the names of the Wall forts such as Magnis are known (or have been deduced) is due to a variety of sources, not all of them literary. The most striking of these are the Rudge Cup and the Amiens Skillet. The cup, found in 1725, is a bronze drinking vessel, which contains an inscription moulded into it detailing the names of five of the forts along Hadrian's Wall, and a stylised representation of the battlements of the Wall itself. Its exact date is unclear, but it may well show the forts along the Wall during the latter part of the reign of Hadrian.[72] Unfortunately, the craftsman seems to have corrupted some of the names, or at least shortened them in order to squash the letters into the confined space available. They therefore do not agree with those on the Amiens Skillet, a Roman cooking pan found in France in 1949, on which are inscribed the names of six forts. A further cooking pan, found in 2003 in Staffordshire, adds another fort at Drumburgh (or Congavata), near the far west of the Wall, which is not represented on either of the previous two vessels.[73] All of these pieces were most likely made as souvenirs for former members of the garrison, and though their accuracy cannot be guaranteed, they must have been made for soldiers who had first-hand experience of the Wall and its forts, and so can be presumed to bear some close approximation to the reality.

The literary sources include the *Antonine Itinerary*, which details more than 200 routes across the Empire, amongst them one showing part of the Wall's system at the time of Caracalla (211–17), which includes the outpost forts at Blatobulgium (Birrens) and Netherby (Castra Exploratorum). The *Ravenna Cosmography*, composed in the early 8th century, and intended to include all the towns and roads of the known world, incorporates details on Britain, and thus the Wall.[74] Finally, the *Notitia Dignitatum*, although a very late source, and which may include elements of the Wall garrison that had already been withdrawn, adds some important elements to the mix. It does, however, miss out forts that are incontrovertibly known to have existed, such as Maia (Bowness). The reconciliation of all these sources is fraught with difficulty, but in general the names of the main forts are now agreed by archaeologists and historians, although always able to be thrown out of kilter by a new discovery on the ground.[75]

From Magnis, the Wall enters its hilly central stretch. For the modern-day walker the way can be punishing, with constant rises and falls, beginning here with the 'Nine Nicks of Thirlwall', but as the Wall snakes up and down, and the higher ground gives enhanced visibility of its course further to the east, the views are truly mesmerising and the restored Wall at some points almost rises up to head height. The crags that punctuate the route from here to Corstopitum (Corbridge) are of whinstone, a dark, hard stone that resisted weathering over the geological ages and thus left exposed outcrops, the spines of which Hadrian and his surveyors used to form the backbone of the Wall.

At Walltown Gap, the crags are dramatically interrupted by a lone Roman turret that keeps watch, providing one of the most spectacular panoramas along the Wall. After this the way leads, via a succession of ascents and descents, past a section of unconsolidated wall, whose weathered and collapsed masonry shows the fate the rest of the Wall would have endured, had it not been for a succession of restorations. The route continues through a small and pleasantly shaded wood, at the entrance to which stands part of the structure of an old gate, an ancient Roman milestone clearly built into it.

Aesica (or Great Chesters), the next fort, lay just about 3 Roman miles east of Magnis, a closer interval than might be expected, and the construction of the fort over the foundations of the preceding milecastle 43 shows that it was something of an afterthought, built to guard the Caw Gap. It is quite modest in area, at about 1.2 hectares and, from an inscription to Hadrian that includes a title (*pater patriae* or 'father of the country')[76] which he took only in 128, must date to after that period. Much of its perimeter is intact, delineating the fort boundaries, although on one side a modern farm has subsumed part of Aesica's interior and encroached upon the walls. The west gate still survives relatively well, its 3rd-century level almost a metre higher than the original Hadrianic part of the structure, showing how the ground rose with successive years of occupation on the fort site.

The interior is mostly empty, pocked by bumps here and there marking unexcavated interior buildings, and patrolled only by the odd tourist and a lazily sprawling cat. In the centre of the site the remains of the strongroom which sat beneath the *aedes* in the *principia* can be made out, very overgrown and neglected. In one corner of the fort a solitary altar stands, much eroded, with its inscription wholly illegible. But upon it passing travellers have set coins, a pile of latter-day votive offerings, which are themselves weathering in the rain and wind, the bronze ones already having acquired a deceptively aged patina of green. The most ancient, however, far from being an original Roman relic, is just twenty years old.

Outside the fort a complex series of ditches (not just the normal single line) gave extra security to Aesica, but its lack of a fresh-water spring, which necessitated the piping of water from some 10 kilometres away, did not make it the most ideal location to site a garrison. Beyond, the Wall proceeds along a series of boot-breaking crags, always taking advantage of the high ground, past Cawfield Crags – chilly in winter and searingly exposed in the summer – where milecastle 42's south gate is preserved to an impressive height of 1.8 metres (almost the highest on the Wall), to the equally vertiginous Peel Crags. At times the view, with the Wall undulating as the landscape rises and falls, creates an almost hypnotic effect, drawing the visitor physically into the past.

Between these peaks and the next set of hills, Highshield Crags, the high ground is interrupted by Sycamore Gap, named for the extremely old tree that spreads its branches here, and which was immortalised by a scene in Kevin Costner's *Robin Hood: Prince of Thieves*. The Wall here is almost all original, up to seven courses high, and not reconstructed, as it mostly is elsewhere in this dramatic section of its line. The next break in the crags, at Milking Gap, opens the way to a wonderfully preserved fort (and one of the few in private hands), Vindolanda. It was also the scene of one of the most spectacular finds and feats of preservation in the annals of Roman archaeology.

Set a couple of kilometres south of the Wall, Vindolanda was one of the Stanegate forts, and did not form part of the defences of Hadrian's Wall proper. A timber fort was constructed here around AD 80[77] although it was rebuilt and enlarged in about 92 and then reconstructed in stone around 124.[78] A new fort was then built on the site in the 220s, which remained in use until the 4th century. As well as the military buildings, the site contains the best-excavated *vicus* (or civilian settlement associated with an auxiliary fort) to be found on the whole of Hadrian's Wall, including a small Romano-Celtic temple (featuring a grotto to a nymph, artfully provided with mood music by the site owners), a military bath-house and a *mansio* (or inn) for officially sanctioned travellers.

The interior buildings of the fort largely date from the 3rd-century phase of Vindolanda, when it was garrisoned by the Fourth Cohort of Gauls. It contained, as well as the regular structures, a series of round huts, an odd feature that has caused much archaeological head-scratching.[79] The foundations of the *principia* of the first stone fort are visible, as well as those of the cross-hall of the 3rd-century incarnation, and the *praetorium*, which was still in use and being restored as late as 370. A set of timber buildings that lay alongside the *via principalis* and probably formed part of the *praetorium* was the site of the find of the first (and the majority) of the so-called Vindolanda Tablets.

These tablets, on thin leaves of wood only a few millimetres thick, were inscribed in ink and seem to have formed a cheap and relatively ephemeral means of record-keeping and the sending of personal letters that were not expected to end up in an official archive. At Vindolanda, the majority of those found seem to have been discarded in some kind of a clear-out, and some show evidence of having been deliberately – but unsuccessfully – burnt.[80]

The survival of the tablets is due mainly to northern England's inclement climate: the waterlogging of the ground into which the tablets had been secreted created an oxygen-poor environment in which the wood did not (as would otherwise have been expected) rot away. The contents of the tablets provide a wealth of incidental detail about military life, the most extensive set of correspondence being that of Flavius Cerealis, who was prefect of the Ninth Cohort of Batavians around 100. A later period, from about 105 to 120, has yielded evidence from the tablets of a new garrison, the First Cohort of Tungrians.

Whatever the information to be gleaned from the stocklists and accounts of garrison duties in which the tablets abound, it is the more personal revelations that are most touching. One tablet huffily complains about the local Britons and their low-down fighting tactics, referring to them by the extremely derogatory term *brittunculi*, which translates approximately as 'filthy little Britons'.[81] Another soldier writing home asks to be sent a quantity of socks and two pairs of underpants, as presumably the military issue was not sufficiently warm in the northern climes, which made frozen toes an unpleasantly real winter hazard.[82]

Flavius Cerealis corresponded with a wide range of fellow-officers in the province. Amongst those to whom he wrote was Aelius Brocchus, another equestrian prefect, whose wife Claudia Severa exchanged letters with Cerealis's own wife Sulpicia Lepidina. By this stage, it was not unusual for the officers in auxiliary units to have their wives and families stationed with them, a privilege that was denied to the troopers, who were not, until the late 2nd century, allowed to make legal marriages.

In one of the most poignant of all the tablets, Claudia Severa writes to Sulpicia Lepidina, inviting her to attend her birthday party on 11 September.[83] It is one of the few surviving letters from antiquity written by one woman to another in very probably her own hand. These are astonishing shafts of light illuminating the otherwise hidden world of day-to-day friendships, of the mundane life of a far-flung garrison. They are all the more precious for the ephemeral nature of their contents, which would not have been judged worthy of preserving in any more permanent form.

After Highshield Crags, weary legs are rewarded by the only section of Hadrian's Wall where it is officially permitted actually to walk along the Wall itself. Through a small wood, marching over the original (but consolidated stones), it is possible for a brief few minutes to visualise oneself as a Roman auxiliary peering over to the north and barbarian territory, wondering when, if ever, an assault might come.

The next fort is but a few hundred metres away, and is preceded by the dramatic span of the arch of milecastle 37's gateway, through which it might be imagined wheeled traffic trundled to and fro as the economic life of the frontier – at least in the early days of the Wall – remained untrammelled by its presence. Unfortunately, this particular gate actually collapsed almost as soon as it was built, since the foundations were inadequate, and so the attractive opening in the Wall visible today existed for only a very short time before the (presumably rather embarrassed) engineers blocked it up, only to reopen a much smaller version in the 3rd century.

Up a slight slope, the eastern wall of Vercovicium, or Housesteads, comes into view. Its name has been tentatively translated (from a Celtic root) as meaning 'hilly place'[84] – a choice, given the local terrain, as unimaginative as it is accurate. Built as part of the Hadrianic decision to move the forts up to the Wall, its early garrison was probably the *Cohors I Tungrorum milliaria*, a double-strength (1,000-man) infantry regiment from what is now Belgium. The fort was abandoned after just two decades, when the frontier moved forward into Scotland, but repairs to the fort (especially to part of the north wall) took place in the late 2nd century, following its recommissioning. Further restoration occurred in about 200 under Septimius Severus, another emperor who gave the northernmost frontier of his realm some personal attention. Occupation here appears to have continued at least until the later 4th century, when a small bathhouse was placed inside the fort to replace an earlier, external complex.

Exactly when Housesteads was abandoned is unclear, but if it remained garrisoned at the end of that century, it would have experienced the last of the attempts by the central political authority in Rome to address its security, initiated by Stilicho, the part-Vandal military commander in the early 5th century.[85]

The barracks in the interior of Housesteads preserve in stone some sense of how the later Roman army deployed its diminishing resources to face new threats from tribes besetting the British frontier. In place of the neat rows of barracks seen earlier, rows of separate 'chalets' were built, in clusters of six, with a larger house at the end, presumably for a senior NCO. The Housesteads *praetorium*, the commander's house in the central range, retains some sense of the more prosperous and secure times, with its impressively large-scale construction, in which the hypocaust tiles of the 4th-century baths are visible alongside the villa's private kitchens.

Next to the *principia*, a strikingly large set of *horrea* is visible, its size showing the difficulty of providing sufficient grain to feed 1,000 hungry soldiers throughout the year. Nearby, the fort's latrines are the best preserved in Roman Britain, with a set of five individual seats surviving, but no partitions in between, for the Roman sense of privacy was not that of the modern age, and modesty did not demand that such bodily functions be regarded as a private act. A large water tank sat close by, for there was no aqueduct to deliver a suitable water supply to flush away the results hygienically.

The walls of Housesteads survive in reasonably good order, patrolled now by large groups of summer tourists peering quizzically north across the border or trying in vain to pronounce *valetudinarium* ('hospital'). As Housesteads did not project north of the wall, as did the other forts, only one of its gates pointed towards 'hostile' territory and the others were not blocked up early, as happened elsewhere. The south gate's basic structure, with two arched entrances and stone piers at the front and back, is clear, with the wear caused to the sill at the front by centuries of use quite obvious. The west gate is, however, even better preserved, its massive blocks of masonry rising above head height, showing just how imposing the basic elements of Roman military architecture could be.

Outside the south gate a *vicus* rose up, as around many of the forts along the Wall. The buildings that clustered around the protection of the Wall included a mix of residential houses, commercial establishments (most notably an inn) and, to minister to the inhabitants' spiritual needs, a variety of temples, including one to the oriental god Mithras and another to a Celtic-Roman hybrid, Mars Thinscus. In one house, set a little further from the fort wall, evidence of an ancient crime was uncovered, for beneath the clay floor were found two skeletons, one of them with part of a knife still embedded in its ribs, evidently victims of a murder, which was then covered up.

The museum at Housesteads contains a good representative collection of the various artefacts found on or near the site, but perhaps its finest piece is a carving of three hooded deities (or *cuculli*), their arms folded within cloaks, staring out with almost identical expressions. These hooded cloaks, of a type called *byrus britannicus*, were a well-known export from the province of Britannia. Strabo, in the 1st century BC, had remarked that the island was renowned for its exports of 'corn, cattle, gold, silver, iron, hides, slaves and dogs' – not, save for the metals, the stuff to set the economic world of the Empire alight.[86]

It is an open question, indeed, whether the occupation of Britain was actually profitable. Here, though, as elsewhere along the frontier, the presence of so many soldiers who were actually paid in (and therefore liable to spend) cash accelerated the development of a monetary economy, and encouraged the development of economic structures slightly different from those elsewhere in the province. Yet, with the exception of Luguvalium and Pons Aeli, no large urban centres developed along the line of the Wall, and there are few examples in this area of the large rural villas that are found elsewhere in Britain. Moreover, once the Wall garrisons were withdrawn, certainly at the start of the 5th century, the economic *raison d'être* of the civilian communities that had grown up around them disappeared, and much of the region would have relapsed into the state of subsistence farming in which the Romans had found it in Hadrian's day.

Around 6 kilometres east along the Wall line from Housesteads lies the fort of Carrawburgh (or Brocolitia). Reaching it on foot involves the negotiation of Sewingshield Crags, one of the Wall country's most pictur-esque and leg-shattering stretches, compensated for by the views north over the enticing blue water of Broomlew Lough. All that remains of the fort itself is a rather unprepossessing grassy mound fenced off and overshadowed by the next-door car park. Home to a cohort of Batavians (*Cohors I Batavorum*) from the 3rd century,[87] its earlier garrison is not definitely established, although the fort was certainly constructed as part of the second wave of Wall defences in the late 120s or early 130s.

Carrawburgh's Latin name, Brocolitia, probably derives from a local Celtic term and may mean 'covered in heather'[88] or, more romantically, 'the place of the badgers'. It also boasts two of the most important reli-gious sites on the wall. Down in a shallow dip around from the fort site itself lie the remains of a *mithraeum*, a temple to Mithras. Probably constructed in the early 3rd century, at a time when such cults were gaining increasing vogue in the Empire, and especially amongst its soldiers, the temple was uncovered in 1949. Lacking a roof and much of its enclosing wall, it is hard to comprehend that this sacred space – now open to the elements – was intended to mimic a cold, dark cave, a place of mystery and awe, from which initiates might be reborn into the light. Originally an ante-chapel screened off the central cult space, which was flanked by stone benches to the side of today's reconstructed concrete pillars, and had a set of altars at the other end. If modern impressions are accurate, all the sculptures would have been painted in colours that stood out in sharp relief against the temple's darkness.

Mithraism has been classified – by modern scholars, not by the Romans – amongst a set of beliefs known as 'mystery cults'. What these cults, which included the worship of Jupiter Dolichenus (who originated in Doliche, near Gaziantep in modern Turkey) and Isis (an Egyptian import), had in common was a closed membership and a reservoir of sacred knowledge, which must not be revealed to the non-initiate. They existed in parallel with mainstream Roman religion, and belonging to one of them did not mean abstinence or exclusion from official rites; there was no 'Great Persecution' of Mithraists, at least not until Christianity achieved official recognition in the 4th century and, with its insistence on exclusive adherence, undermined the position of ambitious pagans.

There has been much speculation about the origin of Mithraism.[89] There is a deceptively obvious connection to be made with the Persian god Mitra, who is attested at least as early as the 5th century BC, and who may have been the god of contracts or oaths (his name means 'contract' or 'treaty'). His popularity in the areas influenced by Persia is evidenced by the royal dynasty of Pontus in modern Turkey, no fewer than six of whom were named Mithridates ('gift of Mithras') between the 3rd and 1st centuries BC. He was part of a religious system that included a personification of supreme good, Ahura Mazda, and of evil, Ahriman, who were engaged in an eternal struggle for mastery. This dualist belief had a long lifespan in the Middle East, influencing a variety of Christian heresies (and the not-quite Christian Manichaeism) and surviving into modern times in the guise of Zoroastrianism. There is, however, no concrete evidence that the Persian Mitra-cult evolved directly into Roman Mithraism, which emerged seemingly fully formed around the start of the 1st century AD. Conscious echoes or borrowings there may have been – something similar happened with the new cult of Serapis in Egypt, which combined Greek and Egyptian elements – but the Roman army was hardly likely to tolerate what was practically the state religion of its greatest adversary, Persia.

Mithraic temples are found throughout the Empire, from Egypt to the Rhine provinces. In Britannia, as well as the Brocolitia Mithraeum, and that at Housesteads, another was found at Rudchester (on the eastern sector of the Wall). This cult seems to have found its greatest number of devotees in the army. Entry was strictly confined to men, and the limited size of its congregations – most *mithraea* probably had space for a congregation of only a score or so – may have given it something of the flavour of a secret military confraternity. Backing of the cult extended quite high up the military hierarchy, however: Marcus Valerius Maximianus, one of Marcus Aurelius's leading generals, dedicated an altar to Mithras at Apulum in Dacia while still a legionary legate, and a further two at Lambaesis in Numidia.[90]

The temples themselves were generally very small – one of the largest, in Rome, is still only about 23 metres long[91] – and in the cities they were often incorporated into private buildings. The ideal *mithraeum*, however, was a subterranean cave, a reference to Mithras as the 'rock-born god', in which guise he is depicted on one of the Carrawburgh altars, his head wreathed in a halo of sunburst, his muscle-bound torso emerging fully formed from the blank rock below. The temples were decorated with statues of a variety of other deities, most commonly Cautopates and Cautes, Mithras's divine attendants, the former holding a flaming torch held downwards to represent sunset and the autumn equinox, and the latter directing his torch upwards, symbolizing sunrise, the spring equinox and rebirth.

The most important depictions, however, related to the mystical narrative of the life of Mithras himself. These included his birth from the rock, a date that Mithraists celebrated on 25 December, which was then identified as the winter solstice. The popularity of this festival of *Sol Invictus* ('the Unconquered Sun') – a name often used by devotees to refer to Mithras – may well have played a role in the early Christians' adoption of it as the birthday of their own saviour. The central drama of Mithraism, though, was the bull-slaying, an event dramatically depicted in temples throughout the Empire: Mithras forces the beast to the ground, pushing it down with his left knee, grasping the animal's struggling head in his left hand, ready to plunge a dagger into its throat with his right. From this death and the sacrifice of the bull's blood, the Mithraists believed, would come rebirth: both literal, in the renewal of the cycle of growth each year, and metaphorical, in guaranteeing the survival of the universe and heavenly salvation.

The *mithraeum* is often adorned with references to the number seven, which seems to have been regarded as sacred, or at least auspicious. Symbols abound of the zodiac and the seven planets – which in the classical world were enumerated as the Sun, the Moon, Mercury, Venus, Mars, Jupiter and Saturn. Many temples were built with seven steps leading down into the sanctuary, and Mithras was sometimes depicted as having seven stars on his cloak.

The importance of seven extended into the organisation of the cult itself, for there were seven graded levels of initiates, although we only have their names from a letter of the Christian writer, Saint Jerome. At the lowest level came the Raven, followed by the Bridegroom, Soldier, Lion, Persian, Sun-Runner and, at the top of the hierarchy, the Father (*Pater*), who seems to have been the congregational leader of each *mithraeum*. What role the others played, and how progression from one rank to another was achieved, is unclear and it seems that, except perhaps informally, there was no system for linking the various temples into groups of more than just one congregation. It was a fatal weakness, and although Mithraists do not seem to have had any conscious ambitions for universality, when they came up against Christianity – a religion that did possess this drive – there was no internal organisation to defend the cult. By the 4th century, coin series at *mithraea* came to an end, statues were carefully concealed or buried, altars overturned. Jerome related with some relish that the urban prefect, one Gracchus, had broken up and caused to be burnt 'all the monstrous images' at a *mithraeum* in Rome.[92] The Brocolitia temple, like so many others, was abandoned and forgotten.

Equally forsaken at Brocolitia was the nearby shrine to a water-nymph, the spring at 'Coventina's Well', which was located a few hundred metres from the *mithraeum*, across a mud-spattered, boggy field. Today there is no evidence of the devotion accorded to this local deity. Indeed, the spring itself dried up in Victorian times as a consequence of lead-mining in the vicinity. In the 2nd and early 3rd centuries, however, believers deposited hundreds of coins and inscribed altars, the dedicators most commonly coming from the Lower Rhine and Netherlands. A stone relief from Brocolitia depicts Coventina bare-chested, a light flowing veil-like garment covering her lower half, looking for all the world like a prototype mermaid. This was a landscape in which the religious options open to the soldiers were far more varied than the official pantheon might suggest.

A couple of kilometres further on, as the Wall itself becomes more sparse, its spectacular stride through the central crags now done, it passes through 'Limestone Corner', which, apart from being the most northerly tip of the Wall, marks the point where even the Roman engineers gave up trying to drive the ditch north of the wall through the solid rock. The end of their endeavours is marked by massive chunks of limestone lying scattered about, already sliced away by the masons, but simply left in place after the decision to give up the ditch over this stretch. That such monumental pieces of rock were broken away without the use of explosives is a sober reflection on the monomania and sheer back-breaking effort that was involved in the construction of such an amazingly ambitious project as the Wall.

Around 3 kilometres further on, the fort of Cilurnum (or Chesters) lies in an attractive position astride the North Tyne River. Across a rather busy and noisy road, a curiously humpbacked modern bridge leads down, via a fenced approach that hems in any straying tourists, to the abutment of the Roman bridge. Down in a dip, it all seems at first a confusing mass of masonry, which resolves itself on inspection into one bridge pier and a tower, with the abutment itself – in the shape of a sundial or radial sun-pattern – lying beneath. Nearby an almost complete column lies prostrate, with a little knob on the side, rather like a bollard. Up the slope caused by the excavators' digging lies a display area for a whole array of miscellaneous fragments, looking rather like a huge jigsaw puzzle abandoned in frustration by the archaeologists.

There were in fact two bridges on the site, the first one (which preceded this more massive structure) being built around 122, at the time the Wall and fort were constructed.[93] It seems that the walkway across the bridge was around 3 metres wide, the same width as the Wall itself at this point, so that it in effect acted as a continuation of the Wall across the river. The second bridge was intended to act as a roadway for wheeled traffic and dates from the early 3rd century, although it is not clear at what point it fell into disuse.

The fort of Cilurnum lies on the other side of the river, and access would have been gained to it in Roman times across the bridge. Its Latin name is associated with a Celtic root, which may mean 'cauldron',[94] a possible reference to the swirling eddy in the river just by the site of the bridge. It was a cavalry fort, variously housing the *Cohors I Augusta* and *Ala II Asturum*. The remains of the walls, gates, *principia* and bathhouse date largely from the Hadrianic phase of Cilurnum, whilst the commander's house and many of the barracks are from the later phase of occupation of the site during the 3rd century. The site seems strangely fragmented, the protective fences and gates around the various internal fort buildings breaking it up and making it difficult to take in as an organic whole. It is an attractive setting, however, set in the lush fields of the Clayton estate, with trees liberally sprinkled outside the perimeter of the fort itself and a gentle slope down to the cooling balm of the Tyne.

The north gate, which projected beyond the line of the Wall, would originally have been 10 metres high, though now less than a metre remains, only fragments of its flanking tower being intact. One side of the gate seems to have been blocked soon after it was built, and indications from the other fort gates point to the unblocked part of this double-entrance being the sole passageway into Cilurnum from beyond the Wall. The west gate, which also projected beyond the Wall, is rather better preserved, and the thresholds and pivot-holes of the original can still be seen. It was from the northern guardpost here that a water tank (fed by an external aqueduct) channelled water to the other parts of the fort, as it represents the highest point on the site.

In the north-east of the fort lie the remains of the barracks, an impressive array of rectangular stone blocks, though the symmetry is rather broken up by the third of the triple barrack blocks, which was later subdivided, possibly to create 'chalets' similar to those of the last phase of Housesteads fort. The *principia* also remains in good shape (although of course mostly only in outline and just a couple of stone-courses high). It is even possible to make out, off the cross-hall leading from the main courtyard, the range of rooms in which the administrative grind of legionary life – all the rosters, stocktaking and details of the soldiers' pay and deductions – would have been worked out and archived. In one corner of the next-door *praetorium*, a small hypocaust indicates that the prefect of the *ala* had his own bath-suite and so did not have to slum it by taking the waters with his troopers.

Outside the east gate, where the Wall met the fort – a section of it survives just a metre or two away – a gentle slope leads down to the river. Sited close by was the soldiers' bath complex. Its position outside the fort meant there was less risk of fire, which might be caused by the furnaces necessary to keep the warm and hot rooms of the baths at a suitable temperature, but such a location – which it shares with many military baths along the frontier in Britannia and elsewhere – had the disadvantage of leaving the soldiers at risk of a surprise attack. The baths seem large for an auxiliary camp, and were reconstructed several times over the years, meaning that the exact shape and purpose of some of the rooms is unclear (and the walls, though still in fair shape, have deteriorated over the years since their initial excavation in 1884–5).

A large rectangular area at the northern end of the bath complex is obviously the *apodyterium* or changing room. The row of seven niches in the west wall here is sometimes interpreted by the overly pragmatic as lockers for the soldiers to place their clothes and valuables in as they bathed. But there are no holes where doors might have been fixed; besides, there would be room only for seven troopers to store their valuables at once, leading to queues or unseemly rows. Instead it is likely that the niches originally contained statues for the seven gods of the week.[95] The baths were provided with all of the normal facilities of *frigidarium* (cold room) – not, presumably a popular choice in the English winter – *tepidarium* (warm room) and *caldarium* (hot room) so that the soldiers could replicate the bathing rituals being enjoyed by their comrades across the Empire, from here to Durostorum on the Danube and Lambaesis in the North African desert.

The Chesters museum is a real old-style relic, containing a mass of stonework crowded together in a manner that is deliberately reminiscent of the customary style of display in the 19th century. Including material found at nearby forts, it is a treasure house in which to browse and take relief from the visual overload of the Wall and from ice-cream-wielding visitors. Its finest piece is a statue of Juno Regina, the consort of Jupiter Dolichenus, who played a central role in a mystery cult imported from Cappadocia in Asia Minor that was popular with the military. There is also a wealth of altar dedications, including some in honour of emperors such as Numerian (283–4) whose reigns were so fleeting as to scarcely have bothered the scorers.

The beginning of the process that would ultimately lead to the public stewardship of the Wall and its scientific study and conservation began in 1796, when Nathaniel Clayton bought the estate on which the Roman fort of Chesters lay. Although Roman studies took a step backwards when he ordered the razing of much of 'this eyesore', as he called the fort – which was then clearly visible to a much greater extent than it is today – he passed on the land to his son in 1832, leaving him a collection of Roman sculpture and monuments that had been preserved from demolition. From 1843 John Clayton began to excavate at Chesters, and assiduously bought up any section of land containing Roman remains that came up for sale. By 1890 he owned no fewer than five of the Wall forts, and had excavated parts of Housesteads, too, and so to him is owed directly the preservation of some of the most splendid Roman monuments in northern Europe.

The Wall as it can be seen today also owes a great deal to John Clayton, for he ordered his workmen to reconstruct large sections of it, using surviving facing stones to build a drystone wall infilled with rubble up to a level of about seven courses, and topped with turf to prevent erosion. Without Clayton there would be no stone barrier snaking its way through the low hills and crags of the central sections of the frontier. In a sense, therefore, he stands alongside Hadrian himself as the 'builder' of the Wall.

Further eastwards there are still sections of Wall surviving, though nothing like the continuous runs of the hilly country in the west. The pathway along the Wall line leads for the most part through fields populated by nothing more threatening than overcurious sheep, soon reaching Brunton turret, just a kilometre from Chesters. Here, a nice section of Wall brackets the remains of one of the watchtowers, complete up to ten courses or so, hidden in a dip beside a row of trees. A further kilometre beyond, in open fields at Planetrees, is one of the most surprising and revealing survivals of the Wall. It is the point at which it changes from being the Narrow Wall, which has been its form in all the stretches west of here, to the Broad Wall, which was the architects' original conception for the whole, though possibly in this case the widening of the Wall is the result of building work around 205 rather than the modifications of the 120s.[96] It is possible to see exactly the point where the change was made, as the stones of the broader foundation, which have hitherto projected outside the curtain of the Wall, disappear underneath it at a rather awkward, but fascinating join.

A few kilometres to the east lie the remains of the Wall fort of Onnum. Unexcavated, and marked by just a few bumps in the ground, it is a convenient point to deviate away from the Wall, back to the line of the Stanegate forts and to one of the best-preserved Roman monuments in the north of England. This area was probably first occupied by the Romans around 79 during Agricola's governorship. They built an early fort around a kilometre from the present one to act as a supply base for the push northwards against the Caledonians. By the mid-80s, however, the new base had been built at Corstopitum, around three kilometres south of the future line of Hadrian's Wall. Today it lies in a neat rectangular enclosure that creates the deceptive impression that the fort was an isolated affair, for the civilian settlement and other diverse buildings that grew up around the military base have either not been dug up or have, over the years, been backfilled by the excavators.

The new fort was destroyed by fire around 105[97] and a replacement built with timber internal buildings. When the Wall was constructed in the 120s, Corstopitum was not initially abandoned, but when the decision was later taken to construct new forts along the line of the Wall, it must have suffered at least a reduction in its garrison, if not outright withdrawal. Corbridge lies in a strategic position close to Dere Street, the main road that led north into Scotland, and so when Antoninus Pius ordered the frontier moved northwards around 139, it actually prospered anew, in contrast to the posts on Hadrian's Wall. A new stone fort was constructed; an inscribed dedication stone of the time records the name of the then governor, Quintus Lollius Urbicus, who was responsible for the work.

By 163 at the latest, however, the Antonine frontier had been abandoned and Hadrian's Wall reoccupied, leading to another reversal of fortune, as Corstopitum again ceased to be a military post; its ramparts may have been thrown down and the site opened up for civilian occupation. For the next century or so it prospered modestly as a regular town, although one exposed to the vagaries of frontier life – it may have been burnt around 180 in a barbarian incursion to which the historian Cassius Dio makes vague reference.[98] Little is known of the subsequent history of the site, although it certainly seems to have been occupied until the later 4th century. How long, if at all, it survived the final Roman evacuation of Britannia is obscure.

The main street of Corstopitum is something of a palimpsest, the surface of the east end much higher, indicating its 4th century level, while towards the centre of the site, where excavation has cleared away most of the subsequent rebuildings, its 1st-century level is almost a metre lower. Interestingly, the 3rd-century reconstruction of parts of the fort contained a large amount of reused sculpture and architectural fragments, indicating that the Romans of the time were much less precious than modern sensibility would allow about putting antique stonework to use, when the practical demands of the time dictated it. To the north side of the road lies a pair of enormous *horrea*. Stone vents that are still visible on the lower level allowed the circulation of air, which prevented the corn from going mouldy, while the top, which presents the appearance of a great stone platform, still retains some of its flagged paving stones. The granaries date from 180, and thus supplied the town once it had been given over to civilian use, but, whether for reasons of bureaucratic impediments or sheer lack of funds is unclear, it took well into the 3rd century to complete them.[99]

Just to the east of the granaries lies a house fronted by the remains of a monumental fountain. Only the basin survives, but it was originally flanked by two statues of winged Victories, with a building dedication by the XX Valeria Victrix legion. Such a showy public fountain or *nymphaeum* was once an essential statement of civic pride in cities throughout the Empire, and Corstopitum was not to be outdone.

One of the most curious areas in the interior of the fort, known as 'Site 11', was at first interpreted by the excavators as a forum. The grassy rectangular area flanked by ranges of buildings does, indeed, initially give this impression, but equally persuasive arguments have been made for its having been a military depot or a storehouse.[100] The history of the occupation of the flanking buildings, however, gives eloquent testimony to the decline of Corstopitum during its later years, for whereas in the 3rd century most of the rooms in both building ranges were being occupied, by the mid-4th century just three rooms were still being used.

The eastern compound of the site, to the south of the main street (the *decumanus*), is more of a jumble of stones, containing a variety of residential complexes, the remains of an old barracks and the former *principia* of the fort, as well as workshops and temples. In the *principia* was found, among the ruins of the temple of the standards, an altar dedicated to 'Imperial Discipline' by the II Augusta legion, which still retained traces of the original red paint used to highlight the lettering. Such dedications to abstract martial virtues – and other edifying concepts such as *Concordia* ('Concord') and *Pax* ('Peace') – were an important part of imperial propaganda. Indeed, it is hard not to suspect that dedications to *Pax* proliferated most in times when war threatened, and those to *Disciplina* multiplied when there had been outbreaks of mutinous behaviour in the ranks of the army.

East of Corstopitum the landscape begins to grow more urban. At Heddon-on-the Wall (some 16 kilometres along the Wall line from Corbridge) and Denton Hall, a stretch of Wall in a field and the remains of a turret can be seen, while on the outskirts of Newcastle the remains of a Mithraic temple poke through in an incongruous suburban setting at Benwell. Newcastle itself, or Pons Aeli, had the signal honour – given to no other installation on the Wall – of being named after Hadrian himself (whose full name was Publius Aelius Hadrianus). Of the fort itself, which guarded a key crossing over the Tyne, nothing survives, Roman Newcastle (and the neighbouring forts) instead being encapsulated within the walls of the Great North Museum.[101]

East of Pons Aeli, the Wall, mostly invisible, wends its way through the industrial landscape of the Tyne's journey towards the sea. Segedunum fort at Wallsend lies squeezed beside the Swan Hunter shipyard, whilst coal-mining in the area since the 18th century further damaged the site, leaving relatively few pieces of original masonry intact. The towers and cranes of the shipyard look over the Roman ruins, and small cruise boats meander by, blaring out music that breaks the calm and reverie of a summer's evening. What it lacks in the grandeur of the surviving remains, though, Segedunum makes up with the imagination with which it has been displayed. A great glass tower gives an eagle's-eye-view over the site, clearly displaying the outline of the fort and the way in which it – and most other typical Roman military bases – were organised, a panorama for which no amount of fort plans on paper can make up. A rebuilt military bathhouse (not on the site of the original) also gives a taste of what the real thing would have been like, when fully decorated and provided with its various pools, mosaics and frescoes, a sensation far removed from that which the bare, but original, stones elsewhere provoke.

The fort housed the Fourth Cohort of Lingones in the 3rd and 4th centuries, a part-mounted unit, and excavations of what is left of the cavalry barracks (marked on the site by stone outlines) revealed that far from there being separate stable blocks in Roman cavalry forts, as had been supposed, the men lived with their horses in the same blocks, the animals being housed in neighbouring cubicles.[102] A little way beyond the fort's car park a 30-metre section of Wall has been reconstructed, with (possibly anomalous) crenellations, fronted by pits inset with wooden spikes, a Roman anti-personnel trap that must have been horribly effective against incautious marauders. Beside it is a low stretch of Wall foundation, the last along the frontier, and almost the final vestige of Hadrian's great project.

Not quite the last, however, for eventually the stretch from Wallsend to the coast some 10 kilometres away, which it had not initially been deemed necessary to defend, was fortified, a decision that was then reversed – taken, presumably, to prevent hostile forces from the north slipping across the Tyne at a point where it was only lightly guarded. At South Shields, just south of the mouth of the Tyne, lies Arbeia, originally constructed in the 2nd century as a regular auxiliary fort, and now surrounded by low, neat terraces, a world away from the sparse rural settings of the remains at Housesteads or Chesters. It has been speculated that the name derives from an Aramaic term for 'Arab', an etymology reinforced to some extent by the presence in the 4th century of a *numerus Barcariorum Tigrisiensium* (a number of Tigris boatmen) as its garrison.[103] Another ancient immigrant to Tyneside is commemorated in Arbeia's museum, where the tombstone of Regina, a native Briton (from the Catuvellauni tribe) is on display. Originally a slave, she was freed by her master, Barates, who came from far-off Palmyra in modern Syria. His tomb, astonishingly, also survived and is in the museum at Corbridge.

Not much remains of the actual wall of the fort at Arbeia, but its western gateway has been reconstructed in its entirety, giving a rare chance in Britain – the habit is much more common along the German sections of the frontier – to see how impressive the Roman monuments must have been in their heyday. Whether it should have been built with crenellations or whether the towers had roofs is the subject of endless debate,[104] but its sheer imposing presence is a reminder that what we now see as jumbles of stone and fragments of defences were once part of complete, towering buildings and continuous, dominating sections of wall. The gateway, too, gives a splendid view over the site, and in particular over the series of *horrea* that were built over the northern third of

Arbeia at the start of the 3rd century. The fort was also extended at this time and, over the course of a decade, more and more granaries were built, so that from 205/8 (when fourteen were built) to about 220, the total reached an astonishing twenty-four grain stores. It was only at the end of the 3rd century that many of these were converted back into use as barracks.

The reason behind this proliferation of granaries was Rome's last serious strike northwards into the Highlands of Scotland. Since the border had been pulled back to Hadrian's Wall in 169, the frontier had been fairly quiet.[105] Following the civil war that brought Septimius Severus to the throne in 193, and which also involved Clodius Albinus (the then governor of Britain) in a failed attempt to become Emperor, a decision was taken to cut Britannia in two – a fate also meted out to Syria, where Septimius's other rival, Pescennius Niger, had been governor. The southern part of Britain became Britannia Superior, with its governor based in London, whilst the north, including Hadrian's Wall, fell to Britannia Inferior, with its capital (and sole legion) at Eboracum (York).[106]

It seems that the northern tribes were keen observers of the Romans' troubles and, when Albinus withdrew part of the garrison for his ill-fated march through Gaul,[107] a confederacy in the Lowlands, known as the Maetae, started to cause trouble. It was only in 207 that the frontier line was restored once more and in a position to take any further punishment the Maetae might want to throw at it. The Emperor, however, was not content, and in 208 Septimius arrived in Britain in person, accompanied by his senior officials and his two sons, Caracalla and Geta. The latter, the younger son, was left in London to administer, with suitable guidance, the province from the rear, whilst Septimius and Caracalla marched north to deal out suitable retribution to the recalcitrant Maetae.

The army seems to have moved rapidly to the Forth–Clyde isthmus and then used Carpow in Fife as a springboard to launch a series of operations further north. Septimius's campaign is said to have taken him almost to the extremities of the island and, wherever he did reach, no Roman force would ever again operate so far north.[108] The Maetae were temporarily cowed, and the Emperor felt sanguine enough to allow the issue of coins with the legend *Victoriae Britannicae*.[109] Yet in summer 210 they once again rose up in revolt, this time in alliance with the Caledonians. Septimius was now too ill to join his legions on their march north and appointed Caracalla to lead the troops instead. The old Emperor's death at Eboracum in February 211, however, brought a rapid end to the campaign. Although the legionaries were still present in Scotland (at Carpow) in 212, Caracalla seems to have done a deal with the Maetae to allow his and Geta's return home to Rome, a necessary move to forestall any attempts at usurpation.

As he lay dying, Septimius had given his two sons a piece of advice, culled from long experience of revolt and government: 'Pay the army, love each other, and forget all else.'[110] Caracalla and Geta stopped their ears to his middle counsel, for they loathed each other, and within months had turned the imperial palace at Rome into a virtual war zone, divided between the contesting parties. Caracalla, the eldest, although less popular with the army, proved the more ruthless, and in December the same year he had his brother murdered at a meeting ostensibly called to effect a reconciliation between them.[111]

The Antonine Wall

Hadrian's Wall almost became the greatest white elephant in Roman military history when the Emperor died barely a decade after its completion. His successor, Antoninus Pius, who was Hadrian's adoptive son (even though just ten years younger),[112] gained a reputation as a peace-loving scholarly type. In stark contrast to Hadrian, he rarely left the confines of Rome or his villas on its outskirts.

It was perhaps, therefore, his desire to gain a reasonably cheap victory that lay behind his decision to move the frontier forward again, this time to the shorter line of the Forth–Clyde isthmus. Interestingly, he made a similar advance in Germany, where he pushed the *limes* in Germania Superior eastward by 30 kilometres; all a case of a few cautious steps forward, which might reap a rich harvest in glorious proclamations. The move 160 kilometres or so north of the line of Hadrian's Wall probably took place within months of Pius's accession in July 138.[113] It seems to have been a great success, meeting no serious resistance, and the Emperor, well satisfied, awarded himself the title *imperator*, normally bestowed only on victorious generals (but, after the very early days of the Empire, the exclusive prerogative of the emperors themselves).

Hadrian's Wall was now abandoned, the Vallum filled in and the garrisons moved to new positions further north. Here, along the Forth–Clyde isthmus, a new wall was constructed, this time entirely of turf. It was just 60 kilometres long, barely half the length of its southern predecessor, and so in many ways was a more defensible proposition. It probably stood around 3 metres in height, on a base of stone about 15 Roman feet (approximately 4.5 metres) in width.[114] Whether there were any plans to relay the Antonine Wall in stone at a later point is unknown, and its subsequent early abandonment meant that it remained for ever a turf construction. Like Hadrian's Wall, it was provided with a ditch, around 4 metres deep, but the Vallum dug behind the southern barrier was not replicated in the Antonine scheme. Just like Hadrian's Wall, it was provided with forts, and these, like their southern counterparts, became subject to a change of plan that left much greater levels of force actually stationed along the Wall line. Whilst initially it seems that the Antonine Wall was only to have six forts, with fortlets (similar to the milecastles on Hadrian's Wall) every Roman mile (or 1.6 kilometres), the number of forts was greatly increased during the actual building process, leading to a dense network with one sited every 3.2 kilometres.

The forts were generally placed against the line of the Wall, and did not project from it, in another variance from the early plan of Hadrian's Wall. They thus had only one gate facing into 'enemy' territory. Like the southern wall, the garrison was composed of a mixture of units, mostly auxiliaries, but with a distinct lack of cavalry, unlike Hadrian's Wall.[115] The construction gangs, as ever drawn from the legions stationed in the province at the time, came from the II Augusta, VI Victrix and XX Valeria Victrix legions, and seem to have worked in blocks of 4 Roman miles (or 6 kilometres) in the western half, with a slightly different division in the east.[116]

From Old Kilpatrick at the far west of the line to Carriden at the eastern end, the legionary working parties placed a distance slab at the end of each section they completed. Whereas plain inscriptions were deemed sufficient on Hadrian's Wall, for the Antonine Wall much more elaborate carvings were set into the fabric of the wall. In one, the goddess Victory awards the legion a laurel wreath in token of its achievement, whilst in the most elaborate, found in the east at Bridgeness, a priest makes a sacrifice of a bull, pig and sheep, the *suovetaurilia* that was normally offered at the start of a military campaign, and which might be evidence that the building of the Wall started from the east and went westwards.[117] As a final component of the defensive system, the legionaries built the Military Way, a road sited to ensure effective communications and rapid movement between the various military installations, and which ran right the way along the frontier, at a distance of 15–40 metres behind the rampart.

Although less easy to trace along the ground than Hadrian's Wall, a reasonable number of the forts and some stretches of the Antonine Wall can be visited today, though the comparatively fragile nature of the material used to build the Wall and the flatter terrain on which it was built have meant that there are none of the spectacular stretches of stone-clad hills which have made Hadrian's Wall the more famous and visited of the two Roman walls in Britain. Beginning at the western extremity, little of the Antonine Wall is visible until Bearsden, which housed the fourth fort along the line in the revised scheme, less than 10 kilometres to the east of Glasgow. A short section of the Wall base is exposed in New Kilpatrick cemetery, but of more interest, the military baths at Bearsden are the Antonine frontier's first major surviving relic. The fort itself is now entombed beneath the housing estate whose low blocks surround the baths on three sides, the fourth bordered by a minor, but busy road. The bath complex is almost complete, and the various rooms stand to a reasonable height, as much as seven courses in places.[118] They include a *laconicum*, a small room whose very name suggests it was a super-heated or sauna room in which lingering for very long was not advised. Hedged about, its survival seems a lucky accident, when so much of the Wall has simply vanished.

About 10 kilometres east, into the central section of the Wall and already practically halfway across the frontier, Bar Hill sits high on a rise above the B802 road, almost entirely hidden behind a screen of trees that blocks off views of the slope where the fort lies. Unlike most of the forts and fortlets on the Wall, the garrison here is known, being made up of the *Cohors I Baetasiorum*, followed by the *Cohors I Hamiorum*, a unit of archers from Syria,[119] who presumably must have found the wet and cold climate distinctly uncomfortable. Faint remains of the *principia* are visible on the slopes, together with a bathhouse that was, unusually, built within the perimeter of the fort. It was a small complex, as befitted such an isolated outpost.

At Seabegs, 4–5 kilometres to the east, a fine section of the Wall rampart and ditch can be seen at the edge of a small wood that obscured it until the overgrown section was cleared away. The ditch strikes in a dramatic V-shape, towered over by the grass hump of the mound, giving a sense, for the first time on the Antonine frontier, of a formidable barrier. Its grassed-over remains also provide a pleasant park-like atmosphere and, even in the impending gloom of mid-autumn, is more populated by the cries of children enjoying a post-picnic play than by the echoes of legionaries cutting out and laying endless sections of turf.

The next fort along the line, a couple of kilometres away at Rough Castle, is perhaps the most spectacular setting along the whole Antonine Wall. Both Wall and ditch here survive in excellent condition, with the tiny fort of Rough Castle itself – barely 0.4 hectares – sitting in a very ruined state on a promontory overlooking the undulating site. Through the turf and the grass, odd pieces of stonework poke through, and to the east of the site parts of an annexe can be discerned in a low mound and vestigial ditch. It is a very up-and-down outpost, with ditch, rampart and mounds in a beautiful wooded setting, but within it a hidden danger lurks, at least for intruders in ancient times. North-west of the ditch, opposite the castle itself, ten rows of pits were uncovered, each of which would have been booby-trapped with wooden spikes and then covered with vegetation. The wounds caused to any unsuspecting intruders would have been horrendous. With grim military humour, the Roman army referred to these silent watchdogs as *lilia* ('lilies').

Three kilometres to the east, on the outskirts of modern Falkirk, a busy town and the largest in the Edinburgh–Glasgow corridor apart from those cities themselves, lies another finely preserved portion of the Wall. Set beside a busy road, a thin strip of a park shaded by a straggly line of trees conceals a section of ditch that has survived to almost its full depth, some 5 metres deep, making a walk along the rampart edge above a precarious business. The latter has not survived quite so well, and had the 3-metre-high lip which it originally formed at the edge of the ditch remained, it would have been possible to gain a truly accurate impression of quite how difficult the scramble down ditch and up rampart would have been, to all but the truly determined. Yet even so, peering down at the ditch bottom, part choked by autumn leaves that render the whole thing a riot of golden orange, one realises why the Caledonians made little serious effort to penetrate the Wall whilst it was still in commission.

At the eastern stretch of the Antonine Wall again little is visible, although the ditch has often remained where the Wall itself has been obliterated. The final relic (apart from the remains of the fort at Cramond, which was not strictly on the Wall line) is at Kinneil, near Bo'ness, where a milefortlet, the only one to have been excavated, sits in an open area screened by a small wood from the rest of the park in which it lies. The fort only really survives at its north-east corner, where the stone base of the rampart has resisted the ravages of time. Elsewhere a couple of the gates have been marked out with posts, while very indistinctly the line of the Wall ditch can be made out. For the most part, however, it seems a forgotten place, ignored even by the procession of dog-walkers sheltering beneath the trees from an unwelcome shower.

The abandonment of the Antonine Wall remains something of a mystery.[120] The consensus of opinion seems to be that it was around 161 that the withdrawal began.[121] Building works were undertaken on Hadrian's Wall at about this time, which would be consistent with a recommissioning of its defences.[122] That the process of withdrawal was

not a simple one is indicated by a coin found at Old Kilpatrick dated
164–9 and some pottery at Castlecary, which would also support a similar
date for occupation. Yet the Romans had always held outpost forts beyond
Hadrian's Wall, such as those at Birrens and Newstead, and it is expecting
too much in the way of a smooth transition for them not to have held
onto at least some positions of the Antonine Wall as long as they found
it convenient.[123]

Exactly why the pull-back took place is obscure. There had been little
obvious strategic reason for the occupation of the Scottish Lowlands in
the first place, and equally little compelling motive for drawing back
from it. Antoninus Pius's successor, Marcus Aurelius, had despatched
Calpurnius Agricola as the new governor to Britannia in 161, as some
kind of war seemed to threaten. Perhaps this rising tension on the frontier led to his recommending a retreat, which might have been viewed
as temporary, as the best way of easing pressure. After Antoninus Pius's
death in 161, there would have been no emotional reason for a reoccupation of his Wall line, and Marcus Aurelius had other preoccupations,
becoming embroiled in a decade-long war against the Sarmatians on the
Danube.[124] Once back on Hadrian's Wall, the Roman army units were
to stay, for the most part, for the rest of the life of the Roman province.

The Saxon Shore

The 3rd century was a time of growing uncertainty for the Empire. The
western provinces, which had known a high level of security and prosperity for 200 years, began to feel the danger of external invasion, which
had been absent for generations. Towns, and particularly those in highly
urbanised Gaul, began to acquire walls, often enclosing only a reduced
area, with their circuit excluding areas that were still populated – but
from which, into the safety of the defences, the people would in due
course remove themselves. The walls were bulky, thick affairs, often
with rounded projecting towers from which crossfire could be rained
down on the heads of assailants. They were platforms from which to
defend, and a far cry from the relatively modest stone ramparts of the
earlier legionary fortresses. Britain was not immune to this development, and in the 3rd century a new frontier opened up far to the south
of Hadrian's Wall, as barbarian raiders – far from trying to breach the
land defences – took to boats and conducted plundering raids aimed at
the comparatively easy pickings to be had along the southern and eastern
coasts of Britannia.

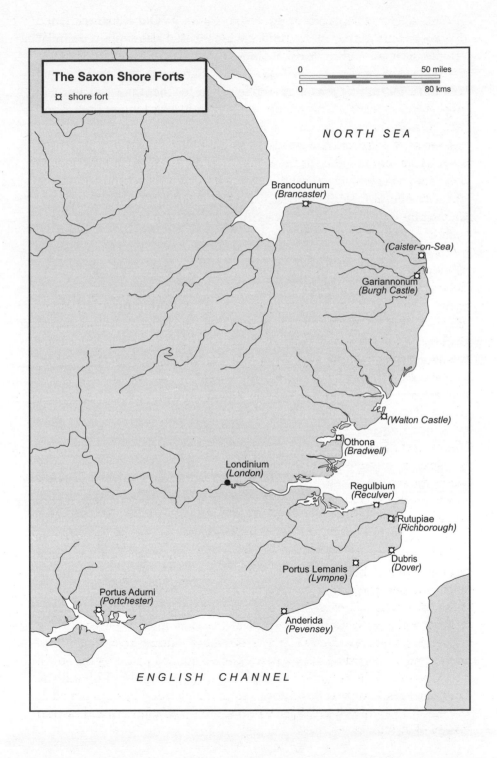

The Saxon Shore Forts

◘ shore fort

0 ____ 50 miles
0 ____ 80 kms

NORTH SEA

Brancodunum
(Brancaster)

(Caister-on-Sea)

Gariannonum
(Burgh Castle)

(Walton Castle)

Othona
(Bradwell)

Londinium
(London)

Regulbium
(Reculver)

Rutupiae
(Richborough)

Dubris
(Dover)

Portus Lemanis
(Lympne)

Portus Adurni
(Portchester)

Anderida
(Pevensey)

ENGLISH CHANNEL

The defence of Britain's south coast had long devolved to the *Classis Britannica*, the British fleet, with its principal stations at Gesoriacum (Boulogne) and Dubris (Dover), and smaller supply bases at ports like Fishbourne. Most evidence of this fleet comes in the 2nd century, such as an altar located at Lemanis (Lympne) set up by Lucius Aufidius Pantera, prefect of the fleet.[125] In the 3rd century, however, the number of coin hoards buried in south-east England seems to increase, often a sign of insecurity, as the owners stashed them in troubled times, hoping to return (but, by definition, never did, enabling their discovery by modern archae-ologists). There is some evidence of destruction by burning in sites in the south such as London and Colchester,[126] although whether this was caused by hostile action or by accident is hard to determine. It seems that the *Classis Britannica* was failing to hold back the raiders; indeed, it may almost have ceased to operate, as the last mentions of it come in the 250s.[127] The historians Eutropius and Aurelius Victor relate that the whole area of northern Gaul had become infiltrated by nests of pirates, who must have caused grave difficulties for the authorities both there and across the Channel in Britannia.[128]

The Roman response was to build a new chain of defences that stretched from roughly the Solent in the south-west to the Wash in the north-east, and which has become known as the 'Saxon Shore'. Whether this came as the result of a single decision by one emperor (or governor) is doubtful, for, although erosion has caused difficulty in dating certain sites (the one at Walton disappeared beneath the waves as the coastline retreated in the 17th century), the architectural style of the individual forts does seem to indicate a spread of more than half a century between the dates of their construction.[129]

The earliest of these forts was most probably that at Caister, which may even have been begun as early as 200, whilst the latest, at Pevensey, was still being worked on in the 290s.[130] What is certain, however, is that the defence of this area was dramatically illuminated in 286 when Britannia broke away from the Empire. From the early 280s Gaul had been suffering the depredations of a group of rebels known as the Bagaudae. The nature of their revolt is unclear, and whether they were merely a bunch of brigands, a proto-nationalist insurrection or a local self-help militia that got out of control has been widely debated.[131] The rebels kept the central state at bay for several decades, particularly in Armorica (modern Brittany), and so they were probably more than just a bunch of ill-disciplined bandits.

In 284, Maximian was appointed co-Emperor by Diocletian, in a move that foreshadowed the system of four cooperating emperors that would be known as the Tetrarchy.[132] As part of this reorganisation, Carausius was promoted to admiral with a special brief to deal with the problem of the pirates still plaguing the narrow straits between Britannia and Gaul. Eutropius dismisses him as 'a man of the lowest birth',[133] although this was an assertion that he was able to make at the safe distance of almost a century. He further alleges that Carausius got into the habit of allowing the barbarians to pillage the coast of Britannia Superior with impunity and only moved to intercept them when they were on their way back home, their ships laden with plunder – which of course the admiral then sequestered for his own personal enrichment.

Whether he was actually engaged in such nefarious activity, came under suspicion for another reason or acted entirely on his own initiative, by 286 or early 287 Carausius had raised the standard of revolt and declared himself Emperor. He thus began a tradition of British breakaway emperors, which would persist right up until the end of the Roman occupation. Maximian was now faced with a serious crisis. His early attempts to deal with the problem were distinctly unsuccessful, and seem to have ended up in 288–9 with the destruction of those elements of the fleet that he still commanded.[134] Carausius remained secure in this possession both of Britannia and of the northern shores of Gaul, including the former *Classis Britannica* base at Gesoriacum.

He apparently ruled his new domain with some discretion, actually increasing the bullion content of the coins, rather than introducing a debasement that would have indicated economic distress.[135] He joined in the imperial propaganda game with great panache, issuing coins with the legends *Pax Auggg* ('the peace of the three Augusti') and incorporating busts of Diocletian and Maximian, thereby hinting visually that he was actually a legitimate member of the college of emperors, rather than a rank usurper, as the other two regarded him to be. He even pinched elements of the official imperial nomenclature, renaming himself Marcus Aurelius Mausaeus Carausius.[136] Diocletian and Maximian were not mollified, and when the Tetrarchy reached its full form in 293, with the appointments of two junior emperors or Caesars, one of them, Constantius I (who became Maximian's deputy), was given the brief of sorting out Carausius once and for all. In the autumn of the same year, however, half of Constantius's job was done for him, when Allectus, who had been Carausius's chief financial minister, assassinated his master and took over as British Emperor himself.[137]

It took until 296 for Constantius to assemble a fleet powerful enough to attempt a crossing of the English Channel.[138] The force was divided into two squadrons, one of which assembled at the mouth of the Seine under Constantius himself, while the other gathered at Gesoriacum, led by his praetorian prefect, Asclepiodotus.[139] Constantius's force was delayed by bad weather, so it was the army of Asclepiodotus that encountered such units as Allectus had been able to cobble together, possibly somewhere in the region of Silchester in Hampshire.[140] Allectus's army was roundly beaten and he himself died on the battlefield. The retreating remnants of his force, which included a large contingent of Franks, decided to make the best of their deteriorating fortunes by heading for London and the good prospect of plunder there, before melting away as best they could. Constantius, however, had finally arrived and reached London just in time to intercept them, thereby getting the restoration of imperial rule in Britain off to a very good start.[141]

By the 360s, matters had deteriorated dramatically, and in 367 the great 'barbarian conspiracy' referred to by Ammianus broke out, combining raids across the line of Hadrian's Wall with seaborne assaults on vulnerable sections of the coastline. By the early 5th century the south coast came under the jurisdiction of the count of the *Litus Saxonicum* (or Saxon Shore), who commanded troops at Dubris (Dover), Lemanis (Lympne), Brancodunum (Brancaster), Regulbium (Reculver), Rutupiae (Richborough) and Anderida (Pevensey), all places that contain fortifications now regarded as part of the 'Saxon Shore' system. Portus Adurni (Portchester), which is included in modern historians' lists, seems to have been abandoned by 369.[142] Whether the name 'Saxon Shore' refers to an area settled by Saxon federates (or allies) or whether, indeed, the name is a convention and the sites are no more than fortified ports, not intended to guard against any specific threat, is also debated.[143] Whatever the original purpose, or the reason for its naming, the end result was that the North Sea and Channel coastlines of southern England, which had not hitherto been heavily defended, were hedged around, by the late 3rd century, with a substantial set of fortifications.

Although their construction spanned more than fifty years, to the modern eye the Saxon Shore forts share a superficial similarity of appearance: bulky walls, which have survived the test of time far better than most of the earlier installations in the British Isles (with the obvious exception of Hadrian's Wall); bonding courses of brick (or tile) and stone, alternating to give a striated effect as the red bricks stand out against the duller stone of the facing and, where exposed, the rubble core; and in most cases large, rounded, projecting towers that prefigure the classic architecture of the early medieval castle (and which on occasion were co-opted to form part of such baronial fortifications). The quantity of material needed to construct the Saxon Shore defences was vast; it has been calculated that for Pevensey alone – albeit one of the larger forts – it amounted to around 1,600 boatloads of building materials.[144]

Today many of these forts do not sit along the coastline, being beached instead some distance inland (or, in the case of Walton, actually under the water). It is therefore hard to gain a sense of the original topography of the land as the Romans would have experienced it. At Brancaster in Norfolk, the most northerly of the forts generally ascribed to the Saxon Shore, the island that blocks off egress from the creek on which the fort sits was simply not there in Roman times.[145] Similarly, the complex series of channels and waterways near Great Yarmouth on which Burgh Castle and Caister-on-Sea forts sit was already being affected by the contrary forces of erosion and silting during Roman times, so that the coastline at Caister-on-Sea actually lay 2 kilometres to the east of its present position.

South of Burgh Castle and Caister-on-Sea, the approaches to the Essex coast were watched over by the now-vanished Walton Castle and Othona (or Bradwell). The Kent and Sussex shorelines were guarded by what are perhaps the most famous – and visually striking – set of castles at Regulbium (Reculver), Rutupiae (Richborough), Dubris (Dover), Anderitum (Pevensey) and Portus Adurni (Portchester). Regulbium, which in ancient times sat alongside the Wantsum Channel that made the Isle of Thanet a true island, was probably one of the earliest of the forts. Although half of it has been washed away, its architecture is more reminiscent of traditional auxiliary-fort construction than its near-neighbour Rutupiae. An inscription attributed the construction of part of the *principia* of the fort to the time of Rufinus, probably the man who was governor between 225 and 230, so the start of building works at Regulbium must have been not too long before that. Its nearly square form, without apparent bastions, now hosts the dramatic silhouette of the ruined 12th-century church of Saint Egbert, its own rectangular towers seeming to offer the protection that Regulbium's robbed walls lack.

Garrisoned by the *Cohors I Baetasiorum* in the 3rd century, the fort may have been abandoned after the time of Carausius[146] and then reoccupied in the 4th. There is little evidence of its being used in the early 5th century, however, and it, and the neighbouring port, had probably lain abandoned for more than a century before Saxons chose it as the site of a church in 669.[147]

Only around 15 kilometres south of Regulbium lies the fort of Rutupiae. There was much less ease of access in ancient times, when the Wantsum Channel meant that to travel between the two forts demanded a boat journey or land trip all the way south-westwards

towards Durovernum (Canterbury) and then back eastwards to
Rutupiae, which then sat on a small coastal island, and not, as today,
4 kilometres inland. The pleasant walk through fields and along the
River Stour to Richborough brings the fort into view at its most attractive, the elongated stretch of its southern wall rising to 8 metres in
height, cut off where its south-western tower would have been, looking
like a great stone boat with its angular prow pointed away from the
sea. These walls, undoubtedly the most impressive feature of the site,
come from its late 3rd-century phase, but Rutupiae has a much longer
history, which is in a way a microcosm of that of the province of
Britannia itself.

The ditch that fronts the wall at a distance of 20 metres or so, cutting
a swathe through the verdant green of the field around, comes from the
very earliest Roman occupation, for Richborough is believed to have
been the main landing place of the invasion force under Aulus Plautius
in AD 43,[148] and an earth rampart would have been built around the site
at that time. The ditch, however, was soon filled in, and for the next
four decades Rutupiae experienced a more humdrum existence as a rear
supply base for the gradual Roman advance across the whole island.

Another curious feature lies in the eastern half of the fort, looking
like a great cruciform mound, raised a metre or more and covered in
grass. Far from being some precocious evidence of early Christianity in
the province, this is the remains of the base of a triumphal arch, which
was erected around 85. The centre of the site was raised and an enormous monument, probably around 25 metres high[149] and possibly topped
with a bronze statue, was constructed. Exactly what shape it took – and
whether it was built to celebrate the victory at Mons Graupius in 83,
which might have been said to mark the final 'conquest' of the island –
is unknown, but it was clad in white Carrara marble imported all the
way from Italy, the only building in Roman Britain known to have received
such a prestigious treatment.[150] When completed, it must have been
visible over a great distance and would have formed a hugely impressive gateway to the province.

The town that grew up around the monument – and whose streets
lie buried in the surrounding fields – prospered and the remains of a
stone *mansio* or inn, complete with small hypocaust, can be seen in the
interior of the fort. However, times changed and in the middle of the
3rd century a new earth fort was built on the site, a token that Kent
needed defending in a way that for almost two centuries had not been
necessary. The monument itself suffered the indignity of being converted
into a watchtower, and the interior of what would become the Saxon

Shore fort was scored with a system of huge triple ditches, which even when partly filled in and grassed over are extremely unkind on the ankle and would have amply broken up the momentum of any concerted charge that an enemy might have cared to launch.

This phase was comparatively short-lived, and some time around 280 the remains of the monument were pulled down and the whole site was cleared. Debris from the demolition was incorporated into a new set of walls, which are those that can be seen so dramatically today. With its huge towers and massive 3-metre-thick walls, the Saxon Shore fort of Rutupiae must have been every bit as impressive a statement of Roman might as the monument had been, but the province was clearly living on reduced means. Only wooden internal structures have been found, presumably of the barracks of the II Augusta legion, the garrison listed for the fort in the *Notitia Dignitatum*.

However, the port continued to be a principal gateway for arrivals to the province, and for high dignitaries whenever Britannia attracted the attention of the central authorities. It was at Rutupiae in 368 that Theodosius landed on his mission to restore order following the barbarian conspiracy of the previous year, but by this time the end was nearly in sight for the Saxon Shore system. In the late 4th or early 5th century a Christian church (of timber) was erected within the fort precinct (its hexagonal stone font can still be seen), but it was about the last structure to be built there under the Romans. By the time Saint Wilfrid visited the area in 687, he went ashore instead at Sandwich, possibly indicating that Rutupiae's harbour had by now silted up.[151] It was not wholly abandoned, for eventually a late-Saxon church was built there, the indistinct remains of which can still be seen alongside the much more dramatic relics of the Roman fort.

The shortest journey across the English Channel between Gaul and Britannia was guarded by the Roman port and fort at Dubris (modern Dover), which was situated close to the medieval Dover castle. It was almost certainly occupied at a very early stage, possibly shortly after the Claudian invasion of 43, and in the 2nd century it became a principal base for the British fleet, the *Classis Britannica*, with a new fort built about 130.[152] Parts of the fort's wall and one of its gates have been unearthed, as well as some internal buildings, but more substantial remains have been found of the Saxon Shore fort, which was constructed around 270. With its wall of tufa and chalk, it lay a little north-east of the by-now-demolished naval fort. Beside it, and possibly preceding it by a few decades, was the building now known as the 'Painted House', which was in turn destroyed to make way for the Saxon Shore defences and in which were discovered, during the 1970s, the most extensive set of Roman wall paintings to be found north of the Alps.

In the grounds of Dover Castle lies the last of Dubris's monuments to survive, the Roman lighthouse, a most unlikely bell tower to the 11th-century church of Saint Mary in Castro (which itself incorporated a great deal of robbed Roman stonework). Although somewhat modified (with the top 5 metres or so being totally rebuilt), a sense can still be gained of the lighthouse's unique octagonal structure (resolving itself into a rectangle in the internal chambers), which tapered to the top where a fire would have been kept burning to guide mariners into the harbour and safety.

About 20 kilometres south-west along the coast from Dubris lay Portus Lemanis (Lympne) on the edge of Romney Marsh, and after this, a further 60 kilometres further on, the Saxon Shore's next major installation was at Anderitum (Pevensey). It is one of the later forts in the system, and was still under construction at the end of the 3rd century. Its massive walls are punctuated by eleven U-shaped towers that still rise for the most part to about 8 metres in height, crowning a hillock that is now several kilometres inland, but to which, in antiquity, a navigable channel existed. Inside the walls a huge grassy oval is surrounded only by the stumps of walls a metre or two high, but halfway along the north wall a deep archaeological trench sunk in the 1930s shows how much lower the ground was during the 3rd century.

A walk around the perimeter, negotiating both a sleepy country lane and the far-less-tranquil avenue of the A27, which bounds the fort on the north, shows the walls off to their true and dramatic height. They are built with the typical late-Roman *opus mixtum* technique, with layers of stonework alternating with bands of coloured tiles and bricks that lent stability to the structure. In places, where these bands do not entirely meet each other, evidence can be seen in the mismatch of the separate working groups of soldiers who constructed the different sections of wall.

Anderitum provides possible evidence for the process by which the garrisons of Britain were evacuated to the Continent, for a unit attested in the *Notitia Dignitatum* with the name of the fort is later listed as being stationed near Paris [153] At each successive crisis of the 4th century, and with each successive British usurper, more and more forts like this one must have been left with only skeleton defence forces, if any at all. The survival of the fort's defences into the 5th century, however, is indicated by a reference in the *Anglo-Saxon Chronicle* under 491, which records the siege by Aelle and Cissa of a force of Britons within a place named

'Andreadsceaster', which must surely be Anderitum. In one sense they were the very last defenders of the Saxon Shore, but, once Aelle had captured the place, they were slaughtered to the last man.'[154]

Even afterwards, the walls stood firm, since a medieval keep, whose first incarnation was built shortly after the Norman conquest of England in 1066,[155] is in places bonded with the stonework of the Roman fort. Anderitum, at some 4 hectares in area, was too large for the Normans to defend and the eastern part of the interior was sectioned off with a wall and ditch. That those defending Pevensey prior to the Norman invasion were the very folk against whose forefathers the Romans had built the 'Saxon Shore' forts in the first place is a rich historical irony, but not one that their king, Harold, who died a few weeks later at the Battle of Hastings, had much leisure to contemplate.

Forming the final link in the chain, Portus Adurni (modern Portchester), 120 kilometres to the west of Anderitum, sits on a low spit of land that projects out into Portsmouth Harbour. Contrary to the case at many of the other forts, the topography here has changed little since Roman times. It must have been an attractive place to be garrisoned, its narrow beach giving spectacular views to the other side of the harbour, with a cooling breeze in summer. The Roman fort's walls survive intact (but reduced in width) almost around the whole circuit. It is a rare pleasure to be able to walk the entire perimeter, gazing up at original Roman masonry all the way, although many of the bastions and some of the gates are missing (at least in their original form). Along the east and south side a water-filled moat, crossed by a modern bridge, harbours a mass of small crabs, which together with the open grassed-over area of the fort's interior attracts large numbers of late-summer visitors, and gives it the air of a tranquil country park, which just happens to have one of Britain's most stunning Roman remains within its bounds.

Enclosing just short of 4 hectares, and lacking internal structures apart from the 12th-century keep built in one corner and the Church of Saint Mary in the north-west (of similar vintage), the interior magnifies the sense of the sheer space and size of the fort. Amidst the ball-playing, kite-flying and picnicking it now hosts, the central area gives an unrivalled vantage point for a look at the whole of an almost intact fort wall. Unusually, the gates (which survive in the Landgate and Watergate, respectively to the east and west of the fort) do not possess projecting towers, with the Watergate – whose central arch retains its original Roman masonry and which was not reconstructed in medieval times – showing this particularly clearly.

The fort seems to have been built in the late 280s or 290s.[156] It was still in use until at least the 350s, with some evidence of rebuilding in the 340s, possibly in association with a visit by Emperor Constans to Britannia in 342.[157] There are very few coins datable after 367, even though a military garrison is listed in the *Notitia*,[158] revealing at best a very light military presence at Portus Adurni in the later 4th century. The next finds at Portchester are of Saxon huts dating from the 5th century, an indication that the life of Roman Britannia and of the Saxon Shore frontier was by that time at an end.

There had certainly still been a Roman army in the province in the second decade of the 5th century, for at that point yet another series of usurpers was raised up by it, the last of whom, Constantine III, was instrumental in the final collapse of Roman authority on the island. With Gaul seemingly lost after a large force of barbarians crossed the Rhine late in 405,[159] Britain was left to its own devices. The army there adopted the tried and tested method of electing its own emperor. It took them several times to get it right, for usurpers named Marcus and Gratian were elevated and murdered in rapid succession, before the poisoned chalice was passed to Constantine, who may have had no better recommendation for the job than his illustrious-sounding name. Constantine III (as he now became) lost no time in assembling the remnants of the army and in 407 or 408 crossed over to Gaul, intending to rescue the province from the barbarians and then either overthrow Honorius or come to some agreement with him over sharing out the rapidly diminishing imperial pie.

The local authorities in Britain were faced with the unpalatable truth that their one last hope, Constantine III, had promptly marched off with the remains of the army supposed to defend them. According to the historian Zosimus, by 410 they had ejected the remaining representatives of Roman authority and begun to govern themselves. Although the coherence of Zosimus's narrative has been disputed,[160] and it has even been suggested that instead of Britannia he was referring to a unilateral declaration of independence by Bruttium in southern Italy, it remains clear that the central government was in no position to reassert its authority in Britain. Northern Gaul was henceforth held by the Romans only intermittently, if at all, and the reduced resources of the Empire were simply not up to launching an expedition to bring Britain back into the fold, and certainly not to supporting a sufficiently strong garrison to maintain order there. With the horizons of the Roman government in Ravenna increasingly those of a regional and not a Europe-wide power, the process of Britain's slipping the Roman leash was probably more extended than Zosimus implies, but the result was nonetheless the same. Constantine himself fared little better than the province he had abandoned. In 411, weakened by a revolt by his own lieutenant, Gerontius, in Spain, he surrendered and was promptly executed.

In many British town and cities, the population diminished, as the economic sophistication and long-distance trade necessary to support large-scale settlement dwindled away. Layers of 'dark-earth' are found within the former urban grids, suggesting to some that there was now agricultural production going on actually within the towns.[161]

Britain did not, however, fall totally outside the cultural sphere, or knowledge, of Rome. In 429 Bishop Germanus of Auxerre visited the island at the request of the British episcopate,[162] who were concerned to staunch the spread of the Pelagian heresy, which taught that mankind had not been irrevocably tainted by original sin when Adam was expelled from the Garden of Eden, and thus, to a great extent, an individual's own actions were responsible for his salvation or damnation. Germanus found there an urban elite still carrying on their lives in a familiar way and encountered officials with recognisably Roman titles, such as a *vir tribunicia potestatis* ('a man of tribunician authority')[163] He also discovered Christian communities (although no bishops).[164] However, the shadow that would finally blot out this post-Roman landscape was already spreading. Germanus was said to have helped the Britons defeat a Saxon war band by simply chanting 'Alleluia', at which their adversaries, believing that the sky was about to fall down upon them, fled.[165]

Once Constantine III had removed the last of the Roman army from Britain in 407–8, the Britons were thrown back on their own resources and these proved pitifully inadequate. In a previous century it might have been expected that one or other emperor might eventually have reincorporated Britannia, but by the second quarter of the 5th century the Empire was struggling even to retain Gaul and Spain in the face of barbarian inroads on a scale it had never before experienced. According to a Gallic chronicler, Britain was 'devastated by an incursion of Saxons',[166] and the 'Groans of the Britons', an appeal to the patrician Aëtius, the Roman military supremo of the moment in 446,[167] went unanswered. Procopius, writing in the 6th century, observes that Britain from this time remained under the rule of 'tyrants'.[168] It is probably petty warlords such as these 'tyrants' that underlie the later legends of Vortigern – who by tradition invited the Saxon brothers Hengist and Horsa to Kent, thereby unleashing a demon he could not control – and Arthur, to whom legend ascribes a last-ditch and ultimately fruitless defence against the newcomers.

What is abundantly clear is that, deprived of a central authority that could fund an effective army and maintain the forts, the Britons found themselves militarily, as well as politically, fragmented. As the defensive systems of Hadrian's Wall and the Saxon Shore effectively ceased to exist, increasing numbers of barbarians breached both frontiers. They came to settle, and over a short time irrevocably changed the societies they invaded, bringing Roman Britannia to an end and starting the slow process by which England, Wales and Scotland would in due course emerge.

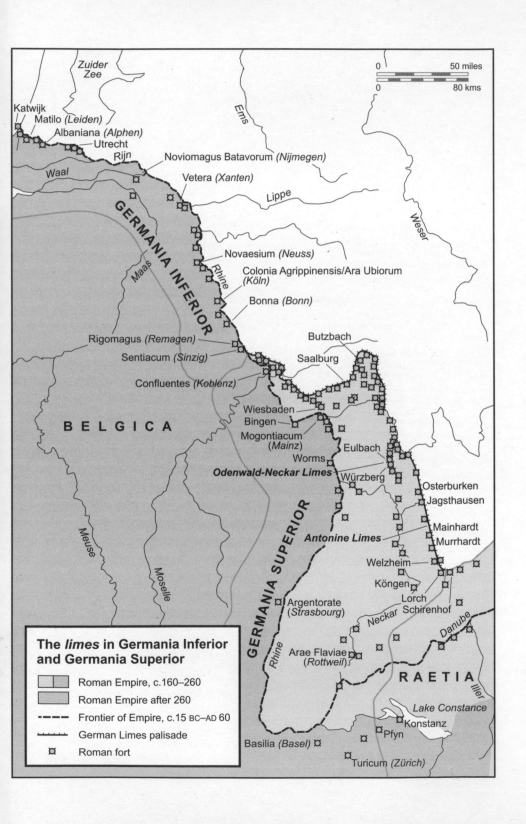

Zuider Zee

Katwijk
Matilo *(Leiden)*
Albaniana *(Alphen)*
Utrecht
Rijn
Ems
Noviomagus Batavorum *(Nijmegen)*
Waal
Lippe
Vetera *(Xanten)*
Weser

GERMANIA INFERIOR

Novaesium *(Neuss)*
Maas
Rhine
Colonia Agrippinensis/Ara Ubiorum *(Köln)*
Bonna *(Bonn)*

Butzbach
Rigomagus *(Remagen)*
Sentiacum *(Sinzig)*
Saalburg
Confluentes *(Koblenz)*

BELGICA

Wiesbaden
Bingen
Mogontiacum *(Mainz)*
Eulbach
Worms
Odenwald-Neckar Limes
Würzberg
Osterburken
Jagsthausen
Meuse
Moselle
GERMANIA SUPERIOR
Antonine Limes
Mainhardt
Murrhardt
Welzheim
Köngen
Lorch
Schirenhof
Argentorate *(Strasbourg)*
Rhine
Neckar
Danube

RAETIA

Arae Flaviae *(Rottweil)*
Iller
Lake Constance
Konstanz
Pfyn
Basilia *(Basel)*
Turicum *(Zürich)*

50 miles
80 kms

The *limes* in Germania Inferior and Germania Superior

Roman Empire, c.160–260
Roman Empire after 260
Frontier of Empire, c.15 BC–AD 60
German Limes palisade
Roman fort

CHAPTER 2

Germania

The peaks of the Alps seemed to collapse upon one another and so send up three columns of fire; the sky in many places seemed ablaze and numerous comets appeared at one and the same time; spears seemed to dart from the north and to fall in the direction of the Roman camps; bees formed their combs about the altars in the camps; a statue of Victory that was in the province of Germany and faced the enemy's territory turned about to face Italy . . .

Cassius Dio, *Roman History*, on omens associated with the German victory against the Romans at Teutoberger Wald.[1]

Germania Inferior

Just like the site of the fort of Maia in the far north of Britannia, Katwijk seems an unlikely spot for the start of a frontier, this time that of Rome's long land border through Europe, a frontier that will stretch for several thousand kilometres through river, plain, mountain and forest, down the great Rhine and Danube rivers, before it touches the Black Sea coast amidst a spider's web of delta waterways far off in Moesia Inferior (in modern Romania). Here on the North Sea coast of the Netherlands, the fort of Lugdunum lay as the first post along this immense string of defensive installations. It was a fortified naval base, which, as well as playing a role in the Rhine fleet, had the task of supervising a section of the North Sea that was particularly vulnerable to raids by the Frisians and Chauci, barbarians who had acquired a naval capability.

Katwijk has, however, long since totally disappeared, finally sinking beneath the waves early in the 17th century, having, most fortuitously, been sketched by the cartographer Abraham Ortelius in the 1580s. Its precise location is unknown and the pretty, unassuming beach resort, with its rows of small grass-tufted dunes, bears only two clues to its past. The first is a bus stop named Brittenburg, which was long the local name for the vanished Lugdunum fort, as though the local transportation company possesses arcane knowledge denied to the archaeologists. More obvious is the large white lighthouse that is Katwijk's most notable landmark.

It may not have been the first lighthouse in the area, for in AD 40 Caligula notoriously took a fancy to finishing off what Julius Caesar had left uncompleted ninety-five years before in his abortive invasion of Britain. Having raised two new legions for the purpose (the XV and XXII Primigenia), Caligula marched north to the coast opposite the island. Once there, he either lost his nerve or there was the threat of a mutiny, resulting in him ordering his soldiers up and down the beach to collect seashells instead. These most unmartial proceedings were accompanied by the erection of a lighthouse that would have guided the invasion fleet on its way. One tradition has it that it was at Lugdunum that this was built, the predecessor of that which stands on the shoreline today.[2]

The two provinces of Germania Inferior and Superior experienced some of the defining crises of the Roman Empire. It was here that the Romans' expansive urge met its first serious check for centuries in the catastrophic defeat by the German tribes in AD 9 at Teutoberger Wald; and here, in 405–6 that the most notorious breach of the Empire's frontiers took place, as barbarians flooded through into Gaul and Spain. In the intervening period, the border stayed largely put on the Rhine, save at the southern end in Germania Superior, where the gap between the Rhine and the Danube was successively occupied from the time of Domitian to Antoninus Pius, creating an additional triangular salient of land (the Agri Decumates) that was only finally abandoned in the mid-3rd century.[3]

The Romans first reached the line of the Rhine during the time of Julius Caesar. The great Roman general's and politician's impulsive urge to obtain glory through (strictly unauthorised) expansion in Gaul brought him across the river twice, in 55 BC and 53 BC.[4] There is, however, little archaeological evidence of the camps he established whilst campaigning there, and he had more than enough to deal with when the great Gaulish revolt led by Vercingetorix broke out in 53 BC than to embark on further trans-Rhenish adventures.

Apart from the integration of the territories on the west bank, and particularly those of the Treveri (around Trier) and the Ubii (in the vicinity of Cologne), the line of the Rhine is largely where matters lay until 16 BC.[5] In that year the Sugambri destroyed a legion under Marcus Lollius, causing Augustus[6] to reassess his policy towards the Rhineland and the Danube in general. It was at about this time that the forts of Vetera (Xanten) and Mogontiacum (Mainz) were first established, together with Novaesium (Neuss), each of which received a garrison of two legions.

A series of campaigns over the next two decades seem to have aimed at securing a buffer zone in western Germany and then pushing this gradually forward. By 9 BC Roman armies under Drusus had reached the Elbe, and the following year a successful campaign by Tiberius may have led the unwary to believe that the whole of Germany was on the point of becoming a Roman province. Whether it was Augustus's intention to engage in a permanent occupation of the territory between the Rhine and the Elbe has, however, been obscured by the disastrous Roman reverse that occurred at Teutoberger Wald in AD 9 and led to the evacuation of the area.[7]

Combining intelligence and ruthless ambition, Augustus had, in the space of two decades, made the transition from a widely underestimated nineteen-year-old to the feared (and respected) master of the Roman world.[8] In addition to extending his own personal powers, he expanded the physical bounds of the Roman state enormously. He could hardly not do so, for his possession of a large (twenty-eight-legion-strong) army meant that he had to find employment for it, and military success was also necessary to avoid unfavourable comparisons with his adoptive father, Julius Caesar. As well as the acquisition of Egypt, which had come with the defeat of Cleopatra, Augustus sent expeditions to Ethiopia and Arabia.[9] In Spain he finished off the resistance of the Cantabrian tribes in the north-west by about 19 BC, and strengthened Rome's grip on North Africa. In the Alps he extended Roman control in modern Switzerland and the mountain passes that led into southern Germany and Noricum (Austria), while in the Balkans he sponsored campaigns into Illyricum, which began to establish a permanent Roman presence north of their existing holdings in Macedonia.[10]

Around AD 7, Publius Quinctilius Varus took command of the enterprise that was Roman Germany. Married to the daughter of Augustus's great friend and lieutenant Marcus Agrippa, Varus had advanced quickly, from a consulate in 13 BC to governorships in Judaea and Syria. In neither had he excelled, and he seems to have been more a capable bureaucrat than an imaginative military commander. Yet Germany was supposed to have been subdued, so perhaps it was assumed that Varus could get on safely with the more mundane business of organising it as a civilian province. Sadly, that was not to be. The Germans were already restive, and Arminius, an aristocrat of the Cherusci tribe who had served in the Roman army and gained citizenship, managed to form a broad coalition of the German tribal nobility opposed to further Roman encroachment. He lulled Varus into a false sense of security by feigning favourable intent and lured him deep into Teutoberg Forest.[11]

There, in September of AD 9, Varus and his three legions (the XVII, XVIII and XIX) were ambushed by the Germans at the Kalkriese Hill near modern Osnabrück. Constricted into a narrow space, the Romans were unable to deploy effectively into battle order and, after a bitter struggle were overwhelmed.[12] Exactly how long the Roman resistance went on during the battle is unclear, but it seems that Varus and his senior officers, sensing that their position was hopeless, committed suicide, leaving the centurions to fight on as best they could. As many as 20,000 Roman soldiers died and, more wounding to Roman pride, the eagle symbols of the three legions fell into tribal hands. The effect of the disaster was electric. Roman positions east of the Rhine were swept away, while Augustus, distraught, was said by Suetonius to have wandered in a dishevelled state about his palace for hours after hearing the news, crying out, '*Quintili Vare, legiones redde*' ('Quinctilius Varus, give me back my legions').[13]

The task of revenging the legions was given to Germanicus, the grandson of Augustus's wife, Livia (and also, as it happened, of Mark Antony). In a series of campaigns from AD 15 to 16 he achieved mixed results, although he recovered one of the eagles from the Bructeri in AD 15. By the time he was recalled in AD 16, the Romans were back in their positions in the forts along the Rhine, and it was here that the frontier coalesced.

The Rhine frontier then seems to have remained relatively quiescent, apart from the further abandonment of territory in the modern Netherlands north of the Rhine in AD 28 following a Frisian revolt[14] and raids by the Chauci in AD 47, which caused damage in the same sector. Some time between 85 and 90, the area west of the Rhine was officially organised into two provinces – up until then it had been under direct military administration. The two new regions, Germania Inferior (or Lower Germany) to the north and Germania Superior (or Upper Germany) in the south, had their mutual border between Bonna (Bonn) and Confluentes (Koblenz). Germania Inferior had its capital at Ara Ubiorum (Cologne), while the governor of Superior had his seat at Mogontiacum (Mainz), an arrangement that was to last for two centuries. The frontier in Germania Inferior would remain the Rhine, but in Germania Superior the border gradually moved forward to the north and east, with an increasingly sophisticated series of defensive works to compensate for the lack of a riverine barrier.

Under Domitian a series of wooden watchtowers were built along a military road designed to supervise the upper German frontier, while in the reign of Hadrian this was supplemented by a wooden palisade erected on the side of the road facing the Germans. In the 2nd century, the wooden towers were replaced by stone versions and a ditch and rampart were constructed. In the Agri Decumates, meanwhile, the Romans gradually moved forward from initial positions around Vindonissa (Windisch) to push into the Swabian forest and up to the River Neckar, reaching their most advanced position under Antoninus Pius in around 160.

There was a scare late in 88, when Antonius Saturninus, the governor of Germania Superior, revolted against Domitian and enlisted the help of the Chatti, but his barbarian allies failed to come to his aid when loyalist troops arrived to put the revolt down. Domitian promptly ordered the abolition of double legionary camps, because the presence of such large concentrations of troops on one spot clearly offered too great a temptation to any generals who harboured treacherous designs.

The German frontier suffered few further shocks during the early 2nd century, apart from raids by the Chatti in Upper Germany and a seaborne assault by the Chauci on the Channel coast of Gaul.[15] In the early 3rd century, however, the appearance of larger tribal confederations amongst the free Germans began to threaten the tranquillity of the *limes*. The Alamanns, who emerged to the south, opposite Germania Superior, are first attested in 213,[16] while the Franks who raided Germania Inferior in 257 began to settle alongside the Rhine in the northern sector.

The process by which these new groups coalesced from pre-existing formations is unclear, but the very presence of the Roman frontier must have played a part. For with an insuperable barrier blocking any further migration westward or southward, and increasing pressure to their rear from other barbarian groups moving towards the Empire, those who reached the frontier had little choice but to establish an uneasy symbiosis with the Romans. Their elites would have recognised the undoubted advantages offered both by some level of cooperation with the Empire, which might manifest itself in subsidies or actual service in the army, and by occasional raiding across the frontier that might result in the acquisition of more immediately tangible benefits. In one sense, of course, the establishment of the tribal confederacies actually aided the Romans, for it meant there were fewer players on the barbarian side with whom they had to deal, and treaties could be made with more powerful rulers who actually stood some chance of making them stick.

Pressure by the Alamanns resulted in the abandonment of positions across the Danube in Raetia, and in the loss of the Agri Decumates some time after 250. The threat became so grave that the Emperor Gallienus was forced to come to Gaul in person in 257 to deal with them. Thus began the tradition of an imperial presence on the Rhine frontier, which would, in some shape or form, survive for around a century until the reign of Julian. By then the frontier had become permeable indeed, and

Julian campaigned against the Alamanns as far west as Senones (Sens), where he was besieged by them in the winter of 356.[17] In the north, a Frankish invasion of 275–6 marked the beginning of a process by which the Roman population was pushed inexorably out of the lands occupied in ancient times by the Batavi. By the end of the 3rd century, the squeeze in the north was total and the area of the modern Netherlands west of the Rhine had largely been abandoned to the Franks.

The last really successful attempts to reinforce the Rhine frontier took place in the 4th century under Constantine I and Valentinian I, both of whom ordered the building of fortifications on the 'barbarian' side of the river. Although the Goths under Alaric – who had traversed the whole of the Balkans, creating havoc both economically and politically – placed the Empire under very great pressure in the late 4th and early 5th centuries, the Rhine frontier itself held until 405. Then, on the last day of the year, a great horde of Alans, Vandals and Sueves poured across the river near Mogontiacum (Mainz), brushing aside the Franks who were manning the river defences in notional alliance with the Romans.[18] Pausing briefly to sack that city, they marauded west towards Augusta Treverorum (Trier) and then took a turn south-westwards, leaving a trail of devastation as far as the Pyrenees. The Alamanns, meanwhile, crossed the frontier near Argentorate (Strasbourg), spreading destruction and despair in equal measure along that sector.

As the situation deteriorated in the 4th and 5th centuries, the Empire came increasingly to rely on *foederati* ('federates') whose obligations were less onerous, still involving military service in exchange for land, but generally fighting under their own war chiefs and thus retaining a higher degree of autonomy.[19] Some historians believe that they actually received a fixed share (*sors*) of the land on which they settled, others that this *hospitalitas* that was imposed on their Roman hosts only extended to a percentage of the income or tax revenue of the estates on which they were foisted.[20] Whichever is the case, over time the temporary billeting of these barbarian federates became indistinguishable from ownership and contributed to the formation of the new Germanic kingdoms that emerged in western and southern Europe in the later 5th and 6th centuries.

Well before the deposition in 476 of Romulus Augustulus, the last Roman Emperor in the West, the frontier on the Rhine had ceased to have any meaning. The Romans did exercise intermittent control over parts of Gaul and fragments of Germania Superior, but it was very much a patchwork, dependent on the resistive qualities of particular strongholds and on local conditions and treaties. In central Gaul the Roman general Syagrius, whose forces must have been largely composed of

barbarian federates, managed to hold out for ten years after the 'fall' of
Rome, being finally defeated by the Frankish King Clovis in 486 at
Soissons.[21] In the southern Gallic provinces a heavily Romanised aristocracy remained loyal to the central government until the 470s, their
faithfulness flying in the face both of reality and prudence. Yet they were
just breakwaters, and the flood that had overwhelmed the *limes* itself
some decades before soon submerged even these hold-outs.

A 10-kilometre drive south-east from Katwijk across flat terrain riven
with dykes and waterways lies Leiden, which in Roman times housed
the small fort of Matilo, and which is situated at the confluence of the
Oude and Nieuwe Rijn (the Old and New Rhine, the manifestations of
the great river in the Netherlands). A pretty town of 100,000, criss-crossed
by canals lined with tall gabled 17th-century houses, Leiden preserves its
Roman past only in the collection of local finds in the museum: principally the graves and altars that would have lined the streets outside the
town and a few telltale signs of the Roman military presence, such as
cavalry helmets and tile stamps.[22]

More important than these paltry remnants is Matilo's position at the
head of one of the most astonishing Roman engineering works in the
north-western provinces, the *Fossa Corbulonis*, or 'Ditch of Corbulo'.
Domitius Corbulo was sent by Claudius in AD 47 to deal with a serious
outbreak of piracy amongst the Chauci that was troubling the Lower
Rhine frontier, and to reimpose Roman authority over Frisia, which imperial forces had evacuated in 28.[23] After defeating Gannascus, the Chaucian
leader, Corbulo set to building a fort in the territory of the Frisians, but
was ordered back to the Roman side of the Rhine by Claudius before
he could make the settlement permanent. Once there, and perhaps to
compensate himself for the opportunities of glory that he had missed,
he set his men to digging a canal between the Rhine and the Meuse that
would enable ships to reach the Meuse estuary, thus avoiding the long
trip up the Rhine to Katwijk.

The other end of the canal stands 15 kilometres to the south-west, near
modern Voorburg, not far from The Hague. Here, from around AD 120,
the small settlement that had grown up was reconstructed in stone and
renamed Forum Hadriani in honour of the then ruling Emperor. It served
as the capital for the district inhabited by the Cananefates, one of the
leading tribes of western Holland, who were later involved in the great
Batavian revolt of 69–70.[24] The west wall of the town ended on the banks
of what is now the Vliet Canal, which in all probability was in antiquity
the *Fossa Corbulonis* itself. On it, river boats ply slowly up and down, while

along its banks small groups lazily take advantage of the summer sun, cycling, walking and lounging, perhaps totally unaware of the canal's original military purpose. On a nearby side-branch a party of schoolboy rowers makes steadier progress along the narrower waterway, its grassy banks dotted with low-hanging willows, while beyond, a small estate of pretty housing gives a clearer indication of the place's Roman heritage, with street names such as Agrippinastraat, Hadriansstraat and, in memory of the great engineer-soldier himself, Corbulokade.

Where the Aar River joined the Oude Rijn at Alphen aan de Rijn, around 12 kilometres east of Leiden and the remains of Matilo, stood the small auxiliary fort of Albaniana, which seems to have been built around 41, possibly in association with Claudius's preparations for his invasion of Britain.[25] Part of one of the gateways has been excavated, but more striking for those on the hunt for echoes of Rome is the Archeon, one of Europe's few archaeological theme parks, which occupies a site not far from that of ancient Albaniana. On a lakeside setting, amidst twisting and winding tracks, the unwary visitor in search of a Roman legionary can find himself trailing alongside a Bronze Age Frisian leading long-horned cattle to pasture, or walking past a virtuoso display of medieval weaving.

The Romans are fully represented by a bath-complex and an open palaestra (gymnasium) area, where, cheered on by a latter-day legionary in impeccably reproduced *lorica segmentata*,[26] an office party of Dutch pharmaceutical workers on an incentive day out practise archery, striking a target some 5 metres off with a worrying level of accuracy. Next door a reproduction amphitheatre, suitably miniature for a provincial backwater such as Albaniana (with seating for just a thousand or so), hosts fake (but oddly compelling) gladiatorial fights. As a trident-wielding *retiarius*[27] falls to the ground, his body prone against the sandy floor of the arena, the crowd of visitors bays for his opponent to finish him off. If ten minutes of athletic mimicry can invoke such a thirst for the gladiatorial sport, no wonder a regular diet of such spectacles instilled a deep-seated taste for such bloody pursuits throughout the Empire.

For those desiring a quieter, more reflective moment, or perhaps expiation for their guilty enjoyment of the gladiator's demise, a Gallo-Roman temple to the goddess Nehalennia, much worshipped in northern Germania Inferior, provides the opportunity. A blue-robed priestess offers the tourists a chance to make their very own burnt offering of fruit and to invoke Nehalennia's good wishes for their future ventures. As an experience it may lack objective authenticity, but in bringing flesh to the bones of what, on many sites, are but bare stones, it makes the point that – for all their distance in time, and in their modes of thought – the Romans were, after all, just human beings.

Ninety kilometres to the east, and almost at the border with modern Germany, Noviomagus, which became the chief administrative town for the Batavi under Roman rule, was occupied early by the armies of Augustus. The Romans took the pre-existing Batavian *oppidum* around 12–9 BC as part of Drusus's campaign to expand Roman control in the area. A legionary base was constructed on a steep plateau a couple of kilometres east of the modern city centre of Nijmegen, but was not finished, and both this and a civil settlement to the west seem to have been destroyed in AD 70 during the Batavian revolt. A new legionary fortress was built between the two older sites for the X Gemina legion, which occupied it from 71. This camp remained in use until about 175, and several of the gates and the *principia* have been explored, though stone-robbing in the Middle Ages erased most traces of the remaining internal buildings.[28] A civil settlement, meanwhile, grew up to the west of the modern town, close to the banks of the Waal River. Although generally referred to as Noviomagus Batavorum, it also bore the name Batavodurum, and there is some confusion as to whether there were in fact twin settlements rather than a single town. It received imperial patronage in 104, when Trajan had it renamed Ulpia Noviomagus Batavorum, thereby awarding it a title that reflected his own family name.

Modern travellers leaving Nijmegen to the east are greeted by a solitary statue of the Emperor, sword in hand, which presides over a ragged band of hitch-hikers hoping for a lift into Germany. More prosaically, this is also the way to the Huneberg Hill, the promontory on top of which the area's first Augustan camp was built, and where a Roman-era necropolis has been found. From around 260, however, when Frankish tribes began to occupy the area in some force, both of these sites were abandoned, and the remaining population clustered together in a more central position on top of the Valkhof Hill; for in the flattish Netherlands, any high ground was regarded as an advantageous place to site a defensive stronghold.

The Valkhof Hill is one of the few places in modern Nijmegen where the transportation mode of choice is not the bicycle, and the pedestrian is king. It seems that it was still retained by the Roman central authorities into the 300s and was refortified under Constantine I and then again by Valentinian I towards the end of the century.[29] The park that now occupies it again housed a fortress in the 9th century and its stones were ransacked once more in 1796, during the Napoleonic occupation of the Netherlands when most of the structures there were dismantled. The nearby remains of the apse of the Church of Saint Martin, probably

dating originally from Carolingian times and then rebuilt by Frederick
Barbarossa in the 12th century, have, however, resisted all these vagaries.
High up on the shell of the second storey, two Roman columns are
embedded in the wall, a stray fragment of what must once have been a
prosperous settlement.

The Romans early on recognised the strategic significance of the point
where, in ancient times, the Lippe probably entered the Rhine – though
their confluence has moved further south over time – and built a double
legionary fortress here as early as 12 BC. This camp, known as Vetera I,
was the first of a series intended to assist infiltration up the Lippe deep
into free Germany and, as the reverse side of the coin, to defend against
any German attacks that might strike the Roman territories on the Lower
Rhine and the less well-fortified hinterland province of Gallia Belgica.
It sits some 50 kilometres south-east of Nijmegen, just outside the modern
German town of Xanten, whose attractive historic centre is dominated
by the soaring spire of the Gothic Cathedral of Saint Victor, which,
though begun in 1263, took nearly three centuries to complete. The
church lies on the site of the shrine that gave the town its modern name,
which is a corruption of *Ad Sanctos* ('at the place of the saints'), for it is
supposed to represent the last resting place of Saint Victor, one of the
martyrs of the 'Theban legion'.

A tradition grew up in early medieval times that an entire legion,
which had been recruited in the Thebaid in Egypt, had converted to
Christianity and, once drafted to Europe in 286, refused to sacrifice to
the Emperor. For this insolent behaviour, it was to a man put to death
at Agaunum (Saint-Maurice in modern Switzerland). The veracity of the
legend is uncertain, and it seems unlikely that an entire military unit of
around 6,000 men could have been executed without provoking a storm
of commentary in the contemporary literary sources, but there really
was a legion that embarked from Egypt at about the time, so the story
may contain a germ of truth.[30]

In 1933, two graves were found beneath the Cathedral, of men in their
thirties who had been killed violently. The burial was dated to around
360, and was thus about eighty years after the time of the Theban legion,
so the skeletons may well represent some unknown early Christian
martyrs to whom the legend became attached.[31] Whatever the reality,
members of the Theban legion were venerated the length of the Rhine,
particularly in Cologne and Xanten, with Saint Victor becoming the
latter's very own military saint.

When it became apparent that a Roman push east, deep beyond the
Rhine, was to be abandoned or postponed indefinitely, the garrison at

Vetera – made up from AD 43 of the V Alaudae and the XV Primigenia legions – settled in for a long stay. Unfortunately for them, their fate was to be very different. The year AD 69 started out as a bad one for the Roman Empire – its subsequent nickname as the 'Year of the Four Emperors' is a good indication of the chaos – and was to turn into an even worse one for the German provinces, threatening for a time to overturn the whole edifice of Roman control, both there and in Gaul.

The crisis had its roots in the final years of the reign of Nero, the last ruling member of the Julio-Claudian dynasty. The latter part of his reign had degenerated into a tedious round of licentiousness, conspiracy and unbridled revenge. Although a revolt in 68 by Julius Vindex, the legate of Gallia Lugdunensis, was put down by a force of Rhineland legions, the tide of power had begun to ebb and the Emperor lost his nerve. He committed suicide on 9 June, dying as flamboyantly as he lived with the bon mots 'What an artist the world loses in me'[32] upon his lips.

His successor Galba, already over seventy at the time of his accession, was soon afterwards murdered in the Forum by the praetorian guard, who had really been rather fond of Nero and nursed a grudge against the man who had supplanted him. The same day, 15 January 69, they declared Otho, who had been governor of Lusitania (in modern Portugal) under Nero, their new Emperor, a move countered by the Rhine army who sought to elevate their own commander, Vitellius, to the throne. Having scavenged imperial power from the corpse of Galba in such an unseemly fashion, neither of the two 'emperors' was to enjoy it for very long. This complex power struggle ended with the triumph of a third military strongman, Vespasian, who from 67 had been entrusted with the task of putting down a serious Jewish revolt in Judaea.[33]

Unfortunately, for Germania things were even more complicated. In a desperate bid to scrabble together reinforcements, Vitellius had ordered the conscription of extra auxiliary troops amongst the Batavians in Lower Germany. Under their leader Julius Civilis, who had backed Galba in the multifaceted civil war, the Batavians refused, declared themselves for Vespasian and set to besieging the pro-Vitellian legion that was based at Vetera (Xanten).[34]

What began as a ploy in a piece of imperial power politics soon took on the colours of a native revolt. For Civilis was a member of the traditional Batavian royal family, and local resentment at the heavy exactions on his people caused by the levies needed to fight the three-way civil war had fuelled nostalgia for the days when the Batavians were independent. Exactly what Civilis hoped to achieve is hard to determine, for much of the evidence for the revolt comes from Tacitus's *Historia*,[35] and it is sometimes hard to disentangle what are commonplace literary themes (such as the barbarian thirsting to throw off the yoke of Roman oppression) from actual motives or events.

What is indisputable is that in March, when the legionaries at Vetera tried to evacuate, they were slaughtered almost to a man by the Batavians. Civilis should now by rights have called off his men, for Vitellius was dead and Vespasian the unchallenged Emperor. Instead he made contact with Julius Classicus, a noble from Augusta Treverorum (Trier) who had been a Vitellian cavalry commander, and with Julius Tutor, who had been Vitellius's commander of the Rhine garrisons. Classicus declared himself Emperor of an independent Gaul and, with the aid of several Rhine legions that defected to him (including IV Macedonica and XXII Primigenia), finally captured Vetera and swept down the Rhine destroying fortresses as far south as Vindonissa (Windisch), which was spared, however, as the insurgents thought its garrison was sympathetic to them.

In the aftermath of these successes, the legate of one of the defeated legions[36] was captured and sent northwards as a present for Veleda, a prophetess of the Bructeri, whose supernatural sight was said to have foretold the Batavian victory. On the way the luckless legate was killed by his captors, and so, when Civilis captured the flagship of the Roman Rhine fleet some time later, it was rowed back and sent to Veleda as compensation for her loss. In the aftermath of the fall of Vetera, Civilis, who had at the start of the revolt sworn to cut neither his hair nor his beard until the Romans had been swept from the Batavians' land – and who therefore probably cut rather an alarming figure with a long, flowing red mane – symbolically cut short his locks, in a potent gesture that suggested there was nothing further to fear from their defeated adversaries.

By spring 70, however, the Romans were on the counter-attack, ably led by Petillius Cerealis,[37] who arrived at Mogontiacum (Mainz) in May. The disloyal I and XVI legions were defeated (and let off with a lecture), Julius Classicus and Julius Tutor fled back to the Batavian heartland, and those Gauls who had thought of joining the revolt were chastened back into cautious compliance with Roman rule. Mopping-up operations took some time, with bitter fighting south of the 'Island of the Batavians' across the Waal. Tacitus's account breaks off just at the point where Civilis is negotiating his surrender on a half-ruined bridge across the river, so it is unclear exactly what fate befell the Batavian leader.[38] If he really fell into the hands of the Romans, it was unlikely to have been a kind one, for his leadership of the revolt had led to the death of at least one legionary legate and the destruction of a swathe of forts. Their reconstruction took years, and the whole affair led to abandonment of the practice by which auxiliary regiments could serve in the province where they were raised; henceforth Batavian units would be drafted elsewhere,[39] far from the theatre in which Civilis had been able to use them to cause such mayhem.

The legionary camp at Vetera was not reconstructed; instead a new fort was built about 1.5 kilometres to the east, close to the Rhine (into which it would eventually collapse during the Middle Ages, rendering excavation practically impossible). This new site housed only a single legion, first the VI Victrix and then the XXX Ulpia, which was stationed there from around 125 until the time of Diocletian. Some way to the north-west of this a civilian settlement, known as Civitas Cugernorum, had grown up before the Batavian revolt. This was refounded under Trajan in about AD 100 under the name Colonia Ulpia Traiana. The new settlement may have been properly speaking a *colonia*, for the settlement of retired veterans of the legion.[40]

Colonia Ulpia Traiana is a little way out of the centre of modern Xanten. A deep ditch leads into a park, in which, on the day of our visit, a Celtic music festival was taking place, with strains of very un-Roman music wafting over the breeze, as though the Batavians and a bunch of their Gallic allies were about to make another attempt on Vetera. Through a crowd of incongruously tartan-clad spectators, the entrance to the archaeological site lay just beyond.

Ulpia Traiana is spectacular in a restrained sort of way, for it is the most complete reconstruction of a Roman city wall to be found anywhere. It emphatically does not pretend to be the original – although it runs along the line of the old perimeter – but its unbroken run of crenellated walls and the imposing bulk of its reconstructed gateways give some authentic sense of quite how imposing Roman urban defence works would have seemed to anyone tempted to have a crack at storming them.

Inside, the latter-day *colonia* is a mix of tree-lined paths striking straight (in true Roman town-planning fashion) between neat, verdant patches of lawn. Interspersed between them are those elements of Ulpia Traiana's major buildings that have been excavated and conserved. As many as 10,000 people lived here, crammed together in the 73-hectare site, which would have made it twice as crowded as modern Hong Kong or Singapore.[41] Despite the relatively advanced sewage systems possessed by Roman towns, the general conditions must have been incredibly unsanitary and the urban centres needed constant replenishment from the countryside to keep their populations stable.[42]

Although Ulpia Traiana possessed a major harbour and base for the Rhine fleet (the *Classis Germanica*), today only a column stump remains of the vast quays that carried vital trade up and down the river. Coastal and riverine communities such as this enjoyed privileged access to a cheaper and wider range of goods, as land transport was extremely expensive – for some non-luxury goods, prohibitively so – and therefore wherever possible merchants would transport their wares as far as they could by water.[43]

The most impressive of the city's reconstructed buildings is the amphitheatre, which had seating for about 10,000 (and so capable of holding the entire population of the town) around its enormous oval. The tiers of seats have been restored for modern spectacles, but standing in the centre of the sand-strewn arena, the entrance gates seem a long way off and the 3-metre internal wall dauntingly high. It inspires a moment of panic that escape might not be possible – just as it was not, without a potentially fatal encounter, for the gladiators who fought in it almost two millennia ago.

The second-largest temple in the colony was the Harbour Temple.[44] To which god it was dedicated is unknown, but its reconstruction is extremely striking. Most of the columns on the temple podium have been left as stumps, with only four restored to their complete height and topped with a portion of the architrave cut off at a 45-degree angle, making it look as if it has been sliced away deliberately and methodically by some very angry deity.

Apart from this, most of the rest of the site slumbers in peace. A reconstructed bathhouse and an unrestored bathing complex just outside the city walls under a large, modern glass protective cover are reflections of the level of amenities that inhabitants in such an important centre could expect, but in times of insecurity on the frontier the economies of the towns were simply not up to supporting them. Ulpia Traiana was still occupied in the 4th century; it was refortified under Constantius I, but by then it no longer seems to have housed a significant civilian population and had become a purely military station. Like all else in the area, it was swept away under Frankish pressure by the 5th century. That it survived as a significant centre of some sort is indicated by its appearance in the *Nibelungenlied*, a medieval Germanic epic (that almost certainly has even earlier oral antecedents) in which the exploits of Siegfried, a prince from a noble family based in Xanten, include the slaying of a dragon in order to win the hand of the princess Kriemhild of Worms.

From Vetera, the Rhine proceeds in a generally south-eastern direction, the modern landscape becoming more populated and visibly prosperous as it goes, this being one of the economic powerhouses of Germany. After around 35 kilometres the river reaches Neuss, which in Roman times was Novaesium, a Roman legionary fortress from about 12 BC until AD 92, when its garrison, the VI Victrix, was transferred to Vetera, and the camp was thenceforth home only to auxiliary units. It was held as late as 359, when Julian reconstructed it, and in 378 one of the last Roman expeditions to venture beyond the Rhine into German territory crossed here.

It is only 35 kilometres from Neuss to Cologne, a major metropolis both of modern Germany and of the Rhineland frontier of the Roman Empire. Now a city of one million people, at the centre of an urban sprawl that houses many times this number and spreads its concrete fingers almost back as far as Neuss, Cologne began its history as the *oppidum* of the Germanic Ubii people, who are first attested at the time of Caesar's conquest of Gaul. Having favoured the Romans, and as a consequence in some danger from their fellow-Germans across the Rhine, the Ubii were resettled on the Roman side of the Rhine by Marcus Agrippa in 38 BC.[45] There they founded the town that would ultimately become modern Cologne. In an interestingly toadying example of street planning, the grid of the new city was laid out in such a way that the east–west axis was diverted a few degrees in order to line up with the direction of the sun on 23 September, the birthday of Augustus. The Emperor, no doubt, would spare a brief smile for this piece of topographic flattery on the part of some of his northernmost subjects. Perhaps in gratitude, around 9 BC the town was allowed to build an altar (*ara*) to honour Rome and Augustus, and because of this became known as Ara Ubiorum.

Although initially only a forward base for the conquest of the rest of Germany, after the Varan disaster of AD 9, the town became the chief centre of the securely pacified area that would later become Germania Inferior. The legionary camp that was built nearby had housed two legions, probably the XVII and XIX, both of which perished in the Battle of Teutoberger Wald.[46] To replace the lost units, the I Germanica and the XX Valeria Victrix were drafted in, but during the reign of Tiberius both were transferred away (to Bonna and Novaesium), and Ara Ubiorum became a purely civilian settlement. In AD 50 it was raised to the status of *colonia* in honour of the marriage of the Emperor Claudius to Agrippina, after whom it received the new name of Colonia Claudia Ara Agrippinensium (or Colonia Agrippinensis for short), from which its modern name derives.

As the capital of Germania Inferior, and hence the seat of the governor, Colonia Agrippinensis was furnished with all the prestige buildings to be expected of a leading Roman provincial centre. Most of them, however, were submerged beneath the modern city, including the walls that it received at the time of its re-establishment as a *colonia*.[47] These were only brought back to light in many areas through the damage done by bombing during the Second World War, destruction that yielded a very small silver lining in permitting the archaeological investigation of ancient strata of the city that had long been inaccessible.

Although it lacked a military garrison, Colonia Agrippinensis experienced a relatively tranquil existence until the mid-3rd century. The only real exception was its central role in the revolt of Aulus Vitellius, as it was here that he was declared Emperor in 69. As he processed through the streets, Vitellius is said to have carried the sword of Julius Caesar, which had been deposited in one of the city's temples.[48] The city experienced the rather more successful making of a new emperor, in 98, when Trajan, who was then governor of Germania Superior, happened to be staying in Colonia Agrippinensis when he received the news that Nerva was dead and that he was now ruler. Fittingly, that news was brought to him by Hadrian, who would in turn – though under rather more controversial circumstances – accede to the throne on Trajan's demise.

During the second half of the 3rd century, however, this part of the Rhine frontier began to suffer severely from Alamannic raids. The response of the central government was strong, if ultimately ineffective. In 257, Gallienus, who had hitherto been more than occupied in stemming a rising tide of barbarian incursions on the Danube, moved to base himself at Augusta Treverorum (Trier), using Colonia Agrippinensis as a forward position from which to strike back at the Alamanns. At this point, a series of appalling disasters struck. Gallienus's elder son, Valerian II, who had been elevated to the rank of Caesar, died; and, when a revolt broke out on the Danube,[49] Gallienus was left with no choice but to appoint his younger son Saloninus to the same rank and leave the inexperienced young man in charge of Colonia Agrippinensis. Meanwhile, Gallienus's father Valerian was captured after a serious defeat by the Persians on the Empire's eastern frontier in 260,[50] and, to make matters even worse, the Alamanns overran the Agri Decumates, while the Iuthungi, not to be left out, poured across the Danube.

Gallienus struggled to deal just with the Iuthungi, who penetrated as far as Rome, before finally being beaten near Milan in the summer of 260. The fear that their raid spread across Italy, which had not known fighting against foreign invaders on its soil for centuries – though it had had more than its fair share of campaigning in a variety of civil wars – led directly to the building by Aurelian, his successor, of a new set of walls around Rome for the first time since Severus (one of the early kings of Rome) in the 6th century BC.

When Gallienus left Saloninus in Colonia Agrippinensis, he had entrusted his safety to the guardianship of a senior official, the Frank Silvanus. Unfortunately, tension developed between Silvanus and Marcus Postumus, the governor of Germania Inferior,[51] and when a quarrel broke out in summer 260 over the distribution of spoils from a successful encounter with a Frankish raiding party, the soldiers mutinied and proclaimed Postumus as Emperor.[52] Gallienus was unable to provide any assistance to his son, and Saloninus and Silvanus were both murdered by the city garrison, their corpses thrown over the ramparts and the gates opened to Postumus.

The newly proclaimed Emperor rapidly secured control of Gallia Belgica, and then over a matter of months extended his rule over Germania Inferior. The rest of Gaul, together with Britain and Spain, and for a time even Raetia, also defected to him.[53] Apart from the personality clash with Silvanus, the revolt may be seen as an example of local self-help, for Gallienus was patently unable to come to the aid of the western provinces, whilst Postumus had shown himself at least modestly successful in holding back Frankish raids (though not the Alamannic ones that engulfed the Agri Decumates).

Having consolidated his position in the west, Postumus made no move to march on Rome, leading to a stand-off in which he remained firmly ensconced in his 'Gallic Empire', while Gallienus controlled the Italian peninsula and the Balkans. It is unclear whether Postumus was intent on the establishment of a permanent breakaway empire, or if he regarded himself in some sense as an (unrecognised) colleague of Gallienus in the imperial office – or, indeed, whether he had designs on absorbing the rest of the Empire, should the opportunity ever present itself. Given that he was based in Gaul, he had neither sought nor received senatorial approval and the constitutional legitimacy that it might bestow. Yet no one much seems to have been bothered by this, and it is clear that in an age of crisis the Roman state was being forced to adapt by whatever means it could to ensure its survival.

Postumus kept the Franks at bay on the Rhine, even though he could do nothing much about the Alamanni in the Agri Decumates. He retained an administration very much along Roman lines, complete with a local senate and representatives who mirrored in their titles those employed by the official imperial regime.[54] Having beaten back an attempt by Gallienus in 264–5 to secure southern Gaul, his regime was sufficiently self-confident that in late 268 he was able to celebrate his *decennalia*, the commencement of his tenth year on the throne, something no 'legitimate' emperor had succeeded in doing for over thirty years.[55]

The next year, Laelianus, who was probably Postumus's governor in Germania Superior,[56] revolted. The uprising was put down, but when Postumus refused his troops permission to pillage Mogontiacum (Mainz), the disgruntled soldiers murdered him. The Gallic Empire did not collapse immediately upon its founder's demise. The central Roman Empire was still too weak, and Claudius II Gothicus and Aurelian too preoccupied, first in the Balkans fighting the Goths, and then in dealing with the revolt of Queen Zenobia of Palmyra in the east, to reabsorb the western separatist empire. Victorinus, who had been head of Postumus's praetorian guard, was proclaimed Emperor by the troops in Trier,[57] but he lasted just two years before his own murder and replacement by Tetricus, who had previously been governor of Aquitania.

By now, the Gallic Empire was seriously weakened, and it was further undermined when Hispania restored its allegiance to the Rome-based Emperor. Once Aurelian had defeated Zenobia in the east, it was only a matter of time before he turned his attention to the reconquest of Gaul.

In early summer 274 Aurelian crossed the Alps and on the Catalaunian Fields, near Châlons, the two armies met. It was, by strange historical coincidence, precisely the same area where, 177 years later, Attila the Hun would suffer his first major defeat.[58] Tetricus was taken prisoner during the course of the fighting and his men panicked and fled, resulting in the predictable slaughter that was inflicted on retreating armies in ancient times. One version of the events has it that Tetricus so despaired of coming out victorious, and was in any case so tired of dealing with troops ever on the point of mutiny, that he had been in secret negotiations with Aurelian before the battle.[59] It is unlikely, however, that his capture was prearranged, for it failed to avert the large-scale loss of life that such a deal would have been expected to broker.[60]

Tetricus certainly did receive merciful treatment at Aurelian's hands. Far from being executed (or left to the mercy of the victorious army, which was tantamount to a death sentence), he was packed off to be the administrator of Lucania, a relatively unimportant district in southern Italy. Aurelian had now achieved the reintegration of the Roman Empire, something that had seemed impossible just a decade before.[61]

Colonia Agrippinensis, too, was by this time back under the authority of the Emperor at Rome. But it was a changed world now, and increasingly rulers had to base themselves in the provinces if they were to have any hope at all of dealing with the multifaceted problems that they could never seem to solve definitively and certainly could not cope with from the safe, but isolating, distance of Rome. Constantine I established himself in Colonia Agrippinensis around 310, when he also engaged in some important refortification works. The city saw a further attempted usurpation in the troubled years after the revolt of Magnentius, who had succeeded in bringing the whole of Gaul to his side and was only defeated in a close-run battle by Constantius II at Mursa (Osijek) in Moesia in 351.

In August 355, Constantius's infantry commander in Gaul, Silvanus, revolted and was proclaimed Emperor by his troops in Colonia Agrippinensis; he had been a former supporter of Magnentius, and had defected at a crucial moment in the Mursa battle, so his double treachery was all the more surprising.[62] Although Silvanus was dealt with inside a month – his supporters were suborned by Constantius's envoy Ursicinus and the usurper dragged from the church within which he had taken refuge, and then murdered – it was clear that the Rhineland provinces could not be left to their own devices. Constantius, in desperate need of a deputy whom he could trust to shore up the imperial position there, turned to his young cousin Julian, one of the last surviving male members of Constantine I's family (most of the others had been killed in a purge probably instigated by one or other of Constantine's sons immediately upon his death in 337, with the aim of eliminating potential rivals).[63]

Constantius had previously entrusted the position of Caesar in the East to Julian's older brother Gallus, but he had proved difficult to manage and was executed for possible treasonous designs in 354. The Emperor consequently tried to restrain his young cousin on a tight leash, and Julian was therefore sent to Gaul in 356 with only a few hundred troops under his command.[64] Colonia Agrippinensis had in the meantime fallen to the Salian Franks, who were busily extending the area under their control from their heartland at the mouth of the Rhine. It took ten months before it could be retaken, and so Julian was probably involved in the campaign that ended in its recapture.[65] He became increasingly assertive and his military senior officers, who believed they had been appointed to act as the inexperienced Caesar's minders, grew disenchanted. They intimated to Constantius that Julian might even be aiming to replace his cousin as the senior Emperor. When Julian came under siege in Sens by a group of Franks in winter 356, the cavalry commander Marcellus made no move to relieve him, and as a result Constantius sacked him at Julian's request.

Henceforth, the young Caesar was given far more leeway in ruling his own affairs in Gaul, and his victories against the Franks and Alamanns over a two-year period of campaigning show the success of this policy. In a later account of his time in Gaul,[66] Julian celebrates his triumph in recovering Colonia Agrippinensis, and proclaims that after this Roman ships were once more able to sail down the Rhine, a vital prerequisite of establishing security in the province. In 356 and 357, Julian engaged in a series of small-scale campaigns against the Franks that recovered many of the smaller towns which had fallen to them and generally restored the security of the countryside.

The next year, a coordinated campaign, which was supposed to have dealt with the Alamanni in conjunction with a thrust from Augusta Raurica (Kaiseraugst) in the south by Constantius's infantry commander Barbatio, faltered when the southern arm got the timing wrong and did not link up with Julian's force. Instead, Julian launched an attack on Chnodomarius, the Alamannic king near Argentorate (Strasbourg). He was probably seriously outnumbered (Ammianus says he had 13,000 men to Chnodomarius's 35,000),[67] but Roman discipline told, and when their battle line failed to buckle under the weight of uncoordinated Alamannic attacks, their adversaries turned tail and fled to the river, where huge numbers drowned, while many of the rest were picked off by Roman arrows and javelins. Chnodomarius, who made a last stand on a nearby hill, was captured and despatched to Constantius's court in Milan.[68]

Flushed with success, Julian defeated several minor Alamannic kings ensconced near Mogontiacum (Mainz) and rooted out a band of Franks who were in possession of two abandoned Roman forts on the Meuse. Over the next two years, he managed to reduce the taxation burden on the Gauls – in the face of dogged resistance from his praetorian prefect Florentius, who felt that a higher tax rate would yield more revenue, Julian implemented the simpler policy of actually collecting more efficiently the tax that was owing.[69] He also mounted two more expeditions against the Alamanns across the Rhine, which in places reached the former line of the *limes* under Antoninus Pius, positions that had been abandoned almost a century earlier.

Julian's victorious career in Gaul, and the security he had brought to the frontier regions, would end with his proclamation as Emperor by his troops in Paris in February 360. The rest of his career was to be bound up in the East, and his fame in subsequent centuries has owed more to his attempt – which failed because of his early death – to restore paganism as the official religion of the Roman Empire.[70]

Although Julian had succeeded in reconquering Colonia Agrippinensis from the Franks, the same group again laid waste to the city in 388, and barely seventy years later, in 455, one of their sub-groups, the Ripuarians, retook it. By now, there was almost no Roman army to speak of anywhere on the Rhine, so there was absolutely no prospect of reclaiming it for the Empire. Colonia Agrippinensis became the Ripuarian capital, which it remained until 507, when Sigebert was defeated by Clovis, the Salian Frankish king, after which the city formed part of the Merovingian and then the Carolingian Frankish kingdoms.

Modern Cologne houses the Römisch-Germanisches Museum, one of Europe's premier collections of Roman archaeological remains, which lies roughly in the north-west corner of the former Roman city. Its master-piece is the Dionysus mosaic, which is preserved in its original position, its vast 7 x 10.5-metre canvas probably saved by the fire that destroyed the roof of the building in which it originally lay, possibly during one of the Frankish sackings of the city in 355 or 388.[71] It is composed of more than one million individual tesserae and is a work of the highest order. Its central panel depicts a youthful Dionysus leaning louchely on a satyr, with an empty wine cup at his feet. Around this, other panels show maenads and satyrs dancing ecstatically, while the outer register of panels portrays a medley of edible animals, including peacocks and ducks.

Amidst a wealth of other survivals of Roman Colonia Agrippinensis, two stand out. The central arch of the city's north gate has been recon-structed in the museum, made up of thirteen heavy slabs of limestone; through here, traffic coming in from Novaesium (Neuss) to the north would have entered directly onto the *cardo maximus*, which today forms Cologne's Hohe Straße. The fragment of inscription on the arch, which reads 'Galliena', is most likely a reference to Gallienus, and so probably dates it to the 250s, before the usurpation of Postumus brought the city into the territory of the Gallic Empire.

At the museum's entrance stands one of the most spectacular and showy items, the reconstruction of the mausoleum of Poblicius, a veteran of the V Alaudae legion, which was based in Vetera. It is a huge multi-storey affair on which the dead man is depicted flanked by his family, standing between the columns of a 4-metre-high temple portico, which forms the mausoleum's centrepiece. Dressed in a toga, and bearing a scroll, Poblicius himself has a sanguine, almost resigned, expression about him. The inscrip-tion at the base of the monument is finished off with the initials 'H.M.H.'; the presumed additional (but missing) letters 'N.S.' would make it stand for *Hoc Monumentum Heredem Non Sequitur* ("This monument is not to fall to the lot of my heir). In other words, Poblicius's sons and successors are to keep their hands off his tomb and not pull it down to replace it with one of their own. Evidently filial piety could only be ensured beyond the grave by the threat of legal sanctions implicit in this formula.[72]

Another of the highlights of the museum is its collection of Roman glassware, the majority of it discovered in one or other of the extensive Roman-era cemeteries that lined the roads out of the ancient city. Most of it is well made but plain, in a variety of colours and shapes; the finest examples, however, are delicately incised with coloured paintwork. One piece, in particular, stands out: the Achilles Goblet, found by chance in the grounds of a student hostel in 1991. In vibrant colours, the myth of Achilles is recounted. The hero has been hidden by his mother Thetis and dressed as a girl to avoid being sent to the war against Troy, but is revealed when, unlike his female companions, he does not run away at the sound of a war trumpet, instead seizing a spear to face down the intruder.

A few hundred metres south of the museum, tucked beneath the modern Rathaus, a rather anonymous-looking square-shaped structure with iron grilles marks the entrance to one of Cologne's most important archaeological relics. It is the *praetorium*, the remains of the Roman governor's palace, and it was probably here or hereabouts that Vitellius was proclaimed Emperor in 69, and that Postumus later had his headquarters. It served all this time as the capital of Germania Inferior and houses a complex series of remains, which represent several stages of building throughout the long centuries of its use. Underground, the light that illuminates the shattered walls ranges from yellow to metallic blue, giving the disorienting effect that the past is refracted as it passes through the various phases of the *praetorium*.

The first stone building on this site, surviving in two parallel walls 4 metres apart, comes from a time before Colonia Agrippinensis and probably represents the headquarters building for Germanicus, who resided here in AD 13–17, using it as a base for his campaigns across the Rhine into Free Germany.[73] It was probably here that his daughter Agrippina was born in AD 15, for whom, after her marriage to Claudius in 50, the city would be renamed. Another structure is clear in the semi-darkness, with two apses and a water basin that come from a phase in the mid-2nd century. The building was then adapted yet again in the later 3rd century, when a galleried hall was created. One of the tile stamps found here can be deciphered to reveal the name 'Didius Julianus', who was governor of Germania Inferior in the early 180s and who, for a brief few months in 193, would become Emperor (having effectively bought the imperial office from the praetorian guards in an auction).[74] A final phase of the building, an octagonal structure, is also clearly discernible amongst the jumbled walls of the various levels. This was built some time in the mid-to late 4th century, although whether it can be ascribed to Julian's stay in the city is unclear.[75]

The building was rediscovered as long ago as 1570, when the foundations for the old Rathaus were dug, and in 1630 a stone was found with the inscription 'Praetorium', resulting in its identification as a Roman governor's palace. Leading off from the main building, a passage that is traversable for a few hundred metres in dark and claustrophobic gloom is in fact a Roman-era sewer. Not a place to linger long, and certainly not in reflecting on its original use, for there are far more edifying Roman remains to be found nearby, beneath the Dom, the cathedral of Cologne.

The soaring Gothic towers of the church, whose current building was begun in 1248, are one of Germany's most famous landmarks. It remained unfinished, however, for more than 400 years, before a fit of antiquarian interest in Germany's medieval heritage and a goodly dose of civic pride caused its completion in the mid-19th century, very much in the spirit of the plans that had been conceived seven centuries earlier.

The cathedral had been a place of Christian worship for 700 years even before that, and so lies on top of one of Germany's earliest attested churches. The city's first recorded bishop, Maternus, attended the synod called by Constantine I in Rome in 313 to adjudicate on the Donatist schism that was afflicting North Africa,[76] but there must have been a Christian community in Colonia Agrippinensis at least a little before this. Beneath the medieval cathedral, an underground world of remains overlies the presumed site of this earliest basilica. Massive blocks mark the foundation stones of the 13th-century church, while scattered around lie walls from its 8th-century predecessor (the Alter Dom or 'Old Cathedral'). The whole is a maze of walls, blocks and rubble, lying silent save for the occasional guided tour, and unknown to the vast majority content to view the huge edifice above.

The very first phase of the building is represented by the remains of a Roman hypocaust, which came from a 1st-century structure, which was, a couple of centuries later, enlarged by the addition of a long atrium, at which point the building could have served as the meeting house for Cologne's Christians – indeed, this may have been the determining factor in the selection of this site for the city's first major Christian construction. The building had an octagonal basin, which may have served as a baptismal font for the community. In the 5th or 6th century the land next to this building was being used as a cemetery, possibly by the Frankish community, which by then occupied the city. Archaeologists currently believe that there was not in fact a temple of Mercury below the deepest level of Christian occupation,[77] a variance from the tradition of siting churches on ancient pagan cult sites.

The cathedral hides yet another secret, for in the treasury a section of the city's north wall protrudes, a massive bulk some 7 metres high and 20 metres long. Although the remains of this wall then disappear under the north transept of the Dom, it is possible in Cologne, unlike in most cities of Roman origin, to follow much of the line of the wall and still see fair sections of it intact. The original circuit, constructed at the time of the *colonia*'s foundation in the mid-1st century, was around 4 kilometres in length and punctuated by nine gates, three to the west, three on the Rhine side of the city, two in the south and only one to the north (which is the one that has been reconstructed in the museum).[78] The outer and inner walls, which rose to almost 8 metres in height, were constructed of small ashlar stone, with a mixture of rubble and tiles forming a supporting core.

To follow the line of the walls today involves a walk of roughly three hours and is one of the most extraordinary experiences that the Roman frontier can offer. It seems, walking along main roads, on alleys between apartment blocks and through squares crowded with traffic, that the city truly is a palimpsest on which the modern version has been inscribed over an incomplete erasure of the ancient. The circuit begins in the most unlikely of settings, an underground car park. A massive section of masonry sits in a quiet corner, just metres away from rows of neatly parked Audis and Volkswagens, the faint smell of petrol fumes the only distraction from the surprise of the place.

Back above ground the remains of the eastern arch of the north gate to the city lie in a small park to the west of the Dom. It survived the dismantling of much of the gate in 1106, as it was then built into the cathedral provost's house, and was moved here from its original position a little to the west in 1971. It seems very precariously perched now, almost skeletal, and totally drowned out by the to-and-fro rush of tourists in search of postcards and ice cream or dashing to catch that last train from the main station just a few hundred metres away.

Westwards on Komedienstraße, which begins unpromisingly with a parade of kebab shops and other cheap snack stalls, a small section of the wall lies, matter of fact in the middle of the pavement, only around a metre tall, but providing a very convenient perch for a pair of local teenagers to lounge and catch a leisurely coffee. Where the road hits a busy junction with the side Nord-Süd-Fahrt stands the most visible tower on this stretch of the wall, known as the Lysolphturm, the outline of its shell complete to over a metre in height, but looking rather beleaguered as the traffic whizzes by its ancient form.

A couple of hundred metres further west, not far from Cologne's history museum, stands the Römerbrunnen or 'Roman Fountain', built in 1915 to commemorate the city's Roman heritage. It was badly damaged during the Second World War, and only an image of the Capitoline She-Wolf suckling Romulus and Remus – a reference to Rome's foundation myth – and six portraits and busts of Roman emperors and empresses remain of the original scheme. As a strictly modern evocation of Cologne's Roman past, it has a self-conscious monumentality of which the Romans would have been proud, and is, therefore, in a way as authentic as the remains of the wall itself.

Just where the north wall ends and the west wall begins, the Römerturm looms into view. This angle tower is the best preserved along the wall circuit, and almost three-quarters of its shape juts out from the junction of the north and west walls. It is richly ornamented in rosettes, triangles and lozenges, and, though the battlements at the top are a reconstruction from a rebuilding undertaken in 1898, its present use as a private residence is certainly far less humiliating than its fate in the early 19th century, when it was employed by the Franciscan nuns of the convent of Saint Clara as their communal lavatory.

Just to the south along Saint Apernstraße lies the Saint Helenturm, a romantic ruin entirely overgrown with a layer of creepers and vegetation so that the tower, although its semicircular outline is clearly visible, is scarcely noticed by modern passers-by. Beyond the Ehrentor, which marked one of the city's western gates, reproductions of murals and parts of the Roman road are visible under glass slabs in the foyer of a savings bank, making them seem like a part of some everyday advertising campaign promoting the virtues of an antique lifestyle.

Just further south, where Im Laach Street bends round to meet Marsilstein, the Roman aqueduct came into the city. Until the late 18th century part of it was still visible, a surviving section of the water channel, which was dubbed in the Middle Ages the Marsilisusstein and believed to be the sarcophagus of an (entirely fictional) local hero named Marsilius who had, it was supposed, saved the city when it was under siege by a Roman emperor.

On this western section of the ancient city's perimeter, several sections of wall are clearly visible in the foundations of modern apartment blocks, sitting below hanging baskets or forming the frame of basement windows. In Bobstraße, a section of the wall pokes into a shop that seems to be a hairdressing salon, matter of factly protruding amongst the clients' chairs, whilst a lady who is doing the wall tour with her small son tries to explain to her disbelieving child that this architectural oddity is not some piece of botched building work, but a precious cultural relic almost two millennia old. A little way further south along the western wall, between two sets of apartment blocks behind Mauritiussteinweg, the wall survives in a section around 50 metres long. Partly overgrown, this precious relic is the most extraordinary everyday footpath of the modern residents.

The wall then becomes more fragmentary and its remains more elusive. Just at the point where it curves east to form the south wall, there once stood a gate that formed the exit point for those citizens on their way to the city's hippodrome, a structure attested in sources but as yet unlocated. Along Alte Mauer am Bach – from which the ditch, at least, of the ancient wall can be seen – lies another interval tower, opposite a heavily graffitoed modern wall, with old, broken-down suitcases and a grubby, discarded mattress piled in a heap beside it.

From such indignities, the wall proceeds north-eastwards past the site of the city's main south gate, which lay at one end of the *cardo*. It now turns north for its final stretch alongside the Rhine. Here lies the tower that has become known as the Ubiermonument. Discovered in 1965, and built on massive oak piles composed of wood felled in AD 4,[79] the huge square structure pre-dates the rest of the walls, possibly by decades, and may have served either as a bulwark for a fortification of the *oppidum* Ubiorum, which preceded Colonia Agrippinensis, or even (according to one interpretation) as a mausoleum, which was later adapted for use in the line of the colony's new walls.

A hundred metres north lay the Capitoline temple, later transformed into the Romanesque church of Saint Maria in Kapitol, preserving its origins in its name. Remains of the *capitolium* were found beneath the lovely round church in the early 20th century, and its heart lay more or less directly under the altar of the current building, a clear sign of the Christians' intent in appropriating the sacred spot of the pagans whom they were displacing. Further north, just by the little square today appropriately called Marspforte, there was by tradition a temple to Mars. It was from here that Vitellius took the sword of Julius Caesar, which played a central role in his proclamation as Emperor in 69. In the 16th century, two statues were erected here, one to Mars and the other to his Christian warrior analogue, the Archangel Michael, and, set in a wall nearby, the stone pedestal of the Saint Michael statue can still be seen.

Along the northernmost section of the eastern wall, the Roman harbour once lay, not far from the Drachenpforte, which was long the city's main passage to reach the Rhine. Until the later Roman period, the Rhine reached almost to the city walls, and an island lay between it and the current riverbank. This, however, silted up some time after the 2nd century, leaving the river's course much as it is today. The wall now finally turns west, liberated from main roads, traffic and apartment buildings, and strikes under the cathedral to appear in the Treasury where the walk began.

Many of Cologne's other surviving Roman buildings lurk around or beneath its collection of Romanesque churches. Beneath the massive tower of the church of Saint Georg, just outside the city's southern gates, stood, for example, a post of the *beneficiarii*, the sub-section of the military that was tasked with protecting the road system and ensuring that tolls owed by travellers carrying goods for sale were handed over to the authorities.

West of the church of Saint Gereon, the outline of a Roman atrium that pre-dated the church is marked out in stones. The church itself marks another of the supposed sites of the martyrdom of a member of the Theban legion. A column fragment inside is alleged to be the stone over which the blood of the martyr flowed at his execution. By tradition, no person who attempted to pass by the column harbouring a guilty secret would find it possible to proceed. The conscience of the few modern Cologners visiting the church seems, mercifully, to be completely clear, and no one is left humiliatingly stuck in the porch.

A more surprising remnant of Colonia Agrippinensis is to be found in the busy shopping street of Schildergasse, which lies on the line of the *decumanus maximus*, the main east–west axis of the ancient city. It was here, in 1995, that the remains of the forum were discovered during the demolition of a brewery. The five pedestals and columns that were unearthed at the time were not preserved and were removed. However, one piece at least of the forum can be seen in its original find-spot. It involves an expedition into the basement of the C&A department store. There, to the side of a McDonald's franchise and just beyond women's swimwear, a section of masonry 1.5 metres high is preserved, lodged beneath the stairs besides the ladies' toilets, access to it partly blocked off by the cleaners' trolleys. It is one of the more unusual settings for Roman ruins on the frontier, but at least one can munch on a burger or try on the latest beach fashion whilst admiring the vestiges of Colonia Agrippinensis's civic heart.

Across the railway bridge that leads over the Rhine (looking back from which the most staggering view of the Dom can be snatched), a confusing spaghetti tangle of roads and pathway leads down to the site of Divitia, the bridgehead fort built around 310 by Constantine I to guard the landing place opposite the main city. It was constructed by the XXII legion[80] as part of a programme to establish fortified positions on the east bank of the Rhine, which would secure traffic along the river, discourage any barbarians who might be so disposed from attempting to cross over directly opposite the main cities, and provide a suitable base from which to launch punitive expeditions into German territory.

It is a rather melancholy site now, sandwiched between the concrete blocks of a Lufthansa administrative building and an old people's home, an unmarked and unloved Roman relic. Two of the east-gate towers survive, extant to about 60 centimetres in height. One of the towers is wholly overgrown in nettles, the other sporting a recent graffito. A small section of the south wall lies hidden in an underground garage, while part of the north wall's central tower is marked in the pavement some way off. The camp originally had fourteen towers and two gates, with sixteen rows of barracks inside the walls to house up to a thousand soldiers. The sole ancient depiction of the fort comes from a medal minted in Trier around 315, which shows Constantine standing inside its wall, as though delivering a speech. On it, seven towers can be made out, together with the 400-metre-long Roman bridge across the river. The Emperor would, no doubt, be most displeased at the fate of his handiwork.

Just as today's Cologne sprawls untidily in every direction, threatening to engulf the countryside and suck the neighbouring towns and villages into its ambit, so ancient Colonia Agrippinensis had suburbs and satellite towns. The old cemeteries that spread out for many kilometres outside the city are one sign of this. Many of the funerary monuments are now visible only in museums, divorced through necessity from their original settings. In the suburb of Weiden, around 9 kilometres west of Cologne (a half-hour ride on the U-bahn), one of Colonia's ancient mausolea can, however, still be seen in place. It lies in the garden of a suburban house, a concrete protective chamber built above it, and a sign for the 'Römergrab' (Roman tomb) the only indications that this is anything other than an overly ambitious shed.

Once led downstairs by the householder, the atmosphere changes. A small display of Roman glass, found after the mausoleum was opened in 1843, leads down to further steps. And there the tomb sits, as though time has utterly passed it by. In the centre lies a partly shattered sarcophagus of white marble, a relief carved on it of winged goddesses flanking a medallion with portraits of the deceased and two youthful figures. To the right and left, niches hold busts, presumably of the deceased; a man with a moustache and curly sideburns and, to the left, two women, one with a severe expression and a garment flung over her shoulder, her hair parted in the middle, and the other seemingly by a different artist, her face more crudely delineated.

Either side of the doorway, precise limestone reproductions of wicker armchairs perch. They were probably for funerary feasts in honour of the deceased, and would be used by the women (men generally reclined on couches to take their meals). Coins found in the chamber indicate that it was probably used from the 2nd century to the mid-4th century, housing several generations of the dead of one family. It is a very striking place. Those who were buried here, and their loved ones, thought they would never be forgotten and that their names and memories would be cherished for ever. Yet although their names and identities are utterly erased, the faces – albeit anonymous – of at least three of them really have survived.

Thirty kilometres south-east of Cologne, the former legionary camp at Bonna (Bonn) has undergone some dramatic swings in fortune during its time. Occupied originally by an auxiliary unit in about 10 BC, it became the home of the I Germanica legion in around AD 30,[81] who then built a wooden fortress there, a construction that was upgraded to stone around 83, some time after its destruction in the Batavian revolt. After Colonia Agrippinensis was effectively demilitarised in 50, Bonna became the main garrison point in the area.

The fortress lay in the middle of the old town of the modern city of Bonn, which was from 1945 until 1990 the capital of West Germany (and very briefly of a unified Germany, before the transfer of the capital back to Berlin), but only the street grid and stray finds betray this heritage. The southern edge of the camp's east wall is recorded by a plaque on a tower that now forms part of a beer garden. Further north and between two apartment blocks in a run-down part of town, the tomb of a soldier indicates the *porta principalis sinistra* of the camp, a lonely marker stuck on the edge of a dual carriageway. The Römerstraße seems a very ordinary busy road in a down-at-heel neighbourhood, but it leads on to what was the south gate of the camp, indicated by yet another tombstone, this time set into the wall of a house. Here the deceased was an auxiliary in the V Asturum cohort who reached the rank of signifer, the standard-bearer for the unit, and died aged just thirty, after six years of service. His monument at least survives, but, rather disrespectfully, it has a yellow wheelie-bin parked beside it for the refuse from the neighbouring houses.

Of the interior buildings of the fort and town, even less is intact, though the old auxiliary fort is believed to have been on the site of the Old Rathaus, a baroque affair, finished in sickly-sweet pink and white, which stands near the central market. Bonn's cathedral, the Münster, also, stands on ancient ground, for it was built on top of a 4th-century *cella memoriae* that honoured two further members of the ubiquitous Theban legion, saints Cassius and Florentinus.

Most of Bonn's Roman memories, however, are entombed in the Rheinisches Landesmuseum, a curious structure, which looks as if the architect despaired halfway through and just encased what he had so far achieved within a glass sarcophagus. Its most famous piece is the tombstone of Marcus Caelius, which was originally discovered embedded in a monastery wall near Xanten.[82] Caelius was a centurion serving in the XVIII legion and died aged fifty-three during Varus's campaign in AD 9, if not at the final disastrous battle itself.[83] Wherever he perished, Caelius stares out from his monument flanked by two freedmen and heavily adorned with military decorations demonstrating his bravery, including *phalerae*, disk-like medallions, one of which is decorated with the head of Medusa. Around his head he wears the *corona civica*, a wreath of oak leaves and acorns, which was only awarded to soldiers who saved the life of a Roman citizen in the heat of battle.

Rigomagus (modern Remagen), some 20 kilometres to the south-east of Bonn, marks the last major defensive position in Germania Inferior. An auxiliary fort was built here in the 1st century, and it remained in use until the 5th century. Perhaps its most unusual relic is an inscription recording the repair in 218 of the camp sundial by the commander Petronius Athenodorus, who was, presumably, fed up of his men turning up late for parades.

Germania Superior

Just a couple of kilometres down the river from Rigomagus, and a little south of Sentiacum (Sinzig), began the province of Germania Superior. Here, the *limes* starts to take on an altogether different quality, as for roughly two centuries the Rhine (and to the east the Danube) did not form the frontier of the Empire at all. Instead, in a complicated series of moves forward, successive emperors pushed away from the line of the rivers, in effect demilitarising them and carving out new provincial territory in the Agri Decumates, whose occupation provided increased security for major centres such as Mogontiacum (Mainz) and Augusta Raurica (Kaiseraugst in Switzerland).

The result is that the frontier here has a series of *limites*. There is the line of the Rhine and Danube, which marked the border until the late 1st century and would do so again from the later 3rd century. Further east of the Rhine and Danube, the first advanced position reached by the Romans is known as the 'Neckar–Odenwald *limes*', whilst a final forward push under Antoninus Pius (138–61) led to a position known – although only to modern scholars of the frontiers – as the 'Antonine *limes*'.

A narrow area of land on the Upper Rhine between the river and the beginning of the Black Forest had probably been under the control of the Roman military since the reign of Augustus. Gradually more permanent forts were established in this area, the Wetterau, a fertile plain that lies between the river and the Taunus mountains to the north-west. Amongst these was Aquae Mattiacorum (modern Wiesbaden), which was first built in timber under Claudius and re-established by Vespasian after its destruction by the Chatti in around AD 50. Vespasian also promoted the building of roads to enhance communications between Mogontiacum and Augusta Vindelicum (Augsburg) in Raetia, necessitating the moving of some forts to the east bank of the river. Finally, in AD 73–4 a large-scale campaign became necessary, led by Cnaeus Pinarius Clemens, legate of the Upper Germany army, which secured the region around the lower Neckar river, so allowing the Romans to build a road through the Black Forest. At the same time, another road was constructed leading from Vindonissa (Windisch) in the south up to Arae Flaviae (Rottweil), and in the south-east control was extended in Raetia beyond the Danube, with the building of a line of forts, including Günzburg.[84]

A further extension of the line was achieved under Domitian, particularly as a result of a major campaign against the Chatti, who were the dominant tribe in the area of modern Hesse. The actual date for the outbreak of the war is frustratingly vague, but it probably began in summer 82 or the winter of 82–3.[85] The Chatti seem to have been a much more organised group than most of the tribes on the *limes* (with the exception of the Batavians in 69) and are said to have elected their officers, and to have drawn up plans for each day's operations in advance, as well as building proper camps each night on Roman lines.[86] The Roman force that undertook the campaign was very large, possibly 50,000–60,000 men including units from at least five legions,[87] and used Mogontiacum as the main base for the assault. The course of the war is uncertain, but it was clearly prolonged and bitter, and on one occasion the Emperor is recorded as having made his cavalry dismount so that they could chase the Chatti into the otherwise impenetrable forest, which the barbarians employed as a refuge.

Exactly how far Domitian's army advanced is unclear; Frontinus in his *Strategemata* maintains that he moved the *limes* forward '120 miles' (equivalent to about 175 kilometres), and although this may be too far, a significant push north-east towards the Taunus mountains was definitely achieved.[88] The major victories seem to have been won in 83, after which Domitian celebrated a triumph, although fighting actually went on until 85. The new frontier was reinforced with a series of watchtowers and timber forts, running into the Taunus and to the south along the Main and then the Odenwald forest, before linking up with the previously secured border line along the central course of the Neckar river.

It was also under Domitian's rule, probably in the years immediately following the end of the Chattian War, that Germania Inferior and Superior were constituted as regular provinces. The system he established remained more or less unchanged along the northern stretches until the middle of the 3rd century, a lasting achievement for which he is often denied credit amidst the welter of accusations that accompanied his later decline into suspicion and paranoia.[89] Domitian had never been expected to be Emperor; it was his older brother Titus, fresh from a successful military career (including the finishing-off of the Jewish revolt in AD 71), who had initially succeeded to the throne, but his early death in 81 of a fever led to the younger brother's unheralded elevation. Possibly as a result of his comparative inexperience, Domitian tended to stress heavily his own military achievements as Emperor – he awarded himself no fewer than twenty-three imperial salutations, more even than Augustus had achieved – and this may have led him into the prosecution of the war against the Chatti[90] (and one against the Dacians in 88–9).

Further fortification of the area took place under Trajan, but it was with his successor Hadrian in the second quarter of the 2nd century that the new frontier was truly consolidated. Many of the watchtowers were rebuilt in stone, and along the whole length of the frontier a palisade of oak stakes was erected. This was placed in front of the military road that led along the frontier on the barbarian side of the line, acting more as a visible marker and obstacle to small-scale incursions than as a fixed point to defend. Thus, to Hadrian, who in northern Britain laid out the most visible frontier defences on the whole *limes*, is also owed an analogous system in Germania.

Finally, under Antoninus Pius, the forts along the Neckar and Odenwald in the central sector were moved around 30 kilometres forward, creating a stretch of frontier that ran 80 kilometres southwards, which in all that distance deviated by only a matter of metres from a dead-straight line, an astonishing achievement on the part of the Roman surveyors. Under Caracalla the defences of the *limes* were again strengthened by the addition of a steep ditch and an earth rampart behind the palisade, improvements that rendered the barrier of more than symbolic significance. In Raetia, the palisade was replaced by a stone wall studded at intervals with watchtowers, very similar in its basic conception to Hadrian's Wall.

Thirty-five kilometres south down the original river line from Sentiacum, the frontier led past Koblenz, where the confluence of the Rhine and the Mosel gave the town its Latin name, Confluentes, and whose Liebfrauenkirche contains a 15-metre-high section of the fortress built here in Constantinian times (although there had been some form of military encampment since very early in the 1st century AD). This section of the Rhine is studded with fairytale castles perched impossibly high up on crags, the most famous of them the 'Pfalz' (or Burg Pfalzgrafenstein) whose pentagonal keep acted as a tollhouse on the river from the 13th century right up until 1867. The river also flows here through the Rhine Gorge, a picturesque 60-kilometre-long section whose soaring cliffs were cut by the erosive action of the river over many millennia. On the east bank the most famous landmark of all, the rock of the Lorelei, rises up. The Lorelei's striking silhouette and the murmuring sound of the Rhine as it rushes against its base gave rise to the legend of the 'Rhine Maidens', monsters who lured sailors to their death against the rocks, in a German reprise of the Greek myth of the Sirens.

Around 25 kilometres south of Koblenz is Boppard – Bodobriga to the Romans – which was probably occupied by them in the 1st century AD, but became demilitarised when the frontier moved east during Flavian times. Once the frontier returned to the river, however, its position blocking any westwards thrust towards Augusta Treverorum (Trier) rendered it worthy of a new fort as late as Valentinian, under whom the extensive wall that can be seen today was constructed. The Roman castle, which was rectangular with 3-metre-thick towers, has become an organic part of the modern town, in many places determining its grid pattern, at others popping up as an integral part of newer buildings or as surprisingly mundane adjuncts to parking lots or municipal parks.

In the Römerpark, a small area of green away from the town centre, lies the largest surviving section, containing a substantial portion of wall and part of the south tower of the fortress; here the remains were integrated in the 10th century into the precinct of a convent. In the 15th century, a dance-hall or tavern was built over the ruins of the convent; the local teenagers hanging out here are possibly in search of a faint hint of the merriment that once rose up on the remains of the Roman town, but really it is a quiet and sombre place, the 6-metre-high silhouette of the tower faintly threatening. In one corner, markers indicate where more than forty 7th-century Frankish graves were found, including one of a high-status lady wearing a silver finger-ring and carrying spindles and two bronze keys.

The *Notitia Dignitatum* lists the garrison here as the *milites balistarii*,[91] an artillery unit, whose speciality must have come in handy when lobbing projectiles into barbarian territory across the Rhine, but which may have been of limited use in actual field campaigns into unfriendly territory. The remains of the north-east wall of the fort are just discernible, built into the Hotel Römerburg, its pretty exterior studded with the telltale herringbone pattern of Roman stonework. Burggrabe, the street that runs southward from this, marks the eastern wall of the fort, and there, lying between numbers 4 and 6 is, if you please, a whole Roman tower (presumably number 5). It sits, minding its own business, intact almost to its complete height, although partly overgrown with creepers and dead branches; the quiet bourgeois houses to either side with their well-tended gardens seem to do their best to ignore their incongruous neighbour. More sections of the wall lie to the rear of houses further down the street, some of it visible, other parts gated off. The south-east tower at the end of the street sits in a small cark park; its facing is medieval, but the core is fundamentally Roman. The south wall occupies the line of Mergstrasse, where another tower sits squarely in the centre of a back garden. If ever for sale, presumably the house (in estate-agent-speak) would be said to 'benefit from the unique amenity of a 4th-century Roman tower'.

Further evidence of Boppard's Roman past comes in the main church of Saint Severus off the old town's main square, its pretty whitewashed exterior and high towers punctuated by single columns set into the wall. This was the site of a 4th-century bathhouse, although the church also includes part of the city wall in its own north wall. During the 5th century, the baths were converted into an early Christian basilica, which incorporated in its structure an *ambo* – a common feature of the liturgy in early Western Christianity – a key-shaped platform along which the clergy would process to perform certain parts of the service. At the back of the current church, which largely dates from the 13th century, the graves of a couple of Bodobriga's earliest Christians are on display, including one Audicia, whose memorial stone is inscribed with doves and Christograms, unmistakable indications of her religious allegiance.

An afternoon's gentle cruise down the Rhine from Boppard, and just opposite the confluence of the river and the Main, lies Mainz, another city whose subsequent success has done much to bury its antecedents, in this case as the Roman city of Mogontiacum. First occupied during the reign of Augustus, at which time a double legionary camp was constructed, it long formed one of the main Roman bases for campaigns into free Germany, although its military importance was reduced after the reduction of its garrison to a single legion after 89. This came about through the revolt of Lucius Antonius Saturninus,[92] who was either governor of Germania Superior or commander of the army there,[93] after the suppression of which Domitian decreed that henceforth no legionary fortress would hold more than a single legion; the total number of legions garrisoned in Germania Superior was reduced to three. The Emperor also forbade the soldiers to keep more than 1,000 sesterces-worth of their savings in the legionary strong-room, since Saturninus had financed his revolt by plundering the troops' savings stashed in the fortress at Mogontiacum.

From 92 until the mid-3rd century Mogontiacum was defended by the

XXII Primigenia Pia Fidelis legion, but the outline of the camp they inhabited is uncertain beneath the modern city. During this period of Roman advance the town was no longer on the frontier, and from the 1st century Mogontiacum's civilian settlement developed rapidly and it became the capital of the province of Germania Superior. In 235, the town saw a key moment in the beginning of the period of 'military anarchy' that would afflict the empire for most of the rest of the 3rd century, when Alexander Severus and his mother, Julia Mamaea, were murdered there by their own soldiers.[94]

Opposition to Alexander had coalesced around Julius Verus Maximinus,[95] a Thracian of peasant origin who had made good in the army. In March, the soldiers declared him Emperor, and Alexander failed to take decisive action. The army defected, and Alexander and his mother met their fate.[96] Thus commenced a half-century in which it was rare in the extreme for an emperor to die naturally, several being killed (and one captured) by barbarians, but most of them falling in battle against 'usurpers' who in turn became Emperor, or at the hands of their own troops. The effect of these five decades of mayhem was debilitating in the extreme for the Empire, and for a while in the middle of the century it looked as though it might not survive at all.

Once the *limes* to the east of the Rhine had been abandoned around 260, Mogontiacum received a stone wall. It was not of sufficient strength to prevent the city from falling briefly into the hands of the Alamanns in the 350s, only being recovered after Julian's victory over them at Strasbourg in 357. The defence of the Mogontiacum sector of the Rhine was by this time in the hands of the *dux Mogontiacensis*, one of the new breed of regional commanders who supervised the defence of the late-Roman frontiers. With the eruption of the Vandals and their allies across the Rhine late in 405, the position of Mogontiacum became well nigh untenable. It was occupied by Burgundians, as Roman federates, who in 411 proclaimed Jovinus, a Gallic notable, Emperor. The city's last moment as an imperial capital in the fading twilight of Roman rule in the West was pitiably brief. Jovinus had to balance the competing interests of Burgundians, Alans and, most notably, the Visigothic chieftain Athaulf. The Visigoth by 413 found a rapprochement with the official Emperor, Honorius, more convenient, and had Jovinus executed, his head sent as a grizzly present to his new ally.

Of all of this comparatively little now survives, but Mainz has become a city of 200,000, the capital of the German Land of Rhineland-Palatinate. Down towards the river on a grandly laid-out square (the Ernst Ludwig Platz) stands a reconstructed Jupiter column, made using casts of the

2,000 or so pieces of the original that were found embedded in the late-Roman wall. Soaring some 15 metres high, it is a richly decorated affair, made up of five drums atop a double-plinth. The original was erected in honour of Nero in around 60 by the *canabari*, the inhabitants of the civilian settlement around Mogontiacum. The plinths and drums are covered in reliefs of various deities, whose exact identities are uncertain, but which include Jupiter himself, Juno, Mars, Neptune, Apollo, Diana, Hercules and Fortuna. The top would have been surmounted by a bronze statue of Jupiter bearing a thunderbolt. Such columns are a phenomenon mainly of eastern France and the Rhineland,[97] but were erected by a wide range of social groups within that area. They seem to represent an integration of existing localised beliefs with Roman religious forms (as expressed by the range of deities that appear upon them).

The religious world of Rome was not a place of comforting certainties and theological absolutes. The clamour of later Christians for the imposition of orthodoxy was not a position much understood by pagans, who – save for the special position of the mystery cults – did not really have an organised 'church' and confined their acts of zealotry to reactive strikes against overenthusiastic bishops or sullen adherence to traditional practices (such as dancing at funerals), which they saw no good reason to abstain from.

So varied, and in some sense accepting, was the pagan world-view that in many cases local deities were simply absorbed into the Roman pantheon by equating them with the nearest appropriate Latin deity and then worshipping such hybrids as Apollo Grannus (very popular in Gaul), Jupiter Ammon (in Egypt) and Juno Caelestis (in Africa). This syncretism suited Roman purposes very well, for the acceptance of local cult practices meant that a potential source of resentment against imperial rule was removed. Only where native cults were seen as possible sources of political resistance, or practised rites that the Romans regarded as abhorrent, were they suppressed. Druidism in Britain suffered such a fate because of its adherents' involvement in the final resistance to the Roman conquest in Wales, and for their alleged performance of human sacrifices.

On the other side of the square, nestled between a playground and a school, a replica of the arch of Dativius Victor was erected in 1962. It commemorates the giving of an arch and colonnades to the city by a former priest of the imperial cult. Dated from the mid-3rd century, and thus after the collapse of the Roman trans-Rhenish territory in the area, it shows that, even in those increasingly uncertain times, the virtue of municipal benefaction did not die out altogether.

The nearby Mittelrheinisches Landesmuseum houses another of Germany's best collection of Roman artefacts. Amongst its finest pieces are the 'Mainz pedestals', which originally made up the supporting columns of a structure near the *praetorium* of the legionary camp. They may perhaps celebrate the victory of Domitian over the Chatti, and, though provincial in execution, their reliefs show a brutal aspect of imperial power. The faces on the carvings are fuller and less well defined than the more refined depictions on Trajan's Column in Rome.[98] In one, a legionary holds a spear, poised to thrust it into a helpless barbarian. In another, two prisoners are held by chains around their neck. In a third, a figure representing Germania sits and weeps at the victory of Rome. The pedestals exude a striking air of raw power and menace, precisely the sort of image the Empire would want to project across the frontier for the consumption of any restive barbarians.

Mogontiacum possessed one of the comparatively rare temples of Isis to be found in the north-western part of the empire. One of the group of mystery cults – most notably including Mithraism – that came into vogue in the 3rd century, Isis-worship had travelled very far west from its Egyptian homeland by the time it reached the Rhine. Its shaven-headed priests might have been more obvious than most of the leaders of its sister cults, and its temples tended to have a more 'public' aspect than those of Mithras or Attis, but to enter the remains of an Iseum today is still to pass into a world that seems more linked to its oriental roots than to the orderly world of the Capitoline Triad.[99] The Mogontiacum Isis temple, however, now sits in the basement of a modern shopping arcade, hung about with the panoply of Christmas decorations and crowded with Saturday shoppers making that essential last-minute purchase.

It seems to have been built under Vespasian, making it one of the very early examples of the genre in the Empire. The remains themselves represent a sanctuary used over several centuries. An atmospheric cloud of smoke provided by the modern guardians of the site drifts over as an evocation of the sacrifices (mostly of burnt fruit and vegetables) that would have taken place here. There seems to have been some kind of official dedication to Vespasian, and on the ceiling of the dimly lit museum that enfolds the site, a representation of the stars on the precise day of the Emperor's accession (21 December 69) is projected.

Among the discoveries made here were curse tablets, a sign of the darker side of Roman religion.[100] Most often scratched on lead, and often scrawled in almost indecipherable script, they were then buried at sacred locations such as this in the hope that the deity present might grant the writer's darkest wishes. At the Mogontiacum shrine were found, in addition, a series of clay figurines that had been mutilated by sticking pins into them or breaking off limbs, as if summoning up some voodoo magic to inflict unbearable pain on the person in whose image the doll was fashioned.

The scant remains of Mogontiacum's legionary camp lie on a high terrace of a modern development in the district of Kästrich. The estate is called 'Am Römer Tor', and is a surprisingly tasteful setting for the ruins. Not many such housing estates can boast mosaic-style insets in the pavement that celebrate Roman warships and emperors or commemorate a legionary garrison. The tower after which the complex is named formed part of a city gate from the 4th century that in turn used stones from the legionary encampment. The stone skeleton of the gate structure survives on the ground, while the tower itself is more complete, intact to around half a metre. In one place part of a carved stone can be seen inset on its outside face. Set down a few metres below the present surface and ringed with residential blocks, the little archaeological corner also presents a section of the Via Praetoria of the camp, in which, many centuries later, the ruts worn in the gate's pavement by decades of use can still be made out.

The Jakobsberg hill, which lies just behind Mainz's main railway station, formed a strategic gap in the city's defences during the Middle Ages, and in the mid-17th century a quadrangular fortress was constructed there, which remained in military use until the Treaty of Versailles forced its slighting in 1919. It served for centuries as the military headquarters of the Electors of Mainz, one of the college of princes and archbishops responsible for the choice of each successive Holy Roman Emperor, and so it retained the ghost of a memory of Mogontiacum's Roman past.

In one corner of the citadel lies the Drusussteine ('Stone of Drusus'), a Roman funerary monument. It is a huge cylindrical structure, partly hidden by an emerald screen of trees to one side, and resembles faintly one of the Martello towers that dotted the south coast of England to defend against an invasion from Napoleon that never came. The tower once had a conical roof, but stone-quarrying at about the time the citadel was built resulted in the removal of this and the loss of several metres in height.

Its alternative name, Eichelstein (or 'Acorn Stone'), was once thought to be derived from the mutilated state of the monument after it had been robbed of so much of its stone, but may well be a variant on the Latin aquila or eagle, from a possible representation of the bird that might have crowned the structure; or even a corruption of aguila, a late Latin word that means, more prosaically, 'obelisk'.[101] It has long been associated with Drusus, an extremely popular and able general, who died in 9 BC after a fall from his horse following a successful campaign against the Chatti and Marcomanni. However enticing the notion that the structure is his memorial, it has been found to contain later stonework, complicating the dating process and preventing any firm conclusion as to the monument's true origin and significance.

Further down the citadel hill, nearly at its base, lies a Roman amphi-theatre. It was the largest Roman auditorium north of the Alps, with a capacity for some 10,000 spectators, and a stage more than 40 metres wide. Not regularly open and hemmed in by building works, it sits just beside Platform 4 of the Sudbahnhof; indeed, the best views of it are to be had as the trains pull out on their meticulously punctual journeys south towards the cathedral cities of Worms and Speier.

Mogontiacum's final visible relic lies on the south-west edge of town, in the suburb of Mainz-Zahlbach. This is the 'Römersteine', part of the aqueduct that once fed the city and the camp. The remains languish in a field to the side of a tree-fringed footpath. In their eroded and ruined state, they seem more like some straightened-out piece of megalithic stone circle than a testament to Roman hydrographic genius. Originally these stumps would have reached 25 metres in height and marched 9 kilometres from the source of the water right to the edge of Mogontiacum. Their survival, though, when almost all of the city they were built to serve has vanished, seems nothing short of miraculous.

Even more astonishing are the remains of several Roman ships dredged up in the Rhine and on display in the Antiker Schiffahrts Museum in the centre of town. Substantial timber sections of these shallow oar-driven vessels (which date from the early 5th century) survived for more than 1,500 years at the bottom of the river, possibly representing part of one of the very last Roman military contingents in the city. Enough remained to recreate the curved shape of the hull of one of the boats, and a more complete reconstruction using modern timbers allows the eye to run over an almost complete late-Roman warship.

The Roman navy was never, under the Empire, the senior service. Although it had played an important role in Rome's victories against Carthage during the Punic Wars, the last naval battle that really decided the issue of a campaign was the defeat of Mark Antony and Cleopatra by Octavian – soon to take on his more familiar name as Augustus – at Actium in 31 BC. Yet thereafter the navy still played a crucial role in the transportation of armies, in securing lines of communication in the Mediterranean and on the north-western coastlines of the Empire, and, most importantly for the frontier, in patrolling the river-stretches of the boundary between Rome and the barbarians.

The fleet had its own hierarchies, with the navarchs very roughly approximating to centurions in the army and acting as squadron commanders, and trierarchs as the captains of individual ships.[102] The sailors in the various imperial fleets had less prestige than their land-based counterparts; indeed, during the reign of Commodus, one legionary was actually transferred to naval duty as a punishment.[103] They were, on the whole, not citizens (though some freedmen served) and, like members of auxiliary regiments, only received citizenship on discharge from the service, in their case after twenty-six years, one year more than their counterparts in the army.[104]

The greatest Roman naval bases were at Misenum (Porto Miseno) and Ravenna in Italy.[105] All of the river sections of the frontiers had their own provincial fleet (with the exception of the Euphrates in the East, where the nature of the threat from the Persians with their large, well-organised land armies made it redundant).[106] The *Classis Germanica*, the German fleet, is the best attested of all the provincial naval units. It had its origins in the Augustan expansion into Germany, and easier passage for it to the North Sea was the motive for Drusus's excavation of yet another waterway, the *Fossa Drusiana* between the Rhine and the Zuider Zee.[107] Drusus exploited this new route in 12 BC to attack the Frisians, but the naval element in his campaign (even though it managed to circumnavigate Denmark) achieved only relatively modest success. In AD 4, the Rhine fleet again sailed along the north coast of Germany, and met with Tiberius on the Elbe, where it resupplied his army, the furthest point the Roman navy ever reached in Germania.

As the advance into Germany faltered in the second decade of the 1st century, the *Classis Germanica* became stationary, stalled at its main base at Colonia Agrippinensis, from where it provided additional security through its patrols on the river. When the Batavian revolt broke out in 69 and the Romans abandoned the forts on the Lower Rhine, the fleet did little good and was swiftly destroyed, with the humiliating capture of the flagship. Thereafter, apart from a possible role in suppressing the revolt of Saturninus in 89, the fleet did not appear in any high-profile operations.[108]

South of Colonia Agrippinensis there were no permanent bases, and once the *limes* was advanced under Domitian, the Rhine in Germania Superior was not the actual frontier, so a strong naval force would have been redundant. In Germania Inferior, however, the situation was different, and there continued to be naval bases at Novaesium (Neuss), at Vetera (Xanten) and probably at Noviomagus (Nijmegen) and in several stations nearer the Rhine delta, such as Lugdunum (Katwijk) and Forum Hadriani (Voorburg). The last mention of an organised fleet comes in

235, when Alexander Severus used a squadron on the Upper Rhine,[109] and it seems that the naval stations were abandoned by the middle of the century. Some kind of naval arm must still have existed, for patrols are mentioned as late as the 4th century,[110] but it was clearly not on the scale of the early Empire, and the disappearance of the *Classis Germanica* must have contributed at least a little to the general decline in security along the Rhine frontier.

The *Classis Germanica*'s northern flank was patrolled by the *Classis Britannica*, whose mission was to protect the Channel crossings and the security of the British coastline. Further to the east, the Danube, too, was patrolled by the Roman navy, in this case the *Classis Pannonica* for the western section and the *Classis Moesica* for the eastern stretch ending at the Danube delta. These two units seem, and particularly in Moesia, to have carried out their duties virtually to the end of Roman rule there, an unsung but vital element in the military system that secured the safety of the frontier, and thus of the provinces in the interior of the Empire.

Set back from the Rhine and the frontier itself (and 120 kilometres south-west of Mainz), but in virtual symbiosis with these, the city of Augusta Treverorum (Trier) in Gallia Belgica provided an important base and vital centre for the supply of the armies that guarded the river. It became one of the most important administrative centres of the Later Empire and, while all about it seemed in decline, was embellished to become a virtual second Rome in the North. Its preserved monuments are grander than those of anywhere else in Germany and it is one of the few places in northern Europe where it is possible to get some sense of the sheer scale of the Roman cities that once dotted the landscape. In the market square of Trier, surrounded by medieval and faux-Gothic gabled shop-fronts, the 'Rotes Haus', a survival from the 14th century, states, in impeccable Latin, that Trier was founded some 1,300 years before Rome.[111] It is a boastful declaration, and the Celtic antecedents of the town probably do not stretch much further back than the 2nd century BC,[112] but the city still has a fair claim to be amongst the oldest in Germany.

The site lies on the road that led from Lugdunum (Lyons) in the interior of Gaul, at the point where it crossed the Moselle and then proceeded across to the Rhine. The local tribe, the Treveri, allied themselves early on with Julius Caesar during his conquest of Gaul, and in 57 BC sent a force of cavalry that served alongside the Roman army.[113] They subsequently caused the conqueror no end of trouble, rising up in 55 BC under the leadership of Indutiomarus, and again in 51 BC (though they remained sullenly on the sidelines during the great revolt of Vercingetorix).

A fort was probably built here under Augustus, and it was then that the settlement that grew up took the name Augusta Treverorum. When the frontier definitively reached the Rhine under Tiberius, the fort was abandoned, and Treverorum never again acquired a military garrison.

Augusta Treverorum seems to have attained the rank of *colonia* under Claudius.[114] His reign signalled the start of an era of great prosperity for the town, but imperial favour was briefly interrupted when the Treveri failed to support Galba's bid for the throne in 69 and instead joined the adherents of Vitellius. Moreover, Julius Classicus and Julius Tutor, the leading lights in the rebel movement that coalesced around Julius Civilis, were both Treverans. However, the revenge of the loyalist general Petillius Cerealis and his troops when they took the city was surprisingly muted. Thereafter the Treverans remained steadfastly loyal to the Emperor (although not always to the official Emperor), and reaped the rewards of the economic development that followed, with the construction of monumental public buildings, such as amphitheatres and some of the most imposing bath complexes to be found outside Rome itself.

The tranquillity of the city was shattered in the late 2nd century, when it seems to have been besieged by forces loyal to Clodius Albinus, the governor of Britain, in his bid to unseat Septimius Severus as Emperor.[115] It was a token of things to come, for, as the *limes* came under threat from the Alamanns and successive emperors failed to provide for the security of Germania and the Gallic provinces, in 259 Augusta Treverorum threw in its lot with the breakaway Gallic empire of Postumus, and, though not ever the leading city in that venture, it was closely associated with Postumus's successor, Victorinus.[116] Once calm (and the unity of the Empire) was restored, however, Treverorum reaped benefits from the new order of things in a way that its leading citizens cannot have dreamt of.

Under the reorganisation of provinces conducted by Diocletian after his accession in 284, the city became the capital of the new province of Belgica Prima. The new Emperor recognised early on that one of the causes of the military anarchy that had afflicted the Empire for the last half-century was that no one man could possibly attend to all the challenges now facing it on the frontiers. Further, the absence of the Emperor on campaign in one direction might very well invite a usurpation by another army strongman in an opposite part of the Empire, precisely the dismal military merry-go-round that had seemed unstoppable since the death of Caracalla in 217.

In 285, Diocletian appointed Maximian, another army officer, whose origins also lay in Illyria, to be his co-Emperor with the rank of 'Caesar'.

It was not the first time there had been joint emperors; this had initially occurred officially with Marcus Aurelius and Lucius Verus in the mid-2nd century. Indeed, the idea of associating a potential successor with the ruling emperor by rendering him certain imperial powers dated back to the very early years of the Empire; Augustus had given Tiberius tribunician power in AD 4. Diocletian's design was of a wholly different order, though it is not clear whether he conceived it all in one go or developed the plan piecemeal as he went along.[117] For in 286, Maximian was raised to the rank of 'Augustus' alongside Diocletian, and then, in 293, each of the two senior emperors appointed a 'Caesar' to assist them, with Constantius serving under Maximian (who was his father-in-law), while Galerius acted as subordinate to Diocletian.

This new system, known as the Tetrarchy, had a number of advantages. It meant that the four emperors could divide in order to face the diverse enemies who beset the Empire, while remaining united (in theory) in terms of policies. The elimination of one of them by any potential opponents would still leave three members of the tetrarchal group to avenge their colleague, and this, for almost a quarter of a century, acted as a powerful disincentive to revolt. What eventually caused the whole complex structure to come crashing down, though, was the thorny matter of succession and whether, as Diocletian thought, it should be on the basis of merit or whether (as various other male members of the four imperial families considered) family ties and a dynastic principle should be the pre-eminent consideration.

Although the Tetrarchy did not involve a simple geographical division of the Empire, with each Emperor ruling over a given set of provinces, in general Diocletian and Galerius held sway over the east, while Maximian and Constantius looked after the western provinces.[118] Each of the Tetrarchs tended to base themselves in regional capitals, closer to the areas in which action was likely to be necessary. Galerius, for example, spent much of his time in Salonica, while Diocletian favoured Nicomedia in Asia Minor (modern Iznik). Maximian chose Augusta Treverorum as one of his preferred residences (the others being Milan and Aquileia in Italy), and the city thus became an imperial capital, a role that it fulfilled during a golden age which spanned around five decades. In 293, Constantius I, Maximian's Caesar, also made Treverorum his capital, and the city then became the centre of the main mint for the Western Empire.

Constantius's son, Constantine I, arrived in Trier in 306, shortly after he had been proclaimed Emperor by the troops in Britain. He would be based here for the better part of the next decade, presiding over a period of rebuilding in the city intended to create a setting appropriate for an imperial capital. It is from this period that the majority of the city's most notable surviving monuments come. Even when Constantine moved on to greater things, his elder son Crispus was based in Trier, and after Crispus fell from grace (and was executed in 326), it remained an imperial residence, first of Constantine II, and then of his brother Constans. After the usurpation of Magnentius in 350, which the Treverans supported, the city's prosperity tailed off, and Julian did not use it as his capital, basing himself instead mainly in the region around modern Paris.

The lure of the city's strategic location and its amenities, however, led to its restoration to favour under Valentinian I, who moved there in 367 and used it as his main base for the next eight years. His son, Gratian, too, would reside here until his death in 383, providing the city with a late Indian summer and a security that most other cities in northern Gaul would have envied. Amongst the residents of the imperial court in these halcyon days was Decimus Magnus Ausonius, doyen of the late flourishing of Latin literary culture.[119]

Many of Ausonius's poems deal with life at court, even referring to individual works of art; one glorifies a painting in which Gratian was shown slaying a lion, both poem and painting being suitably flattering works of art to soothe a sensitive imperial ego[120] Ausonius paints an almost idyllic picture of Treverorum, of its relative security and wealth, despite its proximity to the Rhine and the barbarian dangers beyond. His most celebrated work, the *Mosella*, describes a journey from Bingium (Bingen) to Treverorum, conjuring up a bucolic image of a countryside in which nothing has changed for centuries and all – both prosperous and peasants – live in a state of almost cloying contentment. Yet the mention by the poet of Sarmatians living near Noviomagus (Nijmegen) reminds us that the settlement of barbarians as *laeti* inside the frontiers – including groups of Franks who had been settled near Trier by Probus (276–82) – was changing the demography of the area in quite dramatic ways.[121]

Ausonius's charmed world came to an abrupt end in 383, when Magnus Maximus, who had been the *comes Brittaniarum* in charge of the forces in Britain, rebelled, was proclaimed Emperor by his troops, crossed over into Gaul and suborned the Rhineland legions. After some minor engagements near modern Paris, Gratian's Frankish general Merobaudes defected and the Emperor was compelled to flee with a small force of loyal cavalry. In August, he was caught at Lugdunum (Lyons) and unceremoniously executed. Maximus set himself up at Treverorum, making no initial moves to unseat Valentinian II and absorb Italy. Ausonius, however, caught up in the winds of a very unwelcome change, made haste for his estates in Burdigala (Bordeaux), where he lived out the last decade of his life in the kind of enforced idleness that only the leisured Roman aristocracy knew how to exploit to the full.

Some time after 395 the seat of the praetorian prefect for the north-western provinces of the Empire was transferred from Treverorum to Arelate (Arles) in the south of Gaul, and the city's importance declined. It may have resisted the onslaught of the Vandals and their allies in 406[122] but it seems to have been sacked by the Franks in 411. The city was still serving as a mint in 414–16 when it coined for Attalus, a puppet Emperor installed by Attila the Hun, and for another usurper, Johannes, in 423. Treverorum was then battered by successive barbarian attacks – one writer refers to it being sacked four times between 400 and 450.[123] By the 480s, it was in the hands of one Arbogast, who bore the title *comes* and may have been in some sense a representative of Roman rule,[124] but soon after-wards it was annexed by Clovis's growing Frankish kingdom.

Approaching the city from the Moselle, Roman travellers would have crossed over into Augusta Treverorum on one of two bridges. The south-ernmost still survives in part, carrying buses and cars thundering across the river on a modern bridge, which sits atop the unmistakably massive bulk of some of the original Roman piers. Five of the seven that bear the bridge's weight are of Roman vintage, their pointed shape upstream moulding the water's flow to act as ice-breakers.[125] From here the road led eastwards, eventually arriving at the west façade of the forum, an area that is comparatively little known, but whose construction (prob-ably in the early 2nd century) marks the beginning of the provision of a truly monumental centre for the city.[126] More substantial are Treverorum's places of public and private entertainment, the baths and the amphitheatre.

On a square of middle-class housing set just east of the river between the busy arteries of Südallee and Friedrich-Wilhelmstraße lie the Barbarathermen, one of the city's two grand sets of imperial baths. Probably built during the first quarter of the 2nd century, they are a very tangible symbol of the Romanisation of the area. The ruins still give some idea of the general layout of a Roman bath complex. To the south lay the *caldarium*, a large, elaborate structure set in a position to receive the maximum amount of sun. Beyond it, just to the north, a smaller, cross-shaped structure, the *tepidarium*, was a luke-warm room, and then at the north, a large rectangular building represents the *frigidarium*, along-side which lay various porticoes and a *palaestra* or exercise yard. Now utterly ruined, the Barbarathermen were in use as late as Frankish times, and in the 12th century the *caldarium* was adapted for use by a local noble family as their palace. As late as the 17th century much of the structure still survived, before it was dismantled by the local Jesuits, who used it to construct a college.

Baths have a good claim to be one of the defining elements in the spread of the 'Roman way' throughout the Empire and spanned the whole spectrum from relatively simple establishments in small villages in modern Syria to the grand, fully fledged examples built in Treverorum. They are referred to as *thermae* or *balnea* – the exact distinction is unclear, though *thermae* may have been more elaborate examples.[127] In the increasingly crowded environment of Roman towns, they acted as a social centre in which to meet one's peers, as well as providing a vital hygienic function in the majority of settlements where the provision of private household water supplies was the privilege of a select few. The baths required vast quantities of water, and would normally need to be supplied by an aqueduct. According to Frontinus, who was *curator aquarum* (the official in charge of Rome's water supply) in 97, no less than 45 per cent of the water coming from the city's aqueducts was used for public purposes, which, on the whole, would have meant for the baths.[128]

As well as these more obvious functions, the baths also provided ample opportunity for local notables to publicise their generous benefactions to their native towns by giving funds for a portico here, the reconstruction of a *caldarium* there, or, perhaps the money to provide the oil needed in the baths or the fuel for the furnaces that heated them – all expenses that would otherwise have to be met out of public funds. Such self-conscious generosity (or euergetism) is memorialised in countless inscriptions on baths – and of course on other buildings – throughout the geographic extent of the Empire.

The experience of a visit to the baths of course varied slightly, depending on the nature of the building and the local climate. However, it seems that mixed bathing was (contrary to the confident assertion of guides in the more conservative modern countries) not uncommon at all; the poet Martial sulkily criticises those women who do not want to bath with him, and makes unkind comments about the appearance of some of them naked.[129] It may, of course, be that certain days or sections in bathing complexes were reserved for women, but this was by no means the universal rule.

There were, of course, more nefarious goings-on at the baths, and Ovid refers to them as places where young lovers might meet unmolested,[130] while certain of the graffiti found at Herculaneum (the neighbour of Pompeii) make unmistakable references to prostitution occurring in the baths. Another perennial problem was, apparently, the theft of clothes, an unavoidable hazard when the customers bathed naked, and to guard against which attendants called *capsarii* could be hired to see to the safe-keeping of possessions. The *capsarii* were of course not always themselves to be trusted, and a specific provision in Justinian's law code deals with dishonest members of the profession.[131]

Having disrobed and left their clothes to the tender mercies of the attendants or to the chance of an unguarded corner, bathers would proceed through the series of bathing rooms, many of them with marble or mosaic flooring and decorated with statues and friezes (whose lavish-ness depended on the wealth of the establishment), before returning, cleansed, to collect their possessions. Generally speaking, bathers would first be anointed with oil – a service for which there would be an extra charge – followed by visits to the various hot rooms: first the *tepidarium*, then the *caldarium* and, if feeling intrepid, the *sudarium* (or steam room). In hotter climates, the *frigidarium* and various plunge pools would provide relief from the sticky heat outside. At an intermediate point during the visit, bathers would be scraped with a strigil to remove the oil and dirt that had accumulated on their bodies, a process that undoubtedly added a certain amount of pain to the general pleasure of a visit to the baths, should the tips to the ministering slaves not be large enough.

The baths catered for the whole gamut of society, from senators to the most humble, and there are even records of visits by emperors to public establishments (though they no doubt mostly confined their ablu-tions to the facilities provided for them in the imperial palaces). The most celebrated example comes from the *Historia Augusta*,[132] where Hadrian is said to have caught sight of the veteran of one of his mili-tary campaigns rubbing himself against a wall. When the Emperor asked what his former comrade was doing, the ex-soldier said that he was simply too poor to afford to pay for a slave to rub his back. Hadrian instantly ordered that a number of slaves be given to the man, along with money to house them, so that the old soldier would not in future have to suffer such public indignity. On the Emperor's next visit to the baths, he found a large crowd of men massaging their backs against the wall, hoping that they would receive a similar benefaction. Hadrian, however, was not so easily fooled, and simply remarked that they should get together and rub each other's backs, thereby resolving their respect-ive 'problems'.

Just to the east of the city centre, up a quiet street, lies the city's other early relic, the amphitheatre. Probably built in the early 1st century, it is not a free-standing colossus such as the Flavian amphitheatre at Rome or the one at Arles, but instead made use of the slope of the Petrisberg hill, supplemented by earthworks to create the oval shape required for the building. The banks of seats that were set into this housed up to 20,000 spectators, a huge number even for a place the size of Treverorum. Most of the stone structure has now gone, apart from a section of the southern entrance, and the gates through which the spectators issued out into the seats (the *vomitoria*). Down below in the cellars lies a scattering of stones and a lot of ground water, creating a dank and very dark atmosphere, appropriate for a place where cages for condemned criminals would have been housed. Up above, all is strangely tranquil, as the grassed-over mounds of the auditorium hold little sense of the bloody spectacles that once took place here.

Around 400 metres to the west lies the first evidence of the great building programme of Treverorum's career as a tetrarchic capital, the Kaiserthermen (or 'imperial baths'). The huge shell of the *caldarium* rears up as one of the most prominent landmarks of Roman northern Europe, the massive double-tier of open arches in red brick alternating with lighter tiles that make it seem almost like a massive aqueduct rather than a bath building. Everything about the Kaiserthermen is monumental, and they are indeed the largest baths outside Italy itself (the second-largest being the Barbarathermen). They originally formed part of the palace precinct constructed for Constantine I, and in their skeletal state it requires a great effort to imagine the lavish decoration with which they must have been adorned. The triple-apsed *caldarium* is the best surviving building, with the *tepidarium* and *frigidarium* nearby surviving to a much lower height. Although almost all above is ruined, beneath the rooms, tunnels and drainage channels that made up the sub-structure survive almost complete, creating a claustrophobic underworld in whose maze it is easy to be gripped with a nameless sense of panic.

Astonishingly, the baths seem never to have been completed. Although begun in the early 4th century, work on them seems to have been incomplete by 316, when Constantine left Treverorum for his new capital at Constantinople. No traces of the water-pipes that would have been an absolute necessity in such a structure have been found, and the building seems to have lain neglected for some time. During the reigns of Valentinian I and Gratian, however, an extensive programme of remodelling was undertaken, with the *frigidarium* being completely levelled, leaving the *caldarium* to act as a monumental hall of some kind. Its exact function is unclear, though it could have acted as a meeting place for the *curia*, the municipal council. Bizarrely, considering the genesis of the building, a new, much smaller bathhouse was built just north of the original site.[133]

The other principal remnant of the Constantinian palace lies a couple of hundred metres to the north, in a pretty park attached to the 18th-century palace of the Electors. The Aula Palatina (or 'Basilika' as it was known for centuries) is one of the most complete Roman buildings anywhere and gives a rare chance to experience the sheer size and interior space of a Roman original, largely uncluttered by subsequent accretions or demolitions. At 67 metres long, about 27 wide and 30 high, its long, rectangular shape, studded with arched windows, with a circular apse at the end, is characteristic of late-Roman audience chambers, the function that it performed in Constantine's palace. Much of the brickwork of the outside walls is not in fact original, for in the 17th century the building of a new bishop's palace resulted in the removal of the east wall and the partial demolition of the south wall. Yet a great deal of this has been restored, while on the west wall the original Roman masonry can be clearly discerned. Having served as a barracks in the 18th century, the Aula Palatina owes its restoration to King Friedrich Wilhelm IV of Prussia, who ordered it rebuilt in its original form and gave it to the Evangelical Protestant community at Trier to serve as their church, a function the venerable building still performs today.[134]

Inside, the austerity of the decoration, with just a simple cross on the far wall of the apse, heightens the grandeur of the space. The windows in the apse were made deliberately smaller, an architectural trick that makes it seem more distant and draws the eye towards the space where the platform on which the Emperor, in full pomp, would have sat to receive visitors.[135] It was all part of the tendency under the Later Roman Empire, particularly accentuated from the time of Constantine, for the distance between sovereign and subject to grow. Whilst there had been a kind of suspension of disbelief until the 2nd century, a fiction that the emperors were really a superior kind of senator and that, at a pinch, the Republic might just be restored, the chaos of the 3rd century brought forward a reformed structure that was more dogmatic, much more bureaucratic and in which the Emperor was set apart as an unapproachable ideal.[136]

As the aura of mystique around them grew, of course, those Emperors who were not strong-minded came to be dominated by their civil servants, largely unaware of what was really going on outside the palace walls, and able to command only that which they comprehended, which was really very little. Honorius, who ruled from 395 to 423, is the classic case of this. From his palace in Ravenna, surrounded by miasmic marshes, which protected the imperial person but from whose security he rarely ventured, Honorius seems to have known little and cared less. One of his favourite pastimes, it seems, was to spend a choice hour feeding his pet chickens. When Rome was sacked by Alaric's Goths in 410 and one of the ministers was deputed to tell the Emperor that Rome had fallen, Honorius was, for a brief moment, shocked, believing that he was being informed instead that one of his beloved fowl had died.[137]

More tangible evidence of Constantine's connection with the city was found in a room beneath Trier's cathedral, the Dom. Medieval legend had long held that the church owed its origins to the donation of a palace by Helena, his mother, upon which the predecessor of the Dom was built in the late 4th century. A section of bricked-up Roman masonry can indeed be seen on the north side of the cathedral today. In 1945–6, however, a room from the palace was discovered, containing thousands of plaster fragments. When reassembled, they proved to be a series of wall paintings (now on display in the Diocesan Museum).

The three most striking paintings seem to be of imperial women, clad in purple robes and richly adorned with jewels and golden diadems. One, veiled, may be Helena herself, the other figure with a diadem possibly his wife Fausta. The third and youngest woman, who wears flowers in her hair and toys with a jewel box, her expression quizzical, as though she holds the key to some kind of mystery, could be Helena the Younger, who became Constantine's daughter-in-law by her marriage to his eldest son, and presumptive heir, Crispus in 322.

It has been suggested that the portraits were painted to commemorate the marriage of Crispus and Helena; if so, their subsequent neglect is easily explicable, for it was a match that ended tragically. In 326, Constantine suddenly summoned Crispus, who had been commanding imperial forces on the eastern front, to the Balkans, and there, at Pola, he was summarily executed. The reasons for this were never made public, but it seems that the young Caesar was accused of an illicit affair with his stepmother Fausta. However, the whole thing seems to have been a malicious plot of Fausta's, and once this was discovered the following year she was shut up in an overheated bath where she slowly choked to death. Constantine is said to have suffered remorse for the rest of his life, knowing that he had unjustly put his own child to death at the behest of his conniving wife, who had almost certainly been jealous of Crispus, the product of her husband's first marriage.

Between the 2nd and 4th centuries, Treverorum possessed a city wall. It was certainly built after the second half of the 2nd century, for it cut through a cemetery of that date,[138] and there is a record in 353 of the Treverans shutting the gates of their city to Decentius, the brother of the usurper Magnentius, so a wall must have been in place then. It was probably around 6 metres high and enclosed some 285 hectares within its circuit. Beyond it a ditch was constructed for extra security. To reinforce one section, part of the wall of the amphitheatre was incorporated to act as a bulwark for the fortification, which presumably implied the blocking up of at least some of that building's entrances, and possibly its total disuse as a place of public spectacle.

The one significant relic of the wall, and also Trier's poster child of its Roman heritage, is the Porta Nigra ('Black Gate'), which is the original northern gate of the city. Its twin, rounded arcaded towers, one of them missing a storey, stand either side of the gate and are connected by a two-storey arcade running above the gate's arches. The ground floors of the twin towers lack windows, however, presumably for defensive reasons. Although magnificent and overawing all about it (even the traffic that speeds by, obscuring the efforts of the most assiduous of photographers), the gate was in fact completed rather hurriedly and its finish is rough. The unfaced sandstone then weathered to black over the ages, giving the structure a solemn and austere appearance, which renders it all the more powerful.

The Porta Nigra owes its survival, when all the other gates were dismantled in medieval times, to a hermit named Simeon of Syracuse, who in around 1000 chose the structure as the location of his cell. After he died in 1035, the building was converted into a church, and an apse attached. The remains of several late-medieval religious monuments can still be seen in the interior of the Porta on its first floor. They are what is left of a once-large collection stripped away by Napoleon in 1804, when, after annexing the city, he ordered that the Porta Nigra be restored to its original state, a process that was completed in the 1870s.

It was another piece of misplaced piety that preserved one of the best Roman-era monuments in the vicinity of Trier, the Igelersaüle, standing in the small village of Igel around 8 kilometres south-west of the city. It is in fact the funerary monument of the Secundinii, a rich merchant family who made their money in the cloth trade. A single column surrounded by friezes, it consists of several storeys that soar up to 23 metres. Although weathered, the main scene of the front frieze is quite clear, possibly showing the sons of Lucius Secundinius Securus bidding their father farewell. Another scene shows the transportation of cloth, with bales of the stuff being drawn by mules. More recondite scenes include the rescuing of Andromeda by Hercules, part of a cycle that may be associated with a mystical journey by the soul to heaven.[139] The funerary monument owes its survival to the belief that the figures represented on it were not Secundinius and his wife, but instead Constantius

I and Helena, the parents of Constantine I. As their son had brought Christianity to the Roman Empire, it was therefore perceived as almost sacrilegious to tinker with it, and so the Igel altar survived the ages nearly unscathed.

From Mainz, the pre-Flavian frontier followed the line of the Rhine past Borbetomagus (Worms), down towards the legionary camp at Argentorate (Strasbourg) where the VIII Augusta legion was stationed from AD 70 until at least the 3rd century, while units detached from it may be the ones recorded for the town in the *Notitia Dignitatum* at the start of the 5th century.

The river now enters the hilly territory north of the Alps, and modern Switzerland. There is not a great deal to show in quietly prosperous Basle of its Roman predecessor Basilia. The Roman settlement was established on the Münsterhügel, a promontory above the Rhine on which the modern cathedral sits, and which was also the site chosen by the Celtic Raurici for their *oppidum*, captured by Drusus in 15 BC. Just off the Münsterplatz, under a glass display roof, part of the Celtic wall has been unearthed. It dates from the early 1st century BC, and is constructed using a technique that became known as *murus gallicus*, which involved the building of an earth rampart with a stone or rubble facing reinforced internally by wooden beams. The pile of rubble formed when the wall collapsed can still be seen, close to a section where in medieval times the grave of a small child was set into the ancient wall.

In the nearby museum a fragment of Roman wall lies immured in the basement; after the fall of the *limes* of the Agri Decumates in the 260s, the Münsterhügel was reinforced and fortified as it once again became a link in the frontier defence system on the Upper Rhine. It is from later in this period (374) that the first mention of the name Basilia (or Civitas Basiliensis) comes. By the early 5th century, however, the garrison seems to have abandoned the place, leaving the old *vicus* of the fort to survive unguarded, which then over the centuries developed into a thriving city of more than 150,000.

Just 12 kilometres and a short train ride southwards down the Rhine the *limes* reached Augusta Rauricorum, now in the village of Kaiseraugst, which, not having enjoyed such a glittering existence following the Roman period, has survived in substantially better shape than ancient Basilia. The snow-topped trees and icy fields are a salutary reminder that, though the real barrier of the Alps lies elsewhere, in winter this was still forbidding terrain and campaigning in such weather was an act of desperation or an attempt to spring an unwelcome surprise on the enemy.

An inscription records that Augusta Rauricorum was established around 44 BC as a colony by Lucius Munatius Planus, his aim being to block off any incursions from further east into Caesar's newly conquered provinces in Gaul.[140] It was not until the time of Augustus, however, and the absorption of the central Alps by Tiberius and Drusus in 15 BC, that the town really became important and a building boom ensued. Around AD 40–70 the residential areas were rebuilt in stone, and a rash of public buildings was erected in the 70s, including the theatre, the forum and a large temple. Small army detachments from units based in Vindonissa (Windisch) to the east garrisoned it, and in 73–4 it served as a springboard for Domitian's occupation of the Agri Decumates.[141] After 260, although it lay once more on the frontier, the civilian population appears to have become sparser, and in the 4th century most of the town was abandoned, leaving only the upper section (Kastelen) in occupation. In around 320, the old fort was razed, and a new one built to the north, which took the name Castrum Rauracense. The old colony of Augusta Rauricorum began its descent into ruin, to be rescued only by archaeological investigations that began in Switzerland as early as 1582 under the humanists Andreas Ryff and Basilius Amberbach.[142]

A short walk from the train station, with neat, low modern houses for its neighbours, lies a Roman merchant building, for, although not militarily important (save in exceptional circumstances, such as Domitian's expedition), the town was a prosperous trading centre and derived much of its wealth from the transportation of goods up and down the Rhine. It seems that fulling was carried out in this particular building, and an inn was attached to the complex, for visiting merchants to rest in before selling their wares or pressing on down the road towards Vindonissa. The criss-cross of low stone walls and sequence of rectangular rooms give out little of the secret of the place, and it is the small items such as the cache of five *lares*, or household gods, that carry a real resonance of the past life of Rauricorum.

About five minutes' walk up the gently sloping hill on which the bulk of the town was built lies the Augst museum, with a Roman-style portico out front, its red-tiled roof coldly outlined against a threatening grey sky. Inside, the fine collection features a lovely bronze bust of Minerva, with staring white eyes and a Medusa's-head breastplate, and a consular diptych in ivory, together with a collection of exquisite small votive figurines of a constellation of deities.

The masterpiece is undoubtedly the Kaiseraugst Treasure, a hoard unearthed in the winter of 1961/2 in the late-Roman fortress of Rauracense. It seems to have been buried around 352, and is made up of sixty-eight pieces from an extremely rich table service, largely of silver, together with a large hoard of coins. The mix of coins suggests that the treasure's owner was probably a follower of the usurper Magnentius, but that, in the face of an onslaught of Alamanns who attacked the Magnentian-held fort in 351–2, he buried his portable wealth and was never able to come back to collect it.

The array of pure silver bowls, spoons and large plates is staggering and the story of its discovery a wonderful example of archaeology by accident. During the winter of the discovery the snow lay deep near the fortress walls, and when a mechanical digger tore the hoard out of the ground by chance, it lay unnoticed for some time. When finally the precious pieces were spotted and experts were called in to identify them, many items had already been spirited away. A lovely rectangular silver bowl depicting Ariadne with Dionysus and a group of satyrs was subsequently retrieved from a rubbish pit into which it had been pitched, while a bowl with a portrait of Achilles etched into it was found hidden under the bed of a young boy, who had, no doubt, found an unexpected prize on his way into school that morning.

Just opposite the museum sits the theatre, Switzerland's largest Roman monument, now heavily restored. It was rebuilt on at least three occasions over its three centuries of life, so that little clearly survives from the original structure that was raised in about 70, save some monumental blocks lying deep down beside the refreshments kiosk. Although parts of the stage backdrop can be seen in place, around 110 the theatre was adapted to serve as an amphitheatre for gladiatorial contests rather than the more refined dramas it had hosted hitherto. An oval arena had to be built in place of the hemispherical stage that had preceded it, though most of the seating was kept intact. Around 200, it was restored to its original use and the place became a theatre once more. The seating now seems strangely complete, but this is a function of the theatre's use as a venue for the Pro Augusta Raurica jazz festival rather than any miraculous feat of preservation.

On a small hill opposite the theatre stands the great stone block of the Schönbühl temple, accessed by a flight of modern steps. What survives is actually the base of the 3-metre-high platform of an enormous shrine, part of a complex that included six smaller temples, the outlines of the walls of which can still be seen just south of the massive foundation of the later temple. With nothing surviving on top of the base save the stumps of six pillars, it seems more like an Aztec or other Meso-American construction than a Gallo-Roman shrine. The sanctuary was established around 50–70, just at the time that Augusta Raurica was undergoing its first real building boom, and coins found on the site indicate that it was in use at least until 217.[143] A large hole is evidence of an attempted forced entry into the interior by an overenthusiastic pre-modern excavator, a sign that, even here, plundering of sites was not unknown in the past.

A few hundred metres behind the theatre to the north-east lay the colony's forum. It is now a large, square meadow broken slightly by bumps where the public buildings of the site may lie. As late as 1918 it was still in use for farming, and in that year much of the platform of the monumental temple of Roma and Augustus was torn down. In front of the ruined temple site, there now stands a reconstructed marble altar, with an eagle bearing a thunderbolt. It was the only temple in Augusta Raurica to be built in the purely Italian manner, a rectangular colonnaded affair rather than the square sanctuaries within a walled compound that are more characteristic of the way of temple-building in Celtic-influenced provinces. A wooden framework façade has also been erected; supposed to represent the original, but with nothing behind it but sky, it has the definite air of a Potemkin temple on the Rhine.

At the other end of the forum lies the 1st-century basilica, or law court, nothing now surviving but a few pieces of pillar (as the excavated remains have been covered over), but the nearby *curia* or town hall, where the municipal temple met, has been restored. About five tiers of semicircular rows of seats, where the councillors met, are visible, together with a podium where the *duumvirs*, or two senior magistrates of the city, stood to address the assembly.

Just beyond the *curia* at the foot of a slope (which in turn became the focus of new fortifications in the late 2nd and early 3rd centuries) is a residential area, with a small bathhouse which may have been part of a *mansio*, or inn. The complex is quite small (in contrast to the leviathans of Trier) and so is more easily comprehensible at a casual glance, with the *frigidarium* and the hypocaust for the *caldarium* all still in place. Built in the late 2nd century, it faced onto the street, presumably providing a welcome amenity to local residents and traders.

Steps down beside the baths lead into an underground well-house, in the shaft of which five human skeletons were found together with the remains of a number of dogs. Related finds in the vicinity turned out to be clay moulds used in the counterfeiting of coins,[144] an occupation that became more widespread during the high inflation of the 3rd century when the central mints simply could not (or did not bother to) keep up with the demand for small change. It all adds up to an intriguing and insoluble murder mystery. Down below in the shaft it feels extremely claustrophobic – not a place to linger with the ghosts of the ancient counterfeiters.

From here the way leads back towards the centre of town, along a road fringed by fields that passes by the site of the former central baths south-east of the theatre, now discernible only by the irregular cast of the ground. Built in the mid-1st century AD, and altered and enlarged in the 2nd century, they remained in use until the upper part of the town was abandoned in the 3rd century, but the only remaining portion is a cellar and sewer, which survived because they were filled in with a heap of potsherds around 100. It is possible to follow the sewer, which was intended for drainage from the baths, for about a hundred metres, a passage that provokes a peculiar and alarming sensation as one makes slow, dark progress along a channel for ancient Roman effluent.

On the eastern edge of town, just by the site of a 'Roman zoo' in which modern children have the opportunity to experience ancient breeds of sheep and goats (although most of them seem to be more concerned with impromptu picnic parties at the top of the panorama tower erected nearby), there sit the remains of the eastern gate of Augusta Raurica, lying along a stretch of the town's eastern walls, which have been iden-tified for a length of 500 metres. The gate's projecting round towers, which have been reconstructed to eight or nine layers of the facing bricks, with the rubble core still exposed, were clearly intended as part of a great monumental gateway, but the plans were cut back to something less ambitious several times during its construction. The building seems to have begun around AD 80,[145] but was never in fact completed, an affront to the prestige of the town, which must have been all too visible over the next two centuries.

Perhaps the eye of the citizens was more taken by the massive funerary monument that lies just 50 metres away. Only the stone skeleton of its base now survives, indicating a massive stone cylinder that was 15 metres in diameter, probably topped with a mound of earth on which a statue of the deceased might have stood. It was built around the same time as the east gate, and the human remains, which were cremated on the spot, were probably of a man about thirty-five to forty years in age. He must have been someone of great importance, for it is neither a modest nor a discreet monument, and one that anyone entering or leaving the town in this direction could not fail to have remarked upon.

Moving from the eastern gate to visit the town's second amphitheatre – this time not a conversion – involves a walk beside the modern motorway, a rude awakening from the silence that enfolds most of the ruins. Across the lanes of speeding cars, a small portion of the western wall of Raurica is visible – all that remains, and heavily graffitoed. The amphitheatre, built around 200, and with seating for around 5,000 spectators, was a late addition to the town, but the citizens had been able to enjoy the adapted theatre for blood spectacles, and presumably only when it was turned back over to the dramatic arts was it deemed necessary to acquire a dedicated building. The arena's oval measures about 50 x 30 metres, strewn about with damp leaves, while the slopes upon which the seats once stood are populated by a thin copse of trees. The monumental western entrance survives more intact, with evidence of deep buttresses, which were added in Roman times to halt the slippage of the steep seating slope that has threatened ever since to collapse.

In a valley below, on a stretch of marshy land to one side of the theatre, lies the 'Grienmatt' shrine, a complex of Gallo-Roman temples set on a small plateau. The main one, right in the middle of an open field, is hedged about by an alarming forest of electric fences, clearly erected by a local farmer who is not that keen on visitors to the antiquities. The bold base of a platform survives, surrounded by the vestigial remains of a portico, with two or three columns still in place, and has been variously interpreted as a temple to the healing god Asclepius – in whose honour a number of inscriptions were found – or to the gods of the days of the week.

Back to the centre of town and a short walk north over to the Rhine, in a rather sleepy-looking section of Kaiseraugst (the twin village of Augst), lies the late-Roman fortress of Castrum Rauracense, directly on top of which the medieval settlement grew. It gets several notices in Ammianus Marcellinus (as Rauracum)[146] and is mentioned also in the *Notitia Dignitatum*, for the area was now a lynchpin between the imperial capital at Trier and the Danubian province of Raetia to the east.

Probably built in the early 4th century, it was visited by Julian in 360 and its fortifications may have been strengthened by Valentinian I in 370.[147] At about 3.5 hectares in area, it is the largest of Switzerland's late-Roman forts and housed units of the I Martia legion. The south wall is in fair condition, rising to around 4 metres in height, a section of its facing stones having been neatly restored. Part of the foundation of the south-western round tower is visible and it was close to this point that the Kaiseraugst Treasure was unearthed in 1960. The fort was probably destroyed in about 350, around the time the treasure was buried, but was subsequently rebuilt. Much of the interior of the fort is taken up with the site of a modern primary school, and the neat houses that surround the place and the general air of tranquillity give it more the atmosphere of a village green than a military monument.

Alongside the 'Rhine Baths' that lie in a jumble of ruins a few hundred metres away, a palaeo-Christian church perches just on the banks of the river. Almost hidden away in trees and under a protective shelter, the first building here was erected in the 4th century and remained in use possibly until the 6th century. Inside the apse of the church can just be made out, and it was here that the local bishops presided up to the 7th century, when the see was transferred to the up-and-coming settlement of Basle just down the river.[148] Deprived even of its position as an ecclesiastical centre, Castrum Rauracense went the way of its neighbour Augusta Raurica and dwindled to become a small village.

Just across the river, hidden amongst a deep screen of trees, lie the remains of a bridgehead fort built by Valentinian I, who ordered a general reinforcement of the whole of the Rhine defences right the way from Basilia to Lake Constance. Lying about 40 kilometres to the east of Raurica, and set back around 15 kilometres from the Rhine, the legionary fortress of Vindonissa formed part of this chain of defence. The scenery of low hills seems to have strayed straight off a chocolate box, the cows doing their scenic duty even in the face of a light dusting of snow. Vindonissa, which lies interleaved with the modern town of Brugg, was sited at the confluence of three rivers, the Aare, Reuss and Limmat, and dominated a pass over the Jura mountains, as well as blocking off access southwards to intruders passing beyond the Rhine, so it commanded a position of huge strategic importance.

The first legionary camp was probably constructed here in about AD 16, and until 45 it was the base for the XIII Gemina legion, who were replaced by the XXI Rapax some time before 69. Then, following the civil war of that year, the fort became the home to the XI Claudia. Deprived of much of its military function once the *limes* advanced forward around 75, Vindonissa lost its full legionary garrison around 101, but continued to be the station for elements from the VIII legion based at Argentorate (Strasbourg). Reoccupied when the frontier moved back to the Rhine after 260, a smaller fortress, known as Castrum Vindonissense, retained a garrison into the early 5th century; and, once the Roman army had abandoned its positions on the Rhine, the continuing role of this site as a Christian bishopric indicates that some, at least, of its civilian population stayed put.

A few hundred metres south of the railway station, on a site revealed when a modern building was demolished, a Roman pottery-manufacturing area has been unearthed. This comparatively heavy industry lay outside the main *vicus* of the settlement, enabling it to reach a scale that would have been unimaginable in a residential district. Little can be made out of the structures involved, but in one of the excavated trenches, strata of *terra sigillata* – the high-quality red-glazed ware for which the Rhineland

and parts of Gaul became famous, and which was exported throughout the Roman world – can be seen.[149]

To the extreme south-east of the main settlement lay the amphitheatre, a short way from the main legionary camp. All around are pretty terraces of houses on streets evoking the place's past, with names such as Römerstraße and Arenastraße, and the name indicated on old maps for the site translates as 'place of the bears', a possible folk-memory of the animal displays that may once have taken place here. Intriguingly, though no bones of lions (or other wild beasts) have so far been dug up, archaeologists did find the remains of a camel. The amphitheatre had a capacity of about 5,000 and was rebuilt at the end of the 1st century. The oval of the arena, and the earth banks on which the terraces of seats once stood, are fairly intact and the arena wall itself has been partly reconstructed with a double ring of stones.

The site of the main fort lies on an area known as the Königsfeld, a large open park, in part occupied by a church. The camp perimeter was irregularly shaped, with seven sides rather than the regulation four, in part determined by the difficulty of the terrain, overlooking the river gorge. The few remains to be seen today date from the 3rd-century version of the fort; its monumental west gateway is well preserved in outline, with a triple-entrance, the two at the sides being for pedestrians and the central archway for wheeled traffic. A stone set against one side of the central entrance seems to have been placed there because the road outside branched in two directions, forming a Y-junction, so that carts cutting in to avoid a bottleneck where the roads met must have been forever crashing against the gate and damaging its posts; the stone was to protect the structure and discourage such reckless driving. No other structures are apparent in the camp (though some have been identified by archaeological soundings) apart from the north gate, a smaller affair with square towers and deep rectangular holes set within the stone, which may represent a pre-existing wooden structure that was simply encased within the new building. The gate overlooks the river and a deep cut that was made when the railway was constructed in the 19th century. An earlier stretch of the wall strikes off to the north-east before disappearing into the ravine, much of it lost.

A short way outside the camp, under a protective roof, a 1st-century *mansio* marks the more purely civilian side of life in Vindonissa. It was extended on several occasions, so that it had its own bath-complex, complete with *frigidarium* and a small hypocaust for the warm rooms. In one corner of the complex a water-channel indicates an even earlier bath-house. A few hundred metres from this lies the last major visible relic of

Vindonissa's Roman life, the 'kitchen building'. Accessed through a metal grille at the bottom of a short flight of steps, it sits in the grounds of a primary school, and its entrance feels more like that of a bomb shelter than that of an archaeological site. It may well have formed part of the house of a centurion of the XI Claudia legion, possibly of the *primipilus*, the most senior of all. At one side of it were various inns, and part of the wall of one of these still survives in this subterranean world.

The main body of the ruins comprises the kitchen itself, which was in places built over the walls of the Celtic *oppidum* that existed at Vindonissa before the Roman occupation, and into which part of the Roman level has collapsed. A couple of rooms, quite bare of adornment, survive; in one corner blackening of the brickwork is visible, though whether from the normal sort of accident that might occur in a kitchen or through deliberate destruction is unclear.

Kitchen waste found here indicated a surprisingly high level of imported food being consumed, including oysters, which because of the need to ensure their freshness were a rarity, though a delicacy much in demand amongst Roman gourmands.[150] At the time, however, river transportation was possible all the way from Massilia (Marseilles), so the freshness of the produce in the centurion's kitchen would have been satisfactorily assured. When it was abandoned, the house was stripped and almost nothing left, save items that had been damaged or were considered worthless, such as a few tile stamps and a mortar, which was left behind as it had a hole in it.

Thirty-five kilometres of gentle countryside to the south-east of Windisch, Turicum's Roman past has been totally obscured by its development into the major banking centre of Zurich, but perhaps a precursor of the city's later international financial role was the station of the *beneficiarii*, the military units who collected road tolls, which was situated near here. A fort was also constructed under Valentinian I in the 370s, though abandoned with the rest of the *limes* in the early 5th century. Some thirty minutes by train to the south-east of the city lies a much better-preserved Roman fort, at Pfäffikon.

The landscape here is predominantly of low hills, and it is prime agricultural territory punctuated by crisp-looking villages. Around a kilometre from the centre of Pfäffikon village, set on a low hill at the back of houses, the fort's isolation is accentuated by a blanket of snow, its slopes now home to nothing more martial than a family tobogganing down the hill. Its quadrangular walls were reconstructed early in the 20th century, the dark, smallish bricks making it seem like a rather outmoded office building. Inside, the only hint of an interior structure on the day of our visit was almost totally covered by the snow. It is the outline of a 1st-century *villa rustica*, which occupied the site before the fort was built. Two rooms have been identified along with a hypocaust that sits beneath the fort's south-eastern tower.

Coins found from the reign of Valentinian I suggest that it was under this emperor that the fort was constructed, as part of a building programme to shore up the leaking sieve that the *limes* had become. The site could equally, however, date to the late 3rd or early 4th century and a similar programme by Diocletian, which led to the building of forts at Oberwinterthur, Stein-am-Rhein, Pfyn and Arbon, securing a line leading up to Lake Constance. From there the late-Roman *limes* followed the line of the Iller river, defended by a series of large watchtowers, until it reached the Danube between Lorch and Schirenhof.

The Agri Decumates

North and east of the portions of Switzerland that shelter behind the Rhine, the Agri Decumates – the territory that was occupied as the *limes* advanced from around 74 to 260 – was one of the more ephemeral of Roman conquests, with only Dacia beating it for the brevity of its occupation. According to Tacitus, the area had once been settled by a mixture of Gallic tribes, a fact confirmed by 2nd-century inscriptions that mention the Boii, Mediomatrici and Senones.[151] The exact meaning of the term that came to be applied to this area between the Neckar, Black Forest and Swabian Alps is unclear; it was once believed that it derived from *decuma*, meaning 'tithe', but it is more probable that it comes from a Celtic-term meaning 'ten' and refers to an area comprising ten districts or cantons.

Among the chief towns of the region, which experienced two centuries of prosperity under Roman rule, was Arae Flaviae, whose very name suggests a temple to the Flavian conquerors of this region. Now just outside the modern town of Rottweil, it lies on the banks of the Neckar river. Founded in around AD 73, it owed its existence to a slight realignment of the frontier by Pinarius Clemens, which meant that new forts had to be built to secure a straighter line between the Upper Rhine and the Danube. The town's main Roman remains, the baths, lie almost enclosed by the cemetery to the east of town. They are the biggest in south-western Germany and originally formed part of a legionary camp of the XI Claudia from 75. When this was abandoned after just five years, they were integrated into a smaller cohort camp. The auxiliary troops

who were then stationed at Arae Flaviae thus found themselves in possession of a facility far grander than their numbers (no more than 1,000)
would normally have permitted. Set in a dip a few metres deep and
surrounded by a grassy bank, the bath complex was originally purely
symmetrical, but a part of one wing was lopped off when the camp was
reduced in size (from its original extent of 16 hectares to a mere 5.7).

Just across the river, where the civilian settlement developed, one of
the surprises of the *limes* sits under the church of Saint Pelagius (which,
though much reconstructed, originally dates from the 8th or 9th century).
Down in the basement, behind a barely openable wooden door, is a
section of hypocaust, some 40 metres square, which may have survived
through its later use as living quarters. The pillars of this hypocaust are
particularly tall and so it is possible to walk, or rather to crouch, in this
subterranean interstice. It must, however, have made a very damp
bedroom indeed, with the constant dripping of water creating an atmosphere of foul dankness.

A 50-kilometre drive to the north-east, again along the line of the
Neckar, lies Sumelocenna (modern Rottenburg). The town seems to have
had its origin as part of an imperial estate, for it is known in the earliest
records (in the mid-80s) as the Saltus Sumelocennensis,[152] though it later
became the civilian capital of the region. It had a city wall more than 2
kilometres long built at the end of the 2nd century, of which parts
survive. But the most intriguing relic, over which the local museum has
been built, is probably the largest public latrine to be seen in the Roman
world. Although others can be found along the *limes*, mostly associated
with bathhouses and particularly well preserved in North Africa, none
is as impressive as this. Set around a courtyard, it is provided with individual marble seats, each with its own hole down which urine and faeces
would be deposited. It was very much a public facility, for in performing
this (to modern Western sensibilities, very private) act, the Romans were
surrounded by their fellows. Around the latrine a water channel normally
ran, and the public were provided with sponges, which served in lieu of
the modern predilection for toilet paper. With the remains of impressive pillars set into the middle of the courtyard, this mammoth provision
for a very mundane need seems strangely like a temple.

Behind the latrine a small section of street survives, together with
part of a private villa. Elsewhere, a temple has been located in the area
of the modern gaol, together with two sets of baths. The second of
these sits in the basement of the Eugen Bolz Gymnasium, a school not
far from the museum, and seems to have been built in the mid-2nd to
early 3rd centuries. The area of the ruins is quite small, with a dusty and

neglected air, but from there a fine view can be had of the school library (and, presumably, vice versa), an echo of the ancient habit of siting libraries near bath complexes to cater to those for whom mere pampering of the body was not satisfaction enough.

The Neckar-Odenwald and Antonine Limes

To trace the advances of the *limes* of Germania Superior requires a jump back northwards from the Agri Decumates to the point where (after the time of the Flavian emperors) the *limes* deviated from the line of the Rhine south of Remagen between Hönningen and Rheinbroh. It then proceeded generally south-eastwards, parallel to the river, but around 7 kilometres to the east of its course. It passed into the Taunus mountains, and then around Bad Schwalbach turned east. Soon after this, about 5 kilometres from the modern town of Bad Homburg, stands the Saalburg, one of Germany's most famous Roman forts. That this auxiliary camp should achieve such fame, when it is really no more significant than its fellows to east and west, is in large part due to Kaiser Wilhelm II, who spent a great deal of time in the area as a child, grew fond of the place and, when he ascended to the throne in 1888, ordered that it be reconstructed, a process that was completed in 1907.[153] So fond was he of the Saalburg that, fancying himself, as German Emperor, to be the heir of his Roman counterparts, he had an inscription set above the main gatehouse, which, in impeccable Latin, honoured him as the re-founder of the Saalburg, accompanied by a statue of Antoninus Pius.

Originally an earthwork fort built under Domitian in around 83 as part of his war against the Chatti,[154] it was rebuilt in timber soon afterwards, and sometime between 125 and 139 received a regular garrison of the *Cohors II Raetorum civium romanorum*, a part-mounted auxiliary unit from the neighbouring province to the east. The fort was reconstructed in stone around 139, but seems to have been destroyed during the Alamannic invasion of 233, after which it was briefly restored, only to be abandoned with the rest of the Agri Decumates around 260.

The Saalburg occupies a rectangular ground-plan with rounded corners, each wall punctuated by a gate. With their neat crenellations and perfectly tiled roofs for the towers, the fortifications seem, perhaps, too immaculate – the grey stone and brooding forest around giving a sense that somehow a Roman fort had mated with a Gothic castle and produced this uneasy compromise as offspring. This is perhaps unfair, for everything is meticulously done, and the museum presents an excellent display of finds from the site, including a very large collection of Roman footwear, which was found in waterlogged levels that had preserved the boots' leather. Around the centre of the fort, the *principia* has been reconstructed, including a representation of the Temple of the Standards, complete with legionary flags, although most of the main buildings lie in ruins or still beneath the ground.

Outside to the south-west of the main gate, a *vicus* grew up around the fort, today just a confusing collection of ruined shells. One of these was once an inn, possibly for official visitors, whilst beside it lay the bath-house. Further into the surrounding woods, a Jupiter column has been set up, reconstructed in the 19th century from fragments found nearby, very much along the lines of the one in Mainz. Its particularly fine panel of Hercules wielding an enormous club seems lost in the trees, viewed only by the occasional dog-walker.

Around 200 metres to the north of the Saalburg lies a section of the *limes*: a rather overgrown ditch is backed by an earth rampart some 2 metres high, and in front of this a long, low palisade of wooden stakes has been erected, a small token of a barrier that originally stretched for hundreds of kilometres. Up in the wood-wreathed hills above the Saalburg the *limes* continues, punctuated by the occasional watchtower, one of a string that policed the frontier at surprisingly short intervals. The walk is a pleasant one, shaded by the canopy of the trees from both rain and sunshine. A kilometre or so away, at Fröhlichmannskopf, a small tower, originally of timber, but reconstructed in stone in the mid-1st century after a fire, lies lost in the wood, with only about 20 centimetres of stone poking up above the ground to indicate its plan. The next tower, which is around 500 metres away in the Köpern valley, may originally have been a comparative giant, at three storeys, with the entrance on the middle floor. However, its remains are now only fractionally more complete than those of its neighbour, overgrown with grass and partly concealed by leaves. Here, the *limes* is a very quiet and forgotten place.

From this point the frontier turned north towards Butzbach, then arched round southwards to reach the Main at Hanau, protected by a series of forts on the west bank of that river until it reached Miltenberg. It then cut through the Odenwald, forming two distinct lines, one west of Miltenberg proceeding via Eulbach and Würzberg to reach the Neckar in the south near Köngen, and the other about 30 kilometres to the east, attained during the reign of Antoninus Pius, cutting in a south-easterly direction until it hit the Raetian border near Lorch.

At Eulbach, the unlikely setting of the 'English Garden' of the Counts of Erbach-Erbach's hunting lodge houses some of the best-preserved remains of the pre-Antonine (or Odenwald) *limes* in this section. It was established between 1802 and 1818 by Count Franz I, an inveterate collector of ancient remains and an exponent of the then current fashion of arranging them artfully in a seemingly natural setting. Amongst his other acquisitions was a herd of buffalo, thus providing the nearest connection that the Romans, in a sense, ever made to North America.

The guardian seems rather surprised to see visitors at opening time and surveys me suspiciously as we make our way in search of the Roman castles within. In the slightly muddy maze of pathways, the first sign of Rome is an obelisk, probably a Jupiter stone, placed to the side of the path. Then, beyond a clump of legionary gravestones, the gateway of Eulbach fort lies. It is the east gate of the fort, which housed an irregular unit (or *numerus*) in its 5.5-hectare precinct. It was originally sited to the east of the park, only 80 metres from the *limes*, before the count uprooted it and planted it close to his other antiquities. It only saw military use between 100 and 159, before Antoninus Pius moved the frontier eastwards and the posts on the Odenwald–Neckar *limes* were evacuated. The rest of the fort was subsequently destroyed, so the count's apparent act of vandalism in fact saved this portion, a single gateway rising to a couple of metres. A short distance away sits another, rather more complete gate, from Würzberg fort, though its battlements resemble more the image of a medieval portal than a Roman gateway and seem to have been a later addition. The final piece in the count's collection, beyond the line of the wood's edge, is the remains of a stone watchtower, which was removed from a position south of Eulbach. It is the most complete, placed on a small mound, with a couple of votive altars set inside it for good measure.

The small fort of Würzberg is 3–4 kilometres a little further south, lying alone in the Odenwald. The bathhouse, which is all that remains apart from the gate in the 'English Garden', was built, along with the fort, in the early 140s by a unit from the north of England. The turn-off to the fort is by a car park at the edge of the forest. A few hundred metres within, along a tree-shaded track, lie the Roman remains, but a lorry-load full of rifle-wielding hunters – predominantly dressed in green to blend in with the trees, a few among them wearing a feather in their caps – block the way. Their leader, a belligerent type in late middle age, is aggressive, demanding that we leave the forest at once, for there is a hunt today and access to the Roman ruins is, he insists, forbidden. Appeals to reason fail, and tension mounts. Faced with a dozen or more armed and increasingly irritated men for whom the idea of waiting a quarter of an hour is far too much of an affront to bear, we leave, and Würzberg fort remains elusive. It is, perhaps, the only encounter with genuine 'barbarians' along the whole frontier.

Twenty kilometres to the east, along the line of the *limes* as advanced by Antoninus Pius, the *numerus* fort of Haselburg lies in fields near the village of Reinhardsachsen. Only a small section of tower and wall survives, hemmed in by fields on either side. It was built in around 150, and lies just 60 metres or so from the line of the frontier itself, which can just be made out in a copse of trees to the east. One gate of the wall remains, seemingly pointing into the middle of nowhere in this picturesque but lonely rural setting. A coin of 264/5 was found on the site (an *antonianus* of Gallienus),[155] creating a minor mystery, as it was supposed that the *limes* had been evacuated by this time. But there is no need to suppose that Haselburg was held as an isolated outpost after that point, for Roman troops would continue to have patrolled beyond the new line, engaging in proactive patrols and strikes against any Alamanns who looked foolish or bold enough to penetrate the Rhine, and there was no more natural place to base themselves temporarily than the recently abandoned fort sites.

Not far to the south, the modern town of Walldürn, attractively set in woodlands, lies about 2 kilometres north-west of the point where the *limes* begins a run of 80 kilometres in an almost dead-straight line. It does so with little regard for the terrain it traverses, a testament to the obstinacy (as well as the skill) of the Roman surveyors. There was a fort here, about 30 metres off the main road, but it has almost totally disappeared, marked only by slight undulations in the ground, though down a little incline the military baths have survived in reasonable shape. They were completed in their final form only in 232 – a dedication to the goddess Fortuna provided the date – a bare three decades before the *limes* fell and the Romans abandoned the place for ever. The baths were then destroyed by fire, but whether in an accident or by invading German tribesmen is unknown. The complex is quite small, with just a few stone courses to give the outline of the rooms, but the setting, half-hidden by the higher fields to one side, is pleasantly peaceful.

At Osterburken, around 20 kilometres to the south, an original auxiliary cohort fort that was built around 155 (and garrisoned by a unit from Aquitania) has been totally submerged beneath the modern village. However, under Commodus the auxiliaries were supplemented by a *numerus* and a second fort was built for the newcomers on a slope above the old camp. It is an irregular-shaped trapezium, which employed one wall of the auxiliary fort as its own north-western perimeter. The original fort had in any case been at something of a disadvantage with this high point overlooking its walls, and so the new structure, as well as housing the *numerus*, would have provided additional security for the Aquitanians. As usual, it seems to have been legionaries who were the workhorses of this major building project, and detachments of the VIII Augusta from Argentorate (Strasbourg) were drafted in to erect it.

The west wall of the fort is the best preserved, with a fine view of the roofs of the modern village, but it was in the ditch of the earlier cohort fort that the most interesting finds were dug up (in 1991). Two levels of burning were found, together with pottery and the bones and skulls of two adults showing signs of a violent death. It could be evidence of the final Germanic assault on the place. In the village museum the main items of interest are no fewer than twenty-one altar stones dedicated by *beneficiarii* (customs officers) who had a shrine set up nearby; over successive decades each new head of the station added a new altar. Alongside are the remains of a bathhouse, one of two found at Osterburken (the other lying buried beneath a local bank).

Past the bathhouse of the fort at Jagsthausen, the *limes* now proceeds gently south-east into largely wooded territory. At Pfahldoebel, a section of 200 metres or so of the original earth rampart and ditch survives, hidden deep in the forest. The V-shape of the ditch is clearly visible amongst the fallen leaves and branches; the effect is very much like that of the Antonine Wall in Scotland, hardly surprising given that they both date from the same emperor's programme of works on the frontier. At Gleichen, still deep in the woods, along a kilometre or so of trackway, lies one of the more unusual watchtowers. Its base survives only up to three courses or so, but it is, quite exceptionally, hexagonal, as though the architect had decided in some small way to stand out, or the commander of the unit based there felt he had to be different from the Julii next door. More scientifically based speculation suggests that the six-sided shape gave extra strength, but if so, it is an innovation that was only rarely adopted elsewhere.[156]

Only twenty minutes' drive further south lies the small town of Mainhardt, which housed a fort for the *Cohors I Asturum equitata*, a part-mounted unit from the north-west of Spain. It was transferred here from the Neckar–Odenwald *limes* under Antoninus Pius, but then at the start of the 3rd century was sent to Britain,[157] and its replacement unit in Germany is unknown. The remnants of the fort are very slight, a small stretch lying near the local sports hall, together with a corner tower. The line then disappears into thick undergrowth, although for the truly determined it can be traced further at the base of a tangled hedgerow (and a further section – now invisible – was preserved under the sports field built by the United States army in 1945). The town is also home to one of the frontier's best small museums, including some stone reliefs of a mother goddess suckling a child, which are highly unusual and only found along this small section of the *limes* and in Gaul. Their kinship with later representations of the Madonna and baby Jesus is unmistakable.

The next section of *limes* to the south is thickly populated by watch-towers in the woods. At Grab, around 5 kilometres from Mainhardt, one has been reconstructed in wood, recreating a middle state of the *limes*, with tower, rampart and ditch, and a wooden palisade in front of it. At more than 20 metres tall, the tower provides a good Roman's-eye-view of the wooded *barbaricum* beyond, and shows clearly that to scramble over the palisade and then through the ditch and over the earth banks would have created such a commotion that intruders would have been detected relatively easily, although dealing with them would very much have depended on the numbers in which they came. It seems that the proportion of large trees such as oak and fir in the forest declined in Roman times,[158] so there may have been a deliberate attempt to thin out the forest canopy to encourage better visibility.

Further south at Heidenbuhl in the Murrhardt forest, a watchtower[159] lies up a slight slope. The structure was composed of two separate towers, and the outline of one, really just the stone foundation, can be made out, and next to it a reconstructed but still-ruinous twin, complete to around 4 metres on one side and 2 metres on the other. Utterly surrounded by trees, it bears a most romantic air. The two towers are less than a metre apart, and it seems that the first stage was destroyed in a fire, but then rapidly reconstructed without using the shell of the original. The foundations of this second stage, though, were badly set – proving that the Romans were on occasions poor engineers – and the reconstructors therefore chose to use the older watchtower's founda-tions for their handiwork.

Another series of watchtowers strikes south-east; in one of them a Roman shoehorn was dug up, providing the first evidence that the Romans wore shoes that were closed at the back.[160] Finally, the *limes* emerges from the woods near Welzheim, at the edge of a modern village. Originally there were two forts, but the western one has disappeared, while the smaller eastern one (only 1.6 hectares in extent) has in part survived. Although otherwise not particularly remarkable, the eastern fort does have one curious feature. It lies east of the line of the *limes*, with a gap in the frontier palisade enabling communication and access into 'friendly' territory to the west. The western fort had a cavalry garrison (the *Ala I Scubulorum*),[161] whilst this one was garrisoned by a unit of *exploratores* (or scouts), appropriate for such a forward position. It seems that the eastern fort was established first, and then when the *limes* ended up running as straight as it did, the decision was taken not to abandon it.

The remains now lie in an open field, with few structures standing. The south gateway and a section of the south wall have been impressively rebuilt, though, complete with ditch in front, the 10 metres or so to either side of the single entranceway contrasting with the ruinous state of the rest. The internal buildings have gone, but the field is liberally sprinkled with altars and sculptures, including one of Mithras killing the bull. The low line of the remaining walls is cut in places by water-overflow channels, an indication that the site was not chosen carefully enough and suffered from flooding. In confirmation of this, the south-eastern tower shows evidence of having collapsed several times during the life of the fort.

Just about 10 kilometres further to the south-east lies Lorch, most famous for its abbey, Kloster Lorch. The modern town has completely covered the Roman fort that lay here (part of which is buried beneath the church itself). In compensation, a watchtower has been reconstructed nearby on a site that may have been occupied by a smaller fort. It seems a fairly suburban sort of a tower, neat, manicured and utterly unmilitary, but it provides excellent views over the Rems valley. Just beside Lorch lay the Rotenbachtal, a narrow 3-kilometre-long valley, which from the mid-2nd century marked the border between Germania Superior and Raetia to the east. It was a heavily fortified area both on the German and Raetian sides, marking a strategic trade route as well as a provincial boundary. Amongst the trees and the gentle rush of brooks, it all seems a very long way from Germania's northernmost reaches, far away on the shores of the North Sea.

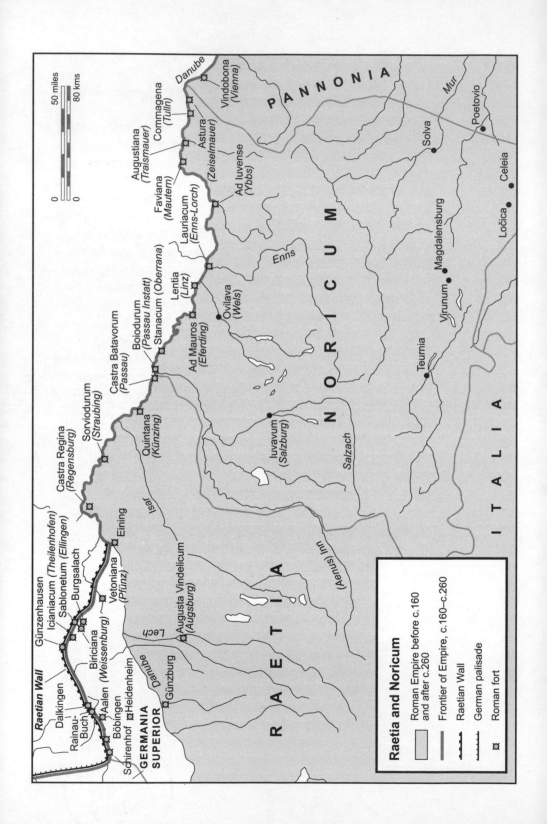

Raetia and Noricum

	Roman Empire before c.160 and after c.260
	Frontier of Empire, c.160–c.260
	Raetian Wall
	German palisade
⌗	Roman fort

50 miles
80 kms

Danube

PANNONIA

Vindobona (Vienna)
Commagena (Tulln)
Astura (Zeiselmauer)
Augustiana (Traismauer)
Ad Iuvense (Ybbs)
Faviana (Mautern)
Lauriacum (Enns-Lorch)
Lentia (Linz)
Boiodurum (Passau Instatt)
Stanacum (Oberrana)
Castra Batavorum (Passau)
Ad Mauros (Eferding)
Ovilava (Wels)

Solva
Poetovio
Celeia
Ločica
Magdalensburg
Virunum
Teurnia

N O R I C U M

Enns
Iuvavum (Salzburg)
Salzach

Mur

I T A L I A

Sorviodurum (Straubing)
Castra Regina (Regensburg)
Quintana (Künzing)
Eining

Augusta Vindelicum (Augsburg)

(Aenus) Inn

Raetian Wall
Günzenhausen
Icianiacum (Theilenhofen)
Sablonetum (Ellingen)
Burgsalach
Vetoniana (Pfünz)
Biriciana (Weissenburg)
Dalkingen
Aalen (Weissenburg)
Rainau-Buch
Böbingen
Schirenhof
Heidenheim

GERMANIA SUPERIOR

R A E T I A

Isar
Lech
Danube
Günzburg

CHAPTER 3

Raetia and Noricum

The troops at Batavis, however, held out. Some soldiers of this troop had gone to Italy to fetch the final pay to their comrades, and no one knew that the barbarians had slain them on the way. One day, as Saint Severinus was reading in his cell, he suddenly closed the book and began to sigh greatly and to weep. He ordered the bystanders to run out with haste to the river, which he declared was in that hour besprinkled with human blood, and straightway word was brought that the bodies of the soldiers mentioned above had been brought to land by the current of the river.

Eugippius, *Vita Sancti Severini, c.20*[1]

Raetia

The transalpine sections of southern Raetia, now in southern Germany, first came into the Roman sphere during the campaigns of Augustus and Tiberius in 15 BC, expeditions that would also result in the conquest of the Norican kingdom to the east. It was occupied by peoples of Celtic origin, and the failure of the Romans to annex this area any earlier had left a salient from which raiders or invaders could cut off Roman access to the Balkans or, indeed, threaten the security of the newly acquired territories along the Rhine. The groups who dwelt there were, however, separated into a number of small tribes, often controlling barely more than the valley that they inhabited, and so the chance of a concerted assault south of the Alps was slight. The territory of Vindelicia – around modern Augsburg – which lay in the north and east of Raetia, was conquered by the Romans at about the same time as southern Noricum, and a legion was stationed there, only to be withdrawn in about AD 16–17. The remaining central portion of Raetia was not then formally constituted a province until about AD 50, and thus had no official governor, being administered by the military.

Although many of the forts south of the Danube in the western part

of Raetia were destroyed in the upheavals that surrounded the complex
civil war of 69 and the revolt of Julius Civilis the same year,[2] by the time
of Vespasian they had been rebuilt. A complicated series of moves forward
– in part in connection with the Roman desire to bridge the gap between
the Rhine and the Danube, and in part to fill holes in the defensive
system further east along the Danube – resulted in an extensive building
programme and a shifting about of military units until the mid-2nd
century. The Marcomannic Wars (166–80) caused some damage in the
east and probably led directly to the stationing of a legion, the III Italica,
in the province.

Throughout this time the Raetian *limes* was, as in Germania Superior,
marked out by a wooden palisade. This was replaced in 205–6[3] by the
building of a stone wall, some 3 metres high, studded with interval
towers. Just like Hadrian's Wall, it was not a suitable platform from which
to mount a fixed defence, but it was a potent statement of intent, and
would seriously have hindered small-scale raids whilst obstructing larger-
scale incursions, at least to the extent of facilitating the passing of warning
messages further back into the province, where reinforcements could
then be mustered. By the mid-3rd century, however, serious damage had
been done by the Alamanns and other barbarian raiders, and some positions north of the Danube may have been evacuated, whilst others were
abandoned when the Agri Decumates to the west were lost and the *limes*
was restored to its 1st-century position in Switzerland.

The early 4th century was surprisingly quiet in Raetia, but serious
raids by the Iuthungi in 357–8[4] led to a sharp retort under Valentinian I
and to the refortification of significant parts of the *limes* both on the
Rhine and the Danube. But the withdrawal of troops by Stilicho, probably in 401, to meet the challenge posed by Alaric and his Goths, led to
the stripping of vital Raetian garrisons, after which it is hardly possible
to talk of a consistently held frontier line at all.

Just east of Lorch in Baden-Württemberg, the border between Raetia
and Germania Superior was a provincial border of administrative convenience, and did not mark out any great shift in landscape or culture. A
covering mantle of conifers closes in along the path through the
Rotenbachtal, the voices of those visitors to the park who are more intent
on forest walks than archaeology fade and the distant past begins to feel
ever more present. After a while, across a shallow brook via a small
modern bridge – the wooden piles of whose Roman ancestor remain
elusive in the free-flowing water – the way leads up a gentle wooded
slope. Here at length the beginning of the Raetian wall comes into view.
At this point it is reconstructed, its stones rebuilt in a stepped fashion,

with one small section rising to a metre or so in height and half a metre thick. Largely concealed by the thin forest canopy, it seems almost impossible to believe that this low and weathered wall was part of one of the most ambitious and extensive Roman defensive works in the entire Empire.

Around 20 metres higher up the rise lies a very weathered altar or dedication stone and part of a worn frieze, possibly originally topped by rosettes. It is an altar to Terminus, the god of frontiers and borders. It is a most appropriate place to find a shrine to this ancient deity, whose worship seems to date from the very beginning of Rome. His birthday was celebrated on 23 February each year with the festival of the Terminalia, when sacrifices were made by landowners at the boundaries of their holdings, and an offering of blood was sprinkled on the stones dividing their fields.[5]

On the southern edge of these woods lie the small Roman baths at Schirenhof, their stones greyed and dulled by the weather, the small park in which they are set surrounded by prim suburban housing. Set on a slight hill, their position gives a wonderful view back down across the wooded valley. The complex was much reduced in size in the 3rd century, possibly as a result of the slighter hold that the Romans then exercised along the *limes*. The wall continued until it met the Danube just north of Eining, some 150 kilometres to the east, from where the river line made such a fortification redundant. Between Zimmer and Böbingen an der Rems (around 8 kilometres east of Schirenhof), where the wall takes a slight detour to the north-east, another section of it is visible, really just a few metres long set on a grassy stretch next to the B29 road. In a laudable demonstration of municipal pride, a locally erected sign declares 'World Heritage Site', a reference to the designation by UNESCO of the German *limes* as such in 2005.[6]

A few kilometres north-east lay the fort of Böbingen, situated on a hill above the Rems river. Originally enclosing an area some 145 x 135 metres in area, the fort was constructed in around 150, and was probably occupied until around 260, when many of the positions in this part of Raetia were abandoned. The ancient site has now largely been gobbled up by the car park of a family restaurant, though its gate towers are still intact, surrounded by a vast array of BMWs and Volkswagens. Both towers of the gateway have been partially reconstructed, though the right-hand one is filled with rubble and seems to have been subjected to some recent damage.

Around 30 kilometres to the east of Böbingen, and in turn about 5 kilometres behind the line of the *limes* wall, is the largest fort along this sector of Raetia and certainly the most spectacular in terms of its visible remains.

Built around 160, Aalen also housed the largest cavalry unit in the Western Empire north of the Alps, the *Ala II Flavia milliaria*, a rare double-strength mounted troop of around 1,000 men. It was one of only seven such milliary *alae* in the Empire (if one includes the camel unit stationed near Palmyra in Syria, a truly unique detachment).[7] Its commander would have been the most senior military officer in the province of Raetia until the stationing of the III Italica legion in Augusta Vindelicorum (Augsburg) around a decade later, although just as with the cavalry commander at Stanwix on Hadrian's Wall, there is no evidence of his exercising any general supervisory capacity over the provincial *limes*.

The western half of the fort's former site has been swallowed up by the Johannis Friedhof, a large cemetery thickly shaded with trees. It seems truly a place of sleep and forgetfulness, many of the crosses commemorating local men who died in the two World Wars, some of them simply 'lost in Russia'. Beyond, at the entrance to the archaeological area proper, lies the remains of the *porta principalis sinistra*, excavated in 1962. It is a double-gate with two passages, each around 3 metres wide – substantial enough, in other words, to let two mounted soldiers pass with relative ease. It leads the way into the Limes Museum, the leading German museum devoted to the study of the Roman frontier, which was founded in 1964. It was not the beginning of study into the *limes*, for in Germany (just as in Britain) a fascination for these ruins that could be seen without excavation was a venerable hobby, and scientific study of the frontier began early with the establishment of the Reichslimeskomission in 1892. This undertook many of the first excavations along the *limes*, and was headed up from its foundation until 1903 by Theodor Mommsen, the redoubtable doyen of German historians of the Roman Empire.[8]

The exhibits include fine examples of all the pieces expected to be associated with a significant Roman military presence: a votive table to Jupiter Dolichenus; from Osterburken, a relief to Mithras, another favoured god amongst the military; and a hoard of silver from Hildesheim, a sobering reminder that, for all the presence of this imposing military unit along the central Danube, instability and the threat of barbarian raiding were never wholly absent.

The main surviving structure of the fort is the *principia*, the outlines of whose stones rise a couple of courses in height, including the apse of the Temple of the Standards and the basilical cross-hall, a rather imposing statue of Marcus Aurelius presiding over it all. There are two dedication inscriptions. One of them, dating from 163–4, uniquely refers to the temple as a *capitolium*, a term more appropriate for a town or city forum than a military camp. The second, from the time of Commodus, may mark some rebuilding of the fort. The other buildings are less well defined, and down towards the *porta principalis dextra*, at the opposite end of the camp to the museum entrance, the ruins dwindle into a grassy patch and a few bumps, the remains of excavations during the 1970s. The Roman presence at Aalen, however, did not survive the tidal wave of Alamannic incursions and the general pull-back to more defensible positions that took place around 260.

From Aalen it is only about 15 kilometres north-east to the next cluster of important Roman Raetian remains at Rainau-Buch, the site of an auxiliary cohort fort, possibly of the *Cohors III Thracum*, posted here from the eastern Balkans. The fort itself lies up a slight slope, surrounded by fields and hedgerows. There is no visible evidence of internal structures, and only the remains of the southern gate and part of the wall give any evidence that the Roman army ever occupied the site. The gate is flanked by two square towers reconstructed to half a metre or so in height. On their own, shorn of most of the original structures, and beaten by late autumn rain, they seem somehow beleaguered, still conscious of being in fundamentally unfriendly country.

As was customary, the fort's bathhouse was sited some way from the main building and now lies by the side of an artificial lake in a kind of country park. A surprisingly grand structure for such a place, it seems more appropriate for a small town than a modest military detachment, but may have undergone some expansion in anticipation of a visit by Caracalla to the *limes* in 219–20; and the outline of a large building just by the water's edge, composed of two stepped terraces and interpreted as residential, may well have been erected as accommodation for the Emperor or some senior member of his entourage.

A short way to the north-west in the Mahdholz woods lurks yet another reconstruction of a *limes* watchtower. It rises two storeys up, its wooden bulk bolstered by a core of concrete, providing an excellent view for many kilometres east and west. The real gem, however, waits in the trees behind it. In a quiet clearing, accessed by a few metres of muddy track, is the most impressive section of the Raetian wall along the whole *limes*.

Although heavily reconstructed, it gives a good sense of how the barrier might have looked. A section around 8–10 metres long, it soars to around 3 metres in height and is around a metre thick. The end-piece where the reconstruction finishes exposes the mass of irregular stones that made up the wall's core, looking as though it has been sliced by some enormous cleaver. Running along 166 kilometres of the boundary, it must have been a truly imposing sight, and only the relative sparseness of its remains rob it of its place next to Hadrian's Wall as the most magnificent of Roman defensive works. Beside it are the remains of the original watchtower (an earlier phase of which the modern version represents). Evidence can be made out here for several phases of reconstruction of the stone-built phase of the *limes*, as the outline of a smaller, square tower is superimposed on the remains of an earlier rectangular watchtower.

A couple of kilometres to the east, at Dalkingen, lie the ruins of another cohort fort, in an isolated location off a minor side-road and thence up a muddy track. The remains are of a rectangular building, walls and gates with two levels, one of them marked out by wooden stakes that indicate the internal buildings of an earlier phase. The history of the *limes* fortifications here is relatively complex, for a hedge barrier under Hadrian was then followed by a watchtower, and in turn by a large stone building. In its fourth stage, however, Dalkingen departed from the normal career trajectory of a Raetian fort, since around 213 part of the building was dismantled and replaced by a façade with 3.5-metre-thick walls and a triumphal arch. The strength and depth of the foundations indicate that this was of a very significant height, and it seems that a larger-than-life statue of the Emperor Caracalla was incorporated within it. It was almost certainly built to honour him during his fighting against the German tribes in this area, although the construction of the arch may have been more about flattery of the Emperor than a true representation of the results of the campaign.

Caracalla had crossed the frontier in August 213, accompanied by Gaius Suetrius Sabinus, intent on punishing the Alamanns, who were only then beginning to threaten the borderlands. Having launched the attack, he proceeded back up the Rhine towards Mainz, where he seems to have defeated the Cenni. After a further victory near the Main river, Caracalla had himself declared *imperator* (for the third time) and *Germanicus Maximus*. Contemporary writers who were almost universally negative towards Caracalla complained that he had bought peace from the Germans and that his comparison of himself with earlier martial emperors was shameful. Perhaps they were thinking in purely territorial terms, for it is true that the Emperor did not actually annex any new land, but the salutary lesson he taught the Alamanns, and the strengthening of sections of the *limes* that he ordered, may have restored peace to the frontier for the best part of two decades – a far more effective use of resources than a showy and expensive acquisition of ultimately indefensible territory.

From Dalkingen to Gunzenhausen, a distance of some 120 kilometres, the frontier curved gently to the north-east, pushing almost to its furthest extent into Free German territory. Nothing remains of the small fort that was situated in Gunzenhausen, though in 1897 part of the ramparts and *principia* were unearthed by the town's main church. It seems only to have been around 80 metres square, and so must have housed a relatively small unit. A coin hoard dated to 241–3 is suggestive of destruction along this sector of the frontier at the time, but little more is known of the site's history.

A little way out of the centre of town, on a high rise behind the cemetery, lies further evidence of the Raetian wall. It is a quiet place, populated almost entirely by deer and the odd winter walker following the confusing complex of waymarked trails. Just at the top of the hill rises an obelisk with a base of cut stones. The face on the attached plaque is not that of a Roman emperor, however, but of Bismarck, the key figure in the 19th-century unification of Germany. The 'Bismarckturm' does, though, incorporate some antique remains, as it was constructed with stones from a primitive ring fortification built on this hill by the Alamanni in the 8th century, which probably in turn borrowed stones from the remains of the nearby Roman watchtowers and wall. Bismarck's obelisk may, therefore, partly be composed of third-hand building material, some of it very ancient indeed.

Beyond the Bismarckturm lie the remains of the small Roman watchtower itself, just the outline now surviving, but laid out with an unusual double-room. Around 4.5 x 6 metres in area, it was constructed in the 1st century AD and at the time would have been protected by a wooden palisade. A reconstruction of this has duly been erected nearby, with a metre-deep ditch underneath it, which was filled with stones to stabilise the sharpened wooden stakes. At around 3 metres high, the barrier was bound together with wooden bands and, just like its later stone successor (wings of which can be seen coming off the watchtower), would have provided just enough of an obstacle to frustrate minor incursions and disrupt the course of major ones.

Around 40 kilometres to the south-east, the Roman fort of Icianiacum at Theilenhofen is, like many other forts, largely represented only by its bathhouse, some of whose walls rise to a metre or so in height. It is set in a slight dip, screened by trees. At some 2 kilometres behind the *limes*, the soldiers here, from the *Cohors III Bracaraugustanorum* (originally all the way from Braga in modern Portugal), were at less danger than most of being surprised by barbarians whilst about their ablutions.

A short way along the frontier, where it begins to curve once more down to the south-west, lies the fort at Ellingen, ancient Sablonetum. It was one of the early excavations by the Reichslimeskomission in 1895, but further work was not possible until the early 1980s when a programme to encourage consolidation by farmers of disparate land-holdings made the site once more available for digging.[9] The building inscription found here refers to a reconstruction in 182, at the start of the reign of Commodus, though it was probably originally built in wood under Hadrian and housed a *numerus* whose identity is unknown. Around 80 metres square, the site has had one wall and a 30-metre section of stone rampart extensively reconstructed. A lower section of wall survives and runs to the east, reaching the the remains of an angle tower. It sits on a very flat area, with good visibility over the fertile farmland all around. The fort was probably abandoned some time before 233, during the Alamannic Wars, an evacuation that may have been planned, as no evidence has been found of destruction.

To the south-west of Ellingen and a few kilometres back from the *limes* is the auxiliary fort of Biriciana, now modern Weissenberg. It was established under Domitian around AD 90 after his campaign against the Chatti had pushed the Roman frontier forward into the Rhine–Danube gap. First built in earth, it was reconstructed in stone around 140 and then renovated again, possibly after 179, when this section of the frontier received new attention after the posting of a legion to nearby Augusta Vindelicum (Augsburg). It was very badly damaged during the Alamannic invasions of 233–4 and, although rebuilt after a campaign by Maximinus Thrax to restore the situation, was definitively abandoned later in the 250s when most positions north of the Danube were evacuated. Biriciana is most notable for its reconstructed north gate, from which two rounded towers project outwards, surmounted by an inscription in which the modern councillors of Weissenberg have fancied themselves as *decuriones*,[10] dating their work using the AUC system (from the foundation of the city of Rome), in the absence of contemporary emperors or consuls to use as reference points.[11] A small portion of the protective wall has been faced with a reflective white stone, supposed to represent the finishing that gave the place its name in early medieval times: 'The White Fortress'.

A few kilometres away to the east, beyond the actual line of the *limes* wall (which continued to curve to the south-east), is Burgsalach. There is another reconstructed wooden watchtower here, five minutes' walk off the road beside some woods, but of more interest is the *burgus*, which lies a kilometre away in a small and muddy wood. A massive square fortification, this style of oversized watchtower was uncommon in earlier times, and its occurrence here is echoed with greater prevalence in several other provinces, including in Pannonia at Lussonium[12] and the *centenaria* of the North African desert. Its life was probably short, for it was most likely abandoned at the time when the territory north of the Danube was given up in the mid-3rd century. Probably originally two storeys high, only the lower level now survives in a deep indentation in the ground. The large semicircular curve that formed part of the monumental façade of the building is clearly visible amongst a jumble of ruins. The blockier, denser and more inward-looking style of the *burgus* seems to be an intimation of a more defensive mentality and an awareness set in stone that the frontiers were under severe stress.

The fortress at Vetoniania (modern Pfunz), which lies 30 kilometres to the east of Burgsalach, was built near the River Altmühl, again when the frontier was moved north across the Danube during the reign of Domitian, and its role was to guard a military road that was constructed from Biriciana to Kösching. Around 2.7 hectares in extent, it housed the *Cohors I Breucorum civium Romanorum equitata*, a unit whose designation indicates that all its serving members at a particular point in time had been granted Roman citizenship (which would normally only have come on completion of their twenty-five years' service) for some unspecified act of bravery. Rebuilt in stone under Antoninus Pius, its final destruction seems to have come in 233 during the severe Alamannic incursion of that year. That the onslaught was sudden is indicated by the skeletons of guards found in the southern tower, bereft of their shields, while a prisoner who was being held in a cell in the *principia* died with a chain still shackled around his shinbone.

The whole of the west wall has been reconstructed, its neat crenellations and just-so towers gracing many a poster and book about the *limes*. The interior of the fort, however, is almost entirely given over to cultivation, and a cabbage patch sits over the remains of all the interior buildings. The line of the field goes to within a few centimetres of the east wall, and stones that have been upcast by ploughing seem to indicate that the remains beneath continue to be degraded by this surprising persistence of agriculture inside an important cultural monument. The eastern gate itself has been partly reconstructed and one other angle tower at the north-east pokes up to about a metre in height, with a small section of wall projecting from it. Somewhere round about must lie the civil settlement in which a temple of Jupiter Dolichenus was uncovered, but this, too, must have been destroyed or at least abandoned in short order at the time of the Alamannic raid which brought the occupation of the fort to an end.

At the junction of the Regen and Danube rivers, 50 kilometres to the east of Vetoniana, lay the legionary fortress of Castra Regina, which, many centuries later, has transmuted into the attractive riverside city of Regensburg. Its alternative name, Ratisbon, probably derives from a Celtic root, which alludes to an earlier Celtic settlement on the site. At the time of Vespasian, an auxiliary fort was built to protect an important crossing of the Danube, which was then reconstructed in stone under Hadrian. The garrison from the time of Trajan appears to have been the *Cohors III Bracaraugustanorum*,[13] a mixed cavalry and infantry unit from Portugal. The original fort, which lay south of the modern city centre at Kumpfmühl, was destroyed during the Marcomannic Wars in the 170s, and this time a legionary camp was built on a site nearer the Danube, which housed the III Italica legion. Although the commander of this legion was governor of Raetia, his official residence remained further south at Augusta Vindelicorum (Augsburg), safely away from the *limes* line.

In an exposed position on the central Danube, Regensburg suffered terribly during Alamannic invasions in 233 and 259–60, and major repairs were needed to the camp after the second assault. The III Italica seems to have remained in place until at least the beginning of the 5th century, although after Diocletian's reign *vexillationes* (detachments) were stationed elsewhere (including at Cambodonum/Kempten), so the effective strength of the Castra Regina garrison was reduced.

Although the Roman city has mostly disappeared beneath the medieval and above all the modern settlements, Castra Regina still peeps out from between the beer-cellars and baroque charm of this Bavarian town. It has retained vestiges of the Roman street grid and the *decumanus* along the line of the modern Fröhliche Türkengasse. At Maximilianstraße, down some steps in a shallow depression, stretches a 15-metre-long section of the south-east Roman fortress wall, with part of a rounded corner tower. The blocks of the tower stand to a couple of metres in places, and give a real sense of how massive the fortifications must have been when fully intact. A few broken column drums lie, partly obscured by an untidy carpet of grass. This little nook retained some defensive importance, for in 1383 another tower was erected on the spot, and its outline partly obliterates that of its Roman predecessor. Overshadowed by a little square lined with an optician's shop and a car park, they both seem largely forgotten.

Next to the chapel of Saint Georg and Afra, on a very busy road junction, lies another section of the Roman wall, but the pride of Roman Regensburg – lying half-concealed on Unter den Schwibbögen, a narrow street of souvenir shops behind the 13th-century cathedral – is the Porta

Praetoria. It consists of a gateway and part of a gate tower, whose semi-circular outline is embedded into a modern hotel. It is the rounded single section of what must have been a double-tower, one entrance having almost totally disappeared save for a few fragments. The left-hand side, however, rises to a second partly arcaded storey, belonging to a structure that was probably built in the 4th century, not dissimilar in style and intent to the great Porta Nigra in Trier.

The capital of Raetia, Augusta Vindelicum (Augsburg), lay on a protected spit of land between the Wertach and Lech rivers some 115 kilometres to the south-west of Regensburg and far behind the safety of the *limes*. It took its name from the Vindelici, the Celtic tribe who had dominated the area before the Roman conquest. During the conquest, it was the first Roman forward base in the area, and the site of a short-lived legionary camp for a quarter of a century from around 10 BC. Although it became the provincial capital, Augusta Vindelicum did not receive a formal constitution until the time of Hadrian, when it became a *municipium*. It remained the administrative centre of the province right up until the 5th century, after which the fate of the town is difficult to trace.

The 'Augsburg Victory Altar', which lies in the city's Roman museum, sheds light on a dark phase in the town's history.[14] It is dated April 260, and shows the taking of Augsburg from the Semnoni and Iuthungi after those barbarians had held it for a while in the face of a Roman siege. Interestingly, it honours not the official emperor at the time, Gallienus, but Postumus, who had declared himself Emperor in the Gallic provinces just a few months before, and whose authority seems, for a time at least, to have extended this far eastwards. But he cannot have held Augusta Vindelicum for long, as this would have resulted in an unacceptable encirclement of the Italian peninsula.

Also in the museum a case of 'hack-silver' dates from this time. This consists of parts of finely decorated plates that have been cut into pieces and divided, probably by barbarian raiders who were not so much concerned with the level of workmanship as with the raw value of the metal of which they were made. There is also a suitably celebratory dedication stone of 281, which commemorates Probus as the *Restitutor provinciarum et operum publicorum* ('Restorer of the provinces and of public works'). After half a century of near-anarchy in which barbarian raiders had not had to dread the full might of the legions, the citizens of Augusta Vindelicum must have breathed a hearty sigh of relief.

The only fragments of Roman Augsburg that can be seen above ground sit outside the Dom, the cathedral, a masterpiece of the German

Gothic style, which was begun around 1275 on the site of a yet earlier Romanesque church, and which lies more or less on the site of the old forum. Set against a wall (the 'Römische Mauer') a miscellany of pieces includes the grave of Marcus Aurelius Carus, who was an Augustal priest, (and so ministered to the imperial cult) in the 2nd century, and an altar of the Romano-Celtic hybrid god Apollo Grannus. Another dedicated to the sun god commemorates Julius Avitus Alexianus, who was the husband of Julia Maesa, and thus the grandfather of the Emperor Elagabalus.[15]

Just opposite the wall lies a jumble of ruins, all that remains of the Johannis chapel, which was demolished in 1808, but which had itself been built on the site of a very early Christian baptistery. It was here, in a small square well-shaft which the Christian community adapted as a font, that Saint Afra was baptised in the early 4th century. According to her *Acta*, Afra had originally come from Cyprus and worked as a prostitute in the Temple of Venus in Augusta Vindelicum.[16] She was converted to Christianity and weaned away from her unseemly profession by the offices of the Spanish bishop Narcissus of Gerona. When the Great Persecution broke out in 303, she and her mother concealed the bishop in their house, but Afra was detected and as a punishment tied to a tree on an island in the Lech river and then burnt to death.

The veneration accorded to Afra in the city is mentioned by Venantius Fortunatus, a 6th-century Bishop of Poitiers, who travelled from Italy to Gaul in 565, and who reported that the cult of Afra was still remembered at Augsburg. He also hints that the Bavarians, then in possession of Augusta Vindelicum, impeded the passage of travellers. However, while his journey may well have been fraught with perils, it does at least provide concrete evidence that a settled community of some kind remained in the city around 150 years after the collapse of Roman rule.

Running alongside the cathedral square is a curious reminder of the history of the study of the *limes*, for the road is named Peutingerstraße, in honour of Martin Peutinger, who was a citizen of Augsburg. His acquisition[17] of the medieval copy of a late-Roman map, which detailed itineraries throughout the Empire, revolutionised scholars' understanding of the detailed topography of the provinces and has proved a fertile quarry ever since for those locating 'lost' Roman sites or seeking to attribute names to those that have long since been found.

Back on the line of the Danube, the stretch to the border of modern Austria was defended by forts at Sorviodurum (modern Straubing), 25 kilometres to the east of Castra Regina, and at Quintana (Künzing), where a timber castle built under Domitian seems to have been destroyed so suddenly by an Alamannic attack around 242–4 that the soldiers were unable to retrieve their weapons from the armoury before disaster struck.[18]

Although there is nothing to see of the fort of Sorviodurum itself, which was built under Vespasian and garrisoned in the 2nd century by a detachment of Syrian archers, excavations at a villa to the west of the town revealed the most extraordinary treasure. Hidden in a bronze basin was a collection of lavish pieces of armour, including seven parade helmets. These were a Roman cavalryman's 'best' display armour, in the form of a bronze mask that concealed the features, reserved for special occasions and very definitely not battlefield wear. At Sorviodurum, four of the masks have wavy Grecian-style hair, lips slightly curled, with an otherwise impassive expression, while the other three sport more tightly curled hair styled in a conical form, which seems almost Persian in effect. The rest of the collection includes barding for the horses, and a series of cuirasses and greaves, one of which shows a fine figure of Mars standing on a giant, a symbol perhaps of the capacity of the wearer to triumph even in the face of enormous odds.

This area of the frontier, Sorviodurum not excluded, suffered grievously from raids by the Alamanns, beginning in the 230s. Despite Caracalla's success against them on the Rhine in 213, by 235/6 they were raiding extensively in Raetia, and in Noricum further to the east. By the late 250s, the Danube frontier and large stretches of the Rhine were in serious danger of being overrun by both the Alamanns and other groups such as the Iuthungi. The Raetian frontier was probably never held in anything like the same strength after 260, and some frontier positions were abandoned to the Alamanns. The tribes were always politically fragmented however, being ruled by a number of *reguli* or sub-kings and so the threat that they posed to the Roman Danube and Upper Rhine provinces remained intermittent.

The final point in the defensive system of Raetia, and indeed the border of the province, was at Castra Batavorum (known in later Roman sources as Batavis), which is buried under modern Passau. It derived its name from its early garrison, the *Cohors IX Batavorum milliaria equitata*, a mixed infantry-cavalry regiment from the lower Rhineland. It lies where the River Inn flows into the Danube, creating a protected spit of land just where the two waterways meet. At the very tip, the Ortsspitze, an early Roman fort was placed under Domitian; it is now a quiet waterside park populated by late-afternoon joggers and those wishing merely to contemplate the counter-flows and eddies caused by the joining together of the two rivers with yet a third, the Ilz, which flows down to here from the Bavarian forests to the north.

For the main, Passau is a picturesque university town, dominated by the bishop's fortress-cum-palace on the north bank of the Danube and the 17th century baroque bulk of St Stephen's Cathedral, which holds the second-largest church organ in the world. A later fort at Castra Batavorum was sited further west, near the Römerplatz, now a rather nondescript piazza with a little park overlooking the main bridge over the Danube. While the rest of the *limes* was collapsing, the Batavian cohort continued to hold the line here, and they seem to have remained in their station until the early 5th century, by which time the fort must have been little more than a refuge for the desperate populations nearby, and an ambivalent symbol of a far away emperor who could, in reality, do little to protect them.

Noricum

The border line between the provinces of Raetia and Noricum lay at modern Passau (Castra Batavorum), on the modern German-Austrian border. The Bavarian Passau lies within the provincial boundary of Raetia, while Passau Instatt (Boiodurum), the Austrian section of the city, sits at the western edge of what was Noricum. The eastern border of that province ran between the modern towns of Zeiselmauer (ancient Astura) and Vienna (Vindobona) much further east along the Danube. It was not one of Rome's most glamorous provinces and its annexation came about not through a series of hard-fought campaigns, but by an almost peaceful process of absorption.

The *Regnum Noricum* that was annexed by Tiberius, probably in 15 BC,[19] had its beginnings in the mid-4th century BC, when Celtic peoples began to filter down from Raetia into the territory of Salzburg and Upper and Lower Austria, and was securely established before 186 BC, when the Noricans sent an embassy to Rome.[20] It was only under the early Empire that Roman attention turned towards securing the alpine passages into Italy and achieving a frontier on the Danube which might block raids that threatened the peninsula, such as the Celtic incursions that had been so troublesome in the early 2nd century BC.

According to Cassius Dio, the pretext for the annexation of Noricum was an attack on Istria in 16 BC, which brought Roman retribution the next year and an end to the Noricans' independence.[21] Not all of the former kingdom was absorbed within the new province: the area north of the Danube was not occupied, while territory in the east was attached to Pannonia. Carnuntum (Petronell), which the Romans established as a legionary base, remained in Noricum until the XV Apollinaris was posted there in AD 14, when it, too, was transferred to Pannonia.

At first Noricum seems to have been garrisoned by small detachments from Pannonia, with the provincial administration based at the Magdalensburg fort in the south of the province. Later, under Claudius, Virunum became the provincial capital, and the normal apparatus of provincial administration was established, with Noricum being governed by a procurator.[22] It was at this time, too, that Noricum, which had previously possessed few towns, began to urbanise, with the establishment of *municipia* at Virunum, Celeia (Celje), Teurnia (Tiburnia), Aguntum and Iuvavum (Salzburg), all of them safely away from the frontier. The interior of the province was now largely demilitarised, with the construction of new forts along the line of the Danube, particularly at Lentia (Linz) and Lauriacum (Enns-Lorch); the forts at Boiodurum, Faviana (Mautern) and Commagena (Tulln) probably came later, possibly during Flavian times.

The province seems, thereafter, to have developed smoothly, but in an unspectacular fashion. As elsewhere in the Empire, (or at least those areas along the frontier that had not previously possessed a flourishing civic culture), Romanisation spread from the urban centres, radiating outwards into the rest of the province. Latin names came to predominate quite rapidly, although many of them are in fact only Latinised versions of Celtic forms, such as Acceptus, Avitus and Ingenuus.[23]

It was only under Hadrian that urban settlement crept further north towards the Danube, with the foundation of Ovilava (modern Wels) in the valley of the Traun, at the point where traditional routes leading down from the Danube and then towards Virunum and Iuvavum crossed. Hadrian did not operate on a blank slate, for there seems already to have been a merchant settlement at Ovilava, but a new street-plan was laid out, which can be dimly discerned in the grid system of the modern town.[24]

The peace of Noricum was only really disturbed during Marcus Aurelius's Marcomannic Wars (166–80), and while it was not a main theatre of that war, some destruction identified in the northern sectors of the province from around 166 to 170 might be ascribable to it, particularly at Lentia, Ovilava and Lauriacum in the west, and at Faviana and Augustiana (Traismauer) in the east. It was in an effort to keep the Marcomanni out of Italy, and to prevent a recurrence of their damaging descent through Pannonia towards the alpine passes, that Noricum received its own legion for the first time, at Ločica, where the II Italica legion – first raised in 166 – was stationed from 171.[25]

Situated west of Celeia, Ločica dominated the road that led south-west towards Emona (modern Ljubljana in Slovenia) and ultimately into Italy. The legion did not stay there long, being moved within three years to Albing, 7 kilometres from Lauriacum and near the mouth of the River Enns. Its new station was short-lived, too, for some time before 191 the unit was transferred to its final posting at Lauriacum. As a result, Noricum's administrative status was promoted, for whereas as a province with only auxiliary troops it could be governed by a man of equestrian rank, now that it had a legion its top official was a legionary legate, and hence of senatorial rank. This situation continued until some time after 255 (when the last attested imperial legate, Macrinius Decianus, served),[26] after which governors of equestrian rank supervised the province.

Alamannic raids began to hit Noricum from the second quarter of the 3rd century, and coin-hoards buried at Iuvavum around 235 may be a sign of this. It seems that Maximinus Thrax had siphoned off elements of the Norican garrisons for campaigns further east along the Danube, and – stripped of the means to fight off the barbarian raids – Noricum paid a heavy price. At the time of the general reforms of provincial administration by Diocletian at the end of the 3rd century, Noricum was split into two, with the northern part becoming Noricum Ripense and the southern (with its capital at Virunum) being reorganised as Noricum Mediterraneum; both of the new provinces came under the Diocese of Illyricum. Most of the army units remained stationed in the Noricum Ripense, with the addition of a new legion (I Noricorum) at Ad Iuvense (Ybbs) to see to the security of the eastern sector of the *limes*.[27]

The frontier was again strengthened under Valentinian I in the 370s, with the construction of new watchtowers, but from the time of Gratian the garrison seems to have been run down and Noricum was debatable territory by the early 5th century. In 407, Alaric and his Gothic followers occupied a large part of the province, formally requesting that the Emperor Honorius officially hand over the territory to them, baldly stating that Noricum was of no worth to the Romans as it was not paying any taxes.[28]

Alaric was a typical product of the late-Roman world, occupying a position of great ambiguity, in which his aims were extremely unclear. It may have been his intent to damage the Empire, extract as much profit from it for himself and his followers as he could, or to obtain a hand-somely rewarded official position within it.

Alaric led a people, the Goths, whose origins are much disputed. Around 150, Ptolemy records a people known as the Gutones settled somewhere between the Danube and the Vistula, but there is no trace of them for the next century. Writing in the 6th century, Jordanes puts their origins somewhere in southern Scandinavia; but attempts to trace the migration of any groups of people from there to the Danube have been problematic.[29]

Probably from the 230s the Goths began to migrate from their then homeland around the western Ukraine and the Black Sea,[30] though whether pushed from behind by tribes in search of land or pulled towards the Roman frontier by the lure of the undoubted riches to be obtained in the Empire is unclear. Only from the mid- to late 3rd century, when they began to raid the Empire, can their progress be traced with anything approaching precision. At the time they were not divided into the groups that would later establish kingdoms in Italy and Spain (the Ostrogoths and Visigoths respectively), but were constituted in a series of tribal confederacies, the principal amongst which were the Tervingi and Greuthingi.

In 238, they had first definitively emerged into the historical record with a raid on Olbia and Tyras. By 255, the Goths had acquired the use of a fleet, and for the next three years raided at will around the Black Sea, capturing Trebizond on the southern coast in 256 when its garrison, alarmed at the appearance of shipborne barbarians, simply turned tail and fled

After a turbulent eruption back into Roman territory in the 370s, which led to their defeat of the Romans at the Battle of Adrianople in 378[31] and the peace treaty four years later, the Goths subside for a time into the background.[32] Alaric first comes to the notice of the sources in around 395, though he may have been active in an attack by Gothic marauders on Theodosius I as he travelled to Constantinople from the west in 391. Four years later, he seems to have been serving in the Roman army that fought at the Frigidus river against the usurper Eugenius, a battle in which the Goths had taken terrible casualties.

Alaric was probably angered that he received neither recognition nor promotion for his role in the conflict, and he rose up in revolt.[33] He proceeded to march on Constantinople, but turned aside – either intimidated by the strength of its defences or, according to the poet Claudian, bribed by the praetorian prefect Rufinus – and set to plundering Macedonia and Thessaly. For the next two years Alaric pillaged at will, his raiding parties reaching as far south as the Peloponnese. Then, in 397, when the western military strongman Stilicho was poised to act against him, Alaric received some kind of recognition in a military position (which may have been that of *magister militum per Illyricum*) from Eutropius, the eunuch who then dominated the eastern government and was not at all keen on Stilicho extending his influence into the Balkans.[34] Until 401, therefore, Alaric's illegal raiding in the Balkans was replaced by the obligation on the citizens of the provinces to provide him, as a lawful representative of the government, with military supplies, which may in the end have amounted to pretty much the same thing. In November 401, for reasons that are not entirely clear,[35] Alaric crossed the Alps into Italy. Stilicho beat him twice, at Pollentia and Verona, but on both occasions the Goth gave the Roman general the slip, finally fleeing into Pannonia, where he rebuilt his forces over a couple of years, smouldering with resentment.

Probably in 404 or 405, Stilicho appointed him to a military office, thereby seeking to co-opt the Goths in the game of tug-of-war between Eastern and Western Empires over the Balkans. In 407, however, Alaric – sensing that Stilicho, weakened by the usurpation of Constantine III in Britain and Gaul, might be amenable to pressure – invaded Italy once more. A complicated series of negotiations with the Senate and Stilicho were interrupted by the latter's murder in August 408 at the hands of Honorius. Stilicho's barbarian followers were massacred in large numbers throughout Italy and the remnants fled to Alaric, who found himself bereft of his principal negotiation partner in the wake of Stilicho's death, and at the same time bolstered by the acquisition of a large number of fresh warriors. He laid siege to Rome in late 408, a blockade during which Serena, the widow of Stilicho, was strangled to death on the orders of the Senate, who could not quite get it into their heads that negotiation and compromise were the only means to avoid disaster.

Finally, at Rimini in 409, the praetorian prefect Jovius[36] agreed to talks, at which Alaric insisted on being appointed to the supreme command of the Roman army (as *magister utriusque militiae*) and receiving a hefty sum in cash. Honorius, needless to say, refused, resulting in a year of increasingly desperate manoeuvres by both sides, in which Alaric raised up a usurper – a senator named Priscus Attalus – found that his new protégé was not nearly as compliant as hoped, deposed him and then discovered that Honorius (given fresh heart by a new draft of reinforcements from the East) was now refusing to negotiate at all.[37] Angry and frustrated, Alaric marched on Rome, and gave his followers free rein for three days to loot and pillage the Eternal City.

The Romans had suffered nothing like it since the capture of the city by the Gauls in 390 BC, and the shock was profound. Yet despite its seeming portentous significance and a collective gnashing of teeth by contemporary writers,[38] the sack of Rome resolved nothing. As Hannibal had six centuries before, Alaric headed to the south of Italy, largely for want of anything better to do, but possibly intending to cross into Africa. There, near Consentia (Cosenza), he contracted a fever and died soon afterwards. Alaric, who had campaigned for two decades across the Balkans and Italy, had in the end achieved little, save landing a few body-blows on his would-be paymaster, the Empire, and taking its prestige down a good few notches by his capture of the capital.

The journey east along the Norican *limes* begins where the River Inn (or Aenus to the Romans) meets the Danube. Here the *castellum* of Boiodurum dominated the Norican side, mirroring its twin of Castrum Batavorum on the Raetian bank. Just as it had been a provincial boundary in Roman times, so this stretch of water continued to mark the separation between realms, marking out the border between German Bavaria and Austria. The footbridge that runs over the German side of the Inn to Austria leads first to the church of Saint Severin, a saint who has a much higher profile in the latter country than elsewhere (and who should not be confused with the Bishop of Cologne, or the 4th-century Bishop of Bordeaux who is remembered in the church of Saint Séverin in Paris). The life of the saint, who operated in Noricum Ripense from around 460[39] is told in the *Vita Sancti Severini*, written by Eugippius around 511, a text that gives a unique portrayal of the twilight of Roman rule in the area.

Severin was said to have come to the province 'at God's command', but from exactly where is not recorded. He would stay in Noricum until his death in 482, travelling widely within the province and acting as a rallying point for the Romanised population in the face of the near-total collapse of the official administration. During the early years of Severin's stay in Noricum, there are scattered references to Roman troops, to the garrison at Boiodorum across the border in Raetia, and to a *tribunus* called Mamertinus who was based at Faviana (Mauern) with a small force at his disposal, but who soon afterwards gave up the military life and became a bishop.[40]

Elsewhere in the province, unlike Mamertinus with his small military force, the people had to rely on their own resources to defend themselves in the late 5th century, and it was not enough. The Rugii occupied Commagena (Tulln); Astura (Zeiselmauer) was destroyed around 460; and by 480 the whole of the western sector of the *limes* had been overrun. The very end of the Roman army in the area is poignantly described by Eugippius in a scene that must have been repeated a number of times throughout the Empire.[41] The pay for the garrison at Batavis had failed to arrive, and some of the soldiers set off towards Italy to see what the problem might be. On their way, they were set upon by barbarians and murdered and some time later their bodies were washed up by the river near Passau. Their former comrades, realising that there would now be no reinforcements or money from the central government in Rome, simply disbanded. In places such as this, the soldiers may have continued to cluster together in the fort, but in the absence of any organised support, their numbers would soon have dwindled away. Some lived off the local populations and their depredations become indistinguishable from those of the barbarians whom they were once supposed to have kept at bay.

With the disappearance of the Batavis garrison, Boiodurum was captured by the Thuringians, and in response Severin organised the evacuation of the whole frontier region and resettled the surviving population in and around Lauriacum, where, however, they were still at the mercy of the local Rugian king. By 476, the Western Empire itself had ceased to exist, and so what remained of 'Roman' Noricum now fell to Odovacar. A leader of the Germanic Scirians, he had led a group of *foederati* in the 470s, and by the middle of the decade was in effect the commander of the Roman army in Italy. When the patrician Orestes tried to pre-empt his authority by setting his own son Romulus on the imperial throne in 475, Odovacer in exasperation deposed the hapless young emperor within a year, and, choosing not to rule the rump of Roman territory in Italy through an imperial puppet, exercised power himself directly as a king. A few years later, Noricum became entangled in the Eastern Empire's first serious attempt to do something about the situation. The Eastern Emperor Zeno (474–5, 477–91) called upon Feletheus, the King of the Rugians, who were in effective control of Noricum, to invade Italy and drive Odovacar out. Odovacar, however, defeated the Rugians in 487, and the following year launched an invasion of Noricum to finish the task. However, his brother Onoulfus, who was in charge of the expedition, decided that the province could not be effectively defended and so ordered all the 'Romani' to leave Noricum and evacuate to Italy. The body of Saint Severin accompanied the refugees, carried by the monks of his monastery of Favianae as far as Naples, where it ultimately came to rest in the Abbey of San Severino.[42]

Amidst the well-kept graveyard, and the memorials of white and sombre black marble enlivened by faded photographs of the deceased, the Passau church is a plain and simple structure, its wall washed with a pretty shade of pink, but to the right of the main door is evidence of the Roman town that lies everywhere underneath. The memorial to Faustinianus, who was a customs officer, conjures up the image of a man who supervised the border between Illyria, which began here (from the fiscal point of view), and the German customs area to the west. He would have reported ultimately to the headquarters of the Norican customs office, which lay in the provincial capital at Virunum.[43] The river crossing and the now-vanished customs house would have marked the point at which tolls due for carrying goods across the provincial border would have to be paid.

The riverside is populated with narrow streets and plain-fronted houses. A stretch of ancient stone wall and the adjacent round bulk of the 'Saint-Severin Tower' are in fact late-medieval constructions, from around 1412. A short way off lies the remains of Boiotro, a late-Roman fort built around 300 to replace an earlier one destroyed by the Alamanns in about 240. This is the place where Saint Severin is reported to have built his monastery in the 5th century. He is not forgotten here, either. Inside the ruined shell of the walls a pleasant garden has been laid out with what looks like Roman foundations adapted as tower-like planters for a variety of shrubs and flowers. In one corner of this rather municipal-seeming place, presiding over it all, is a 20th-century statue of the saint, arm outstretched as though to say, 'Look how well I preserved the land that I sought to protect.'

Much of the interior of the fort has disappeared and the outlines of the buildings are marked out with chalked lines. Small sections of the south-east and south-west towers remain intact, together with a substantial portion of the south tower, the ruins quietly enclosed and hidden by the surrounding houses. It was from a vantage point such as this that the last garrison troops of Noricum would have watched as the administrative infrastructure of the Empire diminished and dwindled to nothing.

Around a kilometre's walk along the line of the Danube lay the earlier Roman fort of Boiodurum. It began its life under Domitian, initially as a wood and earth construction, and probably housed the V Breucorum cohort after the reign of Marcus Aurelius. Later rebuilt in stone, it was destroyed by an Alamannic incursion in the 240s and was not directly rebuilt, as the new site of Boiotro was instead chosen to replace it. The church of Saint Aegid, on whose ground the fort lay, is now a private house, situated besides a car park dotted with some bedraggled-looking recycling bins. A bold 'Privatgrund' sign prevents any latter-day Alamanns from investigation of the former castle ground, while only the oddly basilical shape of the house betrays any hint of its subsequent history as a church.

East of the Passau area, the Danube flows through a thick gorge, which makes crossing perilous, and thus for around 60 kilometres the Romans did not find it necessary to site significant forces, with just small units at Stanacum (Oberanna) and Ad Mauros (Eferding) to defend this whole sector. At Lentia, however, which has mutated into modern Linz, the normal density of fortifications resumed. Here the initial construction was a cavalry fort in open country suitable for a mounted detachment, and was first established under Claudius.[44]

Now Austria's third-largest city, with around 200,000 people, Linz's Roman heritage has suffered the fate of most antique cities that have subsequently thrived and been completely built over. Its principal monuments are pretty baroque churches, topped with green onion domes, and a 20-metre-high column erected in thanks for the delivery of Linz from an outbreak of plague in 1713. The Roman remains that have been found were largely brought to light through the destruction of more modern buildings during the Second World War. A temple complex and a *mithraeum*, together with the *capitolium*, were all identified, but nothing of them can really be seen today. Instead there are only fragments and guesses, but it seems the civil settlement lay beneath today's Hauptplatz. Lentia suffered widespread destruction during the Marcomannic Wars in the 160s, but probably revived before too long. It does not feature in the life of Saint Severin, so its age of prosperity had most likely ended long before the start of the 5th century.

Around 30 kilometres to the south-west of Lentia, in the interior of the province, Ovilava (modern Wels) had become an important road junction, because the route from Aquileia in Italy that led through Virunum crossed here with one that ran parallel to the *limes* from Boiodurum and Lentia to Lauriacum further east. Under Hadrian, Ovilava attained the rank of *municipium*, suitably honouring him by its new name of Municipium Aelium Ovilava, taken from 'Aelius', one of the Emperor's own names. It achieved further promotion as a result of the Marcomannic Wars, when many of the civilian offices of the provincial governor moved here.[45]

Under Caracalla, the town became a *colonia* (as Aurelia Antoniana) and it may have been at this time that it received its city wall. Ovilava reached the summit that a provincial city could hope to achieve when, during the reign of Diocletian, it became the capital of Noricum Ripense. That it continued to flourish, as far as the uncertain times of the 3rd to 5th centuries would permit, is demonstrated by a visit from Gratian in 378 and the town's appearance in the *Vita Sancti Severini* as one of the remaining places where something like normal urban life still staggered on. By the 7th century, however, all vestiges of Rome had gone, and the town was settled by Germanic-speaking Bavarians, the ancestors of today's residents.

Now a modest-sized town of about 50,000 people, Wels's main square is an elongated oval surrounded by lovely plaster façades done up in pastel colours. At the far end lies the Lederturm, the last surviving town gateway, dating from the 14th century, its white rectangular tower soaring above the other buildings. Just a small portion of Roman Ovilava can be viewed in the basement of the Minoritenkirche museum on the main square. Excavations in 1988–90 around the church unearthed part of the Roman layer, though extensively overlaid by the remains of the Romanesque church. Part of a mosaic floor, some water pipes and tile stamps are all that remain. In the main museum, pieces of a large equestrian statue dragged out of the Traun river nearby may have come from the town's forum, possible evidence of the damage caused by barbarian raiders in the 3rd century.

The legionary fortress at Lauriacum (Lorch), around 30 kilometres south-east from Lentia, was situated near the confluence of the Enns and the Danube. It is a position of great strategic importance, lying on the road that ran parallel to the *limes* between Carnuntum and Castra Batavorum in the east of the province, and along the head of the route that led from Aquileia in Istria all the way north across the Danube. The original auxiliary fort here was destroyed during the Marcomannic Wars, and was rebuilt as a legionary fortress. Irregularly shaped, at around 600 x 400 metres, it varied somewhat from the classic 'playing-card' shape and housed the II Italica until the end of the Roman period. The civil settlement that grew up around it may have been granted the status of *municipium* under Caracalla around 212, and the forum of this settlement is believed to have been in the area of the modern Saint Laurenz church.

The church itself is the successor to a basilica that was constructed in the early 4th century on the site of a Gallo-Roman temple that was certainly still standing around 197.[46] It lies down a quiet suburban street, at the end of which lies a section of 2nd- to 3rd-century Roman housing, a few walls and two column fragments representing scant survivals of the Roman civil settlement. Perched on one section of wall is the ubiquitous statue of Saint Severin, still carrying about him a vaguely protective air in case any late and stray barbarians should happen by.

Inside the basilica itself, in a corner of which a charnel house is adorned with a splendid carving of Pontius Pilate dressed in Ottoman gear, the main altar has been moved forward to expose the remains of the church's ancient predecessors. Part of the hypocaust of a Roman heating system and some 2nd-century walls are clearly visible, the latter once believed to belong to a Romano-Celtic temple from 175 to 192 (dated by an altar stone), but now thought more likely to be a private house. Cutting through it is the clear apse shape of an early Christian basilica and, forming a kind of outer ring, another larger apse. The first church is believed to date from around 370, and was destroyed during the Hunnish invasions of the 440s, but rebuilt soon thereafter. A new church was then erected on the site during the 8th century, to be replaced ultimately by the present model. It all provides a neat summary of the career of Lauriacum itself, from Roman legionary fortress to the modern-day Austrian town.

The Christianisation of Noricum is further represented by the life of Saint Florian, who, according to the *Acta* composed about his life, was martyred at Lauriacum. A high-ranking official during the era of the Great Persecution, though whether he was a soldier or civilian is unclear, Florian had converted to Christianity. On hearing of the tribulations suffered by his co-religionists at Lauriacum, where some forty of them had been arrested, he resolved to hand himself over to the authorities in order to share their fate. He was then hauled before the governor, Aquilinus, and provocatively declared that although Aquilinus might have possession of his body, his soul was still in the hands of God. For this he was beaten, his shoulder blades broken, a bonfire lit underneath him and, when none of this dampened his ardour for confessing himself a Christian, Aquilinus ordered a heavy rock to be tied around Florian's neck, and that he then be hurled into the River Enns, where he drowned. The river is said to have thrown up his body the next day. It was found by a devout local Christian widow, Valeria, and transported to a place a short way away from Lentia, where later the Abbey of Saint Florian was built. For his trial by fire, and his immersion in water – and hence, by transference, a presumed ability to douse or protect from flames – Florian later became the patron saint of both firefighters and chimney sweeps.[47]

Lauriacum suffered badly during the uncertainty of the 3rd century, and seems to have been burnt down three times. During the widespread raids by the Alamanni and Iuthungi, which penetrated Raetia to the west in the 270s, Lauriacum was razed once more. However, it recovered and was rebuilt, and in the 4th century both Constantius II (in 341) and Gratian (in 378) stayed here.

To the east of Lauriacum, the land was more open, a broad plain that provided easy access for hostile incursions, especially, in the 2nd century, by the Marcomanni. It was thus more heavily fortified, by posts at Faviana (Mautern) in the west and by Commagena (Tulln) and Astura (Zeiselmauer) in the east. Tulln, around 120 kilometres along the river from Lauriacum (Enns), is an attractive small town on Austria's central stretch of Danube. Down by the riverside walk, a pretty housing estate groups around the Marc-Aurelstraße, while nearby a Mark-Aurel Parc stretches, both named in honour of the 2nd-century emperor. A modern equestrian statue has Marcus pointing his sword out into the Danube in a vaguely menacing gesture, an air that is punctured by the toy train that wends its way by each Saturday half-hour, transporting tourists around Tulln's main sites. A short walk down the Danube shore – the river not exerting itself unduly as it flows lazily by – is the Salzturm (or 'salt tower'), heavily rebuilt in medieval times, but preserving the horseshoe shape of one of the interval towers of the Roman fort's west wall.

The *Ala I Commagenorum*, after whom Commagena took its name, was certainly present here by 96, around fifteen years after the fort itself was built. It came as part of a new draft of troops to Noricum[48] which included the transfer of the *Cohors I Asturum* (originally from Spain) to Astura and of the *Cohors I Aelia Brittonum* to Faviana some time during the reign of Hadrian. Around the back of the town museum under a glass roof are sheltered a few fragments of the camp's *porta principalis dextra*, a gate that was bricked up in about 370, in a sign of increasing insecurity in the area.

Commagena did survive in some fashion, however, as it is mentioned as one of the places that Saint Severin visited. Although only in a later literary fancy, it did play a significant role in the age of migrations, for in one version of the *Nibelungenlied*, the south-German epic saga, it was at Commagena that Attila the Hun proposed to Gudrun, his future wife, who was loosely modelled around Ildico, the real Hun ruler's last spouse; it was not a happy match, for on their wedding night Attila choked to death in bed.

Noricum, meanwhile was left to the successive depredations of the Goths, Huns, Lombards, Avars and Slavs. Only in the former Noricum Mediterraneum to the south did urban life persist in anything like its previous form. However, by 600, even those few places had collapsed and been abandoned; only at Celeia in the far south-east of the province is there any sign of continuous occupation. Noricum now returned to much the state it had been in before the Romans had taken it in 15 BC: a small population, economically unsophisticated and centred around hill fortifications, which were used in (the lamentably frequent) times of trouble.

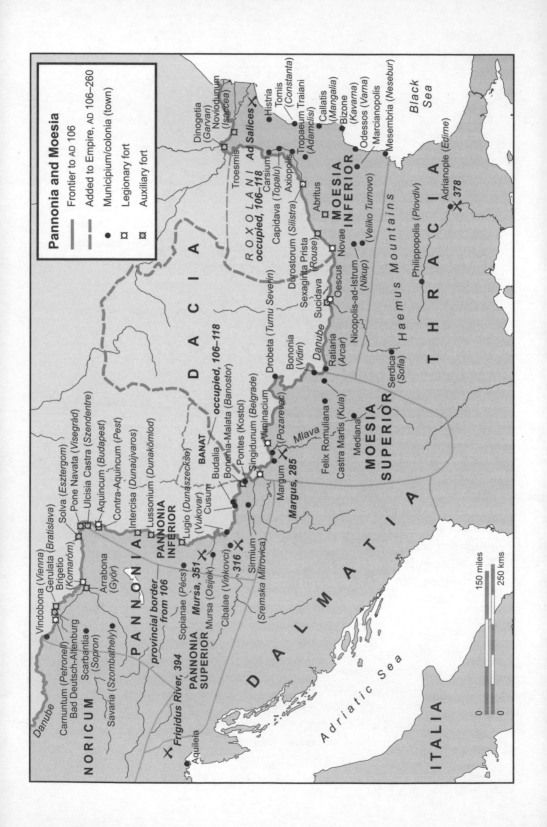

Pannonia and Moesia

Frontier to AD 106
Added to Empire, AD 106–260
● Municipium/colonia (town)
� Legionary fort
� Auxiliary fort

150 miles
250 kms

Danube

NORICUM

Vindobona (*Vienna*)
Carnuntum (*Petronell*)
Bad Deutsch-Altenburg
Gerulata (*Bratislava*)
Brigetio
Scarbantia (*Sopron*)
Arrabona (*Győr*)
Savaria (*Szombathely*)

Solva (*Esztergom*)
Pone Navata (*Visegrád*)
Ulcisia Castra (*Szendentre*)
Aquincum (*Budapest*)
Contra-Aquincum (*Pest*)
Intercisa (*Dunaújvaros*)
Lussonium (*Dunakömlod*)

**PANNONIA
INFERIOR**

*provincial border
from 106*

Sopianae (*Pécs*)
**PANNONIA
SUPERIOR**
X *Frigidus River, 394*
Aquileia
ITALIA

Mursa (*Osijek*)
Cibalae (*Vinkovci*)
Mursa, 351 X
X 316
Sirmium
(*Sremska Mitrovica*)

Lugio (*Vukovar*)
Cusum
Budalia
Bononia-Malata (*Banostor*)
Pontes (*Kostol*)
Singidunum (*Belgrade*)
Viminacium
Margum (*Pozarevac*) X
Margus, 285
Mlava

BANAT
occupied, 106–118

D A C I A

**ROXOLANI
occupied, 106–118**

Dinogetia (*Garvan*)
Noviodunum (*Isaccea*)
Troesmis
X **Ad Salices**
Histria
Tomis (*Constanta*)
Carsium
Capidava (*Topalu*)
Axiopolis
Tropaeum Traiani (*Adamclisi*)
Callatis (*Mangalia*)
Bizone (*Kavarna*)
Odessos (*Varna*)
Marcianopolis
Mesembria (*Nesebur*)

*Black
Sea*

Capidava (*Topalu*)
Durostorum (*Silistra*)
Sexaginta Prista (*Rouse*)
Sucidava
Abritus
**MOESIA
INFERIOR**
Novae
Oescus
Nicopolis-ad-Istrum (*Nikup*)
(*Veliko Turnovo*)

Drobeta (*Turnu Severin*)
Bononia (*Vidin*)
Ratiaria (*Arcar*)
Danube

**MOESIA
SUPERIOR**

Felix Romuliana (*Kula*)
Castra Martis
Mediana
Serdica (*Sofia*)

H a e m u s   M o u n t a i n s

Philippopolis (*Plovdiv*)
Adrianople (*Edirne*)
X 378

T H R A C I A

D A L M A T I A

Adriatic Sea

CHAPTER 4

Pannonia and Moesia

His eyes, his voice, his colour, his gestures, expressed the violence of his ungoverned fury; and, while his whole frame was agitated with convulsive passion, a large blood-vessel suddenly burst in his body, and Valentinian fell speechless into the arms of his attendants. Their pious care immediately concealed his situation from the crowd; but, in a few minutes, the emperor of the west expired in an agony of pain . . .
Edward Gibbon, *Decline and Fall of the Roman Empire*[1]

The Roman provinces of Pannonia and Moesia occupied portions of the modern countries of Austria, Hungary, Slovakia, Croatia, Serbia, Bulgaria and Romania, with Pannonia taking up the western portion from Vindobona (Vienna) to Singidunum (Belgrade in Serbia), and Moesia the eastern section as far as the Danube delta. The river formed the traditional boundary of these provinces in the face of *barbaricum*[2] – a position that was only really modified by the annexation of Dacia by Trajan in AD 106 and the occupation of that new province for a century and a half.

Pannonia and Upper Moesia along the Middle Danube first came to Roman attention following the defeat of Perseus, the last King of Macedonia, at Pydna in 168 BC. Friction now arose with Celtic tribes such as the Scordisci and Boii, whose lands lay further north towards the Danube plain.[3] The Romans were drawn deeper into the Balkans, and during a war against the Dardanians in 76–73 BC a Roman army reached the Danube for the first time, possibly somewhere near the valley of the Oescus.[4] There they encountered a tribe called the Moesi, whose name the Roman province would in time take.

Much of Pannonia and Moesia came under the influence of the Dacian king, Burebista, in the 60s BC, and the expansion of his domains threatened to block off Roman access to the northern Balkans, but after his death in 44 BC (at about the same time as Julius Caesar's assassination) the confederation he had built fell apart. This opened the region to a serious extension of Roman power, and in 35 BC Octavian (as Augustus was still known) marched eastwards from Aquileia in northern Italy and captured the Pannonian stronghold of Siscia (modern Sisak in Croatia). The Romans then pushed further northwards and westwards from their bases in Macedonia; in 29 BC, Marcus Licinius Crassus defeated King Cotiso of the Dacians and subdued a whole swathe of tribal peoples, including the Dardanians and Moesians.

Following a campaign by the young Tiberius in 15 BC, Pannonia was officially annexed in 11 BC – although this had not stopped Octavian, in his morale-raising speech to the troops at Actium in 31 BC claiming that Roman might had reached the Danube two years beforehand. The first governor of Moesia, Poppaeus Sabinus, was not, however, appointed for around half a century after Crassus's 29 BC campaign. The process by which that province was subsumed into the Empire is therefore somewhat obscure,[5] although it was probably characterised by a gradual northwards advance towards the line of the Danube.

In AD 6, Roman armies marched north across the Danube, aiming to stem the rise of the Marcomannic kingdom of Maroboduus which had established a powerful confederacy in the area of modern Bohemia. The Danube force under Tiberius coordinated its attack with a pincer movement from Raetia in the west under Sentennius Saturninus. The campaign – which, if successful, might have established a strong Roman presence across the Danube – failed because of an uprising in the rear by the still-restive Pannonians, which was not finally suppressed until AD 12.[6] The near-catastrophe of the revolt, coupled with the disastrous defeat of Varus in the Teutoberger Wald, in effect put paid to any Roman designs to occupy the area of Germany between the Rhine and the Elbe. These two events probably did more than anything to halt the Roman army in its tracks, and the advances of the previous half-century would prove difficult indeed to replicate.

It was after this campaign that the Romans came to understand the importance of controlling the routes that carried into Dacia and the ancient Amber Trade Road across the Danube, a realisation that led them to the stronger occupation of the river line and the establishment of a military presence at Carnuntum. The acquisition of eastern Pannonia, however, took much longer and may not have been firmly achieved until the reign of Claudius (41–54).[7]

The Roman military presence in Pannonia and Moesia was then substantially strengthened under Domitian, with the establishment of a string of auxiliary forts along the Danube,[8] although the Romans experienced a serious setback when a resurgent Dacian kingdom under Decebalus began to raid south of the river in 85. Having seen this threat off three years later,[9] Domitian faced further trouble from the Sarmatians in the late 80s and in 92–3, although he emerged victorious and celebrated an ovation, a lesser version of a triumph.[10]

Trajan's Dacian Wars in 101–2 and 105–6 also resulted in a significant reorganisation of the Pannonian frontier. In 106, the Emperor divided the province into two, with Pannonia Superior to the west (stretching from Vindobona (Vienna) to Cirpi (modern Dunabogdány) having three legions (initially the XIII Gemina Martia at Vindobona, XV Apollinaris at Carnuntum and XXX Ulpia Victrix at Brigetio)[11] to defend against what was perceived as the greater danger from the Germans; meanwhile the governor of Pannonia Inferior in the east had to make do with a single legion at Aquincum (Budapest). This province reached as far as a point just west of Singidunum (modern Belgrade in Serbia).

A further emergency took place in 118 when the Sarmatians threatened the border but were beaten back.[12] After that, this critical portion of the frontier was largely quiet until the reign of Marcus Aurelius, who fought a prolonged fourteen-year campaign against the Marcomanni and Quadi, peoples who would still be causing trouble on this stretch of the *limes* two centuries later. On the death of Marcus in 180, his son and successor, Commodus, brought the war to an abrupt end, but it was some years before the damage caused by the conflict could be restored. An indication of the disruption is that, as part of the peace settlement, the Iazyges are said to have returned 100,000 prisoners to the Romans.[13]

The frontier remained relatively tranquil for four decades, with only an invasion by Carpi and Vandals in 212 or 213 recorded in the sources. In 214, a slight reorganisation occurred, by which Brigetio[14] was shifted into Pannonia Inferior, resulting in both Pannonian provinces now having two legions. It was part of a process by which the Severans[15] did away with three-legion provinces, which had provided too tempting a platform for overambitious generals to mount bids for the imperial throne, a route to power that Septimius Severus, the founder of the dynasty, had himself followed when he was governor of Pannonia Superior in 192.

In the end, the soldiers and the military governors were to have the last laugh, for in the half-century of disorder following the assassination of Alexander Severus in 235, the majority of emperors came from Pannonia and Moesia, particularly from the area around Sirmium (Sremska Mitrovica). The tradition would be a long-standing one: the last of these military strongmen was Valentinian in the latter part of the 4th century. Although the Pannonian and Moesian provinces achieved a much higher profile politically during this century, it was also a period of great troubles. Wars against the Carpi in 247–8 were followed by a disastrous conflict against the Goths in 250–1 in which the Emperor Decius perished,[16] and in 258–60 attacks by Suebi and Sarmatians caused enormous damage. The latter represented a particularly grave threat, for the eastern provinces were slipping away from Rome after a signal Persian victory in 260, and the Gaulish provinces had broken away in 259, so the loss of control over the Balkans would have left Gallienus, the Emperor unlucky enough to have to deal with these concurrent crises, as a ruler without a realm.

Even after this emergency was overcome, and the imperial administration was placed on a firmer footing under the Tetrarchy, Pannonia was not spared. Diocletian had to spend a great deal of time in the period 289–94 conducting yet another war against the Sarmatians.[17] It was probably shortly after this that the Pannonian provinces were further subdivided, creating four new provinces (Pannonia Prima, Pannonia Secunda, Savaria and Valeria). Moesia Superior had already had a slice of its eastern portion cut off in the 270s to make way for Dacia Ripensis, the Roman state's way of obscuring the fact that it had evacuated (and therefore lost) the real Dacia to the north of the Danube.[18] Under Diocletian, the remaining western part of Moesia Superior was renamed Moesia Prima, and the former Moesia Inferior became Moesia Secunda (with its easternmost portion, the modern Dobrudja, lopped off to become Scythia), while Dacia Ripensis continued to occupy the middle ground. If it was all very confusing, it at least provided additional jobs for the bureaucrats, for each of the provinces needed its own governor and administrators.

The mid-4th century brought further woes, and Constantius II was forced into major operations across the Danube in 358–9 to deal with the Sarmatians and Quadi. By the 370s, the tribes were at it again, and Valentinian I ordered the building of forts in Sarmatian territory to bring them finally to book. One such may have been located as far as 60 kilometres north of the Danube,[19] but generally the refortification was on the Roman side of the river. After the Emperor's death and the influx of Goths across the river in 376, the Romans were never really able to bring Pannonia and Upper Moesia firmly back under their control. Although the Danube remained in formal terms the border of the Empire, the settlement of barbarian federates in the border areas meant that the matter of whether the Romans really controlled the area or could exert any significant level of day-to-day influence there became confused.

In around 400, the poet Claudian praises the half-Vandal patrician Stilicho as restorer of peace to Pannonia,[20] but whether this is mere poetic hyperbole or a reflection of a real consolidation of the frontier is unclear. The migrations of Vandals through Pannonia in 401 and the movement of the Goths under Alaric into Italy the next year must have severely taxed any remnants of the Roman administration that still remained in the province. The invasion of Italy under the Goth Radagaisus in 405 also passed this way, although by then Alaric had been given control of portions of Pannonia by Stilicho, and it had in effect become the prize for competing barbarian groups rather than a part, in any real sense, of the Empire. A *dux* of Pannonia Prima is, however, still listed in the *Notitia Dignitatum* (though his command is a joint one with Noricum Ripensis to the west),[21] and so there may still have been some Roman garrisons operating even in the early 5th century.

In 427, it seems that the eastern Roman army temporarily regained control of Pannonia,[22] although it was lost to the Huns once more in 433. In 437, the enfeebled western government ceded its rights to Sirmium to the Eastern Emperor at Constantinople, but by the 450s such concessions were rendered meaningless, as the Hunnish advance had swept away everything south of the Danube as far as Naissus (Niš). In 455, Avitus did try to recover the province for the Western Empire, but it was a last fitful act of exertion on the part of a hopelessly weakened administration, and it did not succeed.

The situation in Moesia Inferior to the east was somewhat different. The barbarian raids there were never as bad as those that afflicted Pannonia and Moesia Superior, and the Gothic and Hunnish hordes in particular never devoted much attention to the province. Since it fell securely into the domain of the Eastern Emperors, the resources available for its defence were also greater. Nonetheless, by the end of the 6th century, raids by Avars, Slavs and Bulgars had made the Roman hold very insecure and most of the towns were abandoned. The restoration of Byzantine control here in the 9th century was over a much changed political and social landscape, and it makes little sense to speak of a *limes* in the sense of the one that had existed along the Danube until the 5th century.

Pannonia

Just 20 kilometres or so down the Danube from the border with Noricum, lies Pannonia's first significant fortification, and one of its historical success stories. Vindobona – or Vienna, as it has become – survived the fall of the Roman Empire, maintained itself in the early Middle Ages and then flourished to become the capital of another empire, that of the Habsburgs, which self-consciously borrowed some of the symbolism of its Roman predecessor.[23] In one sense, therefore, Vindobona only ceased to be an imperial city in 1918, when the Austro-Hungarian monarchy collapsed in the chaotic conditions following the end of the First World War.

Reminders of this second imperial period are hard to avoid in modern Vienna, from the grandiose bulk of the Hofburg, half-bastion and half-palace, which acted as the seat of the Habsburg sovereigns from 1279, to the rococo masterpiece of Schönbrunn Palace, where Franz Josef I – whose sixty-eight-year reign spanned both the zenith and the nadir of the empire – spent most of his life until his demise in 1916. The Schönbrunn even has its own 'Roman Ruin', a Romantic folly that was installed in the palace grounds in 1778 during a period when enlightened European tastes craved reminders of the classical heritage, which they were just then coming to rediscover and to value – feelings that would, at their most developed, feed into the ideology of Napoleon in his recreation of a Gallic Empire in France in 1804. Referred to commonly at the time as the 'Ruins of Carthage', their construction was supposed to represent Rome's triumph over that city, a reminder that the Habsburgs claimed, as Holy Roman Emperors (an office the dynasty had held, without a break, since 1452), some sense of continuity with the Roman imperial past.

The Schönbrunn ruins, although largely a creation of the craftsmen and artists of the late 18th century, did contain a real nucleus of the Roman past. Elements of a Roman palace that had existed in the centre of Vienna had been reused by Maximilian I in the 16th century for his Neugebaude Palace, and a few Corinthian columns and other architectural features were then transferred to the Schönbrunn's fanciful recreation of the original. The glimpses of more authentic Roman antiquities in Vienna are equally tantalising, peeping out between the Gothic or baroque exteriors, or half-drowned out by the insistent demands of modernity.

Vienna's antecedents, however, are ancient indeed. There were Celtic hill-fort *oppida* on the Leopoldsberg hill next to Vienna, which were occupied by the Boii, although these seem to have been abandoned around 20 BC, some time before the Romans arrived at this point on the Danube. Exactly when they first occupied the area around Vindobona is unclear, but it may well have been in association with Tiberius's abortive expedition against Maroboduus of the Marcomanni in AD 6. A fort for a cavalry unit (the *Ala I Britannica milliaria*) was probably built under Domitian, and soon thereafter Vindobona became a legionary base with the construction of a fortress by the XIII Gemina legion around 89.[24] After the accession of Hadrian, however, the X Gemina became the permanent garrison, and the legion was stationed here from around 115 until the end of Roman rule in Pannonia in the 5th century.

Vindobona remained relatively peaceful, apart from its use as a base by Marcus Aurelius during his Marcomannic Wars. Although the reign of Marcus was later idealised as something of a Golden Age, at least in contrast with what was to come, the cracks were already beginning to show for those who knew where to look, and his years in power were a relentless struggle – in the east, in Germany and on the Rhineland – to hold the line rather than to effect any significant advance in Roman power.

That Marcus has a reputation as a philosopher-statesman as well as a dogged but effective military commander is because, uniquely, he left a kind of private philosophical manifesto, the *Meditations*, which has survived to transmit the Emperor's most private thoughts. They seem to have been composed during the final years of his reign, and were not known to Cassius Dio, who composed the only really contemporary historical account in the first quarter of the 3rd century. Tellingly, Marcus wrote this private work in Greek, for that was widely regarded as the language of philosophy. It is not a diary or journal, and no coherent narrative of his reign can be constructed from it. Yet it does argue powerfully for the virtues of self-control and self-scrutiny, both attributes highly valued by the Stoics.[25]

In the *Meditations* themselves there is much general musing on the futility of struggling against the cares of the world, and on the uselessness of a life that is not spent at least in part in self-examination. There are a few distant echoes, too, of the lessons and consolations that the Emperor must have drawn during the seemingly incessant campaigns on the northern frontier. Individual fame is seen as futile in the face of time itself, which will utterly erase all such vaunted achievements.[26] In the chapters on the deaths of great men, Marcus remarks on how many renowned soldiers and philosophers have died, a telling remark from a man who himself constantly ran the risk of such a fate.[27]

The first Marcomannic War broke out in 166 and lasted, with some intervals, for the best part of a decade and a half, bringing destruction to many areas along the Danube line and exposing the weakness of a frontier that was better placed for forward supervision and the repelling of occasional raids than for such long-term warfare. In the end it seemed that victory was within the Emperor's grasp, for in the campaigning season of 178–9 he achieved the kind of decisive victory over the Bohemians that had long eluded him. It looked as if his plans for the organisation of the new provinces of Quadia and Marcomannia, which would project Roman power far beyond the Danube and perhaps even permit the long-abandoned lands of the German interior to be re-annexed, would come to fruition.[28]

Yet in 180 Marcus fell ill and died at Vindobona. Rumour had it that he was assisted in his passing by Commodus, who choked his ailing father to death with a pillow.[29] Marcus's unstoic attachment to his own flesh and blood in promoting his son to imperial honours (making him co-Emperor in 177) turned out to have been particularly unfortunate. As well as degenerating – in the eyes of contemporary historians – into tyranny, Commodus abandoned his father's plans for a final solution on the Danube. Perhaps he was just making a point that his father would well have understood: that excessive regard for one's own achievements will ultimately end only in disappointment.

In general, however, Vindobona was overshadowed by Carnuntum (Petronell), its neighbour some 40 kilometres to the east, and it may only have reached the status of *municipium* some time in the early 3rd century.[30] The plan of the Vindobona fortress is barely recognisable from the modern street plan of the city. It was sited on the high plateau of the Hohe Markt and at its northern end, which fronted onto the Danube, was protected by a dyke, near which the military harbour was located. The south-eastern edge of the camp lay just near the Stephansdom, the imposing cathedral of Vienna, outside which a series of Roman-inspired stone busts of the Evangelists and the double-headed eagle of the Habsburgs are reminders of the imperial iconography that the Austrian Empire inherited. The *principia* of the camp lay a little to the south of modern Wipplingerstraße, while the *via decumana* prob-ably ran north from the modern Kohlmarkt. The Wipplingerstraße passes on a high road bridge over the Tiefer Graben and marks the point where the legionary camp was defended by additional ditchworks to the west. As traffic whizzes by in a somewhat polluted and untouristed section of the city centre, it is extremely hard to summon up any image of the past.

At the Michaelerplatz, just short of the entrance to the Hofburg Palace, a few foundations have been unearthed from houses of the legionary *cannabae*,[31] that grew up to the south-east of the camp itself. Above the exiguous ruins, the hemispherical sweep of the Hofburg entrance looms, with huge statues of what looks like Heracles and his labours, one with the hero wielding a large club. Alongside the small square, Viennese horse carriages trot by, decked out in mock 19th-century style for the benefit of the tourists. For a brief moment all these times in Vindobona's history seem to telescope and collapse into one.

To the west of the Hohe Markt, close to what would become the forum, lies one of the more unusual settings for Roman remains on the *limes*. The elaborate clock on the market square parades round ornately painted and gilded figures from Vienna's past at set times of the morning and afternoon. For those with Roman interests, ten o'clock is the hour, as Marcus Aurelius makes his round then, while those of a more medieval bent might come at two o'clock when it is Charlemagne's turn. Those nostalgically hankering after the Habsburg apogee should turn up at eleven o'clock to see Empress Maria Theresa, while anyone with more eclectic interests can see the whole parade of historical figures at midday.

Just next door, at No. 3 Hohemarkt, downstairs from an Asian noodle bar, lie the remains of several Roman officers' houses, one of them with a hypocaust visible and the faint remains of plaster still clinging to the walls. The grandest of them was probably the house of a *tribunus lati-clavius*,[32] the senior commander of the legion. Down below the level of the street, the ruins, despite their highly unlikely setting, exude a sense of calm. A few pieces of Mithraic altar, and also one to Neptune, indicate the religious preferences of the senior soldiery, while a gravestone of a camp prefect of the X Gemina from Rimini (later reused as a mill-stone) is evidence of the decline of the site, when the sanctity of such memorials was ignored in favour of their recycling for much more mundane purposes.

The camp was last repaired during the time of Valentinian in the 370s. Some time in the early 5th century it became the base of the section of the Danube fleet that had been stationed previously at Carnuntum, but this was Vindobona's last moment of glory. Presumably, though, the legionary fortress managed to shelter the remains of the city's population against the depredations of successive waves of Germanic barbarians, and so it was that Vindobona was able to re-establish itself in the early Middle Ages and grow into the Vienna of today.

It is barely an hour by car or train east from Vienna to the modern village of Petronell, within which the ruins of the legionary fort and *vicus* of Carnuntum lie. It is fairly flat and unassuming countryside, in which the predominance of viticulture is evident and where the touristic labels of 'Weinstraße' and 'Limesstraße' seem to compete for pre-eminence. The village itself historically depended on agriculture, and every other driveway seems to have a tractor parked in it. Unlike Vienna, it never developed to any great size after the collapse of the Empire, and it was this failure to thrive that has enabled it to preserve so much of its ancient structure.

Situated more or less at the point where the Amber Road crossed the

Danube on its way to the Baltic, and at the crossroads with routes that led to the Adriatic, Carnuntum was of primary strategic importance, and its use as a base by Tiberius for his attacks on Maroboduus in AD 6 confirmed its usefulness to the Romans. As early as AD 14, the XV Apollinaris legion moved here from Emona (Ljubljana) to build the first fortress on the site, at about the same time that Carnuntum, which had fallen to Rome in the conquest of the Norican kingdom, was transferred to the province of Pannonia.[33] After being moved in the early 60s AD and replaced by a succession of short-lived garrisons, XV Apollinaris was back in station in AD 71, and the legion stayed at Carnuntum until it was replaced by the XIV Gemina legion,[34] which then remained here until the end of Roman rule in the 5th century.

Carnuntum's profile was massively raised in 106, when the province was divided by Trajan, as the town became the seat of the governor of Pannonia Superior. The civilian settlement that had arisen west of the camp was raised to the rank of *municipium* by Hadrian in 124 (as Municipium Aelium Carnuntum), and it was while based here that Marcus Aurelius wrote one of the books of his *Meditations*. It was also at Carnuntum in 193 that Septimius Severus, who was then governor of Pannonia Superior, was proclaimed Emperor by his troops,[35] less than two weeks after the murder of his predecessor, Pertinax.

Once he finally reached Rome, the new Emperor summoned the praetorian guard to a meeting on the parade ground of their camp in the centre. They expected a welcoming speech and, no doubt, a handy donative (a 'present' due on the accession of a new emperor or the anniversary of his rule) to add to a massive pay-off they had received from Didius Julianus just eight weeks before. Instead they were disarmed by Septimius's men, who had surrounded the camp, and the former guardsmen were then exiled to beyond the hundredth milestone from Rome on pain of death. Septimius had learnt the lesson of the past twelve months and would brook no mutinous troops subverting his position at the very heart of the Empire. However, it took a further two years for him to be totally secure, as he needed to see off the parallel attempts to seize power by Clodius Albinus and Pescennius Niger, the governors of Britain and Syria.[36]

In memory of the place where his rise to the imperial throne began, Septimius awarded Carnuntum the rank of *colonia*, with the suitably florid title of Colonia Septimia Aurelia Antoniniana Carnuntum. Carnuntum next saw an imperial proclamation in 258 or 260 (the date is uncertain) when the rather less successful usurpation of Regalianus[37] broke out on the Danube. He seems to have struggled to attract support, for coins minted in his name cluster around Carnuntum and Vindobona and are hardly found elsewhere. In the end his demise was swift, possibly in battle against the Roxolani, or even deposed by his own supporters.

The central excavated site at Carnuntum represents part of the civil town; the legionary fort itself lies 2 kilometres further to the east. The gaps between the town *insulae* and the gentle downward slope beside the unearthed buildings are laid out with manicured lawns and pretty flower beds, while the roofs of the reconstructed buildings with their ochre-orange tiles make it seem like a quaintly old-fashioned Mediterranean village transplanted to the Danube, which is in a sense exactly what Carnuntum was.

'House I', near the entrance to the site, demonstrates the longevity of the settlement, for it was in use right up until the 5th century, and sometimes in the early 4th century a mosaic room was installed after the house had been badly damaged by fire. Its outline can still be seen in a geometric pattern, with broken *terra sigillata* used to delineate the outer border of the design. A little garden beside House I is planted with the same flowers whose seeds were found in the Roman-era level of the soil, including *Lilium candidum* (the Madonna lily) and what looks like a pink geranium, creating some sense of the domesticity – rather than just the imposing architectural presence – of the Roman town. 'House II', next door, has been totally reconstructed, and it looks just as if the inhabitants had departed in unseemly haste. Herbs, onions and garlic hang in the kitchen, and the door to the shrine of the *lares*, the household gods, stands open. To the east, Houses III and IV are un-reconstructed and lie, mere outlines of walls and foundations, much as the archaeologists found them.

The baths in the central section of the site are being re-excavacted, and it is hard, therefore, to gain much sense of the shape of this vital civic amenity. Next to it runs a road of large cobbles, roughened with age, left almost as it was the day the settlement was abandoned, the ruts of the cart wheels that plied the Amber Road[38] still visible on the stone. Along the north road, which led to the Danube, a reconstructed portico has been erected, on the site of which were recently found 150 pieces of raw, unworked amber, a sign of the importance of Carnuntum to the trade. Beside the portico lay a temple (in which a head of Diana was found, perhaps indicating the deity to whom it was dedicated), and shops, all part of a busy, noisy commercial quarter.

Much of the rest of the city is lost in fields and woods. On a peaceful country path to the west of the main site sits the brooding baroque bulk of Schloss Petronell. Its peeling plaster and shuttered windows enclose

the shell of an 11th-century castle, which was constructed on the probable site of Carnuntum's old Roman forum and later massively
reconstructed in the 17th century. Although the forum has largely
vanished, some of the buildings associated with it remain, known as the
'Palace Ruins', overgrown with spring flowers in a quiet glade a few
hundred metres away. The ruins are difficult to disentangle, being badly
eroded, but one of them may be a *macellum*, or public market, and others
are certainly associated with the city's largest public baths. The remains
of an octagon and a round building could be a temple or meeting hall.

It was in these unlikely surroundings that the Conference of
Carnuntum, one of the most extraordinary meetings of the Later Roman
Empire, took place in 308, bringing together the retired emperors
Diocletian and Maximian, and Galerius, who had been appointed
Augustus and ruler of the eastern provinces when the two former rulers
had stepped down. It was this abdication of power by Diocletian and
Maximian, carried out in coordinated ceremonies in Milan and Nicomedia
in May 305, that was at the root of the problem, for it had very definitely been Diocletian's idea that he and his co-Augustus should do what
no other Roman emperors had willingly done and stand aside from the
throne. This ignoring of dynastic claims in the new arrangement had
doubtless added to the unease of Maximian's son, Maxentius, who felt
that he was being passed over.

The events following the death of Constantius I, who had been selected
as the new Augustus in the West, which was followed by the troops'
proclamation of his son, Constantine I, as Emperor in July 306, must
have aggravated both Maximian's and Maxentius's sense of grievance.
On 28 October 306, Maxentius engineered his own declaration as Emperor
by a section of the Rome garrison, and at the same time ordered that
his father, who had been skulking in less-than-happy retirement in Lucania
in southern Italy, be conveyed to Rome.[39] In February, Maximian resumed
the purple as co-Augustus with his son, a move as utterly illegitimate as
it was bound to bring down upon him the wrath of both Constantine
and Galerius. After an attempt to dislodge Maxentius from Rome failed,
with fatal consequences for Severus, the Western Augustus, Galerius
tried in person late in 307; but, unable to contemplate storming the walls
of Rome or an extensive siege, his army retreated with its tail between
its legs.

Meanwhile, Constantine took advantage of the constitutional confusion to forge an unlikely alliance with Maximian. The old Emperor came
north across the Alps to Trier to arrange the marriage of his daughter,
Fausta, to Constantine. He also gave his blessing to his new son-in-law's

elevation from Caesar to Augustus, meaning that there were now no fewer than three claimants to this rank in the West: Constantine, Maximian himself and Maxentius. On his return to Rome, however, Maximian quarrelled with his son and attempted to strip him of his imperial robes, fleeing in the ensuing chaos back to Constantine's court. It was all an appalling mess, and Galerius looked on askance as Diocletian's orderly scheme for the imperial succession fell apart in an unseemly outbreak of family quarrels, constitutional coups and over-lapping jurisdictions.

Finally, Galerius turned to the architect of the Tetrarchy to restore his blueprint to working order. Diocletian was coaxed out of retirement at Salonae and travelled to a conference at Carnuntum on 11 November 308. The old Augustus resolutely refused to return to power as Maximian had done, and indeed ordered that his old colleague abdicate once more.[40] Constantine was demoted from Augustus to Caesar, and Licinius, a former colleague of Galerius, became the new Augustus in the West. Maximin Daia, who had been loyally serving Galerius as Caesar in the East, thus failed to gain promotion, a slight that rankled greatly with him. Constantine, too, believing he should have kept the senior rank of Augustus, felt aggrieved, while Maxentius (who had received nothing out of the settlement) and his father Maximian (who resented being pushed back into retirement) resolved immediately to do whatever they could to undermine the Conference's decision.

Within two years, the incorrigible Maximian had declared himself Emperor for a third time, been chased down by Constantine in southern Gaul and forced to commit suicide, while Constantine himself – refusing to accept his demotion from Augustus   was joined in that rank by Maximin Daia, who had his troops acclaim his promotion to the rank of senior emperors. By 310, therefore, there were just as many Augusti as there had been at the time of the Carnuntum Conference, and the confusion and bitterness between the notional imperial partners was, if anything, even more marked. Meanwhile, Diocletian disappeared into obscurity. Despite the recognition he has rightly received for his re-engineering of the Roman state and army, and his establishment of the institution of joint emperorship on a firm basis, even the date of his death is uncertain. It was probably in 316 that he passed away, no doubt disillusioned that the only power he possessed was that to survey the frustration of his designs.[41]

The absolute impotence of the former Emperor is amply demon-strated by the fate of his daughter Valeria (widowed in 311 on the death of Galerius),[42] who roamed the Balkans as a fugitive after the death of her husband before being put to death on the orders of Licinius in 315. Her father – or his memory, if he was already dead – could do nothing to protect her. Diocletian's great palace at Salonae also passes into obscurity. It had one last moment in the limelight, when it formed the headquarters of Julius Nepos, the last lawfully appointed Emperor in the West, who based himself in Illyricum after his expulsion from Italy in 475, claiming, in vain, until his death in 480 – and especially after the deposition of Romulus Augustulus in 476 – that it was he who was still the Emperor.

Carnuntum's civil amphitheatre is a short walk to the south-west of the Palace Ruins. Cutting along narrow country lanes and through fields, the way seems totally divorced from the urban settlement behind, and the building itself is only marked out by the grassy banks where the seats (calculated to hold 13,000 spectators) once lay. Only part of the main supporting walls and some auxiliary buildings to the south remain, though a hexagonal pool was discovered in excavations, composed of reused parts of the original building, and may have been a baptismal font.[43]

Much more resonant of Carnuntum's Roman past is the Heidentor ('Heathen's gate'). Splendidly isolated in fields beyond a railway track, this quadriform arch is all the more striking for being orphaned of its original context. It strikes a dramatic silhouette against the sky, a touch shorter than its original 15-metre height, but still imposing from afar and even more impressive close up. The top of the arch, from which soar the stumps of a second storey, was probably decorated with relief figures in marble. It has been dated to the reign of Constantius II (351–61)[44] and might have had some military function for official parades or the assembly of troops. The arch has long piqued the interest of those with an eye for classical antiquity and was mentioned as long ago as 1551 by the humanist Wolfgang Lazius, while its appealing and mysterious image appears in a prominent position on all of the modern publicity for the Carnuntum site.

The legionary camp itself lies beneath fields halfway between Petronell and the next-door settlement of Bad-Deutsch Altenburg. Situated on a raised plateau, its walls described an irregular quadrilateral, much longer on one of the sides. Although the normal camp buildings have been identified from aerial photography and from a series of excavations in the 1960s and 1970s, there is little to be seen on the ground. The only building that has been restored is the military amphitheatre, just a hundred metres or so from the fortress perimeter and laid out in a slight depression. The original structure was wooden and rebuilt in stone in the 2nd century, with funds donated by a town councillor named Caius Domitius Zmaragdus, who originated from Syria. The grassed-over arena is an oval around 70 x 45 metres, and part of the podium where the legionary legate's box would have stood survives to the west side. All around the stone supports of the seating tiers and the facing of the arena walls are still intact, and an inscription atop the main entrance memorialises the *quattorviri*, or municipal magistrates, of the Municipium Aelium Carnuntum, a name for the city that dates the inscription to before the reign of Septimius Severus.

The amphitheatre's small museum contains an admirable display on the training and life of Roman gladiators, a caste who were alternately lionised and despised by Roman authors. The Christian Tertullian, regarding the whole thing as scandalous, acidly commented that 'Men offer them their hearts and women their bodies.'[45] Gladiatorial contests had their origin in ancient Etruscan funeral rites of the 6th century BC, in which prisoners of war fought to the death to propitiate the shades of departed warriors.[46] The custom was taken over by the Romans, whose very early history included a phase of Etruscan dominance at Rome. They fastidiously made a distinction between *ludi* (processions and chariot-races), which were regarded as genuinely Roman, and *munera* (the gladiatorial version), for whose development the Etruscans were credited (or blamed).[47] By 55 BC, the *ludi* were so well established and elaborate that a set put on by Pompey for his consulship involved the slaughter of a thousand lions and leopards and the first public display of an Indian rhinoceros in Europe.[48]

The gladiatorial *munera* developed more slowly; the funeral of Marcus Aemilius Lepidus in 216 BC featured twenty-two pairs of gladiators, and that for the father of Titus Flaminius in 174 BC had thirty-seven pairs fighting over three days,[49] but these were essentially private affairs. It was only really under the Empire that the gladiatorial games received official sponsorship.[50] By that time amphitheatres, the normal venue for such contests, with their oval shape surrounded on all sides by seats (in contrast to the hemispherical shape of theatres for less bloody spectacles) dotted the Empire, most especially in the western provinces and North Africa.[51] They provided a hugely popular form of entertainment and a vent for the frustrations of the lower orders, who could scream out from the crowd slogans satirising the administration of the day, an act that would in any other context have led to summary punishment.

The gladiators themselves were a mixture of prisoners of war, condemned criminals and slaves, who had often been captured beyond the boundaries of the Empire. Occasionally – producing a particular frisson amongst the Roman chattering classes – free men put themselves into the arena, in effect enslaving themselves to the gladiatorial school to which they had signed up. Even Mark Antony's brother Lucius fought in the arena, in Asia Minor, much to the patrician sneering of Cicero.[52] The most extraordinary manifestation of the desire amongst the well-to-do to experience the thrills and danger of the arena, and the admiration of the baying crowd, was the Emperor Commodus, who spent long days fighting as a 'gladiator' – in little or no danger of being injured, however, so hand-picked, drugged or terrified were his opponents.

Most Roman public officials were forced to put on games as part of their magistracy, and so there was a healthy market in gladiators and a respectable profit to be made. Under Augustus, there were sixty-six days a year given over to some form of public spectacle, and by the reign of Marcus Aurelius this had risen to 135.[53] The greatest games were given by Trajan to celebrate his conquest of Dacia; they lasted more than four months and included the sending of 10,000 gladiators into the arena, together with the slaughter of more than 10,000 wild animals.[54] By no means all contests ended in the death of one of the fighters, but nonetheless the carnage (and the cost) must have been prodigious.

The gladiatorial industry became a highly technical affair, with specialist schools and the fights themselves becoming increasingly ritualised, the appointed equipment of the gladiators sometimes aping that of various of Rome's defeated opponents. The 'Samnite', for example, wore a large oblong shield, a helmet with a visor and prominent crest, and a metal greave on the left; the 'Thracian' sported a curved sickle-shaped sword, a smaller round shield and greaves on both legs; the *retiarius* fought with a trident-shaped harpoon and a net to ensnare his opponent. The shows were overseen by an *editor* who supervised the general organisation, while the pairings of gladiators were generally done by lot. After the day's bloodshed was done, careful lists were made, some of which survive, noting against the names of the gladiators P (for *periit*, 'perished'), V (for *vicit*, 'won') or M (for *missus*, 'spared') – the last-named being those who lost but whom the senior magistrate present had decided should be spared, often at the behest of the crowd.

After Constantine I's acceptance of Christianity, gladiatorial games gradually withered away. An edict of his in 326 purported to abolish them, but its lack of effectiveness is indicated by another law of Constantius II in 357, which forbade soldiers to fight in the arena.[55] The gladiatorial schools were closed by Honorius in 399, but such spectacles sputtered on for a few years, and the last recorded games at Rome took place in 404.[56] The arenas were even then not shut down completely and were used for *venationes* (wild-beast spectacles), in which men hunted ferocious animals, sometimes at the cost of their own lives. By 440, the Christian writer Salvian, in a bitter attack on public shows, mentions *venationes* and chariot-racing, but not gladiatorial shows, implying that by then they had ceased.[57] At Rome, the last such recorded beast-show came as late as 523.[58]

At the Carnuntum amphitheatre, a small troupe of Austrian school-children is decked out in gladiatorial array (with a detachment of mini-legionaries, presumably on guard duty). Someone, however, has forgotten the swords, and there is a great deal of chaotic running backwards and forwards to recover the weapons for the programmed mock-combats. To while away the time the legionaries lock their wooden shields together over their heads to make an impromptu *testudo*, the Roman army's 'tortoise' defensive formation, which protected against projectiles and objects hurled from the battlements of cities under siege. This manoeuvre, it must be presumed, formed part of last week's lesson.

Only a kilometre east of the main legionary camp lay a fort for a cavalry *ala*, originally based here in the 1st century AD, which then occupied the camp until at least the mid-3rd century. Although little save the outline of the camp's ditches can be made out, the positions of the main buildings during its four phases of rebuilding have been established[59] and the situation of another significant military force shows how vitally important the Carnuntum area was.

The next fort along the Pannonian *limes* was around 60 kilometres from Carnuntum at Gerulata, to the south of Bratislava, situated in modern Slovakia's exiguous strip of land south of the Danube. It lies in the quiet village of Rusovce, now in effect a suburb of the Slovak capital, and Gerulata itself never achieved the glorious afterlife of the more substantial army camps at Vindobona (Vienna) and Aquincum (Budapest). It sits down a quiet tree-lined side-street, near a twin-towered baroque church whose peeling frontage has seen better times, and close to the old course of the Danube, which has since shifted a little southwards. It was probably first erected during the reign of Domitian and by the early 2nd century housed a garrison of the *Ala I Milliaria Cananefatium*,[60] who hailed from the far west of the continental *limes* at distant Forum Hadriani (Voorburg) on the coast of the Netherlands.

Relatively little remains of the fort, with its ruins a mixture of the 2nd-century stone phase of the site and a late-antique smaller fortlet, which was subsequently built in the north corner of the earlier walls, cannibalising stones from its predecessor as well as a medley of tombstones, altars and whatever other building material lay easily to hand. A small section of the north-eastern angle of this later fort survives to just a few restored courses, with a peristyle courtyard in the interior of the building. Set asymmetrically in the centre of this lies a deep well, providing the security of water supplies for the soldiers and eliminating the need, in the less secure circumstances of the 3rd and 4th centuries, to leave their camp.

Around 75 kilometres to the south-west of Gerulata lay the important town of Scarbantia, now modern Sopron in Hungary, which was one of Upper Pannonia's chief settlements. It began life as a road station on the route that led from the Adriatic and Istria up to the Danube, and was initially assigned under Tiberius to the province of Noricum, being transferred by the reign of Vespasian to Pannonia, at around the time it reached the rank of *municipium*.[61]

The old town of Sopron is an attractive place with a predominantly baroque feeling, its most impressive monument, the late-medieval Fire Tower, squatting faintly phallus-like over the town centre. Watchers stationed at the neoclassical balustrade towards its summit could spot and warn of any conflagrations before they burnt out of control. Its base is also built in part over the remains of the Roman city wall beside the northern gate. A little further into the old town, butted right against the medieval wall and hemmed in by later, early modern buildings, are the remains of Scarbantia's forum. A couple of *insulae* are clearly demarcated on either side of the remains of a road; in one of them evidence of a bronze workshop was found. From the Roman wall itself one fan-shaped and one horseshoe tower survived, which were built over in the 14th century when the old fortifications were renewed.

Off to the right lay another defensive structure, which again had the remains of a medieval breastwork built over it. An outer ring is early medieval, but then, later in the 15th century, the Roman circuit (which was ignored by the earlier builders) was reused. One round projecting bastion, patrolled by a few cats prowling in the low grassy moat, was incorporated in all the phases. This complex of Roman walls represents the Constantinian defences of the city, at a time when the town defended the northernmost reaches of Pannonia Prima, after Pannonia had been subdivided by Diocletian in 296.

Somewhere nearby, the remains of an amphitheatre, a *horreum* and a Temple of Isis were uncovered by archaeologists, all part of the normal panoply of civic life, and a testament to the high level of Romanisation in the area. Concealed in the basement of a bank building, down a staircase reached by squeezing behind a set of desks and metal filing cabinets, hides another remnant of the forum. Here fragments from a sanctuary to Silvanus, god of the woodlands, sit beside the main roadway into the forum, marked out with a line of reconstructed portico columns. To one side is the base of what must have been a monumental equestrian statue. Its sheer size could only have been appropriate for a person of the highest eminence, and probably it carried an official portrait of one of the emperors. The roadway and another weed-choked portion of it visible through an iron grille above ground on the other side of the square were once – strange though it might seem in their current straitened circumstances – part of an ancient and vital trade route, the Amber Road.

Trade in the attractive fire-coloured gem, with its strange electric qualities, was no easy matter, for the principal source of the stone in ancient times lay along the shores of the Baltic Sea, many days' journey into *barbaricum*. The origin of amber was believed, as far back as the time of Herodotus in the 6th century BC, to be a 'river Eridanus'.[62] Pliny recounts the expressive tale of how, when Phaethon, the son of Helios the sun god, stole his father's chariot and allowed it to veer out of control – incidentally creating the Sahara Desert where it scorched North Africa, and turning the Ethiopians' skins black – Zeus was forced to strike him with a thunderbolt to bring his fiery joyride to an end. So besides themselves with grief were his sisters that they turned into poplars, which each year shed viscous tears on the banks of the Eridanus river, tears that were called *electrum*, in other words, amber.

The best account of the trade in amber and the search for its origins comes from the time of Nero, when a Roman member of the equestrian class was despatched by Julianus, a businessman, to try and transport back a huge quantity of amber.[63] This probably represented an attempt to make direct contact with the tribes at the head of the route and so cut out some of the middlemen along the way. It is unclear whether it was successful, and with the constantly shifting patterns of migrations of peoples to which the central European plain between the Danube and the Baltic was prone, any attempt to reach agreements with the tribes there to allow direct Roman access to the amber sources would have been like trying to tame the wind.

The route in ancient times carried the amber down via the estuary of the Vistula either to the Black Sea or through the Moravian Gate (the flat area between the mountains of the Sudetenland and the Carpathians) on towards the Danube near Carnuntum and Gerulata, and thence south (via Scarbantia) to the Italian peninsula. However, once the *limes* became porous in the late 4th century and collapsed completely in the late 5th century, the settlements that had depended on the trade, such as Scarbantia and Savaria (Szombathely), the provincial capital of Pannonia Prima 40 kilometres to the south, diminished in importance, and the trade in amber dwindled away to nothing.[64]

Scarbantia was vulnerable as early as the 2nd century and, to cap its earlier sacking during the Marcomannic Wars (166–80), it was overrun by the Goths in the early 5th century and was thereafter effectively lost to the Empire. Ninety kilometres to its east, and 60 kilometres to the south-east of Gerulata, Arrabona (modern Györ) lay on a tributary of the Danube. Its pleasant old lanes, baroque-style churches, squares and riverside walks totally conceal its heritage as a Roman *castrum* and a key link in the line between the legionary fortresses of Carnuntum and Brigetio. The earliest fort seems to have been built under Tiberius,[65] and the site, which was later rebuilt in stone, was occupied until late-Roman times by a variety of garrisons, principally cavalry regiments (such as the *Ala I Augusta Ituraeorum sagittariorum* from Syria), which were well placed to take advantage of the flat conditions on the Hungarian plain.

It is a short trip along the river to Brigetio, which began life as an auxiliary camp in the mid-1st century AD, before becoming a legionary fortress in 101 with the posting of the XI Claudia legion there, to be replaced five years later by XXX Ulpia Victrix and then, finally (before 119), by the I Adiutrix. Its very name has a Celtic root (*Brig-*) meaning 'fort'. Despite the subsequent rich history of the camp, and the town that grew up alongside it, there is relatively little left to see.

The fort sits alongside a factory compound in a park of neatly manicured hedges overlooked by an enormous housing estate in the modern settlement of Komárom (a suburb of Szöny), which nestles alongside the Danube, the southern section being in Hungary and the northern part (Komarno) in Slovakia. A few sarcophagi without inscriptions lie scattered around, together with a modern carved stone that marks the visit in 375 by Valentinian during his campaign against the Quadi, which ended in his death after an apoplectic fit. Of the fortress buildings, nothing remains, all backfilled after excavations, while the housing estate, built in the 1940s, has swallowed the southern portion.

More evocative are the wall paintings in the small local museum. One from a peristyle house, dated by a coin of Antoninus Pius to the period after the mid-2nd century, shows a man bearing a tray with a blue background, holding something in his hand, poised as though to bite into it, his curly hair and confident face clearly delineated. Another less clearly outlined figure and a lion-skin stretch out across part of the floor. In another scene, Pegasus and Andromeda are depicted in a central medallion, while at the corners of the painting beautifully refined women's faces represent the Four Seasons, creating a star-shaped composition of great elegance.

Of the line of forts that guarded the Danube *limes* between Brigetio and the next legionary fortress of Aquincum, little has remained, particularly where the situation was of sufficient strategic importance (as at Esztergom, or ancient Solva, 55 kilometres to the east of Brigetio) to encourage continued occupation in medieval times. Solva itself, originally founded in the 2nd century, remained in use until the 430s, but suffered particularly badly as it lay on the site of the palace of the Hungarian kings in the Middle Ages, with further destruction being wrought when a 19th-century basilical church was built on top of the fort mound.

Twenty kilometres east along the Danube towards the modern town of Visegrád, the country becomes hillier and more wooded, differentiating itself from the unbroken plain behind. Here, too, a medieval palace was built, occupying a prime position in the centre of town. Yet elements of the late-Roman castle of Pone Navata have survived, high up on a 170-metre plateau overlooking the river. It is not quite the biggest hill in the vicinity; that honour goes to a slightly higher promontory next door, to which a medieval fortress clings, almost inaccessible, even to its defenders. Pone Navata was one of the more important fortifications in this section during the Later Empire, probably built under Constantine I in the 320s or 330s,[66] and it remained in use at least until the 380s (the *Notitia Dignitatum* lists its garrison as the *auxilia Ursarensia*). Around this time most of the fort was abandoned and only a watchtower built around the main gateway continued in use. From there, the remaining soldiers watched as their hold on the territory of the middle Danube grew ever weaker. By the 5th century, barbarian hut dwellings clustered on the southern side of the fort, as Roman control in this region collapsed for ever.

Of Pone Navata, one main line of walls survives to about 30 centimetres high, running for about 10 metres before disappearing into the ground, together with three horseshoe-shaped projecting towers. One of the fort's gates survives, and beyond it is a curious small, round structure with wall-spurs projecting from it. This section of the Danube, where it changes direction and bends round to flow north–south, rather than east–west, was densely defended, with the auxiliary castle of Ulcisia Castra (modern Szentendre) lying between Pone Navata and the main base on this part of the river, some 35 kilometres to the south at Aquincum.

Both the twin capitals of the Austro-Hungarian monarchy, Budapest and Vienna, owe their existence to their origins as Roman legionary camps, sites whose location was so strategically placed that their associated civil settlements survived the catastrophe of the Empire's fall in the West, continued to grow and eventually became capital cities. It is a singular history, which only Belgrade in Serbia unambiguously shares (although Gerulata near Bratislava at least lies near its successor, even if occupation was not continuous, and Bonna on the Rhine frontier did give birth to what was the capital of West Germany until German reunification). The earliest fort, which would ultimately give rise to Buda, was founded under Tiberius for a cavalry detachment, which was replaced by the fortress of the II Adiutrix legion under Domitian.[67] The second of Budapest's constituent cities, Pest, derives in turn from Contra-Aquincum, which was established as a bridgehead fort across the Danube in the late 2nd century.

The main civil settlement of Aquincum lies to the north-west of the centre of Buda, the rattling ride on the city's HEV light-railway system an incongruous entry into the Roman *municipium*. From its status as mere legionary camp, Aquincum rose to become the capital of Pannonia Inferior at the time of Trajan's division of the province into two parts in 106. The first governor of the province, and therefore a resident of Aquincum for several years, was none other than Trajan's young protégé, the future Emperor Hadrian. It did not, however, reach the rank of *municipium* until 124 (when it took the name Municipium Aelium Aquincum), and had to wait until 194 during the reign of Septimius Severus to reach the level of *colonia*.

Only the eastern section of the ancient town has been extensively excavated, and the consolidated walls of this section, bordering a very busy main road, have a slightly sombre, pensive feel about them. So close to the centre of a capital city, the ruins are well visited and a procession of day-trippers and schoolchildren lounge against urban villa walls or run excitedly along the *decumanus*, barely pausing to examine an altar or explanatory plaque. In the museum the most striking exhibit is a Roman water-organ, a recreation of one found on the site. The original was given by a certain Iulius Victorinus to the firemen's guild in 228. Even though the inscription discovered with it referred to it as a water-organ, its workings (using fifty-two pipes) are in fact pneumatic. An old newsreel plays out a concert given by a reconstructed version of the organ, the music creating a rather haunting and distant atmosphere. Elsewhere in the museum, a statue of a man clad in a toga has a handy stone slot at the neck for screwing on a replacement head, no doubt a very useful fixture in the 3rd century when emperors changed almost every other year and the city could thus economise on commissioning an entirely new statue by simply replacing the old head with the latest imperial bust.

Close to the museum lies the lapidarium (stone repository) of Aquincum, an awesome collection which takes up a stretch several hundred metres long, arrayed with tombs, altars, milestones, sarcophagi, lintels, architraves, statues and all the other stonework and masonry that a provincial capital might produce over several hundred years. It is a veritable graveyard of the city, and in a way more evocative than the ruins themselves, as the hopes, fears and life stories of the citizens are pressed together in a jumble of memories.

Just opposite the museum is the *mithraeum* of Symphorus and Marcus, its central hall with the side-rooms clearly visible, but the middle section now lacking the altars that must once have stood there. It was one of four shrines to the god in the town, a sign of military influence in Aquincum, for the cult was always particularly popular amongst the military, as evidenced by the other *mithraea* along the frontier. Beyond it, a substantial section of the *decumanus* survives, principally in a quarter composed of craftsmen's and traders' shops and dwellings, including a *macellum* for the butchers. The colonnade of the *decumanus* runs alongside a grassy bank all the way back to the site entrance, and beside it sit the 'Great Baths', the largest of half a dozen such complexes found in the city. Part of the building close to the hypocaust seems charred, perhaps evidence of the destruction of Aquincum in the 3rd- and 4th-century disorders.[68]

A small forum at the end of the *decumanus*, the main east–west axis of the city where it crossed the *cardo*, the principal north–south street, possesses a shrine of uncertain dedication, with a very weathered altar still *in situ*, together with the town's *curia* and the fragmentary remains of the basilica and law courts. On the north-west outskirts of town lay the civil amphitheatre, now missing its seats, but with the stone piers that supported them, the entrance gate and enclosing wall still intact. Around 30 metres in length on its longest side, it seems now to serve principally as a pleasant walking and running track.

The legionary camp that gave birth to Aquincum was sited a little way from the Danube. Built in stone under Hadrian to replace the early Domitianic fort, it remained in use until the time of Constantine, when a new stronghold was constructed on the banks of the river. This, in turn, was abandoned and replaced with a simple watchtower under Valentinian I. Although excavated intermittently during the 20th century as the demolition of older buildings permitted, only small parts are now visible. The largest surviving section, wedged under a spaghetti-like complex of flyovers and overpasses, is that housing the camp baths, which were enlarged in 268 and then partly adapted in the 4th century to be the palace of the *Dux Ripae Pannoniae*. To wander through a two-millennia-old bathhouse 10 metres beneath a road over which thunders the heavy traffic of modernity is a surreal experience. Dramatic stripes of shaded and sunlit stones caused by the criss-crossing of the roads above create a confused impression of walls and columns, obscuring any wide-ranging viewpoint of the site.

In an underpass beside the nearby metro stop, the life of the camp fleshes itself out somewhat with the tombstone of an auxiliary soldier tacked to the wall next to a snack bar, with a very unmilitary purple teddy bear perched on a seat propped up against it. Outside the precinct of the metro, on a totally neglected patch of ground, lie the remains of the south gate of the camp and the re-erected pillar of the house of one of the senior officers. As commuters rush to and from their daily office grind, no one at all seems to notice the stones, the earliest evidence of their home city.

Of Contra Aquincum, the great-grandfather of Pest, the remains are even sparser, although it was always a smaller fortress, a mere bridge-head on the barbarian side of the Danube. It now sits in a depression in the centre of Budapest-Eskü Square, the outline of a round projecting tower with wall spurs about 3–4 metres long still visible. Hemmed in by the buildings of the square and overlooked by incurious office-workers consuming their lunchtime snacks, these remains are of a later Roman fort. It was originally about 85 metres square, and probably constructed on the site of a larger 2nd-century fort, as the *limes* was strengthened in the late 3rd or 4th century, but at a point when there were no longer sufficient resources to build or garrison the larger military installations of former times.

After the reforms of the late 2nd-century, the provincial administration moved away from the town, with Sopianae (Pecs) or Gorsium (Tác) becoming the capital of Valeria.[69] The town diminished, and the proconsul's palace was abandoned. The palace of the *dux* of the Pannonian *limes* was moved away to the military camp, and the civil settlement was left bereft of patronage. In the 370s, when Valentinian I passed through on his campaign of refortification of the Danube *limes*, he found Aquincum so impoverished that he could not have his winter quarters in the city.[70] By the time the *Notitia Dignitatum* was composed at the end of the 4th century, Aquincum's legion had been transferred to Gaul, and the town had probably been overrun by Germanic tribes and then by the Huns in the early 5th century. The Romanised civilian population evidently did not evacuate entirely, for it must have formed the core of the settlement that would, many centuries later, evolve into modern Budapest.

From Budapest the Danube strikes in a more or less straight line south-wards. The land here is again very flat and was vulnerable to nomadic incursions, particularly horseborne ones. The principal civilian town in this sector, set around 75 kilometres to the south-west of Aquincum, and 30 kilometres west of the Danube, was Gorsium, where around AD 50 a military camp was built on the banks of the Sárvíz river.[71] Over time it was transformed into a civilian settlement as the main garrison moved up to the line of the river, although a new camp, for the *Cohors Alpinorum equitata*, was built just to the south of it. When Pannonia was parti-tioned by Trajan in 106, Gorsium became the centre for the imperial cult in Pannonia Inferior and a new and more intense phase of construction began. Severely damaged by a Sarmatian raid in 178, the settlement was then completely destroyed by the Roxolani in 260, and had to be entirely rebuilt on the ashes and wreckage of the old town. It was then renamed Herculia, a name very much in keeping with the spirit of the times, for it was with Hercules that the Emperor Maximian was identified in the official ideology of the Tetrarchy.

Far away from any modern settlement, Gorsium has a much more tranquil air to it than Aquincum, set amongst fields and bordered by small clumps of trees, and it is far easier here to gain a sense of the whole life of the ancient city. It is mainly the late-Roman settlement that can now be seen, its predecessor having been so comprehensively erased both by the barbarians and by the rebuilding of the site. At the entrance a rounded projecting angle tower survives, its stones seeming to gleam impossibly white in the mid-afternoon sun. The port that serviced Gorsium was situated nearby, but it seems lost in a tangle of under-growth and mud; the modern river has moved 200 metres or more away, but its ancient course lay much closer to the city. As Gorsium/Herculia was rebuilt, large urban villas were sited within it, a sign perhaps of the growing social division between the *potentes* who possessed power and social distinction and the *humiliores*, who, even if they belonged to groups that had been enfranchised and (certainly after 212) had citizenship, grad-ually slipped into a position of inferiority. This division was even recognised by the law, which, for example, permitted the humbler (but free) classes to be tortured, whereas no such sanction was applicable to their social betters.

The largest of the villas, in the north-west of the town, was some

60 metres long, a maze-like complex of state apartments, baths and work-shops, so grand as to be termed a 'palace'. Several of the rooms have apses, and one in particular has the feeling of an audience chamber. It is possible, once Pannonia Inferior was divided in two by Diocletian, that this was the headquarters of the governor of the new province of Valeria.[72] To the east of it, preserved under a shelter, are the remains of a series of wall frescoes, one preserving the shape of a winged figure, the other a simple geometrical pattern. Around this survives the curve of an early Christian basilica, probably built not long after official govern-ment recognition of the religion under Constantine in 311.

Along the *decumanus*, past a *nymphaeum*, with what looks curiously like a stone trilobite shell placed on top of it as part of the modern restoration, lie the remains of the forum, the only area whose use was conserved intact from the pre-3rd-century phase of the city, bordered by four columns of a pagan-style temple dedicated to Rome and Augustus. As this area seems to have constituted the official provincial religious centre, the remains of a podium to the south of the *decumanus* have been taken to have some purpose associated with the imperial cult.[73]

This cult, exploited in the frontier provinces as a handy agent of Romanisation and a means to promote provincial loyalty to the ruling classes, centred on posthumous worship of the emperors as gods. Deification had an ancient pedigree in Roman tradition, for Romulus – Rome's first founder and first king – was regarded as a god after his death and worshipped under the name Quirinus. Republican leaders underwent no such elevation, although overenthusiastic subjects had occasionally come close to worshipping them,[74] especially in the East, where such cults had a heritage stretching back to Alexander the Great and before. It took until the accession of Augustus as first Emperor for the tradition to be revived at Rome. His adoptive father, Julius Caesar, was posthumously recognised as divine in 42 BC,[75] strengthening Augustus's position as not only the son of a great military leader, but of a god as well. The honorific *divus* ('deified') was accorded to Augustus after his death and the deifica-tion of subsequent emperors became almost routine, although not without an occasional hint of controversy. Antoninus Pius had to threaten to abdi-cate in order to cajole the Senate into deifying Hadrian, with whom that august body had latterly been on bad terms. Similarly, emperors univer-sally regarded with execration, such as Domitian and Caracalla, were denied their immortality as gods. Emperors whose accession could be regarded as of dubious legitimacy, such as Septimius Severus – who, for all his virtues, had taken the throne by force – could try to associate themselves with a previous regime by proclaiming a predecessor to be a god.

Hence, in 193 Septimius tried to acquire a veneer of lawfulness by having the title *divus* accorded to Pertinax, who had received wide support amongst the senate prior to his murder, and pointedly denying it to Didius Julianus, his immediate predecessor whom he had overthrown. Whether the divine status of former emperors was taken particularly seriously is unclear, but it did form a central part of the imperial cult, which focused, as time went on, on the worship of the deified emperors as a group. Only the most notable, such as Augustus himself, received their own individual temples. The role of priest of the imperial cult was an attractive means of social advancement for ambitious provincials, and even more so for the fact that it was one of the few prestigious positions that were not denied to freedmen.[76]

The direct worship of living emperors continued to be frowned upon, but a means around this was found through the veneration of certain aspects of the Emperor's personality, such as his *genius* (or spirit) and his *numen* (or divine presence). Even in relatively conservative Italy, altars were dedicated to the *numen* of Augustus, in which sacrifices to his 'divine presence' would only have been distinguishable from actual worship to the most pedantic.[77]

An arch comment on the whole business came from one of its beneficiaries, Vespasian, who, as he lay dying in AD 79 is reported to have said, 'I can feel myself becoming a god.'[78] More satirically, Seneca penned a piece entitled 'On the Pumpkinification of Claudius', in which the dead Emperor pleads unsuccessfully before a court of the gods to be allowed to join their number.[79] The Christianisation of the Empire in the 4th century rendered deification redundant and Emperor-worship highly suspect. Even so the notion was so embedded in the popular psyche that Constantine himself was referred to in inscriptions as *divus*, although by this time it had more the connotation of 'the late' than any sense that he was in any way the equal of the one God, whose worship he had so greatly promoted on Earth.

In the east of Gorsium, the town walls are less well preserved. Around 378, after the security of the western Balkans had been gravely compromised by the Gothic victory at Adrianople, a large part of the civilian population that had been living in suburbs outside the city walls moved inside the shelter of the fortifications. A great number of poor-quality houses were built, often against the inside of the ramparts, and the southern suburbs of the town were entirely deserted. Sometime between 380 and 430, this area was converted into a cemetery; mingled amongst the ruins of the abandoned buildings are dozens of humble graves, *tegulae*, made of tiles propped together into a triangular shape, with a light infill of earth. They look like a hundred little huts for the dead and, together with the broken-down houses of this former residential quarter, lend to this area of Gorsium a very eerie feeling indeed.

Intercisa, one of the larger auxiliary forts on the Pannonian *limes*, lies around 50 kilometres to the south-east of Gorsium, transformed now into the rather depressing town of Dunaújvaros, its centre almost entirely composed of high-rise blocks, and where the museum has a whole wing still devoted to the glorification of the locality under the communist regime (for a while it even renamed itself for the Soviet dictator as Sztalinvaros). The remains of the camp lie at the edge of one of the huge apartment complexes. Not much of it survives, except the grassy outline of the ramparts and one north-eastern tower overlooking the Danube (and a fetching panorama of an industrial complex packed with cranes).

A few stone outlines of the interior buildings are still intact, one situated near where the camp *principia* should be. Otherwise there are just slight indentations in the ground to indicate the principal buildings of the fort. The baths lay elsewhere, five minutes' walk away, in an older, more agricultural quarter of Dunaújvaros. The surviving section, a rather dusty-looking affair, must be the old *caldarium*, judging from the number of tiles scattered around, which would have been used to raise the floor level, beneath which the hot air used to heat the building circulated. Looking away from the crane-lined riverbank, it all seems very peaceful and tranquil, a couple of sarcophagi quietly sitting in the small lapidary garden next to the guardian's house.

Intercisa did not have a particularly peaceful history, however; it was probably destroyed during an action by the Iazyges in 117–18, and was then burnt again by the Marcomanni during their war against Marcus Aurelius around 178, only to be put to the torch once more by the Roxolani in 260. It was partly reconstructed under the Tetrarchy, but more comprehensively so under Constantine I between 325 and 330. Further repairs were then necessary under Valentinian I, that great refortifier of the Danube *limes*. It is not clear exactly when Intercisa was abandoned, but it was probably some time in the early 5th century. The town had probably been garrisoned in the last years of its existence by Germanic federate troops, and, with the Western Emperors' decreasing ability to guarantee military pay, the army units may simply have dissolved rather than suffered any catastrophic local defeat.

From Intercisa, southward along the river through 40 kilometres of flat fields, woods and a few low hills, the auxiliary fort of Lussonium, near the modern village of Dunakömlőd, sits on a bluff overlooking what was in ancient times the gorge of the Danube, though the river has now moved several hundred metres further to the east. At the north gateway of the fort, a crew of workmen are busily plastering and mortaring, creating a reconstruction of the north entrance, and have just reached part of one projecting tower, so that before too much time has elapsed, Lussonium, or its gate at least, will be restored to its former glory. Although the camp was first occupied by a wooden building in the 1st century, the visible stones date from the late-Roman period.

The western part of the fort collapsed due to erosion caused by the river's course at the foot of the hill and was further damaged by defensive works built on the hill under the Habsburgs in the 18th century. The fort therefore has an elongated strip feeling about it, and the shape of the ruins is further confused by the superimposition of a massive tower at the end of the 4th century when the rest of the fort was demolished. Some 10 metres square, the tower had 2-metre-thick walls and at least two storeys, and was characteristic of the type of fortification built along the Danube in the last years of reasonably secure Roman control here. Its situation atop the hill and the additional height provided by the tower must have given the garrison an excellent view of what was going on across the Danube, though with their presumably limited numbers it is doubtful what, if anything, these border troops could have done to intercept any incursions.

A good example of the fate of many of the forts along the *limes* is to be found at Lugio, around 70 kilometres south on a bend in the river in Dunaszeckslő county. The fort stands (or stood) on top of the Várhegy ('castle') hill, but the crest of this is entirely covered in a vineyard, and the sides of the slope are thickly wooded. Somewhere in here, apparently, are the remains of walls, and a frescoed house and hypocaust were found, but they remain resolutely concealed amongst the trees. On the opposite side of the river a cluster of ruins makes up the remains of the bridge-head fort in *barbaricum*, Contra Florentiam (a name which indicates that Lugio itself was renamed as Florentia during the late-Roman period).

Lugio makes up for the paucity of its remains by its most spectacular find, a bronze statue bust of Marcus Aurelius (now in the museum at Pécs), a masterpiece that depicts the Emperor at about thirty or forty years of age. He sports curly hair and an ample philosopher's beard, his brow furrowed and his eyes cast slightly upwards. He seems just a little weary, but still strong and enduring, his expression at the same time knowing and compassionate. It is an exquisite embodiment of the spirit of the Emperor, which comes across so strongly in his *Meditations*, mired in a seemingly incessant war with the Marcomanni, when he would much rather have been tending to his own inner contemplative life.

Around 40 kilometres almost due west of Lugio lies Sopianae, which was the principal town of the area and evolved in due course into the city of Pécs, Hungary's fifth-largest, with about 150,000 inhabitants. The town's name may perhaps derive from a Celtic root that means 'swamp', but it does not seem to have been a major settlement until Roman times, when it grew on the junction of roads that led north towards Aquincum, and east–west towards Sirmium and the Italian peninsula. The modern town completely overlays ancient Sopianae, and so excavation has only given a partial impression of the antique city.[80]

The majority of the remains that have been located date from the late-Roman period, when the town probably rose in status, and most of these are associated with its Christian cemeteries. These mainly lie clustered around the modern basilical church, indicating that this was early on the nucleus of Christianity's development in Sopianae. The main area is known as the Cella Septichora, from a seven-apsed structure built in the late 4th or early 5th century, which forms the centrepiece of an extensive cemetery complex. With its sterile modern lights, and arrayed with modern metal benches, it still manages to retain an aura of mystery, its walls in some places surviving to greater than head height. In passageways that lead off in each direction are a variety of early Christian tombs, some plain burials, others in carefully crafted mausolea.

The highlight of all is the Saint Peter and Paul burial chamber, its barrel vault visible one level up in the multi-storey catacomb, its interior ceiling decorated with frescoes of the two saints – clad in Roman robes, with wide-bordered tunics – and the Virgin Mary, faded to an almost chalk-like consistency. Across the square from the city's basilica lies another early Christian mausoleum excavated in the 1950s. It is a single vaulted tomb, with one large sarcophagus and a collection of exquisite frescoes from the 4th century. To the left the temptation of Adam and Eve is shown, together with Daniel, in imminent danger of being consumed by the lions.[81]

The Christian burial chapels at Sopianae survived in use into the Age of Migration, (when large numbers of Germanic and other barbarian peoples moved south and westwards into Roman territory), and there are some 8th- or 9th-century frescoes on a few of the tombs. The medieval name of the town, Quinque Basilicae ('Five Churches') probably indicates a continuity of use in the vast Christian complex. In the 9th century, however, a second wave of invaders from the East swept through the

Pannonian plain. By the time the Magyars crossed the Carpathian basin in 895, the Roman province was but a far-off memory.

The journey through the flat Pannonian plain to the south and east of Sopianae crosses agriculturally rich territory dotted with the small, nondescript villages of the eastern Slavonian province of Croatia. It has long been debatable territory between the Balkans (or the steppes) and the lands further west. It lay along the most obvious routes towards the Italian peninsula, and usurpers or legitimate emperors intending to secure Rome from a base in Constantinople (or vice versa) were forced to traverse it. Just a little further east, one of Europe's most persistent fault lines appears. To its west, in Croatia, lies the area that formed, in general, part of the western Roman provinces, largely Latin-speaking, whilst to its east, in Serbia, lay the Eastern Emperor's lands, which were or became predominantly Greek-speaking. The division persisted in the line between the Habsburg Austria-Hungary and the Ottoman Turkish lands in the Balkans, and between the Roman Catholic majority in Croatia and the Eastern Orthodox of Serbia. The passage of time has not erased the area's strategic importance; it was bitterly fought over during the civil wars that accompanied the break-up of Yugoslavia in the 1990s. Empty lots and charred and burnt-out shells of buildings mark the passing of the fighting, while an even more sinister reminder of the conflict lurks to either side of certain stretches of roadway, in the red or black skull-and-crossbones symbols that warn of uncleared mine-fields amongst the gently swaying trees.

Osijek, the regional capital, is a gracious 19th-century city lying near the confluence of the Danube and Drava rivers, its main square scattered with statues honouring the forefathers of Croatian nationalism, the tower of the Saint Peter and Paul Cathedral at one end still pockmarked by bullet and shrapnel holes from the bombardment during the civil war. The remains of Mursa, part-excavated, lie in the eastern section of town around 300 metres south of the hospital on an open lot, though with little to rival the more spectacular finds of sites such as Carnuntum or Viminacium (Kostolac). Granted the status of a *colonia* by Hadrian in 133, Mursa remained a prosperous outpost near the *limes* into the 4th century. Its political life was uneventful, though the area outside the city twice saw major battles that were the undoing of a usurper, with the defeat in 258 or 259 of Ingenuus,[82] and the bloody suppression of the revolt of Magnentius in 351.[83]

To the south-east of Osijek along the highway that leads a short distance later into Serbia, Cibalae (Vinkovci) was badly damaged during the Yugoslav civil war, but not destroyed like its near-neighbour Vukovar.

The scant remains of baths and hypocausted houses that have been exca-vated hardly do justice to its real importance as the birthplace of Valens and Valentinian, brothers who both became Emperor in 363.

The Balkan provinces of Pannonia, Moesia and Illyricum did, indeed, become something of a cradle for emperors from the 3rd century. After the demise of Alexander Severus in 235, emperors were largely made (and as often murdered) by the soldiers. And what better replacement for an unsatisfactory emperor than their own general, whom they most often trusted, sometimes even admired, but from whom they could be absolutely sure of a suitable financial reward for their elevation of him to the highest office? In this fashion Trajan Decius, from the small village of Budalia (Martinci) between Cibalae (Vinkovci) and Sirmium (Sremska Mitrovica), became Emperor in 249, while Aurelian (270–5) may have been from Sirmium, Probus (276–82) was born near the same city, and Diocletian's colleague Maximian (286–305) hailed from the surrounding area. Constantine I (306–37), in turn, was born at Mediana outside Naissus (Nis) in Moesia.

It was, therefore, hardly shocking when Valentinian, born at Cibalae, became Emperor, and eminently predictable that when, urged by the troops to appoint a colleague to support him, his choice fell on his own brother, Valens. He was advised by Dagalaifus, a senior military officer, to choose Valens if his first concern was for his own family, but someone else if his primary loyalty was to the Empire. Blood, as so often, won out over reason.[84] The general was wise not to press the point against his new Emperor, for Valentinian had a notoriously bad temper. Once firmly ensconced in the palace in Constantinople, he is said to have procured two bears, which he had stationed outside his audience chamber, and, should someone cause him too much annoyance, he would allow the beasts literally to tear them apart.[85]

Valentinian had a great deal to keep him occupied. He allocated the government of the eastern provinces to his brother, who had little mili-tary experience, and set off to deal with a renewed threat from the Alamanns in the west. Their king, Vithicabius, had been assassinated and Valentinian took advantage of the confusion in their ranks to lead a pre-emptive expedition into their territories. By 374 the Emperor had brokered a tenuous peace with Macrianus, the new Alamannic ruler, and the Rhine frontier thereafter remained quiescent. Valentinian then turned eastwards to face a new danger threatening his own homeland.

The Quadi and the Sarmatians, the latter an Iranian-speaking people whose mounted warriors fought in chainmail armour, were vexed that Valentinian had ordered the erection of forts in what they regarded as their territory on the northern bank of the Danube. In 374, the barbarians tried to negotiate, but their humour was hardly helped by the murder of their king, Gabinius, at a banquet given by the local Roman commanders.[86] Unsurprisingly, the Quadi streamed across the river and plundered the neighbouring towns. One of their marauding bands very nearly intercepted the carriage transporting Constantia, the granddaughter of Constantine I, to her planned wedding with Gratian, Valentinian's eldest son.

The outrage to imperial dignity was unsupportable, and Valentinian moved his headquarters from Trier into Illyricum to be closer to the frontier and as a means to intimidate the troublesome barbarians. Faced with the full might of the legions, the Sarmatians wisely sent envoys begging for forgiveness. The Emperor merely promised to investigate their claims and sent them away, neither forgiven nor chastised. Valentinian then crossed over into the territory of the Quadi at Aquincum (Budapest) and set enthusiastically to laying waste their lands. The Quadi, seeing that they were beaten, or at least that they would starve if matters were left unchecked, sent a deputation to the Emperor, who was by now in Pannonia at Sirmium. Curious portents attended their arrival; lightning struck the imperial palace, and Valentinian dreamt that he had seen his wife – who was in Gaul – attired in mourning clothes.

At their meeting, it was agreed that in return for supplying recruits to the Roman army, the Quadi would be left to enjoy what was left of their lands in peace. Before departing, the envoys were granted a personal audience with the Emperor. Unwisely, but understandably, they insisted that the cause of the conflict had been the Romans' building of forts on their tribal land. To be addressed in this way was an appalling breach of protocol and Valentinian was enraged – as far the Romans were concerned, all these tribes were subjects of Rome, albeit sometimes rather badly behaved ones. He had a fit of apoplexy, followed by a stroke, and died that very night, 17 November 375. The hapless envoys were rushed away before they could witness Valentinian's death agony.

Colonia Aurelia Cibalae, as Osijek city had become on its elevation to colonial status in the 2nd century,[87] was a modestly prosperous town, some 56 hectares in extent, around which Valentinian's father Gratian had held extensive estates before they were confiscated on the grounds of his suspected involvement in the rebellion of Magnentius. However, it was comprehensively outshone by Sirmium, its neighbour some 70 kilometres to the south-east, which became a favoured imperial residence under Diocletian and the Tetrarchy, as well as at the time of Constantine and his successors.

Sirmium lay just on the edge of two worlds, within striking distance of both East and West, and so it became a location of massive strategic importance for the 3rd- and 4th-century emperors, right up to the time when there was so little left to preserve of the Western Empire that maintaining such a stronghold at its border ceased to have much purpose. Today the medium-sized town of Sremska Mitrovica in Serbia's Vojvodina province, it was first settled by the Romans in the early 1st century AD on the site of a former Pannonian settlement. With its strategic position on the Sava river, it became a *colonia* in Flavian times, and found frequent use as the headquarters for expeditions against the tribes across the Danube.

A short walk from the Sava, where a Roman port was located, lie the excavated remains of a 'trading quarter' set in a small shop-lined square. The buildings are from the 2nd or 3rd century and represent just a couple of *insulae* of the quarter, the stones remaining to about five or six courses high, set in a grassy dip surveyed by a gaggle of inquisitive pensioners seated on the surrounding benches. With its section of roadway, an exposed water channel with brick-built arches, and parts of several small but well-built houses, it is a mundane representation of what was for many years a working imperial capital.

Sirmium's administrative importance long pre-dates the Tetrarchy. In 103, when the province of Pannonia was split into two, the city became the capital of Lower Pannonia, and with Diocletian's further subdivision of Pannonia into four provinces in the 290s, it was made the capital of Pannonia Secunda, and also of the Vicariate of Illyricum. During the 2nd-century it saw frequent imperial visits from Marcus Aurelius, who used it as his headquarters during his decade-long Rhine and Danubian campaigns. During the Tetrarchy itself, Sirmium acted as the capital of Galerius, who, on the retirement of Diocletian and Maximian, became, in effect, the senior emperor. Sirmium, rather than Rome, was thus now the political centre for the whole Empire.

The remains of Galerius's palace lie just a few hundred metres from the trading quarter, split into two sections by the modern street. Set in a deep pit surrounded by a high concrete and wooden fence against the prying of curious eyes, it is really only a section of what must have been a much grander building. These are the baths of the imperial palace, their original function given away by the preservation of the bricks of a hypocaust in one corner and the telltale curved apses of the various pools. Low walls enclose grass-filled interiors, and here and there a few decorated pieces from friezes or pediments lie scattered on the ground, together with fragments of pinky-orange marble and a few bits of deep-purple imperial porphyry. In one section, small hexagonal floor tiles have broken up, leaving their six-sided cylinders as just a thousand pieces in some nightmarish jigsaw puzzle.

The only clue to the former inhabitants is a paw-mark on the border of some floor tiles, imprinted by a dog that ran over them as they dried around 1,800 years ago. It is hard in such an abandoned place, staring down at the ruins and up at the orange-tiled roofs of the surrounding modern houses surmounted by the white, round stains of their satellite dishes, to conjure up the atmosphere of an imperial palace in all its complexity, bustle and backdoors intrigue. However, the place does still excite interest, and a Serbian television crew listen intently as the layout is explained to them, taking panoramic shots to create a broad sweep of the past and as much visual drama as their cameras can muster.

Yet more ruinous is the small section of the palace on the other side of the road, where under a lattice-like wooden framework, its protective sheath of translucent plastic lying shredded in strips all over the ground, are a few more rooms, clothed in grandiose metre thick monumental walls. Somewhere, too, under the houses of Sremska Mitrovica lies one of the largest hippodromes in the ancient world; a section of its central barrier – the *spina* – has been found, and it is calculated that the arena must have been more than 300 metres long.

Sirmium was served by a port at Bononia-Malata (Banoštor), 40 kilometres to the north along the Danube, which also housed a fortress and, according to the *Notitia Dignitatum*, had units of the V Iovia legion as its garrison. Further east along the river, at modern Novi Sad, the massive complex of the Petrovaradin Fortress rears up. Composed of multiple defensive rings around the high point of the citadel hill, it was begun in the late 17th century and, by its completion around 1776, represented the very height of military architectural sophistication. Unfortunately, by this time the threat from the Ottoman Turks, to defend against whom it had been built, had receded so far that they never attacked it in its completed form. Somewhere deep beneath the impressive, pointless stonework may lie the remains of the small Roman fort of Cusum,[88] which, at 16 Roman miles from Bononia, hosted a small cavalry unit of *equites Dalmatae* that saw to the security of this sector in the 4th century.

Moesia Superior

Singidunum (modern Belgrade), some 75 kilometres south-west of Novi Sad, was one of the frontier's most important military stations, and

marks the westernmost point of Moesia Superior. The Roman settlement was situated on the high ground that overlooks the confluence of
the Sava and Danube rivers. The Romans originally established a
legionary fortress here in AD 86 for the IV Flavia Felix legion,[89] and small
parts of it can still be discerned in the bulk of the Kalemegdan fortress
that broods over the city, but the town's very survival as a viable settlement in the Middle Ages, and its growth to become the capital of
Yugoslavia and then of Serbia, have obliterated almost all trace of its
ancient forebear. The Roman Danube fleet, the *Classis Moesica*, had its
base here after its transfer from Viminacium to the north-east, and the
city became a *municipium* in 169, by which time Trajan's conquest of
Dacia meant that it was no longer a frontier position. Singidunum was
finally elevated to become a *colonia* in 239, but was always overshadowed
by Sirmium, its grander neighbour to the west, and by the legionary
fortress of Viminacium to the east. In contrast to Sirmium, it can claim
to be the birthplace of just one emperor, Jovian, the short-lived successor
to Julian in the 360s.

From the 4th century, Singidunum experienced a dizzy series of swings
in fortune and political control. It fell to the Huns in 441,[90] during Attila's
victorious campaign that swept away Roman control along a wide band
of territory south of the Danube. In the chaotic times following the Hun
khan's death, the eastern Roman army recaptured the fortress in 454,
only to be pushed out almost immediately by the Sarmatians. They in
turn were expelled by the Ostrogoths under Theoderic the Amal, who,
when they invaded Italy in 488 at the invitation of Emperor Zeno, ceded
Singidunum to the Gepids. The Byzantine Empire regained the city in
510, and around 535 Justinian rebuilt the fortress, only for it to be sacked
once more by the Avars in 584.[91] Finally, in the 7th century, after a brief
period of Byzantine reoccupation, it was settled by the Slavs, under
whom it became Beograd, the 'White City'. A large and noisy capital,
there is little white about it now; its suburbs are swathed in a band of
undifferentiated grey apartment blocks, the gift of socialist town planning to most cities of the region.

Outside of Belgrade's urban sprawl, the landscape is more rural,
though dotted with the shells of redundant industrial installations and
factories built according to the inscrutable requirements of the socialist
command economy. The sector east of Singidunum was guarded by
the fort at Margum (Dubravica), which, according to Ptolemy,[92] served
as the winter quarters of the VII Claudia legion in the mid-2nd century.
Although destroyed by the Huns in 441, the fort (and the *municipium* of
Aurelium Augustum Margum that had grown up around it) managed

to recover and by 505 was serving as the headquarters of the *magister militum* of Illyricum. It formed a key part of the *limes* of Djerdap, the defensive system in this part of the Danube, for which a significant upgrading of the road network was undertaken during the reigns of Tiberius, Claudius and Domitian. Once the trans-Danubian province of Dacia had been conquered, the fort lost its significance, but nearby another crucial and impressive structure appeared. A massive bridge was constructed between Pontes (Kostol) and Drobeta (Turnu Severin in Romania), where remains of some of the supporting structures can still be seen.[93]

Finally, just near the Danube, and about 12 kilometres from Pozarevac – most notable for being the birthplace of Slobodan Milosevic, Serbia's nationalist leader and the bringer of war to the Balkans – lies Viminacium. Just outside the small modern town of Kostolac, the old legionary fortress is situated on a plain beside the Mlava river, overshadowed by a power-plant whose chimneys pump a constant stream of white vapour-clouds out into the atmosphere, with the view further scarred by a coal mine in the distant hills. Amidst the often underfunded, neglected and badly presented Roman sites in the Balkans, Viminacium stands out as an exception, and it is, paradoxically, precisely the eyesore of a power-station that has been its salvation. The money provided for rescue excavation as a *quid pro quo* for permitting the building of the station on a site of such known archaeological sensitivity meant that there were funds for a modern visitor centre and the effective presentation of finds from the large-scale Roman necropolis that was discovered, in part on the site now obliterated by the power-plant itself.

Viminacium is first mentioned in the sources in Ptolemy's *Geography*. By early in the 1st century the Romans had built a military camp there, which became the base first for the IV Flavia legion and then the VII Claudia legion, one of the two with which Julius Caesar had invaded Britain in 55 BC, and which had subsequently acquired the nickname *pia fidelis*, for its loyalty to Claudius in the face of a revolt in AD 42. Viminacium served as the headquarters for Trajan in 98–9 before his First Dacian War, and, safely behind the shelter of the new province of Dacia, it developed rapidly as a civilian centre during the 2nd century, being granted the status of a *municipium* by Hadrian, in whose honour it became known as Municipium Aelium Viminacium.

Rapid, largely untroubled development followed for Viminacium in the early 3rd century, and under Gordian III it reached the status of *colonia*, at the same time being granted the prestigious right to mint its own copper coins (a right that would be revoked by Gallienus for the town's involvement in the revolt of Ingenuus).[94] During the reign of Philip, Viminacium briefly became the centre of the usurpation of Pacatianus, an officer in the Danube army (whom Zosimus says was of low rank), who persuaded the soldiers to raise him to the imperial eminence, possibly because Philip was seen to be ineffective in countering the threat posed by the Goths across the Danube.[95] They then did away with Pacatianus and threw in their lot instead with Trajan Decius, the very general whom Philip had despatched to suppress the revolt.

Having seen off Philip, who was killed in battle near Verona in 249, Decius enjoyed the position for only about two years before he, in turn, died fighting the Goths near Abritus in Moesia in 251.[96] With him perished his older son, Herennius Etruscus, leaving just his fifteen-year-old younger son Hostilianus, who was declared Emperor in Rome. The Danube armies, by now exercising their practically biennial right to pick a new sovereign, opted instead for the senior general Trebonianus Gallus. He acted cautiously, recognising Hostilianus's right to rule, while also appointing his own son Volusianus as co-Emperor. Shortly afterwards the whole terrible muddle of emperors was greatly simplified by the death at Viminacium of Hostilianus (and his mother, the splendidly named Herennia Cupresennia Etruscilla) in an outbreak of plague.

There is an intriguing possibility that Hostilianus might have been buried at Viminacium, and that one of the 13,000 graves that were located in the eastern necropolis belonged to him. The presentation of the site is spectacular. A modern shell of steel and plastic encloses the whole; inside, a stone wall of large, well-cut and dressed stones surrounds more than a dozen tombs, all grouped around a central mausoleum with an opening formed by a truncated triangle, now closed off with a metal grate. The central tomb is certainly of some prestigious personage, and seems to date from the mid-3rd century, so the theory that it is Hostilianus's grave is a plausible one. Against this, the stock of the former imperial family might not have been so high after his death (and the seizure of power by Trebonianus Gallus and his son) as to attract others to bury their dead near Hostilianus's mausoleum.

In the silence and the slightly grey-brown dust of the floor, it seems a secret, hidden place, despite the open nature of its display. One of the other tombs has a barrel vault that makes it look like a basket, while others have rounded roofs that give them the strange appearance of a dog-kennel. A few more conventional sarcophagi lie around, some of them with lids missing. Other poorer, 'free' burials were discovered, with just the skeleton and no sarcophagus, which it has not been possible, on the whole, to conserve. The earliest grave found here was from about

250, and the cemetery enclosure remained in use for about another century or so after that. Arrayed outside it was another selection of graves, some with the skeletons *in situ*, crouched as though trying to defend themselves from their inevitable fate.

Downstairs in the darkness a member of the site staff plays Charon, hooded cloak and scythe leading the visitor on into the Underworld. Here three tombs were found, complete with their original frescoes (two sets of which had to be moved to the museum at Pozarevac, while one remains in its original position). Two of them incorporate Christian symbolism into the wall decorations: in one a pair of peacocks, in the other a Christogram. The third contains a portrait of the 'Lady of Viminacium', the undoubted masterpiece of the site. She is richly dressed in a draped cloak, her hair in an elaborate coiffure, with pearl earrings, her eyes turned slightly to the right. Analysis of the bones found in the tomb have indicated that the woman – if this was her portrait – was at least partly paralysed in the later years of her life. On the opposite wall is the figure of a young man bearing offerings on a tray. An imaginative interpretation of the frescoes – which one of the archaeologists, in a break from the tangible world of cold, back-breaking digging, made into a film – is that he is the painter of the tomb, and had fallen madly in love with his subject opposite, a love that, because of social differences, could never be requited.

The area around Viminacium (or possibly closer to Margum) saw the denouement of another 3rd-century power struggle, when the armies of Carinus were defeated by those of the 'usurper' Diocletian near the River Margus in April 285. Carinus's father, Carus, had died the previous year fighting the Persians, and his brother Numerian had perished in suspicious circumstances while leading the army back to Constantinople; some pointed the finger of responsibility at Diocles (as Diocletian was then known), head of the palace guard, who had the next day engineered his proclamation as Emperor by the troops. Then, in a theatrical gesture he executed Aper, the praetorian prefect – who might have known the truth behind Numerian's death – by lopping off his head on the podium before the assembled army.

Constantine I is recorded to have visited Viminacium twice, in 321 and 334, while his son Constantius II graced the city with his presence in 338 and 358. From the later 4th century, however, emperors simply travelled less. The death of Valens in battle against the Goths in 378 led to a reaction against the idea that the Emperor should lead his troops in person; the consequences of an imperial death on the battlefield were too grave to risk it occurring again. Henceforth, emperors were largely confined

to their capitals, or the areas around them, and the last to visit Viminacium
was Gratian (the nephew of Valens) in 382. From this 4th-century period
of guarded security dates a section of the legionary camp's *porta praetoria*. It lies across virtually open fields from the necropolis building, the
landscape of the ancient city and fortress visible only in gentle undulations and bumps in the grass that suggest the presence of ancient stones
beneath. In the light early-autumn drizzle, and the first faint hints of a
biting winter wind, it instantly instils a desire to huddle against some
warming camp fire.

Under another cover, fragments of the paving of one tower are visible,
as well as part of a water channel that led down to the Danube. It was
once believed that the area between the fortress and the river was marshy,
but subsequent finds have indicated that it was dry and that the banks
of the river were reasonably accessible. A little way on from the camp
gate lies a shallow bowl-shaped indentation in the grass, which indicates
the location of the amphitheatre. The baths nearby, and under another
cover, are in good condition, but represent several different stages of
building and so are hard to read at first. There are in fact no fewer than
five different floor levels, and two different layers of hypocaust are visible
in what might be the *caldarium*. The whole complex, 30 metres long and
15–20 metres wide, represented a substantial amenity for the citizens.

Viminacium was destroyed by Attila and the Huns in 441, in a campaign
that devastated most of the urban settlements in this part of Moesia.
Although it was reoccupied and refortified as part of Justinian's
programme to strengthen the Danube *limes* in the early decades of the
6th century, within 100 years it had once again been overrun, this time
by Slavic invaders, and it was not reoccupied.

Opposite Drobeta (Turnu-Severin in Romania) the river changes
direction, turning southwards, before kinking east again to form the
border between modern Bulgaria and Romania. Around 100 kilometres south of the river, and so well back from the *limes* itself, lay
ancient Naissus (now modern Niš), the third-largest city in Serbia. The
town was founded in the late 1st century BC after the subjugation of
the indigenous Dardanians, at a relatively early stage in Rome's gradual
absorption of the Balkans. After the establishment of the province of
Moesia Inferior in AD 15, Naissus became one of its most important
centres and experienced several centuries of quiet prosperity before
the crises of the 3rd century.

Naissus's most famous son, the future Constantine I, was born around
273 – his birthday would be later celebrated as 27 February, but the precise
date is uncertain[97] – and spent at least part of his childhood in a villa at

Mediana, just outside Naissus. His mother, Helena, was the daughter of an innkeeper, and the taint of such ignoble ancestry was an early handicap that Constantine struggled to overcome. When his father became Caesar in 293, he was forced to marry his senior colleague Maximian's stepdaughter Theodora and thus divorce Constantine's mother. Helena and her son were then packed off to Byzantium, out of the way, but where a close eye could be kept on their activities.

The remains of the villa are sited around 5 kilometres out of town along a minor highway. Lying on the south bank of the Sava river, this was the main route through the Balkans to Serdica in Thracia, and Mediana became the favoured location for the out-of-town properties of those wishing to escape the bustle and unhealthy atmosphere of the larger Roman settlement. The site lies in a wooded park, separated from the road by low walls. Approaching from a track, the low remains of a peristyle courtyard come into view. The site guardian is clearly not expecting much in the way of visitors and only reluctantly opens the museum, before warming to his task with a torrent of information delivered in Balkan-inflected French. The museum building houses Mediana's star piece, and the object around which the building itself was constructed. A Constantinian-era mosaic occupies a large central roundel several metres across, with three circular apse-shaped extensions creating private corners. Bands of lotus flowers and a series of crosses, swirls, knot-patterns and meanders fill the space of the black-and-white mosaic, whose high quality speaks of the prosperity of the villa's owners. This may indeed have been Constantine's private *triclinium*, a personal retreat when he returned to this place of his childhood.

The main villa complex was clearly very large, with a number of rooms set around the peristyle, but only the outlines and a couple of courses of brickwork have been reconstructed. Further to the east, a long rectangular building with double rows of internal columns and huge jars set into the ground must have been some kind of storage chamber. Nearby, a larger complex represents the imperial baths, with a rectangular room still possessing a hypocaust and a small semicircular apse for a pool. The rest of the site is largely unexcavated, a great expanse of field pitted with excavators' trenches and a few wooden shelters where structures of particular importance have been unearthed. Under one of them lies a recently discovered palaeo-Christian church, the floor of the apse just visible beneath plastic sheeting.

It is scarcely surprising to find an early Christian church in the birthplace of Constantine, who has found everlasting fame as the first Christian emperor. It is hard now to untangle the route by which Constantine reached Christianity and his motives in espousing the new religion, or indeed the real level of his commitment to it. The 2nd and 3rd centuries had seen an increase in the popularity of 'mystery cults' and in the occurrence of inscriptions that invoked gods such as Zeus Hypistos (Zeus the Greatest)[98] – a tendency towards recognising one of the deities in the pantheon as the supreme one, which is referred to as henotheism (as opposed to monotheism, which only accepts the existence of a single god and denies the reality of the rest). Three decades before Constantine, Aurelian seems to have favoured the worship of the Sun (Sol Invictus) as a single unifying cult for the Empire,[99] while under the Tetrarchy the promotion of the cults of Jove and Hercules, the protectors respectively of Diocletian and Maximian, seems to indicate official imperial support for a simplified pantheon, which might help bolster the position of a new imperial system.

Narratives that were written during Constantine's reign, such as the *Vita Constantini* of Eusebius, Bishop of Caesarea, have something of the hagiographical about them, and the bishop even implies that Constantine's father, Constantius Chlorus, was practically a Christian himself. Constantine, though, had shown little evidence of Christian sympathies during the early stages of his rise. The panegyrist who delivered a speech in praise of him in 310 was happily able to claim that the Emperor had received a vision of Apollo, who had offered him a laurel wreath in token of a reign that would last many years,[100] while the coinage of the time depicts him as being associated with Hercules and Mars. Then, from 310 Constantine promoted the image of the sun god, of whom Aurelian had been so fond.

By summer 311, the appalling political mess that had followed Diocletian and Maximian's abdication in 305 had begun to resolve itself somewhat, with the untimely death of Galerius. He had been suffering from some kind of malignant ulcer in his genitals, which may have been associated with bowel cancer and caused him the most indescribable torment – a fact that Christian authors related with unholy relish, ascribing it to God's revenge for the persecutions he had earlier unleashed on their co-religionists.[101] On 30 April 311, as he lay dying, Galerius issued an edict in which he ordered an end to the persecutions and allowed the Christians to return to the worship of their God. It did him no good, for a few days later he died in the utmost agony. Constantine now made a bargain with Licinius, one of the surviving emperors in the East, that in exchange for his support against Maximin Daia there, Constantine would be given a free rein to deal with Maxentius in the West. To seal the alliance, Licinius was to marry Constantine's sister Constantia.

It was at some point during his march against Maxentius that Constantine appears to have received – or believed he had – some kind of vision from the Christian God. Advancing rapidly with a relatively small force, and brushing aside Maxentius's army near Segusio (Susa), he reached Rome in late October 312. It might well have been here that the Constantinian enterprise ended, for he had nothing like the strength to invest Rome completely, so all Maxentius had to do was wait for his opponent's supplies to dry up or for the support of his legions to ebb away. Constantine would then have faced ignominious retreat, or worse. Maxentius had seen off previous challenges by Severus (whom he actually succeeded in capturing) early in 307 and by Galerius later that year, precisely by waiting behind Rome's powerful fortifications and watching the loyalty of his opponents' troops waver.

Yet this time he made the fatal error of marching out of Rome to give battle. Things were not so favourable for him as in 307; he was deprived of the residual loyalty to his father, the former Augustus Maximian, who had committed suicide in 310, and Maxentius had unleashed his praetorian guard on the population of Rome after a fire at the Temple of Fortuna in 309, leading to the death of perhaps 6,000 civilians and irreparably damaging a crucial reservoir of support for his regime. On 28 October, at Saxa Rubra, 14 kilometres from Rome, his army was routed and in its retreat back to the city was caught in the bottleneck over the Milvian Bridge crossing, and huge numbers were slaughtered or drowned, including Maxentius himself, whose body washed up the next day and whose head was then paraded on a pike.

The dedicator of the Arch of Constantine in the Forum at Rome ascribed his victory to 'the inspiration of a divinity' (*instinctu divinitatis*), a suitably vague formulation, which might as well apply to a pagan deity as to a Christian one. Lactantius,[102] however, writes that Constantine received a dream shortly before the Battle of the Milvian Bridge in which he was told to have all his soldiers mark the 'heavenly sign of God' upon their shields in the form of a Cross with a hook that formed a P-shape. This 'Chi-Rho' monogram was subsequently to become a characteristic symbol of those claiming Christian allegiance. According to the version in Eusebius, Constantine – overcome by the weight of the task facing him in dislodging Maxentius from his Roman stronghold – had prayed to the Christian God, asking for a sign.[103] After he did so, he saw a fiery cross in the sky, and alongside it the message *In hoc signo victor eris* ('By this sign you will conquer').

Although accounts of these portents were written down some years later and with the benefit of hindsight, it is clear that Constantine ascribed some role to the Christian God in his victory over Maxentius, for on taking control of Rome he promptly exempted the clergy from civic duties and ordered a lavish programme of construction of new Christian buildings. He ordered the barracks that had housed Maxentius's cavalry guard to be demolished and on the site was erected a grand new basilica – the traditional form of a civic meeting house – as a place of worship for the Christians. This new cathedral, initially known as the Basilica Constantiniana, would later (from its proximity to the imperial Lateran Palace) take on the name of San Giovanni in Laterano. Within a decade, work had also begun on the Church of Saint Peter over the site of the martyr shrine of the apostle, which would, in time, become the head-quarters of the Western Christian Church.

Constantine now cemented his accord with Licinius by celebrating the previously agreed marriage of Licinius and his sister Constantia at Milan. After the festivities the two emperors agreed on the issuing of a decree of religious toleration, which has become known as 'The Edict of Milan'.[104] It was specifically aimed at permitting Christian activity, for it refers to freedom of worship for 'Christians and to all people', and repeals point by point the disabilities under which Christians had laboured since Diocletian had launched the Great Persecution in 303.

Once Constantine had finally disposed of Licinius in 324,[105] he issued further edicts to enforce the restitution of any property in the eastern provinces that had been confiscated from Christian individuals or churches on the grounds of their religion. Christianity was now free of persecution and the unchallenged religion of the victorious ruling clique. Anyone who wanted to curry favour with the Emperor would find it convenient to be a Christian. There would be pagan reactions in the future, most notably under Julian in the mid-360s, but within two gener-ations the Christian Church had established itself so securely that dislodging it from its central religious (and, increasingly, social and polit-ical) role would prove impossible. Within a century the pagan temples had closed, public sacrifice had been forbidden on pain of death and, while there were still pagans in positions of public authority,[106] they had no power – or mostly any intention – to turn back the tide of religious policy in favour of the traditional cults. Rites such as the *Parilia*, the cele-bration of the birthday of Rome, would persist into the early Middle Ages, but more as traditional folk festivals than as any real survival of pagan practice and belief.

Aside from Mediana, precious little survives of ancient Naissus. A curious reminder of the great Emperor stands, however, some kilo-metres from it. Niš airport is officially named 'Constantine the Great' (or Konstantin Veliki in Serbian). It is the only such facility anywhere to have been named after a Roman emperor, and so, uniquely, travellers from the terminal flying off to Switzerland or Montenegro can pause a moment for contemplation of perhaps the most famous Serbian of them all.

The Turkish fortress dominates the older part of town near the river. Its ramparts are forbiddingly high, but only a single ditch protects it. Inside, in the late-afternoon chill, a couple of open-air cafés and souvenir stalls struggle on, and beyond them in a section a few metres square are some Roman remains, parts of brick piers and walls. Another similar area lies scooped out from the basement of a disused mosque. Beyond, up a slight slope leading away from the main path through the fort, is a longer structure with large rectangular rooms or vaults, each one with an arch. Above these a double-arched entrance leads into yet another rubble and rubbish-choked chamber. It is clear that the fortress mound must be honeycombed with Roman remains, but they lie undisturbed beneath the coffee-houses and the tread of locals taking a quick evening stroll before darkness falls. In the centre of the fort-park, a Roman necropolis was unearthed and a selection of the finds has been arrayed in a somewhat neglected lapidary garden. One tombstone memorialises two sisters, both called Attidia, while another sports a delicately carved dolphin-like sea monster.

Naissus was to be the birthplace of two more Roman emperors: Constantius III, one of the West's last really able military commanders,[107] and Justin, one of the first of the renaissance of the Empire in the East, who was born in the nearby settlement of Bederiania. Around 470, he set out from Naissus with two companions, Zimarchus and Dityvistus, to try and seek their fortunes at Constantinople. Of Justin's two friends, nothing further was heard, but he managed to secure himself a position in the *Excubitores*, the new palace guard that Emperor Leo (457–74) was then establishing. Over time Justin rose to be the commander of the unit, and he brought over his young nephew Petrus Sabbatius[108] to take advantage of his good fortune. In due course, and certainly before 520, he adopted the young man, who then changed his name to Justinianus (known, in turn, to historians as Justinian). The accession of his uncle to the throne in 518 opened the way for the young Justinian to become one of the Eastern Empire's most successful rulers.[109]

It was to be Naissus's last moment of glory. The new Emperor refortified the town, though not particularly out of any sense of nostalgia, for he strengthened the Danube defences in general. However, it fell to the Slavs in 578 and then to the Avars in the late 6th century, after which organised occupation of the site ceased. Instead Justinian lavished his imperial building instincts on Constantinople and on the town of Justiniana Prima, which lay near his birthplace. The latter's location is not certain, but is probably the extensive site that lies near Caričin Grad, close to Lescovac in southern Serbia.[110]

From Niš, the road climbs gradually, crossing over the edge of the Stara Planina, the mountain range that strikes across central Bulgaria and which divided Moesia from the plain of Thrace to the south-east. Around 10 kilometres west of modern Zaječar, and about 70 from the line of the Danube, lies the 4th-century palace complex of Felix Romuliana, built by Galerius near the village where he had been born, and which he intended to be his place of retirement. Diocletian had set the precedent in 305 when he stepped down voluntarily from the imperial office, maintaining that he had achieved all that he wished and that he was tired – an unprecedented relinquishing of supreme power. He had the vast fortified palace at Spalato (Split) prepared for this eventuality, and there he spent his last years, tending (as he claimed on his one brief foray back into imperial politics) his cabbages.[111]

From the parking lot, the bulk of two large, round projecting towers greet visitors to the site of Felix Romuliana, a token that this was not just any old imperial residence. The retirement of former emperors had proved a troublesome affair, as Maximian's misbehaviour before and after the Carnuntum Conference in 308 had proven, and the towers are a reminder of the military detachment that would have manned the palace complex; though ostensibly their job would have been to maintain an appropriate sense of dignity and the basic security of such an eminent person, it might equally have been to keep an eye on any intrigues in which he might become involved.

The wall on this side of the palace is almost complete, punctuated by interval towers, presenting a formal obstacle for casual marauders, though not perhaps much of an impediment for more organised forces. The double-gateway has a further interior tower, for additional protection, and, inside a whole array of remains, in a huge area some 6 hectares in extent,[112] presents itself: basilicas, temples and baths. Everything, in short, that an ex-emperor could possibly desire, save the power that he had voluntarily laid down. Now inaccessible on a hillside a kilometre away, the track to it cut off by mud caused by heavy rain and snow, lies the Margura, the mausoleum that Galerius constructed for his mother, Romula, so that, during his declining years, he would be able to gaze upon and visit her last resting place. The name of the palace, too, derives from Galerius's sense of filial piety: Felix Romuliana ('the fortunate place of Romula'), but it was never so lucky for him.

Galerius's rise to fortune had been rapid, one of the almost common-place success stories of the hard school of the Danubian armies in the 3rd century. Having begun his career as a herdsman, an occupation that he inherited from his father, Galerius sought better prospects in the army and fought with some distinction under Aurelius and Probus. When Diocletian established the Tetrarchy, Galerius was well known to him and was an obvious choice to be the Caesar, or junior Emperor, to Maximian in the East. His base was to be Illyricum and the Balkans.

In 305, when Maximian and Diocletian retired and Galerius became Augustus (together with Constantius I in the West), he chose his nephew Maximin Daia, another local lad, to be his Caesar. It was probably Galerius who had been responsible for persuading Diocletian to unleash the Great Persecution against the Christians in 303 and, now that he was answerable to no one, his thirst for targeting them increased. He is, indeed, one of the principal targets of the Christian writer Lactantius in his *De Mortibus Persecutorum* ('On the Death of the Persecutors'). Yet Galerius's ambitions to rule the Empire as the pre-eminent among the four emperors, just as Diocletian had done, were ultimately thwarted by the upstart Constantine. Even Galerius's move to cut off Constantine's route to the top by appointing Licinius (another Moesian) as the second Augustus in 308 was unable to stop his young rival's rise. Galerius never lived to enjoy his peaceful retirement at Felix Romuliana, dying in 311. Once Constantine had eliminated all his rival emperors by 324, the Tetrarchy – and with it the tradition of emperors' retiring once they had reached an appropriate age – was never again revived or proposed.

The little site museum preserves a few architectural fragments; on one the name of the palace is inscribed in a wreath supported by two peacocks sporting crowns and, most notably, a beautiful bust of Galerius in imperial porphyry, its deep-purple colour lightly speckled in white. The Emperor seems stern, and the sketchy, stylised lines of his facial features give him a faintly surprised and suffering air, as though resigned to the trials that overcame him almost the moment he achieved supreme power.

The first section of the palace has a peristyle courtyard, off which leads the unmistakable shape of a basilica. The presence of churches on the site, despite Galerius's persecuting policy, is not a surprise, for the palace remained in use as a garrison and then a small town into the 7th century, and the former palace buildings were adapted, including through the construction of Christian places of worship.

Steps to the west lead up to a largish platform, which is indeed a pagan one, possibly a temple of Cybele.[113] To the side of this lies another hall with an apse, partly cut off, later reduced in size by the building of walls of a different stone from the left and right wings. The far wall of the town, opposite the main entrance, is less impressively preserved, just an earthwork rampart still standing, with only the gateway surviving in stone. Off from this the remains of a colonnade lead to a bulky rectangular structure on a podium with no apparent means of entrance.

With the premature death of Galerius, and the small town that grew up on the palace site suffering so severely from barbarian attacks from the 4th century onwards, Felix Romuliana never acquired the degree of permanency of settlements such as Singidunum, Vindobona or, for that matter, Diocletian's own palace at Salonae (Split). Galerius did at least come home to Felix Romuliana in death, for he was interred in a second mausoleum at Margura, next to his mother. As we leave, a mist descends and a haunting otherworldly lament wafts in from somewhere amongst the hills, sweet, yet chilling. It is probably the song of a shepherdess, but it seems instead to be a lament on the pain endured by an emperor, and the power that brought him no joy.

The road from Serbia passes east along the Danube into Bulgaria not far from the small town of Kula, about 30 kilometres east of Felix Romuliana. The run-down main street is made more attractive by a carpet of snow and swirling wind-blown flakes that promise an even deeper covering. Alongside its main square sits the remains of the fort of Castra Martis, a military station on the ancient road from Naissus to Bononia (Vidin). It never housed a large garrison, nor was it in itself of huge importance, but the loneliness and grandeur of its ruins in such an unlikely setting are one of the secret gems of the Danubian *limes*. Its sides 30 metres long, the square fort in its current form dates from around the late 3rd or early 4th century. Inside the bulky curtain walls, two rows of barracks with a central pier run down the middle. One's eye, though, is immediately drawn to the angle tower to the south-east, which soars to more than 16 metres high in one part, probably lacking only a metre or so of its original height. For three-quarters of its diameter more of the tower's top portions are missing, and the great ruined silhouette pushes out dramatically against the snow-laden sky. It is one of the most striking pieces of military architecture on the frontier.

Castra Martis's efforts to remain a discrete and untroubled garrison fortress were rudely brought to an end in 408, with the first serious irruption of the Huns across the Danube into the Empire. Pushing forward from a homeland somewhere in central Asia, the Huns were involved in a complex movement of peoples that was part domino effect, as one group pushed forward in search of new lands and propelled those in front of them further from the steppes and towards the Mediterranean littoral, and part the magnetic pull of the Roman Empire, which attracted 'barbarian' groups with its promise of easy wealth and an end to the constant struggle for land and food to which they had grown accustomed.

Attempts to link the Huns to the 'Xiongnu' on China's northern frontier in the 1st century BC are somewhat tenuous, but do reveal that the challenges facing the Roman Empire were not dissimilar to those experienced by its late Han Chinese counterpart. Wherever they came from, the Huns became the bogeymen of late antiquity. Ammianus Marcellinus describes them as squat, with thick necks and so ugly that they seemed like figures crudely carved out of wood.[114] They cut the cheeks of their boys to create patterns of scars, and their legs were bowed from constant life on horseback, so that they found it uncomfortable to dismount and walk. Of course, Ammianus most likely had little direct experience of the Huns himself, and his descriptions are purely conventional ones. Yet, real or not, these attributes were melded with a reputation for ferocity that, once they had united under the leadership of Attila, made them the barbarians whom the Romans most feared.

In 395, they had given notice of their future intentions when they rode around the Black Sea and descended on Georgia, Armenia and even into Syria. Saint Jerome in his Bethlehem monastery referred to them as 'wolves of the North', who ranged so widely and rapidly that no one knew where to expect their arrival next.[115] By 400 the Huns were led by Uldin, who is first recorded for his killing in that year of Gainas, the refugee Gothic former *magister militum* and effective head of the government at Constantinople, who had fallen foul of an anti-barbarian coup in the city. In 404–5, Uldin crossed the Danube and ravaged part of Moesia, and then, three years later, he crossed in greater force, capturing Castra Martis, before his raiding band was broken up by a Roman army that was rushed to the scene and he was forced back across the Danube.

Little more was heard of the Huns for some decades, as they seem to have expended their energies on consolidating control over other tribes in central and eastern Europe, rather than on confronting the Romans directly. It was around this time that the teenage Aëtius spent some years as a hostage amongst them, and his subsequent use of them as mercenaries in the 420s may actually have revived their interest in the gain to be had from plundering or blackmailing the Roman state.[116] By the 430s they were led by Ruga, who had expanded Hunnish control over a large area based on a heartland in central Hungary before he was, according to a dramatic account given by the Church historian Socrates, struck dead by lightning.[117] If it was divine retribution for his crimes, then God may later have had cause to reconsider, for Ruga was succeeded by his nephews Bleda and Attila, the latter of whom would become infamous as the *Flagellum Dei* ('scourge of God').

The pretext for the brothers' assault, and the start of a fifteen-year campaign that would almost bring the Empire to its knees, seems to have been a little freelance looting on the part of the Bishop of Margum, who was alleged to have connived in the ransacking of certain royal tombs across the Danube. They were probably not Hunnish graves, but it represented an intrusion into their domain that Attila and Bleda chose not to tolerate. In response, they led a great force south of the Danube, capturing and sacking Viminacium (Kostolac), Singidunum (Belgrade) and a great number of other towns, including Margum itself, whose gates the treacherous bishop left open in return for being allowed to escape. The Huns finally turned back, mollified by the promise of a satisfying stream of tribute.

The respite was strictly temporary, and before long a vast swathe of territory to the south of the Danube was laid waste and the area fell so much under the dominion of the Huns that Attila later claimed that the boundary between the Hunnish and Roman territory lay not, as it traditionally had, on the Danube, but at Naissus, some three days' journey to the south. And so it remained until 449. In that year, an embassy from Attila to Theodosius II arrived in Constantinople.[118] The return embassy included the historian and diplomat Priscus, who left a detailed account of his journey (in a more general history of the Empire of which, unfortunately, only fragments survive).[119] His description of Attila's headquarters, which have been variously located in Hungary[120] or even close to Kula,[121] contains the surprising revelation that it included a bath complex, built in stone by a Roman architect captured at Sirmium.[122]

The impression that Attila's was no mere crude encampment, but had achieved a level of sophistication that belies the Huns' reputation for gross barbarity, is reinforced by Priscus's encounter with a merchant from Viminacium. Captured by the Huns in the recent wars, he had set up business again on the Hunnish side of the *limes* and, even though he had amassed enough wealth to buy his freedom, was doing sufficiently well that he chose not to return to Roman territory and face the oppressive taxation and capricious bureaucracy that he insisted he would find there.[123]

It is just 35 kilometres north-east from Kula to Vidin, which was the settlement of Bononia in Roman times, its Latin name sharing a root with its much more famous cousins of Bologna in Italy and Boulogne in France. The Ottoman-era Baba Vida fortress, its rounded towers and deep moat dominating the riverside section of the old town, incorporates what remains of Bononia – indeed, at the base of the north-west wall traces of much older masonry may hint at the original Roman fort that stood on the site to protect this stretch of the Danube *limes*.

Half an hour to the east along a loop in the river lay Ratiaria, once a legionary fortress, now surviving in much-reduced circumstances near the small village of Arcar, some 25 kilometres to the south-east of Vidin. It started life as a garrison camp in the late 1st century AD, and after Trajan's conquest of Dacia was demilitarised and raised to the rank of a *colonia* as Colonia Ulpia Traiana Ratiaria. After the evacuation of Dacia in the 270s, Ratiaria became the capital of the newly created province of Dacia Ripensis on the south bank of the Danube, and once again received a garrison, this time the XIII Gemina legion. In 441 it was captured and destroyed by the Huns, but restored in the late 5th century under Anastasius, in whose honour it took the name Anastasiana Ratiaria. It was finally overrun by the Avars in 586, following which it was abandoned.

The only evidence today from the road of the formerly prosperous town is a café named 'Ratiaria'. Here enquiries about the ancient fortress are met with blank, self-conscious looks; finally one old lady has no idea about a Roman site, but wonders if we want the place 'where the gold-seekers are digging'. To the north of the road, in dense undergrowth, we still find no trace of the Roman remains, but encounter a boy of about fourteen, dragging behind him a dilapidated-looking metal detector; the contraption itself, rust-caked and mud-spattered, seems to merit the label of antiquity. He rather cagily dismisses the notion of a Roman site and directs us in another direction. Here an aged shepherd, his face lined by years in the outdoors performing an honest occupation, at last knows what we are looking for. He himself had worked as a driver on the excavation of Ratiaria in the 1980s, and had transported a whole sarcophagus down to the national museum in Sofia.

Back on the other side of the road, up a low, sloping side-road, an open area stretches out besides a terrace of single-storey houses. It seems composed of a series of small grassy hummocks stretching out as far as the eye can see. Walking a short way into this field, it is clear that we are not the first visitors. The whole place is pitted with holes and trenches, some shallow, others metres deep. The hummocks we saw at first are simply the areas where the 'gold-seekers' of whom the old lady spoke have not yet dug. The ground is soft underfoot as we step over the spoil of these illicit excavations, the brown mud disturbed by their works caking our boots.

Ratiaria was researched properly in the 1980s, particularly in the south-western corner, where several *insulae* were dug up, including a bath complex, and sections of the 4th-century wall and fortifications were revealed.[124] But in 1992, in the wake of the collapse of the communist regime in Bulgaria, the money for such research dried up. Once the official archaeologists had packed their bags and left the site, unofficial digs began on a grand scale. The result was the total destruction of an antique city, with trenches and holes sunk throughout the area of the original excavations and across an area many times its size – which did reveal, incidentally, that estimates of the area covered by Ratiaria gained from aerial photography were more or less correct.

Everywhere now there are bits of pot and tile, the remains of everyday life in Ratiaria considered by the looters not attractive enough for the international market in stolen antiquities. Here and there a fragment of green marble and a larger piece of white-flecked marble about 15 centi-metres long pokes out from the side of a robber trench. Occasionally pieces of stonework protrude, largely undisturbed, for the skeleton of the city did not interest the treasure-seekers, but only the flesh they could easily strip from its bones. One part seems to be the remains of a rectangular building with four or five courses of stone, but it seems like a stranded survivor amongst the scene of utter devastation.

The pockmarks of the illicit dig stretch for more than a kilometre and some of the trenches seem relatively recent. The destruction of the Roman city stands as one of Europe's cultural disgraces and it is hard not to form the impression that, after destruction by the Huns and the Avars, Ratiaria has suffered its third and most comprehensive sacking only in the last fifteen years.

The Huns were by no means the last nomadic group to arise on the central Asian steppes, sweep westwards and create havoc on the Roman frontier. The Avars first appeared in the area of modern Ukraine around the 550s, viewed by the Byzantines as potentially useful allies in the volatile mix of nomads swirling around the northern Balkans. They were soon apprised of their mistake as the Avars smashed first the Kutrigurs and Utrigurs, and then in 567 proceeded to destroy the Gepids.[125] The Avars' own Lombard allies, afraid that they were to be next, migrated en masse southwards into Italy, knocking over at a stroke the Byzantine control of the peninsula that had been so painfully won in the Gothic Wars just fifteen years previously.

The Avars did not rest on their laurels, pushing south over the Danube

Hadrian's Wall, near Vercovicium (Housesteads) fort, Britannia

Hadrian's Wall, looking towards
Housesteads Crags

The *mithraeum* at
Carrawburgh, Britannia

The chalet-style
barracks at
Cilurnum (Chesters)
fort, Britannia

Interior ditches and wall, Rutupiae (Richborough) fort, Britannia

South wall, Rutupiae (Richborough)

Ditch and embankment of the Antonine Wall at Watling Lodge, Britannia

The Porta Nigra, Augusta Treverorum (Trier), Gallia Belgica

Pfäffikon fort, Germania Superior

Reconstructed watchtower and palisade at Grab, Germania Superior

Caldarium of the Kaiserthermen,
Augusta Treverorum (Trier),
Gallia Belgica

Roman wall tower, Bodobriga
(Boppard), Germania Superior

Reconstructed city gate, Colonia Ulpia Traiana (Xanten), Germania Inferior

Reconstructed west wall and tower, Pfünz, Raetia

The *porta praetoria* at Castra Regina (Regensburg), Raetia

Statue of Saint Severinus, Boiotro (Passau) fort, Noricum

Section of the Raetian wall in Mahdholz woods, Raetia

Castra Martis (Kula) fort, Moesia Superior

The Heidentor, Carnuntum (Petronell), Pannonia Superior

Decumanus maximus of Nicopolis-ad-Istrum, Thracia / Moesia Inferior

Porphyry bust of Galerius from Felix Romuliana, Moesia Superior

Metope from the Tropaeum Traiani (Adamclisi), Moesia Inferior

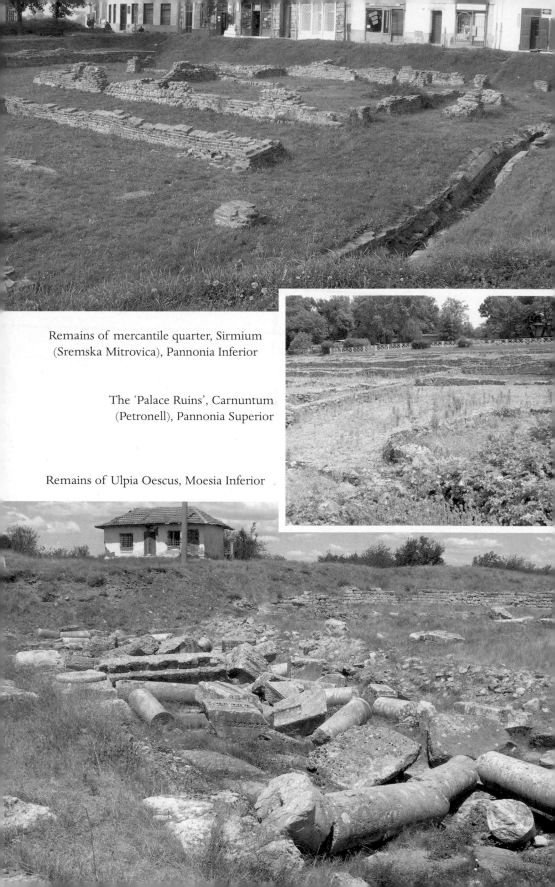

Remains of mercantile quarter, Sirmium
(Sremska Mitrovica), Pannonia Inferior

The 'Palace Ruins', Carnuntum
(Petronell), Pannonia Superior

Remains of Ulpia Oescus, Moesia Inferior

Modern monumental
sculpture of
Decebalus, Dacia

Remains of Roman
bridge, Drobeta
(Turnu-Severin), Dacia

Dacian temple, Sarmizegetusa Regia, Dacia

Amphitheatre, Porolissum, Dacia

The Romans cross the Danube. Trajan's Column, Rome

Church of Our Saviour, Ani, Armenia

Ruins at Satala (Sadagh), Cappadocia

The *Hierothesion* at Nemrud Dagh, Cappadocia

Palace of the Comneni, (Trebizond) Trabzon, Cappadocia

Frescoes at Soumela monastery, Cappadocia

Roman bridge at Cendere, Cappadocia

The 'catapult', Edessa (Sanliurfa), Osroene

Church of Meryemanna in the Tur Abdin, Mesopotamia

and capturing Sirmium in 581–2, thus providing them with a bridgehead from which they could raid at will into the Balkan plains. Their expansion also displaced the Slavs, who had occupied the plain between the lower Danube and the Carpathians in the 6th century, but who now moved southwards in earnest, switching from small-scale raids from their forest hideouts to full-scale ravaging of the southern Balkans. Only in 591 did a peace treaty with the Sassanid Persians enable Emperor Maurice to switch his military resources westwards and begin to repair the much-breached frontier.[126]

The renewed Sassanid invasion in 602 undermined this policy and the Avars resumed their expansion southwards towards the Peloponnese. In 623, Heraclius, desperate for peace on his western flank in order to reverse the devastating Persian advances that had overrun almost the whole of the East, arranged a parley with the Avar leader, the kagan, in Thrace. The Avar ruler, scenting weakness, instead tried to capture the Byzantine Emperor and Heraclius was forced to beat a humiliating retreat to Constantinople, and then watch the Avars as they ravaged the suburbs of the capital. Only a timely payment of 200,000 numismata per year was able to buy off the barbarians. It was not enough, and three years later the kagan moved on the imperial city once more, this time orchestrated with a Persian assault from the east. With Heraclius campaigning far away in Armenia, it looked as if the Empire was finished. But the Avars' attempts at a seaborne assault on the city wall using light canoes were broken up by the Byzantine fleet, and their confused bid to ferry the Persians over ended in a similar disaster. Disenchanted at being robbed of a prize that seemed so easily within their grasp, the Slavs in the Avar force revolted, and the whole army withdrew from Constantinople in disarray.

The Slavs themselves were to prove rather more durable than the Avars, who were finally smashed by Charlemagne's Franks in the early 9th century. They formed part of a second wave of barbarian invasions that threatened to overwhelm the Eastern Roman Empire in the 500s, just as it appeared to have weathered the storm that overcame the western provinces in the previous century. It is possible that there were Slavs in the multi-ethnic confederacy that made up the Hunnish Empire, and some allusions in Priscus (who visited Attila's court in 448) have been taken to refer to them, such as the use of *monoxyles*, or boats scooped out from hollow logs.[127]

By the 6th century, Justinian was having to deal with a group called the Sclavini (most likely the Slavs) who streamed into the Balkan peninsula from their lands north of the Danube;[128] by 528 they were menacing

Thrace, and a particularly severe raid in 550–1 even threatened Constantinople. Tiberius (578–82) was so desperate that he enlisted the kagan Baian of the Avars to push the Sclavini out of the Balkan provinces. Despite cutting a destructive swathe through the Balkans and looting and sacking Slav outposts, the Avars were unsuccessful in their main mission, and within a decade were making common cause with the Sclavini in causing mayhem south of the Danube. Throughout eastern Pannonia, Moesia and Thrace the Sclavini came to stay, forming the nucleus of the modern Slavic-speaking countries in those areas.

In the east they merged with the Bulgars, who had first appeared in the guise of the Kutrigurs and Utrigurs during the reign of Zeno and who were to form the principal challenge to the re-establishment of Byzantine dominance in Thrace during the early medieval period. Although the Byzantines managed to recover the southern Balkans from the Slav tribes by the 8th century, in the areas of modern Serbia and Bulgaria they ever afterwards had to contend with Slav tribal confederacies that ultimately coalesced, in the early Middle Ages, into kingdoms. If there was a victory, it was a cultural one, for in the end the Slav kingdoms – such as Serbia, and most particularly Bulgaria – came to form part of a 'Byzantine commonwealth', influenced in religion, language and expectations by the norms of Constantinople. Ultimately this Byzantine inflection was transmitted even to Russia, which was unashamedly able to declare itself the 'Third Rome' after the fall of Constantinople in 1453.

Moesia Inferior

Around 150 kilometres south-east down the Danube from Vidin, and about 40 kilometres north of modern Pleven, lies the legionary fort of Oescus. It served as one of the two legionary bases for Moesia Inferior, whose western border lay just to the east of Ratiaria (Arcar). To travel along this stretch of the river is truly to take a step back in time. The main roads become an obstacle course of ruts and potholes, the principal traffic on them ceases to be motorised, as horse-drawn carts predominate, and on chimneys and other architectural high-points, families of storks lazily watch the world go slowly by. Oescus itself sits on a low plateau set back a few kilometres from the Danube, and was originally a Thracian settlement, referred to by the geographer Ptolemy as Oescus Triballorum.[129]

The first Roman fortification in stone may have been built here under Domitian about 85–6, at the time of his invasion of Dacia, or else at the start of the 2nd century, shortly before Oescus's garrison (the V Macedonica) departed following Trajan's more successful Dacian campaign. The city, now a civilian settlement, was made a *colonia* by Trajan, and took on his family name of Ulpius to become Ulpia Oescus. It underwent rapid expansion, though it suffered badly during the Gothic invasion of 250–1, and its wall needed to be repaired afterwards. Within twenty years or so, however, Dacia had been evacuated and Oescus got back its legion – much, it must be presumed, to the relief of its inhabitants.

There is little to be seen of the walls now. Backing onto their original location, towards the main gate, lies the 'extra-mural' complex, constructed, as its name suggests, beyond the original city perimeter. It is a massive collection of largely rectangular rooms, with two apsed chambers to one end. The outside walls are solid and bulky, but the inside ones have internal corridors penetrated by pipes. It is unclear what purpose these served, although one plausible theory is to allow for extra ventilation.

The first significant buildings visible in the eastern sector of the city are the baths, built in the 2nd century, of which the only restored section is a rectangular room, bordered by two smaller ones, in which a square stone basin sits. On the day of our visit, the area around is being cleared by teams of local ladies, for a television team is visiting the next day to do a feature on Oescus, and this high-level visit has prompted some fitful hoeing in the almost forty-degree heat.

In the city centre, to the south of what is probably the forum, lie the remains of the Temple of Fortuna, one of Oescus's principal public buildings. Once a splendid affair, some 30 metres long with a Corinthian portico, it was erected under Commodus, but is now utterly ruined. Whether it was destroyed by raiding Goths or as part of one of the outbreaks of temple-sacking by Christians in the late 4th century is unclear, but whichever party was responsible, the job was thorough. Fractured columns lie in heaps, shattered architraves keeping company with bits of pediment and smaller piles of inscrutable fragments. The sole area that retains any sense of order was in fact cleared in the 12th century to create space on which to construct a church. Out of the devastation peep floral designs, garlands, Medusa heads and eagles, all melancholy reminders of the temple at the height of its splendour.

Another structure nearby, more than 70 metres long, occupied a whole city block. There remain just the traces of hypocausts with brick piers and an apsed room more than 20 metres long. Here was found a mosaic showing a scene from the *Achaeans* by the playwright Menander. The chance nature of the survival of ancient manuscripts is highlighted by the fact that, until the mosaic depiction was discovered, the play itself was totally unknown (and its text has been completely lost). To the north lies the forum itself, where huge sections of columns and capitals mark the portico, and beside it the council chamber. This would have been a place humming with life, but apart from the women clearing the weeds beside the baths, Oescus's only inhabitants today are a couple of startled rabbits, which at our approach make a break for the city's gate.

At the edge of the excavated area of the city, a low mound gives a good view over the plain that leads down to the Danube a few kilometres away. It was here that Constantine came in July 328 to inaugurate a new bridge across the Danube, linking Oescus with the bridgehead fort at Sucidava in modern Romania.[130] It was a massive undertaking, at 2,400 metres long the longest bridge in classical antiquity, and indicates that communication with (and possible conquest of) the northern bank was still very much on the Roman agenda. It coincided with a general strengthening of the Danube *limes*, which was experiencing a period of relative stability between the storms of the mid-3rd century invasions and the disastrous Gothic incursions a century later.

Fifty kilometres further east along the river – but, with the lamentable state of the roads in the region, a much longer journey than one might suppose – lies the legionary camp at Novae.[131] For roughly the first two decades of its career, from AD 46 to 69, it housed the VIII Augusta legion, but after that unit's support for Otho during the 'Year of the Four Emperors' the legion was transferred away to the Rhineland, where it then spent the best part of three centuries based at Argentorate (Strasbourg). Its replacement was the I Italica legion, which in turn resided for almost 300 years at its Novae base.

Originally a Thracian settlement – of which nothing survives – Novae was situated at a strategic road junction and in a position to dominate one of the easier crossings over the Danube. Together with Oescus, it marks one of the densest concentrations of legionary force anywhere in the Empire – at least once the double legionary fortresses had been abolished – and is a strong testament to the strategically vital nature of the Danube *limes*.

A recent influx of archaeological investment in Bulgaria, much of it the fruit of European Union funding, has seen Novae build a smart new glass-domed visitor centre, the fort's most significant development in one and a half millennia. The main entrance to the site, through the camp's west gate, was originally a simple affair. In the 4th century, however, gate-towers were added, making it a much grander portal – the largest surviving one in Moesia – its outline still clear amid the carpet of grass and encroaching shrubs that threaten to engulf it. Along part of the curtain wall that joins onto the gate, large holes and indentations betray a vaulted passage, which might be used by the defenders as a sally port to catch attackers unawares and assail them from behind. The path through the site then diverts slightly into a small wood, before cutting north back into the fortress, which lies on a slight incline running down to the Danube. A chaotic jumble of walls, probably of several stages of construction, represents the officers' housing, which was replaced in the early 4th century by some kind of public building and later by a church.

The most splendid surviving vestige of ancient Novae is the *valetudinarium*, the hospital complex, a series of rectangular rooms, their walls restored and consolidated to above a metre high, arrayed around a central (presumably colonnaded) courtyard.[132] With the Danube just a hundred or so metres away and the opposite, Romanian bank, lined with a thin screen of trees, it seems an idyllic setting in which to spend some time recovering from wounds or fever. Beside it, a quick scramble down the 3-metre slope formed by the archaeologists' trenching to uncover the site, are the baths, solidly constructed but with little to indicate their original purpose, save a rectangular stone basin. In the corner of the hospital complex, just by the Danube, is the toilet, which must have had alarming consequences for the legionary water supply if its outflow went straight into the river.

A *municipium* from the time of Marcus Aurelius, Novae first experienced the uncertain times that lay ahead in the middle of the 3rd century, when it saw some fighting associated with the Gothic invasion under Cniva in 250–1. However, it remained throughout a legionary fortress, so the inhabitants of the town that grew up around it must have drawn some comfort from the presence of the troops, while less militarised parts of Pannonia and Moesia were easy prey for barbarian raiding.

Throughout this time, the I Italica stayed at Novae, although units of it had previously taken part in a series of external campaigns, from Trajan's conquest of Dacia in 101–6 to his later Parthian War, and possibly in Hadrian's suppression of the Bar Kochba revolt in Palestine in 132–5. By the end of its career at Novae, the legion had been split, with a portion of it based further east, at the Danube fleet base of Sexaginta Prista (modern Ruse). The pushing of the frontier of the Dacian province 50 kilometres eastward beyond the River Olt under Caracalla then almost created a situation where Novae, south of the Danube, would no longer have been on the frontier. But the Roman holdings in Dacia did not advance beyond its new *Limes Transalutanus*,[133] and Novae remained a military settlement.

Across the modern main road is the southern part of the camp, where the remains are, if anything, more extensive, sitting in a large, almost rectangular clearing about 150 x 200 metres. The portion nearest the road was originally the site of more baths,[134] but these were later supplanted by a huge Christian basilica, one of the largest in the Balkans at over 45 metres in length and about 25 metres or so in width,[135] a bulk that is impressive, even in its current overgrown state. A rank of brick stumps marks the base of the columns that delineated the aisles, but little else of the internal structure of the building is discernible. Novae was indeed the seat of a bishopric in the 5th and 6th centuries,[136] and to warrant a basilica as grand as this, the civilian population of the town must have been reasonably substantial.

Beyond these remains lie an almshouse and a pilgrims' hostel, only the outline remaining in a couple of stone courses, but their existence implies that the grand ecclesiastical complex attracted Christian visitors from far afield. Just visible in one corner, the remains of a furnace survive from the baths submerged beneath the Christian development. Next to the main basilica is a much more modest church, the 'Small basilica', only 12 metres or so in length; in the grass beside it pokes up a column on which the inscription 'SS MARI[A]' is just visible, possibly evidence of a church dedicated to Mary. Off to the east lie the remains of the *principia* of the original legionary camp; now an undifferentiated collection of stones, but a reminder that, whatever its subsequent growth, Novae always remained at heart a military centre.[137]

By the late 5th century the Roman hold on Moesia was growing weak. Already in 441 the Huns had passed through, devastating the area. Although the Hunnish Empire had collapsed into fratricidal squabbling following Attila's death in 453, the Romans were still not able to reassert full control over the area. Consequently, from 476 until 483, Novae served as the capital of the Ostrogothic king, Theoderic the Amal.[138] Once ensconced here, the Goths threatened the north–south routes over the Haemus mountains (the Stara Planina), allowing easy intervention in Thrace and permitting Theoderic a little judicious meddling in imperial politics to advance his cause even further. His large, well-organised barbarian kingdom based to the south of the Danube posed a potentially fatal challenge to the eastern Roman government, and Zeno came up with a cunning and mutually satisfactory ruse to persuade the Ostrogoths to move elsewhere.

It had been more than a decade since Odovacar, the Scirian general, had taken control of Italy. After his coup in 476, he had chosen not to elevate a new emperor; the dizzying succession of ineffectual imperial candidates had by the 470s become something of a nuisance for their barbarian sponsors. Instead, wishing to rule directly himself, but still conscious of diplomatic niceties, he despatched the imperial regalia back to Constantinople, in effect acknowledging Zeno as the sole Emperor, and implying that Odovacar ruled Italy on his behalf.

Zeno, however, muddied the issue by replying that there was still a legitimate Western Emperor, Julius Nepos, who had been pushed out of Italy in 475 and still skulked in the Illyrian province that had been the domain of his father, Count Marcellinus. But Nepos died in 480, and so there was then no obstacle to Zeno's despatch of Theoderic and his Ostrogoths into Italy. The campaign was prolonged, initially held up by the Gepids, who obstructed the Gothic advance near the modern city of Vukovar. But by 493 Theoderic was victorious and had Odovacar murdered at a banquet, displaying his grasp of table manners by cutting his guest in half with a single blow of his sword. More importantly, from Zeno's point of view, it opened the way for the reoccupation of the northern Balkans.

By Justinian's day, a quarter of a century later, Novae was back in eastern Roman hands, and, according to Procopius, new fortifications were built, though there is little evidence of these later defensive structures on the ground. Although most of the Christian buildings date from the late 5th or 6th centuries, and so the city was clearly occupied at the time, it seems that by the 7th century the effort required to hold it against waves of Slav, Bulgar and Avar invaders was just too great, and it was abandoned.

Around 50 kilometres south of the Danube at Novae, and lying just inside the province of Thrace at the foot of the Haemus mountains, the town of Nicopolis-ad-Istrum was founded by Trajan as the 'city of victory' in 102, in celebration of the battle that brought an end to the first Dacian War. It was part of a programme intended to strengthen the urban framework and economy of the Thracian plain. From here roads lead northwards to Novae and to Sexaginta Prista and southwards across the Stara Planina to Philippopolis (Plovdiv) in Thrace. It also stood on a road that led east–west to Odessos (Varna) on the Black Sea. To this day it stands on much more accessible routes than the poorly maintained arteries that sluggishly link the majority of towns along the Danube, and here, unlike the tourist deserts of Oescus or Novae, the occasional accent from Manchester or Manhattan is to be heard.

Close to the modern town of Nikup, in whose main square a few rather dusty and neglected column bases sit in a tiny sculpture garden, the remains of Nicopolis lie near a bend in the Rositsa river, down a country lane that is more pothole than thoroughfare. The main approach is through the remnants of the ancient city's western gate, up the former *decumanus*, its wide slabs smoothed with age. The area to the left is a combination of slightly overgrown grass and trees, with a few mounds and hummocks marking what must have been the southern edge of the city.

A collection of fallen columns, altars and the lids of monumental sarcophagi litter the ground, inscribed in Greek. Away from the influence of the Danube-based army, for whom Latin long persisted as the language of command, this part of Thrace was firmly in the Greek-speaking portion of the Empire, a tendency exacerbated by the pull of the old Greek settlements of the Black Sea coast, which were only a couple of days' journey away. Almost every educated Roman was expected to show some knowledge of Greek, and many were in prac-tice bilingual. From the reign of Hadrian, this tendency became even more pronounced.

The process was not a two-way one, and many in the Greek-speaking East spent their careers, if they were not in the central government, without displaying any evident knowledge of Latin. At many of the church councils in the 4th and 5th centuries the business was clearly done in Greek, and the minority of bishops who turned up from the West required interpreters if they could not, as was becoming more common by then, speak (or at least understand) Greek.[139] In the early 6th century, Justinian recognised the inevitable and decided that the language of governance should henceforth be Greek. It probably did not help his cause in trying to resecure the lost provinces of Italy, North Africa and Spain that they had been (and still were) Latin-speaking terri-tories, and therefore their acquisition by a new set of Byzantine officials might seem all the more alien, and not like the restoration of the old Roman Empire at all. With the loss of Carthage to the Arabs in 698, the Empire held almost no land that had been Latin-speaking in the 5th century, while the Arab conquest of the Syriac-speaking lands on its eastern border (and the Copts of Egypt) meant that it had become a wholly Greek affair.

Accentuating this imperial trend to Greekness, Nicopolis-ad-Istrum was established by Trajan not as a *colonia* or a *municipium*, but as a Hellenistic foundation, mirroring the constitutions of the ancient Greek city-states of the coast (and of Greece proper), rather than being organised on strictly speaking Roman lines.[140] Founded on a low plateau, it was laid out on a traditional grid pattern, with its north-eastern corner truncated as it sloped down to the River Rositsa, forming a rather irregular pentagonal shape. Only the central section around the forum (or *agora*) has been investigated, and an odd-shaped enclosure to the west of the main walls, revealed by aerial photography, might or might not be a fort.[141]

At the point where the *decumanus* crosses the *cardo*, the main excavated area is a large rectangle, scattered with stones, part overgrown with grass and weeds and bordered by straggly copses of low trees. Huge sections of architrave inscribed with floral decorations (and in just a few cases with fragments of inscription) lie everywhere, mostly sculpted from the limestone available in the nearby quarries at Honitsa. The architraves must have formed part of the portico of the forum, and much of this is missing. It seems hard to believe that such huge sections of stone could have been robbed, so sections of it must still lie buried.

Around the northern edge of the forum, a strip of the portico is more intact, with a few pieces of column still lying in place. Ahead, at the east, four great Corinthian columns rear up, forming a *propylaeum*, the monumental entrance to the forum. An inscription revealed that it was set up by Nicopolis in 145 in honour of Antoninus Pius and Marcus Aurelius. Behind lay the council house of the city, the *bouleuterion*, the remains of whose decrees, set in stone, sit now beneath a little shelter, as though stacked and filed in neat rows for easier consultation. The councillors' chambers and their seating, in contrast, lie mostly ruined.

To the south of the *bouleuterion* are the remains of a little theatre or *odeon*, whose orchestra was only a little over 9 metres in diameter. The seating is long gone, and only the semicircle of the raised platform on which it stood survives, rising about a metre from the ground, which makes it most unlikely that the place was ever used for gladiatorial spectacles, as it would have left the audience dangerously exposed. Behind are the ruins of shops and taverns, a few doorways still standing, one of them, in marble, totally unattached to any supporting wall, and looking like a ghostly portal into another world. A little way beyond the *odeon*, the excavated portion of the site peters out. Low mounds from which protrude telltale pieces of stone and the detritus of shattered columns, all tangled in increasingly thick undergrowth, betray the presence of as-yet-uncovered sections of the city.

The evidence of inscriptions from Nicopolis seems to indicate a heavy oriental influence, with immigrants coming predominantly from the eastern portion of the Empire. Votive dedications commemorate cults identified with the East, such as Serapis, Mithras, Magna Mater and Priapus. Interestingly, no Christian churches have so far been discovered here, although this may simply represent mere chance, with so much of the site yet to be excavated.

Already raised to the status of a *municipium* by Hadrian, Nicopolis received further imperial favours under Septimius Severus, who transferred it from the provincial authority of Thrace to that of Moesia,[142] and visited the city in 202, receiving in honour of his stay there a huge gift of 700,000 sesterces from the 'grateful' citizenry. By the mid-3rd century, however, prosperity gave way to uncertainty and then to fear, as the Goths laid siege to Nicopolis in 250 and 270, though they failed to take it on both occasions. There is some evidence that buildings begun at this time were simply not finished, a clear indication of economic retraction.[143] In the troubled times after the Gothic invasion of 376 and the Roman defeat at Adrianople in 378, the countryside in this area of Moesia must have been devastated and the towns, even if they held out, were cut off from their rural hinterlands. Justinian may have ordered the refortification of the city, though, and a bishop is certainly attested in 458.[144] But it seems that the population gradually drifted 20 kilometres southwards to a more defensible position at Veliko Turnovo, where a Byzantine fortress survived into the reign of Heraclius (610–41), and which was later to become one of the most important centres of the Bulgarian kingdom in the Middle Ages.

Around 70 kilometres to the north-east of Nicopolis, the town of Abritus (Razgrad) – some 60 kilometres south of the Danube *limes* – saw the Empire's worst disaster for three centuries, with the first-ever death of a reigning emperor in combat. Decius was almost sixty when he seized power in 249, making him one of the oldest men to assume the purple, but his death just two years later left him far down in the league of ages achieved by emperors.[145] A senator and one who had achieved a modicum of military success on the Danube, Decius might, with better luck and the continued support of the army, have built a coalition of factions that would have put an end to the revolving-door nature of 3rd-century imperial politics. As a token of his intent (ill-omened as it turned out), he took the additional name of Trajan, as if to show his hopes of bringing glory to the Empire to equal those won by the great warrior-emperor more than a century before.

Cniva, the first leader of the Goths whose name is known, headed a host that crossed the Danube in 249. At first trying their hand at plundering Novae, the Goths were repelled by the governor of Moesia Inferior, one Trebonianus Gallus, and they then moved southwards to

Philippopolis (Plovdiv). After Decius's army was badly beaten north-east of the city, its commander, Lucius Priscus, the governor of Thrace, gave the city up. Cniva was left in possession of his prize all winter before seeking the next spring to push back north across the Danube. Decius had ordered the crossing points to be secured to prevent Cniva escaping into *barbaricum*.

At Abritus (modern Razgrad) he cornered his quarry. The Goths hid a portion of their force in a swamp, and the Romans, having defeated a section of the remaining barbarians, advanced incautiously through the marshy ground, believing it to be undefended. Weighed down by their armour and utterly surprised, Decius and most of his army were cut to pieces. The Emperor's body was never found, nor that of his son Herennius Etruscus. The loss of an emperor for the first time in battle created a dangerous moment of crisis. The Moesian legions, casting about for a new ruler, proclaimed Trebonianus Gallus, the same man who had earlier had some success against the Goths at Novae. There were, understandably, some nasty rumours that he might have played a part in Decius's downfall, but to allay these he acknowledged his predecessor's younger son, Hostilianus, as Caesar along with, for the sake of family harmony, his own son Volusianus.

The Abritus fort, set some way back from the frontier itself, was in fact built in the late 3rd or early 4th century,[146] and so was not there at all when Decius met his untimely end. The communist-era authorities in Razgrad thoughtfully permitted the building of an enormous pharmaceutical factory right across the site, slicing it in two, making excavations next to impossible over much of it and gifting it with the eyesore of a 60-metre-high steam-billowing tower.

However, much of the wall survives, solid and thick, typical later imperial work, originally 3 metres thick and 12 metres high, with the regulation four gates at each of the compass points. Only two gates are in place now, and of the interior buildings the most important is a large town house, grand enough to be that of a leading citizen, its reconstructed walls stretching for 400 square metres or more, and with an apsidal room that may have been an audience chamber of some kind. A few hundred metres from the site's central area, overlooked by a set of ramshackle chalets, an indistinct scatter of ruins marks a site that was in use first as a palaeo-Christian basilica and then as an early medieval Bulgarian church.[147]

Back along the Danube and an hour or so east of Novae, Ruse is another of the region's riverside settlements that has clearly seen better days. It was once Bulgaria's third city – after Sofia and Plovdiv – and the peeling, fading remains of the once-splendid opera house on the main square speak eloquently of a town that is rather down on its luck. Local knowledge of its Roman past is rather faded, too, for though a few passers-by seem to remember something about an antique fort, no one actually knows where it is. Finally, in a down-at-heel part of town, just along a slope that leads to the railroad track which hugs the Danube on its slow way eastwards, a tree-covered and unpromising-looking promontory houses what is left of Sexaginta Prista.

A military camp was established here under Vespasian, which was later garrisoned by the *Cohors II Flavia Brittanorum equitata*, a part-mounted detachment, and then by the *Cohors II Mattiacorum* composed of troops from faraway Germania Superior. By the 5th century, at the time of the *Notitia Dignitatum*, a unit of the I Italica legion was stationed here.[148] It was also a base for the Moesian fleet, the *Classis Flavia Moesiana*, and the name of the site derives from a type of fast reconnaissance vessel (*Prista*)[149] and the Latin for sixty (*sexaginta*), presumably referring to the size of the flotilla based here.

Sited as it is on a steep bluff, whose cliffs overlook the Danube far below, the fort would have been fairly impregnable to a river-based assault, though vulnerable from the rear. And so, over time it proved. Now just a narrow strip of the site remains, most of it swallowed up by the growth of Ruse in the 19th and 20th centuries, buried under the foundations of buildings or, in part, by a large copse of trees. The remains of barracks and one of the gates are still visible in a patch some 5 metres or so across. The site guardian, sporting a magnificent walrus moustache and sideburns, is most keen to show us the site's 'surprise'. This turns out to be a reconstruction of a *mithraeum* situated in a bunker of Second World War vintage, whose building must itself have taken another bite out of the Roman fort. A few altar fragments and a rather fetching brown and dark-blue colour scheme attempt to resurrect the air of mystery surrounding the cult. Some votive stelae for Mithras were found during excavations at Ruse, and so the supposition of a *mithraeum* at the fort is not entirely fanciful.

Just where the Danube begins to turn north, protected by wide marshes, Durostorum, some 125 kilometres east of Sexaginta Prista, protected the entrance to the area now known as the Dobrudja, which acted as a Roman-held salient pushing northwards towards the Crimea. Though this wide finger of land was terribly exposed to barbarian attacks, it did not lie on the most direct or accessible routes, either towards Thrace and the Western Empire or to Constantinople itself. The attacks therefore tended to be on a lesser scale and, coupled with the possibility of river- or seaborne reinforcements to the forts and cities here, this helped the lower Danube, which marked out the Dobrudja territory, to remain virtually the last part of the river over which the Byzantine authorities were able to exert control. Generally, the cities around Durostorum resisted conquest by the barbarians until the late 6th or even the 7th century, around a hundred years later than the frontier outposts further to the west.

The modern city of Silistra has long obliterated almost all that remained of Durostorum, but here and there tantalising elements survive. The legionary camp, which became home to the XI Claudia legion following its posting around 102 after Trajan's First Dacian War, was reconstructed during the reign of Aurelian, and its wall strengthened from about 1.5 metres to 2.5 metres in thickness. Already the Dobrudja had felt the chill wind of insecurity coming in from the steppes, for in 170 it had suffered the ravages of the Costobocci, one of the tribes whose incursions Marcus Aurelius struggled for decades to contain.[150] When the V Macedonica legion was transferred from Troesmis, Durostorum was left as the only legionary base along the Danube to the east of Novae, and so was of critical importance to Rome's hold on the section of river nearest the delta. It was probably during the reign of Marcus – or possibly that of Caracalla in the early 3rd century – that the town was elevated to the rank of *municipium*. Further raids by a combined group of Carpi, Goths and Sarmatians occurred during the reign of Gordian III, following the death of Decius in 251 and during the rule of Aurelian.

Close to the town centre of Silistra lie the remains of a *villa urbana*, set on a grassy patch below a couple of apartment blocks. The complex, including parts of a set of baths, dates from the 5th or 6th century, evidence that urban life was still flourishing here at that late stage. Durostorum's most spectacular archaeological discovery came about as a result of a chance find in 1942. It lies to the south-east of the city centre in a nondescript housing estate of low barrack-like concrete blocks, an unbroken forest of grey slabs. The small rectangular structure that sits on top of the late-Roman tomb makes it look more like a miniature church than a mausoleum, but inside and downstairs its purpose is clear.

Visible from a square hole punched into the original tomb chamber when it was opened, a Roman master and his wife stare out, flanked by a male and female slave, with further household slaves arrayed on the right and left walls. The tomb, which is generally dated to the second half of the 4th century, was never actually used, and since the very point on the wall where an inscription might have been located was destroyed when the tomb was first opened, the identity of the mausoleum's owner is something of a mystery. The man's gaze is stern, his clothing that of an aristocrat, a long tunic under a mantle that is fastened at the shoulder with a fibula (a type of brooch). In his hands he bears a codicil, probably commemorating his appointment to some senior official position. Such signs of appointment to high office were so valued and revered that they were often put on public display, set on cushions and bracketed by candles, as a visible token of the eminence of their owner.[151] It has been speculated that the tomb dates to shortly before the disastrous Roman defeat at Adrianople and that the man intended to be buried here was lost in that battle and his body never recovered. The truth will probably never be known.

After 1,600 years, the colours are amazingly vivid; an unused tomb would not have been attractive to grave-robbers, and thus its opening in the 20th century was the first time that the frescoes had been exposed to the air since the chamber was sealed. The mistress of the house seems to have been painted in later, for reasons that are unclear, and her face is obscured by a veil so that her features cannot clearly be seen; the female slaves to her right hold items for her bath, including a mirror and a towel, while the male slaves who flank her husband carry items of his clothing, such as his cloak and a *cingulum*, a badge of military office and a further indication of the man's importance.[152] Four boys and young men are depicted in roundels on the wall, possibly portraits of the master at various stages in his life; in one of them he is shown holding a spear, apparently hunting a bear.

Above the couple's portrait, set in a lunette, two peacocks are shown drinking from a vase. The image is such a commonplace of Christian iconography that it is taken – together with the east–west orientation of the tomb – as an indication that the owners may well have been Christians. Durostorum did have something of a reputation as a citadel of the new religion, producing its own rich crop of martyrs. A curious tale relates the story of Dasius, a legionary who refused to take part in a celebration associated with the feast of Saturnalia. Although well known as a time of inversion when the normal social order was turned upside down, in this extraordinary form of the rite, lots were drawn and the winner became 'king' for a month, during which period he was allowed to indulge in whatever pleasures he chose. At the end of the thirty-day period, the 'king' would be beheaded. Dasius, a staunch Christian (whose actual historical existence is doubtful),[153] is said to have refused to take part after the lot fell upon him, and was thrown into prison and executed.

Durostorum's brand of Christianity was not always orthodox. In 380, it received a new bishop, Auxentius, who was a leading supporter of the

Arian creed. Amongst the tortuous theological controversies that afflicted Christendom in the century after its adoption as an official religion, one of the most bitter was the question of whether God the Father took primacy amongst the members of the Trinity and created the other two, or whether instead Jesus Christ and the Holy Spirit were coeval with him and uncreated.

Arius, a Christian priest from Alexandria who lived in the mid-3rd century, taught the former and acquired a strong body of adherents before he was roundly condemned as a heretic at the Council of Nicaea in 325.[154] His teaching, however, lived on, particularly beyond the borders of the Empire, where his disciples had experienced notable success in evangelising the barbarians. Most prominent was Ulfilas, who preached amongst the Goths from the 340s and translated the Bible into Gothic. His story is muddied by the competing claims of orthodox historians (such as Sozomen and Zosimus) who maintain that Ulfilas actually converted the Goths to orthodox Christianity[155] and only turned to Arianism in the 370s at the behest of the Emperor Valens, who strongly supported that creed. Yet the Goths were certainly Arian by the end of the 4th century, and both the Visigoths in Spain and the Ostrogoths in Italy (together with the Vandals in North Africa) established kingdoms that derived some of their strength from their self-conscious identification with Arianism in opposition to the 'Roman' Nicene Church.

Auxentius – who was, as it happens, Ulfilas's foster son – was certainly a strong partisan of Arianism, and a letter that he wrote around 400 is one of the chief sources from the Arian side for the nature of their theology.[156] Later appointed as the Arian Bishop of Milan, Auxentius had the misfortune to be the contemporary of Saint Ambrose, an exceptionally able and pugnacious defender of the Nicene cause, who comprehensively outplayed his milder opponent in 386 over which of the two creeds had the right to celebrate mass in Milan's principal basilica.

Durostorum's other famous son was Flavius Aëtius, one of the Western Empire's last really capable military leaders. Born a little after 390 from a partly noble background,[157] as a young man Aëtius was held for a time as a hostage at various barbarian courts, first that of the Goths and then, more significantly, in the entourage of Rugila, King of the Huns. There he made important contacts and learnt something of Hunnish organisation and tactics, lessons that would stand him in great stead later in his career. He owed his initial rise to prominence to his reputation as a man who could deal with the Huns, taking advantage of the confused period that followed the death of Honorius in 423.

Castinus, who had been Honorius's *magister militum*, decided, on the death of his master, that his interests would not be best served by the raising of the infant Valentinian III to the imperial throne. Instead he elevated Ioannes, a relatively minor civil servant,[158] to become Emperor. When it was clear that the Eastern Emperor Theodosius I would vigorously oppose this move, Aëtius was despatched to recruit a force of Huns to deal with the inevitable conflict. By the time he returned, having duly mustered a large host, the eastern general Aspar had already captured the western capital, Ravenna, and had Ioannes executed. Aëtius's presence was now menacing rather than fortuitous and he was bought off with a large donative for his Hunnish mercenaries and his own appointment as *magister militum per Gallias*.[159] Valentinian III was installed on the throne, although at the tender age of six he was the plaything of competing factions, one of them led by Aëtius.

It took time for Aëtius to cement his influence at court, but by 430 he had managed to dispose of his first rival Felix, whom he had murdered that year.[160] He then engaged in a violent struggle with Boniface, who had held Africa for the legitimate government of Valentinian III during the usurpation of Ioannes, and who thus held an ace card in his relations with the Emperor's mother, Galla Placidia. It appears that Aëtius attempted to trick Boniface into rebelling, by fabricating letters showing that Galla Placidia was about to execute her former favourite.[161] But in the end the plot came to nothing, and instead, in 432, Boniface was given the title of 'patrician', the most prestigious position short of Emperor. A chastened Aëtius fled to Pannonia and thence to the Hunnish court. There he obtained from Ruga a fresh military force, with which he then marched on Italy, suffering a tactical defeat near Rimini in which Boniface was (luckily for Aëtius) mortally wounded.

Now without effective rivals, Aëtius came to dominate the government of the Empire for the next twenty years, during which time the Emperor, Valentinian III, remained firmly in the background. Aëtius received the almost unparalleled honour – for a non-member of the imperial family – of a third consulate in 446, and struggled with all his might for two decades to hold back the Hunnish genie, which he himself had first unleashed in 423. The principal arena of his activities was in Gaul, against which the Huns, led from 435 by Attila and his brother Bleda (and from 445 by Attila alone), pressed incessantly. Aëtius made able use of other barbarian groups in an effort to create buffers against their growing power. In 440, he settled a number of Alans on lands around Valence that had become deserted, and in 443 he placed the remnants of the Burgundians (whose power had been smashed by the Huns in 437) in Sapaudia (modern Savoy).[162]

The climactic struggle of Attila's career came about as the result of an extraordinary piece of court intrigue. Valentinian III's sister, Honoria, is said to have become pregnant by her household steward Eugenius. In order to avoid a scandal, he was executed and the Emperor's sister betrothed to a senator of consular rank with absolutely no hint of ambition about him. Outraged, Honoria had a ring despatched to Attila, saying that in exchange for a huge quantity of gold, he should come and rescue her; the clear implication was that she would also marry him. At this point the Eastern Emperor, Theodosius, who had advised Valentinian to pack his sister off to Attila and have done with the troublesome princess, died after a bad fall from his horse.[163] He had no male heir, and after the predictable period of jockeying for power, his sister Pulcheria effectively gifted the throne to a senator from Thrace named Marcian by marrying him. The new Emperor adopted a much harsher policy towards the Huns, to whom the Eastern Empire had been paying large subsidies each year, and cut off the supply of gold.

Faced with the drying-up of a handy source of payment for his growing horde, Attila did not (as might have been expected) turn on Marcian and make him pay for his insolence. Instead, he brought up the matter of Honoria, deciding that now was the time to assert his marriage rights over her. At the very least, he might have supposed, a massive payment would be in order to buy him off. In the end, he demanded the whole of Gaul in exchange for turning back his huge army, which was even then marching in the direction of the province. Aëtius, whose power base Gaul had always been, could never countenance such a move. He hastily cobbled together a coalition of all those who stood to lose by Attila's ultimate victory: the Visigoths under Theoderic, the Franks, Saxons and Burgundians, the men of Brittany and a motley collection of other minor barbarian clans. There was even a contingent of genuinely Roman soldiers.

The two armies met in June 451 on the Catalaunian Fields, some 50 kilometres from Châlons (or Catalaunum). The Huns were already somewhat on the defensive, having been forced to withdraw from the gates of Orléans, and they were tired. The Visigoths managed to occupy a slight rise on the plain, giving Aëtius's forces a significant advantage in the bitter hand-to-hand fighting that followed. Gradually Attila was forced back to his army's wagons, stationed in the rear. Just when it looked as if the Visigoths might press home their advantage – despite the death of Theoderic – Aëtius called them off and allowed the bloodied Huns to escape.

He had, perhaps, no intention of allowing any one barbarian group to become dominant and thought that some advantage might still be gained from manipulating the Huns – with whom, after all, he had a long history of involvement – at some later convenient moment. In 452, however, Attila was back, laying siege to Aquileia and blazing a trail through Italy as far as the River Po, where an embassy from Rome, including Pope Leo I, persuaded him to turn back. Attila's departure probably had more to do with the plague and famine then afflicting the Italian peninsula than with any sudden attack of piety on his part, when faced with the papal pleas to leave the Eternal City in peace.[164]

The next year, though, the great Hun was dead and the Hunnish confederacy shattered, its subjects no longer held in check by their almost superstitious fear of Attila's wrath. His sons struggled to keep even a much-diminished realm together, and in the 460s the two survivors, Dengizich and Hernac, asked leave to bring their remaining followers to settle south of the Danube. At first this was summarily refused, and in the end it was only Hernac who was permitted to bring a much-reduced band to settle in the Dobrudja as federates.[165] Thus, within two decades of the death of Attila, the Huns had disappeared almost entirely as a political force.

The ignominious removal of his great rival might have been considered a moment for Aëtius to relish. Yet just as he had first involved the Huns in Roman politics, so their removal from the equation meant that, for a brief moment, he was vulnerable, as his longtime clients-cum-enemies could no longer be invoked either as a threat or as the unlikely saviours of the Roman state. In September 454, Valentinian summoned his overmighty general to a meeting to discuss some accounts, and there stabbed Aëtius to death with his own hand. Procopius acidly remarks that the Emperor had thereby cut off his own right hand with his left.[166] While clearly out to advance his own best interests, Aëtius had also juggled the competing challenges facing the Empire with at least reasonable success. His defeat of Attila may have saved the Gallic provinces from premature loss to the Empire, and though he could not preserve Africa, in Gaul he did at least retain one of the two best revenue-raising areas that the Empire still possessed. From provincial obscurity, Aëtius had risen to the highest rank and truly earnt the epithet often attached to his name, 'the last Roman'.

Apart from its southern extremity, the Dobrudja now lies largely within the territory of modern Romania. The Romans first entered the area in 72–71 BC during their war against Mithridates, ruler of Pontus on the southern Black Sea coast, whose power had grown to encompass a series of Hellenistic cities on the western shores of the sea, such as Tomis (Constanţa), Callatis (Mangalia) and Histria (Istros). The great Pontic ruler, as well as being vexingly hard to unthrone, held two kingly records. The first, his ability to speak all twenty-two of the languages of his subjects and address each soldier in his army by name and in his own tongue, would have left him a wide range of options for a place of exile in which he could converse with ease.[167] The second, much more ambivalent gift was his immunity to all then-known poisons. This tolerance he had, ironically, built up on account of his fear of assassination and consequent self-administration of small doses of venom throughout his adult life, which created an immunity to the otherwise lethal substances. When finally facing capture by the Romans, his attempts to poison himself failed miserably and in the end he had to call on his friend Bituitus to kill him.[168] Although the historians do not record it, one can well imagine him cursing heartily and creatively in all those twenty-two languages.

Marcus Terentius Varro Lucullus, the Roman general who had been victorious against Mithridates, forced a treaty of alliance on a number of cities. This certainly included Callatis (for the text of the inscription survives) and quite possibly Tomis and Histria, too, promising mutual assistance in case of attack, and providing a useful guarantee for Roman expansionist moves in Macedonia and Thrace. A revolt in Macedonia led to the defeat of Gaius Antonius Hybrida in 61 BC near Histria and this, together with the expansion of the native Dacian state that grew up under Burebista in the 60s and 50s BC, led to a temporary diminution of Roman influence in the area. It took a campaign by Marcus Licinius Crassus[169] in 29–28 BC to restore the situation, and the trio of Greek-speaking cities on the coast – Callatis, Histria and Tomis – were now effectively annexed by Rome, although nominally retaining their freedom.

Under Tiberius, the Dobrudja was incorporated into Moesia during the province's formal organisation in AD 15. Apart from an invasion by the Roxolani in 67–8,[170] the area remained relatively tranquil under the early Empire, although, in a token of things to come, Plautius Silvanus Aelianus (governor of Moesia from 57 to 67) is said to have transported 100,000 tribespeople from beyond the Danube to replenish provincial manpower resources,[171] establishing a precedent for the *receptio* of barbarians into the Empire that would become a regular feature during the more troubled times of the 4th and 5th centuries.[172] The Roman authorities always sought to present the settling of barbarians within the Empire in a positive light, rather than as an act into which they had been forced. The settling of the Ubii on the left bank of the Rhine by Augustus in 38 BC had been a model for this, but the process became so frequent from the 2nd century that imperial propagandists struggled to present *receptio* as a positive thing. Marcus Aurelius allowed a large number of Naristae into the Empire around 180, Probus permitting 100,000 Bastarnae to enter the Empire, and Constantine capping it all with the settlement of 300,000 Sarmatians.[173] After the Roman defeat at Adrianople in 378, and the large-scale migration of unintegrated Goths that resulted, the panegyricist Themistius made the best of it by opining that it was far better that Thrace should be filled with barbarian farmers than by hostile warriors.

Even though the province was further enlarged after Claudius annexed the kingdom of Thrace in AD 46, appending to Moesia those parts of it that lay north of the central Balkan range, there is not much evidence for Roman troops being stationed in Dobrudja until the time of Vespasian. Once Dacia was occupied by Trajan by 106, and the central sector of the Danube between Durostorum and Novae (which had hitherto been heavily militarised) no longer lay on an external frontier, troops were released, both for the occupation of Dacia itself and to provide a legionary garrison for the first time for Dobrudja. A string of forts was built at Axiopolis (Cernavoda), Carsium (Hirsova) and Troesmis (Igliţa), which continued to defend the Dobrudja into the reign of Justinian, long after the forts on the central Danube to the west had been overrun by successive waves of barbarian invasions. As well as the V Macedonica legion, which was despatched to Troesmis (only to be withdrawn and sent to Dacia around 167), a number of auxiliary cohorts were sent to reinforce the defence of the area, including the *Cohors I Germanorum* at Capidava.[174]

During the Diocletianic reforms Moesia Inferior was renamed Scythia Minor, and from here on, reinforced by new legionary forces (the I Iovia and II Herculea), it acted as a Romanised bastion. There was some destruction by the Huns, but it was nothing like as severe as the swathe of land south of the Danube towards Naissus had to endure. The area suffered the depredations of the Goths' naval campaign in 257, and a large contingent of Sarmatians was settled in Scythia Minor between 340 and 360 to bolster the security of the province. However, even after the disastrous defeat by the Goths at Adrianople in 378, the Dobrudja remained resolutely Roman. It was only in the late 6th century with the advent of the Avars, and even more so in the 7th and early 8th centuries, that Constantinople's grip on the area finally weakened. Even so, cities in southern Dobrudja and northern Thrace such as Odessos (Varna) and Mesembria (Nesebur) remained Byzantine, with interruptions, almost to the very end of the Empire in 1453.

Some way into the interior of the province, around 100 kilometres east of the Danube at Silistra, along a Roman road that bypasses both the Danube and the Black Sea coast, resolutely refusing both sea and river, lies one of the most extraordinary monuments to Roman imperialism anywhere in the Empire. In a part of Romania where low chalet-style houses and horse-drawn carts seem the height of modernity, somewhat blurring the line between antiquity and the present, the small village of Adamclisi houses a monument of wholly unexpected grandeur. In 109, at a place that became known as Tropaeum Traiani, Trajan erected a stone trophy to celebrate his recent victory over the Dacians. Unlike the refined depictions on the column he set up in his forum in Rome, with its cartoon-strip narrative of the Dacian Wars, this account is rawer and bloodier, the art more provincial, but carrying more power and authenticity for lacking the filter of a refined disdain for the realities of war.

A reconstructed version of the monument stands a little way outside the village. A 40-metre-diameter marble drum some 10–12 metres high is set on a platform, which adds a further 8 metres to the monument. Topping it, a statue of Mars Ultor, the avenging god of war, is festooned with the trophies of battle, arms and armour captured from dead Dacians. It is a reflection of an ancient Roman tradition, by which the arms of slain opponents would be hung from a tree on the battlefield, so sending a grizzly message to anyone who might oppose the young city-state's rise to power, while at the same time glorifying the achievement of the victorious general.[175] All around, on fifty-four panels, were depicted scenes from the execution of the war. Even if the carvings themselves could not have been seen at any great distance, the Tropaeum would have been visible over a huge area, an ever-present – and presumably galling – reminder to the Dacians that they were no longer a free people.

The originals of the panels are held in the Adamclisi museum where, though divorced from their original context, they are more easily comprehensible than the replacements that encircle the reconstructed monument. They are weathered by long exposure to the atmosphere, but their patina of age lends them a disturbing immediacy. Here a bearded Dacian wields a *falx*, the characteristic sickle-shaped sword of his people; there a Roman legionary in chain armour thrusts his *gladius* into the chest of a bearded and kilted warrior, whose stone image writhes and twists in its death agony. On one panel a Dacian seems to hang in the air, almost flying, while on another the *cornicularii*, the legionary trumpeters. sound the advance. Trajan, meanwhile, watches and waits to receive the victorious cohorts at the end of the campaign.

The final panels show Dacian prisoners bound and shackled, with Roman soldiers leading them into captivity, while two Dacian women, one bearing a baby, are depicted standing apart, perhaps watching their husbands being led into slavery. It is all a brutal depiction of the subjugation of a nation and the ugliness of war, made all the more unsavoury for its triumphalist tone. Yet, from the Roman point of view, they had done nothing more than punish the Dacians for breaking a treaty and had brought 'peace' to the new province. Just a few hundred metres away to the east, the Romans erected a more personal monument to the losses they had endured in the taking of Dacia; the names of almost 4,000 soldiers who died in the campaign were set up on a square altar, together with a rectangular mound, presumably the burial tumulus of a senior commander who had fallen in the fighting.[176]

Tropaeum Traiani was not simply the trophy. The place lay at an important crossroads between Tomis and Durostorum, and Trajan settled veterans from his Dacian campaign there, establishing a fortress as well as a civil town, certainly before 115–16 when the inhabitants, the 'Traianenses Tropaeenses' dedicated a statue to their patron emperor. Under Antoninus Pius it became home to a detachment of the XI Claudia legion, and its increasing importance is shown by its promotion to the rank of *municipium* around 180 during the reign of Marcus Aurelius.

Tropaeum Traiani's exposed position, however, meant that it did not prosper during the 3rd century and had to be rebuilt almost from scratch during the time of Constantine the Great and Licinius.[177] A dedication survives to the two emperors, in which Constantine tellingly takes precedence (just a few years later, in 317, he would defeat Licinius in the first of two fratricidal wars between them). The place staggered on until it was destroyed by the Avars at the end of the 6th century. At what point the trophy was thrown down, and what the reactions of the local population might have been to the overturning of this symbol of their subjugation, it is hard to say. They may have been more ambivalent than expected, for Rome's fall did not mean Dacia's rise, and the conditions that prevailed after the collapse of the *limes* on the Danube were hardly conducive to basic survival, let alone fine proto-nationalist sentiment.

The town lies just a couple of kilometres away, on a low rise from which a fantastic view can be had of the trophy itself and on to the high plateau up to the east. It is protected on three sides by a natural slope, which was reinforced in the 4th century by a defensive wall studded with horseshoe-shaped towers. In the mid-afternoon summer sun, it seems an exposed place, the carpet of grass and tangle of weeds threatening to blur and obscure the indistinct outlines of its surviving buildings, while here and there the ground is scarred with the trenches from various archaeological campaigns.

On the town's main street, around 200 metres from the principal gate (which survives only in its rubble core and a few facing blocks), lies the *basilica forensis*, the civilian basilica, marked out by two rows of column bases that formed the portico of the building. The forum, alongside which the basilica must have lain, is obscured by a jumble of ruins. Nearby, four Christian basilicas from the 4th to 6th centuries are evidence of the Christian life of the city. One, the 'Cistern Basilica', was adapted in late-Roman times from a pre-existing water cistern, which provided a convenient and well-built rectangular structure without the need for extensive new building. Across the main street again are the ruins of the 'Marble Basilica', clear only from the shape of its apse, the rest being just an undifferentiated mass of stones.

The east gate of the city and the adjacent wall have been reconstructed and one tower stands incongruously whole. Leaving the site from the south side, a single jagged arch of a gateway survives, divorced from any surviving stones of the walls, from where a slight scramble leads down to the modern roadway. Unvisited and half-shapeless with age, Tropaeum Traiani is a stark reminder that the proud boasts of emperors could do nothing to prevent the collapse of the frontier and the overwhelming of such towns by the tide of time.

The modern road along the Danube is subject to exactly the same vagaries that periodically damaged many of the forts and at the same time contributed to their security. The fort at Capidava (modern Topalu), which lies on the Danube 55 kilometres north of Tropaeum Traiani, was first constructed under Trajan at the start of the 2nd century, but is now rendered somewhat more difficult to find by a flood that has washed away the riverside road, necessitating a slanting detour inland before the mound of the fort appears, unexpectedly, at the side of the new highway around 20 kilometres beyond Cernavodă. The ruins, as at so many places that the Romans occupied for several centuries, are something of a multi-layered prospect, with the Trajanic phase almost entirely built over by a reconstruction under Diocletian or Constantine, which in turn has been obscured by a heavy overlay of buildings from the 8th to the 11th centuries. It is certainly a testament to the obduracy of the Roman and Byzantine hold on the place.

Entering from the western side, parts of one horseshoe-shaped projecting tower have been reconstructed a little further to the east, while the others lie in ruins. Inside the main circuit, many of the buildings are dwellings from the 8th to 10th centuries, when the fort was adapted for civilian use. In the south-west of the wall, an earthwork mound represents the late-Roman fort, which, like many fortifications of the time, occupied a restricted area; partly because the size of garrisons was reduced, and partly because those troops might actually be expected to defend their bases against attack. It all offers a fine view over the Danube, flowing tranquilly by.

The first garrison here (until 243) was the *Cohors I Ubiorum* from near Cologne, which was replaced by the *Cohors Germanorum civium romanorum*, again from Germany. The fort was destroyed by the Goths during an incursion in the mid-3rd-century. It was razed again by the Huns in the mid-4th, and the place was only revived when Justinian built the smaller fort in the 5th century. Capidava was by then the centre of a bishopric, and a basilica with three apses has been unearthed. After being on the receiving end of another sacking, from the Avars in the late 6th century, Capidava was then temporarily abandoned, to be further devastated by an earthquake in the 7th century. It was only reoccupied when Byzantine control returned to this section of the Danube in the 9th century and, from the evidence of the hut-like dwellings half-sunken into the ground that made up the predominant type of housing of this phase in Capidava's history, it was not a very prosperous era. By the 11th century even these petered out, and presumably the site was abandoned.

The lynchpin of the *Limes Scythiae*, which formed the defensive system of Dobrudja, was Troesmis (Igliţa), some 75 kilometres north along the *limes* from Capidava. The V Macedonica legion was based here after its transfer from Oescus around 102 until it was sent to Dacia in the 160s.[178] It gave rise to two civilian settlements, one based around the legionary *cannabae*, the other, a more purely civilian town, a *municipium* under Marcus Aurelius.[179] Its citadel, at a strategic position on the lower Danube around 50 kilometres from the point where it finally bends eastwards for the last stage of its journey to the delta, was first excavated in the 1860s by a Frenchman, Desiré More, who claimed that the local Turks were so hostile to him that one of them even shot off his right thumb.[180]

Situated near this final bend, a few kilometres from modern Garvăn, is the fortress of Dinogetia, which lies on a broad plateau above what was once an ancient tributary of the Danube, and which retained an isolated garrison amidst all the vicissitudes of the ages of invasions, right up until the end of the 6th century. It was built over the remains of a pre-existing Geto-Dacian[181] settlement, and was certainly constructed before the mid-2nd century, when it is mentioned in Ptolemy's *Geographia*.[182] Extensive reconstruction was carried out under Diocletian, and large numbers of tile stamps of the I Iovia legion have been found. It was again rebuilt during the reigns of Anastasius and Justinian, as the part of the general strengthening of the Danube *limes*, but was burnt to the ground during an invasion by the Kutrigurs in 559. Although it was reoccupied, Dinogetia limped on in a fairly poor state. A medieval basilica of the 11th or 12th century occupies part of the central area of the site, evidence of the last stage of its existence.

The fort lies a few hundred metres from the main road, occupying a prime site on a low promontory, its 12-metre-high walls and semicircular towers making it seem as if a siege would still present a formidable challenge. The guardian, who farms in the locality, as did his father for twenty years before him, says that the area was far marshier in ancient times, so the approach to the citadel would have been even more treacherous. Despite the relatively complete state presented by it exterior, Dinogetia is splendidly ruinous inside, grassed over and quietly decaying. Roughly in the centre a square building probably represents the *praetorium*, next to which another structure could have been the house of some local notable built within the fort precincts in the 4th century, and which, in common with the rest, was sacked by the Huns around 375.[183] The gate facing the roadway was blocked up in Byzantine times, evidence of the increasing insecurity experienced by all such outposts as this.

A few hundred metres from the fort, past fields of waving corn, lies the bath-complex. Partly protected by a metal-roofed shelter, the remains are overgrown, although the hypocaust, the best-preserved in Romania, can just be made out. The ruins here are made more confusing by the fact that in the 6th century they were partly cannibalised to make a Christian chapel on the site. Presumably by then, the ritual of bathing was less central to a civic life that was becoming divorced from its classical antecedents. It is a process that continues even today, as the guardian acidly points out that whilst his forebears of Roman times had enough water to run such an establishment, he has lived here for forty years without ever once having access to mains running water.

A further 25 kilometres east along the river, close to modern Isaccea, lies Noviodunum, which was the main base of the *Classis Flavia Moesica*, the Moesian fleet that patrolled the lower section of the Danube.[184] The fort was built to control the last easy crossing point of the river before it begins to divide into the confusing web of waterways that make up the river's delta. The high promontory on which it was erected was later used for an Ottoman-era fortress, and the visible Roman remains are scant, a large part of the northern sector of the walls having simply slid into the Danube. One of the interval towers of the late-Roman stage of the fort, which may originally have been built at the time of Nero, but certainly by the time of the Flavians, can still be made out. On the riverside humps and mounds in the grass probably represent the remains of the fort's interior buildings, but there is little actually visible above the ground. At this point, the Danube forms the border between Romania and the Ukraine, and across the wide expanse of river the wooded bank opposite seems peaceful, although since 2007 it once more represents a kind of boundary with *barbaricum*, as the Romanian side forms part of the economically advantaged club of the European Union, while a few kilometres away the Ukrainians are the wrong side of a tariff barrier, just as they were in Roman times.[185]

Noviodunum's moment of greatest fame came in 369, when the Emperor Valens met the Gothic chieftain Athanaric on a boat moored in the river outside the fortress to agree a treaty between their two peoples. Valens had been engaged in a campaign against the Goths for almost three years, and had earlier the same year crossed over into *barbaricum* on a bridge of boats that he had ordered constructed at Noviodunum.[186] The Goths were tired of fighting, and their supplies were exhausted. Athanaric finally came to sue for peace in person. Yet many years before he had sworn an oath to his father that he would never set foot on Roman territory, and in deference to the aged chieftain's pious wish not to violate his vow, Valens agreed to meet him midstream.

Temporarily, it seemed that the Gothic menace had been turned aside, and that peace might return to the Balkans. Less than ten years later, however, the Eastern Empire was overwhelmed by total catastrophe. Its origin lies precisely in dissatisfaction with the terms of the treaty brokered with Valens. A group of Goths under Fritigern revolted against the rule of Athanaric, who, by suing for peace at the hands of the Romans, had proved himself unworthy as a war leader. As a result the Tervingi, the leading faction of the Goths, which Athanaric had dominated, began to break up into their component sub-tribes. It was particularly unfortunate that this process coincided with aggressive advances by the Huns and their Alan allies, who were pressing in on the Gothic rear from their lands east of the Don.

The Tervingi, having largely abandoned Athanaric, and now under the leadership of Alavivus and Fritigern, flooded towards the Danube.[187] They demanded refuge in the Empire, and the panicked local authorities ordered them to stay put whilst the Emperor, far away in Antioch (Antakya in modern Turkey), was consulted. Eventually, permission was given for the Tervingi to cross, probably in the area of Durostorum, a complicated procedure during which many of them drowned in the swollen river. Once there, they faced terrible privations. Far from giving them adequate supplies, as the Emperor had commanded, the local military leaders

Lupicinus (the *comes per Thracias*) and Maximus (probably the *dux* of Moesia) pocketed the funds intended to pay for the Goths' upkeep and let their new charges simply starve, thus beginning a long and dishonourable tradition of the mistreatment of political refugees. Parents are said to have exchanged their children for dog-meat, and huge numbers of Goths were sold into slavery.[188] In the meantime, the Tervingi were joined on the north bank of the Danube by another Gothic group, the Greuthingi under Alatheus and Saphrax. However, these newcomers were denied entry into imperial territory.

Further embittered by the paltry shelter offered to them in the face of a bitter winter, Gothic hearts turned from gratitude for their sanctuary to burning hatred at the arrogance and cruelty of their hosts. Fritigern restrained his followers from any intemperate violence and directed his Goths south-eastwards towards Marcianopolis, inland from the great port of Odessos (Varna) on the Black Sea coast. Lupicinus, who was still supervising the movements of the Tervingi, invited Fritigern to a banquet inside the town, but forbade the Gothic chieftain's followers to accompany him. Fritigern narrowly avoided assassination, for the feast had been a trap, and in the ensuing battle outside the town walls Lupicinus and his army were roundly defeated. The Goths, who could take no more Roman perfidy, set to plundering Thrace and Moesia with an enthusiasm redoubled by their treacherous treatment.

It took until 378 for Valens to assemble a sufficient force to face down the Goths, who in the meantime had dealt a stinging blow to the local Roman forces at Ad Salices in the summer of 377. The problem was now, if anything, even worse, for the Greuthingi had also crossed the Danube (probably near Noviodunum) and joined up with Fritigern's horde. Held up by trouble in Isauria in Asia Minor, and by a revolt in Palestine, Valens only set out from Constantinople in the second week of June[189] while reinforcements from Gratian in the west were delayed by the need to deal with an Alamannic invasion.[190] Faced with a move by Fritigern to bypass him and block his return route to Constantinople, Valens decided, against the advice of some of his senior generals, to seek battle as soon as possible. On 9 August, he found the Goths camped around 12 kilometres from Adrianople (Edirne in Turkey). Fritigern seems to have played for time, asking for a parley whilst he called back scattered bands of warriors to rejoin his central force; he is even said to have set fires to create a choking blanket of smoke to wear down the Romans' morale.

When fighting did break out, it was confused. Valens was unaware of the true numbers of Goths and ordered an ill-judged attack on their camp, which was thrown back once the large cavalry force led by Alatheus and Saphrax returned to the fray after a foraging expedition. The Roman cavalry broke and the infantry, despite prolonged and dogged resistance, were eventually cut to pieces. Ammianus recounts that the crush was so great that troops slipped on the blood of those who had fallen and were impaled on the weapons of their own comrades.[191] Valens's own bodyguard appears to have fled as resistance crumbled, and a last-ditch stand by the cavalry commander Victor to rescue the Emperor failed. Those Romans who could made a disorderly escape from the battlefield.

The carnage was appalling: two-thirds of the Roman army is thought to have fallen. One estimate gives up to 26,000 Roman dead out of the 40,000 or so who started the battle, including the two *magistri militum* Traianus and Sebastianus and Valens himself, whose body was never found.[192] At a stroke the eastern field army was cut to pieces and, to make matters worse, the Emperor was dead, many of the senior military officers who might be expected to rally the remainder of the army and select a new leader had also perished, while a large force of Goths, fired on by the elation of such a rare and total victory, was on the loose near the imperial capital.

Yet the desperate times called forth the measures necessary to ensure the Empire's survival. Julius, one of the few surviving very senior military officers, summoned the large numbers of Goths who were enrolled in the Roman army and stationed near Constantinople to a special parade. Once assembled, they were tricked into disarming and then massacred to a man, so ensuring that there would be no Gothic fifth column to join up with Fritigern's victorious horde. Gratian, meanwhile, who could easily have kept the job within his family – since he had a seven-year-old cousin, Valentinian II, with whom, nominally, he shared power in the West – chose expediency over the ties of blood. He summoned the capable Spanish army officer Theodosius, who had been in exile on his family's estates since the disgrace and execution of his father in 374,[193] to become *magister equitum*. Then, at Sirmium in January 379, he had Theodosius crowned Augustus, with control of the Eastern Empire. After a series of difficult campaigns, by 382 the Goths sued for peace and were given land on which to settle in Thrace.

Old Athanaric, who had by now been marginalised and deserted by most of his former followers, overcame his qualms and finally entered the territory of the Empire late in 380. Theodosius gave the venerable Goth asylum and welcomed him to Constantinople, where he passed away just two weeks later on 14 January 381 and was given a state funeral. The 'Gothic problem', however, had not been solved, merely shelved, and within fifteen years would erupt again under Alaric with, if anything, even more destructive consequences.[194]

The littoral of the Black Sea coast seems a world away from the winding and twisting river passages of the Danube delta and the forts that fronted the Roman defence against *barbaricum*, yet the ancient Greek cities which lay along it formed the original core of Roman power here and remained the most important settlements in Lower Moesia (and then Scythia Minor). The approach to Istros (or Histria), one of the most important of these, is fringed with reed beds, giving it a much more maritime air than the mound-hugging marsh-beset fortresses to the north. It lies about 100 kilometres to the south-west of Noviodunum (Isaccea), to which it was connected by a direct road that avoided the need to circumnavigate the fringes of the delta.

Istros's beginnings are antique indeed; it was founded by Greek colonists from Miletus in the 7th century BC, and the settlement survived into the 7th century AD, not long after its destruction by the Avars in 586. In between, it experienced alternating periods of prosperity and disaster, suffering a sack by the Getae in the 1st century BC and by the Goths in the mid-3rd century AD. It became Roman in the late 1st century BC, together with its neighbouring Hellenistic cities of Tomis and Callatis.[195]

The outermost set of city walls dates from the period after the Gothic sack in the 3rd century (it was the fourth such circuit, the others being built at the colony's Hellenistic foundation, and under the early Roman occupation). The defences are impressively strong, composed of large blocks, which reused material from earlier phases of the city, including a couple of dedication stones that were incorporated into the gates as lintels. Inside, the city contains remains from throughout its 1,500-year history, creating a confusing jumble of interleaved phases. From its earliest period come a wealth of Greek inscriptions, some one-third of the total found in the Dobrudja,[196] and a sacred area, including the very broken-down remains of a temple of Zeus.

Around the 3rd century BC the harbour at Istros began to silt up, and in 262 BC the city lost a long-running battle with Byzantium over who controlled the harbour at Tomis to the south. A long depression set in, which was compounded after a sacking by Getic allies of the Dacian King Burebista in the 50s BC, and only began to lift once the Romans had securely occupied the city later in that century.

Just inside the town's main gate lies a late-Roman official quarter of the city, with the outlines of several large civic basilicas, a bath building and a small colonnaded square surviving. One of the basilicas sits in a dusty 4-metre-deep depression with just a couple of columns in place. Along an uncertain path, the *palaestra* of the bath-complex with its open space and portico is clear, and the remains of brick arches mark the remaining buildings. Beyond this there is a somewhat poorer quarter, with undifferentiated rectangular dwellings composed of smallish blocks. A larger ecclesiastical district dates from the 4th to 6th centuries and includes the Great Basilica, the largest in the Dobrudja, of which only the outline survives, marking out the nave and the apse, with the rest just architectural shards and fragments, columns and pieces of marble architrave lying hither and thither.

Deeper into the city lies a 6th-century residential area, from the very last years of Istros's existence. Rectangular rubble walls and a small colonnaded square speak of a life that was still at least modestly prosperous, despite the city's reduced circumstances. While in the western Balkans, and the riverine settlements of Upper Moesia, building activity had virtually ceased, here it still went on unabated, and the walls were reinforced several times.[197] Evidence from coins suggest that Istros managed to survive into the reign of Heraclius, though when control over the Danube frontier was achieved once more during the 9th century, the venerable ruins of the city were not reoccupied.

It is only around an hour's journey down the Black Sea coast from Istros to its long-time rival Tomis, but the fate of the two cities since the ending of Roman rule could hardly be more different. While Istros was totally abandoned, settlement at Tomis (or Constanţa as it became) continued. It is now a city of more than 300,000 inhabitants, with the largest harbour on the Black Sea (and one of the biggest in Europe), caught between the competing pulls of a rapid modernisation, the decaying remnants of the heavy industry that communism bequeathed to it and a much more ancient heritage as a Greek foundation of the 6th century BC.

After the Roman annexation in the 1st century BC, Tomis rapidly became the chief town of the Dobrudja, eclipsing its neighbours Istros and Callatis as the centre for the whole region. It is from this period that a unique testament to early-Roman Tomis comes. Publius Ovidius Naso, known to English-speaking posterity as Ovid, was one of the greatest poets of Rome's literary golden age. The author of masterworks such as the *Metamorphoses*, a collection of myths linked together by the theme of transformation, he was sent into exile in AD 8 to the far-flung shores of the Black Sea at Tomis, about as far from the cosmopolitan luxuries of Rome as it was possible to imagine. He spent the rest of his life there, continuing to pen poetry, including the poignant *Tristia*, a set of reflections on exile and pleas for forgiveness.

The slight to the Emperor for which Ovid was banished to his Scythian purgatory has never been securely established. Ovid himself indicated that it was because of a poem (the *Ars Amatoria*) and some kind of political error he had made. It is possible that certain passages in the poem, which seem to promote adultery, may have fallen foul of a new puritanical morality that Augustus was trying to promote, as evidenced by a law he promulgated which decreed severe penalties for adultery; in 2 BC the Emperor even banished his own daughter Julia to a remote island for the crime.[198] Perhaps the most plausible theory for Ovid's exile is that he knew somehow of Julia's adulterous affair with Junius Silanus, that it may even have had more seditious undertones as the basis for conspiracy against the Emperor himself, and that the poet, whilst not directly implicated, chose not to reveal what he knew.[199]

The picture Ovid paints of Tomis is of a city swarming with barbarous types, Getae and Sarmatians, dressed in furs against the winter cold.[200] The inclement weather and the barbarians were a constant preoccupation for the poet during his years of exile, unwelcome contrasts with the world he had left behind for ever at Rome. It took until May of AD 9 for Ovid to arrive in his place of exile, and within a year he was even called upon to don arms as a member of the city militia, to fight off one of the sporadic raids from the neighbouring Getae.

In the end, though, Ovid made the best of it. He carried on a constant stream of correspondence with friends in Rome, as a literary substitute for seeing them on a daily basis, and produced nine volumes of the *Tristia* ('Sadnesses') and of *Epistulae ex Ponto* ('Letters from the Pontus'). He even learnt some Getic, and was capable of conversing in the language – a necessary compromise in a place where, at least according to Ovid, Latin was rarely heard. His exile never ended, for after eight years, and the disappointment of the accession of Tiberius in 14, which did not bring a reversal of Augustus's obdurate refusal to pardon him, Ovid died in 17. His poetry, however, lived on, and neither his unknown crime nor his Pontic exile served to dent his reputation. As the poet himself wrote, '*Tempus edax rerum*' (Time is the devourer of all things).[201]

Ovid still gazes over Tomis, but now in the form of a statue erected on a lofty plinth in front of the city's main museum on Piaţa Ovidiu, the square named in his honour. It is a sad last resting place for a poet in the place of his bitter-sweet exile, as taxis whizz by and groups of adolescents lounge idly, waiting for their tourist coaches to collect them, the odd one curious enough to take a snap of the old bronze statue behind. The museum, from which the poet averts his gaze, houses a collection of priceless relics, mostly from the Greek phase of the city, including a statue of the snake god Glykon, the guardian of temples, his sinuous stone coils taut and ready to spring, whilst around his face fall disturbing, almost dreadlock-like, marble curls of hair. The Roman exhibits peter away around 702, when the city finally fell and was temporarily abandoned, while a run of medieval and modern rooms curiously stutters to a halt in 1939. History resumes in 1989 after the fall of the communist autarch Nicolae Ceaușescu, for, at least in museum circles, a reappraisal of the Second World War years and the communist era is clearly still under way.

The vestiges of ancient Tomis are thin on the ground, unsurprisingly so for a city that has been occupied almost constantly for 2,500 years. Just by the museum, a little sculpture park shares space in a square with a couple of travel agencies, displaying a few of the grave monuments found in the area. Much more spectacular is the 'Roman Edifice' a few metres away, which houses one of the largest extant mosaics in the Roman world, a geometric affair some 100 metres long and 20 metres wide. The building itself has walls some half a metre thick, which still stand to about 3–4 metres on one side. The storey beneath this consisted of around eleven vaulted rooms in which a variety of amphorae were found, indicating some kind of storeroom, but the splendour of the mosaic speaks of a much grander function. The geometric pattern, in black, white and yellow, includes ivy leaves, spirals, vases, shields and double-headed axes in its decoration, although what must once have been a mesmerising expanse of tesserae is now somewhat broken up by the buckling of the floor, caused by the shifting of the earth beneath, perhaps through an earthquake.

The mosaic was laid in the 4th or 5th century AD, by which time the city had been renamed Constantiana, possibly under the Emperor Constantius II (337–61). Down below, fronting the port, sections of the city's sea wall survive, surmounted by modern housing, while nearby fragments of a bath-complex moulder quietly in a green expanse of park beside the harbour road.

A larger section of the late-Roman wall, restored under Diocletian or Constantine, survives inland in a small park, its western gate clear, with a 2-metre-wide opening and the threshold still in place. The south gate also remains, though the section of extant wall here is much lower. Around 50 metres away the 'Butcher's Tower' was originally built during a later, Justinianic refortification, showing that efforts to keep the defences of Tomis in good shape were still under way into the 6th century.

A string of other Hellenistic foundations guarded the Black Sea coast down from Tomis, including Callatis (Mangalia), Bizone (Kavarna in Bulgaria) and the most important city of coastal Thrace, Odessos (modern

Varna). Like Constanţa, Varna boomed in the 19th and 20th centuries, and is now the third-largest city in Bulgaria, counting some 350,000 inhabitants, a mass that has almost wholly effaced its classical heritage. Founded in around 585 BC, again by colonists from Miletus, the town fell under the domination of the Macedonians during the time of Alexander the Great's father, Philip II.

Along with many of the other Greek cities of the Black Sea coast, it came under the suzerainty of Rome in around 27 BC, and then, with the definitive suppression of the Thracian kingdom by Claudius in AD 46, it was attached to the new Roman province of Thrace. After the division of Moesia by Domitian around 85, Odessos was then transferred to the new province of Moesia Inferior. Although Trajan re-established the neighbouring town of Parthenopolis, 30 kilometres away, renaming it Marcianopolis in honour of his sister, Odessos's maritime trade enabled it to continue to flourish, complementing rather than competing directly with its upstart neighbour.

In one of Varna's main pedestrianised streets, half-obscured by the chairs of the neighbouring pavement cafés, sits a small piece of the Roman level roadway, more now the target of those seeking a quick depository for their litter than of any antiquarian curiosity. Somewhere under here, and in the streets leading down to the harbour, lay the original Greek quarter of the city. A section of Roman wall and several buildings sit in a pit by the side of an apartment block, where a tenant has forged an ersatz flowerpot from a very eroded column base. The remains themselves are utterly overgrown with grass and weeds. In the back courtyard of another apartment block, totally cut off from the eye of passers-by, a Roman tower lurks, standing to around half a metre in height, and crowded around by the parked cars of the modern inhabitants of the place.

Nearby are the main Roman baths, some of the finest surviving anywhere in the Balkans. It is a huge complex, some 3–4 metres below present street level, and stretching over some 7,000 square metres, although a section at both ends has been cut off by a later church. Down several flights of steps, part of the subterranean supporting structure survives, its brick vaults dank and water-stained. Up again, the square *apodyterium* or changing room leads into a vestibule with walls surviving up to a height of two storeys, and sections of an arch on both sides creating a hugely impressive silhouette. At the back the normal procession of *frigidarium*, *tepidarium* and *caldarium* is mirrored on both sides of the symmetrical complex. In the rear section of the baths, piles of broken sections of architrave and other architectural fragments lie in heaps. Most impressive of all are the remains of the furnace for the *caldarium* and, down beneath it, a forest of hypocaust tiles and ceramic pipes for moving the hot steam around the building. So intact does the system appear that it seems almost possible that a brief plumbing job might restore the steam room to working order.

The baths were built around the middle of the 2nd century, possibly at the same time as a new aqueduct was constructed for the city in 157.[202] Coins have been found here from the reign of Gordian III (238–44), so the amenities were clearly then still in use, but some time before the end of the 4th century they probably ceased operation. Small, poor dwellings were then constructed around them, making use of the superior-quality masonry, and these in turn collapsed, possibly after an earthquake in 544.[203]

Odessos remained important into the 6th century. In 536, Justinian made it the headquarters of a curious union of the province of Moesia Secunda, Cyprus, the Cyclades and Caria, united by little common interest save their maritime heritages.[204] As late as 595, it was still in use as a military base during a campaign by Peter, the brother of the Emperor Maurice, against the Slavs and Avars. Thereafter it changed hands several times between the Byzantines and the nascent Bulgarian Empire, before falling definitively to the Bulgarians in the 11th century.

Odessos did in fact briefly become a Byzantine city once more in the early 15th century, when it was ceded to Manuel II Palaiologos in 1413, nearly 1,500 years after it had first known Roman administration. The Empire had precious little time left to run, and its territory had shrunk almost to vanishing point, but a few towns further to the south of Odessos represented a continuing hold on the Black Sea coast and a tenuous justification for the continued use of the label 'Empire'.

Mesembria (modern Nesebur in Bulgaria), some 70 kilometres south of Odessos, was almost the last of them, a final outpost on the frontier, when the *limes* had all but collapsed to the front steps of the imperial palace on the Golden Horn. It fell to Mehmet II's Ottoman army in February 1453, just two months before the final siege and fall of Constantinople, a day still referred to by Greeks as the 'Great Disaster'.

In Nesebur a largely reconstructed set of Byzantine city walls encircles part of the old town, in which large numbers of souvenir stalls compete for the attention of day-trippers with a dozen or more medieval churches. The oldest of these churches, the 'Old Metropolitan' constructed between the 5th and 8th centuries, is genuinely Byzantine, rather than a Greek-Bulgarian hybrid. It is a triple-apsed basilica with the nave and aisles separated by massive and still-standing two-storey piers. No decoration survives, though to the right of the principal apse, faint remains of what might be polychrome plaster still cling to the walls. The first church on the site, possibly from the 5th century, was razed and rebuilt in grander fashion in the 7th century, showing a city still able to contemplate major construction projects. A set of Roman baths nearby were, indeed, built only in the 6th century and were still in use as late as the 8th century, when such installations further north in Moesia had long been abandoned.

One of the last inhabitants of Byzantine Mesembria is buried in Saint Spas, a lovely little 15th-century church, whose walls are covered in frescoes of a vast array of saints and holy men. Mataissa Cantacuzina Palaiologina, who combines in her name that of two of Byzantium's last ruling dynasties,[205] died in 1441, and was originally buried in the Old Metropolitan Church, before her tomb was transferred to avoid its being cannibalised by the Turkish authorities for building materials. It seems to have been moved first to a church of the Analepsis, which in turn disappeared by the 1930s, before coming to its final resting place at Saint Spas.[206] Exactly who the princess was is unclear; she was misidentified in the 19th century with a daughter of Tsar John Alexander of Bulgaria, who became the wife of Andronikos IV Palaiologos (1376–9).[207] But she was obviously a woman of great status, laying claim to kinship with two of the families who ruled over the very last years of the Empire, and the survival of her tomb and her name seems almost symbolic, a distorted echo that is virtually inaudible against the tourist hordes of Nesebur.

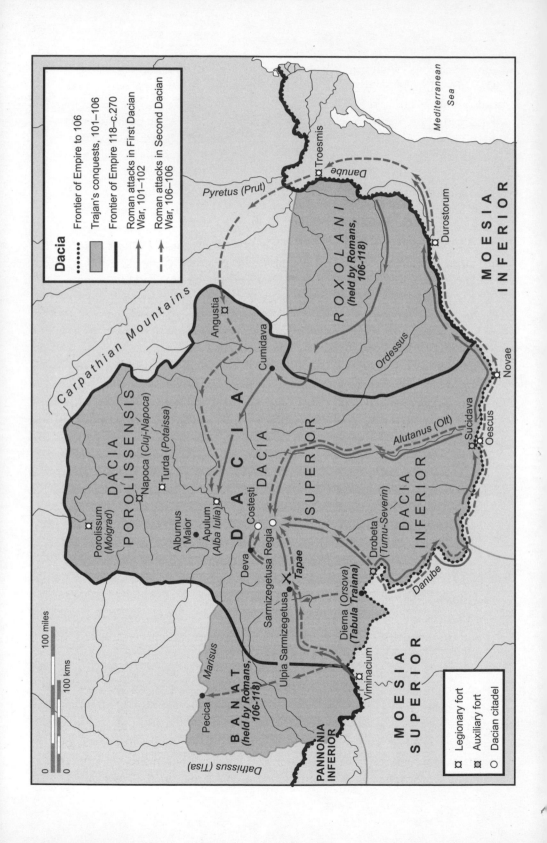

Dacia

- ••••• Frontier of Empire to 106
- Trajan's conquests, 101–106
- — Frontier of Empire 118–c.270
- → Roman attacks in First Dacian War, 101–102
- ⇢ Roman attacks in Second Dacian War, 106–106

Legionary fort
Auxiliary fort
Dacian citadel

100 miles
100 kms

Mediterranean Sea

⊡ Troesmis
Danube

Pyretus (Prut)

MOESIA INFERIOR

Durostorum ⊡

Carpathian Mountains

Angustia ⊡

Cumidava •

R O X O L A N I
(held by Romans, 106–118)

Ordessus

⊡ Novae

Sucidava ⊡
Oescus ⊡

Porolissum
(Moigrad) ⊡

D A C I A   P O R O L I S S E N S I S

Napoca *(Cluj-Napoca)* ⊡
Turda *(Potaissa)* ⊡

Alburnus Maior •
Apulum *(Alba Iulia)* •

Costeşti ○

D A C I A   S U P E R I O R

Alutanus (Olt)

D A C I A   I N F E R I O R

Deva •
Sarmizegetusa Regia ○
Tapae ✕

Drobeta
(Turnu-Severin)

Ulpia Sarmizegetusa •

Dierna *(Orsova)*
(Tabula Traiana)

Danube

Marisus

B A N A T
(held by Romans, 106–118)

Pecica •

Viminacium ⊡

Dathissus (Tisa)

MOESIA SUPERIOR

PANNONIA INFERIOR

CHAPTER 5

Dacia

Trajan constructed over the Ister a stone bridge for which I cannot suffi-
ciently admire him. Brilliant indeed are his other achievements, yet this
surpasses them . . . This too, then is one of the achievements that show
the magnitude of Trajan's designs, though the bridge is of no use to us;
for merely the piers are standing, affording no means of crossing, as if
they had been erected for the sole purpose of demonstrating that there is
nothing which human ingenuity cannot accomplish.

Cassius Dio, *Roman History*[1]

The medium-sized town of Turnu-Severin, far from Romania's political
centre at Bucharest, and long marooned in an awkwardly strategic location
near the point where Bulgaria, Romania and Serbia meet, lies at the root
of the problem that is Dacia and the struggle over the self-identification of
an entire people. It was here, in 101, that one of the columns of Trajan's
expeditionary force crossed into the territory of the Dacians. The army
was intent on teaching a lesson to their overly successful and aggressive
king, Decebalus, who was seen as posing a threat to the neighbouring
Roman provinces of Pannonia and Moesia that was too great to be ignored.
It was a campaign that would ultimately end in the conquest and annexation of Dacia, and the establishment of a Roman presence that would
endure for almost 170 years.

The Dacians and the Romans already had a long history of tension.
Sheltered in the Transylvanian plain behind the high protective cradle
of the Carpathian mountains, the Dacians had prospered, exploiting the
richness of their land in gold and silver resources, and harnessing new
techniques of craftsmanship and engineering that filtered through to
them from the Greek colonies on the Black Sea coast. Out of this they
developed their own indigenous civilisation, which, when united under
a strong political leadership, threatened to pose an awkward block on
any Roman expansive designs north of the Danube and to provide an
alternative power centre for any malcontents south of the river line.

Under King Burebista, the first really unified Dacian state had already expanded into Transylvania and even attacked Olbia in the Crimea.[2] Julius Caesar may have been squaring up to deal with this growing menace of the Dacians before his assassination in 44 BC, particularly as Burebista had offered assistance to his arch-enemy Pompey in 48 BC during the Civil War, but the death of the Dacian king the same year as Caesar reduced the urgency of taking immediate action. Dacia gradually fragmented into a number of warring factions, and what territory Burebista had captured south of the Danube was seized by Marcus Licinius Crassus in 27 BC.[3]

Intermittent raids by the Dacians across the river did continue, but they presented only localised problems, until the kingdom once more united under Decebalus in about AD 86. The previous year, a Dacian raid had resulted in the death of the governor of Moesia, Oppius Sabinus, and the Romans felt that it was high time to revenge him. Domitian therefore despatched his praetorian prefect Cornelius Fuscus to deal with Decebalus. However, at Tapae, about 100 kilometres to the north of Turnu-Severin, the Romans were badly mauled, resulting in the death of Fuscus and the loss of almost an entire legion. So the next year Tettus Iulianus was sent to finish the job, and he defeated Decebalus in more or less the same area.[4] The launching of another campaign against the Suebi and Iazyges to the west of Dacia meant that Domitian had insufficient resources to impose his will fully on Decebalus. The resulting treaty was something of a compromise, and one that the Dacians could even present as a victory, for the Romans handed over a large sum of money to Decebalus to keep him quiet and, possibly more importantly, sent craftsmen and artisans to the royal capital at Sarmizegetusa, some of whom may have been skilled in siegecraft and counter-measures.[5]

Dacia was, therefore, very much unfinished business when Trajan decided to launch his invasion in 101. Exactly what the Emperor's motives were has been the subject of much speculation. Allegedly Decebalus had been harbouring Roman deserters and had employed the engineers provided by the peace in 89 to construct impregnable strongholds; a more likely explanation is simply that he resented the affront to Roman dignity and the expense caused by the continued payment of subsidies to Decebalus,[6] and that he planned a limited campaign to put the Dacian king in his place. It was not in any case a sudden decision, as the logistics necessary to mount such an expeditionary force must have taken several years to arrange, and Trajan appointed safe pairs of hands to govern the neighbouring provinces (and to the command of their legions), including Marcus Laberius Maximus in Moesia Inferior. Estimates of the force involved vary from 50,000 to 100,000.[7] Whatever the true number, it was one of the greatest Roman armies ever gathered together for a single campaign.

The first assault was probably mounted in April. The sources for the campaign are surprisingly slight; the historians Dio Chrysostom and Appian both wrote accounts of the campaign, but they are wholly lost, while of Trajan's own narrative of the Dacian War, but a single sentence survives. Instead, apart from incidental mentions in more general histories, we are forced to rely on one of the most unique military narratives in Roman history. After his final victory in the Second Dacian War in 106, Trajan ordered the erection of a column to commemorate the victory. It was to be the centrepiece of his new forum, which had been started in Rome and sits opposite the older forums of Augustus and Julius Caesar, and adjacent to that of his adoptive father Nerva (the Forum Transitoria). At more than 30 metres high, and made up of seventeen marble drums, Trajan's Column was intended to be the last resting place of the funerary urns for Trajan and his wife Plotina. Whether it was in fact used for this purpose is unclear, but the reliefs, which run in a spiral from the base to the top of the column in around 400 frames, present an official visual history of the Dacian Wars.[8] The column was dedicated in 113 and was originally surmounted by a gilt statue of the emperor; which was replaced by the current portrait of Saint Peter in 1588.

The panels on the column have proved a fertile mine for students of Roman military tactics and equipment, in some cases providing the only really good depiction of such legionary activities as making a camp, entrenching or foraging. But their value in determining a chronological narrative of the Dacian Wars is hard to assess without corroborating evidence, which is, for the most part, lacking. The extent to which it simply depicts commonplace themes that were expected in such a publicly visible glorification of the Emperor is unknowable, but it is likely that, in general terms, the events shown have some relation to the real war, even if attempts to tie down exactly where a skirmish or battle took place are exceedingly difficult. These scenes are, however, a unique resource, and though other emperors (such as Galerius with his arch at Thessaloniki) depicted their campaigns in sequences of panels on stone, none of them approaches the breadth, ambition or completeness of Trajan's Column.

There is other evidence for the engineering work that was necessary for the military operation. Around 40 kilometres west along the river from Turnu-Severin, and 10 kilometres south-west of Orşova on the Serbian side (at ancient Dierna), an inscription records how the Emperor had a roadway excavated out of the bare rock of the cliffs, an extraordinary engineering achievement. A reproduction of the inscription, the *Tabula Traiana* is just visible from the Romanian side, decorated with an architrave as though a temple front; but the original was moved when the Djerdap dam was built and threatened to inundate the monument, and now sits more inaccessibly in a display some way off at Lepenski Vir.[9]

It seems that detachments of at least twelve legions may have been involved in the war,[10] a prodigious number, and – coupled with the large number of auxiliary cohorts and *alae*, plus the allied troops Trajan had assembled – this left Decebalus with very little choice but to fight a fundamentally defensive campaign and avoid full battlefield confrontations. The war as depicted in stone on Trajan's Column seems, therefore, to have an almost leisurely feel about it at first, showing the massing and mustering of the troops and their crossing on pontoon bridges, surveyed benignly by a personification of the Danube. Trajan is depicted on Panel VIII as holding a council of war, seated on a podium surrounded by his personal guard; then, in the next panel, he presides over the sacrifice of an ox and a sheep, a *suovetaurilia*, the proper offering for the successful undertaking of a military campaign. Yet before long, battle scenes appear; in one Jupiter is shown hurling a thunderbolt down against the Dacians, who are duly routed; soon afterwards a Dacian fortress is fired and an embassy composed of long-haired Dacian nobles is seen being received and sent away empty-handed.

Trajan seems to have won a major victory at Tapae, the same location as the two battles in the Domitianic war against the Dacians, but his losses were great enough to mean that he could not press home this advantage and a second year's campaigning was necessary. Further Roman successes led to the taking of at least two fortresses, in the storming of the second of which (on Panel LXVIII) the Romans are seen forming up in the *testudo* (or 'tortoise'), with shields locked together above and to the sides for protection as they near the ramparts.

It appears that Sarmizegetusa, the capital, was now dangerously exposed and Decebalus sued for peace. According to Cassius Dio, he was ordered to surrender the engineers he had previously been allowed by Domitian, to dismantle his forts and to hand over Roman deserters.[11] The Romans did not evacuate the whole of Dacia, retaining an area to the south, the modern Banat, and establishing military camps, possibly including the precursor of the legionary fortress at Sarmizegetusa Ulpia, in a salient threatening Decebalus's capital.[12]

Although Trajan had himself awarded the title Dacicus in honour of his victory and celebrated a triumph in December 102, Decebalus was not content to let things lie. In 103, he invaded the territory of the Iazyges (who had supported the Romans), and began to acquire arms again. In 105, he seems to have launched a direct attack on the Roman garrisons in southern Dacia.[13] There was also an alleged assassination attempt on Trajan and, more tangibly, a senior Roman officer was kidnapped by the Dacians after being tricked into attending peace negotiations in person. It is more than likely that this was the former consul Cnaeus Pompeius Longinus, who had been governor of Pannonia until 98 and so represented a prize hostage indeed.[14] Decebalus offered to parley Longinus's safe return in exchange for a Roman withdrawal south of the Danube. In the true spirit of Roman heroes of earlier times, Longinus took poison, preferring death to a dishonourable part in any exchange of territory for his own survival.

Trajan had had enough. An even larger army was assembled and despatched to Dacia. In the early spring of 106, the army crossed, after the requisite *suovetaurilia* was performed. The target would be the Dacian capital and Decebalus himself. The crossing of the Danube was immeasurably assisted by the construction of a fixed bridge across the river. The architect of the column, Apollodorus of Damascus, a Syrian and a favourite of Trajan, was also responsible for the great bridge (as well as for most of the other elements in Trajan's forum). Unfortunately, he was not so popular with his master's successor, Hadrian, who not only ordered the bridge thrown down, for fear that the Dacians might use it to strike more easily south of the river should they ever rebel, but also did not take kindly to some perceived criticism by Apollodorus concerning his own architectural tastes. The architect was summarily exiled and shortly thereafter Hadrian had him killed.[15]

The bridge was an astonishing feat of engineering. At around 1,100 metres long, it had to be supported by twenty massive piles driven into the river. In order to construct it, the course of the river was diverted by vast dams, which allowed the placing of the piles and arches. Unsurprisingly, its dedication takes pride of place in one of the scenes on Trajan's Column. At the same time the bridge was built, the first Roman stone camp in Dacia was established around the northern bridgehead at Drobeta. First garrisoned by the *Cohors I Antiochensium*, it, together with the bridge, spelled doom for Decebalus.

The second war began with an attempt by Decebalus to cut the Drobeta bridge,[16] and thus sever the vital artery of the entire Roman operation, but it failed. The Roman army then struck north, probably marching through the valley of the Olt to invest Sarmizegetusa from the south and east. Decebalus again avoided direct confrontation where he could, seeking to wear down the Roman through guerrilla-style attacks, hoping that he could survive until winter, and then once again patch up some kind of peace or enlist the support of further allies amongst the neighbouring barbarian tribes. Through hilly defiles and almost inaccessible approaches, the legions and cohorts finally reached Sarmizegetusa. Whether Decebalus defended his capital against a determined Roman assault, or simply fled when his leading warriors looked as if they were losing heart, depends on the interpretation of Trajan's Column.[17] Yet what is clear is that Decebalus escaped the fall of his royal capital in about July 106 alive and fled northwards to carry on the resistance.

Although he continued to defend (and lose) a string of other hill forts, many of his nobles must have defected, including one Biklis, whom Cassius Dio relates betrayed the whereabouts of the royal treasure, a bitter blow for any hopes that Decebalus may have held of buying assistance from outside Dacia.[18] The hoard had been concealed by diverting the Sargetias river, burying it and then rechannelling the river into its old bed.[19] When recovered, it was found (according to one source) to consist of five million pounds of gold and ten million of silver.[20] Even if exaggerated, the true sum must still have been vast, as it went a great deal of the way to defraying the costs of the whole campaign.

Decebalus was by now down to his last few diehard supporters. On 6 September 106, a mounted Roman detachment caught up with him in wooded territory, a scene dramatically depicted on the Column. The Roman cavalrymen desperately try to reach their quarry, but Decebalus, seeing that things are hopeless, slits his throat with his own *falx*, the characteristic curved sword of the Dacians. Astonishingly, corroboration of this account came to light when the tombstone of the very man who had commanded the cavalry in their failed attempt to capture the King was found in 1965 at Philippi in Macedonia.[21] Tiberius Claudius Maximus had been decorated for bravery in Domitian's Dacian War and fought in both of Trajan's campaigns in the *Ala II Pannoniorum*. He was probably about forty-five years old at the time of the exploit that has immortalised his name, and for which he received a further decoration. He would be honoured once more for bravery in Trajan's Parthian War of 115–17, making him one of the most decorated Roman soldiers known. Decebalus's severed head, meanwhile, was sent to Trajan's encampment at an unidentified place named Ranisstorum, together with his two children. The head was later hurled down the Gemonian steps at Rome, a fate reserved for the most heinous amongst Rome's enemies.[22]

Once the Roman conquest was complete, the camp at Drobeta hosted a variety of garrisons, including the *Cohors III Campestris* in the 2nd century, and the *Cohors I sagittariorum milliaria*, a double-strength cohort of archers, in the 3rd.[23] The auxiliary fort grew into a city, which was granted municipal status by Hadrian in 118–19,[24] before becoming a *colonia* under Septimius Severus some time around 200. The remains of the civilian settlement at Drobeta, however, have been wholly swallowed up by the modern town. The square perimeter of the camp is in place, but the several phases of rebuilding have confused somewhat the original neat plan. When the rest of Dacia was evacuated in 270, Drobeta – in common with a couple of other bridgehead forts (including Sucidava (Celei) to the east, opposite Oescus in Moesia) – was retained to provide control over a possible crossing point over the Danube where barbarians might strike southwards, but equally from which Roman armies might more easily launch punitive raids northwards against any troublesome barbarians.

The fort was rebuilt under Constantine I in the early 4th century, but was devastated during the Hunnish invasions of the 440s. It was then restored one last time under Justinian, when a simple defensive tower was constructed here, but so decayed was Drobeta itself by this time that it was given the new name Theodora. Exactly when it was abandoned is unclear, although the other bridgehead fort at Sucidava has yielded finds of coins up until 596–7 in the time of Emperor Maurice, which implies that it was pressure from the Slavs and Avars in the early 7th century that caused the final evacuation of the Byzantine positions to the north of the Danube.

Amongst the ruins, a series of barrack blocks by the river are visible, while the central *praetorium* seems fairly intact, and it is even possible to make out the curved apsidal podium of the temple of the standards. A large, round tower facing the river is of 13th-century vintage, but a less prominent one in the south-west belongs to the reconstruction under Justinian; it even incorporates gravestones from the earlier fort. Of the main fort, part of the gate towers of the *porta principalis dextra* survives, but more impressive by far are the piers of the original bridge that lie beached beside the modern river's course. They sit a little uneasily beyond a railway line, partly encased in modern concrete for protection against erosion. The larger one is as big as a house, part of it torn off, giving it the sinister effect of an insincere smile. Looking across to the Serbian bank, there are further remains towards the southern beachhead at ancient Pontes, but a grey-brown sky, limned with searing flashes of lightning, allows only intermittent glimpses of the point from which Trajan embarked on his invasion of Dacia.

From Turnu-Severin the road northwards is flat at first, but soon starts to climb into the foothills of the Carpathians. The countryside is afflicted by a curious schizophrenia, dotted with abandoned factories, rusting dinosaurs, already half-forgotten testaments to Nicolae Ceauşescu's policy of bringing heavy industry into the countryside. Yet alongside these, horse-drawn carts ply the roads between the villages, an easy and time-tested means of transportation when the money for flash cars or even for fuel is short. And superimposed upon this is a level of new prosperity, as gaudy villas line the roadside and the ever-present hoardings for mobile-phone companies insist on the arrival of a new economic era. Amidst all this, it would be little surprise to encounter a Roman legionary en route to Sarmizegetusa.

Although the Romans tried to lay claim to the Dacian heritage by naming the new town they founded on the lower ground as Sarmizegetusa Ulpia Regia (about 100 kilometres north of Drobeta), they were never really able to claim the uplands, and certainly not its soul. At Oraştie, the nearest main town to the site of Decebalus's capital, known for convenience as Sarmizegetusa Regia, those who do not have fond feelings towards the 170-year-long Roman occupation of Dacia have erected a statue to Burebista, the first of the Dacian kings to cause trouble for Rome.

Whether the Dacians benefited from the Roman occupation, how much native influence survived it, and in turn to what extent Dacia continued to be shaped by the Romans after the Empire evacuated the province have become the subject of a lively and sometimes bitter debate, which verges on the polemic. The traditional standpoint, at least in Romania, has been that the Romanian language (which is quite clearly a Romance tongue, like French or Spanish) is sufficient evidence that a Romanised population persisted in the area after the 3rd century and that today's Dacians are therefore lineal descendants of the settlers who flooded into the province after its annexation. Some neighbouring countries – and this is an attitude particularly prevalent in Hungary – have sniped that this is all nonsense and that Latin could not have survived in the face of widespread barbarian settlement, and without the support of a government infrastructure that Dacia signally lacked after 270. Finally, to add a third corner to a very vexed triangle, there are those in Romania who argue that really the two other camps are asking the wrong questions and that Romanian culture as it emerged into the Middle Ages had a strong component of the original Dacian about it, that the Roman invasion should not be celebrated as a 'liberation', that the Roman abandonment of the province was a good thing, and that in general Romanians should be celebrating Decebalus and his heroic struggle in preference to Trajan and his legionary blitzkrieg.

For the visit to Sarmizegetusa, I am, for the sake of excluding bias (or of including both biases), accompanied by representatives of both pro-Roman and pro-Dacian camps. Really it is a matter of emphasis, and no one doubts that the Dacians were amongst the most advanced of the 'barbarians' that the Romans encountered, and that the imperial occupation of Dacia did leave traces that echo down to the present day. The citadel lies at around 1,200 metres altitude, the first 1,000 metres just about accessible along a very rough road with a four-wheel-drive and a determined driver. Work on a tarmac road, which for the moment makes the ascent even more challenging, will eventually make one of Dacia's most hidden secrets within easy reach of all, with inevitably deleterious effects on the air of mystery that currently shrouds its wood-clad slopes.

The car park, such as it is, is in a narrow glade on a terrace, over-looked by a thin canopy of trees. A few scattered blocks mark the remains of the camp of a *vexillation* of the IV Flavia Felix legion, which occupied a position here for around half a century after the defeat of Decebalus.[25] However, once it was clear that the hill country had been genuinely subjugated and there was to be no Dacian resurgence, such lofty outposts were largely abandoned.[26]

Alongside stands a section of the original Dacian fortress wall, built using a system known as *murus dacicus*, which involved the construction of a double-wall joined together by timber struts with a packed-earth and rubble core between them for extra strength. The grooves and slots along the interior of the stones can still be seen where the timbers were originally laid between the two layers of wall. It was the erection of fortresses using such advanced techniques as this that had so exercised the Romans before the First Dacian War, and that had led to their demands that they be dismantled as part of the peace that resulted in the temporary cessation of hostilities in 102. Reused column drums integrated into the wall also indicate that it was built employing earlier, dismantled structures from the fortress.

A short distance away, the paved stones of a Sacred Way lead further up into the citadel. Sarmizegetusa was primarily a cult site, and the main area that has been investigated by archaeologists relates to its role at the heart of Dacian religious life. The Sacred Way led, originally, to this main sanctuary enclosure a few hundred metres away, which was first used during the time of Burebista. It continued to be maintained and embellished until the end under Decebalus, by which time the political and religious centres of Dacia had been consolidated into this one site, of such vital importance that its capture became the primary focus of Trajan's second war.

The temple enclosure is built on a double-terrace, which holds a series of shrines dating from different stages in Sarmizegetusa's development. The uppermost is the latest, almost certainly dating from the reign of Decebalus. It is composed (as are most of the Dacian temples) of several aisles of columns, which commonly had an upper and lower storey. Here, just the stumps of the columns remain, testament to the comprehensive sacking to which the Romans must have subjected the Dacians' sacred place (and their probable subsequent harnessing of the temple ruins for their own construction needs) – indeed, on the whole site only one more or less complete column is visible. On the lower terrace a number of older aisled temples sit in a wide, open space surrounded by a thick screen of trees.

Among them, one anomalous building stands out. A 7-metre-wide, flat disc, cracked with age, has a tail composed of rectangular blocks leading off from it, making it seem like a great stone lollipop. It is in fact a solar indicator. If a stick is placed in the middle of the disc at noon, its shadow will always fall along the stone 'tail', though the shadow's length will vary depending on the time of year, being shortest at the summer solstice and longest at the winter solstice.

As well as another aisled temple, which represents a pre-Decebelan phase, a curious circular sanctuary sits in the middle of the terrace. It has rows of concentric circles, one of larger stone blocks, then immediately inside this one of smaller stones – almost stone pegs – each seventh one being bigger than the rest. It is believed that these represent the Dacian solar year.[27] Intermediate circles are made up of wooden posts of varying heights, which create a kind of ripple effect. Any speculation that this might have had a particular religious significance is dampened by the revelation that they were in fact placed at Sarmizegetusa by the director of a film made about Burebista in the early 1980s.

At the centre of the temple lies a horseshoe-shaped inner sanctuary with its closed end pointing west, the normal orientation for Dacian temples. Exactly which gods were worshipped here is not clear. The 'Dacian' camp maintains that gods such as Zamolxis and Bendis were honoured at these shrines. Zamolxis is mentioned by Herodotus[28] as the supreme god of the Thracians, who was originally mortal and a disciple of Pythagoras, but who, after his death, was miraculously resurrected and became the subject of a long-lasting cult. Bendis was a goddess of the moon much revered by the Thracians, but to place her and Zamolxis's worship here involves translating the religious practices observed by Herodotus amongst the Thracians of the 5th century BC to those of the Dacians of the 1st century AD, a leap fraught with supposition. It is probable that the reality is much more complex, with groups of mixed Geto-Thracian heritage moving northwards over time and mingling with Celtic influences to create the high 'Dacian' culture of Burebista and Decebalus.

Down below the temple terrace, further sections of *murus dacicus* are visible amongst the trees and undergrowth. Only around 5 per cent of the site has been excavated, and much remains unknown of its governmental buildings and functions, and indeed of the civil population who must have made up the majority of its inhabitants.

Only about 10 kilometres as the crow flies from Sarmizegetusa, but a far longer journey from the summit of one hill fort to the crown of the other to its north-west, lies Costeşti, which was very probably the original capital of the Dacian kingdom under Burebista before its transfer to Sarmizegetusa. The climb here is more modest, a 750-metre hike up a gently sloping track from the guardian's house. The fort was again built using a series of concentric terraces, the topmost of which was surmounted by a palisade of oak logs above an earthwork stronghold and contained the royal palace.

On the second terrace, the grassed-over remnants of a *murus dacicus* defensive wall sit, together with stone blocks forming the outline of one of the gate towers. From a flat section of terrace nearby there is a sublime view of the forested hills opposite. It is an indication of the unfriendliness of the terrain that the Romans had to overcome; the large army groups that Trajan despatched into Dacia must have struggled to make headway in such terrain of wood and hill, yet any smaller units would have risked falling prey to Dacian guerrilla strikes and would have lacked the muscle to invest or storm the hill-fort complexes that dot the Oraştie mountains of the Dacian heartland.

The royal terrace further up retains two towers, one of which originally had an upper storey of brick, but this was badly damaged by fire and has collapsed. A second, larger tower lies 200 metres further off, in which sections of the upper storey survive, together with a porch of four broken columns. It has been interpreted as the royal palace of Burebista, from which he directed the Dacian armies that first threw down the gauntlet against Rome.[29] On a lower terrace nearby, in a quiet, damp glade, sits the largest Dacian temple still in its original location. Many of the smooth, round stones that mark the sites of the columns are covered in little blooms of moss and it seems a very peaceful place, from which the tide of war has long ago receded.

Once Decebalus had been defeated, the Roman armies occupied most of his kingdom, including an area in the east that had been annexed by the Dacians from the Sarmatians in the previous decade; Trajan ignored the latter's protest that their lands should be restored to them, in favour of holding a better defensive line for the Empire. The outline of the new province was dictated very much by the geography of the region. As Jordanes would later say in his *Getica*, 'This country lies across the Danube within sight of Moesia, and is surrounded by a crown of mountains.'[30] The Roman territory formed a rough horseshoe from the Dathissus (Tisa) river on the west, up past the gold-mining centre of Alburnus Maior to Porolissum in the north at the edge of the Apuseni mountains. It then ran along the foothills of the Carpathians to an eastern point at Angustia, at which it was closest to the north-western point of Moesia Inferior in the Dobrudja, though separated by several hundred kilometres of unfriendly territory. A string of fortifications on the Alutus river then took the *limes* to the Danube at a point roughly equidistant between the Moesian forts of Oescus and Novae. An area to the east of the Alutus, which had initially been occupied under Trajan (and attached to Moesia Inferior), was then abandoned by Hadrian in the 130s, before Septimius Severus pushed the frontier 10 or so kilometres east of the river to create a *Limes Transalutanus*. It seems likely that this latter was the first part of the province to be abandoned and was lost by the Romans around the reign of Gordian III (238–44).[31]

A portion of the old Dacian kingdom to the north-west, which was open to the central European plain, was left unoccupied and became known as the land of the 'Free' Dacians. To the north and east of this lay the territory of the Carpi and the route to the Ukraine and the central Asian steppes. It was unfortunate for the Romans that this became a sort of barbarian 'super-highway' along which successive waves of invaders moved. Dacia was thus terribly exposed and required a great outlay of resources to defend it. The province did at least have the merit (apart from its mineral riches in gold and iron) of acting as a lightning conductor, for barbarians would have to travel through it across hundreds of kilometres of Roman territory and past the defending legion and auxiliary units before they ever reached the Danube and the rich pickings of the cities that lay beyond it.

Sarmizegetusa Ulpia Traiana, the most important early centre of Romanisation was about 30 kilometres from modern Hunedoara, and 40 kilometres west of the old Dacian capital of Sarmizegetusa Regia, from which it borrowed its name. It was in fact originally founded (between 108 and 110) as Colonia Dacia, and only acquired its new name under Hadrian. It was the residence of the governor of Dacia, and thus the chief city of the province, before it was divided into three under

Marcus Aurelius. The new subdivisions of Dacia Apulensis (with its capital at Apulum)[32] in the west, of Dacia Porolissensis (with its governor resident at Porolissum) and of Dacia Malvensis in the south (with its centre possibly at Romula) excluded Sarmizegetusa from the direct line of political authority, but it was compensated with a position as metropolis for all Dacia and the focal point for the council of all Dacia (*Tres Daciae*), for which it was the designated meeting point.[33]

The city received a wall as early as the reign of Trajan, a sure sign that it was already recognised that defending the province might prove a challenge. On a rich agricultural plain overlooked by low, forested hills, it encloses an area of some 32 hectares, only part of which has been excavated. Indeed, the site seems like a curious mixture of museum and country park, the buildings infilled with grass, and parts of the ancient city still occupied by orchards and fields dotted with haystacks sculpted in the shape of an upside-down golf tee. The walls have been consolidated with mortar to stop erosion, but this gives them the disturbing appearance that they have been tamed and are now rather sulky. To the left of the main entrance lie a glass workshop and a small temple to the woodland god Silvanus, now with just the fragments of a courtyard and *cella* remaining. Nearby a larger shrine, the 'Great Temple', retains two Corinthian columns of its original colonnade, but the dedication of the god worshipped here is unknown.

Of more interest is the forum, extensively excavated and now a mixture of partly reconstructed and wholly ruinous buildings. The most important of these was the Aedes Augustalium, the palace of the priests of the imperial cult, one of the few such to have been identified throughout the Empire (another example was unearthed at Herculaneum, near Pompeii). The cult, which was ministered to by imperial freedmen (ex-slaves), was a prestigious sign of Romanisation and it is no surprise to find it here, in an area that was subjected to such a heavy military presence.

Among the heaps of fragments and column pieces lying around the forum, one is clearly a dedication by the *duumvirs*, the joint magistrates who presided over the city in provincial imitation of Rome's pair of annual consuls. Just outside the city walls lie the remnants of the Temple of Nemesis, adjacent to the amphitheatre – a juxtaposition of the deity of retribution and the arena that recurs time and again throughout the Roman Empire. The amphitheatre itself, a large curving expanse of brick and stone, seems oddly devoid of soul. There is no seating remaining and it is impossible to make out anything of its internal structure. It was built during the first half of the second century and had a capacity of around 5,000 spectators. It was repaired in 158 and remained in use quite late; the discovery of a 4th-century coin hoard and the conversion of the amphitheatre to some kind of fortress at about that time are rare signs of the residual urban life of Dacia following the Roman withdrawal some decades before.[34]

Most of the defensive installations in Dacia were in fact auxiliary forts (in the north primarily garrisoned by mounted units) or watchtowers, many built during the phase following the initial occupation (except in the *Limes Transalutanus*), but dating them any more precisely than the period 120–200 is difficult, and some at least may have been built later as part of a reorganisation or to fill in gaps in the line. There were, however, probably three legions in Dacia in the immediate aftermath of the Trajanic conquest: XIII Gemina, IV Flavia and I Adiutrix.[35] By 118–20, two of those had transferred to the eastern frontier, where they were needed for the Emperor's new war against the Parthians, and the XIII Gemina remained the sole legionary garrison until 168, when V Macedonica was transferred from Moesia Inferior to Dacia Porolissensis.[36]

Not far from Deva, the regional centre nearest Sarmizegetusa Regia, a large monument in honour of the Dacian king Decebalus, sickle-sword in hand, stands on the way into northern Transylvania. From here it is only around 60 kilometres to Alba Iulia, a handsome town, whose historical centre is in large part based around a Vauban-style fortress that was built by the Austrian Habsburg rulers of Romania in the 18th century. Its bastions and counterscarps lie precisely on top of the presumed fortress of the XIII Gemina legion and the town of Apulum that later developed from it. Under Marcus Aurelius, the town was elevated to become Municipium Aurelium Apulense.[37] It became a *colonia* under Commodus, and inscriptions have been found dating from as late as 253, just two decades before the Roman administration must have evacuated it. Uniquely, Apulum gave rise to two *coloniae*, the second of which, to the north-east of the legionary camp, reached that exalted status under Trajan Decius in the late 240s and was – with singular pragmatism, if not imagination – named Nova Apulensis. It remained long after the Roman era a focus for pan-Dacian (or Romanian) feeling, and it was here that in 1599 the unification of Romania was proclaimed by King Michael the Brave, and the first King and Queen of modern Romania were crowned in 1922. In the Catholic cathedral there, a Gothic structure with soaring barrel vaults, a discreet marble tomb contains the body of Janos Hunyadi (or Ioan de Hunedoara to Romanians) who, as King of Hungary, almost single-handedly held back the Ottoman Turks in the north-western Balkans for the best part of a decade in the 1440s.

The principal visible Roman relic of Apulum is one of the gates of the legionary fortress, the *porta principalis dextra*, which lay in the centre of the right-hand wall of the camp. In the throes of a major restoration, it lies in a grassy area alongside some of the 18th-century ramparts. Part of the Roman wall stands to about 5 metres high, and the two side-towers of the gate (covered in modern protective canopies) and its central arch are visible. Beneath them ditches have been excavated whose purpose looks defensive, but they are more closely associated with archaeological soundings than the original Roman structure. The walkways around the gate are patrolled by a small posse of 'soldiers' dressed in 18th-century Austrian garb, who act as guides to the Vaubanesque fortifications. On the day of our visit there were, unfortunately, no Roman legionaries in evidence.

It is only around 65 kilometres' drive north-east, along what was the Roman military road from Alba Iulia, to Turda, which was in Roman times the town of Potaissa and from 167 to 268 home to the V Macedonica legion.[38] Until then it had been a comparatively small settlement, but soon thereafter was promoted to become a *municipium* under Septimius Severus. Modern Turda is neat and well kept, but its tourism industry depends much more heavily on Dracula tours than it does on Romans, for the lore of the legendary vampire has spawned a large Dracula-themed restaurant and hotel in the centre, while Trajan, Hadrian and Marcus Aurelius merit scarcely a mention.

The site of the Roman camp lies on a plateau up a steep hill just to the south-west of the town centre. On a large rectangular area of grass, on which a couple of cows contentedly munch, and bordered by a row of single-storey houses, a gas holder or storage tower perches besides the Roman remains. The south-west corner tower lies visible in the grass besides the storage tower, then further back towards the east is the consolidated *principia*, really just the outline, though with the apse of what might have been a podium or the temple of the standards clearly discernible. Arrayed alongside it are small rectangular rooms, probably representing offices. Across a track from here are recent excavations, including what seems to be a bathhouse, with a scattering of ceramic pipes. There is clearly still much more to see, for from an obviously artificial mound on which a shrubby bush is growing, large numbers of pieces of tiles peek out, and throughout the fields in which the legionary camp now lies there are small pieces of pottery strewn everywhere.

Potaissa reached the rank of a *colonia* under Caracalla.[39] Coins from the time of Philip I (244–9) indicate that the camp was occupied at least until then, and pottery found on the site, together with indications from burials in a necropolis to the north-east of the town, show signs that Potaissa was not totally abandoned in the wake of the Roman withdrawal.

Some 30 kilometres further north-west lay Napoca, now Cluj-Napoca, the capital of Transylvania. Despite its importance in Roman times, the growth of a thriving medieval town, including the splendid 14th-century church of Saint Michael that dominates the main square, has all but obliterated its ancient parent settlement. It was, however, made a *municipium* by Hadrian in 124, and in common with other towns that their predecessor had raised to that rank, was elevated to *colonia* by Marcus Aurelius or Commodus.

The terminus of the military road that led all the way through the province, coming ultimately from Aquincum (Budapest) in Pannonia, was Porolissum, the administrative centre of the region and the capital of the later province of Dacia Porolissensis. It lies north-west of Zalău, some 80 kilometres to the north-west of Napoca, in countryside populated with low-rise villages with orange-ochre tiled roofs, each one of them with a pretty white- or cream-faced church mounted with metal crosses and almost onion-style domes. Porolissum itself was defended by auxiliary units, including the *Cohors I Brittanorum milliaria Ulpia Torquata pia fidelis civium Romanorum*, a unit from far-off Britain, which must have the honour of one of the longest Roman military names on record.[40] The civilian settlement, amongst whose inhabitants was a strong presence of military veterans, grew up to the south and west of the fort. The possibilities for making a profit from the trade across the border into *barbaricum* must also have drawn merchants and would-be entrepreneurs from much further afield.

The little museum in Zalău maps the seven military forts and sixty-six watchtowers or signal-towers in just this sector alone. The *limes* consisted largely of an earthwork, with a north-facing ditch, studded with strongpoints and observation towers, in distant echo of Britannia's Antonine Wall. The first signs of the camp complex, some 10 kilometres away near Moigrad, are a few vestiges of a rectangular building with a gated entry (now surrounded by barbed wire). This building, outside the camp itself, and just a few kilometres from the military frontier, was the customs house, at which dues could be levied on anyone entering or leaving the Empire, a tax known as *portoria*. The level of this could reach as much as 25 per cent, and it was distinct from any impositions exacted by individual cities (most notably Palmyra in Syria) for goods passing through their territory. *Portoria* dues were also occasionally levied on inter-provincial trade.

It was one of the most effective means of raising revenue that the

Empire possessed, for the government did not, in general, raise taxes based on income (which was difficult to prove), but preferred to attack more tangible assets, such as land and, as in this case, physical goods that were being transported. An additional set of taxes, called *vicesima* and payable at 5 per cent of the value, were levied on the manumission of slaves and as an inheritance duty. One of these, the *vicesima heredi-tatium*, was only payable by Roman citizens, and it is quite possible that Caracalla's decision in 212 to grant citizenship to all free males in the Empire was motivated by a desire to expand the base of this taxation, an argument made all the more plausible by the fact that he simultan-eously increased the rate to 10 per cent.[41]

To the left of the track that leads on towards the fort itself lies another area of remains, with just the foundations and a section of wall surviving. This was originally a sacred enclosure that housed temples to Liber Pater and Baal, the latter evidence of a strong Syrian presence in the town. This structure belonged to the civilian settlement of Porolissum, which, although it became a *municipium* under Septimius Severus, never quite made the final leap to *colonia* status.

The fort sits on Pomet hill, a slight eminence to the north and east of the *municipium*. To the north again a series of wooded ridges formed the actual *limes*, while to the north-west lies a gap in the hills, another 'Iron Gate' into Dacia, analogous to that along the Danube that led Trajan's troops into the province during the war of conquest. It is the need to guard this second opening that explains the heavy Roman mili-tary presence in the area. Across the valley, on Citera hill, another smaller Roman fortlet (probably built under Trajan)[42] stood, but, although exca-vated, the trees and bushes have long since grown back to reclaim the mound as their own.

The *porta principalis* of the main fort has been heavily reconstructed, its two projecting rounded towers somewhat reminiscent of a miniature version of the Porta Nigra at Trier. The surrounding circuit wall, however, is largely gone, leaving just a steep earth bank as a reminder of the once-formidable ramparts. In the centre of the camp the foundations of the *principia* have survived, as well as the podium from which in 214 Caracalla ordered the murder of Gabaromathus, King of the Quadi, who had been invited to Porolissum for peace negotiations.[43] It was a clear indication that Rome's word was best trusted at a very safe distance.

The partly restored *porta decumanus* leads out of the fort to the amphitheatre, which was reconstructed in the late 1990s. It was origin-ally built in stone over an earlier earthen structure in about 157. The level of the original can be made out by a wavy white line in the stones, above which is all modern stonework, albeit quarried locally from the same sources as were used in the Roman building.

Outside the fort to the west, past a partly preserved angle-tower, lies an area that was a tavern and, down some stairs beside it, a shrine to Jupiter Dolichenus. This, and the probable presence of a Temple of Mithras near the *principia*, are evidence of the influence of the military on the religious life of the town. A more mainstream public temple, that of the Imperial Cult, also lay south of the *principia*, which was in turn adapted to become an early Christian basilica once emperor-worship was no longer de rigueur. Porolissum was one of the most exposed outposts on the *limes*, but it still survived right until the end of the Roman period, with coins as late as Gallienus occurring there. It was probably inhabited beyond the withdrawal of the imperial administration, for coins have been found from the reign of Valens (364–78), while in 2007 a large deposit of materials dating to the late 4th and early 5th centuries was discovered.

In the mid-2nd century, persistent pressure by barbarian groups in the Carpathians and along the Danube led to a terrible dilemma for the Roman state. Raids by the Carpi in the 240s and the Goths in the late 240s and 250s had become ever more pressing and there were not the resources to fight on every front at once, particularly when the tax base was subsequently reduced by the breaking away of the Gallic provinces and then of almost the whole of the east during Zenobia of Palmyra's rebellion from 268. Dacia was simply too exposed, vulnerable to attack on three sides, and sometime between the 250s and 270 a pull-out from some of the forts may have begun. The chronology is unclear, but the forts on the Alutus river may have gone first.[44] Porolissum was certainly restored under Trajan Decius (between 248 and 251) and so may have been held comparatively late. Sometime during the reign of Aurelian (270–5), however, the Romans finally evacuated Dacia.[45] It was not a move that the Emperor was particularly disposed to publicise widely; even the slightest success might be celebrated on coins, or trumpeted in triumphs or ovations, but failure was normally quietly forgotten. Indeed, the province of Dacia was 'revived' south of the Danube by Aurelian's establishment of two new provinces of 'Dacia', both carved out of Moesia. Whether any of the population of the abandoned province was transferred to Dacia Ripensis and Dacia Mediterranea is unclear, but it was at least a useful propaganda exercise for the Emperor; it could now be claimed that Dacia had not been lost; it had merely moved a little.

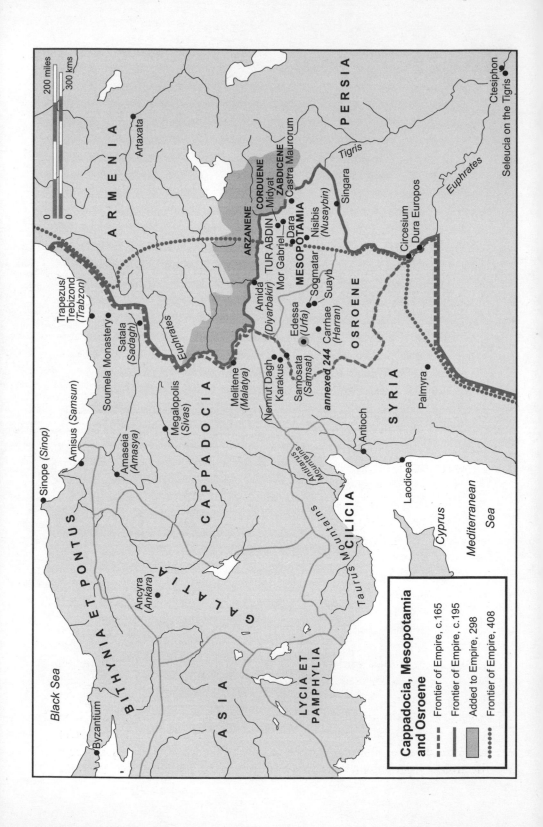

Cappadocia, Mesopotamia and Osroene

- - - Frontier of Empire, c.165
——— Frontier of Empire, c.195
▒▒▒ Added to Empire, 298
⋯⋯⋯ Frontier of Empire, 408

200 miles
300 kms

Black Sea

Byzantium

BITHYNIA ET PONTUS

Sinope (Sinop)

Amisus (Samsun)

Amaseia (Amasya)

ASIA

GALATIA

Ancyra (Ankara)

LYCIA ET PAMPHYLIA

Taurus Mountains

CILICIA

Laodicea

Cyprus

Mediterranean Sea

Antioch

SYRIA

Palmyra

Anti-Taurus Mountains

CAPPADOCIA

Megalopolis (Sivas)

Melitene (Malatya)

Nemrut Dagh
Karakus

Samosata (Samsat)

Samsata (Samsat)

annexed 244

OSROENE

Edessa (Urfa)

Carrhae (Harran)

Suayb

Sogmatar

Circesium

Dura Europos

MESOPOTAMIA

Nisibis (Nusaybin)

Singara

Dara

Mor Gabriel

TUR ABDIN

Midyat

Castra Maurorum

ZABDICENE

CORDUENE

ARZANENE

Amida (Diyarbakir)

Euphrates

Tigris

Euphrates

ARMENIA

Artaxata

Trapezus/ Trebizond (Trabzon)

Soumela Monastery

Satala (Sadagh)

PERSIA

Seleucia on the Tigris

Ctesiphon

CHAPTER 6

Cappadocia

They put arsenic in his meat
And stared aghast to watch him eat;
They poured strychnine in his cup
And shook to see him drink it up:
They shook, they stared as white's their shirt:
Them it was their poison hurt.
– I tell the tale that I heard told.
Mithridates, he died old.
  A. E. Housman, *A Shropshire Lad*, LXII

Rome's long involvement with Asia Minor began in 133 BC with the legacy bequeathed by Attalus III of Pergamum of his kingdom in western Asia Minor to the Roman Republic.[1] Such posthumous gifts – real or concocted – were not uncommon and served as a way of guaranteeing present security against meddling neighbours (or family), all at the expense, of course, of future independence. By the time of Attalus, the hegemony of Alexander the Great's Seleucid successors in the 3rd century BC had long since broken up into a kaleidoscope of fractious Hellenic kinglets, and once Rome was involved, the temptation to them of involving an external power-broker in their quarrels proved both alluring and, ultimately, disastrous.[2] Not particularly keen on annexation, the citizens of Pergamum rose under Aristonicus, and saw off one consul (Publius Licinius Crassus Mucianus), only to be defeated in 130 BC by his successor, Marcus Perperna.[3]

Rome's second acquisition in the area came in a similar fashion when Nicomedes IV of Bithynia (in north-west Asia Minor) willed his kingdom to Rome in 74 BC. From the windfall acquisition of this western coastal region, Rome's tentacles spread gradually inland. But during the next decade the Republic was nearly pushed from Asia by the rising power of Mithridates of Pontus, and it took a hard series of campaigns – and the military prowess of the most famous general of the age, Pompey the Great – to bring him down and in 64 BC establish the structures by which the Romans would dominate the area for a century.

The core of Mithridates's kingdom lay along the Black Sea coast and, extending as far down as the mountainous interior of central Anatolia, became the province of Pontus, while a stretch – including Trebizond (Trabzon) – was handed over to the client king Deiotarus of Galatia; and further south Rome's interests were safeguarded by King Ariobarzanes I of Cappadocia. Under Augustus, the province of Asia became one of the few really prestigious posts left open to senators, and to achieve the proconsulate here – or in Africa – was the summit of many senatorial careers. For the most part Augustus left the minor principalities of Asia untouched, despite the adherence of many of the petty monarchs to the cause of Mark Antony.

Under Tiberius, the huge central kingdom of Cappadocia was annexed to Asia in AD 15,[4] while the kingdom of Commagene – similarly absorbed after the death of its philo-Roman king Antiochos III in 17 – was given to the province of Syria.[5] Cappadocia was initially governed by a procurator (as had been the recent acquisitions of Raetia and Noricum in Europe), so rendering its treasury directly accessible to the Emperor. After a brief experiment under Caligula at reviving the client kingdoms as a means of governing the region,[6] the provincial organisation was finally stabilised by Vespasian, who established Cappadocia as the province covering the greater part of the Anatolian plateau, with Armenia Minor joining it in 72 to guard the north-eastern flank against the Persians.[7]

As the area where Roman power came up against that of Persia, the only state with the resources to truly rival Rome in the long term, expansion beyond the Euphrates, which became marked as an unofficial borderline between the two, was fitful and fraught with difficulties. Despite the strength of the Persians, the Romans did succeed in pushing the frontier forward. Trajan, with brief success in 115–17, and Septimius Severus, with more lasting effect in 197–9,[8] advanced the border to the Tigris, thereby creating the provinces of Mesopotamia and Osroene and an exposed salient into Persian territory to the east and south-east, whose defence would cause far more insecurity than it relieved.

The Cappadocian and Armenian frontier is one of the longest stretches in the Empire, and one of the most rugged. Largely defined by the Euphrates, as the river meanders through modern Turkey and on into Syria, it is comparatively little explored. From the prosperous coastal fringes of the Black Sea, the *limes* snaked, generally southwards, through coastal hills and then through the much more forbidding ranges of the Antitaurus and Taurus mountains, before descending finally into the fringes of the desert in northern Syria. Compared to many of the other sections of the frontier, there are relatively few visible remains in Cappadocia, though the cities that have grown up over the ruins of their Roman (and frequently much older) ancestors have very rich heritages indeed and often played a key role in the history of the Roman East.

Around 150 kilometres south of the Black Sea lay Amaseia (modern Amasya), the capital of the Pontic kingdom for a century after its foundation around 300 BC. It nestles at the foot of a dramatic gorge formed by two sets of cliffs towering above the River Yeşilırmak (the ancient Iris). Its ancient acropolis suffered a vengeful sacking by Lucullus's troops in 70 BC, no doubt frustrated at their inability to run the Pontic King Mithridates to ground. One of Rome's most implacable enemies, Mithridates, having provoked war through a massacre of Roman citizens in western Anatolia in 88 BC[9] – never a wise career move for an oriental despot – saw off Sulla and Lucullus in successive Mithridatic Wars before finally being brought to book by Pompey the Great in 65 BC.

After a brief period of direct occupation, Amaseia fell to a local client king, before being annexed directly to the province of Galatia in 2 BC. The town's most famous son, the geographer Strabo, was born here sometime around 64 BC,[10] just after the initial Roman conquest. An exceptional polymath, Strabo travelled widely, particularly in the Eastern Empire, and lived in Rome for at least nine years, from 44 BC. In 25 BC he travelled down the Nile with Aelius Gallus, the prefect of the province,[11] collecting information for his great seventeen-volume *Geographica*, which combines an account of the geography of the regions he visited with an eclectic mixture of history, mathematics, philosophy and political theorising. It is probable that it was through his relationship with Gallus that Strabo acquired his Roman citizenship (not a given, in an essentially Hellenistic *polis* such as Amaseia).[12] His acute observations included the all-too-true aside that the sun almost never seems to shine in Britain, while about his home town he proudly wrote, 'My city . . . both by human foresight and by nature it is an admirable devised city.'[13] Alongside the riverside walk where Amasyans take an evening stroll to help forget the oppressive midday summer heat, statues have been erected of the town's historic worthies. That for Strabo is robed in distinctly un-Roman garb, making him look like a botched hybrid, half-Oxbridge don, half-Mongol overlord.

The cliff face below the acropolis summit is pockmarked with tombs carved deep into the rock. Known as the 'Tombs of the Pontic Kings', there are five, accessible by staircases leading up the precipitous slope, in one of which an inscription was found dedicated by Metrodoros, the commander of the fort, to Pharnaces I.[14] All that now survive are plain rooms with niches cut into the back, either for the corpses themselves or, more likely, for cult statues. Two of the tombs share a cave, excavated out at the top, with the remains of a carved zigzag pattern in the facing wall to indicate the former presence of steps that would permit access to the roof of the chambers. After the removal of the royal capital to Sinope on the Black Sea coast in the later 2nd century BC, no other kings were buried here. Of Mithridates VI himself, we only know that Pompey ordered a decent funeral and that he was buried 'in the tombs of his forefathers',[15] but as to whether this was at Sinope, or indeed whether the royal necropolis at Amaseia was used for the illustrious last monarch of his line, the Roman historian Appian is studiously vague.

The final Roman frontier lay some 400 kilometres to the east of Amaseia, beginning its long course on the Black Sea coast near the city of Trapezus (later known as Trebizond, and now the modern city of Trabzon).[16] In the first century AD, Trebizond had served the Romans as a vital border conduit for the road over the mountains via the Zigana pass into Armenia, and, although notionally independent under Polemo I of Pontus, it provided a convenient base for Corbulo's campaign against the latter kingdom in AD 58.[17] It was, however, only six years later that the city was formally annexed as part of the province of Galatia.[18] As the frontier pushed eastwards under Vespasian and Hadrian, further roads were built into Persia and Mesopotamia and the city was extensively remodelled under Hadrian. Trebizond then experienced several centuries of quiet prosperity until the Goths, in a surprising eastward extension of their plunderers' progress, sacked it in 256. Finding the garrison drunk and the defences largely unmanned, they were able to break the barbarians' generally bad run at storming walled cities.

By the 13th century Trebizond had fallen to the Comneni, a noble family who since 1204 had presided over a wayward fragment of the greater Byzantine *imperium*, which had escaped the clutches of the Fourth Crusaders and had somehow never quite returned to the fold. Appending the suffix 'Megas' (great) to their family name, the Trapezuntine Comneni survived principally on a diet of absurdly inflated self-belief, cleverly calculated intrigue and an almost inexhaustible supply of princesses whom they used to cement alliances with their predatory neighbours. For all the Comneni's manoeuvring and grandiose statements that it was they, rather than the Palaiologi – the family that had actually recaptured the imperial city of Constantinople from the Crusaders in 1261 – who were the true heirs of Constantine, no one took their Lilliputian empire seriously and their position became ever more parlous.

The total population of the city itself had probably slipped by the 15th century to just 4,000, mainly as a result of the mortality caused by the Black Death. In the early 1450s, a Turkish emir from Erdebil besieged it, and Emperor John IV found only fifty of his subjects remaining, as the rest of the defenders, prizing survival over a valorous end, had simply slipped away.[19]

After the fall of Constantinople to Mehmet II in 1453, the Trapezuntines tried to keep a low profile. David, who came to the throne in 1458, effected an unfortunate change of policy and began to seek salvation through aggressive alliances with the western powers.[20] Being neither particularly interested in the charms of the Comneni daughters, nor in any position to offer concrete assistance, David's new friends – who included Philip the Good, the Duke of Burgundy – were entirely unable to fend off the inevitable denouement, and the offended Ottoman sultan marched on Trebizond in the summer of 1461. In vain David offered one of his daughters in marriage to the sultan, but this traditional gambit had long had its day, and Mehmet, unimpressed, declined.

After a month-long siege, David took the option of dishonourable exile and ordered the gates opened. Mehmet's janissaries streamed in to take possession of the town, and David, his family and most of the surviving nobility were packed off in ships to Constantinople. It was, in a sense, the day the Roman Empire died.

Two years later, angered at a letter that seemed to indicate a plot to restore the Comneni to power, Mehmet had David and seven of his sons beheaded in a single night.[21] The man who betrayed the letter, and who had also undermined David's will to resist the Ottoman siege, was his former treasurer and cousin, George Amoiroutzes. By a bizarre twist of fate, it was Amoiroutzes's son, George, known as Skanderbeg, who would lead decades of resistance to Ottoman advances in the Balkans, in some way making up by his bravery for the perfidy of his father.[22]

Shielded by the Pontic Alps, the Black Sea coast retained a strong and individualistic culture that held back Turkish advances for centuries, and even after the loss of its political independence it retained a vibrant separate identity until its Greek-speaking population was deported wholesale as a result of the Treaty of Lausanne, which formally ended the First World War in the region in 1923. Considered one of the most attractive cities in Asia Minor, Trebizond was described by a panegyricist as 'the apple of the eye of all Asia'.[23] Very little of this splendour now survives. A gate pierces the wall of the lower citadel – there were two – close to a congested square near the former Russian consulate, the immediate interior of old Trebizond being choked with traffic and lined with an unromantic assortment of travel agencies, spare-parts yards and tailors' shops. The square gate bastions project incongruously into another era, much restored and then blackened by the fumes.

Of the 'Golden Palace' of the Comneni there appears to be no trace. Even the most authoritative greybeards shake their heads sadly and offer this mosque or that madrasa as a worthy substitute. Further and further up the citadel slope, where surely the palace must have been sited, its marble great hall decorated with sumptuous portraits of the Grand Comneni,[24] there is still no sign. Finally, a local schoolteacher points us in the direction of the Kraal Köskü ('the King's Pavilion'), which sounds at least as if a dim memory of the palace has survived. So, uphill and past a small mosque, the clear remains of an enclosure wall of some antiquity face the road. In the 1920s, this area was comparatively clear and the palace ruins faced onto an open square called Epiphania, but now a whole suburb has grown around to conceal the ancient secret, making it much trickier to enter.

We plunge down a side-alley, into a kitchen garden with chickens scratching around a collection of ramshackle hutches, and a stand of vegetables struggling away in a gloomy corner. Pulling aside a makeshift barrier of wooden planks, we discover a way into the palace itself. Only shells of rooms now remain, the interior of the structure a shapeless maze of half-collapsed masonry, enclosed by the more substantial exterior walls, which stand in places to around 4 metres high. After a brief ramble around the broken palace interior, egress from the palace precinct is gained by another domestic yard, the modern residences supported in part by the old Byzantine wall. Looking back after another 50 metres, there is nothing to be seen, and the Golden Palace has disappeared behind a screen of modest apartment blocks. It is almost as if the Ottomans had taken until 1461 to storm the Comnenid citadel, for the simple reason that they could never quite find it.

Although at first intent on regaining the great prize of Constantinople, the Comneni soon recognised the practical needs of more localised aspirations by building themselves suitably grand churches in Trebizond. They could not resist, however, giving one the same dedication as the great cathedral of Hagia Sophia in the lost metropolis. Now set in a square well back from the traffic and bustle, the 13th-century monastery church is an island of calm. It is of a cross-in-square design, with a narthex at the west end, along which a gallery of beautiful medieval frescoes are arrayed, while inside, another set includes a very damaged depiction of Pontius Pilate washing his hand, and Saint Thomas feeling Christ's wounds. Although cleaned and restored in recent decades, their survival over seven centuries has something of the miraculous about it.

Hagia Sophia is not, however, Trebizond's oldest surviving church, for that accolade goes to Saint Anne's in the east of the old town. A worn relief slab on its south door depicts a soldier with outstretched sword standing alongside an angel, with an inscription stating that the church was restored in 883/4. The basilica remained a functioning church until 1923,[25] but its once-painted interior has been gutted, and it now remains firmly barred, its courtyard providing handy extra space for the neighbouring parade of coffee-houses.

The city's most important church, the largest of all and the venue for imperial coronations, was the Theotokos Chrysokephalos ('the Golden-headed Mother of Christ'). Its foundation is traditionally attributed to Hannibalianus, nephew of Constantine the Great, and the city's legionary fortress may have occupied an area subsequently used for the building of the church,[26] but its history can really only be traced to the 10th century. Converted soon after the Turkish conquest into a mosque, the Fatih Ortahisar Camii, its plain interior has a pleasing sense of tranquillity about it. Yet in truth the centuries have not been kind to it, and its hidden past jostles for attention in the background. The soaring dome is a reminder of the painting of Christ Pantocrator that must surely once have presided over it. Only a few decades ago, moreover, the walls were plastered over, obliterating a series of wall paintings and mosaics in the apse. Just a section of floor covered in *opus sectile* – cut sections of marble in black and white – gives direct evidence of the original church's decoration. For those intent on further scrutiny, the lower courses of the western wall of the mosque are composed of the original Roman stonework.

South of Trabzon, the road passes high into the Pontic Alps, the way winding through almost alpine forests, increasingly remote from the commercial and urban life of the Greek coastal colonies. Finally, after about 40 kilometres and at about 1,200 metres altitude, there lies the monastery complex of Panayia Soumela, the most spectacular of the many that dotted the Trapezuntine landscape, and among which it is the best representative of the age-old tradition of Christian piety that populated Asia Minor with monastic foundations, both lofty (as here) and (in modern Cappadocia) troglodyte.

From a distance the buildings seem to cling to the rock, as likely to promote vertigo as any sense of religious awe. Said to have been founded in 386, during the reign of Theodosius I, by Barnabas and Sophronius, two Athenian monks,[27] the monastery was long the recipient of high-ranking patronage. Its restoration and enlargement in the 6th century were attributed to Justinian's favourite general, Belisarius. After the establishment of the Empire of Trebizond, the monastery church became if anything an even greater focus for imperial favours, being accessible to Comnenid largesse in a way that the basilicas of Constantinople no longer were. Alexios III Comnenos refortified Soumela in 1360, claiming on his inscription, which survived until 1650 on the monastery's outside gate, the rather overoptimistic title of 'Emperor of all the East and Iberia'.[28]

Soumela survived the Turkish conquest and almost five centuries of Ottoman rule before the transfer of populations in 1923 deprived it of its loyal Greek-speaking flock, and it was abandoned. Today the site is largely based on a remodelling in the 13th century, although many of the buildings were destroyed in a fire in 1929 and have been substantially restored in recent decades. This has not stopped dozens of the fresco panels being defaced by visitors more careful for their own transient fame than the preservation of a priceless cultural heritage. Saints look down amid a score of scrawled names and messages, their frozen stares and stylised poses mercifully betraying no sense of the indignity to which their images have been subjected. Some graffiti pre-date the end of the active life in the monastery in the 1920s, but an upsurge of vandalism in the 1960s was accompanied by predominantly local names, save the proud, neat and disgraceful contribution by a visiting US Air Force man in 1965. Those frescoes sited higher up have largely escaped damage, and the Rock Chapel, which formed the original core of the monastery, retains its biblical scenes mostly intact amid the gloomy half-darkness and distant sensation of a place once drenched in piety, now almost devoid of any hint of the sacred.

The legionary fortress of Satala lay, then, as now, on the route south-wards from Trebizond, which ultimately took travellers skirting the frontier down as far as Antioch, a distance of more than 600 kilometres. The verdant hills of the Black Sea coast gradually become less fertile, browner and more arid in appearance until at length they take on the look of a lunar landscape, scored and furrowed with erosion channels. Finally, the hills descend into the plain of Kelkit, about 90 kilometres south of Soumela, and close by lies the unassuming village of Sadagh, its older houses in part built from stones acquired from the Roman fortress. Until the 1960s, indeed, the former Roman baths were still being used as the village's bakery.[29] Procopius, in his account of Justinian's 6th-century reconstruction of Satala, describes a topography that is instantly recognisable: 'it also lies in a low-lying plain and is dominated by many hills which tower around it'.[30]

Satala seems an unlikely place for a famous Roman victory. Indeed, the fact that it once housed a legionary fortress, a significant civilian settlement, and was the lynchpin of the Roman frontier defences in central Cappadocia seems to risk a severe attack of incredulity. When Alfred Biliotti, the British vice-consul at Trebizond, came here in 1874, there was far more to see.[31] He reported substantial sections of wall remaining, some 6 metres high and more than 4 metres wide. Of all this abundance of remains, most has now vanished.

Upon the annexation of the central Anatolian kingdom of Commagene to the Empire by Vespasian in AD 72, the whole of the upper Euphrates became a frontier area, although in part shielded by the client state of Armenia from direct confrontation with the Parthians. Of the other legionary fortresses that guarded Cappadocia, Zeugma and Samosata, the bases of III Scythica and VI Ferrata respectively, have been inundated by the waters of the Atatürk Dam, while Malatya has been encroached on by the modern city, and so Satala's survival is of unique importance. It became the base of XV Apollinaris, probably under Trajan,[32] who passed through during his Parthian campaign of 115–17, and the legion remained there even after the town's destruction around 256 by the Persian shah Shapur I during his rampage around the Roman East. According to the *Notitia Dignitatum*, they were still on garrison duty there at the end of the 4th century.[33]

The area remained contested by Sassanid Persians and Romans throughout the 3rd century. In 298, Galerius rescued his reputation with his senior colleague Diocletian when he defeated the Persian ruler Narses in the vicinity of Satala, capturing the royal harem and treasury for good measure. He thus made up for a stinging defeat that he had suffered at the Persians' hands two years before, not far from Carrhae (Harran in south-eastern Turkey). So annoyed had Diocletian allegedly been at the damage to Roman prestige on that occasion that he had made Galerius, clad in full imperial regalia, walk on foot in front of his chariot as the two Tetrarchs entered Antioch.[34]

After the Persians suffered a further defeat in 530 in front of Satala, Justinian decided to give it new fortifications, and it is the remains of these that can be seen today. The civilian settlement seems to have been largely swallowed up by the modern village, but perched on a gentle slope that ultimately leads across the fields down to the Kelkit river lies the fort, the surviving banks and stones of its ramparts forming a platform on which a sea of golden wheat ears wave tranquilly in the breeze. The interior of the fort, in part cut away at its western end by the village houses, is impenetrable until harvest time, though Biliotti reported a 'substantial house' there, which a century of agriculture must have eroded away entirely. The rubble-core of the north-east corner towers is substantially intact, standing upright up like a lonely chess piece, its game long over. Just a few courses of stone remain of the rest of the circuit, uncertainly ringing the mound, a scattering of the rest lying at the edge of another field to the east of the fort.

A few hundred metres to the south-east, deep in the middle of another field, sit four arches, only one of them still carrying a channel or lintel on top. A little further on, small piles of stones mark the former site of a fifth arch and, doubtless, further in the agricultural undergrowth lie the remains of many more. After resisting for many centuries, in 1784 the bulk of the structure seems to have been plundered for stones to help repair damage caused by a large earthquake in the regional capital of Erzincan.

There has been a great deal of debate as to whether this is an aqueduct or the remains of a basilical church. Biliotti certainly thought it was a church, but subsequent scholars seem to have favoured the aqueduct, before a recent swing back to regarding it as a religious building.[35] The pair of shepherds who shyly regard our unlikely progress are with Biliotti, and maintain adamantly that it is a former Christian church and that it must be, for their grandfathers told them so. The hillsides, they say, are dotted with tombs and there are inscribed stones to be seen by those who know where to look. People from the government came some years back and took away stones in army helicopters, though whether this was an officially sanctioned excavation or a strictly freelance enterprise they do not know or, diplomatically, will not say.

Biliotti faced similar ambiguities more than a century ago. A bronze head that he had discovered was confiscated by the governor of Erzerum and sent on to Istanbul, where it was sold to a private collector, for which Biliotti received the grand sum of eight Turkish pounds. Immediately after the British consul's departure, the headman of Sadagh set to his own excavations, which apparently yielded him no harvest whatsoever.

The site is still littered with minor treasures. Near the aqueduct or basilica, someone has excavated a deep pit, exposing the remains of an ancient wall. In the debris piled up around the hole lie carved mouldings from friezes with zigzag patterns and a couple of fragmentary tile stamps carved with 'X', which might possibly be part of XV for the Apollinaris legion, Satala's garrison. The fort's final fate is obscure; it was probably abandoned after being sacked by Khusraw II in 607, but what became of its civilian community, which was large enough to send a bishop to the Council of Nicaea in 325, is utterly obscure.

Lying to the south and east of Satala, in a mountainous region of eastern Anatolia bordering the upper Euphrates, the kingdom of Commagene was able for several centuries to exploit its lofty and

inaccessible position to avoid the clutches of its more powerful neighbours. In the second century BC, the Seleucid Empire, one of the successor
states that carved up Alexander the Great's conquests after his death in
323 BC, began to fragment. Ptolemaios, the Seleucid governor, took the
opportunity to declare independence around 162 BC. He founded
Commagene and gradually extended its domain southwards to include
Samosata (300 kilometres south-west of the Kelkit plain),[36] and the
kingdom reached its cultural apogee under Antiochos I, who ruled it
from about 69 BC.[37]

In AD 17, however, Commagene was annexed by Tiberius and appended
to Syria. It was gifted a further three decades of independence by Caligula
in 41, who confirmed Antiochos IV as its ruler. But in 72, Antiochos was
accused by Caesennius Paetus, the governor of Syria, of conspiring with
the Parthians, and Vespasian permitted his legate to annex Commagene
once more. Direct Roman control now extended down the middle
Euphrates, probably as far as its confluence with the Balkh, and Samosata
was renamed Flavia Samosata to indicate its new allegiance. The
Commagene royal family was packed off to Greece, where it regained
a momentary fame when Antiochos's grandson – who rejoiced in the
delightfully Hellenistic-Roman mish-mash name of Gaius Julius
Antiochos Epiphanes Philopappos – was appointed suffect consul in 109.[38]

A much more spectacular legacy lies hidden in the hills to the north
of Samsat, where the Commagene royal house erected a series of memorials and cult installations. The most famous of these is at Nemrud Dagh,
about 100 kilometres to the north-east, where two terraces of decapitated divine heads lie neatly arranged on a platform beneath a massive
tumulus of loose stones. Constructed under Antiochos I, this cult site,
known as a *hierothesion*, involved an enormous effort to carve the terraces
from the living rock and heap up the huge amount of debris to form
the tumulus itself (although whether it actually contains a tomb has not
been determined).[39] The heads propped on the ground and the larger-
than-life-size bodies that once supported them, represent Heracles,
Apollo, Zeus, Tyche (goddess of fortune) and Antiochos, whose divine
nature is thus hinted at by the company he keeps. Most of the gods, in
the syncretistic way of the times, can be identified also with deities from
the Iranian pantheon, such as Mithras for Apollo and Ahuramazda for
Zeus. Elsewhere a set of reliefs shows the illustrious royal ancestry of
Antiochos, from the Achaemenids Darius I and Artaxerxes II, down to
various Seleucids, and also including Alexander the Great, from whom
Antiochos claimed descent on his mother's side.[40] On others the king is
shown greeting various gods in what are charmingly described locally

as 'hand-shaking' scenes,[41] while a relief of a striding lion contains zodiac symbols and a pattern of stars that indicate a precise date, most probably 7 July 62 BC, though both the date and its precise significance have been much disputed.[42]

However, more than any individual piece, it is the ensemble that is striking, and the enormous diversion of resources that must have been necessary to achieve its construction. Antiochos, though, can never have dreamt that his grand project, to which only a limited number of his Commagene subjects can ever have come via a series of difficult processional ways, would become an enormous tourist magnet. At sunrise in particular the slopes are congested with backpackers seeking to witness the first rays touch the sacred sculptures and infuse them with a tint of rosy-yellow. Far more than his Roman conquerors, then, Antiochos has truly achieved immortality.

Around 50 kilometres to the south-west, and on a clear day offering a view of the terraces at Nemrud Dagh itself, is yet another tumulus, this time constructed by Mithridates II, the son of Antiochos I, quite possibly for his sister Laodice. The main feature is two pairs of columns – there were once three – one of which contains the extremely weathered figure of an eagle. It is from a rather creative misinterpretation of the identity of the bird that actually surmounts the column, that the place gets its Turkish name, Karakuş – the tumulus of the blackbird.

As Commagene was absorbed into the Roman provincial structure, it became necessary to provide it with a road network, particularly to reinforce the military spine running down from the Black Sea to Antioch. A few kilometres west of the Commagene royal summer capital of Arsameia (itself about 20 kilometres west of Nemrud Dagh) – where more 'hand-shaking' scenes are visible amidst the tumbled stones – lies the Roman bridge at Cendere, which carried the military road that followed the Cappadocian border via one of the few convenient crossing points over the Kahta river. From the side, as it spans a largely dry riverbed, the awkwardly humped construction with its facing of brick seems to resemble any other bridge of uncertain antiquity, but it still carries traffic, and is thus one of the oldest major river bridges anywhere in the world still in use for vehicles. Coming closer, three columns resolve themselves from the surrounding haze, one at the eastern end and two on the western bank. The bridge was constructed by the legate of the XV Apollinaris legion in the early 3rd century, and the columns (there were originally four) were dedicated for the Emperor Septimius Severus, his wife Julia Domna and sons Caracalla and Geta.

When Caracalla had Geta murdered after their father's death, he decreed that his brother's name be erased from all monuments throughout the Empire, and thus, here at Cendere, one of the columns would have been defaced. Its actual removal, though, is probably more to do with the vicissitudes of time than evidence of a particularly thorough job in removing all trace of Geta's memorial. It is a practice known as *damnatio memoriae*, the Romans' way of literally erasing from history those who had, for one reason or another, fallen into disfavour. It has its antecedents in Greek practice, where as early as the 5th century BC inscriptions were modified to shade out disgraced politicians or remove other unwanted references.[43]

With the extreme political instability and the frequent changes of regime that characterised the later Roman Republic, the use of devices to target opponents posthumously (such as depriving their heirs of the right to inherit or throwing down their statues) became ever more common. Upon the defeat of Mark Antony, the Senate declared that inscriptions mentioning his name should be destroyed (or his name simply erased), the first major example of this type of sanction.[44] They also declared for good measure that the name Marcus should henceforth be banned from use by the Antonii, the disgraced triumvir's family. Thereafter, both those who fell foul of the Emperor, such as Cnaeus Calpurnius Piso[45] (who was convicted of treason under Tiberius), and the emperors themselves if unpopular could find inscriptions in their honour being erased (but the latter only after their deaths). The normal form would be for the Senate, generally at the prompting of the Emperor (but in exceptional circumstance on its own initiative), to vote the target of the *damnatio* as an enemy of the Roman people, and to impose the erasure of inscriptions as an additional sanction.

Emperors who suffered *damnatio* included Nero, Commodus and Caracalla, while during the 3rd-century military anarchy, the ordering of the defacements of a predecessor's monuments became almost a rite of passage. Whilst normally only individuals suffered this penalty, the unique case of an entire legion – the III Augusta – stands out. Its monuments were defaced in the mid-3rd century on the orders of Gordian III, who blamed them for the death of his relatives Gordian I and Gordian II in an uprising that the legion had put down.[46]

To the north and east of Commagene lay the kingdom of Armenia. For the Romans, it was a client state too far. It first came into the sights of Rome through the tacit support of its king Tigranes for Mithridates of Pontus in his own wars against Rome during the 70s BC.[47] Faced with the threat of total occupation of Armenia, Tigranes submitted to Pompey, laying his diadem at the Roman general's feet. He was permitted to retain the core of his kingdom, but his recent acquisitions in Mesopotamia and the borders of Parthia – which were probably what had the Romans worried all along – were handed over.

So began Rome's on–off relationship with Armenia. For more than 600 years the Romans sought to pull Armenia out of the Persian sphere of influence, sometimes shadow-boxing, at other times outright slugging it out. In 20 BC, Augustus intervened to oust a pro-Parthian monarch, Artaxias II, and replace him by his more pliant brother, Tigranes II. And so it continued.

Nero's general Corbulo campaigned here in AD 60, again securing Roman predominance and extracting an agreement that, whilst the Armenian king might be a Parthian and selected by the Parthian shah, he should nonetheless seek Roman confirmation of his rule and receive his crown at Roman hands. The high tide of Roman success in Armenia came in AD 163, when Statius Priscus stormed Artaxata, the northern Armenian capital (now Artashat in modern Armenia), during Lucius Verus's general campaigns against the Parthians.[48] A new capital, Kaine Polis – which means, imaginatively enough, 'New Capital' – was established and a Roman senator, albeit related to the Parthian royal family,[49] placed on the throne.

Armenian-Roman relations were given a further twist in the early 3rd century when the ruling Arsacid Parthian dynasty in Persia was overthrown by the Sassanids. In Armenia, a branch of the Arsacid family clung on to power, so that now, although the territory remained within the Persian cultural sphere, there was an irretrievable cleavage between its own political interests and those of (as the Arsacids saw it) the Sassanid usurpers in Ctesiphon, the capital they established on the east bank of the Tigris (some 30 kilometres south of modern Baghdad). The coming of Christianity to Armenia further accentuated the differences with Persia; the baptism of Tiridates III of Armenia in 314 raised the unpalatable prospect of a permanently pro-Roman state on the Sassanids' northern flank. Under Constantine I, there was even a plan to annex Armenia by declaring his nephew Hannabalianus as king. The Emperor's unexpected death in 337, however, put an end to this, and Hannabalianus was murdered along with most of Constantine's more distant male relatives by his three ambitious sons.

The disastrous death of Julian in 363 on campaign against the Persians,[50] and the subsequent humiliating peace, left the Romans promising not to intervene further in Armenia. Yet under Valens conflict broke out once more, as the Romans placed their nominee, Pap, on the throne in

370. It was an extremely short-lived policy success, as Pap was murdered five years later, leading to the installation of yet another Persian-backed king.[51] The game of royal musical chairs was temporarily halted by a treaty in 387 by which Armenia was in effect partitioned between two kingdoms, one with a pro-Roman king, the other with a Persian-backed ruler. The western portion was soon absorbed into the Empire as the province of Armenia Minor in 428, while the remaining four-fifths became the Persian satrapy of Persarmenia.

Finally, in 590 the forces of Emperor Maurice defeated the Sassanid shah Vahram VI and, with the support of the Armenian nobles, annexed the whole of Armenia. Although they finally had the prize that had long eluded them, the Byzantines had little time to enjoy it. A brief dispossession by the Persians in the 620s was followed by a more definitive expulsion of the Byzantine authorities by the Arabs in the 640s. Brief flickers of independence from 657 to 661 and in the 680s were soon snuffed out.

Arab rule led over time to the destruction of many of the traditional noble class, the *naksharars*, and the consolidation of authority in the hands of a single family, the Bagratunids, culminating in the appointment of one of their number, Ashot I, as 'prince of princes' in 885.[52] For 200 years the Bagratunids performed a delicate juggling act, balancing the competing interests of their nominal Arab suzerains, their religious brothers in the Byzantine Empire, and the fractious squabbling of the resurgent *naksharars*. Ashot, memorialised by the nickname 'the Great', and his son Smbat were reasonably successful, although the latter finally found himself on the losing end of a civil war and was disposed of in 913 by Yusuf, the Arab governor of neighbouring Azerbaijan.[53] Although restored with Byzantine assistance, the Bagratunids were rarely able to reassert their authority over an area as wide as that dominated by Ashot the Great. What Armenia lacked in political unity in the 10th century, however, it made up for in a dazzling cultural and artistic renaissance. In 964, Ashot III 'the Merciful' transferred the Armenian capital to a new site at Ani in the southern portion of the kingdom.

Until the collapse of the Soviet Union in 1991, the site of Ashot's new capital (some 350 kilometres east of Trabzon, and 50 kilometres east of the provincial capital of Kars) was very hard to visit, with the taking of photographs (and even the visible writing of notes) forbidden on pain of confiscation by Turkish border guards; and, for those who strayed too near the Cold War border, the prospect of being shot by their Soviet counterparts. Ani still sits on the frontier, between Turkey and its new neighbour, the Republic of Armenia, divided by the snaking line of the Arpa Cayi river. Relations between the two countries, poisoned by the deaths of huge numbers of Armenians during the chaotic era that followed Ottoman Turkey's defeat in the First World War, are suspicious in the extreme. There have even been accusations from the Armenian side that damage caused to the Ani monuments was connived at by local Turkish authorities, whose attitude to a cultural monument to a people that many accuse the Ottomans of trying to wipe out is decidedly ambivalent.

Passing through the Lion Gate, an Ayyubid gateway – together with the rather too pristine restored walls, the Portakabin ticket office and the gang of juvenile trinket-sellers – gives little promise of what lies ahead. For whether damaged, neglected or unloved, Ani reveals itself as a breathtaking spiritual landscape. Its secular buildings have long ago decayed or are inaccessible, but the remains (in some cases skeletal) of the churches are poignant witnesses to a piety and devotion that sustained this kingdom in its long, and ultimately unsuccessful, defence of its position at the very edge of the Christian world.

At a distance the buildings have the curious appearance of a low, thickset dwelling surmounted by a conical cap, the trademark dome of the characteristic centralised Armenian church architecture. Close to the city's entrance, the church of the Holy Apostles seems curiously chunky and rectangular, but the effect is attributable to a later Seljuk caravanserai bolted onto the ancient church, a building also responsible for the stone portal carved with stalactite-like stone projections at its entrance. Inside, the main church boasts a superb riot of ceiling ribbing, counterpointed with a two-coloured pattern of mosaics and a scattering of Armenian inscriptions. Visible from here, the imposing hill of the town's citadel dominated the skyline, but both this and a monastery beyond lie in a forbidden military zone.

The Menüçehir Camii, towards the southern end of the site, is said to be the earliest Seljuk mosque in Anatolia, dating from the mid-11th century, with a rather funnel-like brick minaret. But inside there is no *mihrab*, save one sculpted out of the bricks of the original gallery, while the same bichromatic black and red work as in the Holy Apostles church, and an inlaid mosaic ceiling, give rise to the suspicion that this was originally an Armenian building, possibly a meeting hall. Climbing of the minaret is strictly forbidden, on account, it is said, of a tourist who some years ago leapt to his death from its summit.

Close to the ravine that delimits the city's plateau on the opposite side from the river gorge lies the church of Saint Gregory of Abughamir, a building restored to its final form in 1040 by a member of the Pahlavuni family, which thrived in the last decades of Ani's independent existence.

Its conical dome is punctuated by mouldings that surround windows in the drum to create blind arcades, a technique which the Armenians made almost their signature flourish. Inside, an arrangement of six apses was intended to focus attention on the central nave, which may have housed the Pahlavuni family tombs.

Ani's main cathedral, near the city's southern edge, lies squat and bulky, very different from the conical structures that otherwise dot the landscape – a little deceptive, for the church did originally have a dome, but it was brought down by an earthquake in 1319, one of a series that have contributed to the generally ruinous state of Ani. Ribs rising up from the arches to support the dome bring to mind the Gothic cathedrals of western Europe, though the process by which it might have influenced Western styles is obscure; perhaps the Crusaders saw Armenian churches in Cilicia, further to the south, and brought back memories of the structures on their return home from the Holy Land.

Nearby lies one of Ani's most famous structures, the church of Our Saviour, known more for the particular nature of its destruction than for the unusually large dimensions of its dome. Built around 1035/6, the church survived (although much decayed through age and general neglect) until the 1950s, when it was struck by lightning during a storm and the façade was literally rent asunder. The surviving half of the church looks, from the correct angle, as if it forms part of a complete whole, yet shift your perspective by a few degrees and it is clear that the other half of the building is simply missing. The stones of the destroyed portion still lie around in a crumpled heap, giving the whole the air of some bizarre Hollywood film set.

Down by the river lies another of Ani's surviving gems, the church of Saint Gregory the Illuminator, named in honour of the saint who brought Christianity to Armenia, himself of a noble Parthian family. It is also known as the Tigran Honents church, for the merchant who dedicated the church in 1215 and paid for its lavish frescoes. Constructed at a late stage in Ani's history, it shows some influence from Georgia, Armenia's Christian neighbour in the Caucasus, which had experienced rather more success in holding back Turkish attempts to absorb it. A pair of saints arched over the baptistery stare out at another trio over the church's main door, their faces gouged out by some unknown iconoclast.

Inside, the frescoes depict scenes from the life of Christ and that of Saint Gregory. Tradition relates that the saint refused to sacrifice to the pagan goddess Anahid – from whom Ani takes its name – and so enraged King Tiridates by his refusal that he was subjected to a brutal sequence of tortures, including suspension upside down over a mound of burning dung, and shredding the flesh on his thighs by gashing them with iron spikes. Finding that Gregory would still not abjure his faith, the King had him consigned to a darkened pit for fourteen years, an ordeal that he survived only because a pious widow threw a loaf of bread down to him each day. Finally, Tiridates went insane, perhaps sent mad by the strain of devising ever more inventive torments for Gregory, and it was only the intervention of the saint, who prayed for his royal tormentor, that cured the King. Suitably impressed, Tiridates released him, became a Christian and began a tradition of royal patronage that would last almost 800 years.

Further down towards the river another little monastery clings, together with the scattered remains of churches that collapsed long ago and sent their stones tumbling down to the edge of the gorge. On the Arpa river itself a pair of end abutments of a bridge that once connected the two sections of Ani sit alone, the void between them a symbol of the fractured relations between Turkey and Armenia, a gulf almost impossible to pass. Over on the other bank, amidst the rumble of machinery and the roar of excavators, in a potent political gesture, the modern Armenians are building a replica Ani, complete with imitations of the principal churches on the Turkish side.

In 1045, Armenian independence was snuffed out by the Byzantine Emperor Constantine IX, keen to reassert Constantinople's influence in the region after a hiatus of some four centuries. But, just as it had so many times in Roman history, the removal of a client state, or at least a sympathetic one, brought direct confrontation with a much more dangerous enemy. With the defensive bulwark of Armenia removed, the Byzantines had to face head-on the depredations of the Seljuk Turks in the region. In 1064, a Seljuk army took Ani after a three-week siege. Sacks by the Mongols in 1237 and by Tamerlane in the 1380s, combined with the effect of a series of earthquakes, consigned the city to a twilight existence in which the inhabitants were scarcely greater in number than the tally of its churches.

Three hundred kilometres to the west of Ani, the main line of the *limes* initially followed the Euphrates southwards. Under Septimius Severus at the end of the 2nd century, however, the border was pushed eastwards, with the annexation of territory between the Euphrates and Tigris. It was a region that the Romans had fought over before, under Trajan, and formed one of the principal approach avenues for expeditions aimed at the Persian heartland and its capital, Ctesiphon.

A hundred kilometres east of the Euphrates and sitting on the Tigris, at the very edge of the territory acqured by Septimius Severus, the great fortress of Amida, modern Diyarbakir, perched on a bluff at the end of the navigable portion of the Tigris. Occupying such a strategic location, it was a frequent target for Persian attacks, particularly after its walls were reinforced by Constantius I while he was still only a Caesar in the 320s. A much-reconstructed version of these still girds the town, the great bastions of black stone exuding a mixture of pride and menace to outsiders.

During Shapur II's campaign of 359, the capture of the town, which together with its southern neighbour Nisibis dominated the region, was a major priority. Its garrison, the V Parthica legion, was boosted by the reinforcement of no fewer than six further legions.[54] The Persians made preparations to besiege the city. However, it soon looked to Shapur as though his cause might be better served by thrusting deeper into the Empire, but fate intervened. A fortunate – although, as it turned out in the end, unlucky – shot from a ballista mounted on the walls of Amida struck the son of one of Shapur's key allies. In order to give the bereaved father satisfaction and save face himself, Shapur could no longer raise the siege and pressed on with it for a further two months.[55]

The defence is vividly chronicled by Ammianus Marcellinus, one of the Later Roman Empire's greatest historians, and one of the few from whom a continuous narrative has survived. Although of Greek descent, born in Antioch, Ammianus wrote in Latin, which was still the language of command in the army. His early career was evidently a success, for by the time his history begins, he was serving on the staff of the general Ursicinus in Asia Minor, and he stayed with him when the senior officer was sent to Gaul and on his despatch back to the East in 357.

Ammianus arrived at Amida to find the siege of the city just beginning. He describes in compelling detail the gradual tightening of the Persian noose, as outlying positions were stormed and defensive artillery had to be employed to repel attacks on the walls themselves.[56] In the end a mound, built by the defenders to reinforce the wall and provide a vantage point from which to fire on the enemy ramps that were approaching the defences, collapsed and enabled the Persians to gain entry. Ammianus and a few companions hid in a deserted corner of the city whilst the Persians engaged in an orgy of unrestrained slaughter. As Ammianus puts it, soldiers and civilians 'without any distinction of age or sex were slaughtered like sheep.'[57] Ammianus and his companions somehow managed to escape, cross the Persian lines and trek, constantly afflicted by thirst, to the comparative safety of Roman-held Melitene (Malatya), nearly 200 kilometres to the west.

For the historiography of the Roman Empire, Ammianus's survival was a fortunate chance, for contemporary reliable accounts of the events of the 4th century are thin on the ground, with alternative sources coming from epitomes, summaries often compiled centuries after the event, or lurking on the pages of saints' lives, rich in anecdote, but failing to provide anything remotely like a coherent political narrative. When Ammianus's account comes to an end after the Battle of Adrianople in 378, Edward Gibbon, the majestic 18th-century chronicler of the Roman Empire, laments, 'It is not without the most sincere regret, that I must now take leave of an accurate and faithful guide, who has composed the history of his own times, without indulging the prejudices and passions, which usually affect the mind of a contemporary.'[58]

Nusaybin, a small Turkish town butted up just against the Syrian border some 120 kilometres south of Diyarbakir, is no stranger to life as a frontier outpost. Like Nisibis, its ancient predecessor, it long sat just at the very edge of the Roman and Persian spheres of control, dominated by one and then the other, before finally ending up under Sassanid Persian control in 363. Although Lucullus had first captured it in the 60s BC, it was not until Trajan marched through here in AD 115 that the Romans made a serious effort to make their presence permanent. As Rome's control over the East had grown tighter, with the annexation of client states such as Commagene, the room for ambiguity in terms of who controlled – or claimed – exactly what grew slighter, and friction between Rome and the ruling Parthian dynasty of Persia grew greater. The Romans had never really forgiven the Parthians for their humiliation of Crassus in 53 BC, and this – combined with the tendency of successive Roman emperors to dream that they would, somehow, recreate the Eastern domains of Alexander the Great – meant that Persia was an obvious target for an emperor in search of a war.

Trajan combined ambition with a good dose of military ability, and the service of effective generals such as the Moorish cavalry commander Lusus Quietus. After softening-up campaigns in 114 and 115, he struck out in 116 for the Tigris, bridging it with a pontoon made of wood stockpiled the previous winter near Nisibis, then pushed south via Dura Europos and captured the twin cities of Seleucia and the Parthian capital of Ctesiphon against relatively light resistance.[59] Then, going further than any Roman emperor before or since, Trajan sailed down the Tigris to the Erythrean Sea (the Persian Gulf), reaching the river mouth at Spasinou Charax (modern Basra in Iraq), where he is said to have caught sight of a ship setting sail east across the sea and lamented – no doubt for public consumption – that had he only been younger, he would have been able to follow in Alexander's footsteps all the way to India.[60]

Pausing on his return journey to pay homage at the house in Babylon where Alexander had died, Trajan found that rebellion had already broken out in the newly captured territories of Mesopotamia and Assyria. Although the initial uprising, under Sanatruces, a nephew of the deposed Parthian king Osroes, was put down and a client king installed on the throne in Ctesiphon, Trajan was too ill to campaign in 117 and died in August while returning on the long voyage to Rome. Although marked on many maps as Roman 'provinces', Mesopotamia and Assyria had no more received a normal Roman provincial government than had Germany between the Rhine and the Elbe early in Augustus's reign, and Roman control of these Parthian territories was most ephemeral.

Having slipped back under the control of Persia, Nisibis was next taken by the Romans in 194 during Septimius Severus's projection of Roman control – this time more permanently – across the Euphrates into Mesopotamia. It was promoted to the rank of *colonia* at some point during Severus's reign[61] and may have been for a short time the base of the newly raised III Parthica legion. The first Sassanid ruler of Persia, Ardashir (224–40), adopted a much more aggressive posture than his Parthian predecessors and captured a number of cities of Roman Mesopotamia, including Nisibis (although the Romans were soon able to recover it). As a token of his intentions, he also seized Spasinou Charax, which had served as a principal entrepôt for trade coming from Roman-controlled Palmyra, thus choking off a major source of wealth entering the Roman Empire.

The Persians took Nisibis again during the reign of Ardashir's successor, Shapur I (241–72). As part of the treaty that followed Galerius's defeat of the Persian shah, Narses, in 298, Nisibis was restored to the Roman Empire and became the designated point for all trade between Persian- and Roman-controlled territory.[62] It was transferred again, however, to the Sassanids in the treaty forced upon Jovian in 363 in order to extricate the battered remnants of the dead Emperor Julian's army from Persian territory. The Romans were permitted to evacuate the inhabitants, so they did not fall into Persian hands, but they were forced to abandon all their property. The Roman interpretation of the treaty was that the city should revert to its former allegiance after 120 years, but in 483 the Persians refused to hand it over, leading to several Roman attempts to wrest back control, most notably in 572 under Justin II (565–78).[63] Nisibis, however, remained stubbornly Persian (and then Arab) until its capture by the Emperor Nicephorus Phocas in 969, after which the Byzantines held a tenuous control over northern Syria for a century.

Ancient Nisibis has all but vanished. Amid the mixture of chaos and enterprise typical of this region of Turkey, almost all memory that it ever was a Roman town has been erased, and enquiries about its antiquities – save for a couple of Jacobite Christian churches – are met with puzzled stares. Yet precisely in no-man's-land between Turkey and Syria, overlooked by a Turkish watchtower and barred off by swathes of barbed wire and a squad of soldiers from the respective sides, sit the remains of a four-way arch, possibly a tetrapylon, or even a triumphal arch. Five columns and three Corinthian capitals remain, all tantalisingly off-limits, as the cross-border traffic shuffles by, eyes focused on the challenges of passport control, and not one casting a sidelong glance at the town's most important monument.

Around 15 kilometres of straight desert highway west of Nisibis, the way turns off into a series of rural backwater roads, more populated by herds of sheep and waddling troupes of ducks than any modern traffic. It was here, 28 stades (5,174 metres) from the Persian border – more or less the same distance that its ruins occupy from the present Syrian frontiers – that Emperor Anastasius decided to solve a tricky strategic problem. Ever since the loss of Nisibis in 363, the Persians had possessed a major fortified base right against Byzantine territory, a most convenient launching pad for raids and outright invasions. Kavadh's success in the war of 503–6, which resulted in the sack of several major cities, including Amida (Diyarbakir), and the extraction of an annual payment of 500 pounds of gold annually for seven years persuaded the Emperor that something had to be done.[64] Work therefore began on converting the little village of Dara into a fortified outpost, which would match and neutralise Nisibis. By 509 the fortress was largely complete, and Kavadh, who had been distracted by a Hunnish attack on his own eastern frontier, was forced to accept a fait accompli. To persuade him to allow the building of such a defensive bulwark, however, took an additional large payment from the Byzantine side as compensation for their violation of the 442 treaty, which had forbidden just such construction of new fortresses in the border regions.[65]

The city, named initially for its founder as Anastasiopolis, was embellished with the normal civic amenities such as baths, churches and – a necessity in this arid clime – water cisterns. It was provided with a strong garrison and became the base for the *dux* of Mesopotamia. But the walls proved inadequate, and, although the Byzantines under the great general Belisarius won a signal victory against the Persians near the city in 530, Justinian decided that Anastasiopolis could do with some serious reconstruction. Never shy at claiming the credit for his building projects – and occasionally those of others – the Emperor permitted the city to be renamed Iustiniana Nova. Although the extent of the work may have been exaggerated by Procopius in his *Buildings* (which was essentially a panegyric for Justinian),[66] the walls of Dara withstood major Persian sieges in 540 and 544, at a time when even Antioch fell to the Sassanids. But in 573, the Persians managed to break their way into the city. For a week the defenders fought inside the walls, behaving quite uncharacteristically for ancient armies, for whom an attempt at surrender or flight would have been more normal at this point.

When he heard of this disaster, Emperor Justin II, at whose behest the war had been initiated in the first place, is said to have lost his mind.[67] His wife Sophia sent the Emperor's doctor to Persia with a message that it would demean Shah Khusraw I's honour to carry on fighting against a defenceless woman. With the addition of a hefty payment, the Persians agreed to a one-year truce, but did not give up possession of Dara. The city remained theirs until 591 when the Byzantines got it back in exchange for giving Khusraw II support to topple Vahram, a usurper who had unseated him. When the Arabs swept through the area in the late 630s, Dara lost its purpose completely. It had risen from being a small village, but, deprived of imperial subsistence and the purchasing power of its garrison, it relapsed once more into that state.

The modern village at Dara seems to have grown organically from the old, and become completely intertwined with it. Every house is in part composed of ancient stones, column drums and friezes, some almost entirely, and it is hard to discern whether a field wall fell down last week or a thousand years ago. Beyond the edge of the village, a huge quarry has been scored into the rock face, the successive campaigns of extraction creating a curious stepped-contour effect, and it is from here that doubtless much of the construction material for the fort and the new city was carried.

The ruins are best preserved in the north-east sector of the walls' irregular perimeter,[68] close to the point at which a barrel-shaped arch carries the defences over the dried-up bed of the Dara Çay stream, itself now strewn with rubble from fallen buildings just inside the city. The bulk of the walls stands intact at this point, punctuated after about 100 metres by a U-shaped tower, still complete with a circular chamber inside topped by a plain pattern of white mosaic tiles.

From the walls the remains of a well-built road strikes straight for 50 metres or so, before coming to a full stop against a later dividing wall. Although now a confusing jumble of ruins, the place has a sense of forlorn grandeur, of an opportunity vanished, that contrasts with the sheer impoverished helplessness of the modern settlement. Further south-west within the old city walls lies a series of ancient cisterns, without whose water storage the place would have become uninhabitable in the heat of summer. The first is exposed to the air, three large vats each at least 20 metres high and 50 long, dwarfing the modern dwellings that surround it.

Further into the village, one of the houses conceals an astonishing secret. The owner – his attention attracted by the crowd of local boys who are making the most of practising their dozen English words over and over again with their eccentrically attired visitors – comes down and offers to show us the 'dungeon'. It is, he attests, a prison used by people in the 'old times' to hold malefactors. At the foot of his house, just visible above the ground, are the tops of arches of some ancient structure, so it seems worth a look. Descending by torchlight down well-cut steps (both staircase and walls slippery from an inflow of water), we reach the 'dungeon'. It is a breathtaking space, the size of a small cathedral, with towering arches creating a triple-aisle and supporting a roof some 40 metres or more above. Far from being a prison, it seems to be another water cistern, but this time staggeringly well preserved. On the floor is a small scattering of column bases, fragments of drums and other worked (but extremely faded) stone. The owner is insistent that his wholly unexpected cellar was used for confining criminals and points out a much smaller side-chamber – which has, however, no door – where he is convinced they were kept.

At the edge of the village lies the necropolis, a complex of rock tombs replete with stone-carved crosses and biblical imagery, for by the 6th century the inhabitants would almost all have been at least nominally Christian. The best of these sits on a carved portal, the arch incised with egg-and-dart patterns, and above it a relief of an angel holding a child and standing above a pile of skulls, to its right a man holding down another child on the point of cutting its throat with a knife. It seems a clear reference to Abraham's sacrifice of Isaac, which the angel has presumably just intervened to prevent. It is speculated that some, at least, of the necropolis complex may have been built in the later 6th century, by citizens of Dara who were deported in 573 after the Persian conquest of the city and then, later, dedicated a series of carvings as an offering of thanks on their safe return.[69]

By this time, the whole plateau to the north of Dara had become a Christian stronghold, and fertile ground for the spread of that late-antique brand of monasticism which seemed to thrive in soil that nurtured little else. Now known as the Tur Abdin, many of its monastic foundations from the 5th and 6th centuries have survived to this day. A small population of the faithful weathered all the vicissitudes of the Islamic conquest, Arab domination, Ottoman rule and then the increasingly unfriendly environment of the later 20th century for the shrinking Christian communities in the Middle East. Latterly, they have been joined by small numbers of the faithful who have begun to drift back, either permanently or to visit their spiritual homeland and, for those who have prospered, to assist in the restoration and upkeep of the churches and monasteries; for those less fortunate, the Tur Abdin still exerts a powerful pull as a place of pilgrimage.[70]

Most of the surviving active monasteries cluster around the regional town of Midyat, 35 kilometres to the north-west of Dara. The monastery of Mar Yakoub, around 25 kilometres north-east of Midyat, is one of the most venerable, founded in the late 4th or early 5th century; it was clearly functioning by 421 when its eponymous founder, Yakoub, died. The current church, however, probably dates from no earlier than the 6th century. On the day of our visit, a couple of aged, black-swathed nuns sit listlessly in a portico, sheltering from the blistering sun, whose heat seems magnified by the white-cream walls of the church and monastery buildings. A couple of stone crosses and a finely carved filigree stone tower shimmer in the heat, as a local Syrian Christian man, who lives in one of the nearby villages, explains something of its history. All, he says, was well until the 15th century when the Christians started to lose their land, only to have it restored in the 1850s. Then, during the First World War, many were massacred, part of the chaos during the break-up of the Ottoman Empire, which brought disaster for the Syrian Christians, although not on the same scale with which it visited the Armenians further to the north.

In the original church, a deliciously cool transverse chamber with three sanctuaries, two crosses flanking a sun are said to represent a solar symbol taken over from the traditional pagan beliefs of the countryside. One part of this ancient church seems still in use, with a Bible set on a stone podium with a red cloth carefully placed beneath it; the rest, with stone crosses carved on the wall, exudes an aura of sacred neglect.

The church of the Virgin, or Meryemanna as it is known locally, sits in the village of Hah, around 3 kilometres north of Mar Yakoub, which for a time until the early 7th century was the seat of the patriarch of the Tur Abdin. It is an isolated place, some 30 kilometres off the main road, and at the entrance to the small settlement a Turkish *jandarma* or police post scrutinises newcomers – intended, presumably, to protect the village's half-dozen or so Christian sites from those inclined to persecute or vandalise evidence of the country's pre-Muslim past. The existing church dates from the 7th century,[71] though the monastery associated with it may date from the 4th century. From the outside its two-storey construction makes it look like an awkwardly placed wedding cake, the niches indenting its exterior, some of them bearing eagles and other symbols of the Evangelists, all adding to the air of nuptial finery. Inside, it is an architectural gem: its walls delicately carved, and a pattern of tiles set in the ceiling to form the outline of a flower or star. The burning of candles lit by the devout and the enveloping gloom of the interior enhance the sense of a place encrusted with centuries-deep layers of devotion.

Around 25 kilometres to the south-east of Midyat, Mor Gabriel, built around 397, is amongst the oldest, and most eminent of the surviving monasteries, being the seat of the Metropolitan bishop of the Tur Abdin.[72] The monastery precinct is ringed around by a high wall, which gives the place even more of a sense of isolation than its position 3 kilometres off the main road on a side-way that seems to lead nowhere and loses itself amid low hills covered in olive groves. Inside, the outer courtyard presents a blank face, little indication of the treasure within, populated mainly by the cars of pilgrims and other visitors; among them is a battered mini-van from Syria, bearing a prominent portrait of President Bashar al-Assad. It takes several rounds of ringing and pleas to be admitted, for there is a service taking place and it is before regular visiting hours, so no one is readily available to show us round. Finally, a volunteer prepared to forego the morning devotions comes forward and we are allowed in.

The monastery was originally founded by Samuel, a monk who may have been from Persia, and a companion, Simeon, who came from the neighbouring village. An angel appeared to Simeon and inspired him to build the monastery on the site of a former pagan temple.[73] The new foundation subsequently received rich endowments from Arcadius (395–408) and particularly from Theodosius II (408–50), who gave the money for a complex of buildings that still survive to the north-west of the monastery. The main church was endowed in 512 by Anastasius and still forms the principal place of worship. The monastery, however, took its name from a 7th-century abbot, Gabriel, who was said to have performed a number of miracles, and whose body was interred in the crypt of the church.

To the north of the main courtyard, the Dome of Theodora, or the 'Octagon', is an unusual eight-sided affair, which probably began life as a baptistery. That it has taken on Theodora's name is a tribute to Justinian's wife, who, despite the strong-willed nature of her husband, adhered stubbornly throughout her life to the non-orthodox, Monophysite creed, which had established a tenacious hold in the south-eastern portions of the Empire, and for which she acted as high-placed sponsor (even sending envoys to proselytise Ethiopia, who got there before Justinian's 'official' party and set the course of the Christian Church there for centuries to come).

The argument about the nature of Christ (whether he was fully human, fully divine or a mixture of the two), although seemingly an abstruse matter to modern eyes, was the question of utmost concern in the early Christian Church and the subject of bitter and prolonged wrangling, which threatened to – and finally did – split the community into rival factions. The 4th-century bishop Gregory of Nyssa (whose see lay in modern Cappadocia) satirised this by remarking that a visitor to Constantinople might ask a local the price of bread and be greeted instead with a discourse on the Trinity.[74] Debates over the nature of the Christian Trinity, God the Father, God the Son (Jesus Christ) and God the Holy Spirit, almost tore the early Church apart. It is hard now to recreate the sense of fervour that could lead to riots over the implication that Mary was not the literal mother of Jesus – and so the cherished epithet *Theotokos* ('Bearer of God') should not be used – or the savage arguments in church councils over the single iota (in the Greek) of difference over whether Jesus was *homoousios* (of the same substance) with God the Father or merely *homoiousios* (of similar substance).[75]

Once Christianity had become in effect the official religion of the Empire and gained access to the benefits of patronage, the problem of defining who exactly made up the orthodox community – and so could benefit from imperial and civic largesse – became more pressing. Particularly bitterly contested was the theology of Arius, a clergyman from Alexandria, who maintained that God the Father preceded all else, that Christ was created, that there was a time when he did not exist. At the Council of Nicaea, called by Constantine in 325 to thrash out a creed to which all orthodox Christians should subscribe, Arius was branded a heretic and excommunicated.[76] For decades, though, the controversy rumbled on, the principal defender of the Nicene cause being Athanasius, the patriarch of Alexandria from 328.

From the early 5th century, the battleground shifted from the relationship between the members of the Trinity to the nature of Christ's humanity – in other words, how it was possible that he could have a divine and a human nature at the same time. In 428, Nestorius, originally from Antioch, was elected Bishop of Constantinople. In his preaching he began to stress the differences between Christ's two natures, maintaining that they needed to be considered as separate.[77] Cyril, the Bishop of Alexandria, responded furiously that Nestorius was reducing

Jesus to a shell behind which separate natures lurk, and not truly a union of divine and human natures. The Council of Ephesus, called in 431 to resolve the issue, broke into Cyrillian and Nestorian counter-councils and only aggravated the division.

It was not until the Council of Chalcedon in 451 that a formula was agreed, that Christ is 'one person in two natures', but critically this point of view was rejected by the bulk of the Egyptian Church, which supported the stance that Christ had only one single nature, a position described (by its opponents) as Monophysite.[78] In Egypt, the Church splintered between Monophysites and Chalcedonians, who accepted the position of the council, but were in a distinct minority. Both groups heartily rejected the extremist Nestorian position, though the Monophysites took great delight in implying that their Chalcedonian opponents were secret followers of the creed of Nestorius.

Successive attempts to bridge the gap between the two factions always foundered, beginning with Emperor Zeno's *Henotikon* in 482, which fudged the matter by stating that while Christ was of the same 'nature' as God the Father, he combined a human nature within him.[79] Efforts at reconciliation gathered pace under Justinian, who, though he may not have had a personal commitment to the Chalcedonian creed – and his wife, Theodora, was an active Monophysite – was most keen to bring the competing Christian factions together for the sake of imperial harmony. They finished with the Council of Constantinople in 553,[80] which ended disastrously as it failed to reconcile the Monophysites and also alienated the Western Church, which considered that its eastern counterpart had backtracked on the doctrinal purity of Chalcedon.[81]

The Monophysite faction gave rise to the Coptic Orthodox Church in Egypt, which derived great strength from the monasteries and the rural areas, and acquired something of the nature of a national Church, a characteristic that enabled it to weather the storm of the Arab Muslim invasion in the 7th century. It also gave birth to many of the local churches of the Near East, including the Syrian Orthodox, whose monasteries dot the hills and valleys of the Tur Abdin. At first a beleaguered if staunch group of believers, the Monophysite cause was permanently bolstered by Theodora's connivance in the consecration of two bishops for the Ghassanid sheikh al-Harith (who was a Monophysite, like many Arabs). One of these, Jacob Baradaeus, who became Bishop of Edessa, traversed the entire Near East from Egypt to Armenia, consecrating priests and ordaining Monophysite bishops, in effect establishing an alternative hierarchy that was to form the backbone of the Monophysite churches of the future (and in honour of whose activities the Syrian Orthodox Church is often termed 'Jacobite').[82]

Down a flight of stairs near the monastery's octagon lies Mor Gabriel's crypt. At its entrance rests the tomb of the last bishop, who died in 1984 and was buried in a crouching position, a burial posture unique to the Syrian Orthodox metropolitans. The plain and simple niches for the remains of further bishops lie nearby, and also somewhere down here are the bones of '10,000 martyrs' resting near the grave of Mor Gabriel himself.

Back in the main church, a service is still going on, the priest officiating from the sanctuary, an apse-like room set away from the main congregation. Those present are a mixture of young and old, predominantly women wearing black-lace mantillas, many of them visiting here from abroad, particularly the United States, where a strong Syrian Orthodox community thrives. The liturgy is given in Syriac, a close relation to the Aramaic that was probably Jesus's mother tongue; the intoning of the prayers in a rhythmic, almost chant-like fashion certainly exerts a tug at the soul similar to that inspired by the few surviving islands of the Latin rite in western Europe.

The canopy over the altar was originally gilded, but this has been almost totally stripped off, leaving just small portions of gold leaf to represent the rest. It happened, says our guide, at the same time that a tree with branches entirely made of gold and silver vanished. It sounds like a recent act of desecration, but when pressed he admits that this happened during the time of Tamerlane, the last Mongol ravager of Asia Minor in the early 15th century. In a place as ancient as this, 500 years ago is regarded almost as recent history.

At the end of the service the forty-strong congregation troops up to kiss the Bible and then an icon concealed behind a curtain, which turns out to depict a military saint saddled on a white charger. As they depart, the church is left deserted, its nave rather bare, with the decorations principally in the three sanctuaries that run off it. In the corner a large stone trough has been placed, but it is not a baptismal font, merely a stone on which dough was made that was brought up from the monastery kitchen some decades ago and left here in the church. That it dates from the 8th century is almost an afterthought, the kind of antique detritus that litters the corridors and courtyards of these ancient places of worship.

It is sites such as the monastery of Tur Abdin that preserved elements of the late-Roman religious culture of the province, long after the central authorities had relinquished it to the conquering waves of Arabs in the 640s. For more than thirteen centuries their rites remained almost unchanged and they clung tenaciously to their lands and churches. Here, above all, it is possible to gain an insight into how life felt, at least on a religious level, and to connect with one aspect of the Roman past in a way that the ruins – however appealing or romantic – cannot inspire.

Around 250 kilometres west of Midyat lies Sanliurfa (also known as Urfa), one of the most important of the Roman possessions east of the Euphrates. The imprint of piety weighs heavily upon the city, Roman Edessa, and successive religions – paganism, Christianity and Islam – have all sought to claim its allegiance as a cornerstone of their presence in the region. At the heart of its mystical life lie two sacred carp pools, great oblong cisterns today surrounded by later mosque buildings, but the fish themselves, grown numerous and fat on the titbits offered by visiting pilgrims, are the descendants of a very ancient cult indeed. High up above the throng of visitors, curious or devout, and the parade of kebab restaurants that minister to them, the steep cliffs of Edessa's citadel soar, and on them perches the city's most curious sight.

Two columns strike up against the skyline, entirely bereft of companions, as though the rest of the colonnade to which they once belonged had simply tumbled down the cliff face.[83] Local legend relates that Abraham came to settle in Urfa, whose similarity in sound – even closer in its Semitic form, Orhai – to his much better-attested residence at Ur may have caused confusion and the assimilation of his legends to Edessa. Nimrod, the local ruler, became angry at Abraham for his piety and refusal to worship idols, a prissiness that rather showed up the dissoluteness of his own lifestyle, and resolved to do away with him. Using the two columns on the citadel hill to create a giant catapult, the citizens of Urfa propelled Abraham towards a fiery death in a furnace which they had lit down below. However, God transformed the fire into water, and the burning pieces of wood into fish, and thus Abraham – far from being incinerated – merely went for a dip in the sacred carp pool.[84]

The city's position, dominating one main route towards Persia, has long been a strategic one, a fact recognised by Seleucus I Nicator around 303 BC when he sited his new foundation of Edessa close to an existing native settlement there.[85] Although it had acquired the name 'Antioch by the Callirhoe' by the mid-2nd century BC, the multiplicity of Antiochs in the region meant that it soon reverted to plain Edessa. About this time, also, it became the capital of an Arab kingdom governed by a succession of rulers who mostly bore the name Abgar. The fifth king of that name features in an early Christian legend, which relates that he engaged in an exchange of letters with Jesus Christ and was so enthused by what he learnt that he passed on the message to the Emperor Tiberius, to the King of 'Assyria' and the ruler of Persia.[86] After the crucifixion, Abgar V is alleged to have converted to Christianity under the influence of Saint Thaddeus, making Edessa by some margin the first Christian country. Sadly, there is no concrete evidence for all this and the correspondence between Jesus and Abgar, apparently still intact in the state archive in the 4th century, has long since vanished. More credible, but still unproven, are claims that Abgar VIII the Great (177–212) became Christian a century before Constantine's conversion heralded the Christianisation of the Roman Empire itself.

Edessa's religious heritage was complex. Long renowned as a centre for the worship of the gods Nebo and Bel, it also hosted large-scale cults of the Sun and Moon, the latter of which had its main centres further east at Harran and Sogmatar. The cult of Atargatis seems even more exotic. Its male devotees were given, at times of ecstatic reverie, to self-emasculation – clearly a once-only act of sacrifice to the goddess, and a practice which caused such controversy that it was outlawed under Abgar the Great. Another of the rites of Atargatis involved the ascent by holy men of two wooden columns at the temple entrance, where they would remain for several days, a practice which foreshadows that of Saint Simeon Stylites and his followers many centuries later.[87] The 'catapult' up on the citadel may, indeed, be the remains of an Atargatis temple, just as the sacred carp pools may originally have been associated with the cult (although other scholars have supposed they were simply a part of Abgar the Great's winter palace).[88] The pools, however, survived both Abgarid and pagan rule, and the 5th-century Christian pilgrim Egeria,[89] who visited on her way to the Holy Land, noted that she had never seen fish 'of so great size, so bright and of so great flavour'.[90] To this day, it is regarded as extremely unlucky to eat one.

The Abgarids were briefly supplanted by a pro-Roman Parthian prince named Parthamaspat in 117–23, in part as a punishment for Edessa's role in the revolt of Trajan's newly acquired Mesopotamian province the moment the Emperor's back was turned. Then in 193, suspected of complicity with Pescennius Niger in his attempt to oppose Septimius Severus's seizure of the imperial throne (or at least of taking advantage of the disorder to make territorial gains), Abgar VIII had his wings firmly clipped and most of his possessions, save a rump around Edessa, were incorporated as the province of Osroene.[91] The King affected the unimpeachably Roman name of Lucius Aelius Aurelius Septimus and feigned at least enough gratitude for his punishment to be allowed, for the time being, to retain his throne.

Edessa's long period of quasi-independence as one of the last Roman client kingdoms came to an end in 213, when Caracalla, in preparation for his expedition against the Parthians, called King Abgar IX to Rome, where he summarily deposed him, annexing Edessa to Osroene, which had for decades completely surrounded it. In compensation, Edessa was given the title of *colonia*, although as this was the very same year of the Antonine Constitution, the grant of citizenship to the free male population of Edessa in practice meant very little. A brief restoration of 'independence' under Gordian III between 239 and 242 brought a new Abgar (X) to the throne, but Gordian had probably only permitted this as a means of recruiting additional support in the East for his attack on Persia in 242–3, and even before this offensive had got under way, Roman municipal administration was restored and the Abgarids were summarily pushed aside once more.[92]

Somewhere outside Edessa, the Romans suffered their worst military setback since Crassus's death at Carrhae. On a rock relief at Bishapur in modern Iran, Shapur I celebrated his victories over three Roman emperors. His horse is shown trampling one, Gordian III, who had, according to the Persian side of the story, been killed in battle against the Sassanid army at Misiche in 244.[93] A second emperor kneels in supplication before Shapur I. This is Philip, who was forced to conclude a highly unfavourable peace to extricate the Roman army from the debacle of Gordian's death. The third of the trio, Valerian, whose wrist Shapur is seen clutching, suffered the worst fate. It seems that, while leading an army to head off Shapur's invasion of Syria in 260, Valerian was defeated in the vicinity of Edessa, and in the aftermath opened negotiations with the Persian side.[94] He made the fateful mistake of turning up in person at the talks and, seeing this, Shapur had him arrested and carried off into a humiliating and unprecedented imprisonment at the Sassanid court.

Tradition relates that Shapur used the captive former emperor as a mounting stool whenever he wished to get on his horse, and, when the hapless Valerian finally died, had his skin flayed, dyed purple and mounted as a trophy. Valerian's son, Gallienus, made absolutely no attempt to rescue his father. A Roman emperor who had endured the loss of dignity that Valerian had suffered was not a man who could remotely expect to inspire the army's loyalty ever again.

A breathless climb up a claustrophobic enclosed staircase inside the citadel cliff leads visitors to the site of the catapult columns. A series of undifferentiated ruins lies scattered about, shaping indistinct outlines of buildings that may once have formed part of Abgar's palace. The columns are the only undamaged structures, topped with weathered Corinthian capitals, the surface of their drums broken by pimple-like protrusions, which make them this close up seem as if they are scarred by the pox. On one of these there survives an inscription in Syriac, the language of Edessa, in which the dedication by Apthtuha the *nuhadra* (a royal official) states that the column bore a statue of Queen Shelmath, daughter of Ma'nu, the *pasgriba* (or heir to the throne). It is all a long way from Abraham and his catapult.[95]

Edessa's religious ferment continued into the age of Christianity. Among the key figures in its early development is Bardaisan.[96] Born into a well-to-do Edessene family around 155, he became a Christian in the 180s and bequeathed to the Syrian Church a rich legacy of more than 150 metrical hymns, set to music by his charmingly named son, Harmonius. His complex theology, later denounced as heretical, denied the bodily resurrection of the dead, and maintained that God had made all the elements of the universe, but that light and darkness had become inextricably muddled up in his new creation. After 6,000 years order would be restored and creation would revert to its pristine state, one in which light would be separated out and the matter of corporeal bodies would have no place. Such original speculations were commonplace in the independent Syriac Christian Church of the time, drawing freely on dualistic notions of great antiquity. But once Edessa was drawn into the Roman mainstream in the 3rd century and the Christian Church began to take on the mantle of an established religion, this free-thinking came to be regarded as unwise or downright dangerous.

Edessa was besieged a number of times by the Persians in the 6th century, as the grip of the authorities in Constantinople on their eastern possessions grew gradually more tenuous. It withstood sieges in 503, 544 and 580,[97] before a brief Persian occupation in 609 during the civil war following the murder of the Emperor Maurice by his successor Phocas. Heraclius recovered the city in 628, just eleven years before his garrison was swept out by the unstoppable tide of the Muslim Arab armies, who in their turn held it until 1032 when the Byzantines managed to retake the citadel and surrounding territory and maintain it for fifty years. Edessa was then incorporated into a Crusader principality during the First Crusade in 1098.

A dusty 40-kilometre drive to the south-east of Edessa, Harran – or, as the Romans knew it, Carrhae – has an ancient heritage indeed. First mentioned in the Bible as the place where Abraham and Sarah dwelt for a while after leaving Ur, the city is still dotted with curious beehive-shaped buildings of mud-brick whose traditional form may date back to the time of the patriarch, although they are now more often used for storage or for impressing tourists. It was later to Harran that Jacob fled from his brother Esau,[98] and his well (or its alleged location) is still there. A jumble of undifferentiated ruins surrounded by an unsympathetic wall enfold a rubbish-choked hole, a few steps leading to a pool of dubious-looking water, on which bob a collection of very unbiblical plastic water bottles.

More resonant of Harran's past is the citadel, sections of wall and a precarious arched gateway surviving, much restored and rebuilt by the town's various ancient, classical and medieval occupiers. Here in a corner that the Crusaders later turned into a redoubt – for the shortest-lived of their Levantine principalities was based here in the 12th century – is the site of the Temple of the Moon or 'Sin'. Ancient already in the 6th century BC, when it was restored by the Babylonian ruler Nabonidus, it was known as E-hul-hul ('the Temple of Rejoicing') and was magnificently roofed in cedar of Lebanon. Nothing remains of this, hidden somewhere deep inside the dusty mound on which the ruined Crusader fortress has imprinted a broken maze of stone. Visitors are so few and far between in the height of summer that our arrival provokes some curiosity and a slightly crazed local enquires over the reason for our presence.

The temple mound long remained a sacred site. Harran was the centre for the group who later became known as the Sabaeans, recidivist pagans who continued the old worship long after others had taken to different faiths. So resistant were the old ways here that when a delegation was sent to negotiate surrender to the Arabs in 639, it was found that all of its members were pagan.[99] The Koran mentions them in the 7th century as a 'people of the book', who were thus entitled to toleration of their beliefs (along with Jews, Christians and Zoroastrians), and around 830 the caliph Marwan is said to have encountered a group who claimed that they were Sabaeans – on the advice of a local jurist – to avoid being slaughtered or converted for their distinctly heterodox beliefs and practices.

The Sabaean religious life, as far as it can be reconstructed, was complex, but much of the information is derived from later Arab sources, such as the 9th-century writer ibn al-Tayyib. They believed in a single, supreme power beyond direct worship, who had delegated the actual running of the universe to the planets. Although this does not sound like classical paganism, in fact there was an increasing tendency in later antiquity to identify one god who was supreme, but not the only god. If Greeks revered Zeus Hypistos ('the highest') and Romans Jupiter Optimus Maximus ('the best and greatest'), than the Sabaeans clearly had their own variant.

Their planetary temples were each said to have been of a special shape and colour; that of Saturn was a black hexagon, while that of

Venus was a rectangle containing a square of green. The shrine of the Moon was in turn a silver octagon. Sabaean festivals seem to have involved much symbolic use of fire; each 26 September the believers would make vows and then tie a flaming torch to a chicken. The hapless fowl would then, naturally, run around, and if it was burnt to death before the torch went out, the vows were deemed accepted by the 'Lord of Luck'. The Sabaeans would never eat the chicken, for this (together with pigeons, fish, garlic and broad beans) was a forbidden food, making them difficult dinner guests.[100]

Further evidence of the Sabaean inhabitants has been found underneath Harran's Great Mosque, where another of their temples once stood. It also seems that the Emperor Caracalla came to the Moon Temple in the Citadel to sacrifice in 217. In common with a number of Roman emperors, he was an admirer of, indeed even modelled himself on, Alexander the Great, and also had his eyes on securing victories to rival those of his illustrious predecessor Trajan. Taking advantage of a split in the Parthian royal house, between Artabanus V and his brother Vologeses V (who controlled the capital, Ctesiphon), Caracalla sowed further dissension by proposing a marriage alliance with Artabanus's daughter.[101]

When his offer was rebuffed, Caracalla used this as a pretext for launching an expedition against Parthia late in 216. At first this came under the command of one of his favourites, a former dancer named Theocritus, and then, when – predictably – little was achieved, under his own personal direction. Even so, no direct gains were made against Parthia, although the buffer state of Osroene was annexed. Retiring for the winter to Edessa, Caracalla ignored the mounting grumbles in the army at his lack of martial prowess and his increasingly erratic behaviour. On 6 April, the Emperor went to pay his devotions at Carrhae. Two days later, during the journey to yet another moon temple a few kilometres from the city, Caracalla left the convoy to relieve himself amongst some bushes beside the road. There he was killed by a soldier named Martialis, who had a grudge against the Emperor, and who had been assigned to Caracalla's personal guard by the praetorian prefect Opellius Macrinus, himself motivated by fear that the Emperor was about to have him murdered.[102] It was an undignified end for the son of the great Septimius Severus, but after four days of feigned reluctance, Macrinus allowed the troops to declare him Emperor, thereby becoming the first member of the equestrian class to reach that position.

Perhaps Caracalla should have known better, as Carrhae was not exactly a well-omened place for the Romans. It was on the plains somewhere outside the city that Rome suffered its most disastrous defeat since the Punic Wars. Marcus Licinius Crassus, one of the triumvirs who shared power with Julius Caesar and Pompey the Great, rather smarting at his rivals' high profile as military leaders, and in particular at Caesar's successes in Gaul, decided to belie his reputation as a financier and little else, and teach the Parthians a lesson. After some initial successes in Upper Mesopotamia in 54 BC, he was lured outside Carrhae the following spring, where the open country made ideal territory for light cavalry, which the Parthian army had in great abundance, and of which Crassus's legions possessed a much more modest complement.

Hails of arrows from horse-mounted archers and repeated probing cavalry attacks broke the Romans' spirit and they fled: 20,000 were killed (including Crassus), 10,000 captured and only a quarter of the original force escaped towards Antioch. Even more humiliatingly, a number of the legionary eagle standards, the emblems of Roman martial glory imbued with an almost sacral symbolism, were also taken by the Parthians. Although their advance into Syria was largely halted by Crassus's surviving legate, Cassius, the Parthians held on to the standards for more than thirty years, and it took some strenuous diplomacy by Augustus to have them finally returned in 20 BC.[103]

Carrhae saw another Roman ruler on his way to hoped-for victories against the Persians, when the Emperor Julian visited in 363. Just like Caracalla, Julian was drawn by the desire to sacrifice at the Temple of the Moon. The Emperor had spent much of the previous year attempting to restore the old gods in their place at the centre of Roman public life, and to undo the Christianisation of the Empire by Constantine and his successors.[104]

Although he could not openly espouse paganism whilst his uncle the Emperor Constantius II lived, once he himself had become Emperor in November 360, Julian set about rolling back the privileges that the Christian Church had been given. In March 362 he ordered that Christian clergy no longer be immune from their civic duty as *curiales*,[105] and he further commanded that the cities have restored to them the public estates that had generated the revenues for the upkeep of the temples. A few months later, in June, he legislated for the appointment of qualified teachers in the cities, no doubt to promote traditional – polytheistic – learning. Christian teachers were forbidden to give lessons on the traditional curriculum, on the grounds that they did not believe in it and, as the Emperor put it, 'they should either show piety towards the gods or withdraw to the churches of the Galileans to expound Matthew and Luke'.[106]

Many saw Julian's measures as unduly divisive, and even the pagan historian Ammianus Marcellinus commented that it was a 'harsh act which should be buried in lasting oblivion'.[107] A certain amount of anti-Christian violence was sparked off by the new regime's policies; in Alexandria, Bishop Athanasius was expelled, and Bishop George of Cappadocia, the Emperor's old tutor, was lynched by a mob. Julian responded with a mere rebuke, and an instruction to the Prefect of Egypt to acquire George's extensive book collection and have it sent to Constantinople.[108] As scattered opposition grew, the Emperor became more resolute. He penned a treatise entitled *Against the Galileans* setting out his position, and he moved against cities that showed too strong an attachment to Christianity. At Bostra in Arabia, the bishop was hounded out. He demoted Caesarea in Cappadocia from its civic status because of its inhabitants' violence against pagan temples, and promoted Gaza to the rank of a *colonia* as a reward for its steadfast polytheist majority.[109] As a further spite to Christian sentiment, in 363 Julian permitted a start to be made on the rebuilding of the Jewish Temple in Jerusalem. An earthquake, the lack of enthusiasm of the rabbinate for a project that would have undermined their authority, and the death of the Emperor meant the project never in fact got very far.

As a counter to the well-organised Christian hierarchies, Julian tried to re-establish the pagan priesthood on a similar, structured and disciplined basis. In some ways, his Christian education was showing through in his attempt to fight spirit with spirit, and the heritage of his early years influenced him in other ways, too. Rumour had it that when the apostate Emperor was scared, he actually made the sign of the cross.[110] Yet Julian's template did not fit very well onto the massive diversity of pagan belief and practice, and in any case it all came much too late. For in March 363, Julian set out from Antioch for a new war against the Persians.

Motivated by the same desire as Caracalla to emulate Alexander the Great, and in particular by a wish for revenge against Shapur for his seizure of the great fortress city of Dara in 359, Julian may not have had clear objectives for his campaign. As emperors before him had done, such as Carus in 283, Julian struck out at Ctesiphon with little apparent idea what he might do once he had captured it. Although a number of towns were taken, the Persians hindered the Roman army's progress by flooding irrigation ditches, and Shapur's army was still undefeated when Julian reached the Persian capital.

A prolonged siege was out of the question, and the Romans marched north to meet another column under the command of Procopius, which was moving via Armenia to reinforce them. Shapur had, however, ordered the area north of Ctesiphon laid waste to deny his enemy supplies, and constant harrying attacks by the Persians added to the

Romans' discomfort. On 26 June, somewhere near modern Samarra in Iraq, the Persians attacked again. Julian, alerted to the danger, rushed out of his tent to rally resistance, but in his haste neglected to don his breastplate. In the ensuing skirmish the Emperor was mortally wounded by a spear-thrust.[111] As he lay dying, Julian is said to have discoursed lucidly with his former philosophy teacher Maximus on the nobility of the soul, but his inevitable end came within hours. Later, jubilant Christian writers would claim that the end of the 'Apostate' came at the hands of a Christian soldier, and indeed that it was the work of a saint, variously identified as Saint Sergius, Theodore or, more commonly, Mercurius.[112]

Whoever was responsible for Julian's death, any real chance of a re-establishment of paganism was ended. The Roman army, meanwhile, found itself leaderless and beleaguered, still far from friendly territory. A rapid council of war offered the crown to the praetorian prefect Secundus Salutius, who declined on the grounds of his advanced age; in some confusion the senior officials than lighted on a compromise candidate, Jovian, the *primicerius domesticorum*[113] of the imperial guard. Desperate to escape back across the borders of the Empire – not least because he needed rapidly to build a coalition of support amongst the power-brokers in Constantinople and the provinces, who might not regard his hasty elevation particularly favourably – Jovian opened nego-tiations with Shapur.

To secure his safe passage, the new Emperor gave up five Roman provinces across the Tigris (Arzanene, Moxoene, Zabdicene, Rehimene and Corduene), the cities of Nisibis (Nusaybin), Singara and Castra Maurorum (Seh Qubba), and further agreed that he would give no mili-tary assistance to Arsaces, King of Armenia.[114] The new Emperor's surrender of these territories was seen as hugely shameful; when a messenger reached Carrhae with the news, the citizenry was so enraged that they killed him.[115] Ammianus Marcellinus bitterly – and wrongly – commented that it was the first time Rome had ever voluntarily given up land it had won in war.[116] Jovian, meanwhile, did not even survive long enough to reach his imperial capital. On the morning of 2 January 364, halfway between Ancyra (Ankara) and Nicaea (Iznik), and still more than 200 kilometres from Constantinople, he was found dead in his bedchamber. Poisoned mushrooms or the fumes from a brazier close to his bed were blamed, but a suspicion lingered that those who did not approve of the army's battlefield choice had Jovian murdered.

It seems a long, hot road from Harran to Sogmatar (if in reality it is only 30 kilometres to the north-east), passing barren dusty hills and parched land from which scratching a living seems scarcely worth the effort. Past Suayb, a village burrowed into the rock for protection from the searing sun, occupied from Roman times – with a jumble of subterranean dwellings, crude steps and niches, which might as well have been abandoned twenty years ago as 2,000 – the way leads on to Sogmatar Harabesi itself. The modern village, a clutch of single-storey mud-brick dwellings at its heart, more modern but no more assuming at its edges, gives little clue to its ancient secret.

The village is ringed by a series of low hills, on at least several of which lie the ruins of ancient structures. Up the nearest of these the remains of a circuit wall of large blocks and possibly a corner tower give a sense of a defended place, but on the crest a jumble of blocks, pillars and a section of frieze lying among the sun-bleached grass are all that is left of the temple. A single ragged-trousered boy stares at the visitors, too amazed that anyone should visit these abandoned stones even to beg for a pen or some small change.

Similar structures visible on the other mounds once ringed a sacred precinct in the heart of the village, with seven hilltop sanctuaries, one for each of the planets. On a shrine here have been found inscriptions in Syriac and a reference to a dedication by 'Tiridates, son of Adona, ruler of the Arabs', who 'built this altar and set a pillar to Marilaha for the life of my lord the king', dated to AD 165,[117] the very year in which the Romans occupied Edessa and began to bring an end to the vitality of this ancient cult.

It is an eerie feeling, that this may have been the last place where prayers were offered to the traditional pagan deities, suppressed elsewhere by the monotheist certainties and intolerance of, first, Christianity, and then Islam. Far away from the mainstream of history, it is in such hidden-away places that the most poignant glimpses of the past can truly be had, and the most immediate insights into the religious feelings which inspired the mass of the population of the Empire, before Christianity swept aside the old beliefs and relegated them to mere folk tales and superstitions.

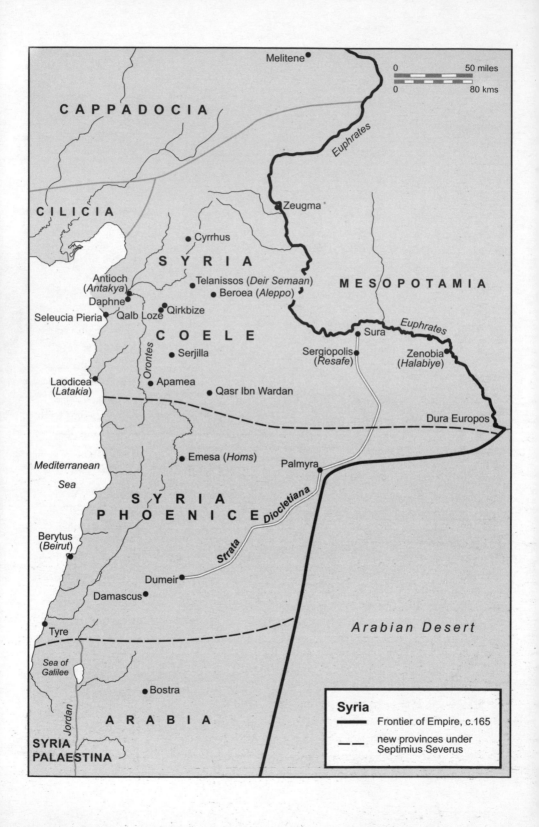

Melitene

CAPPADOCIA

0   50 miles
0   80 kms

Euphrates

CILICIA

Zeugma

Cyrrhus

S Y R I A

MESOPOTAMIA

Antioch
(*Antakya*)
Daphne
Seleucia Pieria
Qalb Loze   Qirkbize

Telanissos (*Deir Semaan*)
Beroea (*Aleppo*)

C O E L E

Euphrates

Serjilla

Sura

Sergiopolis
(*Resafe*)

Zenobia
(*Halabiye*)

Orontes

Laodicea
(*Latakia*)

Apamea

Qasr Ibn Wardan

Dura Europos

Mediterranean

Sea

Emesa (*Homs*)

Palmyra

S Y R I A
P H O E N I C E

Diocletiana

Berytus
(*Beirut*)

Strata

Dumeir

Damascus

Arabian Desert

Tyre

Sea of
Galilee

Jordan

Bostra

A R A B I A

SYRIA
PALAESTINA

Syria

— Frontier of Empire, c.165

– – new provinces under
Septimius Severus

CHAPTER 7

Syria

Cenobia, of Palmyerie queene,
Of Kynges blood of Perce is she descended
I seye nat that she hadde moost fairnesse
But of hir shap she myghte nat been amended . . .
Hir riche array ne myghte nat be told,
As wel in vessel as in hire clothyng,
She was al clad in perree and in gold . . .
Geoffrey Chaucer, *The Canterbury Tales*, 'The Monk's Tale'[1]

Roman Syria swept down in an arc from the edge of Asia Minor and the Euphrates down to the Gulf of Aqaba, always shaped and defined by the desert to the east and in its northern portions by the Mediterranean Sea to the west.[2] It was defined by three principal regions: the fertile coastal strip, which was bordered by a mountainous region, and then to the east and south by the desert. The main towns, such as Antioch (Antakya), Damascus, Emesa (Homs) and Apamea (Afamya), clustered close to the coast or the valley of the Orontes, with a secondary area of dense settlement running from Beroea (Aleppo) down the Euphrates to the south-east.

Although never at the heart of any of the ancient civilisations on the fringes of whose domains it sat, such as the Hittites, Assyrians, Babylonians or Persians, Syria supported cities of time-defying antiquity such as Damascus, and, whenever the central authority of its various suzerains weakened, it gave rise to indigenous kinglets whose aspirations were almost always greater than the reach of their power. Once Alexander the Great had claimed the former domains of the Persian Achaemenids in the 330s BC, Syria fell to him, and then, after his untimely death in 323 BC, it landed in the portion of Seleucus, one of his principal lieutenants.

The large numbers of Greek colonists who, over time, made Syria (and indeed much of the rest of the Near East) their home brought profound changes to the urban landscapes of the area. Many new Greek-style *poleis* (or 'city-states') were founded and others adapted themselves to Greek-style constitutions with citizen-assemblies and annually elected magistrates. Quite how far this process of Hellenisation penetrated into the countryside is hard to say, but when the Romans did eventually arrive in Syria, they ingested the existing arrangements almost wholesale. Their ancient conceit that the Empire was in fact made up of a patchwork of 'independent' cities, which just happened to conform to the wishes of the principal amongst them (in other words, Rome), suited them very well in Syria.

Although the Romans' acquisition of territories in western Asia Minor and then Cappadocia[3] brought them into contact with the Seleucid heartland further to the east and south in Syria, they came at first as diplomats rather than conquerors. The interference in 168 BC by Gaius Popillius Laenas in the Seleucid Antiochus IV's attempt to annex Ptolemaic Egypt established a status quo in which the local potentates had only limited freedom of action, always inviting Roman intervention should they overstep the bounds of their traditional territories.[4] It was really only the expansion of Tigranes of Armenia from 95 BC, who added huge swathes of Cappadocia and Syria (traditionally Seleucid lands) to his kingdom, that upset the balance of power, and, once they had disentangled themselves from the Mithridatic Wars, caused the Romans to enter definitively into Syria.

With the annexation of Antioch in 64 BC, a new province of Syria was established by Ptolemy,[5] although at first a complex patchwork of client states and independent cities obscured the realities of Roman power.[6] Further progress in organising and expanding the Syrian base was hampered by the civil wars between Caesar and Pompey, and then between the leaders of the second triumvirate and Caesar's assassins. The disastrous defeat of Crassus at Carrhae in 53 BC[7] led to the partial occupation of Syria by the Parthians, who even succeeded in seizing Antioch itself.[8] By 50 BC, though, the Parthians had been chased out, and ultimately Syria fell into the domains of Antony, meaning that it once more became entangled in a Roman civil war, this time between him and Augustus, and was only restored to central control after the Battle of Actium in 31 BC.

Once Augustus had established himself in power, he ceded control of some provinces back to the Senate, but only those without a significant military presence, and from which, therefore, no bid to unseat him could be effectively mounted. Syria, as a province with a significant garrison, fell to the Emperor and was governed by a number of distinguished imperial legates, including Varus (the Roman commander at the disastrous defeat at the Teutoberger Wald in Germany) and Calpurnius Piso (who was executed for treason in AD 65). At first client states such as that of the Samsigeramids at Emesa or, more important, that of Herod in Judaea were not absorbed, leading to blocs of Roman provincial territory being surrounded by the domains of those kings, and an administrative system of almost nightmarish complexity.[9] The province initially stretched far to the south, including cities such as Gerasa and Philadelphia that would, once the Nabataean kingdom was annexed by Trajan in 106,[10] form part of the province of Arabia.

After the great Jewish revolt of AD 66–70 had been put down, the new Emperor Vespasian, who had been the commander of the Roman forces in the initial stages of the campaign, set about simplifying the situation. A new province was established in Palestine, while at about this time Emesa was annexed and its royal dynasty deposed.[11] Under Trajan, the province seemed to have reached its final boundaries, with the slicing-off of a section to form the northern reaches of Arabia, but during the reign of Septimius Severus, the province was split into two portions, with the northern part becoming Coele Syria (or 'Hollow' Syria) and the southern part Syria Phoenice, in an effort to avoid the concentration of power in the hands of a single governor that had so threatened Septimius's own bid for imperial power.[12] After the disorders of the 3rd century, which saw Zenobia, Queen of Palmyra, seize almost the whole of the East, the Syrian provinces were further subdivided under Diocletian, who also sponsored a large-scale fortification of the route down from Sura on the Euphrates to Damascus, which formed part of the system that has become known as the Strata Diocletiana.[13]

Although vulnerable to periodic Persian incursions, particularly after the advent of the Sassanids as the ruling dynasty in the mid-3rd century, Syria seemed a bulwark of the Eastern Roman Empire right until the early 7th century, when the invading armies of Arab Muslims swept away in just a few short years what it had taken the Romans almost three-quarters of a millennium to construct.

Antioch-on-the-Orontes, the principal city of Syria, was one of the great cities of the Empire, not on a par with Rome or Constantinople, but equal in size and eminence to Carthage or Alexandria and with a population that, at its height, may have reached several hundred thousand.[14] Its lineal descendant, Antakya, is now a substantial Turkish city, situated in the Hatay, a strip of land that was detached from Syria by the French mandate authorities in the late 1930s.[15] Founded, as so many other towns in the region,[16] by Seleucus I Nicator in the 300s BC,[17] it occupied a sheltered position between the heights of Mount Silpius and the River Orontes in the northern coastal regions of the province. The twin foundation of Seleucia Pieria (Samandaği), some 30 kilometres to the west on the coast, provided a port, for the river was not navigable as far as Antioch itself.

In the 60s BC, Antioch served as the capital of the last two Seleucid kings, Antiochus XIII and Philip II, who squabbled viciously over a rapidly diminishing circle of Syrian land, unaware or uncaring that the world was rapidly moving on and that the Romans were quickly closing in. In 64 BC, following his defeat of Tigranes of Armenia, Pompey the Great arrived in Antioch, and he granted the city *libertas* ('freedom'), a liberty that was to result in seven centuries of Roman rule, regularised by the appointment of Lucius Marcius Philippus as the new province's first governor in 58 BC. He also abolished the previous 'Seleucid' era of the city, which had calculated dates from 312 BC,[18] and replaced it with a modestly named Pompeian era, which, with a deft piece of mathematics, was deemed to begin in 66 BC (when Pompey had defeated Tigranes of Armenia, leaving Syria without alternative patrons and effectively at his mercy). From the time of the early Empire, Antioch came to be the headquarters of the imperial province, with its legate directly in command of several legions and often *de facto* commander of the whole Roman East.

Freed of its rather uncomfortable position as the capital of the collapsing Seleucid state, Antioch then prospered, receiving embellishments such as the building by Julius Caesar of the earliest-known basilica in the region (the Kaisarion),[19] and the establishment of a local Olympic Games under Augustus, which would in due course become one of the most celebrated festivals in the eastern half of the Empire. The city, however, was devastated by a particularly damaging series of earthquakes, starting with one under Gaius Caligula in April 37; it had to be rebuilt by Trajan in 115, by Leo I in 458 and again by Justinian in 526 and 528.

The December 115 earthquake struck whilst Trajan was actually staying in the city before his expedition against the Parthians. The Emperor was only slightly hurt, although one of the consuls, Marcus Pedo Vergilianus, was killed. Trajan was said to have been led safely from his bedroom by a supernatural spirit of extraordinary size,[20] quite possibly, it was believed, Zeus himself. In the aftermath of this earthquake, a spasm of persecution broke out against the Christians, blamed for provoking divine wrath by their impiety, which led the following year to the martyrdom of Ignatius, who had been Bishop of Antioch since around 67. This seismic instability, damage caused by the Persians who seized Antioch in 540 and its loss to the Arabs in 636 eventually deprived Antioch of political significance and it fell into complete decline. When the Byzantines retook the city in 969 under Nicephorus Phocas there was little left worth preserving and they started again on a nearby uninhabited site.

The ancient monuments are thus largely known, not through excavation, but from the testament of ancient texts, principally those by Antioch's most famous son, the orator Libanius.[21] Perhaps the most noted was the colonnaded street, some 3 kilometres long, that ran right through the heart of the city and was rivalled in its magnificence only by the mighty colonnade of Apamea in central Syria. Begun under Augustus, though possibly under the auspices of Herod Antipas, the client king of Judaea, it was completed in the reign of Tiberius and rebuilt in the 2nd century under Trajan and Antoninus Pius.

Control of Antioch acted as a key to the whole Roman East, and it was thus the target for successive attempts by the Persians to capture it.[22] Following Shapur's taking of the city in 260, he deported part of the population to Persia, where he set them to rebuilding the decayed town of Gondeshapur, which he then out of pride – and with a particular eye to annoying the Romans – renamed Beh-az-Andew-i-Sapur[23] or 'Shapur's better-than-Antioch town.'[24] Antioch was also seized by the Palmyrenes under Zenobia in 270, and used by a string of usurpers as a springboard in their attempts to secure imperial power. Avidius Cassius, for instance, found support here and, following his defeat in 175,[25] the city was consequently punished, briefly deprived of the right to stage its games. More seriously, Pescennius Niger, the eastern rival to Septimius Severus in the civil war of 192–3, used Antioch as his base. After his defeat at Issus – site of Alexander the Great's more famous victory against the Persians in 333 BC – Pescennius fled back to Antioch, where he was apprehended and rapidly put to death.[26] As a punishment for its adherence to his opponent's cause, Septimius demoted the city from the rank of metropolis to a mere village under the jurisdiction of Laodicea, its neighbour and bitter rival, whose loyalty to the Severan cause had been notable.

With the increasing tendency of emperors from the Tetrarchy onwards to base themselves closer to the frontiers, Antioch's importance rose dramatically. Diocletian spent several winters here around 298–301 and supervised the construction of a great palace – now lost – on an island in the Orontes. In a sign of the increasing strength and demands of the imperial bureaucracy, an arms factory and granaries were also built, as well as no fewer than five baths.[27]

Amongst Antioch's surviving hidden secrets is evidence of the very earliest emergence of Christianity. It was in Antioch, according to the

Byzantine chronicler John Malalas, that the followers of Jesus were first called Christians, a name given to the faithful by Evodios, who succeeded Peter as bishop around AD 41.[28] As a cosmopolitan city, which had a well-established Jewish community and a heavy veneer of Hellenistic culture, it was receptive to precisely the kind of social and intellectual ferment that gave birth to the new Church in the middle decades of the 1st century.

Set high on a mountainside, with stunning views over the chaos of the modern metropolis, lies the church of Saint Peter. The first Christians are said to have met here secretly, taking advantage of a natural cave, and adapting and extending it for their services. Peter himself spent a year in Antioch, according to the Acts of the Apostles, and he is traditionally credited as the city's first bishop.[29] An unpromising modern courtyard, and a flat Crusader-era façade punctuated with stylised crosses and stars, gives way to the cave itself. It is a simple place, imbued with a deeply spiritual atmosphere, furnished with a bare altar, a statue of Peter – both modern – and the merest hint of wall painting on the back wall, eroded away by the centuries and faint trickles of water, which give the whole a damp as well as holy atmosphere. The tunnel through which the Christians are said to have escaped from would-be persecutors is nowhere in evidence, doubtless long ago blocked up.

As a Christian stronghold, Antioch was perhaps an inauspicious selection for Julian's headquarters in summer 362[30] immediately prior to his assault on Persia. His desire to re-establish pagan shrines and sweep away Christian accretions and usurpations of sacred spots led him to a catastrophic error of judgement. He ordered that the bones of Babylas, the 3rd-century martyr and much-revered Bishop of Antioch, be removed from their resting place at Daphne just outside the city. The Christians responded by putting on a massive show of defiance, as the relics were processed to a newly prepared tomb free of pagan taint or imperial spite. Not long afterwards, the Temple of Apollo at Daphne, from the environs of which Babylas's bones had been so publicly expelled, caught fire and burnt down, an event for which the Emperor understandably – although, as it turned out, mistakenly – blamed the Christians.[31]

Traditionalists were upset by Julian's refusal to attend public spectacles such as the theatre, while the whole populace was affected by the Emperor's attempt to fix the price of grain to dampen the inflation caused by the presence of his army, an intervention that led to landowners refusing to sell their produce, resulting in escalating food shortages. In response to the clear antipathy that his Antiochene subjects felt for him, Julian penned a remarkable, almost self-satirical treatise in his defence, the *Misopogon* ('Beard-Hater'), which he had posted in public outside the imperial palace, and which provoked a grovelling apology from the town council of Antioch.[32]

Antioch's troubled relationship with authority continued in 387, when, after a letter was read out announcing the imposition of additional heavy taxes on the city, a mob pulled down the statues of the Emperor Theodosius and the imperial family that stood outside the governor's palace. Such an act of *lèse-majesté* was intolerable and the perpetrators were immediately arrested, tried and soon afterwards executed by burning or being thrown to the beasts in the amphitheatre.[33] The ruling class of Antioch quailed, fearing that the Emperor's anger at such an unprecedented slight would fall heavily upon them. A deputation was sent off to Constantinople to plead the city's cause, and Libanius tried to deflect responsibility by attributing the 'Riot of the Statues' to the intervention of demons or, almost as heinously one presumes, to foreigners.[34] Theodosius confined his punishment of Antioch to demoting it once more to a village under the jurisdiction of Laodicea. The city's baths and circus also shut down, but the measures were only temporary, for within months the injunctions against it were lifted. Antioch escaped lightly for, just three years later, the same emperor, angered at the murder of the garrison commander in the Greek city of Thessalonica, gave his troops free rein to exact vengeance. Within three hours, around 7,000 people had been slaughtered, while Theodosius himself suffered an eight-month-long excommunication from the Church until he was deemed to have repented sufficiently.[35]

Of Daphne, from which Julian had expelled the remains of Babylas, little survives. It was a favourite, shaded spot for the city's elite, where they built villas and enjoyed the waters of the sacred spring of Castalia. After brief moments of excitement when Zenobia's rearguard fought a delaying action here to permit their queen's escape back to Palmyra, and the crisis caused by Julian's attempt to reopen the holy spring in 363, Daphne relapsed into quiet decay. Indeed, when Julian arrived at such an important pagan shrine, he expected to be greeted by a large crowd and a sumptuous sacrifice, but instead all that came was a single, elderly priest, bearing a rather scrawny duck.[36] It was, the old man explained to the Emperor, all that he could afford. Daphne is still a leafy, comparatively calm retreat from the hustle of Antakya, its pleasant and cool riverside walkways providing a sense, if no direct evidence, of the role it played in Roman times.

Still visible today is the Emperor Titus's impact on the city. Besides giving Antioch a share of the booty taken during the capture of Jerusalem after the Jewish revolt of AD 66–9 (including, it is said, bronze figures of Cherubim looted from the temple itself),[37] he also supervised the building of a canal that connected the area of the port at Seleucia with the Orontes. The construction, known locally as 'the Channel of Titus', is still there, treacherous in rainy weather, scarcely less so in summer. At up to 10 metres in height, the walls of the gorge, now rubble-choked, give way to a tunnel, on occasion eerily lit by the fire of those who fear to tolerate its darkness. The course of the waterwork loses itself in over-grown fields and orchards beyond. A building inscription at the point where the tunnel finally emerges into the light commemorates 'Divus Titus', and so was clearly inscribed after that emperor's death and deifi-cation. The whole, therefore, must still have been under construction during the reign of his brother, Domitian.

Just within the borders of the province of Syria at its north-eastern-most reach, the site of Roman Zeugma (Belkis) is a melancholy place. It lies along the Euphrates, 175 kilometres to the north-east of Antioch, and some 30 kilometres north of the border with modern Syria. Founded around 300 BC by Seleucus I Nicator, a prolific establisher of cities in Syria and its surrounds, its official name was Seleucia-on-the-Euphrates, but it came to be known as Zeugma ('the bridge') for the important river-crossing that it guarded.

The site was almost totally flooded by the rising waters of Turkey's Atatürk Dam Project in the late 1990s and a clear blue expanse of water conceals the temples, forum and markets of the city below – a case where it is man's recent actions rather than the slow chiselling of time that have obliterated the past. A few fragments of buildings, which must have been on the highest parts of Zeugma, cling precariously to slopes at the water's edge: at one point an arch, perhaps part of the supporting structure of a house, at another a fragment of geometric mosaic care-fully preserved on a little jetty that projects beyond the waterline. At the edge of the site, behind a barbed-wire fence, further architectural flotsam, pillars and bases of capitals, have been gathered together, untended, unmarked and disappearing beneath a rapidly growing carpet of grass.

It is hard to credit that this was once a thriving legionary base and city. The Romans controlled it from at least 31 BC, marking the point at which the Euphrates became the commonly accepted boundary of their territory in this region.[38] It first received a legionary garrison in the late 60s, probably initially the X Fretensis,[39] and, after that unit was sent to suppress the Jewish revolt in 66–7, the IV Scythica guarded the crossing until some time in the 3rd century. Only the necropolis at the edge of the city, itself partly cut through by the modern road, survives remotely intact. To gain some sense of the city's ancient life the modern visitor has to go to nearby Gaziantep, where the mosaics rescued from the rapidly sinking site were taken, including the city's finest, from which the piercing-eyed gaze of Zeugma's most-reproduced image seems to follow visitors around the museum. Dubbed the 'gypsy girl', she is, in all likelihood, an embodiment of Gaia, the spirit of the earth.

Around 80 kilometres to the south-west of Zeugma, the Roman road that led south towards Antioch crossed the River Subun just east of the legionary fortress of Cyrrhus (Nabi Khouri). A six-arched Roman bridge still stands, with an exaggerated hump, among low hills planted with a scattering of olive trees on a scarcely frequented route, an ancient artery that carries precious little modern blood. The city was yet another foundation of Seleucus Nicator around 300 BC, named for a town in his Macedonian homeland, and it too fell to Pompey in 64 BC. It became the winter quarters of the Legio X Fretensis in AD 18, retaining its garrison until the aftermath of the Jewish revolt of the late 60s, when the legion was transferred to Judaea.[40]

The final approach to this ancient city, even on a spring day, is a muddy one, the remaining pillars of the south gate mired in deep rainwater pools. From here the *cardo*, once colonnaded, with scattered column fragments a reminder of its former status, leads on into the heart of the city. To the west the brooding massif of the acropolis rears, ringed with late-Roman fortifications, a final sanctuary for the north Syrian populace. The citadel has yielded an inscription of Justinianic date commemorating the construction of the acropolis around 530, but it is probable that by then much of the city had been abandoned and that it had become little more than a hilltop refuge.[41]

In the lee of the hill a cluster of nomad tents clings, threatening at any moment to succumb to the tearing wind. While sheep munch contentedly, and their owners eye any visitors warily from a safe distance, their handiwork (or that of their confederates) is clear. The whole site is pockmarked by holes and small trenches, exposing here an acanthus-leaf-clad column, there a curved section of a well, all marred and spattered by upcast from the illicit excavations. Further to the north a ruin-field lies, stones scattered without apparent form or rhythm. A lonely arch surveys the olive fields, and nearby a still-upstanding structure, itself arched, marks one of Cyrrhus's two located churches, sited just by the remains of a large sanctuary to an unknown god. To the south of this, closer to the city centre lie the most impressive remains by far, those of the theatre. At just over 110 metres in diameter, it has a dozen rows of seating still largely intact, but the stage and *scaenae frons* have been utterly cast down by earthquakes, huge blocks strewn hither and thither as though hurled carelessly by an especially petulant giant.

For much of antiquity the record is silent on Cyrrhus. Its one brief flaring of notoriety came late in the reign of Marcus Aurelius, with the revolt of Avidius Casssius, the governor of Syria, who was a native of the city. Apparently egged on by Faustina, the Emperor's wife – who was concerned that, should her husband die, other factions at Rome might seize the throne and deny her young son, Caracalla – Cassius was considering the merits of assuming the imperial mantle himself. Precipitated into an untimely decision by rumours of Marcus's death that reached the East in April 175, he soon learnt the unfortunate truth that the Emperor still lived. By then it was too late to go back. Declared an enemy of the state by the Senate, Cassius sought and received support from Egypt – where he was recognised as Emperor by 3 May (and an edict has been unearthed rejoicing at his accession)[42] – from Arabia and of course from Syria, giving him the potential support of seven legions. But, critically, he failed to recruit Martius Verus, the governor of Cappadocia, a comrade of his from Marcus's Parthian War.

Cassius's efforts to build a wider coalition were also rebuffed: his letter to the distinguished Athenian senator Herodes Atticus met with the laconic reply 'You are mad!'[43] Marcus gave an emotional speech to his troops, in which he lamented the disloyalty of 'a dear friend' and mused that he would happily have given up the Empire to Cassius if the Senate willed it and it were for 'the common good'.[44] The Emperor was clearly winning the propaganda war, and the usurper's legions succumbed to such grave doubts that a centurion murdered him – probably in early July – and despatched his head on a plate to Marcus. The Emperor, saddened, but no doubt relieved, tastefully refused to receive the trophy and ordered it buried.[45] Martius Verus, meanwhile, marched on Syria, took Cassius's headquarters unopposed and made haste to burn the rebel's correspondence, coincidentally thereby removing any incriminating references to himself or his supporters.[46]

The circuit of walls that girdle the whole site, now largely disappeared, did not keep out the Persians in 256, but this was a fate shared by many Syrian cities at the time and does not speak of any particular vulnerability in Cyrrhus's defences. For a century, little is known, other than that the city acquired a bishopric and sent its prelate to the Council of Nicaea in 325. But in around 423, Cyrrhus received a new bishop, the renowned theologian Theodoret. Born in Antioch around 393, his major work, the *Historia Religiosa*, is an invaluable account of the lives of Syrian ascetics. Theodoret became embroiled in the bitter controversies concerning the nature of Christ that tore apart the Church in the mid-5th century.[47] As a result, the Second Council of Ephesus (449), known to its detractors as the 'Robber Council',[48] deprived him of his see and he went into exile in a monastery at Apamea. Rehabilitated at the Council of Chalcedon in 451, he died six years later, content that his orthodoxy had been established, but little knowing that the Christological controversy would rage for a century yet and claim him as a posthumous victim, for in 553 the Council of Constantinople condemned his writings against Cyril, as part of the last-ditch effort to patch up differences between the contending Monophysite and orthodox Nicene factions.[49]

South from Cyrrhus, the land continues to be fertile, its rural richness an echo of late antiquity, when northern Syria underwent a boom, partly fuelled by the production of olive oil, and prosperous villages and small towns proliferated, only to find themselves in a troubled border-zone after the Arab invasions of the 7th century. They dwindled, were abandoned, but, in the absence of local populations to rob them for building materials, they did not decay.[50] They remain, a shadow-land of 'Dead Cities' strung across the Syrian landscape in two belts, one running north of Beroea (Aleppo) – itself some 80 kilometres south of Cyrrhus – and one to its south-west, forming a collection of stone ghosts, each one with church and solidly constructed houses looking as if a few light repairs might restore them to the state when their residents left just the day before yesterday.

As well as agricultural settlements, the area was highly productive in piety, producing rich harvests of monks and holy men. Theodoret of Cyrrhus enumerated them in the *Historia Religiosa*, but the one who most captured the imagination both then and since is Saint Simeon Stylites. Born somewhere near Antioch around 390, Simeon joined a community of monks at Telanissos around 412, where he made a nuisance of himself by such acts of ascetic athleticism as standing upright on one leg for as long as he could bear his weight, taking no food and drink at all during Lent, and binding a rope of palm fronds so tightly around his waist that the fibres entered the wound and began to fester, an act of self-mortification that resulted in his temporary expulsion from the monastery.

Readmitted to the community, but feeling his spiritual efforts hampered by the increasing throng who came to see him, Simeon adopted the simple but effective expedient of building a pillar and ascending it, thus rendering himself simultaneously closer to God and further from his earthly admirers. At first 3 metres seemed enough, but the clamour below grew ever greater, and he built ever higher, finally reaching a height of

20 metres.[51] The saint lived over thirty years atop this perch, twice daily delivering lengthy and powerful sermons to the stream of visitors for whom, if he himself was out of physical reach, his spiritual message was certainly accessible.

It seems that things could get pretty heated. Theodoret recounts that Bedouin would come to see Simeon in great groups 200–300 strong, smash their idols in front of the pillar and, for good measure, renounce the eating of camel-meat.[52] On one occasion, Theodoret himself was nearly trampled to death by an onrush of enthusiastic nomads, tugging at his beard and cloak in their eagerness to get as close as possible to the holy man on the pillar.[53] Upon Simeon's death, the citizens of Antioch managed to lay claim to his remains and carried them off in a solemn procession to a new resting place in the city. His example spawned a whole series of copycat stylites, among whom the most famous was Simeon the Younger (521–92), who, fittingly, practised his aerial vocation at a monastery between Antioch and the sea, a short journey from the elder Simeon's tomb.[54]

There is little left of the pillar at Deir Semaan now, if indeed the egg-shaped stone about half a metre high perched awkwardly on a column base actually is the remains of Simeon's earthly home. Guides were showing the pillar fragment as early as 1905, when Gertrude Bell spent a contemplative moment seated upon it whilst her Bedouin servants pitched camp.[55] There is no way of telling if it is the genuine article, yet its strange shape does seem almost as if a million believing hands had brushed away a tiny fragment of its sanctity, and it is undeniable that after the saint's death in 459, an enormous complex grew up, for the worship of God, the veneration of the Simeon's remains and the accommodation of the countless pilgrims drawn to the place.

A unique ensemble of four basilicas was constructed, creating a cruciform effect around the central shrine of the pillar. From the south basilica, richly adorned with blown acanthus decorations on the capitals, a typically Syrian flourish, the pilgrim – or modern visitor – gains the first view of the pillar. A whole series of piers and framing arches give extravagant architectural form to the basilicas, but still leave centre stage to the column itself. That four churches were needed is itself evidence of the vast numbers who came to worship here, for evidently they could not be accommodated in just one. The building of the western basilica even involved the effort of levelling off the hillside to enable it to be the same length as the others, its now-ruined state permitting striking views over the plain below that were impossible in the 5th century. The architects were innovators in other ways, too: on the eastern basilica, the apse's curve projects beyond the building to create a *chevet*, possibly the earliest example of such a feature in Syria.

To the south and east of the basilical complex lies a monastery, for those favoured enough to live or lodge so close to the shrine itself. Standing up to three storeys, using blocks and lintels, only the façade remains, giving the impression of a giant monastic noughts-and-crosses board. Beyond, and on the way to Deir Semaan – the lower town, where most had to stay – is the baptistery, containing a font built into the floor with steps to either side, possibly for the more rapid processing of the catechumens in a 'walk-through' baptism.

Deir Semaan, the monastery of Semaan (or Simeon), grew up on the site of the original Telanissos. A shattered monumental arch marks the start of the sacred way that led pilgrims up to the shrine itself. Beyond this lie the churches, monasteries and hostels, which made the place a veritable pilgrim city. In various states of ruination now, their arches alarmingly cracked, keystones wobbling and naves filled with the rubble of earthquake-induced collapse, carpeted in thorn-bushes and spring flowers, they still have the power to awe. The Great Pandocheion, the largest monastery – which also acted as a hostel for travellers – is surrounded by a two-storey portico, and the multiple arcades in the structure give the strange sensation of a building yet to be completed, and not of one in the process of falling down.

Earthquakes had, indeed, damaged the buildings as early as 526 or 528, possibly leading to the collapse of the roof over the pillar shrine itself, and the complex went into a decline after the Arab invasions.[56] A brief Byzantine reoccupation in the 10th century is evidenced by a crude defensive wall around the upper churches, but it was recaptured and sacked by a Muslim Hamdanid army in 985, and thereafter abandoned, leaving the saint's spirit to a final few centuries of silent contemplation.[57]

To enter into the life of a Byzantine holy man is to cross the threshold of a world both similar and yet profoundly different from our own. The ascetic piety, the mortification of the flesh, the longing to be rid of the trammels of a mortal body and to achieve by conspicuous piety the radiant garment of a saint or, better still, of a martyr – all these seem utterly at odds with our materialistic society. Yet the direct appeal over the heads of traditional authorities to the masses, the concern for those dispossessed or left out by the march of 'progress' in the fancy cities, the role of mediator between villages and the elites, the utter unconcern for traditional proprieties and etiquette, these are the hallmarks of the charismatic leader. But for the small matter of a thirty-year stint on top of a stone pillar, Simon Stylites could well, in a modern incarnation, have been a Kennedy or a Castro.

Deir Semaan is not an isolated phenomenon. It sits close to the north-ernmost extension of the Dead Cities, a crown atop a landscape that, though populated only by the deceased, seems curiously alive and vibrant. It is the most vivid witness anywhere to the diversity of rural life in the Later Roman Empire. Much debate has centred over exactly when the villages and small towns that made up this dense network of agricul-tural settlements began to decline, whether they retained their vitality into the 8th century – and thus beyond the Islamic invasion – or were already decaying in the early 7th.[58] That they grew, and flourished, is undeniable. Some 800 villages have been counted, and there may be more, most of them fairly small, with around fifty or so houses, and with no centralised plan, a far cry from the rigid grids – or at least the attempts to impose them on unwilling topography – that are the norm for larger cities in the region. The well-built houses, often with olive presses attached, speak of a comfortable existence, even of prosperity, while the absence of walls, and in general of fortifications save a few watchtowers, indicates a reasonably secure existence untroubled by im-perial crises or external raiders.

Burj Haidar, which lies around 10 kilometres east of Deir Semaan, off a minor road winding south-eastwards towards Aleppo, is not untyp-ical. A settlement first recorded in 298 as Kaprokera,[59] it boasts an unusually large number of churches for a comparatively small place, the most extraordinary of which is a chapel that clings limpet-like to the side of a slope overlooking the modern road. A huddle of bad-tempered dogs guard a tent that has been pitched inside the church, denying entrance. Two walls of a single tower remain, standing to a precarious height and listing at an alarming angle, surveying the rich arable land below, which once supplied the village's wealth.

Dar Qita, 50 kilometres west of Aleppo, seems from the road a small settlement, the walls of its houses merging into a vista of scattered rocks that stretches to the horizon. But on approaching it resolves itself into groups of neat, well-built dwellings, mostly two-storeyed, with the slots for wooden beams to support the upper floors still visible. A spring rain drizzles down, making the stone pathways slippery and treacherous and rendering the exploration of each house a hazardous adventure. Grey stone slabs form the lintels, set on uprights to create doorways that seem like miniature dolmens. In many cases only the roofs have collapsed, the rest of the structure remaining almost totally intact, creating the sensa-tion that the inhabitants stepped out just a minute or two ago and made their way down to the fields with the firm intention of returning quite soon. The village church, complete only on its western side, has a heavily ornamented window decorated with almost spaghetti-like loops of stone. The doorways are all beautifully carved with intricate mouldings of acanthus and other plants. Inside are the remains of a *bema*, a semicircular raised platform of stone, somewhat overgrown, from which the clergy would read the lessons or deliver the sermons to their congregation of prosperous, pious farmers.

Around 20 kilometres further to the south-west lies the church of Qalb Loze. Its Arabic name means 'heart of the almond', though an alternative theory holds that it derives from Qal Baal Uze or 'the light of Baal Uze'. It is in a very poor settlement, at the edge of a village whose general state of repair seems almost worse than that of the 1,500-year-old church. A pile of discarded vaccine packs from the World Health Organisation is a sign that, once agriculturally independent and capable of sponsoring innovative ecclesiastical architecture, this place now very much depends on others for any flicker of prosperity. The church building stands isolated, the rest of the ancient settlement having disappeared, and it probably pre-dates the main church at Saint Simeon by a couple of decades. Around the outside of the rectangular basilica flow three corded bands of decoration, and the outline of the church is broken by a chevet. Inside, three dramatically swept arches divide the space into three aisles, the two at the sides still retaining some of the original flat roofing slabs. As one of the Dead Cities' most ambitious structures, it seems curiously muted and alone.

Just a couple of kilometres north is Qirkbize, in many ways indistinguishable from its many fellow Dead Cities. Yet the solidity of its buildings is still compelling, and on the top of the hill lies a fair-sized 3rd-century private house, converted at some point (probably early in the 4th century) into a church, with the remains of a *bema* still intact in the nave.[60] Incised on a fallen and almost inaccessible slab lies a little cross, a poignant reminder of the village's religious heritage. As we leave, a local imam, splendidly bearded, steps from a nearby van, curious as to what a foreigner is doing quite so far off the beaten track. The response clearly finds favour and he anoints our hands with perfume, kisses our foreheads and duly pronounces upon us sincerely intoned blessings. It is a just reward for a dozen Dead City churches visited.

In the southernmost group of Dead Cities, one more than any other merits the designation of city. Serjilla, around 50 kilometres south of Aleppo, lies in a basin between low hills, whose rocky appearance has been accentuated by their almost total loss of topsoil, long ago blown away and deposited in the valleys, leaving once-fertile slopes barren and lifeless. The settlement seems to flow down the hill, with well-preserved (or, rather, reconstructed) buildings standing tall amidst the debris of their fallen neighbours. In the centre of the site a miniature baths, with the largest room only 15 metres long, butts up against a two-storey building with a double-portico. With its beautifully carved Corinthian columns, this building, the *andron*, or men's meeting house, clearly had a lot of attention and expense lavished on it by the local dignitary who had it built some time in the late 5th century.[61] Even out here, far from the cosmopolitan life of the big cities, life's little luxuries were not neglected.

Around a dozen other houses still stand, some veritable villas; one, just up from the church with a double-frontage and a Corinthian colonnade façade looking out onto a courtyard, must have belonged to a prosperous family indeed; the remains of an olive press behind their residence perhaps give a clue to the source of their wealth. Yet all this passed away. Outside the church lie a couple of stone sarcophagi, hardly decorated save for ornate crosses, with the stone closing slab of one of them pushed slightly ajar, as though its occupant had, at the last moment, tried to flee.

By the 7th century, it seems, there was little chance of escape from the outside forces that were threatening the economic livelihood of these towns and villages. The big cities had been struggling since the 4th century, with little building of new municipal facilities, and by the 6th the decline was palpable. This great rural hinterland needed the possibilities offered by trade and some form of market economy, and, as the arteries of the Empire furred up and were then snapped, first by the Persians and then by Arab invasions, the opportunities for amassing surplus production and converting it into wealth locally disappeared. The monasteries, offering refuge both for the body and the spirit, and a convenient depository to gift what wealth there was, probably survived in more reasonable shape until the 10th century. The villages, too, were inhabited on a lesser scale than before, and it may have been that the final *coups de grâce* were delivered by the disruption caused first by the Crusades in the 11th and 12th centuries, and then by the Mongol invasions of the 13th.

The traveller who moves east from Beroea, rather than south-west towards Serjilla, passes down a road punctuated by villages and small towns, all dependent on the irrigation projects undertaken by the Syrian government over the past decades, tinting the desert fringes with smudges of green. Fifty kilometres to the east the road touches the Euphrates and, 125 kilometres further on, a side-branch leads to the ancient town of Sergiopolis (Resafe), 30 kilometres to the south. It all seems a long way from the modern government in Damascus, and it must have appeared just as distant in Roman times from the authorities in Rome, Constantinople or, at best, Antioch. Sergiopolis formed part of a chain of desert outposts established under Diocletian as part of the Strata Diocletiana, which led from Sura on the Euphrates south to Palmyra and thence as far as Damascus. It created a sort of outer *limes*, a trip-wire, while still retaining the security of a system of fortifications further inside provincial territory.[62] By the 5th century, however, most of the auxiliary and legionary troops had been moved up to this outer line, creating a bristling, threatening border, more like the fixed riverine fron-tiers of the Rhine and Danube than the traditional fluid desert lines of old. But then the outer posts were abandoned, in some cases entrusted to the guardianship of the Romans' Arab allies such as the Ghassanids, in others forsaken completely. It was thus a very thin force indeed that faced renewed Persian thrusts in the late 6th century, and one that depended on the field army or local initiatives to throw back invaders. When either or both of these failed, as they did against Khusraw from 610, the results were catastrophic.

The walls of Sergiopolis enclose a far greater area than was needed for the modest garrison of the 5th century, the brown bulk of the city's buttresses standing out starkly against the desert sands. The reason for this metropolis in the desert was the martyrdom of Saint Sergius, a Roman soldier who refused to make a sacrifice to the gods in 305, during the Great Persecution under Diocletian.[63] Sergius's martyr-shrine soon became a major centre of pilgrimage, drawing crowds from all over Syria and beyond, and churches, hostels and other facilities had to be constructed to service them. Under Anastasius (491–518), the settlement was renamed after the soldier-saint and the mud-brick walls were replaced with stone, using a gypsum that seems to catch the rays of the summer sun and reflect them back at onlookers with intermittent dazzling bursts of white. The walls were further reinforced under Justinian, but inside the arcaded galleries give them a curious light feeling despite their width and bulk. The north gate of the city is one of the finest extant exam-ples of Byzantine military architecture; projecting from the wall, it protects an inner gateway decorated with a complex of arches and vine-branch patterns, more sculptor's tour de force than practical portal.

The principal buildings of Sergiopolis were of course ecclesiastical and the interior of the city is scattered with the skeletal remains of the great pilgrimage basilicas. The most important of these, the church of the Holy Cross, lies in the south-east of the city; some 30 metres long, its sweeping lateral arches are reinforced by smaller arches resting on columns, for the proneness of the region to earthquakes, and the uncertainty of the architects in handling this relatively new technique for dividing nave from side-aisles, meant that remedial reinforcement was necessary. In Basilica B to the west, coloured fragments of fresco have survived against all the odds, depicting indistinct saints' heads, though sadly scarred and obscured by quite recent graffiti. In the northern sector of the city are three huge water cisterns, the largest of which is nearly 60 metres in length, with an estimated capacity of 15,000 cubic metres, proof that Sergiopolis was well equipped to withstand an extended siege or period of drought.[64]

Just outside the north gate of the city lies the building known as the *praetorium* of the Ghassanids, or the palace of al-Mundhir. It is a low rectangular structure, probably an audience chamber, its east wall interrupted by an apse. As early as the end of the 3rd century, with the removal of the buffer that Palmyra had provided,[65] the Roman East became ever more vulnerable to desert raiders or to the depredations of more organised confederacies that began to grow up. The Romans were forced to pay subsidies to Arab allies, a legally sanctioned form of extortion, to make the desert safe, or at least passable, for their troops and merchants. They had had relations with Arab peoples for many centuries, but these were generally settled groups such as the Nabataeans of Petra, the Edessans and the Palmyrenes, which sheltered the Roman provinces from direct dealings with the more fractious nomadic or semi-nomadic groups of the Arabian peninsula itself. Once the Romans annexed the caravan cities of Petra, Edessa and Palmyra – in 106, 244 and 272 respectively – it became necessary to adopt new strategies to cope with the direct responsibility for security of the desert regions over which they had now assumed control.

The success of Diocletian's colleague Galerius in forcing the cession in 298 by the Persians of five satrapies across the Tigris only aggravated the situation. Both Rome and Persia were now in effect forced to recruit the desert Arab tribes directly to their cause. By the early 6th century, the Persians were allied with the Lakhmid confederacy, a group who had its main base at Hira, south-west of the Euphrates in the Iraqi desert, and the Byzantine government placed its faith in the Ghassanids, originally a south Arabian group, which had migrated gradually northwards to the vicinity of Damascus.[66] The chief Ghassanid sheikh was granted the title *phylarch* and substantial payments in exchange for safeguarding imperial interest from the Persians and Lakhmids, and for keeping his own followers from raiding Byzantine towns or convoys. The Ghassanids had converted to Christianity, although to its Monophysite form, a confessional choice that distanced them from the central orthodoxy of Constantinople, although it may have made them more acceptable to the heavily Monophysite populace of rural Syria. Part of their duties must have involved the protection of the pilgrims who came to worship at the shrine of Saint Sergius.

The al-Mundhir named in an inscription at the Sergiopolis palace (his name transliterated into Greek as Alumanduros) ruled over the Ghassanids from 569 to 582 and was arrested and exiled to Sicily by the Emperor Tiberius on suspicion of disloyalty, to be followed in short order by the overthrow of Nu'man, his son and successor.[67] Already in the mid-6th century the Byzantines had grown exasperated at the fickleness of their supposed allies; a treaty of 561 points the finger at the Ghassanids, accusing them of all manner of misdemeanours and threatening them with severe punishment if they transgressed again.[68] Two decades later the relationship had broken down altogether and the Byzantines were content to sit back as the Ghassanid confederation broke up into a score of squabbling factions. By doing so, however, they connived in the removal of the one effective barrier against those Arabs whose domains lay deeper still in the desert. This was not a problem whilst those tribes were disunited and disinclined to anything more damaging than the odd pillaging raid, but when in the early 7th century the advent of Islam gave those groups a new, united purpose, there was little to hold them back.

Sergiopolis had performed its role well as a breakwater against possible Persian incursions, save for its capture by Khusraw II in 616. Against the Arab invasions, however, it was powerless. The city continued to prosper modestly, performing for a time a role as a favoured retreat for the Umayyad caliphs, particularly under Hisham (724–43). But when the Abbasids came to power in 750, their army looted Sergiopolis and ransacked the palace that Hisham had built there – its remains lie beyond the palace of al-Mundhir – sending the city into a steep decline, which became terminal when the Mongols finished the destruction in the 13th century.

Two hundred kilometres further to the south-east down the Euphrates, Dura Europos lies at the very extreme of the Roman Empire, almost its greatest physical projection,[69] a fortress thrust deep into the heart of formerly Parthian territory, and a position that the Romans only held, precariously, for eighty years or so. In many ways, therefore, it is scarcely a Roman city, mingling Hellenistic, Parthian and Semitic influences in a cosmopolitan and unique mixture. The fortress-city lies on the west bank of the Euphrates, just 60 kilometres north-west of the border crossing with Iraq, its huge bulk dominating the view over a wide expanse of river and desert, seeming from a distance as though a mud-flow had spilt over, solidified, baked and then started to crumble back into the dust. It is this great western wall that provides the first, and abiding, impression of the site; on the other three sides Dura was protected by lower walls, steep gorges or the river itself.[70]

The probably founder of Dura was Nicanor, one of the generals of Seleucus I, who named it for Europos, his patron's birthplace in the Macedonian homeland.[71] The other half of its double-barrelled name probably derives from *dur*, a Semitic word meaning 'fort'. From its strategic position on a rocky plateau some 30–40 metres above the river plain below, it was an effective means to control the caravan routes, and consequently attracted the attention of the Parthians, who certainly held it at the time of a treaty with the Romans in 20 BC (which assigned Circesium, 50 kilometres upriver, as the forward Roman position).[72] Trajan's army passed through during his campaign of annexation against Parthia, leading to a brief Roman occupation in 115–17, but all that remains of this stay is a crumbling triumphal arch.

More definitive Roman control began in 164, when Lucius Verus (Marcus Aurelius's less philosophically inclined co-Emperor) captured it, as the Romans pushed ever further down the Euphrates. When the Sassanid dynasty came to power in Persia in 226, it initiated a more aggressive policy against its Roman neighbours, who had largely had their own way in Roman-Persian encounters since the Parthian victory at Carrhae in 53 BC. It seems the city may have been taken in 253, but revolted and, when Shapur recaptured it in 256, he did not permit the inhabitants any second chance to throw off Persian rule; the city was razed and its citizens deported elsewhere in his empire. So total was the destruction that when Julian passed through in 363 on his way to attack Ctesiphon, the Persian capital, there was no trace at all to be found of the town.[73]

It was the desperate efforts to reinforce Dura against this second Sassanid siege that preserved the most important archaeological finds there, for a great earth ramp was thrown up against the walls in a vain attempt to provide greater strength, thereby burying all the buildings at the edge of the city and preserving them from destruction. The intensity of the defenders' struggle was dramatically highlighted by the discovery of a tunnel beneath Tower 19, in which a group of skeletons lay, their armour still in place, three of them with purses full of coins about their bodies, their remains charred by the force of the fire that caused the tunnel supports to collapse.[74] Although it is unclear whether these were Roman defenders digging a countermine to block Persian tunnelling or Sassanid troops trying to undermine the tower, the bitter and fatal fight certainly ended in the city's fall.[75] The nearby bastion is riven by a great crack; though tempting to assign it to destruction during the siege, the damage was as likely caused by subsequent earthquakes.

The main or 'Palmyra' gate leads to the most important finds, a jumble of foundations and wall fragments that housed some of the city's many spectacular religious buildings. The first significant discovery here was made by Captain Murphy, a British soldier in the region as part of the post-First World War carve-up of the Middle East by the western European powers. He wrote to his superior officer that 'The paintings are in the west corner of the fort and consist of life-size figures of three men, one woman and three other figures partly obliterated.'[76] The British hurriedly despatched an archaeological team – for they were about to hand the area over to French control – which found further frescoes, including a depiction of Tyche, but by the time the French were able to commence excavation in earnest in 1922, the local Bedouin had defaced the exposed wall paintings. In a campaign of digs that stretched across fifteen years, Dura yielded an astonishing harvest. There were temples to the Palmyrene gods, a *mithraeum* (probably a legacy of the Roman military occupation) as well as temples to Zeus Kyrios ('the Lord'), Artemis, Zeus Megistos ('the Greatest') and more exotic deities, such as Gaddé, Azzanathkona, Atargatis and Artemis-Nanaia – all now represented by grassed-over walls, indistinct mounds and half-filled excavation pits.

The Durans' eclectic religious life was rounded off by a synagogue and a Christian chapel, both prize examples of their genre. The chapel seems to have been incorporated into a private building (it would have been unwise to advertise a Christian building in public at such an early stage) and is either from the late 2nd century or the first part of the 3rd; a graffito gives the date as 230/1.[77] It is amongst the earliest Christian buildings in the world, and was decorated with biblical scenes including the good shepherd and his flock, the story of Adam and Eve and representations of Jesus and the disciples.

On the other side of the gate lay a Jewish synagogue. The presence of a Jewish community is not in itself unusual, particularly in a cosmopolitan trading post such as Dura, but what is extraordinary is the series of beautifully crafted figurative paintings discovered there, dating from around 244,[78] just a decade before the city's destruction. Judaism would later have an aversion – just as did Islam – to depicting the human form, and so this fresco cycle is highly unusual,[79] perhaps evidence of an accommodation with Hellenistic ideas, perhaps just a sign of the Durans' self-confident individualism. The frescoes have long been removed from the site and can only be viewed in a side-room of the Damascus museum, supervised by a conspiratorial museum guard in a blue-peaked cap. The reds and yellows have survived most strongly, giving the depictions of biblical scenes a warmth and sadness. The whole gamut of stories is present here, from the finding of Moses in the Nile, to King David garbed in a suitably imperial purple robe and the judgement of Solomon.

When the Romans occupied Dura, they very unusually constructed their camp within the walls, sectioning off the whole of the north-west quarter of the city and building a *praetorium* and military baths there. Alongside the Seleucid-era 'new' citadel, the Romans built a fort for the military official who directed the garrison from around 211,[80] the *Dux Ripae* ('Duke of the Shore'). An early example of the *duces* who came to have particular commands along the frontier, the *Dux Ripae* kept watch for any Persian incursions – safe, as he thought, behind the thick, now partly fallen walls.

The archive of the auxiliary unit stationed here, the *Cohors XX Palmyrenorum*, has, thanks to the dry conditions and lack of subsequent occupation, provided a high proportion of the everyday military documents found anywhere in the Empire. These include guard rosters and quartermasters' records, but the most evocative of all is the *Feriale Duranum*, the military calendar of Dura.[81] A corollary of the founding of a permanent standing army under Augustus had been the establishment of an official calendar of religious observances for the soldiers. Aside from major Roman festivals, such as the Vestalia in June,[82] the birthday of Rome was commemorated on 21 April, while on 3 January the soldiers took vows for the health of the Emperor and the security of the Empire, a show of loyalty that, perhaps not coincidentally, took place four days before the army received its first pay-instalment of the year.[83] The date of accession (the *dies imperii*) of former emperors, most of them deified, was also celebrated, including Trajan, Antoninus Pius, Marcus Aurelius and Septimius Severus, but not Commodus, whose memory was universally reviled, or, more surprisingly, Hadrian. Thus from Dura in Mesopotamia to Durostorum in Moesia and Dubris in Britannia, the corporate identity of the army was reinforced by a common round of rituals and sacrifices.

At Dura Europos, the line could not hold, however, and after 256 the Romans never again secured a position quite so far forward on the Euphrates. By the 6th century the Roman border with the Persians ran close to a series of fortified cities further up the river, most notably Zenobia (modern Halabiye, 200 kilometres north-west of Dura Europos), named for the Queen of Palmyra whose territorial ambitions would seriously threaten Rome's control over Syria in the 270s. Here the river runs between two sets of hills, making it a suitable choke-point for blocking waterborne traffic or, indeed, for impeding land forces hugging the course of the Euphrates to take advantage of the ease of resupply that it offered. The set of walls facing the river has long ago been washed way. But the south wall, the longest of Zenobia's irregular triangular perimeter, retains almost all of its bastions, which march like stone pegs high up to the hill on which stands the city's bulky citadel, the last refuge for its defenders. The place is not much visited now; the ticket collector wearily complains that the year's total visitor tally has only just reached a hundred. Immediately below the citadel lies the *praetorium* in this late-Roman incarnation of a military camp, not centrally placed, but squatting at the edge of the city, and, reached by a flight of 120 precipitous steps, not easy of access for those in full armour. Inside, lovely barrel vaulting and clear views of the river compensate for the darkness and the thoughtless defacement of the walls with swastikas.

According to Procopius, the man responsible for the refortification and embellishment of Zenobia was Isidore the younger, the nephew of Isidore of Miletus, the architect of the dome of the great church of Hagia Sophia in Constantinople, and who had himself restored the great church after an earthquake caused its collapse in 558.[84] With such an illustrious architect, Zenobia was clearly a prestige project. Now lost in silence, it is hard to picture the place at the height of its prosperity. The fragments of a bathhouse are evidence of the municipal facilities that all such cities, no matter how remote, demanded, whilst as an outpost dating from the Christian era of the Empire it has its fair share of churches. One basilica, the large blocks of its nave and precarious tower seeming to teeter on the edge of imminent collapse, looks to be principally supported by a warped and buckled old plank.

Zenobia largely fulfilled its purpose, falling to the Persians only in 610 at a time when they seized almost the whole of the Near East. When the Arabs came, the frontier was lightly held, if at all; and, for all the strength of its walls and loftiness of its citadel, Zenobia could not hold them back.

Palmyra is a desert town, lying 300 kilometres across the desert south-west of Zenobia, its wealth derived from the basic need of travellers to rest and stop for water. Its name seems almost impossibly romantic, a distillation of all our preconceptions of the East. Take its alternative name, Tadmor (meaning 'the city of dates'), mix in the story of Queen Zenobia and the cocktail becomes irresistible. Palmyra's glory was built on trade, its sheltered oasis a convenient stopping point on the desert trade routes. Spices, precious metals, slaves – all travelled through here, destined for the insatiable appetite of Rome.

The approach to the town passes through a monotonous, desolate landscape of sand, distant dust-clouds and the debris of past travellers. The journey through the Syrian desert to the refuge of the Palmyrene oasis now takes just four hours from Zenobia, but in ancient times traders would spend days navigating their camel-borne cargoes through the wastelands. It is no wonder that the city was able to grow rich on the tariffs it levied on passing traders – after just an hour in the baking heat of the desert, almost any price for a sip of water sounds a reasonable one. The luscious dates, which gave the town its Palmyrene name and which enthusiastic vendors still hawk today, would have seemed an almost sensuous luxury.

Palmyra's past stretches back into almost unimaginable antiquity. It is first mentioned in records from Mari in the 18th century BC, and the name of Tadmor crops up in Assyrian archives a millennium later.[85] After a stint as a satrapy of the Achaemenid Empire, the city fell into the hands of Alexander the Great's conquering Macedonians around 330 BC. When Alexander died and his subordinates fell (as generals will) to quarrelling over the spoils, Tadmor, in common with much of Syria, found itself in the apportionment of Seleucus. In 64 BC, Pompey the Great, his career still on the upswing before his losing contest with Julius Caesar, lost patience and abolished the Seleucid Empire, at a stroke annexing its territories. It was not until 41 BC, however, that Palymra's enormous wealth tempted the Romans to replace theoretical sovereignty with practical occupation and plunder. Mark Antony tried to seize the oasis in that year, but found all the inhabitants fled and its treasure gone.[86] Disappointed, he left the Palmyrenes in peace and turned his mind to the sensuous delights of Egypt.

The city long formed a kind of buffer zone between Rome and the Parthian Empire to the east, where goods and information could be safely exchanged – needless to say, the Palmyrenes took a cut on each transaction. The bent for commerce and relieving travellers of a portion of their hard-earnt pounds or denarii survives today. Whilst the only real trade now is the tourist business, the ancestors of the modern hoteliers, guides and touts would doubtless be proud of their descendants' ability to mint new money from the distant echo of their forebears' ancient prosperity.

While retaining a neutrality between Parthia to the east and Rome
to the west, Palmyra gradually found itself drawn closer to the Roman
sphere of influence. The city had a studiously vague status that makes
it frustratingly difficult to determine exactly when it became part of
the Empire. Augustus's nephew Germanicus visited in AD 17, and this
is probably the earliest date possible, while a milestone on the road
north to Sura on the Euphrates of AD 75 is taken to indicate that Palmyra
was clearly within Roman territory at this date.[87] Yet whatever the year
of its actual absorption, Palmyra was allowed to keep its own army
and ruling aristocracy and to carry on its business of growing rich on
passing trade for at least another two centuries Ambitious merchants
poured their wealth into the public buildings that make Palmyra, even
in its ruined state, one of the most profoundly impressive sites on the
Roman frontier.

The ruins themselves represent both three centuries of Roman interest
in the town and the strength of local traditions and political power.
Enclosed by the remains of a Roman wall, the site is almost semicircular, bounded to the north by the desert and to the west by rocky hills,
on one of which a ruined Arab castle presides. The modern town of
Tadmor barely intrudes, save in the guise of guides, vendors and hawkers.
Unlike at the pyramids of Giza – where a fixed stare in one particular
direction is needed to ignore the urban sprawl of Cairo – at Palmyra it
needs no conscious effort to turn your eyes towards the past.

The wealth that ambitious local merchants accrued was poured into
grandiose buildings as a public testament to their wealth and a bid for
monumental immortality. Even half-buried under the sands, as they
were for a thousand years, these magnificent ruins impressed later travellers. The first-recorded English visitors, a party from the Levant
Company led by one Dr Huntington in 1678, scarcely had time to enjoy
the ruins because, just after their arrival, they were stripped naked and
chased through the desert by some unsporting local Bedouin.[88] A more
leisurely inspection was achieved by Dr Halifax in 1691, but the most
celebrated visit came in 1751 when the Englishmen James Dawkins and
Robert Wood reached the city – then under Ottoman dominion – and
were struck by 'the quantity of ruins . . . all of white, and beyond them
towards the Euphrates a flat waste, as far as the eye could reach, without
any object which showed either life or motion'.[89] It was as if Palmyra
was the last remnant of some antique disaster that had reduced everything to dust, leaving only the shattered Corinthian pillars and
fragmentary walls as testament.

The pillars and columns – now much restored from Wood's and

Dawkins's time – still seem from afar like the vertebrae of a great beached whale. On drawing closer, the field of ruins distinguishes itself into half-ruined temples, walls, houses and the grid pattern of a Roman town, with the vivid colonnaded gash of the Roman *decumanus maximus* forming the antique cetacean's backbone. The colonnaded street is an unmistakable sign that we are in the East, for it is a form of urban layout that is not found in the Western, Latin part of the Empire and, with its porticoes lined by shops, is probably the ancestor of the bazaar to be found today throughout the Greek and Semitic areas of the former Roman dominions.

Perhaps the most striking and symbolic ruin is the Temple of Bel, its great columns standing on a site that had been occupied for at least a millennium before the Romans came. Until the late 1920s, the temple shared its hallowed grounds with the mud-built houses of the local residents. Its conversion by the Mamelukes into a fortress in the 12th century was the principal reason for its survival in such an intact condition. Now standing alone on the southern edge of the main colonnaded street, it perches on a slight hill formed by the remains of previous sanctuaries – for the site has been regarded as sacred for at least 4,000 years. It was probably begun around AD 17 and was completed by AD 32, as its dedication makes clear.[90]

A massive paved courtyard surrounded by colonnaded porticoes leads to the temple itself, which the Arabs turned into a mosque and a fortress. In the southern chamber of the temple the ceiling decoration still survives in the form of octagons, roses, swastikas and at the centre a huge acanthus leaf. A plate of this was included in Dawkins's and Wood's book of their Eastern travels and was so admired that its reproduction in plaster appeared in a host of grand 19th-century English country houses.[91] Our Roman heritage comes back to us by the strangest of routes.

Guides to the site delight in pointing out a carving of three Syrian women heavily veiled from head to toe – a forerunner, they will say, of the Islamic custom, although these particular women may simply be in mourning.[92] Beside them walks a camel bearing on its back a type of high pavilion, which probably housed the sacred cult idol of the temple. The god worshipped here, Bel (more familiar from the Bible as Baal) shared the crowded Palmyrene pantheon with a host of others – Allat from Arabia, Balshaamin from Phoenicia – but Bel was supreme, and the magnificence of his temple shows it. Ancient gods were certainly not above vanity. Nearby are a series of friezes depicting Bel with a variety of other deities, including Yarhibol (the Sun) and Aglibol (the Moon), for the association of gods into triads was a habit deeply ingrained in the religious observance of the Near East, making the acceptance, if not the precise comprehension, of the Christian Trinity that much easier.

Just a short walk to the north-west lies the Temple of Nebu, a wisdom god from Mesopotamia. Only the podium of the temple really now survives, the rest of the sanctuary – on a much more modest scale than that of Bel – providing a strategic view of the great monumental arch which stands at this point on the colonnaded street. An enormous structure, the arch is in fact slightly wedge-shaped to mask a change of direction in the street, which was needed to preserve the axis based on the Bel Temple. Erected under Septimius Severus at the end of the 2nd century, its richly decorated façade is studded with niches for the exposition of imperial statuary. Even here, it did to pay lip service, at least, to the Emperor.

To the west of the colonnaded street lie two structures without which no city of the Greek-speaking East would have felt itself truly complete, the theatre and the *agora*. The former was probably restored and embellished in the 2nd century. Now complete to nine rows of seating and with an elaborate *scaenae frons*, its extravagant portico and stage entrance with ornate architrave make it look more miniature temple than theatre backdrop.

The *agora*, which was sprinkled, to judge from the column bases found there, with the statues of more than 200 local dignitaries, is adjoined by a much more intriguing space, the Tariff Court. It was here that a decree of AD 137 listing the taxes to be paid by passing trading caravans was displayed. The impression given, however, is hardly one of sumptuousness, for the goods listed are often humdrum. Wheat, wine, olive oil and salt are not the stuff of a despot's dream, but they did ensure the survival of this city, far away from the richer agricultural soils of the Mediterranean littoral. The import of unguent is a more hopeful sign of luxury goods, taxed at 25 denarii the camel-load (or, curiously, at just 13 denarii if carried in goatskins). Slaves, if intended for re-export, were taxed at 12 denarii a head, while, as Palmyra's commerce did not discriminate on moral grounds, prostitutes who charged one denarius or more for their services were themselves to be taxed at one denarius.[93] On how the assessors determined the prostitutes' normal charge, the tariff law is silent.[94]

The Temple of Balshaamin, which lies further to the north of the city, five minutes walk up the *decumanus*, is dedicated to the divine Phoenician import. Its restoration and the tree that has grown up to provide shade for a chirping multitude of local birds give it an almost Gothic quality. Smaller and more ruined than the Temple of Bel, it probably once bore busts of the seven planetary deities and has an inscription recording a three-week visit by the 'divine Hadrian' in AD 129. In gratitude for the hospitality he received there, the Emperor declared Palmyra a 'free city', and, to ensure that his visit was not forgotten, he renamed it Palmyra Hadriana.[95] The Palmyrenes probably breathed a sigh of relief when he left, and they most certainly ignored their city's new imperial nomenclature. Roman control was, for the first few centuries, a relatively light yoke. It was only after the Parthian Wars of 162–7 that a permanent Roman garrison was stationed there, whilst a decline in the caravan trade led to the city gaining more the air of a military encampment and less that of an entrepôt.

As Rome's hold on her eastern provinces weakened in the mid-3rd century against the encroaching power of a new Persian dynasty, the Sassanids, the lifeblood of Palmyra – its control of the trade routes – was slowly strangled. After a Sassanid army defeated and killed the Emperor Valerian in 260, the situation became ever more precarious. The timing could hardly have been worse for Valerian's son, Gallienus, who now took over as sole Emperor. Only the previous year, Postumus had wrested the Gallic provinces away from central control, and there were certainly not sufficient resources to fight on two fronts at once. Meanwhile, the remnants of the defeated Roman army in the East took the understandable view that local self-help was the only viable option and elected as co-Emperors the two sons of Macrianus, one of Valerian's generals, who himself refused the diadem on account of his advanced age.[96]

Although he defeated one of the usurpers' armies in the Balkans (a battle in which the two Macriani were killed), Gallienus still had to rely on Septimius Odaenathus, who had emerged as the exarch of Palmyra around 257–8, to mop up the rebellion in the East. Odaenathus saw the advantage of supporting a Roman emperor desperate enough to show suitable gratitude for his services, yet far enough away not to jib at a little local expansion of Palmyra's power base. He turned his attention to Shapur's Sassanid army, still in possession of large swathes of Roman provincial territory. Despite the modest size of Palmyra's army, he deployed it and co-opted remnants of the Roman eastern legions to great effect, driving the Persians from Armenia and Mesopotamia and almost advancing as far as Ctesiphon, the Persian capital.

Having driven the Persians out of Syria, he was showered by the grateful Romans with high-sounding titles such as 'Corrector of the East'.[97] Odaenathus, for whom modesty was clearly not an issue, styled himself *mlk mlk* – 'King of Kings'. The Romans were probably not unduly concerned by this assumption of a high-sounding indigenous title. More worrying would have been the aping of Roman imperial nomenclature, and this Odaenathus did not do. In fact, it is Shapur who is more likely to have been offended, as the Palmyrene's new style mimicked that of the Persian royal court.[98]

In 267 Odaenathus and his eldest son Herodian were murdered under mysterious circumstances. The chief benefactor, coincidentally, was his widow, Zenobia, who took it upon herself to make her husband's self-given title a reality. For two years, Zenobia's armies carried all before them. It seemed for a time that she might seize the whole of the East and abolish the power of Rome for good. Her armies pushed as far west as Ancyra in Cappadocia and as far south as Egypt, where she defeated the loyalist governor Tenagio Probus in 269. Perhaps in order to arouse local sympathies, she claimed, according to one source, descent from the Ptolemies.

A number of cities turned coat, and it would have seemed preferable for the rest to express, at best, a studied neutrality until the situation became clear. The Empire had seen many usurpations, both failed and successful, over the past half-century, and ending up on the winning side in the various civil wars required a good mixture of foresight, diplomacy, ruthlessness and luck. At first Zenobia, despite the onward march of her armies, did not make the break with Rome official. Exploiting to the full all the opportunities offered by numismatic diplomacy, she initially had coins minted for her son Vaballathus at Antioch, which showed him dressed as a Roman general, and bearing an inscription that can probably be deciphered as 'Rex, Imperator, Dux Imperatorum'.[99] Crucially, Aurelian, who had become Emperor in 270, is depicted on the reverse of the coin with the title Augustus.[100] It seems that Zenobia, believing the new Emperor to have been as unable as Gallienus (and his immediate successor Claudius Gothicus) to reassert his authority in the East, was hoping for some recognition of her position. Only in 271/2 did the title 'Augustus' appear on Vaballathus's coins, showing that Zenobia was now prepared to assert what she could not gain through diplomatic means.[101] She even had her son claim Odaenathus's old title of *Corrector Totius Orientis*, to which he emphatically had no legitimate claim.

Aurelian was a skilled and tough campaigner. Leaving behind him the unfinished business of the breakaway Gallic empire, he marched east. An initial engagement near Antioch went badly for the Palmyrenes. Zenobia's general, Zabdas, only got away by parading an Aurelian look-alike through the streets of the city, claiming that he had captured the Emperor, and thus duping the Antiochenes long enough to make his escape. At Immae, north-west of Antioch, the Palmyrene cavalry was put to flight, and then at Emesa their main force was badly mauled. As quickly as it had appeared, the aura of inevitability about Zenobia's hold on power dissipated and her former allies fell over themselves in the rush to prove that actually they had been loyal to Aurelian all along. The Roman army pursued its royal prey all the way back to Palmyra.

The *Historia Augusta* preserves an exchange of letters between Aurelian and his foe, which, if fictional in its details, may preserve the Emperor's desire to co-opt rather than crush Zenobia, or at least force a bloodless surrender. His demand is peremptory: 'You should have done of your own free will what I now command in my letter. For I bid you surrender, promising that your lives shall be spared, and with the condition that you, Zenobia, together with your children shall dwell wherever I, acting in accordance with the wish of the most noble senate, shall appoint a place.'[102] Zenobia replied with haughty pride: 'From Zenobia, Queen of the East, to Aurelian Augustus. None save yourself has ever demanded by letter what you demand. Whatever must be accomplished in matters of war must be done by valour alone. You demand my surrender as though you were not aware that Cleopatra preferred to die a Queen rather than remain alive, however high her rank. We shall not lack reinforcements from Persia, which we are even now expecting.'[103] Historians' frequent comparisons of Zenobia's career with that of Cleopatra clearly has the most respectable sanction, that of the Palmyrene queen herself.

No aid came from the Sassanids, however, and so, with her Armenian allies having deserted her, the Palmyrene queen went in search of the Persians. She failed to find a boatman to ferry her small party over the Euphrates, and the Romans, to whom her flight had been betrayed, captured her. Taken to Rome, she was displayed to the public in Aurelian's triumph in 274, accompanied in the procession by ten captive Gothic women dressed as Amazon warriors, and by Tetricus, the former Gallic Emperor, whose territory had been recaptured by Aurelian the year before. Rather than suffer strangulation after the triumph, the more traditional fate of defeated chieftains, Zenobia was permitted to live the rest of her life in obscure retirement in a villa near Rome. According to the historian Eutropius – and the less reliable testimony of the *Historia Augusta* – she may have remarried, her descendants still living in Rome at the time of Valens, a century later.[104]

Over the centuries her legend was relayed and embellished by a succession of writers, including Chaucer, becoming more attractive with every retelling. Gibbon wrote of her, with a nice combination of chauvinism and swooning admiration: '. . . Zenobia is perhaps the only female, whose superior genius broke through the servile indolence imposed on her sex by the climate and manners of Asia ... She was of a dark complexion ... Her teeth were of a pearly whiteness, and her large black eyes sparkled with uncommon fire, tempered by the most attractive sweetness.'[105]

In 1813, Lady Hester Stanhope, the niece of Prime Minister William Pitt the Younger, paid a visit to Palmyra during an eccentric progress through the Orient, accompanied by a train of twenty-five camels. In a splendid ceremony, in which Bedouin warriors stood guard on the column brackets, Lady Hester came to believe that she was, in some sense, a reincarnation of Zenobia. 'I have been crowned Queen of the Desert under the triumphal arch at Palmyra,' she wrote. 'I am the sun, the star, the pearl, the Lion, the light from heaven, and the Queen.'[106] In exchange for their paying such extravagant court to her compulsively self-regarding fancies, she awarded the local Arab tribe the 'right' to levy a toll on any subsequent travellers who might pass through Palmyra – a tax that, needless to say, successive sheikhs were more than happy to exact, brandishing in their support a tattered paper of authorisation from the English 'Desert Queen'. When the British naval officers Charles Irby and James Mangles visited the site in 1818, they found that her largesse had set something of a floor on the price to be paid for a safe-conduct through the desert and they were forced to part with 600 piastres, a hundred more than Lady Hester herself.[107]

On the central colonnaded street of the town, close to the Temple of Bel, where old shop doorways can still be made out, is evidence of Palmyra's most famous resident. Just before the tetrapylon – a virtuoso construction of four pedestals, each supporting four huge columns – is a smaller column that originally bore a statue, and an inscription for Zenobia (which the Romans had removed after her defeat). Next to it, the inscription for Odaenathus, her husband and predecessor in power, was left intact by them, an acknowledgement, no doubt, that whilst his wife had done Rome a great disservice, the 'Corrector of the Orient' himself had probably saved the eastern provinces from long-term Persian occupation. Nearby, another dedication commemorates Julius Aurelius Zenobia, who may have been the great queen's father.

After Zenobia's fall, the Romans' military grip became tighter as the Palmyrenes' income from trade fell. The garrison Aurelian had left in the town was massacred in an uprising in spring 273, and, once Palmyra was recaptured, the Emperor showed no second clemency, permitting a large-scale massacre of the inhabitants and the plunder of the Temple of Bel. A wall was built around the city, parts of which still survive, and a legion was permanently based here. Diocletian has given his name to a part of the ruins, known as 'Diocletian's Camp', which houses the remains of the camp for the new garrison, the I Illyricorum legion, its accommodation and temples. A monumental staircase looking as though it has melted in some tremendous furnace into a buckled and folded mass leads up to a massive Temple of the Standards.[108] No inconspicuous shrine such as those found in the legionary camps of the west, this one is huge in scale, the stairs leading up to a platform on which survives a chamber ending in an apse. Here, the sacred eagle and other standards of the legion would be set, in an unmistakable display that the Roman military presence had come to stay, overshadowing the much more modest temple of the south Arabian goddess Allat down below.

Just to the east is the ancient residential quarter of the city. It is an especially broken and desolate place, little more than a field of broken stones, collapsed columns and distant dreams. However, not much has been excavated and it is an almost fitting symbol of the end of Palymra's prosperity, a long, slow decline into night.

For Palmyra the twilight was to be a long one. As the frontier regions that had hosted trade and exchange with the powers further east became military garrisons and closed defensive zones, they became a drain on imperial funds and the city's cultural resources diminished. A few churches were constructed to the north of the city, and the Temple of Baalshamin was converted to Christian use, while under Justinian the walls were strengthened, but already most of the city had collapsed into ruins. In 634, the Roman period came to an end for Palmyra as the armies of the first caliph, Abu Bakr, seized it on their victorious sweep through the province of Syria.[109] Urban life clearly continued for a time, as the Jewish traveller Benjamin of Tudela reports that he found 2,000 Jews living there when he visited in 1192.[110] After that, Palmyra was left to be washed over by a sea of sand and was forgotten, so that when William Halifax visited from Aleppo in 1691, he found just forty families living in hovels crowded together in the Temple of Bel.

To the west of Palmyra's main monuments lies the Valley of the Tombs, a landscape oddly reminiscent of *Star Wars*, peppered with strange funerary towers poking up from amongst the desert dunes. There are underground tombs, too. The whole valley is peopled with the dead and they are still being discovered. A few years ago a lorry skidded off the road and caused the roof of a hidden tomb to collapse, and both vehicle and driver tumbled into the newly revealed necropolis. The driver's thoughts at escaping death only to be confronted by the stylised and faintly smiling statues of his ancestors can only be imagined.

Even in death the Palmyrenes knew how to cut a deal. Inside the tower tombs a central corridor leads onto narrow passages in which the remains of the deceased were stacked, one compartment on top of another, in a kind of bizarre filing cabinet. Some families even funded their own grandiose tombs by selling spaces in these '*loculi*' to others less well-off, but still keen for their stake in immortality. The largest remaining is the Tomb of Elahbel, completed in 103,[III] a solid, soaring tower, which had a capacity for some 300 inmates in an underground *hypogeum*, with four overground storeys stacked on top of it. One of the best preserved of the purely underground structures is the Hypogeum of the Three Brothers, at the foot of whose stairway an inscription unabashedly reports that the necropolis was constructed by the three siblings[112] as a commercial venture. Further into the tomb a fresco shows the fraternal entrepreneurs, depicted in frames supported by winged victories.[113] In death, victory – or at the very least, profit. One of the brothers, Malé, found his rest here in 142, and the tomb remained open for business for more than a century, up to 259.

It is in the tombs that we come face-to-face with the ancient Palmyrenes. They wear carefully arranged tunics and draped cloaks, with their names and ancestry inscribed above their shoulders, almost universally in Palmyrene, for the use of Greek in such private contexts was extremely rare. The men, from the 2nd century generally bearded, often turn their glance to the side, as though not to look visitors in the eye. The women are depicted veiled, wearing an elaborate headdress with a turban, and ornate brooches and earrings. In earlier examples, the women often hold spindles and distaffs, signs of domesticity, or carry a little child. One hand normally holds the two sides of the veils together with the fingers resting against the cheek, a gesture of touching intimacy.

The best time of day to view the tombs and the ruins in general is at sunset and dusk, when the rosy light and deep-hued shadows lend the site an air of melancholy, and the sounds of the desert night give the impression that the gossiping and hawking of the ancient inhabitants are only just out of reach. The finest vantage point is from the hill that towers over the site to the south, from the ramparts of the Arab castle originally built in the 13th century to ward off a Crusader invasion that never quite came. Local Syrian families come to take tea, exchange gossip and watch the sun go down over the final homes of their illustrious ancestors.

The Bedouin still camp in the ruins of Palmyra. Ragged children herd black-fleeced sheep in Diocletian's camp, their refusal to be overwhelmed by the past lending a wistfulness to the imposing marble blocks. Their animals wander through a forum that was once as busy as Rome's or

Antioch's, and by night the barking of their dogs imbues the otherwise tranquil ruins with a sense of threat. Yet any tourist who approaches too closely will be met by demands for money for a photo of shepherd and flock, or even offered a set of grubby postcards of Palmyra for a few pounds a packet. Entrepreneurs come in all shapes and sizes. There is also still an oasis at Palmyra, and its warren-like maze of watered gardens behind low walls exude a timelessness. If *their* walls have fallen and *their* grandeur faded, they seem to say, our Palmyra never changes.

During the last period of Byzantine occupation of Syria, a number of administrative and military complexes were built to secure control over a region that was no longer as heavily militarised as during its 3rd-century heyday. Almost contemporary with the 6th-century stage of Halibiye-Zenobia, the fortified centre at Qasr ibn Wardan lay around 200 kilometres north-west of Palmyra. Completed in 564 – an inscription records the precise day of its dedication – the structures, church, totally ruined barracks and palace have a surprising grace and fragility, surrounded by arid fields that, in antique times, must have produced enough to support at least a small garrison.

It seems that workmen from Constantinople may have been brought in to build Qasr ibn Wardan; the size of its bricks match exactly moulds used in the capital. The main portal of the palace (or *praetorium*) boasts the date inscription which proclaims that all this was made 'for the glory of God', and a surrounding wreath of Alphas and Omegas leaves no doubt as to the Christian allegiances of the workmen. The building is laid out around a central courtyard with a variety of vaulted rooms, which probably ranged from stables to reception halls. The sleeping accommodation was upstairs, now roofless, but providing impressive vistas across the dry scrub of the surrounds.

A short way from the palace lies the church and this is indeed an impressive desert find, entered through a door on which is inscribed (in Greek), 'This is the door which God made through which all the faithful will enter.'[114] Originally two or three storeys tall with a series of internal galleries and arcades lending an illusion of further height, the basic ground plan is square despite the circular dome. Of the latter only one arch survives, pointing heavenwards as though the whole building had been seized and somehow stretched in that direction. A compact gem, its alternating brown and grey levels of brickwork lending it a little the air of a layer cake, the Qasr ibn Wardan church seems to cry out for a larger congregation than the desert, and its Bedouin guardian, can provide.

Emesa (now Homs), Syria's third-largest city, which lies 100 kilometres to the south-west of Qasr Ibn Wardan, back in the more heavily settled western portion of the province, was one Syria's most important cities, and had a venerable pre-Roman past. It was founded far back in the Bronze Age, but achieved prominence under the native Samsigeramid dynasty, who seized control in the mid-2nd century BC as the power of the Seleucids waned. The Romans incorporated it into the province of Syria in AD 78[115] and deposed the last Samsigeramus, his family retreating into the sacred realm, retaining authority as the hereditary high priests of the god Elagabal, symbolised as a black stone that resided in a sumptuous temple, an image renowned throughout the Empire. Of it not the slightest trace has been found, save representations on coins from the time of Antoninus Pius that depict an eagle perched on the black stone.[116]

It was in Emesa that Septimius Severus found his second wife, the formidable Julia Domna, herself a daughter of the high priest. Septimius allegedly married her in 187 because an oracle had declared that she 'would marry a king'[117] and, with an eye for supernatural assistance, he believed this might aid him in one day achieving royal – or imperial – status. A striking woman, Julia Domna and her female relatives were to be an important force in imperial politics for half a century. Of her undoubted charms, Gibbon gushed that she had 'the attractions of beauty, and united to a lively imagination a firmness of mind and strength of judgement, seldom bestowed on her sex'.[118]

It was her great-nephew who would, in effect, be the undoing of her dynastic hopes. Julia Domna died in 217, allegedly starving herself to death in protest at the usurpation of Macrinus following the death of her son Caracalla. Her sister Julia Maesa, and her niece, yet another Julia (Soaemias), contrived to present the troops encamped near Emesa with Julia Soaemias's son, Varius Avitus, who, as the latest high priest of Elagabal, was more commonly referred to by the name of the god he served. Once Macrinus had been disposed of, the thirteen-year-old boy duly took the imperial title of Marcus Aurelius Severus Alexander Augustus, claiming – at the instigation of his mother – to be the illegitimate son of Caracalla,[119] but it is as Elagabalus that he is universally known.

Multiple divorces and remarriages, allegations of open homosexuality and a general collapse of morality in the court eventually undermined any respect for Elagabalus,[120] and in June 221 his grandmother Julia Maesa forced him to adopt his younger cousin Bassianus Alexianus as Caesar.[121] The following year the praetorian guard rioted, murdered Elagabalus and, for good measure, his mother too, and then installed Alexianus as sole Emperor under the name Alexander Severus. The Roman army and aristocracy most probably breathed a collective – if short-lived – sigh of relief and the sacred black stone was despatched back to Emesa, where it remained in place at least long enough for Aurelian to visit it in 272 and (according to the *Historia Augusta*) gain divine assistance from it in his struggle against Zenobia.[122]

One hundred and fifty kilometres to the south of Homs, and almost in the extreme south-west of ancient Syria, Damascus lays claim to being one of the oldest continuously inhabited cities in the world; it is first mentioned as 'Dimashqa' in the archives of Mari around 2500 BC,[123] and remained an important regional centre until its conquest by the Achaemenid Cyrus of Persia in 539 BC. For a time from about 85 BC it marked the northernmost extension of the Nabataeans, the northern Arabian kingdom that had grown rich on the spice trade,[124] and in common with most of the rest of Syria, it became Roman in 64 BC by Pompey's conquest. But it was never the chief city of the Roman province, that honour being accorded to the former Seleucid capital of Antioch on the Orontes.

Although the noise, the urban sprawl and the exuberant chaos of the modern capital city seem utterly to drown out the past, some traces of ancient Damascus still survive, centred around the old walled city. The plan of the ancient town can be detected in the Hellenistic and Roman outline, including the walls – where traces of Roman blocks can be seen at the very bases – and in an underpass just outside Bab Sharqi, the eastern gate, where part of an original Roman angle-tower has been excavated, some 20 metres from the line of the medieval perimeter. The alignment of the gates is closer than the walls to that of the Roman originals, seven of the nine gateways being originally named for the planets: Bab Sharqi itself was the Gate of the Sun, which was numbered among the planets in Roman cosmology.

More resonant of Roman Damascus is its most important holy place, now the site of the Ummayad mosque. Deep inside the old city, it is enclosed within a busy bazaar, selling all those necessities of daily life, from hunks of camel meat to spices, beaten copper trays, wedding dresses and, for the tourists, an almost endless array of carpets. Little has changed over the years, for the mosque's predecessor, the Temple of Jupiter Haddad, also lay within the city's chief market district, while the porticoes of the sanctuary would have been used as classrooms by professional rhetors, just as the columns of the current mosque act as the focus for impromptu Koranic instruction classes. The remains of a *propylaeum* or triumphal arch sit outside the west entrance of the mosque, which may originally have reached to a height of 12 metres. The outer wall of the mosque compound retains, for the most part, that of the *temenos*, the inner temple enclosure of the Jupiter sanctuary.[125] Incorporated within it are several Roman-era inscriptions, including one in Greek declaring that 'Thy Kingdom O Christ is an everlasting kingdom'.[126] Probably during the reign of Theodosius I (379–95) the temple was converted into a Christian church, dedicated to Saint John the Baptist. Almost all trace of this was swept away when, after an uneasy seventy-year cohabitation following the Muslim conquest of Damascus in 636, Caliph al-Walid ordered the building of the present mosque. The reverence for the Baptist, however, survived, and inside the prayer hall is a shrine marking the spot where his head is believed to have been buried after its grizzly presentation by Salome to Herod on a plate.

The Umayyad mosque holds a special place in the development of the mosque's form. Its domed roof vies with the al-Aqsa in Jerusalem as the very earliest example of the type, almost certainly an imitation of the domes of the great Byzantine centralised churches, such as that of Saint Simeon at Deir Semaan. The angle-towers that lined the *temenos* (enclosed sacred space) of the temple, themselves an echo of the ancient Semitic tradition of worship on high places, are said to have influenced the development of the minaret, which was not a feature of the earliest mosques. On the exterior surface of the prayer hall, however, is an embellishment that was not to be replicated so widely, but is nonetheless a sign of the mixed culture within which early Islam flourished in Syria.

The mosaics are the glory of the Umayyad mosque. Against a shimmering golden backdrop, a rich landscape is woven, of fields, orchards, streams, palaces, towers and cities, all bound together with winding trails of acanthus leaves. Much of the surface of the mosaics was lost through fires – most notably in 1893 – and reconstruction, but the original workmen were probably the heirs to a tradition that stretched back to Hellenistic times. They placed the tiny coloured tesserae on the great canvas of the mosque frontage, just as their great-grandfathers had probably done for the adornment of late-Byzantine palaces and churches.

The old town retains other vestiges of its Christian heritage, which was all played out under Roman rule. The 'Street called Straight', which is mentioned by name in the Acts of the Apostles,[127] served as the *decumanus maximus* of the city, cutting westwards through its heart from the Bab Sharqi. It is, as irony demands, not entirely straight, its course changing axis twice along its length, masked in typical Roman fashion by memorial arches, one of which survives as a slightly undignified car-parking space. Mark Twain acerbically commented that the street was 'straighter than a corkscrew, but not as straight as a rainbow'.[128] The pot of gold at its end for anyone braving the traffic that pushes erratically through the congested single-carriage lane is the chapel of Ananias, a subterranean crypt where Saint Paul is said to have taken refuge after his blinding on the road to Damascus. On recovering his sight, Paul took to preaching the new religion in the synagogues of the city, which, as a practice clearly designed to win converts away from their number, angered the Jewish notables of Damascus. The place where tradition holds that he was lowered from the city walls in a basket, to escape their plot to kill him, is marked in a chapel just a few hundred metres away from that of Ananias. For those who have not quite got their bearings, the church has provided a very large (and modern) wicker basket in commemoration of the legend.

In 613, Damascus fell to the Persians. It was one of the first major losses to a resurgent Persia, under the leadership of Khusraw II, which looked set finally to emerge victorious from its seven-century-long struggle with Rome for dominance in the region. Yet in March 630 the Emperor Heraclius made a triumphant ceremonial entrance into Jerusalem. At the head of the procession went the True Cross, the very wood on which Christ had been crucified, seized by Khusraw II when the Persians took the city in 614, and now being restored to its place of honour in the church of the Holy Sepulchre. Negotiations the year before in connection with the restoration of the sacred relic had seemed to presage the conversion of Persia to Christianity,[129] which would have confirmed the Byzantines' absolute victory in religious as well as political terms. Less than a decade later, in 638, the caliph Umar took possession of Jerusalem for Islam, while the final Sassanid opposition to the Muslim armies was swept aside at Nehavand in 641. The age-old rivalry between Persia and Rome was rendered irrelevant and Byzantine control over the Near East and North Africa was swept aside with terrifying rapidity. How had it come to this?

Both principal empires in the Near East were exhausted by thirty years of campaigning, which had seen the Byzantine Empire on the point of collapse before a remarkable swing of fortune left it more able to impose its terms on the prostrate Persians than at any time since Trajan's victories in the early 2nd century.[130] Yet the Byzantines had had just a few years in which to rebuild the administrative structures and re-establish the networks of loyalty that had been swept aside by the Persian occupation. In the meantime, the Arabs of the peninsula had been uniting behind the banner of the religion of Islam, under the inspirational leadership of the prophet Muhammad. The removal in the late 6th century of the buffer presented by the Byzantine and Sassanids' Arab allies, the Ghassanids and Lakhmids, and the previous evacuation of the frontier forts in Syria and Arabia by the Byzantine central army left little to shield those provinces from the new force.

The new religion, by offering tolerance to those Jews and Christians who chose not to convert, and economic benefits – in exemption from the *jizya* or poll-tax – for those who did, undermined what little residual loyalty there was to the central regime in Constantinople. The prevalence of Monophysitism in those provinces bordering on the Arabian peninsula also meant that those Christians who continued to cling to their faith may have felt they were just as well served outside the direct political control of an empire that officially espoused a creed antithetical to their own.

The disastrous defeat of the Byzantine field army at Yarmuk (in the north of modern Jordan) in 636 meant there was no force left to hold the Arab armies back.[131] When a defensive line was finally established in the mid-7th century it was across central Anatolia, where the Empire was able to reorganise the territory into military provinces, or 'themes', and rely on the martial tradition of the mountain tribes to supply them with fresh troops. Syria, Arabia and most of North Africa (save an outlying fragment around Carthage that resisted for a further half-century) were utterly lost.

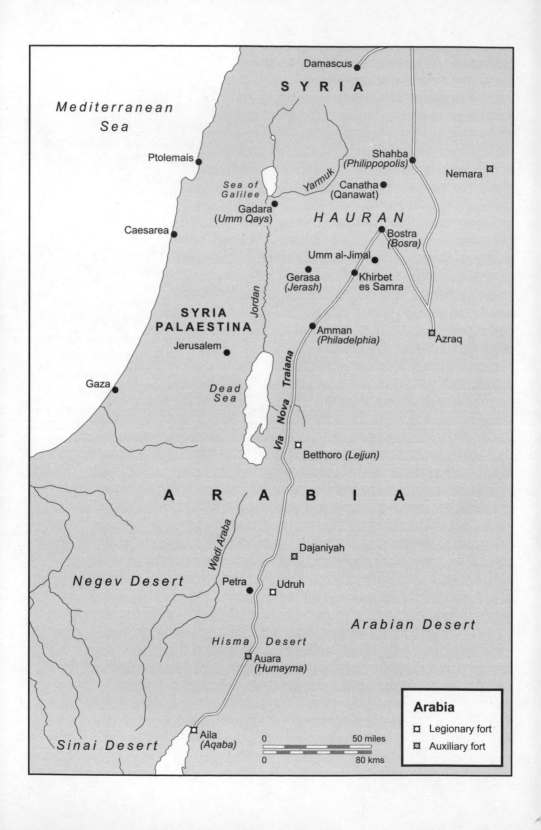

Mediterranean
Sea

S Y R I A

Damascus

Ptolemais

Shahba
(Philippopolis)

Nemara

*Sea of
Galilee*

Yarmuk

Canatha
(Qanawat)

Gadara
(Umm Qays)

H A U R A N

Caesarea

Bostra
(Bosra)

Umm al-Jimal

SYRIA
PALAESTINA

*Gerasa
(Jerash)*

Khirbet
es Samra

Jerusalem

Jordan

Amman
(Philadelphia)

Azraq

Gaza

*Dead
Sea*

Via Nova Traiana

Betthoro *(Lejjun)*

A   R   A   B   I   A

Wadi Araba

Dajaniyah

Negev Desert

Petra

Udruh

Arabian Desert

Hisma   Desert

Auara
(Humayma)

Aila
(Aqaba)

Sinai Desert

0		50 miles
0		80 kms

Arabia

⊠ Legionary fort

⊠ Auxiliary fort

CHAPTER 8

Arabia

They seem no work of Man's creative hand,
Where Labour wrought as wayward Fancy planned;
But from the rock as if by magic grown,
Eternal – silent – beautiful – alone!
Not virgin white – like that old Doric shrine,
Where once Athena held her rites divine:
Not saintly grey – like many a minster fane,
That crowns the hill, or sanctifies the plain:
But rosy-red – as if the blush of dawn
Which first beheld them were not yet withdrawn:
The hues of youth upon a brow of woe,
Which men call'd old two thousand years ago!
Match me such marvel save in Eastern clime,
A rose-red city half as old as time.

John William Burgon 'Petra'[1]

Arabia was amongst the least troublesome of Roman acquisitions. Most of this vast tract of land from the basalt plateau of the Hauran mountains down across the wadi-scored terrain of the Jordan valley and the fringes of the Sinai, Negev and Arabian deserts had been occupied by the Nabataean kingdom, with its capital first at Petra and then latterly at Bostra, and it seems to have fallen without much – if any – of a fight. In AD 106, it was simply annexed by Trajan, its royal family disenfranchised and its territory organised as a new Roman province.

The Nabataeans had occupied at least part of the area since the 4th century BC. Petra was settled originally by the Edomites in the late 8th century BC, but it is not clear what relationship (if any) the Nabataeans had with them. In 312 BC, Antigonus Monopthalmos ('the One-Eyed'), one of Alexander the Great's former generals, sent a raiding force into their territory, since he had heard that they gathered annually at 'a certain rock' (which might have meant Petra).[2] His troops carried off a substantial haul of spices and silver, but the Nabataeans caught up with them somewhere in the desert, mauled the Greeks badly and retrieved their goods. The account of the geographer Strabo, probably relating to a period a century or two later, paints a picture of a more settled folk, whose king lived in a certain style.[3]

The apogee of the Nabataean kingdom ran from the mid-1st century BC to the end of the 1st century AD, or at least the great monuments for which Petra is so justly famous can be dated to that period. It was their command of the spice trade, more than the masterful mausoleums that they constructed at Petra, their capital, that marked out the Nabataeans as the richest of the petty kingdoms of the desert fringe. Exploiting a marginal position between two of the bickering successor kingdoms to Alexander the Great, the Ptolemies and the Seleucids, and lying almost at the head of the spice route that ran from distant Arabia Felix (Yemen), the Nabataeans extracted a suitable cut for permitting the precious cargo to transit northwards to Palmyra and thence to the Roman Empire. Rich, shrewd and adept at balancing the interests of more militarily powerful neighbours, the Nabataeans succeeded for many decades in escaping the avaricious grasp of the legions.

This great wealth enabled the Nabataean monarchs to do more than hold their own against the neighbouring Jewish Hasmonaean state. They faced their first real crisis when it seemed in 63 BC as if Pompey might be looking to add Petra to his list of conquests. He had confidently announced his intention of paying the Nabataeans a visit that year, presumably to extract at least plunder, and possibly even to terminate their independent existence. Fortunately, he was distracted by the opportunities presented by a civil war in the next-door Hasmonaean kingdom and by the far greater prospects for financial gain offered by seizing Jerusalem and taking the Jewish Temple.[4] Two years later, Pompey despatched his lieutenant Aemilius Scaurus against Petra, but – having burnt the harvests and thereby deprived himself, as well as the Nabataeans, of ready sources of food – he settled for extorting a payment of 300 talents to be on his way.[5] At his triumph in Rome, however, the triumvir included Arabia in the list of those areas he had overcome, so that, at least from his point of view, he really had subdued the Nabataeans.

Yet already by the mid-1st century AD, more and more trade was going by sea, either up the Red Sea and along the coast of Africa to Roman Egypt, or heading eastwards to land at the head of the Persian Gulf and thence either east into the Parthian Empire or west via Palmyra, up to the Euphrates and into the Roman Empire. The discovery, around the 1st century, of the monsoon winds, and thus of an all-maritime route to India, accelerated this trend,[6] much to the detriment of the Nabataeans.

After the Roman annexation of Egypt in 30 BC, the Nabataeans faced Roman provinces to the north (in Syria and Judaea) and to the west (in Egypt). It may well be that Augustus planned to annex the kingdom outright, but the Romans were distracted by an expedition in 24 BC against the kingdom of Sabaea in modern Yemen, a land then also known for its legendary wealth as Arabia Felix ('Lucky Arabia'). It could be that the Emperor reasoned that taking control of the source of the precious spices in south Arabia would be even more lucrative than seizing the lands of the Nabataean middlemen, whose role would then be rendered at a stroke superfluous. If so, it may have been a tad unwise for Aelius Gallus, the Prefect of Egypt tasked with the expedition, to choose Syllaeus, the chief minister of Obodas, the Nabataean king, as his advisor and guide to the unfamiliar Sabaean lands.[7]

The whole thing was a fiasco from start to finish. Gallus dallied all winter at the African Red Sea port of Leuke Kome, ordering the construction of warships that were irrelevant to the kind of fighting he would be likely to face. It then took six months to reach the border of the Sabaean kingdom, a journey the historian Strabo alleges was significantly extended by the tortuous route over which Syllaeus led the Romans.[8] By the time Gallus laid siege to the town of Mariaba, his forces were severely weakened by losses to disease and desperately short of water. After just six days, Gallus threw in the towel and retreated, reaching Alexandria in a comparatively speedy seventy-one days, which must have given him at least some pause for thought concerning the prolonged nature of the outward journey. He had also stopped just two days' march short of the spice-producing regions of the Sabaean heartland, the securing of which was presumably the whole purpose of the expedition. As a demonstration of Roman power – which, coincidentally, reached its furthest ever projection south at Mariaba – it was hardly likely to make Rome's neighbours quail.[9]

A gap in the Nabataean coins series in the years 3–1 BC, which coincided with an expedition to Arabia by Gaius Caesar, Augustus's grandson, has been used to suggest a temporary annexation by the Romans, but nothing is proven.[10] At any rate the coinage (and, if the annexation theory really is correct, the monarchy) was restored, and many of the important Nabataean monuments date to the long reign of Aretas IV (8 BC–AD 40). Under Rabbel II, from AD 71,[11] the kingdom seemed to go into a decline; it may be that the spice routes were already shifting eastwards and the Nabataeans' prosperity was fraying at the edges.

The annexation in 106 was a quiet affair, and Trajan failed to order any coins minted to celebrate it until 111.[12] More importantly, work began on the construction of the *Via Nova Traiana*, a defensive road that ran all the way from Bostra – 150 kilometres south of Damascus – to the port of Aila on the Gulf of Aqaba (a southward journey of some 350 kilometres), facilitating any necessary rapid transfer of troops. The Romans annexed territory further south, possibly as far as Ruwaffa, north of the Nabataeans' secondary capital at Medain Saleh in modern Saudi Arabia (and some 250 kilometres to the south of Aqaba). A temple to the emperors Marcus Aurelius and Lucius Verus has been found there, dedicated by a confederation of Arab tribes (the 'Thamud') during the governorship of Claudius Modestus.[13] Here, however, as in the Jordanian desert, the actual border was undefined by any physical features. If the tribes acknowledged Roman power, then they were, in a sense, part of the Empire. Arabia of course received a Roman garrison to shield Judaea and Egypt from attacks from the east. This seems to have been made up of around twelve auxiliary units, including at least one of camel troops (*ala dromedariorium*) and infantry cohorts drafted in from Egypt and Syria.[14] The legionary garrison consisted, at least in the early stages, of III Cyrenaica, which had its main base at Bostra in the very north of the province.

With the disorder caused by successive Persian invasions in the 3rd century, and the temporary loss of control over the whole East during the revolt of Zenobia, the Romans came more and more to depend on dominating or cajoling a succession of Arab allied tribes to take responsibility for the defence of the desert approaches. Although Diocletian defeated the most threatening of the 'Saracen' groups around 290, he was still forced to reorganise Arabia, partitioning the province around 295 to make its separate parts easier to administer, and to construct the Strata Diocletiana, a militarised road system further to the east.[15] During the 6th century, however, a full hundred years before the Arabs swept Byzantine political control away, the military presence on the frontier was drastically reduced, possibly as a result of the financial demands caused by Justinian's campaigns in Italy and North Africa.[16] When the end came, in the 630s, it was terrifyingly swift.

Ninety kilometres south-east of Damascus, and just into the province of Arabia, nestled at the north end of the Hauran mountains, lies the small town of Shahba, a place destined for utter obscurity, had it not been for one of its sons who achieved an improbable elevation to the imperial throne. Marcus Julius Philippus, known to historians as Philip, was a typical product of the military and political turmoil that gripped the Empire in the mid-3rd century. He accompanied the expedition of Gordian III against the Sassanids in 243–4, which aimed to push Shapur I back from the key cities in Syria, such as Carrhae and Edessa, that the Persians had captured in the preceding years. Philip took over as praetorian prefect when Timesitheus fell ill and died late in 243, sharing the post with his brother Julius Priscus.[17]

When the army was defeated somewhere near Ctesiphon and Gordian III was killed, Philip was the most obvious candidate close at hand to succeed him. Paying the whopping ransom of 500,000 denarii for his and the army's safe-passage, he made in haste for the capital before alternative factions could dispute his right to power, leaving Priscus as commander in the east with the *ad hoc* title of *rector orientis*, a kind of deputy Emperor.[18] Philip is commonly nicknamed 'the Arab', and, though probably he was born into a local family with no visible Latin antecedents, there is no sign during his reign of any self-conscious promotion of an Arab identity. Of course he heaped favours on his home regions – few emperors could avoid the temptation – but his ethnic origin is more important as a sign that the hold on power of the traditional senatorial elites, in Italy and the provinces, was fatally weakening.

The most notable feature of his four-year reign were the celebrations for Rome's one-thousandth birthday in 248, an anniversary that also gave rise to unfortunate millenarian currents that may have fed into the revolt of Pacatianus in Moesia, following which Philip was overthrown by his own general, Decius. Philip achieved posthumous fame amongst Christian writers, most notably Eusebius, as the first emperor to convert to the new religion. The evidence for his pre-emption of Constantine is slight, however, and he certainly proclaimed nothing in public.[19] It may well all have been no more than a literary device to contrast him with Decius, who indisputably was an enthusiastic persecutor of Christianity.

Philip's home village thus enjoyed only a few years of glory before construction was stopped, and the place (renamed Philippopolis) was restored to its position as a backwater. Many of the buildings were probably never completed, some not even begun, but what survives makes striking use of the local black basaltic stone, which lends a certain sternness and sombreness to the architecture. Philippopolis is a classic Roman city built in negative, all dark colours that suck in the light instead of reflecting it. Three stumps of a grand triple-gateway draw visitors in along the *cardo*, now a humdrum modern street of low concrete blocks.[20]

A little way up, the street begins to climb and alongside it, perched on the lower storey of a modern building, four bold basalt columns probably mark the site of a temple façade. The street then opens up into a broad square, once the civic heart of Philippopolis, now host to nothing more bustling than an impromptu football match between a crowd of local boys, none of them, assuredly, with their sights set on emulating their imperial forebear. To the west of the square lies a curious structure, a triple façade of basalt almost forming a semicircle inset with deep niches. It is a *kalybe*, a form typical of the province of Arabia and probably having Nabataean antecedents.[21] Most probably the niches were for the exposition of statues of the imperial family, with some form of cult ritual taking place in the open space just in front of the *kalybe*.

Just behind lie the shattered remains of what may have been an imperial palace, but more impressive is the temple at the south end of the square, the Philippeion, erected in honour of the Emperor's father. As the dedication inscription reveals, Philip was not content with his possible elevation to godhead after his death, but saw fit to revere his own father, Julius Marinus, as a god. Not, it must be remarked, the kind of action consistent with his alleged conversion to Christianity. A simple rectangle with a colonnade in front – a prostyle – the temple inside has a quiet, dark dignity. Groups of niches flanked by arches were again probably for the display of family statues, particularly the divine Julius Marinus, while internal steps give the place more the feeling of an intimate theatre than a place of worship.

Philippopolis's real theatre is just a few metres away to the south. It is comparatively small, only about 42 metres in diameter, with seating for just 1,000 spectators, and was one of the last Roman theatres built in the East. In common with the nearby bathhouse, it has a certain starkness. Basalt is a very hard stone and does not lend itself easily to ornate carving, and the stage backdrop here is almost entirely blank. Whether the citizens of Philippopolis were actually able to enjoy extensive theatrical performances, once their imperial patronage was withdrawn so soon after it had been bestowed, is unclear.

The one real insight into the life and wealth of the city comes from the mosaics located in a villa in the town and now housed in the local museum. The vibrant colours of Tethys, the sea goddess, her winding locks surrounded by a swirling crowd of sea creatures, and of Aphrodite and Ares caught in an illicit tryst, as cupids divest the war god of his armour, are of the finest quality. Covered in sand to protect them once the villa was abandoned, some at least seem to date from the early 4th century, so the town did retain some wealthy residents after its brush with imperial fame.

Climbing high up into the Hauran range, the territory becomes more rugged, and some 12 kilometres south of Shahba lies the town of

Qanawat, ancient Canatha. It was a leading member of the Decapolis ('the ten cities'), a grouping of Hellenistic cities, most of them lying further south in modern Jordan. Unfortunately for historians and archaeologists of a precise bent of mind, the exact membership of this grouping is unclear; some counts reach fourteen cities, and some of those mentioned in the lists – such as Dion – have not been identified on the ground. Nor, indeed, is there much evidence for any official federation or formal organisation. It was probably just a convenient term to group together Greek cities in the region, and one that the writer of the Gospel of Matthew took up.[22] Canatha, however, was always regarded as belonging to it, as were Damascus and, further to the south, Gadara (Umm Qays), Gerasa (Jerash) and Pella.

Perched high on a ravine, the city has been extensively built over, and even some of the buildings reported by travellers in the 19th century have since disappeared. In the modern town centre lies a small square fringed by a few coffee shops where impossibly old men and their aged sons while away undifferentiated days smoking, arguing and dreaming. At its centre, railings and a barred gate form a perimeter around the Serail, the 'palace', the principal remaining structure of ancient Canatha. For those fortunate enough to locate the guardian amongst his coffee-sipping peers, entrance reveals a Roman civil basilica, dated by an inscription to AD 124,[23] later converted into a Christian complex. A pre-existing building was adapted in the 5th century by the addition of an apse to change its orientation to east–west. Puddles of melted wax and a few faintly burning candles indicate that someone, at least, still regards the place with reverence. To one side of the Serail lies an atrium, and across it cuts a wall beyond which lies another church, its main entrance beautified with a swirl of floral and vine patterns, the lintel decorated with swastikas, at the time a symbol of good luck and eternity and untainted by the 20th-century associations with anti-Semitic violence. Around the church lie a jumble of chambers that could have been housing for the clergy, almshouses or storerooms. At the far end of the compound is a tower so eroded and ruined that what remains has the air of a rather forlorn arch that would collapse this very minute if only it could muster the energy.

On the south-eastern outskirts of Qanawat, at the edge of the deep ravine of the Wadi al-Ghar,[24] lies the restored outline of a *nymphaeum*, or ornamental fountain, and close by an *odeon*, with about eight or ten rows of seats, both dated to the 3rd century AD.[25] Not far off, next to a busy road just at the edge of town, sits the platform and half a dozen standing columns of the Temple of Helios. Its rubbish-strewn approach and the encroaching concrete skeletons of half-completed apartment blocks mask any sense of mystery or the divine.

Just 30 kilometres south-west of Qanawat and almost into modern Jordan lay the capital of the Arabian province. Although there has been a settlement here since at least the Bronze Age, Bostra – now Bosra in Syrian – only reached real prominence during the later Nabataean period in the 1st century AD, when for a time it supplanted Petra as the capital of the kingdom. It retained its position of primacy in the new Roman province of Arabia, although Trajan granted Petra the title of metropolis as compensation for its downgrading. The Nabataean town originally sprawled slightly to the east of the existing ruins, and to its west the Romans laid out a more orderly grid-like street pattern for the new city, which they named Nova Traiana Bostra. It was favoured with a visit by Hadrian in 129, and was elevated to the rank of a *colonia* under Alexander Severus.

The approach to the site today is unpromising; ringed by the modern town, Bostra appears as an isolated island among the motorcycles, noise and market stalls. The main gate, at its western entrance, is a solidly reconstructed single arch with empty statue niches to either side, constructed in black basalt. From this entry point, the Bab el Hawa ('gate of the winds'), the *decumanus* stretches east, originally colonnaded, with the remains of pillars strewn, stacked and occasionally arranged to either side of it. Proceeding further onwards, it is clear that the ancient town and the new are inextricably intertwined, with columns incorporated into walls and Ionic capitals employed as garden ornaments. Shops selling crisps and chequer-pattern footballs strung up in threes occupy the place of former porticoes and temple precincts, while bicycles are propped up against modern houses whose foundations clearly comprise wholly ancient stonework. It all seems as though the antique city has suffered some great disaster, and in the aftermath the new town has sprung up, scavenging off the old for spare parts. When the government and archaeologists have their way, of course, the residents will be cleared out and the whole restored to a more pristine state, gaining in grandeur what it loses in charm.

An area of ancient shops is marked off by a *cryptoporticus*, an underground colonnade, barred off by grilles, with something of the air of a disused subterranean cloister. The more substantial ruins are further to the east, beginning with the Bab Qandil ('Lantern Arch'), an imposing triple-arch, probably built in the 3rd century and dedicated by the III Cyrenaica legion.[26] It has lost its facing on one side, exposing a cruder brickwork sub-structure, which in contrast to the smooth and polished surface on the other gives it a strange 'before-and-after' look. Around this are grouped most of the city's other major monuments. Four huge columns some 12 metres high and, unusually for basalt work, carved with the more ornate Corinthian capitals, mark the remains of a *nymphaeum*, an ornamental public fountain, while opposite, at the junction with the north–south *cardo*, lies a solid rectangular ruin, whose external walls are punctuated by external niches. This, called locally 'the Palace of the Daughter of the King', is most likely a *kalybe*, similar in purpose to that at Philippopolis further north and intended for the exposition of imperial cult statues. However, the distribution of such *kalybes* in former Nabataean territory gives rise to the suspicion that this was a pre-Roman practice adapted by the new masters as a convenient vehicle for imperial propagandising. Back across the *decumanus* are the city's South Baths, its domed *apodyterium* (changing room) surviving largely intact, but the main bathing areas being far more ruined, both still impressive testaments to the urge to showiness in municipal construction.

Northwards up the *cardo*, flanked by the remains of another colonnade, the way leads to a set of important, early Islamic monuments. The much-reconstructed Mosque of Umar was once attributed to the second caliph, who ruled from 634 to 644, which would make it a relic from the very dawn of Islam. It is now believed to date more probably from the reign of Caliph Yazid II, around 720, still making it a rare survival from the Muslim religion's first century. Indeed, the interior has many reused columns; the position of the mosque may mean that these originally formed part of the portico of the *cardo*. The caretaker proudly points out some of green-streaked *cipollino* (finely veined Italian marble), and a couple with faded, barely legible Greek inscriptions.

A hundred metres or so further east lies another witness to the earliest Islamic period. The basilica probably dates to the 3rd century, and was originally a Roman civic building used by the city magistrates, before being converted in the 4th or 5th century for use as a Christian church. It is an austere and simple place, almost unadorned, its ground-plan broken only by an apse and an old well or cistern long since bricked up. What lends it significance is a meeting alleged to have taken place here around 580 between the Nestorian monk Bahira and the young prophet Muhammad, who was travelling with his uncle as part of a merchant caravan. Bahira noticed stigmata on the youthful trader and predicted that these miraculous marks meant that God had singled him out to become a great prophet. Subsequently a polemic broke out between Christian and Muslim authors as to the significance of this event. As Bahira belonged to a sect that had been condemned as heretical after the Council of Chalcedon in 451,[27] orthodox writers had no hesitation in blackening his name – or, as an alternative approach, doing everything they could to imply that he had taught Muhammad about the Christian faith and that this had been filtered in a distorted form into Islam. Muslim scholars countered with a much more straightforward affirmation of the original story.[28] Whatever the truth about the encounter, this unassuming place may have hosted one of the most portentous meetings in religious history. Bostra went on to become one of the first towns captured by the Muslim armies as they advanced out of the Arabian peninsula, falling to them in 632.

A little to the south sits the cathedral of Bostra, again constructed in dark, subdued shades of basalt. Dedicated to the saints Sergius, Bacchus and Leontius, it was built in 512, and is a transitional type between the earliest rectangular basilicas and the square, centralised form that was to become more fashionable in the eastern Greek-influenced Christian world. The church has lost its roof and most of its interior columns, but part of the walls survives, and in the apse, astonishingly, a few faded frescoes cling on, their colours reduced by sun and rain to red lines and ochre smudges, but with the halo of a saint just visible, and figures seated at a table, possibly portraying the Last Supper.

South again from here, and back on the east–west *decumanus*, lies the Nabataean arch, a rather simpler affair than the other two, with just a single opening, but a complex of niches and columns built into the structure at the sides. It probably formed the eastern end of a processional way, which in Nabataean times ran along what the Romans later converted into the Roman city's *cardo*. Beyond is a much more ruined quarter, which was probably the heart of Nabataean Bostra. The encroachment of modern settlement seems greater here, the dusty streets more rubbish-strewn, the football-playing youths and the grazing sheep look more like the hosts than the guests they appear as further to the west. Another ruined proto-centralised church lies totally neglected nearby, but much more significant is the building referred to locally as the 'governor's palace'. Built around a grand central courtyard, the palace stood at least two storeys high, with official rooms leading off the main court, including the remains of a grand formal dining hall or *triclinium*. It seems possible that this was originally the palace of Rabbel II, the Nabataean king who transferred the capital here from Petra around AD 70, though doubtless as one of the more prestigious buildings in the city it could well have been modified for the use of Roman governors after the annexation of the province.[29]

Almost nothing remains of the legionary camp of III Cyrenaica just to the north of the city, save field walls built from basalt, some of the stones artfully shaped as though they have just been plundered from a more grandiose structure. Of all the fort buildings, its hospital, granaries, barracks, roads and ramparts, nothing can be seen.[30] Bostra's greatest glory is similarly concealed, again just outside the central area of the antique city, this time to the south. The remains of the theatre are preserved within a medieval fortress that encloses it like a jacket, using the bulk of the ancient structure for strength, and at the same time protecting it from stone-robbing and other depredations. It sits now alongside a cleared plaza, frequented largely by postcard-sellers and a huddle of horse-drawn carriages, plying for a trade that never seems to come.

Once through the gloomy passageways of the Ayyubid fort, the theatre's interior is a glorious surprise, all of its forty tiers of seats totally intact (and originally providing places for some 6,000 spectators). The stage backdrop is almost complete, the towering basalt walls dramatically offset by colonnades of white limestone to each side of three stage entrances. From the top row of seating the view is stunning and, albeit in parts restored, this is a perfect gem of an ancient theatre – the ideal place from which to survey one of the more complete remaining Roman provincial capitals.

In the wake of the destruction of Palmyra in 273,[31] the Romans were deprived of a vital ally in their constant struggle to render the desert trade routes secure, and soon other Arab groups had appeared to contest Palmyra's monopoly on extracting wealth from passing traders – which it had done through the legally respectable imposition of tolls, rather than the more traditional mode of simple plunder.

Towards the end of the 3rd century, the Tanukh confederacy emerged as one of the most powerful groups on the desert fringes, gradually migrating north-east towards their final home in the region of Hira in modern Iraq. The Tanukh had a particularly bitter history with the Palmyrans. At the time of Zenobia, their ruler was, according to Arab sources, Jadhima.[32] During the brief period of Palmyrene supremacy, Zenobia's army defeated and captured the Tanukh sheikh and, finely balancing cruelty and refinement, she had his veins cut and the blood gathered into a golden cup. That there was now ill-feeling between the Palmyra and the Tanukh is probably something of an understatement.[33] Arab tradition holds that Jadhima's nephew 'Amr ibn 'Adi avenged his uncle by allying himself with Aurelian against Zenobia,[34] although the claim that he actually killed the Palmyrene queen is contradicted by the Roman historians' narrative that she died in comfortable retirement in Italy.

Whatever the truth, 'Amr ibn 'Adi's son, Imru' al-Qays, seems to have inherited the mantle of leading regional power-broker, this time in alliance with the Sassanids. Yet at the end of a long life he moved southwards, to the edge of the Arabian desert, apparently becoming a Roman ally and participating in the campaigns of Diocletian and Galerius against his former masters.[35] He may even have converted to Christianity, and it is plausible that this caused friction with his former suzerain Shapur II.[36] In any case, it is at Nemara that he settled, at a spot where under Diocletian a fort had been erected for a detachment of the III Cyrenaica legion.

It is in death, however, that Imru' al-Qays achieved his most lasting fame. His tomb inscription, dated 328, discovered at Nemara, some 100 kilometres east of Shahba, is carved in cursive lettering that has been considered a precursor of classical Arabic script. The language itself is undoubtedly Arabic, which here makes its first appearance in the epigraphic record.[37] Imru's epitaph makes the normal kinds of modest claims for his earthly achievements, declaring him to have been 'King of all the Arabs' and reeling off a list of the places under his authority, which might – the inscription is very hard to decipher – include territory as far-flung as the southern Hejaz.[38]

Although only a couple of hours' drive east of Shahba, Nemara seems a totally different world. East of the Hauran hills, the landscape becomes flatter, but the terrain is desolate, the fields increasingly filled with basalt rocks, at first a scattering, then columns, stacks and finally whole mounds of the stuff, which at a distance make the ground look as though it is covered by some black, alien crop. The road snakes through kilometre after kilometre of this harsh, relentless land, which lends true meaning to the term 'lava field' that geologists and archaeologists give it. An enticing well-tarmacked route off to the left leads nowhere, a gift by a local man turned provincial governor to his home village, a few modest houses with no visible livelihood. Finally in the baking heat, just as the road gives out completely, a jumble of basalt-built walls offer the faint impression of an ordered design. Great chunks of dark rock lie strewn around its edges, and, standing either too far away or too close, the structure merges into the sharp tangle of the solidified lava flow. There is no one around to confirm that this is Nemara, and doubtless few ever pass this way, but at just the right distance, one can almost feel the proud exile and clamorous boasts of Imru' al-Qays.

Back to the south of Bostra, but across a tricky international frontier

between Jordan and Syria, the hills of the Hauran begin to impose themselves more fully on the landscape. Buckled and folded outcrops of grim,
tar-black basalt with their hidden reaches, and the isolation of the water-
poor terrain, long provided a refuge for bandits and discontents in a
territory the Romans knew as the Auranitis.

Lying in the heart of this region, Umm al-Jimal – whose expressive
Arabic name 'Mother of the Camels' is a clue to its origins as a Nabataean
post on the trading routes at the northernmost extremity of their
kingdom – is gifted with a multiplicity of modern nicknames, including
'the black gem' and 'the black oasis'. All struggle to capture the real
feeling of these shattered remains of a city built of black basalt, great
blocks scattered about as though in some disorderly giant's dice game,
the jagged silhouettes of its surviving buildings contrasting dramatically
with a blue-on-azure sky. It is as if Tolkien's Mordor had redesigned the
city of Bath.

It is a far cry from the large, cosmopolitan cities of Syria and Arabia.
Very little of note occurred here and, indeed, such is the historical
anonymity of Umm al-Jimal that even its ancient name is unknown.[39]
The nearest it comes to troubling the written records is a Nabataean
inscription hidden on the wall of an anonymous-looking house that
commemorates Fihr, the tutor of Gadhimat, chief of the Tanukh.[40] This
probably refers to Jadhima, the Tanukh sheikh allegedly murdered by
Zenobia for daring to cross her.[41]

The hardness of the basalt made it suitable for constructing multi-
storeyed buildings, with the lower levels often used for storage and stabling
of the animals, and only the upper parts for living accommodation. Access
to these was gained by external staircases, the remains of which hang
outside many buildings here, often leading the way up to ghost floors,
long vanished and collapsed into piles of rubble. To support the weight
of the floors, stone corbels were built out from the walls, or supporting
arches constructed, on top of which wooden beams were laid.

The site was first fortified in about 180, but the original defences may
have been destroyed during the invasion of the area by the Palmyrenes
in 270. The village was rebuilt, using the ruins of the old one as a stone-
quarry, and provided with a remarkable network of churches, some
fourteen of which have been identified for a population estimated at just
8,000 or so. The most remarkable of these is the West Church, a dramatic
arch of piers thrusting outwards towards the modern village, and the
Cathedral, built in 556, of which but a shell remains, preserving a small
patch of polychrome mosaic in its aisle. Everywhere the regular houses
are marked with crosses incised above and alongside their doors.

Around 300 a new fort was built,[42] a great dark rectangular block, with one angle-tower still standing, giving the town a focus that its chaotic layout otherwise lacks. An inscription reused on the door lintel of the Cathedral refers to the building of a watchtower by a detachment of *equites Dalmatorum* (Dalmatian cavalry) and so it is possible that these, for a time, formed the garrison of the town. Scrambling through the ankle-twisting ruins involves a great number of detours, as there is no comforting street-grid to guide travellers, and our wayward progress through the site attracts the attention of the local guardians, who are convinced that we must be in search of some treasure, for why else would anyone come to such a place?

The Romans pushed further east into the desert from the 2nd and 3rd centuries, particularly under Diocletian, building a string of forts to screen the more settled areas of the province's interior from nomadic incursions or, should the eventuality arise, from Persian aggression. One of the most important of these was the fort in the oasis of Azraq, 100 kilometres to the south-east of Umm al-Jimal. Deriving its name from an Arabic word meaning 'blue', Azraq was long famed for the purity of its oasis lake, a boon for thirsty travellers through the Jordanian desert and a useful resource to dominate by means of a military presence. Those days are long past, and water is now scarce, the lake shrunk to a mere collection of muddy puddles. The reinforcement of the Roman frontier here happened under Diocletian, and Azraq is associated with his construction of the Strata Diocletiana.[43]

Today the fort is essentially an Ayyubid construction from the 13th or 14th century, a stolid square of large dark bricks, punctuated by arrow-slits, looking every inch as though the French Foreign Legion were about to emerge to chase down some Arab renegades. Aerial photography has definitely revealed an earlier Roman construction beneath this, however, and a collection of inscribed stones just inside the fort provides some evidence of it. One includes the terms 'Iovii' and 'Herculii', a reference to the symbolic association between Diocletian and his colleague Maximian and those two gods, and also the name of two elite legionary units. Another commemorates the rebuilding of the fort sometime around 326/7 under Constantine I, when it had fallen into considerable disrepair.

The interior of the fort bakes beneath the summer sun, the grey-black dust that carpets it seeming to radiate the heat back into the face of visitors, while the mosque constructed in the centre of the courtyard provides no escape. The most welcoming and shaded spot at Azraq is immediately over the main gate, where a staircase leads to a little room that provides both an unsurpassed view over the oasis and a refreshingly cool refuge. So it was during the First World War, when T. E. Lawrence ('Lawrence of Arabia') used the old fort as a military base during his raising of the Arab Revolt against the Ottoman Turks. The spot is inevitably called by local guides 'Lawrence's Room', but in this case there is for once some justification to their stories, since in *Seven Pillars of Wisdom* (his account of the revolt) Lawrence writes how he established himself in the southern tower, which his Arab helpers obligingly reroofed. So much did Lawrence love the place that he was afflicted by a particularly purple passage in this description of it: 'Azrak's unfathomable silence was steeped in knowledge of wandering poets, champions, lost kingdoms, all the crime and chivalry and dead magnificence of Hira and Ghassan. Each stone or blade of it was radiant with half-memory of the luminous silky Eden, which had passed so long ago.'[44] Of its atmosphere he further opines, 'Numen inest' – that there is a sense of the divine spirit here. Nowadays that sense is much attenuated, and if anyone's spirit can be felt to dwell in the place, it is Lawrence's.

Jerash, ancient Gerasa, around forty kilometres west of Umm al-Jimal is one of the best-preserved Roman cities in the Middle East. Indeed, if appearances were anything to go by, it would seem a much more important place even than Antioch, and of greater significance than Bostra, the capital of Arabia. Yet appearances are deceptive. Massively wealthy Gerasa may have been, but it was of strictly limited political and administrative importance. Yet it is a harsh heart that would deny Gerasa its colonnaded streets, its large temple of Zeus, even grander sanctuary of Artemis, and a host of other partly reconstructed monuments that give – as nowhere else but Palmyra in the region can – a real sense of how a Roman city functioned and was organised.

Gerasa's origins lay far off in the Bronze Age, when a settlement grew up on a nearby hill, but tradition has it that it was refounded by Perdiccas, one of Alexander the Great's generals, who gave it the name Antioch by the Chrysorrhoas ('the golden river'). There seems to have been a major building programme under the Seleucid Antiochos IV Epiphanes (175–164 BC), so it was a town of some grandeur when it fell to Pompey in 64 BC. At first part of Roman Syria, after the annexation of the Nabataean kingdom it was allocated, together with most of the other towns of the Decapolis, to the new province of Arabia.[45]

The main entrance to the city today lies through the Arch of Hadrian, built by the citizens of Gerasa to commemorate a visit by that Emperor in 129/30, the first time the city had been graced by an imperial presence. It is a splendid affair, the central entrance arch matched by two subsidiary passages, both topped by niches (for imperial statues) framed between engaged pillars, above which are a frieze and architrave, a visual reference in miniature to the whole of the arch itself. An inscription in Greek honouring Hadrian is matched by the find of one in Latin – the language of the army – by the *equites singulares*, his personal bodyguard. Coins commemorated his sojourn in the province with the legend *Adventus Aug Arabiae* ('the visit of the Emperor to Arabia').

It may well have been at this time that Hadrian conceived one of his least successful policies, aimed at finally suppressing Jewish resistance to Roman rule in the next-door province of Judaea. The plan was to refound Jerusalem as a *colonia*, a purely Roman establishment, to close down the Jewish Temple and replace it with a temple to Capitoline Jupiter and, for good measure, to ban the practice of circumcision and forbid any Jews from living in their former sacred city. Needless to say, the reaction was furious, and a rebellion broke out in 132. It took three and a half years to suppress the revolt, which was brilliantly directed by the guerrilla leader Simon Bar Kochba ('Son of a Star'),[46] and the involvement of at least four legions, including the local force, the III Cyrenaica from Bostra.

The Gerasenes, too, appear to have been somewhat overoptimistic with their arch. It is possible that they hoped the city would grow to encompass the grand new monument, or at least reach it, but the arch remained outside the municipal bounds, and Gerasa, or Antioch-by-the-Chrysorrhoas (as the inscription, with a resolute antiquarian insistence, continues to name it), remained more or less within the same circuit from the 1st century onwards. Nearby lies the Hippodrome, until quite recently just a grassy collection of earth banks, but now reconstructed for the hourly presentation of shows by a troupe of Jordanian re-enactors. Clutching shiny helmets and sporting polished *lorica segmentata* armour and blunted (one hopes) *gladii*, they mingle among the tourist crowds hoping to drum up business. Late in the day an incongruous crocodile of tired-looking Roman soldiers drifts back towards Hadrian's Arch, weary of the past until tomorrow. The Hippodrome itself has yielded some indication of the late period of Gerasa's history, after the Persians took it in 614 during their victorious sweep through the Byzantine Near East. Evidence has been unearthed that, unimpressed by their conquered enemies' predilection for horse-racing, they converted the Hippodrome into a polo field.[47]

Just inside the city, the Oval Piazza is one of the Roman world's most spectacular urban spaces. Its slightly irregular shape creates a series of curves, which draw the eye onward and seem to enlarge the area far beyond reality. The stones of the piazza's surface bend round too, as does its encircling portico of plain Ionic columns, all accentuating the effect. The unusual shape was used to mask the change of direction of the road between the south entrance gate and the *cardo*, which would otherwise form an awkward dog-leg, an angle caused by the need to preserve an axis oriented on the Temple of Zeus that pre-dated the laying-out of the urban grid on Roman lines. The Oval Piazza, indeed, is not truly a Roman innovation. Such semicircular or oval plazas are characteristic of the East, not appearing in the Western Empire – with the possible exception of Leptis Magna – and they were perhaps associated with processional ways leading to important temples. Once more, the oriental pops out from beneath a seemingly smooth Roman façade.

To the west of the piazza lies the sanctuary of the Temple of Zeus, beneath which evidence of the earliest Macedonian settlers has been found, and beside it Gerasa's Southern Theatre, a highly restored specimen, with a foundation dedication to Domitian. Inside is honoured the gift of 3,000 drachmas by Titus Flavius Dionysius, a magistrate who can hardly have imagined that his beloved theatre would ever be taken over by a Bedouin military band playing a most un-Roman medley of Scottish bagpipe favourites.

Far more ambitious than the Zeus Temple was that of Artemis, further north into the city and, had it ever been completed, one of the largest and most splendid urban sanctuaries anywhere in the Roman world. An elaborate *propylaeum*, a ceremonial gateway now largely vanished, leads up through a broad staircase of seven-times-seven steps to the temple platform itself. It all formed part of a processional Sacred Way, which was cut off in the 6th century by the building of a church right across the area in front of the *propylaeum*. Looking eastwards away from the temple is a melancholy sight now; the *decumanus*, a slightly overgrown forest of pillars, stretches out towards the modern city of Jerash, whose sprawl of apartment blocks seems in imminent danger of engulfing its ancient counterpart.

Around the central *cella* of the Artemis Sanctuary a peristyle six columns wide, each some 13 metres high, makes an unmistakable statement of the wealth of the temple and of Gerasa itself. The columns themselves, with capitals delicately carved despite their immense size, were designed to withstand earthquakes, a fact alarmingly demonstrated by placing a key or spoon in the gaps between the drums, for it will then move up and down as the structure is moved almost imperceptibly by the wind. Lest any visitors be seized by a surfeit of divine ecstasy, a sign beside the main podium warns, 'For the safety of all visitors. Don't pick any of the herbs of the site.'

Once the pagan temples had been closed down or sidelined, the eminence on which the Artemis Sanctuary lies was commandeered by a series of Christian churches, including the Cathedral, amongst whose ruins lies the basin of a fountain where Christians celebrated the miracle of the wedding feast at Cana. During the ceremony, the fountain would, it was alleged, flow with wine instead of water. It is surely no coincidence that the church was built over a former shrine to Dionysus, the pagan god most associated with the vine, and a previous pagan feast was no doubt adapted and continued under the aegis of the Church, a borrowing made much easier by the parallel importance of wine in both belief systems.

Further up the *decumanus* a *tetrakoinion*, a splendid four-way arch used in the East to mark major street intersections, draws the visitor towards the North Theatre, originally a small *odeon* for around 800 spectators, which was enlarged in the 2nd century with the addition of an imposing forecourt bordered by a portico of Corinthian columns. Everything is on a majestic scale for such a modestly important place, a sobering thought when one considers how Antioch, Alexandria or Rome might have looked if their monumental structure had been recoverable to anything like the same extent.

Of Gerasa's final era of prosperity, the Christian churches are ample witness. Towards the northern edge of town lies a cluster of these, including the church of Cosmas and Damian, dedicated in 533 by a Bishop Paul.[48] From the floor stare out portraits of Theodore the *paramonarios* (church-warden) and his wife Giorgia, forever frozen in a pious gesture. The last church seems to have been built around 611, and less than three decades later the Byzantines were swept from this part of Syria. Some occupation did continue under the new masters; pottery kilns and houses of Umayyad date have been found near the North Theatre, the tetrapylon and grouped around the Oval Piazza. Deprived of the comfortable cushion of Roman provincial life, however, there was no real reason for Gerasa to survive, and, damaged beyond the power of its remaining inhabitants to repair, it was finally abandoned by the 10th century.

Further to the east, the Via Nova Traiana snaked down, defended by a series of strongpoints such as Khirbet es Samra and Philadelphia (modern Amman). Sited halfway between today's King's Highway and the Desert Highway, the principal arteries of modern Jordanian travel (the former of which follows roughly the line of the Roman Via Nova Traiana), and roughly 100 kilometres south of Amman, lies the legionary fortress of Lejjun, its name probably a corruption of the Latin *legio* or legion. The Romans knew it as Betthoro and chose the site in around 300 for the construction of a base for the IV Martia legion as part of the general reinforcement of the *limes* in this central section of Arabia. Lying just alongside the Wadi al-Lejjun, with its perennial spring and fertile valley, Lejjun was well situated in a region where the lack of water presented a major difficulty in the long-term supply of large bodies of troops.

On this stretch my guide has given to waving airily at any broken-down buildings of any vintage older than the 1950s and pronouncing, 'Here, ruins!' and at Lejjun he identifies a set of half-collapsed cottages on the hillside beside the road as clear evidence of Roman occupation. They are at least a sign that others recognised the strategic importance of the place, for they are the remains of an Ottoman police post built around 1910,[49] and my guide is only half-wrong, for they were doubtless constructed using stones from the handiest source around, namely the Betthoro fort.

Little remains of the fort save the shattered outlines of the wall, only partly now delimiting the site, although with a lot of patience four corner towers and some of the original twenty interval towers can be made out. The interior is a seeming chaos of disordered stones. Amidst all this archaeologists identified at least the *principia*, the legionary headquarters, though no evidence was found of the great basilical cross-hall characteristic of such buildings,[50] perhaps a sign that during the later Empire less rigorous attention was paid to the old ways of doing things. The barracks buildings, too, are a sign of changing times; divided into six main blocks, they seem to have provided accommodation for around 1,500 men, around one-third of the classic legion's complement of 5,000.[51] IV Martia was probably raised under Diocletian, and although there are clear signs that he increased the overall numbers in the army, the additional legions he raised were probably of this smaller size.[52]

The site suffered badly from natural disasters. The discovery in one building of a level of ash caused by a fire is datable to 502, the same time as an earthquake devastated the fort. Much of the fort collapsed after another earthquake in 551,[53] although the military seem already to have abandoned it twenty years earlier.[54] What subsequent occupation there was seems, to judge from pottery and other artefacts unearthed, to have been non-military, another sign that, after a century of heavy military presence in late-Roman times, the Byzantine authorities retrenched, relying on little more than prestige and the uncertain word of their Arab *phylarch* allies.

Dajaniyah, 80 or so kilometres further south along the desert highway, is a much smaller fort, though dating from the same period and performing in miniature much the same function as Lejjun. Yet it is far more spectacular. From Lejjun the route to Dajaniyah is relentlessly flat and arid, a desert landscape that must have offered the Roman soldiers little in the way of relief. Low, single-storey blocks straggle in untidy clusters alongside the road, many of them Bedouin settlements established as part of the government's programme to encourage the semi-nomadic peoples finally to settle down in one place. Hidden behind one such, the road veers off straight into the desert towards the very distant silhouette of Dajaniyah, one wall visible across the wasteland, a great hole gouged from its central section as though smashed by some massive hammer-blow. My driver will not proceed, his vehicle defeated by the ruts and potholes that bar the way to the fort. I have to rely on the kind service of a local, a former naval officer fortuitously settled in this remote place, to break through the desert barrier. Bones shaken and van's axle buckled, it takes twenty minutes to cover the couple of kilometres to the fort perimeter.

Attached to one corner of the fort is a Bedouin encampment with a couple of tents, presumably inhabited by a few families who wish to retain at least a foothold in their traditional world. The fort is of basalt, the black rock seeming to suck in the burning sun and glow even more darkly for it. The wall circuit is largely intact, but the gateways have gone and entrance now is through the great gash gouged in the south wall, huge chunks of black stone strewn all around. It is still possible to venture onto the parapet walk for an auxiliary's-eye-view of the desert. Looking around, the setting seems the bleakest imaginable, with nothing save the fort itself and the roadside village to break the monotony, while the heat is so severe that it sets up a cruelly inviting haze, suggesting low clouds or even water-courses that are simply not there.

Back in the fort the main artery, the *via principalis*, is reasonably free of debris, and a structure in the middle must be the *principia*, where the *aedes*, the temple of the legionary standards, has been identified – a sign of the military observance that linked desert soldiers at Dajaniyah to their brothers on the Danube and in the chilly northern climes of Britannia. By the 6th century it, too, seems to have been abandoned and left to fall, too far even from major settlements to provide an attractive target for the robbing of stones.

From here the King's Highway continues to mimic the route of the Via Nova Traiana, leading 30 kilometres or so south to Petra, with the landscape, if not exactly inviting, gradually relaxing its relentlessly harsh grip.

William Burgon's poem with its reference to 'a rose-red city half as old as time' has become one of the most-quoted, and misattributed, poetic references to a Roman city. Yet, if not quite half as old as time, Petra is inescapably rose-red. As the rays of the desert sun die in the sandy gloom, the colonnaded and pillared tombs of Petra's city of the dead do absorb the light, become suffused with a golden rosy hue and hold a promise of daylight's return.

The Nabataeans, who inhabited ancient Petra, have become, perhaps unfairly, irredeemably associated with funerary monuments. It is hardly surprising considering the splendour of the final resting places they constructed for their elite, and the paucity of more mundane evidence of their everyday life. It is a narrow passage from the world of mushrooming hotels and the cosmopolitan blandness of tourist menus to the melancholy splendour of the ancient Nabataean capital. Its very name, Petra, may be linked to the Greek for 'rocks', so it is fitting that the entranceway should be a narrow defile through the mountain, the *siq*, a kilometre-long canyon that constricts in places to a mere 2 metres in width, lined all the way with niches that once bore images of the chief Nabataean god, Dusares, whose catch-all portfolio of divine responsibilities included the sky, the rain and the fertility of the soil. His name may mean 'he of the Shara', one of the mountain peaks that tower over Petra. In his earliest incarnation he was worshipped in the form of a betyl ('house of the god'), a solid stone block. Even before modern visitors reach the *siq* a couple of monumental 'god-blocks' are a reminder of the Nabataeans' predilection for aniconic representation of their deities.[55]

In spring 1858, Edward Lear visited Petra in the company of his faithful Greek servant Giorgio. On first sighting the beautifully variegated and striated hues of the rock-tombs, Giorgio was overcome with emotion and exclaimed, 'We have come into a world where everything is made of chocolate, ham, curry powder and salmon',[56] a sentiment worthy of his poetic master. A reaction every bit as extravagant, if perhaps less expressive, is apt to trip off the lips on first sighting Petra's signature monument, which lies exactly at the point where the *siq* opens out into the great valley in which Petra's principal buildings sit. The Khazneh (or 'Treasury') is so named because the local Bedouin believed that it must have contained the treasury of Pharaoh, the semi-mythical personage whose name was liberally sprinkled about the Petra landscape, lending mystery to a culture that subsequent inhabitants of the place simply could not comprehend.

The Khazneh is a tour de force, a classicising extravaganza that is unafraid to borrow local motifs and mix them into what should by rights be a total mish-mash, but in fact holds together to create a façade of arresting power. A colonnade of six columns seems to support a second level (a false impression, for the whole is cut into the rock and is not free-standing at all). Upon this sit three kiosks: to the left and right two rectangular and surmounted by half-pediments, and in the centre a semi-circular drum containing a shattered statue, possibly of Isis, on top of which perches a stone trophy. It was within this that the Bedouin believed the Pharaoh had concealed his fortune and, once the march of progress had blessed them with firearms, they took to taking pot-shots at the monument in the hope of cracking it and causing a shower of gold and jewels to issue forth. A further subterranean level of the Khazneh has recently been discovered by archaeologists, but so far the fabled treasure has remained elusive.

Framed by the rock-face through which the *siq* cleaves and by other promontories that surround and shelter Petra, the Khazneh's location is impossibly romantic, and it is almost hard to criticise those visitors whose pressing schedule for the return to their cruise ships docked at Aqaba means they barely progress any further. The first European since Roman times to see the site was Johann Ludwig Burckhardt, a Swiss orientalist who, intent on travelling in Africa, had decided that passing himself off as a Muslim traveller would be a most useful disguise, and to that end spent several years travelling in the Near East, immersing himself in the culture as thoroughly as he could. When he heard of the Wadi Mousa, the valley outside Petra, and of the nearby antiquities, he feigned a desire to sacrifice a goat at the Shrine of Aaron on the Jebel Haroun, which would involve walking right the way through the monuments.[57] With admirable restraint, Burckhardt describes the Khazneh as 'one of the most elegant remains of antiquity existing in Syria'[58] although his enthusiasm may have been dampened by his Bedouin guides, who were deeply mistrustful of their travelling companion's habit of gawking at ruined buildings. They suspected him of prospecting for treasure and, even more dangerously, of a magical ability to detect hidden gold.

Nonetheless, Burckhardt was able to enter the Khazneh, make draw-ings on a notebook hidden in his robes and visit several of the other Petra ruins, before being struck with a tactical case of weariness when faced with the hard, steep climb to the top of the Jebel Haroun. The goat was sacrificed at the base of the mountain, instead of its top, at 'Aaron's terrace', a place deemed to be of sufficient sanctity and far less onerous to reach than the shrine itself. Unlike Burckhardt, we were able to reach the shrine, though it is a hard slog on horseback in the late-morning heat and on several stretches the horse must walk without a mount, for the footing is treacherous. Past side-valleys scored with the façades of funerary monuments we struggle, many of the structures along the route having Bedouin tents pegged outside them, because, unlike on the main tourist drag, here the authorities have not cleared the local people away from their traditional use of the tombs as additional storage space and a cool refuge from the sun. Most notable amongst these is the 'Snake Monument' near the base of the Jebel Haroun, a squat bulbous stone idol, its ossified coils still looking threatening, as though about to squeeze the life out of any who approach it.

On finally reaching the summit, a small green-domed mosque lies firmly locked, and it is a long way down to find the guardian who might hold the key. The view back over towards Petra, its temple façades just visible as matchstick-like constructions almost lost in the folding mountain valleys, gives a spectacular panorama of the sheer ruggedness of the terrain and helps explain why, in their rocky fastness, the Nabataeans were able to elude the grasp of their more powerful neighbours for quite so long.

From the Khazneh, which has been dated to the time of Aretas IV (9/8 BC–AD 40–1),[59] the 'Outer Siq' opens out, flanked by a number of façades decorated with a characteristic crow's-step pattern of crenellations, a style believed to have originated in Assyria. Around the corner lies the 'Street of Façades', with dozens and dozens more tombs, the strong impression of a City of the Dead broken only by the equally numerous stalls set up to hawk jewellery, trinkets and, on a strictly under-the-counter basis, genuine coins and antiquities that the local people have scavenged from the site. A gaggle of juvenile camel herdsmen offering rides, and a string of donkeys braying with legs buckling under the substantial weight of well-fed tourists, all combine to give some sense of a bazaar, and perhaps, for all its raucous quality, a genuine idea of the past mercantile life of the place.

The theatre rises up to the left, built around the same time as the Khazneh, the *cavea* containing the seats simply slicing through the entrances of several pre-existing tombs. The back rows of seats are very worn now, while the stage backdrop is utterly ruined, having collapsed at the time of an earthquake in 363. To the right the Jebel al-Khubtha, whose heights contain the best vantage points for viewing the Khazneh from above, shelters a series of Petra's finest tombs: the Silk Tomb, the multicoloured striations in whose rock lend it the name; the Corinthian, so called for its use of Corinthian columns in its façade; and the Palace Tomb, an attempt at grandiose classicism whose curiously squat upper level renders the whole effect less than harmonious. The Urn Tomb is a much simpler affair, and inside contains an inscription revealing that the room was converted to use as a church by Bishop Jason in 447.[60]

Though Petra lost its royal family, and the *raison d'être* for its grandest tombs, the life of the city carried on, more modestly than before, but still retaining a certain level of prosperity. Despite no longer being the provincial capital, Petra was still visited by senior officials, and one of them, Titus Aninius Sextius Florentinus, who was governor of Arabia in 127, is buried in a tomb further east, alongside the Jebel al-Khubtha. It exhibits no particularly Roman elements, and could well not have been purpose-built for him at all. Yet, on his death in 129, he (or his family) chose a Nabataean-style burial, lending his name an immortality that neither he nor his successor governors at Bostra could have imagined.

The remains of a colonnaded street, a 300-metre-long artery originally paved with slabs of limestone and marble, much trafficked now by donkeys and camels, leads to Petra's single substantial free-standing monument, the Qasr al-Bint ('Castle of the Daughter of Pharaoh'). This solid rectangular block, with little of the appeal of the tomb façades, was in origin a temple, and the remains of the arch through which the colonnaded street passes probably marks out the road as a processional way to the sanctuary. Exactly which god of the Nabataean pantheon was worshipped here is not clear. It may have been Dusares, the chief deity, or equally the goddess al-'Uzza,[61] equated by the Romans with Aphrodite, and for whom it is known that there was a temple somewhere in Petra. Strabo relates that at the chief temple in Petra – presumably this one – thirteen adepts of the god would preside over banquets and the King himself would serve the guests at the sacred meal.[62] The temple continued in use in Roman times, for an inscription has been found to Zeus Hypistos, as well as a dedication to an unspecified emperor. The earthquake that struck Petra in May 363 severely damaged the sanctuary, and another in the 6th century completed its destruction.

More characteristic of Nabataean worship, and that of the region more generally, was the veneration accorded to 'High Places', and Petra, with its multiplicity of peaks, has a surfeit of these. Ed-Deir ('the Monastery'), sits high up on a promontory at the north-west edge of Petra, requiring an hour's weary climb to reach its summit. It takes its name from the inscribed crosses scratched into the wall in places, but it is without doubt a Nabataean funerary monument. One theory associates it with the last king, Rabbel II, who, though he ruled from Bostra, could have been returned on his death to his ancestral necropolis.[63] The façade, complete with urn and side-kiosks, seems like an attempt to recreate the Khazneh at a higher level, but the columns at ground level are carved into the rock and not free-standing, while the whole, despite its massive scale, contrives to give an impression of brooding squatness totally at variance with the elegant grace of the Treasury. Outside, the great plaza is not natural, but was levelled to accommodate rituals, presumably associated with the cult of the dead king.

Positioned overlooking the Outer Siq is the 'High Place of Sacrifice', Petra's best-known aerial temple, which offers wonderful views over the bleak wilderness valleys of the Wadi Araba. It is a comparatively simple affair, with a stone platform on which sits an altar raised on a podium of four steps, with a basin set beside it. Despite lurid guides' tales of human sacrifice, there is no evidence that the Nabataeans did more than offer animals to their gods here. The Romans, who tended to get huffy about the alleged sacral murder performed by other less-civilised races such as the Celtic Druid priests or the Carthaginians in North Africa, were apt to forget that they themselves were on record as having performed such bloody rites. When Hannibal threatened to march on Rome after his crushing victory at Cannae in 216 BC, the Roman magistrates ordered that two Greeks and two Gauls be sacrificed to ward off the disaster. The poor unfortunates were buried alive in a pit, so that Romans of a more squeamish or moralistic tendency could maintain that they had not actually been killed, but merely left to die.

An alternative way down from the High Place leads through the Wadi Farasa, past a number of other Nabataean tomb façades, most notably the Garden Tomb – an ancient water cistern lying broken and empty in front of it an indication of the nearby residence of the supervisor of the city's water supply. Beside it lies the Roman Soldier's tomb, named for a headless male torso clad in a Roman-style military cuirass, which projects from above its door. Although the dating of the tomb is most likely from the independent Nabataean period and thus the 'Roman' soldier probably served in the local army, it is pleasant to speculate that he may have served as an auxiliary in a Roman cohort and retired to his home town to die, leaving instructions that his military service be remembered in his funerary monument. Whoever he was, he was clearly a man of some substance, as both the tomb itself and the *triclinium* opposite, with carefully carved fluted columns in a riot of mauves and pinks, show a high level of workmanship.

The Petrans dedicated a new temple of Artemis in 150, and Epiphanius, in the 4th century, writes that the inhabitants were still wedded to the cult of Dusares, but these traditional ways did not last for ever and by the 6th century Christianity had established a firm hold here. Up on the north slope from the colonnaded street lie a cluster of churches, evidence of this late phase in Petra's development. The Petra Church, a Byzantine construction of the 5th century, is a fairly typical three-aisled basilica, though enclosed, for its better conservation, in an alarming spider-like sheath of plastic and glass. The floor retains part of its original mosaic covering, on the right a series of beautifully studied personifications of the seasons, on the other side various animals, intended to show the bounty of nature, including a cameleopard, a strange mutant hybrid between a camel and a leopard. A fire at the end of the 6th century caused part of the building to collapse and buried a precious archive of papyrus scrolls, partly carbonised, but containing details of land sales, tax payments and all the other mundane transactions, which shed some light on the minutiae of a community clearly still functioning, if not exactly flourishing.[64]

The Blue Church, named for the blue Egyptian marble columns used in its construction, and the Ridge Church at the highest point of the slope are mostly ruinous, but offer a viewpoint over the very edge of Petra and its perimeter of city walls. Massively built in sandstone blocks, these Nabataean works defended the settlement from attacks to the north. Snaking across the ridges, these unglamorous remains are reminders of a side of Nabataean life about which the grand façades of the Royal Tombs are mute. In the end, it seems they were built in vain, for only one source (Cassius Dio) hints at any kind of fighting during the Roman occupations,[65] and coins issued to commemorate the annexation bear the legend *Arabia Capta* ('Arabia captured') rather than *Arabia Victa* ('Arabia defeated').[66] As the Roman imperial propaganda machine was rarely backward in proclaiming even modest military successes as occasions for celebration, it is safe to presume that its defence was a very brief one.

A dim light on the transition to Roman rule and the early years of the province is shed by an archive of scrolls found in a cave in the Negev desert in the early 1960s. Babatha, to whom the documents belonged, was a rich landowner from a Nabataean-controlled village at Mazoa, south of the Dead Sea. The documents span a period from before the Roman annexation, with the scrolls written in Nabataean, to 132 (when Babatha is presumed to have died), by which time Greek – the language of administration in the eastern portion of the Empire – had taken over. They make reference to a *boule* (town council) at Petra, indicating that a Romanised form of urban administration was then functioning. Interesting, too, are the constant references to Roman soldiers in the region. Babatha goes to the prefect of a cavalry *ala* to register her holding of date-groves during the census carried out in Arabia in 127, while a

Roman centurion is recorded as lending money at an interest rate of 12 per cent to Babatha's second husband, an indication of the army's involvement in the local economy at an informal level.[67]

Babatha's presumed end was not a peaceful one. When the Romans put down the revolt of Simon Bar Kochba in 135, which for three years had torn through Palestine and threatened briefly to herald the restoration of Jewish independence, the surviving fighters scattered into inaccessible hideouts in the desert. Probably caught up somehow in the crisis, and sharing her last days with the rebels, was Babatha, whose remains could be amongst the twenty skeletons unearthed at the cave where her archive was found. Between her death and the establishment of the Petra Church archive, little is known. Then, just forty years after the fire that tore through the Christian complex, the Arabs seized the area. Earthquakes and the shattering of the water-management systems that had allowed the Nabataeans to husband what little moisture the near-desert provided left Petra's astonishing city of the dead as the haunt of just a few Bedouin families.

It is with a certain sadness that one leaves Petra, weary legs carrying the tomb-surfeited visitors away through the *siq* on to the more insistently pressing claims of the modern town. For the most exhausted, a tidy sum in Jordanian dinars claims a place in a carriage, whose clattering wheels break the silence of the route with cries and redoubled echoes. The best way of all to leave the ancient city, however, is on horseback, a mode of transport that requires permission in triplicate and involves incredulous checking of the paperwork by the guards, and jealous stares from those who have been firmly told by their guides that such a practice is strictly forbidden. Yet, a metre above the crowds and the carriages, gently rocked by the sway of the horse's back, it is still possible to feel like a real explorer, and experience just a hint of the wonder with which Burckhardt must first have cast eyes upon the Nabataeans' hidden capital.

Beyond Petra the landscape once more turns arid, transforming into the forbidding Hisma desert of southern Jordan. It was areas such as this that the Romans needed to dominate if they were successfully to hold on to their new Arabian province. Originally a Nabataean settlement, Humayma, 60 kilometres south of Petra, was founded by Aretas III around 80 BC and named Auara, 'the white place', for the vision of a man riding on a white camel that he is said to have seen there.[68] Under the Roman occupation, Auara found itself in a strategic position along the Via Nova Traiana, and one of the earliest Roman forts in Jordan was built here, the first garrison transferring from Egypt, its

presence evidenced by a collection of ankhs and other characteristically Egyptian votive symbols. In the *Notitia Dignitatum* the garrison
of Auara (or Haurae) is listed as the *equites sagittarii indigenae*, a unit
of native horse archers.[69]

The way to Humayma leads through barren limestone outcrops into
a land that somehow provides sustenance to the Bedouin's herds of sheep
and goats, and which, for those like the Nabataeans who were masters
of water husbandry, can actually provide a modest living. Annual rainfall in the area is just 90 millimetres. Yet, set down amid the most
parched-looking landscape fringed by wrinkled and gullied hills, already
baking in the late-winter heat, it seems impossible to conceive of anyone
voluntarily settling here. A short way into the site lies the indistinct
outline of the earlier Roman camp, a square shape possibly indicating
the *principia*, with less-distinct rubble piles to indicate the barracks. A
small building just outside, and equally ruinous, is one of the Byzantine
churches that indicate continuity of settlement in this bleak outpost at
least into the 6th century. Indeed, a tax edict of the mid-5th century indicated that the place was considered prosperous – the levy it was required
to pay, some forty-three gold pieces, being the second-highest in the
Transjordan, an amount exceeded only by Udruh, Arabia's other main
legionary camp, 20 kilometres east of Petra.[70]

A Bedouin shepherdess scrutinises us uncertainly as we approach the
Nabataean reservoir, the cistern still full of water and with intact piping
still leading off from it. Beyond lies another larger, but unroofed, structure marking the Abbasid *qasr*. Arab tradition has it that during the early
Islamic period, the former Byzantine settlement at Auara became the residence of the Abbasid family, who claimed descent from one of the uncles
of the Prophet Muhammad. During the 730s, they used it as a safe base
for their conspiracy against the ruling Umayyad caliphate, and when in
749 they succeeded in seizing power and becoming caliphs themselves,
they abandoned Humayma for the rather more urban delights of Baghdad.

Sited at the northern end of the Red Sea, on the Gulf that bears its
name and just 50 kilometres to the south-west of Humayma, Aqaba has
been an important trading and naval station throughout its history. Even
today it has become a free port, as the Jordanian authorities attempt to
pump life into an economy undermined by successive Middle East crises.
Mentioned in the Bible as a trading post on the way to 'Ophir', the
earliest settlement at Aqaba lies at Tell el-Khuleifa to the west of the
modern centre, and was superseded by a Ptolemaic port at Berenice,
and then, after the annexation of Arabia, by the town of Ailana, which
lies buried beneath the heart of the modern city.

Off the café-fringed cornice, the beach thickly populated with bathers despite the scorching heat, lies Aqaba's partly ruined fort. Originally of late-Abbasid construction (from the mid-12th century), it is most famous for the raid carried out on it by Lawrence of Arabia in July 1917, which drove the Ottoman Turks from the town. Aqaba has been Muslim-held since 630, when its bishop, Yuhanna ibn Ru'ba, brokered a treaty with the Prophet Muhammad, by which the town allowed safe-passage to the Muslim armies and access to its wells, and agreed to pay a tribute of one solidus for each of its non-Muslim inhabitants – which meant, one presumes, virtually the entire population.[71] Such localised agreements and the spirit of self-help and implied disloyalty to the central government's cause must have been typical of the way in which Byzantine control over Arabia and Palestine simply dissolved away. If the government could not protect the towns, the locals would pay tribute to those who could; as for the tribes of the desert fringes, they would fight under the banner of the side that was, in their view, most likely to win.

At such a strategic location, Roman Ailana soon found itself garrisoned by the III Cyrenaica legion, detached from duty in Egypt. The town sat at the southernmost extension of the Via Nova Traiana, and milestones from the construction of that road dated 112 have been found at Aqaba. When Diocletian reorganised the administration of the region, Ailana found itself a part of the new province of Palaestina, with its garrison the X Fretensis legion, which, from the evidence of the *Notitia Dignitatum*, was then stationed there at least until the end of the 4th century. Aqaba remained an important trading centre and a stop on the route for pilgrims making the arduous journey to the monastery of Saint Catherine in the Sinai desert.

But security in the region grew ever shakier. During the reign of Leo (457–74), a tribal sheikh named Amorkesus[72] seized the island of Iotabe in the Gulf of Aqaba and proceeded to levy tolls on all shipping that desired to pass. In order to get rid of this nuisance, the Byzantine government was forced to acquiesce to Amorkesus's demand to be appointed *phylarch* of Palaestina Tertia, the lands around Petra, in effect rewarding his piratical act with an officially recognised position.[73] It took further action on the part of Romanus, *dux* of Palestine, to reassert full control over Iotabe, but by 530 Justinian had in effect demobilised this eastern frontier, handing over primary responsibility for its policing to his Ghassanid Arab allies.

Ailana, therefore, was by 630 hardly defended at all. The remains of the Byzantine walls can be seen around 500 metres from the modern shore, complete with fragments of a projecting tower. It was probably

here that the X Fretensis legion was based. The ruins sit utterly unregarded on a dusty traffic island at the side of a busy road. Over the way,
jumbled fragments of Byzantine Ailana's more domestic life lie in a moul-
dering heap of mud-brick constructions and the more substantial
shattered stones of several churches. The Arab *misr* or fortified encampment – which became known as Ayla – that was set up in the 630s just
by the shore has survived in better condition, although hemmed in by
modern hotels and a yacht club, which has swallowed up part of its
perimeter. The Egypt gate, with two horseshoe-shaped towers intact,
and the ruins of the congregational mosque manage to give at least
some sense of the settlement that finally put an end to the career of
Roman Ailana. Secure in a base such as this, and having acquired the
rest of Palestine with the capture of Jerusalem in 634, the Arabs were
free to turn their attention to the conquest of still-Byzantine Egypt.

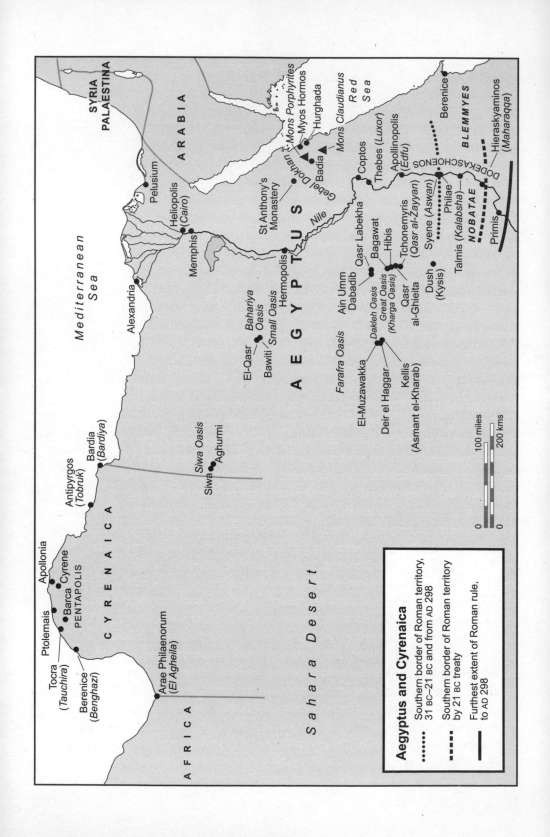

Aegyptus and Cyrenaica

········· Southern border of Roman territory, 31 BC–21 BC and from AD 298

– – – – Southern border of Roman territory by 21 BC treaty

——— Furthest extent of Roman rule, to AD 298

Mediterranean Sea

SYRIA PALAESTINA

A R A B I A

Pelusium
Heliopolis (Cairo)
Memphis
Alexandria
St Anthony's Monastery
Hermopolis

Nile

A E G Y P T U S

Mons Porphyrites
Myos Hormos
Hurghada
Gebel Dokhan
Badia
Gebel el Badia
Mons Claudianus
Red Sea

Coptos
Thebes (Luxor)
Apollinopolis (Edfu)

Berenice

BLEMMYES

Hieraskyaminos (Maharaqqa)

DODEKASCHOENOS

Primis
NOBATAE
Talmis (Kalabsha)
Philae
Syene (Aswan)
Tchonemyris (Qasr al-Zayyan)
Hibis
Dush (Kysis)
Qasr al-Ghieita
Bagawat
Qasr Labekha
Ain Umm Dabadib

Great Oasis (Kharga Oasis)
Dakleh Oasis
Kellis (Asmant el-Kharab)
Deir el Haggar
El-Muzawakka

Farafra Oasis

El-Qasr
Bawiti
Bahariya Oasis
Small Oasis

Siwa
Aghurmi
Siwa Oasis

Bardia (*Bardiya*)
Antipyrgos (*Tobruk*)

C Y R E N A I C A

Apollonia
Cyrene
Barca
PENTAPOLIS
Ptolemais
Tocra (*Tauchira*)
Berenice (*Benghazi*)
Arae Philaenorum (*El Agheila*)

A F R I C A

Sahara Desert

100 miles
200 kms
0
0

CHAPTER 9

Aegyptus and Cyrenaica

The barge she sat in, like a burnished throne
Burned on the water. The poop was beaten gold;
Purple the sails, and so perfumed that
The winds were lovesick with them. The oars were silver,
Which to the tunes of flutes kept stroke, and made
The water which they beat to follow faster,
As amorous of their strokes. For her own person
It beggared all description: she did lie
In her pavilion – cloth of gold, of tissue –
O'erpicturing that Venus where we see
The fancy outwork nature . . .
William Shakespeare, *Antony and Cleopatra*[1]

Egypt always seemed to the Romans a mysterious, atypical place, radically opposed to the 'Roman' way of doing things, a country that entangled, entrapped and mesmerised. During the civil wars of the 1st century BC, it certainly did ensnare such successive aspirants of supreme power as Julius Caesar and Mark Antony. Before this, though, in 210 BC, the Romans had tried to secure grain supplies from Ptolemy IV, and so vital did Egypt subsequently become as a source of food for the teeming populace of Rome that in 168 BC they intervened directly to demand that the Seleucid king of Syria, Antiochus IV, who was trying to annex his neighbour, withdraw his forces and his governor from the country.

Thenceforth, Egypt was always independent more or less at the whim of Rome, and the next century and a half consisted of a 'will they, won't they' diplomatic dance between the Romans and Egyptians, the latter alternately fending off and then inviting Roman occupation. In 55 BC, Pompey was drawn into Egyptian affairs when he had his lieutenant Gabinius restore Ptolemy XIII, who had fled the country following one of the bitter (and quite commonly fatal) feuds that periodically afflicted the Ptolemaic ruling house. If Pompey thought Ptolemy would be grateful, he was rudely disabused when he sought refuge with his old 'ally' following his defeat against Julius Caesar at the Battle of Pharsalus in 48 BC. In an attempt to curry favour with the Caesarian side, Ptolemy – far from sheltering Pompey – had him murdered and sent his head on a dish to Caesar, when he in turn arrived in Egypt. Ptolemy, though, received the just reward for his perfidy, as Caesar had him executed and promoted his half-sister Cleopatra VII to the throne.[2]

Cleopatra, just seventeen at the time of her accession, flirted with and charmed the middle-aged triumvir, seeking thereby to entwine her own ambitions so inextricably with his that her beloved country's independence would be safeguarded. But Caesar finally returned to Rome, leaving as the product of his little adventure a son, dubbed Ptolemy Caesarion. Undeterred, Cleopatra turned her attention, following Caesar's assassination in 44 BC, to the leading star in the rising new generation of Roman strongmen, Mark Antony. A man seemingly of much more volatile temperament than Caesar, Antony appears for a while to have contemplated dismantling the edifice of Roman provincial authority and returning to the system of management through clients which had previously served the Romans so well in the East.

This may have been the motive in 34 BC for the 'Donations of Alexandria', when Antony, seated on a dais in Alexandria and dressed like an oriental potentate, dished out the eastern provinces to Cleopatra and the children he had fathered on her, the twins Cleopatra Selene ('the moon') and Alexander Helios ('the sun') and the youngest, Ptolemy Philadelphos. Even little Caesarion received his share. Needless to say, this did not go down at all well in Rome, where Antony was widely (and hardly inaccurately) regarded as having 'gone native'. It all handed a propaganda coup to Antony's rival Octavian, and Antony's belated pamphlet attempting to defend himself against accusations of betraying Roman morals and interests was tellingly entitled *De sua ebrietate* ('On his Drunkenness').[3] In 31 BC Antony and his Egyptian queen were defeated at the naval Battle of Actium, and in its aftermath both committed suicide, but not before Cleopatra had tried a half-hearted tilt at enticing Octavian into a relationship, an attempt that was firmly rebuffed.

So, in August 30 BC, on the first day of the Egyptian New Year, the country became a Roman province. Octavian – or Augustus, as he would soon become – at once decided that Egypt was too vital to Rome's interests to be treated as just another province. It was not therefore handed over to a governor of senatorial rank, but, uniquely for the time, was to be administered by an equestrian prefect, who would also have command of Egypt's legionary complement – at first three, then reduced to two in AD 23. So tightly held was the rein on Egypt that no senator was even allowed to set foot there without prior authorisation from the Emperor. That the relationship with Egypt was always going to be an ambivalent and occasionally troubled one was presaged when Augustus decided to do a bit of tourism, visiting the tomb of Alexander the Great in Alexandria. He touched the illustrious corpse's face and, most unfortunately, broke off the great man's nose.[4]

Many aspects of Ptolemaic governance were retained, at least for a time, and Roman government officials in Egypt acquired anomalous titles, such as the *strategoi* who supervised the *nomes*, the traditional administrative divisions of the country. The peculiarities of Egypt, combined with the dry desert conditions that have favoured the survival here (as almost nowhere else) of a mass of local archives on papyrus, mean that evidence is almost superabundant, but it cannot always be translated to understand practices elsewhere in the Empire.[5]

After a long period of relative tranquillity, the later 2nd and 3rd centuries brought more troubled times to Egypt. The revolt of Avidius Cassius in 175, although based in Syria, touched Egypt, as he sought to cut off the grain supply from there to Rome, thereby reminding the central government of the vital strategic necessity of keeping a firm grip on the province. Consequently, Septimius Severus visited in 199, implementing an important series of administrative changes, which included the grant of a city council (or *boule*) to Alexandria, a privilege that it had long been denied (and long lobbied vigorously to be awarded).[6] The Emperor must have rather put a dampener on the citizens' celebrations, however, as he also conceded town councils to the chief settlement in each *nome*, some of which the cosmopolitan Alexandrians probably regarded as barely better than native villages.

Egypt, along with much of the rest of the Near East, fell into the hands of Zenobia's Palmyrenes in 269, and a further revolt, under Firmus, demanded the personal attention of Aurelian in 273–4. The province had, therefore, barely been back within the fold of the Empire for two decades when trouble broke out anew. It was probably sparked off by an edict of Diocletian of 297, which reformed the basis of the taxation system, from a purely headcount-based one to a hybrid in which both the productivity of the land and the number of people living there were taken into account (known as *capitatio-iugatio*).[7] Although this was a rational attempt to reform the budgetary system by allowing the central authorities to adjust the amount of revenue raised, depending on the needs of the time (something that, astonishingly, the Empire had not up until that time been able to do), it was seen in many circles as a naked attempt to extort more money out of the long-suffering provincials.

The immediate result was a revolt by one Lucius Domitius Domitianus, probably in the summer of 297, but this was put down early the following year by Diocletian himself.[8] Galvanised by his victory, the Emperor followed his initial reforms with a more radical overhaul of Egyptian bureaucracy and administration generally, which continued with the implementation of a problematic new system of tax assessment. It saw the introduction of a fifteen-year taxation cycle, known as indictions, whose use was to survive in one shape or another into the Middle Ages.[9] Besides these reforms, Diocletian significantly reinforced the military presence in Egypt with units now stationed in the Delta around Pelusium (Tell el-Farama), in the western oases, and at Philae, where the island became a legionary base. In Thebes (Luxor) the main temple complex was converted in part to house a legionary detachment.[10] Egypt was also now for the first time subdivided, first into two (Egypt and the Thebaid), and then later into three or even four provinces.[11]

Egypt escaped the barbarian incursions and occupation that were the fate of Roman North Africa west of Cyrenaica, and the Vandals never sought to penetrate this far east.[12] Although there is evidence of increased activity on the part of nomadic groups such as the Nobatae and Blemmyes in the far south and the eastern desert, and the abandonment of some forward positions, Roman Egypt on the whole remained prosperous (and loyal) throughout the 5th and 6th centuries. The disasters of the 7th century, therefore, must have been a complete shock to the Byzantine emperors who had come to rely so completely on Egyptian taxes, and particularly on the annual shipments of grain from Alexandria to Constantinople.

Roman Egypt fell with barely the shadow of resistance. Heraclius had in fact had little chance to re-establish central authority after the Persian occupation of the province from 617 to 627, before, a bare thirteen years later, a 4,000-strong Arab Muslim army under Amr invaded the province.[13] The imperial army was defeated at Heliopolis in July, and within two months the fortress of Babylon, the Empire's stronghold in Cairo, was under siege. The man chosen by Heraclius to lead the defence was the patriarch, Cyrus, a cleric more adept at theological hair-splitting than military stratagems. He had played a leading role in the propagation of the doctrine of Monothelitism at the Emperor's behest, a belated and ultimately futile attempt to reconcile the Monophysites and the official 'two-nature' Chalcedonians.[14] Christ, Cyrus averred,[15] although he had within him two natures, human and divine, was possessed of but a single united will (or *thelos*).[16]

Those who understood Cyrus's position protested at the unwarranted blurring of their own creeds, while, for the mass of believers, it seemed but a piece of imperially sponsored trickery. Still, his position at the helm of the Roman defence did absolutely nothing to shore up support for Byzantine rule in Egypt, while his vigorous persecution of the Coptic hierarchy undermined what little credibility he possessed. Perhaps recognising this, Cyrus negotiated the surrender of all of Egypt except Alexandria. As the Byzantine troops evacuated Babylon on Easter Day 641, they ensured that any remaining stock of goodwill amongst the Egyptians evaporated by massacring the Coptic prisoners they had been holding in the fortress prison. It took just a year for the final collapse of Alexandria to occur. Cyrus brokered a treaty with Amr in November 641, agreeing an eleven-month armistice after which all Byzantine troops would leave the city and the province would be abandoned to Arab control. In September 642, the imperial fleet weighed anchor and sailed for Constantinople, bringing to an end almost seven centuries of Roman rule.[17] Both Cyrus and Heraclius were by now dead, so neither lived to see Amr take possession of Alexandria, which, he reported to his master Omar, possessed '4,000 palaces, 4,000 baths, 400 theatres, 12,000 sellers of green vegetables, and 40,000 tributary Jews'.[18]

The city lay at the heart of Roman Egypt, as at the core of its Ptolemaic predecessor. It was one of the Empire's great urban centres; indeed, before the rise to prominence of Constantinople it was the only other metropolis that could truly be said to have rivalled Rome in wealth and splendour. However, the centuries have not been kind to the place and, since the Middle Ages, it has been Cairo that has occupied the heart of Egypt's political and cultural life. Alexandria therefore wears its past almost self-consciously, an era of greatness that has slipped frustratingly out of reach, but of which only a fugitive shadow can ever be really grasped.

The history of Alexandria began with a small fishing village named Rakotis, constructed around 1300 BC. When Alexander the Great captured Egypt from the Persians – who had held it for the best part of two centuries – in 332 BC, he at once identified the sheltered harbour as the ideal capital for his new province, one that would look outward to the eastern Mediterranean world, rather than inward to the Nile valley. It became, ultimately, the acropolis of Alexandria. The Roman city, which may have had between 200,000 and 300,000 inhabitants,[19] must have been a truly wondrous as well as a troubled place, becoming as renowned for its boisterousness and riots as for the marvels of its monuments. It was laid out on a grid pattern, with the wide main east–west street known as the Via Canopica. Beside the massive double-harbour – made up of the Great Harbour to the east, and the Eunostos to the west – lay the Caesareum, a temple honouring the memory of the deified Julius Caesar, with three huge obelisks in front, one of which now graces New York's Central Park; the other two sit on London's Embankment and in Paris on the place de la Concorde.[20]

In a bay just north of the Great Harbour lay the Pharos of Alexandria, one of the Seven Wonders of the Ancient World. Its light was visible far out to sea, employing mirrors by day[21] and a fire by night to guide mariners safely to land. It was still intact as late as the 7th century when Arculf, a Frankish pilgrim, described it.[22] Shortly thereafter, the lantern of the lighthouse came crashing down and the Alexandrians used it as a stone quarry, so that by the 12th century only the square base remained. An earthquake in 1365 finished the destruction,[23] and the rubble was removed to provide material for the Mamluk Fort Qait Bey, which now towers up block-like on the promontory. Stonework from the lighthouse still lies in the bay, and locals stroll up and down the promenade here enjoying a cooling ice-cream, surveying the scant remains of one of the ancient world's most celebrated buildings.

Another of the city's prominent landmarks was the Great Library, founded by Ptolemy I Soter as part of his Mouseion, where court-sponsored scholars could pursue philosophical research to the greater glory of the ruling house.[24] It was badly damaged during Caesar's operations against Pompey in 48 BC, although Mark Antony obligingly made matters up to Cleopatra by sequestering the almost-as-renowned collection of the Ionian city of Pergamum. But during the troubles at the end of the 4th century the whole thing was burnt to the ground, destroying a priceless trove of ancient works, the survival of even a fraction of which would have filled many of the huge gaps in our knowledge of antiquity, and the loss of which is enough to make grown classicists weep. Nothing of the old building survives, but down by the sea front, looking more like a beached whale than the 'flowing glass' promised by its publicity, the Biblioteca Alexandrina has been built in an attempt to recreate the spirit of the old. Its current selection of half a million volumes just about matches the level of its ancient model more than 2,000 years ago.

Now sitting in a poor district of the city, the surrounding streets potholed and narrow, encroached upon by a lively array of shops hung with plastic awnings, the main archaeological reserve of Alexandria, dusty and sun-baked, feels more like a building site than a window into Roman Egypt's past. The apartment blocks that crowd about on one side, and the city's public cemetery, which threatens to burst in from the other, complete the hemmed-in, claustrophobic feeling.

Two structures of great importance are located here, one Alexandria's most misnamed relic, the other perhaps its most overlooked. The first, 'Pompey's Pillar', a single towering monolith some 28 metres high, constructed of red Aswan granite and topped with a showy Corinthian capital, dominates the whole hill. Although universally known as such, it has absolutely nothing to do with Pompey.[25] When the Crusaders, in a late attempt to regain a foothold in the Levant, occupied Alexandria in 1365, they found the acropolis almost totally ruined save for the pillar. Since it was clearly of Roman origin, they simply attached to it the identity of a great Roman whose name was familiar to them, and their attractive but erroneous attribution has stuck over the centuries. Local tradition amplified this with the legend that it was put up by Caesar as an honour to his dead foe, slain on the coast not far from here.

The column was in fact erected for Diocletian, possibly around 298, as an inscription on its west side reveals.[26] It probably celebrates his suppression of the revolt of Domitius Domitianus. When the rebel leader died, his deputy, Achilleus, carried on the resistance, specifically around Alexandria, for a further three months. Diocletian was so furious at the delay in taking Alexandria that when the city finally fell, he swore to punish the citizens so severely that the massacre would not cease until the blood reached to his knees – a threat that was thwarted by his horse, which stumbled as it passed the walls, causing the Emperor's legs to touch the ground.[27]

Nearby the foundations of the Serapeum, the temple to Serapis, have been exposed,[28] but now just a jumble of drums and foundations survive, together with a subterranean annex consisting of a passage lined with niches, at one end of which a golden image of the god in the form of the bull Apis was unearthed. These unpromising remains conceal one of the last great pagan shrines in Egypt and, to boot, the final location of the Great Library of Alexandria. The temple was probably built in the time of Ptolemy III Euergetes (246–221 BC), and the worship of Serapis became almost a dynastic cult for the Ptolemaic pharaohs.[29] It seems to have been an attempt to fuse elements of the traditional Greek religious practice with traditional Egyptian beliefs, much as the Ptolemies themselves were Hellenic grafts onto an ancient Egyptian monarchy.

Just as Serapis was associated with the King, so the Ptolemaic queens became identified with Isis, and temples to the two divinities are often, as here, found together. Worship of the 'new' god Serapis spread far and wide throughout the Empire, with a temple to him and Isis being constructed some time in the first century AD on the Campus Martius in Rome. The priests were clearly identified by their shaven heads, and followed what were, to non-believing Romans, rather strange dietary restrictions, being forbidden pork, fish and wine. More startling still was the priestly habit of jumping in the River Tiber.[30] Long after the worship of many of the other traditional gods had ossified, Serapis found favour and, indeed his cult seems to have experienced something of a renaissance in the 3rd century. Amongst diehard pagans, the Serapeum at Alexandria became a symbol of resistance to the seemingly unstoppable advance of Christianity.

After years of obfuscation, some of it disingenuous, about whether private pagan worship was to be tolerated, in 391 Theodosius decided to clamp down once and for all. In a series of constitutions he decreed that sacrifices were to be banned – although this simply repeated earlier laws – at any time, day or night and in any place, including private houses. Even the lighting of fires to the traditional Roman household gods, the *lares* and *penates*, was forbidden, as were a variety of other practices regarded as pagan superstition, such as the tying of ribbons around trees and the building of impromptu altars of turf in rural areas. Theodosius did not specifically decree the destruction of pagan temples – indeed, a law of 399 enjoins their protection as public 'ornaments',[31] – but one of the Emperor's constitutions had been specifically directed to Alexandria, and there Bishop Theophilus interpreted matters quite differently.[32]

Already from 384 to 388 Maternus Cynegius, the praetorian prefect of the East, had connived in or actively encouraged attacks on pagan temples, so in Egypt the groundwork for Theophilus's notionally illegal Christian act of demolition had been well laid. The bishop led round a mob to the Serapeum, into which the pagans had barricaded themselves for protection, though Theophilus accused them of using it as a fortress from which to attack his flock. Finally, the Christians broke into the temple, but, for a brief instant, dared not attack the great cult statue of Serapis itself.[33] The pagans mocked them, saying that if they did assault it, the god would strike them down. Tentative at first, the Christians broke off the statue's jaw and, when no thunderbolt smote them, and the earth failed to open up and swallow them, they levered down the whole great image.[34] Serapis's spell was broken and many of the god's followers instantly accepted baptism. Those that did not tried to turn the whole event round to their own advantage by claiming that Serapis, saddened at the blasphemy of the Christians in violating his sanctuary, had now 'withdrawn' from Alexandria. In the shadowy and persecuted world of late-pagan piety, it may have consoled them, but it did nothing to improve their position or reverse their defeat.

Alexandria saw one of the more shocking (to modern eyes) acts of religiously inspired violence in the ancient world. Cyril, the Alexandrian patriarch from 412, had built up a body of monks, the *parabalani*, who acted as his own private army of enforcers, terrorising all who opposed him, Christian and pagan alike.[35] The city retained an elite, well-educated pagan community into the 5th century, despite all the temple-toppling and the forbidding of traditional rites. Prominent amongst them was the philosopher Hypatia, who was so well 'integrated' that her friends included even Synesius, the Bishop of Cyrene. In 415 a Christian mob that included a sprinkling of pious *parabalani* thugs attacked her carriage and dragged her to the Caesareum, where she was stripped naked, stoned to death and then her body mutilated by the mob.[36] Although the imperial government condemned the atrocity, in practice reprisals were limited to capping the membership of the *parabalani* at 500 and insisting that in future the Prefect of Egypt vet recruits.[37] Hypatia's murder, however, seemed to mark a watershed, at least in Egypt, beyond which to operate as a publicly prominent pagan became next to impossible.

Another victim of the demolition of the Serapeum was the Great Library. After the destruction of the original building in 48 BC, much of the collection that was acquired to replace the destroyed scrolls was housed here (and guides will, improbably, maintain that the whole thing was stored in the niches of the surviving underground section of the temple). When Theophilus's men demolished the rest of the temple in 391, the library's collection, which would have contained many pagan texts, but presumably little or nothing in the way of Christian writings, mostly perished with it. A later, Christian-inspired legend[38] attempted to put the blame on the Arabs in the 7th century, but the subsequent Muslim role in copying and transmitting many precious ancient texts indicates that, had they found the library intact, they would almost certainly have saved it.

The colonnade of the Serapeum was, unlike the temple itself, preserved, and a martyr memorial and small church may have been built outside the area of the original shrine. By the 12th century, however, the whole area was neglected, and in 1167 Saladin removed the pillars from the colonnade to act as an ersatz sea wall against the encroaching waves of the Mediterranean. Only 'Pompey's' (or, rather, Diocletian's) column was left in place.

A few hundred metres south-west of the pillar lies the catacomb of Kom es-Shoqafa ('the hill of potsherds'), a Roman-era necropolis of the 1st or 2nd century AD,[39] and the largest such to be located in Alexandria. The place gets its name from the enormous quantity of broken antique pottery fragments discovered here, believed to be the containers used to transport the elements of funerary (or memorial) feasts and then smashed as being too unlucky to take home because of the association they had acquired with the dead.

The entrance hardly promises much; the hill has been largely cut away to aid the excavations, leaving a flat area dotted with sarcophagi unrelated to the site, which have been gathered together from other locations in Alexandria. Above the way into the catacomb itself sits a kind of glass structure with radial struts, looking more like something out of a 1960s municipal baths than a tomb entrance. The necropolis has three levels (the lowermost flooded), and is accessed by a well down which coffins were lowered by a rope, but where modern steps now obligingly lead in a tight spiral to the first level. Almost immediately a vestibule opens out, with two alcoves to either side topped with conch-shell patterns, and down beyond this another well to allow coffins to be let down onto the second floor. This level is studded with *loculi*, niches for coffins, some hundreds in the complex as a whole. These were for richer folk; the poor were relegated to pit-burials in the floor, while the truly wealthy received memorials such as the elaborate room just to the right of the vestibule.

Two bearded serpents, *Agathodaimones*, guard the way to the left and right of this chamber, above each of them a little Medusa head to transform any intruders into stone. Inside, there are three sarcophagi, although – curiously for such a grand monument – none of them seems ever to have been occupied. The interior walls are decorated with mummification scenes, supervised by two of the gods of the dead: Sobek, the crocodile, dressed in military garb with a cloak and spear, and Anubis, the jackal god, who is robed in a more identifiably Roman military uniform, with cuirass, *gladius* and *pilum* (the Roman legionary's throwing javelin). On the tomb chamber's right-hand niche a man, possibly a prince, is shown wearing the twin crown that represents Upper and Lower Egypt, making an offering to an Apis bull. The intended occupant of the tomb must therefore have been a man with high connections, and it has been speculated that this could have been Tiberius Julius Alexander, the prefect under Nero in 66–9, who was instrumental in the suppression of a Jewish revolt centred on the city, which is said to have cost 50,000 lives.[40]

Adjacent to the main complex, and originally accessed via a separate entrance, is the area known locally as the 'Knights' tomb'.[41] A large quantity of human and equine bones were found interred together here, and it is speculated, without too firm a basis, that these were the victims of an atrocity perpetrated by the Emperor Caracalla when he visited the city in 215. Initially all had gone well, and the Emperor had visited the tomb of Alexander, decreeing that it should be blocked up, so that he himself would be the last person to gaze on the corpse of the great Macedonian. Unfortunately, the Alexandrians' joking references to Caracalla as a fratricide for his (very real) involvement in the murder of his brother Geta were rather too pungent for the Emperor's taste.[42] He ordered a massacre of the citizenry, which even resulted, in the ensuing chaos, in the deaths of a number of his own companions, whom the soldiers indiscriminately slaughtered.

In the 'tomb' itself a series of plain *loculi* and, in one corner, a relief with the remains of four murals are scant reminders of whatever did occur in this place. On the upper register of one there is a mummification scene, the deceased protected by Isis and Nephthys with wings outstretched. Below is a Greco-Roman scene, with three goddesses identified as Hera, Athene and Aphrodite, which could be a reference to the Judgement of Paris. It is not even clearly a funerary scene – though ultraviolet photography has shown the otherwise obscured figure of Persephone, a more appropriate harbinger of the Underworld – and offers no reference or hints to a holocaust of 3rd-century Alexandrians.

None of Alexandria's great public buildings have been excavated, as the sprawl of the modern conurbation makes opportunities for the investigation of its ancient predecessor all but impossible. However, in the Kom el Dikka quarter, about a kilometre through crowded streets north-east of the Serapeum, a collection of the city's more mundane buildings has given an invaluable insight into its everyday life during the 5th and 6th centuries. Its name, 'the Hill of Benches', may be taken from the rows of seats of the partly restored *odeon* (a smaller version of a theatre intended for more intimate, possibly musical, performances), which is its centrepiece. Greek characters on these, intended to show positions reserved for particular divisions of citizens or for notables, are all jumbled up and sometimes upside down, evidence of some long-ago restoration. To one side is a series of rooms, each of which has sets of benches around the wall; it is speculated that these may have served as lecture halls. In a city as famed for scholarship as Alexandria, this is not an idle supposition.[43]

Beyond this again rises the ruined shell of a medium-sized bath-complex, only the brick dome of the *caldarium* really surviving anything like intact. Much of it was badly damaged during the Persian capture of the city in 619.[44] Arrayed on the rim of the valley that has been formed by the excavations are a collection of artefacts unearthed from Alexandria harbour, including some very worn royal heads and sphinxes. The Mediterranean has only just begun to give up the remnants of the northern part of Ptolemaic and Roman Alexandria[45] romanticised as 'the City of

Cleopatra', which were inundated through successive earthquakes, and a hugely ambitious plan to build an underwater museum may one day enable visitors to view the shattered remains of the Pharos as stone fish in an archaeological aquarium.

A world away from the cooling breezes of the Mediterranean coast, the Eastern Desert is an unforgiving place in the summer, when the temperature rises above forty degrees Centigrade and there is little shade to be found. The harsh conditions attracted monks, such as Saint Anthony, the first of the Desert Fathers, who, in the early 4th century, retired deep into the desert, among the hills behind the Red Sea, where the community that grew up still survives as the oldest active monastic community in the world.[46] Save for a harvest of sand and souls, however, there seems precious little reason to linger in such a place. The Roman army must heartily have wished to spend as little time as possible here. Yet come they did, building forts and importing large workforces.

Besides the need to patrol and secure the roads leading from the Nile valley to ports such as Berenice on the Red Sea (far in the south of modern Egypt), the lure that drew the Romans here was the mineral wealth of the Eastern Desert, in particular granite and, most precious of all, porphyry. An igneous rock, formed by the cooling of volcanic magma, its purple form, 'imperial' porphyry, could only be found in a single quarry, Mons Porphyrites, in the shadow of the Gebel Dokhan ('the Hills of Smoke'), some 45 kilometres west of the Read Sea, close to modern Hurghada. An inscription unearthed in the area states that the quarries were found by a certain Caius Cominius Leugas in AD 18, during the reign of Tiberius.[47] So precious was the stone, and the imperial connotations of its colour, that it was used only for prestige projects, such as the statue of the Tetrarchs that stands at the corner of Saint Mark's Cathedral in Venice, the coffin of Constantine's mother Helena, and for imperial statuary, such as the bust of Galerius at Felix Romuliana in Moesia.[48] The imperial birthing chamber at the Palace in Constantinople was also lined in porphyry, giving rise to the term Porphyrogenitus to an imperial prince born there – by definition, after his father had become resident in the palace and thus Emperor – and thus to the English term 'born in the purple'.

From Hurghada (325 kilometres south-east of Suez along the Red Sea coast), with its ultra-modern sprawl of diving resorts and 'family' hotels insulated entirely from Egypt, both ancient and modern, the journey to Mons Porphyrites requires a strong stomach. Twisting, turning and bumping along desert tracks that seem to disappear as soon as they are

found, the way leads past one of the Roman roads that originally facili-
tated the transportation of porphyry, both to the coast and to the Nile
valley. Small piles of stones to either side show its width, and the criss-
cross tracks of four-wheel-drive vehicles mark where modern travellers
have made some use of this partially sand-buried ancient route. More
muttered curses, oaths and frantic discussions lead us finally to the Wadi
Umm Sidri, the gateway to the Gebel Dokhan. Here, in a bleak and
scorched stony desert valley overlooked by the barren jagged peaks of
the Gebel, lies a loading ramp, some 2 metres high and 20 metres long,
looking incongruously like the horse-mounting ramp at Petra. But the
desert is not good horse country, and it would have been camels or mules
that brought the porphyry from the mines, to be transferred here to
larger carts for the far longer stage westwards to the Nile.[49]

Half an hour to the west lies the fort of Badia, which stood guard
on the desert road just south of the main settlements at Mons
Porphyrites. On one side of the fort 'the Hills of Smoke' rise up in the
distance, while to the south the mountains of the Wadi Qattar tower,
giving a sense of grimness and, if this is possible in the wide-open
desert, of claustrophobia. The fort, built of dark local stone, standing
out starkly against the yellow ochre of the desert, is about 40 metres
square, with the remains of eight or nine towers still visible, the stones
used to construct it looking as though they are struggling to keep their
heads above the encroaching sands. The interior buildings are all ruinous,
but pottery and coins indicate that the fort may have been retained as
late as the 6th century.[50]

About 50 metres to the west of the main fort is a curious circular
enclosure, surrounded by a wall around 4 metres high constructed of
small stones. In the centre stands a rocky outcrop, on the top of which
a large hole has been gouged. My guide insists that this was made by
the local Bedouin digging for treasure, but they must have had strong
shovels indeed to dent the rock, and the alternative theory that it was
blasted away with dynamite carries more credibility. Still, quite why the
Romans chose to build a wall around a rock in the first place is unclear.

Finally, a series of upright columns on a rise in the wadi mark the
castle that guarded the settlement at Mons Porphyrites itself. Comforting
plans drawn in the 1950s[51] show a typical square shape with projecting
circular angle-towers, and well-defined rooms. An awkward scramble up
the *castellum*'s mound, which is itself slowly collapsing into the wadi
below, reveals that the five columns are part of the structure of a water
cistern some 2 metres deep. The rest is a chaos of collapsed walls and
maze-like passages.

Descending from the fort, slipping and sliding, we see that the treacherous stones are mixed with a stratum of ancient pottery and even, in
places, with small chunks of the precious porphyry, its white-flecked
purple core standing out clearly against the more subdued colours of
the fort's building material. Just beside the fort lie the shattered remains
of a small Isis temple,[52] while a more substantial testament to the spiritual needs of the original inhabitants, a temple to Serapis, sits on a small
promontory 100 metres down the wadi. Several fallen columns and a
couple of column bases lie scattered around, but the stone itself is bright
and smooth, looking astonishingly as though it was cut only a few weeks
ago. A fallen lintel bears a dedication to 'Zeus Helios Great Serapis' and
carries the name of Rammius Martialis, which dates it to 117–19, when
he was governor of Egypt.[53]

Down on the wadi floor, five pillars ring an ancient well, now dried
up and stuffed full of rubbish and debris. On several of the pillars are
scratched stylised pictures of sailing ships, although from what era they
come is not immediately clear. The place was certainly used as a watering
hole, probably for many centuries after the Romans abandoned the mines
in the 4th century.

Who exactly provided the workforce for Mons Porphyrites and for its
sister quarries at Mons Claudianus 50 kilometres or so to the south has
been the matter of some debate. The theory that the workers were
convicts seems logical to anyone who has spent more than five minutes
in the direct sunlight of the wadi basin, but *ostraka* – discarded pot-sherds
used like notepaper – found at Mons Claudianus indicate that the workers
there, at least, were free.[54] One has to presume that the rates of pay to
attract the miners to this desolate spot must have been significantly over
the norm. They were certainly well provided for in other ways; the
remains of food found at Mons Claudianus indicate a surprisingly rich
diet, including such luxury items as artichokes, walnuts, watermelons
and oysters.

On the way to Mons Claudianus we come across a modern counterpart to the ancient quarry-workers, for the Egyptian government has
opened up mines at several points in the area to exploit the still-rich
mineral seams. He is walking to the nearest café and says it will take
him two hours to get there. Sadly we are going in the opposite direction and can offer him only water and a cigarette. By truck, the 50
kilometres still take more than two hours, for we are cutting south across
the desert roads made by the Romans and so are again caught up in a
confusing succession of switchbacks, false trails and detours to reach
our destination. Every so often we pass by a flimsy lean-to of wood or,

on occasion, of plastic sheeting propped against pillars. A few Bedouin families still live in this wilderness, but diminished rainfall over the last thirty years has made life all but impossible, and only the hardiest or most desperate still eke out a living here.

Although the name of Mons Claudianus implies that it was founded during the reign of Claudius, there is in fact no evidence of settlement before the time of Domitian.[55] The Romans came for the high quality of the white granite to be found here, exporting some of the columns as far afield as Rome itself, where they were used in the construction of Trajan's forum. The fort that guarded the village and quarries sits in the Wadi Umm Hussein, around 70 metres square, and is well preserved, its walls retaining some of the original interval towers. Inside, less is clear; a labyrinthine assortment of rooms wind through the interior, some still with the original stone slabs used as lintels for the door. The roofs, however, are long gone; they may originally have been made from rush matting, providing much-needed shade against the relentless sun.

The outline of wall foundations to the west of the fort, looking like a sun-scorched chequers board, is in fact what remains of the accommodation for those animals unlucky enough to spend their hot and thirsty lives here. To the north, up the slope that leads to the granite quarries themselves, lies a ruined Temple of Serapis. A few fallen column bases and part of the gable end of the building are all that survive, together with a part-buried altar containing an inscription by Annius Rufus, prefect of the XV Apollinaris legion, who was superintendent of the works of Mons Claudianus during the time of Trajan. It was here, in the abandoned stone, that the earliest known mention of the quarry's name was found.[56]

Up the hillside, the remains of the ramp along which the huge granite columns were brought from the quarry are visible, with metre-high cairns of stones to either side, presumably as part of a system to stop the columns rolling away uncontrollably down the ramp and onto the unfortunate camp below. Scattered around this area are more than 100 quarries, and here and there lie the remains of the workings, blocks that were left behind because they cracked during the extraction process or had other defects. Quarrying the stone involved digging trenches into the rock with hammers and picks, and then using chisels to cut wedge-holes into the granite. In one small quarry north-east of the fortress lie the remains of a monumental column, which would have been nearly 20 metres long had it not cracked during its excavation. So determined were the quarrymen to save this leviathan, however, that they used giant iron rods to staple together the cracked section, but it must have split again and they were forced to abandon it for good. Had it not shattered, it must have been destined for a truly massive structure, rivalling that of the Temple of Jupiter in Baalbek, which contains the highest surviving columns in the Roman world.[57]

From the quarry ramps there is a spectacular view over the fort and the wadi below. As the workers here seem to have been free men, they were paid between 28 and 47 drachmae a month, to encourage them to operate in such an unforgiving climate – somewhat more (but not spectacularly so) than the average civilian labourer in the country as a whole.[58] One is again struck by the sheer arid desolation of the place. Indeed, it may have been a shortage of water that caused the Romans to abandon Mons Claudianus some time in the mid-3rd century. It was certainly not the exhaustion of the granite mines, for quarrying still goes on today. Although Mons Porphyrites was probably active for at least a century longer, the cessation of this important economic activity in the Eastern Desert probably also had a connection with a decreasing level of security in the province generally, as nomadic tribes such as the Blemmyes and Nobatae to the south became increasingly emboldened in their raiding.

From Hurghada, it is a hot 240-kilometre drive south-west across the desert to Luxor that brings the convoys of foreigners to the Nile valley, its palm trees and the lush vegetation lining the river coming as a shock to incomers from both east and west. The relief must have been great in antiquity to travellers whose budgeting of food and water to sustain them marked time in days rather than the hours of today's air-conditioned tourists. It is impossible in Luxor not to be conscious of ancient Egypt and its native culture. The huge hypostyle hall of the Karnak temple, with its enormous columns and their mushroom-like capitals and the rows of sphinxes that led in a ceremonial way to the temple entrance; the huge pylon (gateway) to the Luxor temple; not to mention the funerary temples of the Valley of the Kings on the west bank of the Nile – all these (though not of course, the spectacular tomb painting that we now know was contained in pharaonic tombs such as that of Tutankhamun) would have been visible to the Roman rulers of Egypt. It is almost overwhelming, and it is little surprise that in Egypt, of all places, Roman culture and monuments – except in the very latest period – seem to hang back in the shadows, peeping out discreetly, and often deliberately blending themselves in with pre-existing temples and other buildings.

At the back of the Luxor temple lies a temple court that was converted during the late 3rd century to serve as a hall for the imperial cult, with an apse sliced into the back of the pharaonic stone. Barely visible are the remains of frescoes showing four men dressed in rich, late-Roman court costume. Beneath the coloured plaster, the earlier hieroglyphic inscriptions poke through; much was stripped away in the 19th century by souvenir-seekers, who were more interested in the earlier Egyptian layers than the Roman accretions. The modifications were probably made around 298, after the revolt of Domitianus, when Diocletian was keen to stamp his authority (and his image) on the province.

The four figures are in fact the Tetrarchs: Maximian, Galerius, Constantius I and, carrying a golden sceptre, Diocletian himself. Drawings made before the frescoes were destroyed also show an array of richly attired courtiers, with the hems of their robes beautifully decorated and wearing the *cingula*,[59] the elaborate belts that signified senior office (both civilian and military). When Diocletian travelled down the Nile (as Hadrian had before him) in 298, he passed as far as Aswan, although whether he stopped at Luxor is unclear. For the most part, the province rarely saw Roman emperors, although – as the dedication for Constantine I by a *dux* of Thebes (the Roman name of Luxor) reveals – it was as politic here as anywhere to display loyalty to the centre in as public and enduring a fashion as possible.

The principal Roman settlement in the far south of Egypt was (as it had been in pharaonic times) more than 200 kilometres upstream from Thebes, at Syene, which now largely lies under the rapidly growing city of Aswan. This far to the south, the blue strip of the Nile barely cools those sailing upon it, let alone the tired legs of those trudging the corniche beside its banks. Even the hustlers importuning passers-by to attend the Nubian market nearby (which is 'only on today, tomorrow gone') seem to do so with a weary air, calculating that too unmeasured a motion will be punished harshly by the sun's pitiless gaze. Colonisation in this region was a slow business, and the territory between here and Primis (Qasr Ibrim) some 150 kilometres further south, saw an ebb and flow of Roman control over the centuries that caused far less drama than similar adjustments elsewhere in the Empire. The strategic nature of Syene itself stemmed from its location at the first cataract of the Nile, a set of rapids that made river transportation further south impossible without a time-consuming portage to the clear water beyond the obstacle. It served as a most convenient trading centre, and a springboard for expeditions further south; and, though the Romans did maintain garrisons further into Nubia – a general region that included the lands both to the north and south of the provincial border – Syene was as far as their writ could be said to have run securely.

Almost nothing now remains of Roman Syene, although as late as 1839 the artist David Roberts reported that a Roman-era wall could be seen on a promontory on the island of Elephantine, which sits in the Nile just opposite Aswan.[60] To reach it, with its Egyptian settlement pre-dating even that of Syene, requires a short voyage in a felucca, the traditional shallow-bottomed sailboat that plies the Nile around Aswan, whose captains' roguish airs and all-too-expected demands for extra baksheesh are one of the area's less endearing charms. The scattered remains, baking in forty-degree heat, seem to sweat a light dust that cakes both them and any visitors importunate enough to brave the midday blaze. The ancient town of Yebu, which dates from early dynastic times, covers the whole of the south of the island, and its most impressive remains are the Temple of Khnum, dating from the Middle Kingdom (around 1500 BC). Under the Roman occupation the temple was embellished by Antoninus Pius, although Roman troops who were garrisoned on the island also converted part of the area around the temple to act as barracks,[61] and in 391, under Theodosius, a portion of the precinct was converted into a church, in line with that emperor's avowed policy of closing down those pagan places of worship that still functioned.[62]

On the side of the island facing Syene lies a Nilometer down a set of restored steps. This was a device for predicting the rise of the river during its annual inundation, thereby determining the likely abundance (or dearth) of the succeeding harvest and so allowing the government to assess the amount of taxes it was likely to receive. As Pliny the Elder noted, a rise of 5.5 metres meant famine, one of 6.75 metres was pleasing, while one of 7 metres brought great delight; the highest on record was one of 8 metres during the reign of Claudius.[63]

Syene acted as the gateway to Roman Nubia. It was in this region that the only really serious threat to Roman control of southern Egypt lay under the early Empire. The kingdom of Meroë, whose base was several hundred kilometres down the Nile towards the fourth cataract, and whose culture had been strongly influenced by that of later pharaonic Egypt, was at the peak of its power in the 1st century BC and 1st century AD. Relations with its new neighbour to the north were at first quite hostile. In 29 BC, a peace treaty between the two sides established a buffer state between the first and second cataracts,[64] so that the border of Roman Egypt lay officially just south of Syene. The arrangement did not last, and in 25 BC the Meroites invaded Egypt. The Romans were finally victorious, penetrating as far as the Meroite capital of Napata, some 500 kilometres south of Aswan. In the ensuing treaty of 21 BC, which this time did largely hold, the buffer state was abolished and the border transferred further south to lie at Hieraskyaminos (Maharaqqa), at an intermediate point between the first and second cataracts.[65]

The land in this region is much poorer than in the Nile valley to the north. The cliffs of the desert plateau hem in the river, providing little space for agriculture, in contrast to the fertile flood plain that permitted such rich harvests in the lower reaches of Egypt. Between Syene and Hieraskyaminos the Romans built around a dozen settlements and forts in a region they named the Dodekaschoeonos. Much of this area, however, has been inundated by the rise in water level associated with the construction of the Aswan High Dam. This led to the creation of Lake Nasser, beneath whose waters those monuments that were not rescued and transferred elsewhere now lie.

As time wore on, the main threat to Roman control of the region came not from the Meroites, whose centre of political gravity shifted further south, but from the Blemmyes of the Eastern Desert, who exploited the power vacuum that arose. The tribe has received a generally bad press in ancient sources. Pliny the Elder, in his *Historia Naturalis*, reports that they had no heads, and that their eyes, noses and mouths were instead situated on their chests.[66] Subsequent accounts do not confirm Pliny's fantastical physiognomy, but the group remained forever just outside the imperial ken, never as menacing as the tribes of the Rhine or Danube, but posing just enough of a threat to security to make life in the south of Egypt somewhat uneasy.

The Romans' hold on the isolated positions of Hieraskyaminos and Primis was growing tenuous by the mid-3rd century and the Blemmyes launched an invasion at the time of Decius and again during Aurelian's reign, when the Empire's position in the whole of Egypt was critically endangered. At the time of Probus, a Blemmye expeditionary force captured several cities in Upper Egypt and it took a major military effort to dislodge them.[67] It was thus that Diocletian – after his victory over Domitius Domitianus in 298, and a journey to the south that included a series of punitive raids on the Blemmyes and other desert tribes – decided that Roman forces would be withdrawn from Nubia.[68]

Diocletian then tried to use the Nubians as a buffer against the Blemmyes, though the rights of the latter to travel to their traditional cult centre at the Temple of Isis at Philae were guaranteed, presumably as a means of maintaining at least some level of contact with them. Even the most persecuting of Christian emperors, such as Constantius II and Theodosius I, took no action against the Philae temple, when the idols were being overthrown all over the rest of the Empire. It was only in 532 that Justinian finally dared order the doors of the shrine to be shut, snuffing out the last spark of organised paganism in the Empire.

During the latter part of his reign, Theodosius II had been forced to take the radical step of uniting the civilian and military administrations of the province of Thebais, which included all of southern Egypt from Thebes (Luxor) to Syene (Aswan), reversing the tendency since Diocletian to keep them separate. It seems that there must have been something approaching an emergency. Indeed, it was in 450 that the cleric Nestorius wrote of the Blemmye raid that temporarily took him prisoner.[69] The same year the Blemmyes and their neighbours, the Nobatae, were defeated by the *dux* Marcianus and agreed to a peace treaty, but when one of the Roman envoys, Maximianus, died, they took this as an excuse to begin their raids anew.

Other accounts of the Blemmyes are rather sparse, but the poet and diplomat Olympiodorus of Thebes spent a few days among them in 421. The Blemmye chieftains had been so impressed by his reputation that, when they heard he was staying at Syene, they issued an invitation for him to visit in person. The poet asked the tribe's priests, who probably served at the Temple of Isis and Mandulis at Talmis, for permission to see the emerald mines about which he had heard. The Blemmye king, unfortunately, refused to allow it, and after five days Olympiodorus went on his way. His work, which survives only in fragments, also includes an account of an embassy that he accompanied to Donatus, King of the Huns, in 412–13, where he noted the excellent archery ability of the Hunnish warriors. Whether Olympiodorus was accompanied on either occasion by his pet parrot, which he writes about with fondness and which he had taught to sing sea-shanties, dance and say its owner's name, is not recorded.[70]

The temple complex at Philae, the first major archaeological site to the south of Syene and one of Egypt's most splendid relics, lay just beyond the first cataract of the Nile, and was connected to Syene by a road on the east bank, since the rapids made communication by river impossible. Close by was the legionary camp of the I Maximiana, one of the new units established under the Tetrarchs to complement the three auxiliary cohorts that had previously patrolled the area. The camp was enclosed within a protective wall that ran right the way up to Syene, defending the road from marauders. It was not a Roman system in origin, for the walled road may date from the Middle Kingdom, but it was certainly maintained at least until the 4th century AD.[71]

The complex rises up on an island in the Nile, its buildings sharply defined against the river and the searing blue of the sky. This is not in fact the original island, for that was nearly drowned by the Aswan High Dam works, and the archaeologists moved the monuments wholesale to a neighbouring one, which they then landscaped to be as close as possible to the original. It is a little smaller, however, and so the main axis of the temple was not entirely preserved.

Despite the light scatter of early-morning tourists zipping to and fro in motor launches, which rather shatter the fragile tranquillity of the place, it is still a hugely impressive complex. The fancy that the Victorian traveller Amelia Edwards said that a 'procession of white-robed priests bearing aloft the veiled ark of God' might well come round the corner is, though, just a little too whimsical.[72] The Temple of Isis, that last bastion of Blemmye paganism, is of course the most important building, entered by a vestibule constructed under Nectanebo (360–343 BC) during the 30th Dynasty, which features a striking row of columns crowned with capitals in the form of the cow-headed goddess Hathor. To the right of the main pylon, an inscription incised by Napoleon's troops on their victorious entry into Egypt in 1799 defaces the wall, but it is beyond this, in the main part of the sanctuary, that the principal Roman interest lies.

In 9 BC, Augustus permitted a small temple to be built at the north end of the island, thereby beginning the involvement of several emperors in cult worship at Philae. On its walls, Augustus himself is shown in a relief with Buto, goddess of the north. Later, Claudius ordered the erection of a temple to the minor god Harendotes, and successive additions were made under Trajan, Hadrian and as late as Diocletian's reign.

The hypostyle hall – its dark atmosphere, barely penetrated by the sun, offering a cool retreat to visitors and twittering birds alike – was partly converted into a church in Coptic times, with the remains of frescoes of Jesus and Mary just showing, together with more boldly incised crosses on the columns. In the eastern corner of the hall, an altar and a niche have been carved out, evidence that the temple was not completely abandoned in the period after the final suppression of pagan worship in the 530s, and that the adherents of the new religion commandeered it to expunge it of its (to them) demonic connections.

Just outside the main temple to the west is a small gateway overlooking the river, constructed under Hadrian (from whom it takes its popular name of 'Hadrian's gate') near the Claudian Temple of Harendotes. On it is an unusual depiction of the cataract of the Nile, opposite which Isis and Nephthys are seen presenting the two crowns of Upper and Lower Egypt to the falcon-headed sky god Horus, all quite canonical scenes and apparently uninfluenced by the new Roman benefactors, who are themselves immortalised in relief around the corner. On the eastern part of the island lies Philae's most imposing Roman structure, the Kiosk of Trajan – which remained unfinished by the time of the Emperor's death. It is an almost perfect classical-style peripteral temple, but with rather (for a Roman) anomalous acanthus-leaf capitals, its solid and angular bulk gracing a hundred posters of Philae. Inside, the walls are scored by dozens of graffiti from less-than-punctilious travellers, including one, in impeccable Latin, for Tsar Alexander I of Russia.

Off by the waterside, the ruins of a triumphal arch – just the side-entrances now staring out towards the river – represent the 'Gate of Diocletian', the last major Roman construction on the island, commemorating the emperor whose decision to pull out of Nubia and bring the frontier back to Syene left Philae in the hands of the Blemmyes. It was really only the penetration of Christianity further south into Nubia (sponsored by Theodora, Justinian's wife) that neutralised opposition from the desert tribes and permitted the final closure of the Philae temples in the mid-6th century.

It was an inscription at Philae that commemorated the Romans' furthest southward thrust from Egypt, when Caius Petronius was prefect of the province, probably in late 25 BC. Although in the end Petronius's attack on Meroë came to nothing, a curious expedition was despatched in AD 61, during the reign of Nero, consisting of a small number of the praetorian guard, including two centurions.[73] They penetrated even further than Petronius had done, first reaching the city of Meroë itself, only 150 kilometres north of modern Khartoum. On their route they saw parakeets, monkeys and rhinoceroses, and, once at Meroë, were given guides who led them south down the White Nile to an area of 'great marshes', which has been interpreted to mean an area near Malakal, more than 500 kilometres south of Khartoum. The purpose of the expedition is unclear, but there are indications in 68 that Nero had sent additional troops to Egypt to prepare for a campaign in the south, only to be forced to recall them when the revolt of Vindex broke out in Gaul.[74] To have contemplated annexing such a huge swathe of territory would probably have exceeded even the grand designs of the mercurial Nero. Whatever the reason, the little group of praetorians penetrated further into Africa than any Romans before or after them, and probably further than any other European power would reach until the Portuguese in the 16th century.

The Temple of Kalabsha (or Talmis, its ancient name) originally lay about 50 kilometres down the Nile from Philae, but since the construction of the Aswan High Dam it has sat on an island just to the south of the dam itself. The boatman who takes us there on his rather decrepit-looking motor-launch (optimistically named *Cleopatra*, for it is definitely not a thing of beauty) confides that we are the first visitors he has ferried for more than a week, as busy schedules will not permit most tourists more than a cursory look at Philae before they move on elsewhere.

The temple was cut into 13,000 blocks for its transportation north, but does not seem much the worse for it. Approached by a rather precipitous bridge with a steeply angled hump, the main pylon at the front of the temple has a noticeable tilt, leading into an open courtyard, closely set with pillars and decorated with reliefs of Horus and Thoth, the ibis-headed scribe of the gods. Although begun under Tuthmosis III in the 15th century BC, a great deal of it was constructed under Augustus (who is shown standing before Horus), with Caligula and Trajan in turn adding reliefs to the temple decorations. The open court also served as a suitably public place for inscriptions intended for a wider audience. These include one set in the wall facing the main pylon by Silko, King of the Nobatae, in about 543, boasting of his defeat of the Blemmyes.[75] Poor Silko, his inscription is almost always referred to as being in 'bad Greek', with his grammatical infelicities immortalised for all to see. Even worse for his reputation, a papyrus found at Primis (Qasr Ibrim) in the very far south of the province indicates that it was Phonene, King of the Blemmyes, who won the victory and not Silko at all.[76] On the next-door wall is a text by Aurelius Besarion, who was governor around 248,[77] in which he commands the exclusion of all pigs from the temple grounds, an injunction that conjures up a rather strange image of the situation before he had the swine chased out of the shrine. The small hypostyle hall features an image of Trajan offering sacrifice to Mandulis (the Kushite god to whom the temple is dedicated) and a beautiful series of reliefs in a small chapel at the back.

Two hundred and eighty kilometres north-west of Aswan, Kharga was known by the Romans simply as 'The Oasis'. It was the closest to the Nile valley of the settlements in the Western Desert and therefore the easiest of access. Nonetheless, it was still extremely remote and this, and the burning summer heat, made it a favourite place of exile for those who had fallen into imperial disfavour. The satirist Juvenal, who unwisely angered the rather touchy Emperor Domitian, was exiled to Egypt and seems to have spent part of his banishment in Kharga. In the mid-5th century Nestorius, the deposed patriarch of Alexandria, spent some of his years of banishment here, rather than the originally designated and substantially more comfortable place of exile at Petra.[78]

The capital of the oasis in antiquity was Hibis, where one of the most ancient buildings in the oasis, the Temple of Amon-Ra, stands, probably begun by the pharaoh Apries around 588 BC. Discovered here was the official report of a commission sent out in AD 246/9 to investigate the agricultural resources of Egypt. Addressed to Marcellus and Salutaris (the heads of the commission, based in Alexandria), it found that the majority of water sources and reservoirs in the oasis were on land that was uncultivated or had been abandoned. It was a sign, perhaps, of a contracting economy, and a hint of trouble in the oases.[79] By the mid-4th century there were indications of disturbances, with a layer of burning in the Christian buildings that had sprung up outside the Hibis temple. More incontrovertible evidence of insecurity comes in 450 when the Blemmyes invaded and carried off a large number of prisoners, including Nestorius.

Just a kilometre from the temple of Hibis, in the central part of the oasis, lies the early-Christian necropolis at Bagawat, containing hundreds of tombs grouped around a central church. It is a veritable city of the dead, set on a low sandy slope, the landscape studded with low, square blocks of mud-brick. The fancier tombs have arcaded façades and their architectural embellishments make them seem more like a monastic cloister than a graveyard. Between the mausolea run narrow lanes, accentuating the eerie feeling that somewhere, just around the corner, a brown-clad monk will walk by intoning the Coptic liturgy.

The cemetery was in use from pharaonic times, and there are tombs as old as the 6th Dynasty.[80] When the Christians took it over, they did not abandon their ancestral practice of mummification, despite the fact that the religious motivation for embalming the dead had vanished. Perhaps the early-Christian focus on the actual physical resurrection of the body touched a chord with more traditionally minded Egyptians, who considered that they had best ensure that the corpse was kept in good condition for its judgement date with the almighty. The actual graves, which were pits dug into the earth floor of the surrounding mausoleum, were, sadly, mostly robbed and ransacked long ago, but the internal decoration of several survives.

The Chapel of Peace's frescoes, faded now despite the roof and the cool, dry conditions in the tomb, depict Adam and Eve after their expulsion from the Garden, the sacrifice of Isaac and a dozen other biblical scenes. The nearby Chapel of Exodus, one of the oldest of the Christian chapels,[81] contains another wealth of beautifully crafted wall paintings crammed into the dome of a space no greater than 3 metres square. Moses is seen leading the Israelites out of Egypt, pursued by a rather dapper-looking pharaoh sporting a very fine headdress. Jonah, meanwhile, is depicted being swallowed up by the whale, which looks rather more like an irritated dragon than a sea creature. Here, in the deep desert, where temperatures regularly soar over forty degrees, the monkish artists can be forgiven for having their imaginations turned far more to fire than water.

Christianity has a very ancient pedigree in Egypt, and experienced a development all of its own. Egyptian tradition claims Saint Mark as the founder of their church, drawn by a vision to sail from Cyrene, his native town (in modern Libya), to Alexandria, where he preached for two years before the local pagans dragged him through the streets until he died.[82] It is more than likely that Christianity first took hold among the Greek-speaking Jews of Alexandria, but after this community was decimated during the Jewish revolt of 115–117 the new faith was forced to look more widely, and into the countryside, for adherents. Egypt produced more than its fair share of theologians, including one of the very earliest, Origen – whose name actually means 'Born of Horus' – who flourished in the early 3rd century and whose doctrine of the pre-existence of souls before the creation of the physical universe influenced later mysticism, but led to the eventual condemnation of his writings under Justinian in 543.[83]

Egypt suffered, too, at the time of the persecutions ordered by Decius in 250, and by Diocletian in 303. So harsh were conditions during Diocletian's Great Persecution, and so many Christians killed by the authorities, that the Egyptian Coptic Church for ever after dated its calendar, the Era of the Martyrs, from its beginning. The aftermath of the persecution led to a bitter split in the Egyptian Church, not dissimilar to the Donatist schism that simultaneously afflicted the Latin-speaking provinces further west.[84] Its root was the flight of Peter, the Bishop of Alexandria in 304, who was seeking to escape a possible death sentence for refusing to make sacrifice to the Emperor, as decreed by the perse-cuting imperial edicts. The more rigorist Bishop of Lycopolis,[85] Melitius, viewed this as a betrayal of the faith. Even though Peter was in fact eventually martyred in 311, Melitius established what was in effect an alternative Church, which by 327 had as many bishops as the official one. In 334, the Melitians even attempted to depose the orthodox patriarch of Alexandria, Athanasius, by accusing him of murdering a bishop named Arsenius. The patriarch, however, was able to prove incontrovertibly that the charges against him were trumped up, by having his agents seize the still-living Arsenius from his bolthole in Berytus (Beirut). Athanasius was, however, deposed by the Synod of Tyre the next year on charges – quite possibly entirely justified[86] – of having his followers beat up Melitian bishops. On and off over the next forty years he would spend fifteen years in exile, suffering no fewer than five sentences of banishment.[87]

The Melitians, meanwhile – unlike the parallel Donatist movements in the provinces of Numidia and Africa – faded away. There were quite enough Christian viewpoints competing for primacy in the Egyptian Church, with Arians and Monophysites and others all striving to present themselves as national champions in opposition to the central church authorities in Constantinople; and Melitianism, differentiated only in matters of hierarchy rather than doctrine, found insufficient room to take root in the long term.

Around 50 kilometres to the north-west of Bagawat lies Qasr Labekha, one of the chain of forts by which the Romans supervised the desert routes, this one placed strategically athwart the junction between two roads, one leading south towards the capital at Hibis, and the other to the west towards the Dakhleh oasis. Approaching on dirt roads that seem to wend aimlessly across the flat stony ground, the fort comes into sight on the prominent mound on the floor of a wadi. Beyond it, low hills and escarpments stretch red-brown fingers through the desert as far as the eye can see. From a distance the fort's high walls and massive round towers seem complete, save for the part obscured by a huge bank of sand piled up against it by the biting wind. Yet, rounding the corner, this turns out to be an illusion, and on two sides the walls are missing and the interior of the fort consists of mounds of rubble. It is, nonetheless, an impressive site, where conditions for the soldiers would have been difficult on account of the heat, but not as utterly remote as it seems, for it was just 20 kilometres to the west to the neighbouring fort of Ain Umm Dabadib (whose rectangular rather than round towers are unique in the Western Desert).[88]

In the southern portion of the Great Oasis security was provided by the large fort of Qasr al-Ghieita ('Fort of the Little Garden'), which, as was common practice in the Western Desert, was constructed around a much earlier temple, of the gods Amun, Mutt and Khans, that was built during the Persian occupation of Egypt under Darius I (552–486 BC), but was maintained into late-Ptolemaic times. More direct evidence of Roman involvement in the upkeep of the traditional Egyptian cults is provided by Tchonemyris (Qasr al-Zaiyan), a short distance to the south of al-Ghieita. Partly enclosed by a mud-brick wall, the sanctuary has something of the appearance of a small fort from the outside, but a processional way leads through to a much more obviously religious structure, a low kiosk temple, built in Ptolemaic times and dedicated to

'Amun of Hibis'. An inscription commemorates its restoration at the time of Antoninus Pius, during the governorate of Avidius Heliodorus.[89]

Right at the southern edge of the Great Oasis, beyond which to the south there is only desert, lie the temple and fort of Dush (ancient Kysis). Atop a hill the broken remains of the fort may originally date from Ptolemaic times, but it was at the very least adapted and may have been enlarged for Roman use to supervise the route that led eastwards towards the Nile at Edfu, a week's march away, and another that went southwards towards Darfur, a road that in the Middle Ages became known as the Darb al-Arbain, 'the forty days' road', after the length of time it took to traverse it, and which became a principal conduit for the slave trade.

The ground between the fort and the temple contains a scattering of building foundations, but is covered with a mass of pottery remains, from small fragments to almost complete pots, which it takes great concentration on the part of the visitor not to crunch underfoot. The view across the desert here is alluring and disturbing in equal measure, for there is nothing to break the monotony of the endless desolation, save a few minor variations in the intensity of the sand's browny-orange. The temple comes almost as a surprise, for while all else here seems to be subsiding slowly into the earth, or being ground away by the desert winds, the courtyard and hypostyle hall are oddly fresh and complete. Built under Domitian, additions were made by Trajan and Hadrian and the temple, originally for Osiris, also honoured the cult of Serapis.[90]

From the Temple at Hibis, the modern road west roughly follows the line of the traditional route from Kharga to the Dakhleh Oasis. Largely flat, the unremitting desert does not invite travellers to linger, though here and there Roman-era caravan halts existed, a reminder that ancient travellers did not have the luxury of moving from one oasis to the other within a few hours; for them it meant long, hot and thirsty days in the desert – prey, once out of the protective orbit of the nearest forts, to any passing bandit that took a fancy to their goods. Known in ancient times as the 'Small Oasis', Dakhleh – whose eastern reaches lie around 120 kilometres west of Kharga – possessed a reasonably large population supporting four major settlements, and seems to have undergone something of a boom in the early Roman period.

Once a prosperous market town, Kellis, or Asmant el-Kharab ('the ruined'), lies a kilometre down a dirt track off the main road on the eastern edge of the oasis. It looks in ever-present danger of final inundation by the fine sand that blows in from deeper in the desert, its buildings engaged in a constant game of hide-and-seek between concealment by nature and excavation by archaeologists. By the guardian's hut, partly uncovered, a series of barrel vaults seem like the roof of a bath-house. Two low rectangular structures are temples, one with small fragments of wall plaster surviving in yellows and sky-blues, but little trace of the original internal structure. In the main temple complex an inscription was discovered, dedicating it both to Tithoes, the 'Master of the Demons', and to the 'son of the divine Hadrian' – that is to say, Antoninus Pius. One wonders what the sedate and gentle Antoninus would have thought of the juxtaposition.

Nearby, over fields of pottery, abandoned for the many centuries of Kellis's settlement, lies a palaeo-Christian church, newly excavated. Already the desert has begun to reclaim it, and only part of the columns of two aisles and a small apse poke out of the sand. More visible are the remains of the oldest church in the oasis, and one of the most ancient in Egypt, built inside a Ptolemaic-era temple, and occupying around one-third of the original structure's 50-metre length. The later, lower-quality bricks stand out against the fineness of the sandstone used to build its predecessor. The church dates from the middle of the 4th century, and so, although from after the period of the Great Persecution, it is a vener-able place of worship indeed.

It was in a comparatively humble residential area that Kellis gave up its greatest and most unexpected treasure to date.[91] A large quantity of Manichaean documents from the mid-4th century have been found among the houses, including at least eighteen psalms and a number of catechisms in both Greek and Coptic. Their letters, full of phrases such as 'the members of the Holy Church', indicate that they saw themselves as a chosen elect and the true followers of Jesus Christ, in a sense the only real Christians. Other Christians most certainly did not regard the Manichaeans as in any way belonging to their number and particularly reviled them, failing to accord them the same toleration that they them-selves received after the Edict of Milan in 313. It seems that a fair proportion of the towns' populations may have subscribed to the dualist creed, but by the 4th century Manichaeism, which had arrived in Egypt via Alexandria around 260,[92] was very much a community under siege, and Kellis may have been one of its last strongholds in the province. Life there was not all about religion, however, and equally valuable papyri were found detailing a mass of financial and legal transactions, including what is possibly the last-recorded sale of a slave in Egypt, by Aurelius Psais of an unnamed girl to Aurelius Tithoes, a carpenter, in AD 362.[93]

Dakhleh in general lacks the Roman-era forts that dot the rest of the oases, but a section of the town's wall still stands, some 15–20 metres long, with 8 metres or so poking out of the sand, which must have provided some level of security for Kellis. Further exploration of the walls' internal chambers is discouraged by the nest of vipers that do service for the long-departed guards.

The largest Roman necropolis in Dakhleh lies in the west at El-Muzawakka ('the decorated hill'), which takes its name from the painted tombs of Petosiris and Petubastis, the most notable in the cemetery, and in which Petosiris is depicted dressed Roman-style, but otherwise surrounded by Egyptian funerary imagery. The key to the burial chambers has, however, been confiscated by a French archaeologist, afraid of the effect of the breath of too many casual visitors on the fragile wall paintings, and instead the guardian shows us a selection of grizzled mummies and several graves dotted around the hillside that are open to the air, and from which an embalmed hand or a mummified head sticks out, staring balefully through a sand-bleared haze at the modern intruders.

At Magoub, on the western edge of the Dakhleh Oasis, is another of its Roman treasures, once more displaying the accommodation between Roman and traditional beliefs. The temple at Deir el-Haggar (the 'monastery of stone') lies solitary at the edge of the desert, its processional way marked out with the stumps of sandstone columns and a partly reconstructed pylon. It seems every inch the late-pharaonic or late-Ptolemaic temple, but was in fact built under Nero, between AD 54 and 68. As part of the adaptation of their imperial iconography to local Egyptian traditions, the emperors' names frequently appear in temple dedication inscriptions, not in their traditional Latin style, but in the form of a cartouche containing the 'birth' name and 'throne' (or Ra) name of the ruler in Egyptian hieroglyphics. Right from the start, Augustus consented to his depiction as a traditional Egyptian pharaoh, and as the Empire consolidated its hold in North Africa, the establishment of the imperial cult acted as a substitute for the direct worship of the pharaohs that had been the norm in Ptolemaic Egypt.[94] Deir el-Haggar received imperial attention through a number of reigns, and the temple walls also carry cartouches for Vespasian and Titus.[95]

The main gateway, redecorated under Domitian, leads into a small courtyard, and thence to the main temple. The final set of columns on the approach bear a particularly distinguished graffito, that of the German explorer Gerhardt Rolfs, who visited in 1873 (and who, legend has it, made off with a great treasure after placating the temple's spirits by the human sacrifice of one of his servants).[96] The now-unroofed temple is closely decorated with hieroglyphs and faint traces of the colour of the original wall paintings. Better preserved in a small room at one end is an astrological ceiling, set against a deep-blue background; the snake-like god Geb, who represents the Earth, curls around all the other divine beings represented, including a centaur and the constellation of the giant Orion. The ceiling was painted during the reign of Hadrian, whose visit to Egypt in 130 sparked the Emperor's interest in the religious mysteries of the country, which would later be reflected in the decoration of his rural retreat at Tivoli outside Rome.

From Dakhleh, the road passes 200 kilometres north-westwards to Farafra, the most compact of the main oases, and regarded by the Romans as forming part of the 'Small Oasis' (*Oasis Parva*) together with Bahariya. From here on, extreme desert conditions begin to form weird terrains, capricious and colourful flights of fancy for those who have braved the journey this far into the wilds. The 'White Desert', possibly the remains of an ancient lake, is crusted with salt crystals that leach to the surface and make it seem as if the desert has received an impossible coating of snow. In places, the salt has accumulated into strange formations, blasted by the wind and snow, many looking like fantastic mushrooms, or boats beached far out in the sands. Further north-west there is the 'Black Desert', an area of dark, volcanic sand, which stretches for more than 100 kilometres, as if someone has very carefully and evenly sprinkled out volcanic lava from an immense shaker; to the sides of the road small conical mounds sit, for all the world like an array of cadet volcanoes.

Bahariya, 175 kilometres north-east of Farafra, comes as a welcome relief from the visual rigours of the desert, in which a glance in any direction is to be rewarded by a stern and unrelenting beauty. The oasis, first showing itself as a small fence here, a donkey cart there, and then groves of date palms and a dusty main street, was a comparatively poor relation in terms of Roman remains. All that changed in 1996 when an antiquities guard accidentally lighted upon a tomb chamber near the temple he was protecting. It turned out to be part of a huge 1st- and 2nd-century AD Greco-Roman necropolis, which might contain thousands of graves when fully excavated.

Even more extraordinary than this were the richest burials from the cemetery, of mummies encased in cartonnage – layers of plaster and fibre – and with gold leaf and semi-precious stones applied to the topmost layer. A dozen or so of them are now kept in the storehouse of the Antiquities Department in Bawiti, the capital of Bahariya. A strange and nauseating smell pervades the place, literally the stench of death, as decay and preservative chemicals mix in equally unwholesome measure. Some mummies are badly damaged from their sojourn in the tomb or excavation, the faces painted on the coffin lids collapsed into a rather perturbed or worried half-expression, while others are nearly complete, with funereally staring eyes of a more cheerful disposition.

At El-Qasr village in the centre of the oasis lies one of Roman Egypt's unlikeliest gems, a triumphal arch that may have formed part of a larger fortress, long since disappeared. When described by the British anti-quarian G. Hoskins in the 1830s, it was much more complete, with a cornice, attic and other architectural features.[97] Now, even finding it is something of an achievement. Down through the narrow back streets of the village that has utterly concealed it and then into an area of palm gardens, the way is blocked by crowds of children, gently trudging donkeys, and finally by an iron gate. In order to gain access, our guide slides nimbly over an irrigation ditch and scrambles up a slippery slope that leads into one of the palm gardens. And there it sits, utterly engulfed within the village, two piers of stone, their joining arch long since fallen, one side propped up by the trunk of a date palm, as though the locals fear that it too is on the point of tumbling over. Few of the facing stones now remain, so the rubble core of the arch is exposed, slowly crumbling into the garden below. Of the winding staircase, niches and columns that Hoskins also described, there is nothing left.

A couple of kilometres to the north of El-Qasr lies a building which, though not Roman, commemorates perhaps Egypt's most famous ever ruler.[98] The temple at the small village of Qasr al-Migyhbah, probably built in the early Ptolemaic period, seems a very plain structure, a plat-form accessed by a short flight of steps, with walls rising to 5–6 metres. Around this lie the remains of rooms from a much larger complex. The whole is dedicated to Alexander the Great, and once had a cartouche honouring him, the only one to be found in the Western Desert (not even Siwa, much more closely associated with the Macedonian conqueror, had one). The cartouche itself, it is claimed, has been 'eroded' by the elements, but a large hole in the wall where it is said to have been looks as though it has been literally gouged away.

A monotonous and searing stretch of desert makes up the 400-kilometre, eight-hour drive west from Baharia to Siwa, dotted with military checkpoints that aim, in the manner of a fly swatting an elephant, to choke off the smuggling trade through the Western Desert, and which provide for the security of those few travellers allowed down the mili-tary road. Siwa was perhaps the least Romanised of the oases; indeed, it had long resisted integration into the pharaonic kingdom and even now retains a way of life that is distinct from that of the Nile-valley dwellers, if now more closely linked to the centre by transportation and telecommunications than it has been at any time in its history. The people here have stronger ethnic ties with the Berber groups to the west in Libya, Algeria and Morocco. Their isolation is accentuated by the Great Sand Sea to the south, a stretch of nearly impassable dune fields, into which the army of Cambyses of Persia was swallowed in 524 BC when he tried to cross it to conquer the Siwans.[99] Herodotus claims that 50,000 men perished, doubtless something of an exaggeration, but much effort has been expended, fruitlessly, in trying to find any trace at all of the lost Persian host.

Siwa has always had something of an air of mystery about it, principally as the site of one of the ancient world's most renowned oracles, whose existence was recorded as far back as the 18th Dynasty (1550–1292 BC).[100] The most famous visitor of all was Alexander the Great, who came in 331 BC,[101] aided by miraculous desert rains, which ensured that his troops did not perish of thirst like so many before them. The accounts of his visit to the oracle vary frustratingly, but it seems that he asked if the 'empire of the world' was destined to be his, to which the priest's reply was positive. The priest is also said to have referred to Alexander as 'O pais Diou' ('the son of Jupiter'), which pleased the Macedonian despot greatly, even though it may have been an innocent mispronunciation of 'O paidion' ('My child').[102]

The Temple of the Oracle lies today a little way from the central settlement of Siwa, at the end of a palm-fringed road. Over time, the medieval settlement of Aghurmi grew around and over the remains of the temple, much of its mud-brick encrustation not being removed until the second half of the 20th century, and a good deal of it surviving today to obscure the contours of the ancient temple. The inner sanctuary, a large court, adjoined by two smaller courtyards (from which the priests are said to have whispered the responses of the god), is only about 6 x 3 metres and perches on the edge of a cliff-face down which it threatens at any moment to tumble. It is a curiously soulless place now, and it is hard to gain much sense of the awe inspired by the ancient oracle, and the power it wielded through its influence on the judgements of the ancient world's mightiest rulers.[103]

When Strabo visited in 23 BC he reported that the oracle was in a serious state of decline.[104] It was, however, clearly functioning in some form in AD 160, when Pausanias wrote that the priests and oracle were still present. Certainly, by the time of Justinian's order to close the last pagan temples, the oracle must have ceased to operate, and it may well have fallen victim to earlier waves of anti-pagan feeling, such as the bouts of temple-smashing during the reign of Theodosius I. Much earlier, in 48 BC, the Stoic politician Cato the Younger arrived in Siwa, while on the run from Julius Caesar after the death of Pompey at Pharsalus. He tried to provoke the oracle, and no doubt public opinion at home, by asking about the 'freedom of Rome'. The oracle wisely remained silent, in turn not wishing to incur the wrath of Caesar, the almost certain victor in the civil war. On the other hand, perhaps the priest foresaw the collapse of the Republic, the inauguration of the Empire and the fate of Rome under emperors such as Caligula, Commodus and Caracalla, and so his silence expressed most eloquently the amount of freedom that Romans could expect to enjoy in the future.

Once the Siwans had abandoned Aghurmi and left the Temple of the Oracle mute and unregarded, they constructed a new town called Shali, itself now a heap of crumbling mud in the centre of modern Siwa. Built of *kharsif*, a type of mud-brick made using salt, which is extremely suscep-tible to collapse if not maintained, it is a good example of the type of construction that native villages throughout the region would have employed. After severe rains damaged it in 1942, the Siwans left their old home to decay, a confusing maze of alleyways that, given a few decades, will subside back into the mud from which it was created.

Siwa has given rise to one of the more unsavoury spats in the history of modern archaeology. In 1995, a Greek archaeologist who had been excavating in the al-Marqi district of Siwa, some 25 kilometres from the centre, made the astonishing claim that an unprepossessing and out-of-the-way temple was in fact the location of Alexander the Great's tomb, and that inscriptions at the site for Ptolemy I, who had been one of Alexander's chief lieutenants (and went on to be ruler of Egypt), confirmed the connection with Alexander and stated that the Macedonian king had died of poisoning in Babylon. Alexander, it was claimed, had wanted to be buried near his mystical 'father'. After the finding received initial, guarded support from the Egyptian Antiquities Department, a delegation from the Greek Culture Ministry came to investigate. They concluded that the tablets found were not of Ptolemy I, that there was no mention of Alexander or poisoning, and that the temple was not even Macedonian at all.

The available ancient literary evidence all points, in fact, to Alexander being buried in the city named for him, Alexandria. The tomb, which was known as the Soma (from the Greek for 'body'), and which was mentioned by a number of ancient writers, was clearly situated near the centre of the city, and was visited by Augustus, Caligula, Septimius Severus and Caracalla.[105] Thereafter, accounts of the tomb, and know-ledge of its whereabouts, gradually fade from the record. By the Middle Ages, the Arabs of Alexandria were venerating a Prophet Eskander (or

Alexander), and in the early 16th century the traveller Leo Africanus was shown a small building where Eskander was venerated.[106] From then on, visits or searches for the 'tomb' of Alexander became something of a cottage industry, with leading candidates being the Attarine mosque (the former church of Athanasius) and the mosque of Nabi Daniel, where in 1850 a Greek dragoman-interpreter named Scilitzis claimed to have seen a skeleton interred in a secret passage in the crypt, crowned with a golden diadem.[107] The search goes on, and even Venice has been touted as a possible last resting place of Alexander's mortal remains. However, the Siwan theory has generally been discounted, and the Greek archaeologist responsible for announcing the 'discovery' of the tomb there had her licence to excavate revoked.

A short drive west, as the fertility of the soil dwindles to nothing and the green splashes of the oasis seem a distant memory, lies evidence of the late-Roman phase in Siwa's history. Among cliffs dotted with tombs, and rock formations that themselves seem like giant Roman walls, a substantial settlement once stood. All that remains now is a single wall some 7–8 metres high, scarred with a triangular-shaped hole that may once have been an entrance. On the other side, two supporting internal walls may have formed part of a Doric temple some 25 metres long, which was described as being relatively intact by 18th- and 19th-century travellers. An alternative theory is that this is in fact the remains of a church.[108] Christianity came late to Siwa; its location as the centre of a great pagan oracle may have retarded the advance of the new faith, and there is little evidence of Christianisation even by the end of the 3rd century. Having long failed to accept Christianity, the Siwans gained a similar reputation for resisting the advance of Islam, and there are indications that they repulsed an Arab army as late as 708.[109] Balad al-Rum, which means 'Town of the Romans', may, therefore, have been one of the last Christian bastions in the region.

Cyrenaica

From Siwa, it is a further hot 300-kilometre drive to the mercifully cooling waters of the Mediterranean at Mersa Matruh, ancient Paraetonium. It is roughly here that the Roman province of Cyrenaica began, nowadays more normally accessed by a lonely coastal road that runs through the Second World War battlefields at El Alamein and Sidi Barrani. Cut off from Egypt by the Western Desert, and from Africa by the Syrtic Desert to its west, Cyrenaica's narrow coastal fringe failed to share in the massive prosperity of its two agriculturally rich neighbours. Even the relatively large number of secure harbours in the central part of the region provided only a limited boost, for lateral communications between them were difficult in the broken terrain.

Colonised by the Greeks as early as the 7th century, Cyrenaica had five main settlements (Cyrene, Apollonia, Teucheira, Berenice and Barca), from which it acquired its customary designation as the Pentapolis. Just as in Asia Minor, Roman involvement in Cyrenaica came about as the result of a bequest: its last ruler, Ptolemy Apion, bequeathed his kingdom to the Romans, and so they acquired it upon his death in 96 BC.[110] After some decades of muddle over the exact nature of the administration of the new territory, Cyrenaica was formally constituted as a province in 74 BC and a quaestor was despatched to govern it. After the Roman acquisition of Crete in 67 BC, the two areas were normally bundled together as a single province, an odd transmarine pairing, which must have made the life of the governor rather difficult. It was a senatorial province with no permanent legionary garrison under the early Empire.

An abortive Jewish uprising in 73 was a foretaste of much more serious things to come, as the region thrust itself unexpectedly and brutally to the forefront of imperial preoccupations in 115, with the outbreak of a much bigger Jewish revolt. This soon spread into Egypt, where the considerably larger Jewish population of Alexandria, and the closer proximity of Palestine, posed a serious challenge to the Emperor Trajan. Aggravated by long-standing ill-feeling between the Greek and Jewish populations of the Near East, a series of massacres ensued, and 220,000 Greeks are said to have perished.[111] The suppression of the revolt was bloody in the extreme, and thereafter little was heard of the Jewish population of Cyrenaica, which had previously been extremely prosperous (and numerous).

Cyrenaica was then quiet for two centuries apart from an incursion by the nomadic Marmaridae around 268, which required the intervention of the governor of Egypt to put down.[112] In the 280s or 290s, Diocletian reformed the administration of Cyrenaica, as he did in so many other areas of the Empire, dividing the region into two provinces: Libya Superior (or Cyrenaica) based at Ptolemais in the west and Libya Inferior (or Libya Sicca, 'dry Libya') to the east, with its capital at Paraetonium (Mersa Matruh). A screen of forts was constructed south of Berenice (Benghazi).[113] This outer ring of defences for the Pentapolis and signs of increased fortification in the cities[114] mark a struggle to hold back an upsurge of activity by the nomadic tribes of the desert fringe. From the 390s, Cyrenaica suffered particularly badly from the depredations of the Austuriani, a group probably originating from near the Gulf of Sirte, who had expanded their field of operations from initial raiding around Leptis Magna in 363–5. A *dux* 'of the Two Libyas'[115] had already been appointed in the 380s to organise the defence of the region, and by the 470s Cyrenaica had a *dux* of its own.

The principal city of the Greek Pentapolis was Cyrene, nearly 600 kilometres west along the coast from Paraetonium, through terrain both monotonous and forbidding. Cyrene itself has always had a reputation as a green respite from the harsh rigours of the desert; the Arabic name of the prominence on which it sits, Gebel Akhdar, means 'Green Mountain'. Founded by Dorian Greeks in the 630s BC, it was ruled for the first two centuries by kings who, confusingly, alternated between the names Battus and Arcesilaus. Conquered by Alexander the Great in 331 BC, Cyrene fell, save for a few decades of independence, to the Ptolemaic kings of Egypt, and was ruled by a cadet branch of that family from 163 BC to 96 BC.[116] After the Roman acquisition of Cyrenaica in 96 BC, control was light at first, only strengthened after the arrival of the quaestor Cornelius Marcellinus in Cyrene in 74 BC. Thereafter the city enjoyed almost two centuries of uninterrupted growth until the Jewish revolt of 115, when it suffered massive damage. Hadrian gave it the title of metropolis in 134, in recognition of its continued importance, but when the province of Cyrenaica was established, it was Ptolemais and not Cyrene that was made the capital. A severe earthquake in 262 destroyed many buildings, and another in 365 threw down the great sanctuary of Apollo.[117] For the next three centuries there was little building, even after Justinian's reconquest of North Africa had restored a modicum of security, and the city then began a rapid decline into an abandoned backwater.

The first glimpse of the site for modern visitors in the extensive necropolis, a mass of broken stonework and tumbledown tombs that populate the whole of the hillside approach to Cyrene. A few of them retain their pedestals, whilst of others only a sarcophagus survives, creating the eerie and melancholy feeling that something has been sorting through them in search of an unknowable treasure. Close to the site entrance lie the imposing ruins of the Temple of Zeus, with two rows of enormous Doric columns set about its more than 70-metre-long sanctuary. Inside, part of a Latin inscription survives commemorating its partial restoration under Augustus, though, like much of the city, it was destroyed in the Jewish revolt of 115.

The *agora* of Cyrene is a large open square surrounded on two sides by a colonnade, which was then adapted to be a forum in Roman times. The ruinous remains of an altar at one end probably come from a temple built to honour the imperial family during the reign of Tiberius. On the eastern side of the square was erected a victory monument to celebrate Octavian's triumph at the Battle of Actium in 31 BC, which led to his mastery of North Africa (and the rest of the Roman world). Here, so close to Egypt, the battle and its aftermath must have had a particular resonance. The founder of the city, Battus I, was by tradition buried in this area also, and what was believed to be his tomb still survives, down a short flight of steps, with a triangular-shaped roof that has an archaic, almost Mycenaean feel, and which marked a place already ancient by the time the rest of the monuments in the forum were built.

To its east lies the most impressive of the private residences excavated in the city, known as the House of Jason Magnus. Dated to the reign of Commodus, it was owned by an influential priest of Apollo, who also held a number of other public positions, including that of gymnasiarch (the magistrate in charge of public works, who would have been expected to lavish a fair amount of his own personal wealth upon them). Its main surviving feature is a mosaic of the Four Seasons, which gathers dust under a rather unattractive metal protective roof, but the rest of the house, with lovely marble pavements, sections in *cipollino* and yellow marble alternating across an area some metres square, speaks of vast wealth and an unabashed desire to display it.

The road that runs alongside Jason Magnus's house was one of the most prestigious in the city, known as the Skyrota, bordered by a colonnade bearing statues of Hercules and Hermes, alternating at each new column: the former a stout, almost portly hero bearing a club that he seems rather too unfit to carry; the latter a more elegant youth who appears almost ashamed of his proximity to his chubby companion. Alongside the street lie several of the city's five theatres; to one side a very ruinous one, a little beyond it a small gem of an *odeon* for more intimate performances.

Cyrene also contains the normal complement of baths, basilicas and other public buildings appropriate for a city of its wealth and position. Undoubtedly the most impressive of these is the sanctuary of Apollo, approached by a steep flight of steps, which lead down into a spring and fountain dedicated to the god. At the entrance to the cave from which the spring issues, a series of Greek inscriptions can still be made out in his honour. Just beyond, the temple itself has several columns standing and marble slabs laid around, which may have been used for sacrifices. Another fountain for Apollo sits adjacent, made up of two lions, one of which is being strangled and out of whose mouth the water issues.

Cyrene, like many North African towns, succumbed relatively early to the spread of Christianity, after which its new monuments were churches rather than temples or theatres. During the 6th century, two Christian basilicas were constructed in the city centre, whilst a large cathedral was built at the eastern end of the town, although this was not included in the new circuit of walls built in Byzantine times.

Cyrene's most famous and unlikely cleric was Synesius, who was born in the city in 370 and retained close ties with it throughout his career. Close to the house of Jason Magnus lie the ruins of the home of Synesius's friend Hesychius, who was president of the provincial council at the start of the 5th century.[118] As a member of the provincial aristocracy, Synesius would have been expected, along with his peers, to serve on the city council. He received his higher education in Alexandria, and became a pupil of the eminent female philosopher Hypatia, who would later be torn apart by a Christian mob in the city.[119] He must have performed well in his studies, for around 397 he was selected to participate in an embassy from the cities of the Pentapolis, which was to present at court the Cyrenaican cities' *aurum coronarium*, a 'gift' due from the provinces every five years of each imperial reign to honour the Emperor's reaching such an auspicious milestone.[120] By the late 4th century the gift had become an onerous due, and the embassy in which Synesius participated was also intended to plea for a remission from Emperor Arcadius of the general taxation that Cyrene owed. He stayed in the city for four years, only returning home in 401, having composed a treatise *On Kingship*, which was intended for presentation to Arcadius himself.[121]

Synesius returned home, got married and settled into the comfortable life of a provincial aristocrat, taking time off to compose a selection of philosophical treatises heavily influenced by Neoplatonism.[122] As the security situation in Cyrenaica deteriorated, with the increasing frequency of raids by the nomadic Austuriani from the desert fringes, so Synesius became increasingly involved with the defence of Cyrene. In 410, however, he was proclaimed Bishop of Ptolemais, a settlement near his native city, at the behest of Theophilus, the patriarch of Alexandria.[123] It was by no means uncommon for a provincial notable with no previous experience of church leadership to be elevated to the episcopacy. Often, local citizens would take the initiative themselves, seeking to co-opt the network of influences possessed by an influential and successful secular noble and to retain or divert them to the protection of their home town. The phenomenon became particularly prevalent in the later 4th century, when traditional civic leaders seemed to wane in authority, so that, backed by the growing power and geographical reach of the Church, bishops might be more effective and activist guardians of local interests. Such was the fate of Saint Ambrose at Milan and Saint Augustine at Hippo, both of whom were at first most unwilling prelates.

As a condition of accepting the position, Synesius extracted a concession from Theophilus that he would be permitted to retain his personal beliefs about whether or not the soul had been created, and whether the next life meant the literal resurrection of the bodies of the deceased[124] – areas where his Neoplatonist tendencies would normally have led to his being labelled a heretic – as long as his sermons contained a leavening of more orthodox interpretations. Synesius continued to be a tireless advocate for Cyrenaica, organising stout resistance against the depredations of the Austuriani. His letters, many of which survive, recount his standing guard on one occasion on the walls of nearby Ptolemais, awaiting the anticipated arrival of one such raid.[125] However, evidence of any committed conviction to Christianity on an emotional level is sparse indeed in his writings, and so his career acts as a fascinating insight into the transition during late antiquity from a Christianity that was beleaguered, yet fierce in the depth of its belief, to one that became increasingly bureaucratised and subsumed into a parallel hierarchy of power.

Ptolemais lies about 75 kilometres west along the coast road from Cyrene. The settlement, although founded in the 7th century BC, only became really prosperous under Ptolemy III (246–221 BC), who refounded it. It was not until the reign of Diocletian that it became an administrative centre, when it was selected to be the capital of the new province of Libya Superior (or Cyrenaica), thereby promoting it over Cyrene, which had traditionally been the pre-eminent city. Though hugely evocative, Ptolemais is only partly excavated and the approaches are hedged about by the broken-down stone houses of a settlement that grew up here during the Italian colonial occupation of Libya, many of them incorporating the odd arch or column from the ruins of the city and now inhabited by more recent migrants from sub-Saharan Africa.

The museum, among its collection of relics discovered on the site, contains a copy of the Price Edict of Diocletian, a failed attempt by the Emperor to control the raging inflation that was endangering the Empire's prosperity. Published in 301, it sets the maximum prices permitted for a thousand different commodities, as well as fixing wages for labourers and skilled artisans. Its preface expresses exasperation with the 'uncontrolled madmen' whose avarice fleeces the honest citizens of the Empire.[126] Tellingly, the Emperor complains that soldiers are separated from their pay and donative within a single day, so high are the price levels set by the profiteers. Diocletian's edict portrays an idealised world in which a labourer would earn 20 denarii a day, enough to buy himself a couple of pounds of meat or sufficient grain for his family.[127] Of course, since the level that the Emperor sought to impose on prices was probably considerably lower than that prevailing in the marketplace, the new policy served only to throttle the supply of goods that producers were no longer willing to sell, and so it was quietly dropped.[128]

Ptolemais contains several Roman triumphal arches along its *decumanus maximus*, including one dedicated for Constantine, which would originally have been a triple-arch, with two side-ways for pedestrians, and which was made up of twelve columns of black marble that lie strewn about nearby. The *decumanus*, known as the 'Via Monumentale' by the Italian excavators, is littered all the way with a scatter of broken columns and the fragments of Greek inscriptions. The level of the pavement during Byzantine times is clearly visible atop the original paving stones. The prosperity of the town, even at this late stage, is indicated by a set of 6th-century baths, with a large *frigidarium* whose ruins survive nearby, with some of the cracked marble paving still remaining *in situ*, including fine, deep-green-veined *cipollino*.

Around 200 metres down a subsidiary *cardo* lie the solid ruins of a 5th-century structure known as the 'Fortress of Athanasius', named for the eminent Bishop of Alexandria. Next door in an unexcavated building, mosaics are clearly visible under the soil, in black and white, including the indistinct outline of a flower just waiting to be dug up. All around the site, indeed, lie large chunks of tesserae that have broken away from unconsolidated mosaics, as Ptolemais gradually decays away into nothingness.

The cisterns of Ptolemais are among its most impressive monuments. No fewer than seventeen have been unearthed, many of them built during Roman times or adapted from Hellenistic predecessors. The dividing level between the two eras, with the upper portions (the Roman) built in brick and cement, is clearly visible, and the cavernous vaults would have enabled the city to hold out for some time in case of siege or drought. By the 640s and the advent of the Arabs, cities such as Ptolemais were scarcely contested, as the circuit of their walls was too large to be held by the overstretched garrison of the province. At the very end, the governor retired to Tocra (Teucheira), about 40 kilometres further west, a comparatively modest settlement, but one in which he thought (incorrectly) he might be able to resist.[129]

One hundred and twenty-five kilometres to the west of Ptolemais, along the deceptively green coastline, Berenice is the rather more romantic name of modern Benghazi in Libya. Its original and even more evocative designation was Euhesperides, the name given it by the founding Greek fathers some time around 540 BC to evoke the mythical

Alleged column of Saint Simeon, Saint Simeon's monastery, Syria

Temple of the Standards, Palmyra, Syria

Walls of Resafe, Syria

Ruined church, Kaprokera (Burj Haidar), Syria

The theatre, Cyrrhus (Nabi Khouri), Syria

The Valley of the Tombs, Palmyra, Syria

Colonnade of the *decumanus maximus*, Palmyra, Syria

Theatre stage and backdrop, Bostra, Arabia

Colonnade of the *cardo maximus*, Gerasa (Jerash), Arabia

The Oval Piazza, Gerasa (Jerash), Arabia

Dajaniyah
auxiliary fort,
Arabia

Tomb façades at Petra, Arabia

Ed-Deir ('the Monastery'), Petra, Arabia

'Pompey's Pillar', Alexandria, Aegyptus

Qasr Labekha fort,
Kharga Oasis, Aegyptus

Fresco of the Tetrarchs,
the Luxor temple, Aegyptus

Palaeo-Christian church,
Kellis (Asmant el-Kharab),
Dakhleh Oasis, Aegyptus

Fort at Mons Claudianus, Aegyptus

Abandoned granite columns in quarry,
Mons Claudianus, Aegyptus

Remains of triumphal arch,
El-Qasr, Bahariya Oasis,
Aegyptus

Kiosk of Trajan, Philae,
Aegyptus

Temple of Zeus, Cyrene, Cyrenaica

The Sanctuary of Apollo and lower town, Cyrene, Cyrenaica

The amphitheatre,
Thysdrus (El Djem),
Africa Proconsularis

The Severan arch,
Leptis Magna,
Tripolitania

Modern bronze sculpture
of Philaeni brother, Madinat
Sultan, Cyrenaica

Punic tophet, Carthage,
Africa Proconsularis

Ras al-Ghoul fort, Tripolitania

Cuicul (Djemila),
Numidia

Garum vats, Cotta,
Mauretania Tingitana

'Arch of the Basilica',
forum of Banasa,
Mauretania Tingitana

Castellum Tidditanorum
(Tiddis), Numidia

Thamugadi (Timgad), Numidia

western paradise. It is a place full of fabulous connections, for a few kilometres to the north of Benghazi, near the current Libyan Military Academy, lies the site traditionally identified as the beginning of the River Lethe,[130] one of the rivers of the Underworld whose amnesiac draught caused the shades of the dead to forget the cares and triumphs of their former life. Its alleged location was on the edge of the Sebka es-Selmani lagoon, which dried up gradually in antiquity, leading in 246 BC to the moving of the settlement closer to the sea. Benghazi, now Libya's second-largest city and a bustling port, combines fading Italian colonial architecture with a powerfully fetid miasma in the vicinity of the waterfront, but there is precious little in the way of vestiges of its antique past.

Ptolemy III renamed the city for his wife Berenice II in the 3rd century BC. In true Ptolemaic style, she had fabulously unhappy relations with her family. Her mother, Apama (the wife of Magas, King of Cyrene), had set her heart on marrying the young Berenice off to Demetrios the Fair, grandson of Ptolemy I. As ill-luck would have it, Demetrios was not nicknamed the 'Fair' for nothing, and Apama herself fell madly in love with the young prince. On discovering the affair, the sixteen-year-old Berenice had Demetrios put to death, while sparing her mother, who, it must be presumed, resolved firmly never again to mess with her daughter's boyfriends. The city was badly damaged by the Vandals in the 5th century, and, although refortified under Justinian, the brittle hold of the Byzantine authorities had not solidified into sustainable control and prolonged prosperity before it succumbed to Arab invaders in 641–2.

The traditional boundary between the territories of Cyrene and Carthage – the great rival of the Greeks for control of the North African coast – lay at a place named Arae Philaenorum ('the altars of the Philaeni'), somewhere along the south-eastern coastline of the Gulf of Sirte. Legend related that, in order to settle the quarrel between the two cities about where their border lay, it was agreed that two pairs of athletes would set out from their respective home cities and run towards the other; the frontier would be set wherever they met. The Philaeni brothers, the representatives of Carthage, reached much further than the halfway point between the cities, and the Cyrenaicans complained that they had cheated. In response, the Philaeni offered to be buried alive if their run, and the point it had reached, was acknowledged to be legitimate.[131] Their sacrifice on behalf of their mother city was commemorated by an altar, and the spot was, indeed, ever after accepted as the border between Cyrenaica and the Carthaginian lands, becoming the frontier of the Roman province of Africa (and subsequently of Tripolitania).

The precise position of the Arae Philaenorum is unknown,[132] but it certainly lay in the central or eastern sector of the Gulf of Sirte. Undaunted by the problem of its precise location, the Italian dictator Mussolini built a commemorative arch some 40 kilometres west of El Agheila. It was his dream to reconstitute the Roman Empire, or as much of it as his German ally Hitler would permit him, and the mimicking of Roman architectural styles formed a part of his grandiose vision. The new construction, which resembled a high imperial triumphal arch, spanned the coastal road from 1936 until its demolition by the Libyan regime of Colonel Qaddafi in 1973, and was wittily dubbed 'Marble Arch' by the British troops who successively advanced, retreated and advanced again beneath it during the Second World War.

The new Arae, or its remains, is situated in a modest museum near Madinat Sultan, a small jerry-built coastal settlement. Two bronze figures lie in the courtyard, Italian Fascism's representation of the Philaeni brothers, naked, muscular and with expressions both tortured and triumphant at the knowledge that their glorious sacrifice also signifies a terrible death. Lying abandoned in a field, partly overgrown by tiny thorn bushes, are parts of the arch, with the figure of Mussolini taking a salute clearly visible, and representations of the principal buildings of Rome. A frieze of Mussolini shows the *fasces*, the Roman symbol representing the power of magistrates to impose the death sentence, while an inscription proclaims that this is a 'stage in our journey to march in peace towards tomorrow'.[133] At least in its ruination, Mussolini's arch has reached some equality with the broken Roman monuments elsewhere in Africa, but his new Roman Empire lasted but a decade before the Allies swept him out of Libya in 1943.

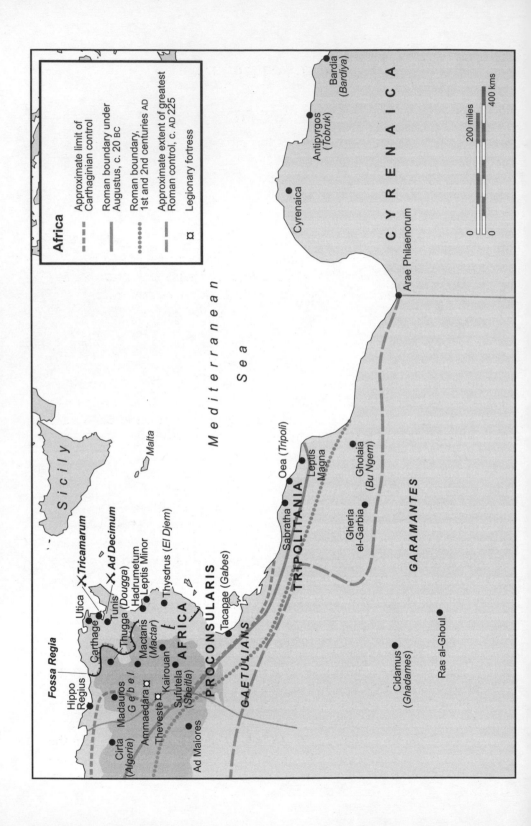

Africa

- – – – Approximate limit of Carthaginian control
- ——— Roman boundary under Augustus, c. 20 BC
- ········· Roman boundary, 1st and 2nd centuries AD
- – – – Approximate extent of greatest Roman control, c. AD 225
- ¤ Legionary fortress

Fossa Regia

Hippo Regius

Cirta (*Algeria*)

Madauros

Gebel

Ammaedara ¤

Theveste ¤

Kairouan

Sufetula (*Sbeitla*)

Ad Maiores

Utica

Carthage

Tunis

Thugga (*Dougga*)

Mactaris (*Mactar*)

X Tricamarum

X Ad Decimum

Hadrumetum

Leptis Minor

Thysdrus (*El Djem*)

Tacapae (*Gabes*)

AFRICA

PROCONSULARIS

GAETULIANS

Sabratha

Oea (*Tripoli*)

Leptis Magna

TRIPOLITANIA

Gheria el-Garbia

Gholaia (*Bu Ngem*)

Cidamus (*Ghadames*)

Ras al-Ghoul

GARAMANTES

Cyrenaica

Antipyrgos (*Tobruk*)

Bardia (*Bardiya*)

C Y R E N A I C A

Arae Philaenorum

S i c i l y

Malta

M e d i t e r r a n e a n   S e a

0   200 miles
0   400 kms

CHAPTER 10

Africa

It was at Megàra, a suburb of Carthage, in the gardens of Hamilcar. The soldiers whom he had commanded in Sicily were having a great feast to celebrate the anniversary of the battle of Eryx, and as the master was away, and they were numerous, they ate and drank with perfect freedom.

Gustave Flaubert, *Salammbô*[1]

It is a considerable irony that the strongest common thread running through Roman Africa is its previous occupation by the Carthaginians, Rome's most dangerous opponents in its earliest expansion in the western Mediterranean. From the Arae Philaenorum in the east, Carthage's writ ran along the coastal strip of Tripolitania, encompassing the rich trading cities of Leptis Magna, Sabratha and Oea (now modern Tripoli in Libya), through to the richer agricultural lands of present-day Tunisia, coming to a halt at the edge of the Algerian plateau, where opposition from native Numidian tribes prevented their further expansion.[2]

The occupation of this territory was Rome's first truly imperial venture. Although the defeat of the great Carthaginian general Hannibal in the Second Punic War (218–201 BC) brought Rome lands in Spain and the Balearics, Africa remained stubbornly under the rule of Carthage. It took until the Roman victory in the Third Punic War (149–146 BC) for them to establish a permanent military presence on the southern shores of the Mediterranean for the first time.

The land the Romans had now acquired was a very varied one, characterised by a fertile strip along the coast, backed by a series of mountain ranges, known in Libya and the east as the Jebel, and behind these the plateau of the Sahara, which in places on its edges permits limited agriculture but, further south, descends into the great sand plains of the deep desert, where only occasional oases allow anything like a settled form of life. In the 'pre-desert' areas between the coastal strip and the desert plateau, semi-nomadic groups continued throughout the Roman period to engage in their age-old practice of transhumance, by which their families and flocks would be moved northwards in late spring to more clement pastures and then southwards in the winter as the bitter heat of the summer abated. The central core of the province, which included Carthage, was much richer, with a broader agricultural hinterland that covered much of modern Tunisia, and possessed a much denser network of urban settlements.

The Roman *limes* in Africa, therefore, is not characterised by long fixed barriers as in Britain, river frontiers as in much of Europe, or even dense networks of forts as in Syria or northern Arabia; the topography of the land could simply not support this. Instead, the Romans concentrated on providing security for the principal settlements on the coast and, inland, on controlling and funnelling the movements of nomadic groups. The viable routes that possessed sufficient water resources were few, and so, throughout most of the Roman period, the whole area west of Egypt was controlled by but a single legion (the III Augusta), together with supporting auxiliary units.[3]

This new province became known as 'Africa', and acted as the nucleus from which Roman territory expanded, surprisingly slowly, over the course of 300 years, until it reached its final extension into the fringes of the Sahara Desert during the reign of Septimius Severus. The frontiers of this first province were defined by a ditch (which became known as the *fossa regia*) dug on the orders of Scipio Aemilianus, the victor in the Third Punic War.[4]

The Roman civil wars of the late Republic brought a further expansion of its territory, as another slice of land was obtained from Numidia to the west, when the Numidian king Juba I chose to ally himself with Pompey instead of Caesar. Two years after his patron had been defeated at Pharsalus in 48 BC, the rump Pompeian forces, including Juba's Numidians, were smashed by Caesar at Thapsus[5] (10 kilometres east of Moknine in modern Tunisia). In the aftermath of this disaster, the eastern part of Numidia was annexed, the new territory being dubbed Africa Nova, to distinguish it from Africa Vetus ('Old Africa'), the existing Roman province.

After Augustus became Emperor in 27 BC, Africa fell amongst those provinces allocated to the Senate, indicating that it was not really viewed as an active frontier region that required a substantial garrison (and therefore direct rule by the Emperor). The two provinces of Africa Vetus and Africa Nova were joined together and assigned to the rule of a proconsul, an official appointed by the Senate. This became known thereafter (until its reorganisation under Diocletian) as Africa Proconsularis. The coastal cities of Tripolitania, which had previously existed in a kind of semi-autonomous state, were now more firmly incorporated into the province. Africa Proconsularis then remained securely in Roman hands, save for the revolt of Tacfarinas in AD 17. Like so many rebellions under the early Empire, this was led by a man who had served as a Roman auxiliary. It took eight years, and a succession of disasters, before the Romans adapted themselves to his guerrilla tactics and Tacfarinas was captured and killed by Publius Dolabella in AD 24.

The security of Africa Proconsularis was greatly enhanced by the annexation in AD 40 of the neighbouring kingdom of Mauretania to the west (which was divided into the provinces of Numidia and Mauretania).[6] The frontier then gradually moved southwards, particularly under Septimius Severus, who ordered the occupation of a string of forward positions deep into the desert, such as Gholaia (Bu Ngem), Gheria el-Garbia[7] and Cidamus (Ghadames) in Libya. Although these advanced positions were largely evacuated at the time of the general imperial crisis of the mid-3rd century, and the coastal cities (deprived of this buffer) began to suffer more from nomadic raids, Africa was one of the most secure regions of the Empire throughout the 4th and early 5th centuries, providing vital revenues and supplies of grain to the beleaguered central administration in Italy. Around 303, Diocletian gave the final administrative form to the Roman possessions in Africa, when he subdivided Africa Proconsularis into Zeugitana (northern Tunisia), Byzacena (southern Tunisia) and Tripolitania (western Libya, including Leptis Magna).

Yet North Africa slipped out of Rome's grasp in the 420s, falling victim to a massive migration by the Vandals. Having broken through the Roman *limes* on the Rhine in 405–6,[8] they pushed through Gaul and on into Spain. Alarmed at the loss of control of such large swathes of territory to the Vandals and their Alan allies, the Roman government had invited the Visigoths to help re-establish central control. In 417/18, the Alans suffered a massive defeat,[9] after which they ceased to be an effective independent political force, and the Vandals – whose Siling sub-group had received similar treatment at the hands of the Visigoths – faced being squeezed into oblivion. It was a particular stroke of luck, therefore, when the power struggle between Aëtius and Count Boniface[10] led, in 429, to the latter's inviting Gaiseric, the Vandal king, to cross over to Africa. Gaiseric did not confine himself to despatching a few hand-picked troops, but instead ferried over – according to Victor of Vita[11] – the whole Vandal nation, some 80,000 men, women and children.

The barbarians swept eastwards through North Africa, and Boniface, by now reconciled with Galla Placidia, sought in vain to persuade them to leave. By summer 430 they had reached the gates of Hippo Regius, blockading the citizenry, including the city's bishop, Saint Augustine, inside its gates. The eminent theologian's principal work, *On the City of God*, is intimately connected to the travails of the later Roman Empire, for it concerns the relationship between Christianity and a secular society, meditations inspired by the fall of Rome to the Goths in 410. As the preface puts it, 'For to this earthly city belong the enemies against whom I have to defend the city of God'.[12] Augustine's City of God remained intact, but the wordly city of Hippo was devastated after the Vandals finally took it in 431 following an eighteen-month siege. Augustine, perhaps mercifully, had died the previous August.

Gaiseric continued to expand the area under his control, until in 435 the Roman government accepted the inevitable and recognised his possession of the less desirable territories of Mauretania (in the far west of North Africa) in exchange for leaving the agricultural heartland of Numidia and Africa alone. The respite lasted for just four years, and in 439 Gaiseric besieged Carthage, taking it with relative ease.

It was a disaster of considerable proportions. The central government's access to grain imports from North Africa was cut off at a stroke. Considering that the grain fleets from Egypt had, since the 4th century, been supplying Constantinople rather than Rome, the ability of the Western imperial authorities to supply the urban populace with the traditional free dole of grain or bread was severely impaired.[13] In addition, the taxation revenues from North Africa dried up. By now Britain had seceded from the Empire, almost all of Gaul save the south was lost, and the imperial government's hold on Spain was precarious in the extreme. With its financial base so weak, Rome was left struggling to marshal the resources necessary to take back the one province that might have saved it.

Understandably, the feeble emperors who oversaw the final collapse of imperial administration in the West looked to their Eastern colleagues for assistance. The prestige of the Constantinople government had itself been dented by Gaiseric's progressive seizure of control over the western Mediterranean – he took Corsica and the Balearic Islands in 456, followed by Sardinia in 468[14] – but the Vandal sack of Rome in 455 was an affront that they could not long leave unavenged. A fleet that was sent in 442 to attempt a reconquest had proceeded no further than Sicily, but another more serious effort was made by Leo I in 468.[15] This was the Empire's largest military effort for decades, comprising more than a thousand vessels, but the Vandals trapped and sank the majority in Carthage harbour by sending fire-ships against them. It was a naval catastrophe on a par with the debacle on land ninety years earlier against the Goths at Adrianople.

In 474, Zeno accepted reality and recognised Vandal control over North Africa. An agreement in 442 had sanctioned the occupation of Carthage in exchange for renewed Roman control over Mauretania,[16] but the imperial government had never reasserted itself in these poorer, western regions of North Africa. Zeno's move to embrace the Vandals as allies therefore made some strategic sense in heading them off from further moves north into the Italian peninsula or eastwards towards Cyrenaica or even Egypt.

The Vandal period of rule in Africa, which extended for almost a century, did not mark, at least on the surface, a dramatic break with the preceding administration. Social ranks such as *illustres* and *clarissimi* continue to be mentioned in Vandal legislation, while in the 480s a *proconsul Carthaginis*, a certain Victorianus of Hadrumentum, is recorded, and the poet Dracontius composed verses very much in the spirit of those that had praised the last emperors.[17]

The Vandal kings set to enjoying the luxuries that a well-developed and rich province could provide. Indeed, Procopius relates that they became so corrupted by luxury (and, in particular, by baths) that their martial spirit was diminished, a key factor in their feeble defence of the province once a Byzantine counter-stroke finally came.[18] At a more humble level, the nature of rural settlements during Vandal times has been revealed by the Albertini tablets, a collection of some forty-five wooden tablets discovered in 1928 in an earthenware pot around 60 kilometres west of Gafsa, near the border between modern Algeria and Tunisia. They date from 493–6 and deal principally with land ownership and the sales of fields. Critically the tablets, which are all written in Latin, make no mention of Vandal names and seem to indicate a thriving agricultural settlement in which there is no obvious evidence of rural decline. They also demonstrate at least a reasonable persistence of literacy into the period of Vandal rule.[19]

In religious policy there was a more definite change, for the Vandals were Arians, espousing a heterodox view of the nature of Christ's humanity[20] that was particularly prevalent amongst those of Rome's barbarian neighbours who had been converted to Christianity. Catholics suffered at best discrimination, with the Catholic see of Carthage being left vacant from 440 to 454 and 457 to 481,[21] and at worst persecution, as when Gaiseric's son Huneric issued edicts against Catholics in 483 and 484. Huneric, however, was married to Eudocia, the daughter of Valentinian III, so that subsequent Vandal kings had a family link to the house of Theodosius, and blood ties to the wider Roman Christian world.

It was this marriage alliance that was to be the Vandals' undoing. For after more than half a century of peace with the Eastern Empire, the deposition by Gelimer in 533 of Huneric's son, Hilderic – who was seen by the Vandal elite as favouring the Catholic, 'Roman' variant of Christianity as opposed to their own Arian creed – provided Justinian with a pretext to intervene.[22] A force of more than 15,000 infantry and cavalry (very large by 6th-century standards) was sent to Africa, under the command of Belisarius.

By ill-chance, Gelimer had sent most of his own fleet and best men to Sardinia to put down a revolt there, and, after the defeat of his army ten Roman miles from Carthage, at a place named Ad Decimum,[23] Vandal resistance folded. Following a further defeat in December at Tricamarum (around 25 kilometres west of Carthage), Gelimer fled to a mountainous refuge even further to the west, but was starved into submission in spring 534 after a three-month siege. He was carted off to Constantinople to grace Justinian's triumph there, and on prostrating himself before the Emperor, exhibited his biblical knowledge and his own take on the transience of earthly power by quoting the Book of Ecclesiastes: 'Vanity of Vanities, all is vanity'.[24]

Hilderic's children received pensions and were sidelined; the victorious Belisarius got a consulship, but was replaced in his command by Solomon; and newly reconquered North Africa settled into prolonged and debilitating border skirmishing with confederations of Moorish tribes that had emerged during the time of Vandal rule. The Byzantine position was hardly strengthened by a law of 534, which permitted those who had had their estates confiscated by the Vandals to regain their property, thus at a stroke alienating the many soldiers who had taken Vandal wives and who had hoped to acquire the land themselves.[25] Although Solomon inflicted a pair of stinging defeats on the Moors in 535, much of Mauretania, save Iol Caesarea, remained wholly outside the control of the Byzantine government.

Over time, the administration of North Africa seemed to have no other purpose than raising the requisite taxation revenues to pay for its own prolongation, and came to take on more the aspect of a military occupation than a civilian government. The Moorish tribes (on fighting whom the Byzantine authorities expended much of their diminished resources) had had centuries to establish themselves. In many areas they had taken responsibility for defending the frontier in the 4th century and, as the Romans evacuated territory or were forced out of it, they occupied the land and saw no good reason to cede it either to the Vandals or to the newly arrived 'lawful' Byzantine conquerors. By the 530s, under such chieftains as Antalas in Byzacena,[26] they posed a well-organised and formidable challenge to the Byzantine authorities. Despite ephemeral successes and intermittent challenges, they were never really overcome, and it is telling that what resistance there was to the Arab invaders in the 7th century came from Moorish or Berber confederacies.

This powerful Moorish presence, coupled with the resumption of war with Persia in the 540s and the consequent division of resources, meant that any further attempt to recapture more of the lost western provinces would be impossible. A devastating outbreak of plague further sapped the vitality of the Eastern Empire (nearly killing Justinian himself), while much of the latter part of his reign was mired in religious controversies and a last-ditch attempt to impose the orthodoxy of the Council of Chalcedon on an increasingly unwilling Monophysite population of Syria and Egypt.[27]

In Africa, as further east in Egypt, there was a very limited store of support for the central government and its representative, the exarch, who, combining civil and military authority, ruled over his precarious realm from the coastal safety of Carthage.[28] After the Arab invasion of Cyrenaica and Tripolitania in 642, it was clear that Zeugitana, Byzacena and Numidia (the provinces into which Diocletian had divided the old Africa Proconsularis) would be next. The exarch Gregory, appealing to sentiments of local self-help, declared himself Emperor in 646 and moved his capital inland to Sufutela (Sbeitla), near the probable line that any invasion would take. It was a purely African usurpation, as Gregory made no attempt to move against Constans II in Constantinople. It was also futile, because the very next year Abdallah ibn Saad's Muslim army swept west, annihilating Gregory's forces. The exarch himself died in a desperate defence of Sufutela, while his daughter, Yasmina, captured by the victorious Arabs, is said to have committed suicide by hurling herself from the camel on which she was being carried back to Arab-held Egypt.[29]

By the 660s, the Byzantine authorities had re-established control over the north-western tip of their former territory, although the rest was largely abandoned to Berber tribal chieftains. The attempt by Constans II (641–68) to reassert religious orthodoxy by the issuing of the *Typos*[30] – which sought to avoid theological controversies associated with Monothelitism[31] by forbidding the open discussion of quite how many wills Christ might have had – did little to win the loyalty of local Christian tribes, who were more confused or outraged than reassured by the changes. In the 660s, the Arab raids were renewed on a larger scale, and in 669 a great army under Uqba took most of Tripolitania and Byzacena,[32] founding a new city at Kairouan (south-west of modern Tunis) to secure Muslim control over the new lands and ensure that the Byzantines could not use Carthage as a bridgehead to take it back.

The final years of Byzantine control over Africa are a story of successive local revolts against the Arab advance; the exarchs themselves did almost nothing to salvage the remains of the province. In 683, Uqba undertook a dramatic and risky expedition westwards into Mauretania and as far as the Atlantic. On his way back he was ambushed and killed at Thabudeos by a Berber army under Kusayla, who had emerged as the leader of a powerful tribal confederacy, and whom Uqba had previously had imprisoned.[33] Kusayla's army then pressed their advantage and drove the Arabs out of Kairouan.

For three years the Berbers dominated the region until Kusayla's death in 687, when an even more dramatic figurehead of Berber independence took up the struggle. Kahina (or 'the Kahina', for it is unclear whether the term is a personal name or the title of her office)[34] – who is described, with the full force of romantic and hopeless nationalist rhetoric, as possessing streaming hair and second sight – is North Africa's answer to Zenobia or Boudicca. After Hasan ibn al-Nu'man had eventually captured the provincial capital of Carthage for the Arabs in 695, she defeated him and drove the Arab armies back towards Egypt. Ultimately, however, Kahina could not resist a renewed campaign by al-Num'an, and she was driven into the desert and finally defeated in 701 or 703 at a place somewhere west of the Aurès mountains of Algeria, which thereafter took the name of 'Kahina's Well'. With no local forces left to save it, Carthage finally and definitively fell to the Arabs in 698, leaving a shadowy hold on several cities in Mauretania Tingitana in the far west as the only Byzantine presence in the whole of North Africa.[35]

Tripolitania

Tripolitania was so named for the three original Phoenician settlements at Leptis Magna, Oea (Tripoli) and Sabratha,[36] which fell to the Carthaginians as their empire expanded in the 4th and 3rd centuries BC. Our first ancient account of it comes from Herodotus, who conjures up a land half-bound in myth, half-emergent into the light of historical scrutiny. Many of the tribes he mentions, such as the Nasamones and Garamantes, still inhabited the region in Roman times, although his description of the Garamantes as a tribe unversed in the arts of war hardly chimes with their bellicose reputation amongst later historians. The most populated area has always been the coastal strip, especially near Sabratha. Between Cyrenaica and Leptis Magna, however, the terrain is extremely harsh and dry. Indeed, Lucan remarked that 'all the expanse of dry sand that divides burning Berenicis from the lesser heat of Leptis knows nothing of leaves'.[37]

The first stage of the occupation by the Romans in Tripolitania was probably limited to Leptis Magna and a few other defensible sites, such as Tacapae (modern Gabes). As more forces were devoted to the region, so the frontier advanced steadily south, despite the setbacks of a war against the Garamantes in 69–70 and a revolt by the Nasamones in 85–6. During the 2nd century, earthworks known as *clausurae* were constructed, to block access north to the better grazing lands closer to the coast and probably to funnel seasonally migrating nomads along routes where they could more easily be controlled and taxed.[38] At the end of the 2nd century, Quintus Anicius Faustus, the legate of the III Augusta legion, projected a new line of defence further into the desert with the construction of forts at Gheria el-Garbia in the east, at Gholaia (Bu Ngem) in the central sector and at Cidamus (Ghadames) in the far west.[39] Gholaia, in partic-ular, has yielded a precious hoard of ostraka, inscriptions on broken pottery, which give details of its military organisation, including daily rosters of the men and their duties and reports on activities and patrols in the vicinity of the fort.

The Romans, however, persistently failed to subdue the Garamantes, who defended with great vigour their capital of Garama, which may equate to the modern village of Germa, north-east of Sabha, deep in the Libyan desert. Herodotus's account of them reveals that they had four-horse chariots with which they chased the hapless Ethiopian cave-dwellers;[40] and, more intriguingly that they possessed 'backward-grazing' cattle, which on account of their great curving horns could not move forwards, for if they did, their horns would get stuck in the ground![41]

The Garamantes first came into real contact with the Romans in the time of Augustus, not long after the unsuccessful expeditions to Arabia Felix and Ethiopia. An expedition in 20 BC led by the proconsul of Africa, Lucius Cornelius Balbus, met with more success. He penetrated some 800 kilometres into the Sahara and reached Garama, teaching the Garamantes a sharp lesson about the reach of Roman power, but not annexing their lands.[42] For his achievements, Balbus was granted a triumph in 19 BC, the last private citizen to be granted this accolade.[43]

The tribe later became involved in the revolt of Tacfarinas from AD 17 to 24, and then sent ambassadors to Rome begging for forgiveness for their transgression, afraid that they would share the fate of their erst-while allies. But their mischief-making did not cease. In AD 68–9 Leptis Magna and Oea (Tripoli) virtually came to blows over a quarrel concerning the boundaries between the two cities.[44] The citizens of Oea called in the Garamantes to help them, and the tribe proceeded with great enthusiasm to ravage the land around Leptis and do untold damage to the precious olive harvest. In retribution, the legate of Numidia, Valerius Festus,[45] was despatched south, discovering a quick route into the Garamantian lands that took only four days and that laid them open to much quicker Roman retaliatory action than hitherto.

Thereafter the Garamantes tended to be more cooperative. In around AD 100, Septimius Flaccus led an expedition, possibly from Leptis Magna, which passed through Garama and then continued three months' march further south to the land of the 'Ethiopians'. Better documented is the expedition of Julius Maternus (which was probably not military in nature), who also journeyed via Garama and was actually escorted for part of his journey by the King of the Garamantes. He then travelled for four months towards the Ethiopians, ending at a place called 'Agysimba' where he observed rhinoceroses.[46] One possibility is that he had reached as far as Darfur or Kordofan in modern Sudan. The extension of the Roman frontier under Septimius Severus by the construction of forts at Bu Ngem, Ghadames and Gheriat el-Garbia may have had an adverse effect on Garamantian power, and thereafter little is heard of them, save as a poetic synonym for the furthest-flung dwellers of the desert.

Around 575 kilometres west along the coast from the provincial border at the Arae Philaenorum, the first of the three cities of Tripolitania, Leptis Magna – it was so called to differentiate it from Leptis Minor near Hadrumetum – sits just over 100 kilometres east of modern Tripoli in Libya.[47] It seems the imperial city par excellence, its extravagant four-way Severan arch and a clutch of other grand monuments sealing its place as the stereotypical 'Roman city'. Leptis is forever associated with Septimius Severus, the local boy made good, whose ascent to the imperial throne in 193 ensured its position as one of the smartest cities in the Empire. Yet the truth is more complex. The city as tourists see it is as much a monument to 'imperialist' archaeology as it is to the Roman Empire. The original excavations, carried out by the Italians during the 1930s, clearly did have scientific aims, but were equally tasked with resurrecting the glory of Rome at its height thus reinforcing Mussolini's plan to use Libya as a springboard for a new 'Roman' Empire of his own. The unfortunate result was that the site was cleared very quickly, and the latest levels of its settlement (particularly the Byzantine) were simply swept away, while the pre-Roman city was neglected entirely.

Founded as a Phoenician trading post no later than 500 BC, Leptis fell firmly under the shadow of Carthage, where for three centuries it remained. With the defeat of its Carthaginian patrons in the second

Punic War, Leptis was absorbed into the Numidian kingdom of Massinissa in 202 BC, becoming a free state in alliance with Rome after the Jugurthine War in 105 BC.[48] The city's production and export of olives was the source of the wealth that permitted the construction of the lavish civic buildings that so impress today. Indeed, so wealthy was Leptis that in 46 BC Julius Caesar imposed an annual tax of three million pounds of oil on it, probably in revenge for the support it had given to his senatorial opponents.[49] It took until AD 203 for Leptis to get a rebate, when Septimius Severus[50] granted it complete exemption from property and land taxes. The Emperor also funded an ambitious building programme in his native city, including the magnificent forum, the mainstay of Libya's postcard industry. Even before him, however, Leptis was a regional centre of some importance and was honoured with a promotion to *municipium* around 75 and to *colonia* in 109.[51]

Leptis never had another imperial patron, and never succeeded in really rivalling its more influential neighbour, Carthage, to the west. It did, however, reach the dizzy heights of provincial capital, when the reorganisation of the imperial administration begun by Diocletian at the end of the 3rd century led to the creation of the province of Tripolitania.[52] But by 363, Leptis was suffering the unwelcome attentions of the Austuriani, a tribe from the local desert fringes. In a massive raid, the surrounding area was laid waste, and only the city's walls preserved it from utter disaster. In desperation, the citizens of Leptis appealed to Romanus, the *comes Africae*, based in Carthage, to come to their rescue. He testily replied that he would provide no aid until they had sent him a huge list of supplies, including 4,000 camels.

After the depredations of the Austuriani, Leptis faced being fleeced by the very authorities meant to protect them, and it simply could not come up with the protection money Romanus demanded. Outraged, the citizens of Leptis sent a delegation to the court of Valentinian I at Trier, only to find that Romanus had higher-placed friends than they. Romanus managed to corrupt Palladius, the envoy sent to Tripolitania to investigate him, and as a result Leptis's own ambassador, Jovinus, was blamed for concocting the whole story and was put to death. The unsavoury tale of corruption reflects badly on Leptis, too, as the city council, also suborned by Romanus, refused to back Jovinus's story. It did them no good, for Leptis never really recovered from the Austuriani raid. Although the story did finally come out a decade later, and Palladius committed suicide, Count Romanus, tellingly, was never punished for either his original dereliction of duty or his subsequent corrupt concealment of the affair.

An earthquake in 365 was followed by the depredations of the Vandals in 455, and topped by the razing of the city by marauding tribesmen in 523. By the time Justinian's forces recaptured Leptis in 533 they must really have wondered whether it was really so 'Magna' after all. Procopius, indeed, relates that Leptis had been so badly damaged by the raids of local tribes that it was abandoned. Yet consider for a moment that, in the aftermath of all these destructions, the magnificence of what remains is astonishing, a mute testament by inference to the even greater glory of those centres such as Carthage, which have been almost totally erased by natural disasters, neglect and wilful destruction.

The Severan arch, at the western edge of the city centre, forms the junction of the *cardo* and *decumanus maximus*. Now largely restored, its four faces all decorated in marble reliefs, it stood as a grandiose state-ment of Leptis's relationship with the imperial house, the bulk of its great Corinthian columns and the broken pediment style of its façade neatly combining local and more traditional architectural styles. Built in 203 to commemorate a visit by Septimius to his native city, its decor-ation ironically included a figure of the Emperor holding the hand of his elder son Caracalla, with his younger, Geta, standing beside him – a public display of family unity that was to survive just months after the old Emperor's death.[53] The panel (the original now in the museum in Tripoli) that portrays a grave Septimius riding in a triumphal chariot, face turned to the front despite the horizontal movement of the scene, is a much more appropriate reminder of North Africa's greatest Roman.

It is easy to be deceived into thinking that before the Severans there was nothing at Leptis, and that after them it instantly collapsed into a small hamlet rattling around in the shell of a grand classical city. Just a hundred metres away from the Severan arch is unambiguous proof of the falsity of this impression. The Hadrianic Baths, built in 126–7, almost seventy years before Septimius Severus's accession, were once a grand symmet-rical complex – one of the first of the great imperial baths – the roof of whose *frigidarium* soared to more than 15 metres, decorated with glass mosaics. Amid the scatter of still-upstanding and reconstructed *cipollino* columns, it is hard to gain a sense of the establishment in full swing, although near the entrance the library and the conveniently situated latrine, with at least thirty seating places in an open court, showed that none of the visitors' needs, physical or intellectual, went unprovided for.

Just beyond the baths, lying beside the Wadi Lebda, the gully that strikes inland from the harbour and severs Leptis into two quarters, is a *nymphaeum*, built as part of the Severan reconstruction of the city. Its semicircular basin would have been backed by an impressive array of Corinthian columns in *cipollino* and red granite, mimicking the stage-back of a Roman theatre, but it has now collapsed into the wadi, great blocks cascading down the slope as though shoved with enormous force. Just a few columns with beautiful vine-leaf detailing remain of a monument both intricate and extravagant. From here a colonnaded street leads on to the Severan forum, Leptis's glory. It is a vast space, imitating the imperial fora of Rome, and was originally surrounded by an immense colonnaded portico. Now the pattern of Medusa heads alternating with busts of victory lies broken, just a few still in place, most scattered in the middle of the forum. Columns lie everywhere, and pieces of capital, fragments of marble, from tiny to huge, mingle with the gorgon's head as though their stony stare had been the cause of all this chaos. The mixture of total devastation and patches of surviving (or reconstructed) decorative masterpieces has caused it to be one of Leptis's most-photographed spots.

Next door is another grandiose Severan construction, this time the basilica, a massive area more than 90 metres long, dominated by the remains of a two-storey colonnade and a huge inscription of Caracalla celebrating the completion of the building in 216, which lies in broken, undulating sections in the centre of the structure. Unlike the basilica at Trier,[54] only a section of this grand civic space was converted for Christian use (under Justinian in the 6th century). The new occupants seem to have been cheerfully undisturbed by the extensive pagan carvings on the pilasters attached to the basilica's end walls, showing the Labours of Hercules at one end and scenes from the life of Dionysus at the other.

Closer to the sea, and to Leptis's old heart, lies the original forum, flanked by the ruins of all the normal municipal buildings, the *curia*, old basilica and temples to Liber Pater, and to Rome and Augustus. An inscription of AD 53–4, in Latin and Punic (for the latter was still very much a living language here), marks improvements made at the expense of one Caius, son of Hanno, who in his name neatly reflects the mixed heritage of the city. Small marks on it indicate where bronze lettering would have been set, giving the original a splendour (and, in the noonday sun, a dazzling quality) that the simple, mute stone now lacks.

Leptis long retained many elements of its pre-Roman Punic culture; those of its citizens named on inscriptions have local, Libyan names, until, in the 2nd century, they lapse into the undifferentiated cultural anonymity of the Roman *praenomen*, *nomen* and *cognomen*.[55] Similarly, inscriptions in neo-Punic, often bilingual with Latin, persist for the first few centuries, with the last of them being found under Domitian towards the end of the 1st century.[56]

Leptis's horizons closed in on it during the late-Roman period, and old taboos about the burial of corpses within the city limits faded away.

A church was built in the forum, and a series of grave-markers associated with it are still in place, their script uncertain and wavering in comparison to the grand dedications of the high classical period. One commemorates the children of a man named Stephanos, who all died young – including Demetria, and a son, Longinus, who lived for just seven months and six days. Many of them exhibit local traits in the spelling of Latin, the stonemasons characteristically confusing b for v and hence writing Berena for the child Verena, and substituting for *vixit* ('he lived') the mistaken form of *bixit*.

Across the *decumanus* from the Old Forum lie the markets, constructed during Leptis's first period of real prosperity under Augustus. Around 8 BC a local notable, bearing the suitably Punic-Latin hybrid name of Annobal (or Hannibal) Tapapius Rufus, paid for the construction of the market. Now, just two octagonal kiosks in sandstone and green *cipollino* marble survive from it, one largely intact, the other a mere shell, inside which the market stalls would have been set up. Outside the northern one is a copy of a stone table, which bears lines marking lengths in Punic feet, Roman feet and Greek feet, for the benefit of the market's multicultural clientele.[57] Sadly for Roman chauvinists, the Roman foot at around 296 millimetres came in much shorter then the Greek-Ptolemaic cubit at 533 millimetres and the Punic cubit at around 515 millimetres, meaning that the Roman legionaries gave their Carthaginian counterparts a 219-millimetre head-start. Tables bearing sculpted indentations served similarly for the verification of different liquid measures; the oil, wine or other commodity could be poured into the basin, which would be stopped at the bottom and, once checked, could be allowed to run through and refill a container placed on the ground beneath it.

To the west of the site lies a less intensively excavated area. The *cardo* leads on to the arch of Antoninus Pius, a relatively simple affair compared to the showy grandeur of the Severan arch, though its remains indicate a quadriform shape. Nearby, the large blocks of the late-Roman wall snake downwards towards the sea, enclosing a much larger area than would its successor, Byzantine perimeter. The imperious stone gateways and procession of massive civic set-pieces give way to low sandy dunes dotted with scrubby bushes. The hurried groups on two-hour tours of Leptis rarely venture here, and in places piles of water bottles moulder, missed (or dumped) by the incongruous yellow truck that screeches around the ruins, oblivious to visitors' photos or shins. In a low hollow 100 metres or so from the shore, the reconstructed concrete domes of its roof making it look like some kind of desert scientific station, are the Hunting Baths, one of Leptis's hidden (and neglected) glories.

Through a splintered wooden door, a small polychrome mosaic of a floral design gives no sense of what is to come. Around a plunge-pool next to the former *frigidarium*, delicate wall paintings depict scenes from rural life: here two men in a boat fishing, their bronze-yellow caps with jutting brims making them look like a pair of aquatic jockeys; there a mother in a blue cloak and a small child walking back from the fields. Next door, however, the scene that gives the whole complex its name springs to life. A series of hunters, their faces vividly drawn and tense, face wild beasts – panthers and leopards. One beast has brought down his attacker and mauls his neck, the wounded hunter desperately seeking to regain his feet and escape. Another animal seems to run straight up the spear that his assailant has run into him, thus seeking in death to despatch his enemy. The hunters have their names painted beside them, Rapidus and Pictor, as though famous athletes or gladiators.

North-west along the seashore, Leptis really does seem to earn its oft-quoted nickname of 'City in the Sand', for from the side of the dunes sprout column capitals, and along the beach worn stones from the city lie alongside more modern rubbish and detritus washed up by the tide. The shoreline leads along past the Byzantine wall into the Wadi Lebda, thick with vegetation at this point, and then past a watchtower to the remains of a Roman lighthouse, surprisingly intact save for a square hole that gives stunning and precarious views over the sea's alluring blue. Beyond the old (and largely dried-up) harbour sit the shattered remains of a Doric temple and beyond that a fort in the Byzantine wall, its stair-case choked with the discarded shells of nuts from impromptu picnics.

Leptis, as befitted a city of its size, did not lack in facilities for public entertainment, and it acquired a theatre comparatively early in its history. A little to the west of the old market, this was dedicated around AD 1 or 2 by the very same Annobal Tapapius Rufus responsible for its neigh-bour. At the top of the auditorium another inscription was found to the goddess Ceres-Augusta, dedicated by Suphunibal, daughter of Annobal Ruso, showing another local family keen to gain public recognition by embellishing the city. Closer to the shore lies the amphitheatre, half of its circle of seats providing a stunning view of the sea. It was probably the largest in Africa, with a capacity of up to 30,000, some two-thirds that of the Coliseum in Rome itself. The holding areas for animals and gladi-ators can still be seen, and to stand in the centre of the arena and imagine the mixture of adrenalin, sweat and terror as the men awaited their next opponent – beast or human – is to experience a real sense of menace.

Nearby is the circus, the horse-racing track, the arches of whose starting cages or *carceres* were still intact in the 19th century, but of which almost nothing now remains except the stump of its central spine. The circuses or hippodromes came to occupy a curiously central role in Roman life, acting, like the amphitheatres, as a place where high officials, and most notably the emperors, might come into regular contact with their subjects. Dangerous undercurrents and opposition to unpopular policies might surface there in the chants of the spectators or, in the most extreme examples, in political rioting. From as early as the Republic, the circus crowds differentiated themselves into four factions, named for the colours favoured by their supporters: the Reds, Whites, Blues and Greens. The latter two seem to have been by far the strongest, and wherever political activism or patronage of the powerful is documented, it is in association with them, and not the Reds or Whites. Many of the emperors are recorded as supporting one or other faction: Caligula, Nero, Domitian, Lucius Verus, Commodus and Elagabalus for the Greens; Vitellius and Caracalla and, most famously, Justinian for the Blues.[58]

At first the factions were most prominent in the West, for chariot-racing was not particularly common in the Eastern Empire, and except at Constantinople really only took place in the context of religious festivals. The few exceptions, such as Gerasa and Bostra (in Arabia),[59] were insufficient to give rise to widespread Blue and Green factions in the cities there.[60] All this changed after the early 5th century, possibly as a result of the eclipse of gladiatorial games and blood-sports in the arena, which left a gap in the provision of public spectacles that successive emperors filled through sponsorship of horse-races.

As the military resources of the Empire became stretched, the Blues and Greens began to take on something of the nature of unofficial militias, with their highly motivated partisans called upon by the authorities in cases of dire emergency. The most popular charioteer of all, Porphyrius, who is memorialised in countless monuments throughout the Eastern Empire,[61] is recorded on one monument as having taken part (together with the Green faction) in the suppression of a 'tyrant' around 500, an event that may refer to the failed usurpation of Vitalian against Anastasius in 515.[62] Further examples include the participation of the factions in the defence of Constantinople against the Kutrigurs in 559, and their manning of the Long Walls in Thrace against the Avars in 583.[63]

The role of the circus factions in crystallising opposition to politicians (under the Republic) and, later, to the Emperor was much more troublesome for the authorities. As early as 44 BC there were, according to Cicero, loud acclamations in favour of Brutus, the murderer of Caesar, during the performance of a play.[64] The most notable example of all, however, came under Justinian, when the factions came perilously close to unseating the Emperor. It all came about as two circus partisans, one from each faction, were due to be executed. On the day appointed for their hanging (12 January), the ropes snapped and both men escaped alive. The Blues and Greens then combined to petition Justinian to allow the pair to live. When the Emperor ignored their pleas, the factions in concert set to pillaging and burning the centre of the city. Their demands grew political, with shouts for the deposition of the widely despised praetorian prefect, John the Cappadocian, and the urban prefect, Eudaemon.

Finally, three days after the riots had broken out, the mob tried to elevate Probus, a nephew of the late Emperor Anastasius, to the throne and when he could not be found, they rousted out Hypatius, another nephew of the dead Emperor and proclaimed him instead. For much of this time, Justinian vacillated and seems to have been on the point of fleeing. It was only the resolve of his wife, Theodora – who flatly insisted that whilst Justinian might try to escape, she was staying firmly put to face her fate – that stiffened the Emperor's resolve. Troops were sent in to quell the riots, and in the end some 30,000 are said to have perished.

The end of the Severan dynasty, with the murder of Severus Alexander in 235, marked the start of Leptis's long decline. The building of the late-Roman wall between 250 and 350 shows an increased concern for the security of the city, and the raiding of the nomadic Austurians in 363–7 badly damaged the city's hinterland. The sand-dunes started to encroach on the city, and a series of floods, as the Wadi Lebda broke its banks, did further damage.

By the end of the 4th century, Tripolitania seems to have had its own duke (*dux*) in charge of the garrison[65] and it resisted absorption by the Vandals longer than any other part of the former Africa Proconsularis. It was only in 455 that it was ceded to Gaiseric's Vandals, who demolished the wall, but they do not seem to have settled at Leptis in any great numbers, since the solitary trace of them is a hoard of coins found in the area of the market. Leptis was reoccupied after Justinian's reconquest, but the much smaller area enclosed within the Byzantine walls indicates that life here was on a much more modest scale than before.

In 544, Leptis played host to a massacre that irrevocably soured Byzantine relations with the local tribes, and greatly hindered the government's attempts at re-establishing financial and military security in the province. A large horde of Leuathae (or Lagutans), a group apparently originating in the Western Desert oases of Egypt,[66] approached the city, promising loyalty to the new rulers in exchange for gifts, particularly the traditional insignia of office (such as a white cloak and gold boots) for their leaders. Sergius, commander of the Byzantine army, invited eighty Leuathae chieftains to a banquet, but an argument over the alleged theft of crops by his soldiers led to a fight, and all but one of the Leuathae were killed.[67] In response, rebellion swept through North Africa, and it took three years and four Byzantine commanders before John Troglita finally put down the uprising in 547.[68] Tripolitania was then largely quiet until the Arab conquest in 643, after which Leptis seems to have continued its inexorable decline. Slowly the dunes and the sea finished their silent work of concealment, leaving the city to await a new wave of incomers from Italy to unearth and reconstruct its past glory.

Oea, 125 kilometres west of Leptis along the coast, has grown subsequently to become Tripoli, the capital of modern Libya, and amid its bustling old town and newer quarter of Italian-era buildings, little remains of the antique past. Almost the sole survivor of the Roman city is a triumphal arch built around 163 during the reign of Marcus Aurelius, surrounded by the fragments of a temple to the Genius of Oea, which was dedicated in 183–5. The layout of the main streets of the bazaar are, however, believed to follow the orientation of part of the Roman grid,[69] a sense of order that it is hard to credit amidst the chaotic crowds of pre-Ramadan shoppers.

A further 75 kilometres west of Tripoli, the coastal route to Sabratha yields little save a scrubby desert, the roadsides carpeted with heaps of discarded rubbish and the wind-swept huddles of black plastic bags that blight the Libyan countryside. It all summons up a profound yearning to dip into the deep blue of the Mediterranean. Sabratha may well have been founded as far back as the 8th century BC, and although it was strongly influenced by Punic culture, it was not actually occupied by the Carthaginians.[70] Evidence of its earliest phase comes from the Mausoleum of Bes, recently reconstructed by Italian archaeologists. Reminiscent of the neo-Punic monument at Dougga,[71] with a needle shape and pointed conical top, it has lions or sphinxes arrayed on each of its four sides, together with an image of Bes, the deformed Egyptian dwarf god, who was seen as the protector of women during childbirth.

Absorbed by Rome near the end of the 1st century BC, the city lived a life of relatively quiet prosperity until the 4th century. Sabratha never produced a claimant, successful or otherwise, to the imperial throne, and so missed out on the type of lavish patronage that Septimius Severus bestowed upon Leptis Magna, though it was elevated to the rank of *colonia* no later than the 180s.[72] In the 360s, the twin disasters of a sack by the Austuriani and the massive earthquake of 363 that devastated the whole of the eastern Mediterranean ruined the city, while the latter flooded much of its shoreline. The 6th-century Byzantine wall here, as in so many other places, excluded much of what had been the civic heart of the city, and by the time the Arabs arrived at Sabratha in 643 (with such suddenness that the inhabitants did not even have time to shut the city gates),[73] the area of the forum had been converted into a cemetery.[74]

Sabratha's gem is without doubt its theatre, whose *scaenae frons* is one of the most complete in the Roman world. Begun around 190, with a capacity for some 5,000 spectators, its 95-metre-diameter auditorium makes it one of the largest in Roman Africa. The concave marble panels in front of the stage, beautifully preserved, represent a variety of scenes appropriate to the dramatic setting, including the three muses, a school-teacher rubbing his beard in meditative contemplation, a personification of Rome and Sabratha with hands joined, comic masks, the judgement of Paris and dancers.[75] Behind them more than 100 Corinthian columns tower, stacked up on a three-tiered colonnade whose grace and beauty must have been in severe danger of distracting spectators from the more mundane performances below.

Although Sabratha's mosaics lie largely entombed in the site museum, some still survive *in situ*. In the Oceanus Baths, so named for a depiction of the sea-deity (now removed), a mosaic of a strigil is still visible at the lintel of the *frigidarium*. At the Theatre Baths, a mosaic inscription originally exhorted those who were a little tentative in their ablutions to '*Bene Lava*' ('Wash Well').

On the south side of the forum stood the basilica, probably originally erected in the mid-1st century BC. The remains are those of a fairly standard civic building of the early Empire, a rectangular hall with an internal colonnade, and at one end an apse-shaped area that acted as the judge's tribunal. A section of it also served as the shrine for the imperial cult. Later on it was extensively remodelled, and around 450 part of it was converted into a Christian church. The building's resonance lies, however, in its being very probably the site of the trial, about 157, of the novelist Apuleius.

Born in Madauros, in the west of Africa Proconsularis, probably in the 120s, Apuleius (though he quite possibly had Punic as his mother tongue) received an elite education and established a flourishing career as a sophist. Having been left, together with his brother, the enormous sum of two million sesterces by their father, Apuleius was in a position to indulge in a life of letters and rhetoric, and served as a magistrate at Madauros some time before 157. He is best known for his novelistic masterpiece – known as *Metamorphoses* in ancient times, but more commonly referred to since as *The Golden Ass* – in which the protagonist is transformed into the eponymous animal and undergoes a series of fabulous adventures, culminating in a life-transforming procession at a Temple of Isis, during which he is mutated back into the form of a man.

Late in 156, Apuleius arrived in Oea (Tripoli) on his way to Alexandria and, while staying there, was joined by Sicinius Pontianus, a friend from his student days in Athens. Pontianus was looking for a husband for his recently widowed mother Pudentilla, in order to prevent her substantial fortune falling into the hands of another family. Pontianus invited Apuleius to stay at his mother's house and encouraged a bond of affection to form between them. The marriage eventually went ahead, but by then Pontianus had begun to accuse Apuleius of using magic to persuade Pudentilla to marry him.

The case was heard at Sabratha before the proconsul Claudius Maximus, and in his speech of defence (the *Apologia*) Apuleius employed the full armoury of a trained rhetor, heaping ridicule on his opponents. Throughout his defence, he persistently implied that his accusers were ignorant, ill-educated folk and that accusations that he used fish to concoct aphrodisiacs or employed a statuette of Mercury to bewitch Pudentilla were simply absurd. Even bearing in mind the inevitable editing of the text for a wider public, the image of the professional sophist defending himself on a plane that the prosecution could simply not counter, or perhaps even comprehend, is a powerful one.[76] Apuleius was probably assisted by the fact that Claudius Maximus may well have been one of the teachers who had instructed Marcus Aurelius in Stoic philosophy, and was therefore quite likely to be favourably disposed towards him. The final verdict is not recorded, but the very fact that Apuleius later published his defence speech is strong evidence for his having won the case.

It could be that Apuleius drew inspiration from Sabratha's own Temple of Isis. With a breathtaking location overlooking the sea, the shrine was originally built in the early 1st century. Eight Corinthian columns still stand guard at the water's edge, a relic of the shrine's colonnaded court-yard. It was damaged both by the encroaching of the sea, after the 4th-century earthquake, and by the late-Roman defensive wall that cut off part of its north-eastern corner.

It is a world away from the rigours of the desert, and as the frontier moved ever further southwards under the Severans, the *limes* and the residual threat from nomadic tribes must have seemed to recede almost to nothingness. One of the forts providing this protection was situated at Cidamus (Ghadames), a baking hot 500-kilometre journey south from Sabratha, a trip that in ancient times must have taken several days of discomfort, hopping between precious water sources in the desert. Here, the landscape is punctuated by fortified Berber granaries – pragmatic mixtures of storage and refuge, and perhaps the lineal descendants of the Roman-era *gsur*, or fortified farms, which acted as fortified posts in the more thinly populated areas. Mostly two-storey square or rectangular constructions, they offered greater security than open farms, with space for tethering animals as well as accommodation for the local population.

While Gholaia, in the eastern desert reaches of Tripolitania, was abandoned around 263, the military occupation of Cidamus may have lasted only until 238. The short-lived Roman fort is as yet unlocated, but must have been at the edge of the 'Old Town' of Ghadames, a medieval mudbrick warren whose permanent occupation was ended several decades ago as part of the Libyan government's programme to move people out of what it saw as unsightly reminders of a past unvarnished by modernity. The lure of traditional oasis life is still a strong one, though, so the narrow claustrophobic streets are not entirely deserted, and the houses are not, as elsewhere in the country, crumbling back into their constituent salt, straw and mud. The small local museum contains what little has been unearthed of Cidamus: a room of column pieces, one heavily carved with palm dates, another with a capital in the shape of a bulbous striated onion. The gravestone of Marcus Varivara, who died aged thirty-five, has very definite straight lines marked upon it to guide the stonemason's uncertain hand in chiselling the inscription.

The Old Town itself is a confusing and delightful labyrinth, composed of twists and turns, shadows and light, squares and tunnels. Running on top of the main alleyways are enclosed passages, used by the women to pass through the town without venturing onto the public street. The walls of the houses, whitewashed with white gypsum interspersed with red gypsum employed as cement, give some brightness to the gloom, reinforced by shafts of sunlight that penetrate weakly into the tunnels. Each quarter of the town has several small squares, traditionally controlled by sub-groups of the two major tribes, the Bani Walid and the Bani Wazid. On one of these, near the town's main entrance, stand four Roman pillars set into the corner of the square, a faint survival of Cidamus, yet somehow contriving to seem more modern than the Old Town itself. At the Yunis mosque, one of the oldest in the city, a few more columns stand in the main prayer hall, though from where they came seems unknown.

Nearby, on the main, neatly whitewashed square, stands the Al-Kadus, the water-clock, where a customary official, the *naib*, would regulate the supply of water to the various gardens in the oasis, counting off time for the running-out of water from four containers, and adding a knot to a tally for each container emptied. At each eighty-eighth knot counted, a waiting farmer could then run to his garden and turn off the sluice from the neighbouring plot to allow the water to irrigate his own. Tight control of the water supply was what enabled efficient exploitation of the oases' exiguous resources, even in Roman times, and evidence of settlement in areas that are not farmed or even inhabited today are explained more by the Romans' (and their predecessors') greater skill at marshalling water supplies than by any significant change in climate or rainfall.

Less tangibly, the *insulae* of the Roman settlement are supposed to have reached the wall of the Old Town, with some names of old Roman structures surviving in terms such as 'Inagdu', though whether this is a corruption of the Latin '*In Augusto*' or a mangling of some other phrase is unclear. Ghadames was reoccupied by the Byzantines in the 6th century, for there is evidence of an episcopal see there, and a basilica may have been built in the town at about this time.[77]

However, like the rest of Tripolitania, Cidamus succumbed to the advance of the Muslim armies in the mid-7th century. A short way out of Ghadames, across rough desert tracks, lies the ruined desert fort of Ras al-Ghoul ('Lord of the Ghosts'), a late-Roman fortification set atop a rocky outcrop. Isolated, but defended by a double-circuit of masonry walls, it commands a wide area, ringed in the distance by the first dunes of the deep desert. It is a place more of desperate defence than of prolonged resistance, but local tradition has it that the last Byzantine garrison of Tripolitania retreated here around 668, and held out for some time. The soldiers were assisted by the presence of a well inside the fort, but in the end made a deal with their attackers to be allowed to leave in peace.

It is a short scramble up the slope to the fort, and determined attackers would surely soon have overrun it, but the well is still there, just inside the inner keep, uncovered, and a hazardous fall for the unwary. Inside the fort are the remains of several structures, one surviving to almost half a metre high, presumably representing the accommodation blocks for the soldiers. The garrison cannot have been large, because the whole area of the upper fort is only about 12 metres in diameter. All around lies a scatter of pottery of indeterminate age, and one stone fragment has a carving roughly incised on it, an eagle, or perhaps a pelican. From here, as the setting sun casts a golden-pinkish shadow over the dune fields, it seems a fitting place for a province to have died.

Africa Proconsularis

Back on the coast, the province of Tripolitania petered out around Gigthis, about 100 kilometres to the west of Sabratha. From here westwards, the bulk of modern Tunisia (apart from the sterile areas to the south of the dried-up salt lakes of the Chott El Jerid) constituted the original core of Africa Proconsularis. The coastline and interior lowlands are dotted with ancient settlements, forming one of the economic powerhouses of the ancient world, and home also to Carthage, one of its most important cities.

Roughly midway between the modern cities of Sfax and Sousse, some 275 kilometres north-west of Gigthis along Tunisia's main arterial route, lies the great amphitheatre at Thysdrus (El Djem). It is one of the most complete in the Roman world, only really rivalled today by the Coliseum and the arena at Arelatum (Arles) in southern Gaul. It was probably the twelfth-largest in the whole Empire.[78] From afar it dominates the skyline, while from nearby it is engulfed by bazaars and shops and all the life and noise of a modern North African town. From outside its arches and engaged columns march in an almost continuous line around the building; from inside, though the seats are largely gone, the arches that supported at least four tiers of them survive intact. The building, the third of its type constructed in Thysdrus, would have been even more complete, had it not been for its bombardment by the Ottoman governor of the region in the 19th century during the suppression of a tax-revolt, a strange irony in view of the amphitheatre's earlier history.

That Thysdrus could have supported such a structure is evidence of its great prosperity during the Severan period. Yet the local landowners were not so rich that the central government could milk them indefinitely without provoking a reaction. The demands of the imperial procurator grew too exacting, and his habit of prosecuting local notables on trumped-up charges so that he could confiscate their properties once they were found guilty further inflamed feelings. By March 238 the local population had had enough, and the procurator was murdered by an angry mob. Realising that they had overstepped a dangerous mark, the rioters then sought out the eighty-year-old governor of the province, Marcus Aurelius Gordianus Sempronianus, at his headquarters in Thysdrus and proclaimed him Emperor – probably much against his better judgement.[79]

Yet the elderly Gordian I, as he is known to history, probably had some reason to hope. Although he had no access to the resources of the army, and could only muster a ragtag assortment of local militias, the 'official'

Emperor, Maximinus Thrax, was not popular, as his role in the murder of Alexander Severus in 235[80] had angered the Senate, whose support could thus be expected for the rebellion. Gordian elevated his son, also called Gordian, to be his co-Emperor (known as Gordian II), and sent an embassy to Rome. The Senate granted its recognition of his position, but the governor of Numidia, Capellianus, who was also the legate of the III Augusta legion, remained loyal to Maximinus. The two Gordians were defeated by Capellianus outside Carthage, the younger perishing in battle, while his father fled into the city and then, in total despair, committed suicide. Until his unwanted proclamation, he had lived a long and blameless life, but he survived his elevation to the imperial office by just twenty-two days.

If Maximinus and Capellianus thought their position was now secure, they were hopelessly wrong. The Senate had declared Maximinus an enemy of the Roman people and elected two new emperors, Pupienus (a former governor of Germania Superior) and Balbinus, in opposition to their 'official' sovereign. Popular opinion, which had favoured the Gordians, did not look favourably on this senatorial carve-up of power, but neither did it relish restoration of the brutal Maximinus to power. The only solution was another Gordian, and there happened to be one available: the young nephew of Gordian II, who was just thirteen years old. Pupienus and Balbinus, not keen on sharing power with this young upstart, compromised by granting him the lesser title of Caesar. Maximinus's attempt to march on Rome then collapsed when he was murdered by his own legionaries, the men of II Parthica, near Aquileia.[81]

Yet the victorious Pupienus and Balbinus fared scarcely better. Once back at Rome, they soon fell to quarrelling and mutual suspicions of the most sanguinary nature. Each feared the other was about to assassinate him. The praetorian guard, not keen on either emperor, then tried to storm the Palatine, where the imperial palaces were sited, and capture both of them. Pupienus's German bodyguard attempted to rescue him, and in the fracas both he and Balbinus were murdered. While the first two Gordians had lasted twenty-two days, Pupienus and Balbinus had survived just a hundred, meaning that, when Gordian III was proclaimed sole Emperor by the soldiers, he became the sixth sovereign in the space of four months. It was the start of the almost comic-opera period of Roman history known as the 'military anarchy' during which emperors came and went so fast that the mint-masters were hard put to keep up with the latest imperial image, and which saw no fewer than fifty emperors (or usurpers) in fifty years,[82] almost none of whom died of natural causes.

Gordian III, barely an adolescent, was hardly in a position to make policy, but his advisors went about vigorously blackening the reputation of the previous regimes. Both Pupienus and Balbinus suffered *damnatio memoriae*,[83] as did, uniquely, the III Augusta legion for its role in the death of Gordian's uncle and grandfather, its name being erased from public monuments as though a corporate public enemy. Africa was not granted another legion and was left to be defended by auxiliary troops, until the III Augusta was reconstituted by Valerian in 253. This meant that the province was dangerously exposed when the Proconsul of Africa, Sabinianus, revolted in 240,[84] but he was defeated, and for a few short years the rot in the body politic of Rome was halted.

As well as its role as a catalyst in the unseating of Maximus Thrax and the 'military anarchy' that followed, Thysdrus also played host to an important moment during the final years of the Roman presence in North Africa. It was in the Thysdrus amphitheatre, around 698, that the Berber Queen Kahina barricaded herself against the Arab army of Hasan ibn al-Nu'man.[85] Her followers mounted a spirited defence, but there was some kind of betrayal or deal done, and, whilst the Queen herself broke out with a small band of followers, her sons were appointed as commanders in the Arab army. Kahina, who had a reputation as a prophetess, was said to have 'foreseen' and approved their seditious behaviour, but it cannot have been an easy pill to swallow. Local tradition tells that the treasure of the Queen is still buried somewhere nearby, but her hidden gold and jewels have remained as elusive as the truth behind her own story.

Perched on Tunisia's north-eastern shore – some 200 kilometres north of Thysdrus – facing equally along the North African shoreline and outwards towards the islands of the Mediterranean, Carthage was Rome's hereditary enemy. The city's foundation is lost in mystery, mirroring nicely the historical haze that obscures the truth behind Rome's own earliest years. The traditional date is 814 BC, thus giving the city sixty years' seniority over its Italian rival. The legend relates that King Pygmalion of Tyre (in the Phoenician homeland of modern Lebanon) murdered the husband of his sister Elissa, who, after her own odyssey around the Mediterranean, landed in Libya. The tale was later taken up by Virgil, who makes Dido (Elissa's nickname, acquired on her voyages) the tragic heroine of his *Aeneid*. He also relates the story that the local king agreed to sell the newcomers as much land as they could cover in the hide of an ox – in other words, very little. The cunning Phoenicians cut the ox hide into very thin strips, thus enabling them to encircle an area 22 stades (around 4 kilometres) in circumference. In honour of this ruse they named their settlement Byrsa (for *bursa* or ox-hide).[86] It later became better known as Kart-asht ('New City') or Carthage.

After the last Punic War in 149–146 BC, more a vengeful campaign to extirpate the Carthaginian identity than a truly equal military struggle, Carthage itself was destroyed, although the legend that its agricultural lands were sowed with salt to render them forever infertile owes more to a Victorian sense of theatricality than to the historical record.[87] '*Carthago delenda est*' – 'Carthage must be destroyed' – intoned Cato the Elder at the close of each of his speeches in the run-up to that war, and so it was. Yet from the rubble emerged eventually, in the time of Augustus, a new Roman city built atop its wholly destroyed Punic predecessor.

Although neighbouring Utica was made the capital of the new province of Africa following the Third Punic War, Carthage, retaining the advantage offered by its unique double-harbour, soon surpassed it once more, first in prosperity and then in political importance. Julius Caesar took the decision to refound it, but his murder in 44 BC meant that it was Augustus who sent the first significant draft of colonists in 29 BC, naming it in honour of his dead adoptive father as Colonia Iulia Concordia Carthago. It became the *de facto* capital of the Latin-speaking portions of Roman North Africa (as Alexandria was for the Eastern Greek-speaking area).

For Carthage, the first three centuries of Roman rule were unremarkable, but in 308, it briefly became the capital of its very own breakaway empire when the Vicar of Africa, Domitius Alexander, briefly threw off the dominion of Maxentius, himself regarded as a usurper by the legitimate Tetrarchs, Galerius, Licinius, Maximin Daia and Constantine.[88] After a period of consolidation later in the 4th century in which it also became a leading centre of learning – attracting the young Saint Augustine, who briefly taught rhetoric there in the 380s – Carthage developed into one of the principal strongholds of Christianity in the West. As the portion of the Empire centred on Rome (and then Milan or Ravenna) weakened in the early 5th century, it grew more and more to depend on the huge grain shipments sent from the rich agricultural lands of Africa via the port of Carthage.

From 423 to 429 Carthage (and Africa) once more became semi-detached from the Empire, ruled as the fiefdom of Count Boniface. After his departure to Italy, and death in 432, no further warlords came to the city's rescue. In 439, when Gaiseric's Vandals swept eastwards from the toehold they had established in Mauretania and besieged Carthage, the frantic population did what little it could to resist and invoke whatever divine aid it could think of. One night, the whole population (Christians included) is reported to have made a sacrifice to Nocturnus, the god of night.[89] Eventually, on 19 October, the city fell, and over the next half-century, the Vandals used the naval resources and maritime knowledge they acquired to terrorise the western Mediterranean and beat back any Roman attempt to send a fleet to recapture North Africa.

Only in 533, with the defeat of the Vandals by the Byzantine general Belisarius, did Carthage re-enter the Roman fold. On the night before he entered the city, the Carthaginians lit lamps throughout the town to welcome him, as the panic-stricken Vandals took refuge in churches and sanctuaries.[90] Yet, as elsewhere in North Africa, it was a very exiguous hold, and the exarch who now administered it was more in the nature of a military governor than an official tasked to restore the province to its former prosperity.

As North Africa succumbed to the westward sweep of the Arab armies from the 640s, Carthage became an island, too strong to be taken, too weak to reclaim lost territory. Many of the suburbs, which had been occupied in the 5th and 6th centuries, were now abandoned. In 669, the foundation of Kairouan, just 150 kilometres to the south-west,[91] virtually sealed its fate. After falling in 695 and being recaptured by the Byzantine authorities two years later, Carthage finally succumbed to the army of Hasan ibn al-Numan in 698.[92] The city was razed and the conquerors chose not to settle there, instead building a new town on the site of modern Tunis.

Carthage continued to exercise a fascination for Western visitors, long after its political eclipse, though its inaccessibility in territory occupied first by the Ottomans, and then by the Barbary Corsairs, made visits rare. The poet François-René de Chateaubriand came to Tunis in 1807 on his way back from Palestine, but found little at Carthage,[93] for it had been used as a stone quarry for the expansion of Kairouan, and then by the Genoese who had occupied nearby La Goulette in 1535. Half a century later, Gustave Flaubert, in the throes of writing *Salammbô*, came to see for himself.[94] The first line of the novel, 'It was in Megara, a suburb of Carthage, in the gardens of Hamilcar',[95] evokes a city and an atmosphere forever lost. Now the buried skeleton of the ancient city sits below the charming leaf-shaded villas built in the French colonial period (and afterwards) for high officials – which line the lanes that lead to what has been unearthed, above all in UNESCO-sponsored excavations since the mid-1970s.

Remains of the late-Punic city have been excavated on the Byrsa hill. Originally, it was a cemetery in the 7th century BC, and then an industrial area. Towards the end, as Roman conquest threatened, housing was constructed here for the richer inhabitants, each dwelling with its own water cistern, the outside originally faced with red stucco. They cling to the slope of the hillside in a surprisingly dense quarter, as if the last generations of independent Carthage clustered here to await their fate. From the hill can also be glimpsed the double-harbours that gifted the city its great commercial wealth and military power, and which in times of trouble could be closed off with iron chains. In the centre of the Military Harbour sits the circle of Admiral's Island, upon which the Carthaginian naval commander had a house, and on which the Romans later built a military base.

The Roman town had the Byrsa hill as its central focus. Below the hill are the Antonine Baths, built in the 2nd century AD, and once one of the largest such complexes in the Empire, now retaining mostly just the substructures that lay beneath the main bath buildings. They are massive enough for all that, and the two huge columns restored from the above-ground complex give some sense of the gigantism of the project.

The most haunting remains of Punic Carthage lie 2 kilometres south-west of the Byrsa hill. Dating from the 8th century BC, the *tophet*, or necropolis, contains a whole field of stelae, disturbed when a Roman-era graveyard was built over the old Phoenician cemetery. Many are carved with stylised fingers or even simple grooves, a sign that they are dedicated to Baal Hammon, while those inscribed with a bottle shape, a female figure or a crescent are for the moon goddess Tanit. Moving down the slope to the left is the original Phoenician level, again filled with an array of grave-markers; along the edge of the cut that the archaeologists made to reach this level, even more stelae are visible, entombed in the soil, one forever entangled in the roots of a palm tree.

Through a small tunnel in an area over which a Roman house and cistern were later constructed, lie several funerary urns and stelae in the darkness, a haunted place, where the ancient Carthaginians feel just a finger's touch away. A disturbing quantity of the graves in the *tophet* contained the remains of very young children, most of them aged just one to three at the time of death.[96] The allegation of infanticidal sacrifices has long dogged the Carthaginians' historical reputation. Tradition claims that at a time of great political uncertainty in 309–308 BC, when Bomilcar overthrew the traditional political order, the city turned to this ancient rite of propitiation. Diodorus Siculus[97] paints a picture of a holocaust in which aristocratic families sacrificed hundreds of children, placing them in the arms of a great statue of Baal Hammon, which then tipped the babies into a flame-filled pit. Yet even Diodorus makes it quite clear that he is referring to an exceptional moment in Carthaginian history, and it may be, with the undoubtedly high level of child mortality, that these were simply infants who died naturally and whose remains were then consecrated to the gods.

Despite the Romanisation of Africa, Punic culture was no more extinguished than the Hellenised Greek civilisation of the Near East. As well as the survival of the Punic language – at least in the countryside, where Saint Augustine commented on the need for clerics to preach in it to their rural flocks as late as the 5th century[98] – Semitic religious beliefs persisted for many years, albeit transmuted into a more acceptably Roman form. The fertility goddess Astarte was often equated with Venus, while Tanit became Juno Caelestis, and, most widespread of all, Baal Hammon transformed into Saturn. A huge number of finds of Tanit stelae have been uncovered in Tunisia, each bearing the stylised symbol of a crescent moon, while from the 3rd century stones bearing the inscription *Saturno sacrum* ('sacred to Saturn') are still widespread.

Just as the history of Carthage was written – with little sympathy – by the Roman victors, so Punic literature was almost entirely suppressed. The only major work that was preserved, the work of Mago, reflected the Romans' long-standing interest in agronomy and, given the agricultural lushness of North Africa at the time, is as fitting a monument as any to the achievement of Carthage. Mago advised that vineyards should be planted on hill slopes facing north, to catch the breeze in such a hot country, and counselled the digging of trenches to let air get at the roots. From Carthage came, in Roman times, not only wine, but vast quantities of olive oil, though it faced stiff competition from Spain, and patriotic writers such as Varro continued to prefer oil produced in Italy. Pomegranates, too, or 'Punic apples' (*Mala Punica*), were a renowned Carthaginian export, as were, above all, African figs. Part of Cato's theatrics in turning the Roman aristocracy in favour of renewed war against the rump of Carthage's North African territory involved bringing a plump, juicy fig into the Senate house and announcing that it had been picked in Carthage just three days before. Not a weapon of mass destruction, perhaps, but it convinced just as well.

From the traffic jams and urban fuss of Tunis, the road leads southwest through increasingly scrub-like territory, lined with olive trees to either side, and begins to climb up into the Tunisian spine of the Atlas mountains. Finally, after around 100 kilometres, on a plateau and steep hillside on the valley of the Wadi Khaled, the city of Thugga (modern Dougga) comes into view, spread out unevenly across a wide area, more like a straggling stone orchard than a meticulously regimented Roman grid. An ancient settlement established well before the Roman province, it fell at first into the territory of the Numidian kings, for whom it served as one of their chief residences, and was not finally annexed by the Romans until 46 BC. At first, the city remained largely self-governing, continuing its traditional ways, and did not reach the status of *municipium* until the start of the 3rd century as Municipium Thuggense.[99] In 261, under Galerius, it finally received the ultimate accolade as a *colonia*, its name transmuting into the hardly laconic Colonia Licinia Septima Alexandriana Thuggenses.

Thugga sits in a rich agricultural area midway between the coast and the great plains of the interior. Though never on the main routes, it is typical of the towns that dotted the province away from the great metropolis of Carthage and provided it with the crops that made Africa the great provider for the hungry mouths of Italy. Sited on a defensible hill, the streets of Thugga wind around uneasily, trying to make the best of the troublesome topography. A number of urban villas give evidence of the unassuming prosperity that must have characterised it for much of the Roman period. From the House of Ulysses came an exquisite mosaic, showing the Trojan hero straining at the mast, muscles taut, eyes alight, desperate to break his bonds and draw closer to the fatally beckoning song of the Sirens. Somewhat lower down the hill the Trifolium House boasts a highly unusual design; the western rooms have a vaulted trefoil shape, with three shell-shaped apses. It is widely pointed out by locals as the site of Thugga's brothel, for no better reason than the number of identical rectangular rooms that run off the central courtyard.

Less puzzling in terms of purpose, and more obviously magnificent, are the forum buildings of Thugga. The entrance to the square is partially blocked off by a massive masonry wall, marking the 6th-century Byzantine perimeter, a sign of the troubled times that followed the Justinianic reconquest, when the government's hold over North Africa was uncertain and very much at the mercy of Berber tribal confederacies that had grown up to the south (and whose descendants are the Berber population of the Maghreb today).

Along the forum's edge, the Capitolium is Dougga's most spectacular building, its four monumental Corinthian columns and the great rectangular block of its sanctuary visible from almost all over the city. Constructed in 166–7 at a time of almost unchallenged prosperity for North Africa, its frieze contains a dedication to Jupiter, Juno and Minerva, the Capitoline Triad, for the salvation of the co-Emperors Marcus Aurelius and Lucius Verus.[100] Above it is a badly damaged carving of an eagle making off with the figure of a man. It almost certainly depicts the apotheosis of Antoninus Pius, the immediate predecessor of the emperors under whom the temple was constructed.[101]

Next to the Capitolium lies the Piazza of the 'Wind-Rose', so named from an unusual wind-compass inscribed into its paving stones, including Auster, the south wind, and Africus, the wind of the south-west. Amongst Dougga's other well-preserved remains are temples to Fortuna, to Liber Pater, to the Piety of Augustus – another example of the worship of emperors, or at least of aspects of their personality or office – to Saturn and, far to the west of the main site, to Juno Caelestis. The last two, the Romanised versions of Baal and Tanit, were perhaps the places of worship closest to the heart of the native population, and today the Caelestis temple still receives surreptitious offerings and the occasional sacrifice of a chicken by locals praying for rain.

Dougga's most venerable relic, however, is the Libyco-Punic mausoleum, a tower-grave down at the edge of the site, standing at the borders of an olive grove. Three storeys high, it is topped with a pyramid on which equestrian statues were carved. Dedicated to an unknown 3rd-century BC Numidian prince, it is a rare survival of such Carthaginian-style tombs. Local guides adamantly insist, particularly to British visitors, that it would have survived even better yet, had the British Consul in Tunis, Thomas Reade, not taken a fancy to the tomb's inscription in 1842 and demolished the edifice in his eagerness to remove it. Consul Reade has been unfairly impugned, however, for visitors in the 18th century already found the tomb in ruins, and when the Frenchman Camille Borgia came in 1840, he discovered the inscription lying on the ground. Reade's sole act of vandalism was to break it in two for easier transportation back to Britain. The inscription itself was bilingual in Punic and Numidian, and acted as a kind of 'Rosetta Stone' for the Numidian language, as Punic was already understood and the parallel texts thus enabled the decipherment of the Numidian alphabet.[102]

Seventy kilometres south of Thugga, along twisting mountain roads, Mactaris's fame rests, rather unfairly, on the testament of a single one of its antique inhabitants. But perhaps, without the inscription of the 'Reaper of Mactar', this medium-sized town of the Numidian hinterland, which lies on a plateau some 900 metres high in the Wadi Saboun valley, might have remained utterly obscure. The Mactar Reaper's inscription, now in the Louvre, relates the story of a poor peasant in the 2nd century – his name is not preserved – who rose from an impoverished start (his father did not own a house) and was forced to work as a farm labourer. After twelve years as an itinerant harvester, he then became a foreman, and finally a landowner, serving on the *curia* of the city; he was even honoured by his appointment as *censor*, the official tasked with the periodic enumeration of the citizenry. It is a rare and explicit example of social mobility and an indication that the lot of the peasant *coloni* labouring on the farm of a rich patron was not completely without hope.

The town, as many others in the region, became a haven for Carthaginians fleeing their final defeat in the Third Punic War in 146 BC, and these incomers constructed a temple and a *tophet* necropolis. Exactly a century later, it fell into Roman hands and was finally made a *colonia* by Marcus Aurelius around AD 180.[103] The place had been ringed with an old Numidian defensive wall, but the Romans demolished this circuit around AD 30.[104] The defensive deficit was made good in Byzantine times when the amphitheatre, built under the Severans, was converted into a fortress. A masonry wall and rather neat archway give, therefore, rather surprisingly onto the former oval of the arena. For those not wishing to be caught unawares, the building obligingly bears the modern label '*Amphitheatre. Gladiateurs chasse d'animaux sauvages.*'

Mactaris's forum, built in 116, preserves the scattered remnants of its portico, and a fine triumphal arch at its southern end, commemorating the victories of Trajan against the Germans, Armenians and Parthians. Just beyond this stand the 'Great South Baths', built in 199 and remarkably well preserved, although sections of white and green geometric mosaic exposed to the air are gradually crumbling away to nothingness.

The town's other unique monument is the *Schola Iuvenum* ('School of Youths'), built around AD 88 as a kind of aristocratic youth association, whose patron was Mars.[105] It therefore had a military character, although it was not directly linked with the army, and may have provided some militia or police functions to Mactaris. The 'club-house' had a large vestibule and courtyard surrounded by the remains of Corinthian columns. There is also a basilica-shaped hall with an apse, which could have been the main meeting place. Curiously, the tomb of one Julia Bennata stands to the south – as a woman, she would have been excluded from membership. Later, the whole thing was converted into a church.

Very little is known, however, of Mactaris's late-Roman existence, save for a reference to a bishop, Victor, in the mid-6th century. Clearly it was occupied in Byzantine times, but thereafter, unmentioned in the sources, it vanishes from sight. It was the fate of many settlements in Africa Proconsularis; once the economic network that had characterised the Roman province collapsed, many of the regional centres simply lost their reason to exist.

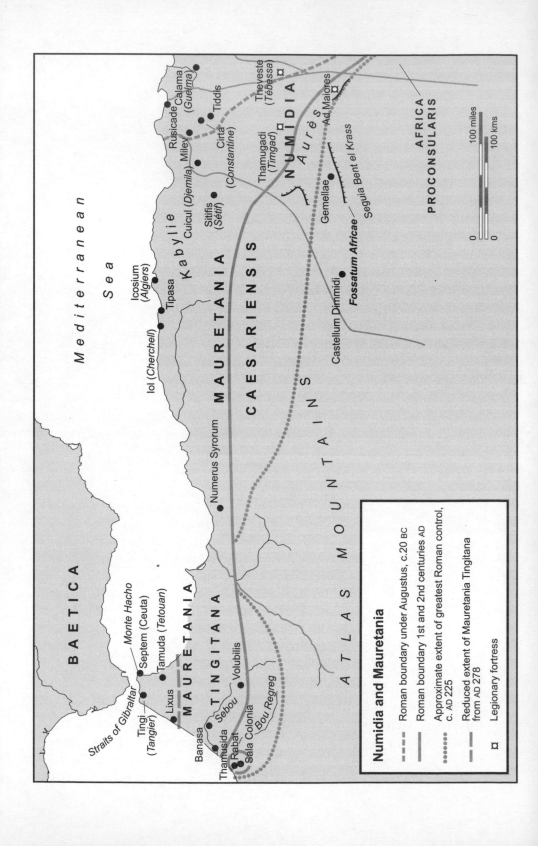

Numidia and Mauretania

- – – – – Roman boundary under Augustus, c. 20 BC
- ———— Roman boundary 1st and 2nd centuries AD
- •••••••• Approximate extent of greatest Roman control, c. AD 225
- – – – Reduced extent of Mauretania Tingitana from AD 278
- ¤ Legionary fortress

Labels on map:

Mediterranean Sea

BAETICA

Straits of Gibraltar
Monte Hacho
Septem (Ceuta)
Tamuda (Tetouan)
Tingi (Tangier)
Lixus
MAURETANIA TINGITANA
Banasa
Thamusida
Rabat
Sala Colonia
Volubilis
Sebou
Bou Regreg

ATLAS MOUNTAINS

Numerus Syrorum

MAURETANIA CAESARIENSIS

Icosium (Algiers)
Tipasa
Iol (Cherchell)
Kabylie

Rusicade
Calama (Guelma)
Milev
Tiddis
Cuicul (Djemila)
Cirta (Constantine)
Sitifis (Sétif)

Theveste (Tébessa)
NUMIDIA
Aurès
Thamugadi (Timgad)
Ad Maiores
Gemellae
Fossatum Africae
Seguia Bent el Krass
Castellum Dimmidi

AFRICA PROCONSULARIS

0   100 miles
0   100 kms

CHAPTER II

Numidia and Mauretania

If a man will wander in Timgad long enough of a spring morning, espe-
cially if he comes late in the season, when the rare visitors no longer reach
the place, he will feel arising in himself two lives, the life of his own time
which he knows and which has made him, and the life of that immemorial
past. It is a terrible, a dangerous, but a fascinating experience.
Hilaire Belloc, Many Cities[1]

That part of North Africa to the west of the areas acquired by Rome
from Carthage in 146 BC was divided into two broad zones, Numidia
(the eastern portion) and Mauretania (further west), occupied by a succession of native kingdoms (but whose area was somewhat different from
the later Roman provinces bearing the same names). It was a war
involving Jugurtha, the ruler of Numidia, that ultimately led to the end
of his kingdom's independence and a further extension of Roman power
in North Africa. Having murdered one of his brothers and seized the
throne, Jugurtha made the mistake, in 112 BC, of sacking Cirta (in modern
Algeria), which had been sheltering his surviving sibling and rival
Adherbal, and failing to prevent his victorious troops from murdering
the colony of Roman merchants that had been settled there. The subsequent war ended in Jugurtha's defeat and a new carve-up of Africa, which
still preserved a Numidian kingdom (under Jugurtha's half-brother
Gauda), but left it reduced in extent. It was only after the end of the
Roman civil war in 46 BC that the rump kingdom of Numidia, which
ran roughly from the borders of modern Tunisia to a point east of Sitifis
(Sétif) in modern Algeria, was abolished and joined to the Roman
province of Africa Nova.[2]

To the west of Jugurtha's former kingdom, the pre-eminent tribe were
the Mauri, who from around 200 BC had taken control of most of the
area of modern Morocco and western Algeria, pushing the Phoenicians
out of their footholds in towns such as Lixus (close to Larache) and
Tingi (Tangier).[3] By 105 the Mauri were ruled by Bocchus, who married

Jugurtha's daughter, but ultimately betrayed the Numidian king and was rewarded with a slice of the monarch's territory and continued independence under the watchful eye of Rome. By the 40s BC the kingdom of Mauretania was split into two, ruled by Bocchus II and Bogud, the former of whom initially supported Pompey in the civil war, but later made up for this indiscretion by adhering to the party of Octavian. As a result, he was allowed to maintain his throne and was rewarded with the territory of his rival, Bogud, who had unwisely supported Mark Antony against Octavian. Bocchus died, childless, in 33 BC and it then looked as though the whole of Mauretania would be annexed as Roman territory. That was until, after a brief period of direct rule, Augustus chose to give the kingdom of Mauretania back its independence.

The family of Juba II, who then became King of Mauretania, boasted a breathtaking and rather dangerous pedigree. His father, Juba I, as King of Numidia, had sided with Pompey against Julius Caesar in 46 BC and had lost his life for it. The young Juba, however, was spared and brought up in Rome in the household of Octavia, Augustus's sister. In 25 BC, the Emperor then presented him with the throne of the newly minted client kingdom of Mauretania. Juba II's wife, who had also been an orphan ward of Augustus, was Cleopatra Selene. Her mother was Cleopatra VII of Egypt, and her father Mark Antony. Juba II's son Ptolemy would, then, count a king of Numidia, a queen of Egypt and a triumvir among his grandparents, a heritage that would later prove his undoing.

Juba presided over a glittering court, although, as a Roman client, his freedom of action outside his own domain was strictly confined. His realm ran from the east of present-day Algeria right to the Atlantic coast of modern Morocco. Volubilis, which lay in the far west of his kingdom, had been the traditional Mauretanian capital, but Juba based his court at Iol (modern Cherchell), which he renamed Caesarea after the patriarch of his foster family. Juba's reputation in the ancient world relied as much on his literary endeavours and his tastes as an artistic patron as on his skills as a ruler. Among his works were *On Arabia*, which he wrote as a result of the experiences he gained in Gaius Caesar's expedition of AD 1,[4] as well as a history of Rome, a *Libyka*, which dealt with subjects closer to home, and works on painting, the history of the theatre and a variety of other topics.

Inevitably he became entangled with Rome's affairs in North Africa. In about AD 3, the proconsul Cornelius Lentulus was killed while on an expedition deep in the desert. The guilty party were the Nasamones, a tribe with a particular reputation for barbaric ferocity, and the incident precipitated a general uprising that brought in the Gaetulians, another

of the pastoral tribes of the desert fringes.[5] Juba joined his Roman patrons
in suppressing the revolt – his territory, too, had been invaded by the
marauding tribesmen. On his coins for AD 6 Juba had triumphal regalia
shown, but there is no evidence that he was awarded the honour by the
Senate.[6] He assisted the Romans once more, during the revolt of
Tacfarinas (AD 17–24), though he died just before the revolt was finally
put down.[7]

After its cultural and political renaissance under Juba II and Cleopatra
Selene, Mauretania retained its independence for just a few years. Their
son Ptolemy angered Gaius Caligula, who was his cousin through their
mutual descent from Mark Antony, and the Emperor had him executed
in 40 or 41. Suetonius relates that Ptolemy had worn a purple robe in
public, a prerogative by now reserved for the Emperor alone, but it is
possible that he was simply sporting the garb of a high priest of the Isis
cult at the dedication of a new temple at Campestris. Ptolemy's death
sparked a revolt in Mauretania under Aedemon, who was said to have
been a freedman of the murdered king. By 42, though, the war was over,
brought to a successful conclusion by Hosidius Geta, who campaigned as
far as the Atlas mountains. Mauretania was now incorporated as a province,
completing Roman control of the whole of the North African coast.

The administrative organisation of the region was not quite complete,
however, for it took until the late 190s, under Septimius Severus, for
Numidia – which had been attached to Africa Nova since 46 BC, but had
long been regarded as its own region, and had for more than a century
been governed separately from Africa by the legionary legates at its principal centre at Lambaesis – to be made officially a distinct province.

Numidia

In its geography, the province of Numidia mirrored much of the rest
of Roman North Africa, with a fertile coastal plain including such
thriving cities as Hippo Regius, backed by the high plateau of the Tell,
and then the descent into near-desert and total desert conditions in the
south. The most far-flung outpost in this region was Ad Maiores, a
station established under Trajan in 105,[8] in an isolated oasis some 140
kilometres to the south of Theveste (Tébessa). Occupied at least until
its destruction by an earthquake in 267, it guarded the junction of a
north–south road from Theveste with an east–west one that led from
Capsa in Africa Proconsularis all the way to Gemellae, another desert
fort in the south-east of Numidia.

This fort, just like Ad Maiores, was guarded by a series of defensive works, which have become known as the *Fossatum Africae*.[9] Composed of a network of earthworks and ditches, and largely built under Hadrian,[10] this does not run in a continuous line across the Algerian desert and so cannot be compared to the fixed defensive positions in northern Britain or, indeed, the *limes* in Germania and Raetia. The defences were probably sited both to provide some kind of shield for the forts slightly to the north and to channel the movements of desert nomads by dominating the routes along which they would have to travel when moving their flocks in search of pasture.[11] Nonetheless, those stretches that still survive, such as a 50-kilometre section south of Gemellae (known as the Seguia bent el-Krass), show that an enormous investment in time and labour would still have been required to construct this system of desert barriers.

The III Augusta legion, North Africa's only legionary garrison west of Egypt, led a fairly peripatetic existence under the early Empire. Despatched to the region in 30 BC, it was at first based at Ammaedara in Tunisia, before a westward move to Thevestis (Tebessa) in the AD 70s, finally coming to rest at Lambaesis (near Batna, 200 kilometres further to the west), probably around AD 81.[12] Around 100 kilometres south of Constantine in Algeria, this lies on a high plain at the edge of the Aurès mountains. There, in compensation for its earlier wanderings, the legion stayed for more than three centuries, until at least the early 5th century, when it was still listed as the garrison in the *Notitia Dignitatum*. From the reign of Diocletian it was also the capital of Numidia Militiana, when the old province was split into two (the northern half becoming Numidia Cirtensis).

Much of the earliest Flavian camp here has now disappeared under the civilian town that grew up on it after the military base was moved a couple of kilometres to its present site. The remains that can be seen date largely from the time of Hadrian, around 129.[13] It seems very austere, set – as befits a military camp – on a rigid grid, but the survival of most of the buildings to just a few courses gives it a stylised chequerboard feel, just a skeleton, with the life of the place long gone. However, it preserves the ideal ground plan of a Roman fort better than almost anywhere else in the Empire. Or at least it did, until the French colonial authorities thoughtfully constructed a prison across the south-western corner of the camp, destroying a part of the fortress. Those areas of the monument that were not obliterated were rendered totally inaccessible for many years, because the Algerian government still maintains the place as a high-security prison; even the pointing of cameras in the direction of the gaol is strictly forbidden. As we inspect the ruins we are accompanied, naturally at a discreet distance, by a squad of local policemen who squawk on walkie-talkies and seek to feign just the slightest pretence of interest in the Roman remains.

Looking down the camp's *via principalis*, the bulky structure of Lambaesis's most famous monument is clearly visible. The 'basilica' is a grand, showy, covered four-way arch at the intersection of the camp's main roads. A winged Victory decorates the central vault, and all around are niches, presumably for the exposition of imperial statues. The specific purpose of the basilica is not clear, but it certainly makes a statement of the legion's power and its permanence. The III Augusta legion's sojourn of more than 300 years at Lambaesis was also surely long enough to permit the construction of buildings whose utilitarian function was outweighed by their grandeur. Beyond the basilica, the camp commander's headquarters, the *praetorium*, lies in a very fragmented state, but the plan of the barrack blocks that take up much of the site is so well preserved that the larger rooms for centurions can be made out at the end of each row. The serried ranks of stones are at once both compelling and monotonous – much as, indeed, the life of the legionaries was, alternating long months of drill and construction work with only occasional bouts of campaigning.

To the west of the site lies a large military amphitheatre, used for both entertainment and military exercise. All the seats have gone, but the banked edges are largely intact, and to one side a fine double-arch survives. The central part of the arena has collapsed, exposing the pillars of the substructure, where stores were kept and prisoners who were to fight or be executed in the arena were held.

A couple of kilometres north-west lies another camp, sometimes known as 'the camp of the auxiliaries' (as distinct from the legionary camp, with its basilica). Little is visible, save from the air, but it was here that Hadrian delivered a famous address to the III Augusta legion in 128 on the occasion of a visit he made to Lambaesis while on his way to Mauretania. He praised the soldiers for their skill in javelin-throwing and for how well they had constructed a camp in a single day, when it would have taken other soldiers twice the time.[14] So pleased was the legion at these imperial plaudits that the whole speech was set down in stone, to be discovered by archaeologists in the civilian town, the *canabae*.

More than one-third of soldiers whose place of birth is listed on funerary monuments at Lambaesis or other inscriptions have it given as *castris*, or 'in the camps', an indication that their father had been a legionary, and it was here that they would have spent their early years.

Many of the tombstones sit in a garden outside the Lambaesis museum, a garden of stelae and eternal hopes. The guardian of the site and the guardian of the museum, however, seem to have a difference of opinion on the day of our visit, and the latter, who has possession of the key – a very important matter in Algeria – declares, in a funk, that not only is the key 'lost', for the moment, but that photography of the grave-stones is not permitted without special permission from the ministry. Charon could not have been more strict with those lacking a coin to secure his services.

A large part of the civilian town, which grew up close to the legionary camp, is taken up by a temple to the healing god Asclepios, which, with its five standing pillars, catches the eye far more than the shattered remains of the *capitolium* or the two bathhouses. Just on the border of this site, a small portion of the wall and part of the tower of the earliest, Flavian-era camp from the 80s has been excavated, the earliest stage of the 300-year Roman military occupation here. On the Asclepios temple itself an inscription in which the name of the III Augusta legion has been scratched out and then restored shows that even here, in its base, it was not immune to its memory being erased from the official epigraphic record. Even when the III Augusta had become but a distant memory, there was still clearly a settled population here as late as 683, for in that year the Arab forces of 'Uqba fought a battle near Lambaesis, and the local peoples, defeated, shut themselves into the fortress.

Forty kilometres east of Lambaesis, the town of Thamugadi (modern Timgad) – which lay at the junction of the north–south road with the west–east highway that ran through Lambaesis and its predecessor legionary camp at Tebessa, and ultimately on to Carthage – was the furthest south of the principal Roman settlements in Numidia. It is set on a high fertile plain, at the edge of the Aurès mountains, a range that the Romans never subdued, but instead elected to ring with fortified posts and settlements in an effort to contain what they could not conquer. There were army bases far off in the desert, the most remote being Castellum Dimmidi, isolated and baking in the Algerian desert; but, as Hilaire Belloc remarked of Timgad '. . . the Romans rightly thought that upon placing their town here, they had an outpost and would go no further, for the life lived further south is not natural to our race'.[15]

Thamugadi was founded around 100 by Minucius Gallus, legate of the III Augusta, as a *colonia* in the true spirit of the word, to house veterans of the legion after their retirement. Rejoicing in the full name of Colonia Marciana Traiana Thamugadi, it was planned on a precise grid, some 1,200 Roman feet square, and in its design it replicated rather rigidly, although on a grander scale, the design of a legionary fortress, making it the Milton Keynes or Chandigarh of Roman Africa. Indeed, its forum is pretty much where a legionary camp's *principium* might be expected to lie, and the other buildings are similarly deployed. The population has been estimated at some 15,000, which, given that a legionary served twenty-five years and so a maximum of 200 were discharged each year, represented many years of time-served veterans, even when their families were taken into account. The population must, therefore, have included a significant non-military element from the start.

Looking at the city from outside the remains of the wall – which was largely demolished as the population outgrew its bounds – the uprights of the buildings (the architectural feature that has survived best) create the image of a particularly orderly cemetery interspersed with the odd more grandiose funerary monument. Serving the citizenry were no fewer than fourteen baths; one of them by the *cardo* on the north side of town was bordered by a library donated, according to an inscription, by Marcus Flavius Rogatianus, at a cost of some 400,000 sesterces. More evidence of the municipal prosperity of Thamugadi came from the forum, which was ringed with monuments. A variety of graffiti survives etched into its blue limestone, including the digits of a sundial and the inscription *Venari, Lavari, Ludere Ridere, Hoc est Vivere* (which translates as 'Hunting, bathing, gambling and laughing, now *that* is living'). The forum was bordered by the only temple built at the time of the original foundation, which was dedicated to Trajan and had in its basement a vaulted room that acted as the city treasury, much as the Temple of the Standards in a legionary camp would have housed the unit's strongroom.

It was here that the *album* of Thamugadi was found, dating from 363–4.[16] It was intended as a list of all the town's dignitaries, including the decurions (the members of the curial order). In effect, it listed all those men who were liable to compulsory service – which mainly involved the expenditure of money on a variety of public projects and duties. It is a constant complaint in the sources, and one that much late-Roman imperial legislation sought to correct, that the decurions were seeking to evade their civic obligation by any means open to them. This included outright flight from the cities, the acquisition of titles or offices locally that might exempt them, and the payment of fines which, though burdensome in themselves, were far less so than actually taking up the onerous magistracies that they were seeking at all costs to avoid.[17] After the bureaucratic reforms of Diocletian and his successors, and the establishment of something resembling a centralised civil service, not to mention the multiplication of offices when the number of provinces was greatly increased, and an extra layer of governance added at the level of the vicariate, the opportunities for central service, and thus exemption – temporary or permanent – from town duties dramatically increased.

The distress of the decurial class is often cited as evidence for the decline of towns, but, as the nature of the Empire's government changed, so too did the relationship between the traditional urban ruling classes and the centre. Officials such as *correctores* appeared[18] charged with the reform of the administration of this or that town, and cities increasingly looked to a patron (*patronus*) to protect their interests, as the base of those willing or able to devote their own personal financial resources to power on a purely local scale diminished. Finally, those families who had traditionally been eager to memorialise themselves by donating public buildings, or services such as the provision of free oil at the baths, found, after the advent of Christianity in the 4th century, a much better spiritual bargain. In giving money for the foundation of churches, and in having this liberality commemorated in stone or mosaic inscriptions, they gained immortality both for their memory amongst the living and for their souls in the next life.

The first ten on the Thamugadi list are given the title *illustrissimi*, which in the inflationary world of late-Roman honorifics gave them exemption from civic service. The next rank includes *perfectissimi*, who were exempt until 354 and may have tried to cling on to this privilege even after that date.[19] There then follows a list of various priests, including thirty-two *flamines perpetui*, four *pontifices* and three *augures*, for service in a municipal priesthood or as part of the imperial cult was one of the more prestigious ways to serve one's city. A number of the men listed who did not have a specific title are given as *excusati*, and it is probable that they had paid some kind of fine to avoid the exacting financial toll of municipal office.

At the bottom of the heap are those fifty unfortunates who are *non excusati* and therefore liable to serve as magistrates, and to pay the hefty price involved. Interestingly, the Thamugadi album lists eleven Christian clergy (*clerici*). Christian priests had been exempted by Constantine in 319 from compulsory civic duties, but the acquisition of clerical status had become such a popular way of evading public service that subsequent emperors chafed at their predecessor's liberality, and as part of the pagan reaction under Julian the priests were restored to their place in the curial order and the concomitant obligation to carry out municipal duties.

Beyond the forum of Thamugadi lies the Arch of Trajan, a curiously muted affair compared to the triumphal arches in other North African towns. It was, despite its name, actually built around 166. Its large main entrance flanked by two smaller openings and the rounded attics of the arch's architrave are said to be typical of Eastern influence, which could say something about the origins of the legionary architects responsible for its construction. On the outer side, an inscription of Severan date originally had the word 'Auggg' with the three 'g's representing the three emperors (Septimius Severus, Geta and Caracalla). But here, as elsewhere, the agents of Caracalla were ruthless in erasing one 'g' after their master's murder of his brother Geta.

To the south of the forum, with a capacity for some 3,500 spectators, lies the city's theatre, its seating largely intact, but with the stage backdrop missing to permit spectacular views over the city from the auditorium's rearmost rows. If the theatre seems out of proportion to Thamugadi's orderly layout, the *capitolium*, in the south-west of the original town, is even more so. On a 53-metre-wide podium, only four of its original six columns now standing, it is erected on an axis at variance with the main grid pattern of the city, and so was clearly not part of the original plan. Whatever the motives for its addition, it was obviously being maintained comparatively late in Thamugadi's history, for an inscription dedicated to Valens and Valentinian (and hence between 364 and 378) commemorates the restoration of the building's portico.

Around the end of the 2nd century, the city burst its bounds, much of the wall was demolished and new suburbs built, particularly to the west of the original settlement. Amongst these are two entirely separate Christian complexes, one Catholic and one Donatist, mirroring the religious strife that divided North Africa throughout the 4th and most of 5th centuries.[20] The Donatist quarter lies to the southwest, and was the powerbase of one of the most notorious of the sect's leaders, Bishop Optatus of Thamugadi.[21] His cathedral church, originally a huge construction preceded by an atrium, survives only in ruins, though it was identified by a mosaic inscription that named Optatus and then, modestly, added: 'how great the praise to his name'.[22] The whole complex also included a further chapel, the bishop's house and, a few metres away, a baptistery with a hexagonal font decorated by a fine zigzag-patterned mosaic.

The Catholic area, situated well away in the south-west suburbs, is of poorer construction reflecting, presumably, its lower status at Thamugadi. In the end, Catholicism won, a pyrrhic victory that would be entirely undone by the advent of Islam just two centuries later. Between those events, however, came the Byzantine reoccupation of Thamugadi, represented by the fort to the south of the city.

Thamugadi seems to have been destroyed by tribes from the Aurès, who razed it at the time of the Justinianic invasion 'so that the Romans would have no excuse to come near us again'.[23] But the imperial general Solomon reused some of the ruins to construct new defences, using as his base the site of a Severan temple. It stands block-like some 110 metres long and 65 metres wide, its walls still standing in places to more than 15 metres in height. A simple gateway gives access to the interior beside a building inscription commemorating Solomon's work that lies in the undergrowth. Inside, the former barracks are a jumble of stones and a Byzantine chapel, all arranged around the original *piscina* (pool) of the Severan temple.

The fact that settlement at Thamugadi continued to the very end is shown by an inscription found in a Christian cemetery near the fort, which commemorates the building of a chapel by the patrician Gregory, whose term of office ran from 641 to 647, expiring after an ill-fated attempt to establish an independent Empire in the African provinces. Thereafter Thamugadi lost its *raison d'être*. No longer an outpost against the desert tribes, who were themselves largely incorporated into the Islamic empire, and with its role as an administrative and market centre disappeared, it soon withered away, decaying into the faded skeleton of today's site.

The Donatists, who had taken such a hold in Thamugadi, were a peculiarly African breakaway group. In the way of all good sectaries, they regarded themselves as the members of the true Catholic Church, and all the rest as excommunicants – not strictly heretics, for they differed from the official Church principally in whose authority they recognised, rather than in matters of dogma. The schism had its origins in the Great Persecution of Diocletian in 303–5. The initial edict, which reached Africa in mid-May 303,[24] ordered the handing over of Christian Scriptures and the destruction of some church buildings, but it was not reinforced by a general order to make a sacrifice to the gods until the following year. The initial reaction of some bishops, such as Paulus of Cirta, was to hand over some Scriptures, while others such as the Primate of Africa Proconsularis, Mensurius of Carthage – a nice piece of casuistry this – gave up heretical writings, which surely could not count as a sinful act.[25] By the end of 304, the persecution was beginning to wane in its intensity, and those who had refused to hand over Scriptures and had been imprisoned – though many had been martyred – for their obduracy, began to turn on those who had been weaker, labelling them as *traditores*, or traitors to the Christian faith.

In 311 or 312, Mensurius died, leaving the see of Carthage empty. The senior clergy, anxious for a quick succession, chose Mensurius's archdeacon, Caecilian, to replace him. Unfortunately, Caecilian had offended a leading member of the congregation, a Spaniard named Lucilla, by scolding her for kissing the bone of a martyr before communion. In revenge, she encouraged the populace of Carthage to name one of her servants, Majorinus, as the rightful bishop. At a council held in Carthage, the African bishops sought to mend the rift.[26] Yet feelings were running too high, and once Caecilian was accused of having been consecrated by a *traditor* and thus not really, in the eyes of the extremists, a priest at all, the council fell apart and the rival factions could not be reconciled.

By 313, Majorinus had died and the anti-Caecilianist faction came to be led by Donatus of Casae Nigrae, whose acuteness and able leadership over forty years meant that the schismatics grew in strength and could not simply be bullied back into the fold. He also gave his name to the movement, which was thenceforth known as Donatism. The 'official' Catholic Church remained strong in the large cities, in the smaller towns and particularly in the villages of the hinterland – and most especially in Mauretania – but Donatism took root and thrived, though the Catholics were to take great delight over subsequent years in accusing the Donatists of being bishops of mere estates (*fundi*) or manors (*villae*) and not of real towns at all.

It had been just a few short years since Constantine I's conversion to Christianity, and the Edict of Milan that put an end to the persecutions throughout the Empire, was issued, the same year that Donatus rose to prominence. The Emperor had heard murmurs of the troubled state of the Church in Africa, and was not best pleased, for he did not wish to have subscribed to the Christian religion only to find his new faith beset by squabbling and disharmonious factions that would undermine, rather than bolster, the unity of the Empire. Constantine gave his support to Caecilian without hesitation or, it seems, much thought, authorising the imperial procurator in Africa to restore to the Catholic faction any estates that had been confiscated during the persecutions.[27]

The howls of Donatist protest were heard all the way to Rome, and a petition was sent to Constantine demanding justice. It was a pivotal moment, not only in the schism, but for Christian history in general, because now, for the first time, Christians were appealing to a Christian emperor, the supreme secular authority, to make a ruling on Church discipline.[28] Constantine, infuriated that his initial decision had been questioned, nonetheless ordered the summoning of a council at the Lateran Palace in September 313.[29] At this Pope Miltiades condemned Donatus for his schismatic ways, and in particular for insisting on the rebaptism of clergy who had originally been baptised by *traditores*. The Donatists responded by accusing Miltiades himself of being a *traditor* and demanding another judgement. Constantine, showing admirable restraint, summoned a new council at Arles for August 314, at which the Donatists were condemned once more.[30]

In 317, persecution of the Donatists began with orders that their churches were to be confiscated. In a spasm of violence unleashed by the *dux* Leontius, a crowd of Donatists was massacred in Carthage,[31] while the bishops of Advocata and Sicilabba were murdered. This served only to provide the anti-Catholic cause with a rich crop of martyrs, and in 321 Constantine granted the Donatists toleration, hoping that by ignoring them their self-righteous sense of persecution might wither away and cause them to regret their error. Far from begging for re-admission, however, Donatus used the new latitude granted by the removal of the threat of official intervention to consolidate the African Church, so that by the 340s it was the Catholics who were on the defensive, under pressure from Donatist congregations almost everywhere.[32]

In 346, so confident was Donatus that he asked the Emperor Constans for official recognition of his position as Bishop of Carthage. Constans sent two imperial notaries, Paul and Macarius, to investigate, but rumours swirled around the African provinces that they had come to condemn Donatism afresh.[33] Riots broke out in Carthage, and the more extreme elements among the Donatists played into their opponents' hands. Known as the circumcellions – possibly from their habit of hanging around country shrines (*circum cellas*) – they acted as the muscle of Donatism, actively seeking martyrdom by attacking those who opposed them (including officials) swinging clubs and crying '*Laus Deo*' ('Praise to God'). In extreme cases, when they could find a martyr's death in no more satisfactory fashion, they threw themselves, lemming-like, off the edge of cliffs. In some mountainous areas, heaps of stones lying at the foot of such precipices, each carved with the word *reditum* ('ransom' or 'offering'), are believed to represent a commemoration of such mass suicides.[34]

The result, predictably, was that Donatism was outlawed once more. The decision was reversed in 361 when the Emperor Julian, mischievously seeking to sow dissent amongst his Christian opponents, permitted the return of all those who had been exiled on account of their religious beliefs, the Donatists included.[35]

The pendulum swung yet again in 364 with the accession of Valentinian and Valens, whose restoration of Christianity as the official creed carried implicit in that decision the need to crack down once more on schismatics and heretics. In the end it was the involvement, or at least the perception of involvement, in the revolts of Firmus in 372 and Gildas in 397[36] that fatally undermined support for Donatism in Africa. The tireless campaigning of Saint Augustine against the Donatists in the early 5th century also drew supporters away from them. Although ably defended by their very own theologian, Petilian[37] – who accused Augustine of bad faith, and implied (as it happens correctly) that the Bishop of Hippo had been at one point a Manichaean (and thus not a Christian at all) or was at least sympathetic to them – Donatist congregations continued to be pressurised. But the anti-Donatist coalition was too strong by now, and in a dramatic denouement at the Council of Carthage in 411, Donatism was condemned, its clergy exiled and adherence to their cause made a crime. Although the Donatists had mustered 279 bishops at Carthage (against the Catholics' 286, which included the rousing of a number of invalids from their sick-beds), their threat faded away in the last twenty years of Roman rule in Africa, but they had represented a very real local challenge to the hegemony of a Church centralising in the West around the see of Rome.

For the Donatists, Africa was the 'Bride of Christ' and, as they made no headway in persuading others outside their provinces of the justice of their cause, they came simply to ignore them. They were nourished in their belief in a salvation reserved only to Donatist true believers by a martyrology of their own. They prayed to saints such as Maxima, Secunda and Donatilla, who around 304 were tortured by being made to lie on a bed of crushed shells, then thrown into the amphitheatre, where a savage bear piously declined to devour them, and were finally beheaded.[38] Dedications to such martyrs, whose names are rarely found elsewhere, are a crucial indicator for archaeologists that a North African Church was occupied by a Donatist, rather than a Catholic, congregation.

Once the Vandals had captured North Africa in 429, however, the very notion of a separatist Church opposed to Rome came to have no sense, for Africa itself was now in opposition to the Roman Empire. The Vandals' Arianism, moreover, which led them intermittently to persecute those of a more orthodox bent, drove former Donatists and Catholics together. Separated from the political control of Rome and persecuted by their barbarian overlords in Carthage, the former foes were left more united in their common adversity than at any time since the Great Persecution.

Constantine (Cirta to the Romans) lay 105 kilometres north of Timgad, through intractable mountainous terrain. The city has antecedents stretching even further back. Now Algeria's second city, a bustling, crowded, traffic-choked metropolis, it is recorded as early as the 3rd century BC, when it was the capital of the Numidian King Syphax. Later it became the chief centre of Massinissa, the base from which he encroached steadily into the former territory of Carthage. In the confused period after Julius Caesar's victory against the Pompeian forces at Thapsus in 46 BC, Cirta and its territory were handed over to Publius Sittius, a mercenary adventurer and favourite of Caesar, who, with his band of followers, occupied a territory between the new province of Africa Nova and the lands of King Bocchus of Mauretania.[39]

Although Sittius himself was killed around 44–43 BC, the land around Cirta managed, together with nearby Rusicade, Chullu and Milev, to retain a separate identity for nearly a century and a half, as the confederation of 'Four Colonies', until the abolition of their privileges by Trajan and the elevation of Cirta to the rank of a more standard *colonia*. Although it was an important town in Roman times (and became the seat of the *dux Numidiae* in 534),[40] its very success in surviving into the Arab period and then beyond to become a thriving modern city has meant that almost nothing remains from the Roman era. Somewhere in the deep gorge that dramatically slashes through Constantine – dividing it into two parts connected by a precariously wobbling bridge built by the French in 1912 – lie two arches of a Roman bridge. More tangible are the five arches of an aqueduct, which lie largely forgotten in an open area above the city, part of the system that provided water to it.

Only 15 kilometres or so north-west of Cirta, but already mired deep in hill country, lies Tiddis or, to give the settlement its full name, Castellum Tidditanorum. The term *castellum* was generally applied in the North African provinces to those indigenous settlements that already acted as a focal point for their vicinities, but which were not formally organised as a *municipium* (or *colonia*) with a Roman constitution. The town lies precariously attached to a crag overlooking the gorge of the Rhumel river, as if waiting for some seismic wobble to send it tumbling into the valley below. Even relatively recently it was no easy matter to find the site, and it long remained remote from the attentions either of archaeologists or of stone-robbers. In 1893, the French historian Alfred Baraudon, hearing of some worthwhile Roman ruins there, spent a torrid day scouring the hills around in search of it, but finally gave up, declaring Tiddis to be *'vraiment introuvable'* and signing off with a bitter warning against having too much confidence in the veracity of local guides or foreign guidebooks.[41]

Had Baraudon persisted, he would have seen a town that mimicked the classical ideal in spirit, while varying from it as much in form as the vertiginous topography of the place dictated. The rosy-red barrenness of the surrounding hills makes the town's grey stones stand out more starkly as its roads and alleyways turn and switch sharply back in twists and hairpins to reach, after a half-hour's breathless climb, Tiddis's highest point. In places the slope is just too much and the walkways are replaced by flights of stairs to encourage tired travellers upwards. It has something of the character of the modern Berber villages that dot the Kabylie mountains, but actually to term it a 'Berber town' is to telescope history unduly.[42]

The site has no natural spring and is generally not well provided with water, so its innate defensibility must have outweighed this otherwise severe disadvantage. The deficit was made up by a large number of cisterns that dot the town, thristily capturing whatever rainwater the gods might provide. Tiddis's north gate has its very own monumental arch, dedicated by Quintus Memmius Rogatus, which imitates in miniature the grander affairs to be found at Timgad, Leptis or Dougga. On the arch's keystone is carved the image of a sword, as if an indication of the military purpose of the town, from the Romans' point of view – intended to defend and supervise the only partly Romanised inhabitants of the interior. Roman ways did, however, penetrate Tiddis; only a short way from the north gate lies a *mithraeum*, its shallow grotto excavated into the hillside, and with a few broken altars now lying about, some with the unmistakable image of a bull's head incised into them. The door jambs of the shrine bear a good-luck symbol of a double-winged phallus.

The city was defended in those areas accessible to intruders by a pre-Roman wall built of large cyclopean blocs, which was retained in Roman times and, much later, during the Arab period, repaired and reinforced, using demolished buildings and cutting across existing paths and edifices (including the immurement of a baptistery at the foot of the forum's retaining wall).[43]

A few bends further on lies Tiddis's tiny forum, at just 30 metres long and 10 metres wide the smallest in North Africa, and hardly the place for any but the most self-conscious mingling. Its purpose, then, was purely ceremonial. As Tiddis took on the aspect of a Roman town, so a Roman forum it had, perforce, to have. Among the altars and memorials erected in this tiny space was one to *Fortuna Augustae*, the Fortune of the Emperor, and a number to individual emperors, particularly the Severans from Septimius Severus to Alexander Severus. The last emperor honoured by name was Gordian III in 239, while the rulers of the mid-3rd-century are remembered only in a plaque attached to the baths constructed further uphill by Marcus Cocceius Anicius Faustus in 251, which states that he employed 'ruined buildings' to construct the cisterns and baths,[44] implying that the town, exposed in the hills, had suffered difficult times after the dissolution of the III Augusta legion in 238.

Here also stands a memorial to Quintus Lollius Urbicus, a local man whose family probably originated from Cirta, and whose career shows the astonishing heights to which someone from even a small hill settlement such as this could reach. Born around 100, he reached the praetorship in 129, commanded a legion in Noricum on the Danube, and was then instrumental in the suppression of the Bar Kochba revolt in Palestine in 132–5, was awarded a consulship between 136 and 138, and was then despatched to be governor of Britain in the early 140s, where he oversaw the initial construction of the Antonine Wall in 142–3.[45] Short of becoming Emperor, he had achieved everything an ambitious aristocrat could dream of. The inscription commemorates the consulate, the high-point of his career, and names him as the town's 'patron': Urbicus clearly was (or his home town hoped him to be) in a good position to swing favours on its behalf. That he did continue links with his native land is indicated by the well-appointed mausoleum that he erected for his parents at El Heri, 4 kilometres to the north of Tiddis.[46]

Christianity seems to have come late to Tiddis. There is no evidence of a bishop before the 5th century, and there is only one small Christian basilica. Indeed, the governor of Numidia at the end of the 4th century, Publius Ceionius Caecina Albinus, seems to have been responsible for the installation of a cult shrine to Vesta at Tiddis, which implies at least some residual pagan resistance to Christianisation even at that late stage. Apart from the *mithraeum*, the Christian baptistery and a small ruined Christian chapel near the north gate, the religious life of Tiddis was very varied. A substantial shrine to the harvest goddess Ceres clings halfway up the city slopes, keeping company with a nearby Temple to Asclepios, the healing god, while right at the top among a jumble of ruins and dry, parched vegetation lie the scattered remains of a shrine to that perennial North African favourite god, Saturn.[47]

From here the view down into the valley is spectacular. A series of blue ant-like figures gradually wend their way towards the summit, not taking the 'easy' way up the twisting decumanus, but cutting straight up the hillside. It is a platoon of the village militia, for Tiddis, or at least those few who visit it, still need defending from local insurgents. With their ages spanning the full range of active life and their vintage rifles glinting dully in the midday sun, they seem the rightful heirs of the last Roman defenders of the place, whose best hope of survival was probably to avoid being attacked in the first place.

The last coins found in Tiddis date from 406, during the reign of Arcadius. It seems, therefore, that regular economic activity and trade had ceased even before the Vandal invasion and normal life was not restored under Byzantine rule. In this latest period of Tiddis, a pottery kiln was installed on the site of a former villa and another in the *caldarium* of the baths. If not abandoned, the town was certainly transformed. There is evidence, indeed, from pottery found here of some sort of settlement as late as the 11th century, making it one of the most long-lived of the native towns of the region. Perhaps the mountain air encourages longevity, for one of Tiddis's monuments records thirty-one Tidditan citizens who lived to be centenarians, one of whom, Cutruvia Urbana, is said to have survived a very creditable, if scarcely believable, 130 years.[48]

The last resting place for the Roman Tidditans was a series of necropolises to the north, south and east of the town. The eastern cemetery lies close to the road, an exposed and abandoned jumble of sarcophagi, many of them commemorating deceased with the family name of the mercenary Sittius, for the Campanian *condottiere* was remembered in the region of Cirta long after his demise. Here – honour satisfied that no one has come to grief while inspecting the ruins – our guards thirstily accept a gift of water, for Tiddis's cisterns are long fallen into disrepair, and then wave us on through the 'safety' of the mountain road.

This route leads some 60 kilometres to the west, through the *bled*, the high plain ringed by mountains (here the Lesser Kabylie) that produces a surprisingly great yield in crops. Finally, nestling in a valley surrounded by almost lunar-like hills, lies Cuicul. Its Arabic name Djemila, 'the fair', accurately reflects the stern beauty of its setting. Although comparatively near to the coast, there was little ease of north–south communications, and so Cuicul's connections were largely to the east and west. Founded under Nerva as a veteran colony,[49] the town lay on a rocky outcrop between two wadis and began as a classic planned settlement on a grid pattern. Thereafter, as the population expanded, new districts had to be constructed further down, and so the lower levels seem as if they have been poured out of the original city bounds and then congealed in ten thousand dragon's teeth strewn about the hillside. Down past the remains of Cuicul's colonnaded *cardo*, an archway leads into the North Forum, the city's original civic centre, which preserves an enormous number of statue bases and inscriptions intact, giving a real sense of its role as the focus of local government, trade and self-publicity for the ruling clans. One of them preserves the tongue-twisting original name of Djemila, 'Colonia Cuiculitanorum', which must have given even native Italians pause for thought.

A series of steps run behind the forum, leading up to the raised podium on which sits the Temple of Venus Genetrix, the goddess of mother-hood, only three of its columns still standing, giving it a curiously fractured feeling. This version of Venus was traditionally seen by the Romans as the mother of Aeneas, who fled the burning ruins of Troy and, after many travails, ended up in Italy, where his descendant, Romulus, would found their city. Aeneas, crucially, was also viewed as the ancestor (through his son, Iulus) of the Julian *gens*, of which Julius Caesar was a member, and to which Augustus became attached by virtue of adop-tion. The worship of Venus Genetrix, although not particularly widespread,[50] thus became almost an adjunct to the imperial cult, and for a city to have such a splendid temple to her – mirroring that estab-lished by Caesar himself at Rome – was a formidable statement of loyalty.

Also bounding the North Forum is the market of Cosinius, dedicated in the 2nd century by two brothers, Lucius Cosinius Primus and Caius Cosinius Maximus. They were of Carthaginian origin, for Cosinius Primus had held various magistracies at that city before in turn becoming a *duumvir* at Cuicul. Still standing beside the twenty or so shops are the stone basins (one with a stone plug still intact) in which liquid measures were assayed, and an inscription showing that the construction of the complex cost the Cosinii brothers the princely sum of 30,000 sesterces.[51]

Nearby is situated a series of rich urban villas – the House of the Ass, the House of Europa and the House of Amphitrite – each named for the most splendid of the mosaics found there. The last-named was the site of one of the most spectacular of all, now in the site museum. It shows a brilliant array of Nereids depicted by the artist around a triumphant figure of Amphitrite, the consort of Poseidon, who is surrounded by dolphins and seals, the sea-creatures seen as her children, together with a very spider-like octopus. Nearby, a curious mosaic (from the House of the Ass) portrays a donkey looking rather pleased with itself, together with a variety of animals and naked figures clutching grapes; it bears the inscription *Asinus nika* ('The Ass conquers'), a mixture of Greek and Latin, which might refer to a victory of some sort by the owner of the place (who may therefore have been named Asinius).[52] Many of the mosaics were comparatively late additions, from the 4th or even 5th centuries, showing that the villas were occupied for more than 200 years after their establishment in the 2nd century.

To the south of Cuicul lies the principal area of the city's develop-ment in its middle phase. The Severan Forum, a huge irregular space, has a certain overpowering monumentality to it, just as the Empire itself was displaying a certain self-conscious effort by the late 2nd century, far removed from the easy-going expansiveness of the late Republic and the early emperors. Along one side stands a temple dedicated to the Severan family, constructed in 229, at almost the end of their rule, with two podiums stacked one atop the other, the central sanctuary being reached by a double flight of steps. Even in its partially ruined state it is the city's most imposing edifice, a statement of might by a dynasty whose rule would crumble within a decade.

Here, too, lies Cuicul's theatre, again part of the Severan reconstruction, partly scooped out of the hillside, which meant that elaborate substructures to support it were not necessary. Three curved stone sections of the backdrop survive, remnants of the three stage entrances that would have conventionally represented buildings or locations away from the main scene of the action, and through which the actors would have come onto the stage, depending on their supposed point of departure.[53] The topmost of the twenty-four rows of seats provides a wonderful vantage point to the hills beyond, the nearer ones partly wooded, then the higher peaks beyond brown and arid-looking, folded in and back over themselves in a confused muddle of slopes and wadis.

At the exit from the forum, at the start of the road that led west towards Sitifis (modern Sétif), a monumental arch (of Caracalla) built in 216 completes the collection of Severan buildings. Its single span towers high above the roadway, flanked by niches set in double-columns for the exposition of the imperial images. It was only mere chance that Cuicul preserved this magnificent arch, for in 1839 the Duc d'Orléans passed this way during an expedition against the desert tribes. So impressed was he with the monument that he decided to have it dismantled and removed to Paris. Fortunately (for Cuicul, at least), he died at the critical moment, so the structure was left in place.[54]

As in the majority of North African towns, the most visible buildings of the city's later phase are Christian in purpose. Two main basilicas, one of the 4th and one of the 5th century, together with a circular baptistery, mark the centre of the Christian quarter set on a hillside at a discreet distance from the original urban heart. The confused skeletons of the buildings are less interesting than the mosaic placed in one of them by Bishop Cresconius, which, if it was the same man as the one who attended the Council of Constantinople in 553, represents the last visible evidence for the occupation of the city.

The Council itself was called by Justinian as a means of settling the 'Three Chapters Controversy', which the Emperor himself had caused by having the works of three theologians (Theodoret of Cyrrhus, Theodoret of Mopsuestia and Ibas of Edessa) anathematised in an effort to reconcile Monophysites to the official Chalcedonian position on the nature of Christ's humanity.[55] This set off a storm of controversy, particularly in the Western Church, where many of the protagonists could neither read Greek (and so were at rather a loss as to what Justinian was trying to achieve), nor particularly welcomed continued imperial meddling in what they thought was the done deal of Chalcedon. A series of petty schisms broke out, with some bishops (such as Elias of Aquileia) point-blank refusing to have anything do with the condemnation of the Three Chapters.[56]

Ecclesiastical politics was not a pretty thing in late-Roman or Byzantine times, and Pope Vigilius, who travelled to Constantinople on an imperial summons in 546, was held a virtual hostage there for eight years, whilst the Emperor alternately tried cajoling and threats in order to get him to condemn the anathematised Chapters. Vigilius was even forced at times to take sanctuary in one or other of Constantinople's basilicas, issuing an anguished encyclical letter protesting at the outrageous treatment to which he had been subjected. Finally, after a cat-and-mouse game of acceptance, retraction and counter-retraction of the Three Chapters, Vigilius was allowed home in 555, only to die at Syracuse in Sicily before he reached Rome.[57]

Bishop Cresconius of Cuicul seems to have suffered no such indignities, but his home town had less than a century left of rule by Christian sovereigns. Here, unlike other places such as Timgad, the Byzantines did not build a fortress, but whether this was because the region was, for some reason, felt to be more secure or, just the opposite – that it could not easily be held and was not therefore worth defending – is unclear. The final fate of the city, too, is obscure. It is no longer mentioned in the sources, and presumably its population drifted away, leaving its colonnaded avenues, its arches and its splendid hilltop site untenanted and unregarded.

Mauretania

Just to the west of Cuicul, the province of Mauretania began. After the Romans acquired it in AD 40–2, it was initially governed as a single unit, but, during the reign of Claudius, around 60, this was divided into two, with the eastern part becoming Mauretania Caesariensis (whose western border was around Numerus Syrorum, modern Maghnia, 50 kilometres west of Tlemcen in Algeria), and the western portion – which covered roughly the north-west of modern Morocco – being organised as Mauretania Tingitana. Much as its Numidian neighbour to the east,

Mauretania had a comparatively densely populated coastal zone, a hilly, but still-fertile hinterland in which prosperous agricultural settlements clustered, and an arid southern portion, home to few save the odd patrol of Roman auxiliaries.

From Cuicul in Numidia, the road leads south-westwards to Sétif (ancient Sitifis), a town that lay inside the boundaries of Mauretania Caesariensis (with its capital at Iol Caesarea, modern Cherchell), but which from the 290s was the chief centre of its own miniature province of Mauretania Sitifensis.[58] The city that in fact became the capital of modern Algeria lies 225 kilometres to the north-west, on the coast. Of ancient Iconium, Algiers (its modern descendant) preserves almost nothing. The warren-like kasbah, clinging to the hill that leads down into the city's port, is crumbling through a mixture of studied neglect and programmed demolition to cleanse its teeming streets of the taint of Islamic radicalism that touched it during Algeria's vicious civil war in the 1990s. The pacification campaign that brought an end to this conflict, in which thousands died, has left an uneasy calm in places such as this, and in the regional towns to the south-east of Algiers intermittent bomb blasts are a sign that, as far as tourism and archaeological investigation go, this is a country that very much still lies on the frontier.

The kasbah sits on the site of the original Punic settlement, and its Roman successor stretched also along the coast, leaving only the traces of three bathhouses and parts of a necropolis. According to the 3rd-century Latin grammarian Solinus, the city derives its name from the Greek 'Eikosi' (meaning 'twenty', a reference to the legendary travels of Heracles in the area, during which he is said to have founded Icosium with the help of twenty companions).[59] Solinus's *Polyhistor*, however, is so stuffed with tall stories – such as the grasshoppers of Rhegium who emit no sound because Heracles was so irritated by their clicking and whirring that he told them to be silent – that the tale of the twenty founders of Icosium is probably equally fantastic.

Around 50 kilometres west along the coastal road from Icosium lies Tipasa. Its spectacular seaside setting and sheltered harbour attracted the attention of the Phoenicians as early as the 6th century BC, and there was already a thriving Punic community here by the time Mauretania became a Roman province. It was made a *municipium* under Claudius, and in the mid-1st century, Tipasa received a new circuit of city walls, some 2 kilometres in circumference, intended to guard against a Moorish attack that never came. It was made a colony under Hadrian or Antoninus Pius,[60] but never achieved outstanding pre-eminence.

It is the beauty of Tipasa's location, more than its historical standing, that makes it unique, and its remaining buildings acquire their grandeur more from its topography than their undoubted architectural virtuosity.[61] The place has inspired many to raptures, including Albert Camus in his *Noces à Tipasa*.[62] With its shaded pathways drawing the traveller's eyes into a pleasing struggle between the closed green world of the trees and the open blue expanse of the sea, the monuments seem but a series of fleeting stone-grey impressions. Close to the site entrance, the colonnaded *cardo* leads down first to a set of baths, where two fractured lines of brickwork standing to 14 metres indicate the remains of the *caldarium*. Beyond, the road, with many of its cobblestones still surviving, smoothed with age, gives on to the 'New Temple', a shrine to an unknown god, whose cult is now commemorated only by a few orphaned columns. Then it passes by the amphitheatre, some 80 metres long, where clear evidence of the concrete tapering vaults to support the now-disappeared upper levels show that the capacity of the place must have been large. Now, in the grassy oval, where formerly blood, fear and violence ruled, a clump of sheep tranquilly graze.

The city's forum lies on a peninsula about a kilometre from its port, complete with civic basilica and Capitoline temple. However, its most significant find was the House of the Mosaics, a rich private villa, whose floors were lavishly decorated with mosaics and its walls with sumptuous frescoes. Built on a pre-Roman cemetery, it was occupied from the reign of Antoninus Pius until the Byzantine era. One set of rooms was converted in the late 2nd or early 3rd century into private baths, with a summer dining room that gave a spectacular view over the bay. Later on, the north of the villa was converted for the manufacture of *garum*, the fish paste so beloved of the Romans.[63] In one room, three large storage jars can still be seen, the upper portions broken away, but the cracked bases still set into the concrete floor. The smell of the fish as they decayed and putrefied to just the right consistency must have tempered somewhat the later inhabitants' enjoyment of their idyllic surroundings.

Unlike many Mauretanian and Numidian towns, Tipasa does not seem to have been a bastion of Donatism – in fact quite possibly the opposite. After the relaxation of strictures on the sect by Constans in 347, Tipasa suffered the wrath of the Donatists and was sacked by a mob that included two of their bishops.[64] In 372, a revolt led by Firmus, a local aristocrat who was alleged to have received succour from the Donatists, suffered its fatal defeat outside the walls of the city. The inhabitants attributed their salvation to the miraculous intervention of Saint Salsa, a thirteen-year-old Christian girl who had angered the local pagans by stealing the most venerated of their idols, a bronze serpent with a

gilded head, and casting it into the sea. Infuriated, they beat Salsa, stoned
her to death and then flung her corpse to lie with their lost snake statue
at the bottom of the bay. However, a miraculous storm, blew up and
the waves deposited her body on the shore, where a sea-captain from
Gaul rescued it and buried the saint on the eastern promontory of the
bay, at a spot where in later years a basilica was constructed and a great
pilgrimage shrine sprang up.

The church lies there still, beyond the settlement walls, for the practice of not burying the dead within the city boundaries continued to be
adhered to. Within the burial ground's circular enclosure, its walls
embedded with decorative columns, dozens of lidless sarcopaghi cluster,
as though all jostling to reach as close as possible to the city's patron
saint, hoping that her sanctity would aid their own pleading on the Day
of Judgement. Beyond, a thick copse of sturdy trees girdles the necropolis in soothing green. The tomb of Salsa itself borrowed a pagan
sarcophagus, on which scenes were carved from the legend of Endymion,
a shepherd with whom Selene the moon goddess became so enamoured
that she entreated Zeus to preserve his beauty by granting him everlasting sleep – all hardly fitting for a Christian saint. In her own eternal
slumber, Saint Salsa seems nonetheless to have aged, for when the
sarcophagus was opened, it was found to contain the bones, not of a
teenage girl, but of a middle-aged woman.

Christianity clearly took a very firm hold here. The city boasts a
number of other early Christian basilicas, most notably the 'Great
Basilica', also by the sea, with no fewer than seven naves (later extended
to nine) and more than 50 metres long, with a series of reconstructed
arches on the side facing the sea, which make the church look as if it
has subsumed a miniature aqueduct within its precinct.[65]

A few kilometres west of Tipasa, the town is most dramatically highlighted against the surrounding massif of the Chenoua, whose form is
imaginatively compared – as so many such low hills are – to the form of
a sleeping giant. Here a road leads off towards an extraordinary funerary
monument, known most widely as Le Tombeau de la Chrétienne (the tomb
of the Christian woman). The huge beehive-shaped structure, visible across
the plain for many kilometres, is clearly no such thing, and dates from
the 2nd or 3rd century BC. Its soaring steps of brick, shorn of their covering,
sit on a base more than 50 metres in diameter composed of some sixty
engaged Ionic columns, making it look a little as if a Mesopotamian ziggurat
had merged with the Parthenon. False double-doors set a few metres up
the edifice, with stone beads and scrollwork, give a cross-like effect, which
is how the popular name of the building arose.

Another, even more fanciful legend is that this was the tomb of 'Florinda La Cava', said to have been the daughter of Count Julian, the Byzantine governor of Ceuta (in the far northern tip of Mauretania Tingitana, opposite Gibraltar) at the beginning of the 8th century. When the Visigothic King Roderick caught sight of her bathing naked, he was so inflamed with lust that he raped her, leading her irate father to take revenge by allowing the Muslim army of Tariq free passage over the Straits of Gibraltar to destroy the Visigothic kingdom.[66] Other legends held that the mound was the repository of a great treasure, guarded by a fiercesome djinn. So convinced of this were the Turkish rulers of Algiers in the 19th century that they had the mound bombarded in an effort to outflank the djinn's sorcery and secure the gold, but, when the French effected a more scientific excavation, they found the central burial chamber deep inside the mound empty of valuables or, for that matter, of bones. The high grade of the masonry, however, and the immense effort required to bring such a mass of stone up the mountainside suggest that it was probably a royal burial. Precisely who was interred here is unknown, but favoured candidates are one of Mauretania's glittering royal couple, Juba II or Cleopatra Selene.[67]

It is hard now to recapture the glory of Iol Caesarea, their capital, for time has not been kind to the ruins, which have been engulfed by the modern city of Cherchell, 25 kilometres to the west of Tipasa. The annexation of Juba's former kingdom in AD 40 did not mean the immediate eclipse of Iol, for it became the capital of the new province of Mauretania Caesariensis, and was promoted to the rank of *colonia* under Claudius. The remains of all this glory now require the modern visitor to hunt around the busy, crowded streets of Cherchell. The first relic, at least, is clear, for outside the city museum an array of orphaned columns stand in a piazza shaded by the umbrella-like foliage of delicious shade-providing trees.

The rest of the Roman city lies stranded amidst the traffic-choked narrow streets. The theatre, which has had most of the stone from its seats robbed, lies, rather forlorn, in the centre of a scruffy square. Most probably completed in about 13 BC,[68] it was at a late stage in its antique career converted into an oval shape and the stage façade removed, as civic taste came to prefer the bloody spectacle to the refined literary set-piece. The forum, which originally stretched almost as far as the theatre, now lies truncated in another down-at-heel little square. The remains of a flight of steps on which rested marble capitals can be seen turning a corner and then disappearing beneath a modern building. As late, though, as the 6th century economic life still sputtered on in Iol and a large bazaar of shoddily built stalls was excavated here.[69]

Further to the west lies a two-way arch, forming the centrepiece of a dusty traffic island, rubbish-strewn and now host mainly to some focused milling-around by underemployed Cherchellites and to the screeching of motorcycle tyres. It would have formed one of the main axes of the city, but now, shorn of any decorative motifs, it seems a rather desolate relic. The city baths, a few hundred metres away, were originally more splendid, modelled self-consciously on the Baths of Agrippa in Rome. They were constructed on a monumental scale, with soaring brick vaults, but today piles of marble columns lie in the undergrowth, and the gate to the little park in which they reside is firmly locked.

Mauretania Caesariensis petered out around Numerus Syrorum, near Maghnia in the far north-west of Algeria; and beyond, stretching to the Atlantic coast of modern Morocco, lay Mauretania Tingitana. It is by no means clear that land communication between the two provinces was possible (or at least regular),[70] and travel by sea may have been necessary between them. Indeed, for much of its career as a Roman province, Mauretania Tingitana was attached administratively to Spain rather than North Africa, from the time of Diocletian forming part of the Diocese of Hispania rather than that of Africa.

On the province's far western coast, Rabat, the capital of modern Morocco, has ancient antecedents indeed. Behind the façade of the 17th-century royal capital, all gorgeously tiled doorways and stately palace gardens, lies a Punic foundation from around the 7th century BC. At 4 kilometres from the sea, on the Oued Bou-Regreg, it was not typical of the earliest Punic settlements, which tended to be trading posts clustered for safety on the shore. In the area of the city now known as Chellah, which became the royal centre of the Merinids dynasty in the 14th century, a Roman-style city was constructed under Juba II, which, in about AD 50, was remodelled with the building of a forum, basilica and baths. About this time, most of the monuments of the previous town were razed and covered in earth banks, although whether during the revolt of Aedemon or as a deliberate act on the part of the rebuilders is unclear.

The site, known as Sala Colonia, lies on a slope above the Bou-Regreg river, its buildings sitting on a series of terraces set into the slope. Dry, parched and neglected, there is no delicacy in its state of preservation; a mass of stones and a couple of columns here; a hint of geometric mosaic peeking out from underneath a dusty tarpaulin there. Amidst the jumble of ruins the easiest area to read, the forum, is a large rectangular space, off which the little cubicle-like shops can still be discerned, a single headless statue in a toga welcoming any 21st-century visitors.

The *colonia*'s *capitolium* sat nearby, identified by a monumental statue of Jupiter excavated there. The mid-2nd-century garrison of this outpost, the *Ala II Syrorum*, was memorialised in an inscription of 144 in honour of its prefect, Sulpicius Felix.[71] In it, thirty-eight of the members of the city council thank him for his work in bringing peace and security to the town and rescuing them from the 'normal lawlessness' (*solitis iniuriis*) that had afflicted the town. That both provinces of Mauretania were under one governor at this time has been adduced as a sign that there were particularly severe security problems, but the evidence is by no means conclusive.[72]

In 288, the Bavares, Quinquigentanaei and other Mauretanian tribes rose up in revolt and were beaten back by the governor Aurelius Litua, but they continued to cause trouble and in 297 Maximian had to come in person to finish the suppression of the rebellion.[73] The Emperor stayed in Africa for eighteen months putting the provinces in order. He then decided that Mauretania Tingitana was simply not worth the expense of defending, and withdrew to an enclave around Tingis (Tangier) in the north. Almost all of the rest of Tingitana was left to the indigenous tribes, who had contested it for so long with the Romans.

Uniquely in the southern area of Mauretania Tingitana, Sala Colonia was not abandoned by the Romans at the time of the Tetrarchy. A mini *limes* of ditch and wall was erected some 10 kilometres east of the town and a Roman garrison retained there, which is mentioned in the *Notitia Dignitatum*.[74] Yet remains from this later era are sparse; an inscription of Constantine I, a Christian mosaic and a few tombs. Sometime in the 4th century, the forum was abandoned and turned into a rubbish dump; thereafter Sala was in effect an impoverished village, and its adherence to the Empire purely nominal. However, the ruins were still sufficiently impressive to be commented on by the Arab geographer El Bekri in the 11th century.[75] In the 13th century, the Merinids erected an encircling wall around the remains of the site, whose crenellated outline, pockmarked with square indentations, its mud-brick facing partly peeled off, still girdles Sala Colonia. The Merinids made use of what little remained of the Roman town, too, for in the mosque that they constructed to act as guardian to their royal tombs they employed several thin, delicately refined Roman columns. Now abandoned for a second time, they are a fitting symbol of one of Rome's most far-flung and forgotten outposts.

Northwards from Sala Colonia, the road leads towards the heart of Mauretania Tingitana. Here, on the banks of the Sebou river, lies Thamusida, 10 kilometres upstream from the modern city of Kenitra (and 50 kilometres north-east of Rabat). Although a reasonably prosperous place, it was never one of any great political importance. Its main source of visitors now are pilgrims to the shrine of the Muslim saint Sidi Ali ben Ahmed, a white domed square on the site's most prominent mound. Amidst the remains of the Roman *decumanus*, baths and temples, their children run and play, while the women in gaily coloured headscarves enjoy a picnic beneath one of the few shade-giving trees.

The city seems to have undergone its most significant growth from the time of the Flavians, when it became the location of a garrison, and had several temples, only the barest of whose outlines can be determined amongst the low grass, scrubby bushes and thistles. A larger camp was constructed under Marcus Aurelius to the south-west of the town,[76] this time big enough to hold a whole cohort or cavalry *ala*. Very eroded steps lead up to a podium, upon which most probably lay the *praetorium*, which was adapted by the addition of a large basilical hall under the Severans.

Further towards the river a series of rectangular pits arrayed in orderly rows represent vats for the production of *garum*, the fish paste that was a mainstay of Roman gourmands, and whose export was a significant source of revenue for the towns of North Africa. The defensive circuit that encloses Thamusida is a melancholy reminder that, for all the bourgeois prosperity, the garrison and the walls with their semicircular towers, it suffered the same fate as the rest of the southern part of the province, being abandoned in the 280s. Thereafter, there seems evidence only of 'squatter' occupation and a few huts, huddled together in the shell of their ancestors' much grander past.

Around 100 kilometres south-east of Thamusida, Volubilis is Morocco's most spectacular site, and the fine state of preservation of its Roman ruins creates the enticing impression that it must have been a centre of the greatest importance. For, compared to Carthage, Antioch or Alexandria – and even, at a pinch, to Constantinople itself – the remains are more splendid. Yet for all its baths, basilica and grand urban villas, for all the magnificence of its surviving mosaics, Volubilis was a place of strictly local importance, and one that the Romans abandoned relatively early.

The site lies at the foot of the Jebel Zarhoun, and it is a slight climb uphill before Volubilis really reveals itself, the remaining standing columns of the basilica gradually coming into view in a tantalising archaeological tease. The first traces of settlement on the site come from around the middle of the 3rd century BC, and the Punic influence here was strong; for the city long retained the title *suffete* for its magistrates, along the Carthaginian model.

Long before the Roman annexation and eventual division of the province, Volubilis was the western capital of the kingdom of Mauretania under Juba II. An untidy mound at the centre of the site represents the acropolis, the strong- (though not particularly high-) point around which pre-Roman Volubilis clustered. Some other elements of this stage of the city's development still survive, including a monumental altar near to the Capitoline Temple, and a shrine (often wrongly attributed to Saturn) which lies to the east of the city.

After Caligula had the Mauretanians' last king, Ptolemy, murdered in AD 40, Volubilis seems to have taken the side of Rome in the subsequent rebellion, and its reward was to be incorporated into the Empire as a *municipium*, with rights of citizenship and a ten-year tax exemption. The city, as a consequence of Juba's rule, was already partly Romanised, and under Nero and his successors development was rapid. The whole centre of the city is a grid of rich houses, many of them incorporating olive presses, evidence that even the grandest of families derived their wealth from the rural hinterland, the agro-barons of antiquity. Many of the villas, which otherwise survive in the barest outline, their walls standing to 50 centimetres or so and retaining only the odd pillar, do come to life because here, unlike so many other sites in North Africa, a large proportion of the mosaics have been left *in situ*. Dusty and fading from the effect of the summer's intense sunlight, they nonetheless give a focus and intensity to the houses, which would otherwise be bare and sterile skeletons.

An exception, however, is the House of the Voyage of Venus, whose main mosaic has been transported to Tangier. It was one of the largest of the villas, and originally had mosaics in at least eight of the rooms. The principal one, from which the house gains its modern name, showed the goddess of love, with heavily kohled eyes, impossibly perched on the prow of the boat, a series of bare-chested Graces in attendance tugging at the oars. But they are not propelling the boat, which is in fact carried along by a troupe of sea nymphs and tritons, whose strands of straggly seaweed hair stand out in contrast to the blue of the water.

Up from here runs the *decumanus*, alongside which another impressive range of houses is arrayed, leading eventually to the simple arch of the Tangier gate at the city's north-eastern end. The House of the Wild Beasts is named for the striking mosaic of wild animals on its floor, including a snarling tiger, a leopard and a somewhat damaged lion, while other villas cover the whole gamut of the classical visual repertoire, including the Four Seasons, bathing nymphs, Bacchus and the Labours of Heracles.

At the southern end of the *decumanus* lies Volubilis's most famous monument, the Arch of Caracalla, dating from around 216–17. At about 20 metres high, with a 9-metre opening, it overpowers almost everything else around it. Originally the arch would also have had an image of the Emperor riding a four-horse chariot, or *quadriga*. It may lack the grandeur of the arch at Leptis Magna, or the delight of that at Palmyra, but it is nonetheless hugely impressive.

Nearby lies the forum, which was completely renewed during the Severan era. Its squat basilica rises up dramatically beside it, double-apsed, but now lacking the two rows of columns that once ran down the middle. In the central area a semicircular depression has been cut into the floor. It is possible that this represents a baptistery and that it is evidence that this basilica – in origin a purely civil affair – was later adapted to Christian use. To the south, a small open area and steps lead up to a podium with a few columns still standing, and in front of it the bulky block of an altar. This is the *capitolium*, and the porticoed colonnade that stands beside it was dedicated under Macrinus, for even in the briefest of reigns time was found for imperial self-promotion, and it would not do for him to leave the field in North Africa entirely to the monuments of the Severan dynasty which he had supplanted.

Back on the *decumanus*, amongst the mosaic villas, lies a complex that has been dubbed 'The Palace of the Gordians'. It is in fact a collection of buildings, which was most likely the residence of the imperial procurator Ulpius Victor.[77] A unique series of inscriptions was found here on a set of altars, apparently giving details of negotiations between the Roman authorities and the local tribes, the Bavares and Baquates. Known as *colloquia*, and dated in a series that begins in 140 and ends in 280, it is difficult to determine whether they represent troubled relations with the neighbouring group, which necessitated a quick succession of peace treaties, or whether quite the contrary: that the tribes were accustomed to settle their differences with (or to seek favours from) the Romans through diplomatic means rather than warfare. The intervals between the *colloquia* grow shorter in the 3rd century, when there are eight within eighty years, as compared to the three in sixty years of the 2nd century, so whatever the reason for the dialogues, it seems to have grown more pressing. The chief of the Baquates, Iulius Matif, is referred to as *rex* in one of the inscriptions, dated 277, and his people are termed *gens foederata* ('federate peoples'). They were clearly thus outside the formal control of the Empire. There were no further *colloquia* after this, for the imperial government soon afterwards evacuated the southern portion of Mauretania Tingitana and such discussions were then rendered rather redundant.

Volubilis did not disappear, but among the indications of uncertainty is the superb bronze bust of Cato the Younger that was buried under the floor of the House of Venus at about this time. The city seems to have contracted to the south and east, into the quarter beyond the Arch of Caracalla, although some new buildings were erected there, including a late Christian basilica.

Of Volubilis, Hilaire Belloc mused, 'Here the impression is rather one of history and of contrast. Here you see how completely the new religion of Islam flooded and drowned the classical and Christian tradition.'[78] Volubilis was clearly still of sufficient importance in 788 that Moulay Idriss – in effect the founder of the Islamic Moroccan kingdom – used the much-diminished city as his capital for a time, before decamping to a new (and thus suitably pristine Islamic) settlement nearby,[79] which later took his name and played Tunis to the now-abandoned Volubilis's Carthage.

Around 150 kilometres' drive north-west of Volubilis, the road to Banasa seems to lead to nowhere, passing through sparsely populated rural territory south of the Sebou river and up a small side-route that cuts along the edge of fields of waving corn. For a city that became a *colonia* in the 2nd century, there is not a great deal to show. At first sight, even the grid pattern is hard to discern amongst the jumble of ruins covered with a low carpet of dry, parched grass and a species of thistle that snaps noisily when stepped upon. The only things that seem to be flourishing are a small group of palm trees, sucking water from the soil where all else finds only dust. The remaining stones of the city are lightly encrusted with spots of a rust-red algae that make them seem in the grip of some iron-based pox.

On the site of a pre-existing Mauretanian village, Augustus planted a veterans' colony – Iulia Valentia Banasa – some time before the region was briefly given back its independence under Juba II in 33 BC.[80] The settlement does not seem to have prospered and could well have been damaged or destroyed during the revolt of Aedemon, for the buildings that have been excavated date largely from the end of the 1st century AD or later. It was reorganised as Colonia Aurelia Banasa during the reign of Marcus Aurelius, but was devastated during the late 3rd century, probably during one of Mauretania's perennial tribal revolts, and was abandoned, together with the rest of the south of the province, during the reign of Diocletian.

To the left of the main site entrance, the ruins of a series of small buildings include a bakery, where a hoard of 457 coins was unearthed (the latest of them dating from around 259), buried in the panic before the final destruction. Further down a slight slope are the well-preserved and partly reconstructed remains of a bath with the dome of one room still half in place and a curious tower-like structure in the middle.

To the north, more substantial walls stand, though the general standard of construction is not good, for the nearest quarries are quite some distance away, and even then the quality of the stone found there is inferior. In the centre of town, the indistinct remains of the forum are situated. At its edge lies the 'Arch of the Basilica', which seems very precarious indeed, the keystone of its thin span nudged slightly out of position, fit to tumble down at the slightest tremor. Looking back into the forum from the arch, a few broken columns mark its portico, while at the south end stone steps lead up to a platform on which stand three altars, one of which has a dedication to Juno, another to Minerva, so that, although far less grand than its counterparts elsewhere in North Africa, it is clearly the Capitoline temple of the colony.[81]

The most important find from Banasa was the so-called Tabula Banasitana, a bronze tablet which – under the authority of twelve members of the imperial council, including three former proconsuls of Africa – grants citizenship to Julianus, chieftain of the Zegrenses tribe, to his wife Ziddina and their four sons (all of whom bore Latinised names). It preserves several imperial letters, the first from 168, which notes that, while it is not customary to grant citizenship to the tribespeople, in the case of Julianus an exception will be made.[82] The second letter, from 177, bestows citizenship on another Julianus, who is presumed to be the son of the first, together with his wife and children.

The grant to the wives is of some importance, for according to Roman law the children of mixed marriages did not automatically become citizens, but rather inherited the status of their non-citizen parent. The Tabula is a sign of the efforts the authorities made, through selective use of such privileges, to involve the native tribes in the dirty business of Roman patronage, and create a delicate balance in which revolt would be followed by the instant removal of the favours granted. Within half a century, however, the award of citizenship to all by the Antonine Constitution would remove this particular tool of imperial policy; and within a century the withdrawal of the *limes* north to the enclave around Tingis would render such manipulations irrelevant.

Closing on Morocco's north-western tip, Lixus (40 kilometres northwest of Banasa, and a few kilometres north of modern Larache), where the Atlantic breezes provide a pleasing respite from thousands of kilometres of North African desert heat, has some claim, at least in fable, to be the oldest settlement in Morocco. Legend relates that it was founded around 1100 BC, although archaeology has only revealed traces as far back as the 6th or 7th century BC, and no substantial buildings earlier than the 4th century BC have come to light.[83] The place first appears in the literary sources around 500 BC in the *Periplus* of the Carthaginian navigator Hanno. His extraordinary expedition sailed far down uncharted territory on the west coast of Africa, incidentally providing the first recorded description of gorillas. Quite how far he got – whether to Senegal, Cameroon or even further – is not completely clear. He was accompanied by interpreters referred to as 'Lixitae', who probably came from what was later known as Lixus, although, most unfortunately, it turned out that they were not familiar with the languages of the people who lived along the far southern shores to which Hanno brought them.

The land of the Lixitae was closely associated with the legend of Heracles. One of the traditional sites of the Gardens of the Hesperides – a rival being Euhesperides (Benghazi) in Cyrenaica[84] – lay along the banks of the Loukkos river, whose loops were said to represent the coils of the unconquerable dragon that guarded the garden's precious golden apples.

Lixus's political history was troubled. It seems to have been first destroyed during the early 1st century BC, possibly in connection with the raid by Sertorius, a Roman renegade who chose the wrong side in a civil war and who had taken refuge in Spain.[85] He invaded North Africa in 81 BC with a small expeditionary force, wreaking havoc and eventually capturing Tingis, before his successes led the Lusitanians to invite him back to Spain.[86] It then seems to have been sacked again in the turmoil that followed Gaius Caligula's assassination of Ptolemy of Mauretania. As some compensation for its travails, Claudius granted it the title of *colonia*, and thereafter it developed all the standard appurtenances of a prosperous provincial town. It was razed yet again in the middle of the 3rd century, presumably during one of the province's native uprisings. It was then rebuilt on a smaller site to the south and garrisoned by the *Cohors I Herculea*.[87] Unlike the towns and forts further south, Lixus was retained into the 4th century, but all traces of organised activity disappear before the 7th century, so that by the time the Muslims arrived, there was no one left to oppose them.

An ancient sanctuary to Heracles-Melkart (the guise in which he was worshipped most widely in Mauretania) sat atop the acropolis mound that formed the original settlement nucleus at Lixus, but before reaching it the path through the site loops like the sinuous coils of the dragon around and around the hillside's slopes. Passing by the lounging junior *gardiens*, none of them seeming a day above sixteen years old, the path leads first to the *garum* vats, laid out in a chequerboard pattern, each separated by thin stone walls for those brave enough to walk between the pools of fermenting fish. The place is safely downhill from the main settlement, which seems to some extent to bear out the almost universally bad press that *garum* has had since ancient times.

Yet for Lixus, it was a vital source of wealth. Around a hundred sites for the production of the sauce have been identified in southern Spain and northern Mauretania, but this was one of the most important, with a complex of about ten buildings devoted to the task. The industry drew much of its raw material from the annual migration of tuna, which the currents of the Mediterranean around the Straits of Gibraltar pushed close enough to the shore for teams of fishermen to catch the enormous fish (sometimes weighing up to 300 kilograms) and then to bludgeon them to death, in a ritual repeated into modern times off the coast of Sicily.

Ancient authors differed in their view of the *garum sociorum*, the finest grade of fish sauce. Pliny the Elder noted that it was as expensive as perfume,[88] while Seneca warned that gullible purchasers were simply buying rotten fish guts at inflated prices.[89] The basic production method was to remove the intestines and other parts that could not be consumed directly, then add salt to the rest of the fish and place the resulting mush in a jar, or *garum* vat, seal it and leave it for a couple of months to ferment. The exact type of fish (sometimes a mixture of several), the amount of salt paste and whether wine was added all had an effect on the final quality. Every so often the vat would be opened for stirring by strong-nosed workers.

The liquid that resulted at the top of the vat was most prized, and was drawn off to make the *garum* itself. The residue was referred to as *allex*, while a medium-quality product gathered from the paste beneath this was termed *muria* (and recommended for the treatment of burns!). The price of the best-quality sauce was extremely high; Pliny claims that two amphoras of the stuff could sell for 4,000 sesterces, an exorbitant amount that could equally have purchased a dozen top-quality slaves. Yet he may have been exaggerating somewhat, for of around 200 fish-sauce vessels unearthed in Pompeii, nearly 60 per cent were for *garum* (as opposed to *muria* or *allex*) and so it was clearly within the budget of the average citizen.[90]

From the *garum* vats and the accompanying cisterns that provided the necessary water for the process, the path leads up to the north-west and here, around a slight curve, lies the undoubted pearl of Lixus, its amphitheatre. Set in a bowl between two shallow hills, it was originally a conventional theatre; it is clear where it has been converted by building a wall some 4 metres high to protect the lower-range seats from the dangers of escaping beasts or resentful gladiators. The stage backdrop, the three upright stumps still standing, was cut off and a crude masonry oval created. Just to the east of the amphitheatre and butting against it was a small bath-complex, in which until recently stood the remains of a mosaic of Oceanus; allegedly a local youth was caught trying to dig out the face, presumably to sell it on, an ever-present temptation in countries where cultural budgets and wages are low in comparison to the lure of the international antiquities-smuggling market.

The town's river wall is composed of absolutely monumental stone blocks, from which a spectacular view over a bend of the Loukkos river is possible, lazily wending its way across the plain. From here the rest of the city is revealed, partly overgrown with low, tough bushes: the outline of a peristyle house; an almost intact cistern, with just one end of the structure broken; a small church; and a cluster of temples largely of Severan date, with now just a few columns from the porches and colonnades surviving. It is a quiet and contemplative place, little visited and mostly abandoned to the ministrations of goats and other domestic animals.

Of Tingi, the ancient capital of Mauretania Tingitana, and from which the province took its name, only hints remain. It now lies under modern Tangier, some 80 kilometres north-east along the coast from Lixus, and almost all of it has been swallowed up by the city's kasbah, where some baths and a possible Christian basilica were excavated. Once again Heracles plays a role in the city's legendary foundation. After the hero had bested the giant Antaeus in a wrestling match before seizing the golden apples of the Hesperides, which the Titan was guarding, he is said to have settled down with his defeated opponent's mother, Tingi, and sired the race which then populated north-western Mauretania. The enormous body of Antaeus was rumoured to have been buried in a nearby mound, which Sertorius ordered dug up during his expedition in the area in 81 BC. Gigantic bones were duly unearthed, to the great wonderment of the Roman general.[91] No doubt they were the bones of a dinosaur or mammoth, but the legend of Antaeus and Tingi was greatly enhanced by the discovery, and Juba II of Mauretania would later claim descent from Heracles and Tingi. The inhabitants of Tingi then had the good sense to side with Octavian against Antony and received Roman citizenship as a reward; their city became Colonia Iulia Tingi and remained quietly loyal to the Empire until the very end of Byzantine rule in North Africa.

At the northernmost tip of Morocco, just where it touches the territory of the Spanish enclave of Ceuta, another Punic settlement turned

Roman town lies on the outskirts of modern Tetouan, some 60 kilometres south-east of Tangier. Tamuda is situated 4–5 kilometres out of town, along roads lined with advertising hoardings and smart new developments that draw their finances from the money remitted by Moroccan migrants and businessmen operating in the much more lucrative markets of Spain. It sits in open ground on a dusty promontory ringed on one side by anonymous village houses; on the other by a water-filled wadi and groves of trees, with the foothills of the Rif mountains looming in the middle distance.

Piles of stones heaped up cairn-like at the entrance to the site promise little, but the line of a rise of ramparts soon becomes apparent, revealing the army camp that was constructed in the 2nd century AD. It seems not to be of the highest quality, but was modified in the next century with the addition of projecting semicircular towers that are still evident, broken shells rising to a metre or so. Tamuda may be identical with the Tamuco listed in the *Notitia Dignitatum*,[92] in which case its garrison was the *Ala Herculaea*, a cavalry detachment. At least four gates, at the cardinal points, survive, one a double-portal, where one of the entrances was blocked up at some point before the fort's demise.

The camp sat on part of the grid of the pre-Roman town, which had been abandoned during the mid-1st century AD, a destruction blamed, as elsewhere, on the unrest following the murder of Mauretania's last king by Caligula in AD 40. About 100–200 metres to the south a large rectangular piazza represents the heart of this pre-Roman stage, while arrayed around it are small square buildings that were probably shops. Everywhere, a covering of low, dry grass, further thinned by the attentions of a small herd of sheep, gives the place an abandoned feel.

It is a short forty-five-minute drive north along the coast from Tetouan to the border with the Spanish enclave of Ceuta. The coastal road seems incongruously wide, the developments of apartments and hotel complexes a long way from the chaotic hustle of Tetouan or Tangier. The status of modern Ceuta, controlled by Spain since its cession by Portugal in 1680 (before which it had been Portuguese since 1415), curiously mirrors that of its ancient antecedent, Roman Septem. Like Ceuta, Septem was long governed as part of North Africa (or Mauretania), but, from the late 3rd century, after the evacuation of southern Tingitana, it was attached administratively to Spain, whose fate it then shared for several centuries.

It was in fact the last fragment of the North African mainland to be held by the Byzantine Empire, and thus the last piece in the long history of Roman Africa. Its defences had been left to decay by the Vandals, but

John, one of the lieutenants of Belisarius (who had led the Byzantine reconquest of North Africa for Justinian), retook it in 533–4 and had a new city wall built, also decreeing the construction of a large basilica to the Mother of God. The Visigoths tried to retake it in 546, and managed to storm the army camp, but the Byzantines, belying their reputation for sometimes self-defeating piety, attacked the invaders whilst they were at their Sunday prayers and drove them off.

Thereafter it remained under tenuous Byzantine control until the early 8th century, the walls protecting the settlement when the rest of North Africa had succumbed to the Arabs. Its final governor was Count Julian, a shadowy figure, whose allegiances – caught between the Arabs, the Visigothic rulers in Spain and the far-away Emperor in Constantinople – are hard to pin down. In 706, Musa ibn Nusayr attacked the town, which again held out.[93] However, Julian became caught up in a power struggle between contenders for the Visigothic kingdom of Spain, taking the side of Witiza, the legitimate king, against the upstart Roderick, whom he accused of violating his daughter.[94] In revenge, he assisted the Arab commander Tariq ibn Ziyad, who was based at Tingi, to cross into Spain, and then, having disturbed the delicate balance of power by which Septem survived, finally opened the gates to the Arabs in July 711.

The gates of Ceuta are still not open to all. Just as for a time Septem formed the boundary between the empire and *barbaricum*, so today it lies along the border between the European Union and the outside world. Just as most of the cross-border moves in Roman times were by groups seeking a share in the economic resources of the Empire, sometimes to plunder, but more often simply to gain access to a more prosperous way of life, so Ceuta is beset by their modern-day counterparts, trying to enter Spanish territory by any means possible, legal or otherwise. The scene at the border is pandemonium; young men and aged market women wander up and down seemingly at random, vaulting over fences that define queues of indistinguishably separate purpose, or playing grandmother's footsteps with the border guards. Some lines breeze through the immigration checks, while others seem like holding pens for those without the agility or wit to argue their way through. At the border points of the Empire, or the gates into Hadrian's Wall, it must have been like this; not so much an invasion as an insistent throng arguing and cajoling its way to be allowed to engage in some peaceful (and lucrative) commerce. A genuine invasion must at times have seemed like an orderly relief from the daily repetition of such noisy theatre.

Beyond, all seems deceptively calm. The tranquil Ceuta coastal road gives a clear view of the bulky promontory of Monte Hacho, topped by a medieval fortress, which has a strong claim to be the southern of the mythical Pillars of Hercules (with the pillar on the northern side being universally agreed to be the Rock of Gibraltar).[95] Legend relates that Heracles, seeking a shortcut on his way to fetch the Cattle of Geryon as one of this Twelve Labours, smashed through the mountain formed by the body of the giant Atlas, and so separated Europe from Africa, with the two pillars being formed to either side. Monte Hacho was known in ancient times as Abila, and was settled by the Phoenicians as a trading post and salting factory.

The Roman name for the settlement, Septem, or Septem Fratres ('Seven brothers'), was a reference to its having, like Rome, its own seven hills. The Phoenician installations for the salting of fish carried on being used into Roman times, and a variety have been found, from the 2nd to the early 5th century. An inscription found with the word *Ordo* on it has been taken to mean that the city was at some stage elevated to the rank of *municipium*. From the 4th century, though, Septem seems to have fallen into a sharp decline, and around the time of the Vandal invasion may have been abandoned entirely. What Justinian retook and transformed into a strategic naval base in 534 was probably but a shell.

Nonetheless, Septem did recover and is mentioned by the 7th-century Spanish bishop and encyclopaedist Isidore of Seville in his *Etymologiae* under the name Septe.[96] The city walls that guarded Byzantine Septem lie roughly along the line of the early modern Murales Reales, which cut off the isthmus from incursions from the south and west. An impressive series of bastions and counter-bastions (designed to deflect artillery strikes and make undermining more difficult) harbours a minute section of the Byzantine walls, and a larger portion of those built under the rule of the caliphs.

Fifteen minutes' walk from the walls the Plaza de Africa, overlooked by the imposing baroque frontage of Ceuta's cathedral, seems to have marked the heart of old Septem. Beside it, under glass, lie sections of the walls of a 7th-century house. The most substantial remains, however, are of the palaeo-Christian basilica, a few hundred metres away. Enclosed within the shell of a modern museum, the remains are thus well protected from the ravages of sun and moisture. Around 25 metres long and 10–12 metres wide with an apse in the east, it was under construction in the late 4th century, but was never completed. By the 6th century it had been converted into a necropolis – the low level of life expectancy in Septem is indicated by the fact that more than 55 per cent of burials here were of infants, while only 2 per cent of the deceased were over fifty years old.

Within the basilica walls, the burials cluster together, some of them just interments in amphoras, others with simple brick structures as grave-markers. The nave of the basilica has been cut across with low sectioning walls, and the bare earth of the floor is pitted with holes, mostly shallow, some seemingly lined with bricks. A few of the graves sit in ordered rows, many others in disordered clusters. It seems almost as if the latter are the last survivors of some catastrophe, huddling together against a force that they could never hope to understand or overcome.

And in a way, so it was; for, if not for the contemporaries of Count Julian, these graves may have been the last resting place of their grand-parents. The place is an apt symbol of the resistance of the Empire, continuing against all the odds, holding the line in such a remote outpost, at the very end of the *limes*, when all else around them had fallen.

By the early 8th century, Maia, at the western edge of Hadrian's Wall, was well into its post-Roman phase, with the imperial troops having departed three centuries before. All of the western European provinces had been lost, while the Danube line seemed fatally breached by the Slavs and Avars. In the East, the Arabs had swept aside the *limes* in Syria and Arabia and had overwhelmed Byzantine resistance in Egypt, Africa and Numidia. Of all those countless forts, town and cities that had shared in the life of the Roman frontier, it was, unaccountably, Ceuta that was practically the last to resist. It is, therefore, a fitting place to take leave of the *limes*, or, for those travelling the other way, to begin the tracing of its course.

CONCLUSION

The long expanse of the Roman frontier was not an end in itself. Its thousands of kilometres, hundreds of forts and scores of major towns and cities did not, for all that they developed an autonomous and vibrant life of their own, exist in a political vacuum. They served – whatever the individual circumstances of their position or the history of their fall – to defend what lay within. The interior provinces of the Empire, and for that matter the frontier provinces for most of the time until the late 4th and 5th centuries, experienced centuries of peace and reached a level of economic development that they simply could not have attained in less settled regions or more troubled times.

At the heart of this *pax Romana* (spiritually if not quite geographically) was the capital, Rome itself. At the core of this lay the Forum (or rather Fora, for the original was gradually embellished and supplemented by new spaces laid out under Julius Caesar, Augustus, Nerva and Trajan), and at the centre of this was the *omphalos*,[1] a small, round brick structure marking the very centre of Rome and thus of the Empire. It is utterly drowned out by the showy marble façade of the Senate house, and the imposing bulk of the arches of Septimius Severus and Titus at opposite ends of the Forum. Yet from here[2] distances all the way to the periphery of the Empire were measured and, just a few paces away beneath the *lapis niger* (or 'black stone'), the grave of Romulus himself was believed to lie.[3] It is a curiously neglected spot, the broken black marble that marked it out cracked and surrounded by an unsteady rope barrier to prevent the tourists from trampling on one of the ancient city's most sacred spaces.

The Romans' expansion from small city-state to ancient superpower was characterised by a supreme pragmatism and an ability to muddle through and adapt. From the start, Romulus accepted slaves and runaways into his new statelet, and his successors incorporated, through citizenship or bargains with the local elites, more and more people into the Roman enterprise. First the people of Latium, the territory around Rome, and then, after the Social War in 91–88 BC, the inhabitants of the

Italian peninsula gained citizenship, while, up to the Antonine Constitution of 212, a steady creep of urban magistrates and discharged auxiliaries added to the total of those who had a personal stake in the Roman Empire. There is an instructive comparison to be made with Athens, the most successful of the Greek city-states, which denied citizenship to foreigners, even long-standing residents (or *metics*) and, while it overawed a selection of other Greek-speaking cities, never managed to establish an empire of more than limited reach, in time or territory. Roman pragmatism even extended to the watering down of the importance of the city of Rome itself, when, in the late 3rd century, the tetrarchal emperors established their fixed bases elsewhere – in Antioch, Sirmium or Thessalonica – and finally, from the 4th century, Constantinople completely eclipsed Rome as a political centre.

The study of the Roman frontier has been bedevilled by a concern for fixed and traceable lines, which is why an early concentration on phenomena such as Hadrian's Wall or the Germanic *limes* seemed to provide a set of pleasing certainties, which, on closer examination, turned into a muddle of provisos, hedges and exceptions. The obsession with fixed (and often immutable) borders probably has its origin in the European psyche with the terms of the Peace of Westphalia, which brought an end to the Thirty Years War in 1648. Before, the centre of Europe was a mess of overlapping jurisdictions and untidy conflicting sovereignties, a situation that did not seem to perturb the medieval mindset, but which played unhappily on early modern monarchs, who instead craved definites and absolutes in their quest to order and unite their countries.

The Roman *limes* was in reality a much more untidy affair, only reaching anything approximating the ideal of a fixed line on the stretch that fronted Persia. Here, there existed a power of similar status to the Romans, with whom cities could be shared out in precise measure. Yet elsewhere there was none of this neatness, and a vague mist envelops discussion about exactly where the Romans viewed their territory as ending. If anything it was a zone of influence, and the garrisons and walls marked the point from which that control was projected both inwards and outwards, largely by means of the army.

The matter of frontiers has become ever more topical in Europe at the start of the 21st century, with agonised discussions about where exactly Europe should end, what the 'purpose' of Europe is, what its constitution should be, and how the borders of the European Union should be policed and controlled. If there is anything that modern Europe (and the wider world) can learn from the Roman Empire, it is that adaptation is all. Augustus solved his dilemma by stretching the constitutional norms to their limit and establishing an imperial office, while still quite happily maintaining that the Republic survived. For all the enormous expenditure on the vast frontier armies, Rome gained centuries of peace in the interior, and the Empire spread cultural homogeneity not through force, but through the convenience of economic and social interchange. Large numbers of people were accepted into the Empire, notably through conquest, but also by means of controlled migration and through the settling of federates, so that the *limes* was never the uncrossable barrier that some might imagine it to have been.

The reign of Augustus to that of Honorius (the period within which the Roman frontier, as classically defined, existed) spans four centuries. For any political entity to survive that long – and Rome in fact in one sense did so for a millennium more – and for its frontier regions to remain largely intact throughout is an astonishing achievement. For today's political settlement in Europe to reach even a fraction of this longevity would be a triumph indeed. In the end, though, all the count-less pages of speculation about why the border collapsed, particularly in the West, amount to one simple fact: the Empire grew old. Adapt though it might, its mechanisms for dealing with change gradually became set and atrophied, its military 'immune system' needed more and more help from outside, and finally – faced with new generations of more vigorous neighbours, who had borrowed from the Empire what they needed to give their political systems and their cultures strength and coherence – it died of old age.

The Roman Empire gave rise to a culture with many elements in common, but still containing an astonishing diversity among its 200 million-plus inhabitants. To travel along its frontier, through more than twenty different countries and cultures, is to gain just a dim sense of this. The *limes* crosses modern political boundaries and through regions that are judged to belong today to different and conflicting geo-strategic spheres. Yet in the past Serbia and Britain, Turkey and Libya (and even Syria and Israel) all formed part of the same political entity. As well as the pleasure of tracing the ancient connections between all these countries, and the sheer richness of the remains along the frontier, to travel along the Roman frontier is to be touched by two emotions: wonder that after close to 2,000 years so much can survive, and sadness that for all our sophistication, we are unlikely ever again to create something so enduring.

ACKNOWLEDGEMENTS

I would like to express my very great thanks to all those who have helped me with a project which has been long in the making and whose scope seemed to grow every time I examined it. In particular, the team at Jonathan Cape: Dan Franklin, who was persuaded enough of the merits of the Roman frontier to take the book on; Alex Bowler, who has been a discerning and diplomatic editor; and Mandy Greenfield, the copy-editor, for her careful scrutiny of the text. Martin Brown's wonderful and clear cartography will, I hope, help guide the reader where mere words fail. Thank you also to my wonderful agent, Gill Coleridge, for all her support in a process which took longer in time and far longer in miles covered than I had ever suspected at the outset.

Many people assisted me along the way, either in travel arrangements, as guides, or simply through their kindness. Many of them did not even know of my self-appointed task to visit the whole Roman *limes* and would surely have dissuaded me if they had. To those I have omitted, or whose names I simply do not know, my apologies. In rough provincial order, thanks to: Douglas Moody for his hospitality in Falkirk; Susanne Dambacher at the Verein Deutsche Limes Straße for her assistance in arranging my tour of the German *limes*; Michaela Köhler for a delicious Roman meal at Mainhardt; Christian Weiss for showing me Vindonissa; András Bereznay for his sterling efforts in making contacts for me in Hungary; Professor Zsolt Visy for facilitating my visit there; and Máté Varga for shepherding me around the Pannonian *limes*; Mihaela Simion at the National Museum of Romania, Bucharest, for kindly showing me the collection; Edouard Popescu for his wonderful efforts in guiding me aroud Romania; Iosif Ferencz and Vladimir Brilinski for giving me such contrasting yet complimentary views of Sarmizegetusa Regia; 'Papa Bear' and 'Mama Bear' at Oreshak in Bulgaria for the heartiest meals a weary traveller could wish for; Snezana Golubović for showing me around the site at Viminacium in Serbia; Ana Wild at the Museum of Slavonia, Osijek; Tolun Cerkes for acting as the most determined and knowledgeable guide to eastern Turkey one could wish for; Nigel Fisher and Tanya Evans at Silk Road Travel for facilitating my visit to Syria; Ma'an al-Sabagh, whose enthusiasm for Syrian history and calm and pleasant companionship made my visit to the country such a pleasure; Dougan, who guided me in Jordan; Saddam at Petra, who kept me from falling off his horse more than once; Mohammed at Dajaniyah, whose kindness meant I got to see the fort close up; Rob Hitchings at Nomadic Travel for his help in arranging my visit to Egypt; Hussein Mersel for enabling me to reach Mon Claudianus and Mons Porphyrites in the Eastern Desert; Esra for showing me Alexandria; Ghada for guiding me in Aswan; and Mohammed for his assurance and determination during a gruelling summer trip in the Western Desert; Alaeddin for guiding me in Libya; Wadia in Tunisia; Renira Rutherford at The Traveller for her help in arranging my trip to Algeria; Hussein in Morocco for stepping in when others had failed me.

It is probably iniquitous to single anyone out, but I would like to express particular thanks to Torsten Pasler, one of Germany's wonderful *Limes-Cicerones*, who in four days showed me more of the German *limes* than I thought possible, as well as being an excellent companion; and Patrick Penev in Bulgaria, whose enthusiasm for my project seemed to exceed even my own, and who, in a series of long trips through Bulgaria, Croatia and Serbia, showed himself to be a wonderful guide and a true friend.

I'd like also to thank Amanda Faber, for her encouragement over many months and for making me sit down and think about the book's title. Further in the past, I owe a debt of gratitude to those who encouraged my love of history – they are many – but in particular the late Richard Rottenbury at Dover College Junior School, Tim Connor at Eton College and Professor Rosamond McKitterick at Newnham College, Cambridge.

All of these in their own way steered me from errors I might otherwise have made, but any which remain are entirely of my own commission.

Finally, my thanks are due to my partner, Tania, who endured my long absences with boundless patience, and my daughter, Livia, who shares my love for the Romans, principally because of their penchant for purple. Without them to return home to, I might well have given up at Hadrian's Wall.

NOTES

INTRODUCTION

1 For an account of the sources for the foundation of Rome, see T.J. Cornell, *The Beginnings of Rome, Italy and Rome from the Bronze Age to the Punic Wars (c.1000–264 BC)* (London 1995), pp. 10–76

2 And a very early phase of occupation by the Etruscans, a much more developed culture, to whom the Romans probably owe many of their traditions. For a discussion of Etruscan influence on Rome, see Cornell, *The Beginnings of Rome*, pp. 156–70

3 Caesar raided Britain again the following year, see p. 16

4 L. Richardson Jr *A New Topographical Dictionary of Ancient Rome*, (Baltimore 1992), pp. 293–5

5 Tacitus, *Annals*, 12.23.2–24, and 'Tacitus on Claudius and the Pomerium, Annals 12.23.2–24' by Mary Taliaferro Boatwright in *Classical Journal*, Vol. 80, No. 1 (Oct.–Nov. 1984), pp. 36–44, for a discussion of the Claudian extension

6 Tacitus, *Annals*, 1.11; see also the discussion in 'The Nature and Function of Roman Frontiers' by W.S. Hanson in *Barbarians and Romans in North-West Europe from the later Republic to late Antiquity*, ed. John C. Barrett et al. (BAR International Series 471, Oxford), pp. 55–63

7 *imperium sine fine dedi* (*Aeneid* I, 279)

8 'The Meaning of the Terms Limes and Limitanei' by Benjamin Isaac in *Journal of Roman Studies* 78 (1988), pp. 125–47

9 See Peter the Patrician, fr. 14, in Michael H. Dodgeon and Samuel N.C. Lieu, *The Roman Eastern Frontier and the Persian Wars (AD 226–363)* (London 1991), p. 133

10 See, for example, the discussion in W.S. Hanson, 'Why did the Roman empire cease to expand?' in Freeman et al., *Proceedings of XVIIIIth International Congress of Roman Frontier Studies* (Sep. 2002) (Limes XVIII BAR S 1084), pp. 25–34

11 On the economic argument for the borders, see the discussion in 'Supplying the System, Frontiers and Beyond' by C.R. Whittaker in Barrett et al. (eds) (above note 6), pp. 64–75

12 Most nearly after their victory over the Caledonians at Mons Graupius, possibly in Aberdeenshire, in 83

13 See the contribution by Benjamin Isaac in *The Limits of Empire: The Roman Army in the East* (Oxford 1992)

14 A.D. Lee, *Information and Frontiers: Roman Foreign Relations in Late Antiquity* (Cambridge 1993)

15 See p. 466

16 C.R. Whittaker, *Rome and its Frontier: The Dynamics of Empire* (London 2004), p.51

17 Ammianus Marcellinus, 31, 8.5, trs C.D. Yonge (London 1911)

18 Former slaves who were still beholden to their former masters by ties of reciprocal obligations. The 'imperial freedmen', who were former slaves of the Emperor, formed a particularly powerful group under the very early Empire. See Ramsay McMullen, *Roman Social Relations 50 BC–AD 284* (New Haven 1974), pp. 100–4. The number of imperial civil servants is estimated to have risen from only around 200–300 under the very early Empire to possibly around 30,000 in the Later Empire. In contrast, Han China in the 1st century BC had more than 130,000 bureaucrats. See Peter Garnsey and Caroline Humfress, *The Evolution of the Late Antique World* (Cambridge 2001), p. 36

19 Although these provinces in turn were the result of a previous subdivision under Septimius Severus (193–211) or Caracalla (211–217)

20 In the very early days, each of the Tetrarchs – the college of four emperors established under Diocletian to spread the burdens of power – had their own praetorian prefect, with the division on territorial grounds only becoming established a little later. R. Malcolm Errington, *Roman Imperial Policy from Julian to Theodosius* (Chapel Hill 2006), pp. 80–1

21 See, for example, Christopher Kelly, *Ruling the Later Roman Empire* (Cambridge, MA, 2004), pp. 138–86

22 Kelly, *Ruling the Later Roman Empire*, pp. 115–16

23 O.A.W. Dilke, *Greek and Roman Maps* (London 1985), pp. 112–29

24 See, for example, the discussion in *Aspects of the Notitia Dignitatum*, ed. J.C. Mann et al. (BAR Supplementary Series 15, Oxford 1976), esp. 'What is the Notitia for?' by J.C. Mann, pp. 1–11

25 Although it was in fact a joint decree with his then co-Emperor Licinius

26 Byzantium is the term generally applied to the eastern portion of the Empire from the later 5th century. Although in many ways anachronistic, as it was not the term employed at the time, it is so universally understood that I have chosen to use it to refer to the Eastern Empire after the fall of the last Western Roman Emperor in 476. For the eastern provinces between the permanent political split with the West in 395 and the deposition of Romulus Augustulus in 476, I have used 'Eastern Empire', and similarly 'Western Empire' for the western provinces.

CHAPTER I: BRITANNIA

1 Rudyard Kipling, *Puck of Pook's Hill* (London, 1906), Chapter 6, p. 173

2 Roger J.A. Wilson, *A Guide to the Roman Remains in Britain* (4th edition, London 2002), pp. 415–24

3 See, for example, David J. Breeze and Brian Dobson, *Hadrian's Wall* (4th edition, London 2000), pp. 39–43; Malcolm Todd (ed.), *A Companion to Roman Britain* (Oxford 2007), pp. 130–1; and J. Collingwood Bruce, *A Handbook to the Roman Wall* (14th edition, by David J. Breeze, Newcastle 2006), pp. 107–13

4 In his own account (known in modern times as the *Gallic Wars*), Caesar uses technical terms such as *deditio*, which imply the formation of a province. See Sheppard Frere, *Britannia: A History of Roman Britain* (London 1991), p. 27

5 In general throughout this book I have chosen to follow the Latin place-name forms given in the *Barrington Atlas of the Greek and Roman World*, ed J.A. Talbert (Princeton 2000)

6 The invasion force was made up of four legions: the II Augusta, IX Hispana, XIV and XX, together with a number of auxiliary units

7 During its course, both St Albans and London were burnt, the latter with the alleged loss of 70,000 lives

8 He served on the staff of Suetonius Paullinus, and may have been present at the final assault on Anglesey in AD 61, which broke the back of Druidic power in Britain

9 He probably arrived in the summer of 78, and served until his recall in 83. See Frere, *Britannia*, pp. 87–102

10 Frere, *Britannia*, p. 95

11 Tacitus, *Agricola*, 30. Calgacus also picturesquely (and, some might say, accurately) called the Romans 'the plunderers of the world'

12 Of course they did not, and could not, have actually thought of it as 'Scotland' for there was no such entity until the late Middle Ages. Indeed, tribal boundaries straddled what is now the border with England, while, later on (under Hadrian), parts of what is now England lay outside the Roman province of Britannia, and for a time (under Antoninus Pius) much of the lowlands of modern Scotland lay definitely within it

13 The date is not clear, and it may have been as late as 88. See Peter Salway, *A History of Roman Britain* (Oxford 1993), p. 112

14 Wilson, *A Guide to the Roman Remains in Britain*, p. 597

15 *Perdomita Britannia et statim missa*, Tacitus, *Histories*, I, 2. See also Frere, *Britannia*, p. 102

16 See Frere, *Britannia*, p. 107, for an outline account of the evacuation

17 At Carlisle, Brampton Old Church, Nether Denton, Carvoran, Vindolanda, Newbrough and Corbridge

18 A dynasty known collectively as the 'Flavian' Emperors

19 *Historia Augusta*, Hadrian, 11, 2. Also Birley, *Hadrian*, p. 123. The *Scriptores Historiae Augustae* (SHA), or *Augustan Histories*, is one of the few continuous sources for the period 117–284. It purports to be the work of six authors, each of whom tackled the biographies of several emperors. However, it is clear that it is almost certainly the work of a single author, who posed as multiple writers as a literary affectation or imposture, probably sometime in the last quarter of the 4th century. Whilst much of the material in the earlier biographies is probably accurate, for later emperors (and particularly those during the period of the military anarchy of the 3rd century), a great deal of it is unreliable and some outright fiction. See Sir Ronald Syme, 'Controversy Abating and Credulity Curbed' in *Historia Augusta Papers* (Oxford 1983), pp. 208–23, and for a very early contribution to the debate, Norman Baynes, *The Historia Augusta, Its Date and Purpose* (Oxford 1926)

20 Probably with him arrived a new governor, Q. Pompeius Falco, to whom would be entrusted the ambitious plan that Hadrian now conceived.

21 *Historia Augusta*, Hadrian, 11, 2 (trs David Magie, London 1922)

22 One of Hadrian's first concrete actions, however, had been to order the total evacuation of the Parthian conquests. On his way back to Italy, he also ordered that part of Trajan's Dacian conquests should be relinquished to the barbarian Roxolani. It probably made defensive sense, but to senators brought up on the diet of unrelenting success under Trajan, it may have seemed shocking.

23 See p. 78

24 See p. 140

25 Birley, *Hadrian*, pp. 78–80

26 The Roman mile is 1,618 imperial yards or 1,480 metres, around 9 per cent shorter than the modern British imperial mile. The wall is in total 70 British imperial miles, or 113 kilometres, in length. See Breeze and Dobson, *Hadrian's Wall*, p. 29

27 Breeze and Dobson, *Hadrian's Wall*, p. 40

28 Todd, *Companion to Roman Britain*, p. 120

29 Todd, *Companion to Roman Britain*, p. 120; Frere, *Britannia*, p. 117, twelve forts

30 Even where no inscription has been found, subtle differences in the construction techniques of the various structures on the Wall (such as the shape of the gateways) indicate the handiwork of the different legions. See Breeze and Dobson, *Hadrian's Wall*, p. 67, and Collingwood Bruce (ed. Breeze), *Handbook to the Roman Wall*, pp. 72–3, for more details. The milecastles in particular are susceptible to such differentiation

31 For the general order and date of the building works, see Collingwood Bruce (ed. Breeze), *Handbook to the Roman Wall*, pp. 102–4

32 See Breeze and Dobson, *Hadrian's Wall*, p. 78, for details of the chronology

33 See David Mattingley, *An Imperial Possession: Britain in the Roman Empire* (London 2006), p. 157

34 See the account in Breeze and Dobson, *Hadrian's Wall*, p. 82

35 Collingwood Bruce (ed. Breeze), *Handbook to the Roman Wall*, p. 465

36 'Hadrian's Wall: A History of the Problem' by R.G. Collingwood in *Journal of Roman Studies* 11 (1921), pp. 37–66

37 In the aftermath of the Batavian revolt. See p. 78

38 A Roman centurion, therefore, commanded not 100, but 80 men

39 There is some evidence that the first cohort was a double-strength one, at least in the 1st century, leading to a slightly higher estimate of legionary strength, at 5,500–6,000 men

40 At least until the mid-3rd century, when members of the equestrian order, the next rank down in the social hierarchy, came to command legions

41 The quingenary infantry cohort consisted of six centuries, each of 80 men, and the milliary cohort of ten centuries of 80 men. The cavalry quingenary ala of 512 men was divided into 16 troops (*turmae*), each of 32 men, while the milliary ala had 24 *turma*, making 768 men

42 For the camel units or *dromedarii*, see Karen Dixon, *The Roman Cavalry from the First to the Third Century AD* (London 1992), p. 32

43 The praetorian guard, however, amongst their other privileges, served for only sixteen years. See J.B. Campbell, *The Emperor and the Roman Army 31 BC–AD 235* (Oxford 1984), pp. 110–11

44 Paul Erdkamp (ed.), *A Companion to the Roman Army* (Oxford 2007): The Augustan Reform and the Structure of the Imperial Army', Kate Gilliver, pp. 187–200; Richard Duncan-Jones, *Money and Government in the Roman Empire* (Cambridge 1994), p. 35

45 Until 140, the children of discharged auxiliaries had their marriages to non-Roman women recognised and their children became citizens, but this privilege was then withdrawn. See 'Marriage, Families, and Survival: Demographic Aspects' by Walter Schiedel in Paul Erdkamp (ed.), *A Companion to the Roman Army* (Oxford 2007), pp. 417–34. This also had the unfortunate consequence that, technically, soldiers could not transmit property to their (illegitimate) sons, a disability that was ameliorated under Julius Caesar, who granted soldiers the same right as married citizens to make wills granting goods and property to their sons. This concession then fell into abeyance and was not revived until the time of Domitian; Campbell, *The Emperor and the Roman Army*, p. 210

46 David J. Breeze, *The Antonine Wall* (Edinburgh 2006), p. 103. The Antonine Wall would be held by around 5,000 men covering roughly half the distance of Hadrian's Wall (William S. Hanson and Gordon S. Maxwell, *Rome's North West Frontier: The Antonine Wall* (Edinburgh 1983), p. 158)

47 The normal size was 500 men. See p. 25

48 W. Hutton, *The History of the Roman Wall* (London 1802), p. 265. Hutton ascribed the Vallum to Hadrian, and believed it should be called 'Hadrian's Bank' and that the Wall itself should be attributed to Septimius Severus and

thus be named 'Severus's Wall'. He rather melodramatically said of the Wall that 'This Place has been the scene of more plunder and murders, than any part of the Island, of equal extent. During four hundred years, while the Wall continued a barrier, this was the grand theatre of war, as well as during ages after its destruction.' (p. 5). The first person to provide a decent account of the Wall, however, was John Leland, whose *Itineraries*, a record of his travels throughout England and Wales in the 1540s, include material on the Roman frontier works. William Camden's *Britannia*, published in 1600, gives a far fuller account of Hadrian's Wall, though at a time when travel was still fairly hazardous in a countryside infested by bandits and cattle-rustlers. The Reverend John Horsley's *Britannia Romana* in 1732 provided the first comprehensive account of the ruins, including descriptions of elements that have disappeared since his time

49 The numbering system was established in the early 1930s. See Collingwood Bruce (14th edition, ed. Breeze), *Handbook to the Roman Wall*, pp. 10–11

50 For the Turf Wall in general, see Collingwood Bruce (14th edition, ed. Breeze), *Handbook to the Roman Wall*, pp. 58–62. For the size of the turves, see Vegetius, *De Re Militari*, III, 8. Vegetius wrote a military manual sometime in the period 383–450 addressed to the Emperor of the time (who quite probably never read it), aimed at 'restoring' the legions to the glory days of old. Part of his solution was to reduce reliance on barbarian troops by recruiting more citizens to the armed forces. He seems to have collected together and summarised the works of earlier military writers, such as Julius Frontinus's *Strategemata*, and is an invaluable resource for all kinds of Roman military tactics, such as how to reinforce walls, how the legions were supposed to march out of camp, and even, in the case of siege, what to do if the salt ran out. See Vegetius, *Epitome of Military Science* (trs N.P. Milner, Liverpool 1996)

51 Tony Wilmott, *Birdoswald Roman Fort* (London 2005), p. 28

52 A geophysical, resistivity and partial magnetometry survey in 1997 tentatively identified several of the concealed structures in the interior of the fort. See J. Alan Biggins et al., 'A Survey of the Roman Fort and Settlement at Birdoswald, Cumbria' in *Britannia* 30 (1999), pp. 91–110

53 During the governorship of Alfenus Senecio

54 See p. 52

55 See Collingwood Bruce (14th edition, ed. Breeze), *Handbook to the Roman Wall*, p. 300

56 See p. 57

57 This was carried out by the governor Aurelius Arpagius in the time of Diocletian and Maximian, when Constantius and Maximian Daia were Caesars, and thus between 296 and 305. Flavius Martinus, the centurion in charge, supervised the works. See Collingwood Bruce (14th edition, ed. Breeze), *Handbook to the Roman Wall* pp. 298–9

58 Vegetius, *De Rei Militari*, II 23

59 Later to find fame on the eastern front, where his mistreatment of the Goths contributed to the Empire's disastrous defeat at Adrianople in 378. See p. 243

60 In the words of the historian Ammianus Marcellinus; Ammianus Marcellinus, XXVII 8, 4–9

61 Possibly the *Comes Litoris Saxonici* in charge of the 'Saxon Shore' forts in southern and eastern England. See Peter Salway, *Roman Britain* (Oxford 1981), p. 378

62 *Dux* (or 'duke') was a senior rank that became common in the Later Roman Empire, particularly referring to the commander across a stretch of the frontier

63 In passing he put down a revolt by Valentinus, the brother-in-law of the praetorian prefect Maximinus, who had been sent to Britain when his death sentence for an unspecified (but presumably very serious) crime was commuted to one of exile. Such usurpations by provincial notables – or by influential outsiders co-opted to a local cause – became increasingly common in the Later Empire; as the central authorities seemed impotent to provide for the security of the provinces, local leaders often simply raised up their own 'emperor', who would, they hoped, be much more attuned to solving problems in their own back yard.

Valentinus was not the last British usurper, and certainly not the most serious one. Around 380, Magnus Maximus, a Spaniard who had been a close companion of the Emperor Theodosius I, was appointed *comes Britanniarum* ('count of Britain'). Just three years later, his troops declared him Emperor, a role that he may have taken less than unwillingly, since Theodosius's appointment of his son Arcadius as co-Emperor in January 383 had removed any lingering hope that Maximus's distinguished career might be rewarded by the ultimate prize. Unlike Valentinus, Maximus struck outside Britain, removing part of the garrison for a campaign in Gaul against the Western Emperor Gratian (367–83). So successful was Maximus that, after capturing and executing Gratian near Lyons in August, the following year he received official recognition from Theodosius as co-Emperor. It took four more years, and a rash attack on Italy by Maximus, before he was finally captured near Aquileia and in his turn executed after a salutary lecture on his crimes by his former comrade Theodosius. The troops he had withdrawn from Britain for his continental adventure were probably not returned. The effects that this had on the local economy in the north may have been as damaging as any immediate reduction in security. The number of coin finds in Britain datable to after 378 – and thus the presumed level of supply – falls sharply. As the troops' possession of cash is what had driven the local economy, here as elsewhere on the frontier, their withdrawal probably caused a dramatic localised economic depression.

64 The situation is muddied by the existence of *ripenses*, first found sometime after 325, who seem to have been a superior grade of *limitanei* with somewhat greater privileges, but not as highly regarded as the *comitatenses*, while later-still units of *limitanei* were stripped from the frontier as the central field army weakened and were upgraded to become *pseudocomitatenses*. Southern and Dixon, *The Late Roman Army*, pp. 36–7

65 Under the early Empire, the *cursus honorum* set out a defined career path for ambitious aristocrats, beginning, for young men of the senatorial order, with minor magistracies known as the *vigintivires* in their early twenties, and then leading on to a position as the junior tribune of a legion, followed by further political positions as quaestor, aedile and praetor, then by command of a legion and then, for the truly successful, a consulate. The equestrian class had its own *cursus*, known as the *tres militiae*, which began with a prefecture of an auxiliary cohort, then a position as legionary tribune, then the prefect of an *ala* (auxiliary cavalry regiment). After this, the top equestrians could serve in positions such as Urban Prefect of Rome or Prefect of Egypt

66 Augustus raised the qualification for senators from 800,000 sesterces. See Matthias Gelzer (trs Robin Seager), *The Roman Nobility* (Oxford 1969), p. 22. The equestrians or *equites* were originally those who were liable for draft into the Roman cavalry as opposed to the infantry. The figure of 400,000 is first recorded in AD 49 (see Seager, p. 10). The process by which equestrians gained a monopoly over military commands is slightly obscure, and it is not clear whether the change came about through a conscious decision by any one emperor or as a matter of expediency to open out a career path to a wider group of serving officers. In any case, the junior officers of the legion, the *tribuni laticlavii* (they were known as this for the *laticlavius* or broad purple stripe on their togas, as opposed to the *angusticlavius* or narrow stripe allowed to equestrian officers), were also generally equestrians from about this time. It also now became possible for senior centurions to rise to the very top of the military, and, coupled with instability at the centre, the influence of the army became ever greater

67 See the discussion in Alan K. Bowman, Peter Garnsey and Averil Cameron (eds), *Cambridge Ancient History* XII (Cambridge 2005), pp. 115–20

68 See 'Strategy and Army Structure between Septimius Severus and Constantine the Great' in Erdkamp (ed.), *A Companion to the Roman Army*, pp. 267–86

69 *Cambridge Ancient History* XII, p.123; Agathias, *The Histories*, V.13.7 (trs Joseph D. Frendo, Berlin 1975), who gives this as the level the army ought to have been at, but that by the latter part of the reign of Justinian it had fallen to around 150,000 men; John Lydus, *De Mensibus*, 1.27

70 Zosimus, II.33.3

71 When their commander Flavius Secundus set up an altar. See Collingwood Bruce (14th edition, ed. Breeze), *Handbook to the Roman Wall*, p. 280

72 Breeze and Dobson, *Hadrian's Wall*, p. 291, and Collingwood Bruce (14th edition, ed. Breeze), *Handbook to the Roman Wall*, pp. 34–5. All three objects almost certainly date to the 2nd century

73 The Staffordshire skillet, confusingly, omits Aballava. Collingwood Bruce (14th edition, ed. Breeze), *Handbook to the Roman Wall*, p. 35

74 Collingwood Bruce (14th edition, ed. Breeze), *Handbook to the Roman Wall*, p. 38

75 Breeze and Dobson, *Hadrian's Wall*, pp. 291–8, and their list of forts on p.298; also J.C. Mann, 'Birdoswald to Ravenglass' in *Britannia* 20 (1989), pp. 75–9

76 This title was commonly the last of the major honorifics that were awarded to each emperor, and tended to be taken up late in an imperial reign (in the case of Augustus only in 2 BC). The first person recorded as having received the award was in fact not an emperor at all, but Marcus Tullius Cicero, for his role in suppressing the Catiline Conspiracy in 63 BC. Tiberius is said to have been offered, but refused, the title

77 For further discussion of the date, see Alan K. Bowman, *Life and Letters on the Roman Frontier, Vindolanda and its People* (London 1998), p. 15

78 Roger J.A. Wilson, *A Guide to the Roman Remains in Britain* (4th edition, London 2002), p. 499

79 They could have been for prisoners of war or as a temporary refuge for un-Romanised local inhabitants. See Wilson, *A Guide to the Roman Remains in Britain*, p. 504

80 Bowman, *Life and Letters on the Roman Frontier*, pp. 16–17

81 Tab. Vindol. II 164, see Bowman, *Life and Letters on the Roman Frontier*, p. 106

82 Tab. Vindol. II 346, see Bowman, *Life and Letters on the Roman Frontier*, p. 139

83 Tab. Vindol. II 291, see Bowman, *Life and Letters on the Roman Frontier*, pp. 71, 127

84 J.G. Crow, *Housesteads Roman Fort* (London 1989), p. 43

85 Flavius Stilicho, who was the architect of this policy, was a typical product of the Later Roman Empire; half-Roman and half-Vandal, he was, despite his part-barbarian heritage, unswervingly loyal in his service to the Empire. For almost a decade and a half, from the death of Theodosius I in 395 to his execution on charges of treason in 408, he dominated the politics of the Western Empire, though never, despite his earnest hopes and best endeavours, managing to insinuate himself into an analogous position in the East. Part powerful warlord and part skilful politician, it was men such as he who held the West together, though his consummate skill in solving immediate problems and pressing crises may have blinded him to the danger that the compromises he was forced to make might undermine the very existence of the Empire in the longer term.

In between seeking to assert his own ambitions, and dealing with the

challenge posed by Alaric and the Goths, who in the later 4th century threatened alternately to establish themselves in the Balkans or to march on the
Italian peninsula, Stilicho did at least find some time to spare for Britain.
The poet Claudian, who as an official panegyrist could hardly be expected
to criticise his master, sang his praises: 'His was the care which ensured
Britain should not fear the spears of the Scot, nor tremble at the Pict, nor
watch along the shore for the arrival of the Saxon.' Stilicho clearly seems
to have won some sort of victory against the tribes besetting the British
frontier, and the very fact that, with all his other problems, he had chosen
to deal with the crisis there in person shows that it must have been grave.
Claudian, moreover, claims that Stilicho fortified Britain against her barbarian
enemies, which could either be a poetic turn of phrase or refer to some
actual repairs to the frontier system on Hadrian's Wall.

Whatever the truth of the matter, the respite was short-lived. In 401,
desperate for troops to defend Italy against Alaric, Stilicho withdrew yet
another draft of troops from Britain. By now the line must have been very
thin, and it could have been at about this time that a British field army,
under the *comes Britanniae*, was established. With six cavalry units and
perhaps a handful of others, this miniature force was perhaps intended to
make up a mobile rapid-reaction unit to compensate for the decreasing
force levels along the frontier itself.

86 See Todd (ed.), *Companion to Roman Britain*, p. 309; 'Economic Structures',
  Michael Fulford in; Strabo, *Geographia*, IV.v.2
87 It arrived there sometime before 222, and possibly even in 213; John Spaul,
  *Cohors²: The Evidence for and a short history of the auxiliary infantry units of
  the Imperial Roman Army* (BAR International Series 841, Oxford 2000)
88 Wilson, *A Guide to the Roman Remains in Britain*, p. 485
89 See, for example, 'Mithraism and Christianity in Late Antiquity' by Engelbert
  Winter in *Ethnicity and Culture in Late Antiquity* (ed. Stephen Mitchell and
  Geoffrey Greatrex, London 2000), pp. 173–82
90 Manfred Clauss, *The Roman Cult of Mithras: The God and his Mysteries*
  (Edinburgh 2000), pp. 34–5
91 Clauss, *The Roman Cult of Mithras*, p. 43
92 Jerome, *Epistolae*, 107.2 (trs F. A. Wright, Loeb Classical Library, London
  1933); Clauss, *The Roman Cult of Mithras*, p. 170. Gracchus, the kinsman of
  the letter's addressee, is said to have destroyed this *mithraeum* whilst he was
  Prefect of Rome
93 J.S. Johnson, *Chesters Roman Fort* (London, 1990), pp. 2–9, and Collingwood
  Bruce (14th edition, ed. Breeze), *Handbook to the Roman Wall*, pp. 191–4
94 Johnson, *Chesters Roman Fort*, p. 37, and Collingwood Bruce (14th edition,
  ed. Breeze), *Handbook to the Roman Wall*, p. 195
95 Namely Sol (the sun) for Sunday, Luna (the moon) for Monday, and Mars,
  Mercury, Jupiter, Venus and Saturn (for Saturday). The names for Tuesday

to Friday are better preserved in Romance languages than in English (e.g. *Martedi* in Italian for Tuesday)

96 Wilson, *A Guide to the Roman Remains in Britain*, p. 476

97 J.N. Dore, *Corbridge Roman Site* (London 1989), p. 19

98 Cassius Dio, *Roman History*, LXXII, 8 (trs Earnest Cary, London 1927)

99 Dore, *Corbridge Roman Site*, p. 6

100 Dore, *Corbridge Roman Site*, p. 10, and Wilson, *A Guide to the Roman Remains of Britain*, pp. 474–5

101 The collections of the former Museum of Antiquities were moved in spring 2009 into a new home in the Great North Museum

102 Collingwood Bruce (14th edition, ed. Breeze), *Handbook to the Roman Wall*, p. 138

103 Collingwood Bruce (14th edition, ed. Breeze), *Handbook to the Roman Wall*, p. 115

104 Wilson, *A Guide to the Roman Remains of Britain*, p. 451

105 Apart from the brief notice given by Cassius Dio of tribes crossing the frontier during the reign of Commodus. A general is said to have died, but it is not clear who he was or, indeed, even if the 'wall' that Dio mentions was the old Antonine Wall or Hadrian's Wall itself; David Mattingley, *An Imperial Possession, Britain in the Roman Empire 54 BC – AD 409* (London 2006), p. 122. Todd (ed.), *A Companion to Roman Britain*, p. 139. Also Cassius Dio, LXII.8.2

106 The division may not actually have come into effect on the ground until the reign of Caracalla, however, as late as 213. See Frere, *Britannia*, p. 164

107 See p. 174, note 36

108 Peter Salway, *A History of Roman Britain* (Oxford 1981), pp. 176–7

109 Frere, *Britannia*, p. 162

110 Cassius Dio, LXXVI, 15, 2. See also Anthony R. Birley, *Septimius Severus: The African Emperor* (London 1988), p. 257

111 Birley, *Septimius Severus*, p. 189. In the aftermath of Geta's assassination, up to 20,000 of his supporters were also murdered

112 It was all part of a complex scheme to ensure the eventual successions of Marcus Aurelius and Lucius Verus in 161. Hadrian's initially preferred heir, Lucius Ceionius Commodus, was adopted in 136 (and renamed Lucius Aelius), but he was in bad health and died early in 138, just six months before Hadrian's own demise

113 Breeze and Dobson, *Hadrian's Wall*, p. 90

114 Breeze and Dobson, p. 94, and David J. Breeze, *The Antonine Wall* (Edinburgh 2006), p. 72

115 Breeze and Dobson, *Hadrian's Wall*, p. 112

116 Breeze, *The Antonine Wall*, p. 65. In the East the ratios were 4⅔ Roman miles to 3⅔ and 3

117 Because in a sense the building campaign might be said to be a sort of

military campaign, and thus merited a *suovetaurilia*. Breeze, *The Antonine Wall*, p. 70

118 Wilson, *A Guide to the Roman Remains in Britain*, p. 582

119 For the garrisons at Bar Hill, see 'The Garrison of the Antonine Wall: Some New Evidence from Bar Hill' in *Studien zu den Militargränzen Roms* III (Stuttgart 1986), pp. 53–7

120 The *Historia Augusta* records that in 161 the Emperor sent Calpurnius Agricola to deal with an impending war against the Britons, whilst the next major literary mention of the province is the cryptic remark of Cassius Dio concerning the transgression of the northern tribes across 'the wall' around 180. By this time, however, it is fairly clear that the Antonine Wall had been evacuated

121 Breeze, *Antonine Wall*, p. 167, for example

122 Such as at Chesters, and at Corbridge a little later in 163. See Breeze and Dobson, *Hadrian's Wall*, p. 167

123 Breeze and Dobson, *Hadrian's Wall*, p. 129

124 In 175, Marcus Aurelius had more than 5,000 Sarmatians deported to Britain to form part of the provincial army, although whether this was because it was the furthest-flung place to which he could deport his former enemies, or whether Britannia was indeed so hard-pressed at the time as to be in need of such substantial reinforcements, is unknown

125 Stephen Johnson, *Roman Forts of the Saxon Shore* (2nd edition, London 1979), p. 13

126 Johnson, *Roman Forts*, p. 16

127 Johnson, *Roman Forts*, p. 18. An inscription from Arles mentioning the prefect of the *Classis Britannica Philippiana*

128 Although they both wrote in the 390s, and it is possible that they may have been influenced by subsequent insecurity in the intervening century. Eutropius, *Breviarium* X, 21, and Aurelius Victor, *Epitome De Caesaribus*, xxxix, 20, and Johnson, *Roman Forts*, p. 199

129 Andrew Pearson, *The Roman Shore Forts, Coastal Defences of Southern Britain* (Stroud 2002), pp. 55–8

130 Pearson, *The Roman Shore Forts*, p. 66

131 See, for example, E.A. Thompson, *Romans and Barbarians, The Decline of the Western Empire* (Madison 1982), pp. 31–6

132 See p. 111

133 Eutropius, *Breviarium* IX, 21 (trs H.W. Bird, Liverpool 1993)

134 A panegyric of Maximian hints that this was because of bad weather (Johnson, *Roman Forts*, p. 28, and *Panegyrici. Latini* X, 119–21), but this probably conceals a reason that could not even be hinted at in such a public forum of praise for the Emperor

135 Johnson, *Roman Forts*, p. 28

136 Pearson, *The Roman Shore Forts*, p. 46

137 Eutropius, *Breviarium* IX, 22, and Johnson, *Roman Forts*, p. 31

138 He had in the meantime dealt a series of crushing blows to the barbarian Franks on the Lower Rhine, who had been in alliance with Carausius and had in effect sheltered his northern Gaulish possessions from recapture by the central authorities. Constantius was then able to capture Bononia, leaving Allectus's weakened regime isolated on the island of Britain

139 Johnson, *Roman Forts*, p. 31; Pearson, *The Roman Shore Forts*, p. 46; and Frere, *Britannia*, p. 331

140 Frere, *Britannia*, p. 331

141 It was probably at about this time that the British provinces were again reorganised, as part of a programme of subdivisions of existing units, which Diocletian ordered implemented in almost all regions of the Empire. The existing provinces of Britannia Superior and Inferior were split into two, being replaced by Britannia Secunda (with its capital at Eboracum) and Flavia Caesariensis in the north and north-east, and by Britannia Prima and Maxima Caesariensis (with its governor based at Londinium) in the south and south-east. Another province, Valentia, is also mentioned by later writers, but, rather than being a subdivision of one of the others, it may have been a new name for Maxima Caesariensis. Roger White, *Britannia Prima, Britain's Last Roman Province* (Stroud 2007), p. 37

142 Johnson, *Roman Forts*, p. 149

143 See the discussion in Pearson, *The Roman Shore Forts*, pp. 130–8

144 Pearson, *The Roman Shore Forts*, p. 85, who calculates that, again for Pevensey, this meant seventeen ships operating over 280 days, and that it would have taken a building force of 120 men working continuously three years to complete the fort

145 See the map in Pearson, *The Roman Shore Forts*, p. 106

146 Johnson, *Roman Forts*, p. 107

147 Susan Harris, *Richborough and Reculver* (London 2001), p. 34, and Valerie Maxfield (ed.), *The Saxon Shore, A Handbook* (Exeter Studies in History No. 25, 1989), pp. 136–7

148 Frere, *Britannia*, pp. 48–9

149 Harris, *Richborough and Reculver*, p. 8

150 Maxfield, *The Saxon Shore*, p. 142

151 Maxfield, *The Saxon Shore*, p. 145

152 Maxfield, *The Saxon Shore*, p. 147

153 Maxfield, *The Saxon Shore*, p. 159. There is a *Praefectus Classis Anderetianorum* (Prefect of the Anderetian fleet) listed in *Notitia Dignitatum* XLIII

154 'In this year Aelle and Cissa besieged Andreadsceaster and slew all the inhabitants; there was not even one Briton left there.' *Anglo-Saxon Chronicle*, 491 (trs G.N. Garmonsworthy, London 1953)

155 William the Conqueror landed near Pevensey, so Anderitum was in a sense his first foothold on English soil

156 John Goodall, *Portchester* (London 2003), p. 27, but see also Maxfield, *The Saxon Shore*, p. 160

157 By 342, however, Constantine's son, Constans, was forced to make an unscheduled winter visit to Britannia to sort out an unspecified problem with the barbarians. There are indications that the *areani*, who performed something of the function of scouts far out into enemy territory, were actually colluding with the barbarians, and they had to be disbanded – thus, presumably, robbing the Roman army of a vital source of intelligence. Goodall, *Portchester*, p. 27

158 Richard Stilwell (ed.), *Princeton Encyclopedia of Classical Sites* (Princeton, NJ, 1976), p. 731

159 For the date of 31 December 405, as opposed to 406 for the crossing, see Michael Kulikowski, 'Barbarians in Gaul, Usurpers in Britain' in *Britannia* 31 (2000), pp. 325–45

160 The early parts of Zosimus's history borrow extensively from earlier writers, such as Dexippus, Eunapius and Olympiodorus, but as a consequence sometimes muddle or misunderstand the original source. Nonetheless, as one of the few pagan historians writing on the 5th century, his history is invaluable

161 See Guy de la Bédoyère, *Roman Towns in Britain* (London 1992), pp. 121–9, and John Wacher, *The Towns of Roman Britain* (London 1975), pp. 411–22

162 His *Vita*, by Constantius of Lyon, is, as most hagiographies of the time, frustratingly short of the kind of detail that would really clarify the political situation in Britain just two decades after Roman rule collapsed there (and was, moreover, written some fifty years after the events it describes). See E.A. Thompson, *Saint Germanus of Auxerre and the End of Roman Britain* (Woodbridge, Suffolk, 1984)

163 See Thompson, *Saint Germanus of Auxerre and the End of Roman Britain*, p. 11, and *Vita Sancti German*, s.15 (261,23)

164 Thompson, *Saint Germanus of Auxerre and the End of Roman Britain*, p. 19

165 Thompson, *Saint Germanus of Auxerre and the End of Roman Britain*, p. 41

166 Gallic Chronicler of 452 (442). See Maxfield, *The Saxon Shore*, p. 81

167 Gildas, *De Excidio Britanniae*, 20

168 Procopius, *History of the Wars*, 3.2.31 and 38a

CHAPTER 2: GERMANIA

1 Cassius Dio, *Roman History* (trs Earnest Cary, London 1914–27), Book LVI, 4–5

2 An alternative (and probably more likely) theory for the lighthouse's location is Boulogne. See Alan K. Bowman, Edward Chaplin and Andrew Lintott (eds), *Cambridge Ancient History* X (Cambridge 2006), p. 228

3 See p. 129

4 Julius Caesar, *Gallic Wars*, IV.2 and VI.4 (trs S.A. Handford, Harmondsworth 1963); H. Schönberger, 'The Roman Frontier in Germany: An Archaeological Survey' in *Journal of Roman Studies* 59 (1969), pp. 144–97

5 There does, though, seem to have been a deliberate Roman policy of allowing friendly tribes to settle on the right bank of the Rhine, creating a buffer between Gaul and trans-Rhenish Germany. See Bowman, Champlin and Lintott (eds), *Cambridge Ancient History* X, p. 522

6 Augustus, or Gaius Octavius as he was known in his childhood (and to historians as Octavian), had a long, though privileged, route to become the first Emperor of Rome. Julius Caesar spotted his promise early and adopted him, thus gifting him simultaneously the strong legacy of the brilliant general's military prestige and the more problematic accusations that Octavian, just as his adoptive father, was intent on undermining the very basis of the Roman Republic. This suspicion about Octavian turned out, of course, to be entirely true. Although he accepted a role as a member of the Second Triumvirate (with Mark Antony and Marcus Lepidus, the latter more financier than politician or general), Octavian clearly saw himself as pre-eminent among the three, a position that Mark Antony, fresh from his victory against the forces of the Senate at Philippi in 42 BC, was wholly unwilling to concede. The domains of Rome were not big enough to accommodate the towering ambitions of both Antony and Octavian, and a decade of bitter political struggle, failed reconciliations and outright military confrontation ended with Mark Antony's defeat at Actium in 31 BC at the side of Cleopatra, his treacherous Egyptian paramour.

The Senate at Rome clamoured to shower honours on the young 'Caesar' – as he called himself, deriving propaganda advantage from the fact that Julius had been declared a god in 42 BC – and awarded him the title *imperator*, the accolade for a victorious general, which was to become a permanent epithet of the later emperors. Octavian had also been consul every year from 31 to 28 BC, and it is quite possible that he might have chosen to occupy that position on a quasi-permanent basis or to have himself appointed dictator, as Julius Caesar had done. Instead, in 27 BC he abolished all the emergency powers he had accrued during the civil war, but then allowed the Senate to grant him a ten-year command over Spain, Gaul, Syria and Egypt, the most strategically important of Rome's provinces. He also permitted himself to be known as *princeps*, a term that carried the informal sense of the leading statesman of the Republic. Also that year he acquired the title 'Augustus', the name that historians have subsequently used to refer to him.

Gradually, over the next decade, Augustus accrued further powers, acquiring in 23 BC the right to intervene in all matters of state, even those not formally under his power (*imperium proconsulare maius*) and the right to veto all legislation (*tribunicia potestas*). Without actually declaring the

Republic abolished, Augustus therefore established a position for himself of such primacy that, in control of all the levers of power, he made it next to impossible for any ambitious general or politician to follow the same path that he had done.

7 See C.M. Wells, *The German Policy of Augustus, An Examination of the Archaeological Evidence* (Oxford 1972), pp. 149–232

8 For Augustus's rise to power, see also Werner Eck, *The Age of Augustus* (trs Deborah Lucas Schneider, Oxford 2003), esp. pp. 41–67

9 See p. 406 and p. 355

10 See Wells, *German Policy of Augustus*, pp. 35–88

11 See Cassius Dio, LVI.18–22.2 for an account of the battle and Augustus's reactions. The catastrophe was accompanied by all sorts of ill omens, such as a statue of Victory that had faced towards Germany, which then did an about-turn to look instead into Italy

12 See Adrian Murdoch, *Rome's Greatest Defeat: Massacre in the Teutoburg Forest* (Stroud 2006), pp. 99–123

13 Suetonius, *Lives of the Twelve Caesars*, Augustus 23 (trs Robert Graves, London 1962)

14 See note 23 below

15 On the developing threat in the northern Rhine area, see Alan K. Bowman, Peter Garnsey and Averil Cameron (eds), *Cambridge Ancient History* XII (Cambridge 2005), pp. 414–15

16 In connection with Caracalla's campaigns against them. See Bowman, Garnsey and Cameron (eds), *Cambridge Ancient History* XII, p. 442

17 Ammianus Marcellinus, XVI, 3–4

18 For a discussion of this, see Averil Cameron and Peter Garnsey (eds), *Cambridge Ancient* History XIII (Cambridge 1993), pp. 122–3

19 The Alan, Vandal and Sueve force broke into Spain later in 407, but this did not lead to a restoration of the situation further north, and the Roman government came to rely on the use of one barbarian group of 'federates', such as the Visigoths in Aquitaine from 418, to counterbalance the demands of others. The exact terminology used to describe Roman allies is problematic, but in general *laeti* had been the earlier term to denote barbarian allies, who were settled in a particular area (often farming it), but were obliged to provide troops for the Roman army and would serve under regular Roman officers. Normally, they are only found described as such in Gaul and Italy. See E.A. Thompson, *Romans and Barbarians*, pp. 23–7 (The Settlement of Barbarians in southern Gaul); Southern and Dixon, *The Late Roman Army*, pp. 48–50. On *laeti*, see Southern and Dixon, *The Late Roman Army*, pp. 48–9

20 See in general W. A. Goffart, *Barbarians and Romans AD 418–584: The Techniques of Accommodation* (Princeton, NJ, 1980) and the refinement of his ideas in *Barbarian Tides: The Migration Age and the Later Roman Empire* (Philadelphia 2006), esp. pp. 119–86

21 Syagrius succeeded Aegidius, who had been *magister militum* in Gaul and then in effect set himself up as a semi-independent warlord, with a domain probably centred around Soissons. See Penny MacGeorge, *Late Roman Warlords* (Oxford 2002), pp. 115–64

22 These were essentially makers marks stamped into the tiles before they dried. As a large part of tile production was controlled or supplied to the military, most of the tiles which have been discovered bear the mark of a legion (or cohort) and provide invaluable evidence as to which legions may have been involved in the construction of a particular fort

23 Tacitus, *Annals*, 4.72–4. The Frisians had been relatively content under arm's-length Roman control. The tax levied on them had been tied to the value of a certain number of ox-hides. However, Olennius, the relatively junior army officer entrusted with collecting it, decided this meant the hide of an auroch, a much larger and rarer beast, thus vastly increasing the tax due. A detachment under Lucius Apronius sent to deal with the revolt was almost wiped out, after which the Romans cut their losses and withdrew from Frisia

24 See p. 79

25 See p. 16

26 The banded leather armour typical of legionaries in the early Empire

27 See pp. 178–81 for a further discussion of the types of gladiator

28 See C.F.C. Hawkes in *Journal of Roman Studies* 22, Part 2 (1932), pp. 251–2, review of Professor F.J. de Waele, *Noviomagus Batavorum (Romeinsch Nijmegen)*, (Nijmegen-Utrecht 1931)

29 See J. Thyssen, 'The late Roman fort at the Valkhof in Nijmegen at the transition from the Roman period to the middle ages' in Philip Freeman, Julian Bennett, Zbigniew T. Fiema and Birgitta Hoffmann (eds), *Proceedings of the XVIIIth International Congress of Roman Frontier Studies* (BAR International Series 1084 (i), Oxford 2002), pp. 453–9

30 See 'The Theban Legion of St Maurice' by Donald F. O'Reilly in *Vigiliae Christianae*, Vol. 32, No. 3 (Sep. 1978), pp. 195–207 for further discussion of the legend

31 Joachim von Elbe, *Roman Germany, A Guide to Sites and Museums* (Mainz, 1975), p. 473

32 *Qualis artifex pereo.* (see Suetonius, *Lives of the Twelve Caesars*, Nero 49). His very last words were '*Haec est fides*' ('That is fidelity'), to his slave, Sero, who had obeyed his master's command and stabbed him to death

33 In 69, one of Vespasian's former legions (the III Gallica) had been transferred to Moesia, where, seeing at first hand the chaos gripping the Empire after Otho (defeated in a series of battles by Vitellius) had taken his own life, its soldiers declared their old commander Emperor. Bolstered by the predictable support of his own Syrian legions and recognition from Tiberius Alexander, the governor of Egypt, Vespasian's allies in the Danube legions

then marched on Rome, where by 20 December they had secured Rome for their master. Whilst Vitellius was dragged into the Forum and beaten to death by a mob, Vespasian's son Domitian, who had escaped the Vitellian forces the day before disguised as a priest of Isis, tried to restore some order to the imperial government.

34 See Tacitus, *Histories*, 4.12–18

35 See Tacitus, *Histories*, 4.20–37, 54–79, 5.14–26

36 Municius Lupercus

37 The same Cerealis who had been so badly beaten by Boudicca's forces in Britain in 60 and later returned as governor in the early 70s, suppressing the Brigantes. See p. 16

38 The narrative in Tacitus, *Histories*, breaks off at Book 5, 16, with the final result of the rebellion (and the fate of Civilis) unclear

39 Including to Hadrian's Wall in Britannia

40 The development of Roman administrative terms for towns outside Italy was complex. In general, those native centres that continued to run their own affairs (under Roman supervision, of course) were termed *civitas*, and their inhabitants were not Roman citizens. Where a settlement had developed further, and was judged worthy of recognition, it might be promoted to a *municipium*, receiving a constitution based on a Roman model and, in general, replacing whatever form of city governance it had previously possessed with two annually elected magistrates (normally called *duumvirs*), backed up by a *curia*, an assembly of the leading local notables. Those who held the position of *duumvir* (and occasionally other, lesser positions in the city government) would be awarded Roman citizenship, together with their families. Gradually, therefore, the proportion of Roman citizens in the provincial urban elite crept up and, with it, their loyalty to the Roman cause. A *municipium* might ultimately be promoted to *colonia*, an urban status that gave all its free male inhabitants the right to Roman citizenship. Strictly speaking, a *colonia* should have been a fresh foundation composed of former legionary veterans, but quite quickly under the Empire the reserves of such men proved insufficient to stock many new cities, and the temptation to the emperors of having the gift of *colonia* status in their armoury proved difficult to resist. By the late 2nd and early 3rd centuries, under Septimius Severus and his successors, the number of these grants became very high, though by the mid-3rd century, with a more general extension of Roman citizenship throughout the Empire, the status of *colonia* became less obviously attractive and the awards much rarer

41 10,000 inhabitants in 73 hectares (or 0.73 square kilometres) is equivalent to 13,698 per square kilometre as against 6,422 for Hong Kong and 6,336 for Singapore. See *United Nations World Populations Prospects Report* (2006 revision, New York 2007). Figures are for 2005 estimated populations

42 An epidemic of an unspecified sickness in Rome in AD 65 is said to have

killed 30,000 people, while in an outbreak of plague in 189 some 2,000 people a day died in the capital. See Ralph Jackson, *Doctors and Diseases in the Roman Empire* (London 1988), p. 173

43 At the time of Diocletian, the cost of a cartload of hay was 600 denarii, and the cost to transport it a mile was 20 denarii, meaning that for distances of more than 30 miles the cost was prohibitive (though of course for higher-value goods, such as silk, this may not have been the case). See 'The Evolution of Land Transport in the Middle Ages' by R.S. Lopez in *Past and Present* 9 (Apr. 1956), pp. 17–29

44 The largest temple was the Capitoline, which has not been so extensively restored

45 Gerta Wolff, *Roman-Germanic Cologne* (Cologne 2003), p. 8

46 See p. 71

47 Wolff, *Roman-Germanic Cologne*, p. 144

48 Suetonius, *Lives of the Twelve Caesars*, Vitellius, 8

49 Led by Ingenuus

50 See p. 304

51 For Postumus's position, see *Cambridge Ancient History* XII, p. 45. He may also have been Gallienus's praetorian prefect, see J.F. Drinkwater, 'The Gallic Empire, Separatism and Continuity in the North-Western Provinces of the Roman Empire AD 260–7', *Historia* 52 (Stuttgart 1987), p. 25

52 Drinkwater, 'The Gallic Empire', p. 24

53 Alaric Watson, *Aurelian and the Third Century* (London 1999), p. 35

54 Drinkwater, 'The Gallic Empire', pp. 28–9

55 Since Alexander Severus in 232

56 Drinkwater, 'The Gallic Empire', pp. 34–5

57 After a brief reign by Marius (268). See Eutropius, *Breviarium*, 9.9–10, and Watson, *Aurelian and the Third Century*, pp. 89–90

58 See p. 234

59 Eutropius, *Breviarium*, 9.13.2, and Aurelius Victor, *Epitome de Caesaribus*, 35.4. Also Watson *Aurelian and the Third Century*, 93. He sent a verse of Virgil (*eripe me his, invicte, malis* – 'Rescue me, unconquered one, from these ills': Virgil, *Aeneid*, VI, 365)

60 Bowman, Garnsey and Cameron (eds), *Cambridge Ancient History* XII, p. 55

61 He did not live long enough, however, to enjoy the fruits of his signal achievement. After some unspecified mopping-up operations in Gaul, he was murdered in Thrace in 275, possibly whilst on his way to renew the war against the Persians; Bowman, Garnsey and Cameron (eds), *Cambridge Ancient History* XII, p. 53

62 Silvanus was in fact cornered into revolt by allegations against him that he was going to lead a rebellion. Once these were believed at court, he had little choice but to follow through with the plan that his enemies had devised for him. Ammianus Marcellinus, XV, 5.31

63 Cameron and Garnsey (eds), *Cambridge Ancient History* XIII, p. 3. Edward Gibbon called this a 'promiscuous massacre' and it involved the murder of no fewer than nine of the future Emperor Julian's male relatives

64 Shaun Tougher, *Julian the Apostate* (Edinburgh, 2007), p. 31

65 Ammianus Marcellinus, 15.8.19, and Tougher, *Julian the Apostate*, p. 32

66 Julian, *Letter to the Athenians*, 278–81 (trs in *The Works of the Emperor Julian* by Wilmer Cave Wright, London, 1913) and Tougher, *Julian the Apostate*, p. 33

67 Ammianus Marcellinus, XVI, 12.6. The Romans are said to have lost just 243 men to the Alamanns' 6,000 dead

68 He was then drafted into a Roman army unit, but died soon afterwards in Rome; Adrian Murdoch, *The Last Pagan: Julian the Apostate and the Death of the Ancient World* (Stroud 2003), p. 62

69 Ammianus Marcellinus, XVII, 3.5

70 See p. 308

71 Wolff, *Roman-Germanic Cologne*, p. 136

72 Wolff, *Roman-Germanic Cologne*, p. 23

73 Wells, *German Policy of Augustus*, p. 136, and Tacitus, *Annals*, I, 23–42, II, 5–28

74 See Chapter 4, note 35

75 Wolff, *Roman-Germanic Cologne*, p. 190

76 See p. 472

77 Wolff, *Roman-Germanic Cologne*, pp. 198–224

78 Wolff, *Roman-Germanic Cologne*, p. 144

79 Wolff, *Roman-Germanic Cologne*, p. 169

80 Wolff, *Roman-Germanic Cologne*, p. 260

81 The I Germanica was involved in a mutiny in AD 13 that demanded higher pay and a shorter term of service. It escaped serious punishment on that occasion, but Vespasian disbanded the legion in 70 for their involvement in the Batavian revolt

82 And indeed a reproduction of the monument can be seen just outside the Cathedral of Saint Victor in Xanten

83 The inscription says '*in bello Variano*', which may mean just during the war. There are indications that the stone was not a cenotaph, but formed part of the outer wall of an actual burial chamber. Von Elbe, *Roman Germany*, p. 79

84 Barbara Levick, *Vespasian* (London 1999), p. 163

85 Pat Southern, *Domitian: Tragic Tyrant* (London 1997), pp. 79–80

86 Tacitus, *Germania*, 30 (trs R.B. Townshend, London 1895) and Pat Southern, *Domitian*, p. 82

87 I Adiutrix, XIV Germina, VIII Augusta, XI Claudia from Germania Superior and XXI Rapax (from Bonna in Lower Germany)

88 Levick, *Vespasian*, p. 85. See also Brian W. Jones, *The Emperor Domitian* (London 1992), p. 150

89 Domitian's character seems to have degenerated in the last years of his reign and life, for those with any level of political involvement, became dangerous in the extreme; Pliny describes him as *demens* ('mad'). Finally a plot was hatched, possibly involving the two praetorian prefects, Secundus and Norbanus, but carried out by members of the Emperor's household staff, who stabbed him to death. The Senate – once his demise was made known – lost no time in declaring a *damnatio memoriae*, and his name was carefully chiselled out of as many inscriptions as the authorities could lay their hands on. Thus, for all his achievements in stabilising the *limes*, Domitian fell firmly (as far as Roman and subsequent historians were concerned) into the camp of 'bad' emperors, and certainly suffered the most unfavourable comparisons with his immediate successors

90 Alan K. Bowman, Peter Garnsey, Dominic Rathbone (eds), *Cambridge Ancient History* XI (Cambridge 2000), p. 63

91 *Notitia Dignitatum*, occ. XLI, which lists a *praefectus militum balistarorum* at Bodobrica

92 News of the uprising reached Rome in January 89, and Domitian hurried to the scene with but a single legion, the VII Gemina from Spain, to face Saturninus's potential four: the two of the Mainz garrison and those from Vindonissa and Argentorate (Strasbourg). In the event, the XI Claudia at Vindonissa and the VIII Augusta at Argentorate did not defect. With the tide not flowing in his favour, Saturninus was defeated by Aulus Lappius Maximus, the governor of Germania Inferior, in a battle somewhere near Remagen. Lappius is said to have burnt all Saturninus's correspondence, suggesting that he himself may have been implicated in the rebellion, or that he was trying to protect others

93 The provinces may not have been formally created yet, hence the uncertainty. See Southern, *Domitian*, p. 101

94 Alexander Severus, who had been only thirteen at the time of his accession in 222, had struggled to escape the influence of his strong-minded mother, Julia Mamaea. On the influence of Julia Mamaea, see 'Studies in the Lives of Roman Empresses: Julia Mamaea' by Mary Gilmore Williams in Henry A. Sanders (ed.), *Roman Historical Sources and Institutions* (London 1904). The Emperor, moreover, never succeeded in gaining authority over the army; indeed, his praetorian prefect, the leading jurist Ulpian, was murdered in 223 and the soldiers responsible went unpunished. In 233, Alexander, who had been in the midst of prosecuting a war against the Persians, was forced to hurry west at the news of a serious Alamannic threat in the region of the Taunus. The Emperor and his mother arrived at Mogontiacum in 234, but failed to take decisive action, and resentment smouldered amongst the troops, to whom this smacked of indecision (not to mention that the Illyrian legionaries were concerned that their families might be exposed to barbarian attacks in the Balkans in their absence)

95 See Pat Southern, *The Roman Empire from Severus to Constantine* (London 2001), pp. 62–3

96 Maximinus, meanwhile, faced immediate counter-uprisings by supporters of Alexander, but, once these had been put down, he did not march (as might have been expected) straight on Rome. In fact he never made it there at all, dying in 238 during the siege of Aquileia in northern Italy, while attempting to put down the revolt that would lead to the elevation of Gordian III (238–44) to the throne

97 See Mary Beard, John North and Simon Price, *Religions of Rome: A History*, Vol 1(Cambridge 1998), pp. 146–7

98 See p. 255

99 On Isis worship in general, see Beard, *Religions of Rome*, pp. 264–6 and 308

100 Such a curse was blamed for the death of Tiberius's adoptive son, the general Germanicus, in AD 19. See Beard, *Religions of Rome*, p. 234

101 Von Elbe, *Roman Germany*, p. 256

102 Chester G. Starr, *The Roman Imperial Navy*, (2nd edition, Cambridge 1960), pp. 38–40

103 Starr, *The Roman Imperial Navy*, p. 67

104 Starr, *The Roman Imperial Navy*, p. 70

105 For the Roman navy in general, see Starr, *The Roman Imperial Navy*

106 There were, however, fleets in the East. The *Classis Pontica* patrolled the Black Sea from its base in Trapezus, while a *Classis Syriaca* was based at Seleucia Pieria and is presumed to have existed from at least AD 93. In Egypt, the *Classis Alexandrina* patrolled the Nile and Mediterranean coast, while there is some scant evidence for an African fleet, the *Classis Nova Libyca*; Paul Erdkamp, *A Companion to the Roman Army* (Oxford 2007)

107 Starr, *The Roman Imperial Navy*, p. 142

108 Starr, *The Roman Imperial Navy*, p. 147

109 Starr, *The Roman Imperial Navy*, p. 151

110 Starr, *The Roman Imperial Navy*, p. 152

111 *Ante Roman Treviris stetit annis mille tercentis. Perstet, et aeterna pace fruatur, amen*

112 Edith Wightman, *Roman Trier and the Treveri* (London 1970), p. 16

113 Caesar, *Gallic Wars*, II.4

114 For a discussion of the date and significance of evidence, see Wightman, *Roman Trier and the Treveri*, pp. 40–1

115 The sources speak of an *obsidio*, a siege of the town or possibly just a threatened attack (Wightman, *Roman Trier and the Treveri*, p. 52)

116 A mosaic panel bearing Victorinus's name has been found (Wightman, *Roman Trier and the Treveri*, p. 52)

117 Stephen Williams, *Diocletian and the Roman Recovery* (London 1985), pp. 102–14

118 Williams, *Diocletian and the Roman Recovery*, pp. 64–5

119 Ausonius was a member of a leading family in Aquitania, who spent the

early part of his career teaching rhetoric at Bordeaux. Around 366, he was summoned by Valentinian I to Trier to act as the tutor to the young Gratian (the precise date is not clear). Whilst there, he accompanied the Emperor on an expedition against the Alamanns in 369 (the last time a Roman emperor campaigned across the Rhine), but it was at court that his influence was most keenly met. He rose to the rank of *comes*, and then praetorian prefect in 378, a giddy height indeed for a poet and rhetor. In 379, he even became consul, whilst his many relatives shared in his good fortune – an almost inevitable feature of the world of Roman patronage – with his son-in-law Thalassius becoming vicar of the diocese of Macedonia in 377 and his nephew Arborius being appointed *comes sacrarum largitionum* (the senior minister in charge of the imperial finances). See 'The Academic Career of Ausonius' by Alan D. Booth in *Phoenix* 36, No. 4 (Winter 1982), pp. 329–43; John Matthews, *Western Aristocracies and the Imperial Court, AD 364–425* (Oxford 1975), pp. 70–1

120 Wightman, *Roman Trier and the Treveri*, p. 65

121 Wightman, *Roman Trier and the Treveri*, p. 66, and Ausonius, *Mosella*, 9 (trs Hugh G. Evelyn Wright, London 1921)

122 There is a story in the *Chronicle of Fredegar* of a last stand in the amphitheatre. Wightman, *Roman Trier and the Treveri*, p. 68, and Fredegar, 2.60

123 Merobaudes (*Mon. Germ. Auct. Antiq* 14.1, pp. 11–18) in Wightman, *Roman Trier and the Treveri*, pp. 69–70

124 John Rich and Graham Shipley, *War and Society in the Roman World* (London 1993), p. 285

125 Von Elbe, *Roman Germany*, p. 396

126 Wightman, *Roman Trier and the Treveri*, p. 78. This possibly took place under Hadrian

127 This is what is implied in Martial. See Garrett G. Fagan, *Bathing in Public in the Roman World* (Ann Arbor 1999), pp. 14–20

128 Fagan, *Bathing in Public in the Roman World*, pp. 69–71

129 For example, Martial, *Epigrams*, 3.51 (to Galla). See Fagan, *Bathing in Public in the Roman World*, p. 28, for a discussion

130 Ovid, *Ars Amatoria*, 3.638–40 (trs Rolph Humphries, London 1958); Fagan, *Bathing in Public in the Roman World*, p. 40

131 Fagan, *Bathing in Public in the Roman World*, p. 38

132 *Historia Augusta*, Hadrian, 17.5–7

133 Wightman, *Roman Trier and the Treveri*, p. 114

134 See von Elbe, *Roman Germany*, p. 403

135 See Wightman, *Roman Trier and the Treveri*, p. 108

136 See, for example, Christopher Kelly, *Ruling the Later Roman Empire* (Cambridge, MA, 2004), pp. 23–4

137 Procopius, *History of the Wars*, III 2.22–5 (trs H.B. Dewing, London 1916)

138 Wightman, *Roman Trier and the Treveri*, p. 73

139 Wightman, *Roman Trier and the Treveri*, p. 239

140 Alex R. Furger, *Augusta Raurica* (trs Cathy Aitken and Christoph Maier, Augst 1995), p. 12

141 See p. 99

142 *Princeton Encyclopaedia of Classical Sites*, p. 116 (citing CIL x, 6087) and also Furger, *Augusta Raurica*, p. 12

143 Furger, *Augusta Raurica*, p. 23

144 Furger, *Augusta Raurica*, p. 4 (2nd-edition supplement)

145 Furger, *Augusta Raurica*, p. 53

146 Ammianus Marcellinus, XIV, 10.6

147 Furger, *Augusta Raurica*, p. 61

148 Furger, *Augusta Raurica*, p. 66

149 This is the characteristic fine ware of the early Roman Empire, with a typical red glaze, which is found throughout Roman territory and beyond. The main workshops were located in Gaul and in Roman Germany, and the productions of each workshop are generally distinct enough to enable the tracing of pots to particular regions of origin

150 Trajan is said to have had oysters despatched to him on his campaign in Persia, and they were so fresh they were still alive on arrival, while the usurper Clodius Albinus is said to have been so fond of them that he was capable of downing 400 at a single sitting. See 'Oysters as a Food in Greece and Rome' by Alfred C. Andrews in *Classical Journal* 43 (1948), pp. 299–303

151 'Whatever happened to the Agri Decumates' by J.G.F. Hind in *Britannia*. 15 (1984), pp. 187–92

152 *Saltus* was the normal term for an imperial estate, which was usually (at least initially) in rural areas. Only later did some of them begin to develop the characteristics of urban settlements, as in the case of Sumelocenna. Over time the emperors acquired huge estates, by inheritance from their predecessors and by confiscation

153 Von Elbe, *Roman Germany*, p. 343

154 See p. 99

155 The *antoninianus* was introduced by Caracalla in 213 as part of a currency reform. Worth twice the denarius, it was only one and a half times its weight and had just 80 per cent of the silver of two individual denarii pieces, thus providing a useful windfall for the treasury, if only a temporary one because the expedient, once detected, had the inevitable consequence of fuelling inflation. See Kenneth W. Harl, *Coinage in the Roman Economy 300 BC to AD 700* (Baltimore 1996), p. 128

156 Just three others on the German *limes* are hexagonal (Wp 1/26, Wp 1/48 and Wp 4/11), making four out of some 1,000 watchtowers along the frontier

157 Probably for Septimius Severus's campaign against the Caledonians; Spaul, *Cohors²*, pp. 72–4

158 For oak from 15 to 5 per cent, for fir from 13 to 5 per cent

159 Number 9/96 in the German numbering system

160 This is Tower Wp 9/98 a few hundred metres north of Murrhardt

161 The unit had been at Canstatt in the reign of Domitian and was then probably transferred to Welzheim. In the 3rd century, the *ala* would be stationed at Mainz; John E.H. Spaul, *ALA²: The Auxiliary Cavalry Units of the Pre-Diocletianic Imperial Roman Army* (Andover 1994), p. 192

CHAPTER 3: RAETIA AND NORICUM

1 Eugippius, *Vita Sancti Severini* (trs George W. Robinson, Cambridge, MA, 1914)

2 See p. 78

3 In November 2008, dendrochronological research on the wood used in the foundations of the wall in the marsh of Ehinger–Dombach resulted in the first clear date of the building of the Roman wall; the wood was cut in the winter of 205–6

4 Ammianus Marcellinus, XVII, 6

5 W. Warde Fowler, *The Roman Festivals of the Period of the Republic* (London 1899), pp. 224–6. On the earliest Roman religion and festivals, see Beard, North and Price (eds), *Religions of Rome*, Vol. 1, esp. pp. 171–80

6 A distinction it shares with Hadrian's Wall and (since July 2008) the Antonine Wall in Scotland

7 For a list of the milliary *alae*, see P.A. Holder, 'Roman auxiliary cavalry in the second century AD' in *Archaeology Today* 8 (June 1987), pp. 12–16. The *Ala Augusta Galliorum Petriana milliaria civium Romanorium bis torquata* was the unit at Stanwix, while the camel unit was the *Ala Ulpia dromedariorum milliaria* raised under Trajan. See Karen Dixon and Pat Southern, *The Roman Cavalry from the First to the Third Century AD* (London 1992), p. 32

8 Born in 1817, Mommsen's long and distinguished career was most marked by his ground-breaking works on the Roman world, including an unfinished history of Rome and the *Corpus Inscriptionum Latinarum*, intended to be a collection of all known Latin inscriptions (and which has been updated periodically since his day). He also found time to serve as a member of parliament in the German Reichstag and as the first head of the Reichslimeskomission. He was the second recipient of the Nobel Prize for Literature in 1902, and died the following year

9 A process known as *Flurbereinigung*

10 The class of councillors in Roman towns

11 As Rome was traditionally founded in 753 BC, AD 2008 would therefore be AUC 2761

12 See p. 192

13 Confusingly, another unit with precisely the same name was based in Britain at the time. It is believed, though, that they were two distinct cohorts (Spaul, *Cohors²*, pp. 92–5. Another unit, the *Cohors II Aquitanorum equitata*, was also

based in Raetia and may have served in or around Regensburg (Spaul, *Cohors²*, p. 146 and Von Elbe, *Roman Germany*, p. 322)

14 Bowman, Garnsey and Cameron (eds) *Cambridge Ancient History* XII, p. 66

15 For the career of Elagabalus, see p. 347, note 20

16 *Conversio Beatae Afrae* (Migne, *Patrologia Latina*, Vol. 142)

17 The map was in fact discovered by a Konrad Celtes, a friend of Peutinger's, in 1507. A copy was made before Peutinger's death in 1547, and then another one in 1598 by Marcus Velser. As most of the original has almost disappeared, modern reproductions are based on these copies. Although the exact date of the original is disputed, and what Celtes found was in turn a medieval copy, the route network shown is believed to date from sometime between the mid-4th and mid-5th centuries. See 'The Peutinger Table' by R.A. Gardner in *Geographical Journal* Vol. 136, No. 3 (Sept. 1970), pp. 489–90

18 Von Elbe, *Roman Germany*, p. 234

19 Herbert Schutz, *The Romans in Central Europe* (New Haven 1985), p. 6

20 Géza Alföldy, *Noricum* (trs Anthony Birley, London, 1974), p. 32

21 Cassius Dio, *Roman History*, LIV 20, 2 (trs Earnest Cary, London 1917)

22 Alföldy, *Noricum*, p. 80

23 Alföldy, *Noricum*, p. 135

24 Alföldy, *Noricum*, p. 96

25 Alföldy, *Noricum*, pp. 155–6

26 Alföldy, *Noricum*, p. 162

27 Alföldy, *Noricum*, p. 201–2

28 Alföldy, *Noricum*, p. 214

29 Southern, *The Roman Empire from Severus to Constantine*, p. 220

30 Bowman, Garnsey and Cameron (eds), *Cambridge Ancient History* XII, p. 445

31 See p. 243

32 See p. 244. See also Michael Kulikowski, *Rome's Gothic Wars from the Third Century to Alaric* (Cambridge 2007), pp. 154–78, for a general discussion of Alaric and the Goths

33 Kulikowski, *Rome's Gothic Wars*, p. 165

34 Bowman, Garnsey and Cameron (eds), *Cambridge Ancient History* XII, p. 512

35 Kulikowski, *Rome's Gothic Wars*, p. 170

36 Thomas S. Burns, *Barbarians within the Gates of Rome* (Indiana University Press 1994), p. 227

37 See Kulikowski, *Rome's Gothic Wars*, pp. 173–4

38 Such as Orosius, *History against the Pagans*, and Saint Augustine in *The City of God*

39 'The End of Noricum' in E.A. Thompson, *Romans and Barbarians, The Decline of the Western Empire* (Madison 1982), pp. 113–33; 'Eugippius and the Closing Years of Noricum Ripense' by Charles Christopher Mierow in *Classical Philology*, Vol. 10, No. 2 (Apr. 1915), pp. 166–87

40 Alföldy, *Noricum*, p. 222. One of his men, Avitus, accompanied Mamertinus on his journey into the ecclesiastical life, becoming a priest

41 *Vita S Severini*, 20.1

42 Near Naples. Confusingly, there is another Saint Severin, who was actually a native of Naples, but who became Bishop of Septempeda in the modern Marche region of Italy

43 Alföldy, *Noricum*, p. 117

44 Alföldy, *Noricum*, p. 104

45 Alföldy, *Noricum*, pp. 160, 199

46 Alföldy, *Noricum*, p. 186

47 'Six Saints of Sweepdom' by George Lewis Phillips in *Folklore*, Vol. 74, No. 2 (Summer 1963), pp. 377–86

48 The *I Commagenorum* had previously served in Egypt; Spaul, *ALA²*, p. 95

CHAPTER 4: PANNONIA AND MOESIA

1 Edward Gibbon, *Decline and Fall of the Roman Empire* (ed. David Womersley, London 2005), Chapter XXV

2 Although Marcus Aurelius pushed Roman positions across the river into Slovakia in preparation for an expansion of Roman territory into Bohemia, this was not consolidated by his son, Commodus

3 András Mócsy (trs Sheppard Frere), *Pannonia and Upper Moesia. A History of the Middle Danube Provinces of the Roman Empire* (London 1974), pp. 10–14

4 Mócsy, *Pannonia and Upper Moesia*, p. 14, and Eutropius, *Breviarium*, vi, 2

5 Mócsy, *Pannonia and Upper Moesia*, p. 33

6 Zsolt Visy (ed.), *The Roman Army in Pannonia, An Archaeological Guide of the Ripa Pannonica* (Budapest 2003), p. 21

7 Mócsy, *Pannonia and Upper Moesia*, pp. 41–2

8 Mócsy, *Pannonia and Upper Moesia*, p. 83

9 See p. 254

10 A triumph was the parade through the streets of Rome awarded to successful generals in honour of their victory. A frequent award for generals in the late Republic, under the Empire it became rapidly confined to members of the imperial house and particularly the emperors, in many cases for campaigns in which their participation had been at best a token one

11 Visy, *The Roman Army in Pannonia*, p. 25

12 By a force under Hadrian's friend, Quintus Marcius Turbo

13 Mócsy, *Pannonia and Upper Moesia*, p. 194

14 See p. 196

15 The general term for Septimius Severus and his successors up to Alexander Severus

16 See p. 226

17 Mócsy, *Pannonia and Upper Moesia*, p. 268

18 See p. 270

19 Mócsy, *Pannonia and Upper Moesia*, p. 293, though see Lynn F. Pitts, 'Relations between Rome and the German "Kings" on the Middle Danube in the First to Fourth Centuries AD' in *Journal of Roman Studies* 79 (1989), pp. 45–58

20 Mócsy, *Pannonia and Upper Moesia*, p. 347, citing Claudian, *De Consolatu Stilichonis*, ii, 191–207

21 *Notitia Dignitatum* V

22 Mócsy, *Pannonia and Upper Moesia*, p. 350

23 Including most particularly its double-headed eagle symbol, which mirrors the eagle standards of the Roman legions

24 Visy, *The Roman Army in Pannonia*, p. 53

25 That an emperor should espouse the doctrines of Stoicism was in itself something of a paradox, for the first of the distinguished line of Roman Stoics was Cato the Younger, whose involvement with Brutus and Cassius, the murderers of Julius Caesar, might hardly have recommended him to the lineal successor of Augustus, Caesar's adoptive son. The Stoics continued to have a hard time of it, acting as a kind of principled but impotent opposition to the more extreme manifestations of imperial tyranny. Under Nero, Thrasea Paetus was executed for writing a biography that portrayed Cato in a favourable light, while Domitian had two other Stoics put to death: Arulenus Iunius Rusticus, who had in turn written a biography of Thrasea; and Herennius Senecio. By the 2nd century and the era of the adoptive emperors, rulers and philosophers were somewhat more in tune, and the Greek sophist Dio Chrysostom lavished effusive (and it seems sincere) praises on Trajan. Marcus's adoptive 'grandfather' Hadrian was well known to be interested in all things Greek, and especially philosophy, and he chose Cornelius Fronto, a well-known rhetor, to be one of his young protégé's tutors

26 Marcus Aurelius, *Meditations*, vii, 10 and vii, 19 (trs. Gregory Hays, London 2003)

27 Marcus Aurelius, *Meditations*, vi, 47

28 See Anthony Birley, *Marcus Aurelius* (London 1966), pp. 284–7. An inscription at Trenčin in Slovakia, some 125 kilometres north of the Danube, and known to the Romans as Leugaricio, records a stay there by the II Adiutrix legion

29 Although Cassius Dio says that the Emperor's doctors were responsible for his death (Cassius Dio, *Roman History*, LXII 33, 4–34). One classical authority (Tertullian) gives Marcus's place of death as Sirmium and not Vindobona. See Birley, *Marcus Aurelius*, p. 288

30 *Princeton Encyclopaedia of Classical Sites*, p. 982

31 Another type of settlement that grew out of the military camps, this one being used only in the context of a legionary fortress, while the villages that grew up next to auxiliary forts were called *vicus*; Erdkamp, *A Companion to the Roman Army*, p. 410

32 In all, there were six officers' houses on the site. *Römische Ruinen unter dem Hohen Markt* (Wien Museum, Vienna [undated]), pp. 7–8

33 Mócsy, *Pannonia and Upper Moesia*, pp. 80, 89, 92

34 Mócsy, *Pannonia and Upper Moesia*, p. 99

35 The insurrection, which in the end proved to be successful, had its origins in events in Rome the previous year. The regime of Commodus, the son of Marcus Aurelius, had grown increasingly unpopular and even those close to the Emperor had come to fear his mercurial nature and the increasingly evident instability that had led him, amongst other eccentricities, to spend most of his time in the amphitheatre. There, on one occasion, he is said to have shot the heads of ostriches and then waved the bloody trophies in the direction of those senators present, as if to imply that they would be next. He even fought as a gladiator, though needless to say his opponents never had any chance of laying a sword upon him. A conspiracy headed by the praetorian prefect, Aemilius Laetus, arranged for Commodus's mistress Marcia to have him poisoned (and then, when this did not work, strangled). The reins of power were picked up by Pertinax, a senior senator, but the murdered Commodus had been popular with the army, and within days of his accession an attempted coup by the praetorian guard had to be put down. Exactly when news of Pertinax's accession reached Pannonia is unclear, but Septimius duly swore allegiance to the new Emperor and made the customary sacrifice. Soon afterwards, on 28 March, some 200 members of the praetorian guard arrived at the palace just as Pertinax was inspecting the palace slaves. They set upon the Emperor and killed him after a reign of just eighty-seven days. There then followed one of the most inglorious (at least up to that point) episodes in the history of the imperial office. The troops, having murdered the Emperor, had no clear plan and retired to consider their positions. Pertinax's father-in-law, Sulpicianus, who had been Urban Prefect, tried to have himself proclaimed Emperor, and as he was in charge of the Urban Cohorts he possessed at least some muscle with which to enforce his will. Unfortunately, several tribunes of the praetorian guard, fearing the family link between Pertinax and Sulpicianus might lead the Urban Prefect to exact revenge for the assassination of his son-in-law, persuaded the eminent senator Didius Julianus to make his own bid for power. When he arrived at the camp of the praetorians, he found the gates barred, and that Sulpicianus had arrived there as well. The two senators then engaged in an unseemly auction as to who would award the guard the higher donative on his accession as Emperor. Sulpicianus put in a final offer of 20,000 sesterces, but Julianus trumped this by raising the odds to 25,000 sesterces, yelling out his bid and indicating the increased amount with hand-signals. It got him his day as Emperor, but it did not win him the Empire.

Julianus had the support of the governor of Pannonia Inferior,

Valerius Pudens, which gave him another legion, and he also sought the assistance of the six legions in Moesia and Dacia. In parallel, however, Clodius Albinus, the governor of Britain, who had three legions, and Pescennius Niger, governor of Syria, who had an equal number and the support of more from neighbouring provinces, declared themselves Emperor. Septimius, who soon won over the Rhine legions, could by now call on sixteen legions to Niger's probable ten and, moreover, took advantage of his comparative proximity to the centre of power by launching a rapid march on Rome. Julianus's supporters defected as rapidly as was seemly, and the lame-duck Emperor had a decree passed making Septimius his co-Emperor. On 1 June, Julianus was murdered in the palace, just two months after Pertinax had suffered a similar fate.

36 Septimius neutralised Albinus by offering him the subordinate post of Caesar, and he then defeated Pescennius Niger in a series of campaigns culminating at Issus in northern Syria in April 194, after which Niger was killed fleeing for the imagined safety of Antioch. Septimius then turned on Albinus, who, short of troops, tried to make a dash for Rome, but was finally defeated on 19 February 197 near Lugdunum (Lyons) and then committed suicide. The battle was hard fought, and at the critical moment (according to Herodian) Septimius actually threw off his purple cloak and tried to flee the battlefield, but Septimian reinforcements arriving at the last minute drove Albinus's men off the field

37 The background of the would-be Emperor is unclear; the *Historia Augusta* attributes to him descent from the great Dacian king Decebalus, but this seems a fanciful fabrication. The Emperor Gallienus had recently lost his son (Valerian II) who had been in nominal control of the Danube provinces, whilst the real power there, the governor Ingenuus, had himself revolted shortly beforehand. Matters had been made worse by a serious Gothic raid along the coasts of the Black Sea in 257, increased pressure from the Alamanns along the Rhine front, and a mounting threat from Persia in the East, which meant that reinforcements from his father, Valerian, were unlikely

38 See p. 183

39 Charles Matson Odahl, *Constantine and the Christian Empire* (London 2004), p. 87

40 Odahl, *Constantine and the Christian Empire*, pp. 90–1

41 'Diocletian's Palace at Split' by A. J. Brothers in *Greece & Rome*, Second Series 19, No. 2 (Oct. 1972), pp. 175–86

42 See p. 206

43 F. Humer, *Carnuntum, The Roman City Quarter in the Open Air Museum*, (Petronell 2004), p. 15

44 Humer, *Carnuntum*, p. 16

45 Tertullian, *De spectaculis*, 22

46 Michael Grant, *Gladiators* (London 1967), p. 10

47 Thomas Wiedemann, *Emperors and Gladiators* (London 1992), p. 2

48 Pliny the Elder, *Natural History*, VIII, 20 for the rhinoceros

49 Wiedemann, *Emperors and Gladiators*, p. 6

50 Wiedemann, *Emperors and Gladiators*, p. 7, who dismisses the story that the first were in 105 BC at the time of the consul P. Rutilius Rufus

51 Although rarer, there were amphitheatres in the eastern provinces such as at Antioch and Berytus (Beirut) in Syria and at Caesarea in Palestine

52 Grant, *Gladiators*, p. 32

53 Grant, *Gladiators*, p. 35

54 Wiedemann, *Emperors and Gladiators*, p. 11

55 Grant, *Gladiators*, pp. 122–3

56 Grant, *Gladiators*, p. 123. When Telemachus, a monk from Asia Minor, rushed into the arena to push the fighters apart and was torn to pieces by the angry crowd, leading Honorius finally to stamp out the practice

57 Salvian, *De gubernatore Dei*, 6 cited in Wiedemann, *Emperors and Gladiators*, p. 158

58 This was provided for by the Ostrogothic king Theoderic; Wiedemann, *Emperors and Gladiators*, p. 154

59 Visy, *Roman Army in Pannonia*, pp. 58–60

60 Visy, *Roman Army in Pannonia*, pp. 61–2

61 *Princeton Encyclopedia of Classical Sites*, p. 812

62 Review of Spekke (see note 64 below), by Marija Gimbutas in *American Slavic and East European Review*, Vol. 17, No. 4 (Dec. 1958), pp. 571–2

63 Pliny the Elder, *Natural History*, XXXVII, 45

64 Arnolds Spekke, *The Ancient Amber Routes and the Geographical Discovery of the Eastern Baltic*, (Stockholm 1957), p. 33

65 Visy, *Roman Army in Pannonia*, p. 69

66 Visy, *Roman Army in Pannonia*, pp. 93–4

67 Visy, *Roman Army in Pannonia*, pp. 97–9

68 *Princeton Encyclopedia of Classical Sites*, pp. 80–1

69 Mócsy, *Pannonia and Upper Moesia*, p. 273

70 Ammianus Marcellinus, 19.11.8

71 A. Lengyel and G.T.P. Radan, *The Archaeology of Roman Pannonia*, (Budapest 1900) p. 261

72 Visy, *Roman Army in Pannonia*, p. 186, though an alternative view is that the governor's headquarters were at Gorsium

73 Visy, *Roman Army in Pannonia*, p. 187

74 In 86 BC, for example, the plebs at Rome set up a statue in honour of Marius Gratidianus, a praetor responsible for a popular currency reform, and made offerings of incense and wine to it. Lily Ross Taylor, *The Divinity of the Roman Emperor* (Philadelphia 1975), pp. 48–9

75 'Apotheosis of the Roman Emperor' by Larry Kreitzer in *Biblical Archaeologist*, Vol. 53, No. 4 (Dec. 1990), pp. 211–17

76 Essentially former slaves freed by their masters, who in many cases possessed significant personal wealth, but little means of expressing it through the holding of traditional offices

77 See Beard et al., *Religions of Rome (volume I)*, p. 354

78 Suetonius, *Lives of the Twelve Caesars*, Vespasian 23 (trs Robert Graves, London 1962). According to Suetonius, Vespasian could not resist another series of death-bed jokes. On seeing a comet, a clear portent of his demise, he remarked, 'Look at that long hair! The King of Parthia must be going to die.'

79 Seneca, *Apocolocyntosis Divi Claudii*

80 For a more complete account of the excavations, see Ference Fülep, *Sopianae, The History of Pécs during the Roman era and the Problem of Continuity of the Late Roman Population* (Budapest 1984), esp. pp. 24–35

81 Visy, *Roman Army in Pannonia*, p. 160

82 Ingenuus, a senior officer in the Pannonian legions, persuaded his troops to raise him to the purple. It was a critical moment for the Empire; Gallienus had been hard-pressed to restore the Rhine frontier in the face of serious Frankish incursions, and restlessness amongst the soldiers there would lead, within a year, to the breaking away of the British and Gaulish provinces, while in the East a serious Persian invasion had been pushed back in 253 and, again within a year or so, Gallienus's father Valerian would be captured in battle against the Persians, a catastrophe that led to virtually the whole of the East breaking away. However, at Mursa, Gallienus's cavalry commander defeated Ingenuus, who died in the battle, ensuring that when the storm broke next year, the centre, at least, would hold

83 By 350, the sons of Constantine had been ruling the Empire for nearly fifteen years, exhibiting a strictly limited level of fraternal affections amongst themselves. Constans, the youngest, to whom had fallen rule of the West, created a great deal of discontent amongst both provincials and officials for the financial exactions he imposed to fund his campaigning against the German frontier tribes. Eventually, in 350, Flavius Magnus Magnentius, the commander of the elite field regiments, the Joviani and Herculiani, rose up in revolt at Autun in Gaul, securing the adherence of many of Constans's senior civil and military officers. Constans, taken by surprise at the widespread support for the rebellion, fled south and was captured and murdered at Helena in southern Gaul.

Magnentius, having first taken Rome in the face of a counter-usurpation by the luckless Nepotianus (a nephew of Constantine I who lasted just twenty-eight days), then sought to move east and expand the area under his control into the Danubian provinces. It was at Mursa that he received a double-check, the second of them fatal. First, Vetranio, who had been the *magister peditum* of Constans, was proclaimed Emperor in the city, though there is some suggestion that this was a put-up job to obtain the loyalty of the Pannonian army under a trusted general until Constantius could with fresh troops. Duly, Vetranio went over to Constantius in December 350 and the two armies united at Naissus (Niš). Second, by appointing his cousin Gallus as Caesar and sending him to Antioch to hold the line in Syria, Constantius made it clear to Magnentius that there was no hope of a rapprochement between them. Having managed to suborn one of Magnentius's leading supporters, the Frankish general Silvanus, Constantius went on the offensive and, on 28 September 351, the two armies met just outside Mursa. It was an extremely bloody clash; according to Zonaras, two-thirds of Magnentius's men perished and half of Constantius's. If there was one force that a Roman legion could not outmatch in fighting ability, it was another Roman legion, and so, whenever the opposing forces in the civil wars of the 3rd and 4th centuries chose to stand and fight, rather than broker a deal to get rid of one or other contending emperor, the losses could be truly terrible, and the damage to the Empire's longer-term ability to keep the frontiers secure might be serious indeed. Magnentius survived the battle and fled westwards, but his power was broken and he soon lost control of Italy, committing suicide near Lugdunum (Lyons) in August 353.

84 Ammianus Marcellinus, XXVI, 4

85 One of the bears rejoiced in the name of 'Innocence'. Ammianus Marcellinus, XXIX, 3.9

86 Ammianus Marcellinus, XXIX, 6.5

87 Probably in 133, under Hadrian. Visy, *Roman Army in Pannonia*, p. 161

88 Visy, *Roman Army in Pannonia*, p. 145

89 *Princeton Encyclopedia of Classical Sites* p. 831; Mócsy, *Pannonia and Upper Moesia*, pp.82–3

90 Mócsy, *Pannonia and Upper Moesia*, p. 350

91 For further discussion of the Avars, see p. 217

92 Claudius Ptolemaeus (or Ptolemy) was an Alexandrian geographer, who lived from around 86 to 161. His *Geography* included an account of the whole known world, and may originally have been illustrated with maps – those now reproduced as 'Ptolemaic maps' are reconstructions. He estimated the circumference of the world at 500 stades, around one-sixth too small. He also wrote treatises on mathematics (the *Al-Magest*) and on astrology (*Tetrabiblos*).

93 See p. 216 below

94 Pat Southern, *The Roman Empire from Severus to Constantine* (London 2001), pp. 96–7. On the history of mints in the 3rd century in general, see Harl, *Coinage in the Roman Empire*, p. 144

95 See Bowman, Garnsey and Cameron, *Cambridge Ancient History* XII, pp. 37–8

96 See p. 227

97 Some sources indicate 276 and arguments have been made for a date as late as 288. See *Cambridge Companion to the Age of Constantine*, ed. Noel Lenski (Cambridge 2006), p. 9

 98 On religious practice under the Empire, see Mary Beard, John North and
    Simon Price, *Religions of Rome, Volume I: A History* (Cambridge 1998), pp. 313–62
 99 Alaric Watson, *Aurelian and the Third Century* (London 1999), pp.188–98;
    Southern, *The Roman Empire from Severus to Constantine*, p. 124
100 Odahl, *Constantine and the Christian Empire*, p. 94
101 Orosius, *Seven Books of History against the Pagans*, VI, 28
102 Odahl, *Constantine and the Christian Empire*, pp. 104–6
103 For a discussion of the Constantinian conversion, see Lenski, *Cambridge
    Companion to the Age of Constantine*, pp. 110–14
104 The surviving copy, however, comes from the eastern provinces and is that
    promulgated by Licinius
105 Although Licinius paid lip service to the idea of the *summus deus* ('highest
    god'), the Empire was not big enough for both his and Constantine's ambi-
    tions and, once he had disposed of Maximin Daia in late 313, the inevitable
    frictions came to the surface. They first came to blows in 316 in a quarrel
    over the appointment of Bassianus, Constantine's brother-in-law, to be Caesar
    with authority in Italy. Licinius was defeated at Cibalae on 8 October 316,
    but managed to preserve part of his army intact. A new peace was patched
    up at Serdica in 317, by which Constantine took control of Pannonia and
    Moesia in addition to his original possessions. In 324, the uneasy concord
    broke down once more, and this time Licinius's defeat, at Chrysopolis
    (Scutari), was final. He surrendered to Constantine, who feigned clemency
    and let his former imperial colleague retire as a private citizen to
    Thessalonica. There, the next year, Licinius was conveniently executed on
    suspicion of treasonous plotting
106 Such as Symmachus, who was urban prefect in 384
107 Flavius Constantius was a career army officer, who by the 410s had risen
    to a high army command, and who in 414 managed to push the Visigoths
    out of the province into Spain, thereby raising the prospect of a Roman
    reoccupation of the revenue-rich southern area of Gaul. Despite the fact
    that by 417 the Visigoths were filtering back, Constantius was seen by many
    as providing the Empire's greatest hope of a military leader who might
    revive the glories of Constantine, Diocletian or even Trajan, and in that
    year he married Galla Placidia, the sister of the Western Emperor, Honorius.
    It was not a particularly happy marriage; Galla's previous husband had been
    the Visigothic king Athaulf and after his murder she had been traded by
    the new ruler, Wallia, in exchange for a treaty that allowed the Visigoths
    back into Aquitaine. It was as a very unwilling bride that she was forced by
    Honorius to wed Constantius. The marriage did at least produce a son,
    Valentinian III, who presided in total ineffectiveness over the dwindling of
    the empire from 425 to 455. His much more able father Constantius was
    proclaimed Augustus and co-Emperor by Honorius in 421, but sickened and
    died after enjoying the imperial office for just over six months

108 Odahl, *Constantine and the Christian Empire*, p. 114

109 When Anastasius died in 518, after a reasonably successful reign of twenty-seven years in which he had fought off the Slavs in the Balkans and kept the Persians at bay, he had failed to nominate an heir. Justin took advantage of his position at the centre of power, and his possession of the enforcement muscle of the imperial guard, to have himself declared Emperor. He advanced his nephew rapidly, giving him the title *comes* in 519 and promoting him to *magister equitum* (commander of the cavalry) the following year.

Justin's rule was largely uneventful; in 524–5 he gave support to an expedition by the (Christian) Ethiopian Axumites against the (Jewish) Himyarite kingdom of Yemen, and he dabbled in the politics of the Laz kingdom in the Caucasus by sponsoring the baptism of King Tzath, a move that sparked a small-scale war with Persia. In 525, Justin passed a curious law permitting women who had been actresses to marry lawfully if they showed repentance for their former profession – which was regarded as tantamount to prostitution. The measure was directed in favour of Theodora, a woman of doubtful background whom Justinian had met and fallen madly in love with. The daughter of a courtesan and a bear-tamer, no less, she followed in her mother's footsteps by becoming a mime in a theatre troupe. Much of the information about her comes from Procopius, who, although he wrote an ostensibly pro-regime account of Justinian's wars, also penned a vitriolic denunciation of the court and its mores in his *Secret History*, a manuscript that was never intended to see the light of day during his imperial master's lifetime. He accuses Theodora of all kinds of immorality: of night-long orgies with ten men at a time, of a long-running affair with the governor of Libya, and of already possessing an illegitimate daughter. After Justin's change to the law, and the death of the Empress Euphemia, who had bitterly opposed the match, Justinian and Theodora were married. In 527, Justin raised his nephew to be co-Augustus, and six months later he was dead, leaving Justinian as sole Emperor.

110 John Moorhead, *Justinian* (London 1994), p. 149

111 Williams, *Diocletian and the Roman Recovery*, p. 196

112 See *Gamzigrad, An Imperial Palace of Late Classical Times* (Belgrade 1983), p. 194

113 See *Gamzigrad, An Imperial Palace*, p. 195

114 Ammianus Marcellinus, XXXI, 2.1–2

115 Jerome, *Epistolae*, 60

116 For a more detailed account of the career of Aëtius, see p. 231

117 Socrates, *Historia Ecclesiastica*, VII, 43.3

118 Included in its number, by a strange historical coincidence, were Ediko, a former leader of the Scirian peoples and a vassal of Attila, and Orestes, a Roman from the lands south of the Danube now occupied by the

Huns. Their children were both to play key roles in the final disappearance of the Roman Empire in the West, for Orestes's son would become the Emperor Romulus Augustulus, whose brief reign in 475–6 was brought to an abrupt end by his deposition by Ediko's son, Odovacar, who then chose not to install another puppet emperor, but to rule Italy as a king on his own authority

119 Priscus of Panium was born sometime between 410 and 420. He was probably a professional civil servant, and in this capacity accompanied the embassy to Attila. After the mid-450s, nothing further is known of him. See R.C. Blockley, *The Classicising Fragmentary Historians of the Later Roman Empire* (Liverpool 1981), pp. 48–50

120 John Man, *Attila* (London 2005), p. 178

121 *Cambridge Companion to the Age of Constantine*, p. 65, citing Eusebius, *Vita Constanti*, 1.35.1

122 Priscus fr 11, 355–370 (trs R.C. Blockley *The Classicising Fragmentary Historians of the Later Roman Empire* (Liverpool 1981)

123 Priscus, fr 11, 405–505 (trs Blockley, *Classicising Fragmentary Historians*). The embassy finally ended in disaster as a plot to assassinate Attila was uncovered. Attila then held as hostage Vigilius, the Roman ambassador who had been sent with the gold to pay Ediko (who was to arrange the killing) for his services. In exchange for his release, Attila extorted a further 50 pounds of gold from Theodosius. Having learnt a salutary lesson about the faithlessness of Romans – something he was not backward in lecturing the Emperor about through the medium of Orestes, who appeared at the court in Constantinople with a bag containing Ediko's gold theatrically hung around his head – Attila now turned his attention westwards

124 See 'Résultat des fouilles de la ville antique de Ratiaria au cours des années 1976 à 1982', Jordana Atanassove-Georgieva in *Studien zu Den Militärgrenzen Roms* III (Stuttgart 1986), pp. 437–40

125 Stephen Mitchell, *A History of the Later Roman Empire AD 284–641* (Oxford 2007), pp. 405–6

126 Mitchell, *A History of the Later Roman Empire*, p. 398

127 Marija Gimbutas, *The Slavs* (London 1971), p. 98

128 P.M. Barford, *The Early Slavs: Culture and Society in Early Medieval Eastern Europe* (London 2001), pp. 45–66

129 Mócsy, *Pannonia and Upper Moesia*, pp. 2, 25

130 Odahl, *Constantine and the Christian Empire*, p. 226

131 About 4 kilometres east of modern Svištov in Bulgaria

132 See 'Valetudinarium at Novae' by Ludwika Press in *Studien zu den Militargränzen Roms* III (Stuttgart 1986), pp. 529–35

133 See p. 264

134 For more on Novae's baths, see Andrezej B. Biernacki, 'The Roman legionary bath from the C2nd AD in Novae (Moesia Inferior)' in *Proceedings of the*

XVIIIth International Congress of Roman Frontier Studies, ed. Philip Freeman, Julian Bennett, Zbigniew T. Fiema and Birgitta Hoffmann (BAR International Series 1084 (i), Oxford 2002), pp. 649–61

135 In its final form it was 46.4 metres long and 24.3 metres wide; Stefan Parnicki-Pudelko, *The Episcopal Basilica in Novae, Archeological Research 1976–1990* (Poznan 1995)

136 The lists of bishops of Novae carries on into the 10th century (Parnicki-Pudelko, *The Episcopal Basilica in Novae*, p. 55)

137 Indeed, evidence of destruction in the *principia* of the camp from around 316/17 has been interpreted as the result of some kind of mutiny or military revolt (the ceiling of the *principia* collapsed after being bombarded by stone catapult balls); T. Sarnowski, 'La Destruction des principa à Novae vers 316/317 de notre ère. Révolte militaire ou invasion gothique?' in *Archaeologia* 30 (1979), pp. 119–28

138 Peter Heather, *The Goths* (Oxford 1996), p. 158

139 Fergus Millar, *A Greek Roman Empire, Power and Belief under Theodosius II (408–450)* (Berkeley 2006), pp. 21–5

140 Andrew Poulter, *Nicopolis ad Istrum: A Roman, Late Roman and Early Byzantine City* (Society for Promotion of Roman Studies, Journal of Roman Studies Monograph 8, London 1995), p. 11

141 Poulter, *Nicopolis ad Istrum*, pp. 22–5

142 Poulter, *Nicopolis ad Istrum*, p. 12

143 R.F. Hoddinott, *Bulgaria in Antiquity, an Archaeological Introduction* (London 1975), p. 149

144 Poulter, *Nicopolis ad Istrum*, p. 16

145 Augustus was seventy-five at the time of his death and Tiberius seventy-nine. Nerva and Pertinax were older than Decius at their respective accessions, both being sixty-six years old

146 Possibly under Diocletian around 292, see Teofil Ivanov and Stojan Stojanov, *Abritus* (Razgrad, 1985), p. 13

147 There is a certain irony in Abritus, the place where Decius met his end, playing host to an important Christian complex. For Decius's greatest fame came not as a soldier or administrator, but as one of the most infamous persecutors of Christians. The new religion had come to the attention of the Roman authorities before: Nero had tried to deflect responsibility on them for the great fire in Rome in AD 69, and Pliny the Younger had tried to get instructions from Trajan as to whether it was right to take action against Galatian Christians who had committed no other crime (Pliny, *Letters*, 10.96–7). Yet it was Decius who set off the first Empire-wide and consistent attack on the Christian Church. Late in 249 or at the start of 250, new orders were issued from Rome to all provincial governors. There was to be a universal ceremony of sacrifice to the gods, in which a libation had to be poured and a tasting made of sacrificial meat.

Certificates, *libelli*, were to be issued as proof of compliance with the directive and those unable to produce them on demand were to be put on trial. (J.B. Rives, 'The Decree of Decius and the Religion of Empire' in *Journal of Roman Studies* 89 (1999), pp. 135–54). Christians could not, of course, perform the rite without being considered to have apostatised and so many refused. Some purchased false *libelli* as a way of avoiding their obligations, while a few actually did make the sacrifice. Many prominent Christians, including bishops, simply fled; others were seized by the authorities. In Alexandria, no fewer than eighteen victims are known (Bowman, Garnsey & Cameron (eds), *Cambridge Ancient History* XII, p. 633) and in Rome the most prominent victim of the persecution, Pope Fabian, was martyred (Southern, *The Roman Empire from Severus to Constantine*, p. 74). Yet in Ephesus the bishop himself apostatised, while in Alexandria many socially eminent Christians took the easier course of sacrificing and awaiting easier times. The result was a legacy of bitterness and divisions against the *lapsi* – those who had either bought their freedom through obtaining false certificates or who had actually performed the damnable pagan rituals. The competition to be among the purest and most unsullied, who had refused all engagement with Decius's project, was an ominous portent of the even worse trials that the Christian Church would face fifty years later, under Diocletian.

148 *Notitia Dignitatum*, XL

149 Erdkamp, *Companion to the Roman Army*, p. 214

150 See p. 171

151 The ceremony of presentation of the codicils, the supreme moment in a bureaucrat's career, is shown on the Missorium of Theodosius I. The emperor is depicted wearing a pearl diadem, and the official who has received the codicil is shown with his hands veiled (to avoid the offence of actually touching the imperial fingers). Kelly, *Ruling the Later Roman Empire*, p. 19

152 Kelly, *Ruling the Later Roman Empire*, pp. 20–1

153 One problem with the whole story is that the day of Dasius's martyrdom, 20 November, is actually a month *before* the date of Saturnalia ('The Testament of the Piglet', Edward Chaplin in *Phoenix*, Vol. 41, No. 2 (Summer 1987), pp. 174–83)

154 Maurice Whiles, *Archetypal Heresy, Arianism through the Centuries* (Oxford 1996), pp. 1–4

155 As defined at the Council of Nicaea

156 Whiles, *Archetypal Heresy*, pp. 43–4

157 Penny MacGeorge, *Late Roman Warlords* (Oxford 2002), p. 9

158 Ioannes had been *primicerius notariorum*, or head of the notaries' department

159 Bowman, Garnsey and Cameron (eds), *Cambridge Ancient History* XII, p. 136

160 Mitchell, *A History of the Later Roman Empire*, p. 111

161 Procopius, *History of the Wars*, III, iii, 21–2. Averil Cameron, Bryan Ward-Perkins and Michael Whitby, *Cambridge Ancient History* XIV (Cambridge 2000), p. 6

162 Cameron, Ward-Perkins and Whitby, *Cambridge Ancient History* XIV, p. 13; *Gallic Chronicler of 452*, (trs Richard Burgess, 'The Gallic Chronicle of 452: A New Critical Edition with a Brief Introduction' in Ralph W. Mathisen, Danuta Shanzer *Society and Culture in Late Antique Gaul: Revisiting the Sources*, Aldershot 2001)

163 Cameron, Ward-Perkins and Whitby, *Cambridge Ancient History* XIV, p. 15; John Man, *Attila, the Barbarian King who Challenged Rome* (London 2005), pp. 200–4

164 Man, *Attila*, pp. 250–6

165 Man, *Attila*, pp. 277–8

166 Procopius *The Secret History* III, iv.28

167 Pliny the Elder *Natural History*, VII, 24

168 Appian, *History of Rome* XII, 16.111–12 (trs Horace White, London 1899)

169 The son of the *triumvir*

170 Mócsy, *Pannonia and Upper Moesia*, p. 42

171 Mócsy, *Pannonia and Upper Moesia*, p. 41

172 See Thomas S. Burns, *Rome and the Barbarians* 100 BC–AD 400 (Baltimore 2003), pp. 172, 202, 345, 348–9

173 Ramsay McMullen, *Changes in the Roman Empire* (Princeton 1990), pp. 48–9

174 Which was replaced under Diocletian by a detachment of the II Herculea legion. See Paul MacKendrick, *The Dacian Stones Speak* (Chapel Hill 1975), p. 169

175 Augustus also built himself a 'trophy' in stone at La Turbie, near Nice, to commemorate his victory over the Alpine tribes in 7–6 BC. The origins of the 'trophy' are, however, lost in time. The historian Florus says that the first example was that dedicated by Fabius Maximus and Domitius Ahenobarbus following their victory against the Gauls in 121 BC, but alternative traditions associate the practice with Tarpeia. She was custodian of the citadel at Rome at the time of Romulus and was said to have opened the gates to a party of Sabine invaders, who promised her all the jewels they carried. But on being admitted, they threw not only the gems and gold, but all their shields on top of her, crushing her to death and creating a grizzly 'trophy'. It was the same Tarpeia for whom the Tarpeian rock was named, from which traitors to Rome were hurled. See Gilbert Charles Picard, *Les Trophées Romains, Contributions à l'histoire de la Religions et de l'Art triumphal de Rome* (Paris 1957), pp. 103–48

176 The identity of this officer is unclear. It has even been suggested that the altar was erected after Domitian's campaigns and that the officer was Cornelius Fuscus, who perished in that war. See 'The Lower Moesian Limes and the Dacian Wars of Trajan' by Andrew G. Poulter, in *Studien zu den Militärgränzen Roms* III (Stuttgart 1986), pp. 519–28

177 MacKendrick, *The Dacian Stones Speak*, pp. 172–4

178 MacKendrick, *The Dacian Stones Speak*, p. 115

179 MacKendrick, *The Dacian Stones Speak*, p. 182

180 MacKendrick, *The Dacian Stones Speak*, p. 182

181 A mixed culture of Getae and Dacians

182 Ptolemy, *Geographia*, III, 8, 2. It is also mentioned in the Antonine Itinerary (225,5) as Diniguttia and in the *Notitia Dignitatum* (XXXIX 24) as Dirigothia. For a general account of the site, see 'La forteresse de Dinogetia à la lumière des dernières fouilles archéologiques' by Alexandru Barnea in *Studien zu den Militargränzen Roms* III (Stuttgart 1986), pp. 447–50

183 MacKendrick, *The Dacian Stones Speak*, p. 169

184 MacKendrick, *The Dacian Stones Speak*, p. 149

185 There was in fact a bridgehead fort at Alobrix/Aliobrix on the Ukrainian side

186 Ammianus Marcellinus, XXVII, 5.6. C. Scorpan, *Limes Scythiae: Topographical and stratigraphical research on the late Roman fortifications on the Lower Danube* (BAR International Series 99, 1980), p. 18

187 Cameron and Garnsey (eds), *Cambridge Ancient History* XIII, pp. 507–9

188 Ammianus Marcellinus, XXXI, 4.10–11

189 Lenski, *Failure of Empire*, p. 336

190 Ammianus Marcellinus, XXXI, 10

191 Ammianus Marcellinus, XXXI, 13.1–8

192 Ammianus Marcellinus, XXXI, 13.12–19

193 See p. 36

194 See p. 156

195 MacKendrick, *The Dacian Stones Speak*, p. 146

196 MacKendrick, *The Dacian Stones Speak*, p. 23

197 MacKendrick, *The Dacian Stones Speak*, p. 184

198 Tacitus, *Annals*, I, 53

199 Hermann Fränkel, *Ovid, A Poet between Two Worlds* (Berkeley 1945), p. 113

200 Alessandro Barchiesi, *The Poet and The Prince, Ovid and Augustan Discourse* (Berkeley 1997), p. 14

201 Ovid, *Metamorphoses*, XV, 234

202 Hoddinott, *Bulgaria in Antiquity*, pp. 228–9

203 Hoddinott, *Bulgaria in Antiquity*, p. 229

204 Michael Maas (ed.), *Cambridge Companion to the Age of Justinian* (Cambridge 2005), p. 50

205 The very last ruling Emperor in Constantinople, Constantine XI, was a Palaiologos

206 Review of *The Kantakouzenoi* by Anthony Bryer in *Classical Review*, New Series, Vol. 20, No. 2 (Jun. 1970), pp. 219–22

207 Donald M. Nicol, *The Byzantine Family of Kantakouzenos ca 1100–1460, A Genealogical and Prosopographical Study* (Dumbarton Oaks 1968), p. 229

CHAPTER 5: DACIA

1 Cassius Dio, *Roman History* (trs Earnest Cary, London 1914–27), Book LXVIII, 13.1,5

2 Julian Bennett, *Trajan Optimus Princeps* (London 1997), p. 86

3 Mócsy, *Pannonia and Upper Moesia*, pp. 21, 22–4

4 MacKendrick, *The Dacian Stones Speak*, p. 149

5 MacKendrick, *The Dacian Stones Speak* p. 149

6 Bennett, *Trajan Optimus Princeps*, p. 87, and Cassius Dio 68.6.1

7 MacKendrick, *The Dacian Stones Speak*, p. 71, gives 100,000–150,000. Bennett, *Trajan Optimus Princeps*, p. 89, has 50,000

8 Lino Rossi *Trajan's Column and the Dacian Wars* (trs J.M.C. Toynbee, London 1971), p. 13

9 Lepenski Vir is also one of Europe's most important Mesolithic sites, the home of a culture that produced characteristic stone sculptures in the shape of stylised fish

10 Bennett, *Trajan Optimus Princeps*, p.93 (I Italica, I Minervia, I Adiutrix, IV Flavia Firma, V Macedonica, VII Claudia Pia Fidelis, XII Fulminata, XIII Gemina, XV Apollinaris, XX Valeria Victrix, XXI Rapax, XXX Ulpia)

11 Bennett, *Trajan Optimus Princeps*, p. 94, and Cassius Dio, *Roman History* LXVIII 9.4–7

12 Bennett *Trajan Optimus Princeps*, p. 95. See also discussion in Ioana Bogdan Cătăniciu, *Evolution of the system of defence works in Roman Dacia* (trs Etta Dumitrescu, BAR International Series 116, Oxford 1981), pp. 9–10

13 Bennett, *Trajan Optimus Princeps*, p. 97

14 Bennett, *Trajan Optimus Princeps*, p. 98

15 Cassius Dio, 69, 4

16 Trajan's Column, Panel LXXXVI–LXXXVII, Rossi, *Trajan's Column and the Dacian Wars*, p. 181

17 See Rossi, *Trajan's Column and the Dacian Wars*, pp. 202–4, vs Bennett, *Trajan Optimus Princeps*, p. 100

18 Cassius Dio, 68, 14.3–5

19 This is the same trick that is said to have been used to conceal the grave of Alaric and is a sufficiently common ruse that it may be a mere literary topos rather than a true account of the concealment of Decebalus's hoard

20 Bennett, *Trajan Optimus Princeps*, p. 101

21 'The Captor of Decebalus: A New Inscription from Philippi' by Michael Speidel in *Journal of Roman Studies* 60 (1970), pp. 142–53

22 Bennett, *Trajan Optimus Princeps*, p. 101

23 Cataniciu, *Evolution of the system of defence works in Roman Dacia*, p. 11

24 *Princeton Encyclopedia of Classical Sites*, p. 285

25 MacKendrick, *The Dacian Stones Speak*, p. 133

26 The fort at Orăştioara de Sus, however, was retained until the 3rd century; Cătăniciu, *Evolution of the system of defence works in Roman Dacia*, p. 14

27 MacKendrick, *The Dacian Stones Speak*, p. 64

28 Herodotus, *Histories*, 4, 94–6 and see the discussion in 'Zalmoxis' by Mircea

Eliade and Willard R. Trask in *History of Religions*, Vol. 11, No. 3 (Feb. 1972), pp. 257–302

29 MacKendrick, *The Dacian Stones Speak*, p. 55

30 Jordanes, *Getica* 74 (trs. Charles Christopher Microw, Princeton 1915)

31 MacKendrick, *The Dacian Stones Speak*, p. 142

32 See p. 266

33 MacKendrick, *The Dacian Stones Speak*, p. 114. It occupied this role from at least the reign of Alexander Severus (222–35)

34 MacKendrick, *The Dacian Stones Speak*, p. 112

35 MacKendrick, *The Dacian Stones Speak*, p. 123

36 'The Defensive System of Roman Dacia' by Nicolae Gudea in *Britannia* 10 (1979), pp. 63–87

37 See *Princeton Encyclopedia of Classical Sites*, p. 74

38 MacKendrick, *The Dacian Stones Speak*, p. 126

39 MacKendrick, *The Dacian Stones Speak*, p. 126

40 *Princeton Encyclopedia of Classical Sites*, p. 729. The *Torquata* refers to a torque or decoration for valour that must have been given to the unit, whilst *civium Romanorum* shows that at some time those serving in the unit had been granted citizenship, again for some act of great bravery or loyalty

41 Birley, *Septimius Severus*, p. 190. Note that a group called *dediticii* was specifically excluded; the meaning of this is never clearly defined, but equates more or less to enemy who had surrendered or been captured, and their descendants

42 Cătăniciu, *Evolution of the system of defence works in Roman Dacia*, p. 17

43 Cassius Dio, 78, 20.3–4

44 Cătăniciu, *Evolution of the system of defence works in Roman Dacia*, p. 58, although there may simply be evidence that has been missed, and it is never entirely safe to use a *terminus post quem* from coins as an absolutely final date

45 Watson, *Aurelian and the Third Century*, pp. 255–8

CHAPTER 6: CAPPADOCIA

1 See David Magie, *Roman Rule in Asia Minor to the End of the Third Century After Christ* (Princeton, NJ, 1950), pp. 3–33

2 The Roman defeat of the Seleucid Antiochus III had led to the potential acquisition of lands in Asia Minor by the Treaty of Apameia in 188 BC. But the Romans gifted their share to Eumenes of Pergamon, their ally in the war, as the Senate did not wish at that stage to become involved. It fell to them anyway in 133 BC. See Magie, *Roman Rule in Asia Minor*, p. 16

3 On the course of the war, see Magie, *Roman Rule in Asia Minor*, p. 152

4 Following the death of King Archelaus of Cappadocia, who had been summoned to Rome to face a trial on charges of treason and who, at the

age of eighty, seems simply to have expired of old age or exhaustion brought on by the long journey before the trial actually began. See Magie, *Roman Rule in Asia Minor*, p. 491

5 On the death of Antiochus, rival factions sent embassies to Rome, one arguing for the continued independence of Commagene, the other lobbying for its annexation by Rome. The pro-Roman lobby, unsurprisingly, won out. See Magie, *Roman Rule in Asia Minor*, p. 496

6 This included the restoration of Commagene independence under Antiochus III's son, Antiochus IV

7 This involved the deposition of Aristobulus, who had been given the kingdom under Nero in 54. Initially it included the whole of eastern Asia Minor. See Magie, *Roman Rule in Asia Minor*, p. 574

8 See Magie, *Roman Rule in Asia Minor*, pp. 670–82

9 On the Mithridatic Wars, see Magie, *Roman Rule in Asia Minor*, pp. 177–230, 321–50

10 For uncertainty about Strabo's date of birth, see Daniela Dueck, *Strabo of Amaseia* (London 2000), pp. 2–3

11 He was later to become involved in an abortive invasion of Yemen. See p. 355

12 Dueck, *Strabo of Amaseia*, p. 7

13 Strabo, *Geographia* (trs H.C Hamilton and W. Falconer, London 1854), 12.3.39

14 His exact dates are uncertain, but he reigned in the second quarter of the 2nd century BC

15 Appian, *History of Rome*, XII, 16.113

16 Intermittently during the early Empire and more definitively from the 6th century. Roman power did extend further east into the Caucasus, leaving such remains as the castle of Apsarus in modern Georgia. Roman diplomacy from the time of Justinian onwards centred on the struggle to influence or control minor kingdoms such as that of the Laz, which steered an awkward course between absorption by the Romans and falling under the sway of Persia. The furthest-flung evidence of Roman advances to the north-east is the inscription at Gobustan in modern Azerbaijan, left by a centurion from the XII Fulminata, probably in the reign of Domitian

17 See Magie, *Roman Rule in Asia Minor*, pp. 554–9

18 This was on the enforced 'retirement' of Polemo II. Cassius Dio, 63, 6.5; Magie, *Roman Rule in Asia Minor*, p. 561

19 William Miller, *Trebizond: The Last Greek Empire* (London 1926), p. 84

20 Miller, *Trebizond*, p. 98

21 Miller, *Trebizond*, pp. 108–9

22 Miller, *Trebizond*, p. 112

23 Ioannides, *Historia kai Statistike Trapezountos*, 59 (cf. Miller, *Trebizond*, pp. 8–13)

24 'Trebizond, A Medieval Citadel and Palace' by D. Talbot Rice in *Journal of*

Hellenic Studies, Vol. 52, Part I (1932), pp. 47–54

25 Anthony Bryer, *The Byzantine Monuments and Topography of the Pontos* (Dumbarton Oaks 1995), p. 218. The tomb of Theodora, daughter of John IV, who married Uzin Hasan, was once to be seen in Saint George's church in Diyarbarkir

26 See Roger Matthews (ed.), *Ancient Anatolia, Fifty Years of Work by the British Institute of Archaeology of Ankara* (London 1999) p. 271

27 Miller, *Trebizond*, p. 61

28 Miller, *Trebizond*, p. 62

29 Matthews (ed.), *Ancient Anatolia*, p. 268

30 Procopius, *Buildings* (trs H.B. Dewing, London 1940), III.4

31 'Biliotti's Excavation at Satala' by T.B. Mitford in *Anatolian Studies* 24 (1974), pp. 221–44

32 Replacing XVI Flavia Firma, which had been there since about 75. See C.S. Lightfoot, 'Survey Work at Satala' in Matthews (ed.), *Ancient Anatolia*, pp. 273–84

33 *Notitia Dignitatum*, XXXVIII

34 Beate Dignas and Engelbert Winter, *Rome and Persia in Late Antiquity, Neighbours and Rivals* (Cambridge 2007), p. 28

35 See Lightfoot in Matthews (ed.), *Anatolia*, p. 279

36 The modern settlement of Samsat is no longer on the site of ancient Samosata, which was indundated by the rising waters caused by the Atatürk Dam. The inhabitants of the old Samsat, which had sat on the Roman site, were moved to a newly constructed town, which was also called Samsat

37 Antiochos appears for the first time during the Third Mithridatic War. Wise to the new diplomatic realities, he offered support to Lucullus and Pompey in their campaigns in Asia Minor and adopted the unmistakably ingratiating title 'Just and manifest God, friend of the Romans and friend of the Greeks'. Even so, an accusation of complicity with the Parthians in the invasion by Pacorus in 51 BC resulted in Antiochos having to pay a massive bribe to persuade the Romans to desist from a siege of the royal capital. His successor Mithridates II then made the tactical error of supporting Mark Antony against Octavian in the civil war, but somehow managed to get away with his life and his kingdom

38 After the early Empire, the main consuls (or *ordinarii*) for the year would often resign and be replaced by additional (or suffect) consuls, who would serve the rest of the year, sometimes being themselves replaced by a new pair (or pairs) of suffects. The position was still prestigious, if not as highly regarded as the position of main consul for the year. The height of the practice was reached under Commodus in 190, when no fewer than twenty-five men served as consul, one of them being the future Emperor Septimius Severus

39 'The Excavation of the "Hierothesion" of Antiochus I of Commagene on

9 Millar, *The Roman Near East*, p. 39

10 See p. 356

11 Sartre, *The Middle East under Rome*, p. 77

12 See p. 174

13 See Millar, *The Roman Near East*, pp. 181–4. Although, strictly speaking, the road may have been called Strata Diocletiana only in certain stretches and, for example, from Khan el-Qattar to Khan el-Trab may have been called Strata Diocletiani et Maximiani. See Ariel Lewin, 'Diocletian: Politics and limites in the Near East' in *Proceedings of the XVIIIth International Congress of Roman Frontier Studies*, Philip Freeman, Julian Bennett, Zbigniew T. Fiema and Birgitta Hoffmann (eds.), (BAR International Series 1084 (i), Oxford 2002), pp. 91–102

14 Glanville Downey, *Ancient Antioch* (Oxford 1972), pp. 92–3, calculates in the region of 150,000

15 The precise legal position of the Hatay is the subject of a dispute between Syria and Turkey, the former maintaining that the French (then in control of Syria) illegally ceded the territory to Turkey, the latter that the 1939 plebiscite which confirmed the change of political allegiance was an entirely fair and free reflection of the wishes of the population of Hatay

16 Confusingly, no fewer than fifteen towns founded by Seleucus received the name Antioch. See Downey, *Ancient Antioch*, p. 31

17 In fact the port of Antioch, at Seleucia Pieria, was founded a month earlier, but the flight of a sacred eagle that made off with the sacrificial meat at the foundation celebrations for Pieria and then landed on the future site of Antioch persuaded Seleucus that, to be on the safe side, he had better establish a city there too, which then became the royal capital. See Downey, *Ancient Antioch*, p. 31

18 See 'Notes on Seleucid and Parthian Chronology' by Elias J. Bickerman in *Berytus* 8 (1943), pp. 73–84

19 See Downey, *Ancient Antioch*, p. 75

20 See Downey, *Ancient Antioch*, p. 98

21 See, in general, J.H. Liebeschuetz, Antioch, *City and Imperial Administration in the Later Roman Empire* (Oxford 1972)

22 Which were successful in 256, 260 and 540

23 See Downey, *Ancient Antioch*, p. 113

24 On deportations from Roman territory into Persia in general, see 'Captives, Refugees and Exiles: A Study of Cross-border civilian movements and contacts between Rome and Persia from Valerian to Jovian' by Samuel, N.C. Lieu in *The Defence of the Roman and Byzantine East*, Philip Freeman and David Kennedy (eds), (BAR International Series 297 (ii), Oxford 1986), pp. 475–505

25 See p. 321

26 He was caught on the outskirts of the city by Septimius's commander-in-chief

Anullinus. He had, it seems, intended to flee into the Parthian Empire. Birley, *Septimius Severus*, p. 113

27 See Downey, *Ancient Antioch*, pp. 118–19

28 See Acts of the Apostles 11,26

29 See Downey, *Ancient Antioch*, p. 126, who points out that Peter is said to have been the bishop in Rome for twenty-five years before his martyrdom in AD 65, thus making it difficult for him to have been bishop in Antioch in the AD 40s

30 See Downey, *Ancient Antioch*, p. 162

31 See Downey, *Ancient Antioch*, p. 169

32 See Downey, *Ancient Antioch*, p. 175

33 For the 'Riot of the Statues', see Potter, *The Roman Empire at Bay*, pp. 515–16; John Chrysostom, *Homily on Saint Babylas*; Socrates, *Historia Ecclesiastica* 3.18; John Matthews, *The Roman Empire of Ammianus* (London 1989), pp. 429–31. See also Stephen Williams and Gerard Friell, *Theodosius, the Empire at Bay* (London 1984), pp. 67–8

34 'The Riot of 387 in Antioch: The Role of the Theatrical Claques in the Later Empire' by Robert Browning in *Journal of Roman Studies* 42 (1952), pp. 13–20

35 Williams and Friell, *Theodosius*, p. 67. Theodosius's personality was marked, throughout his reign, by a quickness to anger, followed by bouts of guilt, which – coupled with a straightforward devotion to the orthodox Catholic position as defined by the Council of Nicaea – rendered him peculiarly intolerant of pagans and heretics. It was Theodosius who overtly established the Catholic Church as the official one, and who, in 391, forbade conversion from Christianity to paganism (Williams and Friell, *Theodosius*, p. 121). Although both praetorian prefects in that year were pagan, the active approval or tacit connivance of the Emperor led to an outburst of destruction of pagan temples, particularly in the East, from Heliopolis to Gaza and, most notably, in Alexandria. In 392, Theodosius issued an even sterner edict, criminalising any form of sacrifice or divination, on pain of death, and decreeing the confiscation of property for anyone displaying pagan symbols, whether in private or in public (Williams and Friell, *Theodosius*, pp. 122–3). Henceforth, although it was perfectly possibly to hold pagan beliefs, it was next to impossible to engage openly in pagan practices (save in exceptional cases such as Philae in Egypt) and, since paganism had always been more of a way of life and of practice than a theology, its final withering away was only a matter of time

36 Julian, *Misopogon*, 361; Downey, *Ancient Antioch*, p. 167

37 Downey, *History of Antioch in Syria*, p. 206

38 Millar, *Roman Near East*, p. 29

39 'Legions in the East from Augustus to Trajan' by Lawrence Keppie in *The Defence of the Roman and Byzantine East*, Freeman and Kennedy (eds) pp. 411–29

40 See 'Legions in the East from Augustus to Trajan' by Lawrence Keppie in *The Defence of the Roman and Byzantine East*, Freeman and Kennedy (eds) pp. 414–15

41 Ross Burns, *Monuments of Syria, An Historical Guide* (London 1999), p. 530

42 Bowman, Garnsey and Rathbone (eds), *Cambridge Ancient History XI*, p. 177

43 Birley, *Marcus Aurelius*, p. 256

44 Cassius Dio, 72, 24.1–3

45 Cassius Dio, 72, 28.1

46 The rebellion had more unfortunate consequences for some: although Marcus wrote to the Senate asking that his reign not be stained by the blood of others, one of Cassius's sons, Maecianus, had already been murdered. The Empress Faustina died near Tyana in Cappadocia, accompanying her husband en route to Syria. There were rumours that she had committed a diplomatic suicide, shamed by her complicity with Cassius. The Emperor carried on his journey, spending a year in the East before returning to Rome – the whole experience resulting in an edict that henceforth no governor should serve in the province of his birth

47 Although not supporting the position of Nestorius, who maintained that Christ had two fully independent natures (human and divine) not joined together in one person, Theodoret felt that Cyril of Alexandria's 'Twelve Chapters' anathematising the Nestorian position went too far. Christopher Baumer, *The Church of the East, an Illustrated History of Assyrian Christianity* (London 2006), pp. 42–8; István Pásztori-Kupán, *Theodoret of Cyrrus* (Oxford 2006), pp. 10–12

48 During the course of which Roman soldiers entered the council chamber, shaking manacles as a warning to any bishops considering voting the 'wrong' way. As an additional incentive the bishops were forced to sign voting forms in front of the soldiers. W.H. Frend, *The Rise of the Monophysite Movement* (Cambridge 1972), pp. 39–43

49 Pásztori-Kupán, *Theodoret of Cyrrus*, pp. 26–7

50 Warwick Ball, *Rome in the East, the Transformation of an Empire* (London 2000), pp. 229–32; Kevin Butcher, *Roman Syria and the Near East* (London 2003), pp. 145–53

51 Robert Doran, *The Lives of Simeon Stylites* (Spencer, MA, 1992), p. 16

52 Theodoret, *Historia Religiosa* 13 (in Doran, *The Lives of Simeon Stylites*, p. 77)

53 Ramsay McMullen, *Christianizing the Roman Empire* (New Haven 1984), p. 2, and Theodoret *Historia Religiosa* 14

54 The last stylite, however, was recorded as late as 1848 in Djgqondidi in Georgia by the traveller Brosset. Atiyah, *A History of Eastern Christianity*, p. 189

55 'While the servants pitched my tents, I went out and sat upon St Simon's column – there is still a little bit of it left – and considered how very different he must have been from me. And there came a big star and twinkled at me

through the soft warm night, and we agreed together that it was pleasanter to wander across the heavens and the earth than to sit on top of a pillar all one's days.' 31 March 1905, from Kalaat Simaan; Florence Bell (ed.), *The Letters of Gertrude Bell* (London 1927), Vol. 1, pp. 207–8

56 Burns, *Monuments of Syria*, p. 216

57 For the durability of the monastery, see Tchalenko, *Villages antiques de la Syrie du Nord*, p. 206

58 Ball, *Rome in the East*, pp. 229–32; Kevin Butcher, *Roman Syria and the Near East* (London 2003), pp. 145–53

59 Burns, *Monuments of Syria*, pp. 69–70

60 Tchalenko, *Villages antiques de la Syrie du nord*, pp. 320–42

61 The nearby baths are dated to 473. Burns, *Monuments of Syria*, p. 219

62 Williams, *Diocletian*, pp. 94–5; Southern and Dixon, *The Late Roman Army*; but for a contrary view, see G.W. Bowersock, 'Limes Arabicus' in *Harvard Studies in Classical Philology* 80 (1976), pp. 219–29

63 Burns, *Monuments of Syria*, p. 207

64 Burns, *Monuments of Syria*, p. 209

65 See p. 343

66 Irfan Shahid, *Byzantium and the Arabs in the Sixth Century* (Dumbarton Oaks 1995), pp. 32–6

67 Shahid, *Byzantium and the Arabs in the Sixth Century*, pp. 439–78

68 Shahid, *Byzantium and the Arabs in the Sixth Century*, pp. 266–82

69 The Romans also held the town of Kifrin and built a fort on the Euphrates island of Bijan, some 150 kilometres further downriver from Dura, which were the very furthest outposts, only around 200 kilometres from Ctesiphon, the Persian capital

70 There were walls on these sides, but the topography meant they did not need to be strong, and in places in the north-east of the city the original mud-brick was never replaced; Ann Perkins, *The Art of Dura Europos* (Oxford 1973), p. 12

71 Nicanor was a Macedonian general who governed Syria for a while, but as cities were normally referred to as being founded by a ruler, the reference to Nicanor in the chronicle of Isidore of Charax could possibly be a mistake for 'Nicator' – in other words, King Seleucus I; Perkins, *The Art of Dura Europos*, p. 4

72 Dignas and Winter, *Rome and Persia in Late Antiquity*, p. 13

73 Ammianus Marcellinus, 24, 1.5

74 Clark Hopkins, *The Discovery of Dura Europos* (New Haven, 1979), p. 242; Clark Hopkins, 'The Siege of Dura' in *Classical Journal*, Vol. 42, No. 5 (Feb 1948), pp. 251–9

75 In January 2009, Dr Simon James of Leicester University presented evidence that the dead tunnellers were Roman and that, more fascinatingly, they may well have died as a result of the earliest identified use of chemical warfare:

their Persian opponents may have lit braziers laced with bitumen and sulphur crystals which would have emitted choking fumes and rendered the Roman soldiers unconscious within minutes

76 Hopkins, *The Discovery of Dura Europos*, p. 1

77 Hopkins, *The Discovery of Dura Europos*, p. 92

78 The current version was a reconstruction of an earlier synagogue, which was originally founded sometime between 165 and 200 (Perkins, *The Art of Dura Europos*, pp. 26, 29)

79 Though not unprecedented for this era; there are figurative representations in the 6th-century synagogue of Beth Alpha in Galilee (Nicholas de Lange, 'Jews in the Age of Justinian' in Michael Maas (ed.), *The Cambridge Companion to the Age of Justinian* (Cambridge 2005), p. 416)

80 This is the date of the dedication of the *praetorium* of the new camp (Perkins, *The Art of Dura Europos*, p. 26)

81 'The Roman Military Feriale' by J.F. Gilliam in *Harvard Theological Review*, Vol. 47, No. 3 (Jul. 1954), pp. 183–96

82 This was the festival in honour of Vesta, the goddess of the hearth, during which, at Rome, the inner sanctum of her temple would be opened to Roman women, and the Vestal Virgins would bake special cakes in her honour

83 The soldiers were paid three times a year, a practice that lasted from the early Empire at least until the 3rd century

84 Unfortunately his work lasted for only five years, before another earthquake brought it down in 563

85 When Tiglath-Pileser I mentions that the people of Tadmor were amongst the many other peoples he had defeated. Iain Browning, *Palmyra* (London 1979), p. 19

86 Sartre, *The Middle East Under Rome*, pp. 51, 69

87 Browning, *Palmyra*, pp. 24–6

88 Browning, *Palmyra*, p. 53

89 James Dawkins and Robert Wood, *The Ruins of Palmyra* (London 1753), p. 35

90 Browning, *Palmyra*, p. 114

91 Dawkins and Wood, *The Ruins of Palmyra*, Plate 19. As well as the purely architectural plates, Dawkins's and Wood's book includes beautiful panoramas of the site as it appeared in the mid-18th century, unencumbered by site clearances, reconstructions or the general tidying up that has enhanced the accessibility, yet diminished the romantic appeal of many sites on the Roman frontier. Plates 35 and 42 are particularly fine examples

92 The habit of veiling women was fairly prevalent in the Near East even before the advent of Islam in the 7th century. An Assyrian law code of the 20th century BC enjoins that free women must be veiled if outside their

house (though slave girls and concubines could go uncovered). The Christian writer Tertullian in his *De Virginibus Velandis* also advised pious women to veil themselves in public. See Browning, *Palmyra*, p. 32

93 Browning, *Palmyra*, p. 15

94 The original of the tariff, which contains the longest text yet discovered in Palmyrene, now resides in the Hermitage Museum in St Petersburg

95 Browning, *Palmyra*, p. 27

96 Sartre, *The Middle East under Rome*, p. 354

97 *Corrector Totius Orientis*. See Browning, *Palmyra*, p. 45

98 Richard Stoneman, *Palmyra and its Empire, Zenobia's Revolt against Rome* (Ann Arbor 1992), pp. 78–9

99 Sartre, *The Middle East under Rome*, p. 355

100 Stoneman, *Palmyra and its Empire: Zenobia's revolt against Rome*, p. 117

101 Sartre, *The Middle East under Rome*, p. 356

102 *Historia Augusta*, Aurelian, (trs David Magie, London 1954) XXVI, 7

103 *Historia Augusta*, Aurelian, XXVII, 1

104 *Historia Augusta*, Thirty Pretenders, XXX, 7. Zosimus, however, relates the far less romantic version that Zenobia died (or committed suicide) on the way back to Rome and so never appeared in Aurelian's triumph, let alone lived out the rest of her days as a dutiful Roman wife

105 Edward Gibbon, *The History of the Decline and Fall of the Roman Empire*, (ed. David Womersely, London 2005), Vol. I, Chapter XI, p. 313

106 Letter to H.W. Wynn, 30 June 1813 (*The Life and Letters of Lady Hester Stanhope* by the Duchess of Cleveland (London 1914), p. 159)

107 Six hundred piastres was at least a lot less than the 3,000 piastres initial asking price. When they finally did arrive, Mangles and Irby were ambivalent about the place, much as they would be about Petra. Although, taken together, they deemed the ruins as 'presenting altogether the most imposing sight of the kind we have ever seen . . .', their final verdict was far less favourable: 'Take any part of the ruins separately, and they excite but little interest; and altogether, we judged the visit to Palmyra hardly worthy of the time, expense, anxiety, and fatiguing journey through the wilderness, which we had undergone to visit them . . . The sculpture, as well of the capitals of the columns, as of the other ornamental parts of the door-ways and buildings, is very coarse and bad.' (Irby and Mangles, *Travels in Egypt and Nubia, Syria and Asia Minor*, pp. 268–9)

108 See the discussion of its function in Browning, *Palmyra*, p. 188

109 Browning, *Palmyra*, p. 50

110 Malcolm A.R. Colledge, *The Art of Palmyra* (London 1976), p. 22

111 Browning, *Palmyra*, p. 196

112 Named Malé, Saadai and Naamain, with the construction being in the mid-2nd century. Browning, *Palmyra*, p. 205

113 On tomb reliefs; Colledge, *The Art of Palmyra*, pp. 68–9

114 Burns, *The Monuments of Syria*, pp. 201–2

115 Cameron and Garnsey (eds), *Cambridge Ancient History* XI, p. 659

116 Butcher, *Roman Syria and the Near East*, pp. 343–4

117 Birley, *Septimius Severus*, p. 72

118 Gibbon, *Decline and Fall of the Roman Empire*, Vol. I, Chapter XI, p. 150

119 Southern, *The Roman Empire from Severus to Constantine*, p. 58

120 The teenager took his position as priest very seriously and refused to dress in a Roman toga, continuing to affect the robes of a Syrian priest, and even going so far as to send the Senate a portrait of himself in this garb so that the august fathers could become better acquainted with their new imperial master. This disregard of traditional forms did not go down well, nor did his installation of the sacred black stone of Elagabalus in the Temple of Capitoline Jupiter, once he finally arrived in Rome in September 219. Things went from bad to worse: the young Emperor took up the title of 'most magnificent priest of the sun god Elagabalus' on coins, and relegated or dropped the revered appellation of *Pontifex Maximus*. He declared his own deity to be the supreme one of the pantheon, and even married Julia Aquila Severa, a Vestal Virgin, the normal penalty for having sexual relations with whom should have been death; Bowman, Garnsey and Cameron (eds), *Cambridge Ancient History* XII, p. 21

121 David S. Potter, *The Roman Empire at Bay* (London 2004), p. 157

122 *Historia Augusta*, Aurelian, 25.2

123 Burns, *Monuments of Syria*, p. 25

124 Jean Starcky, 'The Nabataeans: A Historical Sketch' in *Biblical Archaeologist*, Vol. 18, No. 4 (Dec. 1955), pp. 81–106

125 Burns, *Monuments of Syria*, pp. 79–80

126 From Psalm 145, 13. Burns, *Monuments of Syria*, p. 84

127 Acts of the Apostles 9, 11

128 Mark Twain, *Innocents Abroad*, Chapter 44

129 Dignas and Winter, *Rome and Persia in Late Antiquity*, pp. 47, 230

130 The peace that Khusraw II had accepted in 591 as the price for being restored to his throne had left the Sassanids smarting at the loss of Dara and other strategic positions (Dignas and Winter, *Rome and Persia in Late Antiquity*, p. 43). When Khusraw's 'benefactor' Maurice was slaughtered in the palace revolution that placed Phocas on the imperial throne in 602, the Persian found the perfect pretext to avenge his dead ally through a series of campaigns in the Byzantine borderlands. Much-contested Dara fell first in 604, and by 610 Khusraw's armies had taken Amida, Edessa and Mardin, opening the way to Syria and Palestine (Mitchell, *A History of the Later Roman Empire*, p. 412). By 609, the line had been breached in Armenia and Cappadocia too, with the loss of Satala and Theodosiopolis (modern Erzerum). Phocas's critically weak position was further undermined by the revolt of Heraclius, the exarch of Africa. Egypt was lost to the rebels in

609, and the following October Heraclius's fleet – led by his similarly named son – cruised into the Bosphorus. The citizens of Constantinople, clearly seeing which way the wind was blowing, showed their contempt for Phocas by murdering him and dragging his mutilated body through the streets. The younger Heraclius, who was now declared Emperor, was at first unable to turn the Persian tide, having to acquiesce in the loss of Damascus in 613 and Jerusalem the following year. By 620, not only had eastern Asia Minor fallen, but Khusraw's forces had captured Egypt, cutting off the supply of grain on which Constantinople depended. By 626 a Persian army was camped at Chalcedon, but the lack of an effective naval arm, and the failure of the Avar kagan to ferry them over, meant it had to withdraw. Heraclius, meanwhile, had taken the risky decision to strike at the Persian capital rather than defending his own. In December 627, he decisively defeated the Persians near Nineveh, and within three months Khusraw had been deposed by his son Kavadh, who himself died six months later. In the confusion, Heraclius opened negotiations with a Persian general, Shahbaraz, who, in return for support in gaining the throne, offered to evacuate all the recently conquered territories, return the True Cross and even allow his eldest son to be baptised. That Shahbaraz was in turn assassinated within three months only added to utter chaos engulfing the Sassanid state (Dignas and Winter, *Rome and Persia in Late Antiquity*, p. 48)

131 Mitchell, *A History of the Later Roman Empire*, p. 420

CHAPTER 8: ARABIA

1 John William Burgon, *Poems (1840 to 1878)* (London 1885), pp. 25–6
2 G.W. Bowersock, *Roman Arabia* (Cambridge, MA, 1983), p. 13
3 Bowersock, *Roman Arabia*, p. 16
4 Whilst there, unable to temper his curiosity, Pompey desecrated the Holy of Holies by entering it, but came out again declaring that it was entirely empty
5 Bowersock, *Roman Arabia*, p. 33
6 Maria Giulia Amadasi Guzzo and Eugenia Equini Schneider, *Petra* (trs Lydia G. Cochrane, Chicago 2002), p. 51. The traditional view that the monsoon was discovered by a mariner named Hippalus was rather spoilt when it was realised this was probably a corruption of Hypalos, the Greek name for the south-west monsoon wind
7 Bowersock, *Roman Arabia*, pp. 46–8
8 Strabo, *Geography*, XVI, 4.23–4
9 The Nabataeans escaped punishment, so perhaps Augustus was more exasperated with his bumbling prefect than suspicious of any connivance by the royal court in Petra. Syllaeus eventually got his come-uppance in 5 BC, when, during a possible bid to seize power, he became implicated in a nasty

series of assassinations of high-ranking opponents and was summoned to Rome, where he was decapitated on the personal orders of the Emperor; Bowersock, *Roman Arabia*, pp. 52–3

10 Bowersock, *Roman Arabia*, pp. 55–6

11 For the dates of Nabataean kings, see G.W. Bowersock, 'A Report on Arabia Provincia' in *Journal of Roman Studies* 61 (1971), pp. 219–42

12 And when he did, they bore the legend *Arabia Adquista* (the Acquisition of Arabia) rather than *Arabia Capta* (the Conquest of Arabia), again implying a more peaceful absorption. See S. Thomas Parker. 'The Roman Frontier in Jordan: an overview' in *Proceedings of the XVIIIth International Congress of Roman Frontier Studies*, Philip Freeman, Julian Bennett, Zbigniew T. Fiema and Birgitta Hoffmann (eds) (BAR International Series 1084 (i), Oxford 2002), pp. 77–84

13 S. Thomas Parker, 'History of the Late Roman Frontier East of the Dead Sea' in *The Roman Frontier in Central Jordan, Interim Report on the Limes Arabicus Project*, S. Thomas Parker (ed.) (BAR International Series 340 (ii), Oxford 1987), pp. 793–825

14 Bowersock, *Roman Arabia*, pp. 78–9

15 S. Thomas Parker, 'History of the Late Roman Frontier East of the Dead Sea' in *The Roman Frontier in Central Jordan*, pp. 793–825

16 Irfan Shahid, *Byzantium and the Arabs in the Sixth Century* (Dumbarton Oaks 1995), pp. 307–73

17 Southern, *The Roman Empire from Severus to Constantine*, p. 70

18 Southern, *The Roman Empire from Severus to Constantine*, p. 71

19 For an account of the evidence (which concludes that he might have been Christian), sec Irfan Shahid, *Rome and the Arabs – A Prolegomenon to the Study of Byzantium and the Arabs* (Dumbarton Oaks, 1984), pp. 65–95

20 The area was even more built over until 1974, when the Jordanian General Directorate of Antiquities and Museums decided to clear away all the modern housing that had obscured much of the complex until then. See Hassan Hatoum, *Canatha and Philippopolis* (Damascus, 2001) p. 105; Arthur Segal, 'Roman Cities in the Province of Arabia' in *Journal of the Society of Architectural Historians*, Vol. 40, No. 2 (May 1981), pp. 108–21

21 Although opinions vary and M.G.H. Amer and M. Gawlikowski (1985) believe that it should not be classified as a *kalybe*, but as a temple of the imperial cult

22 Matthew 4, 25

23 Hatoum, *Canatha and Philippopolis*, p. 16

24 Which picturesquely translates into English as 'the torrent of the bay-tree'

25 The *odeon* cost 10,000 denarii, donated by Marcus Ulpius Lysias. See Hattoum, *Canatha and Philippopolis*, p. 19

26 Burns, *Monuments of Syria*, p. 66

27 See p. 300

28 Such as al-Tabari in his *Tarikh al-Tabari*

29 It could also have been used as the later residence of a Christian bishop. Burns, *Monuments of Syria*, p. 69

30 For a description of the archaeological soundings, see Maurice Lenoir, 'Le camp de la légion IIIa Cyrenaica à Bostra. Recherches récentes' in *Proceedings of the XVIIIth International Congress of Roman Frontier Studies* (BAR International Series 1084 (i)), pp. 175–9

31 See p. 343

32 Millar, *The Roman Near East*, pp. 433–5

33 On relations between Zenobia and the Arabs, see 'Zenobia and the Arabs' by David F. Graf in *The Eastern Frontier of the Roman Empire*, D.H. French and C.S. Lightfoot (eds) (BAR International Series 553 (i), 1989), pp. 143–67

34 See Tabari, *Tarikh al-Tabari*, 1.621–7, quoted in Graf, 'Zenobia and the Arabs' in *The Eastern Frontier*

35 Bowersock, *Roman Arabia*, p. 140

36 Irfan Shahid, *Byzantium and the Arabs in the Fourth Century* (Dumbarton Oaks 1983), pp. 33, 414–15

37 Shahid, *Byzantium and the Arabs in the Fourth Century*, pp. 31–53

38 Bowersock, *Roman Arabia*, p. 138

39 Bert de Vries, 'Umm el-Jimal in the First Three Centuries AD' in Freeman and Kennedy, *The Defence of the Roman and Byzantine East*, pp. 227–41; Bert de Vries, 'What's in a Name: The Anonymity of Ancient Umm el-Jimal' in *Biblical Archaeologist*, Vol. 57, No. 4 (Dec. 1994), pp. 215–19

40 See Bowersock, *Roman Arabia*, p. 237

41 See p. 363

42 See de Vries, 'Umm-el Jimal in the First Three Centuries AD' p. 231

43 See p. 356

44 T.E. Lawrence, *Seven Pillars of Wisdom* (London 1935), Chapter LXVV

45 Millar, *Roman Arabia*, pp. 412–13

46 Cassius Dio, 69, 12–15

47 G.W.L. Harding, *The Antiquities of Jordan* (London 1959), p. 88

48 *Princeton Encyclopedia of Classical Sites*, p. 349

49 S. Thomas Parker, 'Preliminary Report on the 1980 Season of the Central Limes Arabicus Project' in *Bulletin of the American Schools of Oriental Research* 247 (Summer 1982), pp. 1–26

50 S. Thomas Parker, 'Preliminary Report on the 1980 Season', p. 5. The building also seemed to lack a *valetudinarium* or hospital.

51 See S. Thomas Parker, 'Retrospective on the Arabian Frontier after a Decade of Research' in Freeman and Kennedy, *Defence of the Roman and Byzantine East*, p. 644

52 See p. 30

53 For a summary of the history of the site, see S. Thomas Parker, 'Research

on the Central *Limes Arabicus, 1980–1982'* in *Studien zu den Militargränzen Roms* III (Stuttgart 1986), pp. 641–8

54 S. Thomas Parker, *The Roman Frontier in Central Jordan, Interim Report on the Limes Arabicus Project, 1980–1985* (BAR International Series 340 (i), Oxford 1987), p. 258

55 Guzzo and Schneider, *Petra*, pp. 79–82

56 'Edward Lear in Petra' by G.W. Bowersock in *Proceedings of the American Philosophical Society*, Vol. 134, No. 3 (Sep. 1990), pp. 309–20

57 Guzzo and Schneider, *Petra*, p. 133

58 John Lewis Burckhardt, *Travels in Syria and the Holy Land* (London 1822), p. 424. In contrast, the next group of visitors, the British naval officers Irby and Mangles, found Nabataean architecture to be 'loaded with ornaments in the Roman manner, but in a bad taste, with an infinity of broken lines and unnecessary angles and projections, and multiplied pediments and half pediments, and pedestals set upon columns that support nothing. It has more the air of a fantastical scene in a theatre than an architectural work in stone; and for unmeaning richness and littleness of conception, Mr Bankes seemed to think, might have been the work of Boromini himself.' (Charles Leonard Irby and James Mangles, *Travels in Egypt and Nubia, Syria and Asia Minor during the years 1817 and 1818* (London 1823), Letter V, pp. 413–14). Irby and Mangles further noted the damage caused by musket shots, which was visible on the Khazneh façade even at this early date

59 Guzzo and Schneider, *Petra*, p. 33

60 Guzzo and Schneider, *Petra*, p. 178

61 Guzzo and Schneider, *Petra*, p. 75

62 Strabo, *Geography*, XVI, 4.26

63 Guzzo and Schneider, *Petra*, p. 176

64 Guzzo and Schneider, *Petra*, pp. 47–8

65 Cassius Dio, 68, 14.5

66 Bowersock, *Roman Arabia*, p. 83

67 Bowersock, *Roman Arabia*, pp. 76–82

68 John W. Eadie and John Peter Oleson, 'The Water-supply Systems of Nabataean and Roman Humayma' in *Bulletin of the American Schools of Oriental Research* 252 (May 1986), pp. 49–76

69 Eadie and Oleson, 'The Water-supply systems of Nabataean and Roman Humayma', p. 51

70 Eadie and Oleson, 'The Water-supply systems of Nabataean and Roman Humayma', p. 52

71 Philip Mayerson, 'The First Muslim Attacks on Southern Palestine' in *Transactions of the American Philological Association* 95 (1964), p. 173

72 Also known by the Arabic form of his name as Imru' al-Qays, but not to be confused with the 4th-century ruler whose inscription was found at Nemara (see p. 364)

73 See Irfan Shahid, *Byzantium and the Arabs in the Fifth Century* (Dumbarton Oaks, 1989), pp. 59–90

CHAPTER 9: AEGYPTUS AND CYRENAICA

1 William Shakespeare, *Antony and Cleopatra*, Act II, Scene 2, 200–11
2 Strabo *Geographia*, XVII, 1.12
3 'Octavian's Propaganda and Antony's *De Sua Ebrietate*' by Kenneth Scott in *Classical Philology*, Vol. 24, No. 2 (Apr. 1929), pp. 133–41
4 Cassius Dio, 51, 16.5
5 Bowman, Garnsey and Cameron (eds), *Cambridge Ancient History* XII, pp. 320–2
6 Bowman, Garnsey and Cameron (eds), *Cambridge Ancient History* XII, p. 318
7 Bowman, Garnsey and Cameron (eds), *Cambridge Ancient History* XII, pp. 175–6. In essence the combination of the *iugum* (the size of the plot of land) and the *caput* (the amount of labour to work it) would yield a value in notional units. The amount of tax per unit was then varied up and down, depending on the government's needs. This was vastly more efficient than a fixed tax on a piece of land, or per head of population, but understandably those faced with the new system may have believed that it was yet another attempt to extract extra revenue from them
8 'Lucius Domitius Domitianus Augustus' by Allan Chester Johnson in *Classical Philology*, Vol. 45, No. 1 (Jan. 1950), pp. 13–21
9 Williams, *Diocletian*, pp. 120–5. There is some evidence for the taxation cycle originating earlier than Diocletian, possibly as early as the 2nd century (Duncan-Jones, *Money and Government in the Roman Empire*, p. 59)
10 See 'L'enceinte du camp militaire romain de Louqsor' by Jean-Claude Golvin and Michel Reddé in *Studien zu den Militargränzen Roms* III (Stuttgart 1986), pp. 594–9
11 The sequence is complex. In about 314, the new province of Egypt was split into two (Herculia and Iovia), with Herculia being further divided in 322 with the creation of a new province of Mercuriana. In 324, however, the two-province division into Egypt and Thebaid was restored, only for a tripartite division to be restored in 357. Roger S. Bagnall, *Egypt in Late Antiquity* (Princeton 1993), p. 63
12 On the Vandal Kingdom of North Africa, see p. 432
13 J.D. Fage (ed.), *Cambridge History of Africa*, Vol. 2 (Cambridge 1978), pp. 495–500; E.M. Forster, *Alexandria: A History and a Guide* (Alexandria 1938), pp. 48–9
14 On the Monophysite controversy, see p. 299–300
15 In 638 the Emperor Heraclius promulgated the *Ecthesis*, an attempt to reconcile the question of whether Christ had one or two natures, by affirming that within him there was only one will (*thelos*). Cyrus was a key figure in the failed attempt to impose this compromise on Egypt.

Frend, *The Rise of the Monophysite Movement*, p. 352. Forster, *Alexandria: A History and a Guide*, p. 49. See also Cyril Hovorun, *Will, Action and Freedom, Christological Controversies in the Seventh Century* (Leiden 2008), pp. 55–76

16 Heraclius had previously had a go with a short-lived doctrine, which became known as Monoenergism, which held that, though having two natures, Christ had only one 'energy'. Having failed with his single energy, the Emperor then moved on to Christ's single will

17 Alan K. Bowman, *Egypt after the Pharaohs* (London 1986), p. 52

18 Forster, *Alexandria: A History and a Guide*, p. 50; Theodore Vretto, *Alexandria, City of the Western Mind* (New York 2001), pp. 212–13

19 Christopher Haas, *Alexandria in Late Antiquity: Topography and Social Conflict* (Baltimore 1997), pp. 45–7

20 They had originally been erected by Thutmosis III in Heliopolis around 1450 BC, but were uprooted and moved to Alexandria when the Caesareum was built

21 Judith Mackenzie, *The Art and Architecture of Alexandria and Egypt c. 300 BC to AD 700* (New Haven 2007), p. 252

22 Arculf's account of this and the Holy Places of Palestine was written down by Adomnan, the Bishop of Iona from 679 to 704, in a compilation known as *Holy Places*. See John Wilkinson, *Jerusalem Pilgrims before the Crusades* (Warminster 1977), p. 9

23 Mackenzie, *The Art and Architecture of Alexandria and Egypt*, p. 10

24 Roy MacLeod (ed.) *The Library of Alexandria, Centre of Learning in the Ancient World* (London 2000), p. 96

25 On the name of 'Pompey's Pillar', see Forster, *Alexandria: A History and a Guide*, p. 136; Alfred Butler, *The Arab Conquest of Egypt* (2nd edition, Oxford 1978), p. 368

26 The column was dedicated by Publius, the Prefect of Egypt, on the occasion of Diocletian's recapture of the city; Jean-Yves Empereur, *Alexandria Rediscovered* (trs. Margaret Maehler, London 1998), p. 102

27 Bowman, *Egypt after the Pharaohs*, p. 44; John Malalas, *Chronographia*, 308–9

28 The original Ptolemaic temple in fact burnt down in a fire in AD 181 and was rebuilt by the Romans around 216. Thus the temple that was destroyed in 391 had been in place for only 175 years (Mackenzie, *The Architecture of Alexandria and Egypt*, p. 149)

29 Empereur, *Alexandria Rediscovered*, pp. 90–3

30 Beard, North and Price, *Religions of Rome*, Vol. 1, p. 264

31 Law of 399, in *Cambridge Ancient History* XIII, p. 553 (*Codex Theodosiana*, XVI.10.15)

32 The Temple of Philae in the south of Egypt, near Aswan, survived for more than a century these waves of anti-paganism. See p. 404

33 David Franfkurter, *Religion in Roman Egypt, Assimilation and Resistance* (Princeton, NJ, 1998), pp. 281–2; Empereur, *Alexandria Rediscovered*, pp. 94–5

34 Haas, *Alexandria in Antiquity*, pp. 162–3

35 Empereur, *Alexandria Rediscovered*, p. 206

36 Mary Beard, John North and Simon Price, *Religions of Rome* (Cambridge 1998), p. 264

37 Vretto, *Alexandria, City of the Western Mind*, pp. 204–5

38 It may first have appeared in the works of the Jacobite Syrian bishop Bar Hebraeus in the late 13th century, who relates a story that 'Amr sent a message back to the Caliph Umar asking what he should do about the library. The reply came back that if the books disagreed with the Qu'uran they should be burnt, but that if they agreed with its message, then they were not needed and should be burnt anyway.' Atiyah, *A History of Eastern Christianity*, p. 81

39 Empereur, *Alexandria Rediscovered*, p. 156

40 Vretto, *Alexandria, City of the Western Mind*, pp. 84–5

41 Or even 'The Tomb of Caracalla'. See Empereur, *Alexandria Rediscovered*, p. 170

42 See Cassius Dio, 78, I 22–3; *Historia Augusta*, Caracalla, 6

43 Mackenzie, *The Art and Architecture of Alexandria and Egypt*, p. 214

44 Roger S. Bagnall (ed.), *Egypt in the Byzantine World, 300–700* (Cambridge 2007), p. 203

45 Empereur, *Alexandria Rediscovered*, pp. 155–75

46 Founded in AD 356, just after the saint's death

47 Robert B. Jackson, *At Empire's Edge, Exploring Rome's Egyptian Frontier* (New Haven 2002), p. 4

48 See p. 211

49 On this and Mons Porphyrites and Mons Claudianus in general, see 'The Roman Remains in the Eastern Desert of Egypt' by David Meredith in *Journal of Egyptian Archaeology* 38 (1952) pp. 94–111. The large granite columns from Mons Claudianus were transported to the Nile on enormous twelve-wheeled carts for shipment to the Nile delta and thence across the Mediterranean to their ultimate destinations (including far-off Rome). See Marijke van der Veen, 'High living in Rome's distant quarries' in *British Archaeology* 28 (October 1997)

50 Jackson, *At Empire's Edge*, pp. 24–7

51 Meredith, 'Roman remains in the Eastern Desert of Egypt', pp. 94–111, plan by Leo Tregenza

52 The temple probably dates to 113. See Meredith, 'Roman Remains in the Eastern Desert of Egypt', p. 107

53 Jackson, *At Empire's Edge*, pp. 7–8

54 Jackson, *At Empire's Edge*, pp. 46–50

55 See Meredith, 'Roman Remains in the Eastern Desert of Egypt', p. 107. Pliny says that Vitrasius Pollo brought statues made of imperial porphyry to Rome from Egypt during the reign of Claudius, and so from this it was presumed that the mines were being worked then

56 Jackson, *At Empire's Edge*, p. 37

57 Although not the largest monolithic columns of ancient times, as the obelisks in the Karnak Temple at Luxor, erected by Hatshepsut, are 27.5 metres tall, while the broken unfinished obelisk at Aswan is more than 40 metres long

58 Hélène Cuvigny, 'The Amount of Wages Paid to the Quarry-Workers at Mons Claudianus' in *Journal of Roman Studies* 86 (1996), pp. 139–45

59 Kelly, *Ruling the Later Roman Empire*, p. 21, for a description of this and its significance

60 Jackson, *At Empire's Edge*, p. 112.

61 Jackson, *At Empire's Edge*, p. 114

62 See pp. 392–393

63 Pliny the Elder, *Historia Naturalis*, V.10.58; Jackson, *At Empire's Edge*, p. 119

64 J.D. Fage (ed.), *Cambridge History of Africa*, Vol. 2, p. 193

65 Jackson, *At Empire's Edge*, p. 130

66 Pliny, *Historia Naturalis*, V.8.46

67 Fage (ed.), *Cambridge History of Africa*, Vol. 2, p. 206

68 Fage (ed.), *Cambridge History of Africa*, Vol. 2, p. 424; Jackson, *At Empire's Edge*, p. 152

69 Jackson, *At Empire's Edge*, p. 146

70 'Olympiodorus of Thebes' by E.A. Thompson in *Classical Quarterly* Vol. 38, No. 1/2 (Jan.–Apr. 1944), pp. 43–52; see also R.C. Blockley, *The Fragmentary Classicising Historians of the Later Roman Empire* (Liverpool 1981), pp. 27–47

71 Jackson, *At Empire's Edge*, p. 218

72 Amelia B. Edwards, *A Thousand Miles up the Nile* (London 1877), p. 308

73 'Chronology of the Campaigns of Aelius Gallus and C. Petronius' by Shelagh Jameson in *Journal of Roman Studies*, Vol. 58, Parts 1 and 2 (1968), pp. 71–84; L.P. Kirwan, 'Rome Beyond the Southern Egyptian Frontier' in *Geographical Journal*, Vol. 123, No. 1 (Mar. 1957), pp. 13–19

74 See p. 79

75 Jackson, *At Empire's Edge*, p. 137

76 Jackson, *At Empire's Edge*, p. 145, and T.C. Skeat, 'A Letter from the King of the Blemmyes to the King of the Noubades' in *Journal of Egyptian Archaeology* 63 (1977), pp. 159–70

77 Jackson, *At Empire's Edge*, p. 137

78 On Juvenal and Nestorius's exile, see Jackson, *At Empire's Edge*, p. 164

79 'The Wells of Hibis' by Peter J. Parson in *Journal of Egyptian Archaeology* 57 (1971), pp 165–80

80 Ahmed Fakhry, *The Necropolis of El-Bagawat in Kharga Oasis* (Cairo 1951), p. 4

81 Dating from the early 4th century; see Fakhry, *Necropolis of El-Bagawat*, p. 2

82 Fage (ed.), *Cambridge History of Africa*, Vol. 2, p. 412

83 Frend, *The rise of the Monophysite Movement*, p. 279

84 See p. 472

85 Fage (ed.), *Cambridge History of Africa*, Vol. 2, p. 425

86 William Harmless, SJ, *The Desert Christians* (Oxford 2004), p. 35

87 Athanasius was sentenced in 335, 338, 339, 349 and 351 and spent the years 335–7, 339–46 and 356–63 in exile (G.W. Bowersock, Peter Brown and Oleg Grabar, *Late Antiquity, A Guide to the Postclassical World* (Cambridge, MA, 1999), p. 320)

88 Jackson, *At Empire's Edge*, pp. 190–5

89 Jackson, *At Empire's Edge*, p. 175

90 Jackson, *At Empire's Edge*, p. 167

91 I.M.F. Gardner and S.N.C. Lieu, 'From Narmouthis (Medinet Madi) to Kellis (Asmant el-Kharab): Manichaean Documents from Roman Egypt' in *Journal of Roman Studies* 86 (1996), pp. 146–69

92 A merchant named Scythianus, who travelled with his goods to Berenice on the Red Sea coast, was instrumental in the early spread of the Manichaeist sect in Egypt. See Samuel N.C. Lieu, *Manichaeism in the Later Roman Empire and Medieval China, a Historical Survey* (Manchester 1985), pp. 71–2

93 Jackson, *At Empire's Edge*, p. 209, for the slave sale

94 On the imperial cult, see pp. 190–191

95 Jackson, *At Empire's Edge*, p. 216

96 Jackson, *At Empire's Edge*, p. 220

97 G.A. Hoskins, *Visit to the Great Oasis of the Libyan Desert* (London 1837), pp. 225–6, although Hoskins is relating second-hand material from the French traveller Cailliaud. He reports that the arch then sat on a platform 128 feet long and was itself 25 feet high and equipped with a staircase to the upper levels. Only the central arch was still standing, the rest having long collapsed, a fate that much of the rest of the structure has since endured

98 Ahmed Fakhry, *Baharia Oasis*, Vol. II (Cairo 1950), pp. 41–8

99 Ahmed Fakhry, *Siwa Oasis, its History and Antiquities* (Cairo 1944), p. 29

100 Fakhry, *Siwa Oasis*, p. 41

101 For Alexander's visit, see Fakhry, *Siwa Oasis*, pp. 36–40

102 Ian Worthington (ed.), *Alexander the Great: A Reader* (London 2003), pp. 237–40

103 On oracle shrines in Roman Egypt in general, see Frankfurter, *Religion in Roman Egypt*, pp. 147–97

104 Strabo, *Geographia*, 17, 1.43

105 Caracalla had the place reopened in 215 and, instead of purloining any further treasures as his predecessor emperors had done, laid his own purple cloak and precious rings upon the body as an offering

106 Empereur, *Alexandria Rediscovered*, p. 148

107 Forster, *Alexandria: A History and a Guide*, p. 96

108 Jackson, *At Empire's Edge*, pp. 250–1

109 Jackson, *At Empire's Edge*, p. 251

110 Fage (ed.), *Cambridge History of Africa*, Vol. 2, p. 198

111 Fage (ed.), *Cambridge History of Africa*, Vol. 2, p. 198

112 See 'Africa' by Charles Daniels in John Wacher (ed.), *The Roman World*, Vol. 1 (London 1987), pp. 223–65

113 See 'Roman and Byzantine "Limes" in Cyrenaica' in *Libyan Studies: Select Papers of the late R.G. Goodchild* (ed. Joyce Reynolds, London 1976), pp. 195–209

114 Such as the use of the former forum at Cyrene as a type of citadel. See Goodchild, *Libyan Studies*, p. 204

115 He had responsibility for the Thebaid in Egypt too. His full title was *Dux Aegypti Thebaidos utrarumque Libyarum*. See Goodchild, *Libyan Studies*, p. 195

116 MacKendrick, *The North African Stones Speak*, pp. 121–3

117 MacKendrick, *The North African Stones Speak*, pp. 125, 129

118 MacKendrick, *The North African Stones Speak*, p. 129

119 See p. 393

120 The *aurum coronarium* or 'crown gold' had originally been a gift voted to victorious generals after a major victory (particularly if they had been awarded a triumph), and did actually involve the presentation of a golden crown, but by the 3rd century it had become simply another tax imposition

121 Jay Bregman, *Synesius of Cyrene, Philosopher-Bishop* (Berkeley 1982), pp. 52–3. Synesius's reference in it to the heretical Aryan religion of the Goths – who were then highly influential at court, and threatened to reduce the authority of the Eastern Emperor to the same ineffectual state as that of his brother Honorius – may have been an opportune one. Anti-Gothic sentiment was on the rise and finally erupted in 401, leading to the downfall of Gainas, the leading Gothic official, the murder of many of his countrymen and the breaking of the Gothic monopoly on power. Gainas managed to flee, but as he made his way north of the Danube, he was killed by the Hun Uldin and his head sent back to Arcadius as a little present to the Emperor

122 Bregman, *Synesius of Cyrene*, pp. 60–78

123 Bregman, *Syncsius of Cyrene*, p. 155

124 Bregman, *Synesius of Cyrene*, p. 159. Synesius also refused to affirm that the world would be destroyed, since in Neoplatonic belief there is no time when the cosmos will not be, whilst similarly the soul is regarded as an immortal entity divorced from time, and so not created by God

125 Claudia Rapp, *Holy Bishops in Late Antiquity: The Nature of Christian Leadership in an Age of Transition* (Berkeley 2005), pp. 158–9

126 Williams, *Diocletian*, p. 129

127 See Williams, *Diocletian*, pp. 128–32

128 Simon Corcoran, *The Empire of the Tetrarchs: Imperial Pronouncements and Government AD 284–324* (revised edition, Oxford 2000), pp. 205–33

129 Graeme Barker, John Lloyd and Joyce Reynolds, *Cyrenaica in Antiquity* (BAR International Series 236, Oxford 1985), pp. 36–8

130 Barker, Lloyd and Reynolds, *Cyrenaica in Antiquity*, pp. 30–2

131 Robert Wheeler, *Roman Africa in Colour* (London 1966), p. 14

132 Though the best candidate is Ras el Aali, 6 kilometres inland, where there are the remains of a boundary monument set up under Diocletian. See 'Boreum of Cyrenaica', RG. Goodchild, *Journal of Roman Studies*, Vol. 41, Parts 1 and 2 (1951), pp. 11–16

133 'Una tappa di nostra cammina a marciare nella pace per [. . .] domani'

CHAPTER 10: AFRICA

1 Gustave Flaubert, *Salammbô* (trs J.C. Chartres, London 1956)

2 See Chapter 11

3 This is in stark contrast to Britain with two legions, Germania Inferior alone with four legions at the peak of its garrison, and little Noricum, which still had one

4 It may have been along the line of, or in part based on, an earlier ditch, which been dug in 202 BC on the orders of Scipio Africanus following the defeat of Hannibal in the Second Punic War, and which had been intended to mark out the borders of the territory to which Carthage was then reduced; Dexter Hoyos, *Hannibal's Dynasty: Power and Politics in the western Mediterranean* (London 2003), pp. 180–1

5 See Fage (ed.), *Cambridge History of Africa*, Vol. 2, p. 192

6 See p. 465

7 Its Roman name is unknown

8 See p. 74

9 Cameron, Ward-Perkins and Whitby (eds), *Cambridge Ancient History* XIV, p. 121

10 See p. 232

11 *Historia persecutionis africanae provinciae*, 1.2 (trs John Moorhead, Liverpool 1992). The figure of 80,000 is one often used in the ancient sources simply to mean 'a huge number' and may not be intended to represent anything like a precise figure (see Whittaker, *Rome and its Frontiers*, p. 54)

12 Augustine, *The City of God*, Book I, 1 (trs Marcus Dods, London 2000), p. 3

13 Already there had been portents of what this might mean; the attempted usurpation of Heraclian, the *comes Africae*, in 413 had been accompanied by the blocking of the grain fleets bound for Italy

14 Cameron, Ward-Perkins and Whitby (eds), *Cambridge Ancient History* XIV, p. 125

15 Cameron, Ward-Perkins and Whitby (eds), *Cambridge Ancient History* XIV, p. 125

16 Fage (ed.) *Cambridge History of Africa*, Vol. 2, p. 479

17 His *Laudes Dei* were particularly admired. See Susan Raven, *Rome in Africa*, p. 197

18 Raven, *Rome in Africa*, pp. 196–200

19 Peter Pentz, *From Roman Proconsularis to Islamic Ifriqiyah* (Göteborg 2002), p. 89. See also Raven, *Rome in Africa*, pp. 200–4; A.H. Merrills (ed.), *Vandals, Romans and Berbers: New Perspectives on Late Antique North Africa* (Ashgate 2004), pp. 200–14. Around 68 per cent of the male sellers of land are recorded as illiterate, with only 16 per cent signing with an autograph, leading to a literacy rate of somewhere between one-third and one-sixth

20 See p. 231

21 Fage (ed.), *Cambridge History of Africa*, Vol. 2, p. 480

22 Justinian, the man who had conceived and directed the reconquest of North Africa, was one of the Empire's most extraordinary rulers and perhaps its greatest law-giver. The first decade of his reign saw a string of astonishing achievements and successes. As well as recapturing North Africa from the Vandals, in 535 Justinian sent Belisarius to Italy, where with astonishing rapidity he overthrew Ostrogothic control in the south of the peninsula, capturing Naples and Rome itself the following year. Visigothic Spain in turn followed in 551 or 552, but this time Justinian's armies contented themselves with taking a broad band of territory in the south-west centred on Cartagena. The following decades brought little but disappointment; the last stages of the war in Italy were mishandled, and it took until 554 to suppress the last Ostrogothic resistance, leaving a country ravaged and to which the war of reconquest had done far more damage to the Romanised institutions of the peninsula than had eighty years of 'barbarian rule'. Yet despite the troubles there, at the time of his death in 565, it seemed that Justinian had at least restored the Empire's partial control over North Africa and Italy. Justinian's other and much more enduring legacy was his reform of the Roman legal system, an achievement that Edward Gibbon could still refer to more than 1,200 years later as 'a fair and everlasting monument'. Under the Empire, Roman law had been essentially reactive, with the emperors issuing responses to problems that were placed before them, which then achieved the force of law (as 'rescripts' or 'constitutions'). A very limited legislative role had originally been assigned to the Senate, but this was, by the Later Empire, all but redundant as a law-making body. The result was that, although the laws provide an interesting insight into the kinds of challenges that faced the imperial administration, there was a chaotic assemblage of legislation, often contradictory and, crucially, with no central archive that held all of the rulings. Lawyers, unsurprisingly, made hay out of the confusion, and legal cases could often turn on which of two contradictory (but apparently equally valid) laws was accepted by the judge to be the relevant one. The situation was aggravated even further after 395, when the Eastern and Western parts of the Empire were finally separated politically, and so it was unclear whether a law passed by the Eastern Emperor had validity in the West or vice versa; and the absence of any central archive meant that lawyers in each half did not necessarily

have access to copies of laws passed in the other half, even when they were supposedly binding in all parts of the Empire. An attempt to clear up the muddle was made by Theodosius II, who appointed a commission in 429 to collect all laws made since the reign of Constantine I and codify them. The resulting Theodosian Code was published in 438 in the East, and a copy that was sent to the Western Emperor, Valentinian III, was promul-gated in his domains the following year, restoring a semblance of harmony between the legal systems in the two parts of the Empire.

In 528, a century after Theodosius II had begun his project, Justinian tried again. He appointed a commission led by the praetorian prefect John of Cappadocia to collect all the imperial constitutions from the reign of Hadrian to that of Justinian himself. The sources for this included a wide range of legislative texts, from private letters of the emperors to officials to more public pronouncements and decisions. The Code of Theodosius and a yet earlier set of rationalised laws from the reign of Diocletian (the Codex Gregorianus and Codex Hermogenianus) provided a principal quarry for the work of Justinian's legal team. It took just a year for the resulting Codex of Justinian to be promulgated (in April 529), although such was the pace of legislation and the need to refine the original that it was replaced within five years by a second edition. Yet this and the succeeding Digest – which was intended to collect together, sift and simplify the mass of deci-sions and commentaries by five centuries of Roman jurists – finally created a solid benchmark for Roman law and established the Emperor once and for all as the sole fount of valid legislation.

23 Meaning 'at the tenth milestone'

24 Ecclesiastes 1, 2

25 Raven, *Rome in Africa*, p. 213; R. Denys Pringle, *The Defence of Byzantine Africa from Justinian to the Arab Conquest* (BAR International Series 99 (i), Oxford 1990) pp. 23–4

26 Pringle, *Defence of Byzantine Africa*, pp. 28–9

27 See p. 299

28 Raven, *Rome in Africa*, pp. 218–22

29 Raven, *Rome in Africa*, p. 225; Fage (ed.), *Cambridge History of Africa*, Vol. 2, p. 505; Charles-André Julien, *A History of North Africa – Tunisia, Algeria, Morocco* (trs John Petrie, London 1970), p. 3

30 Cyril Hovorun, *Will, Action and Freedom* (Leiden 2008), p. 82

31 See p. 388

32 Raven, *Rome in Africa*, p. 226

33 Brett and Fentress, *The Berbers*, pp. 84–5; 'Historiography, Mythology and Memory in Modern North Africa: The Story of the Kahina' by Abdelmajid Hannoum in *Studia Islamica* 85 (1997), pp. 85–130

34 'Historiography, Mythology and Memory in Modern North Africa', pp. 85–130

35 Fage (ed.), *Cambridge History of Africa*, Vol. 2, p. 505

36 See David Mattingly, *Tripolitania* (London 1995), p. xiii

37 Lucan, *The Civil Wars* (trs J.D. Duff, London 1928), IX, 524

38 See MacKendrick, *The North African Stones Speak*, pp. 240–41

39 Elizabeth W.B. Fentress, *Social, Military and Economic Aspects of the Frontier Zone* (BAR International Series 53, Oxford 1979), pp. 82–119

40 Herodotus *Histories* (trs George Rawlinson, London 1927) IV, 183, 4

41 Charles Daniels, *The Garamantes of Southern Libya* (Stoughton, WI, 1970); Herodotus, *Histories*, IV, 183; Pliny the Elder, *Natural History*, VIII, 178

42 Balbus's route, as related by Pliny the Elder (Pliny, *Natural History*, V, v.34) led through Phazania (the Fezzan) and the cities of Alele, Cillaba, towards Sabratha and Cidamus (Ghadames), before crossing the Black Mountains and the desert to Garama. It is not totally clear which of the towns that his army passed through were actually controlled by the Garamantes, but, as well as Garama itself, they seem to have dominated Bu Ngem

43 Although Aulus Plautius did receive an ovation (a lesser form of triumph) in AD 47 for his part in the Claudian conquest of Britain. See Mary Beard, *The Roman Triumph* (Cambridge,MA, 2007), pp. 290–1, 296–7

44 Fage (ed.), *Cambridge History of Africa*, Vol. 2, p. 200

45 Daniels, *The Garamantes of Southern Libya*, p. 22

46 'The Garamantes and Trans-Saharan Enterprise in Classical Times' by R.C.C. Law in *Journal of African History*, Vol. 8, No. 2 (1967), pp. 181–200; Fage (ed.), *Cambridge History of Africa*, Vol. 2, p. 285

47 It is often spelled Lepcis, which may in fact be a better transliteration of the original Phoenician name LPQY. See Mattingley, *Tripolitania*, p. xiii

48 Fage (ed.), *Cambridge History of Africa*, Vol. 2, p. 186

49 'The Oil of Leptis' by Richard Haywood in *Classical Philology* (1941), pp. 65–76

50 Septimius Severus is regarded as one of Rome's great military emperors. He was born in Leptis in 146, and though his uncles Publius Septimius Aper and Caius Septimius had become senators and held consulates in the 150s, he himself was brought up in Africa. The *Historia Augusta* claims that he spoke with an African accent even in his old age, and he is certainly recorded as having been embarrassed that his first wife Paccia Marciana, a local woman, could scarcely speak Latin, and that his sister, Octavilla, had an even worse grasp of the language (Anthony R. Birley, *Septimius Severus* (London 1999), p. 35). By 164, Septimius was in Rome, seeking the first steps on the *cursus honorum* that would lead to his advancement as commander of the IV Scythica legion in Antioch in 182. After a brief fall from grace, when his patron Pertinax fell out of favour with Commodus, Septimius was successively governor of Gallia Lugdunensis, proconsul of Sicily and governor of Upper Pannonia. Here he had command of three legions and, with his brother Geta occupying the governorship of neighbouring Lower

Moesia with its complement of two legions, this left the family well placed when Commodus was assassinated in 192 to make a bid for the imperial throne itself. The Emperor's pathological tendency to kill those nearest him, and his disturbing propensity for appearing in the gladiatorial arena where he fancied himself a new Heracles, led his closest advisors to murder him. But the new Emperor, Pertinax, angered the praetorian guard (who had rather liked Commodus and the favours he showered on them) by his meanness with the level of the donative he bestowed upon them to mark his accession. After Pertinax's murder in the imperial palace, and the undignified bidding war for the throne that led to the accession of Didius Julianus, the prestige of the Emperor sank to a new low. With the office so demeaned, the various large concentrations of troops in the Empire had no compunction in declaring emperors of their own. After his successful execution of the civil war, Septimius would rule largely unchallenged and, for the most part, respected, apart from the embarrassing affair of his over-reliance on the long-serving prefect of the praetorian guard, Fulvius Plautianus, which ended in the latter's murder in 205

51 See Mattingly, *Tripolitania*, p. 116

52 D.E.L. Haynes, *The Antiquities of Tripolitania* (Tripoli 1955) mentions that it was only under Maxentius that the province was first actually recorded

53 See p. 52

54 See p. 117

55 These were the *tria nomina* that marked out the full Roman citizen in Republican and early imperial times. The *nomen* usually indicated the clan to which the person belonged, such as the Julii or Claudii

56 Fergus Millar, 'Local Cultures in the Roman Empire: Libya, Punic and Latin in Roman Africa' in *Journal of Roman Studies* 58, Parts 1 and 2 (1968), pp. 126–34

57 'Doric Measure and Architectural Design 1: The Evidence of the Relief from Salamis' by Mark Wilson Jones in *American Journal of Archaeology*, Vol. 104, No. 1 (Jan. 2000), pp. 73–93

58 Alan Cameron, *Circus Factions: Blues and Greens at Rome and Byzantium* (Oxford 1976), p. 62; J.H.W. Liebeschuetz, *The Decline and Fall of the Roman City* (Oxford 2001), pp. 210–18

59 See Chapter 8

60 Cameron, *Circus Factions*, pp. 203–4

61 Alan Cameron, *Porphyrius the Charioteer* (Oxford 1973)

62 Cameron, *Circus Factions*, p. 107

63 Cameron, *Circus Factions*, p. 108

64 The circus factions also came to be represented at the theatre, so that there, too, there were Blue and Green cliques. See Cameron, *Circus Factions*, pp. 195–229

65 Mattingly, *Tripolitania*, p. 173

66 Mattingly, *Tripolitania*, p. 175

67 Procopius, *History of the Wars*, IV, 21.4–10

68 Denys Pringle, *The Defence of Byzantine Africa from Justinian to the Arab Conquest* (BAR International Series 99 (i), Oxford 1981), pp. 33–9

69 Mattingly, *Tripolitania*, pp. 123–4

70 MacKendrick, *The North African Stones Speak*, p. 165

71 See p. 459

72 Mattingly, *Tripolitania*, p. 125

73 Pringle, *Defence of Byzantine Africa*, p. 223

74 Pentz, *From Roman Proconsularis to Arab Ifriqiyah*, p. 39

75 Haynes, *The Antiquities of Tripolitania*, p. 131

76 S.J. Harrison, *Apuleius, A Latin Sophist* (Oxford 2000), pp. 38–86

77 Isabella Sjöström, *Tripolitania in Transition, Late Roman to Early Islamic Settlement* (Aldershot 1993), pp. 203–4

78 'Amphitheatres of the Roman World' by Herbert W. Benario in *Classical Journal* (1981), pp. 255–9

79 Raven, *Rome in Africa*, p. 142

80 See p. 103

81 Bowman, Garnsey and Cameron (eds), *Cambridge Ancient History* XII, p. 33

82 Bowman, Garnsey and Cameron (eds), *Cambridge Ancient History* XII, p. 28

83 See p. 285

84 Bowman, Garnsey and Cameron (eds), *Cambridge Ancient History* XII, p. 34

85 See p. 436

86 Virgil, *Aeneid* (trs Frederick Ahl, Oxford 2007) I, 360–70

87 See Lance Sergel, *Carthage, A History* (trs Antonia Nevill, Oxford 1995), p. 428. The story may initially have appeared in the very first edition of the *Cambridge Ancient History*

88 In the confused power-politics of the time, Domitius seems to have gained some support from Constantine, who saw him as a means to weaken Maxentius and lever him out of Italy. Around 311, however, Maxentius sent an expeditionary force to Carthage under the command of his praetorian prefect Volusianus, and Domitius, who had managed to expand his diminutive domain only as far as Sardinia, was captured and executed

89 Frank M. Clover, *The Late Roman West and the Vandals* (Aldershot 1993), p. 14

90 Procopius, *History of the Wars*, III, 21.25

91 Raven, *Rome in Africa*, p. 226

92 Raven, *Rome in Africa*, p. 228

93 See Sergel, *Carthage*, p. 439

94 See Sergel, *Carthage*, p. 441

95 See Sergel, *Carthage*, p. 442

96 See Sergel, *Carthage*, p. 249

97 Diodorus Siculus, *Library of History* (trs Russell Geer, London 1954), XX, 14, 4–7

98 Raven, *Rome in Africa*, p. 146

99 *Princeton Encyclopedia of Classical Sites*, p. 918

100 *Princeton Encyclopedia of Classical Sites*, p. 918

101 For more on the imperial cult and the deification of dead emperors, see pp. 190–191

102 The site was also visited in 1765 by James Bruce and Luigi Balugani, who already found the monument in ruins. When Camille Borgia visited in 1840, the top three levels of the monument had gone and the inscription was lying on the ground. There were originally two inscriptions, which were clearly mounted on the outside (they were too big to go on the inside). In 1842 Thomas Reade simply removed them from where they lay

103 MacKendrick, *The North African Stones Speak*, p. 76

104 MacKendrick, *The North African Stones Speak*, p. 75

105 MacKendrick, *The North African Stones Speak*, pp. 76–7; *Princeton Encyclopedia of Classical Sites*, pp. 540–1

CHAPTER II: NUMIDIA AND MAURETANIA

1 Chapter XVI, p. 128

2 See Chapter 10. An area around Cirta (Constantine in Algeria) was given to the independent Roman general Sittius, which he ruled until his assassination by the Libyan prince Arabion in 44 BC. Arabion was in turn chased out by Octavian's general T. Sextius and the area returned to the control of the central Roman government

3 Fage (ed.), *Cambridge History of Africa*, Vol. 2, pp. 188–90

4 G.W. Bowersock, *Roman Arabia*, p. 56

5 Mattingly, *Tripolitania*, pp. 29–30, 33, 52

6 Duane W. Roller, *The World of Juba II and Kleopatra Selene* (London 2003), p. 111

7 Mattingly, *Tripolitania*, p. 71

8 See *Princeton Encyclopedia of Classical Sites*, p. 9

9 Jean Baradez, *Fossatum Africae* (Paris 1949); Mattingly, *Tripolitania*, pp. 79, 106–7, 114; Raven, *Rome in Africa*, pp. 76–8

10 David Cherry, *Frontier and Society in Roman North Africa* (Oxford 1998), pp. 45–7

11 See MacKendrick. *The North African Stones Speak*, p. 241; Cherry, *Frontier and Society in Roman North Africa*, p. 63

12 See MacKendrick, *The North African Stones Speak*, p. 221

13 See MacKendrick, *The North African Stones Speak*, p. 222

14 ILS 2487, reproduced in Brian Campbell, *The Roman Army 31 BC–AD 337: A Sourcebook* (London 1994), p. 18

15 Hilaire Belloc, *Many Cities* (London 1928), pp. 126–7

16 'Decurions and Priests' by Michael G. Jarrett in *American Journal of Philology* (1971), pp. 513–38

17 Peter Garnsey, *Social Status and Legal Privilege in the Roman Empire* (Oxford 1970), pp. 274–6

18 J.H.W Liebeschuetz, *The Decline and Fall of the Roman City* (Oxford 2001), pp. 111–23

19 Jarrett, 'Decurions and Priests', pp. 521–2

20 See p. 472

21 He engaged in a prolonged polemic with Saint Augustine, the champion of the orthodox cause. Optatus's attempt to secure his and the Donatists' power base ended when he was executed – or, as the Donatists would have it, 'martyred' – for alleged involvement in the rebellion of Gildo

22 MacKendrick, *The North African Stones Speak*, p. 236

23 Procopius, *History of the Wars*, IV xiii 26; Michael Brett and Elizabeth Fentress, *The Berbers* (Oxford 1997) p. 79

24 W.H.C. Frend, *The Donatist Church, A Movement of Protest in North Africa* (Oxford 1952), pp. 8–9

25 Frend, *The Donatist Church*, p. 6

26 Frend, *The Donatist Church*, p. 18

27 Frend, *The Donatist Church*, pp. 145–46

28 It was not the very first appeal to an emperor, as Aurelian (albeit not a Christian) had been sent a petition in 271 regarding the activities of the heretical bishop Paul of Samosata; Philip Hughes, *A History of the Church* (London 1979), p. 168

29 Frend, *The Donatist Church*, p. 149

30 Frend, *The Donatist Church*, pp. 150–51

31 Frend, *The Donatist Church*, p. 159

32 Frend, *The Donatist Church*, pp. 168–74

33 Frend, *The Donatist Church*, p. 178

34 Frend, *The Donatist Church*, pp. 175–76; Fage (ed.), *Cambridge History of Africa*, Vol. 2, p. 472

35 Frend, *The Donatist Church*, pp. 187–91

36 The political eclipse of Donatism began in 397, when Gildo, the *comes Africae*, made the seemingly extraordinary move of offering to transfer the allegiance of Africa from the Western Emperor in Italy, in whose territory it had traditionally sat, into the domain of the Eastern Emperor at Constantinople. In doing so, he was trying to exploit a tricky piece of dynastic rivalry. For on the death of Theodosius, the Empire had fallen to his two young sons, with Honorius inheriting the West and Arcadius the East. The ten-year-old Honorius was firmly under the thumb of Theodosius's overmighty *magister militum*, the half-Vandal Stilicho, who was married to the late Emperor's niece Serena. Stilicho maintained that Theodosius had appointed him guardian to both his sons, a claim that Arcadius's advisors in Constantinople vigorously opposed

(Cameron and Garnsey (eds), *Cambridge Ancient History*, p. 113). In the West, however, Stilicho was without serious rivals, cementing his position by marrying his own daughter Maria to Honorius. Gildo's offer, therefore, was a cunning one, enabling him to dissemble loyalty to the Empire at least on the surface, while using Arcadius's antipathy to Stilicho as a shield to protect him from the consequences of his previous involvement with the supporters of the usurper Eugenius in 392–4. He withheld the grain supplies from Rome, threatening to topple Stilicho by starving Italy. Had he succeeded, his reward from a suitably grateful Eastern government might have been immense. It all turned out, however, to be too clever by half. Just as Gildo had exploited a family quarrel, so too did Stilicho, and he sent Gildo's brother Mascezel with a modest force from Italy. No assistance arrived from the East for Gildo, and when the two sides met near Theveste in 398, his troops melted away, and he fled, dying a hunted fugitive. (Raven, *Rome in Africa*, p. 184). The principal result of the revolt was that the Donatists became tarred with the taint of treason. The leading, and extremist, Donatist bishop Optatus of Thamugadi (Timgad) was on friendly terms with Gildo, and his own private army of circumcellions in turn offered pious and thuggish support for the Count of Africa. Once Gildo was defeated, the tendency that had become established over the past half-century just to leave the Donatists well alone was replaced by more deliberate action to uproot them and favour more strongly their Catholic opponents.

37 Frend, *The Donatist Church*, pp. 253–57. Petilian had in fact originally been an orthodox Catholic, but around 395 was kidnapped by Donatists who rebaptised him in their creed. Petilian became convinced this was the will of God and ever after served the Donatist cause faithfully and effectively.

38 *Donatist Martyr Stories: The Church in Conflict in North Africa* (trs Maureen A. Tilley, Liverpool 1996)

39 Raven, *Rome in Africa*, pp. 53–4

40 Pringle, *Defence of Byzantine Africa*, p. 194

41 André Berthier, *Tiddis, Antique Castellum Tidditanorum* (1952, reissued Algiers 1991) p. 18

42 Pentz, *From Roman Proconsularis to Islamic Ifriqiyah*, p. 48

43 Berthier, *Tiddis*, p. 52

44 Jean Marie Blas de Roblès and Claude Sintes, *Sites et monuments antiques de L'Algérie*, (Aix-en-Province 2003), p. 131

45 See p. 52

46 Berthier, *Tiddis*, p. 263

47 Blas de Roblès and Sintes, *Sites et monuments antiques de L'Algérie*, p. 134

48 Berthier, *Tiddis*, p. 276

49 MacKendrick, *The North African Stones Speak*, p. 221

50 'Venus Genetrix outside Rome' by James Rives in *Phoenix*, Vol. 48, No. 4 (Winter 1994), pp. 294–306

51 Blas de Roblès and Sintes, *Sites et monuments antiques de l'Algérie*, p. 109

52 MacKendrick, *The North African Stones Speak*, p. 229

53 Richard C. Beacham, *The Roman Theatre and its Audience* (London 1991), pp. 60–2

54 Blas de Roblès and Sintes, *Sites en monuments antiques de l'Algérie*, p. 110; Wood, *Roman Africa in Colour*, p. 128

55 See p. 300

56 The resulting schism in which the northern Italian Church broke from Rome lasted for more than a century. See John Moorhead, *Justinian* (London 1994), p. 137

57 Frend, *The Rise of the Monophysite Movement*, pp. 281–2

58 B.H. Warmington, *The North African Provinces from Diocletian to the Vandal Conquest* (Cambridge 1954), p. 1

59 'The Myth of Numidian Origins in Sallust's African Excursus (Iugurtha 17.7–18.12)' by Robert Morstein-Marx in *American Journal of Philology* (2001), p. 188

60 *Princeton Encyclopedia of Classical Sites*, p. 925

61 Tipasa is, however, a UNESCO World Heritage site and of undoubted architectural and cultural importance

62 Camus began, '*Au printemps, Tipasa est habitée par les dieux et les dieux parlent dans le soleil et l'odeur des absinthes, la mer cuirassée d'argent, le ciel bleu écru, les ruines couvertes de fleurs et la lumière à gros bouillons dans les amas de pierres*'. Albert Camus, *Noces à Tipasa* (Paris 1976), p. 9

63 See p. 495

64 Raven, *Rome in Africa* p. 180

65 Blas de Roblès and Sines, *Sites et monuments antiques de L'Algérie*, p. 59

66 See p. 498

67 See Brett and Fentress, *The Berbers*, p. 43. Alternative theories are that the tomb was built for Bocchus of Mauretania or even for an unknown potentate as late as the 5th or 6th century AD. Blas de Roblès and Sintes, *Sites et monuments antiques de L'Algérie*, pp. 74–6

68 Roller, *The World of Juba II* and Kleopatra Selene, p. 123

69 T.W. Potter, *Towns in Late Antiquity: Iol Caesarea and its Context* (Oxford 1995), pp. 48–61

70 MacKendrick, *The North African Stones Speak*, p. 224

71 MacKendrick, *The North African Stones Speak*, p. 299

72 MacKendrick, *The North African Stones Speak*, p. 299

73 Raven, *Rome in Africa*, p. 162

74 *Notitia Dignitatum*, XXVI

75 *Princeton Encyclopedia of Classical Sites*, p. 714

76 See 'La fortification des villes de Tingitane au second siècle' by Gilbert Hallier, in *Studien zu den Militargränzen Roms III* (Stuttgart 1986), pp. 605–24

77 Raymond Thouvenot, *Maisons de Volubilis: Le Palais dit de Gordien et la Maison a la Mosaïque de Vénus* (Rabat 1958)

78 Hilaire Belloc, *Many Cities*, p. 129. However, Belloc made the contrast between the two towns as 'that between a Poussin or a David and an arabesque of Toledo. It is the contrast between the superbly simple replica of Inigo Jones which forms the façade of the English School at Rome and the Mosque of Cordova – two worlds wholly distinct; the one that pagan and late Christian world of which we are the children; we live by our return to its noble classic lines; the other, the fantasy which the Mohammedan developed from the Byzantine.'

79 *Princeton Encyclopedia of Classical Sites*, p. 989

80 *Princeton Encyclopedia of Classical Sites*, p. 140

81 Although this is not universally accepted. *Princeton Encyclopedia of Classical Sites*, p. 140

82 A.N. Sherwin-White, 'The Tabula of Banasa and the Constitutio Antoniniana' in *Journal of Roman Studies* 63 (1973), pp. 86–98; MacKendrick, *The North African Stones Speak*, pp. 294–5

83 MacKendrick, *The North African Stones Speak*, pp. 287–9

84 See p. 425

85 Sertorius was a partisan of Marius, who fought a bitter civil war against Sulla in the 80s BC, which prefigured the later wars between Julius Caesar and Pompey, and Mark Antony and Octavian (Augustus), but which did not have such immediately catastrophic consequences for the institutions of the Roman Republic.

86 Sertorious then fought a long campaign against Pompey and conspired with Mithridates of Pontus, before finally being assassinated at a banquet in 72 BC.

87 *Princeton Encyclopedia of Classical Sites*, p. 521

88 Pliny the Elder, *Natural History*, XXXI, 42, 93–4

89 Seneca, *Letters to Lucilius* (trs E. Phillips Barker, Oxford 1932), 95.25

90 Pliny, *Natural History*, XIII 42, 94, and Robert I. Curtis, 'In Defense of Garum' in *Classical Journal*, Vol. 78, No. 3 (Feb.–Mar. 1983), pp. 232–40; Thomas H. Corcoran, 'Roman Fish Sauces' in *Classical Journal*, Vol. 58, No. 5 (Feb. 1963), pp. 204–10

91 Robin Lane Fox, *Travelling Heroes* (London 2008), p. 193

92 *Notitia Dignitatum*, XXVI; *Princeton Encyclopedia of Classical Sites*, p. 876

93 Pringle, *The Defence of Byzantine Africa*, p. 50

94 Whom one legend related was buried in the 'Tombeau de la Chrétienne' (see p. 485)

95 The other candidate in Morocco is Jebel Musa

96 Isidore of Seville, *Etymologiae*, XV, 1.73

CONCLUSION

1 This is the Greek form of the name. In Latin, it was also known as the *Umbilicus Urbis* (or 'navel of the city'), and it seems it was also known in the earliest times as the *Mundus*. Here, according to Plutarch, the inhabitants of the new cities threw sods of earth from their original homes in a symbolic abjuration of their places of origin; Filippo Coarelli, *Il Foro Romano* (Rome 1983), pp. 214–16

2 Or, more precisely, from the *Miliarium Aureum*, the golden milestone, a bronze column set at the opposite end of the stairs beside which both it and the *omphalos* stood

3 Alternative theories are that it was the tomb of Hostus, father of Rome's third king, Tullus Hostilius, or of a shepherd who was said to have brought up Romulus and Remus. Found beneath it was the oldest-known inscription in Latin, dated to about 525 BC, which contains a curse against anyone who defiled this most sacred of spots; Michael Grant, *The Roman Forum* (London 1970), pp. 49–53

APPENDIX A

Roman Emperors, 27 BC–AD 711

Dates are of reign as Augustus (dates of joint rule or, under the Tetrarchy, rule as Caesar are shown in brackets). Usurpers are shown in italics. Note that not all usurpers are indicated, particularly during the 'Military Anarchy' of the 3rd century.

27 BC–AD 14	Augustus
AD 14–37	Tiberius
37–41	Gaius Caligula
41–54	Claudius
54–68	Nero
68–69	Galba
69	Otho
69	Vitellius
69–79	Vespasian
79–81	Titus
81–96	Domitian
96–98	Nerva
98–117	Trajan
117–138	Hadrian
138–161	Antoninus Pius
161–180	Marcus Aurelius
161–169	Lucius Verus (co-Emperor)
180–192	Commodus
193	Pertinax
193	Didius Julianus
193–194	*Pescennius Niger*
195–197	*Clodius Albinus (officially recognised as Caesar 193–195)*
193–211	Septimius Severus
198–217	Caracalla (co-Augustus with Septimius Severus 198–211)
209–211	Geta (co-Augustus with Septimius Severus 209–211)
217–218	Macrinus
218	Diadumenianus (co-Augustus)
218–222	Elagabalus
222–235	Alexander Severus

235–238	Maximinus Thrax
238	Gordian I and Gordian II
238	Pupienus and Balbinus
238–244	Gordian III
244–249	Philip I
247–249	Philip II (co-Augustus)
249–251	Decius
251	Herennius Etruscus (co-Augustus)
251–253	Trebonianus Gallus
251	Hostilianus (co-Augustus)
251–253	Volusianus (co-Augustus)
253	*Uranius Antoninus*
253	Aemilianus
253–260	Valerian
253–268	Gallienus
	(co-Augustus 253–260)

		Gallic Empire		Empire of Palmyra	
258–259	*Ingenuus*				
260	*Regalianus*	259–269	Postumus	267–272	Zenobia and Vaballathus
260–262	*Macrianus*				
260–262	*Quietus*				
268	*Aureolus*				
268–270	Claudius Gothicus				
270	Quintillus				
270–275	Aurelian	*268*	*Laelianus*		
275–276	Tacitus	*268*	*Marius*		
276	Florian	*269–271*	*Victorinus*		
276–282	Probus				
282–283	Carus	*271–274*	*Tetricus*		
283–284	Numerian				

283–285	Carinus (co-Augustus 283–284)
284–305	Diocletian*
297	*Domitius Domitianus*
297–298	*Aurelius Achilleus*
286–305	Maximian (Caesar 285–286, co-Augustus 286–305)*
286–293	*Carausius (British Emperor)*
293–296	*Allectus (British Emperor)*
305–306	Constantius I Chlorus (Caesar 293–305, co-Augustus 305–306)*
305–311	Galerius (Caesar 293–305, co-Augustus 305–311)*
306–307	Severus (Caesar 305–306, co-Augustus 306–307)†
306–308	*Maximian (reinstated)*
306–312	*Maxentius*
	L. Domitius Alexander (usurper against Maxentius in Africa)

308–324	Licinius†
310–313	Maximin Daia (Caesar 305–310, co-Augustus 310–313)†
306–337	Constantine I (Augustus 306, Caesar 306–307, co-Augustus 307–324)†
337–340	Constantine II (Caesar 317–337, co-Augustus 337–340)
337–361	Constantius II (Caesar, 324–337, co-Augustus 337–350)
337–350	Constans (Caesar 333–337, co-Augustus 337–350)
350	*Vetranio*
350–353	*Magnentius*
355	*Silvanus*
360–363	Julian (Caesar 355–360)
363–364	Jovian
364–375	Valentinian I
372–375	*Firmus*
364–378	Valens
365–366	*Procopius*
367–383	Gratian (co-Augustus 367–383)
383–388	*Magnus Maximus*
375–392	Valentinian II (co-Augustus 375–392)
392–394	*Eugenius*
379–395	Theodosius I (co-Augustus 379–392)

Western Empire

395–423	Honorius (co-Augustus 393–395)	**Eastern Empire**		
		395–408	Arcadius (co-Augustus 383–395)	
408–411	*Constantine III*			
409–410/		408–450	Theodosius II (co-Augustus 405–408)	
414–415	*Priscus Attalus*			
411–413	*Jovinus*			
421	Constantius III (co-Augustus)			
423–425	*Johannes*			
425–455	Valentinian III			
455	Petronius Maximus	450–457	Marcian	
455–456	Avitus			
457–461	Majorian			
461–465	Libius Severus	457–474	Leo I	
467–472	Anthemius			
472	Olybrius			
473–474	Glycerius			
474–475	Julius Nepos (reigned in Illyricum to 480)	474–475	Zeno (deposed)	
		475–477	Basiliscus	
475–476	Romulus Augustulus			

Eastern/Byzantine Empire

477–491	Zeno (restored)
488–494	*Leontius*
491–518	Anastasius
518–527	Justin I
527–565	Justinian
565–578	Justin II
578–582	Tiberius II
582–602	Maurice
602–610	Phocas
610–641	Heraclius
641	Heraclonas
641	Constantine III
641–668	Constans II
646–647	*Gregory*
668–685	Constantine IV
685–695	Justinian II (deposed)
695–698	Leontius
698–705	Tiberius III
705–711	Justinian II (restored)

* First Tetrarchy
† Second Tetrarchy

APPENDIX B

Chronology

BC	
814	Traditional date of foundation of Carthage
753	Traditional date of foundation of Rome
509	Roman Republic established
390	Gaulish victory at Allia; Gauls capture Rome
331	Alexander the Great visits oracle of Ammon at Siwa
323	Alexander the Great dies at Babylon
264–241	1st Punic War, after which Romans gain Sicily
221	Philip V becomes king of Macedonia
218	2nd Punic War begins; Hannibal invades Italy
216	Disastrous Roman defeat at Battle of Cannae
210	Massinissa of Numidia allies with Carthage
206	Massinissa defects to Rome
203	Scipio Africanus lands in Africa at Utica
202	Battle of Zama ends 2nd Punic War
190	Battle of Magnesia (Romans defeat Seleucid Antiochus III)
168	Roman ultimatum forces Antiochus IV to evacuate Egypt; Romans defeat Perseus of Macedonia at Pydna
149	Rome declares war on Carthage, beginning 3rd Punic War
148	Death of Massinissa of Numidia
146	Carthage captured by Romans after a seige and destroyed; province of Africa formed; Romans sack Corinth
133	Attalus III of Pergamum dies and bequeaths his kingdom to Rome
120	Province of Transalpine Gaul created
c.113	Mithridates VI comes to power in Pontus
111–105	Jugurthine War
105	Jugurtha captured, ending war
101	Battle of Vercellae, Roman victory over the Cimbri
96	Tigranes I becomes king of Armenia; Ptolemy Apion bequeaths Cyrene to Rome; Sulla is proconsul of Cilicia
91	Tigranes I occupies Cappadocia; Mithridates VI seizes Bithynia; beginning of Social War in Italy (to 88 BC)

89	1st Mithridatic War begins
88	Massacre of Roman citizens in Asia
83	2nd Mithridatic War begins
74	Nicomedes of Bithynia wills his kingdom to Rome
73	3rd Mithridatic War begins; Slave Revolt of Spartacus (to 72 BC)
72	C. Scribonius Curio celebrates Triumph over Dardanians
71	Mithridates flees to court of Tigranes of Armenia
69	Lucullus invades Armenia; Battle of Tigranocerta
68	Lucullus campaigns in northern Armenia; Nisibis captured; Mithridates returns to Pontus
67	Romans defeated by Mithridates at Zela; Tigranes retakes Cappadocia
66	Pompey given command against Mithridates
65	Mithridates flees to Crimea
64	Pompey annexes Syria; birth of geographer Strabo at Amaseia
63	Death of Mithridates; Pompey captures Jerusalem; Aemilius Scaurus makes unsuccessful attack on Petra; Julius Caesar becomes *pontifex maximus*
61	Pompey's Triumph over Mithridates and Tigranes celebrated
60	First Triumvirate of Caesar, Pompey and Crassus established
57	Gallic Wars begin; campaigns of Caesar against Helvetii, Belgae and Nervii
55	Campaigns of Caesar against Veneti; Caesar crosses the Rhine; Caesar's first expedition to Britain
54	Caesar's second expedition to Britain
53	Crassus defeated and killed by Parthians at Carrhae; Gallic rebellion under Vercingetorix; Caesar's second Rhine crossing
52	Siege and capture of Alesia, defeat of Vercingetorix
51	Cleopatra VII (and Ptolemy XIII) succeed to Egyptian throne; Parthians invade Syria
49	Julius Caesar leads army across Rubicon into Italy; Caesar appointed Dictator
48	Caesar defeats Pompey at Pharsalus; Pompey flees to Egypt and is assassinated
47	Caesar defeats Pharnaces of the Crimea at Zela
45	Caesar defeats Pompeian army at Munda; Parthians invade Syria
44	Caesar assassinated (15 March); Brutus and Cassius flee to the East; Lucius Munatius Planus founds Augusta Rauricorum; death of Burebista of Dacia
43	Octavian appointed consul; Second Triumvirate established (Octavian, Mark Antony and Lepidus)
42	Deification of Julius Caesar; Battle of Philippi (Brutus and Cassius defeated and commit suicide)
41	Antony meets Cleopatra in Alexandria; Antony fails to capture Palmyra

40	Parthians under Pacorus invade Syria
38	Second Triumvirate renewed for five years; Agrippa resettles the Ubii on the Roman side of the Rhine
37	Appointment of client kings in Cappadocia, Galatia and Pontus
36	Antony's failed campaign against the Parthians
35–33	Octavian's campaigns in Balkans (captures Siscia in 35)
34	Antony invades Armenia; the 'Donations of Alexandria'
33	Bocchus of Mauretania dies
32	Antony divorces Octavian's sister, Octavia
31	Battle of Actium (2 September)
30	Octavian captures Alexandria; suicide of Antony and Cleopatra
29–28	Campaigns of Licinius Crassus in Thrace
28	Campaign of Cornelius Gallus beyond First Cataract of the Nile
27	Octavian receives name Augustus and grant of a *provincia* for ten years
26–25	Campaign of Aelius Gallus in Arabia Felix
25	Juba II becomes king of Mauretania; Galatia annexed; Meroites invade Egypt
23	Augustus receives tribunician power for life
21	Treaty with Meroites
20	Recovery from Parthia of Roman standards seized after Battle of Carrhae; expedition of Lucius Balbus reaches Garma
19	Campaign of Cornelius Balbus against Garamantes
15	Tiberius and Drusus campaign in Raetia, reach Danube; Regnum Noricum annexed
13	Campaign of Agrippa in Pannonia; Augustus awarded *imperium proconsulare maius*
12–9	Campaigns of Tiberius in Balkans and of Drusus in Germany
12	First legionary camp built at Vetera (Xanten); Rhine fleet circumnavigates Denmark
11	Official annexation of Pannonia
9	Drusus reaches Elbe in Germany, dies after accident; altar to Augustus and Rome set up at Ara Ubiorum (Cologne)
2	Augustus given title *pater patriae*
AD	
4	Tiberius campaigns in Germany
5	Tiberius reaches Elbe
6	Outbreak of revolt in Pannonia and Illyricum
8	Ovid banished to Pontus
9	Pannonian revolt suppressed; Varus defeated at Teutoberger Wald with loss of three legions

14	Mutinies in Rhine and Danube armies; death of Augustus, succeeded by Tiberius
15	Cappadocia made a province, Moesia organised as a province
15–16	Germanicus's campaigns in Germany
17	War against Tacfarinas begins in Numidia; death of Ovid
c.18	Establishment of quarries at Mons Porphyrogenitus
19	Death of Germanicus
21	Revolt of Sacrovir in Gaul
24	Final defeat of Tacfarinas
28	Revolt of the Frisians
31	Tiberius's praetorian prefect Sejanus dies
37	Tiberius dies; accession of Caligula
40	Caligula's abortive invasion of Britain; murder of Ptolemy of Mauretania, Mauretania revolts
40–43	Mauretania reconquered by Hosidius Geta and annexed as a province
41	Caligula murdered, succeeded by Claudius
43	Invasion of Britain
46	Thrace annexed
47	Corbulo orders construction of *Fosso Corbulonis*
c.50	Raetia constituted as a province
53	Parthians seize Armenia
58	Corbulo invades Armenia
59	Capture of Armenian capital Tigranocerta by Corbulo
60	Romans appoint Tigranes king of Armenia; Corbulo governor of Syria; revolt of Iceni in Britain
62	Caesennius Paetus surrenders to Parthian king Vologaeses
66	Outbreak of Jewish revolt
67	Vespasian appointed legate in Judaea
68	Revolt of Vindex in Gaul; Galba proclaimed Emperor by army in Spain (April); suicide of Nero (June)
69	Year of the four Emperors: Otho proclaimed Emperor by praetorian guard (January); Galba murdered; Vitellius proclaimed Emperor (April); Otho commits suicide; Vespasian proclaimed Emperor (July); Vespasian's forces defeat Vitellius at Cremona; Vitellius murdered (December); Vespasian sole Emperor
69–70	Batavian revolt
69–70	War against the Garamantes
70	Capture of Jerusalem, end of Jewish revolt
71	Accession of Rabbel II, last Nabataean king
72–73	Commagene annexed; Armenia Minor joined with Cappadocia
73–74	Campaign of Pinarius Clemens in Agri Decumates
c.75	Emesa annexed

77–84	Agricola's governorship of Britannia
81	Domitian becomes Emperor
82–83	Domitian's war against the Chatti
83	Caledonians defeated at Battle of Mons Graupius
85–88	War against the Dacians
85–90	Organisation of provinces of Germania Inferior and Germania Superior
85–96	War against Nasamones in North Africa
86	Legionary fortress at Inchtuthill in Scotland evacuated
89	Revolt of Antonius Saturninus in Germania Superior
98	Trajan becomes Emperor
100	Thamugadi founded
101–102	Trajan's 1st Dacian War
c.104	Withdrawal from advanced positions in Scotland
105–106	Trajan's 2nd Dacian War
106	Annexation of Nabataean kingdom and establishment of province of Arabia
107/108	Tropaeum Traiani set up at Adamklissi
114–116	Trajan's Parthian War; Armenia, Mesopotamia and Assyria annexed
115	Serious earthquake strikes Antioch; Jewish uprising in Cyrene
116–118	Revolt in the East; Mesopotamia and Assyria break away from Empire
117	Hadrian becomes Emperor
122	Hadrian visits Britannia; beginning of work on the Wall
132–135	Bar Kochba revolt
c.136–137	Last fort on Hadrian's Wall (Carvoran) built
138	Antoninus Pius becomes Emperor
139–142	Construction of Antonine Wall
c.150	Antoninus Pius advances the *limes* in Germany
159	Dacia divided into three provinces
161	Marcus Aurelius and Lucius Verus become co-Emperors
c.161	Evacuation of Antonine Wall frontier
162–166	Lucius Verus's Parthian War
163	Statius Priscus captures Artaxata
166–170	Plague strikes the Empire
166–180	Marcommanic Wars
175	Revolt of Avidius Cassius
180	Commodus becomes Emperor
192	Murder of Commodus; Pertinax becomes Emperor
193	Pertinax murdered; Didius Julianus becomes Emperor (murdered in June); Pescennius Niger declared Emperor by troops in Antioch; Septimius Severus declared Emperor by Danube armies, takes Rome; Clodius Albinus, governor of Britannia, made Caesar by Septimius

194	Niger defeated at Issus
195	Clodius Albinus declares himself Emperor
197	Clodius Albinus defeated and killed near Lyons
197–202	Septimius Severus's eastern campaigns
198	Caracalla made Augustus; Severus takes Ctesiphon
199–201	Septimius Severus visits Egypt
208	Septimius Severus, Caracalla and Geta arrive in Britain
211	Septimius Severus dies at York; Caracalla and Geta return to Rome, where Geta is murdered
212	*Consitutio Antoniniana* grants near-universal citizenship
213	Caracalla's campaigns against Alamanns; Caracalla annexes Edessa
215	Caracalla invades Parthia; massacre in Alexandria ordered by Caracalla
217	Caracalla assassinated near Carrhae; Macrinus appointed Emperor
218	Elagabalus declared Emperor; Macrinus makes peace with Parthia, then is defeated and killed near Antioch
221	Elagabalus adopts cousin Alexianus
222	Elagabalus murdered; succeeded by Alexianus (as Alexander Severus)
226	Ardashir, first Sassanid ruler, becomes shah of Persia
230	Persians invade Mesopotamia and besiege Nisibis
234	Maximinus Thrax declared Emperor by Pannonian army
235	Murder of Alexander Severus; Maximinus campaigns against Alamanns; Persians again invade Mesopotamia
238	Gordian I and Gordian II declared Emperor; they are defeated and killed near Carthage. Senate elects Balbinus and Pupienus Emperors; after their murder Gordian III appointed Emperor; Maximinus murdered during siege of Aquileia (June)
241	Shapur I becomes shah of Persia; invades Mesopotamia
239–242	Edessa again independent under Abgar X
242	Gordian III and praetorian prefect Timesitheus begin campaign to counter Persian invasion
244	Shapur defeats Romans, death of Gordian III; Philip 'the Arab' becomes Emperor, makes peace with Shapur
244–246/ 248–253	Goths and Carpi invade Balkans
248	Philip organises celebrations for Rome's 1000th birthday; Decius campaigns successfully in Balkans
249	Philip dies in battle against Decius near Verona; Decius becomes Emperor; Decian persecution of Christians
251	Decius dies in battle against Goths at Abritus; Trebonianus Gallus Emperor

253	Valerian becomes Emperor; Gothic seaborne attacks in Asia Minor; Shapur invades Syria and takes Dura Europos; usurpation of Uranius Antoninus
254	Marcomanni attack Pannonia; Alamanni ravage Raetia; Shapur takes Nisibis; Valerian retakes Dura
255	Renewed Gothic seaborne attacks on Asia Minor
256	Shapur again takes (and destroys) Dura Europos
257	First Frankish raids recorded; Gallienus campaigns against Alamanns from base at Trier
258/259	Usurpation of Ingenuus in Pannonia put down by Gallienus
259	Alamanns invade Illyricum; Iuthungi attack Italy
260	Valerian defeated and captured by Shapur at Edessa; Macrianus and Quietus declared emperors in East; Persians capture parts of eastern provinces; usurpation of Postumus in Gaul and establishment of Gallic Empire; Augsburg Victory Altar dedicated
c.260	Evacuation of Agri Decumates
261	Macrianus killed in Illyricum; execution of Quietus; Odaenathus of Palmyra given title of *corrector totius Orientis*
262	Successful campaign of Odaenathus against Persians
266	Death of Odaenathus; his wife Zenobia takes power at Palmyra
267	Goths invade Greece and Balkans; revolt of Gallienus's cavalry commander Aureolus
268	Gallienus murdered; succeeded by Claudius II (Gothicus)
269	Claudius II defeats Goths at Naissus; assassination of Postumus in Gaul; succeeded by Victorinus; Zenobia extends Palmyrene territory
270	Claudius II dies of plague at Sirmium; Aurelian proclaimed Emperor; Zenobia annexes Egypt, Syria and much of Asia Minor
271	Tetricus becomes Emperor in Gaul; evacuation of Dacia; Vaballathus (son of Zenobia) declared Augustus
272	Defeat and capture of Zenobia
273	New revolt in Palmyra suppressed
274	Defeat of Tetricus and reabsorption of Gallic Empire
275	Alamanns invade Gaul; murder of Aurelian
276	Probus declared Emperor by army in the East
278	Probus campaigns against Vandals and Burgundians in Raetia
282	Probus murdered; Carus declared Emperor; campaigns against Sarmatians and Quadi
283	Carus dies near Ctesiphon; succeeded by Carinus and Numerian; Carinus campaigns against Germans in Gaul
284	Diocletian becomes Emperor after murder of Numerian
285	Battle of Margus; Diocletian defeats Carinus
286	Maximian declared Augustus; revolt of Carausius in Britain

293	Constantius I and Galerius declared Caesars, establishment of the Tetrarchy; Carausius killed by Allectus
296	Constantius I recaptures Britain; Diocletian defeats Quadi
297	Maximian in Africa to suppress revolt; Narses of Persia defeats Galerius near Carrhae; revolt of Domitius Domitianus in Egypt
298	Galerius takes Ctesiphon; end of Egyptian revolt; Diocletian pulls back border in Egypt to Syene
298	Treaty with Persia
301	Edict of Maximum Prices
303	Start of Great Persecution of Christians
305	Diocletian and Maximian abdicate; Constantius I and Galerius replace them as Augusti, with Severus and Maximin Daia as Caesars
306	Constantius I dies at York; Constantine I declared Emperor by soldiers; usurpation of Maxentius (son of Maximian) at Rome
307	Constantine recognised as Augustus by Maximian; Severus attacks Rome, forced to retreat and abdicates
308	Carnuntum Conference; Maximian retires again, Licinius appointed Augustus; revolt of Domitius Alexander in Africa
310	Death of Maximian
311	Galerius issues Edict tolerating Christians; death of Galerius
c.312	Death of Diocletian
312	Constantine defeats Maxentius at Battle of Milvian Bridge (28 October)
313	Licinius defeats Maximin Daia at Adrianople; Edict of Milan recognises freedom of religious belief; Council at Rome on Donatist problem
314	Council of Arles condemns Donatists; Constantine campaigns in Germany
315	Arch of Constantine constructed at Rome
316	Constantine defeats Licinius at Cibalae
324	Constantine defeats Licinius at Chrysopolis; foundation of Constantinople
325	Council of Nicaea
326	Execution of Constantine's eldest son Crispus
328	Death of Imru' al-Qays at Nemara
332	Constantine campaigns against Goths
334	Constantine campaigns against Sarmatians
336	1st Council of Constantinople
337	Death of Constantine I; Constans, Constantine II and Constantius II co-Emperors
337–350	Wars of Constantius II against Persia
340	Death of Constantius II
343/344	Battle of Singara
343	Council of Serdica

350	Persian siege of Nisibis; Magnentius proclaimed Emperor in Gaul; death of Constans
353	Death of Magnentius
355	Silvanus declared Emperor in Gaul (and assassinated)
357	Battle of Strasbourg, Julian defeats Alamanns; raids by Iuthungi in Raetia
359	Persians capture Amida after siege
360	Julian declared Caesar in Gaul
361	Death of Constantius II
362–363	Julian resident at Antioch
363	Julian dies on campaign against Persia; Jovian declared Emperor, makes treaty with Persia, ceding several districts across Euphrates and Nisibis
363–364	Album of Thamugadi inscribed
364	Death of Jovian; Valentinian I declared Emperor, with Valens as co-Emperor
365–366	Revolt of Procopius
367	'Barbarian Conspiracy' in Britannia
367–369	Valens's campaigns across the Danube
369	Valens makes peace with Gothic chieftain Athanaric
372	Revolt of Firmus in Africa
375	Valentinian I dies of apoplexy after campaign against Quadi and Sarmatians
376	Tervingi Goths cross Danube in great numbers
378	Battle of Adrianople; Valens defeated and killed by Goths
379	Theodosius I declared Emperor
381	2nd Council of Constantinople
382	Peace treaty with Goths
383	Revolt of Magnus Maximums; Gratian killed by his army
387	Riot of the Statues at Antioch; Persian-Roman treaty partitions Armenia
388	Revolt of Magnus Maximus suppressed
391–392	Anti-pagan edicts of Theodosius I
391	Temple of Serapis at Alexandria destroyed
392	Suicide of Valentinian II; usurpation of Eugenius
394	Battle of Frigidus River, Eugenius killed
395	Death of Theodosius I; Honorius and Arcadius Emperors in West and East (effective political separation of two parts of Empire)
395	Augustine becomes bishop of Hippo; first major Hunnish incursions
396	Armies of Alaric ravaging Balkans
397	Alaric recognised as *magister militum* by Eastern Empire
397–398	Revolt of Gildo in Africa
397–398	Visit of Synesius to Constantinople

400	Gainas killed by Hun Uldin
404	Last recorded gladiatorial games at Rome
405–406	Vandals, Alans and Sueves cross Rhine
407	Alaric and Goths invade Italy; death of Stilicho
410	Alaric sacks Rome
410	Britannia secedes from Empire after usurpation of Constantine III; Synesius becomes bishop of Ptolemais
411	Council of Carthage condemns Donatism
412	Simeon Stylites joins community at Telanissos
415	Murder of philosopher Hypatia in Alexandria
421	Olympiodorus of Thebes visits the Blemmyes
423	Death of Honorius
427	Eastern Empire regains control of Pannonia
429	Vandals cross over into Africa under Gaiseric; first visit of Bishop Germanus of Auxerre to Britain
430	Death of Saint Augustine
431	Vandals capture Hippo Regius; 1st Council of Ephesus deposes Nestorius
433	Pannonia lost to the Huns
438	Theodosian code issued
439	Vandals capture Carthage
440	Persians under Yezdegird attack Mesopotamia
441	Attila ravages Balkans
443	Aëtius settles Burgundians in Savoy
446	'Groans of the Britons', appeal for aid by British notables to patrician Aëtius
449	2nd Council of Ephesus ('the Robber Council'); Embassy to Attila and failed assassination attempt
451	Attila defeated at Catalaunian Fields by Aëtius; Council of Chalcedon
452	Attila invades Italy, turns back without attacking Rome
453	Death of Attila
454	Murder of Aëtius
455	Vandals sack Rome
456	Vandals capture Corsica and Balearics
460–482	Saint Severinus active in Noricum
468	Eastern fleet fails to defeat Vandals
475	Orestes revolts and appoints his son Romulus (Augustulus) as Western Emperor
476	Odovacer deposes Romulus Augustulus; end of Western Roman Empire
476–483	Theoderic the Amal based at Novae
482	Acacian schism breaks out; Zeno's *Henotikon*

486	Syagrius defeated by Frankish king Clovis in Soissons, collapse of 'Roman' enclave in Gaul
488	Theoderic the Amal invades Italy
491	Anglo-Saxons capture Anderitum, last 'Saxon Shore' fort
493	Theoderic takes Ravenna and kills Odovacer
502	Persians under Kavadh invade
505	Truce with Persians; Dara constructed
518	Acacian schism ends
527	Justinian becomes Emperor
528	Justinian appoints commission to codify laws
529	First edition of Justinian's Code
530	Persians defeated at Satala
532	Nika Riot; 'Endless Peace' signed with Persia
533	Hilderic deposed by Gelimer as Vandal king, gives pretext for Byzantine intervention; Vandals defeated by Belisarius in battles at Ad Decimum and Tricamarum; Digest of Justinian completed
534	Gelimer surrenders; end of Vandal War
536	Belisarius invades Italy, captures Rome
540	Khusraw I of Persia invades and sacks Antioch; Jacob Baradaeus becomes bishop of Edessa
544	Massacre of Leuthae chiefs at Leptis Magna
546	Gothic king Totila recaptures Rome
552	Totila defeated at Busta Gallorum
553	Council of Constantinople, condemnation of 'Three Chapters'
562	Fifty-Year Peace with Persia
568	Lombards invade Italy
572	War with Persia begins
573	Persians capture Dara; Justin II becomes insane
574	Truce with Persia
581	Ghassanid sheikh al-Mundhir arrested
582	Avars capture Sirmium
602	Emperor Maurice murdered; Phocas becomes Emperor
609	Revolt of Heraclius in Africa
610	Heraclius captures Constantinople, becomes Emperor
613	Persians capture Damascus
614	Persians capture Jerusalem
616	Persians take Egypt
622	The Hegira (flight of Prophet Muhammad from Mecca)
623	Persians and Avars fail to take Constantinople
627	Heraclius defeats Persians at Nineveh
636	Arab Muslims defeat Byzantine army at Yarmuk
638	Jerusalem captured by Arabs
640	Arab Muslims conquer Armenia

640–641	Arab Muslims conquer Egypt
642	Final Byzantine evacuation of Alexandria; Arabs invade Cyrenaica and Tripolitania
646	Usurpation of Gregory, the exarch of Africa
648	Constans issues *Typos* in attempt to restore unity to Christian Church
669	Arabs under Uqba take most of Tripolitania and Byzacena
674–678	First Arab siege of Constantinople
683	Uqba killed by Berber chieftain Kusayla
695	First Arab capture of Carthage; the Arabs are driven out by Kahina
698	Final Arab capture of Carthage
717–718	Second Arab siege of Constantinople
701/703	Death of Kahina
711	Arabs take Septem (last Byzantine possession in North Africa)
726	Beginning of Iconoclast controversy
750	Beginning of Abbasid caliphate
751	Ravenna falls to Lombards; effective end of Byzantine presence in northern Italy
787	2nd Council of Nicaea restores icons
800	Charlemagne crowned Emperor at Rome (first 'Holy Roman Emperor')
863	Mission of Constantine and Methodios to the Slavs
864	Khan Boris of Bulgaria baptised
913	Khan Symeon of Bulgaria reaches walls of Constantinople; crowned 'Emperor' by the patriarch
944	John Kourkouas takes Amida, Dara and Nisibis for Byzantine Empire; besieges Edessa
968	Nikephoros Phocas retakes Antioch and Aleppo, annexing northern Syria
970s	John Tzimiskes captures Damascus, Tiberias and Caesarea
976	Basil II becomes Emperor
995	Basil II's victorious campaign in the East
1014	Basil II defeats Bulgarians at Kleidion
1045	Byzantines conquer Armenia
1064	Seljuk Turks take Armenian capital Ani
1071	Battle of Manzikert; disastrous defeat of Romanos IV by Seljuk Turks under Alp Arslan
1096	First Crusaders reach Constantinople
1098	Crusaders take Antioch
1099	Crusaders take Jerusalem
1147	Second Crusaders reach Constantinople
1176	Battle of Myriokephalon; Manuel I Komenos defeated by Seljuk Turks
1189	Third Crusade begins

1204   Fourth Crusaders take Constantinople (12 April); beginning of
           Latin Empire
1214   Treaty between Latin Empire and Greek Empire of Nicaea
1261   Michael VIII captures Constantinople; end of Latin Empire
1389   Battle of Kosovo Polje; Serbs defeated by Ottoman Turks, opening
           Balkans to Turkish domination
1402   Battle of Ankara; Timur's Mongols destroy Ottoman army,
           temporarily reprieving Byzantine Empire
1453   Ottoman sultan Mehmed II captures Constantinople (29 May)
1460   Ottomans occupy Despotate of Morea (Peloponnese)
1461   Emperor David surrenders the city of Trebizond to Ottomans
           (15 August), thus ending last Byzantine (and Roman) state

BIBLIOGRAPHY

ANCIENT SOURCES

Ammianus Marcellinus *Res Gestae* (trs C.D. Yonge, London 1911)

The Anglo-Saxon Chronicle (trs G.N. Garmonsworthy, London 1953)

Appian, *History of Rome* (trs Horace White, London 1899)

Augustine, *The City of God* (trs Marcus Dods, London 2000)

Aurelius Victor, *Epitome De Caesaribus* (trs H.W. Bird, Liverpool 1994)

Ausonius, *Mosella* (trs Hugh G. Evelyn Wright, London 1921)

Cassius Dio, *Roman History* (trs Earnest Cary, London 1914–27)

Claudian, *De Consolatu Stilichonis* (trs Maurice Platnauer, London 1922)

Diodorus Siculus, *Library of History* (trs Russell Geer, London 1954)

Eutropius, *Breviarium* (trs H.W. Bird, Liverpool 1993)

Gildas, *De Excidio Britanniae* (trs Michael Winterbottom, London 1978)

Herodotus, *Histories* (trs George Rawlinson, London 1927)

Historia Augusta (trs David Magie, London 1954)

Isidore of Seville, *Etymologiae* (trs Stephen A. Barney, Cambridge 2006)

Jerome, *Epistolae* (trs C.C. Mierow, Westminster, MD, 1963)

John Malalas, *Chronographia* (trs Elizabeth Jeffreys, Michael Jeffreys and Roger Scott, Melbourne 1986)

Jordanes, *Getica* (trs Charles Christopher Mierow, Princeton, NJ, 1915)

Julian, *Misopogon* (trs Wilmer Cave Wright, London 1913)

Julius Caesar, *Gallic Wars* (trs S.A. Handford, Harmondsworth 1963)

Lucan, *The Civil Wars* (trs J.D. Duff, London 1928)

Marcus Aurelius, *Meditations* (trs Gregory Hays, London 2003)

Martial, *Epigrams* (trs Walter C.A. Kerr, London 1919–20)

Orosius, *History against the Pagans* (trs Irving Woodworth Raymond, New York 1936)

Ovid, *Ars Amatoria* (trs Rolph Humphries, London 1958)

Pliny the Younger, *Letters and Panegyricus* (trs Betty Radice, London 1969)

Pliny the Elder, *Natural History* (trs H. Rackham, W.H.S. Jones, D.E. Eichholz, London 1949–67)

In Praise of Later Roman Emperors: The Panegyrici Latini (trs R.A.B. Mynors, C.E.V. Nixon and Barbara Saylor Rodgers, London 1994)

Procopius, *History of the Wars* (trs H.B. Dewing, London 1914–35)

Procopius, *Buildings* (trs H.B. Dewing, London 1940)

Procopius, *Secret History* (trs Richard Atwater, Ann Arbor 1961)

Seneca, *Letters to Lucillus* (trs E. Phillips Barker, Oxford 1932)

Strabo, *Geographia* (trs H.C Hamilton and W. Falconer, London 1854)

Suetonius, *Lives of the Twelve Caesars* (trs Robert Graves, London 1962)

Tacitus, *Germania* (trs R.B. Townshend, London 1895)

Tacitus, *Annals* (trs A.J. Woodman, Indianapolis 2004)

Vegetius, *De Re Militari* (trs N.P. Milner, Liverpool 1996)

Victor of Vita, *Historia persecutionis africanae provinciae* (trs John Moorhead, Liverpool 1992)

Virgil, *Aeneid* (trs Federick Ahl, Oxford 2007)

Zosimus, *Historia Nova* (trs James J. Buchanan and Harold T. Davies, San Antonio, Texas 1967)

GENERAL WORKS

Andrews, Alfred C., 'Oysters as a Food in Greece and Rome' in *Classical Journal* 43 (1948), pp. 299–303

Antaya, Roger, 'The Etymology of Pomerium' in *The American Journal of Philology*, Vol. 101, No. 2 (Summer 1980), pp. 184–9

Atiyah, A.S., *A History of Eastern Christianity* (London 1968)

Austin, N.J.E. and Rankov, N.B., *Exploratio: Military and Political Intelligence in the Roman world from the Second Punic War to the Battle of Adrianople* (London 1995)

Ball, Warwick, *Rome in the East, the Transformation of an Empire* (London 2000)

Barchiesi, Alessandro, *The Poet and The Prince, Ovid and Augustan Discourse* (Berkeley 1997)

Barnes, Timothy D., *The New Empire of Diocletian and Constantine* (Harvard 1982)

Barnwell, P.S., *Emperors, Prefects & Kings: The Roman West, 395–564* (London 1992)

Beacham, Richard C., *The Roman Theatre and its Audience* (London 1991)

Beard, Mary, *The Roman Triumph* (Cambridge, MA, 2007)

Beard, Mary, North, John and Price, Simon, *Religions of Rome: A History*, Vol. 1, (Cambridge 1998)

Benario, Herbert W., 'Amphitheatres of the Roman World' in *Classical Journal* (1981), pp. 255–9

Bennett, Julian, *Trajan Optimus Princeps* (London 1997)

Biggins, J. Alan et al., 'A Survey of the Roman Fort and Settlement at Birdoswald, Cumbria' in *Britannia* 30 (1999)

Birley, Anthony R., *Marcus Aurelius* (London 1966)

Birley, Anthony R., *Septimius Severus: The African Emperor* (London 1988)

Birley, Anthony R., *Hadrian, The Restless Emperor* (London 1997)

Blockley, R.C., *The Classicising Fragmentary Historians of the Later Roman Empire* (Liverpool 1981)

Blockley, R.C., *East Roman Foreign Policy: Formation and Conduct from Diocletian to Anastasius* (Leeds 1992)

Boatwright, Mary Taliaferro, 'Tacitus on Claudius and the Pomerium, Annals 12.23.2–24' in *Classical Journal*, Vol. 80, No. 1 (Oct–Nov. 1984), pp. 36–44

Bowersock, G.W., Brown, Peter and Grabar, Oleg, *Late Antiquity, A Guide to the Postclassical World* (Cambridge, MA, 1999)

Bowman, Alan K., Garnsey, Peter and Rathbone, Dominic (eds), *The Cambridge Ancient History, Volume XI, The High Empire, AD 70–192* (Cambridge 2000)

Bowman, Alan K., Garnsey, Peter and Cameron, Averil (eds), *The Cambridge Ancient History, Volume XII, The Crisis of Empire, AD 193–337* (Cambridge 2005)

Brauer, George C. Jr, *The Age of the Soldier Emperors AD 244–284* (Park Ridge, NJ, 1974)

Braund, David, *Rome and the Friendly King: The Character of Client Kingship* (London 1984)

Brown, Peter, *The World of Late Antiquity* (London 1971)

Brown, Peter, *Society and the Holy in Late Antiquity* (London 1982)

Brown, Peter, *Authority and the Sacred: Aspects of the Christianization of the Roman World* (Cambridge 1995)

Burns, Thomas S., *Barbarians within the Gates of Rome: A Study of Roman Military Policy and the Barbarians, ca. 375–425 AD* (Bloomington 1994)

Burns, Thomas S., *Rome and the Barbarians 100 BC–AD 400* (Baltimore 2003)

Cameron, Alan, *Porphyrius the Charioteer* (Oxford 1973)

Cameron, Alan, *Circus Factions: Blues and Greens at Rome and Byzantium* (Oxford 1976)

Cameron, Averil, *The Mediterranean World in Late Antiquity, AD 395–600* (London 1993)

Cameron, Averil and Garnsey, Peter (eds), *The Cambridge Ancient History, Volume XIII, The Late Empire, AD 337–425* (Cambridge 1993)

Cameron, Averil, Ward-Perkins, Brian and Whitby, Michael (eds), *The Cambridge Ancient History, Volume XIV, Late Antiquity: Empire and Successors, AD 425–600* (Cambridge 2000)

Campbell, Brian, *The Roman Army 31 BC–AD 337: A Sourcebook* (London 1994)

Campbell, J.B., *The Emperor and the Roman Army 31 BC–AD 235* (Oxford 1984)

Casson, Lionel, *Travel in the Ancient World* (Baltimore 1974)

Clauss, Manfred, *The Roman Cult of Mithras: The God and his Mysteries* (Edinburgh 2000)

Coarelli, Filippo, *Il Foro Romano* (Rome 1983)

Collins, Roger, *Visigothic Spain 409–711* (Oxford 2004)

Corcoran, Simon, *The Empire of the Tetrarchs: Imperial Pronouncements and Government AD 284–324* (revised edition, Oxford 2000)

Cornell, T.J., *The Beginnings of Rome, Italy and Rome from the Bronze Age to the Punic Wars (c. 1000–264 BC)* (London 1995)

Cornell, Tim and Matthews, John, *Atlas of the Roman World* (Oxford 1982)

De Serviez, J.R., *The Roman Empresses* (Vol. 2, London 1899)

Dignas, Beate and Winter, Engelbert, *Rome and Persia in Late Antiquity, Neighbours and Rivals* (Cambridge 2007)

Dilke O.A.W., *Greek and Roman Maps* (London 1985)

Dixon, Karen, *The Roman Cavalry from the First to the Third Century AD* (London 1992)

Dodgeon, Michael H. and Lieu, Samuel N.C., *The Roman Eastern Frontier and the Persian Wars (AD 226–363)* (London 1991)

Drummond, Steven K. and Nelson, Lynn H., *The Western Frontiers of Imperial Rome* (New York 1994)

Dunbabin, Katherine M.D., *Mosaics of the Greek and Roman World* (Cambridge 1999)

Duncan-Jones, Richard, *Money and Government in the Roman Empire* (Cambridge 1994)

Dyson, Stephen L., *The Creation of the Roman Frontier* (Princeton 1985)

Eck, Werner (trs Deborah Lucas Schneider), *The Age of Augustus* (Oxford 2003)

Elton, Hugh, *Warfare in Roman Europe 350–425* (Oxford 1996)

Erdkamp, Paul (ed.), *A Companion to the Roman Army* (Oxford 2007)

Errington, R. Malcolm, *Roman Imperial Policy from Julian to Theodosius* (Chapel Hill 2006)

Evans, J.A.S., *The Age of Justinian: The circumstances of imperial power* (London 1996)

Everitt, Anthony, *The First Emperor: Caesar Augustus and the Triumph of Rome* (London 2006)

Fagan, Garrett G., *Bathing in Public in the Roman World* (Ann Arbor 1999)

Ferrill, Arthur, *The Fall of the Roman Empire: The Military Explanation* (London 1986)

Finley, M.I., *Atlas of Classical Archaeology* (London 1977)

Flower, Harriet I., *The Art of Forgetting* (Chapel Hill 2007)

Fränkel, Hermann, *Ovid, A Poet between Two Worlds* (Berkeley 1945)

Freeman et al. (eds), *Proceedings of XVIIIIth International Congress of Roman frontier studies (Sep. 2002)* (BAR International Series 1084 (i), Oxford 2002)

Frend, W.H.C., *The Rise of the Monophysite Movement, Chapters in the History of the Church in the Fifth and Sixth Centuries* (Cambridge 1972)

Gardner, R.A, 'The Peutinger Table' in *The Geographical Journal*, Vol. 136, No. 3 (Sept. 1970), pp. 489–90

Garnsey, Peter, *Social Status and Legal Privilege in the Roman Empire* (Oxford 1970)

Garnsey, Peter and Humress, Caroline, *The Evolution of the Late Antique World* (Cambridge 2001)

Geffcken, Johannes (trs Sabine MacCormack), *The Last Days of Greco-Roman Paganism* (Oxford 1978)

Gelzer, Matthias (trs Robin Seager), *The Roman Nobility* (Oxford 1969)

Gibbon, Edward, *The History of the Decline and Fall of the Roman Empire* (ed. David Womersley, London 2005)

Goffart, W.A., *Barbarians and Romans AD 418–584: The Techniques of Accommodation* (Princeton, NJ, 1980)

Goffart, W.A., *Barbarian Tides: The Migration Age and the Later Roman Empire* (Philadelphia 2006)

Goldsworthy, Adrian, *Roman Warfare* (London 2000)

Goldsworthy, Adrian, *The Complete Roman Army* (London 2003)

Goodman, Martin, *The Roman World 44 BC–AD 180* (Oxford 1997)

Grant, Michael, *Gladiators* (London 1967)

Grant, Michael, *The Roman Forum* (London 1970)

Grant, Michael, *The Severans, The Changed Roman Empire* (London 1996)

Harl, Kenneth W., *Coinage in the Roman Economy 300 BC to AD 700* (Baltimore 1996)

Holder, P.A., 'Roman auxiliary cavalry in the second century AD' in *Archaeology Today* 8 (June 1987), pp. 12–16.

Honoré, Tony, *Emperors and Lawyers* (London 1981)

Hovorun, Cyril, *Will, Action and Freedom, Christological Controversies in the Seventh Century* (Leiden 2008)

Hughes, Philip, *A History of the Church* (London 1979)

Isaac, Benjamin, 'The Meaning of the Terms Limes and Limitanei' in *Journal of Roman Studies* 78 (1988), pp. 125–47

Jones, A.H.M., *The Later Roman Empire* (Oxford 1964)

Jones, Brian W., *The Emperor Domitian* (London 1992)

Kean, Roger Michael and Frey, Oliver, *The Complete Chronicles of the Emperors of Rome* (Ludlow 2005)

Kelly, Christopher, *Ruling the Later Roman Empire* (Cambridge, MA, 2004)

Kelly, J.N.D., *Early Christian Doctrines* (revised edition, London 1980)

Kennedy, David and Riley, Derrick, *Rome's Desert Frontier from the Air* (Austin, TX, 1990)

Kreitzer, Larry, 'Apotheosis of the Roman Emperor' in *The Biblical Archaeologist*, Vol. 53, No. 4 (Dec. 1990), pp. 211–17

Kulikowski, Michael, *Rome's Gothic Wars from the Third Century to Alaric* (Cambridge 2007)

Lane Fox, Robin, *Pagans and Christians* (London 1986)

Lane Fox, Robin, *Travelling Heroes* (London 2008)

Lee, A.D, *Information and Frontiers: Roman Foreign Relations in Late Antiquity* (Cambridge 1993)

Lenski, Noel, *Failure of Empire, Valens and the Roman State in the Fourth Century AD* (Berkeley 2002)

Lenski, Noel (ed.), *Cambridge Companion to the Age of Constantine* (Cambridge 2006)

Levick, Barbara, *Vespasian* (London 1999)

Liebeschuetz, J.H.W., *The Decline and Fall of the Roman City* (Oxford 2001)

Lieu, Samuel N.C., *Manichaeism in the Later Roman Empire and Medieval China, a Historical Survey* (Manchester 1985)

Lopez, R.S., 'The Evolution of Land Transport in the Middle Ages' in *Past and Present*, No. 9 (Apr. 1956), pp. 17–29

Luttwak, Edward N., *The Grand Strategy of the Roman Empire from the First Century AD to the Third* (Baltimore 1976)

McClue, M.L. and Feltoe, C.L., *The Pilgrimage of Etheria* (New York 1919)

MacGeorge, Penny, *Late Roman Warlords* (Oxford 2002)

MacMullen, Ramsay, *Roman Social Relations 50 BC–AD 284* (New Haven 1974)

MacMullen, Ramsay, *Roman Government's Response to Crisis AD 235–337* (New Haven 1976)

MacMullen, Ramsay, *Christianizing the Roman Empire (AD 100–400)* (New Haven 1984)

MacMullen, Ramsay, *Corruption and the Decline of Rome* (New Haven 1988)

MacMullen, Ramsay, *Changes in the Roman Empire* (Princeton 1990)

MacMullen, Ramsay, *Christianity and Paganism in the Fourth to Eighth Centuries* (New Haven 1997)

Mann, J.C. et al. (eds), *Aspects of the Notitia Dignitatum* (BAR Supplementary Series 15, Oxford 1976)

Mann, J.C., 'The Notitia Dignitatum – Dating and Survival' in *Britannia* 22 (1991), pp. 215–19

Mathisen, Ralph W. and Sivan, Hagith S., *Shifting Frontiers in Late Antiquity* (Aldershot 1996)

Matthews, J.M., *Western Aristocracies and the Imperial Court AD 364–425* (Oxford 1975)

Matyszak, Philip, *The Enemies of Rome* (London 2004)

Millar, Fergus, *The Roman Empire and its Neighbours* (London 1967)

Millar, Fergus, *The Emperor in the Roman World (31BC–AD 337)* (London 1977)

Millar, Fergus, *A Greek Roman Empire, Power and Belief under Theodosius II (408–50)* (Berkeley, 2006)

Millar, Fergus, 'Emperors, Frontiers and Foreign Relations, 31 B.C. to A.D. 378' in *Britannia* 13 (1982), pp. 1–23

Mitchell, Stephen, *A History of the Later Roman Empire AD 284–641* (Oxford 2007)

Mitchell, Stephen and Greatrex, Gregory (eds), *Ethnicity and Culture in Late Antiquity* (London 2000)

Momigliano, Arnold (ed.), *The Conflict between Paganism and Christianity in the Fourth Century* (Oxford 1970)

Moorhead, John, *Justinian* (London 1994)

Murdoch, Adrian, *The Last Pagan: Julian the Apostate and the Death of the Ancient World* (Stroud 2003)

Nicasie, M.J., 'The Borders of the Roman Empire in the Fourth Century' in *Roman Frontier Studies 1995* (ed. W. Groenman-van Waateringe, B.I. van Beek, W.J.H. Willems, S.L. Wynia, Oxford 1997)

Odahl, Charles Matson, *Constantine and the Christian Empire* (London 2004)

Pohl, Walter, Wood, Ian and Reimitz, Helmut, *The Transformation of Frontiers from Late Antiquity to the Carolingians* (Leiden 2001)

Potter, David S., *The Roman Empire at Bay* AD *180–395* (London 2004)

Rapp, Claudia, *Holy Bishops in Late Antiquity: The Nature of Christian Leadership in an Age of Transition* (Berkeley 2005)

Rees, Roger, *Diocletian and the Tetrarchy* (Edinburgh 2004)

Rich, John (ed.), *The City in Late Antiquity* (London 1992)

Rich, John and Shipley, Graham, *War and Society in the Roman World* (London 1993)

Richardson, L. Jr, *A New Topographical Dictionary of Ancient Rome* (Baltimore 1992)

Rutherford, R.B., *The Meditations of Marcus Aurelius: A Study* (Oxford 1989)

Sanders, Henry A. (ed.), *Roman Historical Sources and Institutions* (London 1904)

Sanford, Eva Matthews, 'Nero and the East' in Harvard Studies in Classical Philology 48 (1937), pp. 75–103

Saradi-Mendelovic, Helen, 'Christian Attitudes toward Pagan Monuments in Late Antiquity and Their Legacy in Later Byzantine Centuries' in Dumbarton Oaks Papers 44 (1990), pp. 44–61

Southern, Pat, *Domitian: Tragic Tyrant* (London 1997)

Southern, Pat, *The Roman Empire from Severus to Constantine* (London 2001)

Southern, Pat and Dixon, Karen Ramsay, *The Late Roman Army* (London 1996)

Spaul, John E.H., *ALA²: The Auxiliary Cavalry Units of the Pre-Diocletianic Imperial Roman Army* (Andover 1994)

Starr, Chester G., *The Roman Imperial Navy* (2nd edition, Cambridge 1960)

Stilwell, Richard (ed.), *Princeton Encyclopedia of Classical Sites* (Princeton, NJ, 1976)

Swain, Simon and Edwards, Mark, *Approaching Late Antiquity* (Oxford 2004)

Talbert, J.A., *Barrington Atlas of the Greek and Roman World* (Princeton 2000)

Taylor, Lily Ross, *The Divinity of the Roman Emperor* (Philadelphia 1975)

Thompson, E.A., *Romans and Barbarians: The Decline of the Western Empire* (Madison 1982)

Todd, Malcolm, *The Northern Barbarians* 100 BC–AD *300* (London 1975)

Tougher, Shaun, *Julian the Apostate* (Edinburgh 2007)

Wacher, John (ed.), *The Roman World* (London 1987)

Ward-Perkins, Brian, *The Fall of Rome and the End of Civilization* (Oxford 2005)

Ward-Perkins, John B., *Roman Imperial Architecture* (London 1981)

Ward-Perkins, John B., *Roman Architecture* (London 1988)

Warde Folwer, W., *The Roman Festivals of the Period of the Republic* (London 1899)

Watson, Alaric, *Aurelian and the Third Century* (London 1999)

Whiles, Maurice, *Archetypal Heresy, Arianism through the Centuries* (Oxford 1996)

Whitby, Michael, *Rome at War* AD *293–696* (Oxford 2002)

Whittaker, C.R., *Rome and its Frontier: The Dynamics of Empire* (London 2004)

Whittow, Mark, *The Making of Orthodox Byzantium, 600–1025* (Basingstoke 1996)

Wiedemann, Thomas, *Emperors and Gladiators* (London, 1992)

Wilkinson, John, *Jerusalem Pilgrims before the Crusades* (Warminster 1977)

Williams, Derek, *Romans and Barbarians: Four Views from the Empire's Edge* (London 1998)

Williams, Stephen, *Diocletian and the Roman Recovery* (London 1985)

Williams, Stephen and Friell, Gerard. *Theodosius: The Empire at Bay* (London 1998)

Wilson Jones, Mark, 'Doric Measure and Architectural Design 1: The Evidence of the Relief from Salamis' in *American Journal of Archaeology*, Vol. 104, No. 1. (Jan. 2000), pp. 73–93

Witt, R.E., *Isis in the Ancient World*, Baltimore 1997

Yarshater, Ehsan (ed.), *The Cambridge History of Iran, Volume 3, The Seleucid, Parthian and Sasanian periods* (Cambridge 1983)

Yegül, Fikret, *Baths and Bathing in Classical Antiquity* (Cambridge, MA, 1992)

CHAPTER 1: BRITANNIA

Alcock, Leslie, *Arthur's Britain* (London 1989)

Bidwell, Paul (ed.), *Hadrian's Wall 1989–1999: A Summary of Recent Excavations and Research* (Newcastle upon Tyne 1999)

Biggins, J. Alan et al., 'A Survey of the Roman Fort and Settlement at Birdoswald, Cumbria' in *Britannia* 30 (1999), pp. 91–110

Birley, Anthony, *Garrison Life at Vindolanda* (Stroud 2002)

Birley, Robin, *Magna and Carvoran – The Fort at the Rock* (Carlisle 1998)

Bowman, Alan K., *Life and Letters on the Roman Frontier, Vindolanda and its People* (London 1998)

Breeze, David, *The Northern Frontiers of Roman Britain* (London 1982)

Breeze, David J., *Roman Forts in Britain* (Princes Risborough 2002)

Breeze, David J., *The Antonine Wall* (Edinburgh 2006)

Breeze, David J. and Dobson, Brian, *Hadrian's Wall*, (4th edition, London 2000)

Collingwood Bruce, J., *A Handbook to the Roman Wall* (14th edition, by David J. Breeze, Newcastle 2006)

Collingwood, R.G., 'Hadrian's Wall: A History of the Problem' in *Journal of Roman Studies* 11 (1921)

Carroll, Kevin K., 'The Date of Boudicca's Revolt' in *Britannia*, Vol. 10 (1979), pp. 197–202

Cleary, A.S. Esmonde, *The Ending of Roman Britain* (London 1989)

Crow, J.G., *Housesteads Roman Fort* (London 1989)

Dark, Ken, *Britain and the End of the Roman Empire* (Stroud 2000)

Dark, K.R., 'A Sub-Roman Re-Defence of Hadrian's Wall?' in *Britannia* 23, (1992), pp. 111–20

De la Bédoyère, Guy, *Roman Towns in Britain* (London 1992)

De la Bédoyère, Guy, *Eagles over Britannia* (London 2001)

Dore, J.N., *Corbridge Roman Site* (London 1989)

Faulkner, Neil, *The Decline and Fall of Roman Britain* (Stroud 2000)

Fields, Nic, *Rome's Saxon Shore: Coastal Defences of Roman Britain* (Oxford 2006)

Frere, Sheppard, *Britannia: A History of Roman Britain* (London 1991)

Goodall, John, *Portchester* (London 2003)

Green, Miranda J., *The Gods of Roman Britain* (Princes Risborough, 2003)

Hanson, William S. and Maxwell, Gordon S., *Rome's North West Frontier: The Antonine Wall* (Edinburgh 1983)

Harris, Susan, *Richborough and Reculver* (London 2001)

Heurgon, Jacques, 'The Amiens Patera' in *Journal of Roman Studies* 41, Parts 1 and 2 (1951), pp. 22–4

Hill, Peter, *The Construction of Hadrian's Wall* (Stroud 2006)

Ireland, S., *Roman Britian, A Sourcebook* (London 1986)

Johnson, J.S., *Chesters Roman Fort* (London, 1990)

Johnson, Stephen, *Roman Forts of the Saxon Shore* (London 1979)

Jones, Michael E., *The End of Roman Britain* (Ithaca 1986)

Mann, J.C., 'The Northern Frontier after AD 368' in *Glasgow Archaeological Journal* 3 (1974), pp. 34–42

Mann, J.C., 'Birdoswald to Ravenglass' in *Britannia* 20 (1989), pp. 75–9

Mattingly, David, *An Imperial Possession: Britain in the Roman Empire* (London 2006)

Maxfield, Valerie (ed.), *The Saxon Shore, A Handbook* (Exeter Studies in History No. 25, 1989)

Maxwell, Gordon S., *The Romans in Scotland* (Edinburgh 1989)

Miller, M., 'Stilicho's Pictish War' in *Britannia* 6 (1975), pp. 141–5

Pearson, Andrew, *The Roman Shore Forts, Coastal Defences of Southern Britain* (Stroud 2002)

Philip, Brian, *The Roman Fort at Reculver* (Dover 1970)

Robertson, Anne S., *The Antonine Wall: A Handbook to the Surviving Remains* (3rd edition, Glasgow 1990)

Salway, Peter, *A History of Roman Britain* (Oxford, 1993)

Shotter, David, *The Roman Frontier in Britain* (Preston 1996)

Thompson, E.A., *Saint Germanus of Auxerre and the End of Roman Britain* (Woodbridge, Suffolk, 1984)

Todd, Malcolm (ed.), *A Companion to Roman Britain* (Oxford 2007)

Wacher, John, *The Towns of Roman Britain* (London 1975)

Wacher, John, *Roman Britain* (London 1978)

Wilmott, Tony, *Birdoswald Roman Fort* (London 2005)

Wilson, Roger J.A., *A Guide to the Roman Remains in Britain*, (4th edition London 2002)

CHAPTER 2: GERMANIA

Alföldi, Andreas, 'The moral barrier on Rhine and Danube' in *The Congress of Roman Frontier Studies 1949* (ed. Eric Birley, Durham 1952), pp. 1–16

Barrett, John C., Fitzpatrick, Andrew P., Macinnes, Lesley, *Barbarians and Romans in North-West Europe from the later Republic to late Antiquity* (BAR International Series 471, Oxford 1989)

Blandt, Roel and Slofstra, Jan, *Roman and Native in the Low Countries, Spheres of Interaction* (BAR International Series 184, Oxford 1983)

Booth, Alan D., 'The Academic Career of Ausonius' in *Phoenix*, Vol. 36, No. 4 (Winter 1982), pp. 329–43

Carroll, Maureen, *Romans, Germans and Celts* (Stroud 2001)

Drinkwater, J.F., 'The Gallic Empire, Separatism and Continuity in the North-Western Provinces of the Roman Empire AD 260–7' in *Historia* 52 (Stuttgart 1987)

Furger, Alex R., *Augusta Raurica* (trs Cathy Aitken and Christoph Maier, Augst 1995)

Hawkes, Christopher and Hawkes, Sonia (eds), *Greeks, Celts and Romans: Studies in Venture and Resistance* (London 1973)

Hind, J.G.F., 'Whatever happened to the *Agri Decumates*' in *Britannia* 15 (1984), pp. 187–92

Johnson, Anne, *Roman Forts of the 1st and 2nd Centuries AD in Britain and the German Provinces* (London 1983)

King, Anthony, *Roman Gaul and Germany* (London 1990)

Kulikowski, Michael, 'Barbarians in Gaul, Usurpers in Britain' in *Britannia* 31 (2000), pp. 325–45

MacKendrick, Paul, *Roman France* (London 1971)

Murdoch, Adrian, *Rome's Greatest Defeat: Massacre in the Teutoburg Forest* (Stroud 2006)

O'Reilly, Donald F., 'The Theban Legion of St Maurice' in *Vigiliae Christianae*, Vol. 32, No. 3 (Sep. 1978), pp. 195–207

Rieche, Anita, *Guide through the Archaeological Park Xanten* (Xanten 1994)

Roymans, Nico, *Ethnic Identity and Imperial Power: The Batavians in the Early Roman Empire* (Amsterdam 2004)

Schönberger, H., 'The Roman Frontier in Germany: An Archaeological Survey' in *Journal of Roman Studies* 59 (1969), pp. 144–97

Springer, Lawrence A., 'Rome's Contact with the Frisians' in *Classical Journal*, Vol. 48, No. 4 (Jan. 1953), pp. 109–11

Verwers, W.J.H., *North Brabant in Roman and Early Medieval Times* (Amersfoort 1998)

Von Elbe, Joachim, *Roman Germany, A Guide to Sites and Museums* (Mainz 1975)

Von Petrikovits, Harold, 'Fortifications in the North-Western Roman Empire from the Third to the Fifth Centuries AD' in *Journal of Roman Studies* 61 (1971), pp. 178–218

Wells, C.M., *The German Policy of Augustus, An Examination of the Archaeological Evidence* (Oxford 1972)

Wightman, Edith Mary, *Roman Trier and the Treveri* (London 1970)

Wightman, Edith Mary, *Gallia Belgica* (London 1985)

Wolff, Gerta, *Roman-Germanic Cologne* (Cologne 2003)

CHAPTER 3: RAETIA AND NORICUM

Alföldy, Géza (trs Anthony Birley), *Noricum* (London 1974)

Mierow, Charles Christopher, 'Eugippius and the Closing Years of Noricum Ripense' in *Classical Philology*, Vol. 10, No. 2 (Apr. 1915), pp. 166–87

Phillips, George Lewis, 'Six Saints of Sweepdom' in *Folklore*, Vol. 74, No. 2 (Summer 1963), pp. 377–86

Pitts, Lynn F., 'Relations between Rome and the German Kings on the Middle Danube in the First to Fourth Centuries A.D.' in *Journal of Roman Studies* 79 (1989), pp. 45–58

Schutz, Herbert, *The Romans in Central Europe* (New Haven 1985)

CHAPTER 4: MOESIA AND PANNONIA

Aricescu, Andrei, *The Army in Roman Dobrudja* (BAR International Series 86, Oxford 1980)

Atanassove-Georgieva, Jordana, 'Résultat des fouilles de la ville antique de Ratiaria au cours des années 1976 à 1982' in *Studien zu Den Militargränzen Roms III* (Stuttgart 1986), pp. 437–40

Barford, P.M., *The Early Slavs: Culture and Society in Early Medieval Eastern Europe* (London 2001)

Brothers, A.J., 'Diocletian's Palace at Split' in *Greece & Rome*, Second Series, Vol. 19, No. 2 (Oct. 1972), pp. 175–86

Carter, Francis W. (ed.), *An Historical Geography of the Balkans* (London 1977)

Champlin, Edward, 'The Testament of the Piglet' in Phoenix, Vol. 41, No. 2, (Summer 1987), pp. 174–83

Gamzigrad, An Imperial Palace of Late Classical Times (Belgrade 1983)

Gimbutas, Marija, *The Slavs* (London 1971)

Heather, Peter, *The Goths* (Oxford 1996)

Hind, J.G.F., 'Greek and Barbarian Peoples on the Shores of the Black Sea' in *Archaeological Reports*, No. 30 (1983), pp. 71–97

Hoddinott, R.F., *Bulgaria in Antiquity, an archaeological introduction* (London 1975)

Humer, F., *Carnuntum, The Roman City Quarter in the Open Air Museum* (Petronell 2004)

Ivanov, Teofil and Stojanov, Stojan, *Abritus* (Razgrad, 1985)

Lengyel, A. and Radan, G.T.P., *The Archaeology of Roman Pannonia* (Budapest 1980)

Man, John, *Attila the Barbarian King who Challenged Rome* (London 2005)

Mócsy, András (trs Sheppard Frere), *Pannonia and Upper Moesia. A History of the Middle Danube Provinces of the Roman Empire* (London 1974)

Nicol, Donald M., *The Byzantine Family of Kantakouzenos ca 1100–1460, A Genealogical and Prosopographical Study* (Dumbarton Oaks 1968)

Oliva, P., *Pannonia and the Onset of Crisis in the Roman Empire* (Prague 1962)

Parnicki-Pudelko, Stefan, *The Episcopal Basilica in Novae, Archeological Research 1976–1990* (Poznan 1995)

Petulescu, Liviu, 'The Roman Army as a Factor of Romanisation in the North-Eastern Part of Moesia Inferior' in *The Roman and Late Roman City* (International Conference, Veliko Turnovo 26–30 July 2000) (Sofia 2002), pp. 31–42

Pitts, Lynn F., 'Relations between Rome and the German Kings on the Middle Danube in the First to Fourth Centuries AD' in *Journal of Roman Studies 79* (1989), pp. 45–58

Popović, Vladislav (ed.), *Sirmium – Archaeological Investigations in Sirmian Pannonia* (Belgrade 1971)

Poulter, A.G. (ed.), *Ancient Bulgaria: Papers presented to the International Symposium on the Ancient History and Archaeology of Bulgari* (Nottingham 1981, 1983)

Poulter, Andrew, *Nicopolis ad Istrum: A Roman, Late Roman and Early Byzantine City* (Society for Promotion of Roman Studies, Journal of Roman Studies Monograph 8, London 1995)

Press, Ludwika, 'Valetudinarium at Novae', in *Studien zu den Militargränzen Roms* (III Stuttgart 1986), pp. 529–35

Rives, J.B., 'The Decree of Decius and the Religion of Empire' in *Journal of Roman Studies 89* (1999), pp. 135–54

Schutz, Herbert, *The Romans in Central Europe* (New Haven 1985)

Spekke, Arnolds, *The Ancient Amber Routes and the Geographical Discovery of the Eastern Baltic* (Stockholm 1957)

Syme, Ronald, 'Lentulus and the Origin of Moesia' in *Journal of Roman Studies 24* (1934), pp. 113–37

Visy, Zsolt (ed.), *The Roman Army in Pannonia, An Archaeological Guide of the Ripa Pannonica* (Budapest 2003)

CHAPTER 5: DACIA

Cătăniciu, Ioana Bogdan, *Evolution of the system of defence works in Roman Dacia* (trs Etta Dumitrescu, BAR International Series 116, Oxford 1981)

Bichir, Gh. (trs Nubar Hampartumian), *The Archaeology and History of the Carpi from the Second to the Fourth Century AD* (BAR Supplementary Series 16 (i), Oxford 1976)

Eliade, Mircea and Trask, Willard R., 'Zalmoxis' in *History of Religions*, Vol. 11, No. 3 (Feb. 1972), pp. 257–302

Gudea, Nicolae, 'The Defensive System of Roman Dacia' in *Britannia* 10, (1979), pp. 63–87

MacKendrick, Paul, *The Dacian Stones Speak* (Chapel Hill 1975)

Picard, Gilbert Charles, *Les Trophées Romains, Contributions à l'histoire de la Religions et de l'Art triumphal de Rome* (Paris 1957)

Poulter, Andrew G., 'The Lower Moesian Limes and the Dacian Wars of

Trajan' in *Studien zu den Militargränzen Roms* III (Stuttgart 1986), pp. 519–28

Rossi, Lino (trs J.M.C. Toynbee), *Trajan's Column and the Dacian Wars* (London 1971)

Scorpan, C., *Limes Scythiae: Topographical and Stratigraphical Research on the late Roman fortifications on the Lower Danube* (BAR International Series 99, Oxford 1980)

Speidel, Michael, 'The Captor of Decebalus: a New Inscription from Philippi' in *Journal of Roman Studies* 60 (1970), pp. 142–53

CHAPTER 6: CAPPADOCIA

Akurgal, Ekrem, *Ancient Civilizations and Ruins of Turkey* (London 2002)

Barnard, L. W. 'The Origins and Emergence of the Church in Edessa during the First Two Centuries AD' in *Vigiliae Christiane* Vol. 22 No. 3 (Sept. 1986), pp. 161–175

Baumer, Christopher, *The Church of the East, an Illustrated History of Assyrian Christianity* (London 2006)

Baynes, Norman H., 'The Death of Julian the Apostate in a Christian Legend' in *Journal of Roman Studies* 27, Part 1, pp. 22–9

Bell, Gertrude, *Churches and Monasteries of the Tur Abdin and Neighbouring Districts* (Heidelberg 1913)

Bryer, Anthony, *The Empire of Trebizond and the Pontus* (London 1980)

Bryer, Anthony and Winfield, David, *The Byzantine Monuments and Topography of the Pontos*, Vols 1–2 (Washington 1985)

Croke, Brian and Crow, James, 'Procopius and Dara' in *Journal of Roman Studies* 73 (1983), pp. 143–59

Dueck, Daniela, *Strabo of Amaseia* (London 2000)

Freeman, Philip and Kennedy, David, *The Defence of the Roman and Byzantine East* (BAR International Series 297 (ii), Oxford 1986), pp. 737–83

French, D.H. and Lightfoot, C.S. (eds), *The Eastern Frontier of the Roman Empire* (BAR International Series 533 (i), Oxford 1989)

Goell, Theresa B., 'The Excavation of the "Hierothesion" of Antiochus I of Commagene on Nemrud Dagh (1953–1956)' in *Bulletin of the American Schools of Oriental Research*, No. 147 (Oct. 1957)

Jones, A.H.M., *Cities of the Eastern Roman Provinces* (Oxford 1937)

Magie, David, *Roman Rule in Asia Minor* (Princeton 1950)

Matthews, Roger (ed.), *Ancient Anatolia, Fifty Years of Work by the British Institute of Archaeology of Ankara* (London 1999)

Miller, William, 'The Chronology of Trebizond' in *English Historical Review*, Vol. 38, No. 151 (July 1923), pp. 408–10

Miller, William, *Trebizond: The Last Greek Empire* (London 1926)

Mitford, T.B., 'The Euphrates Frontier in Cappadocia' in *Studien zu den Militargränzen Roms* II (Bonn 1977), pp. 502–10

Mitford, T.B., 'Biliotti's Excavations at Satala' in *Anatolian Studies* 24 (1984), pp. 221–44

Payaslian, Simon, *The History of Armenia from the Origins to the Present* (London 2007)

Ross, Steven K., *Roman Edessa, Politics and Culture on the Eastern Fringe of the Roman Empire 114–242 CE* (London 2001)

Sanders, Donald H. (ed.), *Nemrud Daği, The Hierothesion of Antiochus I of Commagene*, Vol. 1: Text (Winona Lake, IN, 1996)

Segal, J.B., *Edessa: The Blessed City* (Oxford 1970)

Segal, J.B., 'The Planet Cult of Ancient Harran' in E. Bacon (ed.), *Vanished Civilizations* (London 1963)

Sinclair, T.A., *Eastern Turkey, an Architectural and Archaeological Survey*, Vols I–IV (London 1989)

Stark, Freya, *Rome on the Euphrates* (London 1966)

Talbot Rice, D., 'Trebizond, a Medieval Citadel and Palace' in *Journal of Hellenic Studies*, Vol. 52, Part 1 (1932), pp. 47–54

Wheeler, R.E.M., 'The Roman Frontier in Mesopotamia' in *The Congress of Roman Frontier Studies 1949* (ed. Eric Birley, Durham 1952), pp. 112–29

CHAPTER 7: SYRIA

Balty, Jean, 'Apamea in Syria in the Second and Third Centuries AD' in *Journal of Roman Studies* 78 (1988), pp. 91–104

Bell, Florence (ed.), *The Letters of Gertrude Bell*, Vol. 1 (London 1927)

Bickerman, Elias J., 'Notes on Seleucid and Parthian Chronology' in *Berytus* 8 1943 pp. 73–84

Browning, Iain, *Palmyra* (London 1979)

Browning, Iain, *Jerash and the Decapolis* (London 1982)

Browning, Robert, 'The Riot of AD 387 in Antioch: The Role of the Theatrical Claques in the Later Empire' in *Journal of Roman Studies*, Vol. 42, Parts 1 and 2 (1952), pp. 13–20

Burns, Ross, *Monuments of Syria, An Historical Guide* (London 1999)

Butcher, Kevin, *Roman Syria and the Near East* (London 2003)

Colledge, Malcolm A.R., *The Art of Palmyra* (London 1976)

Dawkins, James and Wood, Robert, *The Ruins of Palmyra* (London 1753)

De Vries, Bert, 'What's in a Name: The Anonymity of Ancient Umm el-Jimal' in *Biblical Archaeologist*, Vol. 57, No. 4 (Dec. 1994), pp. 215–19

Doran, Robert, *The Lives of Simeon Stylites* (Spencer, MA, 1992)

Downey, G., 'Aurelian's Victory over Zenobia at Immae, AD 272' in *Transactions and Proceedings of the American Philological Association* 81 (1950), pp. 57–68

Downey, Glanville, *A History of Antioch in Syria from Seleucus to the Arab Conquest* (Princeton, NJ, 1961)

Downey, Glanville, *Ancient Antioch* (Oxford 1972)

Frankfurter, T.M., 'Stylites and Phallobates: Pillar Religions in Late Antique Syria' in *Vigiliae Christianae*, Vol. 44, No. 2 (June 1990), pp. 168–98

Gilliam, J.F., 'The Roman Military Feriale' in *Harvard Theological Review*, Vol. 47, No. 3 (Jul. 1954), pp. 183–96

Hopkins, Clark, *The Discovery of Dura Europos* (New Haven 1979)

Hopkins, Clark, 'The Siege of Dura' in *Classical Journal*, Vol. 42, No. 5 (Feb. 1948), pp. 251–9

Isaac, Benjamin, *The Limits of Empire: The Roman Army in the East* (revised edition Oxford 1992)

Kennedy, David, *The Roman Army in Jordan* (revised edition, London 2004)

Liebeschuetz, J.H., *Antioch, City and Imperial Administration in the Later Roman Empire* (Oxford 1972)

Matthews, J.F., 'The Tax Law of Palmyra: Evidence for Economic History in a City of the Roman East' in *Journal of Roman Studies* 74 (1984), pp. 157–80

Millar, Fergus, *The Roman Near East, 31 BC–AD 337* (Cambridge, MA, 1993)

Nicasie, M.J., *Twilight of Empire: The Roman Army from the Reign of Diocletian until the Battle of Adrianople* (Amsterdam 1998)

Nicolle, David, *Yarmuk AD 636* (Westport 1994)

Pasztori-Kupán, István, *Theodoret of Cyrrus* (Oxford 2006)

Perkins, A., *The Art of Dura-Europus* (Oxford 1973)

Pollard, Nigel, *Soldiers, Cities and Civilians in Roman Syria* (Ann Arbor 2000)

Richmond, I.A., 'Palmyra under the Aegis of Rome' in *Journal of Roman Studies*, Vol. 53, Parts 1 & 2 (1963), pp. 43–54

Rostovtzeff, M., *Caravan Cities* (Oxford 1932)

Rostovtzeff, M., *Dura-Europos and its Art* (Oxford 1938)

Sartre, Maurice, *The Middle East Under Rome* (Harvard 2007)

Segal, Arthur, *From Function to Monument: Urban Landscapes of Roman Palestine, Syria and Provincia Arabia* (Oxford 1997)

Sha'ath, Shawqi (trs Dorothy Stele, Yahya Abu Risha), *Qal'at Sim'an (and other sites): An Archaeological and Historical Guide* (Aleppo)

Stanhope, Lady Hester (ed. The Duchess of Cleveland), *The Life and Letters of Lady Hester Stanhope* (London 1914)

Stoneman, Richard, *Palmyra and its Empire – Zenobia's revolt against Rome* (Ann Arbor 1992)

Tchalenko, Georges, *Villages antiques de la Syrie du Nord* (Paris 1953)

Vasiliev, Alexander A., 'Notes on some Episodes concerning the Relations between the Arabs and the Byzantine Empire from the Fourth to the Sixth Century' in *Dumbarton Oaks Papers* 9 (1956), pp 306–16

Zahran, Yasmine, *Zenobia between Reality and Legend* (BAR International Series 11669, Oxford 2003)

CHAPTER 8: ARABIA

Bowersock, G. W., 'A Report on Arabia Provincia' in *Journal of Roman Studies* 61 (1971), pp. 219–42

Bowersock, G.W., 'Limes Arabicus' in *Harvard Studies in Classical Philology* 80 (1976), pp. 219–29

Bowersock, G.W., *Roman Arabia* (Cambridge, MA, 1983)

Bowersock, G.W., 'Edward Lear in Petra' in *Proceedings of the American Philosophical Society*, Vol. 134, No. 3 (Sep. 1990), pp. 309–20

Browning, Iain, *Jerash and the Decapolis* (London 1982)

Burckhardt, Johann Ludwig, *Travels in Syria and the Holy Land* (1822, reprinted London 1992)

Damiani, Anita, *Enlightened Observers: British Travellers to the Near East* (Beirut 1979)

Eadie, John W. and Oleson, John Peter, 'The Water-supply Systems of Nabataean and Roman Humayma' in *Bulletin of the American Schools of Oriental Research* 252 (May 1986), pp. 49–76

Guzzo, Maria Guilia Amadasi and Schneider, Eugenia Equini (trs Lydia G. Cochrane), *Petra* (Chicago 2002)

Harding, G.W.L., *The Antiquities of Jordan* (London 1959)

Hatoum, Hassan, *Canatha and Philippopolis* (Damascus 2001)

Jameson, Shelagh, 'Chronology of the Campaigns of Aelius Gallus and C. Petronius' in *Journal of Roman Studies*, Vol. 58 Parts 1 and 2 (1968), pp. 71–84

Lander, James and Parker, S. Thomas, 'Legio IV Martia and the Legionary Camp at El-Lejjun' in *Byzantinische Forschungen, Internationale Zeitschrift für Byzantinistik* 8 (1982), pp. 185–211

Khouri, Rami G., *Jerash: A frontier city of the Roman East* (London 1986)

Khouri, Rami G. and Whitcomb, Donald, *Aqaba* (Amman 1986)

Lawrence, T. E., *Seven Pillars of Wisdom* (London 1935)

MacAdam, Henry Innes, *Studies in the History of the Roman Province of Arabia* (BAR International Series 295, Oxford 1986)

Mayerson, Philip, 'The First Muslim Attacks on Southern Palestine', *Transactions of the American Philological Association* 95 (1964), p. 173

Nicholson, Oliver, 'Two Notes on Dara' in *American Journal of Archaeology*, Vol. 89, No. 4 (Oct. 1985), pp. 663–71

Parker, S. Thomas 'Preliminary Report on the 1980 Season of the Central *Limes Arabicus* Project' in *Bulletin of the American Schools of Oriental Research* 247 (Summer 1982), pp. 1–26

Parker, S. Thomas, *The Roman Frontier in Central Jordan, Interim Report on the Limes Arabicus Project* (BAR International Series 340 (i & ii), Oxford 1987)

Segal, Arthur, 'Roman Cities in the Province of Arabia' in *Journal of the Society of Architectural Historians*, Vol. 40, No. 2 (May 1981), pp. 108–21

Shahid, Irfan, *Rome and the Arabs – A Prolegomenon to the Study of Byzantium and the Arabs* (Dumbarton Oaks 1984)

Shahid, Irfan, *Byzantium and the Arabs in the Fourth Century* (Dumbarton Oaks 1989)

Shahid, Irfan, *Byzantium and the Arabs in the Fifth Century* (Dumbarton Oaks 1989)

Shahid, Irfan, *Byzantium and the Arabs in the Sixth Century* (Dumbarton Oaks 1995)

Starcky, Jean, 'The Nabataeans: A Historical Sketch' in *Biblical Archaeologist*, Vol. 18, No. 4 (Dec. 1955), pp. 81–106

Stoneman, Richard, *Palmyra and its Empire, Zenobia's Revolt against Rome* (Ann Arbor 1992)

Welsby, Derek A., 'Qasr al-Uwainid and Da'ajaniya: Two Roman Military Sites in Jordan' in *Levan* 30 (1998), pp. 195–8

CHAPTER 9: AEGYPTUS

Alston, Richard *Soldier and Society in Roman Egypt: A Social History* (London 1995)

Bagnall, Roger S., *Egypt in Late Antiquity* (Princeton 1993)

Bagnall, Roger S., 'Archaeological Work on Hellenistic and Roman Egypt, 1995–2000' in *American Journal of Archaeology*, Vol. 105, No. 2 (Apr. 2001), pp. 227–43

Bagnall, Roger S. (ed.), *Egypt in the Byzantine World, 300–700* (Cambridge 2007)

Barnard, L.W., 'Athanasius and the Meletian Schism in Egypt' in *Journal of Egyptian Archaeology* 59 (1975), pp. 181–9

Barnes, T.D., 'The Career of Abinnaeus' in *Phoenix*, Vol. 39, No. 4 (Winter 1985), pp. 368–74

Bowman, Alan K., *Egypt after the Pharaohs* (London 1986)

Butler, Alfred, *The Arab Conquest of Egypt and the last thirty years of the Roman Dominion* (2nd edition, Oxford 1978)

Cuvigny, Hélène, 'The Amount of Wages paid to the Quarry-Workers at Mons Claudianus' in *Journal of Roman Studies* 86 (1996), pp. 139–45

Edwards, Amelia B., *A Thousand Miles up the Nile* (London 1877)

Empereur, Jean-Yves (trs Margaret Maehler), *Alexandria Rediscovered* (London 1998)

Fakhry, Ahmed, *Siwa Oasis, its History and Antiquities* (Cairo 1944)

Fakhry, Ahmed, *Baharia Oasis* Vol. II (Cairo 1950)

Fakhry, Ahmed, *The Necropolis of El-Bagawat in Kharga Oasis* (Cairo 1951)

Forster, E.M., *Alexandria: A History and a Guide* (Alexandria 1938)

Franfkurter, David, *Religion in Roman Egypt, Assimilation and Resistance* (Princeton, NJ, 1998)

Gardner, I.M.F. and Lieu, S.N.C., 'From Narmouthis (Medinet Madi) to Kellis (Asmant El-Kharab): Manichaean Documents from Roman Egypt' in *Journal of Roman Studies* 86 (1986), pp. 146–9

Golvin, Jean-Claude and Reddé, Michel 'L'enceinte du camp militaire romain de Louqsor' in *Studien zu den Militargränzen Roms* III Stuttgart 1986, pp 594–9

Haas, Christopher, *Alexandria in Late Antiquity: Topography and Social Conflict* (Baltimore 1997)

Harmless, William, *The Desert Christians* (Oxford 2004)

Jackson, Robert B., *At Empire's Edge, Exploring Rome's Egyptian Frontier* (New Haven 2002)

Jameson, Shelagh, 'Chronology of the Campaigns of Aelius Gallus and C. Petronius' in *Journal of Roman Studies*, Vol 58, Parts 1 and 2 (1968), pp. 71–84

Johnson, Allan Chester, 'Lucius Domitius Domitianus Augustus' in *Classical Philology*, Vol. 45, No. 1 (Jan. 1950), pp. 13–21

Kirwan, L.P., 'Rome Beyond the Southern Egyptian Frontier' in *Geographical Journal*, Vol. 123, No. 1 (Mar. 1957), pp. 13–19

Mackenzie, Judith, *The Architecture of Alexandria and Egypt c. 300 BC to AD 700* (New Haven 2007)

Mackenzie, Judith S., Gibson, Sheila Reyes, A.T., 'Reconstructing the Serapeum in Alexandria from the Archaeological Evidence' in *Journal of Roman Studies* 94 (2004), pp. 73–121

MacLeod, Roy (ed.), *The Library of Alexandria, Centre of Learning in the Ancient World* (London 2000)

MacQuitty, William, *Island of Isis: Philae, Temple of the Nile* (London 1976)

Meredith, David, 'The Roman Remains in the Eastern Desert of Egypt I' in *Journal of Egyptian Archaeology* 38 (Dec. 1952), pp. 94–111

Parson, Peter J., 'The Wells of Hibis' in *Journal of Egyptian Archaeology* 57 (1971), pp. 165–80

Peacock, D.P.S., *Rome in the Desert: A Symbol of Power* (Southampton 1993)

Peacock, David and Maxfield, Valerie, 'On the Trail of Imperial Porphyry' in *Egyptian Archaeology* 5 (1994), pp. 24–226

Scott, Kenneth, 'Octavian's Propaganda and Antony's De Sua Ebrietate' in *Classical Philology*, Vol. 24, No. 2 (Apr. 1929), pp. 133–41

Sidebottom, S.E., 'The Roman Frontier in the Eastern Desert of Egypt' in *Roman Frontier Studies 1995* (ed. W. Groenman-van Waateringe, B.L. van Beek, W.J.H. Willems, S.L. Wynia, Oxford 1997), pp. 503–9

Skeat, T.C., 'A Letter from the King of the Blemmyes to the King of the Noubades' in *Journal of Egyptian Archaeology* 63 (1977), pp. 159–70

Thompson, E.A., 'Olympiodorus of Thebes' in *Classical Quarterly*, Vol. 38, No. 1/2 (Jan.–Apr. 1944) pp. 43–52

Van der Veen, Marijke, 'High living in Rome's distant quarries' in *British Archaeology* 28 (October 1997)

Vivian, Cassandra, *The Western Desert of Egypt* (Cairo 2000)

Vretto, Theodore, *Alexandria, City of the Western Mind* (New York 2001)

CHAPTER 10: AFRICA

Barker, Graeme, Lloyd John and Reynolds, Joyce, *Cyrenaica in Antiquity* (BAR International Series 236, Oxford 1985)

Barton, I.M., *Africa in the Roman Empire* (Accra 1972)

Bregman, Jay, *Synesius of Cyrene, Philosopher-Bishop* (Berkeley 1982)

Broughton, T.R.S., *The Romanization of Africa Proconsularis* (New York 1968)

Buck, D.J. and Mattingly, D.J., *Town and Country in Roman Tripolitania – Papers in Honour of Olwen Hackett* (BAR International Series 174, Oxford 1985)

Caffarelli, Ernesto Vergara and Giacomo, *The Buried City: Excavations at Leptis Magna* (London 1966)

Cherry, David, *Frontier and Society in Roman North Africa* (Oxford 1998)

Clover, Frank M., *The Late Roman West and the Vandals* (Aldershot 1993)

Daniels, Charles, *The Garamantes of Southern Libya* (Stoughton, WI, 1970)

Fage, J.D., *Cambridge History of Africa* Vol. 2 (Cambridge 1978)

Fentress, Elizabeth W.B., *Social, Military and Economic Aspects of the Frontier Zone* (BAR International Series 53, Oxford 1979)

Goodchild, R.G., 'The Roman and Byzantine Limes in Cyrenaica' in *Journal of Roman Studies* 43 (1953), pp. 65–76

Goodchild, R.G., 'Boreum of Cyrenaica' in *Journal of Roman Studies*, Vol. 41, Parts 1 and 2 (1951), pp. 11–16

Hannoum, Abdelmajid, 'Historiography, Mythology and Memory in Modern North Africa: The Story of the Kahina' in *Studia Islamica*, No. 85 (1997), pp. 85–130

Harrison, S.J., *Apuleius, A Latin Sophist* (Oxford 2000)

Haynes, D.E.L., *The Antiquities of Tripolitania* (Tripoli 1955)

Haywood, Richard, 'The Oil of Leptis' in *Classical Philology* (1941), pp. 65–76

Hoyos, Dexter, *Hannibal's Dynasty: Power and Politics in the western Mediterranean* (London 2003)

Hurst, H.R. and Roskams, S.P., *Excavations at Carthage: The British Mission. Volume 1, The Site and Finds other than Pottery* (Sheffield 1984)

Julien, Charles-André (trs John Petrie), *A History of North Africa – Tunisia, Algeria, Morocco* (London 1970)

Law, R.C.C., 'The Garamantes and Trans-Saharan Enterprise in Classical Times' in *Journal of African History*, Vol. 8, No. 2 (1967), pp. 181–200

MacKendrick, *The North African Stones Speak* (London 1980)

Manton, E. Lennox, *Roman North Africa* (London 1988)

Mattingly, David J., 'A Tribal Confederation in the Late Roman Empire' in *Libyan Studies* 14 (1983), pp. 6–108

Mattingly, D.J., *Tripolitania* (London 1995)

Mattingly, David J. and Hitchener, Bruce, 'Roman Africa: An Archaeological Survey' in Journal of Roman Studies 85 (1995), pp. 165–213

Merrills, A.H. (ed.), *Vandals, Romans, Berbers: New Perspectives on Late Antique North Africa* (Ashgate 1994)

Millar, Fergus, 'Local Cultures in the Roman Empire: Libya, Punic and Latin in Roman Africa' in *Journal of Roman Studies*, Vol. 58, Parts 1 & 2 (1968), pp. 126–34

Oost, Stewart Irvin, 'Count Gildo and Theodosius the Great' in *Classical Philology*, Vol. 57, No. 1 (Jan. 1962), pp. 27–30

Pentz, Peter, *From Roman Proconsularis to Islamic Ifriqiyah* (Göteborg 2002)

Pringle, R. Denys, *The Defence of Byzantine Africa from Justinian to the Arab Conquest* (BAR International Series 99 (i), Oxford 1990)

Raven, Susan, *Rome in Africa* (3rd edition, London 1993)

Reynolds, J. (ed.), *Libyan Studies: Selected Papers of R.G. Goodchild* (London 1976)

Rives, J.B., 'Imperial Cult and Native Tradition in North Africa' in *Classical Journal*, Vol. 96, No. 4 (Apr.–May 2001), pp. 424–36

Scott, Kenneth, 'Mussolini and the Roman Empire' in *Classical Journal*, Vol. 27, No. 9 (Jun. 1932), pp. 645–57

Sergel, Lance (trs Antonia Nevill), *Carthage, A History* (London 1997)

Shaw, Brent D., *Rulers, Nomads and Christians in Roman North Africa* (Aldershot 1995)

Sjöström, Isabella, *Tripolitania in Transition, Late Roman to Early Islamic Settlement* (Aldershot 1993)

Warmington, B.H., *The North African Provinces from Diocletian to the Vandal Conquest* (Cambridge 1954)

Wheeler, Robert, and Wood, Roger, *Roman Africa in Colour* (London 1986)

CHAPTER II: NUMIDIA AND MAURETANIA

Baradez, Jean, *Fossatum Africae* (Paris 1949)

Belloc, Hilaire, *Many Cities* (London 1928)

Berthier, André, *Tiddis, Antique Castellum Tidditanorum* (1952, reissued, Algiers 1991)

Blas de Roblès, Jean Marie and Sintes, Claude, *Sites et monuments antiques de l'Algérie* (Aix-en-Provence 2003)

Brett, Michael and Fentress, Elizabeth, *The Berbers* (Oxford 1997)

Camus, Albert, *Noces à Tipasa* (Paris 1976)

Corcoran, Thomas H. 'Roman Fish Sauces' in *Classical Journal*, Vol. 58, No. 5 (Feb. 1963), pp. 204–10

Curtis, Robert I., 'In Defense of Garum' in *Classical Journal*, Vol. 78, No. 3 (Feb.–Mar. 1983), pp. 232–40

Euzennat, Maurice, 'Le Limes de Volubilis' in *Studien zu den Millitargränzen Roms, Vortrage des 6 Internationalen Limeskongresses in Süddeutschland* (Cologne 1967), pp. 194–9

Fentress, Elizabeth W. B., *Numidia and the Roman Army; Social, Military and Economic Aspects of the Frontier Zone* (BAR International Series 53, Oxford 1979)

Ferguson, John, 'Roman Algeria' in *Greece & Rome*, 2nd Ser, Vol. 13, No. 2. (Oct. 1966), pp. 169–87

Fishwick, Duncan, 'The Annexation of Mauritania' in *Historia* 20 (1971), pp. 467–87

Fred, W.H.C, *The Donatist Church: A Movement of Protest in North Africa* (Oxford 1952)

Hallier, Gilbert, 'La Fortification des villes de Tingitane au second siècle' in *Studien zu den Militargränzen Roms* III (Stuttgart 1986), pp. 605–24

Jarrett, Michael G., 'Decurions and Priests' in *American Journal of Philology*, Vol. 92, No. 4 (Oct. 1971), pp. 513–38.

Lixus – Actes du colloque organisé par l'Institut des sciences de l'archéologie et du patrimoine du Rabat avec le concours de l'École française de Rome, Larache, 8–11 novembre 1989 (Rome 1992)

Lugan, Bernard, *Histoire du Maroc, des origines à nos jours* (Paris 1992)

Morstein-Marx, Robert, 'The Myth of Numidian Origins in Sallust's African Excursus (Iugurtha 17.7–18.12)' in *American Journal of Philology* (2001), p. 188

Potter, T.W., *Towns in Late Antiquity: Iol Caesarea and its Context* (Oxford 1995)

Pringle, R.D., *The Defence of Byzantine Africa* (BAR International Series 99, Oxford 1989)

Rives, James, 'Venus Genetrix outside Rome' in *Phoenix*, Vol. 48, No. 4 (Winter 1994), pp. 294–306

Roller, Duane W., *The World of Juba II and Kleopatra Selene* (London 2003)

Sherwin-White, A.N., 'The Tabula of Banasa and the Constitutio Antoniniana' in *Journal of Roman Studies* 63 (1973), pp. 86–98

Sigman, Marlene C., 'The Romans and the Indigenous Tribes of Mauritania Tingitana' in *Historia* 26 (1977), pp. 415–39

Spaul, John, 'Across the Frontier in Tingitana' in *Roman Frontier Studies 1995* (ed. W. Groenman-van, Waateringe, B.l. van Beek, W.J.H. Willems, S.L Wynia, Oxford 1997), pp. 253–58

Thouvenot, Raymond, *Maisons de Volubilis: Le Palais dit de Gordien et la Maison à la Mosaïque de Vénus* (Rabat 1958)

Tilley, Maureen A., *Donatist Martyr Stories: The Church in Conflict in North Africa* (Liverpool 1996)

Watkins, Thomas H., 'Colonia Marciana Traiana Thamugadi: Dynasticism in Numidia' in *Phoenix*, Vol. 56, No. 1/2 (Spring–Summer 2002), pp. 84–108

Weech, W.N., 'Rambles in Mauretania Caesariensis' in *Greece & Rome*, Vol. 1, No. 1 (Oct. 1931), pp. 3–12

INDEX

www.rbooks.co.uk